RECTANGULAR GRID

COORDINATE SYSTEM

(Copy for use in Exercises and Problems 2.2, 11.2, and 11.3)

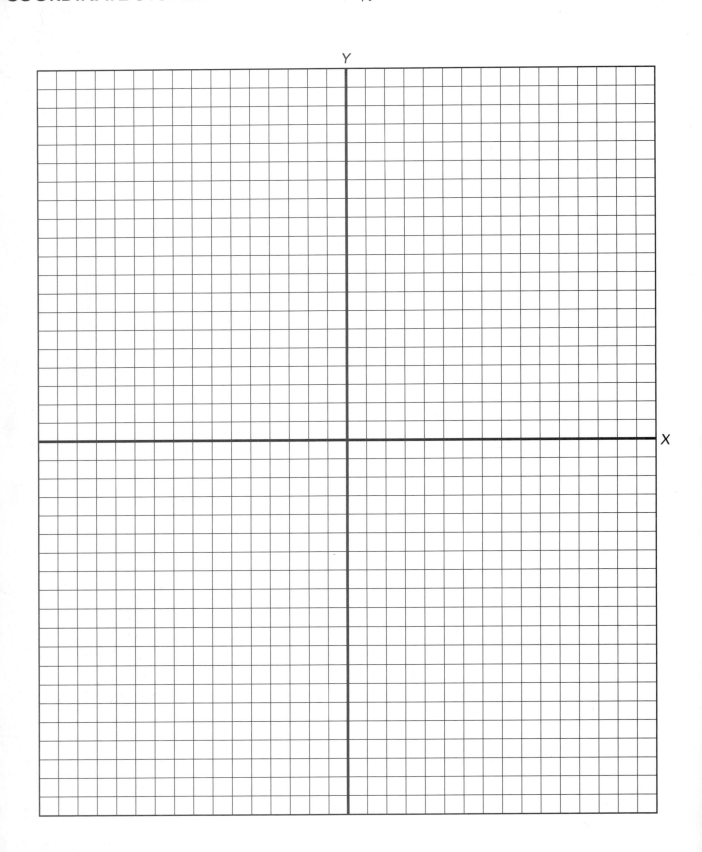

IMPORTANT:

HERE IS YOUR REGISTRATION CODE TO ACCESS
YOUR PREMIUM McGRAW-HILL ONLINE RESOURCES.

For key premium online resources you need THIS CODE to gain access. Once the code is entered, you will be able to use the Web resources for the length of your course.

If your course is using **WebCT** or **Blackboard**, you'll be able to use this code to access the McGraw-Hill content within your instructor's online course.

Access is provided if you have purchased a new book. If the registration code is missing from this book, the registration screen on our Website, and within your WebCT or Blackboard course, will tell you how to obtain your new code.

Registering for McGraw-Hill Online Resources

TO gain access to your McGraw-Hill web resources simply follow the steps below:

1. USE YOUR WEB BROWSER TO GO TO: **http://www.mhhe.com/bennett**
2. CLICK ON **FIRST TIME USER**.
3. ENTER THE REGISTRATION CODE* PRINTED ON THE TEAR-OFF BOOKMARK ON THE RIGHT.
4. AFTER YOU HAVE ENTERED YOUR REGISTRATION CODE, CLICK **REGISTER**.
5. FOLLOW THE INSTRUCTIONS TO SET-UP YOUR PERSONAL UserID AND PASSWORD.
6. WRITE YOUR UserID AND PASSWORD DOWN FOR FUTURE REFERENCE. KEEP IT IN A SAFE PLACE.

TO GAIN ACCESS to the McGraw-Hill content in your instructor's **WebCT** or **Blackboard** course simply log in to the course with the UserID and Password provided by your instructor. Enter the registration code exactly as it appears in the box to the right when prompted by the system. You will only need to use the code the first time you click on McGraw-Hill content.

Thank you, and welcome to your McGraw-Hill Online Resources!

REGISTRATION CODE

EF2U-J8BZ-TQN7-V3H3-H3OZ

Mc Graw Hill Higher Education

0-07-293165-5 BENNETT/NELSON, MATHEMATICS FOR ELEMENTARY TEACHERS: A CONCEPTUAL APPROACH, 6E

Sixth Edition

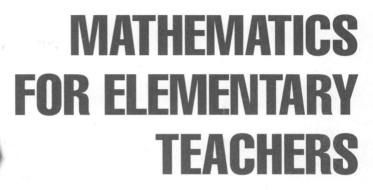

MATHEMATICS FOR ELEMENTARY TEACHERS

A CONCEPTUAL APPROACH

Albert B. Bennett, Jr.
University of New Hampshire

L. Ted Nelson
Portland State University

Higher Education

Boston   Burr Ridge, IL   Dubuque, IA   Madison, WI   New York   San Francisco   St. Louis
Bangkok   Bogotá   Caracas   Kuala Lumpur   Lisbon   London   Madrid   Mexico City
Milan   Montreal   New Delhi   Santiago   Seoul   Singapore   Sydney   Taipei   Toronto

MATHEMATICS FOR ELEMENTARY TEACHERS: A CONCEPTUAL APPROACH
SIXTH EDITION

Published by McGraw-Hill, a business unit of The McGraw-Hill Companies, Inc., 1221 Avenue of the Americas, New York, NY 10020. Copyright © 2004, 2001, 1998, 1992, 1985, 1979 by The McGraw-Hill Companies, Inc. All rights reserved. No part of this publication may be reproduced or distributed in any form or by any means, or stored in a database or retrieval system, without the prior written consent of The McGraw-Hill Companies, Inc., including, but not limited to, in any network or other electronic storage or transmission, or broadcast for distance learning.

Some ancillaries, including electronic and print components, may not be available to customers outside the United States.

This book is printed on acid-free paper.

2 3 4 5 6 7 8 9 0 VHN/VHN 0 9 8 7 6 5 4

ISBN 0–07–293164–7

Publisher: *William K. Barter*
Senior sponsoring editor: *David Dietz*
Developmental editor: *Christien A. Shangraw*
Executive marketing manager: *Marianne C. P. Rutter*
Senior marketing manager: *Mary K. Kittell*
Senior project manager: *Vicki Krug*
Production supervisor: *Sherry L. Kane*
Senior media project manager: *Tammy Juran*
Media technology producer: *Jeff Huettman*
Coordinator of freelance design: *Rick D. Noel*
Cover design and artwork: *Rokusek Design*
Illustration concept: *Rebecca Bennett*
Lead photo research coordinator: *Carrie K. Burger*
Supplement producer: *Brenda A. Ernzen*
Compositor: *GAC—Indianapolis*
Typeface: *10/12 Caslon 224 Book*
Printer: *Von Hoffmann Corporation*

The credits section for this book begins on page 860 and is considered an extension of the copyright page.

Library of Congress Cataloging-in-Publication Data

Bennett, Albert B.
  Mathematics for elementary teachers : a conceptual approach / Albert
B. Bennett, Jr., L. Ted Nelson. — 6th ed.
      p.   cm.
  Includes bibliographical references and index.
  ISBN 0–07–253294–7 (hard copy : alk. paper)
  1. Mathematics. I. Nelson, Leonard T. II. Title.

QA39.3 .B457   2004
510—dc21   2002015191
                                                                CIP

www.mhhe.com

TO THE STUDENT

You are preparing to enter an exciting profession, one in which there are many changes taking place in content, methodology, and technology. In the past, elementary school mathematics programs stressed computational rules and speed and accuracy in computing. The focus is now changing, and today's children need to develop conceptual understanding, the ability to reason and communicate through mathematics, and the ability to solve problems. When estimations and approximations are not sufficient, computations can be done with calculators and computers. Children who are able to see mathematics conceptually have a better chance of solving problems and acquiring confidence in their ability to reason.

During your career as a teacher, you will have far-reaching influence on the lives of your students; a huge responsibility! As a teacher you will be among energetic and enthusiastic young people who will need your support and understanding to build their confidence.

Over the years that the authors of this book taught mathematics courses to prospective elementary school teachers, they asked their students to write about their mathematical background, including special experiences and influences. It was not uncommon to receive statements such as, "My math teacher was awesome and changed my attitude toward mathematics. Because of this influence I decided to become a teacher." Unfortunately, negative comments about teachers and teaching practices were also common, and students discussed the fears and anxieties resulting from such experiences. If you have a school teacher that you thought was outstanding, you might want to write a note of thanks. If you do enter the teaching profession, you may find that such notes and words of appreciation are among your most prized possessions.

ONE-PAGE MATH ACTIVITIES

CONTENTS

The opening paragraph in NCTM's *Principles and Standards for School Mathematics* (Standards 2000) states that its recommendations are grounded in the belief that all students should learn important mathematical concepts and processes with understanding. This belief has guided and influenced the writing of the first six editions of *Mathematics for Elementary Teachers: A Conceptual Approach*, which continues to place emphasis on the use of models and processes for providing insights into mathematical concepts before generalizations.

Standards 2000 contains frequent references to the dual need for acquiring *conceptual understanding* and *procedural fluency*. It states that conceptual understanding is essential in learning to solve new kinds of problems. *Mathematics for Elementary Teachers: A Conceptual Approach* develops conceptual understanding and models mathematical procedures through its extensive use of diagrams, applications, and problem solving.

The primary objective of *Mathematics for Elementary Teachers: A Conceptual Approach* is to present mathematics in a format that prepares teachers to teach elementary school mathematics. Teachers need a firm foundation in the theory of mathematics as it pertains to the elementary school curriculum. They also need ideas and methods for teaching mathematics to elementary school children in a way that will provide an understanding of concepts and generate interest and enthusiasm.

This edition of *Mathematics for Elementary Teachers: A Conceptual Approach* contains several features to help future teachers see connections between their college mathematics courses and the mathematics they envision teaching to elementary school students. There is a one-page **Math Activity** at the beginning of each section which involves materials and ideas that can be adapted to teaching elementary school mathematics. New to this edition are **sample pages from elementary school texts** that show the close relationship between some of the mathematical content and processes in *Mathematics for Elementary Teachers: A Conceptual Approach* and the elementary school curriculum. There are also **statements from research** about learning and teaching mathematics in elementary and middle schools that suggest good practices and show some of the common learning difficulties of students. Finally, numerous **statements from Standards 2000** have been added to highlight recommendations for teaching mathematics with conceptual understanding.

NCTM's Process Standards

Standards 2000 has five Content Standards: **Number and Operations, Algebra, Geometry, Measurement,** and **Data Analysis and Probability.** It also has five Process Standards: **Problem Solving, Reasoning and Proof, Communication, Connections,** and **Representation.** The Process Standards discuss ways of acquiring and using content knowledge, and the following outline shows how this is accomplished in *Mathematics for Elementary Teachers: A Conceptual Approach.*

PROBLEM SOLVING

Several problem-solving strategies are illustrated in Chapter 1 and additional strategies are introduced in each chapter of the text.

Problem Openers at the beginning of each section provide opportunities for using the problem-solving strategies.

Problem-Solving Applications in each section illustrate specific strategies using Polya's four-step approach.

Reasoning and Problem Solving in each exercise set require explanations and justifications.

REASONING AND PROOF

Inductive reasoning and conjecture forming are introduced in Chapter 1 for extending patterns.

Deductive reasoning and Venn diagrams are introduced in Chapter 2, and both inductive and deductive reasoning are used throughout the text.

Puzzlers occur in each section and provide opportunities to grapple with problems that require extra effort.

Reasoning and Problem Solving in the exercise sets require both inductive and deductive reasoning.

COMMUNICATION

One-page *Math Activities* at the beginning of each section provide problems employing manipulative materials for small group discussions of strategies and solutions.

Research Statements in the margins of the text relate the mathematical content to school-student performance.

Problems for discussion and writing in mathematics for each section of the text are on the website for the text (see following pages).

Problem Openers at the beginning of each section provide opportunities for class or small group discussions of strategies and solutions.

Statements from Standards 2000 have been placed in the margins to relate the content, models, and pedagogy of the text to the proposals in the standards.

CONNECTIONS

Spotlights on Teaching at the beginning of each chapter contain examples from NCTM's standards which show connections to school mathematics.

Elementary School Text Pages relate the content and models of elementary school mathematics to key topics from the text.

Numerous photographs throughout the text of crystals, buildings, and many other types of objects illustrate connections to the real world.

An abundance of models and visuals illustrate mathematical concepts and provide insights and connections across number systems. For example, models help to show that the underlying concepts of the basic operations on numbers remain the same regardless of the type of numbers being used.

Techniques for estimation and mental calculation provide another common thread across the number system chapters.

Historical Highlights show the evolution of key ideas and provide background on some of the world's outstanding mathematicians.

REPRESENTATION

One-page *Math Activities* at the beginning of each section represent concepts with models and diagrams.

Mathematical concepts throughout the text are illustrated with models and diagrams before introducing definitions and generalizations.

Mathematical statements and relationships are represented throughout the text by tables, graphs, equations, and algebraic expressions.

Instruction and exercises for using calculators occur throughout the text and are marked by icons.

Graphing Calculator and Computer Investigations for specific topics are contained on the website. The *Mathematics Investigator* software on the website illustrates the power and convenience of computers in quickly generating large amounts of data.

Models and diagrams provide opportunities for representing relationships at the concrete level, then describing relationships verbally, and finally expressing them by algebraic statements.

Suggestions for Active Student Participation

NCTM's *Curriculum and Evaluation Standards for School Mathematics* (1989) and Standards 2000 recommend that students develop mathematics by looking for patterns, making conjectures, and verifying hypotheses. Many instructors have been influenced by such recommendations and are using instructional methods which involve more active student participation and less time in the lecture format. Following are a few suggestions involving the special features of the text which encourage active student participation.

MATH ACTIVITIES

The one-page Math Activities preceding each section of the text are augmented by the Manipulative Kit of colored, perforated cardstock materials which can be packaged with the text, if requested by the instructor (ISBN 0-07-287392-2). These Math Activities serve as: homework assignments to provide background for a section of the text; ideas for projects or papers involving the design of an elementary school activity; small group instruction for introducing sections of the text. They are designed to: introduce students to activities that develop concepts and mathematical reasoning; provide opportunities for students to look for patterns, form conjectures, and express their thinking; familiarize students with activities that can be adapted to the elementary school curriculum.

PROBLEM OPENERS

Each section of the text begins with a Problem Opener related to the content of that section. Problem Openers may be used for small, group problem solving and class discussions. They can be used to open a lesson before the content of the section is introduced and to motivate interest in the topic. The solution to each Problem Opener and the problem-solving strategies required are contained in the Instructor's Resource Manual. The manual also includes one or more ideas for looking back and extending each Problem Opener for additional problem solving in class or on assignments and tests.

INVESTIGATIONS

The National Council of Supervisors of Mathematics has stated, "Students need to explore mathematics using manipulatives, measuring devices, models, calculators, and computers."* At the end of each section of the text there is a website reference for a mathematics investigation that is designed specifically for the mathematical content of the section. These investigations pose open-ended questions that require collecting data, looking for patterns, and forming and verifying conjectures. The investigations can be used for student papers or class reports. There are three types of investigations: computer, calculator, and laboratory. Some of the computer investigations are designed for discovering relationships in geometry with one of several interactive geometry software packages; and some are designed for numerical discoveries with the software Mathematics Investigator which is on the text's Online Learning Center located at www.mhhe.com/bennett-nelson. This software is described on the following pages under Supplements.

PROBLEM-SOLVING APPLICATIONS

Each section of the text contains one or more Problem-Solving Application, which applies the subject matter of the section and is analyzed with Polya's four-step plan. These problems can be posed to the class for small group problem solving. A follow-up discussion can involve comparing students' plans for solving a problem and their solutions with those suggested in the text.

Special Approaches and Features

Reasoning and **Problem Solving** exercises marked by PS icon
Math Activities at the beginning of each section that employ the
   Manipulative Kit of colored, perforated materials
Parity of Exercises for all skills and concepts
Problem-solving Strategies introduced throughout the text
Statements from Standards 2000 in margins of text
Elementary School Text Pages set within the text to illustrate practical
   application of concepts
Problem Openers at the beginning of each section
Research Statements throughout the margins of the text
Calculator Paragraphs and Exercises marked with an icon
Problem-solving Applications developed by Polya's four-step plan
Spotlights on Teaching from NCTM's Standards at the beginnings of chapters
Puzzlers for challenges and reasoning
Historical Highlights for origins of important ideas
Mental Calculating and Estimating are required in number systems chapters
Chapter Reviews and Chapter Tests at the end of each chapter
Numerous Photographs to illustrate connections and applications
Boxed Features for key definitions, rules, properties
Answer Secton with selected answers for the section-opening Math
   Activities (marked with ★), odd-numbered exercises, puzzlers, and
   chapter tests

---

*National Council of Supervisors of Mathematics, "Essential Mathematics for the 21st Century" (Minneapolis, MN: NCSNI Essential Mathematics Task Force, 1988), 3–4.

Supplements

ONLINE LEARNING CENTER

The Bennett/Nelson Online Learning Center for the sixth edition of *Mathematics for Elementary Teachers*, located at www.mhhe.com/bennett-nelson includes improved and updated versions of the Bennett/Nelson online material, in addition to many NEW features developed especially for the sixth edition. Online Learning Centers are also compatible with a number of full-service online course delivery systems or outside educational service providers.

Digital Manipulative Kit A new, digitally interactive version of the Bennett/Nelson manipulative kit is now provided on the website for carrying out activities.

Interactive Mathematics Applets Content-specific interactive applets demonstrate key mathematical concepts.

Writing/Discussion Problems Correlated directly to the 34 sections of the text, these exercises raise classroom teaching issues and require explanations of mathematical concepts.

Color Transparencies Color copies of the materials from the Manipulative Kit may be downloaded and used for printing color transparencies.

Grids and Dot paper Black and white masters of geoboards, regular polygons, blank Decimal Squares, base-ten grid, coordinate system, random number chart, and a wide variety of grids, dot paper, and spinners are available to students and instructors.

Math Investigations 34 investigations that are classified as computer, calculator, and laboratory. Data for 14 of these investigations may be generated by the user-friendly, browser-based Mathematics Investigator software. Updated with a new design especially for this edition.

Bibliography An expanded set of bibliographies and Internet links for each of the 34 sections of the text.

Logo Instruction Instruction in Logo, including special commands, worked examples, and exercises. Answers for the odd-numbered exercises are included in the website and answers for the even-numbered exercises are included in the Instructor's Manual.

Network Graphs Instruction Instruction in Network Graphs, including worked examples and exercises. Answers for the odd-numbered exercises are included here on the Online Learning Center and answers for the even-numbered exercises are included in the Instructor's Resource Manual.

NetTutor NetTutor is a revolutionary system that enables students to interact with a live tutor over the World Wide Web. Students can receive instruction from live tutors using NetTutor's Web-based, graphical chat capabilities. They can also submit questions and receive answers, browse previously answered questions, and view previous live chat sessions.

INSTRUCTOR'S RESOURCE MANUAL

The *Instructor's Resource Manual* to accompany *Mathematics for Elementary Teachers: A Conceptual Approach* (ISBN 0-07-253298-X) contains extensions for all problem openers and answers for the problem openers and extensions; answers for all even-numbered Exercises and Problems; answers for the Online Mathematics Investigations, chapter tests with answers (two tests for each chapter); transparency masters (various grids and dot paper); and a description of the *Mathematics Investigator* website software.

STUDENT'S SOLUTION MANUAL

(ISBN 0-07-253297-1) Newly revised for this edition by its author, Joseph Ediger of Portland State University, this manual contains detailed solutions to the even-numbered exercises and problems and the chapter tests.

MATHEMATICS INVESTIGATOR

The *Mathematics Investigator* is software containing 14 programs (see list below) designed to demonstrate the computer investigations on the website. Students may use this software to gather data and run simulations for the investigations. These investigations pose questions to generate interest in various mathematical topics and encourage students to formulate and investigate their own conjectures. Instructors may use this software to demonstrate computer simulations and the process of forming conjectures and looking for counterexamples. This newly-updated, browser-based software is compatible with both Macintosh and PC platforms. Functionality such as editing, cutting, pasting, copying text to other files, and printing can be used with the programs on this software.

MATHEMATICS INVESTIGATOR

Triangular Numbers   Factorizations
Palindromic Sums   Frequency of Primes
Palindromic Differences   Number Chains
Palindromic Decimals   Integer Differences
Consecutive Numbers   Standard Deviations
Differences of Squares   Dice Roll Simulations
Repeating Decimals   Coin Toss Simulation

ACTIVITY BOOK

(ISBN 0-07-253307-2) *Mathematics for Elementary Teachers: An Activity Approach,* Sixth Edition, contains an activity set corresponding to each section of the text. Each activity set is a sequence of inductive activities and experiments that enable the student to build an understanding of mathematical ideas through the use of models and the discovery of patterns. The activity sets augment the ideas presented in the corresponding sections of the text. Over 50 Material Cards, some with colored manipulatives are packaged with *Mathematics for Elementary Teachers: An Activity Approach.* A section on *Ideas for the Elementary Classroom* at the end of each chapter includes a suggested elementary school activity and a list of selected sources. There are puzzlers throughout the book and the activity sets are followed by *Just for Fun* enrichment activities. The text, *Mathematics for Elementary Teachers: A Conceptual Approach,* may be packaged with the activity book, *Mathematics for Elementary Teachers: An Activity Approach,* and the Manipulative Kit (ISBN 0-07-287392-2).

Acknowledgments

We thank the many students and instructors who have used the first five editions of this book and have supported our efforts by contributing comments and suggestions. In particular, significant improvements were suggested by Professors Judy Carlson at Indiana University/Purdue and Danny Breidenbach of Purdue University. Portland State University Teaching Assistants Steve Blair, Dan Canada, and Matt Ciancetta also contributed valuable suggestions. The following students in the Geometry for Teachers class at the University of New Hampshire used the fifth edition of the text and merit special thanks for their suggestions: Karen Astell, Alicia Briggs, Megan Haldemen, Lauren Magner, Amy Schmidt, and Tayna Welsh.

We especially acknowledge the following reviewers who contributed excellent advice and suggestions for the sixth edition.

Danny Breidenbach, *Purdue University*
Laurie Burton, *Western Oregon University*
Judy Carlson, *Indiana University-Purdue University, Indianapolis*
John Drury, *Indiana University-Purdue University, Indianapolis*
Fe Evangelista, *University of Wisconsin, Whitewater*
Kim Hagens, *Louisiana State University, Baton Rouge*
Jean Marie Grant, *Bradley University*
Elizabeth Gray, *Southeastern Louisiana University*
Joyce Griffin, *Auburn University*
Joan Cohen Jones, *Eastern Michigan University*
Janet Melancon, *Loyola University*
Kathleen Miller, *California State University, Long Beach*
Carole Phillips-Bey, *Cleveland State University*
Virginia Powell, *University of Louisiana, Monroe*
Fary F. Sami, *Harford Community College*
Susan Schibel, *New Mexico State University, Las Cruces*

Special thanks go to Jane Bennett for devoting many hours to reading various stages of the manuscript and the galleys. We are grateful to Joe Ediger for his valuable suggestions and his writing and revising the Student's Solution Manual, and to Albert B. Bennett, III, for the initial programming of the *Mathematics Investigator* software. We also wish to acknowledge the following University of New Hampshire reference librarians for providing assistance on so many occasions: Louise Buckley, Peter R. Crosby, Valerie Harper, David Severn, Deborah E. Watson, and Dianna Wood. We wish to express our gratitude to the following members of McGraw-Hill Higher Education: Senior Sponsoring Editor David Dietz for his vision and leadership; Developmental Editor Christien Shangraw and Senior Project Manager Vicki Krug for their many excellent decisions in guiding this book through the revision and production process; Marketing Manager Mary Kittell for her professional judgment; Designer Rick Noel for imaginative and interesting interior text and cover designs; and Media Producer Jeff Huettman for recognizing the potential of the *Digital Manipulative Kit* and for overseeing the development of this kit, the Interactive Mathematics applets, and the revised *Mathematics Investigator* software. Finally we thank copyeditor Pat Steele for her meticulous attention to detail in this and the previous edition.

PROBLEM SOLVING

SPOTLIGHT ON TEACHING

Excerpts from NCTM's Standards for School Mathematics Prekindergarten through Grade 12*

Problem solving can and should be used to help students develop fluency with specific skills. For example, consider the following problem, which is adapted from the *Curriculum and Evaluation Standards for School Mathematics* (NCTM 1989, p. 24):

I have pennies, nickels, and dimes in my pocket. If I take three coins out of my pocket, how much money could I have taken?

This problem leads children to adopt a trial-and-error strategy. They can also act out the problem by using real coins. Children verify that their answers meet the problem conditions. Follow-up questions can also be posed: "Is it possible for me to have 4 cents? 11 cents? Can you list all the possible amounts I can have when I pick three coins?" The last question provides a challenge for older or more mathematically sophisticated children and requires them to make an organized list, perhaps like the one below.

PENNIES	NICKELS	DIMES	TOTAL VALUE
0	0	3	30
0	1	2	25
0	2	1	20
0	3	0	15
1	0	2	21
⋮	⋮	⋮	⋮

Working on this problem offers good practice in addition skills. But the important mathematical goal of this problem—helping students to think systematically about possibilities and to organize and record their thinking—need not wait until students can add fluently.

*Principles and Standards for School Mathematics (Reston, VA: National Council of Teachers of Mathematics, 2000), p. 52.

MATH ACTIVITY 1.1

TOWER PUZZLE PATTERNS

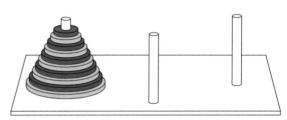

Puzzle: One of the three towers shown here has 10 disks of increasing size. What is the least number of moves needed to transfer these 10 disks from one tower to a different tower if only one disk can be moved at a time and a disk cannot be placed on top of a smaller one?

NO. OF DISKS	NO. OF MOVES
1	1
2	—
3	—
4	—
5	—

1. **Use a model** by drawing three towers on a sheet of paper and placing a quarter, nickel, penny, and dime on one of the towers (or disks can be cut from paper). Experiment.

*2. **Solve a simpler problem** by using fewer disks. What is the smallest number of moves needed to transfer 2 disks? Then try 3 disks.

*3. **Make a table** and record the smallest number of moves for 2, 3, and 4 disks. Try to predict the number of moves for 5 disks.

*4. **Find a pattern** in the table and extend the table for up to 10 disks.

NO. OF DISKS	NO. OF MOVES
6	1
7	—
8	—
9	—
10	—

5. You may have noticed a pattern in transferring the disks in the first three activities. The sequence of four figures below shows 3 disks being transferred from one tower to another. Three moves are needed to go from *(a)* to *(b)* because it takes 3 moves to transfer the top 2 disks from one tower to another. Then 1 move is used from *(b)* to *(c)* to transfer the third disk, and 3 more moves are needed from *(c)* to *(d)* to place the 2 smaller disks on top of the third disk.

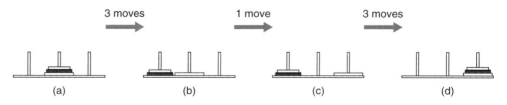

Notice how these figures show that the number of moves for transferring 2 disks can be used to determine the number of moves for transferring 3 disks. Draw a similar sketch, and explain how the number of moves for transferring 3 disks can be used to determine the number of moves for transferring 4 disks.

---

*A star indicates an activity is answered or suggestions are given in the Answer Section.

SECTION 1.1

INTRODUCTION TO PROBLEM SOLVING

There is no more significant privilege than to release the creative power of a child's mind.
Franz F. Hohn
Courtesy of International Business Machines Corporation

PROBLEM OPENER

Alice counted 7 cycle riders and 19 cycle wheels going past her house. How many tricycles were there?

"Learning to solve problems is the principal reason for studying mathematics."* This statement by the National Council of Supervisors of Mathematics represents a widespread opinion that problem solving should be the central focus of the mathematics curriculum.

A **problem** exists when there is a situation you want to resolve but no solution is readily apparent. **Problem solving** is the process by which the unfamiliar situation is resolved. A situation that is a problem to one person may not be a problem to someone else. For example, determining the number of people in 3 cars when each car contains 5 people may be a problem to some elementary school students. They might solve this problem by placing chips in boxes or by making a drawing to represent each car and each person (Figure 1.1) and then counting to determine the total number of people.

Problem solving is the hallmark of mathematical activity and a major means of developing mathematical knowledge.

Standards 2000, p. 116.

Figure 1.1

You may be surprised to know that some problems in mathematics are unsolved and have resisted the efforts of some of the best mathematicians to solve

*National Council of Supervisors of Mathematics, *Essential Mathematics for the 21st Century* (Minneapolis, MN: Essential Mathematics Task Force, 1988).

them. One such problem was discovered by Arthur Hamann, a seventh-grade student. He noticed that every even number could be written as the difference of two primes.* For example,

$$2 = 5 - 3 \qquad 4 = 11 - 7 \qquad 6 = 11 - 5 \qquad 8 = 13 - 5 \qquad 10 = 13 - 3$$

After showing that this was true for all even numbers less than 250, he predicted that every even number could be written as the difference of two primes. No one has been able to prove or disprove this statement. When a statement is thought to be true but remains unproved, it is called a **conjecture.**

Problem solving is the subject of a major portion of research and publishing in mathematics education. Much of this research is founded on the problem-solving writings of George Polya, one of the foremost twentieth-century mathematicians. Polya devoted much of his teaching to helping students become better problem solvers. His book *How to Solve It* has been translated into 18 languages. In this book, he outlines the following four-step process for solving problems.

Understanding the Problem   Polya suggests that a problem solver needs to become better acquainted with a problem and work toward a clearer understanding of it before progressing toward a solution. Increased understanding can come from rereading the statement of the problem, drawing a sketch or diagram to show connections and relationships, restating the problem in your own words, or making a reasonable guess at the solution to help become acquainted with the details.

Devising a Plan   The path from understanding a problem to devising a plan may sometimes be long. Most interesting problems do not have obvious solutions. Experience and practice are the best teachers for devising plans. Throughout the text you will be introduced to strategies for devising plans to solve problems.

Carrying Out the Plan   The plan gives a general outline of direction. Write down your thinking so your steps can be retraced. Is it clear that each step has been done correctly? Also, it's all right to be stuck, and if this happens, it is sometimes better to put aside the problem and return to it later.

Looking Back   When a result has been reached, verify or check it by referring to the original problem. In the process of reaching a solution, other ways of looking at the problem may become apparent. Quite often after you become familiar with a problem, new or perhaps more novel approaches may occur to you. Also, while solving a problem, you may find other interesting questions or variations that are worth exploring.

Polya's problem-solving steps will be used throughout the text. The purpose of this section is to help you become familiar with the four-step process and to acquaint you with some of the common strategies for solving problems: *making a drawing, guessing and checking, making a table, using a model,* and *working backward.* Additional strategies will be introduced throughout the text.

Doing mathematics involves discoverey. Conjecture—that is, informed guessing—is a major pathway to discovery. Teachers and researchers agree that students can learn to make, refine, and test conjectures in elementary school.

Standards 2000, p. 57

---

*M. R. Frame, "Hamann's Conjecture," *Arithmetic Teacher* 23, no. 1 (January 1976): 34–35.

Objective: Solve problems by drawing a diagram.

7·4 Problem Solving: Strategy
Draw a Diagram

Read

Read the problem carefully.

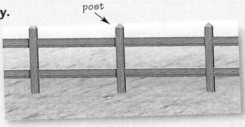

post

In the Falkland Islands, south of Argentina, Armando, a sheepherder's son, is helping his father build a rectangular pen to keep their sheep from getting lost. The pen will be 24 meters long, 20 meters wide, and have fence posts 4 meters apart. How many fence posts do they need?

- **What do you know?** The enclosure is rectangular; the two long sides are 24 m long and the two short sides are 20 m long; the posts are to be 4 m apart.

- **What are you asked to find?** The number of fence posts needed

Plan

One way to solve the problem is to draw a plan of the enclosure, including the points at which the fence posts will be placed. It is a good idea to place the corner posts first.

Solve

Draw a diagram.

Show that the length of the rectangle is 24 meters and the width is 20 meters.

Show that the fence posts are 4 meters apart in your diagram.

Count the fence posts.

Armando needs 22 fence posts.

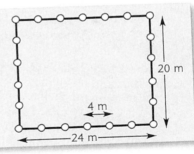

20 m

4 m

24 m

Look Back   How can you solve the problem another way?

   How does drawing a diagram help you solve a problem?

Making a Drawing

One of the most helpful strategies for understanding a problem and obtaining ideas for a solution is to *draw sketches and diagrams.* Most likely you have heard the expression "A picture is worth a thousand words." In the following problem, the drawings will help you to think through the solution.

PROBLEM

For his wife's birthday, Mr. Jones is planning a dinner party in a large recreation room. There will be 22 people, and in order to seat them he needs to borrow card tables, the size that seats one person on each side. He wants to arrange the tables in a rectangular shape so that they will look like one large table. What is the smallest number of tables that Mr. Jones needs to borrow?

Of the many descriptions of problem-solving strategies, some of the best known can be found in the work of Polya (1957). Frequently sited strategies include using diagrams, looking for patterns, listing all possibilities, trying special values or cases, working backward, guessing and checking, creating an equivalent problem, and creating a simpler problem.

Standards 2000, p. 53

Understanding the Problem   The tables must be placed next to each other, edge to edge, so that they form one large rectangular table. **Question 1:** If two tables are placed end to end, how many people can be seated?

One large table

Devising a Plan   Drawing pictures of the different arrangements of card tables is a natural approach to solving this problem. There are only a few possibilities. The tables can be placed in one long row; they can be placed side by side with two abreast; etc. **Question 2:** How many people can be seated at five tables if they are placed end to end in a single row?

Carrying Out the Plan   The following drawings show two of the five possible arrangements that will seat 22 people. The X's show that 22 people can be seated in each arrangement. The remaining arrangements—3 by 8, 4 by 7, and 5 by 6—require 24, 28, and 30 card tables, respectively. **Question 3:** What is the smallest number of card tables needed?

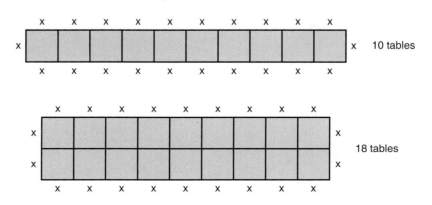

Looking Back   The drawings show that a single row of tables requires the fewest tables because each end table has places for 3 people and each of the remaining tables has places for 2 people. In all the other arrangements, the corner tables seat only 2 people and the remaining tables seat only 1 person. Therefore, regardless of the number of people, a single row is the arrangement that uses the smallest number of card tables, provided the room is long enough. **Question 4:** What is the smallest number of card tables required to seat 38 people?

Answers to Questions 1–4   **1.** 6   **2.** 12   **3.** 10   **4.** There will be 3 people at each end table and 32 people in between. Therefore, 2 end tables and 16 tables in between will be needed to seat 38 people.

Guessing and Checking

Sometimes it doesn't pay to guess, as illustrated by the cartoon at the left. However, many problems can be better understood and even solved by trial-and-error procedures. As Polya said, "Mathematics in the making consists of guesses." If your first guess is off, it may lead to a better guess. Even if guessing doesn't produce the correct answer, you may increase your understanding of the problem and obtain an idea for solving it. The *guess-and-check* approach is especially appropriate for elementary school children because it puts many problems within their reach.

PROBLEM

How far is it from town *A* to town *B* in this cartoon?

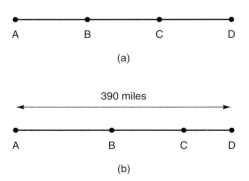

Peanuts © UFS. Reprinted by Permission.

Understanding the Problem   There are several bits of information in this problem. Let's see how Peppermint Patty could have obtained a better understanding of the problem with a diagram. First, let us assume these towns lie in a straight line, so they can be illustrated by points *A, B, C,* and *D,* as shown in (*a*). Next, it is 10 miles farther from *A* to *B* than from *B* to *C,* so we can move point *B* closer to

point C, as in (b). It is also 10 miles farther from B to C than from C to D, so point C can be moved closer to point D. Finally, the distance from A to D is given as 390 miles. **Question 1:** The problem requires finding what distance?

Devising a Plan   One method of solving this problem is to make a reasonable guess and then use the result to make a better guess. If the 4 towns were equally spaced, as in (a), the distance between each town would be 130 miles (390 ÷ 3). However, the distance from town A to town B is the greatest. So let's begin with a guess of 150 miles for the distance from A to B. **Question 2:** In this case, what is the distance from B to C and C to D?

Carrying Out the Plan   Using a guess of 150 for the distance from A to B produces a total distance from A to D that is greater than 390. If the distance from A to B is 145, then the B-to-C distance is 135 and the C-to-D distance is 125. The sum of these distances is 405, which is still too great. **Question 3:** What happens if we use a guess of 140 for the distance from A to B?

Looking Back   One of the reasons for *looking back* at a problem is to consider different solutions or approaches. For example, you might have noticed that the first guess, which produced a distance of 420 miles, was 30 miles too great. **Question 4:** How can this observation be used to lead quickly to a correct solution of the original problem?

Answers to Questions 1–4   **1.** The problem requires finding the distance from A to B.   **2.** The B-to-C distance is 140, and the C-to-D distance is 130.   **3.** If the A-to-B distance is 140, then the B-to-C distance is 130 and the C-to-D distance is 120. Since the total of these distances is 390, the correct distance from A to B is 140 miles.   **4.** If the distance between each of the 3 towns is decreased by 10 miles, the incorrect distance of 420 will be decreased to the correct distance of 390. Therefore, the distance between town A and town B is 140 miles.

Making a Table

A problem can sometimes be solved by listing some of or all the possibilities. A *table* is often convenient for organizing such a list.

PROBLEM

Sue and Ann earned the same amount of money, although one worked 6 days more than the other. If Sue earned $36 per day and Ann earned $60 per day, how many days did each work?

Understanding the Problem   Answer a few simple questions to get a feeling for the problem. **Question 1:** How much did Sue earn in 3 days? Did Sue earn as much in 3 days as Ann did in 2 days? Who worked more days?

Devising a Plan   One method of solving this problem is to list each day and each person's total earnings through that day. **Question 2:** What is the first amount of total pay that is the same for Sue and Ann, and how many days did it take each to earn this amount?

Carrying Out the Plan   The complete table is shown on page 9. There are three amounts in Sue's column that equal amounts in Ann's column. It took Sue 15 days to earn $540. **Question 3:** How many days did it take Ann to earn $540, and what is the difference between the numbers of days they each required?

NO. OF DAYS	SUE'S PAY	ANN'S PAY
1	36	60
2	72	120
3	108	(180)
4	144	240
5	(180)	300
6	216	(360)
7	252	420
8	288	480
9	324	(540)
10	(360)	600
11	396	660
12	432	720
13	468	780
14	504	840
15	(540)	900

Looking Back   You may have noticed that every 5 days Sue earns $180 and every 3 days Ann earns $180. **Question 4:** How does this observation suggest a different way to answer the original question?

Answers to Questions 1–4   **1.** Sue earned $108 in 3 days. Sue did not earn as much in 3 days as Ann did in 2 days. Sue must have worked more days than Ann to have earned the same amount.   **2.** $180. It took Sue 5 days to earn $180, and it took Ann 3 days to earn $180.   **3.** It took Ann 9 days to earn $540, and the difference between the numbers of days Sue and Ann worked is 6.   **4.** When Sue has worked 10 days and Ann has worked 6 days (a difference of 4 days), each has earned $360; when they have worked 15 days and 9 days (a difference of 6 days), respectively, each has earned $540.

Using a Model

Models are important aids for visualizing a problem and suggesting a solution. The recommendations by the Committee on the Undergraduate Program in Mathematics (CUPM) contain frequent references to the use of models for illustrating number relationships and geometric properties.*

The next problem uses **whole numbers** 0, 1, 2, 3, . . . and is solved by *using a model*. It involves a well-known story about the German mathematician Karl Gauss. When Gauss was 10 years old, his schoolmaster gave him the problem of computing the sum of whole numbers from 1 to 100. Within a few moments the young Gauss wrote the answer on his slate and passed it to the teacher. Before you read the solution to the following problem, try to find a quick method for computing the sum of whole numbers from 1 to 100.

PROBLEM

Find an easy method for computing the sum of consecutive whole numbers from 1 to any given number.

*Committee on the Undergraduate Program in Mathematics, *Recommendations on the Mathematical Preparation of Teachers* (Berkeley, CA: Mathematical Association of America, 1983).

Understanding the Problem   If the last number in the sum is 8, then the sum is $1 + 2 + 3 + 4 + 5 + 6 + 7 + 8$. If the last number in the sum is 100, then the sum is $1 + 2 + 3 + \cdots + 100$. **Question 1:** What is the sum of whole numbers from 1 to 8?

Devising a Plan   One method of solving this problem is to cut staircases out of graph paper. The one shown in *(a)* is a 1-through-8 staircase: There is 1 square in the first step, there are 2 squares in the second step, and so forth, to the last step, which has a column of 8 squares. The total number of squares is the sum $1 + 2 + 3 + 4 + 5 + 6 + 7 + 8$. By using two copies of a staircase and placing them together, as in *(b)*, we can obtain a rectangle whose total number of squares can easily be found by multiplying length by width. **Question 2:** What are the dimensions of the rectangle in *(b)*, and how many small squares does it contain?

> Problem solving is not only a goal of learning mathematics but also a major means of doing so.
>
> Standard 2000, p. 52

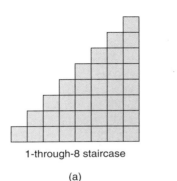

1-through-8 staircase

(a)

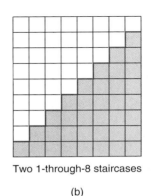

Two 1-through-8 staircases

(b)

Carrying Out the Plan   Cut out two copies of the 1-through-8 staircase and place them together to form a rectangle. Since the total number of squares is 8×9, the number of squares in one of these staircases is $(8 \times 9)/2 = 36$. So the sum of whole numbers from 1 to 8 is 36. By placing two staircases together to form a rectangle, we see that the number of squares in one staircase is just half the number of squares in the rectangle. This geometric approach to the problem suggests that the sum of consecutive whole numbers from 1 to any specific number is the product of the last number and the next number, divided by 2. **Question 3:** What is the sum of whole numbers from 1 to 100?

Looking Back   Another approach to computing the sum of whole numbers from 1 to 100 is suggested by the following diagram, and it may have been the method used by Gauss. If the numbers from 1 to 100 are paired as shown, the sum of each pair of numbers is 101.

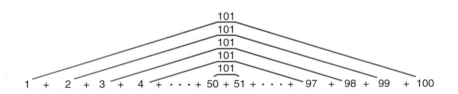

Question 4: How can this sum be used to obtain the sum of whole numbers from 1 to 100?

Answers to Questions 1–4 **1.** 36 **2.** The dimensions are 8 by 9, and there are $8 \times 9 = 72$ small squares. **3.** Think of combining two 1-through-100 staircases to obtain a rectangle with 100×101 squares. The sum of whole numbers from 1 to 100 is $100(101)/2 = 5050$. **4.** Since there are 50 pairs of numbers and the sum for each pair is 101, the sum of numbers from 1 to 100 is $50 \times 101 = 5050$.

HISTORICAL HIGHLIGHT

Hypatia
370–415

Athenaeus, a Greek writer (ca. 200), in his book *Deipnosophistoe* mentions a number of women who were superior mathematicians. However, Hypatia in the fourth century is the first woman in mathematics of whom we have considerable knowledge. Her father, Theon, was a professor of mathematics at the University of Alexandria and was influential in her intellectual development, which eventually surpassed his own. She became a student of Athens at the school conducted by Plutarch the Younger, and it was there that her fame as a mathematician became established. Upon her return to Alexandria, she accepted an invitation to teach mathematics at the university. Her contemporaries wrote about her great genius. Socrates, the historian, wrote that her home as well as her lecture room was frequented by the most unrelenting scholars of the day. Hypatia was the author of several treatises on mathematics, but only fragments of her work remain. A portion of her original treatise *On the Astronomical Canon of Diophantus* was found during the fifteenth century in the Vatican library. She also wrote *On the Conics of Apollonius*. She invented an astrolabe and a planesphere, both devices for studying astronomy, and apparatuses for distilling water and determining the specific gravity of water.*

*L. M. Osen, *Women in Mathematics* (Cambridge, MA: MIT Press, 1974), pp. 21–32.

PROBLEM

Working Backward

A businesswoman went to the bank and sent half of her money to a stockbroker. Other than a $2 parking fee before she entered the bank and a $1 mail fee after she left the bank, this was all the money she spent. On the second day she returned to the bank and sent half of her remaining money to the stockbroker. Once again, the only other expenses were the $2 parking fee and the $1 mail fee. If she had $182 left, how much money did she have before the trip to the bank on the first day?

Understanding the Problem Let's begin by guessing the original amount of money, say, $800, to get a better feel for the problem. **Question 1:** If the businesswoman begins the day with $800, how much money will she have at the end of the first day, after paying the mail fee?

Devising a Plan Guessing the original amount of money is one possible strategy, but it requires too many computations. Since we know the businesswoman has

$182 at the end of the second day, a more appropriate strategy for solving the problem is to retrace her steps back through the bank (see the following diagram). First she receives $1 back from the mail fee. Continue to work back through the second day in the bank.   **Question 2:** How much money did the businesswoman have at the beginning of the second day?

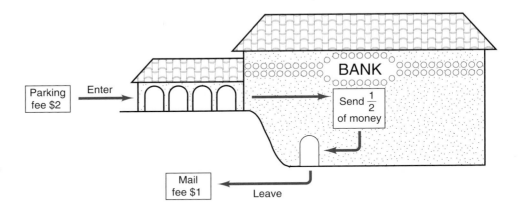

> The goal of school mathematics should be for all students to become increasingly able and willing to engage with and solve problems.
>
> Standards 2000, p.182

Carrying Out the Plan   The businesswoman had $368 at the beginning of the second day. Continue to work backward through the first day to determine how much money she had at the beginning of that day. **Question 3:** What was this amount?

Looking Back   You can now check the solution by beginning with $740, the original amount of money, and going through the expenditures for both days to see if $182 is the remaining amount. The problem can be varied by replacing $182 at the end of the second day by any amount and working backward to the beginning of the first day. **Question 4:** For example, if there was $240 at the end of the second day, what was the original amount of money?

Answers to Questions 1–4   1. $398   **2.** The following diagram shows that the businesswoman had $368 at the beginning of the second day.

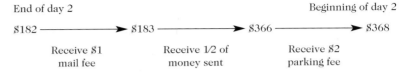

3. The diagram shows that the businesswoman had $740 at the beginning of the first day, so this is the original amount of money.

4. $972

Sometimes the main difficulty in solving a problem is knowing what question is to be answered.

EXERCISES AND PROBLEMS 1.1

Problems 1 through 20 involve strategies that were presented in this section. Some of these problems are analyzed by Polya's four-step process. See if you can solve these problems before answering parts a, b, c, and d. Other strategies may occur to you, and you are encouraged to use the ones you wish. Often a good problem requires several strategies.

MAKING A DRAWING (1–4)

1. A well is 20 feet deep. A snail at the bottom climbs up 4 feet each day and slips back 2 feet each night. How many days will it take the snail to reach the top of the well?

 a. Understanding the Problem   What is the greatest height the snail reaches during the first 24 hours? How far up the well will the snail be at the end of the first 24 hours?

 b. Devising a Plan   One plan that is commonly chosen is to compute 20/2, since it appears that the snail gains 2 feet each day. However, 10 days is not the correct answer. A second plan is to *make a drawing* and plot the snail's daily progress. What is the snail's greatest height during the second day?

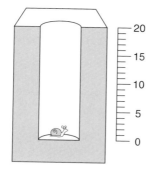

 c. Carrying Out the Plan   Trace out the snail's daily progress, and mark its position at the end of each day. On which day does the snail get out of the well?

 d. Looking Back   There is a "surprise ending" at the top of the well because the snail does not slip back on the ninth day. Make up a new snail problem by changing the numbers so that there will be a similar surprise ending at the top of the well.

2. Five people enter a racquetball tournament in which each person must play every other person exactly once. Determine the total number of games that will be played.

3. When two pieces of rope are placed end to end, their combined length is 130 feet. When the two pieces are placed side by side, one is 26 feet longer than the other. What are the lengths of the two pieces?

4. There are 560 third- and fourth-grade students in King Elementary School. If there are 80 more third-graders than fourth-graders, how many third-graders are there in the school?

MAKING A TABLE (5–8)

5. A bank that has been charging a monthly service fee of $2 for checking accounts plus 15 cents for each check announces that it will change its monthly fee to $3 and that each check will cost 8 cents. The bank claims the new plan will save the customer money. How many checks must a customer write per month before the new plan is cheaper than the old plan?

 a. Understanding the Problem   Try some numbers to get a feel for the problem. Compute the cost of 10 checks under the old plan and under the new plan. Which plan is cheaper for a customer who writes 10 checks per month?

b. Devising a Plan   One method of solving this problem is to make a table showing the cost of 1 check, 2 checks, etc., such as that shown below. How much more does the new plan cost than the old plan for 6 checks?

CHECKS	COST FOR OLD PLAN, $	COST FOR NEW PLAN, $
1	2.15	3.08
2	2.30	3.16
3	2.45	3.24
4	2.60	3.32
5	2.75	3.40
6		
7		
8		

c. Carrying Out the Plan   Extend the table until you reach a point at which the new plan is cheaper than the old plan. How many checks must be written per month for the new plan to be cheaper?

d. Looking Back   For customers who write 1 check per month, the difference in cost between the old plan and the new plan is 93 cents. What happens to the difference as the number of checks increases? How many checks must a customer write per month before the new plan is 33 cents cheaper?

6. Sasha and Francisco were selling lemonade for 25 cents per half cup and 50 cents per full cup. At the end of the day they had collected $15 and had used 37 cups. How many full cups and how many half cups did they sell?

7. Harold wrote to 15 people, and the cost of postage was $4.08. If it cost 20 cents to mail a postcard and 32 cents to mail a letter, how many postcards did he write?

8. I had some pennies, nickels, dimes, and quarters in my pocket. When I reached in and pulled out some change, I had less than 10 coins whose value was 42 cents. What are all the possibilities for the coins I had in my hand?

GUESSING AND CHECKING (9–12)

9. There are two two-digit numbers that satisfy the following conditions: (1) Each number has the same digits, (2) the sum of the digits in each number is 10, and (3) the difference between the two numbers is 54. What are the two numbers?
   a. Understanding the Problem   The numbers 58 and 85 are two-digit numbers which have the same digits, and the sum of the digits in each number is 13. Find two two-digit numbers such that the sum of the digits is 10 and both numbers have the same digits.
   b. Devising a Plan   Since there are only nine two-digit numbers whose digits have a sum of 10, the problem can be easily solved by guessing. What is the difference of your two two-digit numbers from part a? If this difference is not 54, it can provide information about your next guess.
   c. Carrying Out the Plan   Continue to guess and check. Which pair of numbers has a difference of 54?
   d. Looking Back   This problem can be extended by changing the requirement that the sum of the two digits equal 10. Solve the problem for the case in which the digits have a sum of 12.

10. When two numbers are multiplied, their product is 759; but when one is subtracted from the other, their difference is 10. What are these two numbers?

11. When asked how a person can measure out 1 gallon of water with only a 4-gallon container and a 9-gallon container, a student used this "picture."
   a. Briefly describe what the student could have shown by this sketch.
   b. Use a similar sketch to show how 6 gallons can be measured out by using these same containers.

12. Carmela opened her piggy bank and found she had $15.30. If she had only nickels, dimes, quarters, and half-dollars and an equal number of coins of each kind, how many coins in all did she have?

USING A MODEL (13–16)

13. Suppose that you have a supply of red, blue, green, and yellow square tiles. What is the fewest number of different colors needed to form a 3 × 3 square of tiles so that no tile touches another tile of the same color at any point?
   a. Understanding the Problem   Why is the square arrangement of tiles shown on page 15 not a correct solution?

b. **Devising a Plan** One plan is to choose a tile for the center of the grid and then place others around it so that no two of the same color touch. Why must the center tile be a different color than the other eight tiles?

c. **Carrying Out the Plan** Suppose that you put a blue tile in the center and a red tile in each corner, as shown here. Why will it require two more colors for the remaining openings?

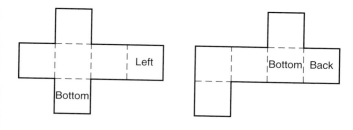

d. **Looking Back** Suppose the problem had asked for the smallest number of colors to form a square of nine tiles so that no tile touches another tile of the same color along an entire edge. Can it be done in fewer colors; if so, how many?

14. What is the smallest number of different colors of tile needed to form a 4 × 4 square so that no tile touches another of the same color along an entire edge?

15. The following patterns can be used to form a cube. A cube has six faces: the top and bottom faces, the left and right faces, and the front and back faces. Two faces have been labeled on each of the following patterns. Label the remaining four faces on each pattern so that when the cube is assembled with the labels on the outside, each face will be in the correct place.

Left
Bottom

Bottom
Back

16. At the left in the following figure is a domino doughnut with 11 dots on each side. Arrange the four single dominoes on the right into a domino doughnut so that all four sides have 12 dots.

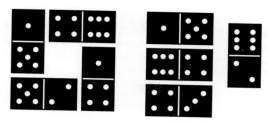

Domino doughnut

WORKING BACKWARD (17–20)

17. Three girls play three rounds of a game. On each round there are two winners and one loser. The girl who loses on a round has to double the number of chips that each of the other girls has by giving up some of her own chips. Each girl loses one round. At the end of three rounds, each girl has 40 chips. How many chips did each girl have at the beginning of the game?

a. **Understanding the Problem** Let's select some numbers to get a feel for this game. Suppose girl *A*, girl *B*, and girl *C* have 70, 30, and 20 chips, respectively, and girl *A* loses the first round. Girl *B* and girl *C* will receive chips from girl *A*, and thus their supply of chips will be doubled. How many chips will each girl have after this round?

b. **Devising a Plan** Since we know the end result (each girl finished with 40 chips), a natural strategy is to work backward through the three rounds to the beginning. Assume that girl *C* loses the third round. How many chips did each girl have at the end of the second round?

	A	*B*	*C*
Beginning			
End of first round			
End of second round			
End of third round	40	40	40

c. **Carrying Out the Plan** Assume that girl *B* loses the second round and girl *A* loses the first round. Continue working back through the three rounds to determine the number of chips each of the girls had at the beginning of the game.

d. **Looking Back** Check your answer by working forward from the beginning. The girl with the most chips at the beginning of this game lost the first round. Could the girl with the fewest chips at the beginning of the game have lost the first round? Try it.

18. Sue Ellen and Angela both have $510 in their savings accounts now. They opened their accounts on the same day, at which time Sue Ellen started with $70 more than Angela. From then on Sue Ellen added $10 to her account each week, and Angela put in $20 each week. How much money did Sue Ellen open her account with?

19. Ramon took a collection of colored tiles from a box. Amelia took 13 tiles from his collection, and Keiko took half of those remaining. Ramon had 11 left. How many did he start with?

20. Keiko had 6 more red tiles than yellow tiles. She gave half of her red tiles to Amelia and half of her yellow tiles to Ramon. If Ramon has 7 yellow tiles, how many tiles does Keiko have?

Each of problems 21 to 24 is accompanied by a sketch or diagram that was used by a student to solve it. Describe how you think the student used the diagram, and use this method to solve the problem.

21. There are three numbers. The first number is twice the second number. The third is twice the first number. Their sum is 112. What are the numbers?

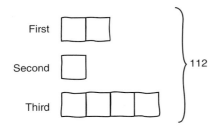

22. Mike has 3 times as many nickels as Larry has dimes. Mike has 45 cents more than Larry. How much money does Mike have?

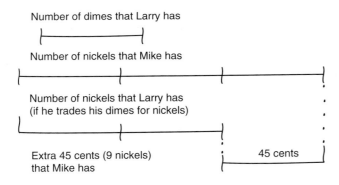

Number of dimes that Larry has

Number of nickels that Mike has

Number of nickels that Larry has
(if he trades his dimes for nickels)

Extra 45 cents (9 nickels) that Mike has   45 cents

23. At Joe's Cafe 1 cup of coffee and 3 doughnuts cost $0.90, and 2 cups of coffee and 2 doughnuts cost $1.00. What is the cost of 1 cup of coffee? 1 doughnut?

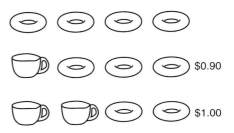

$0.90

$1.00

24. One painter can letter a billboard in 4 hours and another requires 6 hours. How long will it take them together to letter the billboard?

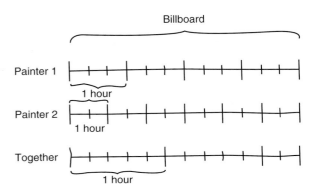

Problems 25 through 34 can be solved by using strategies presented in this section. While you are problem-solving, try to record the strategies you are using. If you are using a strategy different from those of this section, try to identify and record it.

25. There were ships with 3 masts and ships with 4 masts at the Tall Ships Exhibition. Millie counted a total of 30 masts on the 8 ships she saw. How many of these ships had 4 masts?

26. When a teacher counted her students in groups of 4, there were 2 students left over. When she counted them in groups of 5, she had 1 student left over. If 15 of her students were girls and she had more girls than boys, how many students did she have?

27. The video club to which Lin belongs allows her to receive a free movie video for every three videos she rents. If she pays $3 for each movie video and paid $132 over a 4-month period, how many free movie videos did she obtain?

28. Linda picked a basket of apples. She gave half of the apples to a neighbor, then 8 apples to her mother, then half of the remaining apples to her best friend, and she kept the 3 remaining apples for herself. How many apples did she start with in the basket?

29. Four people want to cross the river. There is only one boat available, and it can carry a maximum of 200 pounds. The weights of the four people are 190,

170, 110, and 90 pounds. How can they all manage to get across the river, and what is the minimum number of crossings required for the boat?

30. A farmer has to get a fox, a goose, and a bag of corn across a river in a boat which is only large enough for her and one of these three items. She does not want to leave the fox alone with the goose nor the goose alone with the corn. How can she get all these items across the river?

31. Three circular cardboard disks have numbers written on the front and back sides. The front sides have the numbers shown below.

By tossing all three disks and adding the numbers that show face up, we can obtain these totals: 15, 16, 17, 18, 19, 20, 21, and 22. What numbers are written on the back sides of these disks?

32. By moving adjacent disks two at a time, you can change the arrangement of large and small disks shown below to an arrangement in which 3 big disks are side by side followed by the 3 little disks. Describe the steps.

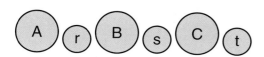

33. How can a chef use an 11-minute hourglass and a 7-minute hourglass to time vegetables that must steam for 15 minutes?

34. The curator of an art exhibit wants to place security guards along the four walls of a large auditorium so that each wall has the same number of guards. Any guard who is placed in a corner can watch the two adjacent walls, but each of the other guards can watch only the wall by which she or he is placed.
   a. Draw a sketch to show how this can be done with 6 security guards.
   b. Show how this can be done for each of the following numbers of security guards: 7, 8, 9, 10, 11, and 12.
   c. List all the numbers less than 100 that are solutions to this problem.

35. Trick questions like the following are fun, and they can help improve problem-solving ability because they require that a person listen and think carefully about the information and the question.
   a. Take 2 apples from 3 apples, and what do you have?
   b. A farmer had 17 sheep, and all but 9 died. How many sheep did he have left?
   c. I have two U.S. coins that total 30 cents. One is not a nickel. What are the two coins?
   d. A bottle of cider costs 86 cents. The cider costs 60 cents more than the bottle. How much does the bottle cost?
   e. How much dirt is in a hole 3 feet long, 2 feet wide, and 2 feet deep?
   f. A hen weighs 3 pounds plus half its weight. How much does it weigh?
   g. There are nine brothers in a family and each brother has a sister. How many children are in the family?
   h. Which of the following expressions is correct? (1) The whites of the egg are yellow. (2) The whites of the egg is yellow.

ONLINE LEARNING CENTER   www.mhhe.com/bennett-nelson
   • Math Investigation 1.1   *Four-Digit Numbers*
   Section Related: • Links   • Writing/Discussion Problems   • Bibliography

MATH ACTIVITY 1.2

PATTERN BLOCK SEQUENCES

Materials: Pattern block pieces in the Manipulative Kit.

1. Here are the first four pattern block figures of a sequence composed of trapezoids (red) and parallelograms (white).

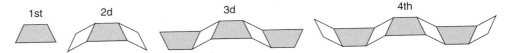

1st   2d   3d   4th

*a. Find a pattern and use your pattern blocks to build a fifth figure. Sketch this figure.

*b. If the pattern is continued, how many trapezoids and parallelograms will be in the 10th figure?

c. What pattern blocks are on each end of the 35th figure in the sequence, and how many of each shape are in that figure?

d. Determine the total number of pattern blocks in the 75th figure, and write an explanation describing how you reached your conclusion.

2. Figures 1, 3, 5, and 7 are shown from a sequence using hexagons, squares, and triangles.

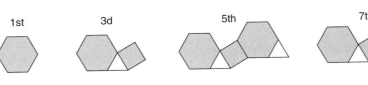

1st   3d   5th   7th

a. Find a pattern and use your pattern blocks to build the eighth and ninth figures.

*b. Write a description of the 20th figure.

c. Write a description of the 174th, 175th, and 176th figures, and include the number of hexagons, squares, and triangles in each.

3. Use your pattern blocks to build figures 8 and 9 of the following sequence.

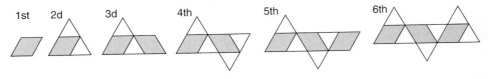

1st 2d 3d 4th 5th 6th

*a. Describe the pattern by which you extend the sequence. Determine the number of triangles and parallelograms in the 20th figure.

b. How many pattern blocks are in the 45th figure?

c. The fifth figure in the sequence has 7 pattern blocks. What is the number of the figure which has 87 blocks? Explain your reasoning.

SECTION 1.2

PATTERNS AND PROBLEM SOLVING

The great spiral galaxy Andromeda

PROBLEM OPENER

This matchstick track has 4 squares. If the pattern of squares is continued, how many matches will be needed to build a track with 60 squares?

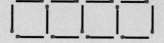

Patterns play a major role in the solution of problems in all areas of life. Psychologists analyze patterns of human behavior; meteorologists study weather patterns; astronomers seek patterns in the movements of stars and galaxies; and detectives look for patterns among clues. Finding a pattern is such a useful problem-solving strategy in mathematics that some have called it the *art of mathematics*.

To find patterns, we need to compare and contrast. We must compare to find features that remain constant and contrast to find those that are changing. Patterns appear in many forms. There are number patterns, geometric patterns, word patterns, and letter patterns, to name a few. Try finding a pattern in each of the following sequences, and write or sketch the next term.

Example A

1, 2, 4,

Solution One possibility: Each term is twice the previous term. The next term is 8.

Example B

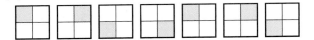

Solution   One possibility: In each block of four squares, one square is shaded. The upper left, upper right, lower left, and lower right corners are shaded in order. The next term in this sequence has the shaded block in the lower right corner.

Example C

Al, Bev, Carl, Donna

Solution   One possibility: The first letters of the names are consecutive letters of the alphabet. The next name begins with E.

> Historically, much of the mathematics used today was developed to model real-world situations, with the goal of making predictions about those situations. Students in grades 3–5 develop the idea that a mathematical model has both descriptive and predictive power.
>
> Standards 2000, p. 162

Finding a pattern requires making educated guesses. You are guessing the pattern based on some observation, and a different observation may lead to another pattern. In Example A, the difference between the first and second terms is 1, and the difference between the second and third terms is 2. So using differences between consecutive terms as the basis of the pattern, we would have a difference of 3 between the third and fourth terms, and the fourth term would be 7 rather than 8. In Example C, we might use the pattern of alternating masculine and feminine names or of increasing numbers of letters in the names.

Patterns in Nature

The spiral is a common pattern in nature. It is found in spider webs, seashells, plants, animals, weather patterns, and the shapes of galaxies. The frequent occurrence of spirals in living things can be explained by different growth rates. Living forms curl because the faster-growing (longer) surface lies outside and the slower growing (shorter) surface lies inside. An example of a living spiral is the shell of the mollusk chambered nautilus (Figure 1.2). As it grows, the creature lives in successively larger compartments.

Figure 1.2
Chambered nautilus
Courtesy of the American Museum of Natural History.

A variety of patterns occur in plants and trees. Many of these patterns are related to a famous sequence of numbers called the **Fibonacci numbers.** After the first two numbers of this sequence, which are 1 and 1, each successive number may be obtained by adding the two previous numbers.

$$1, 1, 2, 3, 5, 8, 13, 21, 34, 55, \ldots$$

Research Statement

Teachers need to provide all students with experiences in which they identify the underlying rules for a variety of patterns that embody both constant and nonconstant rates of change.

Blume and Heckman 1997

The seeds in the center of a daisy are arranged in two intersecting sets of spirals, one turning clockwise and the other turning counterclockwise. The number of spirals in each set is a Fibonacci number. Also, the number of petals will often be a Fibonacci number. The daisy in Figure 1.3 has 21 petals.

Figure 1.3

HISTORICAL HIGHLIGHT

Month
1st
2d
3d
4th
5th

Fibonacci numbers were discovered by the Italian mathematician Leonardo Fibonacci (ca. 1175–1250) while studying the birthrates of rabbits. Suppose that a pair of baby rabbits is too young to produce more rabbits the first month, but produces a pair of baby rabbits every month thereafter. Each new pair of rabbits will follow the same rule. The pairs of rabbits for the first 5 months are shown here. The numbers of pairs of rabbits for the first 5 months are the Fibonacci numbers 1, 1, 2, 3, 5. If this birthrate pattern is continued, the numbers of pairs of rabbits in succeeding months will be Fibonacci numbers. The realization that Fibonacci numbers could be applied to the science of plants and trees occurred several hundred years after the discovery of this number sequence.

Number Patterns

Number patterns have fascinated people since the beginning of recorded history. One of the earliest patterns to be recognized led to the distinction between **even numbers**

$$0, 2, 4, 6, 8, 10, 12, 14, \ldots$$

and **odd numbers**

$$1, 3, 5, 7, 9, 11, 13, 15, \ldots$$

The game Even and Odd has been played for generations. To play this game, one person picks up some stones, and a second person guesses whether the number of stones is odd or even. If the guess is correct, the second person wins.

PASCAL'S TRIANGLE   The triangular pattern of numbers shown in Figure 1.4 is Pascal's triangle. It has been of interest to mathematicians for hundreds of years, appearing in China as early as 1303. This triangle is named after the French mathematician Blaise Pascal (1623–1662), who wrote a book on some of its uses.

Figure 1.4

```
Row 0                      1
Row 1                  1      1
Row 2              1      2      1
Row 3          1      3      3      1
Row 4      1      4      6      4      1
```

Example D

1. Find a pattern that might explain the numbering of the rows as 0, 1, 2, 3, etc.

2. In the fourth row, each of the numbers 4, 6, and 4 can be obtained by adding the two adjacent numbers from the row above it. What numbers are in the fifth row of Pascal's triangle?

Solution   1. Except for row 0, the second number in each row is the number of the row.   2. 1, 5, 10, 10, 5, 1

ARITHMETIC SEQUENCE   Sequences of numbers are often generated by patterns. The sequences 1, 2, 3, 4, 5, . . . and 2, 4, 6, 8, 10, . . . are among the first that children learn. In such sequences, each new number is obtained from the previous number in the sequence by adding a selected number throughout. This selected number is called the **common difference**, and the sequence is called an **arithmetic sequence**.

Example E

$$7, 11, 15, 19, 23, \ldots$$
$$172, 256, 340, 424, 508, \ldots$$

The first arithmetic sequence has a common difference of 4. What is the common difference for the second sequence? Write the next three terms in each sequence.

Solution   The next three terms in the first sequence are 27, 31, and 35. The common difference for the second sequence is 84, and the next three terms are 592, 676, and 760.

GEOMETRIC SEQUENCE   In a geometric sequence, each new number is obtained by multiplying the previous number by a selected number. This selected number is called the **common ratio**, and the resulting sequence is called a **geometric sequence**.

Example F

$$3, 6, 12, 24, 48, \ldots$$
$$1, 5, 25, 125, 625, \ldots$$

Objective: Find a pattern to solve a problem.

5·7 Problem Solving: Strategy
Find a Pattern

Read ➤ **Read the problem carefully.**

Tamara arranged pine cones into different groups. She started with one pine cone in the first group. In the next group she put 2 pine cones. She put 4 pine cones in the third group, 8 pine cones in the fourth, and so on. If the number in each row continues to increase in the same way, how many pine cones does she put in the eighth group?

- **What do you know?** The number in the first four rows
- **What do you need to find?** The number to put in the eighth group

Plan ➤ One way to solve the problem is to find a pattern. Look at how the number of pine cones in each group changes.

Solve ➤ The number of pine cones doubles each time.

$$1 \xrightarrow{\times 2} 2 \xrightarrow{\times 2} 4 \xrightarrow{\times 2}$$

Continue the pattern to find how many pine cones will be in the eighth group.

$$1 \xrightarrow{\times 2} 2 \xrightarrow{\times 2} 4 \xrightarrow{\times 2} 8 \xrightarrow{\times 2} 16 \xrightarrow{\times 2} 32 \xrightarrow{\times 2} 64 \xrightarrow{\times 2} 128$$

Tamara puts 128 pine cones in the eighth group.

Look Back ➤ Is there another way to describe the pattern above?

Sum it Up! What other strategies could you use to solve this problem?

210 Cluster B

Initially, students may describe the regularity in patterns verbally rather than with mathematical symbols (English and Warren 1998). In grades 3–5, they can begin to use variables and algebraic expressions as they describe and extend patterns.

Standards 2000, p. 38

The common ratio in the first sequence is 2. What is the common ratio in the second sequence? Write the next two terms in each sequence.

Solution   The next two terms in the first sequence are 96 and 192. The common ratio for the second sequence is 5, and the next two terms are 3125 and 15,625.

TRIANGULAR NUMBERS   The sequence of numbers illustrated in Figure 1.5 is neither arithmetic nor geometric. These numbers are called **triangular numbers** because of the arrangement of dots that is associated with each number. Since each triangular number is the sum of whole numbers beginning with 1, the formula for the sum of consecutive whole numbers can be used to obtain triangular numbers.*

Figure 1.5

1   3   6   10   15

Example G   The first triangular number is 1, and the fifth triangular number is 15. What is the sixth triangular number?

Solution   The sixth triangular number is 21.

HISTORICAL HIGHLIGHT

Karl Friedrich Gauss
1777–1855

Archimedes, Newton, and the German mathematician Karl Friedrich Gauss are considered to be the three greatest mathematicians of all time. Gauss exhibited a cleverness with numbers at an early age. The story is told that at age 3, as he watched his father making out the weekly payroll for laborers of a small bricklaying business, Gauss pointed out an error in the computation. Gauss enjoyed telling the story later in life and joked that he could figure before he could talk. Gauss kept a mathematical diary, which contained records of many of his discoveries. Some of the results were entered cryptically. For example,

$$\text{Num} = \Delta + \Delta + \Delta$$

is an abbreviated statement that every whole number greater than zero is the sum of three or fewer triangular numbers.*

*H. W. Eves, *In Mathematical Circles* (Boston: Prindle, Weber, and Schmidt, 1969), pp. 111–115.

There are other types of numbers that receive their names from the numbers of dots in geometric figures (see 28–30 in Exercises and Problems 1.2). Such

*The computer program Triangular Numbers in the *Mathematics Investigator* software (see website) prints sequences of triangular numbers.

numbers are called **figurate numbers,** and they represent one kind of link between geometry and arithmetic.

FINITE DIFFERENCES   Often sequences of numbers don't appear to have a pattern. However, sometimes number patterns can be found by looking at the differences between consecutive terms. This approach is called the method of **finite differences.**

Example H

Consider the sequence 0, 3, 8, 15, 24, ... Find a pattern and determine the next term.

Solution   Using the method of finite differences, we can obtain a second sequence of numbers by computing the differences between numbers from the original sequence, as shown below. Then a third sequence is obtained by computing the differences from the second sequence. The process stops when all the numbers in the sequence of differences are equal. In this example, when the sequence becomes all 2s, we stop and work our way back from the bottom row to the original sequence. Assuming the pattern of 2s continues, the next number after 9 is 11, so the next number after 24 is 35.

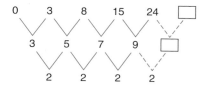

Example I

Use the method of finite differences to determine the next term in each sequence

1. 3, 6, 13, 24, 39

2. 1, 5, 14, 30, 55, 91

Solution   **1.** The next number in the sequence is 58.   **2.** The next number in the sequence is 140.

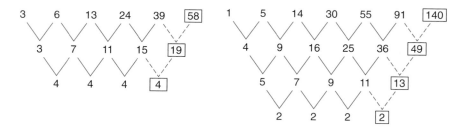

Inductive Reasoning

The process of forming conclusions on the basis of patterns, observations, examples, or experiments is called **inductive reasoning.**

Identifying patterns is a powerful problem solving strategy. It is also the essence of inductive reasoning. As students explore problem situations appropriate to their grade level, they can often consider or generate a set of specific instances, organize them, and look for a pattern. These, in turn, can lead to conjectures about the problem.*

Example J

Each of these sums of three consecutive whole numbers is divisible by 3.

$$4 + 5 + 6 = 15 \qquad 2 + 3 + 4 = 9 \qquad 7 + 8 + 9 = 24$$

If we conclude, on the basis of these sums, that the sum of any three consecutive whole numbers is divisible by 3, we are using inductive reasoning.

Inductive reasoning may be thought of as making an "informed guess." Although this type of reasoning is important in mathematics, it sometimes leads to incorrect results.

Example K

Consider the number of regions that can be obtained in a circle by connecting points on the circumference of the circle. Connecting 2 points produces 2 regions, connecting 3 points produces 4 regions, and so on. Each time a new point on the circle is used, the number of regions appears to double.

Because many elementary and middle school tasks rely on inductive reasoning, teachers need to be aware that students might develop an incorrect expectation that patterns always generalize in ways that would be expected on the basis of the regularities found in the first few terms.

Standards 2000, p. 265

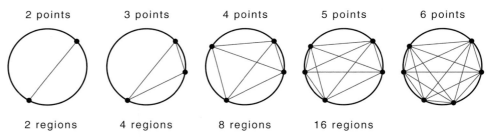

The numbers of regions in the circles above are the beginning of the geometric sequence 2, 4, 8, 16, . . . , and it is tempting to conclude that 6 points will produce 32 regions. However, no matter how the 6 points are located on the circle, there will not be more than 31 regions.

COUNTEREXAMPLE   An example that shows a statement to be false is called a **counterexample.** If you have a general statement, test it to see if it is true for a few special cases. You may be able to find a counterexample to show that the statement is not true, or that a conjecture cannot be proved.

Example L

Find two whole numbers for which the following statement is false: The sum of any two whole numbers is divisible by 2.

Solution   It is not true for 7 and 4, since $7 + 4 = 11$, and 11 is not divisible by 2. There are pairs of whole numbers for which the statement is true. For example, $3 + 7 = 10$, and 10 is divisible by 2.

Curriculum and Evaluation Standards for School Mathematics (Reston, VA: National Council of Teachers of Mathematics, 1989), p. 82.

However, the counterexample of the sum of 7 and 4 shows that the statement is not true for all pairs of whole numbers.

Counterexamples can help us to restate a conjecture. The statement in Example L is false, but if it is changed to read "The sum of two odd numbers is divisible by 2," it becomes a true statement.

Example **M**

For which of the following statements is there a counterexample? If a statement is false, change a condition to produce a true statement.

1. The sum of any four whole numbers is divisible by 2.

2. The sum of any two even numbers is divisible by 2.

3. The sum of any three consecutive whole numbers is divisible by 2.

Solution   1. The following counterexample shows that statement 1 is false: $4 + 12 + 6 + 3 = 25$, which is not divisible by 2. If the condition "four whole numbers" is replaced by "four even numbers," the statement becomes true. **2.** Statement 2 is true. **3.** The following counterexample shows that statement 3 is false: $8 + 9 + 10 = 27$, which is not divisible by 2. If the condition "three consecutive whole numbers" is replaced by "three consecutive whole numbers beginning with an odd number," the statement becomes true.

HISTORICAL HIGHLIGHT

Leaning Tower of Pisa, Pisa, Italy

Aristotle (384–322 B.C.), Greek scientist and philosopher, believed that heavy objects fall faster than lighter ones, and this principle was accepted as true for hundreds of years. Then in the sixteenth century, Galileo produced a counterexample by dropping two pieces of metal from the Leaning Tower of Pisa. In spite of the fact that one was twice as heavy as the other, both hit the ground at the same time.

Problem-Solving Application

The strategies of **solving a simpler problem** and **finding a pattern** are introduced in the following problem. Simplifying a problem or solving a related but easier problem can help in understanding the given information and devising a plan for the solution. Sometimes the numbers in a problem are large or inconvenient, and finding a solution for smaller numbers can lead to a plan or reveal a pattern for solving the original problem. Read this problem and try to solve it. Then read the following four-step solution and compare it to your solution.

PROBLEM

There are 15 people in a room, and each person shakes hands exactly once with everyone else. How many handshakes take place?

Understanding the Problem   For each pair of people, there will be 1 handshake. For example, if Sue and Paul shake hands, this is counted as 1 handshake. Thus, the problem is to determine the total number of different ways that 15 people can be paired. **Question 1:** How many handshakes will occur when 3 people shake hands?

Sue   Paul

Devising a Plan   Fifteen people are a lot of people to work with at one time. Let's simplify the problem and count the number of handshakes for small groups of people. Solving these special cases may give us an idea for solving the original problem. **Question 2:** What is the number of handshakes in a group of 4 people?

Carrying Out the Plan   We have already noted that there is 1 handshake for 2 people, 3 handshakes for 3 people, and 6 handshakes for 4 people. The following figure illustrates how 6 handshakes will occur among 4 people. Suppose a fifth person joins the group. This person will shake hands with each of the first 4 people, accounting for 4 more handshakes.

Fifth person

Similarly, if we bring in a 6th person, this person will shake hands with the first 5 people, and so there will be 5 new handshakes. Suddenly we can see a pattern developing: The 5th person adds 4 new handshakes, the 6th person adds 5 new handshakes, the 7th person adds 6 new handshakes, and so on until the 15th person adds 14 new handshakes. **Question 3:** How many handshakes will there be for 15 people?

Looking Back   By looking at special cases with numbers smaller than 15, we obtained a better understanding of the problem and an insight for solving it. The pattern we found suggests a method for determining the number of handshakes for any number of people: Add the whole numbers from 1 to the number that is 1 less than the number of people. You may recall from Section 1.1 that staircases were used to develop a formula for computing such a sum. **Question 4:** How can this formula be used to determine the number of handshakes for 15 people?

Answers to Questions 1–4   1. 3   2. 6   3. $1 + 2 + 3 + 4 + 5 + 6 + 7 + 8 + 9 + 10 + 11 + 12 + 13 + 14 = 105$ 4. The sum of whole numbers from 1 to 14 is $(14 \times 15)/2 = 105$.

EXERCISES AND PROBLEMS 1.2

NCTM's K–4 Standard *Patterns and Relationships* notes that identifying the *core* of a pattern helps children become aware of the structure.* For example, in some patterns there is a core that repeats, as in exercise 1a. In some patterns there is a core that grows, as in exercise 2b. Classify each of the sequences in 1 and 2 as having a core that repeats or that grows, and determine the next few elements in each sequence.

1. a.
(PS)
   b. ✗ ✗ + ✗ ✗ ✗ + ✗ ✗ ✗ + ✗ · · ·

   c. ○ ✳ ○○○ ✳ ○○○○ ✳ ○○○○ · · ·

2. a.
(PS)
   b. 1, 2, 1, 1, 2, 3, 2, 1, 1, 2, 3, 4, 3, 2, 1, . . .
   c. 2, 3, 5, 7, 2, 3, 5, 7, 2, 3, 5, 7, . . .

Some sequences have a pattern, but they do not have a core. Determine the next three numbers in each of the sequences in exercises 3 and 4.

   3. a. 2, 5, 8, 11, 14, 17, 20, 23, . . .
(PS) **b.** 13, 16, 19, 23, 27, 32, 37, 43, . . .
   c. 17, 22, 20, 25, 23, 28, 26, 31, . . .

   4. a. 31, 28, 25, 22, 19, 16, . . .
(PS) **b.** 46, 48, 50, 54, 58, 64, 70, 78, 86, . . .
   c. 43, 46, 49, 45, 41, 44, 47, 43, 39, . . .

One method of stacking cannonballs is to form a pyramid with a square base. The first six such pyramids are shown. Use these figures in exercises 5 and 6.

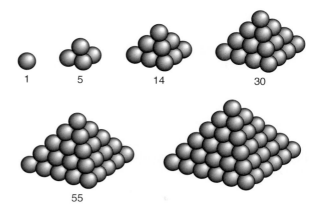

1   5   14   30

55

5. a. How many cannonballs are in the sixth figure?
(PS) **b.** Can the method of finite differences be used to find the number of cannonballs in the sixth figure?
   c. Describe the 10th pyramid, and determine the number of cannonballs.

6. a. Describe the seventh pyramid, and determine the
(PS)   number of cannonballs.
   b. Do the numbers of cannonballs in successive figures form an arithmetic sequence?
   c. Write an expression for the number of cannonballs in the 20th figure. (*Note:* It is not necessary to compute the number.)

Curriculum and Evaluation Standards for School Mathematics (Reston, VA: National Council of Teachers of Mathematics, 1989), p. 61.

Use the following sequence of figures in exercises 7 and 8.

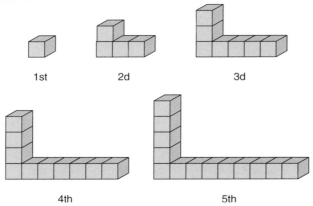

1st   2d   3d

4th   5th

7. a. What type of sequence is formed by the numbers of cubes in successive figures?
   b. Describe the 20th figure and determine the number of cubes.

8. a. Can the method of finite differences be used to determine the number of cubes in the 6th figure?
   b. Describe the 100th figure and determine the number of cubes.
   c. Write an expression for the number of cubes in the nth figure, for any whole number n.

There are many patterns and number relationships that can be easily discovered on a calendar. Some of these patterns are explored in exercises 9 through 11.

NOVEMBER 2002

Sun	Mon	Tue	Wed	Thu	Fri	Sat
					1	2
3	4	5	6	7	8	9
10	11	12	13	(14)	(15)	(16)
17	18	19	20	21	22	23
24	25	26	27	28	29	30

9. The sum of the three circled numbers on the preceding calendar is 45. For any sum of three consecutive numbers (from the rows), there is a quick method for determining the numbers. Explain how this can be done. Try your method to find three consecutive numbers whose sum is 54.

10. If you are told the sum of any three adjacent numbers from a column, it is possible to determine the three numbers. Explain how this can be done, and use your method to find the numbers whose sum is 48.

11. The sum of the 3 × 3 array of numbers outlined on the preceding calendar is 99. There is a shortcut method for using this sum to find the 3 × 3 array of numbers. Explain how this can be done. Try using your method to find the 3 × 3 array with sum 198.

12. Here are the first few Fibonacci numbers: 1, 1, 2, 3, 5, 8, 13, 21, 34, 55. Compute the sums shown below, and compare the answers with the Fibonacci numbers. Find a pattern and explain how this pattern can be used to find the sums of consecutive Fibonacci numbers.

$$1 + 1 + 2 =$$
$$1 + 1 + 2 + 3 =$$
$$1 + 1 + 2 + 3 + 5 =$$
$$1 + 1 + 2 + 3 + 5 + 8 =$$
$$1 + 1 + 2 + 3 + 5 + 8 + 13 =$$
$$1 + 1 + 2 + 3 + 5 + 8 + 13 + 21 =$$

13. The sums of the squares of consecutive Fibonacci numbers form a pattern when written as a product of two numbers.
   a. Complete the missing sums and find a pattern.
   b. Use your pattern to explain how the sum of the squares of the first few consecutive Fibonacci numbers can be found.

$$1^2 + 1^2 = 1 \times 2$$
$$1^2 + 1^2 + 2^2 = 2 \times 3$$
$$1^2 + 1^2 + 2^2 + 3^2 = 3 \times 5$$
$$1^2 + 1^2 + 2^2 + 3^2 + 5^2 =$$
$$1^2 + 1^2 + 2^2 + 3^2 + 5^2 + 8^2 =$$
$$1^2 + 1^2 + 2^2 + 3^2 + 5^2 + 8^2 + 13^2 =$$

A Fibonacci-type sequence can be started with any two numbers. Then each successive number is formed by adding the two previous numbers. Each number after 3 and 4 in the sequence 3, 4, 7, 11, 18, 29, etc. was obtained by adding the previous two numbers. Find the missing numbers among the first 10 numbers of the Fibonacci-type sequences in exercises 14 and 15.

14. a. 10, _____, 24, _____, _____, 100, _____, _____, _____, 686
   b. 2, _____, _____, 16, 25, _____, _____, _____, _____, 280
   c. The sum of the first 10 numbers in the sequence in part a is equal to 11 times the seventh number, 162. What is this sum?
   d. Can the sum of the first 10 numbers in the sequence in part b be obtained by multiplying the seventh number by 11?
   e. Do you think the sum of the first 10 numbers in any Fibonacci-type sequence will always be 11 times the seventh number? Try some other Fibonacci-type sequences to support your conclusion.

15. a. 1, _____, _____, 11, _____, _____, _____, _____, 118, _____

  b. 14, _____, 20, 26, _____, _____, 118, _____, _____, 498

  c. The sum of the first 10 numbers in part a is equal to 11 times the seventh number. Is this true for the sequence in part b?

  d. Is the sum of the first 10 numbers in the Fibonacci sequence equal to 11 times the seventh number in that sequence?

  e. Form a conjecture based on your observations in parts c and d.

16. The products of 1089 and the first few digits produce some interesting number patterns. Describe one of these patterns. Will this pattern continue if 1089 is multiplied by 5, 6, 7, 8, and 9?

$$1 \times 1089 = 1089$$
$$2 \times 1089 = 2178$$
$$3 \times 1089 = 3267$$
$$4 \times 1089 = 4356$$
$$5 \times 1089 =$$

17. a. Find a pattern in the following equations, and use your pattern to write the next equation.

  b. If the pattern in the first three equations is continued, what will be the 20th equation?

$$1 + 2 = 3$$
$$4 + 5 + 6 = 7 + 8$$
$$9 + 10 + 11 + 12 = 13 + 14 + 15$$

In Pascal's triangle, which is shown below, there are many patterns. Use this triangle of numbers in exercises 18 through 21.

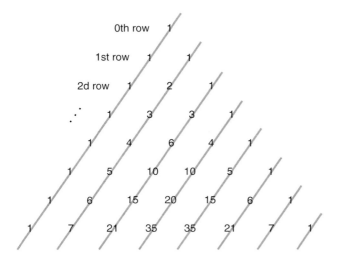

18. Add the first few numbers in the first diagonal of Pascal's triangle (diagonals are marked by lines),

starting from the top. This sum will be another number from the triangle. Will this be true for the sums of the first few numbers in the other diagonals? Support your conclusion with examples.

19. The third diagonal in Pascal's triangle has the numbers 1, 3, 6, ...

  a. What is the 10th number in this diagonal?

  b. What is the 10th number in the fourth diagonal?

20. Compute the sums of the numbers in the first few rows of Pascal's triangle. What kind of sequence (arithmetic or geometric) do these sums form?

21. What will be the sum of the numbers in the 12th row of Pascal's triangle?

Identify each of the sequences in exercises 22 and 23 as arithmetic or geometric. State a rule for obtaining each number from the preceding number. What is the 12th number in each sequence?

22. a. 280, 257, 234, 211, . . .

  b. 17, 51, 153, 459, . . .

  c. 32, 64, 128, 256, . . .

  d. 87, 102, 117, 132, . . .

23. a. 4, 9, 14, 19, . . .

  b. 15, 30, 60, 120, . . .

  c. 24, 20, 16, 12, . . .

  d. 4, 12, 36, 108, . . .

The method of finite differences is used in exercises 24 and 25. This method will sometimes enable you to find the next number in a sequence, but not always.

24. a. Write the first eight numbers of a geometric sequence, and try using the method of finite differences to find the ninth number. Will this method work?

  b. Repeat part a for an arithmetic sequence. Support your conclusions.

25. a. Will the method of finite differences produce the next number in the diagonals of Pascal's triangle? Support your conclusions with examples.

  b. The sums of the numbers in the first few rows of Pascal's triangle are 1, 2, 4, 8, ... Will the method of finite differences produce the next number in this sequence?

Use the method of finite differences in exercises 26 and 27 to find the next number in each sequence.

26. a. 3, 7, 13, 21, 31, 43, . . .

  b. 215, 124, 63, 26, 7, . . .

27. a. 1, 2, 7, 22, 53, 106, . . .

  b. 1, 3, 11, 25, 45, 71, . . .

As early as 500 B.C., the Greeks were interested in numbers associated with patterns of dots in the shape of geometric figures. Write the next three numbers and the 100th number in each sequence in exercises 28 through 30.

28. Triangular numbers:

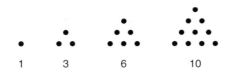

29. Square numbers:

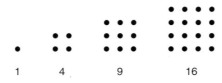

30. Pentagonal numbers. (After the first figure these are five-sided figures composed of figures for triangular numbers and square numbers.)

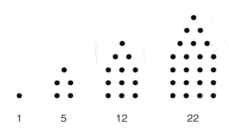

The Greeks called the numbers represented by the following arrays of dots **oblong numbers.** Use this pattern in exercises 31 and 32.

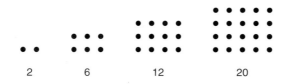

31. a. What is the next oblong number?
   b. What is the 20th oblong number?

32. a. Can the method of finite differences be used to obtain the number of dots in the 5th oblong number?
   b. What is the 25th oblong number?

33. The numbers in the following sequence are the first six pentagonal numbers: 1, 5, 12, 22, 35, 51.
   a. If the method of finite differences is used, what type of sequence is produced by the first sequence of differences?
   b. Can the method of finite differences be used to obtain the next few pentagonal numbers from the first six?

34. Use the method of finite differences to create a new sequence of numbers for the following sequence of square numbers.

$$1, 4, 9, 16, 25, 36, 49, 64, 81$$

   a. What kind of a sequence do you obtain?
   b. How can a square arrays of dots (see exercise 29) be used to show that the difference of two consecutive square numbers will be an odd number?

What kind of reasoning is used to arrive at the conclusions in the articles in exercises 35 and 36?

35.

Vitamin C student finds a little is best

By Nancy Hicks
New York Times News Service

NEW YORK – A Canadian researcher has reported finding therapeutic value in using Vitamin C to treat symptoms of the common cold in much lower doses than had been previously recommended.

Dr. Terence W. Anderson, an epidemiologist at the University of Toronto, reported a 30 per cent reduction in the severity of cold symptoms in persons who took only a small amount of Vitamin C – less than 250 milligrams a day regularly, and one gram a day when symptoms of a cold began.

Anderson's conclusion was based on a study of 600 volunteers.

36.

> ## Operating room work may have health hazards
>
> WASHINGTON (UPI) – There is an increase in cancer and other disease rates among hospital operating room personnel and a report Monday said regular exposure to anesthetic gases appears to be the most likely cause.
>
> A survey of 49,585 operating room personnel indicated that female anesthetists and nurses are the most vulnerable, particularly if they are pregnant.
>
> "The results of the survey strongly suggest that working in the operating room and, presumably, exposure to trace concentrations of anesthetic agents entails a variety of health hazards for operating personnel and their offspring."

37. Continue the pattern of even numbers illustrated below.

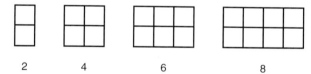

2   4   6   8

a. The fourth even number is 8. Sketch the figure for the ninth even number and determine this number.

b. What is the 45th even number?

38. Continue the pattern of odd numbers illustrated below.

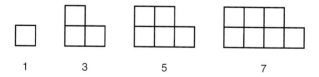

1   3   5   7

a. The fourth odd number is 7. Sketch the figure for the 12th odd number.

b. What is the 35th odd number?

39. If we begin with the number 6, then double it to get 12, and then place the 12 and 6 side by side, the result is 126. This number is divisible by 7. Try this procedure for some other numbers. Find a counterexample which shows that the result is not always evenly divisible by 7.

Find a counterexample for each of the statements in exercises 40 and 41.

40. a. Every whole number greater than 4 and less than 20 is the sum of two or more consecutive whole numbers.

b. Every whole number between 25 and 50 is the product of two whole numbers greater than 1.

41. a. The product of any two whole numbers is evenly divisible by 2.

b. Every whole number greater than 5 is the sum of either two or three consecutive whole numbers, for example, $11 = 5 + 6$ and $18 = 5 + 6 + 7$.

Determine which statements in exercises 42 and 43 are false, and show a counterexample for each false statement. If a statement is false, change one of the conditions to obtain a true statement.

42. a. The product of any three consecutive whole numbers is divisible by 2.

b. The sum of any two consecutive whole numbers is divisible by 2.

43. a. The sum of any four consecutive whole numbers is divisible by 4.

b. Every whole number greater than 0 and less than 15 is either a triangular number or the sum of two or three triangular numbers.

REASONING AND PROBLEM SOLVING

44. Featured Strategy: Solving a Simpler Problem
PS You are given 8 coins and a balance scale. The coins look alike, but one is counterfeit and lighter than the others. Find the counterfeit coin, using just 2 weighings on the balance scale.

a. Understanding the Problem If there were only 2 coins and 1 were counterfeit and lighter, the bad coin could be determined in just 1 weighing. The balance scale below shows this situation. Is the counterfeit coin on the left or right side of the balance beam?

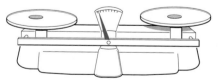

b. Devising a Plan One method of solving this problem is to guess and check. It is natural to begin with 4 coins on each side of the balance beam. Explain why this approach will not produce the counterfeit coin in just 2 weighings. Another method is to simplify the problem and try to solve it for fewer coins.

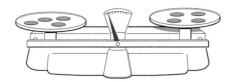

c. **Carrying Out the Plan**   Explain how the counterfeit coin can be found with 1 weighing if there are only 3 coins and with 2 weighings if there are 6 coins. By now you may have an idea for solving the original problem. How can the counterfeit coin be found in 2 weighings?

d. **Looking Back**   Explain how the counterfeit coin can be found in 2 weighings when there are 9 coins.

45. Kay started a computer club, and for a while she was the only member. She planned to have each member find two new members each month. By the end of the first month she had found two new members. If her plan is carried out, how many members will the club have at the end of the following periods?
a. 6 months   b. 1 year

46. For several years Charlie has had a tree farm where he grows blue spruce. The trees are planted in a square array (square arrays are shown in exercise 29). This year he planted 87 new trees along two adjacent edges of the square to form a larger square. How many trees are in the new square?

47. In the familiar song "The Twelve Days of Christmas," the total number of gifts received each day is a triangular number. On the first day there was 1 gift, on the second day there were 3 gifts, on the third day 6 gifts, etc., until the 12th day of Christmas.
a. How many gifts were received on the 12th day?
b. What is the total number of gifts received during all 12 days?

48. One hundred eighty seedling maple trees are to be set out in a straight line such that the distance between the centers of two adjacent trees is 12 feet. What is the distance from the center of the first tree to the center of the 180th tree?

49. In a long line of railroad cars, an Agco Refrigeration car is the 147th from the beginning of the line, and by counting from the end of the line, the refrigeration car is the 198th car. How many railroad cars are in the line?

50. If 255 square tiles with colors of blue, red, green, or yellow are placed side by side in a single row so that two tiles of the same color are not next to each other, what is the maximum possible number of red tiles?

51. A card is to be selected at random from 500 cards which are numbered with whole numbers from 1 to 500. How many of these cards have at least one 6 printed on them?

52. A deck of 300 cards is numbered with whole numbers from 1 to 300, with each card having just one number. How many of these cards do not have a 4 printed on them?

ONLINE LEARNING CENTER   www.mhhe.com/bennett-nelson

• Math Investigation 1.2   *Triangular Numbers*
Section Related: • Links   • Writing/Discussion Problems   • Bibliography

---

PUZZLER

The background in this photograph produces an illusion called the *Fraser spiral*. Can you explain what is wrong with this "spiral"?

MATH ACTIVITY 1.3

EXTENDING TILE PATTERNS

Materials: Color tiles in the Manipulative Kit.

1. Here are the first three figures in a sequence. Find a pattern and build the fourth figure.

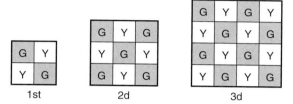

1st   2d   3d

*a. For each of the first five figures, determine how many tiles there are of each color.
   b. Find a pattern and determine the number of tiles of each color for the 10th figure.
   c. What is the total number of tiles for the 10th figure?
   d. Write a description of the 25th figure so that someone reading it could build the figure. Include in your description the number of tiles with each of the different colors and the total number of tiles in the figure.

2. Extend each of the following sequences to the fifth figure, and record the numbers of different-colored tiles in each figure. Find a pattern that enables you to determine the numbers of different-colored tiles in the 10th and 25th figures of each sequence. Describe your reasoning.

*a.

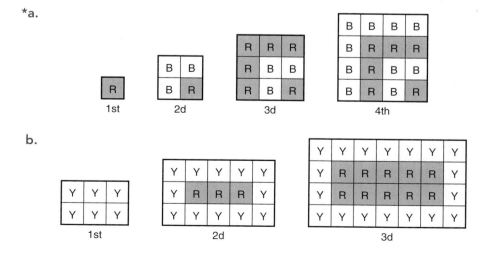

1st   2d   3d   4th

b.

SECTION 1.3

PROBLEM SOLVING WITH ALGEBRA

"If he could only think in abstract terms"

A whole brick is balanced with $\frac{3}{4}$ pound and $\frac{3}{4}$ brick. What is the weight of the whole brick?

> By viewing algebra as a strand in the curriculum from prekindergarten on, teachers can help students build a solid foundation of understanding and experience as a preparation for more-sophisticated work in algebra in the middle grades and high school.
>
> Standards 2000, p. 37

Algebra is a powerful tool for representing information and solving problems. It originated in Babylonia and Egypt more than 4000 years ago. At first there were no equations, and words rather than letters were used for variables. The Egyptians used words that have been translated as *heap* and *aha* for unknown quantities in their word problems. Here is a problem from the Rhind Papyrus, written by the Egyptian priest Ahmes about 1650 B.C.:

Heap and one-seventh of heap is 19. What is heap?

Today we would use a letter for the unknown quantity and express the given information in an equation.

$$x + \tfrac{1}{7}x = 19$$

You may wish to try solving this equation. Its solution is in Example D on the following pages.

Emmy Noether

Germany's Amalie Emmy Noether is considered to be the greatest woman mathematician of her time. She studied mathematics at the University of Erlangen, where she was one of only two women among nearly a thousand students. In 1907 she received her doctorate in mathematics from the University of Erlangen. In 1916, the legendary David Hilbert was working on the mathematics of a general relativity theory at the University of Göttingen and invited Emmy Noether to assist him. Although Göttingen had been the first university to grant a doctorate degree to a woman, it was still reluctant to offer a teaching position to a woman, no matter how great her ability and learning. When her appointment failed, Hilbert let her deliver lectures in courses that were announced under his name. Eventually she was appointed to a lectureship at the University of Göttingen. Noether became the center of an active group of algebraists in Europe, and the mathematics that grew out of her papers and lectures at Göttingen made her one of the pioneers of modern algebra. Her famous papers "The Theory of Ideals in Rings" and "Abstract Construction of Ideal Theory in the Domain of Algebraic Number Fields" are the cornerstones of modern algebra courses now presented to mathematics graduate students.*

*D. M. Burton, *The History of Mathematics,* 4th ed. (New York: McGraw-Hill, 1999), pp. 660–662.

Research indicates a variety of students have difficulties with the concept of variable (Kuchmann 1978; Kieran 1983; Wafner and Parker 1993) . . . A thorough understanding of variable develops over a long time, and it needs to be grounded in extensive experience.

Standards 2000, p. 39

Variables and Equations

A letter or symbol that is used to denote an unknown number is called a **variable**. One method of introducing variables in elementary schools is with geometric shapes such as $\square$ and $\triangle$. For example, students might be asked to find the number for $\square$ such that $\square + 7 = 12$, or to find some possibilities for $\triangle$ and $\square$ such that $\triangle + \square = 15$. These geometric symbols are less intimidating than letters. Students can replace a variable with a number by writing the numeral inside the geometric shape, as if they were filling in a blank.

To indicate the operations of addition, subtraction, and division with numbers and variables, we use the familiar signs for these operations; for example, $3 + x$, $x - 5$, $x \div 4$, and $x/4$. A product is typically indicated by writing a numeral next to a variable. For example, $6x$ represents 6 times x, or 6 times whatever number is used as a replacement for x. An expression containing algebraic symbols, such as $2x + 3$ or $(4x)(7x) - 5$, is called an **algebraic expression**.

Example A

Evaluate the following algebraic expressions for $x = 14$ and $n = 28$.

1. $15 + 3x$

2. $4n - 6$

3. $\dfrac{n}{7} + 20$

4. $6x \div 12$

Solution   **1.** $15 + 3(14) = 15 + 42 = 57$. Notice that when the variable is replaced, parentheses are used; $3(14)$ means 3 times 14.   **2.** $4(28) - 6 = 112 - 6 = 106$.   **3.** $28/7 + 20 = 4 + 20 = 24$.   **4.** $6(14) \div 12 = 84 \div 12 = 7$.

The elementary ideas of algebra can be presented early in school mathematics. Consider the following problem.

Example B

Eleanor wins the jackpot in a marble game and doubles her number of marbles. If later she wins 55 more, bringing her total to 127, how many marbles did she have at the beginning?

Solution   One possibility is to work backward from the final total of 127 marbles. Subtracting 55 leaves 72, so we need to find the number that yields 72 when doubled. This number is 36. A second approach is to work forward to obtain 127 by guessing. A guess of 20 for the original number of marbles will result in $2(20) + 55 = 95$, which is less than 127. Guesses of increasingly larger numbers eventually will lead to a solution of 36 marbles.

Example B says that if some unknown number of marbles is doubled and 55 more are added, the total is 127. This numerical information is stated in the following *equation* in which the variable x represents the original number of marbles.

$$2x + 55 = 127$$

An **equation** is a statement of the equality of mathematical expressions; it is a sentence in which the verb is *equals* ($=$).

A *balance scale* is one model for introducing equations in the elementary school. The idea of *balance* is related to the concept of *equality*. A balance scale with its corresponding equation is shown in Figure 1.6. If each chip on the scale has the same weight, the weight on the left side of the scale *equals* (is the same as) the weight on the right side. Similarly, the sum of numbers on the left side of the equation *equals* the number on the right side.

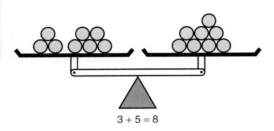

$3 + 5 = 8$

Figure 1.6

The balance scale in Figure 1.7 models the *missing-addend* form of subtraction, that is, what number must be added to 5 to obtain 11. The box on the scale may be thought of as *taking the place of*, or *hiding*, the chips needed to balance the scale.

One approach to determining the number of chips needed to balance the scale is to *guess and check*. Another approach is to notice that by removing 5 chips from both sides of the scale in Figure 1.7, we obtain the scale shown in Figure 1.8. This scale shows that the box must be replaced by (or is hiding) 6 chips.

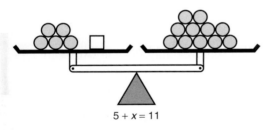

$5 + x = 11$

Figure 1.7

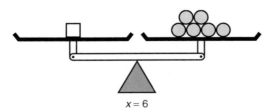

$x = 6$

Figure 1.8

Similarly, the equation $5 + x = 11$ can be simplified by subtracting 5 from both sides to obtain $x = 6$. This simpler equation shows that the variable must be replaced by 6.

Solving Equations

To **solve an equation** or **find the solution(s)** means to find all replacements for the variable that make the equation true. The usual approach to solving an equation is to replace it by a simpler equation whose solutions are the same as those of the original equation. Two equations that have exactly the same solution are called **equivalent equations.**

The *balance-scale model* is used in the next example to illustrate solving an equation. Each step in simplifying the balance scale corresponds to a step in solving the equation.

Example C

Solve $7x + 2 = 3x + 10$, using the balance-scale model and equations.

Solution

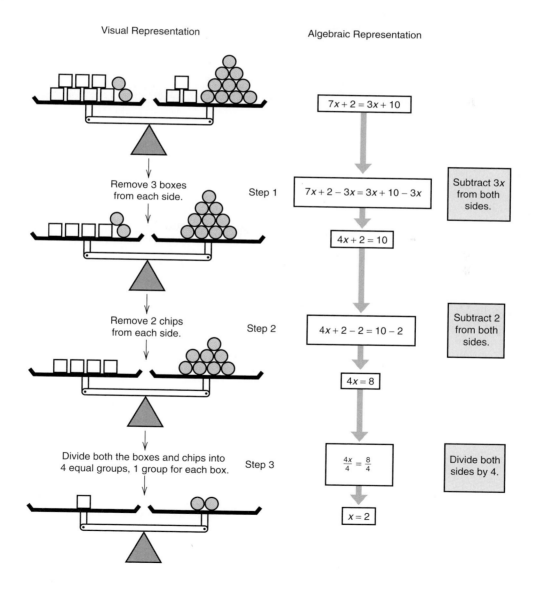

Visual Representation

Algebraic Representation

$$7x + 2 = 3x + 10$$

Remove 3 boxes from each side. **Step 1**

$$7x + 2 - 3x = 3x + 10 - 3x$$

Subtract $3x$ from both sides.

$$4x + 2 = 10$$

Remove 2 chips from each side. **Step 2**

$$4x + 2 - 2 = 10 - 2$$

Subtract 2 from both sides.

$$4x = 8$$

Divide both the boxes and chips into 4 equal groups, 1 group for each box. **Step 3**

$$\frac{4x}{4} = \frac{8}{4}$$

Divide both sides by 4.

$$x = 2$$

Check: If each box on the first scale is replaced by 2 chips, the scale will balance with 16 chips on each side. Replacing x by 2 in the equation $7x + 2 = 3x + 10$ makes the equation a true statement and shows that 2 is a solution to this equation.

The notion of equality also should be developed throughout the curriculum. They [students] should come to view the equals sign as a symbol of equivalence and balance.

Standards 2000, p. 39

When the balance-scale model is used, the same amount must be *put on* or *removed from* each side to maintain a balance. Similarly, with an equation, the *same operation* must be performed on each side to maintain an equality. In other words, *whatever is done to one side of an equation must be done to the other side.* Specifically, three methods for obtaining equivalent equations are stated below as properties of equality.

PROPERTIES OF EQUALITY

1. **Addition or Subtraction Property of Equality:** Add the same number or subtract the same number from both sides of an equation.

2. **Multiplication or Division Property of Equality:** Multiply or divide both sides of an equation by the same nonzero number.

3. **Simplification:** Replace an expression in an equation by an equivalent expression.

These methods of obtaining equivalent equations are illustrated in the next example.

Example D

Solve these equations.

1. $5x - 9 = 2x + 15$

2. $x + \frac{1}{7}x = 19$ (This is the problem posed by the Egyptian priest Ahmes, described on the opening page of this section.)

Research Statement

Students' difficulties in constructing equations stem in part from their inability to grasp the notion of the equivalence between the two expressions in the left and right sides of the equation.

MacGregor 1998

Solution   1.

$5x - 9 = 2x + 15$	
$5x - 9 - 2x = 2x + 15 - 2x$	subtraction property of equality; subtract $2x$ from both sides
$3x - 9 = 15$	simplification
$3x - 9 + 9 = 15 + 9$	addition property of equality; add 9 to both sides
$3x = 24$	simplification
$\dfrac{3x}{3} = \dfrac{24}{3}$	division property of equality; divide both sides by 3
$x = 8$	simplification

Check: When x is replaced by 8 in the original equation (or in any of the equivalent equations), the equation is true.

$$5(8) - 9 = 2(8) + 15$$
$$31 = 31$$

2.

$x + \frac{1}{7}x = 19$	
$7(x + \frac{1}{7}x) = 7(19)$	multiplication property of equality; multiply both sides by 7
$8x = 133$	simplification; $7(x + \frac{1}{7}x) = 7x + \frac{7}{7}x = 8x$. This is an example of the **distributive property.***
$\dfrac{8x}{8} = \dfrac{133}{8}$	division property of equality; divide both sides by 8
$x = 16\frac{5}{8} = 16.625$	simplification

*For examples of the distributive property, as well as several other number properties, see pages 162–166.

Check: When x is replaced by 16.625 in the original equation, the equation is true.

$$16.625 + \tfrac{1}{7}(16.625) = 16.625 + 2.375 = 19$$

Solving Inequalities

Not all algebra problems are solved by equations. Consider the following problem.

Example E

John has $19 to spend at a carnival. After paying the entrance fee of $3, he finds that each ride costs $2. What are the possibilities for the number of rides he can take?

Solution   This table shows John's total expenses with different numbers of rides. John can take any number of rides from 0 to 8 and not spend more than $19.

NUMBER OF RIDES	EXPENSE
0	$ 3
1	5
2	7
3	9
4	11
5	13
6	15
7	17
8	19

Example E says that $3 plus some number of $2 rides must be less than or equal to $19. This numerical information is stated in the following *inequality*, where x represents the unknown number of rides:

$$3 + 2x \le 19$$

An **inequality** is a statement that uses one of the following phrases: *is less than* ($<$), *is less than or equal to* ($\le$), *is greater than* ($>$), *is greater than or equal to* ($\ge$), or *is not equal to* ($\ne$).

The *balance-scale model* can also be used for illustrating inequalities. Figure 1.9 illustrates the inequality in Example E. The box can be replaced by any number of chips as long as the beam doesn't tip down on the left side. Some elementary school teachers who use the balance-scale model have students tip their arms to imitate the balance scale. Sometimes the teacher places a heavy weight in one of a student's hands and a light weight in the other. This helps students become accustomed to the fact that the amount on the side of the scale that is tipped down is *greater than* the amount on the other side of the scale.

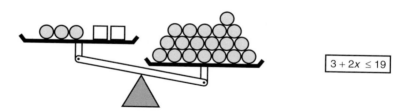

$$\boxed{3 + 2x \le 19}$$

Figure 1.9

One method of finding the number of chips that can be used in place of the box in Figure 1.9 is to think of replacing each box on the scale by the same number of chips, keeping the total number of chips on the left side of the scale less than or equal to 19. Another method is to simplify the scale to determine the possibilities for the number of chips for the box. First, we can remove 3 chips from both sides to obtain the scale setting in Figure 1.10.

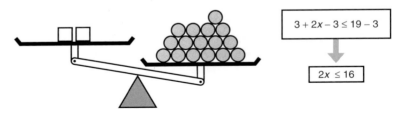

Figure 1.10

Next, we can divide the chips on the right side of the scale into two groups, one group for each box on the left side of the scale. The simplified scale in Figure 1.11 shows that replacing the box by 7 or fewer chips will keep the scale tipped down on the right side and that with 8 chips the scale will be balanced.

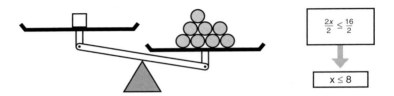

Figure 1.11

To the right of each balance scale above, there is a corresponding inequality. These inequalities are replaced by simpler inequalities to obtain $x \le 8$. To make this inequality true, we must replace the variable by a number less than or equal to 8.

To **solve an inequality** means to find all the replacements for the variable that make the inequality true. The replacements that make the inequality true are called **solutions.** Like an equation, an inequality is solved by replacing it by simpler inequalities. Two inequalities that have exactly the same solution are called **equivalent inequalities.**

Equivalent inequalities can be obtained using the same steps as those for obtaining *equivalent equations* (performing the same operation on both sides and replacing an expression by an equivalent expression), with one exception: Multiplying or dividing both sides of an inequality by a negative number *reverses the inequality.* For example, $8 > 3$; but if we multiply both sides of the inequality by $^-1$, we obtain $^-8$ and $^-3$, and $^-8$ is less than $^-3$ ($^-8 < {}^-3$). These inequalities are illustrated in Figure 1.12.

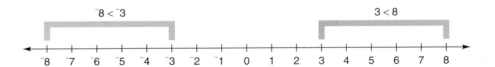

Figure 1.12

Three methods for obtaining equivalent inequalities are stated below as the properties of inequality. (These properties also apply to the inequalities $\leq$, $>$, and $\geq$.)

PROPERTIES OF INEQUALITY

1. **Addition or Subtraction Property of Inequality:** Add the same number or subtract the same number from both sides of an inequality.

2. **Multiplication or Division Property of Inequality:** Multiply or divide both sides of an inequality by the same nonzero number; and if the number is negative, reverse the inequality sign.

3. **Simplification:** Replace an expression in an inequality by an equivalent expression.

Example F

In the middle grades it is essential that students become comfortable in relating symbolic expressions containing variables to verbal, tabular, and graphical representations or numerical and quantitative relationships.

Standards 2000, p. 223

Solve the inequality $4(3x) + 16 < 52$.

Solution $4(3x) + 16 < 52$

$\qquad 12x + 16 < 52 \qquad$ simplification

$\qquad 12x + 16 - 16 < 52 - 16 \qquad$ subtraction property for inequality; subtract 16 from both sides

$\qquad 12x < 36 \qquad$ simplification

$\qquad \dfrac{12x}{12} < \dfrac{36}{12} \qquad$ division property for inequality; divide both sides by 12

$\qquad x < 3 \quad$ simplification

Check: We can get some indication of whether the inequality was solved correctly by trying a number less than 3 to see if it is a solution. When we replace x in the original inequality by 2 we can see that the inequality holds.

$$4[3(2)] + 16 = 4(6) + 16$$
$$= 24 + 16$$
$$= 40$$

and 40 is less than 52.

The solutions for an inequality in one variable may be visualized on a number line. The solutions for the inequality in Example F are shown in Figure 1.13. The circle about the point for 3 indicates that this point is not part of the solution. So the solution includes all the points on the half-line extending to the left of the point for 3.

Figure 1.13

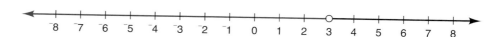

Example G

Solve the inequality $11x - 7 \leq 3x + 23$, and illustrate its solution by using a number line.

Solution $\quad 11x - 7 \leq 3x + 23$

$$11x - 7 + 7 \leq 3x + 23 + 7 \qquad \text{addition property for inequality; add 7 to both sides}$$

$$11x \leq 3x + 30 \qquad \text{simplification}$$

$$11x - 3x \leq 3x - 3x + 30 \qquad \text{subtraction property for inequality; subtract } 3x \text{ from both sides}$$

$$8x \leq 30 \qquad \text{simplification}$$

$$\frac{8x}{8} \leq \frac{30}{8} \qquad \text{division property for inequality; divide both sides by 8}$$

$$x \leq 3\tfrac{3}{4} \qquad \text{simplification}$$

Every number less than or equal to $3\tfrac{3}{4}$ is a solution for the original inequality, and these solutions can be shown on a number line by shading the points to the left of the point for $3\tfrac{3}{4}$.

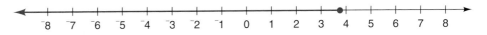

Using Algebra for Problem Solving

One application of algebra is solving problems whose solutions involve equations and inequalities.

Example H

The manager of a garden center wants to order a total of 138 trees consisting of two types: Japanese red maple and flowering pears. Each maple tree costs $156 and each pear tree costs $114. If the manager has a budget of $18,000, which must all be spent for the trees, how many maple trees will be in the order?

Solution If x equals the number of maple trees, then $138 - x$ will equal the number of pear trees. The following equation shows that the total cost of both types of trees is $18,000. Notice the use of the distributive property in going from the first to the second equation.

$$156x + 114(138 - x) = 18,000$$
$$156x + 15,732 - 114x = 18,000$$
$$42x = 2268$$
$$x = 54$$

There will be 54 Japanese red maple trees in the order.

The next problem is a variation of Example H, but its solution requires an inequality.

Example I

The manager of a garden center wants to place an order for Hawthorne trees and Service Berry trees so that the number of Service Berry trees is 6 times the number of Hawthorne trees. Each Hawthorne tree costs $250 and each Service Berry tree costs $125. If the budget requires that the total cost of the trees be less than $30,000 and that there be at least 20 Hawthorne trees, what are the different possibilities for the number of Hawthorne trees in the order?

Solution   If x equals the number of Hawthorne trees, then $6x$ is the number of Service Berry trees, and the following inequality shows that the total cost of the two types of trees is less than $30,000.

$$250x + 125(6x) < 30,000$$
$$250x + 750x < 30,000$$
$$1000x < 30,000$$
$$x < 30$$

Since there is a requirement that the order contain at least 20 Hawthorne trees, the possibilities for the number of Hawthorne trees is 20, 21, 22, . . . 29.

Another application of algebra is in analyzing number tricks and so-called magic formulas. Select any number and perform the following operations:

Add 4 to any number; multiply the result by 6; subtract 9; divided by 3; add 13; divide by 2; and then subtract the number you started with.

If you performed these operations correctly, your final answer will be 9, regardless of the number you started with. This can be proved using the variable x to represent the number selected and performing the following algebraic operations:

1. Select any number x

2. Add 4 $x + 4$

3. Multiply by 6 $6(x + 4) = 6x + 24$

4. Subtract 9 $6x + 24 - 9 = 6x + 15$

5. Divide by 3 $(6x + 15)/3 = 2x + 5$

6. Add 13 $2x + 5 + 13 = 2x + 18$

7. Divide by 2 $(2x + 18)/2 = x + 9$

8. Subtract the number x $x + 9 - x = 9$

The preceding steps show that it doesn't matter what number is selected for x, for in the final step x is subtracted and the end result is always 9.

Problem-Solving Application

The problem-solving strategy of *using algebra* is illustrated in the solution to the next problem.

PROBLEM

A class of students is shown the following figures formed with tiles and is told that there is a pattern which, if continued, will result in one of the figures having 290 tiles. Which figure will have this many tiles?

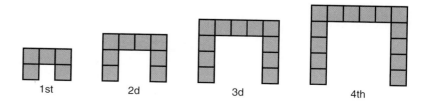

1st   2d   3d   4th

Understanding the Problem The fourth figure has 14 tiles. Find a pattern in the formation of the first few figures, and sketch the fifth and sixth figures. **Question 1:** How many tiles are in the fifth and sixth figures?

Two central themes of algebraic thinking are appropriate for young students. The first involves making generalizations and using symbols to represent mathematical ideas, and the second is representing and solving problems (Carpenter and Levi 1999).

Standards 2000, p. 93

Devising a Plan One approach to solving this problem is to use a variable and write an algebraic expression for the nth term. This expression can then be used to determine which figure has 290 tiles.

Notice that the third figure has 3 tiles in each "leg," 3 tiles in the middle of the top row, and 2 corner tiles. The fourth figure has 4 tiles in each leg, 4 in the middle of the top row, and 2 corner tiles. **Question 2:** By extending this reasoning, how many tiles are in the 20th figure? the 100th?

Carrying Out the Plan The nth figure will have n tiles in each leg, n tiles in the middle of the top row, and 2 corner tiles. So the algebraic expression for the number of tiles in the nth figure is $n + n + n + 2$, or $3n + 2$. **Question 3:** What number for n gives the expression $3n + 2$ a value of 290?

Looking Back Perhaps you saw a different way to group the tiles in the first four figures. **Question 4:** If you saw the pattern developing as follows, what would be the algebraic expression for the nth figure?

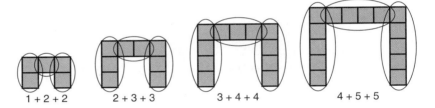

1 + 2 + 2   2 + 3 + 3   3 + 4 + 4   4 + 5 + 5

Answers to Questions 1–4   **1.** The fifth figure has 17 tiles and the sixth has 20.   **2.** The 20th figure has 20 + 20 + 20 + 2 = 62 tiles, and the 100th figure has 100 + 100 + 100 + 2 = 302 tiles. **3.** $n = 96$. **4.** $n + (n + 1) + (n + 1)$ or $n + 2(n + 1)$.

EXERCISES AND PROBLEMS 1.3

"I THINK YOU SHOULD BE MORE EXPLICIT HERE IN STEP TWO."

1. a. At a depth of x feet under water, the pressure in pounds per square inch is $.43x + 14.7$. What is the pressure in pounds per square inch for a depth of 10 feet? 100 feet? 0 feet (surface of the water)?
   b. The temperature (Fahrenheit) can be approximated by $x/4 + 40$, where x is the number of cricket chirps in one minute. What is the temperature for 20 chirps per minute? 100 chirps per minute?
   c. A person's normal blood pressure increases with age and is approximated by $x/2 + 110$, where x is the person's age. The blood pressure for people between 20 and 30 years old should be between what two numbers?

2. a. A woman's shoe size is given by $3x - 22$, where x is the length of her foot in inches. What is a woman's shoe size for a length of 9 inches? 11 inches?
   b. The number of words in a child's vocabulary for children between 20 and 50 months is $60x - 900$, where x is the child's age in months. What is the number of vocabulary words for a child whose age is 20 months? 35 months? 4 years?
   c. A person's maximum heart rate is $220 - x$, where x is the person's age, and the heart rate for aero-bic activity should be between $.7(220 - x)$ and $.8(220 - x)$. A 20-year-old person's heart rate for aerobic activity should be between what two numbers?

3. Tickets for the historical review of ballroom dancing at the Portsmouth Music Hall cost $28 each for the main-floor seats and $19 each for the balcony seats. Let m represent the number of tickets sold for main-floor seats and let b represent the number of tickets sold for balcony seats. Write an algebraic expression for the following amounts.
   a. The cost in dollars of all the main-floor seats that were sold
   b. The total number of seats that were sold for the performance
   c. The difference in dollars in the total amount of money paid for all main-floor seats and the total amount paid for all balcony seats, if the total for all main-floor seats was the greater of the two amounts

4. At the Saturday farmers' market, melons cost $1.20 each and coconuts cost $1.45 each. Let m represent the number of melons sold during the day, and let c represent the number of coconuts sold. Write an algebraic expression for each of the following.
   a. The total number of melons and coconuts sold
   b. The cost of all the coconuts sold
   c. The total cost of all the melons and coconuts sold

5. In research conducted at the University of Massachusetts, Peter Rosnick found that $37\frac{1}{3}$ percent of a group of 150 engineering students were unable to write the correct equation for the following problem.* Write an equation using variables s and p to represent the following statement: "At this university there are 6 times as many students as professors." Use s for the number of students and p for the number of professors.
   a. What is the correct equation?
   b. The most common erroneous answer was $6s = p$. Give a possible explanation for this.

Determine the number of chips needed to replace each box in order for the scales in exercises 6 and 7 to balance. Then using x to represent the number of chips for each box, write the corresponding equation that represents each scale and solve the equation.

*Peter Rosnick, "Some Misconceptions Concerning the Concept of a Variable," *The Mathematics Teacher* 74 (September 1981): 418–420.

6. a.

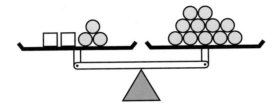

b.

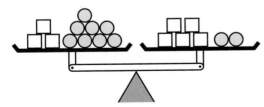

7. a.

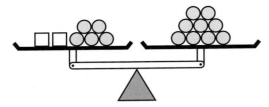

b.

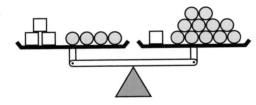

Each of the equations in exercises 8 and 9 has been re-placed by a similar equivalent equation. Write the property of equality that has been used in each step.

8. a.
$$6x - 14 = 2x$$
$$6x - 14 + 14 = 2x + 14 \quad \text{(step 1)}$$
$$6x = 2x + 14 \quad \text{(step 2)}$$
$$6x - 2x = 2x + 14 - 2x \quad \text{(step 3)}$$
$$4x = 14 \quad \text{(step 4)}$$
$$\frac{4x}{4} = \frac{14}{4} \quad \text{(step 5)}$$
$$x = 3\tfrac{1}{2} \quad \text{(step 6)}$$

b.
$$42x + 102 = 6(3x + 45)$$
$$42x + 102 = 18x + 270 \quad \text{(step 1)}$$
$$42x + 102 - 18x = 18x + 270 - 18x \quad \text{(step 2)}$$
$$24x + 102 = 270 \quad \text{(step 3)}$$
$$24x + 102 - 102 = 270 - 102 \quad \text{(step 4)}$$
$$24x = 168 \quad \text{(step 5)}$$
$$\frac{24x}{24} = \frac{168}{24} \quad \text{(step 6)}$$
$$x = 7 \quad \text{(step 7)}$$

9. a.
$$6(2x - 5) = 7x + 15$$
$$12x - 30 = 7x + 15 \quad \text{(step 1)}$$
$$12x - 30 + 30 = 7x + 15 + 30 \quad \text{(step 2)}$$
$$12x = 7x + 45 \quad \text{(step 3)}$$
$$12x - 7x = 7x + 45 - 7x \quad \text{(step 4)}$$
$$5x = 45 \quad \text{(step 5)}$$
$$\frac{5x}{5} = \frac{45}{5} \quad \text{(step 6)}$$
$$x = 9 \quad \text{(step 7)}$$

b.
$$11(3x) + 2 = 35$$
$$33x + 2 = 35 \quad \text{(step 1)}$$
$$33x + 2 - 2 = 35 - 2 \quad \text{(step 2)}$$
$$33x = 33 \quad \text{(step 3)}$$
$$\frac{33x}{33} = \frac{33}{33} \quad \text{(step 4)}$$
$$x = 1 \quad \text{(step 5)}$$

Solve each equation in exercises 10 and 11.

10. a. $2x + 30 = 18 + 5x$
b. $3x - 17 = 22$
c. $13(2x) + 20 = 6(5x + 2)$

d. $8\left(\dfrac{x}{2} - 5\right) = 2x - 6$

11. a. $43x - 281 = 17x + 8117$
b. $17(3x - 4) = 25x + 218$
c. $56(x + 1) + 7x = 45{,}353$
d. $3x + 5 = 2(2x - 7)$

Determine the number of chips for each box that will keep the scales in exercises 12 and 13 tipped as shown. Then, using x for a variable, write the corresponding inequality for each scale and solve the inequality.

12. a.

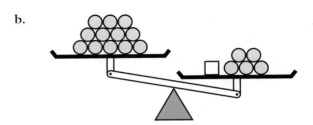

b.

13. a.

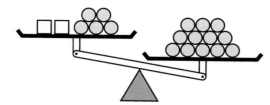

b.

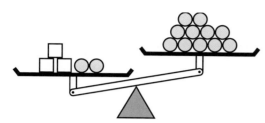

Each of the inequalities in exercises 14 and 15 has been replaced by a similar equivalent inequality. Write the property of inequality that has been used in each step.

14. a.
$$3x + 14 < 55$$
$$3x + 14 - 14 < 55 - 14 \quad \text{(step 1)}$$
$$3x < 41 \quad \text{(step 2)}$$
$$\frac{3x}{3} < \frac{41}{3} \quad \text{(step 3)}$$
$$x < 13\tfrac{2}{3} \quad \text{(step 4)}$$

b.
$$10x < 55$$
$$\frac{10x}{10} < \frac{55}{10} \quad \text{(step 1)}$$
$$x < 5\tfrac{1}{2} \quad \text{(step 2)}$$

15. a.
$$6x + 11 > 2x + 19$$
$$6x + 11 - 2x > 2x + 19 - 2x \quad \text{(step 1)}$$
$$4x + 11 > 19 \quad \text{(step 2)}$$
$$4x + 11 - 11 > 19 - 11 \quad \text{(step 3)}$$
$$4x > 8 \quad \text{(step 4)}$$
$$\frac{4x}{4} > \frac{8}{4} \quad \text{(step 5)}$$
$$x > 2 \quad \text{(step 6)}$$

b.
$$2x > 3x - 12$$
$$2x - 3x > 3x - 12 - 3x \quad \text{(step 1)}$$
$$^-x > ^-12 \quad \text{(step 2)}$$
$$(^-1)(^-x) < (^-1)(^-12) \quad \text{(step 3)}$$
$$x < 12 \quad \text{(step 4)}$$

Solve each inequality in exercises 16 and 17, and illustrate the solution by using a number line.

16. a. $3x + 5 < x + 17$
  b. $3(2x + 7) > 36$

17. a. $6(x + 5) > 11x$
  b. $5(x + 8) - 6 > 44$

18. Mr. Dawson purchased some artichokes for 80 cents each and twice as many pineapples for 95 cents each. Altogether he spent $18.90. Let x represent the number of artichokes, and write an algebraic expression for each item in parts a through c.
  a. The total cost in dollars of the artichokes
  b. The number of pineapples
  c. The total cost in dollars of the pineapples
  d. The sum of the costs in parts a and c is $18.90. Write and solve an equation to determine the number of artichokes Mr. Dawson bought.

19. It cost Marci 20 cents to mail a postcard and 33 cents to mail a letter. She sent either a postcard or a letter to each of 18 people and spent $4.38. Let x represent the number of postcards she wrote, and write an algebraic expression for each item in parts a through c.
  a. The total cost in dollars of the postcards
  b. The number of letters
  c. The total cost in dollars of the letters
  d. The sum of the costs in parts a and c is $4.38. Write and solve an equation to determine the number of postcards Marci mailed.

20. Teresa purchased pens for 50 cents each and pencils for 25 cents each. She purchased 10 more pencils than pens and gave the clerk a five-dollar bill, which was more than enough to pay the total cost. Let x represent the number of pens, and write an algebraic expression for each item in parts a through c.
  a. The total cost in dollars of the pens
  b. The number of pencils
  c. The total cost in dollars of the pencils
  d. The sum of the costs in parts a and c is less than $5.00. Write and solve an inequality to determine the possibilities for the number of pens and pencils that Teresa purchased.

21. Merle spent $10.50 for each compact disk and $8 for each tape. He purchased three more tapes than compact disks, and the total amount of money he spent was less than $120. Let x represent the number of compact disks he purchased, and write an algebraic expression for each item in parts a through c.
  a. The total cost in dollars of the compact disks
  b. The number of tapes
  c. The total cost in dollars of the tapes
  d. The sum of the costs in parts a and c is less than $120. Write and solve an inequality to determine the possibilities for the number of compact disks Merle purchased.

REASONING AND PROBLEM SOLVING

Solve word problems 22 to 24 by writing an equation with a variable to represent the given information and then solve the equation.

22. Jeri spends $60 of her paycheck on clothes and then
PS spends one-half of her remaining money on food. If she has $80 left, what was the amount of her paycheck?

23. Marcia has 350 feet of fence. After fencing in a
PS square region, she has 110 feet of fence left. What is the length of one side of the square?

24. Rico noticed that if he began with his age, added 24,
PS divided the result by 2, and then subtracted 6, he got his age back. What is his age?

Solve word problems 25 and 26 by writing an inequality with a variable and then solve the inequality.

25. If you add 14 to a certain number, the sum is less
PS than 3 times the number. For what numbers is this true?

26. The length of the first side of a triangle is a whole
PS number greater than 3. The second side is 3 inches longer than the first, and the third side is 3 inches longer than the second. How many such triangles have perimeters less than 36 inches?

27. How can 350 be written as the sum of four consecu-
PS tive whole numbers?
   a. Understanding the Problem   If 75 is the first of four consecutive numbers, then the others are 76, 77, and 78. If n is the first number, write an algebraic expression for each of the other three.
   b. Devising a Plan   One plan is to let n be the first of four consecutive numbers, write an algebraic expression for their sum, and determine which number for n gives that expression a value of 350. If n is the first of four consecutive numbers, what is an algebraic expression for their sum?
   c. Carrying Out the Plan   What number for n gives a sum of 350?
   d. Looking Back   Can 350 be written as the sum of other consecutive whole numbers? Use algebraic expressions to determine if 350 can be written as the sum of three consecutive numbers or five consecutive numbers.

28. The teacher asks the class to select a 4 × 4 array of
PS numbers from a 10 × 10 number chart and to use only those numbers for the four-step process described here.

1	2	3	4	5	6	7	8	9	10
11	12	13	14	15	16	17	18	19	20
21	22	23	24	25	26	27	28	29	30
31	32	33	34	35	36	37	38	39	40
41	42	43	44	45	46	47	48	49	50
51	52	53	54	55	56	57	58	59	60
61	62	63	64	65	66	67	68	69	70
71	72	73	74	75	76	77	78	79	80
81	82	83	84	85	86	87	88	89	90
91	92	93	94	95	96	97	98	99	100

1. Circle any number and cross out the remaining numbers in its row and column.
2. Circle another number that has not been crossed out and cross out the remaining numbers in its row and column.
3. Repeat step 2 until there are four circled numbers.
4. Add the four circled numbers.

No matter what sum a student comes up with, the teacher will be able to predict the number in the upper left corner of the student's square by subtracting 66 from the sum and dividing the result by 4. Show why this formula works.
   a. Understanding the Problem   Let's carry out the steps on the 4 × 4 array shown above. The first circled number is 46, and the remaining numbers in its row and column have been crossed out. The next circled number is 38. Continue the four-step process. Does the teacher's formula produce the number in the upper left corner of this 4 × 4 array?
   b. Devising a Plan   This problem can be solved by algebra. If we represent the number in the upper left corner by x, the remaining numbers can be represented in terms of x. Complete the next two rows of the 4 × 4 array of algebraic expressions shown here.

x	$x + 1$	$x + 2$	$x + 3$
$x + 10$	$x + 11$	$x + 12$	$x + 13$

   c. Carrying Out the Plan   Carry out the four-step process on the 4 × 4 array of algebraic expressions you completed in part b. Use the results to show that the teacher's formula works.

d. Looking Back   One variation on this number trick is to change the size of the array that the student selects. For example, what formula will the teacher use if a 3×3 array is selected from the 10×10 number chart? (*Hint:* Use a 3×3 algebraic array.) Another variation is to change the number chart. Suppose that a 3×3 array is selected from a calendar. What is the formula in this case?

29. Many number tricks can be explained by algebra. Select any number and perform the steps below to see what number you obtain. Add 221 to the number, multiply by 2652, subtract 1326, divide by 663, subtract 870, divide by 4, and subtract the original number. Use algebra to show that the steps always result in the same number.

30. Ask a person to write the number of the month of his or her birth and perform the following operations: Multiply by 5, add 6, multiply by 4, add 9, multiply by 5, and add the number of the day of birth. When 165 is subtracted from this number, the result is a number that represents the person's month and day of birth. Try it.

   Analysis: Let d and m equal the day and month, respectively. The first three of the preceding steps are represented by the following algebraic expressions. Continue these expressions to show that the final expression is equal to $100m + d$. This shows that the units digit of the final result is the day and the remaining digits are the month.

$$5m$$
$$5m + 6$$
$$4(5m + 6) = 20m + 24$$
$$\vdots$$

31. Use the information from the first two balance beams shown in the next column to determine the number of nails needed to balance one cube.*

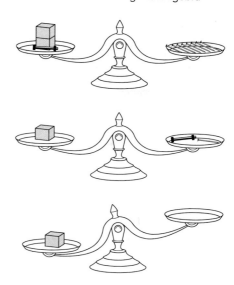

32. Use the information from the first two balance beams to determine the number of marbles needed to balance a cube.

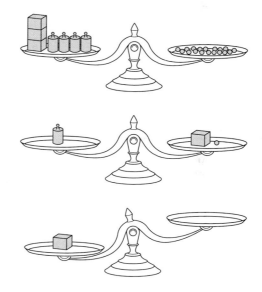

33. In driving from town A to town D, you pass first through town B and then through town C. It is 10 times farther from town A to town B than from towns B to C and 10 times farther from towns B to C than from towns C to D. If it is 1332 miles from towns A to D, how far is it from towns A to B? (Let the variable x represent the distance from towns C to D.)

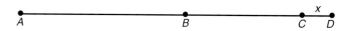

*Balance beam art from *The Arithmetic Teacher* 19 (October 1972): 460–461.

34. The cost of a bottle of cologne, $28.90, was determined from the cost of the bottle plus the cost of the perfume. If the perfume costs $14.10 more than the bottle, how much does the bottle cost? (Let the variable x represent the cost of the bottle.)

35. If the following tile figures are continued, will there be a figure with 8230 tiles? If so, which figure will it be? If not, what figure has the number of tiles closest to 8230? (*Hint:* Write an algebraic expression for the nth figure and set it equal to 8230.)

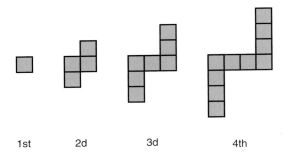

1st   2d   3d   4th

36. Find a pattern to extend the toothpick figures. Determine the number of toothpicks in the 50th figure, and write an algebraic expression for the number of toothpicks in the nth figure.

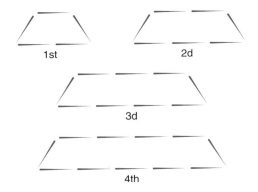

1st   2d

3d

4th

37. Here are the first three figures of a sequence formed by color tiles.

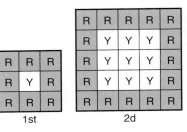

1st   2d   3d

a. Find a pattern and describe the next two figures in the sequence. Then determine how many tiles of each color are used in the fifth figure. Answer this question for each of the first four figures.

b. Describe the 100th figure. Include the number of each color of tile and the total number of tiles in the figure.

c. Write algebraic expressions for the nth figure for (1) the number of yellow tiles, (2) the number of red tiles, and (3) the total number of tiles.

38. These three figures were formed by color tiles.

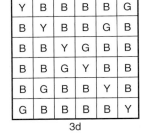

1st   2d   3d

a. Find a pattern and describe the next two figures in the sequence. How many tiles of each different color are in the fifth figure? Answer this question for each of the first four figures.

b. Describe the 100th figure and determine (1) the number of yellow tiles, (2) the number of green tiles, (3) the number of blue tiles, and (4) the total number of tiles.

c. Write algebraic expressions for the nth figure for (1) the number of yellow tiles, (2) the number of green tiles, (3) the number of blue tiles, and (4) the total number of tiles.

- -

ONLINE LEARNING CENTER   www.mhhe.com/bennett-nelson

• Math Investigation 1.3   *Palindromic Sums*
Section Related: • Links   • Writing/Discussion Problems   • Bibliography

CHAPTER REVIEW

1. Problem Solving
   a. **Problem solving** is the process by which an unfamiliar situation is resolved.
   b. **Polya's Four-Step Process**
      Understanding the problem
      Devising a plan
      Carrying out the plan
      Looking back
   c. **Problem-Solving Strategies**
      Making a drawing
      Guessing and checking
      Making a table
      Using a variable
      Using a model
      Working backward
      Finding a pattern
      Solving a simpler problem

2. Unsolved Problems
   a. There are many unsolved problems in mathematics.
   b. A **conjecture** is a statement that has not been proved, yet is thought to be true.

3. Patterns and Sequences
   a. There are many kinds of patterns. They are found by comparing and contrasting information.
   b. The numbers in the sequence 1, 1, 2, 3, 5, 8, 13, 21, . . . are called **Fibonacci numbers.** The growth patterns of plants and trees frequently can be described by Fibonacci numbers.
   c. **Pascal's triangle** is a triangle of numbers with many patterns. One pattern enables each row to be obtained from the previous row.
   d. An **arithmetic sequence** is a sequence in which each term is obtained by adding a **common difference** to the previous term.
   e. A **geometric sequence** is a sequence in which each term is obtained by multiplying the previous term by a **common ratio.**
   f. The numbers in the sequence 1, 3, 6, 10, 15, 21, . . . are called **triangular numbers.**
   g. **Finite differences** is a method of finding patterns by computing differences of consecutive terms.

4. Inductive Reasoning
   a. **Inductive reasoning** is the process of forming conclusions on the basis of observations, patterns, or experiments.

   b. A **counterexample** is an example that shows that a statement is false.

5. Variables
   a. A letter or symbol that is used to denote an unknown number is called a **variable.**
   b. An expression containing algebraic symbols is called an **algebraic expression.**

6. Equations
   a. An **equation** is a sentence in which the verb is "equals" ($=$). It is a statement of the equality of mathematical expressions. The following are examples of equations; no variables, $17 + 5 = 22$; and one variable, $15x + 3 = 48$.
   b. To **solve an equation** means to find values for the variable which make the equation true.
   c. Two equations that have exactly the same solutions are called **equivalent equations.**
   d. **Properties of Equality**
      (1) Addition or Subtraction Property of Equality: Add the same number to or subtract the same number from both sides of an equation.
      (2) Multiplication or Division Property of Equality: Multiply or divide both sides of an equation by the same nonzero number.
      (3) Simplification: Replace an expression in an equation by an equivalent expression.

7. Inequalities
   a. An **inequality** is a sentence that contains $<$, $\leq$, $>$, $\geq$, or $\neq$. It is a statement of the inequalities of mathematical expressions. The following are examples of inequalities: no variables, $12 < 50$; and one variable, $13x + 5 \geq 28$.
   b. To **solve an inequality** means to find all the values for the variable that make the inequality true.
   c. Two inequalities that have exactly the same solutions are called **equivalent inequalities.**
   d. **Properties of Inequality**
      (1) Addition or Subtraction Property of Inequality: Add the same number to or subtract the same number from both sides of an inequality.
      (2) Multiplication or Division Property of Equality: Multiply or divide both sides of an inequality by the same nonzero number; and if this number is negative, reverse the inequality sign.
      (3) Simplification: Replace an expression in an inequality by an equivalent expression.

CHAPTER TEST

1. List Polya's four steps in problem solving.

2. List the eight problem-solving strategies that were introduced in this chapter.

3. The numbers in the following sums were obtained by using every other Fibonacci number (circled).

$\quad$ ① $\;$ 1 $\quad$ ② $\;$ 3 $\quad$ ⑤ $\;$ 8 $\quad$ ⑬ $\;$ 21 $\quad$ ㉞

$$1 + 2 =$$
$$1 + 2 + 5 =$$
$$1 + 2 + 5 + 13 =$$
$$1 + 2 + 5 + 13 + 34 =$$

Compute these sums. What is the relationship between these sums and the Fibonacci numbers?

4. What is the sum of numbers in row 9 of Pascal's triangle, if row 2 has the numbers 1, 2, and 1?

5. Find a pattern in the following sequences, and write the next term.
   a. 1, 3, 9, 27, 81
   b. 3, 6, 9, 12, 15
   c. 0, 6, 12, 18, 24
   d. 1, 4, 9, 16, 25
   e. 3, 5, 11, 21, 35

6. Classify each sequence in problem 5 as arithmetic, geometric, or neither.

7. Use the method of finite differences to find the next three terms in each sequence.
   a. 1, 5, 14, 30, 55
   b. 2, 9, 20, 35

8. What is the fifth number in each of the following sequences of numbers?
   a. Triangular numbers
   b. Square numbers
   c. Pentagonal numbers

9. Find a counterexample for this conjecture: The sum of any seven consecutive whole numbers is evenly divisible by 4.

10. Determine the number of chips needed for each box in order for the beam to stay in the given position.
    a.

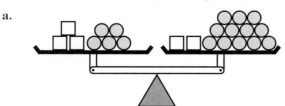

b.

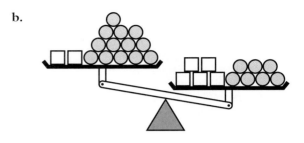

11. Solve each equation.
    a. $3(x - 40) = x + 16$
    b. $4x + 18 = 2(441 - 34x)$

12. Solve each inequality.
    a. $7x - 3 < 52 + 2x$
    b. $6x - 46 > 79 - 4x$

13. Name the property of equality or inequality used to obtain the new expression in each step.

    a. $\quad\quad 15x - 217 = 2x + 17$
    $$15x - 217 - 2x = 2x + 17 - 2x \quad \text{(step 1)}$$
    $$13x - 217 = 17 \quad \text{(step 2)}$$
    $$13x - 217 + 217 = 17 + 217 \quad \text{(step 3)}$$
    $$13x = 234 \quad \text{(step 4)}$$
    $$\frac{13x}{13} = \frac{234}{13} \quad \text{(step 5)}$$
    $$x = 5 \quad \text{(step 6)}$$

    b. $\quad\quad 38x < 5(23 + 3x)$
    $$38x < 115 + 15x \quad \text{(step 1)}$$
    $$38x - 15x < 115 + 15x - 15x \quad \text{(step 2)}$$
    $$23x < 115 \quad \text{(step 3)}$$
    $$\frac{23x}{23} < \frac{115}{23} \quad \text{(step 4)}$$
    $$x < 5 \quad \text{(step 5)}$$

Solve problems 14 through 19, and identify the strategy or strategies you use.

14. A 2000-foot-long straight fence has posts that are set 10 feet on center; that is, the distance between the centers of two adjacent poles is 10 feet. If the fence begins with a post and ends with a post, determine the number of posts in the entire fence.

15. In a game of chips, Pauli lost half her chips in the first round, won 50 chips, then lost half her total, and finally won 80 chips. She finished with 170 chips. How many chips did she have at the beginning of the game?

16. The following tower has 5 tiles along its base and 5 rows of tiles. How many tiles will be required to build a tower like this with 25 tiles along its base and 25 rows of tiles? Write an algebraic expression for the number of tiles in a tower with n tiles along its base and n rows of tiles.

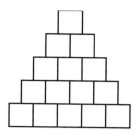

17. Shown below are the first three squares in a pattern. Each square has one more dot on each side than the previous square.

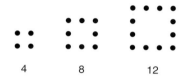

4   8   12

a. How many dots are there in the fourth square?
b. How many dots are there in the 50th square?
c. Write an algebraic expression for the number of dots in the nth square.

18. There are 78 people around a table. Each person shakes hands with the people to his or her immediate right and left. How many handshakes take place? Write an algebraic expression for the number of handshakes, if there are n people around the table.

19. Two men and two boys want to cross a river, using a small canoe. The canoe can carry two boys or one man. What is the least number of times the canoe must cross the river to get everyone to the other side?

20. Find a pattern to extend the following figures of tiles.
   a. How many tiles will there be in the 5th figure? The 150th figure?
   b. Write an algebraic expression for the number of tiles in the nth figure.

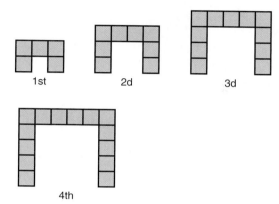

1st   2d   3d

4th

SETS, FUNCTIONS, AND REASONING

SPOTLIGHT ON TEACHING

Excerpts from NCTM's Standards 2 and 3 for Teaching Mathematics in Grades 5–8*

Reasoning is fundamental to the knowing and doing of mathematics. . . . To give more students access to mathematics as a powerful way of making sense of the world, it is essential that an emphasis on reasoning pervade all mathematical activity. Students need a great deal of time and many experiences to develop their ability to construct valid arguments in problem settings and evaluate the arguments of others.

. . . As students' mathematical language develops, so does their ability to reason about and solve problems. Moreover, problem-solving situations provide a setting for the development and extension of communication skills and reasoning ability. The following problem illustrates how students might share their approaches in solving problems:

The class is divided into small groups. Each group is given square pieces of grid paper and asked to make boxes by cutting out pieces from the corners. Each group is given a 20×20 sheet of grid paper. See figure [below]. Students cut and fold the paper to make boxes sized $18 \times 18 \times 1$, $16 \times 16 \times 2$, . . . , $2 \times 2 \times 9$. They are challenged to find a box that holds the maximum volume and to convince someone else that they have found the maximum. . . .

Building a grid-paper box.

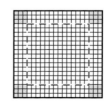 

Curriculum and Evaluation Standards for School Mathematics (Reston, VA: National Council of Teachers of Mathematics, 1989), p.80.

MATH ACTIVITY 2.1

SORTING AND CLASSIFYING ATTRIBUTE PIECES

Materials: Attribute pieces in the Manipulative Kit.

*1. Each attribute piece in the following sequence differs from the preceding piece by exactly one of the attributes of shape, color, or size. As examples, the large blue square differs from the large blue hexagon by shape; the large red square differs from the small red square by size; and so forth. Place five of your attribute pieces in a sequence that continues the one-difference pattern and does not repeat any piece that has been used. List your five pieces in order. (You may wish to abbreviate large blue hexagon as LBH, small red triangle as SRT, etc.)

LBH LBS LRS SRS SRT SYT SYH

2. In the following sequence, each attribute piece differs from the preceding one by exactly two attributes. Use as many of your attribute pieces as possible to continue this sequence. List your pieces in order, and note the ones, if any, that did not fit at the end of the sequence.

LYH LRS SBS SRH

*3. Draw two large circles on paper (or form them with string), and label them as shown here. The circle labeled *Blue* should have only blue attribute pieces inside. The circle labeled *Hexagon* should contain only hexagonal pieces. The overlapping region should have the attribute pieces which are both blue and hexagonal. Place your attribute pieces in the appropriate regions of the circles. List the attribute pieces for each region. Place the remaining pieces outside the circles and list them.

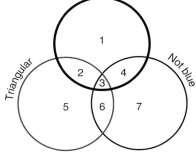

4. Draw three large circles, labeled as shown. Place the appropriate attribute pieces in the seven numbered regions and the remaining pieces in the region outside the circles. List the attribute pieces for each of the eight regions.

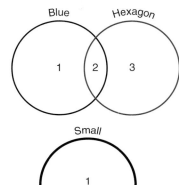

SECTION 2.1

SETS AND VENN DIAGRAMS

Two views of the Ishango bone, found on the shores of Lake Edward in the Congo

PROBLEM OPENER

What is the sum of the numbers in the 10th row of this triangle?

$$0$$
$$1 + 2$$
$$3 + 4 + 5$$
$$6 + 7 + 8 + 9$$
$$10 + 11 + 12 + 13 + 14$$

Long before numbers were invented, numerical records were kept by means of tallies. Archaeologists have unearthed thousands of animal bones marked with groups of notches, which date from prehistoric times. Some anthropologists conjecture that many of these ancient bones are records of days, months, and seasons. One example is the 8000-year-old Ishango bone, which was discovered in East Africa. The marks on this bone occur in several groups that are arranged in columns (see exercises 3 and 4 in Exercises and Problems 2.1).

Art symbols dating from 12,000 B.C. found in the El Castillo caves in Spain

During the Old Stone Age (10,000–15,000 B.C.), figures of people and animals and abstract symbols were painted in caves in Spain and France. The symbols were composed of many geometric forms: straight lines, spirals, circles, ovals, and dots. The rows of dots and rectangular figures in this photograph were discovered on the walls of the El Castillo caves, in Spain, and date from 12,000 B.C. Some scholars conjecture that these symbols made up a system for recording the days of the year. It seems likely that numbers were in existence by this time. At first, it may only have been necessary to distinguish among one, two, and many objects. The first words for numbers were probably associated with specific things. This influence can be seen in the expressions we have for *two,* such as a *couple* of people, a *brace* of hens, and a *pair* of shoes. Eventually the concepts of twoness, threeness, etc., were separated from physical objects, and the abstract notion of *number* developed.

Young children are motivated to count everything . . . and through their repeated experience with the counting process, they learn many fundamental number concepts.

Standards 2000, p. 79

Keeping a tally involves matching sets of objects and marks and is the beginning of the idea of counting. The importance of counting to sets was first recognized by the nineteenth-century mathematician Georg Cantor. He created a new field of mathematics called **set theory.** Cantor used sets to define numbers and, in particular, to develop the theory of infinite sets. Today, sets are one of the major unifying ideas in mathematics, and set terminology is commonly found in elementary school texts.

Sets and Their Elements

There are many words for sets: a *flock* of birds, a *herd* of cattle, a *collection* of paintings, a *bunch* of grapes, a *group* of people, and a *pride* of lions, to name a few. Intuitively, we understand a **set** to be a collection of objects called **elements.**

There are two common methods of specifying a set. One is to **describe the elements** of the set with words.

Example A

1. "The capitals of the six New England states"
2. "The multiples of 10 from 10 to 500"

The other method of specifying a set is to **list the elements** of the set. When this is done, the elements of the set are written between braces.

Example B

1. {Augusta, Concord, Boston, Hartford, Providence, Montpelier}
2. {10, 20, 30, 40, 50, 60, 70, . . . , 490, 500}

If the set of elements is large, as in the set of numbers in Example B, we sometimes begin the list and then use three dots to show that the pattern continues.

It is possible to have a set with no elements. This set is called the **empty set** or **null set** and is denoted by the set braces with no elements between them, { }, or by the null set symbol Ø.

Example C

The set of all whole numbers between 16 and 28 that can be divided evenly by 15 has no elements, so it can be denoted by { } or Ø.

It is customary to name sets using uppercase letters and to denote elements of sets by lowercase letters. If k is an **element of** set S, we write $k \in S$, and if it is **not an element of** S, we write $k \notin S$. As an example, if we use T to denote the set of numbers in Example B, $60 \in T$ and $55 \notin T$.

VENN DIAGRAMS   Sets are often pictured by using rectangles, circles, or other convenient figures. For example, in Figure 2.1, all whole numbers less than 100 are represented by the region inside the rectangle. All even whole numbers less than 100 are represented by the region inside one circle, and all whole numbers less than 100 that are multiples of 5 are represented by the region inside the other circle. Notice there is an overlap of the two circles that could be described as the set of all even whole numbers less than 100 that are multiples of 5. That is, the numbers 0, 10, 20, 30, . . . , 90 are common to both sets. Such figures for representing sets were first used by the Englishman John Venn (1834–1923) and are called **Venn diagrams.**

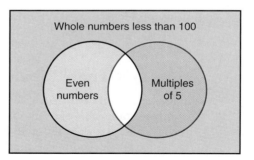

Figure 2.1

ATTRIBUTE PIECES   Attribute pieces are geometric models of various shapes, sizes, and colors that are commonly used in elementary schools for illustrating sets. As an example, the attribute pieces in Figure 2.2 have three attributes: size, shape, and color. There are three different shapes: triangular (t), rectangular (r), and hexagonal (h). There are two sizes: large (l) and small (s). There are two colors: black (b) and white (w).

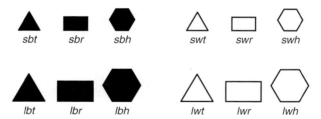

Figure 2.2

These objects can be classified into sets in many different ways. Here are a few possibilities:

Example D

S is the set of small attribute pieces.
L is the set of large attribute pieces.
T is the set of triangles.
H is the set of hexagons.
W is the set of white attribute pieces.
BT is the set of black triangles.

Sorting, classifying, and ordering facilitate work with patterns, geometric shapes, and data. Given a package of assorted stickers, children quickly notice many differences among the items. They can sort the stickers into groups having similar traits such as color, size, or design and order them from smallest to largest.

Standards 2000, p. 91

The attribute pieces will be used in the following paragraphs to illustrate set relationships and operations. You may find it helpful to copy and cut out the 12 pieces for use with the examples.

Relationships between Sets

There are several ways in which sets may be related to one another. For example, two sets may have no elements in common (disjoint) or all elements in common (equal), or one set may be contained in another (subset). Let's look at some examples.

DISJOINT SETS   The two sets of attribute pieces in Figure 2.3 have no elements in common. When two sets do not have any of the same elements, we say the two sets are **disjoint**. Thus the sets in Figure 2.3 are disjoint. The two sets in Figure 2.1, the even numbers and the multiples of 5, are *not disjoint* because they have elements in common.

Figure 2.3

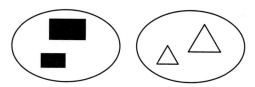

Example E

Which of the following pairs of sets of attribute pieces are disjoint? (*Hint:* List the elements of each set, and check to see if they have any elements in common.)

1. L (large pieces), S (small pieces)

2. S (small pieces), W (white pieces)

3. SH (small hexagons), BT (black triangles)

Solution   1. Sets L and S are disjoint. 2. Sets S and W have small white pieces in common; they are not disjoint. 3. Sets SH and BT are disjoint.

SUBSETS   Figure 2.4 shows that every attribute piece in set BT (black triangles) is also in set T (triangles). In this case we say that BT is a **subset** of T.

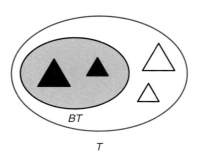

Figure 2.4

If every element of set *A* is also an element of set *B*, then set *A* is a *subset* of *B*. This relationship is written $A \subseteq B$.

Example F

In which of the following pairs of sets of attribute pieces is the first set a subset of the second?

1. *LR* (large rectangles), *R* (rectangles)

2. *T* (triangles), *S* (small pieces)

Solution   **1.** *LR* is a subset of *R*, $LR \subseteq R$. **2.** *T* is not a subset of *S* because *T* has both large and small triangles, $T \nsubseteq S$.

According to the definition of subset, every set is a subset of itself. For example, $BT \subseteq BT$, $T \subseteq T$, and $H \subseteq H$, because every element in the first set is also in the second set. If we know that $A \subseteq B$ and that one or more elements of *B* are not in *A*, then *A* is called a **proper subset** of *B* and we write $A \subset B$. As examples, *BT*, the set of black triangles in Figure 2.4, is a proper subset of *T*, the set of black and white triangles.

EQUAL SETS   Sets that contain the same elements are called **equal sets.** Sometimes two sets may look different or have different descriptions, but they may represent the same elements. Consider the set *E* of even whole numbers and the set *D* of whole numbers that are divisible by 2. Since every even whole number is divisible by 2, the numbers in set *E* are contained in set *D*. Conversely, since every whole number that is divisible by 2 is an even number, the numbers in set *D* are contained in set *E*. Thus, the two sets have the same elements and are equal.

If *A* is a subset of *B* and *B* is a subset of *A*, then both sets have exactly the same elements and they are **equal.** This relationship is written $A = B$. In this case *A* and *B* are just different letters naming the same set.

ONE-TO-ONE CORRESPONDENCE   It is possible to match the elements in the set *SB* (small black) in Figure 2.5 with those in the set *LW* (large white) so that for each element in *SB* there is exactly one element in *LW* and, conversely, for each element in *LW* there is exactly one element in *SB*. We refer to this fact by saying that the two sets can be put into **one-to-one correspondence,** or that they are **equivalent sets.**

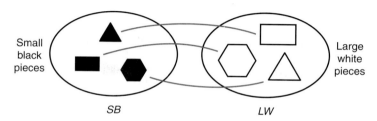

Figure 2.5

The concepts of number and counting are extensions of the idea of one-to-one correspondence. If two sets can be put into one-to-one correspondence, we say they have the **same number** of elements. To **count** the elements of a set, we match these elements with the whole numbers 1, 2, 3, 4, ... Adults will often point to the objects being counted, and children will sometimes touch each object as they match the objects and whole numbers.

The number of elements in the set of small black pieces in Figure 2.5 is 3, because this set can be put into one-to-one correspondence with {1, 2, 3}. If there is a whole number n such that the elements of a set can be matched one to one with the whole numbers 1, 2, 3, . . . , n, the set has n **elements** and the set is called **finite.** For example, the set of small black attribute pieces is a finite set. If a set is not finite, it is called **infinite.** Informally, a set is infinite if its elements go on without end. The set of all whole numbers is an example of an infinite set.

> A set is **finite** if it is empty or if it can be put into one-to-one correspondence with set {1, 2, 3, . . . , n}, where n is a whole number. A set is **infinite** if it is not finite.

Operations on Sets

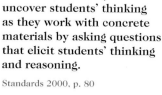

There are operations that replace two sets by a third set, just as there are operations on numbers that replace two numbers by a third number. *Addition* and *multiplication* are examples of operations on whole numbers; *intersection* and *union* are operations on sets.

INTERSECTION OF SETS Figure 2.6 shows that the set of small attribute pieces and the set of black attribute pieces have three elements in common. If we form a third set containing these common elements, it is called the **intersection** of the two sets.

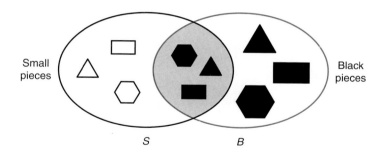

Figure 2.6

The **intersection** of two sets A and B is the set of all elements that are in both A **and** B. This operation is written $A \cap B$.

The intersection of the two sets in Figure 2.6 is the set of attribute pieces that are small and black. This new set is indicated by shading the common region inside the curve. The intersection of these sets is written as $S \cap B$.

Example G

Find the intersection of these sets of attribute pieces. (You may find it helpful to form two large overlapping circles and place attribute pieces inside the appropriate regions.)

1. L (large pieces), H (hexagons)

2. ST (small triangles), BH (black hexagons)

3. SR (small rectangles), S (small pieces)

Solution   1. $L \cap H = \{lbh, lwh\}$ **2.** $ST \cap BH = \emptyset$, because these sets are disjoint.   **3.** $SR \cap S = SR$, because SR is a subset of S.

The key word in the definition of intersection is *and*. In everyday use, as well as in mathematics, the word ***and*** means that two conditions must be satisfied. For example, if you are required to take the Graduate Record Examination (GRE) *and* the Miller Analogies Test (MAT), you must take both tests.

Research Statement

Developing meaning for mathematical symbols is essential for using these symbols effectively.

Hiebert and Carpenter 1992

UNION OF SETS   The set of small attribute pieces and the set of black attribute pieces have three pieces in common (Figure 2.7). A new set containing these three pieces and all other pieces within either set is called the **union** of the two sets.

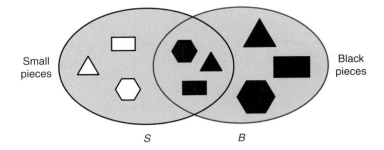

Figure 2.7

The **union** of two sets A and B is the set of all elements that are in A **or** in B **or** in both A and B. This operation is written $A \cup B$.

The union of the two sets in Figure 2.7 is the set of all attribute pieces that are small or black or both small and black. This new set is indicated by shading the total region inside the two curves. We write the union of these two sets as

$$S \cup B = \{swr, swh, swt, sbt, sbr, sbh, lbt, lbr, lbh\}$$

Example H

Find the union of these sets of attribute pieces.

1. *L* (large pieces), *H* (hexagons)

2. *ST* (small triangles), *BH* (black hexagons)

Solution   1. {*lbt, lwt, lbr, lwr, lbh, lwh, sbh, swh*}   2. {*sbt, swt, lbh, sbh*}

Notice that the solution for 1 in Example H contains *lbh* and *lwh* only once, even though these two attribute pieces are contained in both sets.

The key word in the definition of union is *or*. This word has two different meanings. In everyday use, *or* usually means that it is necessary to satisfy one condition or the other, *but not both*. For example, "You must take the course *or* pass the qualifying exam" means that you must do one of these two things but that not both are necessary. This is called the **exclusive *or*.** In mathematics, however, the word *or* usually means that one condition or the other condition, or both, may be satisfied. This is called the **inclusive *or*.** The inclusive *or* is used in defining the union of sets because an element in the union of two sets may be in the first set or in the second set or in both sets.

Sometimes we wish to consider more than two sets at a time. The Venn diagram in Figure 2.8 shows three sets of attribute pieces: *W* (white pieces), *S* (small pieces), and *H* (hexagonal pieces). This diagram can be used to determine the combinations of operations in the next example.

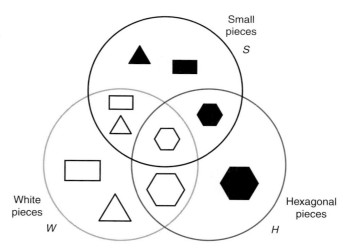

Figure 2.8

Example I

Use Figure 2.8 to list the elements in each of the following sets. (First determine the set in parentheses. You may find it helpful to shade the regions of the diagram in Figure 2.8.)

1. $(W \cup S) \cup H$

2. $(W \cap S) \cap H$

3. $(W \cup S) \cap H$

4. $W \cup (S \cap H)$

Solution   1. {*lwt, lwr, lwh, lbh, swt, swr, swh, sbt, sbr, sbh*}   2. {*swh*}   3. {*lwh, swh, sbh*}
4. {*swh, sbh, swt, swr, lwh, lwt, lwr*}

COMPLEMENT OF A SET   The word *complement* has the same meaning in mathematics as in everyday use. If you know that 11 people are on their way to your house and only 7 arrive, you might ask, "Where is the complement?" That is, where are the rest of the people who make up the whole group? Consider the set of small black attribute pieces and the set of remaining pieces in Figure 2.9. The small black pieces are inside the circle, and the others are outside. These two subsets are called **complements** of each other because their union is the whole set.

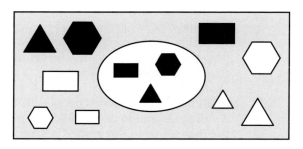

Figure 2.9

> For any given set *U,* if two subsets *A* and *B* are disjoint and their union is *U,* then *A* and *B* are *complements* of each other. This is written $A = B'$ or $B = A'$.

Example J

Set *SB* is the set of small black attribute pieces. The set of all the other attribute pieces—i.e., those that are not (small and black)—is the complement of *SB* (Figure 2.9). This set is denoted by *SB'*.

$$SB = \{sbr,\ sbt,\ sbh\}$$
$$SB' = \{lbt,\ lbh,\ lbr,\ lwt,\ lwh,\ lwr,\ swt,\ swr,\ swh\}$$

The "given set *U*" referred to in the previous definition is sometimes called the **universal set.** We have been using a universal set of 12 attribute pieces. In word problems involving whole numbers, the universal set is often the set of whole numbers.

Example K

Use the set of whole numbers as the universal set to determine the following complements.

1. What is the complement of the set of even whole numbers?

2. What is the complement of the set of whole numbers that are less than 10?

Solution   1. The set of odd whole numbers   2. The set of whole numbers greater than or equal to 10

The universal set can be any set, but once it is established, each subset has a unique (one and only one) complement. In other words, *complement* is an operation that assigns each set to another set, namely, its complement.

Problem-Solving Application

Drawing Venn diagrams is a problem-solving strategy for sorting and classifying information. Try solving the following problem by using the information given in the table and drawing three overlapping circles, one for each of the three networks.

PROBLEM

A survey of 120 people was conducted to determine the numbers who watched three different television networks. The results are shown in the following table. How many of the 120 people did not watch any of the three networks?

NETWORKS	NUMBERS OF PEOPLE
ABC	55
NBC	30
CBS	40
ABC and CBS	10
ABC and NBC	12
NBC and CBS	8
NBC and CBS and ABC	5

Understanding the Problem The Venn diagram in the following figure shows three circles, one to represent each of the three networks. Each of the seven regions inside the circles represents a different category of viewers. For example, people in region *y* watched NBC and CBS but not ABC. **Question 1:** What region represents the people who did not watch any of the three networks? We need to find the number of people in this region.

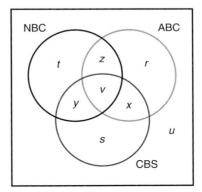

Devising a Plan We can find the number of people who did not watch any of the three networks by first finding the numbers for the seven regions inside the circles and then subtracting this total from 120. It is generally useful to begin with the innermost region and work outward. For example, *v* is the intersection of all three circles, and the table shows that $v = 5$. Using this number and the fact that there are eight people in the intersection of NBC and CBS, we can determine the value of *y*. **Question 2:** What is the value of *y*?

Carrying Out the Plan Continuing the process described in the previous paragraph, we can determine that $z = 7$ and $x = 5$. Now since there are 40 people

Objective: Solve problems by making Venn diagrams.

13·8 Problem Solving: Strategy
Logical Reasoning

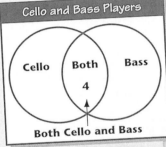

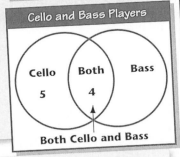

Math Word

Venn diagram

Read

Read the problem carefully.

Have you ever thought of becoming a professional musician? In a group of 12 professional musicians, all of them play cello or bass or both. Nine play cello and 4 play both cello and bass. How many play cello but not bass?

- What do you know?   **12 musicians; 9 play cello; 4 play both**

- What do you need to find? **number who play cello but not bass**

Plan

One way to organize the problem is to draw a Venn diagram. A **Venn diagram** is a diagram that uses overlapping circles to organize and show data.

Cello and Bass Players

Cello   Both   Bass
        4

Both Cello and Bass

Solve

Draw two overlapping circles. Label the circles *Cello* and *Bass*.

Write the number of musicians who play cello **and** bass in the overlapping section.

The 4 who play both cello and bass are part of the 9 who play cello. How many of the 9 play just cello?

Number of cello players	**Number who play both**	**Number who play cello only**
9	− 4	= 5

Show this number in the Venn diagram.

Of the 12 musicians, 5 play just cello.

Cello and Bass Players

Cello   Both   Bass
5   4

Both Cello and Bass

Look Back

How can you check that your answer is reasonable?

Sum It Up

How many musicians play bass altogether, including those musicians who play both bass and cello? Explain.

630 Cluster B

From *McGraw-Hill Mathematics, Grade Six*, by Macmillan/McGraw-Hill. Copyright © 2002 by The McGraw-Hill Companies, Inc. Reprinted by permission of The McGraw-Hill Companies, Inc.

represented inside the CBS circle and $v + y + x = 13$, we know that $s = 40 - 13 = 27$. In a similar manner we can determine that $r = 38$ and $t = 15$. So the total number of people represented by the seven regions is

$$\begin{array}{ccccccc} v & y & z & x & s & r & t \\ 5 + & 3 + & 7 + & 5 + & 27 + & 38 + & 15 = 100 \end{array}$$

Question 3: How many people did not watch any of the three networks?

Looking Back   We solved this problem by finding the number of people in the union of three sets and then finding the number of people in the complement. In addition to solving the original problem, the Venn diagram provides much more information. For example, since $s = 27$, we know 27 people watched only CBS.
Question 4: How many people watched both NBC and ABC but not CBS?

Answers to Questions 1-4   1. The region labeled u, which is inside the rectangle but outside the union of the three circles   **2.** $y = 3$ ($y + v = 8$, so $y + 5 = 8$)   **3.** 20 ($120 - 100 = 20$)
4. 7 ($12 - 5 = 7$)

HISTORICAL HIGHLIGHT

Grace Chisholm Young
1868–1944

Grace Chisholm Young was born in England at a time when education for women was restricted to Bible reading and training in the homely arts. Mathematics and the classics were considered unsuitable subjects for women. Young's only formal education was the tutoring she received at home, but this was sufficient for her to pass the Cambridge Senior Examination. In 1893, she completed her final examinations and qualified for a first-class degree at Cambridge. Since women were not yet admitted to graduate schools in England, Young went to the university of Göttingen, Germany, the major center for mathematics in Germany, where Felix Klein was her adviser. Her outstanding work earned her a doctorate in mathematics, the first official degree granted to a woman in Germany on any subject. Her subsequent mathematical work was productive and creative. With her husband she coauthored the first textbook on set theory, a classic work in its field. Her *First Book of Geometry,* although published in 1905, looks surprisingly contemporary. She advocated that three-dimensional geometry be taught earlier in schools and that students fold patterns to form solids as an aid in visualizing theorems in solid geometry.*

*T. Perl, *Math Equals* (Reading, MA: Addison-Wesley Publishing Company, 1978), pp. 149–171.

EXERCISES AND PROBLEMS 2.1

The notches in the 30,000-year-old Czechoslovakian wolf bone are arranged in two groups. There are 25 notches in one group and 30 in the other. Within each series the notches are in groups of 5. Use this information in exercises 1 and 2, and give reasons for your conclusions.

1. Could this system have been devised without number names?

2. Could this system have been devised without number symbols?

Both sides of the 8000-year-old Ishango bone are sketched below. There is one row of marks on one side of the bone, and there are two rows of marks on the other side. Anthropologists have questioned the significance of the number of marks: Could they be records of game killed or of belongings? Maybe they are intended to show a relationship between numbers. Write the number of marks in each group in these rows, and use the results to answer exercises 3 and 4.

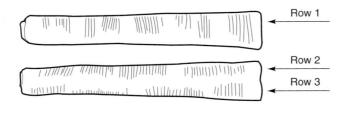

3. **a.** Which of these rows suggests a knowledge of multiplication by 2?
   b. Find some other number relationships.

4. In his book *The Roots of Civilization,* Alexander Marshack correlates these marks* with the phases of the moon and the days of a lunar calendar. Using 28 for the number of days in a lunar month, how many months are represented by the total number of marks on this bone?

*For a discussion of these marks, see A. Marshack, *The Roots of Civilization* (New York: McGraw-Hill, 1972), pp. 21–26.

Use the universal set of 12 attribute pieces below and the following sets to answer questions 5 through 14: W, white attribute pieces; H, hexagonal attribute pieces; SW, small white pieces; SB, small black pieces; and L, large pieces. (You may find it helpful to copy and cut out the attribute pieces and place them in large circles.)

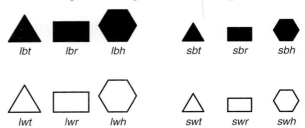

5. Which pairs of sets, if any, can be put into one-to-one correspondence?

6. Which pairs of sets, if any, are equal?

7. Which pairs of sets, if any, are disjoint?

8. Which set is a proper subset of another?

9. Which attribute pieces are in $W \cap L$?

10. Which attribute pieces are in $W \cup L$?

Which of the statements in exercises 11 and 12 are true?

11. **a.** $lbh \in L \cap W$
    b. $lwt \in H \cup L$
    c. $swr \in H'$

12. **a.** $swh \in W \cap H$
    b. $lwt \in L'$
    c. $lbr \in SB \cup W$

List the pieces described in exercises 13 and 14. (Use the *inclusive or.*)

13. **a.** Hexagonal and small
    b. Not (hexagonal and small)
    c. Small or white

14. **a.** Triangular or large
    b. White and triangular
    c. Not (small or white)

Given the universal set $U = \{0, 1, 2, 3, 4, 5, 6, 7, 8\}$ and sets $A = \{0, 2, 4, 6, 8\}$, $B = \{1, 3, 5, 7\}$, and $C = \{3, 4, 5, 6\}$, list the elements in the sets described in exercises 15 and 16.

15. **a.** $A \cap C$ **b.** $C' \cup B$
16. **a.** $C' \cap A$ **b.** $(A \cap C) \cup B$

Draw a Venn diagram for each part of exercises 17 and 18 so that for sets A, B, and C, all the given conditions are satisfied.

17. a. $A \subseteq B, B \subseteq C$
  b. $C \cap B = \varnothing, A \subseteq C$
  c. $(B \cup C) \subseteq A, B \cap C = \varnothing$

18. a. $A \cap B \neq \varnothing, B \cap C \neq \varnothing, A \cap C = \varnothing$
  b. $(B \cup C) \subseteq A, B \cap C \neq \varnothing$
  c. $C \subseteq A, (B \cap C) \subseteq A, A' \cap B \neq \varnothing$

Sketch a three-circle Venn diagram like the one shown here for each of the sets in exercises 19 and 20, and shade the region represented by the set.

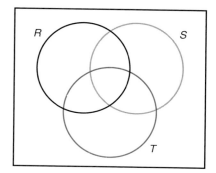

19. a. $R \cap S$
  b. $T \cup R$
  c. $(R \cup S) \cap T$

20. a. $(T \cap S) \cup R$
  b. $(R \cup T)'$
  c. $(R \cap T) \cap S'$

Given that set A has 15 elements and set B has 13 elements, answer exercises 21 and 22. Draw a sketch of each set.

21. What is the maximum number of elements in $A \cup B$? in $A \cap B$?

22. What is the minimum number of elements in $A \cup B$? in $A \cap B$?

Illustrate the set given under the figure in exercises 23 through 25 by shading the figure.

23.

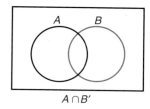

$A \cap B'$

24.

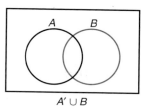

$A' \cup B$

25.

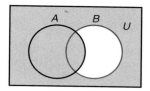

$A' \cup B'$

Use set notation to identify the shaded region in each of the sketches in exercises 26 through 28.

26.

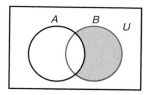

27.

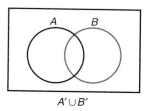

28.

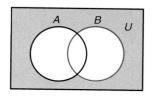

The following diagram of human populations was used in investigations correlating the presence or absence of B27+ (a human antigen), RF+ (an antibody protein), spondylitis (an inflammation of the vertebrae), and arthritis (an inflammation of the joints) with the incidence of various rheumatic diseases.

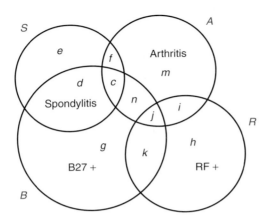

Find the letter(s) of the region(s) in the above diagram corresponding to each set in exercises 29 and 30.

29. a. $S \cap B$ **b.** $A \cap R$

30. a. $(S \cap B) \cap A$ **b.** $(R \cup A) \cap B$

REASONING AND PROBLEM SOLVING

31. In a music club with 15 members, 7 people played piano, 6 people played guitar, and 4 people didn't play either of these two instruments. How many people played both piano and guitar?

32. There were 55 people at a high school class reunion. If 16 people had college degrees, 12 people had college degrees and were married, and 14 people were single and did not have college degrees, how many people were married and did not have college degrees?

Use the following information in problems 33 and 34. In a survey of 6500 people, 5100 had a car, 2280 had a pet, 5420 had a television set, 4800 had a TV and a car, 1500 had a TV and a pet, 1250 had a car and a pet, and 1100 had a TV, a car, and a pet.

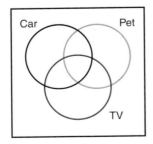

33. How many people had a TV and a pet, but did not have a car?

34. How many people did not have a pet or a TV or a car?

Use the following information in problems 35 and 36. A class survey found that 25 students watched television on Monday, 20 on Tuesday, and 16 on Wednesday. Of those who watched TV on only one of these days, 11 chose Monday, 7 chose Tuesday, and 6 chose Wednesday. Every student watched TV on at least one of these days, and 7 students watched on all three days.

35. If 12 students watched TV on both Monday and Tuesday, find the number of students in the class.

36. If 8 students watched TV on Tuesday and Wednesday, how many students watched TV on Monday or Tuesday but not on Wednesday?

37. An elementary school class polled 150 people at a shopping center to determine how many read the *Daily News* and how many read the *Sun Gazette*. They found the following information: 129 read the *Daily News*, 34 read both, and 12 read neither. How many read the *Sun Gazette*?

38. Of the 22 fast-food businesses in a small city, the number that have a drive-up window, outside seating, or delivery service is summarized as follows: 7 have delivery service; 15 have outside seating; 13 have a drive-up window; 9 have a drive-up window and outside seating; 3 have outside seating and delivery service; 3 have delivery service and a drive-up window; and 2 have all three services. How many of these businesses have only a drive-up window?

39. During spring registration at a midwestern liberal arts college, 442 students registered for English, 187 registered for history, and 234 registered for mathematics. What is the greatest possible total number of different students who could have registered for these courses, if it is known that only 96 registered for both English and mathematics?

40. The police records of a city contain the following statistics on offenses for the month of May: 430 assaults, 146 robberies, and 131 felonies. The records also show that 26 people were involved in both assault and robbery and that 33 people were involved in assault and felony. What is the greatest possible number of offenders for May who satisfy these statistics?

Use the following information in problems 41 and 42. There are eight blood types, shown by the Venn diagram. Each circle represents one of three antigens: A, B, or Rh. If A and B are both absent, the blood is type O. If Rh is present, the blood is positive; otherwise, it is negative. The following table represents the blood types of 150 people.

ANTIGENS	NUMBER OF PEOPLE
A	60
B	27
Rh	123
A and B	12
B and Rh	17
A and Rh	46
A and B and Rh	9

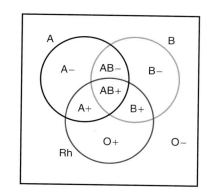

How many people have the blood types given in 41 and 42?

41. a. B+   **b.** A+

42. a. O+   **b.** O−

ONLINE LEARNING CENTER   www.mhhe.com/bennett-nelson

• Math Investigation 2.1   *Consecutive Numbers*
Section Related: • Links   • Writing/Discussion Problems   • Bibliography

---

PUZZLER

During a vacation it rained on 13 days; but when it rained in the morning, the afternoon was fine, and every rainy afternoon was preceded by a fine morning. There were 11 fine mornings and 12 fine afternoons. How long was the vacation?

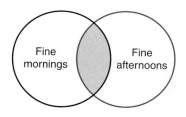

MATH ACTIVITY 2.2

SLOPES OF GEOBOARD LINE SEGMENTS

Materials: Geoboard paper (copy Dot Grid from inside cover pages of text or from website to form geoboard paper)

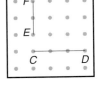

Slope of $\frac{2}{3}$

*1. The slope of the line from point A to B on the geoboard at the left is $\frac{2}{3}$. Notice that you can move from A to B by moving horizontally 3 spaces (called the **run**) and vertically 2 spaces (called the **rise**). These distances are the lengths of the legs of a right triangle. The **slope** of a line is the *rise* (vertical distance) divided by the *run* (horizontal distance) in moving from one point to another on the line. Sketch the following line segments on geoboard paper. Label a run, rise, and slope for each line segment. As the lines get "steeper," what happens to their numerical slopes?

a. 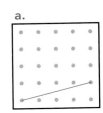 b. 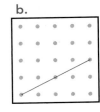 c. 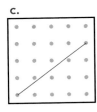 d.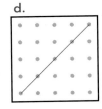

2. Sketch line segments on geoboard paper for the following slopes: $\frac{1}{3}, \frac{3}{2}, 2, \frac{4}{3}$.

3. The line through points C and D on the geoboard at the left is horizontal, that is, has no "steepness." Using points C and D, we find its run is 3 and its rise is 0, and since $0/3 = 0$, the slope of this line is 0. The line through points E and F has a rise of 2 and a run of 0 (there is no horizontal movement from point E to F). Since the formula for the slope is rise/run and 2/0 is not defined, we say that the slope of such line segments is not defined. Sketch line segments on geoboard paper which satisfy the following conditions.

a. Length of 4 and slope of 0
b. Length of 3 and undefined slope
c. Length of 1 and undefined slope
d. Length of 5 and slope of $\frac{3}{4}$

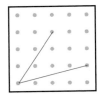

4. There are 24 line segments that have the lower left corner of the geoboard as an end point and 12 have different slopes. Sketch these 12 line segments and label them with their slopes. You may find it helpful to use more than one geoboard for your sketches. (Remember, vertical line segments cannot be used.) Make a list of the 12 slopes, and write them in increasing order from smallest to greatest.

SECTION 2.2

FUNCTIONS AND GRAPHS

Nine-person star with five people making approaches for slots, over California

PROBLEM OPENER

In a guessing game called What's My Rule? team *A* makes up a rule, such as "double the number and add 1," and team *B* tries to guess the rule. To obtain information about the rule, team *B* selects a number *x* and members of team *A* use their rule on the number to obtain a second number *y*. Find a rule for each table of numbers.

x	1	2	8	5	0
y	8	13	43	28	3

x	5	1	6	2	9
y	26	2	37	5	82

x	20	8	3	7	1
y	59	23	8	20	2

Two concepts underlie every branch of mathematics: One is the *set,* and the other, which will be defined in this section, is the *function. The Curriculum and Evaluation Standards for School Mathematics* comments on the importance of functions:

One of the central themes of mathematics is the study of patterns and functions. This study requires students to recognize, describe, and generalize patterns and build mathematical models to predict the behavior of real-world phenomena that exhibit the observed pattern. The widespread occurrence of regular and chaotic pattern behavior makes the study of patterns and functions important.*

Functions

The distance a skydiver falls is related to the time that elapses during the jump. By the end of 1 second, a skydiver has fallen 16 feet, and after 2 seconds, the distance is 62 feet. The distances for the first 10 seconds are shown in the following table.

Curriculum and Evaluation Standards for School Mathematics (Reston, VA: National Council of Teachers of Mathematics, 1989), p. 98.

Distance Fallen in Free-Fall Stable-Spread Position

SECONDS	DISTANCE, FEET	SECONDS	DISTANCE, FEET
1	16	6	504
2	62	7	652
3	138	8	808
4	242	9	971
5	366	10	1138

Figure 2.10

The table in Figure 2.10 matches each time from 1 to 10 seconds with a unique (one and only one) distance. Since the distance fallen depends on time, distance is said to be a *function* of time. A **function** is *two sets* and a *rule* that assigns each element of the first set to an element of the second set so that no element of the first set is assigned to more than one element of the second set.

The two sets for a function have names. The first set is called the **domain,** and the second set is called the **range.** In the skydiving example, the *domain* is the set of whole numbers from numeral 1 to 10, and the *range* is the set of distances.

One visual method of illustrating the assignment of elements from the domain to their corresponding elements in the range is with **arrow diagrams,** as shown in Example A. Such diagrams indicate the dynamic relationship between the elements of the two sets and show why we sometimes speak of an element of the range that gets "hit" by an element of the domain.

Example A

Describe a rule for assigning each element of the domain to an element of the range for the following functions.

Students' observations and discussions of how quantities relate to one another lead to initial experiences with function relationships, and their representations of mathematical situations using concrete objects, pictures, and symbols are the beginnings of mathematical modeling.

Standards 2000, p. 91

1.

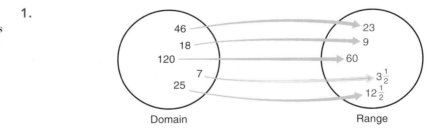

2.

3.

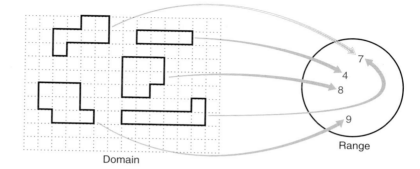

Domain

Range

4.

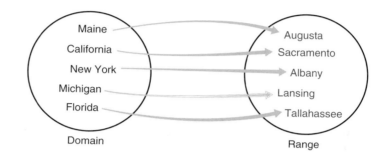

Domain

Range

Solution **1.** Each number in the domain is assigned to one-half its value in the range. **2.** Each pair of numbers in the domain is assigned to its sum in the range. **3.** Each figure in the domain is assigned to its area in the range. **4.** Each state in the domain is assigned to its capital city in the range.

Example A shows that the elements in the domain and range of a function may be different types of objects: numbers, geometric figures, etc. This example also shows that sometimes two or more elements in the domain can be assigned to the same element in the range. The important requirement for a function is that each element in the domain be assigned to not more than one element of the range. Example B will help you become familiar with this requirement. For each part of this example, ask yourself, Can the first element be assigned to more than one second element? If so, the correspondence of elements is not a function.

Example B

Determine which of the following rules for the given sets are functions. If the rule is not a function, explain why.

1. Each person is assigned to his or her social security number.

2. Each amount of money is assigned to the object it will buy.

3. Each person is assigned to a person who is older.

4. Each pencil is assigned to its length.

Solution **1.** Function. **2.** Not a function because two or more objects may cost the same amount. **3.** Not a function because many people are older than a given person. **4.** Function.

The rule for a function is often defined by an algebraic formula. It is customary to refer to an arbitrary element of the domain by a variable, such as x, and the corresponding element of the range by $f(x)$, as shown in Figure 2.11 [or $g(x)$, $s(x)$, etc.]. The symbol $f(x)$ is read as "f of x." Note that $f(x)$ does *not* mean f times x. For a domain element x, the corresponding range element is also denoted by the variable y.

Figure 2.11

Domain   Range

Consider the rule that assigns each x from the set of whole numbers to $3x + 1$ in the range. This rule can also be written as $f(x) = 3x + 1$. Thus, the equation is the rule that specifies what each element of the domain is assigned to: $f(5) = 3(5) + 1 = 16$, so 5 is assigned to 16; $f(0) = 3(0) + 1 = 1$, so 0 is assigned to 1; etc.

Example C

Write an algebraic rule for each of the following functions, where the domain is all whole numbers and x represents an element in the domain.

1. $f(x)$ is an element in the range, and each element in the domain is assigned to 3 more than twice its value.

2. $g(x)$ is an element in the range, and each element in the domain is assigned to 1 more than 4 times its value.

3. $h(x)$ is an element in the range, and each element in the domain is assigned to 10 times its value.

4. Evaluate $f(45)$, $g(56)$, and $h(84)$.

Solution   1. $f(x) = 2x + 3$ 2. $g(x) = 4x + 1$ 3. $h(x) = 10x$ 4. $f(45) = 93$, $g(56) = 225$, $h(84) = 840$

Rectangular Coordinates

Graphs provide a visual method for illustrating functions. A **horizontal axis,** called the x *axis,* is used for the elements of the domain, and a **vertical axis,** called the y *axis,* is used for the elements of the range. Each point on a graph is located by two numbers; their order is significant. The first number is called the x *coordinate* and indicates the distance to the right or left of the vertical axis. The second number is called the y *coordinate* and indicates the distance above or below the horizontal axis. These numbers are called the **coordinates** of the point. Figure 2.12 illustrates the coordinates of four points. The intersection of the two axes is called the **origin** and has coordinates $(0, 0)$.

This method of locating and describing points is called the **rectangular (or Cartesian) coordinate system.** The name *Cartesian* is in honor of René Descartes, the French mathematician and philosopher who first used this system for graphing geometric figures.

10·4

Objective: Represent situations and patterns with tables, words, and equations.

Functions

Algebra & functions

Learn

Math Words

function a relationship in which one quantity depends on another quantity

equation a mathematical statement with an equal sign in it

A fifth-grade student helps reduce trash by recycling. Each week she collects 10 pounds of newspaper from her family. Each neighbor gives her an additional 3 pounds of newspaper each week. What is the relationship between the amount of newspaper she collects and the number of neighbors she collects from?

Example

You can make a table to show the relationship.

Number of neighbors	0	1	2	3	4	5
Pounds of newspaper collected	10	13	16	19	22	25

- The amount of newspaper collected is equal to 10 plus 3 times the number of neighbors. This relationship is an example of a **function**.

- You can represent a function with an **equation**.

  > Think: $3c$ is the same as $3 \times c$.

  let n = pounds of newspaper collected
  let c = number of neighbors

  Then $n = 3c + 10$ is an equation that represents the function.

- Evaluate this equation if 5 neighbors give newspapers.

  > Think: Follow the order of operations.

  Evaluate $n = 3c + 10$ for $c = 5$
  $n = 3 \times 5 + 10$
  $n = 15 + 10$
  $n = 25$

Try It

Write an equation to describe each situation. Tell what each variable represents.

1. Ellie's family recycles 20 pounds of newspaper each week. Each neighbor recycles 5 pounds.

2. It costs $2.00 to dispose of recycling materials plus $0.25 a pound.

Sum It Up Explain what an equation is and how it is used.

440 Cluster A

From *McGraw-Hill Mathematics, Grade Five,* by Macmillan/McGraw-Hill. Copyright © 2002 by The McGraw-Hill Companies, Inc. Reprinted by permission of The McGraw-Hill Companies, Inc.

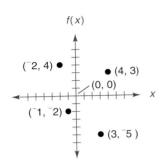

Figure 2.12

HISTORICAL HIGHLIGHT

René Descartes
(1596–1650)

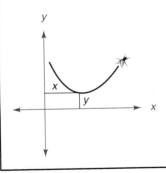

The French mathematician René Descartes is sometimes referred to as the father of modern mathematics. Although he made important contributions in the fields of chemistry, physics, physiology, and psychology, he is perhaps best known for his creation of the rectangular coordinate system. Legend has it that the idea of coordinates in geometry came to Descartes while he lay in bed and watched a fly crawling on the ceiling. Noting that each position of the fly could be expressed by two distances from the edges of the ceiling where the walls and ceiling met, Descartes realized that these distances could be related by an equation. That is, each point on a curve has coordinates that are solutions to an equation, and conversely, every two numbers *x* and *y* that are solutions to an equation correspond to a point on a curve. This discovery made it possible to study geometric figures by using equations and algebra. This link between geometry and algebra is one of the greatest mathematical achievements of all times.*

*H. W. Eves, *In Mathematical Circles* (Boston: Prindle, Weber, and Schmidt, 1969), pp. 127–130.

Linear Functions and Slope

Consider the function that relates time and distance as sound travels through the air. An observer can estimate the distance to an approaching thunderstorm by counting the seconds between a flash of lightning and the resulting sound of thunder. Every 5 seconds sound travels approximately 1 mile. If you count up to 10 seconds before hearing the thunder, the storm is approximately 2 miles away. In this example, *distance is a function of time.* Here are a few times in seconds and their corresponding distances in miles using function notation.

x	5	10	15	20	25
$f(x)$	1	2	3	4	5

As they progress from preschool through high school, students should develop a repertoire of functions. In the middle grades, students should focus on understanding linear relationships.

Standards 2000, p. 38

Since each member in the domain is multiplied by $\frac{1}{5}$ to obtain the corresponding number for the range, the equation for this function is $f(x) = \frac{1}{5}x$, and its graph is the line shown in Figure 2.13.

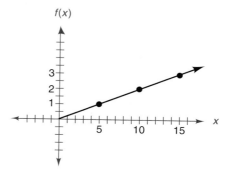

Figure 2.13

Sound travels faster in water than in air. In water it travels about 1 mile per second. In 2 seconds it travels 2 miles; in 3 seconds, 3 miles; etc. This is another example in which distance is a function of time. The equation for this function is $f(x) = x$, and its graph is the line shown in Figure 2.14.

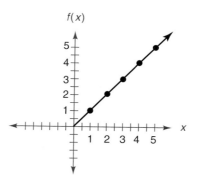

Figure 2.14

Notice that the graph of $f(x) = x$ has a greater slope than the graph of $f(x) = \frac{1}{5}x$. In general, the equation of a line through the origin is $f(x) = mx$, where the constant m is the slope of the line.

The concept of slope occurs in many applications of mathematics. For example, highway engineers measure the slope of a road by comparing the vertical rise to each 100 feet of horizontal distance. The Federal Highway Administration recommends a maximum vertical rise of 12 feet for each 100 feet of horizontal distance (Figure 2.15). Many secondary roads and streets are much steeper. Filbert

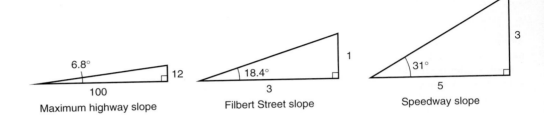

Figure 2.15

Maximum highway slope

Filbert Street slope

Speedway slope

Street in San Francisco has a vertical rise of approximately 1 foot for each 3 feet of horizontal distance. By comparison, the walls at the ends of the Daytona International Speedway have a vertical rise of 3 feet for each 5 feet of horizontal distance.

The slope of a line segment is defined in much the same way as the steepness of highways: Two points on a line are selected, and the **slope** of the line connecting these points is the difference between the two y coordinates (the **rise**) divided by the difference between the two x coordinates (the **run**). Two examples are shown in Figure 2.16. In part a, the ordered pairs (5, 3) and (9, 11) are used to compute the slope.

$$\text{Rise:} \quad 11 - 3 = 8 \qquad \text{run:} \quad 9 - 5 = 4 \qquad \text{slope:} \quad \tfrac{8}{4} = 2$$

Notice that we started with the coordinates of (9, 11) and subtracted the coordinates of (5, 3). The same slope will be obtained by starting with (5, 3) and subtracting the coordinates of (9, 11).

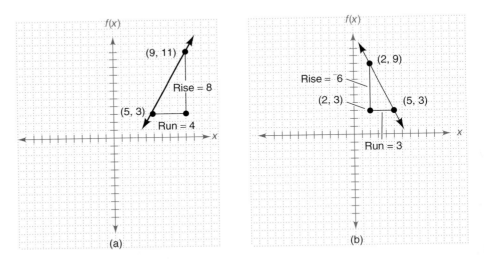

Figure 2.16

In part b, the slope is determined from the ordered pairs (2, 9) and (5, 3)

$$\text{Rise:} \quad 3 - 9 = {}^{-}6 \qquad \text{run:} \quad 5 - 2 = 3 \qquad \text{slope:} \quad \tfrac{-6}{3} = {}^{-}2$$

Example D

Find the rise and run for each pair of points, and determine the slope of the line, if it exists.

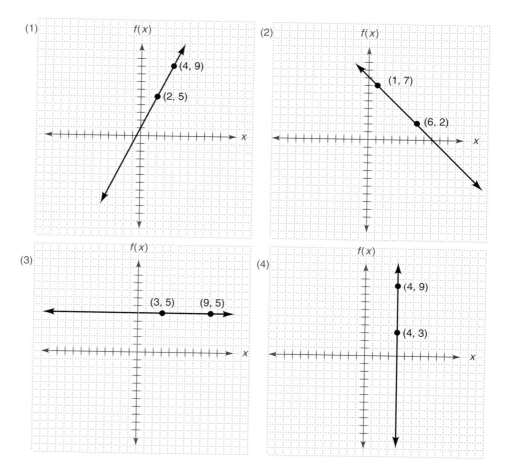

Solution   **1.** Rise: $9 - 5 = 4$; run: $4 - 2 = 2$; slope: $4/2 = 2$ **2.** Rise: $2 - 7 = {}^-5$; run: $6 - 1 = 5$; slope: ${}^-5/5 = {}^-1$ **3.** Rise: $5 - 5 = 0$; run: $9 - 3 = 6$; slope: $0/6 = 0$ **4.** Rise: $9 - 3 = 6$; run: $4 - 4 = 0$; slope: undefined.

Notice that the line in graph 3 in Example D is parallel to the horizontal axis. All lines that are parallel to the horizontal axis will have a rise of zero and, therefore, a slope of zero. The line in graph 4 in Example D is parallel to the vertical axis. All lines that are parallel to the vertical axis will have a run of zero, and since division by zero is undefined, the slope for such lines is undefined. That is, lines parallel to the vertical axis *do not have a slope.* Graphs 1 and 2 in Example D show lines with positive and negative slopes. In general, lines that extend from lower left to upper right have a **positive slope,** and lines that extend from upper left to lower right have a **negative slope.**

Next, consider the three lines and their equations in Figure 2.17. Notice that for pairs of points on these lines, each rise/run equals 2; and this slope can also be seen from the equations of the lines (below the graphs). Furthermore, the *y* coordinate of the point at which each line crosses the vertical axis, the **y intercept,**

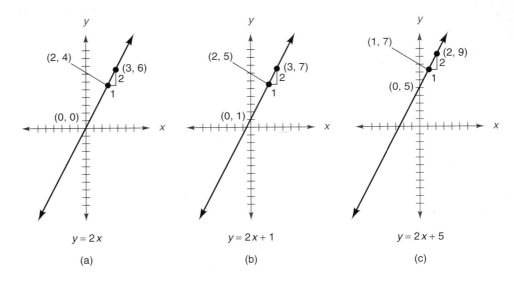

Figure 2.17

can be seen from the equation. It is zero for the line in part a, 1 for the line in b, and 5 for the line in c. The y intercept also can be easily obtained from these equations by setting $x = 0$.

In general, every line (except those parallel to the vertical axis) has an equation of the form

$$y = mx + b$$

where m and b are constants: and conversely, the graphs of such equations are lines. In this equation m is the slope of the line, and b is the y intercept. If a line is parallel to the vertical axis, its equation has the form $x = k$. For example, $x = 6$ is the line passing through $(0, 6)$ and parallel to the vertical axis. Functions whose graphs are lines that are not parallel to the vertical axis are called **linear functions.** When the equation of a line is written in the form $y = mx + b$, it is said to be in **slope-intercept form,** because the slope m of the line and the y intercept b can be read from the equation.

When the slope and the y intercept of a line are known, the equation can be written immediately. This information is often given in applications. Consider **rates,** such as *miles per hour* or *cost per unit.* These are examples of linear functions. Suppose it costs $8 per hour to rent a lawn mower. It will cost $16 for 2 hours, $24 for 3 hours, etc. If x denotes the number of hours and $f(x)$ the total cost, this information is described by the equation

$$f(x) = 8x$$

Now, if there is an initial fee of $5 in addition to the hourly rate, the equation becomes

$$f(x) = 8x + 5$$

In general, the *rate* is the slope of a line, and the *initial cost* is the y intercept.

With strong middle-grades focus on linearity, students should learn about the idea that slope represents the constant rate of change in linear functions and be ready to learn in high school about classes of functions that have nonconstant rates of change.

Standards 2000, p. 40

Example E

A taxi meter starts at $1.60 and increases at the rate of $1.20 for every minute. Let x represent the number of minutes and $f(x)$ represent the total cost. Write an equation for the total cost as a function of the number of minutes.

Solution   The initial fee is $1.60, and each minute costs $1.20. The total cost in dollars is $f(x) = 1.2x + 1.6$.

Many of the examples of linear functions from everyday life occur in rates we pay for services, such as electrical rates, phone rates, cable rates.

Example F

A copy center has the following rates for sending a fax of pages: in-state, $4 for the first page and $1 for each additional page; out-of-state, $5 for the first page and $1 for each additional page. The graphs of the functions defined by these rates are shown below.

1. What is the domain of these functions?

2. What is the range of the in-state function? the out-of-state function?

3. Find the points on the graph which show each cost for faxing 8 pages. What are the coordinates of these points? What is each cost?

4. What patterns do you see for these graphs?

5. If x represents a number from the domain of these functions and $f(x)$ and $g(x)$ are the corresponding numbers from the range for the in-state and the out-of-state function, respectively, write formulas for $f(x)$ and $g(x)$.

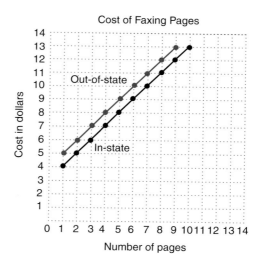

Cost of Faxing Pages

Solution   1. The set of whole numbers: 1, 2, 3, 4, ...   2. Range of in-state function: 4, 5, 6, ... Range of out-of-state function: 5, 6, 7, ...   3. These are the two points above the number 8 on the horizontal axis. The coordinates are (8, 11) and (8, 12). The corresponding costs are $11 and $12. 4. Possible patterns: The points on each graph lie on a straight line; to move from one point on the graph to the next point to the right, move one space right and up one space; the two graphs lie on lines that are parallel; the vertical distance between the graphs is 1.   5. $f(x) = 3 + x$ and $g(x) = 4 + x$.

The graph of each line in Example F is called a **discrete graph** because the points of the graph are separate. The faxing rate is for a whole number of sheets; so, for example, there are no numbers in the domain between 1 and 2. Often however, as in Example F, the points of a discrete graph are connected to help us visualize changes in the graph and to distinguish between two or more graphs.

Nonlinear Functions

The graphs of the functions up to this point have been lines, or separate points on a line, because they have involved constant rates. The function in the next example illustrates a rate of change which is not constant, and its graph is not a straight line. This is an example of a nonlinear function.

Example G

Fold a sheet of paper in half, then fold the resulting sheet in half again, and continue this process of folding in half. The number of regions formed is a function of the number of folds.

1. What are the numbers of regions for the following numbers of folds?

Number of folds	0	1	2	3	4
Number of regions	1				

Students should learn to distinguish linear relationships from nonlinear ones. In the middle grades, students should also learn to recognize and generate equivalent expressions, solve linear equations, and use simple formulas.

Standards 2000, p. 223

2. Find a pattern in the numbers of regions, and predict the number of regions for five folds. Then determine the number of regions by folding paper.

3. Graph this function for the first five folds. (Use a copy of the graphing grid from the inside cover or the website.)

4. If x is an arbitrary number of folds and $f(x)$ is the corresponding number of regions, what is the algebraic rule for the function?

5. The graph shows that the number of regions appears to be doubling for each new fold. How can the paper-folding activity be used to explain why the number of regions will continue to double?

Solution   1.

Number of folds	0	1	2	3	4
Number of regions	1	2	4	8	16

2. The numbers of regions for the first few folds are doubling; 5 folds, 32 regions.

3.

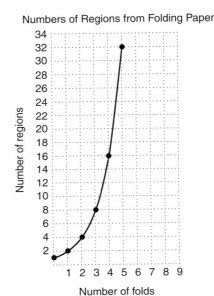

Numbers of Regions from Folding Paper

(vertical axis: Number of regions; horizontal axis: Number of folds)

$\overbrace{}^{x \text{ times}}$

4. $f(x) = 2^x$ or $f(x) = 2 \times 2 \times 2 \times \ldots \times 2$ **5.** After any given number of folds, the next fold will
fold each of the existing regions in half.

The graph in the preceding example curves upward because for each unit increase along the horizontal axis, the increase in the vertical direction is greater. A similar but opposite effect is seen in the next example.

Example H

The fourth-graders at King Elementary School conducted an experiment to observe the rate at which water cools. They placed a thermometer in a beaker of water and heated the water to boiling (212°F). They recorded the water temperature every minute until the temperature dropped to just below 168°F. Then they plotted the results on a grid like the one shown below. Notice that this is not a discrete graph because there is a temperature for each instant of time. The points of the graph can now be connected to form what is called a **continuous graph.**

1. How many degrees did the temperature drop during the first 2 minutes?

2. Did the temperature drop more in the first 2 minutes or in the second 2 minutes?

3. Often the variable t is used to represent time. If t represents the time in minutes and $f(t)$ is the corresponding temperature, use the graph to determine $f(0), f(1.5), f(4), f(4.5), f(8), f(10), f(12), f(14),$ and $f(16)$.

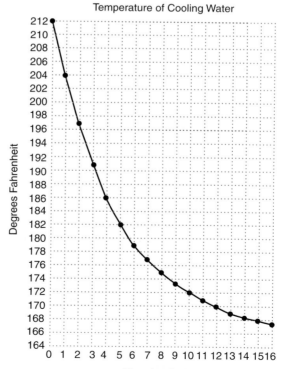

Temperature of Cooling Water

4. Approximately how much did the temperature drop during the first 8 minutes compared to the last 8 minutes?

5. What conclusion does the graph suggest about the rate of cooling during this 16-minute period?

Solution   **1.** 15°F   **2.** First 2 minutes   **3.** $f(0) = 212°F$, $f(1.5) = 200°F$, $f(4) = 186°F$, $f(4.5) = 184°F$, $f(8) = 175°F$, $f(10) = 172°F$, $f(12) = 170°F$, $f(14) = 168.5°F$, $f(16) = 167.5°F$ **4.** 37°F for the first 8 minutes and 7.5°F for the second 8 minutes. The temperature decrease for the first 8 minutes was about 5 times the decrease for the second 8 minutes.   **5.** The rate of cooling is more rapid at first and then slows down.

Interpreting Graphs

The NCTM Standards note that students frequently have experience graphing functions expressed in symbolic form, but that it is equally important that they be given opportunities to interpret graphs and translate from a graphical representation of a function to the symbolic form.* The following examples focus on interpreting graphs.

Example 1

The middle school sponsored a dance, and the graph of their revenue as a function of the number of tickets sold is shown below. After the sale of the first 100 tickets, the cost of the tickets increased, as shown by the steeper portion of the graph.

Research Statement

To provide effective instruction, teachers need to increase their knowledge of graphs and how to teach graphs.

Friel, Curcio, Bright 2001

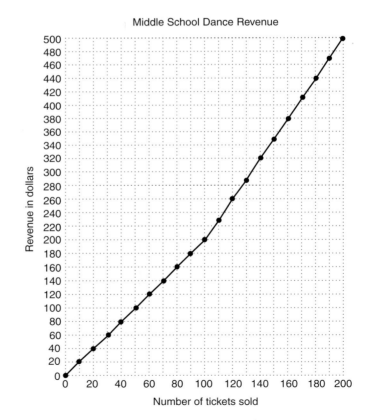

Curriculum and Evaluation Standards for School Mathematics (Reston, VA: National Council of Teachers of Mathematics, 1989), p. 155.

1. What was the revenue for the sale of the first 100 tickets?

2. What was the cost of each ticket for the first 100 tickets?

3. What was the revenue for the sale of the second 100 tickets?

4. What was the cost of each ticket for the second 100 tickets?

5. If $f(x)$ represents the revenue for the sale of x tickets, find $f(50)$ and $f(150)$.

Solution 1. $200   2. $2 per ticket   3. $500 − $200 = $300   4. $3 per ticket   5. $f(50) = 100$, $f(150) = 350$

Example J

The graph below shows distance in meters as a function of time over a 15-second period for a roller-blader's trip through the park.

1. What distance did the roller-blader travel during the first 8 seconds?

2. What distance did the roller-blader travel from the fifth to the eighth second?

3. What information does the graph indicate from the 8th to the 11th second?

4. What can be said about the roller-blader's speed from the 11th to the 15th second compared to the speed for the first 8 seconds?

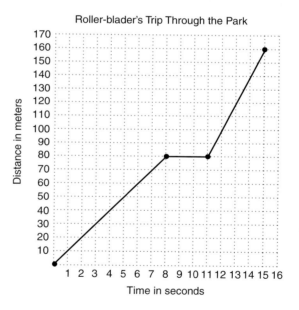

Roller-blader's Trip Through the Park

Solution 1. 80 meters   2. 30 meters   3. There was no increase in distance during this time.
4. It's faster—twice as fast.

Problem-Solving Application

The introduction to functions and graphs provides a new problem-solving strategy, **drawing a graph.**

PROBLEM

Students in the City Center School who live in the direction of Dolan Heights commute from school to home by taking bus 17 or the Dolan Heights subway. The bus leaves when school is over, and every 3 minutes it travels 1 mile. The subway leaves 7 minutes later, and every 3 minutes it travels 2 miles. What advice would you give to students who live in the direction of Dolan Heights and who want to use the method of travel that gets them home more quickly at the end of the school day? Is there a distance from the school which is reached at the same time by bus 17 as by the Dolan Heights subway?

Understanding the Problem   Try a few numbers of minutes to find the distances that students could travel by taking bus 17 or the Dolan Heights subway. For example, in the first 6 minutes after school is out, students would travel 2 miles on the bus and 0 miles on the subway. **Question 1:** What are the distances covered by bus and by subway at the end of 10 minutes?

Even before formal schooling, children develop beginning concepts related to patterns, functions, and algebra. The recognition, comparison, and analysis of patterns are important components of a student's intellectual development.

Standards 2000, p. 91

Devising a Plan   One method of solving the problem is to *form a table* for different numbers of times. Another method is to *draw a graph* of the times and distances for travel by bus and by subway. **Question 2:** If there is a time for which the distances covered by bus and by subway are equal, how will this be shown by the two graphs?

Carrying Out the Plan   The graph of the distances traveled by bus can be plotted by repeatedly moving horizontally 3 spaces (3 minutes) and vertically 2 spaces (1 mile). Similarly, the graph of the distances traveled by subway is plotted by repeatedly moving horizontally 3 spaces (3 minutes) and vertically 4 spaces (2 miles). **Question 3:** What is the amount of time for which the distances traveled by bus and by subway are equal? What is this distance? How might students be advised in selecting the method of travel which gets them home more quickly?

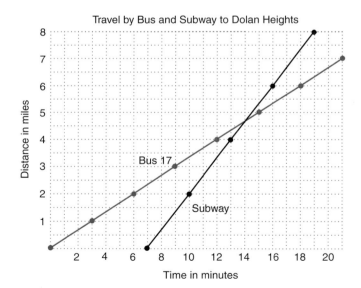

Looking Back   The graphs show that the bus traveled the greater distance for the first 14 minutes, and for times after 14 minutes the subway traveled the greater distance. The vertical distances between the graphs show how much greater the distance by one method of travel is than the other. For example, after 11 minutes the bus has traveled approximately 1 mile farther than the subway. **Question 4:** What is the time at which the subway will have traveled approximately 1 mile farther than the bus?

Answers to Questions 1–4   1. Bus, $3\frac{1}{3}$ miles; subway, 2 miles.   **2.** The time for which the distances are equal is shown by the intersection of the two graphs.   **3.** 14 minutes; $4\frac{2}{3}$ miles. Students traveling less than $4\frac{2}{3}$ miles could be advised to take the bus, and those traveling greater distances could be advised to take the subway   **4.** 17 minutes

EXERCISES AND PROBLEMS 2.2

Copies of the rectangular grid from the inside cover of the text or the website can be used for these exercises.

1. Experiments with rats at the University of London tested the conjecture that the motivation level for learning a task is a function of the difficulty of the task.* What does this graph show about the motivation level as the difficulty level of the task increases? decreases?

*P. L. Broadhurst, "Emotionality and the Yerkes-Dodson Law," *Journal of Experimental Psychology* 54 (1957): 345–352.

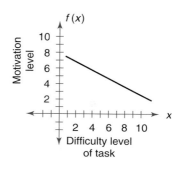

2. This graph shows the relationship between repeated exposure to learning and retention. Explain what this graph shows when the same topic is repeatedly reviewed and used over a period of time.

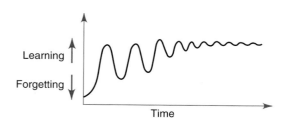

3. Describe in words a rule for assigning each element of the domain to an element of the range for the arrow diagram.

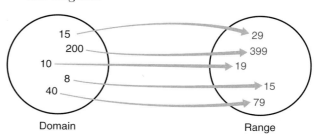

a. Write an algebraic rule for $f(x)$ that describes what each x in the domain corresponds to in the range.

b. Complete this table.

x	1	2	3	4	5	6	7	8	9	10
$f(x)$										

c. Using a rectangular grid, plot the points whose coordinates are given in the table in part b.

4. Describe in words a rule for assigning each element of the domain to an element of the range for the arrow diagram.

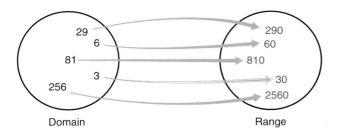

Domain   Range

a. Write an algebraic rule for $g(x)$ that describes what each x in the domain corresponds to in the range.

b. Complete this table.

x	1	2	3	4	5	6	7	8	9	10
$g(x)$										

c. Using a rectangular grid, plot the points whose coordinates are given in the table in part b.

In exercises 5 and 6, determine which rules are functions. If the rule is not a function, explain why.

5. a. People assigned to their birthdays
 b. Numbers assigned to numbers which are 10 times greater
 c. People assigned to their telephone numbers

6. a. Circles assigned to their areas
 b. Numbers assigned to any numbers which are greater
 c. Pairs of numbers assigned to their products

In exercises 7 and 8, write an algebraic rule for each function.

7. a. Each whole number is assigned to the whole number which is 17 greater.
 b. Each whole number is assigned to the number which is 2 less than 3 times the number.

8. a. Each whole number is assigned to the number which is 3 more than 4 times the number.

b. Each whole number greater than 10 is assigned to the number which is 6 less than the number.

9. Consider the function that relates the length x of the side of a square to the area $f(x)$ of the square.
 a. Determine the range value $f(x)$ for each of the following domain values: 1, 2, 3, 4, and 5.
 b. Use the coordinates in part a or a graphing calculator to sketch the graph of this function. (Copy the coordinate system from the inside cover or the website.)
 c. What is the equation of this function?
 d. Is this function linear or nonlinear?

10. Consider the function that relates the length x of the side of a square to the perimeter $f(x)$ of the square.
 a. Determine the range value $f(x)$ for each of the following domain values: 1, 2, 3, 4, and 5.
 b. Use the coordinates in part a or a graphing calculator to sketch the graph of this function.
 c. What is the equation of this function?
 d. Is this function linear or nonlinear?

In exercises 11 and 12, determine the slope and equation of each line (*Hint:* The slope and y-intercept are all that are needed to write the equation of a line.)

11. a.

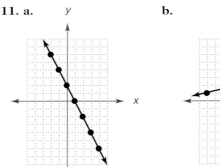

b.

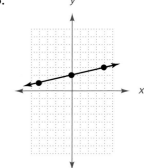

12. a.

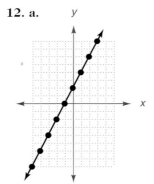

b.

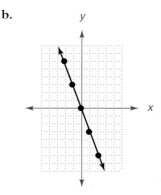

13. The equations of two linear functions and their graphs are shown below.

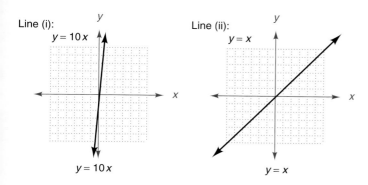

Line (i): $y = 10x$

$y = 10x$

Line (ii): $y = x$

$y = x$

a. What is the slope of each line?

b. Can a line be drawn whose slope is greater than the slope of line i? If so, write the equation of such a line.

c. Is there any limit to how large the slope of a line can become? Explain your reasoning.

14. The equations of two linear functions and their graphs are shown below.

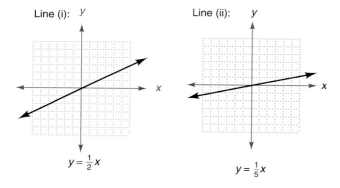

Line (i): y

Line (ii): y

$y = \frac{1}{2}x$

$y = \frac{1}{5}x$

a. What is the slope of each line?

b. Can another line be drawn whose slope is positive and less than the slope of line ii? If so, write the equation of such a line.

c. For any line with a positive slope, is it possible to have another line with a smaller positive slope?

REASONING AND PROBLEM SOLVING

15. During the past few years Great Britain's pound has been worth between $1 and $2 in U.S. currency. Suppose the rate of exchange is $1.50 for each pound.

a. What is the value in dollars for 5 pounds?

b. What is the value in pounds of $25.50?

c. The value in dollars is a function of the number of pounds. Letting x represent the number of pounds and $c(x)$ represent the value in dollars, write the equation for this function.

d. Sketch a graph of the function on a rectangular grid.

16. In recent years the Mexican peso has been worth between 10 cents and 20 cents in U.S. currency. Suppose the rate of exchange is 15 cents for each peso.

a. What is the value in dollars of 200 pesos?

b. What is the value in pesos of $300?

c. The value in dollars is a function of the number of pesos. Letting x represent the number of pesos and $d(x)$ represent the value in dollars, write the equation for this function.

d. Sketch a graph of the function on a rectangular grid.

17. Leaky Boat Club charges $1 per hour to rent a canoe. If you are a member of the club, there is no initial fee. Nonmembers who are state residents pay an initial fee of $2, and out-of-state people pay an initial fee of $5. The graphs of these rates are shown below.

a. Which line (upper, middle, or lower) represents the cost for state residents who are nonmembers?

b. How much more will it cost an out-of-state resident than a club member to rent a canoe for 8 hours? for 11 hours?

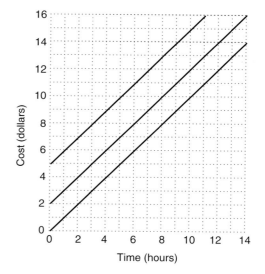

c. Using a rectangular grid, sketch these graphs and indicate the portions that correspond to the differences in part b.

d. How much more will it cost a state resident than a club member to rent a canoe for 9 hours? Mark the portion of the copied graphs that indicates this difference.

18. One rabbit at the Morse Research Labs will be given a diet to lose approximately 2 grams each day, and another rabbit will be put on a diet to lose approximately 3 grams each day. The graphs of their weights (below) for a 10-day period show the weights at the end of each day.
  a. What is the weight of each rabbit at the beginning of the experiment?
  b. How much weight will each rabbit lose after 5 days? Use a rectangular grid to sketch these graphs, and indicate the portion of the graphs that corresponds to the difference in their weights at the end of 5 days.
  c. What is happening to the differences between the weights of the rabbits over the 10-day period?

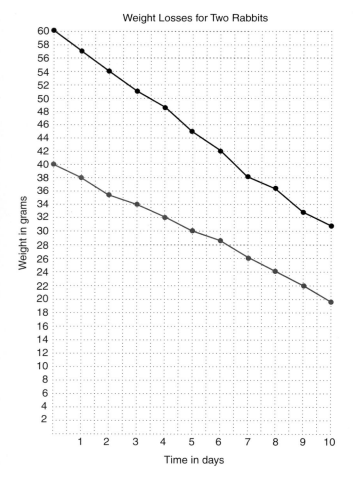

Weight Losses for Two Rabbits

19. In one location the telephone company charges an initial fee of $40 for visiting a house plus $12 for each telephone jack installed. Let x be the number of jacks and $c(x)$ the total cost.
  a. Write an equation for the cost of having the telephone company visit a house and install a total of x jacks.
  b. What is the value of $c(5)$?
  c. Graph this function.

20. A bus transportation company charges a $200 flat rate for a one-day trip (500 miles or less) plus $25 for each person. Let x be the number of people taking a bus trip and $f(x)$ the total cost.
  a. Write an equation for the cost of a bus trip for x people.
  b. What is the value of $f(23)$?
  c. Graph this function.

21. A racquetball club charges $15 per month plus $6 for each hour of court time, and only whole numbers of hours of court time can be purchased. Let x be the number of hours of playing racquetball in a given month, and $g(x)$ the total cost.
  a. Write an equation for the cost per month of playing racquetball.
  b. What is the value of $g(14)$?
  c. Graph this function.

22. A cable television company charges $20 per month plus $5 for each additional channel. Let x be the number of additional channels and $p(x)$ the total cost per month.
  a. Write an equation for the total monthly cost of the television cable service with x additional channels provided.
  b. What is the value of $p(4)$?
  c. Graph this function.

Use the following graph in problems 23 and 24. This graph shows a student's speed during a 20-minute bike ride.

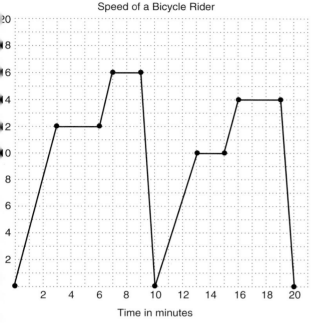

Speed of a Bicycle Rider

Time in minutes

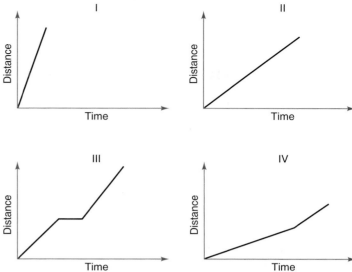

23. a. What was the student's speed from the third to the fifth minute?
b. At what times during the bike ride did the student come to a stop?
c. During what time intervals was the student's speed increasing?

24. a. What was the student's speed from the 16th to the 19th minute?
b. During what time intervals was the student's speed constant, that is, not changing?
c. During what time intervals was the student's speed decreasing?

25. Four children go to school along the same road. Joel walked half the distance and then jogged the rest of the way. Joan jogged all the way to school. Mary rode her bicycle but stopped to talk to a friend. Bob's father drove him to school in the family car.
a. The graphs in the next column show distance as a function of time for each of these students. Match each student with a graph.
b. Which student took the longest to get to school?
c. Which student lives the farthest from school?
d. Which student took the least time to get to school?
e. Which student lives closest to school?

26. Sally, Tom, Bette, and Howard have jobs on weekends at the supermarket. The graphs on the next page show their distances traveled from home to work on a given day as functions of time. Tom walked halfway and then jogged the rest of the way. Sally jogged halfway and then walked the remaining distance. Bette roller-bladed all the way but stopped to enjoy the view for 3 minutes. Howard rode his bike, but had to stop 1 minute at a stoplight.
a. Determine the graph which corresponds to each person's distance as a function of time.
b. Which student took the longest to get to work?
c. Which student lives the farthest from the supermarket?
d. Which student took the least time to get to work?
e. Which student lives closest to the supermarket?

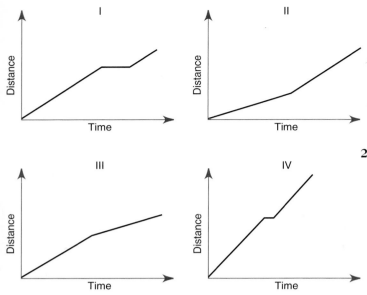

27. Each of the following graphs represents the temperature of an oven as a function of time.

   a. Which graph indicates that the oven door was opened once for a brief time during the cooking period? Mark the portion of the graph which indicates the open door.

b. Which graph indicates the oven was initially heated to a higher temperature than needed for the cooking?

c. Which graph shows the oven maintaining a more or less constant temperature during the cooking period with slight variations due to cooling and reheating? Mark this portion of the graph.

d. Which graph shows that the oven was on at a low temperature for a time before the heat was increased? Mark this portion of the graph.

28. Each of the following graphs represents the speed of a biker as a function of time.

   a. Which graph shows that the biker pedaled up a hill? Mark the portion of the graph which indicates the biker was pedaling up a hill.

   b. Which graph shows the biker's constant speed was not interrupted? Mark the portion of the graph which indicates the speed was constant.

   c. The biker stopped a few minutes for a repair. Which graph shows this? Mark the portion of the graph which indicates the time period for the repair.

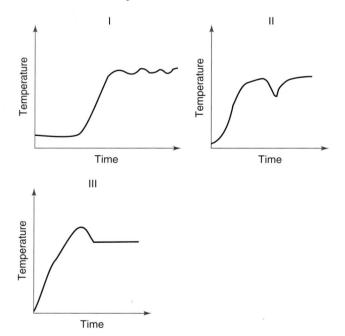

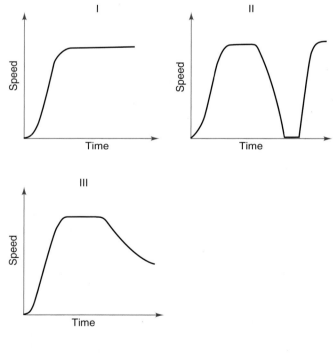

Use the following sketch of a roller coaster in problems 29 and 30 to draw the graphs.*

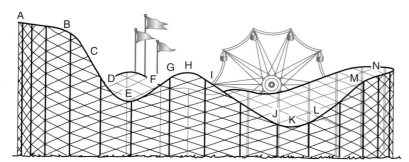

29. Draw a graph of the speeds of the roller coaster from *A* to *H* as a function of the lettered locations on the roller coaster, without using numbers.

30. Draw a graph of the speeds of the roller coaster from *H* to *N* as a function of the lettered locations on the roller coaster, without using numbers.

31. Pat ran a 200-meter race from the swing set to the soccer goal net with her younger brother Hal. Pat runs 4 meters per second, and Hal runs 3 meters per second, so Pat gives her brother a 40-meter head start from the swing set.
   a. Use a rectangular grid to form a graph for each person's distance run as a function of time. (Copy the rectangular grid from the inside cover or the website.)
   b. Mark the points on the graphs which show each person's distance from the swing set after 30 seconds.
   c. How much time will have elapsed when they are both the same distance from the swing set?
   d. Who will win the race?
   e. When the winner wins the race, how far will the other person be from the soccer goal net?

32. At First National Bank the consumer pays a monthly checking account fee of $2 plus 10 cents for each check. At States Saving Bank there is a $1.50 monthly fee for checking accounts with a charge of 15 cents apiece for the first 15 checks and 10 cents apiece for each additional check beyond the 15th.
   a. Use a rectangular grid to form a graph for both types of checking accounts. Label the costs on the grid for the first 15 checks.
   b. Which bank charges more for 15 checks?
   c. For what number of checks will the cost to the consumer be the same?
   d. Determine which bank charges more for 30 checks, and then determine how much greater this cost is than that charged by the other bank.

33. Electrical impulses that accompany the beat of the heart are recorded on an electrocardiogram (EKG). The electrocardiograph measures electrical changes in millivolts (1 millivolt is 1/1000 volt). The graph below shows the changes in millivolts as a function of time for a normal heartbeat.

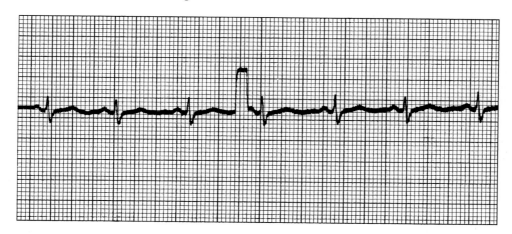

Curriculum and Evaluation Standards for School Mathematics (Reston, VA: National Council of Teachers of Mathematics, 1989), p. 83.

a. How much time is represented on this graph if each small space on the horizontal axis represents .04 second?

b. The tall rectangular part of the graph was caused by a 10-millivolt signal from the EKG machine. Such a signal is called a *calibration pulse.* How long did this signal last?

c. This graph shows 7 heartbeats, or pulses. Approximately how much time is there between each pulse (from the end of one pulse to the end of the next pulse)? At this rate how many pulses will there be per minute?

34. Featured strategy: Drawing a graph Suppose the average annual cost of heating a home with solar energy is $100, with an initial investment of $8000, and the average annual cost of heating a home with oil is $700, with an initial investment of $2000. Find the number of years before the cost of heating with solar energy will equal the cost of heating with oil.

a. Understanding the Problem Let's look at the total costs for the first few years. In the first year, heating with oil costs $2700 and heating with solar energy costs $8100 (including the initial costs). What is the cost of each system for the first 3 years?

b. Devising a Plan One approach to solving this problem is to write and graph equations for the cost of oil heat and solar heat as functions of time. The equation for heating with oil is $c(x) = 700x + 2000$, where $c(x)$ is the total cost for the first x years. In terms of the variables x and $s(x)$, what is the equation for heating with solar energy?

c. Carrying Out the Plan Graph the functions for heating with oil and heating with solar energy, and use these graphs to determine the number of years before the costs of oil heat and solar heat are equal. What is this cost?

d. Looking Back The vertical distances between the cost lines for oil heat and solar heat represent the differences in costs of these two systems. Use the graph to determine the first year for which the total cost of oil heat will be at least $2000 greater than the total cost of solar heat. Label the part of the graph which represents this difference.

35. Following are the first four figures in a sequence which uses square tiles.

a. Let $f(n)$ represent the number of tiles in the nth figure. Complete the table for this function.

Figure number	1	2	3	4	5	6	7	8
$f(n)$	3							

b. Graph the points of the function whose coordinates are in the table. What patterns do you see in the graph?

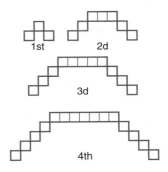

c. Find a pattern in the numbers of tiles, and determine the value of $f(20)$.

d. Write an algebraic rule for $f(n)$. Use this rule to find $f(350)$.

36. Here are the first four figures in a sequence that uses square tiles.

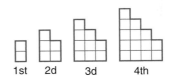

a. Let $g(n)$ represent the number of tiles in the nth figure. Complete the table for this function.

Figure number	1	2	3	4	5	6	7	8
$g(n)$	2							

b. Graph the points of the function whose coordinates are in the table. What patterns do you see in the graph?

c. Find a pattern in the numbers of tiles, and determine the value of $g(18)$.

d. Write an algebraic rule for $g(n)$. Use this rule to find $g(475)$.

37. Consider the following two sequences of figures.
Sequence 1:

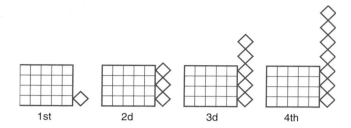

1st   2d   3d   4th

Sequence 2:

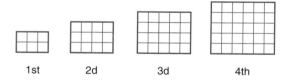

1st   2d   3d   4th

a. Find patterns in sequence 1 and sequence 2, and write an algebraic rule for the number of tiles in the nth figure of each sequence.
b. Use a rectangular grid to graph both functions defined by these rules.
c. Find the value of n for which the graphs intersect.
d. What information about these sequences is obtained by knowing the point of intersection?

38. Consider the following two sequences of figures.
Sequence 1:

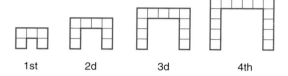

1st   2d   3d   4th

Sequence 2:

126 tiles   124 tiles   122 tiles   120 tiles

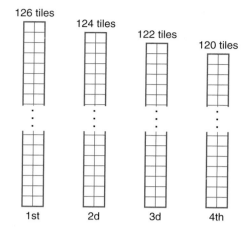

1st   2d   3d   4th

a. Find patterns in sequence 1 and sequence 2, and write an algebraic rule for the number of tiles in the nth figure of each sequence.
b. Use a rectangular grid to graph both functions defined by these rules.
c. Find the values of n for which the graphs intersect.
d. What information about these sequences is obtained by knowing the point of intersection?

· ·

ONLINE LEARNING CENTER   www.mhhe.com/bennett-nelson

• Math Investigation 2.2   *Graphs of Functions*
Section Related: • Links   • Writing/Discussion Problems   • Bibliography

MATH ACTIVITY 2.3

DEDUCTIVE REASONING GAME

Pica-Centro is a game for two players (or groups) in which one player uses **deductive reasoning** (obtaining conclusions from given information) to determine the digits of a number which is selected by the other player.* The game begins with player A choosing a three-digit number that contains no zeros and recording it on a slip of paper without showing it to player B. Player B then tries to determine this number by asking questions. Player B records all guesses and player A's responses in the table. Player B's first attempt is a guess, but after this, deductive reasoning is used based on Player A's replies.

Beginning in the elementary grades, children can learn to disprove conjectures by finding counterexamples. At all levels, children will learn to reason inductively from patterns and specific cases. Increasingly over the grades, they should also learn to make effective deductive arguments.

Standards 2000, p. 59

*1. Suppose player A chooses 574 and player B's first guess is 123 (see table below). Then player A responds by saying 0 pica and 0 centro, and player B records this response in the first row of the table. A pica is a digit that is correct but not in the correct position, and a centro is a digit that is both correct and in the correct position. What does player B know from this response?

*2. Player B's second guess is 456 (see table) and player A responds with 2 pica and 0 centro, which player B records in the second row of the table. What does player B know from this response?

*3. A logical third guess for player B is 654 or 546 or 465. Explain why.

*4. Suppose player B chooses 654 (see table). Then player A would say 1 pica and 1 centro. What can player B deduce from this information? Explain your reasoning. Can player B conclude that the digit 4 is in the correct position? Can player B conclude that 5 is one of the digits in player A's number?

GUESSES			RESPONSES	
DIGITS			PICA	CENTRO
1	2	3	0	0
4	5	6	2	0
6	5	4	1	1

5. Make a Pica-Centro table and play this game with another person. Then reverse roles so that both players have a chance to use deductive reasoning. The player who requires the fewest guesses to determine the number is the winner.

*D. B. Aichele, "Pica-Centro, A Game of Logic," *The Arithmetic Teacher* 19, no. 5 (May 1972): 359–361.

SECTION 2.3

INTRODUCTION TO DEDUCTIVE REASONING

"When do you want it?"

PROBLEM OPENER

Mike won't take part in the school play if Sue is in it. Tim says that in order for him to participate in the play, Sue must be in it. If Mike is in the play, then Rhonda refuses to be part of it. The director insists that only one of the two girls and only one of the two boys be in the play. Who will be chosen?

Lewis Carroll, well-known author of *Alice's Adventures in Wonderland*, also wrote books on logic. At the beginning of his *Symbolic Logic,** he states that logic will give you

. . . the power to detect fallacies, and to tear to pieces flimsy illogical arguments which you will so continually encounter in books, in newspapers, in speeches, and even in sermons, and which so easily delude those who have never taken the trouble to master this fascinating Art. Try it. That is all I ask of you!

As Lewis Carroll noted, examples of illogical reasoning are common. Consider the following statement:

If the world ends tomorrow, then you will not have to pay for the printing.

Suppose this statement is true. Does this mean that if the world does not end tomorrow, there will be a charge for the printing? This question will be answered in this section.

*Lewis Carroll, *Symbolic Logic and the Game of Logic* (New York: Dover Publications, Inc., 1958).

Deductive Reasoning

There are two main types of reasoning, *inductive* and *deductive,* and both are common in forming conclusions in our everyday activities. In Chapter 1 we saw that inductive reasoning is the process of forming conclusions on the basis of patterns and observations.

Example A

Observation   An office clerk notices that a patient has never been on time for an appointment.

Conclusion   This person will be late for his or her next appointment.

This conclusion may be true, but we cannot be sure from the given information. Perhaps you can see why a conclusion based on inductive reasoning is sometimes called an *informed guess.* **Deductive reasoning,** however, is the process of forming conclusions from one or more given statements.

Example B

Given statements

1. The sum of two numbers is 243.

2. One of the numbers is 56.

Conclusion   The other number is 187.

Students should discuss their reasoning on a regular basis with the teacher and with one another, explaining the basis for their conjectures and the rational for their mathematical assertions. Through these experiences, students should become more proficient in using inductive and deductive reasoning appropriately.

Standards 2000, p. 262

Examples A and B illustrate the difference between inductive and deductive reasoning: With *inductive reasoning* we form a conclusion that is probable or likely, and with *deductive reasoning* we form a conclusion based on given statements.

The *Curriculum and Evaluation Standards for School Mathematics* discusses the importance of both types of reasoning:

Both inductive and deductive reasoning come into play as students make conjectures and seek to explain why they are valid. Whether encouraged by technology or by challenging mathematical situations posed in the classroom, this freedom to explore, conjecture, validate, and to convince others is critical to the development of mathematical reasoning in the middle grades.*

Venn Diagrams

Circles, rectangles, etc. to represent sets were used by John Venn (1834–1923) as a visual aid in deductive reasoning. The following examples illustrate the convenience of *Venn diagrams* in representing information and drawing conclusions. Each given statement is called a **premise.**

Curriculum and Evaluation Standards for School Mathematics (Reston, VA: National Council of Teachers of Mathematics, 1989), p. 81.

Example C

Premises

1. All dolphins are whales.

2. All whales are mammals.

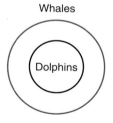

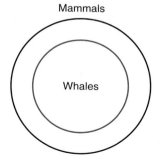

Conclusion   All dolphins are mammals.

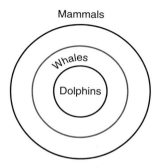

The diagram in Example C illustrates that the dolphins are a subset of the whales and the whales are a subset of the mammals. So the dolphins are a subset of the mammals. Example C also shows something important about deductive reasoning; namely, it is possible to obtain conclusions from given statements without necessarily having an understanding of the subject matter.

One of the conventions in using Venn diagrams is that if a region inside a circle represents a given set, then the region outside the circle represents all elements that are not in the set. In the next example, the region outside the amphibian circle represents all nonamphibians.

Example D

Premises

1. All salamanders are amphibians.

2. Animals that develop an amnion are not amphibians.

Being able to reason is essential to understanding mathematics. Building on the considerable reasoning skills that children bring to school, teachers can help students learn what mathematical reasoning entails.

Standards 2000, p. 56

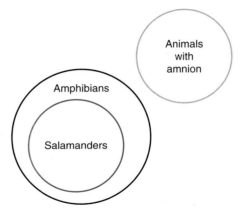

Conclusion   Salamanders do not develop an amnion.

In Example D, premise 2 tells us that animals with an amnion are outside of the amphibian circle, and since the salamanders are inside the amphibian circle, we can conclude that salamanders do not develop an amnion.

The next example involves the word *some*, which means *at least one*. To illustrate with Venn diagrams that at least one element is in two different sets, we place a dot in the overlapping region of the two sets.

Example E

Premises

1. All customs officials are government employees.

2. Some college graduates are customs officials.

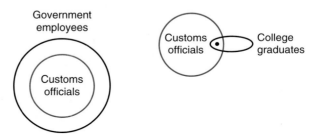

Conclusion   Some college graduates are government employees.

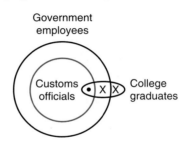

Notice that the diagram for the conclusion in Example E shows that some of the region for the college graduates overlaps the region of the government employees' circle and some of this region is outside the government circle. However, from the given information we cannot conclude that there are college graduates who are outside the government employees' circle, or that there are college graduates inside the government employees' circle but outside the customs officials' circle (see regions marked **X**).

In Examples B, C, D, and E, we have illustrated deductive reasoning. When a conclusion follows from the given information, as in these examples, we say that the conclusion is **valid** and that we have used **valid reasoning.** When a conclusion does not follow from the given information, we say that the conclusion is **invalid** (or **not valid**) and that we have used **invalid reasoning.** Invalid reasoning is illustrated in the next example. Notice the use of dots to indicate there is at least one person in the intersection of two pairs of these sets.

Example F

Premises

1. Some members of the Appropriations Committee are Republicans.

2. Some Republicans are on the Welfare Committee.

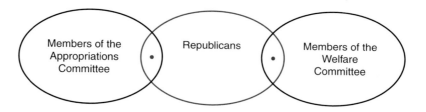

Conclusion   Some members of the Appropriations Committee are members of the Welfare Committee. (invalid)

It is possible in Example F that there are members of the Appropriations Committee who are also members of the Welfare Committee, but from the given information we are not forced to accept this conclusion. Therefore, the conclusion is invalid.

Conditional Statements

The *given information* in deductive reasoning is often a statement of the form "if . . . , then. . . ." A statement of this form has two parts: the "if" part is called the **hypothesis,** and the "then" part is called the **conclusion.** For example,

Hypothesis   Conclusion

If a number is less than 3, then it is less than 8.

A statement in this form is called a **conditional statement.** Many statements that are not in if-then form can be rewritten as conditional statements.

Example G

Students need to explain and justify their thinking and learn how to detect fallacies and critique others' thinking. They need to have ample opportunity to apply their reasoning skills and justify their thinking in mathematics discussions.

Standards 2000, p. 188

Write the following statements in if-then form.

1. All courses completed with a grade of C will not count for graduate credit.

2. Every public beach must have a lifeguard.

3. You will stay in good condition by exercising every day.

4. Students will not be admitted after 5 p.m.

5. The patient will have a chance of recovering if he goes through the treatment.

Solution   1. If a course is completed with a grade of C, then it will not count for graduate credit. 2. If a beach is public, then it must have a lifeguard.   3. If you exercise every day, then you will stay in good condition.   4. If you are a student, then you will not be admitted after 5 p.m.   5. If he goes through the treatment, then the patient will have a chance of recovering.

Every conditional statement "if p, then q" has three related conditional statements that can be obtained by negating and/or interchanging the *if part* and the *then part.* The new statements each have special names that show their relationship to the original statement.

Statement	If p, then q.
Converse	If q, then p.
Inverse	If not p, then not q.
Contrapositive	If not q, then not p.

Example H

Write the converse, inverse, and contrapositive of the following conditional statement.

Statement: If a person lives in Maine, then the person lives in the United States.

Solution   Converse: If a person lives in the United States, then the person lives in Maine. **Inverse:** If a person does not live in Maine, then the person does not live in the United States. **Contrapositive:** If a person does not live in the United States, then the person does not live in Maine.

The statement in Example H, "If a person lives in Maine, then the person lives in the United States," is diagrammed in Figure 2.18. Notice that the *if part* (hypothesis) is the inner of the two circles. The people who do not live in the United

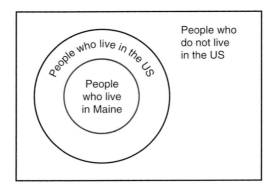

Figure 2.18

States are outside the larger circle. The same diagram also illustrates the information in the contrapositive of the statement in Example H: If a person does not live in the United States, then the person does not live in Maine. So the diagram in Figure 2.18 illustrates an important fact about if-then statements: A conditional statement and its contrapositive are **logically equivalent.** That is, if one is true, so is the other, and if one is false, so is the other.

Figure 2.18 also illustrates another important fact: If a conditional statement is true, its *converse* and *inverse* are not necessarily true. Consider the converse in Example H: If a person lives in the United States, then the person lives in Maine. The region outside the small circle and inside the large circle shows that it is possible for a person to live in the United States and not live in Maine. Consider the inverse in Example H: If a person does not live in Maine, then the person does not live in the United States. If a person does not live in Maine, this person is outside the small circle, but not necessarily outside the large circle. So we cannot conclude that the person does not live in the United States.

Example H illustrated that a conditional statement and its converse are not logically equivalent. That is, a conditional statement may be true, and its converse may be false. However, when it does happen that a conditional statement and its converse are both true, the two statements are often combined into a single statement by using the words *if and only if.* When this is done, the new statement is called a **biconditional** statement.

Example I

The following statement and its converse are both true. Combine them into one statement by using the words if and only if.

Statement: If one of two numbers is zero, then the product of the two numbers is zero.
Converse: If the product of two numbers is zero, then one of the two numbers is zero.

Solution   **Biconditional:** The product of two numbers is zero *if and only if* one of the numbers is zero. Or, it can be written: One of two given numbers is zero if and only if the product of the two numbers is zero.

Reasoning with Conditional Statements

The given information (premises) in the following examples contains conditional statements. Venn diagrams will be used to show whether the conclusions are valid or invalid.

Example J

Premises

1. If a person challenges a creditor's report, then the credit bureau will conduct an investigation for that person.

2. Ronald C. Whitney challenged a creditor's report.

During grades 3–5, students should be involved in an important transition in their mathematical reasoning . . . formulating conjectures and assessing them on the basis of evidence should become the norm.

Standards 2000, p. 188

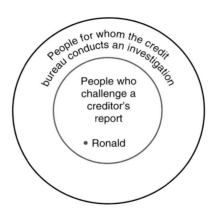

Conclusion The credit bureau will conduct an investigation for Ronald C. Whitney. (valid)

The diagram above shows why the reasoning in Example J is valid. The two circles represent the information in statement 1. Since statement 2 says that Ronald C. Whitney challenged a creditor's report, he is represented by a point inside the small circle, which means that he is also in the large circle. So the credit bureau will conduct an investigation for Ronald C. Whitney.

Example J illustrates a characteristic of conditional statements: When a conditional statement is given (see premise 1) and the *if part* is satisfied (see premise 2), the *then part* will logically follow. This principle is known as the **law of detachment.** This law can be stated symbolically as follows:

LAW OF DETACHMENT

Premises

1. If p, then q
2. p

Conclusion q (valid)

Example K illustrates a different situation involving a conditional statement and valid reasoning.

Example K

Premises

1. If the temperature drops below 65°F, then the heat rheostat is activated.
2. The heat rheostat was not activated on Wednesday.

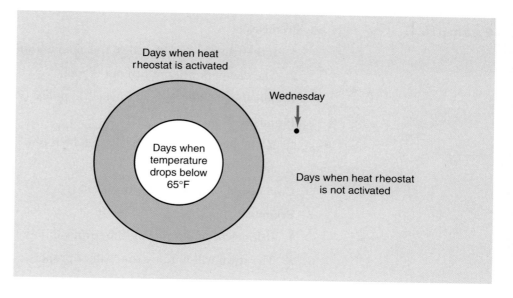

Days when heat rheostat is activated

Wednesday

Days when temperature drops below 65°F

Days when heat rheostat is not activated

Conclusion   The temperature did not drop below 65°F on Wednesday. (valid)

The shaded region outside the inner circle in Example K represents the days when the temperature did not drop below 65°F. Since the dot representing a Wednesday when the heat rheostat was not activated is outside the inner circle, the conclusion is valid.

Example K illustrates another law of reasoning: When a conditional statement is given (see premise 1) and the negation of the *then part* is given (see premise 2), the negation of the *if part* will logically follow. This principle is known as the **law of contraposition.**

LAW OF CONTRAPOSITION	**Premises**
	1. If p, then q
	2. Not q
	Conclusion Not p (valid)

Notice that the law of contraposition follows by replacing the premise "if p, then q" by its contrapositive, "If not q, then not p," and then using the law of detachment.

Premises   1. If p, then q 1. If not q, then not p

2. Not q 2. Not q

Conclusion   Not p (valid)

Determine which of the two laws, *the law of detachment* or *the law of contraposition,* is used in each of the following examples of deductive reasoning.

Example L

1. Premises

   1. If the trip is over 300 miles, the campers will run out of fuel.

   2. The campers will not run out of fuel.

   Conclusion   The trip is not over 300 miles. (valid)

2. Premises

   1. If Jan applies for the job, she will be hired.

   2. Jan applies for the job.

   Conclusion   Jan will be hired. (valid)

3. Premises

   1. If Jones becomes mayor, the town will buy the Walker property.

   2. The town will not buy the Walker property.

   Conclusion   Jones will not become mayor. (valid)

Solution   The law of contraposition is used for 1 and 3 and the law of detachment for 2.

Examples M and N illustrate types of invalid reasoning which commonly occur when using conditional statements.

Example M

Premises

   1. If a company fails to have an annual inspection, then its license will be terminated.

   2. The Samson Company's license was terminated.

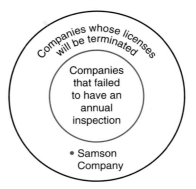

Conclusion   The Samson Company failed to have an annual inspection. (invalid)

The diagram in Example M shows that it is possible for the Samson Company to be inside the large circle (satisfying premise 2) but outside the small circle. Since we are not forced to accept the conclusion, it is invalid. Symbolically, the type of invalid reasoning in Example M is written as

Premises

1. If *p,* then *q*

2. *q*

Conclusion　*p* (invalid)

The next example answers the question posed on the first page of this section.

Example **N**

Premises

1. If the world ends tomorrow, then you will not have to pay for the printing.

2. The world does not end tomorrow.

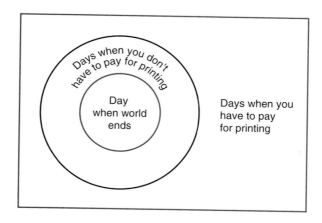

Conclusion　You will have to pay for the printing. (invalid)

The two circles in the diagram for Example N represent the information in premise 1. Notice that the days when you have to pay for the printing are all outside the large circle. The days when the world does not end tomorrow are outside the small circle, but these days may be inside the large circle. Thus, we are not forced to conclude that you will have to pay for the printing. The type of invalid reasoning in Example N is written symbolically as

Premises

1. If *p,* then *q*

2. Not *p*

Conclusion　Not *q* (invalid)

Example **O**

Determine whether the following conclusions are valid or invalid. If valid, state whether the law of detachment or the law of contraposition is being used.

1. Premises

　a. If a person is a Florida resident, he or she will qualify for the supplemental food plan.

　b. Mallory is not a Florida resident.

Conclusion   Mallory will not qualify for the supplemental food plan.

2. Premises

    a. If Jansen does not retire, the piano will be tuned.

    b. The piano will not be tuned.

Conclusion   Jansen will retire.

3. Premises

    a. If the grant is approved, then the Antarctica expedition will be carried out.

    b. The Antarctica expedition will be carried out.

Conclusion   The grant will be approved.

4. Premises

    a. If the new canoes arrive on time, the canoe races will be held.

    b. The new canoes will arrive on time.

Conclusion   The canoe races will be held.

Solution   1. Invalid   2. Valid, law of contraposition   3. Invalid   4. Valid, law of detachment

> Systematic reasoning is a defining feature of mathematics. It is found in all content areas and, with different requirements of rigor, at all grade levels.
>
> Standards 2000, p. 57

Problem-Solving Application

What Is the Name of This Book? by Raymond M. Smullyan has many original and challenging problems in recreational logic.* The following problem from his book is solved using the problem-solving strategies of *drawing Venn diagrams* and *guessing and checking.*

PROBLEM

An enormous amount of loot has been stolen from a store. The criminal (or criminals) took the loot away in a car. Three well-known criminals *A*, *B*, and *C* were brought to Scotland Yard for questioning. The following facts were ascertained.

1. No one other than *A*, *B*, or *C* was involved in the robbery.

2. *C* never pulls a job without using *A* (and possibly others) as an accomplice.

3. *B* does not know how to drive.

Is *A* innocent or guilty?

Understanding the Problem   Statement 1 says that no one other than *A*, *B*, or *C* was involved in the robbery, but it does not say that all three were involved.

Devising a Plan   One approach is to draw a Venn diagram of the given information to see what conclusions can be reached.

Carrying Out the Plan   Statement 2 can be diagrammed by placing the jobs done by *C* inside the circle representing jobs done by *A* (see the following figure)

*Raymond M. Smullyan, *What Is the Name of This Book?* (Englewood Cliffs, NJ: Prentice-Hall, 1978), p. 67.

to show that any time *C* pulls a job, *A* is also involved. The jobs not done by *A* are represented by points outside the large circle. Since we are trying to determine whether *A* is guilty, let's guess and check the results from the diagram. If we guess that *A* is not guilty and select a point outside the large circle, then we know that *C* was not involved. **Question 1:** What does this line of reasoning show?

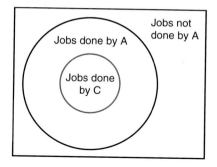

Looking Back   Sometimes it is helpful to write a given statement in if-then form and then write its contrapositive. Statement 2 can be written as "If *C* pulls a job, then *A* pulls a job." **Question 2:** What is the contrapositive of this statement, and how does it help to solve the problem?

Answers to Questions 1–2   **1.** If *A* and *C* are not involved, this leaves only *B*, but *B* does not drive and could not have done the job alone. Therefore, *A* must be guilty.   **2.** If *A* does not pull the job, then *C* does not pull the job. The contrapositive tells us that if *A* is not involved in the job, then *C* is not involved, which leaves only *B*. But *B* cannot do the job alone. Therefore, *A* must be guilty.

EXERCISES AND PROBLEMS 2.3

The diagram and statements at the left were made by an elementary school student.* Use these statements in exercises 1 and 2.

1. If the first statement is true, is the second statement necessarily true? Explain how the diagram supports your conclusion.

2. If the second statement is true, is the first statement necessarily true? Use the diagram to explain your reasoning.

Rewrite each of the statements in exercises 3 and 4 in if-then form.

3. a. Taking a hard line with a bill collector may lead to a lawsuit.

*Nuffield Mathematics Project, *Logic* (New York: John Wiley & Sons, Inc., 1972).

b. All employees in Tripak Company must retire by age 65.

c. There must be 2-hour class sessions if the class is to meet only twice a week.

d. Every pilot must have a physical examination every 6 months.

4. a. The parade will be on Thursday if Flag Day is on Thursday.

b. People under 13 years of age cannot obtain a driver's license.

c. A person who files a written application within 31 days of a termination notification will be issued a new policy.

d. All students in the Moreland district will be bused to the Horn Street School.

In exercises 5 and 6, draw a Venn diagram to illustrate each statement.

5. a. All truck drivers are strong people.

b. Some vegetables are green.

c. If an animal is a duck, then it has two legs.

d. If a person was born before 1980, then the person is more than 10 years old.

6. a. Every member of the Hillsville 500 Club is an alumnus of Hillsville High School.

b. A tree over the Forest Service's size limit will not be cut.

c. Some computers have monitors with color graphics.

d. An animal is a mammal if it is a bat.

Write the converse, inverse, and contrapositive of each statement in exercises 7 through 10.

7. If you take a deduction for your home office, then you must itemize your deductions.

8. If the Democrats take California, they will win the election.

9. If switch B is pressed, the camera focus is on manual.

10. If the weather is fair, the opera will be sold out.

11. Consider the statement "There will be economic sanctions if they do not agree to U.N. inspections." Which of the following statements is logically equivalent to this statement?

a. If there are economic sanctions, then they will not agree to U.N. inspections.

b. If they do agree to U.N. inspections, then there will not be economic sanctions.

c. If there are no economic sanctions, then they will agree to U.N. inspections.

12. Consider the statement "If a number is less than 15, then it is less than 20." Which of the following statements is logically equivalent to this statement?

a. If a number is not less than 15, then it is not less than 20.

b. If a number is not less than 20, then it is not less than 15.

c. If a number is less than 20, then it is less than 15.

Write the contrapositive of each of the statements in exercises 13 and 14.

13. a. If you subtract $750 for each dependent, then the computer will reject your income tax return.

b. The cards should be dealt again if there is no opening bid.

c. If you are not delighted, return the books at the end of the week's free sing-along.

14. a. If this door is opened after 10 p.m., an alarm will sound.

b. This crate of oranges came from the Johnson farm if it is not marked with JJ.

c. The common cold, flu, and other viral diseases occur when the immune system is weak.

Combine each statement and its converse in exercises 15 and 16 into a biconditional statement.

15. If you pay the Durham poll tax, then you are 18 years or older. If you are 18 years or older, then you pay the Durham poll tax.

16. If Smith is guilty, then Jones is innocent. If Jones is innocent, then Smith is guilty.

Write each biconditional statement in exercises 17 and 18 as two separate statements—a conditional statement and its converse.

17. Robinson will be hired if and only if she meets the conditions set by the board.

18. There will be negotiations if and only if the damaged equipment is repaired.

In exercises 19 through 22, sketch Venn diagrams to determine whether each conclusion follows logically from the premises. Explain your reasoning.

19. **Premises:** All flowers are beautiful. All roses are flowers. **Conclusion:** All roses are beautiful.

20. **Premises:** All teachers are smart. All nice people are smart. **Conclusion:** Some nice people are teachers.

21. **Premises:** Some truck drivers are rich. All musicians are rich. **Conclusion:** Some musicians are truck drivers.

22. **Premises:** All good students are good readers. Some math students are good students. **Conclusion:** Some math students are good readers.

Use the law of detachment or the law of contraposition to form a valid conclusion from each set of premises in exercises 23 through 26. Draw a Venn diagram to support your conclusion.

23. **Premises:** If anemia occurs, then something has interfered with the production of red blood cells. The production of red blood cells in this patient is normal.

24. **Premises:** If poison is present in the bone marrow, then production of red blood cells will be slowed down. This patient has poison in her bone marrow.

25. **Premises:** If there is insufficient vitamin K in the body, there will be a prothrombin deficiency. Mr. Keene does not have a prothrombin deficiency.

26. **Premises:** You are not eligible for a prize if you did not sign up for the steamboat trip. The boating club members are eligible for a prize.

Advertisements are often misleading and tempt people to draw conclusions that are favorable to a certain product. Determine which of the ads in exercises 27 through 31 present valid conclusions based on the first statements. Draw a diagram and explain your reasoning.

27. Great tennis players use Hexrackets. Therefore, if you use a Hexracket, you are a great tennis player.

28. If you follow our program, you will lose weight. You are not following our program if you do not lose weight.

29. It has been proved that the new double-shaft clubs result in longer drives. So if your drives are longer, then you are using these clubs.

30. People who use our aluminum siding are satisfied. Therefore, if you don't use our aluminum siding, you won't be satisfied.

31. If you take Sleepwell, you will have extra energy. Therefore, if you don't have extra energy, you are not taking Sleepwell.

REASONING AND PROBLEM SOLVING

32. **Featured strategy: Making a table** Janet Davis, Sally Adams, Collette Eaton, and Jeff Clark have occupations of architect, carpenter, diver, and engineer, but not necessarily in that order. You are told: (1) The first letters of a person's last name and occupation are different. (2) Jeff and the engineer go sailing together. (3) Janet lives in the same neighborhood as the carpenter and the engineer. Determine each person's occupation.
   a. **Understanding the Problem** Each person has a different occupation. Janet can't be the diver. Why can't Sally be the architect?

   b. **Devising a Plan** One approach to this type of problem is to make a table with the names along one side and the occupations along another. Then *yes* or *no* can be written in the boxes of the table to record the given information. Explain why *no* can be written four times as shown in the following table.

	ARCHITECT	CARPENTER	DIVER	ENGINEER
Janet Davis			No	
Sally Adams	No			
Collette Eaton				No
Jeff Clark		No		

   c. **Carrying Out the Plan** Each row and column of the table should have exactly one *yes*. Continue filling out the table to solve this problem.
   d. **Looking Back** One advantage of using such a table is that once *yes* is written in a box, *no* can be written in several other boxes. Each *yes* provides a maximum of how many *no* boxes?

33. Dow, Eliot, Finley, Grant, and Hanley have the following occupations: appraiser, broker, cook, painter, and singer.
   (1) The broker and the appraiser attended a father-and-son banquet.
   (2) The singer, the appraiser, and Grant all belong to the same-gender club.
   (3) Dow and Hanley are married to two waiters.
   (4) The singer told Finley that he liked science fiction.
   (5) The cook owes Hanley $25.

   If three of these people are men, determine each person's gender and occupation.

34. Lee has the flu, and he is concerned that he will not pass the mathematics exam. If the following three statements are true, will Lee pass the exam?
   (1) Lee will not fail the mathematics exam if he finishes his computer program.
   (2) If he goes to the theater, he does not have the flu.
   (3) If he does not go to the theater, he will finish his computer program.

35. Huiru reads the proof of a theorem and finds it easy. Does it follow from the following four statements that the proof is not arranged in logical order?
   (1) Huiru can't understand a proof if it is not arranged in logical order.
   (2) If Huiru has trouble with a proof, it is not easy.

(3) If Huiru studies a proof without getting dizzy, it is one she understands.

(4) A proof gives Huiru trouble if she gets dizzy while studying it.

36. The morning after the big football game, the school guard found the goal posts missing! With better-than-average luck, the guard had three red-hot suspects by midmorning. The suspects—Andy, Dandy, and Sandy—were questioned, and they made the following statements.

Andy: (1) I didn't do it.
      (2) I never saw Dandy before.
      (3) Sure I know the football coach.

Sandy: (1) I didn't do it.
       (2) Andy lied when he said he never saw Dandy before.
       (3) I don't know who did it.

Dandy: (1) I didn't do it.
       (2) Andy and Sandy are both pals of mine.
       (3) Andy never stole anything.

One and only one of the three suspects is the prankster. One and only one of each person's three statements is false. Who lifted the posts?*

*Copyright 1977, Creative Publications, Mountain View, California.

ONLINE LEARNING CENTER   www.mhhe.com/bennett-nelson

- Math Investigation 2.3   *Differences of Squares*
  Section Related: • Links   • Writing/Discussion Problems   • Bibliography

---

PUZZLER

Lewis Carroll popularized logic by writing comically worded statements and conclusions. The following examples are from his book *Symbolic Logic.* Determine whether the following conclusions are valid or invalid.

No professors are ignorant. All ignorant people are vain.
Conclusion: No professors are vain.

Babies are illogical. Nobody is despised who can manage a crocodile. Illogical persons are despised.
Conclusion: Babies cannot manage crocodiles.

CHAPTER REVIEW

1. Sets and Venn Diagrams
  a. A **set** is described as a collection of objects called **elements.**
  b. The elements of a set may be described with **words,** or they may be **listed.**
  c. An **empty set,** or **null set,** is a set with no elements.
  d. To show that k is an **element of** set S, we write $k \in S$.
  e. **Venn diagrams** use circles, rectangles, or other shapes to illustrate sets.

2. Set Relations
  a. Two sets are **disjoint** if they have no elements in common.

  b. If every element of A is an element of B, then A is called a **subset** of B, written $A \subseteq B$.
  c. If A is a subset of B and B has elements not contained in A, then A is called a **proper subset** of B.
  d. Two sets are **equal** if they are subsets of each other.
  e. Two sets can be put into **one-to-one correspondence** if it is possible to match each element in one set to exactly one element in the other set and conversely.
  f. Two sets have the **same number** of elements if they can be put into one-to-one correspondence.

3. Set Operations
  a. The **intersection** of sets A and B is the set of elements that are in both A and B, written as $A \cap B$.

b. The **union** of sets A and B is the set of elements that are in A or in B or in both A and B, written as $A \cup B$.

c. If A and B are disjoint subsets of a given set U, where $A \cup B = U$, then A and B are **complements** of each other, written as $A' = B$ and $B' = A$.

d. A **universal set** is the set that contains all the elements being considered in a given situation.

e. **Venn diagrams** are used to illustrate set relations and operations.

4. Finite and Infinite Sets

a. A set is **finite** if it is empty or can be put into one-to-one correspondence with the set $\{1, 2, 3, \ldots, n\}$, where n is a whole number.

b. A set is **infinite** if it is not finite.

5. Functions and Graphs

a. A **function** is two sets and a rule that assigns each element of the first set to a unique element of the second set.

b. The first set of a function is called the **domain**, and the second set is called the **range**.

c. A function is a **linear function** if its graph has an equation that can be written in the form $y = mx + b$, where m and b are real numbers.

d. A function is **nonlinear** if its graph is not a line, that is, its graph does not have an equation of the form $y = mx + b$.

e. If the graph of a function consists of only separate points, it is called a **discrete graph.**

6. Rectangular Coordinate System

a. The **rectangular coordinate system** is a method for locating the points on a plane by reference to a pair of perpendicular lines called the **x axis** and **y axis.**

b. The first number in the ordered pair (x, y) is called the **x coordinate** and the second number is called the **y coordinate.**

c. The **slope** of a line containing points whose coordinates are (a, b) and (c, d) is the rise $(b - d)$ divided by the run $(a - c)$, for $a \neq c$.

d. An equation in the form $y = mx + b$ is called the **slope-intercept form** because the slope m and the y intercept b can be seen from the equation.

7. Deductive Reasoning

a. **Deductive reasoning** is the process of obtaining conclusions from one or more given statements, called **premises.**

b. When a conclusion follows from the given information, it is said to be **valid,** and the process of deriving the conclusion is called **valid reasoning.**

c. When a conclusion does not follow from the given information, the conclusion and the reasoning process are said to be **invalid.**

8. Conditional Statements

a. A statement in if-then form is called a **conditional statement.**

b. Every conditional statement "if p, then q" has three related statements:
Converse: If q, then p.
Inverse: If not p, then not q.
Contrapositive: If not q, then not p.

c. Two statements are said to be **logically equivalent** if when the first statement is true, the second statement is true and when the first statement is false, the second statement is false.

d. When a conditional statement is given (premise 1) and the *if part* is satisfied (premise 2), the *then part* will always follow. This principle is known as the **law of detachment.**

e. When a conditional statement is given (premise 1) and the negation of the *then part* is given, the negation of the *if part* will always follow. This principle is called the **law of contraposition.**

f. When a conditional statement and its converse are combined into one statement by using *if and only if*, the new statement is called a **biconditional statement.**

CHAPTER TEST

1. Use the attribute pieces shown below to determine the sets satisfying the given conditions.

sbt   sbr   sbh   swt   swr   swh

a. Hexagonal and white

b. Triangular or black

c. Not (white or rectangular)

2. Given the universal set $U = \{0, 1, 2, 3, 4, 5, 6\}$ and the sets $A = \{2, 4, 6\}$ and $B = \{1, 2, 3, 4\}$, determine the following sets.
   a. $A \cap B$ b. $A \cup B$
   c. $A' \cap B$ d. $A \cup B'$

3. Sketch a Venn diagram to illustrate each of the following conditions.
   a. $E \cap F \neq \emptyset$
   b. $E \subseteq G$
   c. $F \cap G = \emptyset$ and $E \subseteq F$
   d. $E \cap G \neq \emptyset$ and $(E \cup G) \cap F = \emptyset$
   e. $E \subseteq G$ and $F \subseteq E$
   f. $E \subseteq F$, $G \subseteq F$, and $E \cap G = \emptyset$

4. Use set notation to name the shaded regions below.

   a.

   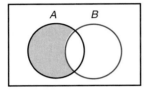

   b.

   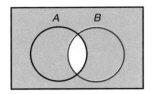

5. Answer each question, and draw a diagram to support your conclusion.
   a. If $k \in R \cup S$, is $k \in R \cap S$?
   b. If $x \in T \cap W$, is $x \in T \cup W$?
   c. If $y \in R \cap S$, is $y \in S'$?

6. Consider the function that relates the length x of each line segment to $f(x)$, which is half of the length of the segment.
   a. Determine the range value $f(x)$ for each of the following domain values: 1, 2, 3, 4, and 5.
   b. Use the coordinates in part a or a graphing calculator to sketch the graph of this function. (Copy the coordinate system from the inside cover or from the website.)
   c. What is the equation of this function?
   d. Is this function linear or nonlinear?

7. Determine the slope of each line.

   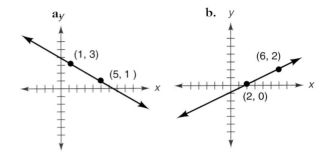

8. Write the equation of the line through the points $(0, 4)$ and $(3, 13)$ in the slope-intercept form.

9. A travel company charges $120 for insurance and $55 a day to rent a trailer. Let x represent the number of days and y the total cost of renting a trailer.
   a. Write an equation for the total cost of renting the trailer.
   b. What is the total cost of renting the trailer for 10 days?
   c. If the travel budget allows $850 for trailer rental and a trailer can only be rented for a whole number of days, for how many days could you afford to rent the trailer?

10. An electrician normally charges $15 per hour but on holidays the charge is $24 per hour. During a certain period the electrician worked 60 hours and received $1062. Let x represent the number of holiday hours worked and write an algebraic expression for the items in parts a to c.
    a. The total amount of money received for the holiday hours worked.
    b. The number of hours worked on non-holidays.
    c. The total amount of money received for working on non-holidays.
    d. How many holiday hours did the electrician work?

11. Alanna used the following types of transportation to go to school on each of 4 days: biking, walking, roller-blading, and jogging. On the day she jogged, she stopped for 3 minutes at a construction site, and on the day she roller-bladed, she stopped for 6 minutes to talk with a friend. The graphs of her distances as functions of time are shown on the next page. Determine which type of transportation she used each day if she only used each type of transportation once.

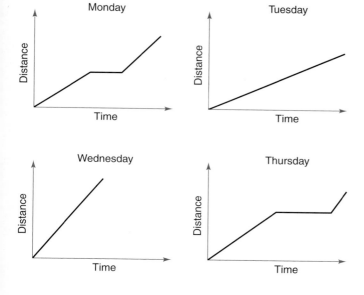

12. Of 75 cars that were inspected, 12 needed brake repair and 18 needed exhaust system repair. If the brakes or exhaust systems on 50 of the cars did not need repair, how many cars needed both brake and exhaust system repairs?

13. In a certain town there live 150 men: 85 are married, 70 have a telephone, 75 own a car, 55 are married and have a telephone, 35 have a telephone and a car, 40 are married and have a car, and 30 are married, have a car, and have a telephone. How many men are single and do not have either a car or a telephone?

14. Rewrite each statement in if-then form.
  a. People who are denied credit have a right to protest to the credit bureau.
  b. All the children who were absent yesterday were absent again today.
  c. Everybody at the party received a gift.

15. Write the converse, inverse, and contrapositive of each of the following statements.
  a. If Mary goes fishing, then her husband goes with her.
  b. If you join the book club, you will receive five free books.

16. "If the temperature drops below 10°F, the culture dies." This statement is logically equivalent to which of the following statements?
  (1) If the culture dies, the temperature drops below 10°F.
  (2) If the temperature does not drop below 10°F, the culture does not die.
  (3) If the culture does not die, the temperature does not drop below 10°F.

17. Combine the following statement and its converse into a biconditional statement: If there are peace talks, then the prisoners will be set free. If the prisoners are set free, then there will be peace talks.

18. Determine whether each conclusion below is valid or invalid.
  a. Premises: All mallards are aggressive birds. Some black ducks are aggressive birds. **Conclusion:** Some black ducks are mallards.
  b. Premises: All geometry classes are interesting. Some math classes are geometry classes. **Conclusion:** Some math classes are interesting.
  c. Premises: If people are happy, then they have enough to eat. All rich people have enough to eat. **Conclusion:** Some rich people are happy.

19. Use each set of premises to form a valid conclusion.
  a. Premises: If a person is healthy, then the person has about 10 times as much lung tissue as necessary. The people in ward B have less lung tissue than necessary.
  b. Premises: If an illegal move is made, the game pieces should be set up as they were before the move. An illegal move was made.

20. Determine whether each conclusion is valid or invalid.
  a. Premises: You may keep the books if you like everything about them. John kept the books. **Conclusion:** John liked everything about the books.
  b. Premises: If this year's tests are successful, the United States will be using laser communications by 1999. This year's tests were successful. **Conclusion:** The United States will be using laser communications by 1999.

WHOLE NUMBERS

SPOTLIGHT ON TEACHING

Excerpts from NCTM's Standards for School Mathematics Grades Pre-K through 2*

Teachers have a very important role to play in helping students develop facility with computation. By allowing students to work in ways that have meaning for them, teachers can gain insight into students' developing understanding and give them guidance. . . . Consider the following hypothetical story, in which a teacher poses this problem to a class of second graders:

We have 153 students at our school. There are 273 students at the school down the street. How many students are in both schools?

    As would be expected in most classrooms, the students give a variety of responses that illustrate a range of understandings. For example, Randy models the problem with bean sticks that the class has made earlier in the year, using hundreds rafts, tens sticks, and loose beans.

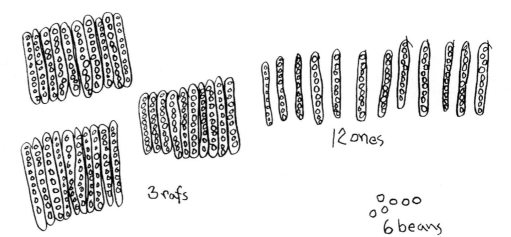

3 rafs

12 ones

6 beans

Principles and Standards for School Mathematics (Reston, Va: National Council of Teachers of Mathematics, 2000), p. 86.

MATH ACTIVITY 3.1

NUMERATION AND PLACE VALUE WITH BASE-FIVE PIECES

Materials: Base-five pieces in the Manipulative Kit.

1. The four base-five pieces shown here are called **unit, long, flat,** and **long-flat.** Examine the numerical and geometric patterns of these pieces as they increase in size, and describe how you would design the next larger piece to continue your pattern.

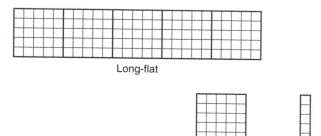

> Concrete models can help students represent numbers and develop number sense, . . . , but using materials, especially in a rote manner, does not ensure understanding.
>
> Standards 2000, p. 80

*2. The two collections shown here both contain 36 units, but collection 2 is called the **minimal collection** because it contains the smallest possible number of base-five pieces. Use your base-five pieces to determine the minimal collection for each of the following numbers of units.

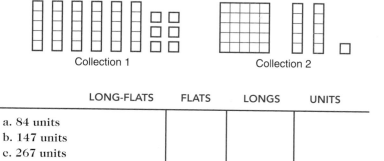

	LONG-FLATS	FLATS	LONGS	UNITS
a. 84 units				
b. 147 units				
c. 267 units				

3. In base-five numeration, 3 flats, 2 longs, and 4 units are recorded by 324_{five}. Sketch the base pieces for each of the following numerals, and determine the total number of units in each collection.

   a. 1304_{five} **b.** 221_{five} **c.** 213_{five} **d.** 1023_{five}

*4. Starting with the unit, sketch the first four base-three pieces.

   a. What is the minimal collection of base-three pieces for 16 units?

   b. What is the total number of units represented by 2112_{three} (2 long-flats, 1 flat, 1 long, 2 units)?

SECTION 3.1

NUMERATION SYSTEMS

Egyptian stone giving an account of the expedition of Amenhotep III in 1450 B.C.

A 7 is written at the right end of a two-digit number, thereby increasing the value of the number by 700. Find the original two-digit number.

There are no historical records of the first uses of numbers, their names, and their symbols. Written symbols for numbers are called **numerals** and probably were developed before number words, since it is easier to cut notches in a stick than to establish phrases to identify a number.

A logically organized collection of numerals is called a **numeration system.** Early numeration systems appear to have grown from tallying. In many of these systems, 1, 2, and 3 were represented by **❘, ❘❘**, and **❘❘❘** . By 3400 B.C. the Egyptians had an advanced system of numeration for numbers up to and exceeding 1 million. Their first few number symbols show the influence of the simple tally strokes (Figure 3.1).

❘	❘❘	❘❘❘	❘❘❘❘	❘❘❘❘❘	❘❘❘❘❘❘	❘❘❘❘❘❘❘	❘❘❘❘❘❘❘❘	❘❘❘❘❘❘❘❘❘
1	2	3	4	5	6	7	8	9

Figure 3.1

Their symbol for 3 can be seen in the third row from the bottom of the stone inscriptions shown above. What other symbols for single-digit numerals can you see on this stone?

Grouping and Number Bases

As soon as it became necessary to count large numbers of objects, the counting process was extended by grouping. Since the fingers furnished a convenient counting device, grouping by 5s was used in some of the oldest methods of counting. The left hand was generally used to keep a record of the number of objects being counted, while the right index finger pointed to the objects. When all 5 fingers had been used, the same hand would be used again to continue counting. In certain parts of South America and Africa, it is still customary to "count by hands": 1, 2, 3, 4, hand, hand and 1, hand and 2, hand and 3, etc.

Example A

Use the "count by hands" system to determine the names of the numbers for each of the following sets of dots.

Solution   1. 2 hands and 2   2. 3 hands and 4   3. 4 hands and 3

> Young children's earliest mathematical reasoning is likely to be about number situations, and their first mathematical representations will probably be of numbers.
>
> Standards 2000, p. 32

The number of objects used in the grouping process is called the **base**. In Example A the base is five. By using the numerals 1, 2, 3, and 4 for the first four whole numbers and *hand* for the name of the base, it is possible to name numbers up to and including 24 (4 hands and 4).

BASE TEN   As soon as people grew accustomed to counting by the fingers on one hand, it became natural to use the fingers on both hands to group by 10s. In most numeration systems today, grouping is done by 10s. The names of our numbers reflect this grouping process. *Eleven* derives from the medieval German phrase *ein lifon,* meaning *one left over,* and *twelve* is from *twe lif,* meaning *two over ten.* The number names from 13 to 19 have similar derivations. *Twenty* is from *twe-tig,* meaning *two tens,* and *hundred* means *ten times ten.** When grouping is done by 10s, the system is called a **base-ten numeration system.**

Ancient Numeration Systems

EGYPTIAN NUMERATION   The ancient Egyptian numeration system used picture symbols called **hieroglyphics** (Figure 3.2). This is a base-ten system in which each symbol represents a power of ten.

HISTORICAL HIGHLIGHT

There are many traces of base twenty from different cultures. The Mayas of Yucatán and Aztecs of Mexico had elaborate number systems based on 20. Greenlanders used the expression *one man* for twenty, *two men* for 40, and so on. A similar system was used in New Guinea.

Evidence of grouping by 20 among the ancient Celtics can be seen in the French use of *quatre-vingt* (four-twenty) for 80. In our language the use of *score* suggests past tendencies to count by 20s. Lincoln's familiar Gettysburg Address begins, "Four score and seven years ago." Another example occurs in a childhood nursery rhyme: "Four and twenty blackbirds baked in a pie."

*H. W. Eves, *An Introduction to the History of Mathematics,* 3d ed. (New York: Holt, Rinehart and Winston, 1969), pp. 8–9.

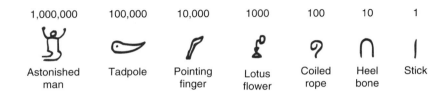

Figure 3.2

Example B

Write the following numbers, using Egyptian numerals.

1. 2342   **2.** 14,026

Solution   1.   𓆼𓆼𓍢𓍢𓍢𓎆𓎆𓎆𓏤𓏤   2.   𓆐𓆼𓆼𓆼𓆼𓎆𓎆 𓏤𓏤𓏤𓏤𓏤𓏤

The Egyptian numeration system is an example of an *additive numeration system* because each power of the base is repeated as many times as needed.

> **ADDITIVE NUMERATION SYSTEM**   In an **additive numeration system,** some number b is selected for a base and symbols representing $1, b, b^2, b^3$, etc., for powers of the base. Numbers are written by repeating these powers of the base the necessary number of times.

In the Egyptian numeration system, $b = 10$ and the powers of the base are 1, 10, 10^2, 10^3, etc. In an additive numeration system, the symbols can be written in any order. In Example B the powers of the base are descending from left to right, but the Egyptian custom was to write them from right to left in descending powers, as shown in the stone inscriptions on page 122.

Example C

Notice the numeral for 743 in the third row from the bottom of the Egyptian stone on page 122. The symbols for 3 ones, 4 tens, and 7 hundreds are written from left to right. What other Egyptian numerals can you find on this stone?

Solution   It appears that the third row up contains 45 and the fourth row up has 150. Parts of many other numerals can be seen.

ROMAN NUMERATION   Roman numerals can be found on clock faces, buildings, gravestones, and the preface pages of books. Like the Egyptians, the Romans used base ten. They had a modified additive numeration system, because in addition to the symbols for powers of the base, there are symbols for 5, 50, and 500. The seven common symbols are

I	V	X	L	C	D	M
1	5	10	50	100	500	1000

Historical evidence indicates that C is from *centum,* meaning *hundred,* and *M* is from *milli,* meaning *thousand.* The origin of the other symbols is uncertain. The Romans wrote their numerals so that the numbers they represented were in decreasing order from left to right.

Example D

Write the following numbers, using Roman numerals.

1. 2342   **2.** 1996

Solution   **1.** MMCCCXXXXII   **2.** MDCCCCLXXXXVI

When a Roman numeral is placed to the left of a numeral for a larger number, as in IX for 9, XL for 40, XC for 90, CD for 400, or CM for 900, its position indicates subtraction. The subtractive principle was recognized by the Romans, but they did not make much use of it.* (In fact, the subtractive principle has only been in common use for about the past 200 years.) Compare the preceding Roman numeral for 1996 with the following numeral written using the subtractive principle:

MCMXCVI

The Romans had relatively little need for large numbers, so they developed no general system for writing them. In the inscription on a monument commemorating the victory over the Carthaginians in 260 B.C., the symbol ⌒ for 100,000 is repeated 23 times to represent 2,300,000.

BABYLONIAN NUMERATION   The Babylonians developed a base-sixty numeration system. Their basic symbols for 1 through 59 were formed additively by repeating ▼ for 1 and ◀ for 10. Four such numerals are shown here.

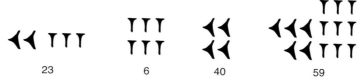

23   6   40   59

To write numbers greater than 59, the Babylonians used their basic symbols for 1–59 and the concept of *place value.* **Place value** is a power of the base, and the Babylonian place values were 1, 60, 60^2, 60^3, etc. Their basic symbols had different values depending on the position or location of the symbol. For example, 135 = 2(60) + 15, so the Babylonians wrote their numeral for 2 to represent 2×60 and their numeral for 15 for the number of units, as shown next. Generally, the first position from right to left represented the number of units, the second position the number of 60s, the third position the number of 60^2s, etc.

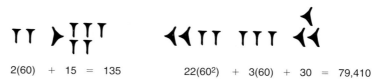

2(60) + 15 = 135   22(60^2) + 3(60) + 30 = 79,410

Example E

Write the following numbers using Babylonian numeration.

1. 47   **2.** 2473   **3.** 10,821

Solution   **1.**   **2.**   **3.**

*D. E. Smith, *History of Mathematics,* 2d ed. (Lexington, MA: 1925), p. 60.

The solution to the third part of Example E illustrates a weakness in the Babylonian system. The number 10,821 is equal to $3(60^2) + 0(60) + 21$, but because there was no symbol for zero, there was no way to indicate a missing power of 60. The numeral shown for the third part of Example E could have represented $3(60) + 21$, or $3(60^3) + 21$, or larger numbers. A larger gap was sometimes used to indicate that a power of the base was missing, but this sometimes led to confusion.

MAYAN NUMERATION   The Mayas used a modified base-twenty numeration system that included a symbol for zero. Their basic symbols for 0 through 19 are shown in Figure 3.3. Notice that there is grouping by 5s within the first 20 numbers.

Figure 3.3

To write numbers greater than 19, the Mayas used their basic symbols from 0 to 19 and place value. They wrote their numerals vertically with one numeral above another, as shown in Example F, with the powers of the base increasing from bottom to top. The numeral in the bottom position represented the number of units. The numeral in the second position represented the number of 20s. Because the Mayan calendar had 18 months of 20 days each, the place value of the third position was 18×20 rather than 20^2. Above this position, the next few place values were 18×20^2, 18×20^3, etc.

Example F

These three Mayan numeral represent the following numbers: $16(20) + 6$, which equals 326; $7(18 \times 20) + 12 \times 20 + 16$, which equals 2776; and $9(18 \times 20^2) + 2(18 \times 20) + 0(20) + 6$, which equals 65,526.

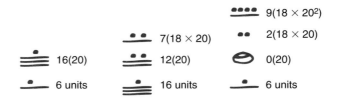

Example G

Write the following numbers using Mayan numerals.

1. 60   **2.** 106   **3.** 2782

Solution **1.** ••• (3 twenties)   **2.** —— (5 twenties)   **3.** •• (7 × 18 × 20)

⬯ (0)   • (6)   ••• (13 × 20)
—

•• (2 units)

Notice the necessity in the Mayan system for a symbol that has the same purpose as our numeral zero. In part 1 of Example G, their symbol for zero occupies the lower place and tells us that the three dots have a value of 3 × 20 and there are zero 1s.

There is archaeological evidence that the Mayas were in Central America before 1000 B.C. During the Classical Period (300 to 900), they had a highly developed knowledge of astronomy and a 365-day calendar with a cycle going back to 3114 B.C. Their year was divided into 18 months of 20 days each with 5 extra days for holidays. Because their numeration system was developed mainly for calendar calculations, they used 18 × 20 for the place value in the third position, rather than 20 × 20.

HINDU-ARABIC NUMERATION   Much of the world now uses the Hindu-Arabic numeration system. This positional numeration system was named for the Hindus, who invented it, and the Arabs, who transmitted it to Europe. It is a base-ten numeration system in which place value is determined by the position of the **digits** 0, 1, 2, 3, 4, 5, 6, 7, 8, and 9. Each digit in a numeral has a name that indicates its position.

Example H

Here are the names and values of the digits in 75,063.

It is absolutely essential that students develop a solid understanding of the base-ten numeration system and place-value concepts by the end of grade 2.

Standards 2000, p. 81

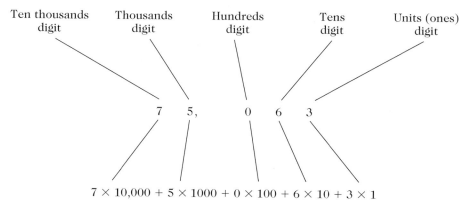

$$7 \times 10,000 + 5 \times 1000 + 0 \times 100 + 6 \times 10 + 3 \times 1$$

When we write a number as the sum of the numbers represented by each digit in its numeral (see Example H), we are writing the number in **expanded form.** Another common method of writing a number in expanded form is to write the powers of the base using exponents. For example, $7 \times 10^4 + 5 \times 10^3 + 0 \times 10^2 + 6 \times 10 + 3$.

The Hindu-Arabic numeration system is an example of a positional numeration system. In general,

> **POSITIONAL NUMERATION SYSTEM**   In a positional numeration system, a number is selected for a base and basic symbols are adopted for 0, 1, 2, . . . up to one less than the base. (In our numeration system these basic symbols are the 10 digits 0, 1, 2, . . . , 9.) Whole numbers are represented in a positional numeration system by writing one or more basic symbols side by side with their positions indicating increasing powers of the base.

Example I

Determine the value of each underlined digit and its place value.

1. 7<u>0</u>24   **2.** 3<u>7</u>0,189   **3.** 49,<u>2</u>38

Solution   **1.** The value is 0, and the place value is hundreds.   **2.** The value is 70,000, and the place value is ten thousands.   **3.** The value is 200, and the place value is hundreds.

Reading and Writing Numbers

In English the number names for the whole numbers from 1 to 20 are all single words. The names for the numbers from 21 to 99, with the exceptions of 30, 40, 50, etc., are compound number names that are hyphenated. These names are hyphenated even when they occur as parts of other names. For example, we write *three hundred forty-seven* for 347.

Numbers with more than three digits are read by naming the **period** for each group of three digits. Within each period, the digits are read as we would read any number from 1 to 999, and then the name of the period is recited. The names for the first few periods are shown in the following example.

Example J

Read the following number.

$$\underbrace{2\quad3,}_{\text{Trillion}}\quad\underbrace{4\quad7\quad8,}_{\text{Billion}}\quad\underbrace{5\quad0\quad6,}_{\text{Million}}\quad\underbrace{0\quad4\quad2,}_{\text{Thousand}}\quad3\quad1\quad9$$

Solution   This number is read as twenty-three trillion, four hundred seventy-eight billion, five hundred six million, forty-two thousand, three hundred nineteen. *Note:* The word *and* is not used in reading a whole number.

HISTORICAL HIGHLIGHT

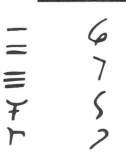

There are various theories about the origin of our digits. It is widely accepted, however, that they originated in India. Notice the resemblance of the Brahmi numerals for 6, 7, 8, and 9 to our numerals. The Brahmi numerals for 1, 2, 4, 6, 7, and 9 were found on stone columns in a cave in Bombay dating from the second or third century B.C.* The oldest dated European manuscript that contains our numerals was written in Spain in 976. In 1299, merchants in Florence were forbidden to use these numerals. Gradually, over a period of centuries, the Hindu-Arabic numeration system replaced the more cumbersome Roman numeration system.

*J. R. Newman, *The World of Mathematics* (New York: Simon and Schuster, 1956), pp. 452–454.

Rounding Numbers

If you were to ask a question such as "How many people voted in the 1988 presidential election?" you might be told that in "round numbers" it was about 89 million. Approximations are often as helpful as the exact number, which in this example is 88,930,371.

Research Statement

Research on students' number sense shows that students continue to have difficulty representing and thinking about large numbers.

Sowder and Kelin 1993

One method of **rounding** a number to the nearest million is to write the nearest million greater than the number and the nearest million less than the number and then choose the closer number. Of the following numbers, 88,930,371 is closer to 89,000,000.

$$89,000,000$$
$$88,930,371 \text{ rounds to } 89,000,000 \longrightarrow$$
$$88,000,000$$

The more familiar approach to rounding a number uses place value and is stated in the following rule.

RULE FOR ROUNDING WHOLE NUMBERS

1. Locate the digit with the place value to which the number is to be rounded, and check the digit to its right.

2. If the digit to the right is 5 or greater, then each digit to the right is replaced by 0 and the digit with the given place value is increased by 1.

3. If the digit to the right is 4 or less, each digit to the right of the digit with the given place value is replaced by 0.

Example K

Round 88,930,371 to the following place values.

1. Ten thousands   **2.** Thousands   **3.** Hundreds

Solution   1. Ten thousands place
↓
88,930,371 rounds to 88,930,000
⟶

2. Thousands place
↓
88,930,371 rounds to 88,930,000
⟶

3. Hundreds place
↓
88,930,371 rounds to 88,930,400
⟶

Models for Numeration

NCTM's K–4 Standard, *Number Sense and Numeration,* says that place value is a critical step in the development of children's understanding of number concepts:

Since place-value meanings grow out of grouping experiences, counting knowledge should be integrated with meanings based on grouping. Children are then able to use and make sense of procedures for comparing, ordering, rounding, and operating with larger numbers.*

Curriculum and Evaluation Standards for School Mathematics (Reston, VA: National Council of Teachers of Mathematics, 1989), p. 39.

There are many models for illustrating positional numeration and place value. The bundles-of-sticks model and base-ten number pieces will be introduced in Examples L, M, and N and then used to model operations on whole numbers in the remainder of this chapter.

BUNDLES-OF-STICKS (OR STRAWS) MODEL   In this model, units and tens are represented by single sticks and bundles of 10 sticks, respectively. One hundred is represented by a bundle of 10 bundles.

Example L

The following figure shows the bundle-of-sticks model for representing 148.

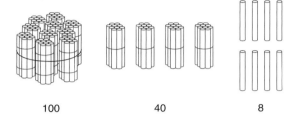

100   40   8

Using concrete materials can help students learn to group and ungroup by tens. For example, . . . to express "23" as 23 ones (units), 1 ten and 13 ones, or 2 tens and 3 ones.

Standards 2000, p. 81

BASE-TEN PIECES   In this model, the powers of 10 are represented by objects called **units, longs,** and **flats:** 10 units form a long, and 10 longs form a flat (Figure 3.4). Higher powers of the base can be represented by sets of flats. For example, 10 flats placed in a row are called a **long-flat** and represent 1000.

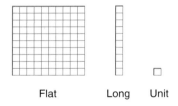

Flat   Long   Unit

Figure 3.4

Example M

Sketch base-ten pieces to represent 536.

Solution

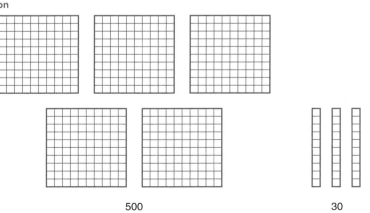

500   30   6

Bundles of sticks and base-ten pieces can be used to illustrate the concept of **regrouping:** changing one collection to another that represents the same number.

Example N

Sketch the minimum number of base-ten pieces needed to replace the following collection. Then determine the base-ten number represented by the collection.

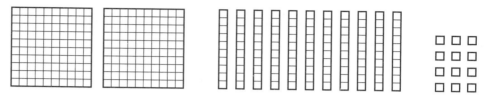

Solution   The new collection will have 3 flats, 2 longs, and 2 units. This collection of base-ten pieces represents 322.

BASE-FIVE NUMERATION   The base-five pieces are models for powers of 5, and as in the case of base ten, there are pieces called **units, longs,** and **flats:** 5 units form a long, and 5 longs form a flat. The next higher power of 5 is represented by placing 5 flats end to end to form a **long-flat.**

Example O

Sketch the minimum number of base-five pieces to represent the following number of units.

1. 39 units   **2.** 115 units   **3.** 327 units

Solution   **1.** A collection with 1 flat, 2 longs, and 4 units

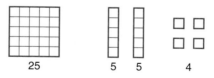

Representing numbers with various physical materials should be a major part of mathematics instruction in the elementary school grades.

Standards 2000, p. 33

2. A collection with 4 flats, 3 longs, and 0 units

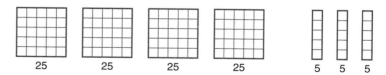

3. A collection with 2 long-flats, 3 flats, 0 longs, and 2 units

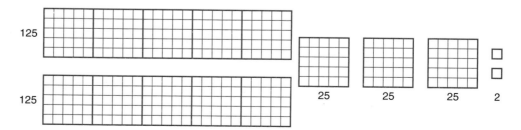

Positional numeration is used to write numbers in various bases by writing the numbers of long-flats, flats, longs, and units from left to right, just as we do in base ten. From Example O, 39 in base-ten numeration is written as 124_{five} in base-five numeration. Similarly, 115 is written as 430_{five}, and 327 is written as 2302_{five}. Since base ten is the standard base, we do not write the subscript to show that a number is being written in base-ten numeration.

Problem-Solving Application

The next problem introduces the strategy of **reasoning by analogy,** which involves forming conclusions based on similar situations. For example, we know that when we add two numbers, *the greater the numbers, the greater the sum.* Reasoning by analogy, we might conclude that *the greater the numbers, the greater the product.* In this case the conclusion is true. This type of reasoning, however, is not always reliable; the conclusion *the greater the numbers, the greater the difference* would be false. The problem-solving strategies of *reasoning by analogy* and *using a model* are used below to solve a problem involving base-twelve positional numeration.

PROBLEM

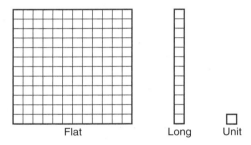

Flat   Long Unit

How can numbers be written in base-twelve positional numeration?

Understanding the Problem The count-by-hands method of counting, which was introduced in the opening pages of this section, is a base-five system. **Question 1:** In that system, what digits are needed to name any number from 1 to 24?

Devising a Plan Consider a similar problem: Why are 0, 1, 2, 3, . . . , 9 the only digits needed in base ten? Referring to the base-ten pieces, we know that if there are more than nine of one type of base-ten piece, we can replace each group of 10 pieces by a piece representing the next higher power of 10. This suggests using similar pieces for base twelve. The first three base-twelve pieces are shown above. **Question 2:** How can this model be extended?

Carrying Out the Plan To count in base twelve, we can say 1, 2, 3, 4, 5, 6, 7, 8, 9, but then we need new symbols for ten and eleven because 10 in base twelve represents 1 long and 0 units, which equals twelve units; and 11 in base twelve represents 1 long and 1 unit, which equals thirteen units. One solution is to let T represent the number 10 and E represent the number eleven. Then the first few numerals in base twelve are 1, 2, 3, 4, 5, 6, 7, 8, 9, T, E, 10, 11, 12, 13, . . . , where 12 represents 1 long and 2 units (fourteen units), etc. In base-twelve positional numeration, 3 flats, 2 longs, and 8 units are written as 328_{twelve}. **Question 3:** Why does any base-twelve numeral require only the twelve symbols 0, 1, 2, 3, 4, 5, 6, 7, 8, 9, T, and E?

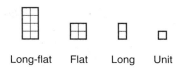

Long-flat   Flat   Long   Unit

Looking Back   These models suggest ways to visualize other number bases, such as base two, base seven, or base sixteen. **Question 4:** What digits are needed in base two, and what would the base-two pieces look like?

Answers to Questions 1–4   1. 0, 1, 2, 3, and 4. For example, 2 hands and 1, 3 hands and 4, etc. **2.** The next base-twelve piece has a row of 12 flats.   **3.** Whenever there are 12 of any base-twelve piece, they can be replaced by the next larger base-twelve piece. If there are no pieces of a given type, the 0 is needed in the numeral to indicate this.   **4.** The only digits needed in base two are 0 and 1. The first four base-two pieces are shown above.

One skill in helping children acquire number sense and familiarity with place value is counting up by 10s from a given number. This can be practiced with a calculator that has a constant function key or is programmed to achieve this function. On such calculators, which are designed for elementary school students, the following key strokes will produce a sequence of numbers, with each number being 10 more than the preceding number.

KEYSTROKES	VIEW SCREEN
26	26
+ 10 =	36
=	46
=	56

In a similar manner, a calculator with a constant function enables students to practice counting down by 10s. Whether or not a calculator has a constant function, the above sequence 26, 36, 46, . . . can be generated on most calculators by entering 26 and repeatedly pressing + 10 = . Similarly, the keystrokes below will produce the decreasing sequence 54, 44, 34, ...

KEYSTROKES	VIEW SCREEN
64 − 10 =	54
− 10 =	44
− 10 =	34
− 10 =	24

HISTORICAL HIGHLIGHT

In the fifteenth and sixteenth centuries, there were two opposing opinions on the best numeration system and methods of computing. The *abacists* used Roman numerals and computed on the abacus and the *algorists* used the Hindu-Arabic numerals and place value. The sixteenth century print at the left shows an abacist competing against an algorist. The abacist is seated at a reckoning table with four horizontal lines and a vertical line down the middle. Counters, or chips, placed on lines represented powers of 10. The thousands line was marked with a cross to aid the eye in reading numbers. If more lines were needed, every third line was marked with a cross. This practice gave rise to our modern custom of separating groups of three digits in a numeral by a comma.*

*D. E. Smith, *History of Mathematics,* 2d ed. (Lexington, MA: Ginn, 1925), pp. 183–185.

EXERCISES AND PROBLEMS 3.1

The chips on the lines of this reckoning table each represent one of the indicated powers of 10. Use this table to answer 1 and 2.

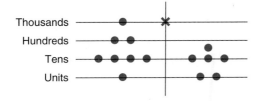

1. What number is represented on the left side of the reckoning table?

2. Each chip in a space between the horizontal lines represents half as much as it would on the line above. What number is represented on the right side of this reckoning table?

Use the following counting system of a twentieth-century Australian tribe to answer exercises 3 and 4.

Neecha	Boolla	Boolla Neecha	Boolla Boolla
1	2	3	4

3. If this system were continued, what would be the names for 5 and 6?

4. How would even numbers differ from odd numbers in a continuation of this system?

5. In the base-five system of counting by fingers and grouping by hands, the name for 7 is *1 hand and 2.*
   a. What is the name for 22 in this system?
   b. If 25 is called a *hand of hands,* what is the name for 37 in this system?

6. The following number names are literal translations of number words taken from primitive languages in various parts of the world.* Follow this pattern, and write in the missing names.

5	whole hand
6	one on the other hand
8	
10	
11	1 on the foot
15	
16	
20	person
21	1 on the hands of the next person
25	
30	
40	

*D. Smeltzer, *Man and Number* (London: A and C. Black, 1970), pp. 14–15.

Sketch the minimum number of base-ten pieces needed to replace each set in 7 and 8.

7.

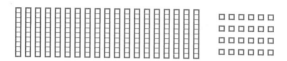

8.

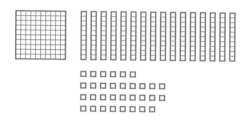

Sketch base pieces for the unit, long, and flat for each of the bases in exercises 9 and 10.

9. a. Base seven
   b. Base three

10. a. Base five
   b. Base twelve

Sketch the minimum number of base pieces for the bases given in exercises 11 and 12 to represent the following set of units. Then write the number of units in positional notation for the given base.

11. a. Base seven
   b. Base five

12. a. Base twelve
   b. Base three

In exercises 13 and 14, determine the total number of units to which the base pieces are equivalent for the given base.

13. a. Base five: 3 flats, 4 longs, 3 units
   b. Base eight: 6 flats, 0 longs, 5 units

14. a. Base twelve: 8 flats, 7 longs, 8 units
   b. Base three: 2 long-flats, 1 flat, 2 longs, 1 unit

15. The following numeration systems were used at different times in different geographic locations. Compare these sets of numerals for the numbers 1 through 10. What similarities can you find? What evidence is there of grouping by 5s?

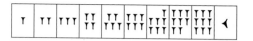

Babylonian numerals

Roman numerals

Mayan numerals

Egyptian numerals

In exercises 16 and 17, write each number in the given system.

16. a. Egyptian numeration: 3275
   b. Roman numeration: 406
   c. Babylonian numeration: 8063
   d. Mayan numeration: 48

17. a. Egyptian numeration: 40,208
   b. Roman numeration: 1776
   c. Babylonian numeration: 4635
   d. Mayan numeration: 172

18. The Greek numerals shown below date from about 1200 B.C. Use these symbols and the additive numeration system to write 2483.

1	10	100	1000

19. The Attic-Greek numerals were developed sometime prior to the third century B.C. and came from the first letters of the Greek names for numbers. Use the clues in the following table to find the missing numerals. What base is used in this system?

1	4	8		26
		ΓΙΙΙ	ΔΓΙ	

32	52	57	206	
ΔΔΔΙΙ		ΓΓΙΙ	ΗΗΓΙ	ΓΔΙ

Write each number in exercises 20 and 21 in two different ways, using expanded form.

20. a. 256,049   **b.** 7088

21. a. 7,082,555   **b.** 57,020

Determine the value of each underlined digit and its place value in exercises 22 and 23.

22. a. 3<u>7</u>2,089
  b. <u>5</u>55,555
  c. <u>9</u>2,441,000

23. a. 1<u>4</u>78
  b. 700,<u>0</u>00
  c. <u>2</u>,947,831

Write the names of the numbers in exercises 24 and 25.

24. a. 5,438,146
  b. 31,409
  c. 816,447,210,361
  d. 62,340,782,000,000

25. a. 4040
  b. 793,428,511
  c. 30,197,733
  d. 5,210,999,617

Round the numbers in exercises 26 and 27 to the nearest given place value.

26. 375,296,588
  a. Million
  b. Hundred thousand
  c. Ten million
  d. Thousand

27. 43,668,926
  a. Hundred thousand
  b. Ten thousand
  c. Thousand
  d. Hundred

Make a sketch of the given model for each number of units in exercises 28 and 29.

28. a. 136, using base-ten pieces
  b. 47, using the bundle-of-sticks model
  c. 108, using base-five pieces
  d. 35, using base-three pieces

29. a. 108, using the bundle-of-sticks model
  b. 570, using base-ten pieces
  c. 93, using base-five pieces
  d. 70, using base-twelve pieces

In exercises 30 and 31, enter the number in the top view screen into your calculator. What numbers and operations can be entered to change the screen to the one under it without changing the digits that are the same in both screens?

30. a.   1034692.
          1834692.

  b.   938647.
          908047.

  c.   36859.
          3859.

31. a.   72913086.
          78913086.

  b.   3270521.
          3470821.

  c.   7496146.
          749146.

In exercises 32 and 33, assume that the calculator view screen displays nine digits and that numbers are entered into the calculator by using only the keys 1, 2, 3, 4, 5, 6, 7, 8, and 9.

32. a. What is the greatest whole number that can be formed in the calculator view screen if each of these keys is used exactly once?
  b. What is the greatest whole number that can be formed in the calculator view screen if a key can be used more than once?

33. a. What is the smallest whole number that can be formed to fill the calculator view screen if each of these keys is used exactly once?
  b. What is the smallest whole number that can be formed to fill the calculator view screen if a key can be used more than once?

If each number and operation in exercises 34 and 35 is entered into a calculator in the order in which it occurs from left to right, and the calculator follows the *order of operations,* what number will appear in the calculator view screen?

34. a. $3 \times 1000 + 4 \times 100 + 0 \times 10 + 7$
  b. $8 \times 10{,}000 + 3 \times 10 + 1$

35. a. $7 \times 100{,}000 + 7 \times 1000 + 7$
  b. $12 \times 1000 + 8 \times 100 + 3 \times 10 + 2$

REASONING AND PROBLEM SOLVING

36. Featured Strategies: Making a Drawing, Making a Table, and Finding a Pattern   A single-elimination basketball tournament has 247 teams competing for the championship. If the tournament sponsors must pay $20 to have each game refereed, what is the total cost of referees for the tournament?

a. Understanding the Problem For every two teams that play each other, there is a winner and a loser. The loser is eliminated from the tournament, and the winner plays another team. The following brackets for a four-team tournament show that three games are needed to determine a champion.

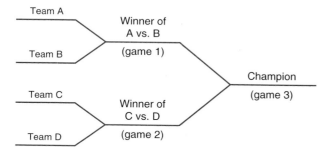

If the number of teams entered in the tournament is not a power of 2, byes are necessary. That is, some teams will be unopposed in the first round so that the number of teams for the second round will be a power of 2. Draw a set of brackets for a seven-team tournament. How many teams will be unopposed in the first round?

b. Devising a Plan One approach to solving this problem is to use small numbers and to look for a pattern. Complete the following table.

No. of teams	2	3	4	5	6	7	8
Total no. of games	1		3				

c. Carrying Out the Plan To solve this problem, use the approach suggested in part b and inductive reasoning, or use your own plan. What is the total cost of referees for the tournament?

d. Looking Back The brackets in part a directed our attention to the winning teams. The total number of games played can be more easily determined by thinking about the losing teams. Each game that is played determines one loser. How many losing teams will there be in the tournament?

37. Powers of 2 are used in base-two numeration systems. These powers are called **binary numbers.** Here are the first few.

1	2	4	8	16	32	64
2^0	2^1	2^2	2^3	2^4	2^5	2^6

Amy and Joel found that the first 25 whole numbers either are binary numbers or can be written as a sum of binary numbers so that each binary number is used only once or not at all. For example, $25 = 16 + 8 + 1$. Is this true for whole numbers greater than 25? Try a few such numbers and form a conjecture.

38. What four-digit whole number satisfies the following conditions? The sum of the digits is 6; the number is less than 1200; none of the four digits are equal; and the tens digit is an odd number.

39. A three-digit number satisfies the following conditions: The digits are consecutive whole numbers; the sum of each pair of digits is greater than 4 and less than 10; and the tens digit is an even number. What is the number?

40. What is Jared's favorite six-digit number if the tens digit is his favorite digit, the sum of the hundred thousands digit and the thousands digit is his favorite digit, and the digits in his number from the largest place value to the smallest place value are consecutive numbers?

41. The third, fourth, and fifth floors of a business building are being remodeled. The rooms will be numbered using all the whole numbers from 300 to 599. The front door of each room will be numbered with bronze digits. How many bronze numerals for the digit 3 will be needed to number these rooms?

42. What is the two-digit number which satisfies the following conditions? The tens digit is larger than the units digit; the sum of the digits is 11; and if the digits are reversed and the resulting two-digit number is subtracted from the original number, the difference is 27.

ONLINE LEARNING CENTER   www.mhhe.com/bennett-nelson

• Math Investigation 3.1   *The Number 6174*
Section-Related: • Links   • Writing/Discussion Problems   • Bibliography

MATH ACTIVITY 3.2

ADDITION AND SUBTRACTION WITH BASE-FIVE PIECES

Materials: Base-five pieces in Manipulative Kit and two dice.

*1. **Trading-Up Game** (two to four players)   On a player's turn two dice are rolled. The product (or the game can be played with sums) of the two numbers on the dice is the number of units the player wins. At the end of a player's turn, the pieces should be traded (regrouped) so that the total winnings are represented by the *minimal collection* (smallest possible number of base-five pieces). The first player to get 1 long-flat or more wins the game.

  Example: On a player's first turn, two 6s were rolled on the dice. The product of 36 is represented by the base-five pieces shown here. On the player's second turn, a 4 and 5 were rolled on the dice. What is the player's minimal collection after the second turn?

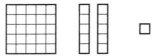

2. The following tables show the numbers of base-five pieces that were won in the Trading-Up Game by three players after each player had seven turns. (LF, F, L, and U denote long-flat, flat, long, and unit, respectively.) Use your base-five pieces to determine the minimal collection each player had at the end of the game. Who won the game?

Player 1

LF	F	L	U
		3	3
		4	4
		3	0
		2	2
		4	4
		4	0
		2	2
Total			

Player 2

LF	F	L	U
		2	0
		2	2
		4	0
		3	3
		4	0
	1	1	0
		2	0
Total			

Player 3

LF	F	L	U
		1	0
		2	2
	1	0	0
		3	1
	1	1	0
		3	3
		1	1
Total			

*3. In the first three turns of a Trading-Up Game, a player won 124_{five} units and in the next three turns won a total of 134_{five} units. Use your base-five pieces to represent each number, and determine the minimum collection of flats, longs, and units the player had after six turns. In the remaining turns, what is the minimal collection of base-five pieces the player will need to obtain one long-flat? Explain how you arrived at your answer.

4. **Trading-Down Game**   Each player begins this game with one long-flat and removes the number of units determined by the product of the numbers on the dice. The object is to be the first player to get rid of all base-five pieces. Suppose that after four turns in this game a player has 3 flats, 1 long, and 0 units. If the player rolls double 6s on the fifth turn, what is the minimal collection of base-five pieces the player will have after the fifth turn?

SECTION 3.2

ADDITION AND SUBTRACTION

PROBLEM OPENER

Use each of the digits 0 through 9 exactly once to obtain the smallest whole-number difference.

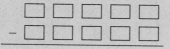

Children learn addition at an early age by using objects. If 2 clams are *put together* with 3 clams, the total number of clams is the **sum** 2 + 3. The idea of *putting sets together*, or *taking their union*, is often used to define addition.

ADDITION OF WHOLE NUMBERS   If set **R** has **r** elements and set **S** has **s** elements, and **R** and **S** are disjoint, then the **sum of r plus s,** written $r + s$, is the number of elements in the union of **R** and **S**. The numbers **r** and **s** are called **addends.**

In the definition of addition, R and S must be disjoint sets. Otherwise, you could not determine the total number of elements in two sets by adding the number of elements in one set to the number of elements in the other set.

Example **A**

There are eight people in a group who play the guitar and six who play the piano. These are the only people in the group.

1. What is the minimum number of people in this group?

2. What is the maximum number of people in this group?

3. What is the total number of people if two people play both the guitar and the piano?

Solution   1. 8 if the 6 piano players also play the guitar   2. 14 if the sets of piano players and guitar players are disjoint   3. 12, as illustrated on the next page

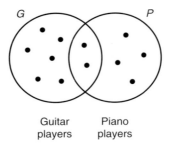

Guitar
players

Piano
players

Models for Addition Algorithms

An **algorithm** is a step-by-step procedure for computing. Algorithms for addition involve two separate procedures: (1) adding digits and (2) regrouping, or "carrying" (when necessary), so that the sum is written in positional numeration. The term *carrying* probably originated back at a time when a counter, or chip, was actually carried to the next column on a counting board. Traditionally, a substantial portion of the school mathematics curriculum has involved practice with pencil-and-paper algorithms. As calculators and computers are readily available, there will be less emphasis on written algorithms. It will always be important, however, to understand algorithms and their use in mental mathematics and estimation.

There are many models for providing an understanding of addition algorithms. Example B shows how to illustrate the sum of two numbers by using the bundle-of-sticks model. The sticks representing these numbers can be placed below each other, just as the numerals are in the addition algorithm. The sum is the total number of sticks in the bundles plus the total number of individual sticks.

Example B

The numbers 26 and 38 are represented in the following figure. To compute 26 + 38, we must determine the total number of sticks. There is a total of 5 bundles of sticks (5 tens) and 14 sticks (14 ones). Since there are 14 single sticks, they can be regrouped into 1 bundle of 10 sticks and 4 more. Thus there are a total of 6 bundles and 4 sticks. In the addition algorithm, a 4 is recorded in the units column and the extra 10 is recorded by writing a 1 in the tens column.

Research Statement

Elementary school students often incorrectly employ a "when in doubt, add" strategy. This is attributed to an aspect of poorly developed conceptual knowledge.

Kroll and Miller 1993

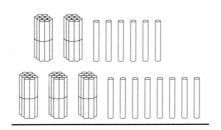

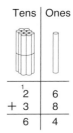

Tens	Ones
$\overset{1}{2}$	6
+ 3	8
6	4

The use of concrete materials such as the base-ten pieces or the bundle-of-sticks model provides opportunities for students to develop their own methods of computing. The *Curriculum and Evaluation Standards for School Mathematics* recognizes the value of such activities:

As they begin to understand the meaning of operations and develop a concrete basis for validating symbolic processes and situations, students should design their own algorithms and discuss, compare, and evaluate them with their peers and teacher.*

Students using the model in Example B might find it natural to combine all the single sticks first, next combine the bundles of 10, and then do the regrouping. This can lead to an algorithm called **partial sums.** In this method, the digits for each place value are added, and the partial sums are recorded before there is any regrouping.

Two methods of writing partial sums are shown in Example C. In part 1 there is seldom a need for regrouping, because if there is more than one digit in the partial sum, the digits are placed in different columns. In part 2 the regrouping can be done beginning with any partial sum with more than one digit.

Example C

1.
$$
\begin{array}{r}
345 \\
+\,278 \\
\hline
13 \\
11 \\
5 \\
\hline
623
\end{array}
$$

2.
$$
\begin{array}{rl}
345 = & 3 \text{ hundreds} + 4 \text{ tens} + 5 \\
+278 = & 2 \text{ hundreds} + 7 \text{ tens} + 8 \\
\hline
& 5 \text{ hundreds} + 11 \text{ tens} + 13 \\
\text{Regrouping:} & 6 \text{ hundreds} + 2 \text{ tens} + 3 \\
= & 623
\end{array}
$$

LEFT-TO-RIGHT ADDITION   Some students might begin the process of combining the sticks in Example B by first combining the bundles of 10. Since children learn to read from left to right, some may find it natural to add in this direction. The next example illustrates this process in computing the sum of two three-digit numbers.

Example D

To compute 897 + 537 from left to right, we first add 8 and 5 in the hundreds column (see below). In the second step, 9 and 3 are added in the tens column, and because regrouping (carrying) is necessary, 3 in the hundreds column is scratched out and replaced by 4. In the third step, we add the units digits. Again regrouping is necessary, so 2 in the tens column is scratched out and replaced by 3.

First step	Second step	Third step
897	897	897
+537	+537	+537
13	1̸3̸2	1̸3̸2̸4
	4	43

The early Hindus and later the Europeans added from left to right. The Europeans called this algorithm the **scratch method.**

*Curriculum and Evaluation Standards for School Mathematics (Reston VA: National Council of Teachers of Mathematics, 1989), p. 95.

Number Properties

A few fundamental properties for operations on whole numbers are so important that they are given special names. Four properties for addition are introduced here, and the corresponding properties for multiplication are given in Section 3.3.

Research has shown that learning about number and operations is a complex process for children. (e.g., Fuson [1992])

Standards 2000, p. 32

CLOSURE PROPERTY FOR ADDITION   If you were to select any two whole numbers, their sum would be another whole number. This fact is expressed by saying that the whole numbers are **closed for the operation of addition.** In general, the word *closed* indicates that when an operation is performed on any two numbers from a given set, the result is also in the set, rather than outside the set. For example, the set of whole numbers is not closed for subtraction, because sometimes the difference between two whole numbers is a negative number. Consider another example. If we select any two numbers from the set of odd numbers {1, 3, 5, 7, . . . }, the sum is not another odd number. So the set of odd numbers is not closed for addition. To test for closure, students sometimes find it helpful to draw a circle and write a few of the numbers from a given set inside. Then if the given operation produces *at least one* result that is outside the circle, the set is not closed for the given operation.

> For every pair of numbers in a given set, if an operation is performed, and the result is also a number in the set, the set is said to be **closed for the operation.** If one example can be found where the operation does not produce an element of the given set, then the set is **not closed for the operation.**

Example E

Determine whether the set is closed or not closed for the given operation.

1. The set of odd numbers for subtraction.

2. The set of odd numbers for multiplication.

3. The set of whole numbers for division.

Solution   1. The set of odd numbers is not closed for subtraction. For example, $23 - 3$ is not an odd number.   2. The set of odd numbers is closed for multiplication.   3. The set of whole numbers is not closed for division.

IDENTITY PROPERTY FOR ADDITION   Included among the whole numbers is a very special number, zero. Zero is called the **identity for addition** because when it is added to another number, there is *no change.* That is, adding 0 to any number leaves the identity of the number unchanged. For example,

$$0 + 5 = 5 \qquad 17 + 0 = 17 \qquad 0 + 0 = 0$$

Zero is unique in that it is the only number that is an identity for addition.

> For any whole number *b,*
>
> $$0 + b = b + 0 = b$$
>
> and 0 is a unique identity for addition.

ASSOCIATIVE PROPERTY FOR ADDITION   In any sum of three numbers, the middle number may be added to (associated with) either of the two end numbers. This property is called the **associative property for addition.**

Example F

$$147 + (20 + 6) = (147 + 20) + 6$$

Associative property for addition

For any whole numbers a, b, and c,

$$a + (b + c) = (a + b) + c$$

When elementary school students compute by breaking a number into a convenient sum, as in the next example, the *associative property of addition* plays a role. Arranging numbers to produce sums of 10 is called *making 10s.*

Example G

$$8 + 7 = 8 + (2 + 5) = (8 + 2) + 5 = 10 + 5 = 15$$

Associative property for addition

COMMUTATIVE PROPERTY FOR ADDITION   When two numbers are added, the numbers may be interchanged (commuted) without affecting the sum. This property is called the **commutative property for addition.**

Example H

$$257 + 498 = 498 + 257$$

For any whole numbers a and b,

$$a + b = b + a$$

As the addition table in Figure 3.5 shows, the commutative property for addition roughly cuts in half the number of basic addition facts that must be memorized. Each sum in the shaded part of the table has a corresponding equal sum in the unshaded part of the table.

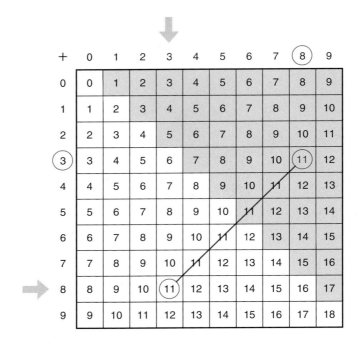

Figure 3.5

Example I

If we know that $3 + 8 = 11$, then, by the commutative property for addition, $8 + 3 = 11$. What do you notice about the locations of these sums in the addition table?

Solution   The sums of $3 + 8$ and $8 + 3$ are in opposite parts of the table. If the shaded part of the table is folded onto the unshaded part of the table, these sums will coincide. That is, the table is symmetric about the diagonal from upper left to lower right.

The commutative property also enables us to select convenient combinations of numbers when we are adding.

Example J

The numbers 26, 37, and 4 are arranged more conveniently on the right side of the following equation than on the left, because $26 + 4 = 30$ and it is easy to compute $30 + 37$.

$$26 + \underbrace{37 + 4} = 26 + \underbrace{4 + 37} = (26 + 4) + 37 = 30 + 37$$

Commutative property
for addition

Inequality of Whole Numbers

The inequality of whole numbers can be understood intuitively in terms of the locations of numbers as they occur in the counting process. For example, 3 is less than 5 because it is named before 5 in the counting sequence. This ordering of numbers can be illustrated with a number line. A **number line** is formed by beginning with any line and marking off two points, one labeled 0 and the other labeled 1, as shown in Figure 3.6. This **unit segment** is then used to mark off equally spaced points for consecutive whole numbers. For any two numbers, the one that occurs on the left is less than the one that occurs on the right.

One method of marking off unit lengths to form a number line is to use the edges of base-ten pieces—such as the *long* for marking off 10 units (see Figure 3.6). This use of base-ten pieces provides a link between the region model and the linear model for illustrating numbers.

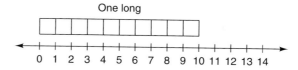

Figure 3.6

The inequality of whole numbers is defined in terms of addition.

> **INEQUALITY OF WHOLE NUMBERS**   For any two whole numbers m and n, m is less than n (written $m < n$) if and only if there is a nonzero whole number k such that $m + k = n$.

An inequality can be written with the inequality symbol opening to the right or to the left. For example, $4 < 9$ means that 4 is **less than** 9; and $9 > 4$ means that 9 is **greater than** 4. Sometimes the inequality symbol is combined with the equality symbol: $\leq$ means **less than or equal to**, and $\geq$ means **greater than or equal to**.

HISTORICAL HIGHLIGHT

The symbols $<$ and $>$ were first used by English surveyor Thomas Harriot in 1631. There is no record of why Harriot chose these symbols, but the following conjecture is logical and will help you to remember their meanings. The distances between the ends of the bars in the equality symbol are equal, and in an equation (for example, $3 = 1 + 2$) the number on the left of the equality symbol equals the number on the right. Similarly, $3 < 4$ indicates that 3 is less than 4, because the distance between the bars on the left is less than the distance between the bars on the right. The reasoning is the same whether we write $3 < 4$ or $4 > 3$. These symbols could easily have evolved into our present notation, $<$ and $>$, in which the bars completely converge to prevent any misjudgment of the distances.*

*This is one of two conjectures on the origin of the inequality symbols, described by H. W. Eves in *Mathematical Circles* (Boston: Prindle, Weber and Schmidt, 1969), pp. 111–113.

Research Statement

For students in grades K–2, learning to see the part to whole relations in addition and subtraction situations is one of their most important accomplishments in arithmetic.

Resnick 1983

Models for Subtraction Algorithms

Subtraction is usually explained as the *taking away* of a subset of objects from a given set. The word *subtract* literally means *to draw away from under*.

The process of taking away, or subtraction, may be thought of as the opposite of the process of putting together, or addition. Because of this dual relationship, subtraction and addition are called **inverse operations**. This relationship is used to define subtraction in terms of addition.

> **SUBTRACTION OF WHOLE NUMBERS**   For any whole numbers r and s, with $r \geq s$, the **difference** of r minus s, written $r - s$, is the whole number c such that $r = s + c$. The number c is called the **missing addend**.

By the end of grade 2, children should know the basic addition and subtraction combinations, should be fluent in adding two-digit numbers, and should have methods for subtracting two-digit numbers.

Standards 2000, p. 33

The definition of subtraction says that we can compute the difference $17 - 5$ by determining the **missing addend**, that is, finding the number that must be added to 5 to give 17. Store clerks use this approach when making change. Rather than subtracting 83 cents from \$1.00 to determine the difference, they pay back the change by counting up from 83 to 100.

After negative numbers are introduced, there is no need to require r to be greater than or equal to s in the definition of subtraction. In the early school grades, however, before negative numbers appear, most examples involve subtracting a smaller number from a larger one.

Three concepts of subtraction occur in problems: the **take-away concept**, the **comparison concept**, and the **missing addend concept**.

TAKE-AWAY CONCEPT   Suppose that you have 12 stamps and give away 7. How many stamps will you have left? Figure 3.7 illustrates $12 - 7$ by showing 7 objects being taken away from 12 objects.

Take-away concept showing 12 − 7 = 5

Figure 3.7

COMPARISON CONCEPT   Suppose that you have 12 stamps and someone else has 7 stamps. How many more stamps do you have than the other person? In this case we compare one collection to another to determine the difference. Figure 3.8 shows that there are 5 more stamps in one collection than in the other

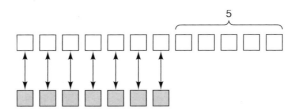

Comparison concept showing 12 − 7 = 5

Figure 3.8

MISSING ADDEND CONCEPT   Suppose that you have 7 stamps and you need to mail 12 letters. How many more stamps are needed? In this case we can count up from 7 to 12 to determine the missing addend.

There are two types of examples to consider in explaining the steps in finding the difference between two multidigit numbers: examples in which regrouping (borrowing) is not needed and those in which regrouping (borrowing) is needed.

The bundle-of-sticks model and the take-away concept of subtraction are used in Example K to illustrate the subtraction algorithm with regrouping.

Example K

To illustrate 53 − 29, we begin with 5 bundles of sticks (5 tens) and 3 sticks (3 ones), as shown. To take away 9 sticks, we must regroup one bundle, to form 13 single sticks. Once this has been done, we can take away 2 bundles of sticks and 9 sticks, leaving 2 bundles of sticks and 4 single sticks. In the algorithm, the regrouping is recorded by crossing out 5 and writing 4 above it.

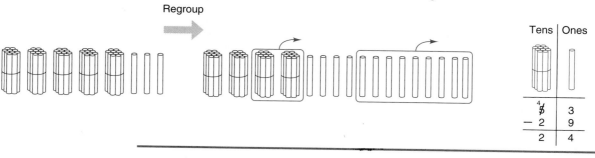

Regroup

Tens	Ones
$\overset{4}{\cancel{5}}$	3
− 2	9
2	4

Sums and differences can be computed on calculators with algebraic logic by entering the numbers from left to right as they occur in equation form. For instance, 475 + 381 − 209 is computed by the following key strokes.

KEYSTROKES	VIEW SCREEN
475	475
+	475
381	381
−	856
209	209
=	647

When numbers and operations are entered into some calculators, such as the one in Figure 3.9, they are displayed on the view screen from left to right as illustrated.* If more numbers and operations are entered than can be displayed on the view screen of this calculator, previous entries are pushed off the left end of the screen but are retained internally in the calculator's memory.

Figure 3.9

Calculators can be used to strengthen students' understanding of place value and algorithms for computing. Earlier in this section we discussed partial sums and left-to-right addition. The next keystrokes illustrate these methods for computing 792 + 485 + 876. Notice that the first view screen shows the sum of the hundreds; the second screen shows the sum of the hundreds and tens; and the last screen shows the sum of the original three numbers.

*SHARP EL-300.

2·8

Explore Subtracting Whole Numbers

Learn

You can use place-value models to explore subtracting whole numbers.

What is 423 − 255?

Work Together

▶ Use the place-value models to find 423 − 255.
- Show 423 using the hundred blocks.
- You will need to regroup to subtract.
- Regroup 1 hundred as 10 tens.
- Regroup 1 ten as 10 ones.

> **You Will Need**
> - place-value models

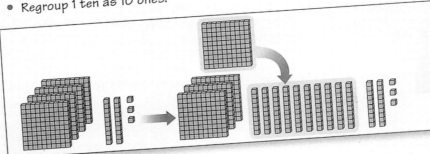

- Use the place-value models to subtract 255.
  Record your work and answer the question at the top of the page.
▶ Use the place value models to subtract. Record your work.

354 − 148   234 − 52   500 − 317   228 − 154   314 − 176

```
        KEYSTROKES              VIEW SCREEN
  700 + 400 + 800 +            [  1900  ]
    90 +  80 +  70 +           [  2140  ]
     2 +   5 +   6 =           [  2153  ]
```

Mental Calculations

Mental calculations are important because they often prove the quickest and most convenient method of obtaining an answer. Performing mental computations requires us to combine a variety of skills: the abilities to use various algorithms, to understand place value and base-ten numeration, and to use number properties. Mental calculations are useful in obtaining exact answers, and they are a prerequisite to estimating. Let's consider a few techniques for performing mental calculations.

COMPATIBLE NUMBERS   One mental calculating technique is to look for pairs of numbers whose sum or difference is easy to compute. For example, it is convenient to combine 17 and 43 in the following computation.

$$17 - 12 + 43 = 17 + 43 - 12 = 60 - 12$$

Using pairs of numbers that are especially easy to compute with is the calculating technique called **compatible numbers.**

Example L

Do the following computations in your head.

1. $17 + 12 + 23 + 45$

2. $12 - 15 + 82 - 61 + 55$

Solution   1.   One possibility is to notice that $17 + 23 = 40$; then $40 + 45 = 85$, and adding 12 produces 97. Another possibility is to notice that $12 + 23 = 35$. Then $35 + 45 = 80$, and adding 17 produces 97.   2.   Here is one possibility: $55 - 15 = 40$ and $82 - 61 = 21$. Then $40 + 21 = 61$, and adding 12 produces 73.

SUBSTITUTIONS   Another method of mental calculation is the method of **substitutions,** in which a number is broken down into a convenient sum or difference of numbers. You can easily compute the sum $127 + 38$ in your head in many ways. Here are three possibilities:

$$127 + (3 + 35) = (127 + 3) + 35 = 130 + 35 = 165$$
$$127 + (30 + 8) = (127 + 30) + 8 = 157 + 8 = 165$$
$$(125 + 2) + 38 = 125 + (2 + 38) = 125 + 40 = 165$$

Example M

Do each computation mentally by substituting a convenient sum or difference for one of the given numbers.

1. $57 + 24$

2. $163 - 46$

Solution   Here is one possibility for each computation: 1. $57 + 20 + 4 = 77 + 4 = 81$ 2. $163 - 40 - 6 = 123 - 6 = 117$

EQUAL DIFFERENCES   Another type of substitution that works for subtraction is the method of **equal differences,** which uses the fact that the difference between two numbers is unchanged when both numbers are increased or decreased by the same amount. Figure 3.10 illustrates why this is true when both numbers are increased. No matter how many tiles are adjoined to the two rows in this figure, the difference between the numbers of tiles in the two rows is $11 - 7 = 4$.

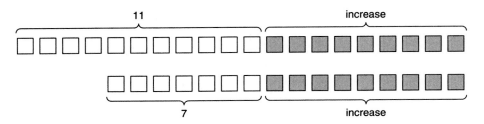

Figure 3.10

Replacing a difference by an equal but more convenient difference can be very useful.

Example N

To compute $47 - 18$, first find a more convenient difference by increasing or decreasing both numbers by the same amount.

Solution   Here are several differences that are more convenient for computing $47 - 18$.

$49 - 20$	(both numbers were increased by 2)
$50 - 21$	(both numbers were increased by 3)
$30 - 1$	(both numbers were decreased by 17)
$40 - 11$	(both numbers were decreased by 7)

The difference, 29, is easy to compute in any of these forms.

ADD-UP METHOD   A convenient mental method for subtracting is to **add up** from the smaller to the larger number.

Example O

Compute each difference by adding up from the smaller to the larger number.

1. $53 - 17$

2. $135 - 86$

Solution   1. From 17 to 20 is **3,** and from 20 to 53 is **33.** So the difference is $3 + 33 = 36$.   2. From 86 to 100 is **14,** and from 100 to 135 is **35.** So the difference is $14 + 35 = 49$.

Estimation of Sums and Differences

In recent years the teaching of estimation has become a top priority in school mathematics programs. Often in everyday applications we need to make a quick calculation that does not have to be exact to serve the purpose at hand. For example, when shopping, we may want to estimate the total cost of the items selected in order to avoid an unpleasant surprise at the checkout counter. Estimation is especially important for developing "number sense" and predicting the reasonableness of answers. With the increased use of calculators, estimation helps students to determine if the correct keys have been pressed.

There are some difficulties in teaching estimation. First, the best estimating technique to use often depends on the numbers involved and the context of the problem. Second, there is no correct answer. An estimate is a "ballpark" figure, and for a given problem there will often be several different estimates.

There are many techniques for estimating. Three common ones—*rounding, using compatible numbers,* and *front-end estimation*—are explained below. After obtaining an estimation, we sometimes need to know if it is less than or greater than the actual answer. This can often be determined from the method of estimation used.

ROUNDING   If an approximate sum or difference is all that is needed, we can round the numbers before computing. The type of problem will often determine to what place value the numbers will be rounded. The following estimates are obtained by rounding to the nearest hundreds or thousands. The symbol $\approx$ means **approximately equal to.**

Example P

Obtain an estimation by rounding each number to the place value of the leading digit.

1. $624 - 289 - 132$

2. $4723 + 419 + 1040$

3. $812 - 245$

Solution   1. $\approx 600 - 300 - 100 = 200$ 2. $\approx 5000 + 400 + 1000 = 6400$ 3. $\approx 800 - 200 = 600$

Some people prefer rounding each number to the same place value. If each number in part 2 of Example P were rounded to the nearest thousand, 419 would be rounded to 0 and the approximate sum would become $5000 + 0 + 1000 = 6000$. Even when numbers have the same number of digits, they do not have to be rounded to the same place value. A different estimation could be obtained in part 3 of Example P by rounding 245 to 250 (the nearest ten). We could then use the add-up method to obtain a difference of 550.

$$812 - 245 \approx 800 - 250 = 550$$

COMPATIBLE NUMBERS   Sometimes a computation can be simplified by replacing one or more numbers by approximations in order to obtain *compatible numbers.* For example, to approximate $342 + 250$, we might replace 342 by 350.

$$342 + 250 \approx 350 + 250 = 600$$

Using compatible numbers is a common estimating technique.

Example Q

Use compatible numbers to obtain each estimate. Without computing the actual answer, predict whether your estimate is too small or too big.

1. $88 + 37 + 66 + 24$

2. $142 - 119$

3. $127 + 416 - 288$

Solution   Here are some estimations. Others may occur to you.   **1.** $90 + 40 + 70 + 20 = 220$, which is greater than the actual answer.   **2.** $140 - 120 = 20$, which is less than the actual answer.   **3.** $130 + 400 - 300 = 230$, which is less than the actual answer.

FRONT-END ESTIMATION   The method of **front-end estimation** is similar to left-to-right addition, but involves only the leading digit of each number.

Suppose you have written checks for $433, $684, and $228 and wish to quickly estimate the total. Using front-end estimation, we see that the sum of the leading digits is 12, so the estimated sum is 1200.

$$433 + 684 + 228 \approx 400 + 600 + 200 = 1200$$

This method of estimation is different from rounding to the highest place value. For example, in the preceding sum, 684 is replaced by 600, rather than the rounded value of 700.

The next example shows how front-end estimation is used when the leading digit of each number in a sum does not have the same place value.

$$3827 + 458 + 5031 + 311 \approx 3000 + 400 + 5000 + 300 = 8700$$

Notice that in estimating the sums in these two examples, the digits beyond the leading digit of each number are not used. Thus, when front-end estimation is used for sums, the estimation is always less than or equal to the exact sum.

Front-end estimation is used for estimating both sums and differences in Example R.

Example R

Use front-end estimation to estimate each sum or difference.

1. $1306 + 7247 + 3418$

2. $4718 - 1335$

3. $527 + 4215 + 718$

4. $7316 - 547$

Solution   **1.** $1306 + 7247 + 3418 \approx 1000 + 7000 + 3000 = 11{,}000$ **2.** $4718 - 1335 \approx 4000 - 1000 = 3000$ **3.** $527 + 4215 + 718 \approx 500 + 4000 + 700 = 5200$ **4.** $7316 - 547 \approx 7000 - 500 = 6500$

Large errors from computing on a calculator, such as those produced by pressing an incorrect key, can sometimes be discovered by techniques for estimating. Suppose, for example, that you wanted to add 417, 683, and 228, but that you entered 2228 on the calculator rather than 228. The sum of the three numbers you intended to add when rounded to the nearest hundred is 1300, but the erroneous calculator sum will be 3328. The difference of more than 2000 between the estimation and the calculator sum indicates that the computation should be redone.

Sum		Estimation
	(rounding)	
417	$\longrightarrow$	400
683	$\longrightarrow$	700
+ 228	$\longrightarrow$	+ 200
		1300

Problem-Solving Application

The following problem introduces the strategy of **making an organized list.** This problem-solving strategy is closely associated with another strategy called *eliminating possibilities.* Next to guessing and checking, one of the most common approaches to solving problems is to systematically search for or eliminate possibilities.

PROBLEM

Karen and Angela are playing darts on the board shown below. Each player throws three darts on her turn and adds the numbers on the regions that are hit. The darts always hit the dartboard, and when a dart lands on a line, the score is the larger of the two numbers. After four turns Karen and Angela notice that their sums for each turn are all different. How many different sums are possible?

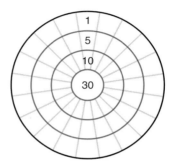

Understanding the Problem   Question 1: What are the largest and smallest possible sums?

Devising a Plan   Here are two approaches to finding all the sums. Since the lowest sum is 3 and the highest sum is 90, we can list the numbers from 3 through 90 and determine which can be obtained. Or we can *make an organized list* showing the different regions the three darts can strike. Question 2: For example, if the first two darts land in regions 1 and 5, what are the possible scores after the third dart is thrown?

Carrying Out the Plan   Use one of the above approaches or one of your own to find the different sums and determine how each can be obtained from the dartboard. Question 3: How many different sums are possible?

Looking Back   Instead of four regions, suppose the dartboard had three regions. Question 4: How many different sums would be possible on a dartboard with three regions numbered 1, 5, and 10?

Answers to Questions 1–4   1. The largest sum is 90, and the smallest is 3.   2. The possible sums are 7, 11, 16, and 36.   3. 20 different sums   4. 10 different sums

EXERCISES AND PROBLEMS 3.2

Use the following information in exercises 1 and 2. To compute $854 + 629$, using the adding machine described above, we first turn the hundreds, tens, and units wheels 8, 5, and 4 notches, respectively. We then dial these same wheels 6, 2, and 9 more notches. The sum will appear on indicators at the top of the machine.

1. a. Which of these wheels will make more than 1 revolution for this sum?
   b. Can this sum be computed by left-to-right addition, that is, by turning the hundreds wheel for both hundreds digits, 8 and 6; turning the tens wheel for 5 and 2; and turning the units wheel for 4 and 9?

2. a. Which two wheels will be advanced one digit because of carrying?
   b. Can this sum be computed by turning the wheels in different orders, such as the tens wheel 5, the units wheel 9, the hundreds wheel 8, the units wheel 4, the hundreds wheel 6, and the tens wheel 2?

Determine the minimum number of flats, longs, and units for the bases in exercises 3 and 4 if the pieces in set A are combined with the pieces in set B. (*Reminder:* In some cases regrouping will be needed.) Then write numbers in positional numeration for sets A and B and the number for their sum in the given base.

3. a. Base five
   A: 2 flats, 3 longs, 2 units
   B: 1 flat, 2 longs, 3 units
   b. Base twelve
   A: 8 flats, 5 longs, 2 units
   B: 2 flats, 9 longs, 5 units

4. a. Base three
   A: 2 flats, 2 longs, 2 units
   B: 2 flats, 1 long, 2 units
   b. Base ten
   A: 5 flats, 7 longs, 7 units
   B: 2 flats, 6 longs, 5 units

Determine the minimum number of pieces in exercises 5 and 6 that need to be combined with set B to obtain set A for the given base. Then write numbers in positional numeration for sets A and B and the number for their difference in the given base.

5. a. Base eight
   A: 5 flats, 2 longs, 3 units
   B: 2 flats, 6 longs, 5 units
   b. Base five
   A: 3 flats, 4 longs, 2 units
   B: 1 flat, 3 longs, 4 units

6. a. Base twelve
   A: 7 flats, 9 longs, 6 units
   B: 5 flats, 8 longs, 9 units
   b. Base ten
   A: 6 flats, 6 longs, 2 units
   B: 2 flats, 9 longs, 3 units

Sketch base pieces for exercises 7 and 8 to illustrate each computation. Show regrouping.

7. a. $106 + 38$
   b. $41_{five} - 23_{five}$, using the take-away concept of subtraction
   c. $161 - 127$, using the comparison concept of subtraction
   d. $142_{five} + 34_{five}$

8. a. $46 + 27$

b. $52 - 36$, using the take-away concept of subtraction

c. $35 - 18$, using the comparison concept of subtraction

d. $33_{\text{five}} + 43_{\text{five}}$

Addition is illustrated on a number line by a series of arrows, as shown here. Use a number line to illustrate the equalities in exercises 9 and 10.

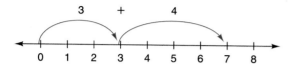

9. a. $2 + 5 = 5 + 2$

b. $(2 + 4) + 1 = 1 + (2 + 4)$

10. a. $(3 + 4) + 1 = (4 + 1) + 3$

b. $(2 + 3) + 4 = 2 + (4 + 3)$

Subtraction is illustrated on a number line by arrows that represent numbers. The number being subtracted is represented by an arrow from right to left, as shown here. Use a number line to illustrate the equations in exercises 11 and 12.

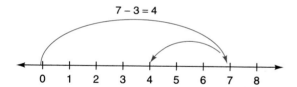

11. a. $(6 - 3) - 2 = 1$

b. $6 - 6 = 0$

12. a. $(4 + 5) - 7 = 2$

b. $(9 - 2) - 6 = 1$

Compute the sums in exercises 13 and 14, using the given method. Describe an advantage of each method.

13. a. Left-to-right addition
$$\begin{array}{r} 726 \\ +508 \\ \hline \end{array}$$

b. Partial sums
$$\begin{array}{r} 974 \\ +382 \\ \hline \end{array}$$

14. a. Left-to-right addition
$$\begin{array}{r} 4763 \\ +9607 \\ \hline \end{array}$$

b. Partial sums
$$\begin{array}{r} 476 \\ +947 \\ \hline \end{array}$$

Which number property shows that the two sides of each equation in 15 and 16 are equal?

15. a. $(38 + 13) + 17 = 38 + (13 + 17)$

b. $(47 + 62) + 12 = (62 + 47) + 12$

16. a. $2 \times (341 + 19) = 2 \times (19 + 341)$

b. $13 + (107 + 42) = (13 + 107) + 42$

Try some whole numbers in exercises 17 and 18 to determine whether the properties hold.

17. a. Is subtraction commutative?

$$\square - \triangle \stackrel{?}{=} \triangle - \square$$

b. Is the set of even numbers closed for addition?

18. a. Is subtraction associative?

$$(\square - \triangle) - \diamond \stackrel{?}{=} \square - (\triangle - \diamond)$$

b. Is the set of odd numbers closed for subtraction?

Error analysis: Some types of student errors and misuses of addition are very common. Describe the types of errors illustrated in exercises 19 and 20.

19. a.
$$\begin{array}{r} 47 \\ +\ 86 \\ \hline 123 \end{array}$$

b.
$$\begin{array}{r} 16 \\ +48 \\ \hline 91 \end{array}$$

20. a.
$$\begin{array}{r} 56 \\ +\ 78 \\ \hline 1214 \end{array}$$

b.
$$\begin{array}{r} 35 \\ +46 \\ \hline 171 \end{array}$$

Error analysis: One common source of elementary school students' errors in subtraction is adding rather than subtracting. When addition is taught first, the students' responses become so automatic that later on they write 8 for the difference $5 - 3$. Try to detect the reason for the error in each computation in 21 and 22.

21. a.
$$\begin{array}{r} 84 \\ -36 \\ \hline 52 \end{array}$$

b.
$$\begin{array}{r} 52 \\ -38 \\ \hline 24 \end{array}$$

22. a.
$$\begin{array}{r} 46 \\ -27 \\ \hline 73 \end{array}$$

b.
$$\begin{array}{r} 94 \\ -37 \\ \hline 12 \end{array}$$

In exercises 23 and 24, compute exact answers mentally by using *compatible numbers or substitutions.* Show your method.

23. a. $23 + 25 + 28$

b. $128 - 15 + 27 - 50$

c. $83 + 50 - 13 + 24$

24. a. $208 + 554$

b. $1398 + 583$

c. $130 + 25 + 70 + 10$

In exercises 25 and 26, use the *equal-differences method* to find a difference which is more convenient for mental computation. Show your work.

25. a. $6502 - 152$
b. $894 - 199$
c. $14,200 - 2700$

26. a. $435 - 198$
b. $622 - 115$
c. $245 - 85$

In exercises 27 and 28, use the *add-up method* to compute exact differences. Record the numbers you use in the add-up process.

27. a. $400 - 185$
b. $535 - 250$
c. $135 - 47$

28. a. $92 - 56$
b. $842 - 793$
c. $2310 - 2105$

In exercises 29 and 30, *round* each number in the table to the place value of its leading digit and then compute the sum of each row of numbers, as shown in the example at the top of the table.

	83 (Think 80)	47 (Think 50)	112 (Think 100)	APPROXIMATE SUM 230
29. a.	102	38	21	
b.	26	43	59	
30. a.	25	212	81	
b.	27	68	18	

In exercises 31 and 32, estimate each sum or difference by replacing one or both numbers by *compatible numbers*. Show your replacements.

31. a. $359 - 192 \approx$ **b.** $712 + 293 \approx$
c. $882 + 245 \approx$ **d.** $1522 - 486 \approx$

32. a. $3906 + 1200 \approx$ **b.** $684 - 317 \approx$
c. $918 - 366 \approx$ **d.** $2243 - 1589 \approx$

In exercises 33 and 34, use front-end estimation to estimate each sum.

33. a. $362 + 408 + 978$
b. $16 + 49 + 87 + 33$
c. $7215 + 5102 + 8736$

34. a. $472 + 821 + 306 + 512$
b. $4721 + 2015 + 3681$
c. $62 + 85 + 31 + 24 + 88$

A home owner has the following bills to pay for the month of March. Use this information in exercises 35 and 36.

Electricity	$86	Food	$541
Heat	$128	Doctor's bills	$477
Water and sewage	$94	Gas and oil	$73
Property taxes	$163	Car payments	$148
Life insurance	$230	Home mortgage	$570
Car insurance	$65	Dentist's bills	$109
House insurance	$58	Recreation	$14

35. a. Obtain an estimation of how much she owes by rounding each bill to the nearest hundred.
b. Can the home owner pay these bills with a monthly salary of $1800?

36. a. Estimate the amount owed by rounding each bill to the nearest $10.
b. What is the difference between the actual amount of the bills and the estimation obtained in part a?

Calculators for students in the early grades often have a constant function as illustrated in exercises 37 and 38. A sequence of numbers is generated by beginning with the first number entered into the calculator and repeatedly carrying out the given keystrokes. Beginning with the first number entered, write each sequence which is produced by the given keystrokes.

37. a. Enter 8723 and repeat the keystrokes ⊞ 100 🟰 seven times.
b. Enter 906 and repeat the keystrokes ⊟ 10 🟰 six times.

38. a. Enter 4337 and repeat the keystrokes ⊞ 1000 🟰 seven times.
b. Enter 8004 and repeat the keystrokes ⊟ 100 🟰 six times.

The constant function on some calculators will repeatedly carry out addition or subtraction of the second number entered by repeated pressing of the 🟰 key. For example, 1 7 3 ⊞ 8 2 🟰 🟰 🟰 will produce the sequence 255, 337, and 419. Assume that such a calculator is used in exercises 39 and 40.

39. a. If the keys 2 7 1 4 ⊞ 1 4 5 are pressed and then 🟰 is pressed six times, what are the next six numbers in the sequence after 2714?
b. What is the 10th number after 2714 in the sequence from part a?
c. If ⊞ is replaced by ⊟ in part a, what are the next six numbers of the sequence after 2714?

40. a. If the keys 7 9 3 ⊞ 2 8 are pressed and then 🟰 is pressed five times, what are the next five numbers in the sequence after 793?
b. What is the eighth number after 793 in the sequence in part a?
c. If ⊞ is replaced by ⊟ in part a, what are the next five numbers of the sequence after 793?

Calculators with constant functions (see exercises 39 and 40) can be used by school children to practice counting forward or backward by various numbers. Assume that such a calculator is used in exercises 41 and 42.

41. List the keys to be pressed on a calculator with a constant function to obtain the first six numbers of the following sequences by counting:
   a. Forward by 2s, beginning with 2
   b. Backward by 3s, beginning with 30
   c. Forward by 5s, beginning with 20

42. List the keys to be pressed on a calculator with a constant function to obtain the first six numbers of the following sequences by counting:
   a. Forward by 10s, beginning with 10
   b. Backward by 2s, beginning with 100
   c. Forward by 3s, beginning with 6

REASONING AND PROBLEM SOLVING

43. A dealer has 30 cars with air conditioning and 22 cars with standard transmissions. These are the only cars on the lot.
   a. What is the minimum number of cars the dealer has on the lot?
   b. What is the maximum number of cars?
   c. What is the total number of cars if there are 17 cars with both air conditioning and standard transmissions?
   d. In which case above can the answer be found by adding the number of cars with air conditioning to the number of cars with standard transmissions?

44. Featured Strategy: Working Backward   This is a two-person game called *Force Out*. An arbitrary number is selected, and from it the players take turns subtracting any single-digit number greater than zero. The player who is forced to obtain zero loses the game. Describe a strategy for winning this game.
   a. Understanding the Problem   On each player's turn only one single-digit number (1, 2, 3, 4, 5, 6, 7, 8, or 9) may be subtracted. If you can get the remaining number to be 1, then you will win. Select a number and play the game to become familiar with the rules. If the number is 15 and it is your turn to play, what number should you subtract?
   b. Devising a Plan   One approach to solving this problem is to play the game for small numbers to see if you can hit upon an idea for a winning strategy. Another approach is to *work backward* to find the numbers that will guarantee you a win. Explain how you can win if the remaining number is greater than 1 and less than 11, and it is your turn.

   c. Carrying Out the Plan   Select an approach to look for a solution to this problem. Explain why you can win if you get the remaining number to be 11 and it's your opponent's turn to play. Describe a strategy for winning the game if it's your turn to play and the final digit in the number is not a 1 (1, 11, 21, 31, 41, etc.).
   d. Looking Back   Let's revise the game so that the players subtract any number from 1 to 19. Suppose you are to take the first turn and the starting number is 76. Describe a strategy for winning the game.

45. A class survey found that 26 students watched the Olympics on television Saturday and 21 watched on Sunday. Of those who watched the Olympics on only one of these days, 11 chose Saturday and 6 chose Sunday. If every student watched at least one of these days, how many students are in the class?

46. Calculators with a constant function can be programmed to add a constant number to any number that is entered into the calculator. Let's assume that a certain stock has paid a bonus of $164 to each stockholder and that this amount is to be added to their accounts.

STOCKHOLDER
ACCOUNTS

$4,728
$13,491
$6,045
$21,437
$10,418
$9,366

The first step shown for one such calculator adds 164 to 4728. To add 164 to the remaining accounts, it is necessary only to enter the next number and press $=$. Find the new account balances for these view screens.

	KEYSTROKES	VIEW SCREEN
a.	4728 $+$ 164 $=$	
b.	13491 $=$	
c.	6045 $=$	
d.	21437 $=$	
e.	10418 $=$	
f.	9366 $=$	

47. Slate and brick are sold by weight. At one company the slate or brick is placed on a loading platform which weighs 83 kilograms. A forklift moves the slate or brick and the platform onto the scales. The weight of the platform is then subtracted from the total weight to obtain the weight of the slate or brick.

Assume that a calculator with a constant function which subtracts a constant from any number entered is used to determine the weight of the slate or brick below. Find the resulting weights for the following calculator view screens, if 83 is subtracted from the weights in lines b–f by entering a number and pressing $\boxed{=}$.

	KEYSTROKES	VIEW SCREEN
a.	748 $\boxed{-}$ 83 $\boxed{=}$	
b.	807 $\boxed{=}$	
c.	1226 $\boxed{=}$	
d.	914 $\boxed{=}$	
e.	1372 $\boxed{=}$	
f.	655 $\boxed{=}$	

48. This circle contains the whole numbers from 1 to 7. By adding two or more *neighbor numbers* (numbers that are next to each other), we can get every number from 8 to 28. How can the numbers 1, 2, 3, 4, 5, and 6 be placed around a circle to obtain all sums from 7 to 21?

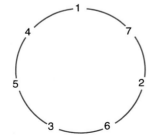

49. How can the whole numbers from 1 to 19 be placed into the 19 circles of the diagram below so that any three numbers on the same line through the center will give the same sum?

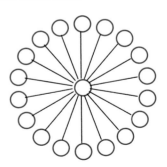

50. Use every digit from 1 to 9 exactly once to compute this sum.

51. The values of C, K, G, and F in this number puzzle are four different digits from 0 to 9. What are these digits?

$$\begin{array}{r} CCC \\ + \quad K \\ \hline GFFG \end{array}$$

ONLINE LEARNING CENTER   www.mhhe.com/bennett-nelson

• Math Investigation 3.2   *Palindromic Differences*
Section-Related: • Links   • Writing/Discussion Problems   • Bibliography

MATH ACTIVITY 3.3

MULTIPLICATION WITH BASE-FIVE PIECES

Materials: Base-five pieces in the Manipulative Kit.

1. Use your base-five pieces to represent 213_{five}. Then determine the minimal collection for a group of four of these sets to illustrate $4 \times 213_{\text{five}}$. This activity illustrates multiplication as *repeated addition.*

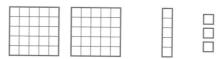

*2. Use your base-five pieces to determine the minimal collection for each of the following products. Then write the base-five numeral for each product.

   a. $2 \times 444_{\text{five}}$ b. $4 \times 234_{\text{five}}$ c. $3 \times 1042_{\text{five}}$

3. In base five, the numeric value *five* is written as 10_{five}. Thus a product such as $10_{\text{five}} \times 13_{\text{five}}$ can be computed by forming five collections of 1 long and 3 units.

   a. Use your base-five pieces to determine the minimal collection for $10_{\text{five}} \times 13_{\text{five}}$, and then write the base-five numeral for the product.

   b. Repeat part a for the product $10_{\text{five}} \times 123_{\text{five}}$.

   c. Explain, in terms of base-five pieces, why multiplication of a number by 10_{five} has the effect of affixing a zero onto the right of the numeral.

4. In base four, the numeric value *four* is written as 10_{four}. Draw a sketch of base-four pieces to illustrate the products $10_{\text{four}} \times 13_{\text{four}}$ and $10_{\text{four}} \times 322_{\text{four}}$, and write the base-four numeral for each product beneath its sketch.

*5. What base is illustrated by the set of multibase pieces shown here? Determine the minimal collection for a group of six of these sets. Write the product which is illustrated by this activity.

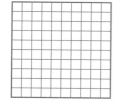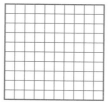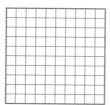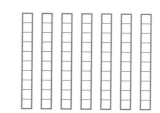

SECTION 3.3

MULTIPLICATION

State office buildings at the Empire State Plaza, Albany, New York

PROBLEM OPENER

Lee has written a two-digit number in which the units digit is her favorite digit. When she subtracts the tens digit from the units digit, she gets 3. When she multiplies the original two-digit number by 21, she gets a three-digit number whose hundreds digit is her favorite digit and whose tens and units digits are the same as those in her original two-digit number. What is her favorite digit?

The skyscraper in the center of the preceding photo is called the Tower Building. There is an innovative window-washing machine mounted on top of this building. The machine lowers a cage on a vertical track so that each column of 40 windows can be washed. After one vertical column of windows has been washed, the machine moves to the next column. The rectangular face visible in the photograph has 36 columns of windows. The total number of windows is 40 + 40 + 40 + . . . + 40, a sum in which 40 occurs 36 times. This sum equals the product 36 × 40, or 1440. We are led to different expressions for the sum and product by considering the rows of windows across the floors. There are 36 windows in each floor on this face of the building and 40 floors. Therefore, the number of windows is 36 + 36 + 36 + . . . + 36, a sum in which 36 occurs 40 times. This sum is equal to 40 × 36, which is also 1440. For sums such as these in which one number is repeated, multiplication is a convenient method for doing addition.

Historically, multiplication was developed to replace certain special cases of addition, namely, the cases of *several equal addends*. For this reason we usually see **multiplication** of whole numbers explained and defined as **repeated addition**.

> **MULTIPLICATION OF WHOLE NUMBERS**   For any whole numbers r and s, the **product** of r and s is the sum with s occurring r times. This is written as
>
> $$r \times s = \underbrace{s + s + s + \ldots + s}_{r \text{ times}}$$
>
> The numbers r and s are called **factors**.

One way of representing multiplication of whole numbers is with a **rectangular array** of objects, such as the rows and columns of windows at the beginning of this section. Figure 3.11 shows the close relationship between the use of *repeated addition* and *rectangular arrays* for illustrating products. Part (a) of the figure shows squares in 4 groups of 7 to illustrate $7 + 7 + 7 + 7$, and part (b) shows the squares pushed together to form a 4×7 rectangle.

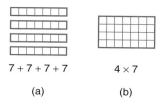

$$7 + 7 + 7 + 7 \qquad\qquad 4 \times 7$$

Figure 3.11   (a)   (b)

In general, $r \times s$ is the number of objects in an $r \times s$ rectangular array.

Another way of viewing multiplication is with a figure called a **tree diagram.** Constructing a tree diagram is a counting technique that is useful for certain types of multiplication problems.

E x a m p l e A

A catalog shows jeans available in cotton, brushed denim, or stretch denim and in stonewash (s), acid wash (a), bleached (b), or regular color (r). How many types of jeans are available?

Solution   A tree diagram for this problem is shown below. The tree begins with 3 branches, each labeled with one of the types of material. Each of these branches leads to 4 more branches, which correspond to the colors. The tree has $3 \times 4 = 12$ endpoints, one for each of the 12 different types of jeans.

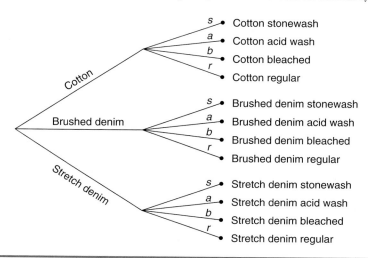

Models for Multiplication Algorithms

Research provides evidence that students will rely on their own computational strategies (Cobb et al. 1991). Such inventions contribute to their mathematical development (Gravemeijer 1994; Steffe 1994).

Standards 2000, p. 86

Physical models for multiplication can generate an understanding of multiplication and suggest or motivate procedures and rules for computing. There are many suitable models for illustrating multiplication. Base-ten pieces are used in the following examples.

Figure 3.12 illustrates 3 × 145, using base-ten pieces. First 145 is represented as shown in (a). Then the base-ten pieces for 145 are tripled. The result is 3 flats, 12 longs, and 15 units, as shown in (b). Finally, the pieces are regrouped: 10 units are replaced by 1 long, leaving 5 units; and 10 longs are replaced by 1 flat, leaving 3 longs. The result is 4 flats, 3 longs, and 5 units, as shown in (c).

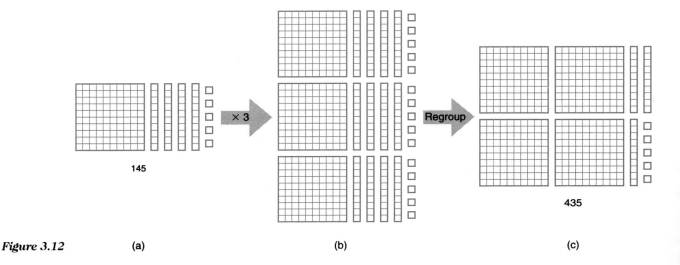

145

× 3

Regroup

435

Figure 3.12   (a)   (b)   (c)

Base-ten pieces can be used to illustrate the pencil-and-paper algorithm for computing. Consider the product 3 × 145 shown in Figure 3.12. First a 5, indicating the remaining 5 units in part (c), is recorded in the units column, and the 10 units that have been regrouped are recorded by writing 1 in the tens column (see below). Then 3 is written in the tens column for the remaining 3 longs, and 1 is recorded in the hundreds column for the 10 longs that have been regrouped.

Flats	Longs	Units
1	1	
1	4	5
	×	3
4	3	5

The next example illustrates how multiplication by 10 can be carried out with base-ten pieces. Multiplying by 10 is especially convenient because 10 units can be placed together to form 1 long, 10 longs to form 1 flat, and 10 flats to form 1 long-flat (row of flats).

To multiply 34 and 10, we replace each base-ten piece for 34 by the base-ten piece for the next higher power of 10 (Figure 3.13). We begin with 3 longs and 4 units and end with 3 flats, 4 longs, and 0 units. This illustrates the familiar fact that the product of any whole number and 10 can be computed by placing a zero at the right end of the numeral for the whole number.

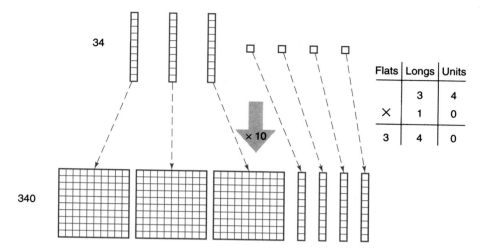

Figure 3.13

Computing the product of two numbers by repeated addition of base-ten pieces becomes impractical as the size of the numbers increases. For example, computing 18 × 23 requires representing 23 with base-ten pieces 18 times. For products involving two-digit numbers, rectangular arrays are more convenient.

To compute 18 × 23, we can draw a rectangle with dimensions 18 by 23 on grid paper (Figure 3.14). The product is the number of small squares in the rectangular array. This number can be easily determined by counting groups of 100 flats and strips of 10 longs. The total number of small squares is 414. Notice how the array in Figure 3.14 can be viewed as 18 horizontal rows of 23, once again showing the connection between the repeated-addition and rectangular-array views of multiplication.

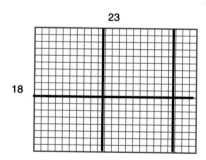

Figure 3.14

The pencil-and-paper algorithm for multiplication computes **partial products**. When a two-digit number is multiplied by a two-digit number, there are four partial products.

The product 13 × 17 is illustrated in Figure 3.15. The four regions of the grid formed by the heavy lines represent the four partial products. Sometimes it is instructive to draw arrows from each partial product to the corresponding region on the grid.

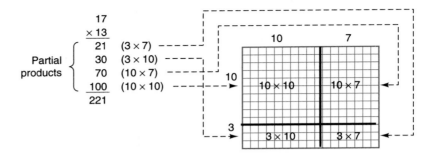

Figure 3.15

One of the earliest methods of multiplication is found in the Rhind Papyrus. This ancient scroll (ca. 1650 B.C.), more than 5 meters in length, was written to instruct Egyptian scribes in computing with whole numbers and fractions. Beginning with the words "Complete and thorough study of all things, insights into all that exists, knowledge of all secrets . . . ," it indicates the Egyptians' awe of mathematics. Although most of its 85 problems have a practical origin, there are some of a theoretical nature. The Egyptians' algorithm for multiplication was a succession of doubling operations, followed by addition. To compute 11 × 52, they would repeatedly double 52, then add *one* 52, *two* 52s, and *eight* 52s to get *eleven* 52s.

Number Properties

Four properties for addition of whole numbers were stated in Section 3.2. Four corresponding properties for multiplication of whole numbers are stated below, along with one additional property that relates the operations of addition and multiplication.

CLOSURE PROPERTY FOR MULTIPLICATION   This property states that the product of any two whole numbers is also a whole number.

For any two whole numbers a and b,

$$a \times b \text{ is a unique whole number}$$

IDENTITY PROPERTY FOR MULTIPLICATION   The number 1 is called an **identity for multiplication** because when multiplied by another number, it leaves the identity of the number unchanged. For example,

$$1 \times 14 = 14 \qquad 34 \times 1 = 34 \qquad 1 \times 0 = 0$$

The number 1 is unique in that it is the only number that is an identity for multiplication.

For any whole number **b**,

$$1 \times b = b \times 1 = b$$

and 1 is a unique identity for multiplication.

COMMUTATIVE PROPERTY FOR MULTIPLICATION   This number property says that in any product of two numbers, the numbers may be interchanged (commuted) without affecting the product. This property is called the **commutative property for multiplication**. For example,

$$347 \times 26 = 26 \times 347$$

For any whole numbers **a** and **b**,

$$a \times b = b \times a$$

The commutative property is illustrated in Figure 3.16, which shows two different views of the same rectangular array. Part (a) represents 7×5, and part (b) represents 5×7. Since part (b) is obtained by rotating part (a), both figures have the same number of small squares, so 7×5 is equal to 5×7.

Using area models, properties of operations such as commutativity of multiplication become more apparent.

Standards 2000, p. 152

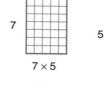

7×5 5×7

(a)   (b)

Figure 3.16

As the multiplication table in Figure 3.17 shows, the commutative property for multiplication approximately cuts in half the number of basic multiplication facts that must be memorized. Each product in the shaded part of the table corresponds to an equal product in the unshaded part of the table.

Example B

Since $3 \times 7 = 21$, we know by the commutative property for multiplication that $7 \times 3 = 21$. What do you notice about the location of each product in the shaded part of the table relative to the location of the corresponding equal product in the unshaded part of the table?

Solution   If the shaded part of the table is folded onto the unshaded part, each product in the shaded part will coincide with an equal product in the unshaded part. In other words, the table is symmetric about the diagonal from upper left to lower right.

×	1	2	3	4	5	6	7	8	9
1	1	2	3	4	5	6	7	8	9
2	2	4	6	8	10	12	14	16	18
3	3	6	9	12	15	18	(21)	24	27
4	4	8	12	16	20	24	28	32	36
5	5	10	15	20	25	30	35	40	45
6	6	12	18	24	30	36	42	48	54
7	7	14	(21)	28	35	42	49	56	63
8	8	16	24	32	40	48	56	64	72
9	9	18	27	36	45	54	63	72	81

Figure 3.17

Notice that the numbers in the rows of the multiplication table in Figure 3.17 form arithmetic sequences, for example, 2, 4, 6, 8, . . . and 3, 6, 9, 12. . . . One reason that children learn to count by 2s, 3s, and 5s is to acquire background for learning basic multiplication facts. The keystrokes in the next two diagrams will produce a sequence which increases by 2s and a sequence which decreases by 5s on most calculators.

KEYSTROKES	VIEW SCREEN		KEYSTROKES	VIEW SCREEN
2	2		35	35
+ 2 =	4		− 5 =	30
+ 2 =	6		− 5 =	25
+ 2 =	8		− 5 =	20

ASSOCIATIVE PROPERTY FOR MULTIPLICATION   In any product of three numbers, the middle number may be associated with and multiplied by either of the two end numbers. This property is called the **associative property for multiplication.** For example,

$$6 \times (7 \times 4) = (6 \times 7) \times 4$$

Associative property
for multiplication

For any whole numbers *a*, *b*, and *c*,

$$a \times (b \times c) = (a \times b) \times c$$

Figure 3.18 illustrates the associative property for multiplication. Part (a) represents 3×4, and (b) shows 5 of the 3×4 rectangles. The number of small squares in (b) is $5 \times (3 \times 4)$. Part (c) is obtained by subdividing the rectangle (b) into 4 copies of a 3×5 rectangle. The number of small squares in (c) is $4 \times (3 \times 5)$, which, by the commutative property for multiplication, equals $(5 \times 3) \times 4$. Since the numbers of small squares in (b) and (c) are equal, $5 \times (3 \times 4) = (5 \times 3) \times 4$.

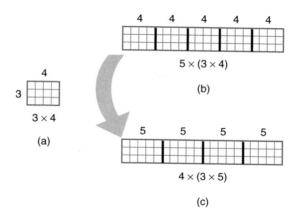

Figure 3.18

The commutative and associative properties are often used to obtain convenient combinations of numbers for mental calculations, as in the next example.

Example C

Try computing $25 \times 46 \times 4$ in your head before reading further.

Solution   The easy way to do this is by rearranging the numbers so that 25×4 is computed first and then 46×100. The following equations show how the commutative and associative properties permit this rearrangement.

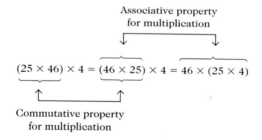

DISTRIBUTIVE PROPERTY   When multiplying a sum of two numbers by a third number, we can add the two numbers and then multiply by the third number, or we can multiply each number of the sum by the third number and then add the two products.

For example, to compute $35 \times (10 + 2)$, we can compute 35×12, or we can add 35×10 to 35×2. This property is called the **distributive property for multiplication over addition.**

$$35 \times 12 = 35 \times (10 + 2) = (35 \times 10) + (35 \times 2)$$

Distributive property

For any whole numbers a, b, and c,

$$a \times (b + c) = a \times b + a \times c$$

One use of the distributive property is in learning the basic multiplication facts. Elementary school children are often taught the "doubles" ($2 + 2 = 4$, $3 + 3 = 6$, $4 + 4 = 8$, etc.) because these number facts together with the distributive property can be used to obtain other multiplication facts.

Example D

How can $7 \times 7 = 49$ and the distributive property be used to compute 7×8?

Solution
$$7 \times 8 = 7 \times (7 + 1) = 49 + 7 = 56$$
Distributive property

The distributive property can be illustrated by using rectangular arrays, as in Figure 3.19. The dimensions of the array in (a) are 6 by $(3 + 4)$, and the array contains 42 small squares. Part (b) shows the same squares separated into two rectangular arrays with dimensions 6 by 3 and 6 by 4. Since the number of squares in both figures is the same, $6 \times (3 + 4) = (6 \times 3) + (6 \times 4)$.

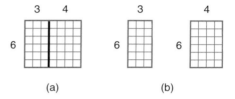

(a)   (b)

Figure 3.19

The distributive property also holds for multiplication over subtraction.

Example E

Show that the two sides of the following equation are equal.
$$6 \times (20 - 8) = (6 \times 20) - (6 \times 8)$$

Solution $6 \times (20 - 8) = 6 \times 12 = 72$ and $(6 \times 20) - (6 \times 8) = 120 - 48 = 72$

Mental Calculations

In the following paragraphs, three methods are discussed for performing mental calculations of products. These methods parallel those used for performing mental calculations of sums and differences.

COMPATIBLE NUMBERS   We saw in Example C that the commutative and associative properties permit the rearrangement of numbers in products. Such rearrangements can often enable computations with compatible numbers.

Example F

Find a more convenient arrangement that will yield compatible numbers, and compute the following products mentally.

1. $5 \times 346 \times 2$

2. $2 \times 25 \times 79 \times 2$

Solution   1. $5 \times 2 \times 346 = 10 \times 346 = 3460$ 2. $2 \times 2 \times 25 \times 79 = 100 \times 79 = 7900$

SUBSTITUTIONS   In certain situations the distributive property is useful for facilitating mental calculations. For example, to compute 21×103, first replace 103 by $100 + 3$ and then compute 21×100 and 21×3 in your head. Try it.

$$21 \times 103 = 21 \times (100 + 3) = 2100 + 63 = 2163$$

Distributive property

Occasionally it is convenient to replace a number by the difference of two numbers and to use the fact that multiplication distributes over subtraction. Rather than compute 45×98, we can compute 45×100 and subtract 45×2.

$$45 \times 98 = 45 \times (100 - 2) = 4500 - 90 = 4410$$

Distributive property

Example G

Find a convenient substitution, and compute the following products mentally.

1. 25×99

2. 42×11

3. 34×102

Solution   1. $25 \times (100 - 1) = 2500 - 25 = 2475$ 2. $42 \times (10 + 1) = 420 + 42 = 462$ 3. $34 \times (100 + 2) = 3400 + 68 = 3468$

Other relationships can be seen by decomposing and composing area models. For example, a model for 20×6 can be split in half and the halves rearranged to form a 10×12 rectangle, showing the equivalence of 10×12 and 20×6.

Standards 2000, p. 152

EQUAL PRODUCTS   This method of performing mental calculations is similar to the *equal differences* method used for subtraction. It is based on the fact that the product of two numbers is unchanged when one of the numbers is divided by a given number and the other number is multiplied by the same number. For example, the product 12×52 can be replaced by 6×104 by dividing 12 by 2 and multiplying 52 by 2. At this point we can mentally calculate 6×104 to be 624. Or we can continue the process of dividing and multiplying by 2, replacing 6×104 by 3×208, which can also be mentally calculated.

Figure 3.20 illustrates why one number in a product can be halved and the other doubled without changing the product. The rectangular array in part (a) of the figure represents 22×16. If this rectangle is cut in half, the two pieces can be used to form an 11×32 rectangle, as in (b). Notice that 11 is half of 22 and 32 is twice 16. Since the rearrangement has not changed the number of small squares in the two rectangles, the products 22×16 and 11×32 are equal.

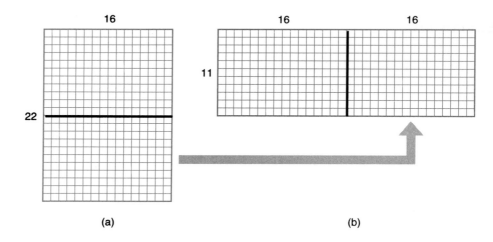

Figure 3.20   (a)   (b)

The equal-products method can also be justified by using number properties. The following equations show that $22 \times 16 = 11 \times 32$. Notice that multiplying by $\frac{1}{2}$ and 2 is the same as multiplying by 1. This is a special case of the inverse property for multiplication, which is discussed in Section 5.3.

$$22 \times 16 = 22 \times 1 \times 16 \qquad \text{identity property for multiplication}$$

$$= 22 \times \left(\frac{1}{2} \times 2\right) \times 16 \qquad \text{inverse property for multiplication}$$

$$= \left(22 \times \frac{1}{2}\right) \times (2 \times 16) \qquad \text{associative property for multiplication}$$

$$= 11 \times 32$$

Example H

Use the method of equal products to perform the following calculations mentally.

1. 14×4

2. 28×25

3. 15×35

Solution   1. $14 \times 4 = 7 \times 8 = 56$ 2. $28 \times 25 = 14 \times 50 = 7 \times 100 = 700$ 3. $15 \times 35 = 5 \times 105 = 525$

Estimation of Products

The importance of estimation is noted in NCTM's K–4 Standard, *Estimation:*

Instruction should emphasize the development of an estimation mindset. Children should come to know what is meant by an estimate, when it is appropriate to estimate, and how close an estimate is required in a given situation. If children are encouraged to estimate, they will accept estimation as a legitimate part of mathematics.*

Curriculum and Evaluation Standards for School Mathematics (Reston, VA: National Council of Teachers of Mathematics, 1989), p. 115.

The techniques of *rounding*, using *compatible numbers*, and *front-end estimation* are used in the following examples.

ROUNDING   Products can be estimated by rounding one or both numbers. Computing products by rounding is somewhat more risky than computing sums by rounding, because any error due to rounding becomes multiplied. For example, if we compute 47 × 28 by rounding 47 to 50 and 28 to 30, the estimated product 50 × 30 = 1500 is greater than the actual product. This may be acceptable if we want an estimate greater than the actual product. For a closer estimate, we can round 47 to 45 and 28 to 30. In this case the estimate is 45 × 30 = 1350.

Example I

Use rounding to estimate these products. Make any adjustments you feel might be needed.

1. 28 × 63

2. 81 × 57

3. 194 × 26

When students leave grade 5, . . . they should be able to solve many problems mentally, to estimate a reasonable result for a problem, . . . and to compute fluently with multidigit whole numbers.

Standards 2000, p. 149

Solution   Following is one estimate for each product. You may find others.   1. 28 × 63 ≈ 30 × 60 = 1800. Notice that since 63 is greater than 28, increasing 28 by 2 has more of an effect on the estimate than decreasing 63 to 60 (see Figure 3.21). So the estimate of 1800 is greater than the actual answer.   2. 81 × 57 ≈ 80 × 60 = 4800   3. 194 × 26 ≈ 200 × 25 = 5000

Figure 3.21 shows the effect of estimating 28 × 63 by rounding to 30 × 60. Rectangular arrays for both 28 × 63 and 30 × 60 can be seen on the grid. The gray region shows the increase from rounding 28 to 30, and the red region shows the decrease from rounding 63 to 60. Since the gray region (2 × 60 = 120) is larger than the red region (3 × 28 = 84), we are adding more than we are removing, and so the estimate is greater than the actual product.

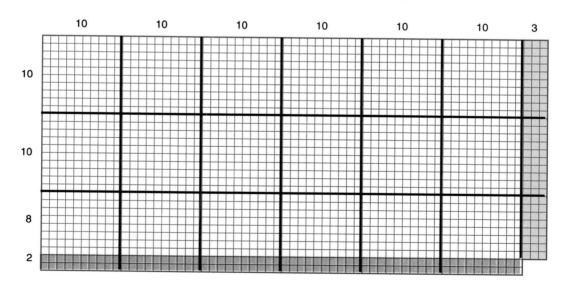

Figure 3.21

COMPATIBLE NUMBERS   Using compatible numbers becomes a powerful tool for estimating products when it is combined with techniques for performing mental calculations. For example, to estimate $4 \times 237 \times 26$, we might replace 26 by 25 and use a different ordering of the numbers.

$$4 \times 237 \times 26 \approx 4 \times 25 \times 237 = 100 \times 237 = 23{,}700$$

Example J

Use compatible numbers and mental calculations to estimate these products.

1. $2 \times 117 \times 49$

2. $34 \times 46 \times 3$

Solution   1. $2 \times 117 \times 49 \approx 2 \times 117 \times 50 = 100 \times 117 = 11{,}700$ 2. $34 \times 46 \times 3 = (3 \times 34) \times 46 \approx 100 \times 46 = 4600$

FRONT-END ESTIMATION   This technique is similar to that used for computing sums. The leading digit of each number is used to obtain an estimated product. To estimate 43×72, the product of the leading digits of the numbers is $4 \times 7 = 28$, so the estimated product is 2800.

$$43 \times 72 \approx 40 \times 70 = 2800$$

Similarly, front-end estimation can be used for estimating the products of numbers whose leading digits have different place values.

$$61 \times 874 \approx 60 \times 800 = 48{,}000$$

Example K

Use front-end estimation to estimate these products.

1. 64×23 2. 68×87 3. 237×76 4. $30{,}328 \times 419$

Solution   1. $64 \times 23 \approx 60 \times 20 = 1200$ 2. $68 \times 87 \approx 60 \times 80 = 4800$ 3. $237 \times 76 \approx 200 \times 70 = 14{,}000$ 4. $30{,}328 \times 419 \approx 30{,}000 \times 400 = 12{,}000{,}000$

Order of Operations

Special care must be taken on some calculators when multiplication is combined with addition or subtraction. The numbers and operations will not always produce the correct answer if they are entered into the calculator in the order in which they appear.

Example L

Compute $3 + 4 \times 5$ by entering the numbers into your calculator as they appear from left to right.

Solution   Some calculators will display 35, and others will display 23. The correct answer is 23 because multiplication should be performed before addition:

$$3 + 4 \times 5 = 3 + 20 = 23$$

To avoid confusion, mathematicians have developed the convention that when multiplication occurs with addition and/or subtraction, the multiplication should be performed first. This rule is called the **order of operations.**

Some calculators are programmed to follow the order of operations. On this type of calculator, any combination of products with sums and differences and without parentheses can be computed by entering the numbers and operations in the order in which they occur from left to right and then pressing ⊟ . If a calculator does not follow the order of operations, the products can be computed separately and recorded by hand or saved in the calculator's memory.

Example M

Use your calculator to evaluate $34 \times 19 + 82 \times 43$. Then check the reasonableness of your answer by using estimation and mental calculations.

Solution   The exact answer is 4172. An estimate can be obtained as follows:

$$34 \times 19 + 82 \times 43 \approx 30 \times 20 + 80 \times 40 = 600 + 3200 = 3800$$

Notice that the estimation in Example M is 372 less than the actual product. However, it is useful in judging the reasonableness of the number obtained from the calculator: It indicates that the calculator answer is most likely correct. If $34 \times 19 + 82 \times 43$ is entered into a calculator as it appears from left to right and if the calculator is not programmed to follow the order of operations, then the incorrect result of 31,304 will be obtained, which is too large by approximately 27,000.

Problem-Solving Application

There is an easy method for mentally computing the products of certain two-digit numbers. A few of these products are shown here.

$$25 \times 25 = 625 \qquad 24 \times 26 = 624 \qquad 71 \times 79 = 5609$$
$$37 \times 33 = 1221 \qquad 35 \times 35 = 1225 \qquad 75 \times 75 = 5625$$

The solution to the following problem reveals the method of mental computation and uses *rectangular grids* to show why the method works.

PROBLEM

What is the method of mental calculation for computing the products of the two-digit numbers shown above, and why does this method work?

Understanding the Problem   There are patterns in the digits in these products. One pattern is that the two numbers in each pair have the same first digit. Find another pattern. Question 1: What types of two-digit numbers are being used?

Devising a Plan   Looking for patterns may help you find the types of numbers and the method of computing. Another approach is to represent some of these products on a grid. The following grid illustrates 24×26; the product is the number of small squares in the rectangle. To determine this number, we begin by counting large groups of squares. There are 6 hundreds. Question 2: Why is this grid especially convenient for counting the number of hundreds?

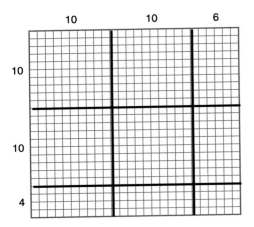

Carrying Out the Plan   Sketch grids for one or more of the products being considered in this problem. For each grid it is easy to determine the number of hundreds. This is the key to solving the problem. Question 3: What is the solution to the original problem?

Looking Back   Consider the following products of three-digit numbers:

$$103 \times 107 = 11{,}021 \qquad 124 \times 126 = 15{,}624$$

Question 4: Is there a similar method for mentally calculating the products of certain three-digit numbers?

Answers to Questions 1–4   1. In each pair of two-digit numbers, the tens digits are equal and the sum of the units digits is 10.   2. The two blocks of 40 squares at the bottom of the grid can be paired with two blocks of 60 squares on the right side of the grid to form two more blocks of 100, as shown below. Then the large 20 × 30 grid represents 6 hundreds. The 4 × 6 grid in the lower right corner represents 4 × 6.

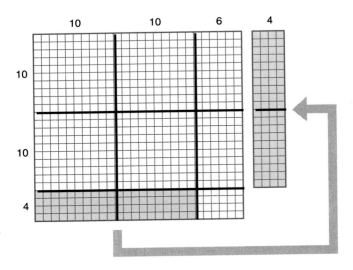

3. The first two digits of the product are formed by multiplying the tens digit by the tens digit plus 1. The remaining digits of the product are obtained by multiplying the two units digits.   4. Yes. For 124 × 126: 12 × 13 = 156 and 4 × 6 = 24, so 124 × 126 = 15,624.

HISTORICAL HIGHLIGHT

As late as the seventeenth century, multiplication of large numbers was a difficult task for all but professional clerks. To help people "do away with the difficulty and tediousness for calculations," Scottish mathematician John Napier (1550–1617) invented a method of using rods for performing multiplication. Napier's rods—or *bones* as they are sometimes called—contain multiplication facts for each digit. For example, the rod for the 4s has 4, 8, 12, 16, 20, 24, 28, 32, and 36. This photograph of a wooden set shows the fourth, seventh, and ninth rods placed together for computing products that have a factor of 479. For example, to compute 6 × 479 look at row VI of the three rods for 479. Adding the numbers along the diagonals of row VI results in the product of 2874.

PUZZLER

Supply the missing digits in this faded document puzzle.

```
        4 □ □
      × □ □ 7
      ┌─────────
        □ □ 8 2
    1 2 □ □
    ┌───────────
    □ □ □ □ □ □
```

EXERCISES AND PROBLEMS 3.3

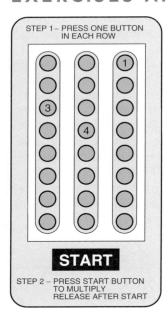

STEP 1 – PRESS ONE BUTTON
IN EACH ROW

START

STEP 2 – PRESS START BUTTON
TO MULTIPLY
RELEASE AFTER START

An exhibit illustrating multiplication at the California Museum of Science and Industry.

The children in the picture above are computing products of three numbers from 1 through 8. Each time three buttons are pressed on the switch box, the product is illustrated by lighted bulbs in the $8 \times 8 \times 8$ cube of bulbs. Buttons 3, 4, and 1 are for the product $3 \times 4 \times 1$. The 12 bulbs in the upper left corner of the cube will be lighted for this product, as shown in the following figure. Whenever the third number of the product is 1, the first two numbers determine a rectangular array of lighted bulbs on the front face of the cube (facing children).

The third number in a product illustrated by the cube of bulbs determines the number of times the array on the front face is repeated in the cube. The 24 bulbs in the upper left corner of the next figure will be lighted for $3 \times 4 \times 2$.

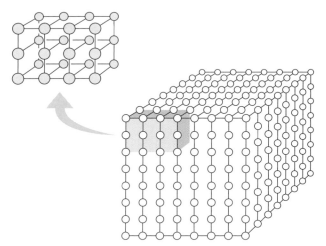

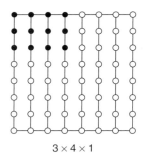

$3 \times 4 \times 1$

Describe the bulbs that will be lighted for the products in exercises 1 and 2.

  1. a. $7 \times 3 \times 1$ **b.** $2 \times 8 \times 1$

  2. a. $5 \times 4 \times 1$ **b.** $8 \times 8 \times 1$

Describe the bulbs that will be lighted for the products in exercises 3 and 4.

  3. a. $6 \times 4 \times 3$ **b.** $1 \times 8 \times 8$

  4. a. $2 \times 2 \times 2$ **b.** $8 \times 1 \times 8$

Sketch a new set of base pieces for each product in exercises 5 and 6, and then show regrouping.

5. a. Multiply 168 by 3.

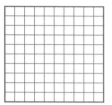

b. Multiply 209 by 4.

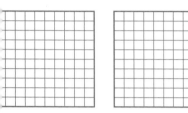

c. Multiply 423$_{\text{five}}$ by 3.

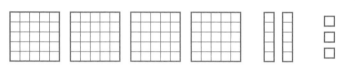

d. Multiply 47$_{\text{eight}}$ by 5.

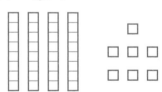

6. a. Multiply 247 by 2.

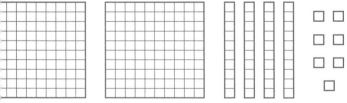

b. Multiply 38 by 5.

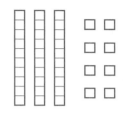

c. Multiply 36$_{\text{seven}}$ by 5.

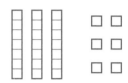

d. Multiply 123$_{\text{five}}$ by 4.

Multiplication of whole numbers can be illustrated on the number line by a series of arrows. This number line shows 4×2.

Draw arrow diagrams for the products in exercises 7 and 8.

7. a. 3×4 **b.** 2×5
   c. Use the number line to show that $3 \times 4 = 4 \times 3$.

8. a. 2×6 **b.** 6×2
   c. Use the number line to show that $2 \times (3 + 2) = 2 \times 3 + 2 \times 2$.

Error analysis. Students who know their basic multiplication facts may still have trouble with the steps in the pencil-and-paper multiplication algorithm. Try to detect each type of error in exercises 9 and 10, and write an explanation.

9. a.   2
            27
          $\times\ 4$
          ‾‾‾‾‾
            48

b.   2
            18
          $\times\ 3$
          ‾‾‾‾‾
            34

10. a.   4
            54
          $\times\ 6$
          ‾‾‾‾‾
           342

b.   1
            34
          $\times\ 24$
          ‾‾‾‾‾
            76

In exercises 11 and 12, use base-ten grids to illustrate the partial products that occur when these products are computed with pencil and paper. Draw arrows from each partial product to its corresponding region on the grid. (Copy the base-ten grid from the inside cover or the website.)

11. a.
$$\begin{array}{r} 24 \\ \times\ 7 \\ \hline \end{array}$$
b.
$$\begin{array}{r} 56 \\ \times 43 \\ \hline \end{array}$$

12. a.
$$\begin{array}{r} 34 \\ \times 26 \\ \hline \end{array}$$
b.
$$\begin{array}{r} 39 \\ \times 47 \\ \hline \end{array}$$

Which number property is being used in each of the equalities in exercises 13 and 14?

13. a. $3 \times (2 \times 7 + 1) = 3 \times (7 \times 2 + 1)$
   b. $18 + (43 \times 7) \times 9 = 18 + 43 \times (7 \times 9)$
   c. $(12 + 17) \times (16 + 5)$
      $= (12 + 17) \times 16 + (12 + 17) \times 5$

14. a. $(13 + 22) \times (7 + 5) = (13 + 22) \times (5 + 7)$
   b. $(15 \times 2 + 9) + 3 = 15 \times 2 + (9 + 3)$
   c. $59 + 41 \times 8 + 41 \times 26 = 59 + 41 \times (8 + 26)$

Determine whether each set in exercises 15 and 16 is closed for the given operation.

15. a. The set of odd whole numbers for multiplication
   b. The set of whole numbers less than 100 for addition
   c. The set of all whole numbers whose units digits are 6 for multiplication

16. a. The set of even whole numbers for multiplication
   b. The set of whole numbers less than 1000 for multiplication
   c. The set of whole numbers greater than 1000 for multiplication

In exercises 17 and 18, compute the exact products mentally, using *compatible numbers*. Explain your method.

17. a. $2 \times 83 \times 50$ **b.** $5 \times 3 \times 2 \times 7$

18. a. $4 \times 2 \times 25 \times 5$ **b.** $5 \times 17 \times 20$

In exercises 19 and 20, compute the exact products mentally, using substitution and the fact that multiplication distributes over addition. Show your use of the distributive property.

19. a. 25×12 **b.** 15×106

20. a. 18×11 **b.** 14×102

In exercises 21 and 22, compute the exact products mentally, using the fact that multiplication distributes over subtraction. Show your use of the distributive property.

21. a. 35×19 **b.** 30×99

22. a. 51×9 **b.** 40×98

In exercises 23 and 24, use the method of *equal products* to find numbers that are more convenient for making exact mental calculations. Show the new products that replace the original products.

23. a. 24×25 **b.** 35×60

24. a. 16×6 **b.** 36×5

In exercises 25 and 26, *round* the numbers and mentally estimate the products. Show the rounded numbers, and predict whether the estimated products are greater than or less than the actual products. Explain any adjustment you make to improve the estimates.

25. a. 22×17 **b.** 83×31

26. a. 71×56 **b.** 205×29

In exercises 27 and 28, use *compatible numbers* and mental calculations to estimate the products. Show your compatible-number replacements, and predict whether the estimated products are greater than or less than the actual products.

27. a. $4 \times 76 \times 24$ **b.** $3 \times 34 \times 162$

28. a. $5 \times 19 \times 74$ **b.** $2 \times 63 \times 2 \times 26$

In exercises 29 and 30, estimate the products, using *front-end estimation* and mental calculations. Show two estimates for each product, one using only the tens digits and one using combinations of the tens and units digits.

29. a. 36×58 **b.** 42×27

30. a. 62×83 **b.** 14×62

In exercises 31 and 32, *round* the given numbers and estimate each product. Then sketch a rectangular array for the actual product, and on the same figure sketch the rectangular array for the product of the rounded numbers. Shade the regions that show increases and/or decreases due to rounding. (Copy the base-ten grid from the inside cover or the website.)

31. a. 18×62 **b.** 43×29

32. a. 17×28 **b.** 53×31

In exercises 33 and 34, circle the operations in each expression that should be performed first. Estimate each expression mentally, and show your method of estimating. Use a calculator to obtain an exact answer, and compare this answer to your estimate.

33. a. $62 \times 45 + 14 \times 29$
   b. $36 + 18 \times 40 + 15$

34. a. $114 \times 238 - 19 \times 605$
   b. $73 - 50 + 17 \times 62$

In exercises 35 and 36, a geometric sequence is generated by beginning with the first number entered into the calculator and repeatedly carrying out the given keystrokes. Beginning with the first number entered, write each sequence which is produced by the given keystrokes.

35. a. Enter 5 and repeat the keystrokes ☒ ③ ▣ eight times.
b. Enter 20 and repeat the keystrokes ⊞ ⑤ ▣ nine times.

36. a. Enter 91 and repeat the keystrokes ⊟ ② ▣ fourteen times
b. Enter 3 and repeat the keystrokes ☒ ② ▣ six times.

An elementary school calculator with a constant function is convenient for generating a geometric sequence. For example, the sequence 2, 4, 8, 16, 32, . . . , will be produced by entering 1 ☒ 2 and repeating pressing ▣. Write the first three terms of each sequence in exercises 37 and 38.

37.

KEYSTROKES	VIEW SCREEN
a. 81 ☒ 5 ▣	
▣	
▣	
b. 119 ☒ 4 ▣	
▣	
▣	

38.

KEYSTROKES	VIEW SCREEN
a. 17 ☒ 3 ▣	
▣	
▣	
b. 142 ☒ 6 ▣	
▣	
▣	

In exercises 39 and 40, estimate the second factor so that the product will fall within the given range. Check your answer with a calculator. Count the number of tries it takes you to land in the range.

	Product	Range
Example	22 × _____	(900, 1000)
	22 × 40 = 880	Too small
	22 × 43 = 946	In the range in two tries

39. a. 32 × _____   (800, 850)
b. 95 × _____   (1650, 1750)

40. a. 103 × _____   (2800, 2900)
b. 6 × _____   (3500, 3600)

41. There are many patterns in the multiplication table (page 166) that can be useful in memorizing the basic multiplication facts.
a. What patterns can you see?
b. There are several patterns for products involving 9 as one of the numbers being multiplied. Find two of these patterns.

REASONING AND PROBLEM SOLVING

42. A student opened her math book and computed the sum of the numbers on two facing pages. Then she turned to the next page and computed the sum of the numbers on these two facing pages. Finally, she computed the product of the two sums, and her calculator displayed the number 62,997. What were the four page numbers?

43. Harry has $2500 in cash to pay for a secondhand car, or he can pay $500 down and $155 per month for 2 years. If he doesn't pay the full amount in cash, he knows he can make $150 by investing his money. How much will he lose if he uses the more expensive method of payment?

44. Kathy read 288 pages of her 603-page novel in 9 days. How many pages per day must she now read in order to complete the book and return it within the library's 14-day deadline?

45. A store carries five styles of backpacks in four different sizes. The customer also has a choice of two different kinds of material for three of the styles. If Vanessa is only interested in the two largest backpacks, how many different backpacks would she have to chose from?

46. Featured Strategy: Making An Organized List
The five tags shown below are placed in a box and mixed. Three tags are then selected at a time. If a player's score is the product of the numbers, how many different scores are possible?

a. Understanding the Problem   The problem asks for the number of different scores, so each score can be counted only once. The tags 6, 5, and 1 produce a score of 30. Find three other tags that produce a score of 30.
b. Devising a Plan   One method of solving the problem is to form an organized list. If we begin the list with the number 3, there are six different possibilities for sets of three tags. List these six possibilities.

c. **Carrying Out the Plan**   Continue to list the different sets of three tags and compute their products. How many different scores are there?

d. **Looking Back**   A different type of organized list can be formed by considering the scores between 6 (the smallest score) and 90 (the greatest score). For example, 7, 8, and 9 can be quickly thrown out. Why?

Find patterns in problems 47 and 48 and determine if they continue to hold for the next few equations. If so, will they continue to hold for more equations? Show examples to support your conclusions.

47. $1 \times 9 + 2 = 11$
  $12 \times 9 + 3 = 111$
  $123 \times 9 + 4 = 1111$

48. $1 \times 99 = 99$
  $2 \times 99 = 198$
  $3 \times 99 = 297$

49. a. Select some two-digit numbers and multiply them by 99 and 999. Describe a few patterns and form some conjectures.

   b. Test your conjectures on some other two-digit numbers. Predict whether your conjectures will continue to hold, and support your conclusions with examples.

   c. Do your conjectures continue to hold for three-digit numbers times 99 and 999?

50. a. Select some two-digit numbers and multiply them by 11. Describe some patterns and form a conjecture.

   b. Test your conjecture on some other two-digit numbers. Predict whether your conjectures will continue to hold, and support your conclusions with examples.

   c. Does your conjecture hold for three-digit numbers times 11?

51. Samir has a combination lock with numbers from 1 to 25. This is the type of lock which requires three numbers to be opened: turn right for the first number, left for the second number, and right for the third number. Samir remembers the first two numbers, and they are not equal; but he can't remember which one is first and which is second. Also, he has forgotten the third number. What is the greatest number of different combinations that must be tried to open the lock?

52. When 6-year-old Melanie arrived home from school, she was the first to eat cookies from a freshly baked batch. When 8-year-old Felipe arrived home, he ate twice as many cookies as Melanie had eaten. When 9-year-old Hillary arrived home, she ate 3 fewer cookies than Felipe. When 12-year-old Nicholas arrived, he ate 3 times as many cookies as Hillary. Nicholas left 2 cookies, one for each of his parents. If Nicholas had eaten only 5 cookies, there would have been 3 cookies for each of his parents. How many cookies were in the original batch?

53. A mathematics education researcher is studying problem solving in small groups. One phase of the study involves pairing a third-grade girl with a third-grade boy. If the researcher wants between 70 and 80 different boy-girl combinations and there are 9 girls available for the study, how many boys are needed?

54. A restaurant owner has a luncheon special which consists of a cup of soup, half of a sandwich, and a beverage. She wants to advertise that a different combination of the three can be purchased 365 days of the year for $4.99 apiece. If she has 7 different kinds of soup and 6 different kinds of sandwiches, how many different kinds of beverages are needed to provide at least 365 different luncheons?

In problems 55 and 56, use the following system of finger positions to compute the products of numbers from 6 to 10. Here are the positions for the digits from 6 to 10.

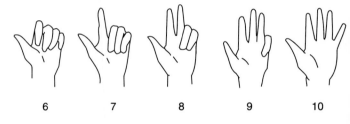

6   7   8   9   10

The two numbers that are to be multiplied are each represented on a different hand. The sum of the raised fingers is the number of 10s, and the product of the closed fingers is the number of 1s.

55. Explain how the position illustrated below shows that $7 \times 8 = 56$.

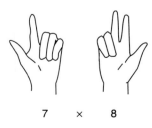

7   ×   8

56. Describe the positions of the fingers for 7×6. Does the method work for this product?

One of the popular schemes used for multiplying in the fifteenth century was called the **lattice method.** The two numbers to be multiplied, 4826 and 57 in the example at the right, are written above and to the right of the lattice. The partial products are written in the cells. The sums of numbers along the diagonal cells, beginning at the lower right with 2, 4 + 4 + 0, etc., form the product 275,082.

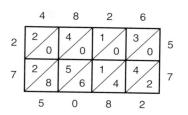

Show how the lattice method can be used to compute the products in exercises 57 and 58.

57. 34×78

58. 306×923

ONLINE LEARNING CENTER   www.mhhe.com/bennett-nelson

• Math Investigation 3.3   *Number Chains*
Section-Related: • Links   • Writing/Discussion Problems   • Bibliography

PUZZLER

One night three men registered at a hotel. They were charged $30 for their room. The desk clerk later realized that she had overcharged them by $5 and sent the refund up with the bellboy. The bellboy knew it would be difficult to split the $5 three ways.

Therefore, he kept a $2 "tip" and gave the men only $3. Each man had originally paid $10 and was given back $1. Thus the room cost each man $9, and together they paid $27. This total plus the $2 tip is $29. What happened to the other dollar?

MATH ACTIVITY 3.4

DIVISION WITH BASE-FIVE PIECES

Materials: Base-five and base-ten pieces in the Manipulative Kit.

*1. Form the set of base-five pieces shown here. If these pieces are divided equally into four sets, regrouping as necessary, what is the minimal collection for each set? This is an example of the **sharing concept** of division.

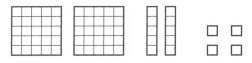

2. Use the *sharing concept* of division and base-five pieces to compute the following quotients. Write the answer in base-five notation.

    *a. $33_{five} \div 2$ **b.** $344_{five} \div 3$ **c.** $34_{five} \div 4$

3. Compute the following quotients by using the *sharing concept* of division and the base-five pieces. For example, the numeral 11_{five} represents 6, so to compute $220_{five} \div 11_{five}$, the base-five pieces for 2 flats and 2 longs can be divided into six equal collections.

    *a. $220_{five} \div 11_{five}$ **b.** $330_{five} \div 20_{five}$ **c.** $434_{five} \div 12_{five}$ **d.** $430_{five} \div 10_{five}$

4. a. Form the collection shown below with the base-ten pieces. Determine the minimal collection each person would receive if these pieces were divided equally among twelve people. Show a sketch of the solution.

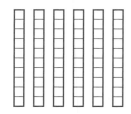

    b. Using the preceding collection of pieces, and regrouping as necessary, determine the number of people who could receive 12 units each, if the total number of units are divided into equal collections of 12. Show a sketch of the solution.

    c. Notice in 4a and 4b theat the sketches are different, but both illustration division. Do they both provide an answer to 168 ÷ 12? Explain why or why not.

SECTION 3.4

DIVISION AND EXPONENTS

*General Motors
Terex Titan and
Chevrolet Luv
pickup*

**PROBLEM
OPENER**

Using exactly four 4s and only addition, subtraction, multiplication, and division, write an expression that equals each of the numbers from 1 to 10. You do not have to use all the operations, and numbers such as 44 are permitted.*

One common use of division is to compare two quantities. In the photograph above, consider the relative sizes of the Terex Titan dump truck and the Luv pickup, which is on the Titan's dump body. The Terex Titan can carry 317,250 kilograms; the Luv pickup has a limit of 450 kilograms. We can determine the number of Luv loads it requires to equal one Titan load by dividing 317,250 by 450. The answer is 705, which means the Luv pickup will have to haul 705 loads to fill the Titan just once! Sitting in the back of the Luv pickup is a child holding a toy truck. If the toy truck holds 3 kilograms of sand, how many of its loads will be required to fill the Titan?

The division operation used in comparing the sizes of the Terex Titan and the Luv pickup can be checked by multiplication. The load weight of the smaller truck times 705 should equal the load weight of the larger truck. The close relationship between division and multiplication can be used to define division in terms of multiplication.

DIVISION OF WHOLE NUMBERS   For any whole numbers r and s, with $s \neq 0$, the quotient of r divided by s, written $r \div s$, is the whole number k, if it exists, such that $r = s \times k$.

---

*Similar equations exist for five 5s, six 6s, etc. See R. Crouse and J. Shuttleworth, "Playing with Numerals," *Arithmetic Teacher* 1, no. 5 (May 1974): 417–419.

Example A

Mentally calculate each quotient.

1. $18 \div 3$ **2.** $24 \div 6$ **3.** $35 \div 5$

Solution   **1.** $18 \div 3 = 6$ since $18 = 3 \times 6$ **2.** $24 \div 6 = 4$ since $24 = 6 \times 4$ **3.** $35 \div 5 = 7$ since $35 = 5 \times 7$

The definition of division, along with Example A, shows why multiplication and division are called **inverse operations.** We arrive at division facts by knowing multiplication facts.

There are three basic terms used in describing the division process: *dividend, divisor,* and *quotient.* In problem 1 of Example A, 18 is the **dividend,** 3 is the **divisor,** and 6 is the **quotient.** Over the centuries, division has acquired two meanings or uses. David Eugene Smith, in *History of Mathematics,* speaks of the twofold nature of division and refers to the sixteenth-century authors who first clarified the differences between its two meanings.* These two meanings of division, known as *sharing (partitive)* and *measurement (subtractive),* are illustrated in the following examples.

Example B

Suppose you have 24 tennis balls, which you want to divide equally among 3 people. How many tennis balls would each person receive?

Solution   The answer can be determined by separating (partitioning) the tennis balls into 3 equivalent sets. The following figure shows 24 balls divided into 3 groups and illustrates $24 \div 3$. The divisor 3 indicates the number of groups. This problem illustrates the **sharing (partitive) concept** of division.

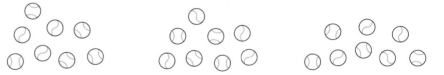

Example C

Suppose you have 24 tennis balls and want to give 3 tennis balls to as many people as possible. How many people would receive tennis balls?

Solution   The answer can be determined by subtracting, or measuring off, as many sets of 3 as possible. The following sketch of 24 tennis balls shows the result of this measuring process and illustrates $24 \div 3$. The divisor 3 is the number of balls in each group, and the quotient 8 is the number of groups. This problem illustrates the **measurement (subtractive) concept** of division.

In prekindergarten through grade 2, students should begin to develop an understanding of the concepts of multiplication and division. . . . They can investigate division with real objects and through story problems, usually ones involving the distribution of equal shares.

Standards 2000, p. 84

Models for Division Algorithms

Of the four basic pencil-and-paper algorithms, the algorithm for division, called **long division,** is the most difficult and has traditionally required the most classroom time to master. As the use of calculators in schools increases, long division,

*D. E. Smith, *History of Mathematics,* 2d ed. (Lexington, MA: Ginn, 1925), p. 130.

especially for three- and four-digit numbers, will be deemphasized. However, an understanding of division and of algorithms for determining quotients will remain important for mental calculations, estimation, and problem solving.

There are several physical models for illustrating division. Base-ten pieces are used in the following examples.

Example D

By creating and working with representations (such as diagrams or concrete objects) of multiplication and division situations, students can gain a sense of the relationships among the operations.

Standards 2000, p. 33

Compute $48 \div 4$ by sketching base-ten pieces.

Solution   1. One possibility is to use the sharing (partitive) concept of division, placing 1 long in each of four groups and then 2 units in each group, as shown in the following figure. The *size* of each group, or 12, is the quotient of $48 \div 4$.

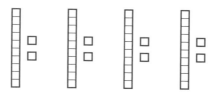

2. Another approach is to use the measurement (subtractive) concept of division to form as many groups of 4 units as possible. In this case there are 12 groups of 4 units each, as shown in the next figure. The *number* of groups, namely 12, is the quotient of $48 \div 4$.

3. A third possibility is to use 4 longs and 8 units to form a rectangular array with one dimension of 4, as shown next. The other dimension is 12, the quotient of $48 \div 4$.

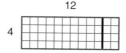

Notice in solution 3 of Example D that by viewing the rectangular array as 4 rows of 12 units each, we are making use of the sharing (partitive) concept of division for computing $48 \div 4$, and by viewing the array as 12 columns of 4 units each, we are making use of the measurement (subtractive) concept of division for computing $48 \div 4$.

Example E shows how base-ten pieces can be used to illustrate the steps in the long-division algorithm.

Example E

This example illustrates $378 \div 3$ by using the sharing (partitive) concept of division. Four steps are described. In each step, as the base-ten pieces are divided into groups, the groups are matched to the quotient of the long-division algorithm.

Step 1. Begin with 3 flats, 7 longs, and 8 units to represent 378.

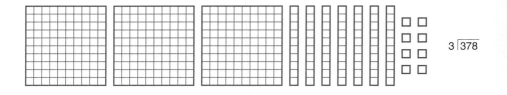

Step 2. Share the flats by placing 1 flat in each of 3 groups. This leaves 7 longs and 8 units.

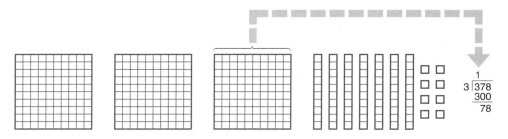

Step 3. Share the longs by placing 2 longs in each of the 3 groups, leaving 1 long and 8 units.

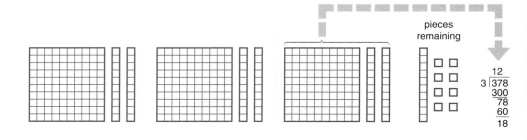

Step 4. Regroup the remaining long into 10 units and share the 18 units by placing 6 units in each of the 3 groups.

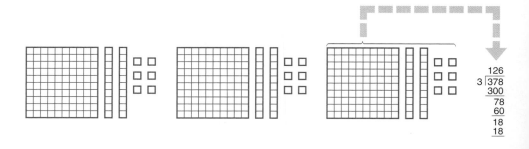

Notice that each of the final groups of base-ten pieces represents the quotient 126.

For small divisors, as in Example E, the sharing concept of division is practical because the number of groups is small. For larger divisors, rectangular arrays are convenient. In recent years, the rectangular-array approach to illustrating division has become more common.

Example F

This example illustrates $336 \div 12$ by using a rectangular array. Three steps are described, and each step is related to the quotient of the long-division algorithm.

Step 1. Begin with 3 flats, 3 longs, and 6 units to represent 336.

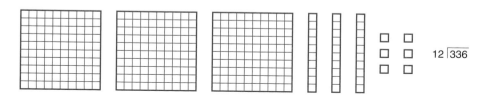

As students move from third to fifth grade, they should consolidate and practice a small number of computational algorithms for addition, subtraction, multiplication, and division that they understand well and can use routinely.

Standards 2000, p. 155

Step 2. Start building a rectangle with one dimension of 12. This can be done by beginning with 1 flat and 2 longs (see shaded region). Then a second flat and 2 more longs can be added by regrouping the third flat into 10 longs. This leaves 9 longs and 6 units.

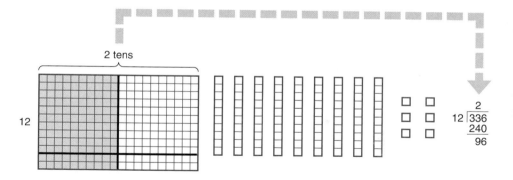

Step 3. Continue building the rectangle by extending it with the remaining 9 longs and 6 units. To accomplish this, regroup one of the longs into 10 units.

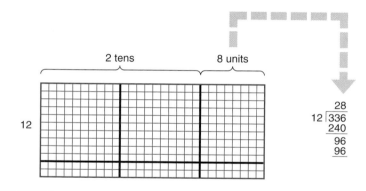

The final dimension of the rectangle in Example F is 28, the quotient of 336 ÷ 12. Notice that the rectangular-array illustration of division is a visual reminder of the close relationship between division and multiplication: The product of the two dimensions, or 12 × 28, is 336, the number represented by the original set of base-ten pieces.

Division Theorem

We have seen that the sum or product of two whole numbers is always another whole number and that this fact is called the *closure* property. Subtraction and division of whole numbers, on the other hand, are not closed. That is, the difference or quotient of two whole numbers is not always another whole number.

Example G

1. $12 - 15$ is not a whole number because there is no whole number c such that $12 = 15 + c$.

2. $38 \div 7$ is not a whole number because there is no whole number k such that $38 = 7 \times k$.

At times we want to solve problems involving division of whole numbers even though the quotient is not a whole number. In the case of $38 \div 7$, we can determine that the greatest whole number quotient is 5 and the remainder is 3.

$$38 = 7 \times 5 + 3$$

 Calculators intended for school children are sometimes designed to display the whole number quotient and remainder when one whole number is divided by another. The view screens for three such calculators are shown in Figure 3.22. These screens show the quotient and remainder for $66,315 \div 7$. Notice that these calculators have a special key to indicate division with a whole number remainder.

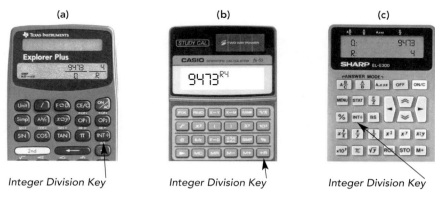

| (a) | (b) | (c) |

Figure 3.22

Integer Division Key   Integer Division Key   Integer Division Key

If you do not have such a calculator, whole number quotients and remainders can be obtained from any calculator. The following view screen shows the quotient in terms of a whole number and a decimal.

$$66315 \;\boxed{\div}\; 7 \;\boxed{=}\; \boxed{9473.571429}$$

The whole number quotient is 9473, and the whole number remainder can be determined as follows: $66,315 - 7 \times 9473 = 4$.

Another approach to obtaining whole number quotients and remainders is to use repeated subtraction. This approach has the added advantage of reinforcing the measurement (subtractive) concept of division, and it can be used on most calculators. The following steps and displays show that $489 \div 134$ has a quotient of 3 (because 134 has been subtracted 3 times) and a remainder of 87. The process of subtracting 134 continues until the view screen shows a number which is less than 134 and greater than or equal to 0.

KEYSTROKES	VIEW SCREEN
489	489
− 134 =	355
− 134 =	221
− 134 =	87

The teacher plays an important role in helping students develop and select an appropriate computational tool (calculator, paper-and-pencil algorithm, or mental strategy).

Standards 2000, p. 156

Calculators which display whole number quotients and remainders help children to see that whenever one whole number is divided by another nonzero whole number, the quotient is always greater than or equal to 0; and the remainder is always less than the divisor. The fact that such quotients q and remainders r always exist is guaranteed by the following theorem.

DIVISION THEOREM   For any whole numbers a and b, with divisor $b \neq 0$, there are whole numbers q (quotient) and r (remainder) such that

$$a = bq + r$$

and $0 \leq r < b$.

This theorem says that the **remainder** r is always less than the divisor b. If $r = 0$, then the quotient $a \div b$ is the whole number q.

Example H

Use a calculator and one of the preceding approaches to determine the whole number quotient and remainder.

1. $81{,}483 \div 26$ **2.** $37{,}641 \div 227$

3. $707{,}381 \div 112$ **4.** $51{,}349 \div 57$

Solution **1.** Quotient 3133 and remainder 25   **2.** Quotient 165 and remainder 186   **3.** Quotient 6315 and remainder 101   **4.** Quotient 900 and remainder 49

Mental Calculations

A major strategy in performing mental calculations is replacing a problem by one that can be solved more easily. This approach was used in Sections 3.2 and 3.3 for mentally calculating sums, differences, and products; it is described here for division.

EQUAL QUOTIENTS   In calculating a quotient mentally, sometimes it is helpful to use the method of **equal quotients,** in which we divide or multiply both the divisor and the dividend by the same number.

Example ▌

1. The quotient $144 \div 18$ can be replaced by $72 \div 9$ by dividing both 144 and 18 by 2. We know from our basic multiplication facts that $9 \times 8 = 72$, so

$$144 \div 18 = 72 \div 9 = 8$$

2. The quotient $1700 \div 50$ can be replaced by multiplying both 1700 and 50 by 2. Then dividing by 100 can be done mentally to obtain a quotient of 34.

$$1700 \div 50 = 3400 \div 100 = 34$$

Figure 3.23a illustrates why both numbers in a quotient can be divided by 2 (cut in half) without changing the quotient (the relative sizes of the two numbers). The number of tiles in the 6×7 array is 3 times the number of tiles in the 2×7 array. After these arrays are both cut in half to obtain 3×7 and 1×7 arrays, the number of tiles in the 3×7 array is still 3 times the number of tiles in the 1×7 array. That is, the relative sizes of the two sets of tiles have not changed. Similarly, Figure 3.23b shows that tripling the number of tiles in two sets to obtain two larger sets does not change the relative sizes of the two original sets of tiles. The 6×7 array is 3 times the size of the 2×7 array, and after we enlarge both sets of tile by a factor of 3, the 6×21 array is 3 times the size of the 2×21 array.

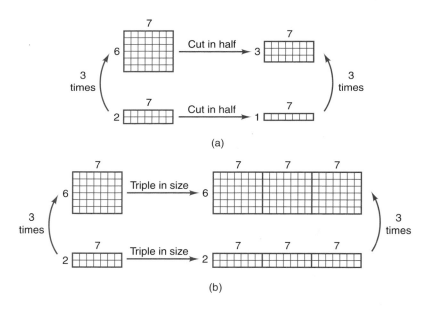

Figure 3.23

(b)

Usually when mentally computing the quotient of two whole numbers, we want to divide both numbers by the same number to obtain smaller numbers. However, when we use the *equal-quotients* technique for mentally computing quotients of fractions and decimals, it is often more convenient to multiply both numbers in the quotient to obtain compatible numbers. (See the use of *equal quotients* in Sections 5.3 and 6.2.)

Example J

Replace each quotient by equal quotients until you can calculate the answer mentally.

1. $180 \div 12$

2. $900 \div 36$

3. $336 \div 48$

Solution   Here are three solutions. Others are possible.   **1.** $180 \div 12 = 60 \div 4 = 15$ (Divide by 3)   **2.** $900 \div 36 = 300 \div 12 = 100 \div 4 = 25$ (Divide by 3 twice)   **3.** $336 \div 48 = 112 \div 16 = 56 \div 8 = 7$ (Divide by 3, then by 2)

Estimation of Quotients

ROUNDING   Often we wish to obtain a rough comparison of two quantities in order to determine how many times bigger (or smaller) one is than the other. This may require finding an estimation for a quotient. *Rounding* numbers is one method of estimating a quotient.

Example K

Estimate each quotient by rounding one or both numbers.

1. $472 \div 46$

2. $145 \div 23$

3. $8145 \div 195$

Solution   Here are some possibilities.   **1.** $472 \div 46 \approx 460 \div 46 = 10$; or $472 \div 46 \approx 500 \div 50 = 10$ **2.** $145 \div 23 \approx 150 \div 25 = 6$ **3.** $8145 \div 195 \approx 8000 \div 200 = 40$

HISTORICAL HIGHLIGHT

Emile de Breteuil
1706–1749

France, during the post-Renaissance period, offered little opportunity for the education of women. Emile de Breteuil's precocity showed itself in many ways, but her true love was mathematics. One of her first scientific works was an investigation regarding the nature of fire, which was submitted to the French Academy of Sciences in 1738. It anticipated the results of subsequent research by arguing that both light and heat have the same cause or are both modes of motion. She also discovered that different-color rays do not give out an equal degree of heat. Her book *Institutions de physique* was originally intended as an essay on physics for her son. She produced instead a comprehensive textbook, not unlike a modern text, which traced the growth of physics, summarizing the thinking of the philosopher-scientists of her century. The work established Breteuil's competence among her contemporaries in mathematics and science.*

*L. M. Osen, *Women in Mathematics* (Cambridge, MA: The MIT Press, 1974), pp. 49–69.

Rounding to obtain an approximate quotient can be combined with the process of finding equal quotients (dividing or multiplying both the divisor and the dividend by the same number).

Example L

Find approximations by *rounding* and using *equal quotients*.

1. $427 \div 72$

2. $139 \div 18$

Solution   **1.** $427 \div 72 \approx 430 \div 70 = 43 \div 7 \approx 6$ **2.** $139 \div 18 \approx 140 \div 18 = 70 \div 9 \approx 8$; or $139 \div 18 \approx 140 \div 20 = 14 \div 2 = 7$

COMPATIBLE NUMBERS   Replacing numbers with *compatible numbers* is a useful technique for mentally estimating quotients.

Example M

Find one or two compatible numbers to replace the given numbers, and mentally estimate the quotient.

1. $92 \div 9$

2. $59 \div 16$

3. $485 \div 24$

Solution   Here is one possibility for each quotient: **1.** $92 \div 9 \approx 90 \div 9 = 10$ **2.** $59 \div 16 \approx 60 \div 15 = 4$ **3.** $485 \div 24 \approx 500 \div 25 = 20$

FRONT-END ESTIMATION   This technique can be used to obtain an estimated quotient of two numbers by using the leading digit of each number. Consider the following example, where both *front-end estimation* and *equal quotients* are used.

$$783 \div 244 \approx 700 \div 200 = 7 \div 2 = 3\tfrac{1}{2}$$

In the example just shown, the two numbers being divided have the same number of digits. A front-end estimation also can be obtained for the quotient of two numbers when the leading digits have different place values, as in $8326 \div 476$.

$$8326 \div 476 \approx 8000 \div 400 = 80 \div 4 = 20$$

Example N

Use front-end estimation to estimate each quotient.

1. $828 \div 210$

2. $7218 \div 2036$

3. $4128 \div 216$

Solution   **1.** $828 \div 210 \approx 800 \div 200 = 8 \div 2 = 4$ **2.** $7218 \div 2036 \approx 7000 \div 2000 = 7 \div 2 = 3\tfrac{1}{2}$ **3.** $4128 \div 216 \approx 4000 \div 200 = 40 \div 2 = 20$

Estimation techniques can help check the reasonableness of results from calculator computations:

Estimation is especially important when children use calculators. If they need to compute 4783 ÷ 13, for example, a quick estimate can be found by using "compatible numbers." In this case 4783 is about 4800 and 13 is about 12, so 4783 ÷ 13 is about 4800 ÷ 12. The dividing can be done mentally, since 48 and 12 are "compatible numbers" for division. Thus 4783 ÷ 13 is about 400. This rough estimate provides children with enough information to decide whether the correct keys were pressed and whether the calculator result is reasonable.*

Exponents

The large numbers used today were rarely needed a few centuries ago. The word *billion,* which is now commonplace, was not adopted until the seventeenth century. Even now, billion means different things to different people. In the United States it represents 1,000,000,000 (one thousand million), and in England it is 1,000,000,000,000 (one million million).

Our numbers are named according to powers of 10. The first, second, and third powers of 10 are the familiar ten, hundred, and thousand. After this, only every third power of 10 has a new or special name: million, billion, trillion, etc.

10^0 = 1   one
10^1 = 10   ten
10^2 = 100   one hundred
10^3 = 1000   **one thousand**
10^4 = 10,000   ten thousand
10^5 = 100,000   one hundred thousand
10^6 = 1,000,000   **one million**
10^7 = 10,000,000   ten million
10^8 = 100,000,000   one hundred million
10^9 = 1,000,000,000   **one billion**
10^{10} = 10,000,000,000   ten billion
10^{11} = 100,000,000,000   one hundred billion
10^{12} = 1,000,000,000,000 **one trillion**

The operation of raising numbers to a power is called **exponentiation.**

EXPONENTIATION   For any number b and any whole number n, with b and n not both zero,

$$b^n = \underbrace{b \times b \times b \times b \times \ldots \times b}_{b \text{ occurs } n \text{ times}}$$

where b is called the **base** and n is called the **exponent.** In case $n = 0$ or $n = 1$, $b^0 = 1$ and $b^1 = b$.

Curriculum and Evaluation Standards for School Mathematics (Reston, VA: National Council of Teachers of Mathematics, 1989), p. 37.

Example O

Evaluate each expression.

1. 3^4 **2.** 2^5

3. 5^0 **4.** 3^1

Solution   1. 81   2. 32   3. 1   4. 3

A number written in the form b^n is said to be in **exponential form.** In general, the number b^n is called the ***n*th power** of b. The second and third powers of b, b^2, and b^3, are usually called ***b* squared** and ***b* cubed.** This terminology was inherited from the ancient Greeks, who pictured numbers as geometric arrays of dots. Figure 3.24 illustrates 2^2, a 2 × 2 array of dots in the form of a square, and 2^3, a 2 × 2 × 2 array of dots in the form of a cube.

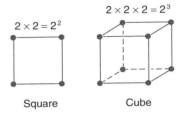

Figure 3.24

Square   Cube

A number greater than or equal to 1 that can be written as a whole number to the second power is called a **square number** or a **perfect square** (1, 4, 9, 16, 25, . . .), and a number greater than or equal to 1 that can be written as a whole number to the third power is called a **perfect cube** (1, 8, 27, 64, 125, . . .).

LAWS OF EXPONENTS   Multiplication and division can be performed easily with numbers that are written as powers of the same base. To multiply, we add the exponents; to divide, we subtract the exponents.

Example P

Evaluate each product or quotient. Write the answer in both exponential form and positional numeration.

1. $2^4 \times 2^3$ **2.** $2^8 \div 2^3$

Solution   1. $2^4 \times 2^3 = (2 \times 2 \times 2 \times 2) \times (2 \times 2 \times 2) = 2^7 = 128$

2. $2^8 \div 2^3 = \dfrac{2 \times 2 \times 2 \times 2 \times 2 \times 2 \times 2 \times 2}{2 \times 2 \times 2} = 2^5 = 32$

The equations in Example P are special cases of the following rules for computing with exponents.

LAWS OF EXPONENTS   For any number a and all whole numbers m and n, except for the case where the base and exponents are both zero,

$$a^n \times a^m = a^{n+m}$$

$$a^n \div a^m = a^{n-m} \qquad \text{for } a \neq 0$$

The primary advantage of exponents is their compactness, which makes them convenient for computing with very large numbers and (as we shall see in Chapter 6) very small numbers.

Example Q

1. In our galaxy there are 10^{11} (100 billion) stars, and in the observable universe there are 10^9 (1 billion) galaxies. If every galaxy had as many stars as ours, there would be $10^9 \times 10^{11}$ stars. Write this product in exponential form.

2. If 1 out of every 1000 stars had a planetary system, there would be $10^{20} \div 10^3$ stars with planetary systems. Write this quotient in exponential form.

3. If 1 out of every 1000 stars with a planetary system had a planet with conditions suitable for life, there would be $10^{17} \div 10^3$ such stars. Write this quotient in exponential form.

Solution   1. 10^{20} 2. 10^{17} 3. 10^{14}

Numbers raised to a whole-number power can be computed on a calculator by repeated multiplication, provided the products do not exceed the capacity of the calculator's view screen. On most calculators the steps shown in Figure 3.25 will produce the number represented by 4^{10}, if the process is carried out to step 10. Try this sequence of steps on your calculator.

KEYSTROKES	VIEW SCREEN
4	4
× 4 =	16
× 4 =	64
× 4 =	256

Figure 3.25

The number of steps in the preceding process can be decreased by applying the rule for adding exponents, namely $a^n \times a^m = a^{n+m}$. To compute 4^{10}, first compute 4^5 on the calculator and then multiply the result, 1024, by itself.

$$4^{10} = 4^5 \times 4^5 = 1024 \times 1024 = 1,048,576$$

Some calculators have exponential keys such as $\boxed{y^x}$, $\boxed{x^y}$, or $\boxed{\wedge}$ for evaluating numbers raised to a power. To compute a number y to some exponential power x, enter the base y into the calculator, press the exponential key, and enter the exponent x. The steps in evaluating 4^{10} are shown in Figure 3.26.

KEYSTROKES	VIEW SCREEN
4 (base)	4
$\boxed{y^x}$	4
10 (exponent)	10
=	1048576

Figure 3.26

Since 10 is a common base when exponents are used, some calculators have a key such as $\boxed{10^x}$ or $\boxed{10^n}$. Depending on the brand of calculator, the exponent

5·2

Explore Multiplying by 1-Digit Numbers

Learn

You can use graph paper to explore multiplying by 1-digit numbers. What is 6 × 29?

Work Together

Find 6 × 29 using graph paper.

▶ Draw a rectangle that is 6 squares high and 29 squares wide.

▶ How many squares are inside the rectangle? How did you find the number of squares?

You Will Need
• centimeter graph paper

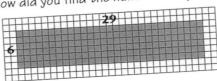
29
6

▶ Use graph paper to multiply. Record your work.

4 × 17	5 × 32	8 × 27
3 × 43	6 × 37	7 × 23
2 × 18	5 × 21	3 × 13
4 × 17	9 × 12	1 × 16

may have to be entered before pressing the exponential key or after, as shown by the following keystrokes.

5 $\boxed{10^x}$ $\boxed{100000}$ or $\boxed{10^x}$ 5 $\boxed{100000}$

Numbers that are raised to powers frequently have more digits than the number of places in the calculator's view screen. If you try to compute 4^{15} on a calculator with only eight places in its view screen, there will not be room for the answer in positional numeration. Some calculators will automatically convert to scientific notation when numbers in positional numeration are too large for the view screen (see Section 6.3), and others will print an error message such as *Error* or *E*.

Order of Operations

The rules for *order of operations,* discussed in Section 3.3, can now be extended to include division and raising numbers to powers. The order of operations requires that numbers raised to a power be evaluated first; then products and quotients are computed in the order in which they occur from left to right; finally, sums and differences are calculated in the order in which they occur from left to right. An exception to the rule occurs when numbers are written in parentheses. In this case, computations within parentheses are carried out first.

Example R

Evaluate the following expressions.

1. $4 \times 6 + 16 \div 2^3$

2. $4 \times (6 + 16) \div 2^3$

3. $220 - 12 \times 7 + 15 \div 3$

4. $24 \div 4 \times 2 + 15$

Solution   **1.** 26 (First replace 2^3 by 8; then compute the product and quotient; then add.)   **2.** 11 (First replace $6 + 16$ by 22; then replace 2^3 by 8; then compute the product and quotient.)   **3.** 141 (First replace 12×7 by 84 and $15 \div 3$ by 5; then compute the difference and sum.)   **4.** 27 (First compute $24 \div 4$; then multiply by 2; then add 15.)

 Calculators that are programmed to follow the order of operations are convenient for computing expressions involving several different operations. You may wish to try problem 3 in Example R on your calculator, entering in the numbers and operations as they appear from left to right and then pressing the equality key, to see if you obtain 141.

Problem-Solving Application

The following problem involves numbers in exponential form and is solved by using the strategies of *making a table* and *finding a pattern.*

PROBLEM

There is a legend that chess was invented for the Indian king Shirham by the grand visier Sissa Ben Dahir. As a reward, Sissa asked to be given 1 grain of wheat for the first square of the chessboard, 2 grains for the second square, 4 grains for the third square, then 8 grains, 16 grains, etc., until each square of the board had been accounted for. The king was surprised at such a meager request until Sissa informed him that this was more wheat than existed in the entire kingdom. What would be the sum of all the grains of wheat for the 64 squares of the chessboard?

Understanding the Problem   The numbers of grains for the first few squares are shown in the following figure.

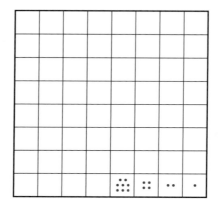

The numbers 1, 2, 4, 8, 16, 32, . . . form a geometric sequence whose common ratio is 2. Sometimes it is convenient to express these numbers as powers of 2.

$$1 \quad\quad 2 \quad\quad 2^2 \quad\quad 2^3 \quad\quad 2^4 \quad\quad 2^5 \quad\quad . . .$$

Question 1: How would the number of grains for the 64th square be written as a power of 2?

Devising a Plan   Computing the sum of all 64 binary numbers would be a difficult task. Let's form a table for the first few sums and look for a pattern. Compute the next three totals in the following table. **Question 2:** How is each total related to a power of 2?

SQUARE	NO. OF GRAINS	TOTAL
1	1	1
2	$1 + 2$	3
3	$1 + 2 + 2^2$	7
4	$1 + 2 + 2^2 + 2^3$	
5	$1 + 2 + 2^2 + 2^3 + 2^4$	
6	$1 + 2 + 2^2 + 2^3 + 2^4 + 2^5$	

Carrying Out the Plan   Find a pattern in the preceding table, and use it to express the sum of the grains for all 64 squares. **Question 3:** What is this sum, written as a power of 2?

Looking Back   King Shirham was surprised at the total amount of grain because the number of grains for the first few squares is so small. There is more grain for each additional square than for all the preceding squares combined. **Question 4:**

Why is the number of grains for the 64th square greater than the total number of grains for the first 63 squares?

Answers to Questions 1–4   1. 2^{63} 2. The total in each row is 1 less than a power of 2.   3. The total number of grains is $2^{64} - 1$.   4. The total number of grains for the first 63 squares is $2^{63} - 1$, but there are 2^{63} grains for the 64th square.

· ·

PUZZLER

Supply the missing digits in this faded document puzzle.

EXERCISES AND PROBLEMS 3.4

In exercises 1 and 2, circle groups of chips to illustrate each concept of division.

1. a. $28 \div 7$ using the *sharing (partitive) concept*

b. $28 \div 7$ using the *measurement (subtractive) concept*

2. a. $30 \div 6$ using the *sharing (partitive) concept*

b. $30 \div 6$ using the *measurement (subtractive) concept*

In exercises 3 and 4, write each division as a multiplication.

3. a. $68 \div 17 = 4$ **b.** $414 \div 23 = 18$

4. a. $288 \div 8 = 36$ **b.** $a \div b = c$

In exercises 5 and 6, write each multiplication as a division.

5. a. $14 \times 24 = 336$ **b.** $9 \times 8 = 72$

6. a. $360 \times 10 = 3600$ **b.** $r \times s = t$

Illustrate each quotient in exercises 7 and 8 by using the *sharing (partitive) concept* of division and circling groups of base pieces. Sketch any new pieces that are necessary to show regrouping.

7. a. $396 \div 3$

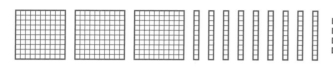

b. $301_{\text{five}} \div 4$

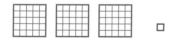

8. a. $76 \div 4$

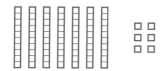

b. $271_{\text{eight}} \div 5$

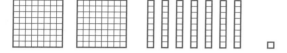

In exercises 9 and 10, use base-ten pieces to illustrate the long-division algorithm for each quotient. In separate steps show which base-ten pieces correspond to each digit in the quotient.

9. a. $7\overline{)392}$ quotient 56 **b.** $5\overline{)320}$ quotient 64

10. a. $4\overline{)96}$ quotient 24 **b.** $3\overline{)426}$ quotient 142

In exercises 11 and 12, use a rectangular array of base-ten pieces to illustrate each quotient. (Copy the base-ten grid from the inside cover or the website.)

11. a. $72 \div 12$ **b.** $286 \div 26$

12. a. $238 \div 14$ **b.** $391 \div 23$

In exercises 13 and 14, show a rectangle that uses all the base-ten pieces and has the given dimension. Regrouping may be needed. Label both dimensions of the rectangle. Write a multiplication fact and a division fact illustrated by each rectangle. (Copy the base-ten grid from the inside cover or the website.)

13. a. 6 flats, 0 longs, and 8 units, with one dimension of 32

   b. 2 flats, 2 longs, and 1 unit, with one dimension of 13

   c. 2 flats, 9 longs, and 4 units, with one dimension of 21

14. a. 1 flat, 1 long, and 7 units, with one dimension of 13

   b. 3 flats, 3 longs, and 0 units, with one dimension of 15

   c. 5 flats, 1 long, and 8 units, with one dimension of 14

In exercises 15 and 16, determine which quotients can be computed and what they equal. Try these quotients on a calculator.

15. a. $0 \div 4$ **b.** $4 \div 0$ **c.** $0 \div 0$

16. a. $39 \div 0$ **b.** $(14 - 14) \div (7 - 7)$ **c.** $0 \div 10$

17. a. What division fact is illustrated by the arrows on the number line?

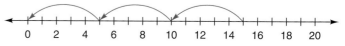

   b. Draw an arrow diagram for $18 \div 6$, using the *measurement (subtractive) concept* of division.

18. a. What division fact is illustrated by the arrows on the number line?

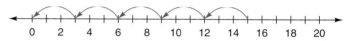

   b. Draw an arrow diagram for $16 \div 8$, using the *measurement (subtractive) concept* of division.

The examples of long division in exercises 19 and 20 illustrate different types of errors. Locate and explain each type of error.

19. a.
$$\begin{array}{r} 56 \text{ R4} \\ 8\overline{)4052} \\ \underline{40} \\ 52 \\ \underline{48} \\ 4 \end{array}$$
   b.
$$\begin{array}{r} 68 \\ 3\overline{)258} \\ \underline{24} \\ 18 \\ \underline{18} \end{array}$$

20. a.
$$\begin{array}{r} 370 \\ 7\overline{)2149} \\ \underline{21} \\ 49 \\ \underline{49} \end{array}$$
   b.
$$\begin{array}{r} 29 \text{ R20} \\ 4\overline{)136} \\ \underline{8} \\ 56 \\ \underline{36} \\ 20 \end{array}$$

Try some numbers for the variables in each equation in exercises 21 and 22. Does the right side equal the left side? Can you find a case in which the equation does not hold? It takes only one counterexample to show that a property does not hold.

21. a. $(\square + \triangle) \div \diagup \overset{?}{=} (\square \div \diagdown) + (\triangle \div \diagup)$

b. $\square \div \triangle \overset{?}{=} \triangle \div \square$

22. a. $\square \div (\triangle \div \diagup) \overset{?}{=} (\square \div \triangle) \div \diagup$

b. $(\square - \triangle) \div \diagup \overset{?}{=} (\square \div \diagdown) - (\triangle \div \diagup)$

Determine whether each set in exercises 23 and 24 is closed or not closed for the given operation.

23. a. The set of odd whole numbers for addition
   b. The set of whole numbers for division
   c. The set of odd whole numbers for multiplication

24. a. The set of even whole numbers for subtraction
   b. {0, 1} for addition
   c. {0, 1} for multiplication

Find the greatest whole number quotient and the remainder in exercises 25 and 26.

25. a. $47,208 \div 674$
   b. $2018 \div 17$
   c. $1,121,496 \div 465$

26. a. $13,738 \div 24$
   b. $107,253 \div 86$
   c. $988,604 \div 236$

In exercises 27 and 28, use the method of *equal quotients* to replace the divisor and the dividend with smaller numbers. Show the new quotient that replaces the original quotient. Repeat this process, if necessary, until you can mentally calculate the exact quotient.

27. a. $90 \div 18$ **b.** $84 \div 14$

28. a. $400 \div 16$ **b.** $144 \div 16$

In exercises 29 and 30, round or use *compatible numbers* to mentally estimate the quotient. Show the new quotient, and predict whether it is greater than or less than the exact quotient.

29. a. $250 \div 46$
   b. $82 \div 19$
   c. $486 \div 53$

30. a. $203 \div 50$
   b. $8145 \div 195$
   c. $241 \div 31$

In exercises 31 and 32, use *front-end estimation* to mentally estimate the quotient.

31. a. $623 \div 209$ **b.** $7218 \div 1035$

32. a. $938 \div 31$ **b.** $5634 \div 713$

Compute the products and quotients in exercises 33 and 34. Leave your answers in exponential form.

33. a. $5^{14} \times 5^{20}$ **b.** $10^{12} \div 10^{10}$

34. a. $10^{32} \div 10^{15}$ **b.** $3^{22} \times 3^{8}$

Evaluate the expressions in exercises 35 and 36.

35. a. $6 + 4 \times 8 - 3$
   b. $5 \times 10 - 2 \times 6$
   c. $5 \times (10 - 2) \times 6$
   d. $45 \div 3 \times 5 - 2$

36. a. $8 - 5 + 2 + 9$
   b. $15 \times (80 + 170) \div 5^{2}$
   c. $160 \div 2^{4} + 2^{7} - 75$
   d. $1440 \div 12 \times 10 + 18$

The chart below shows the approximate frequencies of some common types of waves. Visible light waves, for example, have a frequency between 10^{14} and 10^{15} cycles per second. Exercises 37 and 38 involve the frequency of waves from this table.

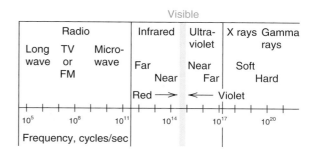

37. a. If a radio frequency is 10^{8} cycles per second and gamma rays have a frequency of 10^{21} cycles per second, the gamma-ray frequency is how many times the radio frequency?
   b. The frequency of a gamma ray at 10^{20} cycles per second is how many times the frequency of a long wave at 10^{5} cycles per second?

38. a. The frequency of television is 10^{8} cycles per second. If a type of x-ray has a frequency that is 10^{11} times the television frequency, what is the x-ray frequency?
   b. If the frequency of infrared is 10^{13} cycles per second and it is 1000 times the frequency of microwaves, what is the microwave frequency?

Beneath each equation in exercises 39 to 41 is a sequence of calculator steps. Determine whether the sequence produces the correct answer. If not, revise the steps so that the correct answer is obtained from a calculator.

39. $8 \times (12 \div 3) = 32$

1. Enter 8
2. $\times$
3. Enter 12
4. $\div$
5. Enter 3
6. $=$

40. $3 \times 4 + 7 = 19$

1. Enter 3
2. $\times$
3. Enter 4
4. $+$
5. Enter 7
6. $=$

41. $17 - 3 \times 5 = 2$

1. Enter 17
2. $-$
3. Enter 3
4. $\times$
5. Enter 5
6. $=$

42. Some calculators for students in grade school have a division key $\boxed{INT \div}$ which determines the whole number quotient and remainder when dividing one whole number by another. Assume an elementary school class has such calculators and the students wish to determine the number of buses needed by six schools in the district, if each bus holds 30 students.

a. For each calculator view screen, determine the whole-number quotient (first bracket of the screen) and remainder (second bracket of the screen) for the given numbers of students.

b. Determine the total number of buses needed by the school district if buses do not pick up children at more than one school.

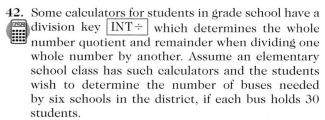

	KEYSTROKES				VIEW SCREEN
1.	132	$INT \div$	30	$=$	
2.	171	$INT \div$	30	$=$	
3.	83	$INT \div$	30	$=$	
4.	227	$INT \div$	30	$=$	
5.	168	$INT \div$	30	$=$	
6.	200	$INT \div$	30	$=$	

43. Six classes in a middle school will go on a field trip in vans that each hold seven students. To determine the total number of vans needed, the students will use a calculator with a whole number division key $\boxed{INT \div}$ as illustrated in the screens below.

a. For each calculator view screen, determine the whole-number quotient (first bracket of the screen) and the remainder (second bracket of the screen) for the given numbers of students.

b. If each class rides only in vans driven by parents of students in the class, what is the total number of vans that will be needed?

	KEYSTROKES				VIEW SCREEN
1.	32	$INT \div$	7	$=$	
2.	26	$INT \div$	7	$=$	
3.	34	$INT \div$	7	$=$	
4.	30	$INT \div$	7	$=$	
5.	27	$INT \div$	7	$=$	
6.	24	$INT \div$	7	$=$	

Calculators with a constant function can be used to generate a geometric sequence by dividing by a common ratio. The second number entered in step 1 in exercises 44 and 45 is the *common ratio* for each sequence, and pressing $=$ in each succeeding step divides the number in the view screen by the common ratio.

a. What are the numbers for the six view screens?

b. How many numbers are there in the sequence that begins with the first number in the view screen before obtaining a number less than 1?

44.

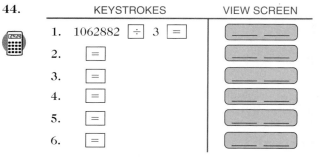

	KEYSTROKES			VIEW SCREEN
1.	1062882	$\div$	3 $=$	
2.			$=$	
3.			$=$	
4.			$=$	
5.			$=$	
6.			$=$	

45.

	KEYSTROKES	VIEW SCREEN
1.	11529602 ÷ 7 =	
2.	=	
3.	=	
4.	=	
5.	=	
6.	=	

The key INT÷, which is used in exercises 46 and 47, displays a whole-number quotient (first bracket of the screen) and remainder (second bracket of the screen) in the calculator's view screen. Determine each quotient and remainder.

46. a. 25684 INT÷ 58 = _____

   b. 6551 INT÷ 112 = _____

47. a. 8683 INT÷ 17 = _____

   b. 7666 INT÷ 605 = _____

Assume that in exercises 48 and 49 a calculator is used that follows the *order of operations* and that pressing the keys 6 10^x produces 1000000 in the view screen and pressing 2 y^x 3 = produces 8. Determine the number which will appear in the view screen for each set of keystrokes.

48. a. 18 + 4 10^x =

   b. 2 × 7 y^x 3 =

49. a. 14 + 6 10^x ÷ 2 =

   b. 251 + 9 y^x 4 =

REASONING AND PROBLEM SOLVING

50. Featured Strategy: Finding a Pattern The chart below illustrates a repeating pattern. If this pattern continues, what symbol will be in the 538th square?

$	$	*	#	#	#	$	$	*	#	#	#	$	. . .

a. Understanding the Problem To become more familiar with the problem, extend the pattern a few more squares. What symbol will be in the 19th square?

b. Devising a Plan Because the pattern repeats itself after six squares, it is suggestive of a clock with six symbols. What symbol occurs in squares 6, 12, 18, etc.? Alternatively, you could think of the pattern as pieces of tile 6 squares long. To make the length 32 squares, how many tiles and squares would you need?

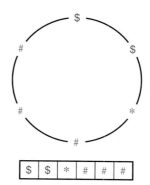

$	$	*	#	#	#

c. Carrying Out the Plan Choose a method for finding the symbol on the 538th square. Explain your method.

d. Looking Back The lengths and symbols of repeating patterns vary. What will be the 345th digit in the following number if the pattern continues? 142,857,142,857 . . .

Find a pattern in each set of equations in exercises 51 and 52, and use inductive reasoning to predict the next equation. Evaluate both sides of your new equation to check the results. Use your pattern to determine the 12th equation.

51. $1^2 + 2^2 + 2^2 = 3^2$
   $2^2 + 3^2 + 6^2 = 7^2$
   $3^2 + 4^2 + 12^2 = 13^2$

52. $1^3 + 2^3 = 3^2$
   $1^3 + 2^3 + 3^3 = 6^2$
   $1^3 + 2^3 + 3^3 + 4^3 = 10^2$

Look for some patterns in the following triangle of numbers. Use these patterns in exercises 53 and 54.

1	= 1
3 + 5	= 8
7 + 9 + 11	= 27
13 + 15 + 17 + 19	= 64
21 + 23 + 25 + 27 + 29	= 125

53. What is the 12th row of this triangle, and what is its sum?

54. What is the 10th row of this triangle, and what is its sum?

If each number in exercises 55 and 56 is expanded and written in positional numeration, what is the digit in the units place?

55. a. 2^{103} **b.** 6^{52}

56. a. 17^{65} **b.** 14^{81}

57. Suppose you had a chance to work for 22 weeks and could choose one of two methods of payment. You could choose to be paid $1 the first week, $2 the second week, $4 the third week, $8 the fourth week, etc., with the amount doubling each week; or you could choose to receive $2 million in one lump sum.

    a. Which method would result in the greater payment?

    b. What is the difference in the amounts between these two types of payments?

58. A school district receives a grant with the stipulation that the money be divided equally among the city's seven elementary schools. Each school is to divide its money equally among grades K through 5, and each grade is to divide its money equally for furniture, books, and science equipment. If each grade obtained $1345.20 for science equipment from the grant, what was the original amount of the grant?

59. Parker let his neighbor tap his 15 sugar maple trees to obtain sap for making maple syrup. In return, his neighbor agreed to divide the maple syrup equally between himself, Parker, and another person who would help to collect the sap. The sap was collected over a 30-day period during March and April. Parker was given 2 quarts of syrup, but he wondered if he had been cheated. He learned that each sugar maple tree gives approximately 1 gallon of sap every 5 days and that 40 gallons of sap must be boiled down to obtain 1 gallon of maple syrup. Given this information, how many quarts of maple syrup should have been given to Parker?

60. You have rented a car for one day at a cost of $28 per day. You also buy the insurance which is $12 per day. When you begin your trip, the tank is full with 12 gallons of gasoline. When you return the car, the gas gauge shows nearly empty. The clerk argues that you should pay for 12 gallons of gasoline, but you think this is unfair. You know that the odometer read 24,140 when you started the trip and 24,425 when you returned. So you ask the clerk how many miles this car gets for each gallon of gasoline. The clerk says 30 miles per gallon. How much gasoline should you pay for?

. . . .

ONLINE LEARNING CENTER   www.mhhe.com/bennett-nelson

    • Math Investigation 3.4   *Sums and Differences of Square Numbers*
    Section-Related: • Links   • Writing/Discussion Problems   • Bibliography

. . . .

PUZZLER

Krypto is a commercially produced game containing cards numbered from 1 through 25. The object is to combine the numbers on five cards that are randomly selected so as to obtain the number on a sixth card, the target number. Any of the four basic operations may be used, but each of the five cards must be used once and only once. How can each of the following sets of cards be used with all four operations to obtain the target numbers?

$$\boxed{22}\ \boxed{19}\ \boxed{2}\ \boxed{14}\ \boxed{10} \longrightarrow 7$$

$$\boxed{21}\ \boxed{2}\ \boxed{3}\ \boxed{12}\ \boxed{7} \longrightarrow 20$$

CHAPTER REVIEW

1. **Numeration systems**
   a. A logically organized collection of numerals is called a **numeration system.**
   b. The number of objects used in the grouping process is called the **base.**
   c. In an **additive numeration system,** each symbol is repeated as many times as needed.
   d. The **Egyptian** and **Roman numeration systems** are additive numeration systems.
   e. In a **positional numeration system,** the position of each digit indicates a power of the base.
   f. In a base-ten positional numeration system, the power of 10 associated with each digit is called its **place value.**
   g. The **Mayan** and **Hindu-Arabic numeration systems** are positional numeration systems.

2. **Reading and rounding numbers**
   a. Numbers with more than three digits are read by naming **periods.** Each period has three digits.
   b. The next three periods after the ones, tens, and hundreds digits are called **thousands, millions,** and **billions.**
   c. To **round** a number to the nearest million means to choose the million that is closest to the number.

3. **Models for numeration**
   a. The **bundle-of-sticks model** and **base-ten pieces** are two models for numeration systems.
   b. **Regrouping** is replacing one collection of pieces in a model by another collection that represents the same number.

4. **Whole-number operations**
   a. **Addition** is defined in terms of sets.
   b. **Subtraction** is defined as the inverse operation of addition.
   c. **Multiplication** is defined as repeated addition.
   d. **Division** is defined as the inverse operation of multiplication.
   e. There are three concepts of subtraction: the **take-away concept,** the **comparison concept,** and the **missing addend concept.**
   f. There are two concepts of division: the **sharing (partitive) concept** and the **measurement (subtractive) concept.**
   g. The operation of raising numbers to a power is called **exponentiation.**
   h. A number written in the form b^n is said to be in **exponential form;** b^n is called the **nth power** of b.

   i. For any whole numbers a, n, and m, not allowing 0^0, $a^n \times a^m = a^{n+m}$ and $a^n \div a^m = a^{n-m}$, for $a \neq 0$.

5. **Algorithms for operations**
   a. An **algorithm** is a step-by-step procedure for computing.
   b. The algorithms for addition and multiplication involve computing **partial sums** and **partial products.**
   c. **Left-to-right addition** is an algorithm that begins with the digits on the left (digits of greatest place value).

6. **Models for operations**
   a. The **bundle-of-sticks model** and **base-ten pieces** are two models for the four basic operations on whole numbers.
   b. A **rectangular array** is a visual method of illustrating the product of two whole numbers.
   c. Constructing a **tree diagram** is a counting technique that involves products of whole numbers.

7. **Number properties**
   a. **Closure property for addition:** For any whole numbers a and b, $a + b$ is a unique whole number.
   b. **Closure property for multiplication:** For any whole numbers a and b, $a \times b$ is a unique whole number.
   c. **Identity property for addition:** For any whole number b, $0 + b = b + 0 = b$, and 0 is a unique identity for addition.
   d. **Identity property for multiplication:** For any whole number b, $1 \times b = b \times 1 = b$, and 1 is a unique identity for multiplication.
   e. **Commutative property for addition:** For any whole numbers a and b, $a + b = b + a$.
   f. **Commutative property for multiplication:** For any whole numbers a and b, $a \times b = b \times a$.
   g. **Associative property for addition:** For any whole numbers a, b, and c, $a + (b + c) = (a + b) + c$.
   h. **Associative property for multiplication:** For any whole numbers a, b, and c, $a \times (b \times c) = (a \times b) \times c$.
   i. **Distributive property for multiplication over addition:** For any whole numbers a, b, and c, $a \times (b + c) = (a \times b) + (a \times c)$.

8. **Inequality of whole numbers**
   a. For any whole numbers m and n, m is **less than** n if and only if there is a nonzero whole number

k such that $m + k = n$. This property is written as $m < n$ or $n > m$.

b. The inequality symbol and the equality symbol can be combined as $\geq$, which means **greater than or equal to**, or as $\leq$, which means **less than or equal to**.

9. **Mental calculations**
   a. **Compatible numbers** is the technique of using pairs of numbers that are especially convenient for mental calculations.
   b. **Substitution** is the technique of breaking a number into a convenient sum, difference, or product.
   c. **Equal differences** is the technique of increasing or decreasing both numbers in a difference by the same amount. With such a change, the difference between the two numbers stays the same.
   d. **Adding up** is the technique of finding a difference by adding up from the smaller number to the larger number.
   e. **Equal products** is a type of substitution that uses the fact that the product of two numbers remains the same when one of the numbers is divided by a given number and the other number is multiplied by the given number.
   f. **Equal quotients** is a type of substitution that uses the fact that the quotient of two numbers

remains the same when both numbers are divided by the same number.

10. **Estimation**
    a. **Rounding** is the technique of replacing one or both numbers in a sum, difference, product, or quotient by an approximate number to obtain an estimation.
    b. **Compatible numbers** is the technique of computing estimations by replacing one or more numbers with convenient approximate numbers.
    c. **Front-end estimation** involves computing with only the leading digit of each number and is used for obtaining estimation of sums, differences, products, and quotients.

11. **Order of operations**
    a. The **order of operations** requires that when combinations of operations occur in an expression, numbers raised to a power be evaluated first, next products and quotients in the order in which they occur from left to right, then sums and differences in the order in which they occur from left to right.
    b. When parentheses are used in an expression, computations within the parentheses should be performed first.

CHAPTER TEST

1. How would 226 be written in each of the following numeration systems?
   a. Egyptian
   b. Roman
   c. Babylonian
   d. Mayan

2. Determine the value of each underlined digit and its place value.
   a. 14,702,301   b. 36,007,285

3. Round 6,281,497 to the nearest
   a. Hundred thousand   b. Hundred
   c. Thousand

4. Represent 123, using the given model.
   a. Bundle-of-sticks model   b. Base-ten pieces
   c. Base-five pieces   d. Base-seven pieces

5. Sketch base-ten pieces to illustrate each computation.
   a. 245 + 182   b. 362 − 148

6. Compute the sum, using the given method.
   a. *Left-to-right addition*   b. *Partial sums*
      483   864
     +274   +759

7. Use *equal differences* to find a replacement for each number that is more convenient for mental calculation. Show the new numbers and determine the answer.
   a. 65 − 19   b. 843 − 97

8. Use *front-end estimation* to estimate the value of each computation.
   a. 321 + 435 + 106   b. 7410 − 2563 + 4602
   c. 32 × 56   d. 3528 ÷ 713

9. Use *equal products* to find a replacement for each number that is more convenient for mental computation. Show the new numbers and determine the answer.
   a. 18 × 5   b. 25 × 28

10. Compute 43×28 by showing the partial products. Sketch a rectangular grid to illustrate the product, and draw arrows from each partial product to its corresponding region on the grid.

11. Evaluate the following expressions.
    a. $6 \times 4 \times 5 - 3$ b. $48 \div 4 + 2 \times 10$
    c. $(8 + 3) \times 5 - 2$

12. Compute the product or quotient. Leave your answer in exponential form.
    a. $3^{12} \div 3^4$ b. $7^4 \times 7^6$

13. Show how to compute $452 \div 4$ by sketching base-ten pieces and using the *sharing (partitive)* concept of division.

14. *Round* or use *compatible numbers* to mentally compute an estimation. Show your number replacements.
    a. $473 + 192$ b. $534 - 203$
    c. 993×42 d. $350 \div 49$

15. Determine whether each statement is true or false for operations on the set of whole numbers.
    a. If the differences involved are whole numbers, multiplication is distributive over subtraction.
    b. Addition is commutative.
    c. If the differences involved are whole numbers, subtraction is associative.
    d. For nonzero whole numbers, division is commutative.
    e. The set of whole numbers is closed for subtraction.

16. Find a pattern in the equations below, and use inductive reasoning to predict the right side of the third equation. Then predict the fourth equation. Evaluate both sides of the fourth equation and determine if the pattern holds for this equation.

$$3^2 + 4^2 = 5^2$$
$$10^2 + 11^2 + 12^2 = 13^2 + 14^2$$
$$21^2 + 22^2 + 23^2 + 24^2 =$$

17. There were 61 athletes at the annual sports banquet who played on either the football team or the baseball team. If 49 were on the football team and 18 were on the baseball team, how many players were on both teams?

18. If pizza is sold in four different sizes and can be ordered plain or with any one of five different toppings, how many different types of pizza are there?

NUMBER THEORY

SPOTLIGHT ON TEACHING

Excerpts from NCTM's Standard 6 for Grades 5–8*

Number theory offers many rich opportunities for explorations that are interesting, enjoyable, and useful. These explorations have payoffs in problem solving, in understanding and developing other mathematical concepts, in illustrating the beauty of mathematics, and in understanding the human aspects of the historical development of number.

Challenging but accessible problems from number theory can be easily formulated and explored by students. For example, building rectangular arrays with a set of tiles can stimulate questions about divisibility and prime, composite, square, even, and odd numbers. [See the figure below.]

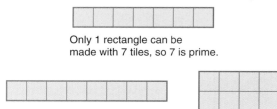

Only 1 rectangle can be
made with 7 tiles, so 7 is prime.

More than 1 rectangle can be made
with 8 tiles, so 8 is composite.

This activity and others can be extended to investigate other interesting topics, such as abundant, deficient, or perfect numbers; triangular and square numbers; cubes; palindromes; factorials; and Fibonacci numbers.

*Curriculum and Evaluation Standards for School Mathematics (Reston, VA: National Council of Teachers of Mathematics, 1989), p. 93.

MATH ACTIVITY 4.1

DIVISIBILITY WITH BASE-TEN PIECES

Materials: Base-five and base-ten pieces in the Manipulative Kit.

*1. The following diagram shows that the base-five pieces representing 143_{five} can be divided evenly into groups of 4. Each flat and long is divided into groups of 4 with 1 unit remaining (marked by arrows). The 8 remaining units $(1 + 4 + 3)$ can be evenly divided into two groups of 4.

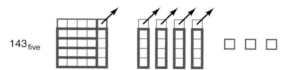

a. Explain how the diagram above illustrates the following divisibility rule: A three-digit base-five number is divisible by 4 if the sum of its digits is divisible by 4. Form an arbitrary collection of base-five pieces to illustrate your reasoning.

b. Use your base-five pieces to form the following collection. Show whether or not the divisibility rule from part a works for the four-digit number 1232_{five}. Write a general statement for determining when a base-five number is divisible by 4.

2. Form some collections of base-ten pieces and show how divisibility by 3 and 9 in base ten is similar to divisibility by 4 in base five.

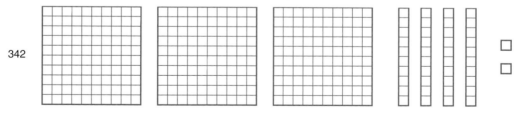

a. Based on your examples, state a rule for divisibility by 3 and a rule for divisibility by 9. Draw diagrams to support your conclusions.

b. Are all base-ten numbers which are divisible by 3 also divisible by 9, and vice versa? Explain.

3. Use your base-ten pieces to form the collection shown in activity 2. Look for an easy method of determining if these pieces can be evenly divided into four equal groups. Try your method on other collections of base-ten pieces. Show diagrams. Write a general statement describing a method for determining when a base-ten number can be divided by 4.

SECTION 4.1

FACTORS AND MULTIPLES

Fifty pennies are placed side by side. Each second penny is replaced by a nickel, each third coin is replaced by a dime, each fourth coin is replaced by a quarter, and each fifth coin is replaced by a half-dollar. What is the value of the 50 coins?

The Pythagoreans (ca. 500 B.C.), a brotherhood of mathematicians and philosophers, believed that numbers had special meanings that could account for all aspects of life. For example, the number 1 represented reason, 2 stood for opinion, 4 was symbolic of justice, and 5 represented marriage. Even numbers were considered weak and earthly, and odd numbers were viewed as strong and heavenly. The numbers 1, 2, 3, and 4 also represented fire, water, air, and earth, and the fact that $1 + 2 + 3 + 4$ equals 10 had many meanings. When only 9 heavenly bodies could be found, including the earth, sun, moon, and the sphere of stars, the Pythagoreans imagined a tenth to "balance the earth."*

*M. Kline, *Mathematics in Western Culture* (New York: Oxford University Press, 1953), p. 77.

Number theory is the study of nonzero whole numbers and their relationships. Historically, certain numbers have had special attraction. Perhaps you have a favorite number. Seven is a common favorite number; 3 is also popular. There may be historical reasons for the preference for 3. For example, in the French phrase *très bien,* which means very good, *très* is derived from the word for 3. One of the oldest superstitions is that odd numbers (1, 3, 5, 7, 9, 11, . . .) are lucky. One exception is the common fear of 13, called **triskaidekaphobia.** Often hotels will not have a floor numbered 13, and motels will not have a room 13. Is this true where you live? Some people have a particular fear of Friday the 13th. Do you know someone with triskaidekaphobia?

Models for Factors and Multiples

One important type of relationship in number theory is that between a factor and a multiple. If one number is a **factor** of a second number or divides the second (as 3 is a factor of 12), then the second number is a **multiple** of the first (as 12 is a multiple of 3).

FACTOR AND MULTIPLE   If a and b are whole numbers and $a \neq 0$, then a is a **factor of b** if and only if there is a whole number c such that $ac = b$. We can say that a **divides b** or that b **is a multiple of a.**

Let's look at two models for illustrating this relationship: the *linear model* and the *rectangular model.* Rods such as those shown in Figure 4.1 are one type of **linear model.** To determine whether one number is a factor of another, or divides another, we mark off the rod representing the second number, using a rod representing the proposed factor.

In Figure 4.1, the rod for 4 units can be marked off 8 times on the rod that represents 32 units. This shows that $8 \times 4 = 32$. So 8 and 4 are factors of 32, and 32 is a multiple of both 8 and 4.

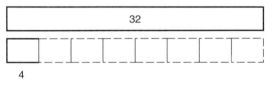

Figure 4.1   8 and 4 are factors of 32   32 is a multiple of 8 and 4

Figure 4.2 illustrates the **rectangular model.** In this model, one number is represented by a rectangular array of squares or tiles, and the two dimensions of the rectangle are factors of the number. One way to determine whether a whole number k is a factor of a whole number b is to try building a rectangular array of b tiles such that one dimension of the array is k.

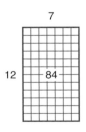

Figure 4.2   12 and 7 are factors of 84   84 is a multiple of 12 and 7

In Figure 4.2, the rectangular array of 84 tiles has 12 rows of tiles. That is, the 84 tiles are divided evenly into 12 rows, so 12 is a factor of 84. Since the 84 tiles are also divided evenly into 7 columns of tiles, 7 is also a factor of 84. Thus the two dimensions of the rectangle, 7 and 12, are factors of 84, and 84 is a multiple of both 12 and 7.

Another way of indicating 12 divides 84 (is a factor of 84) is to write 12|84, where the vertical line means *divides*.

> If a and b are whole numbers such that a **divides** b (a is a **factor** of b), we write $a|b$. If a does not divide b, we write $a \nmid b$.

Example A

To become more familiar with the *divides* relationship, classify the following statements as true or false.

1. 15|60

2. 8|30

3. 3 ∤ 19

4. 18|18

5. 2|0

Solution   **1.** True   **2.** False   **3.** True   **4.** True   **5.** True

Notice that *divides* signifies a *relationship* between two numbers; it indicates that one number is divisible by another. It does not indicate the operation of division, that is, dividing one number by another. For example, 3|15 tells us that *3 divides 15* and should not be confused with the fraction $\frac{3}{15}$, which means *3 divided by 15* and is equal to the fraction $\frac{1}{5}$.

Problem-Solving Application

The following problem is solved by using factors and multiples and features the strategies of *guessing and checking* and *making an organized list.*

PROBLEM

A factory uses machines to sort cards into piles. On one occasion a machine operator obtained the following curious result. When a box of cards was sorted into 7 equal groups, there were 6 cards left over; when the box of cards was sorted into 5 equal groups, there were 4 left over; and when it was sorted into 3 equal groups, there were 2 left. If the machine cannot sort more than 200 cards at a time, how many cards were in the box?

Understanding the Problem   Sorting the cards into groups of 7 is like dividing by 7. Since there were 6 cards left, we know 7 is not a factor of the original number of cards. **Question 1:** How can we be sure that 5 and 3 are not factors of the number of cards in the box?

Devising a Plan   One approach is to *guess and check* a few numbers to become more familiar with the problem. Even as you start to guess, you can throw out certain numbers. For example, there could not have been 100 cards, because 5 divides 100. Another approach is to find numbers satisfying one of the conditions. For example, since dividing by 7 leaves a remainder of 6, we can *make an organized list* of numbers satisfying this condition:

$$13, 20, 27, 34, 41, 48, 55, 62, 69, 76, 83, 90, 97, 104, 111, 118, \ldots$$

Then we can find the numbers in this list that leave a remainder of 4 when divided by 5 and a remainder of 2 when divided by 3. **Question 2:** What is the smallest number in this list that leaves a remainder of 4 when divided by 5?

Carrying Out the Plan   The numbers 34, 69, and 104 leave a remainder of 4 when divided by 5. **Question 3:** Which of these numbers leaves a remainder of 2 when divided by 3? The answer to this question is the solution to the original problem.

Looking Back   Another approach is to change the original problem by noticing that if there had been 1 more card in the box, then 7, 5, and 3 would have been factors of the number of cards. Once this number has been found, the number 1 can be subtracted to obtain the original number of cards. **Question 4:** What is the smallest nonzero whole number that is divisible by 7, 5, and 3?

Answers to Questions 1–4   1. When the total number of cards was divided by 5, there was a remainder of 4; and when it was divided by 3, there was a remainder of 2. If these numbers were factors, there would be no remainders.   2. 34   3. 104   4. 105

Divisibility Tests

During the gasoline shortage of 1974, Oregon adopted an "odd and even" system of gas rationing. Drivers with odd-numbered license plates could get gasoline on

the odd-numbered days of the month, and those with even-numbered plates could get gasoline on the even-numbered days. Some people whose license plate numbers ended in zero were confused as to whether their numbers were odd or even. The solution to this problem lies in the definition of odd and even numbers.

ODD AND EVEN NUMBERS   Any whole number that has 2 as a factor is called an **even number,** and any whole number that does not have 2 as a factor is called an **odd number.**

Example B

Would a person with the following license plate have purchased gasoline on the odd-numbered or even-numbered days?

Solution   On even-numbered days, because 1080 has 2 as a factor ($2 \times 540 = 1080$).

In the following paragraphs we will examine a few simple tests for determining whether a number is divisible by 2, 3, 4, 5, 6, or 9 without carrying out the division. Before looking at these tests, we present three divisibility properties.

DIVISIBILITY PROPERTIES

1. If a number divides each of two other numbers, then it divides their sum. If $a|b$ and $a|c$, then $a|(b + c)$.

2. If a number divides one of two numbers but not the other, then it will not divide their sum. If $a|b$ and $a \nmid c$, then $a \nmid (b + c)$.

3. If one number divides another number, then it will divide the product of that number with any other whole number. If $a|b$, then $a|kb$.

Figures 4.3 through 4.5 illustrate three divisibility properties. There are other divisibility properties in Exercises and Problems 4.1.

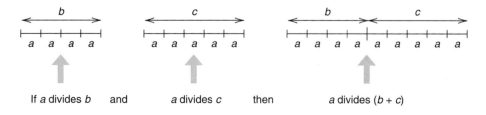

Figure 4.3

If a divides b and a divides c then a divides $(b + c)$

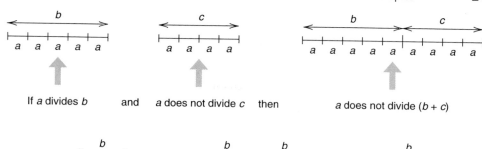

Figure 4.4   If *a* divides *b*   and   *a* does not divide *c*   then   *a* does not divide (*b* + *c*)

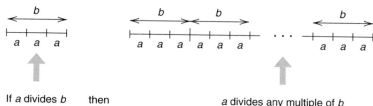

Figure 4.5   If *a* divides *b*   then   *a* divides any multiple of *b*

Example C

Here are examples of the three divisibility properties.

1. Since 6|54 and 6|48, we can conclude that 6|(54 + 48). That is, 6|102.

2. Since 7|42 but 7∤50, we can conclude that 7∤(42 + 50). That is, 7∤92.

3. Since 13|26, we can conclude that 13 divides any multiple of 26. For example, 13|(9 × 26), or 13|234.

TEST FOR DIVISIBILITY BY 2 OR 5   A number is divisible by 2 if the number represented by the units digit is divisible by 2. This means that a number is divisible by 2 if its units digit is 0, 2, 4, 6, or 8. A number is divisible by 5 if the number represented by the units digit is divisible by 5. Thus, a number is divisible by 5 if its units digit is 0 or 5.

Example D

Classify each statement as true or false and explain why.

1. 2|13,776   2. 5|3135   3. 2|2461

Solution   1. True. Since 2|6, we know that 2|13,776.   2. True. Since 5|5, we know that 5|3135.   3. False. Since 2∤1, we know that 2∤2461.

Let's look at a base-ten representation of 2573 to see why these tests work. Figure 4.6 shows that each long-flat, flat, and long can be divided into two equal parts (see dotted lines). So whether 2 divides 2573 depends on whether 2 divides 3. Since 3 units cannot be divided into two equal groups of units, 2 does not divide 2573.

Similarly, we can use Figure 4.6 to see that 2573 is not divisible by 5. Think about how you would divide each long-flat, flat, and long into 5 equal parts. Since 3 units cannot be divided into 5 equal groups of units, 5 does not divide 2573.

Now we will consider the same example, using the divisibility properties which were illustrated in Figures 4.3 to 4.5. The expanded form of 2573 is

$$2573 = \underbrace{2 \times 10^3 + 5 \times 10^2 + 7 \times 10}_{} + 3$$

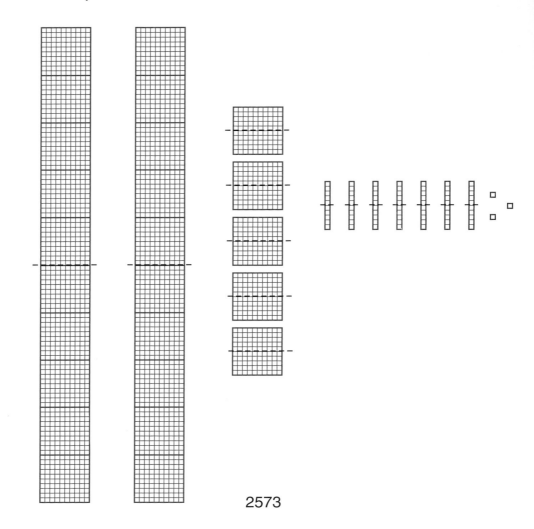

Figure 4.6

2573

Since 2 divides 10^3, by divisibility property 3 it also divides any multiple of 10^3 and, in particular, it divides 2×10^3. Similarly, since 2 divides 10^2 and 10, it also divides 5×10^2 and 7×10. Then, by divisibility property 1, 2 divides the sum of these numbers, which is the portion of the preceding equation indicated by the brace. Therefore, by divisibility property 1, 2 will divide the right side of the equation if 2 divides 3; by divisibility property 2, if 2 does not divide 3, it will not divide the right side of the equation. Since 2 does not divide 3, it does not divide 2573. Similarly, since 5 divides 10^3, 10^2, and 10, it divides the portion of the equation indicated by the brace. However, since 5 does not divide 3, it does not divide 2573. A general proof of the divisibility tests for 2 or 5 for any arbitrary whole number follows the same reasoning.

TEST FOR DIVISIBILITY BY 3 OR 9   A number is divisible by 3 if the sum of its digits is divisible by 3. Similarly, a number is divisible by 9 if the sum of its digits is divisible by 9.

Example E

Classify each statement as true or false, and explain why.

1. 3|2847   **2.** 9|147,389   **3.** 3|270,415

Solution   **1.** True, because 3 divides 2 + 8 + 4 + 7 = 21.   **2.** False, because 9 does not divide 1 + 4 + 7 + 3 + 8 + 9 = 32.   **3.** False, because 3 does not divide 2 + 7 + 0 + 4 + 1 + 5 = 19.

To visualize why the tests for divisibility by 3 and 9 work, consider the base-ten piece representation for 2847 in Figure 4.7. If 1 unit is removed from a long-flat, the remaining 999 units can be divided into 3 equal groups. Similarly, if 1 unit is removed from each flat, the remaining 99 units can be divided into 3 equal groups; and if 1 unit is removed from each long, the remaining 9 units can be divided into 3 equal groups. Thus, whether 3 divides 2847 depends on whether 3 divides the remaining units, which consist of 2 units from the long-flats, 8 from the flats, 4 from the longs, and 7 from the units. Since 3 divides 2 + 8 + 4 + 7 = 21, it also divides 2847.

Tasks, such as the following, involving factors, multiples, prime numbers, and divisibility can afford opportunities for problem solving and reasoning: (1) Explain why the sum of the digits of any multiple of 3 is itself divisible by 3; and (2) A number of the form *abcabc* always has several prime-number factors. Which prime numbers are always factors of a number of this form? Why?

Standards 2000, p. 217

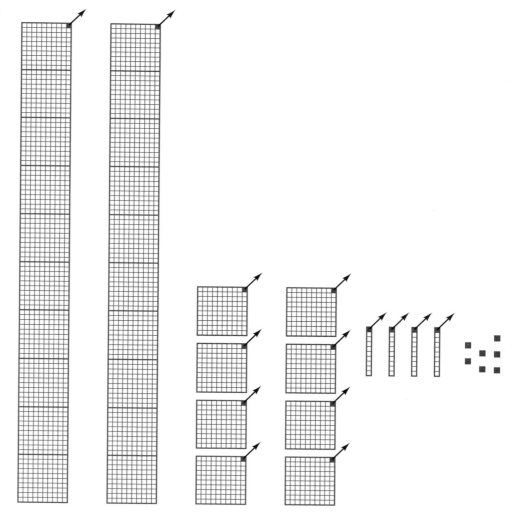

Figure 4.7

Figure 4.7 shows why 2847 is not divisible by 9. Once a unit piece is removed from each long-flat, flat, and long, 9 will divide the remaining number of units in each of these base-ten pieces. Thus, whether 9 divides 2847 depends on whether 9 divides $2 + 8 + 4 + 7$. Since 9 does not divide 21, we can conclude that 9 does not divide 2847.

Let's examine the divisibility tests for 3 and 9 on 2847 by using the divisibility properties from Figures 4.3 to 4.5. The expanded form of 2847 is shown below. Notice the use of the distributive property to obtain the third equation from the second equation. The commutative and associative properties for addition are also needed to obtain the arrangement of numbers in the third equation.

$$2847 = 2 \times 10^3 + 8 \times 10^2 + 4 \times 10 + 7$$
$$= 2 \times (999 + 1) + 8 \times (99 + 1) + 4 \times (9 + 1) + 7$$
$$= \underbrace{2 \times 999 + 8 \times 99 + 4 \times 9} + (2 + 8 + 4 + 7)$$

Since 3 divides 9, 99, and 999, by divisibility properties 3 and 1 it also divides the portion of the equation indicated by the brace. Therefore, because of divisibility properties 1 and 2, to determine if 2847 is divisible by 3, it is necessary only to determine if the remaining portion of the equation containing the sum $2 + 8 + 4 + 7$ is divisible by 3. Since 3 does divide this sum, we know that 3 divides 2847.

The expanded form of 2847 in the preceding equation also shows why a similar test works for divisibility by 9. Since 9 divides the portion of the equation indicated by the brace, it will divide 2847 if and only if it divides $2 + 8 + 4 + 7$. In this case, 9 does not divide this sum, so it does not divide 2847. A general proof of the divisibility tests for 3 or 9 for any arbitrary whole number follows essentially the same reasoning.

TEST FOR DIVISIBILITY BY 6   If a number is divisible by both 2 and 3, then it is divisible by 6. If it is not divisible by both 2 and 3, then it is not divisible by 6.

Example F

Apply the preceding test to determine which of the following numbers are divisible by 6.

1. 561,781   **2.** 2,100,000,472   **3.** 123,090,534

Solution   1. 561,781 is not divisible by 2 (because it is odd), so it is not divisible by 6. 2. 2,100,000,472 is not divisible by 3 (because the sum of its digits is 16), so it is not divisible by 6. 3. 123,090,534 is even and divisible by 3, so it is divisible by 6.

TEST FOR DIVISIBILITY BY 4   If the number represented by the last two digits of a number is divisible by 4, then the original number will be divisible by 4.

Example G

Use the above test to determine which of the following numbers are divisible by 4.

1. 65,932   **2.** 476,025,314   **3.** 113,775,920

Solution   1. $4|65{,}932$ because $4|32$ 2. $4\nmid476{,}025{,}314$ because $4\nmid14$ 3. $4|113{,}775{,}920$ because $4|20$

The following expanded form shows why the test for divisibility by 4 works for 65,932.

$$65{,}932 = \underbrace{6 \times 10^4 + 5 \times 10^3 + 9 \times 10^2} + 3 \times 10 + 2$$

Since 4 is a factor of 10^4, 10^3, and 10^2, by divisibility properties 3 and 1 it will divide the portion of the expanded form indicated by the brace. Thus whether 4 divides 65,932 depends only on whether 4 divides 32. Similar reasoning can be used to prove the test for divisibility by 4 for any arbitrary whole number. (There are questions in Exercises and Problems 4.1 requiring the use of base-ten pieces to illustrate the divisibility-by-4 test.)

Prime and Composite Numbers

NCTM's K–4 standard on number operations recommends that terms such as *factor* and *multiple* be introduced informally:

The notions of factors and multiples can prompt interesting explorations. Children can find the factors of a number using tiles or graph paper. This can lead to an investigation of numbers that have only two factors (prime numbers) and numbers with two equal factors (square numbers).*

Research Statement

Mathematics achievement is increased through the long-term use of concrete instructional materials and students' attitudes toward mathematics are improved when they have instruction with concrete materials provided by teachers knowledgeable about their use.

Sowell 1989

One way to classify whole numbers is to examine their factors. It is possible to find all factors of a number by building rectangular arrays. Figure 4.8 shows rectangular arrays for 16 and 30 by increasing widths. What observations and conjectures can be made from these rectangles?

Here are a few observations: (1) The factors of the numbers occur in pairs (two for each rectangle) except when a number has a square array, as in the case of 16. (2) The numbers 1, 2, 4, 8, and 16 are factors of 16; and 1, 2, 3, 5, 6, 10, 15, and 30 are factors of 30. (3) There is a duplication of rectangles for the number 16 after a width of 4 is reached for the 4×4 square array. There is a duplication for the number 30 after a width of 5 is reached for the 5×6 array.

Figure 4.8 suggests that square arrays, or rectangles which are close to square arrays, are the turning point about which further rectangles have dimensions (or factors) that repeat. To find the factors of 16, we need to consider only arrays with widths up to 4 because 4 is the width of the square array. For the number 30, we know we have passed the turning point for finding its factors when we get to the width of 6 because the second factor must be less than 6 if the product of the two factors is to be 30.

Consider the preceding observations for finding the factors of 188. We first notice that 188 is not a square number because $13 \times 13 = 169$ and $14 \times 14 = 196$. Thus all rectangles for 188 will have at least one dimension (factor) less than 14. Systematically checking arrays with widths less than 14, we find rectangular arrays with these dimensions: 1×188, 2×94, and 4×47. So the factors of 188 are 1, 2, 4, 47, 94, and 188.

Curriculum and Evaluation Standards for School Mathematics (Reston, VA: National Council of Teachers of Mathematics, 1989), p. 42.

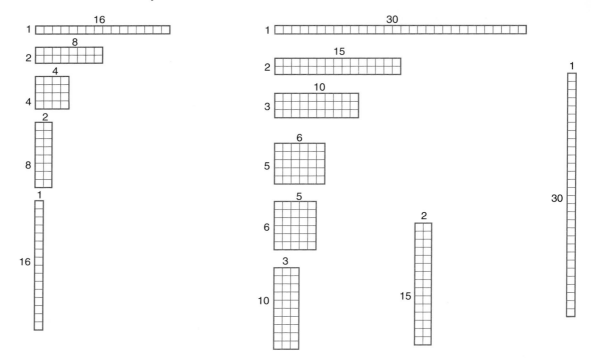

Figure 4.8

Figure 4.9 shows the arrays for 11 and 10. There is only one array for 11, and its factors are 1 and 11. There are two arrays for 10, and its factors are 2, 5, 1, and 10.

Figure 4.9

Arrays can also be sketched for the numbers from 1 to 9. The table in Figure 4.10 lists the factors for the numbers from 1 to 12. Notice that the numbers 2, 3, 5, 7, and 11 have exactly two factors. These numbers are called **prime numbers.** Nonzero whole numbers with more than two factors are called **composite numbers.** Since 1 has only one factor, it is classified as *neither prime nor composite.*

Students should recognize that different types of numbers have particular characteristics; for example square numbers have an odd number of factors and prime numbers have only two factors.

Standards 2000, p. 151

Figure 4.10

NO.	FACTORS	NO. OF FACTORS (DIVISORS)
1	1	1
2	1, 2	2
3	1, 3	2
4	1, 2, 4	3
5	1, 5	2
6	1, 2, 3, 6	4
7	1, 7	2
8	1, 2, 4, 8	4
9	1, 3, 9	3
10	1, 2, 5, 10	4
11	1, 11	2
12	1, 2, 3, 4, 6, 12	6

Example H

The table in Figure 4.10 suggests some questions.

1. Will there be numbers other than 1 with only one factor?

2. What kinds of numbers have an odd number of factors?

3. Are there numbers with more than six factors?

Solution 1. No 2. Square numbers. For a square number, there will be a square array, which contributes only one factor. So for a square number, the total number of factors will always be odd. 3. Yes. Any number of factors is possible.

Example I

List the numbers from 13 to 20, and determine whether they are prime or composite.

Solution The numbers 13, 17, and 19 are prime (each can be represented by only one rectangular array), and 14, 15, 16, 18, and 20 are composite (each has two or more rectangular arrays).

There is no largest prime because there are an infinite number of prime numbers. Some very large primes have been discovered. From 1876 to 1951, this 39-digit number was the largest known prime:

$$170,141,183,460,469,231,731,687,303,715,884,105,727$$

Now computers make it possible to find a larger prime every few months. In November 2001, for example, the team of Michael Cameron, George Woltman, Scott Kurowski, et al. discovered a prime number with over 4 million digits.*

Prime numbers are difficult to locate because they do not occur in predictable patterns. In fact, there are arbitrarily large stretches of consecutive whole numbers that include no primes. For example, between the numbers 396,733 and 396,833 there are 99 composite numbers.

HISTORICAL HIGHLIGHT

Knowing the factors of numbers has long been valuable in research involving prime numbers. In 1659 J. H. Rahn published a table listing the factors for all numbers up to 24,000, and in 1668 John Pell of England extended this table to 100,000. The greatest achievement of this sort is the table by J. P. Kulik (1773–1863) from the University of Prague. His table covers all numbers up to 100,000,000.* Finding the factors of numbers is currently of major interest to cryptographers and intelligence agencies, whose code solutions are often based on the prime factors of very large whole numbers.

*H. W. Eves, *An Introduction to the History of Mathematics*, 3d ed. (New York: Holt, Rinehart and Winston, 1969), p. 149.

Prime Number Test

One method of determining if a number is prime is to check whether it has any factors other than itself and 1. This is where the divisibility tests can be useful.

*For updated information on the largest prime numbers use the URL: http://www.utm.edu/research/prime/largest.html.

Objective: Determine whether a number is prime or composite. Express composite numbers as a product of primes.

Explore Primes and Composites

Math Words

prime number
composite number
prime factorization
factor tree

Learn

You can use counters to explore which numbers are prime and which are composite.

Work Together

You Will Need
• counters

▶ Use counters to model each number.

▶ Arrange the counters in as many ways as possible. Record the dimensions of each arrangement.

▶ Copy and complete the table.

Here are the arrangements for 12 counters.

▶ Continue the activity for 2–11 counters.

Number of Counters	Dimension of Arrangements	Number of Counters	Dimension of Arrangements
2		7	
3		8	
4		9	
5		10	
6		11	

Example J

Which of the following numbers are prime?

1. 43,101   2. 24,638   3. 53

Solution   1. Since $3|(4 + 3 + 1 + 0 + 1)$, we know that $3|43,101$, so this number is not prime. 2. Since $2|8$, we know that $2|24,638$, so this number is not prime.   3. 53 is prime.

To determine if a number has factors other than itself and 1, we need only try dividing by prime numbers (2, 3, 5, 7, . . .). There is no need to divide by composite numbers (4, 6, 8, 9, . . .). For example, if 4 divides a number, then 2 divides the number. In other words, if 2 does not divide a number, then 4 will not divide the number.

Let's consider how we might determine whether 53 is a prime number. The divisibility tests show that 53 is not divisible by 2, 3, or 5, and we know from basic multiplication facts that 7 is not a factor of 53. This means that rectangles whose dimensions are 2, 3, 5, or 7 cannot be built with 53 tiles. Now by the observations from Figure 4.8, we need to consider only arrays up to 8×8, since this is the first square array that has more than 53 tiles. Since there are no arrays for 53 with widths less than 8, 53 is a prime number. This example suggests the following theorem.

> **PRIME NUMBER TEST**   Suppose n is a whole number and k is the smallest whole number such that $k \times k$ is greater than n. If there is no prime number less than k that is a factor of n, then n is a prime number.

This theorem tells us which primes we should try as divisors to determine if a number is prime or composite.

Example K

1. Is 421 prime or composite?   2. Is 667 a prime number?

Solution   1. Since $23 \times 23 > 421$ and $19 \times 19 < 421$, we need only consider 2, 3, 5, 7, 11, 13, 17, and 19 as possible factors of 421. Since none of these primes are factors, 421 is a prime number. 2. No, it is divisible by 23.

Sieve of Eratosthenes

One way of finding all the primes that are less than a given number is to eliminate those numbers that are not prime. This method was first used by the Greek mathematician Eratosthenes (ca. 230 B.C.) and is called the **sieve of Eratosthenes.** Figure 4.11 illustrates the use of this method to find the primes that are less than 120.

We begin the process by crossing out 1, which is not a prime, and then circling 2 and crossing out all the remaining multiples of 2 (4, 6, 8, 10, . . .). Then 3 is circled and all the remaining multiples of 3 are crossed out (6, 9, 12, . . .). This process is continued by circling 5 and 7 and crossing out their multiples. Since every composite number less than 120 must have at least one prime factor less than 11 ($11 \times 11 = 121$), it is unnecessary to cross out the multiples of primes greater than 7. The numbers in the table that are not crossed out are prime.

1	②	③	4̶	⑤	6̶	⑦	8̶	9̶	1̶0̶
11	1̶2̶	13	1̶4̶	1̶5̶	1̶6̶	17	1̶8̶	19	2̶0̶
2̶1̶	2̶2̶	23	2̶4̶	2̶5̶	2̶6̶	2̶7̶	2̶8̶	29	3̶0̶
31	3̶2̶	3̶3̶	3̶4̶	3̶5̶	3̶6̶	37	3̶8̶	3̶9̶	4̶0̶
41	4̶2̶	43	4̶4̶	4̶5̶	4̶6̶	47	4̶8̶	4̶9̶	5̶0̶
5̶1̶	5̶2̶	53	5̶4̶	5̶5̶	5̶6̶	5̶7̶	5̶8̶	59	6̶0̶
61	6̶2̶	6̶3̶	6̶4̶	6̶5̶	6̶6̶	67	6̶8̶	6̶9̶	7̶0̶
71	7̶2̶	73	7̶4̶	7̶5̶	7̶6̶	7̶7̶	7̶8̶	79	8̶0̶
8̶1̶	8̶2̶	83	8̶4̶	8̶5̶	8̶6̶	8̶7̶	8̶8̶	89	9̶0̶
9̶1̶	9̶2̶	9̶3̶	9̶4̶	9̶5̶	9̶6̶	97	9̶8̶	9̶9̶	100
101	1̶0̶2̶	103	1̶0̶4̶	1̶0̶5̶	1̶0̶6̶	107	1̶0̶8̶	109	1̶1̶0̶
1̶1̶1̶	1̶1̶2̶	113	1̶1̶4̶	1̶1̶5̶	1̶1̶6̶	1̶1̶7̶	1̶1̶8̶	1̶1̶9̶	120
121	122	123	124	125	126	127	128	129	130

Figure 4.11

Example L

Examine the locations of the primes in Figure 4.11.

1. What patterns can you see?

2. What is the longest sequence of consecutive numbers that are not prime?

Solution   1. Several primes occur in pairs, with one composite number between them: 3 and 5, 5 and 7, and 11 and 13 are the first few such pairs, and 107 and 109 are the largest such pair in this table. Such primes are called **twin primes.** You might also notice that except for 2 and 5, all the primes occur in columns 1, 3, 7, and 9.   **2.** There are two sequences of seven consecutive numbers that are not prime; the first sequence is the numbers from 90 to 96, and the second sequence is the numbers from 114 to 120. *

---

*The computer program Frequency of Primes on the *Mathematics Investigator* software (see website) prints the prime numbers between two numbers that are entered and counts the number of primes in the interval. There is also an option for printing twin primes.

PUZZLER

EXERCISES AND PROBLEMS 4.1

Use the following information in exercises 1 and 2. Some skyscrapers have double-deck elevators to minimize the number of elevator shafts required. People entering the building use the bottom deck of the elevator to arrive at odd-numbered floors, or they may take an escalator to and from a mezzanine to use the top deck of the elevator, which stops at even-numbered floors.

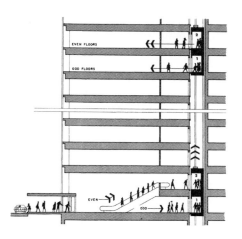

1. a. Suppose you had to deliver packages to floors 11, 26, 35, and 48. How could you do so with the least amount of elevator riding and walking only one flight of stairs?

   b. Describe an efficient scheme for delivering to the 11 floors from 20 to 30.

2. a. Suppose the escalator was not operating and you had to deliver to floors 32, 19, 47, 28, and 50. How could this be done with the least amount of elevator riding and walking only two flights of stairs?

   b. Describe an efficient scheme for delivering to any number of odd- and even-numbered floors if the escalator is working.

Classify each of the statements in exercises 3 and 4 as true or false.

3. a. $3 \mid 4263$
   b. $15 \mid 1670$
   c. $12 \nmid 84$

4. a. $5 \nmid 49$
   b. $1 \nmid 17$
   c. $13 \mid 315$

There are several ways of expressing in words the relationship between two numbers when one divides the other. Rewrite each statement in exercises 5 and 6 in the form $a|b$, using the *divides* relationship.

5. **a.** 7 is a factor of 63.
   b. 40 is a multiple of 8.
   c. 13 is a divisor of 39.
   d. 36 is divisible by 12.

6. **a.** 322 is divisible by 23.
   b. 13 is a divisor of 403.
   c. 30,000 is a multiple of 3000.
   d. 34 is a factor of 6324.

In exercises 7 and 8, illustrate statement **a** with a linear model and statement **b** with a rectangular model.

7. **a.** $6|54$ **b.** $12|60$

8. **a.** $7|42$ **b.** $43|516$

Color rods such as the Cuisenaire Rods shown below are often found in elementary schools.* They may be used as linear models to illustrate the concepts of factors and multiples.

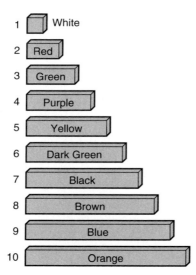

A row in which all the rods are the same is called a **one-color train**. Here is a red one-color train representing 12. Use this model in exercises 9 and 10.

---

*Cuisenaire Rods is a registered trademark of Cuisenaire Company of America, Inc.

9. **a.** What other Cuisenaire Rods can be used to form a one-color train for 12? What information do these trains provide for the number 12?
   b. What one-color trains can be used to represent 15? What information is illustrated by these trains?
   c. How many different one-color trains of two or more rods will there be for each of the numbers 2, 3, 5, and 7? What information does this illustrate for prime numbers?

10. **a.** If an all-brown train is equal in length to an all-orange train, what can be said about the number of brown rods?
    b. If a number can be represented by an all-red train, an all-green train, and an all-black train, it has at least eight factors. Name these factors.
    c. What is the smallest number of red rods for which an all-red train is equal in length to an all-blue train?

Each rectangular array of squares (see Figures 4.8 and 4.9) gives information about the number of factors of a number. Two rectangles can be formed for the number 6, showing that 6 has factors of 2, 3, 1, and 6.

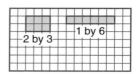

Copy the rectangular grid from the inside cover or the website and use it to sketch as many different rectangular (including square) arrays as possible for each of the following numbers: 15, 16, 30, 25, 17. Use these arrays for exercises 11 and 12.

11. **a.** What kinds of numbers will have only one rectangular array?
    b. Which three of the given numbers have an even number of factors? Use your sketches to explain why.
    c. If a number does not have a square array, explain why its factors will occur in pairs.
    d. If a number has eight factors, how many different arrays will it have? Find the smallest such number.

12. **a.** Two of the given numbers have square arrays. Make a conjecture about the number of factors for square numbers. Explain how your sketches support your conjecture.
    b. What kind of a number will have five factors? Find the smallest such number.
    c. If any nonsquare number has four different rectangular arrays, how many factors does it have?

Which of the numbers in exercises 13 and 14 are divisible by 3? Determine the remainder when the number is divided by 3.

13. a. 465,076,800   **b.** 100,101,000

14. a. 907,116,341   **b.** 477,098,304

Which numbers in exercises 15 and 16 are divisible by 9? Determine the remainder when the number is divided by 9.

15. a. 48,276,348,114
 b. 206,347,166,489

16. a. 2,136,479,180,022
 b. 7,302,511,648,591

Explain your reasoning or give a counterexample to answer each question in exercises 17 and 18.

17. a. If a number is divisible by 3, is it divisible by 9?
 b. If a number is divisible by 9, is it divisible by 3?

18. a. If a number is divisible by 12, is it divisible by 6?
 b. If a number is divisible by 6, is it divisible by 12?

Which of the numbers in exercises 19 and 20 are divisible by 4? Determine the remainder when the number is divided by 4.

19. a. 47,382,729,162
 b. 512,112,911,576

20. a. 14,710,816,558
 b. 4,328,104,292

21. Sketch base-ten pieces for a four-digit number, and explain how they can be used to illustrate the divisibility-by-4 test.

22. Sketch base-ten pieces for a four-digit number that is not divisible by 4, and explain how the divisibility-by-4 test can be used to obtain the remainder when dividing by 4.

Write each statement in 23 and 24 in words, and classify it as true or false. If the statement is true, show a sketch to illustrate the divisibility property. (See illustrations of divisibility properties on pages 214–215.) If the statement is false, show a counterexample.

23. a. If $a|b$ and $a \nmid c$, then $a \nmid (b - c)$
 b. If $a \nmid b$ and $a \nmid c$, then $a \nmid (b + c)$.
 c. If $a|b$ and $b|c$, then $a|c$.

24. a. If $a|c$ and $b|c$, then $(a + b)|c$.
 b. If $a|b$ and $a \nmid c$, then $a \nmid bc$.
 c. If $a|b$ and $a|c$, then $a|(b - c)$.

25. The numbers 2, 3, 5, 7, 11, and 13 are not factors of 173. Explain why it is possible to conclude that 173 is prime without checking for more prime factors.

26. The first 10 prime numbers are 2, 3, 5, 7, 11, 13, 17, 19, 23, and 29.
 a. Which of these prime numbers would you have to consider as possible factors of 367 in order to determine whether 367 is a prime or composite number?
 b. Is 367 prime or composite?

Which of the numbers in exercises 27 and 28 are prime?

27. a. 231   **b.** 277   **c.** 683

28. a. 187   **b.** 431   **c.** 391

Suppose Figure 4.11 was extended for answering questions 29 and 30.

29. Explain how the sieve of Eratosthenes can be used to determine all the prime numbers less than 300.

30. Explain how the sieve of Eratosthenes can be used to determine all the primes less than 400.

In exercises 31 and 32, test each number for divisibility by 11 by alternately adding and subtracting the digits from right to left, beginning with the units digit—that is, units digit minus tens digit plus hundreds digit, etc. If the result is divisible by 11, then the original number will be divisible by 11. (*Note:* Zero is divisible by 11.)

31. a. 63,011,454
 b. 19,321,488
 c. 4,209,909,682
 d. Will the test for divisibility by 11 work if the digits are alternately added and subtracted from left to right?

32. a. 9,874,684,259
 b. 8,418,470,316
 c. 7,197,183,232
 d. Sketch base-ten pieces for 739, and explain how they can be used to illustrate the divisibility-by-11 test.

33. The numbers in the following sequence increase by 2, then by 4, then by 6, etc. Continue this sequence until you reach the first number that is not a prime.

$$17 \quad 19 \quad 23 \quad 29 \quad 37$$

It is likely that no one will ever find a formula that will give all the primes less than an arbitrary number. The formulas in exercises 34 and 35 produce primes for awhile, but eventually they produce composite numbers.

34. For which of the whole numbers $n = 2$ to 7 is $2^n - 1$ a prime?

35. The formula $n^2 - n + 41$ will give primes for $n = 1$, 2, 3, . . . , 40 but not for $n = 41$. Which of the primes less than 100 are given by this formula?

Two of the many conjectures involving primes are given in exercises 36 and 37.

36. The mathematician Christian Goldbach (1690–1764) conjectured that every odd number greater than 5 is the sum of three primes. Verify this conjecture for the following numbers: 21, 27, 31.

37. In 1845 the French mathematician Bertrand conjectured that between any whole number greater than 1 and its double there exists at least one prime. After 50 years this conjecture was proved true by the Russian mathematician Pafnuty Chebyshev. For the numbers greater than 5 and less than 15, is it true or false that there are at least two primes between every number and its double?

REASONING AND PROBLEM SOLVING

38. Featured Strategies: Using a Model, Making a Table, and Solving a Simpler Problem. In a new school built for 1000 students, there were 1000 lockers that were all closed. As the students entered the school, they decided on the following plan. The first student who entered the building opened all 1000 lockers. The second student closed all lockers with even numbers. The third student changed all lockers that were numbered with multiples of 3 (that is, opened those that were closed and closed those that were open). The fourth student changed all lockers numbered with multiples of 4, the fifth changed all lockers numbered with multiples of 5, etc. After 1000 students had entered the building and changed the lockers according to this pattern, which lockers were left open?

a. Understanding the Problem To better understand this problem, think about what will happen as each of the first few students enters. For example, after the first three students, will locker 6 be open or closed?

b. Devising a Plan Simplifying a problem will sometimes help you to strike on an idea for the solution. Suppose there were only 10 lockers and 10 students. We could number 10 markers to represent the lockers and turn them upside down for open and right side up for closed.

| 1 | 2 | 3 | 4 | 5 | 6 | 7 | 8 | 9 | 10 |

Or we could form a table showing the state (open or closed) of each locker after each student passes through.

LOCKERS

	1	2	3	4	5	6	7	8	9	10
Student 1	O	O	O	O	O	O	O	O	O	O
Student 2		C		C		C		C		C
Student 3										

Which of the 10 lockers would be left open after 10 students passed through?

c. Carrying Out the Plan Solving the problem for small numbers of students and lockers will help you to see a relationship between the number of each locker and whether it is left open or closed. What types of numbers will be on the lockers that are left open?

d. Looking Back How many times will a locker be changed if it is numbered with a prime number?

39. The sum of the even numbers between 31 and 501 is how much less than the sum of the odd numbers between 32 and 502?

40. If a collection of pencils is placed in rows of 4, there are 2 pencils left; if placed in rows of 5, there are 3 left; and if placed in rows of 7, there are 5 left. What is the smallest possible number of pencils in the collection?

41. From the numbers 3, 5, 6, 7, 10, 11, 12, and 13, select five numbers that produce 15,015 when multiplied together.

42. Joan's age was a factor of her grandfather's age for 6 consecutive years. What were her grandfather's ages during this time?

43. There are long sequences of consecutive whole numbers that include no primes. For example, the following five consecutive numbers are not prime. Can you see why without computing the products?

$$2 \times 3 \times 4 \times 5 \times 6 + 2$$
$$2 \times 3 \times 4 \times 5 \times 6 + 3$$
$$2 \times 3 \times 4 \times 5 \times 6 + 4$$
$$2 \times 3 \times 4 \times 5 \times 6 + 5$$
$$2 \times 3 \times 4 \times 5 \times 6 + 6$$

a. Construct a sequence of 10 consecutive whole numbers with no primes.

b. Explain how to construct a sequence of 100 consecutive whole numbers with no primes.

ONLINE LEARNING CENTER   www.mhhe.com/bennett-nelson

• Math Investigation 4.1   *Frequency of Primes*
Section-Related: • Links   • Writing/Discussion Problems   • Bibliography

MATH ACTIVITY 4.2

FACTORS AND MULTIPLES FROM TILE PATTERNS

Materials: Color tiles in the Manipulative Kit.

*1. Find a pattern in this sequence, and use your tiles to build the seventh and eighth figures.

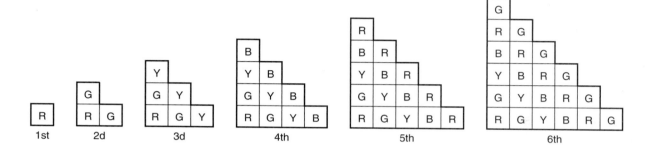

a. The diagonal edge of the fifth figure has red tiles, and the diagonal edge of the sixth figure has green tiles. Determine the color of the diagonal edge of the 20th figure and the 35th figure.

b. Describe a method for determining the color of the diagonal edge for any given figure in the sequence.

c. How many of each color of tile are required to build the 20th figure? The 35th figure? Describe your method.

2. Use your tiles to build the next figure in the following sequence.

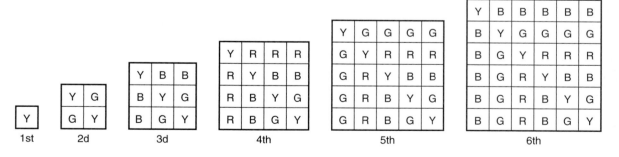

a. Look closely at the sequence, and describe at least three patterns within the figures as the squares become larger.

b. How many of each color of tile will be needed to build the 10th figure? The 13th figure?

SECTION 4.2

GREATEST COMMON DIVISOR AND LEAST COMMON MULTIPLE

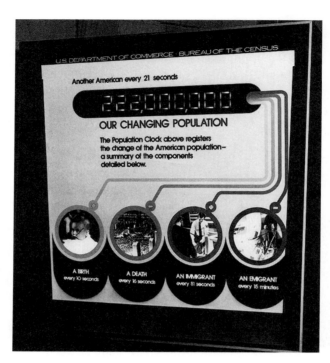

Census Clock, United States Department of Commerce Building, Washington, D.C.

One thousand raffle tickets for a school function are numbered with whole numbers from 1 to 1000. Each winning ticket has a number satisfying the following conditions: The number is even; there is one 7 in the numeral; the sum of the tens and units digits is divisible by 5; and the hundreds digit is greater than the units digit, which is greater than the tens digit. What are the numbers on the three winning tickets?

The census clock pictured above was once located in the lobby of the U.S. Department of Commerce Building and regulated by the Bureau of Census. It showed the estimated population of the United States at any given moment. Four illustrated clock faces displayed the components of population change: births, deaths, immigration, and emigration. Plus and minus signs above the clock faces lighted to indicate when one of these components changed. The clock shows a birth every 10 seconds, a death every 16 seconds, the arrival of an immigrant every 81 seconds, and the departure of an emigrant every 15 minutes.

The times when these lights flashed together can be determined by using multiples of the different time periods of the various clocks.

Example A

The plus sign above the birth clock lighted at intervals of 10 seconds, and the minus sign for the death clock lighted every 16 seconds. If these two indicators both flashed at the same time, when would they flash together again?

Solution   Using a *linear model* for multiples, we can draw a time line showing the flashing periods for each clock. The following line shows that 80 is a common multiple of 10 and 16 and that the clocks would again flash together after 80 seconds.

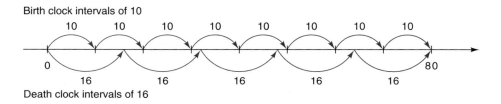

Birth clock intervals of 10

Death clock intervals of 16

The purpose of this section is to develop the mathematical theory and skills to solve problems involving *common factors* and *common multiples* of numbers. Prime factorization is one approach used to solve such problems.

Prime Factorizations

Composite numbers can always be written as a product of primes. Such a product is called the **prime factorization** of a number. For this reason, prime numbers are often referred to as the *building blocks of the whole numbers*.

Example B

Find the prime factorization of each number.

1. 30   **2.** 142   **3.** 429

Solution   **1.** $2 \times 3 \times 5$ **2.** 2×71 **3.** $3 \times 11 \times 13$

The primes in the prime factorization of a composite number are unique except for their order. For example, any prime factorization of 30 will contain the factors 2, 3, and 5, although possibly not in that order. The uniqueness of prime factors for composite numbers is stated in the following important theorem.

> **FUNDAMENTAL THEOREM OF ARITHMETIC**   Every composite whole number can be expressed as the product of primes in exactly one way (the order of the factors is disregarded).

This theorem enables us to find the prime factorization of a number by first finding any two factors of the number and then continuing, if necessary, to find the factors of these numbers. Once we have only prime factors, the fundamental theorem of arithmetic assures us that this is the only prime factorization.

Example C

Find the prime factorization of 300.

Solution   One approach is to note that 300 is even and then divide by 2: $300 = 2 \times 150$. Then since 150 is even, divide by 2 again: $300 = 2 \times 2 \times 75$. When it is no longer possible to divide by 2, try dividing by larger primes in order: 3, 5, 7, etc. In this case 3 divides 75, so $300 = 2 \times 2 \times 3 \times 25$, and from this we can see that the prime factorization is $2 \times 2 \times 3 \times 5 \times 5$.

Another approach is to replace 300 by the product of any two of its factors, not necessarily prime factors. For example, $300 = 10 \times 30$. Then each of these factors can be replaced by its factors, and so on. Since $10 = 2 \times 5$ and $30 = 3 \times 10$, we know $300 = 2 \times 5 \times 3 \times 10$. Finally, 10 can be replaced by 2×5, so

$$300 = 2 \times 5 \times 3 \times 2 \times 5 = 2^2 \times 3 \times 5^2$$

Notice that both approaches to the solution of Example C yielded the same prime factors.

Finding the prime factors of a number by first obtaining any two factors and then obtaining their factors is illustrated in Figure 4.12 with a diagram called a **factor tree**. Through a series of steps, a number is broken down into smaller and smaller factors until all the final factors are prime numbers. Three factor trees are shown, with their primes circled at the ends of the "branches."

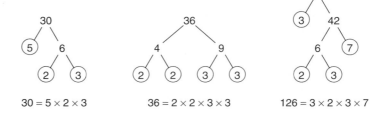

Figure 4.12

$30 = 5 \times 2 \times 3$ $36 = 2 \times 2 \times 3 \times 3$ $126 = 3 \times 2 \times 3 \times 7$

Example D

Sketch a factor tree to find the prime factors of 84.

Solution The fundamental theorem of arithmetic guarantees that the prime factorization is unique, so a factor tree can be started with any two factors of a number. In the factor tree on the left, the first two factors are 7 and 12. In the factor tree on the right, the first two factors are 2 and 42.

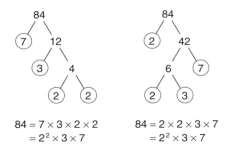

$$84 = 7 \times 3 \times 2 \times 2 \qquad 84 = 2 \times 2 \times 3 \times 7$$
$$= 2^2 \times 3 \times 7 \qquad\qquad = 2^2 \times 3 \times 7$$

Factors of Numbers

In Section 4.1 we classified numbers as *prime* or *composite* depending on their number of factors: prime numbers have only two factors, whereas composite numbers have three or more factors. We also saw that the factors of a number can be visualized by sketching rectangular arrays. The rectangles representing the factors of 24 are shown in Figure 4.13. Notice that since 24 is not a square number, each rectangle produces a pair of factors. There are four pairs and a total of eight factors.

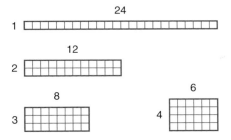

Figure 4.13

A list of *all* the factors of a number can be obtained by starting with 1 and then considering each whole number—2, 3, 4, etc.—in turn as a possible factor. For small numbers this can easily be done with mental calculations.

Example E

List all the factors of each number.

1. 20   **2.** 34

Solution   1. 1, 2, 4, 5, 10, 20   2. 1, 2, 17, 34

Notice that the solutions for Example E list *all* the factors of each number, not just the prime factors.

Another approach to finding the factors of a number is to first find its prime factorization and then use combinations of primes to find all the factors other than 1.

Example F

The prime factorization of 273 is $3 \times 7 \times 13$. List all its factors.

Solution   Since 1 is always a factor and each prime is a factor, we can begin the list with 1, 3, 7, and 13. Then we find the products of all pairs of primes: $3 \times 7 = 21$, $3 \times 13 = 39$, and $7 \times 13 = 91$. Finally, the product of all three primes $3 \times 7 \times 13 = 273$ is also a factor. So the factors of 273 are 1, 3, 7, 13, 21, 39, 91, and 273.

The fact that prime numbers can be used to obtain all the factors of a number is another reason why the prime numbers are called the building blocks of the whole numbers.*

Problem-Solving Application

The following problem can be solved by *guessing and checking* or by finding the *prime factorization* of a number. Try to solve this problem before you read the solution.

PROBLEM

The product of the ages of a group of teenagers is 10,584,000. Find the number of teenagers in the group and their ages.†

Understanding the Problem   As a first step, it is helpful to list all the possible ages. Question 1: What are these ages?

Devising a Plan   One approach is to *guess and check*. We might try dividing 10,584,000 by 13, then 14, etc. Another approach is to find the prime factorization of 10,584,000, since the prime factors can be used to build other factors. Question 2: What is the prime factorization of this number?

Carrying Out the Plan   Expressed as a product of prime factors,

$$10,584,000 = 2 \times 2 \times 2 \times 2 \times 2 \times 2 \times 3 \times 3 \times 3 \times 5 \times 5 \times 5 \times 7 \times 7$$

The ages of the teenagers can now be obtained by using combinations of these factors. Each 7 must be multiplied by 2, which means that there are two 14-year-olds, and each 5 must be multiplied by 3, which results in three 15-year-olds. Question 3: Using the remaining 2s, what is the age of the sixth teenager?

Looking Back   The original problem can be varied by changing the number of teenagers to obtain a new product of ages. The prime factors suggest ways of obtaining new products. For example, we can cross out one 7 and one 2 or two 5s and two 3s. Question 4: Why can we not change the problem by crossing out only one 3 (or one 2)?

Answers to Questions 1–4   1. 13, 14, 15, 16, 17, 18, 19   2. The prime factorization is

$$2 \times 2 \times 2 \times 2 \times 2 \times 2 \times 3 \times 3 \times 3 \times 5 \times 5 \times 5 \times 7 \times 7$$

---

*The computer program Factorizations on the *Mathematics Investigator* software (see website) tests any whole number less than 10 million to determine if it is prime or composite. If the number is composite, the computer prints the prime factorization and lists all its factors.

†"Problems of the Month," *The Mathematics Teacher* 82, no. 3 (March 1989): 189.

3. 16   4. Crossing out only one 3 would leave a factor of 5 with which no number could be paired: 5×2 and 5×7 are not in the teens. Similarly, crossing out one 2 would leave a factor of 7 with which no number could be paired.

**Sophie Germain
1776–1831**

Sophie Germain (1776–1831), a Frenchwoman who won distinction in mathematics in the 1700s, has been called one of the founders of mathematical physics. She was self-educated in mathematics and physics from reading books in her parents' library. In 1801, when Gauss published *Disquisitiones arithmeticae,* a masterpiece on the theory of numbers, Germain sent him some of the results of her own mathematical investigations. Gauss was impressed with this work, and the two entered into an extensive correspondence. In 1816, her *Memoir on the Vibrations of Elastic Plates* earned her the prize offered by the French Academy of Sciences for the best essay on the mathematical laws of elastic surfaces. Winning the grand prize of the Academy elevated Germain to the ranks of the most noted mathematicians of the world. Germain published several other works dealing with the theory of elasticity, but she is best known for her work in the theory of numbers. Here she demonstrated the impossibility of solving Fermat's last theorem (see page 231) if x, y, and z are not divisible by an odd number.*

*L. M. Osen, *Women in Mathematics* (Cambridge, MA: The MIT Press, 1974), pp. 83–93.

Greatest Common Factor

For any two numbers, there is always a number that is a factor of both. The numbers 24 and 36 both have 6 as a factor. When a number is a factor of two numbers, it is called a **common factor** or **common divisor.**

Example G

1. List all the factors of 24.

2. List all the factors of 36.

3. What are the common factors of 24 and 36?

Solution   1. The factors of 24 are 1, 2, 3, 4, 6, 8, 12, and 24.   2. The factors of 36 are 1, 2, 3, 4, 6, 9, 12, 18, and 36.   3. The common factors of 24 and 36 are 1, 2, 3, 4, 6, and 12.

Among the common factors of two numbers there will always be a largest number, which is called the **greatest common factor.** The greatest common factor of 24 and 36 is 12. This is sometimes written GCF(24, 36) = 12.

> For any two nonzero whole numbers a and b, the **greatest common factor,** written GCF(a, b), is the greatest factor (divisor) of both a and b.

The concept of common factor can be illustrated by using separate rods to represent two numbers and then cutting both rods into pieces of common length. In this model, the GCF of the two numbers is the greatest common length that can be used in the cutting. Figure 4.14 shows three possible ways of cutting rods that have lengths of 20 and 30 units. The pieces of common length have lengths of 2, 5, and 10. Since there is no greater common length, 10 is the greatest common factor of 20 and 30.

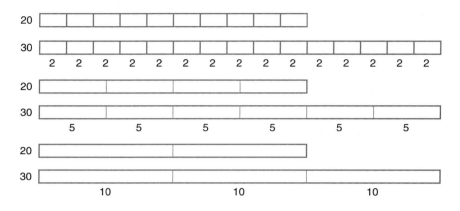

Figure 4.14

One method of finding the greatest common factor of two numbers is to list all the factors of both numbers and select the greatest one. A more convenient approach, especially for larger numbers, is to use prime factorizations. The GCF of two or more numbers can be built by using each prime factor the minimum number of times it occurs in each of the numbers.

Example H

The following factor trees for 60 and 72 show the prime factors for both numbers.

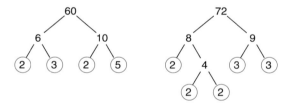

Use these prime factors to obtain GCF(60, 72).

Solution   We can see that 2 occurs as a prime factor at least twice and 3 occurs at least once in both 60 and 72. Therefore, we can use these factors to build the GCF, which is $2 \times 2 \times 3 = 12$.

Notice in Example H that 2 occurs as a factor 3 times in 72 but only twice in 60. So the greatest common factor of 60 and 72 can have 2 as a factor only twice. If 2 occurs 3 times as a factor of a number, that number will not be a factor of 60.

Example I

Find the greatest common factors.

1. GCF(180, 220)   **2.** GCF(92, 136)   **3.** GCF(14, 34, 60)

Solution   1. $180 = 2 \times 2 \times 3 \times 3 \times 5$ and $220 = 2 \times 2 \times 5 \times 11$. So GCF(180, 220) $= 2 \times 2 \times 5 = 20$, since 2 occurs as a factor twice in both 180 and 220 and 5 occurs as a factor once in both numbers.   2. $92 = 2 \times 2 \times 23$ and $136 = 2 \times 2 \times 2 \times 17$. So GCF(92, 136) $= 2 \times 2 = 4$.   3. $14 = 2 \times 7$ and $34 = 2 \times 17$ and $60 = 2 \times 2 \times 3 \times 5$. So GCF(14, 34, 60) $= 2$, since 2 is the only factor common to all three numbers.

Calculators which display fractions and have a key for simplifying fractions can be used to determine the GCF of two numbers.* Let's see how this can be done by finding the GCF of 525 and 546. The keystrokes below show this process on a calculator that has the simplification key $\boxed{\text{SIMP}}$. In the first step, 525 is entered as the numerator of a fraction and 546 as the denominator. When $\boxed{\text{SIMP}}$ is pressed the first time, the common factor 3 of 525 and 546 flashes briefly on the view screen and the fraction $\frac{525}{546}$ is replaced by $\frac{175}{182}$. When $\boxed{\text{SIMP}}$ is pressed the second time, the common factor 7 of 175 and 182 flashes on the screen and the fraction $\frac{175}{182}$ is replaced by $\frac{25}{26}$. Further pressing of $\boxed{\text{SIMP}}$ does not change $\frac{25}{26}$ because there are no common factors greater than 1 of 25 and 26. Since 3 and 7 are the only common factors greater than 1 of 525 and 546, their product, 21, is the GCF of 525 and 546.

KEYSTROKES	VIEW SCREENS
525 $\boxed{\text{b/c}}$ 546	$\frac{525}{546}$
$\boxed{\text{SIMP}}$	3 $\quad \frac{175}{182}$
$\boxed{\text{SIMP}}$	7 $\quad \frac{25}{26}$

If two whole numbers are entered into a calculator as the numerator and denominator of a fraction and the simplification key does not result in a fraction with smaller numbers, then the numbers have no common factor greater than 1. Two numbers whose GCF is 1 are **relatively prime**.

Example J

Use a fraction calculator or a factor tree to determine the GCF of each pair of numbers. Which pairs are relatively prime?

1. 245, 315 **2.** 550, 189 **3.** 232, 186 **4.** 156, 198

Solution 1. GCF(245, 315) = 35 2. GCF(550, 189) = 1, so 550 and 189 are relatively prime. 3. GCF(232, 186) = 2 4. GCF(156, 198) = 6

Fraction calculators such as those described above can be helpful in determining whether a number is prime. For example, rather than making separate checks to see if the primes 2, 3, 5, 7, or 11 are factors of 463, we can try simplifying the fraction $\frac{463}{2310}$, where 2310 is the product of 2, 3, 5, 7, and 11. The following keystrokes show that 463 and 2310 do not have a common factor greater than 1 because the $\boxed{\text{SIMP}}$ key does not replace the fraction by a fraction having smaller numbers. In particular, this shows that 2, 3, 5, 7, and 11 are not factors of 463.

463 $\boxed{\text{b/c}}$ 2310 $\boxed{=}$ $\quad \frac{463}{2310}$ $\boxed{\text{SIMP}}$ $\quad \frac{463}{2310}$

Similarly, since the product of the next three primes (13, 17, and 19) is 4199, the next step is to see if $\frac{463}{4199}$ can be replaced by a fraction having smaller numbers. The following keystrokes show that 463 and 4199 have no common factors other than 1.

*Two fraction calculators with simplification keys are the CASIO fx-55 and the TI Explorer Plus.

463 $\boxed{\text{b/c}}$ 4199 $\boxed{=}$

Since 23 × 23 is greater than 463 and there are no primes less than 23 which are factors of 463, we know that 463 is a prime.

Least Common Multiple

Every number has an infinite number of multiples. Here are the first few multiples of 5.

5   10   15   20   25   30   35   40   45   50   55   60   65   70   75

Example K

Write the first few multiples of 7.

Solution   7   14   21   28   35   42   49   56   63   70   77   84   91   98   105

A number is called a **common multiple** of two numbers if it is a multiple of both. Notice that 35 and 70 occur in both of the preceding lists, so they are common multiples of 5 and 7. The first few multiples of 5 and 7 are shown on the number line in Figure 4.15. Beginning at zero, intervals of 5 units and intervals of 7 units do not coincide again until point 35 on the number line.

Figure 4.15

The next few common multiples of 5 and 7 are 70, 105, 140, 175, and 210. Every pair of nonzero whole numbers has an infinite number of common multiples. Among these common multiples will always be a smallest number, which is called the **least common multiple**. The least common multiple of 5 and 7 is 35. This is sometimes written LCM(5, 7) = 35.

> For any two nonzero whole numbers a and b, the **least common multiple**, written LCM(a, b), is the smallest multiple of both a and b.

Figure 4.16 uses rods to illustrate the concept of least common multiple. Notice that 5 rods of length 4 are required to equal 4 rods of length 5, and that 20 is the smallest length that can be formed by rods of both sizes. The fact that the vertical lines indicating the end of each rod line up only at the left end and the right end of Figure 4.16 shows that the least common multiple of 4 and 5 is 4 × 5 = 20.

Figure 4.16

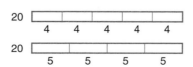

Example L

Sketch rods for the following pairs of numbers to illustrate their least common multiple.

1. 3, 10   2. 4, 14   3. 6, 18

Solution   1. LCM(3, 10) = 30

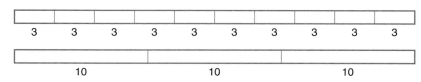

Research Statement

Because students often confuse factors and multiples, the greatest common factor and the least common multiple are difficult topics for students to grasp.

Graviss and Greaver 1992

2. LCM(4, 14) = 28

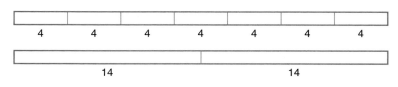

3. LCM(6, 18) = 18

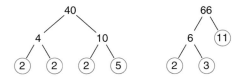

The least common multiple for small numbers can be found by listing the multiples of both numbers. We found the least common multiple of 5 and 7 by listing the first few multiples of 5 and the first few multiples of 7. Another approach, which is more convenient for large numbers, is to use prime factorizations. The LCM of two or more numbers can be built from their prime factors by using each prime factor the maximum number of times it occurs in each of the numbers.

Example M

Factor trees for 40 and 66 are shown below. Use the prime factors to find LCM(40, 66).

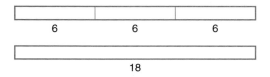

Solution   The factor trees show that 2 occurs three times as a factor of 40 and only once as a factor of 66, so 2 will have to occur three times as a factor in the LCM. Similarly, 5 is a factor of 40, and 3 and 11 are factors of 66, so these numbers will need to be included in the prime factors of the LCM. Therefore, the LCM of 40 and 66 is

$$2 \times 2 \times 2 \times 3 \times 5 \times 11 = 2^3 \times 3 \times 5 \times 11 = 1320$$

Notice in Example M that 2 occurs three times as a factor in 40 and only once as a factor in 66, but it is necessary to have 2 occur three times as a factor in the LCM of 40 and 66.

Example N

Find the least common multiples.

1. LCM(28, 44)   2. LCM(21, 40)   3. LCM(15, 36, 55)

Solution   1. $28 = 2 \times 2 \times 7$ and $44 = 2 \times 2 \times 11$, so LCM(28, 44) $= 2 \times 2 \times 7 \times 11 = 308$ 2. $21 = 3 \times 7$ and $40 = 2 \times 2 \times 2 \times 5$, so LCM(21, 40) $= 2 \times 2 \times 2 \times 3 \times 5 \times 7 = 840$ 3. $15 = 3 \times 5$, $36 = 2 \times 2 \times 3 \times 3$, and $55 = 5 \times 11$, so LCM(15, 36, 55) $= 2 \times 2 \times 3 \times 3 \times 5 \times 11 = 1980$

You may have noticed some special relationships in Example N for the LCM of two numbers. In part 1 of the example, the LCM of 28 and 44 could have been obtained by using all the factors in 28 and 44 and then dividing by the common factors of both numbers. That is,

$$\text{LCM}(28, 44) = \frac{(2 \times 2 \times 7) \times (2 \times 2 \times 11)}{2 \times 2} = \frac{28 \times 44}{\text{GCF}(28, 44)}$$

Similarly, you may have noticed in part 2 of Example N that 21 and 40 have no common prime factors—that is, they are relatively prime—so their LCM is the product of the prime factors from both numbers.

$$\text{LCM}(21, 40) = (3 \times 7) \times (2 \times 2 \times 2 \times 5) = 21 \times 40$$

These relationships are stated as a theorem for the LCM of two numbers.

For positive integers a and b,

$$\text{LCM}(a, b) = \frac{a \times b}{\text{GCF}(a, b)}$$

and when GCF(a, b) = 1,

$$\text{LCM}(a, b) = a \times b$$

Example O

Determine the least common multiples.

1. LCM(17, 20)   2. LCM(20, 33)   3. LCM(138, 84)

Solution   1. GCF(17, 20) = 1, so LCM(17, 20) $= 17 \times 20 = 340$ 2. GCF(20, 33) = 1, so LCM(20, 33) $= 20 \times 33 = 660$ 3. GCF(138, 84) = 6, so LCM(138, 84) $= (138 \times 84)/6 = 1932$

Once you have found the prime factors of two or more numbers, you may find the following schemes helpful for determining their greatest common factor and least common multiple. Notice that the common factors of 198 and 210 are placed under each other in both schemes.

$$
\begin{array}{ll}
198 = 2 \times 3 \times 3 \qquad \times 11 & \qquad 198 = 2 \times 3 \times 3 \qquad\qquad \times 11 \\
210 = 2 \times 3 \qquad \times 5 \times 7 & \qquad 210 = 2 \times 3 \qquad \times 5 \times 7 \\
\hline
\text{GCF} = 2 \times 3 & \qquad \text{LCM} = 2 \times 3 \times 3 \times 5 \times 7 \times 11
\end{array}
$$

Problem-Solving Application

The U.S. Census clock described at the beginning of this section used flashing lights to indicate birth, death, immigration, and emigration rates. If all four lights flashed at the same moment, how much time would pass before they would all flash together again?

Understanding the Problem   The birth, death, immigration, and emigration lights flashed every 10, 16, 81, and 900 seconds, respectively. It will take at least 900 seconds (15 minutes) for all four lights to flash together again, because the emigrant light flashed only every 900 seconds. **Question 1:** Which of the other lights flashed every 900 seconds?

Devising a Plan   To obtain an idea for a plan, we can look at a *simpler problem*. At the beginning of this section, a sketch was used to show multiples of 10 and 16 on a number line and to determine that the birth and death lights flashed together every 80 seconds. This suggests visualizing a number line with multiples of 10, 16, 81, and 900.

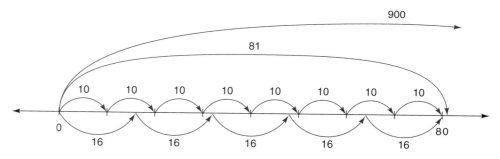

To find the first point beyond zero at which multiples of 10, 16, 81, and 900 coincide, we need to obtain the LCM of these numbers. This requires finding their prime factorizations. **Question 2:** What are the prime factorizations of 10, 16, 81, and 900?

Carrying Out the Plan   The LCM of 10, 16, 81, and 900 can be built from the prime factors of these numbers.

$$10 = 2 \times 5, 16 = 2 \times 2 \times 2 \times 2, 81 = 3 \times 3 \times 3 \times 3$$
$$900 = 2 \times 2 \times 3 \times 3 \times 5 \times 5$$

The LCM must contain 2 as a factor four times, 3 as a factor 4 times, and 5 as a factor twice. So the LCM of 10, 16, 81, and 900 is

$$2 \times 2 \times 2 \times 2 \times 3 \times 3 \times 3 \times 3 \times 5 \times 5 = 32{,}400$$

Thus every 32,400 seconds all four lights would flash together. **Question 3:** How long is this in hours?

Looking Back   The number of people born in 32,400 seconds would be 32,400 ÷ 10 = 3240. Similarly, in 32,400 seconds the number of people who die would be 32,400 ÷ 16 = 2025, the number immigrating would be 32,400 ÷ 81 = 400, and the number emigrating would be $32{,}400 \div 900 = 36$. **Question 4:** What would be the total gain in population for each 32,400 seconds (9 hours)?

Answers to Questions 1–4   **1.** The birth light, since 10 is a factor of 900   **2.** The prime factorizations are

$$10 = 2 \times 5$$
$$16 = 2 \times 2 \times 2 \times 2$$
$$81 = 3 \times 3 \times 3 \times 3$$
$$900 = 2 \times 2 \times 3 \times 3 \times 5 \times 5$$

3. 32,400 seconds is equal to 9 hours. ($32400 \div 60 = 540$ minutes, and $540 \div 60 = 9$ hours.)

4. $3240 - 2025 + 400 - 36 = 1579$ people

EXERCISES AND PROBLEMS 4.2

Find the prime factorization of each number in exercises 1 and 2.

1. a. 126   **b.** 308   **c.** 245

2. a. 663   **b.** 442   **c.** 858

Sketch a factor tree to find the prime factors of each number in exercises 3 and 4.

3. a. 400   **b.** 315   **c.** 825

4. a. 112   **b.** 385   **c.** 390

5. It has been estimated that life began on earth 1,000,000,000 (one billion) years ago. How can the Fundamental Theorem of Arithmetic be used to show that 7 is not a factor of this number?

List all the factors of each number in exercises 6 and 7.

6. a. 60   **b.** 182   **c.** 180

7. a. 500   **b.** 231   **c.** 245

List all the common factors for each pair of numbers in exercises 8 and 9.

8. a. 23, 64   **b.** 112, 84   **c.** 62, 116

9. a. 30, 40   **b.** 15, 22   **c.** 14, 56

Find the greatest common factor in exercises 10 and 11.

10. a. GCF(65, 60)
    b. GCF(8, 30)
    c. GCF(118, 7, 24)

11. a. GCF(280, 168)
    b. GCF(12, 15, 125)
    c. GCF(198, 165)

List the first five common multiples for each pair of numbers in exercises 12 and 13.

12. a. 50, 35   **b.** 14, 42   **c.** 19, 10

13. a. 4, 14   **b.** 6, 8   **c.** 12, 17

Find the least common multiple in exercises 14 and 15.

14. a. LCM(10, 40)
    b. LCM(14, 15)
    c. LCM(14, 5, 26)

15. a. LCM(22, 56)
    b. LCM(6, 38, 16)
    c. LCM(30, 42)

Determine whether the rods in exercises 16 and 17 provide information about common factors or common multiples, and explain what information is illustrated by each diagram.

16. a.

b.

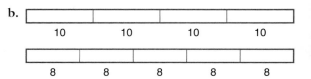

17. a.

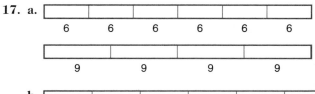

b.

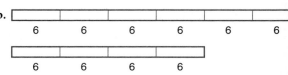

Cuisenaire Rods (see Exercises and Problems 4.1, exercises 9 and 10) are used in exercises 18 and 19 to illustrate common factors and common multiples.

18. **a.** These all-green and all-yellow trains have the same length. Do these rods provide information about common factors or common multiples? What information do they provide?

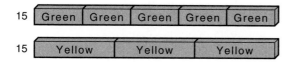

b. If the purple rods (4 units) and the black rods (7 units) are each used to form the shortest possible one-color train of matching length, how many purple rods and how many black rods will be required?

19. **a.** If the length of an all-brown train (brown rods represent 8 units) equals the length of an all-orange train (orange rods represent 10 units), what can be said about the number of brown rods?

b. If the two trains in part **a** are the shortest possible, how many brown rods will be required?

For a U.S. Census clock based on the 1990 census, the birth light would flash every 7 seconds, the death light every 15 seconds, the immigration light every 81 seconds, and the emigration light every 900 seconds, to indicate gains and losses in population.

20. **a.** If the birth and death lights flashed at the same time, how many seconds would pass before they flashed together again?

b. During the time period calculated in part **a**, what is the gain in population due to births and deaths?

c. If the immigration light and the emigration light flashed together at the same time, how many hours and minutes would pass before they would flash together again?

21. **a.** If the birth, death, and immigration lights flashed at the same time, how many seconds would pass before they flashed together again? Is this less than or greater than 1 hour?

b. For the time period in part **a**, what is the gain in population due to births, deaths, and immigration?

c. If all four lights flashed at the same time, what is the shortest time before they would all flash together again?

REASONING AND PROBLEM SOLVING

22. **Featured Strategy: Drawing Venn Diagrams** How many whole numbers from 1 to 300 are not multiples of 3 or 5?

a. Understanding the Problem The number of multiples of 3 from 1 to 9 is $9 \div 3 = 3$.

$$1 \quad 2 \quad ③ \quad 4 \quad 5 \quad ⑥ \quad 7 \quad 8 \quad ⑨$$

How many multiples of 3 are there from 1 to 300? How many multiples of 5 are there?

b. Devising a Plan Since some of the multiples of 3 are also multiples of 5, we need to consider the intersection of the set of multiples of 3 and the set of multiples of 5. How many numbers less than or equal to 300 are multiples of both 3 and 5?

c. Carrying Out the Plan The following Venn diagram helps us to visualize the information. Record the numbers of multiples in the appropriate regions of the diagram, and then determine how many numbers are not multiples of 3 or 5.

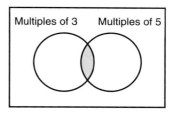

d. Looking Back The Venn diagram helps to answer other questions. How many numbers less than or equal to 300 are multiples of 3 but not multiples of 5?

23. A school principal plans to form teams from 126 third-graders, 180 fourth-graders, and 198 fifth-graders so that there is the same number of students from each grade level on each team. If all students participate, what is the largest possible size of the teams and how many teams will there be?

24. Shane has 72 inches of copper wire and 42 inches of steel wire.

a. What are the largest pieces he can cut these wires into so that each piece is the same length?

b. How many pieces of wire will he have?

25. A bakery has 300 chocolate chip cookies and 264 peanut butter cookies. The bakers wish to divide the chocolate chip cookies into piles and the peanut butter cookies into piles so that each pile has only one type of cookie, there is the same number of cookies in each pile, and each pile has the largest possible number of cookies.

a. How many cookies will there be in each pile?

b. How many piles of chocolate chip cookies will there be?

c. How many piles of peanut butter cookies will there be?

26. Janice and Bob both work night shifts. When they have the same night off, they go dancing together. If Janice has every fourth night off and Bob has every seventh night off, how often does Janice go dancing with Bob?

27. A clock shop has three cuckoo clocks on display. The cuckoos appear at different time intervals. One comes out every 10 minutes, one comes out every 15 minutes, and one comes out every 25 minutes. If they all appear at 5 o'clock, what is the next time they will all come out together?

28. For science day, a school is showing two films: one on volcanoes which is 24 minutes long and one on tornadoes which is 40 minutes long. If they both begin at 8 a.m. and run continuously until 3 p.m., at which times during the day will they both start at the same time?

29. Two sisters, Cindy and Nicole, bought a special 180-day health club membership. Cindy will use the club on every second day (days 2, 4, . . .), and Nicole will use the club on every third day (days 3, 6, . . .). If they go together on day 1, for how many of the 180 days will neither sister use the club?

30. A scientist receives signals from three quasars (distant sources of radio energy). The first quasar sends signals every 84 seconds, the second quasar every 42 seconds, and the third quasar every 30 seconds.
a. The scientist wishes to divide each of the three time intervals into the largest possible equal-size parts so that these parts are equal for all three time intervals. What is the size of these parts?
b. If all three signals are received at the same moment, what is the shortest length of time from that moment before two of the signals will again be received at the same time?

Determine the number of zeros at the right end of the numerals for the products in exercises 31 and 32.

31. $1 \times 2 \times 3 \times \cdots \times 98 \times 99 \times 100$

32. $50 \times 51 \times 52 \times \cdots \times 198 \times 199 \times 200$

The **proper factors** of a number are all its factors except the number itself. The Pythagoreans classified a number according to the sum of its proper factors. A number is **deficient** if the sum of its proper factors is less than the number, a number is **abundant** if the sum of its proper

factors is greater than the number, and a number is **perfect** if the sum of its proper factors is equal to the number.

33. a. Are there any perfect numbers less than 25? If so, what are they?
b. Among the whole numbers less than 25, are there more deficient numbers or abundant numbers?

34. a. Are there any perfect numbers between 25 and 50? If so, what are they?
b. Are there more deficient numbers or abundant numbers between 25 and 50?

Some calculators for middle school students have a SIMP key (see exercises 35 and 36), that replaces a fraction by an equal fraction having smaller numbers, if the numerator and denominator of the fraction have a common factor greater than 1. Find the missing fraction for each of the view screens. Find the GCF of the numerator and denominator of the original fraction entered into the calculator, and determine whether the pairs of numbers are relatively prime.

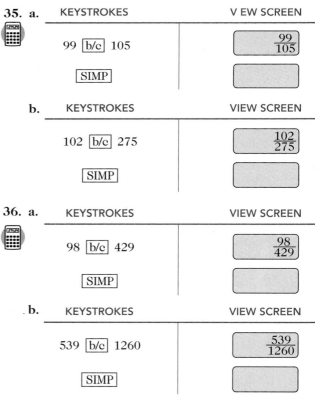

35. a.

KEYSTROKES	V EW SCREEN
99 b/c 105	$\frac{99}{105}$
SIMP	

b.

KEYSTROKES	VIEW SCREEN
102 b/c 275	$\frac{102}{275}$
SIMP	

36. a.

KEYSTROKES	VIEW SCREEN
98 b/c 429	$\frac{98}{429}$
SIMP	

b.

KEYSTROKES	VIEW SCREEN
539 b/c 1260	$\frac{539}{1260}$
SIMP	

37. Selene entered the fraction $\frac{211}{30,030}$ into a fraction calculator and pressed the SIMP key (see exercises 35 and 36). Explain why she can conclude from the following view screens that 211 is a prime number.

KEYSTROKES	VIEW SCREEN		KEYSTROKES	VIEW SCREEN
211 [b/c] 30030	$\dfrac{211}{30030}$		143 [b/c] 2310	$\dfrac{143}{2310}$
[SIMP]	$\dfrac{211}{30030}$		[SIMP]	$\dfrac{13}{210}$

38. Javier entered the fraction $\frac{143}{2310}$ into a fraction calculator and pressed the [SIMP] key (see exercises 35 and 36). Explain why he can conclude from the following view screens that 143 is *not* a prime number.

· ·

ONLINE LEARNING CENTER   www.mhhe.com/bennett-nelson

• Math Investigation 4.2   *Factorizations*
Section-Related: • Links   • Writing/Discussion Problems   • Bibliography

· ·

PUZZLER

This faded document puzzle uses only the prime digits 2, 3, 5, and 7. How can these numbers be placed in the boxes to create a valid product?

CHAPTER REVIEW

1. Number theory relationships
   a. Number theory is the study of whole numbers and their relationships.
   b. If one number is a **factor** of a second, then the second number is a **multiple** of the first.
   c. If a and b are whole numbers such that a is a factor of b, then a **divides** b, and we write $a|b$. If a does not divide b, we write $a \nmid b$.

2. Models for factors and multiples
   a. The **linear model** uses number lines or rods to represent factors and multiples.
   b. In the **rectangular array** model, a number is represented by the number of squares or tiles in an array, and the dimensions of the array are factors of the number.

3. Divisibility properties
   a. For whole numbers a, b, and c, if $a|b$ and $a|c$, then $a|(b + c)$.
   b. For whole numbers a, b, and c, if $a|b$ and $a \nmid c$, then $a \nmid (b + c)$.
   c. For whole numbers a, b, and k, if $a|b$, then $a|bk$.

4. Divisibility tests
   a. A number is **divisible by 2** if and only if its units digit is divisible by 2.
   b. A number is **divisible by 3** if and only if the sum of its digits is divisible by 3.
   c. A number is **divisible by 4** if and only if the number represented by its tens and units digits is divisible by 4.

d. A number is **divisible by 5** if and only if its units digit is divisible by 5.

e. A number is **divisible by 6** if and only if it is divisible by 2 and 3.

f. A number is **divisible by 9** if and only if the sum of its digits is divisible by 9.

g. A number is **divisible by 11** if and only if the number obtained by alternately adding and subtracting its digits is divisible by 11.

5. **Prime and composite numbers**

a. A number with exactly two factors is a **prime number.**

b. A number with more than two factors is a **composite number.**

c. The number 1 has only one factor and is neither prime nor composite.

d. The **prime number test** guarantees that for any whole number n and prime p such that $p^2 > n$, if there is no smaller prime that divides n, then n is a prime number.

e. The **sieve of Eratosthenes** is a systematic method of eliminating all the numbers less than a given number that are not prime.

f. The product that expresses a number in terms of primes is called its **prime factorization.**

g. The **Fundamental Theorem of Arithmetic** states that every composite whole number has one and only one prime factorization (if the order of the factors is disregarded).

h. A **factor tree** is a diagram for finding the prime factors of a number.

i. A list of all the factors of a number can be obtained by beginning with 1, listing the prime factors, and then multiplying combinations of the prime factors.

6. **GCF and LCM**

a. The **greatest common factor** of two nonzero whole numbers a and b, written GCF(a, b), is the greatest factor the two numbers have in common.

b. The **least common multiple** of two nonzero whole numbers a and b, written LCM(a, b), is the smallest multiple the two numbers have in common.

c. If the GCF of two nonzero whole numbers is 1, the numbers are **relatively prime.**

d. If two numbers are relatively prime, then their LCM is the product of the two numbers.

e. Number lines and rods are common **linear models** for illustrating the concepts of GCF and LCM.

CHAPTER TEST

1. Determine whether the following statements are true or false.
   a. 3|48,025
   b. 2|3776
   c. 6 ∤ 7966
   d. 9|4576

2. Rewrite each statement below in the form $a|b$.
   a. 45 is divisible by 3.
   b. 12 is a factor of 60.
   c. 20 divides 140.
   d. 102 is a multiple of 17.

3. Illustrate the fact that 78 is a multiple of 6, using:
   a. A linear model
   b. A rectangular array model

4. Rectangular arrays whose dimensions are whole numbers can be used to illustrate the factors of a number. What can be said about the number of rectangular arrays for each of the following types of numbers?
   a. Prime number
   b. Composite number
   c. Square number

5. Determine whether the following statements are true or false.
   a. If 3 divides the units digit of a number, then 3 divides the number.
   b. If a number is divisible by 8, then it is divisible by 4.
   c. If 2 divides the sum of the digits of a number, then 2 divides the number.
   d. If a number is not divisible by 6, then it is not divisible by 3.

6. Which one of the following numbers is prime?
   a. 331
   b. 351
   c. 371

7. Write the prime factorization of 1836.

8. List all the factors of 273.

9. Determine whether the following statements are true or false. If a statement is false, show a counterexample.
   a. If $a|b$, then $a|(13 \times b)$.
   b. If $a|(b + c)$, then $a|b$ or $a|c$.
   c. If $a|b$ and $a ∤ c$, then $a ∤ (b + c)$.
   d. If $a|bc$, then $a|b$.

10. List the following.
   a. Four common factors of 30 and 40
   b. Four common multiples of 15 and 20
   c. Four common factors of 195 and 255
   d. Five common multiples of 13 and 20

11. Find each GCF or LCM.
   a. GCF(17, 30)   **b.** LCM(14, 22)
   c. LCM(12, 210)   **d.** GCF(280, 165)
   e. GCF(18, 28, 36)   **f.** LCM(6, 15, 65)

12. Sketch linear models to illustrate:
   a. The least common multiple of 3 and 8
   b. The greatest common factor of 15 and 24

13. One lighthouse light flashes every 10 seconds, and a second lighthouse light flashes every 12 seconds. If they both flash at the same moment, how long will it be until they will flash together again?

14. How many whole numbers between 1 and 1000 are multiples of either 3 or 7?

15. Mike has 20 strips of wood molding that are each 70 inches long and 6 pieces that are each 28 inches long. He wants to cut all these strips so that each piece has the same length and no wood is left. What is the longest possible length that can be cut?

INTEGERS AND FRACTIONS

SPOTLIGHT ON TEACHING

Experts from NCTM's Standards for School Mathematics Grades 6–8*

In the lower grades, students should have had experience in comparing fractions between 0 and 1 in relation to such benchmarks as $0, \frac{1}{4}, \frac{1}{2}, \frac{3}{4}$, and 1. In the middle grades, students should extend this experience to tasks in which they order or compare fractions, which many students find difficult. For example, fewer than one-third of the thirteen-year-old U.S. students tested in the National Assessment of Educational Progress (NAEP) in 1988 correctly chose the largest number from $\frac{3}{4}, \frac{9}{16}, \frac{5}{8}$, and $\frac{2}{3}$ (Kouba, Carpenter, and Swafford 1989). Students' difficulties with comparison of fractions have also been documented in more recent NAEP administrations (Kouba, Zawojewski, and Strutchens 1997). Visual images of fractions as fraction strips should help many students think flexibly in comparing fractions. As shown in figure 6.2, a student might conclude that $\frac{7}{8}$ is greater than $\frac{2}{3}$ because each fraction is exactly "one piece" smaller than 1 and the missing $\frac{1}{8}$ piece is smaller than the missing $\frac{1}{3}$ piece. Students may also be helped by thinking about the relative locations of fractions and decimals on a number line.

Figure 6.2
A student's reasoning about the sizes of rational numbers

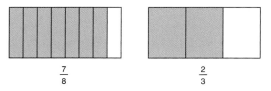

The $\frac{7}{8}$ portion is one piece less than a whole, and so is $\frac{2}{3}$. But the missing piece for $\frac{7}{8}$ is smaller than the missing piece for $\frac{2}{3}$. So $\frac{7}{8}$ is bigger than $\frac{2}{3}$.

$\frac{7}{8}$ $\frac{2}{3}$

Principles and Standards for School Mathematics (Reston, VA: National Council of Teachers of Mathematics, 2000), p. 216.

MATH ACTIVITY 5.1

ADDITION AND SUBTRACTION WITH BLACK AND RED TILES

Materials: Black and red tiles in the Manipulative Kit.

Black and red tiles are used to illustrate the integers . . . , $^-5$, $^-4$, $^-3$, $^-2$, $^-1$, 0, 1, 2, 3, 4, 5, ... Black tiles represent positive numbers, and red tiles negative numbers. Each pair of 1 black tile and 1 red tile represents 0, so each integer can be represented in many ways. The set shown at the right has 10 tiles, but the value of the set is $^-4$, since 3 black tiles can be matched with 3 red tiles.

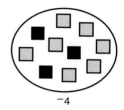

1. Select a small handful of black and red tiles, and drop them on the table. Record the numbers of black and red tiles and the value of the set.
   a. Form a second set with a different number of black and red tiles that has the same value as the original set.
   b. For each set you formed above, turn over each tile to its opposite side and determine the new value of the set. How is the value of the original set related to the value obtained by using the opposite sides of the tiles? Experiment with some other sets of tiles.

2. The sum of two integers can be computed by forming a set of tiles for each integer, combining the sets, and determining the value of the new set. The sum $^-8 + 5$ is illustrated here. Use your tiles to represent the following pairs of integers and to compute their sum. Show sketches both before and after you combine sets of tiles.

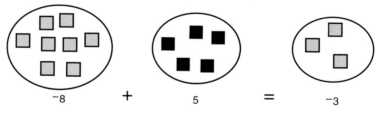

   a. $^-7 + 5$ b. $12 + {}^-9$ c. $^-7 + {}^-6$ d. $^-8 + 8$

*3. The difference of two integers can be computed by representing one of the integers by a set of tiles and using the *take-away* concept of subtraction. Use your tiles to form the set shown here, or some other set for $^-3$, and compute the following differences. Write subtraction equations for each difference.

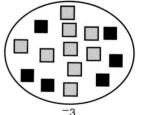

   a. $^-3 - 4$ (remove 4 black tiles)
   b. $^-3 - {}^-2$ (remove 2 red tiles)
   c. $^-3 - {}^-6$ (remove 6 red tiles)   d. $^-3 - 5$ (remove 5 black tiles)

4. Form the minimum collection of tiles to represent $^-3$. Explain how you can alter this set without changing its value, so that you can take away 2 black tiles to determine $^-3 - 2$. Use this example to show why taking away 2 black tiles is the same as adding 2 red tiles.

SECTION 5.1

INTEGERS

© Field Enterprises, Inc. 1975   6-14

PROBLEM OPENER

Keeping the single-digit numbers from 1 to 9 in order,

$$1 \quad 2 \quad 3 \quad 4 \quad 5 \quad 6 \quad 7 \quad 8 \quad 9$$

and inserting plus and/or minus signs, we can obtain a sum of 100 in several ways. For example,

$$1 + 2 + 3 - 4 + 5 + 6 + 78 + 9 = 100$$

Find another way.

The need for negative whole numbers ($^-1$, $^-2$, $^-3$, . . .) originated over 2000 years ago. As trading became more common, whole numbers were needed for two distinctly different uses: to indicate *credits* (or *gains*) and to indicate *debts* (or *losses*). Conventions were developed to permit the use of whole numbers in both cases. About 200 B.C. the Chinese were computing credits with red rods and debts with black rods (Figure 5.1). Similarly, in their writing they used red numerals and black numerals.*

Today it is customary to reverse the color scheme used by the Chinese. Banks often use red numerals to represent amounts below zero ("in the red" is negative). Black numerals are used to represent accounts above zero ("in the black" is positive). This is the convention that is used in this text.

---

*D. E. Smith, *History of Mathematics,* 2d ed. (Lexington, MA: Ginn, 1925), pp. 257–258.

Rods for computing
credits and debits

Figure 5.1

Positive and Negative Integers

Research Statement

The premature use of the number line as a representation of positive integers can lead children to develop the incorrect notion that there are no numbers between the marked points.

Dufour-Janvier, Bednarz, and Belanger 1987

When whole numbers became inadequate for the purposes of society, this number system was enlarged to include negative numbers. The whole numbers, 0, 1, 2, 3, 4, . . . , together with the negatives of the whole numbers, ⁻1, ⁻2, ⁻3, ⁻4, . . . , are called **integers.** A number line with a fixed reference point labeled 0 is a common model for visualizing the integers. The integers are assigned points on the number line that have been marked off in unit lengths to the right and left of 0. For each integer to the right of 0, there is a corresponding integer to the left of 0. These pairs of integers, 2 and ⁻2, 5 and ⁻5, 7 and ⁻7, etc., are called **opposites** or **negatives** of each other (Figure 5.2).

Sometimes the integers to the right of zero are labeled ⁺1, ⁺2, ⁺3, etc. to emphasize that they are **positive integers** as opposed to **negative integers** (⁻1, ⁻2, ⁻3, etc). Since minus signs are also used to represent *subtraction,* raising the signs to indicate negative numbers helps to avoid confusion between the two uses of these symbols.

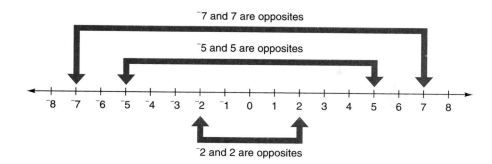

Figure 5.2

Example **A**

Determine the opposite for each integer.

1. 14   2. 0   3. 1   4. ⁻8

Solution   1. ⁻14   2. 0   3. ⁻1   4. 8

Most calculators have a change-of-sign key that can be used to obtain the opposite of the number in the view screen. For example, if 35 is in the view screen, pressing the change-of-sign key changes the number to ⁻35, and pressing the key again produces 35. Here are some of the ways this key is marked: $\boxed{+\rightleftarrows}$, $\boxed{+/-}$, and $\boxed{(-)}$.

HISTORICAL
HIGHLIGHT

Traditionally, it has taken hundreds of years for a new type of number to prove itself necessary and earn a place beside the commonly accepted older numbers. This is especially true of negative numbers. By the seventh century, Hindu mathematicians were using these numbers on a limited basis. They had symbols for negative numbers, such as ⑤ and 5̊ for ⁻5, and rules for computing with them. However, it was another 1000 years before the Italian mathematician Jerome Cardan (1501–1576) gave the first significant treatment of negative numbers. Cardan called these new numbers *false* and represented each number by writing m: in front of the numeral. For example, he wrote m:3 for ⁻3. Other writers of this period called negative numbers *absurd numbers.* The resistance to negative numbers can be seen as late as 1796, when William Frend, in his text *Principles of Algebra,* argued against their use.

Uses of Integers

The concept of number opposites in the form of positive and negative integers, also referred to as **positive and negative numbers,** is useful whenever we wish to count on both sides of a fixed point of reference. The positive integers indicate one direction, and the negative integers indicate the opposite direction.

CREDITS AND DEBTS   One common example of opposites is *credits,* which are represented by positive numbers, and *debts* or *deficits,* which are represented by negative numbers. The graph in Figure 5.3 shows the U.S. merchandise trade balance, which is the difference between exports and imports.*

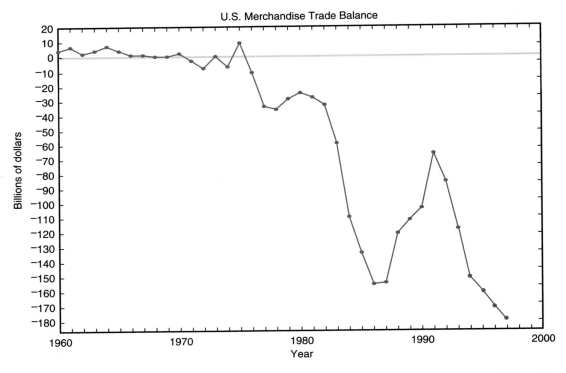

Figure 5.3

Statistical Abstract of the United States, 118th ed. (Washington, DC: Bureau of the Census, 1998), p. 801.

Example B

1. Determine whether the U.S. trade balance was positive or negative for the following periods:

   a. 1960 to 1970   b. 1976 to 1993

2. Determine whether the U.S. trade balance was increasing or decreasing for the following periods:

   a. 1980 to 1986   b. 1986 to 1991   c. 1991 to 1997

Solution   1. a. Positive   b. Negative   2. a. Decreasing   b. Increasing   c. Decreasing

TEMPERATURE   Measuring temperature is another familiar use for positive and negative numbers. The fixed reference point on the Celsius thermometer is 0, the temperature at which water freezes. On the Fahrenheit scale, water freezes at 32. On both scales, temperatures *above* zero are *positive* and those *below* zero are *negative.*

Example C

Write the integer for each of the following temperatures.

1. 10° below zero on the Celsius thermometer

2. 20° below 32° on the Fahrenheit thermometer

3. 20° below zero on the Fahrenheit thermometer

Solution   1. ⁻10° Celsius, or ⁻10°C   2. 12° Fahrenheit, or 12°F   3. ⁻20°F

SPORTS   In several sports there are special reference points from which it is convenient to measure with positive and negative numbers. In golf this reference point is *par,* and a score of ⁻4 represents four strokes *below par.* In football, the yard line at which plays begin is the reference point, and a *loss of yardage* is referred to as *negative yardage.*

TIME   Scientists often find it convenient to designate a given time as *zero time* and then refer to the *time before* and *time after* as being negative and positive, respectively. This practice is followed in the launching of rockets. If the time with respect to blastoff is ⁻15 minutes, then it is 15 minutes before the launch.

ALTITUDE   Sea level is the common reference point for measuring altitudes. Charts and maps that label altitudes below and above sea level use negative and positive numbers. The chart in Figure 5.4 uses negative numbers to show altitudes above the floor of the Atlantic Ocean between South America and Africa.

Figure 5.4

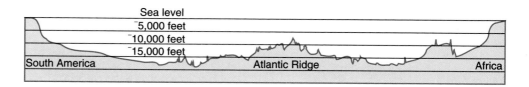

Example D

Write each altitude as an integer

1. 8500 feet below sea level

2. 300 feet above sea level

3. Sea level

Solution   1. ⁻8500 feet   2. 300 feet   3. 0 feet

Models for Integers

There are many models for illustrating integers and operations on integers. The *number line model* and the *black and red chips model* will be used on the following pages.

BLACK AND RED CHIPS MODEL   The red and black rods used by the Chinese for positive and negative integers suggest a physical model for the integers. In place of rods we will use chips, and the color scheme will be reversed; that is, black chips will represent positive integers, and red chips negative integers. By establishing that each black chip together with a red chip represents 0 (think of each black chip as a $1 credit and each red chip as a $1 debt), we can represent every integer in an infinite number of ways. Three different sets that illustrate the number 3 are shown in Figure 5.5. In part b, the red chip is canceled by 1 black chip; in part c, 2 red chips are canceled by 2 black chips.

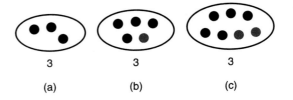

| 3 | 3 | 3 |
| (a) | (b) | (c) |

Figure 5.5

Example E

Describe four different sets of chips that represent ⁻4.

Solution   Here are four possibilities: 4 red chips; 5 red chips and 1 black chip; 6 red chips and 2 black chips; 7 red chips and 3 black chips.

Addition

Addition of integers can be illustrated by putting together (taking the union of) sets of black and red chips. Figure 5.6 shows sets for ⁻5 and 2 and their union, which contains 5 red chips and 2 black chips. The resulting set represents ⁻3, since 2 black chips can be matched with 2 red chips. This shows that ⁻5 + 2 = ⁻3.

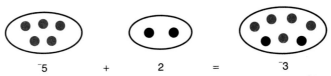

⁻5   +   2   =   ⁻3

Combining a debt of $5 with a credit of $2 reduces the debt to $3.

Figure 5.6

Example F

Sketch sets of chips to illustrate and compute $^-4 + ^-3$.

Solution

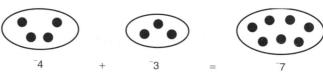

Combining a debt of $4 with a debt of $3 produces a debt of $7.

The usual rules for addition can be discovered by using black and red chips to compute sums of positive and negative integers. For example, when a positive and a negative integer are added, the sum will be positive or negative depending on whether there are more black or red chips. The rules of signs for addition are shown below. In each of the three cases, a and b represent positive integers. Notice that in each of these cases sums involving negative integers can be obtained by computing sums or differences of positive integers.

RULES OF SIGNS FOR ADDITION   Let a and b be positive integers:

1. Negative plus negative equals negative.
$$^-a + ^-b = ^-(a + b)$$
$$^-3 + ^-7 = ^-(3 + 7) = ^-10$$

2. Positive plus negative equals positive if $a > b$.
$$a + ^-b = a - b$$
$$13 + ^-5 = 13 - 5 = 8$$

3. Positive plus negative equals negative if $a < b$.
$$a + ^-b = ^-(b - a)$$
$$6 + ^-11 = ^-(11 - 6) = ^-5$$

The number line is a more abstract model for illustrating the addition of positive and negative numbers. To add two numbers, we begin by drawing an arrow from 0 to the point that corresponds to the first number. Then, if the second integer is positive, we move from that point to the right on the number line; and if it is negative, we move to the left. Two examples are shown in Figure 5.7.

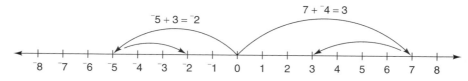

Figure 5.7

 Most calculators are designed to compute with negative as well as positive numbers. Some calculators have a key such as $\boxed{(-)}$ for entering a negative number.* To compute $^-148 + ^-315$ on such a calculator, the numbers and the addition operation are entered as they occur from left to right.

*SHARP EL-E300 and Texas Instruments' TI-80 and TI-82 have this key.

KEYSTROKES	VIEW SCREEN
(−) 148	-148
+	-148
(−) 315	-315
=	-463

Other calculators have a change-of-sign key such as $\boxed{+/-}$ or $\boxed{+\rightleftarrows -}$ to replace any number in the view screen by its opposite.* For instance, if 713 is on the view screen, pressing $\boxed{+/-}$ will display ⁻713; and if ⁻713 is on the view screen, pressing $\boxed{+/-}$ will display 713. Here is an example of the use of this key.

KEYSTROKES	VIEW SCREEN
148 +/−	-148
+	-148
315 +/−	-315
=	-463

Computational fluency should develop in tandem with understanding of the role and meaning of arithmetic operations in number systems (Hiebert et al., 1997; Thornton 1990).

Standards 2000, p. 32

Or, you may prefer to compute with positive numbers and use the *rule of signs for addition* to choose the correct sign for the sum. In particular, using the rule ⁻a + ⁻b = ⁻(a + b), you can determine ⁻715 + ⁻643 by computing 715 + 643 = 1358 and using its opposite, ⁻1358.

Subtraction

The *take-away model* can be used for subtraction of integers. Figure 5.8 illustrates ⁻6 take away ⁻2. We begin by representing ⁻6 by 6 red chips and then take away 2 red chips.

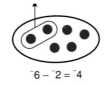

⁻6 − ⁻2 = ⁻4

Taking away a debt of $2 from a debt of $6 leaves a debt of $4.

Figure 5.8

In the early grades, the take-away model for subtraction is used only when one whole number is subtracted from a larger one. However, it is still possible to use this model in cases such as 3 − 5, where the number being subtracted is the larger one. This can be accomplished by using a suitable representation for 3. For example, instead of representing 3 by 3 black chips, as in set A of Figure 5.9, we can represent 3 by 5 black chips and 2 red chips, as in set B. Then 5 black chips can be taken away, leaving 2 red chips: 3 − 5 = ⁻2.

*CASIO fx-55 and TI Explorer Plus have this key.

change to

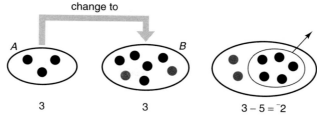

3   3   3 − 5 = ⁻2

Figure 5.9

Having a credit of $3 and taking away a credit of $5 leaves a debt of $2.

ADDING OPPOSITES   One common method of subtracting an integer is to add its opposite. If, instead of removing 5 black chips from set *B* in Figure 5.9, we put in 5 red chips, as in Figure 5.10, the final set will still represent ⁻2. In other words, *putting in 5 red chips* has the same effect as *taking away 5 black chips*. This suggests that subtracting 5 is the same as adding its opposite, ⁻5.

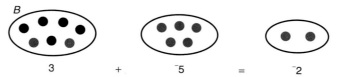

3   +   ⁻5   =   ⁻2

Figure 5.10

Having a credit of $5 taken away is like incurring a debt of $5.

This approach to subtraction is called **adding opposites**. It enables us to compute the difference of any two integers by computing a sum, as stated in the following definition.

SUBTRACTION OF INTEGERS   For any two integers a and b, $a − b$ is the sum of a plus the opposite of b,

$$a − b = a + {}^-b$$

Example G

Compute the following differences:

1. $15 − 7$ **2.** $^-14 − 3$ **3.** $22 − {}^-5$

Solution   **1.** $15 − 7 = 15 + {}^-7 = 8$ (The opposite of 7 is ⁻7.)   **2.** $^-14 − 3 = {}^-14 + {}^-3 = {}^-17$ (The opposite of 3 is ⁻3.)   **3.** $22 − {}^-5 = 22 + 5 = 27$ (The opposite of ⁻5 is 5.)

    A calculator change-of-sign key such as $\boxed{+/-}$ and $\boxed{+\rightleftarrows}$ is handy if you wish to subtract negative integers. Here are the key strokes to compute $^-243 − {}^-109$:

KEYSTROKES	VIEW SCREEN
243 $\boxed{+/-}$	-243.
$\boxed{-}$	-243.
109 $\boxed{+/-}$	-109.
$\boxed{=}$	-134.

Notice that the definition, $a - b = a + {}^-b$, allows us to replace ${}^-243 - {}^-109$ by ${}^-243 + 109$, which can be computed on a calculator by using the change-of-sign key to enter ${}^-243$ $\boxed{+}$ 109, or by commuting the numbers to compute $109 - 243$.

Multiplication

The familiar rules for multiplying with negative numbers, such as "a negative times a negative is a positive," are easy enough to remember but difficult to illustrate. There are many different approaches that attempt to justify the rules for multiplying with negative numbers in an intuitive manner. Two of these methods are explained in the following paragraphs, and a third approach using patterns is contained in Exercises and Problems 5.1.

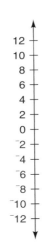

Figure 5.11

NUMBER LINE MODEL   Products of positive and negative integers can be illustrated on a number line. One number line model uses temperatures. Figure 5.11 shows a thermometer scale, a portion of a vertical number line. To illustrate products, we will use the following common conventions:

1. Temperature increases are represented by positive integers and temperature decreases by negative integers.

2. Time in the future is represented by positive integers and time in the past by negative integers.

Example H

Compute each product by determining the new or old temperature. You may find it helpful to sketch a vertical number line.

1. If the temperature is now 0°, what will it be 4 hours from now if it increases 3° each hour?

$$\underset{\substack{\text{4 hours from now}\\\text{(time in future)}}}{4} \qquad \times \qquad \underset{\text{3° increase}}{3} \qquad = \quad \underset{\text{Temperature will be \_\_\_\_\_}}{\Box}$$

2. If the temperature is now 0°, what will it be 5 hours from now if it decreases 2° each hour?

$$\underset{\substack{\text{5 hours from now}\\\text{(time in future)}}}{5} \qquad \times \qquad \underset{\text{2° decrease}}{{}^-2} \qquad = \quad \underset{\text{Temperature will be \_\_\_\_\_}}{\Box}$$

3. If the temperature is now 0°, what was it 3 hours ago if it has been increasing 5° each hour?

$$\underset{\substack{\text{3 hours ago}\\\text{(time in past)}}}{{}^-3} \qquad \times \qquad \underset{\text{5° increase}}{5} \qquad = \quad \underset{\text{Temperature was \_\_\_\_\_}}{\Box}$$

4. If the temperature is now 0°, what was it 4 hours ago if it has been decreasing 2° each hour?

$$\underset{\substack{\text{4 hours ago}\\\text{(time in past)}}}{{}^-4} \qquad \times \qquad \underset{\text{2° decrease}}{{}^-2} \qquad = \quad \underset{\text{Temperature was \_\_\_\_\_}}{\Box}$$

Negative integers should be introduced at this level [3–5] through the use of familiar models such as temperature or owing money. The number line is also an appropriate and helpful model.

Standards 2000, p. 151

Solution 1. The temperature will be 12°:

$$4 \times 3 = 12$$

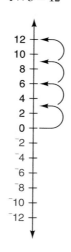

2. The temperature will be ⁻10°:

$$5 \times {}^-2 = {}^-10$$

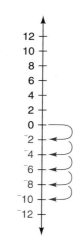

3. The temperature was ⁻15°:

$$^-3 \times 5 = {}^-15$$

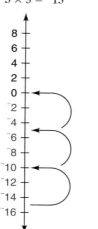

4. The temperature was 8°:

$$^-4 \times {}^-2 = 8$$

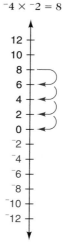

BLACK AND RED CHIPS MODEL Multiplication by a positive integer can be illustrated by putting in groups of chips. Suppose that on 4 occasions you incur debts of $2. This is represented in Figure 5.12 by 4 groups of 2 red chips; the figure illustrates $4 \times {}^-2$. Since there are 8 red chips, $4 \times {}^-2 = {}^-8$.

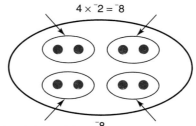

Receiving 4 debts of $2 each is like receiving a debt of $8.

Figure 5.12

Multiplication by a negative integer can be illustrated by removing groups of chips. First let us assume you have $6 and you incur 2 debts, each for $3. These are represented in Figure 5.13 by 6 black chips and 2 groups of 3 red chips. Now suppose that these 2 debts are removed. Removing the 2 groups of 3 red chips illustrates the product ⁻2 × ⁻3. Notice that removing 6 red chips changes the value of the set from zero to 6. This suggests that ⁻2 × ⁻3 = 6.

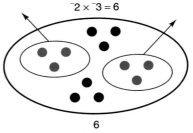

Figure 5.13   Removing 2 debts of $3 each is like removing a debt of $6 or receiving a credit for $6.

Example ❙

Sketch sets of chips to illustrate each computation. Describe the product in terms of debts and credits.

1. $2 \times 4 = 8$ 2. $4 \times {}^-3 = {}^-12$ 3. ${}^-5 \times {}^-3 = 15$

Solution   1. $2 \times 4 = 8$ (Put in 4 black chips 2 times)

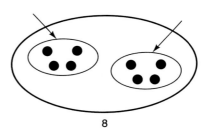

Removing 2 credits of $4 each is like receiving a credit for $8.

2. $4 \times {}^-3 = {}^-12$ (Put in 3 red chips 4 times)

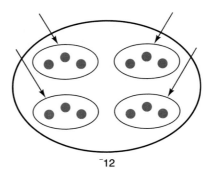

Receiving 4 debts of $3 each is like receiving a debt for $12.

3. $^-5 \times ^-3 = 15$ (Remove 3 red chips 5 times)

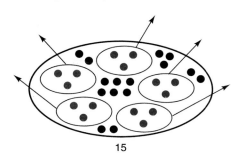

15

Removing 5 debts of $3 each is like removing a debt of $15 or receiving a credit for $15.

The black and red chips model and the number line model illustrate the reasonableness of the rules for multiplying with negative integers, which are shown in the following table. Notice these rules show that products involving negative integers can be obtained by computing products of positive integers.

RULES OF SIGNS FOR MULTIPLICATION   Let a and b be positive integers:

1. Positive times negative equals negative.

$$a \times ^-b = ^-(a \times b)$$
$$5 \times ^-2 = ^-(5 \times 2) = ^-10$$

2. Negative times positive equals negative.

$$^-a \times b = ^-(a \times b)$$
$$^-7 \times 3 = ^-(7 \times 3) = ^-21$$

3. Negative times negative equals positive.

$$^-a \times ^-b = a \times b$$
$$^-4 \times ^-5 = 4 \times 5 = 20$$

 Products involving negative integers can be computed on a calculator by using the $\boxed{(-)}$ key or a change-of-sign key. The next example illustrates the use of $\boxed{+/-}$ to compute $^-44 \times ^-16$:

KEYSTROKES	VIEW SCREEN
44 $\boxed{+/-}$	-44
$\boxed{\times}$	-44
16 $\boxed{+/-}$	-16
$\boxed{=}$	704

However, it is much more convenient, even with a calculator, to use the rule of signs for multiplication to first compute the product of positive integers and then choose the correct sign. In particular, the rule $^-a \times ^-b = a \times b$ allows us to determine the product $^-44 \times ^-16$ by computing $44 \times 16 = 704$.

Example J

Compute each product.

1. $^-426 \times 83$ **2.** $47 \times {}^-2876$ **3.** $^-106 \times {}^-17$

Solution 1. Since $426 \times 83 = 35{,}358$ and a negative times a positive equals a negative, $^-426 \times 83 = {}^-35{,}358$. 2. Since $47 \times 2876 = 135{,}172$ and a positive times a negative equals a negative, $47 \times {}^-2876 = {}^-135{,}172$. 3. Since $106 \times 17 = 1802$ and a negative times a negative equals a positive, $^-106 \times {}^-17 = 1802$.

Division

Both the *sharing (partitive)* and *measurement (subtractive)* concepts of division will be used in the following illustrations of division with the black and red chips model.

To show $^-8 \div {}^-2$, we begin with 8 red chips and then measure off, or subtract, as many groups of 2 red chips as possible (see Figure 5.14). Since there are 4 such groups, $^-8 \div {}^-2 = 4$. This illustration uses the *measurement* concept of division.

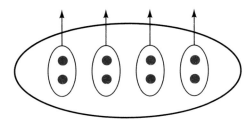

$$^-8 \div {}^-2 = 4$$

A debt of $2 can be measured off (subtracted from) a debt of $8 a total of 4 times.

Figure 5.14

To show $^-6 \div 3$, we divide 6 red chips into 3 equal groups (see Figure 5.15). Since there are 2 red chips in each group, $^-6 \div 3 = {}^-2$. In this illustration the divisor 3 indicates the number of equal parts into which the set is divided. This illustration uses the *sharing* concept of division.

$$^-6 \div 3 = {}^-2$$

Sharing a debt of $6 among 3 people gives each person a debt of $2.

Figure 5.15

In the preceding two examples we showed how two different concepts of division are meaningful for division involving negative and positive integers. In the following definition of division with integers, division is defined in terms of multiplication, just as it was for whole numbers.

DIVISION OF INTEGERS For any integers a and b, with $b \neq 0$,

$$a \div b = k \qquad \text{if and only if} \qquad a = b \times k$$

for some integer k. In this case, b and k are factors of a.

Example K

Calculate each quotient mentally, using the definition of division of integers.

1. $^-24 \div ^-4$ **2.** $18 \div ^-3$ **3.** $^-30 \div 6$

Solution **1.** $^-24 \div ^-4 = 6$, since $^-24 = ^-4 \times 6$ **2.** $18 \div ^-3 = ^-6$, since $18 = ^-3 \times ^-6$ **3.** $^-30 \div 6 = ^-5$, since $^-30 = 6 \times ^-5$

The inverse relationship between division and multiplication of integers accounts for the similarity between the *rules of signs* for these two operations. These rules of signs are shown below. Notice that quotients involving negative integers can be obtained by computing quotients of positive integers.

RULES OF SIGNS FOR DIVISION   Let *a* and *b* be positive integers:

1. Positive divided by negative equals negative.
$$a \div ^-b = ^-(a \div b)$$
$$24 \div ^-6 = ^-(24 \div 6) = ^-4$$

2. Negative divided by positive equals negative.
$$^-a \div b = ^-(a \div b)$$
$$^-14 \div 2 = ^-(14 \div 2) = ^-7$$

3. Negative divided by negative equals positive.
$$^-a \div ^-b = a \div b$$
$$^-30 \div ^-6 = 30 \div 6 = 5$$

As with multiplication of integers, division of integers can be performed on a calculator which displays negative numbers, or on any calculator by using the *rules of signs for division* to replace quotients involving negative integers by quotients of positive integers.

Inequality

For any two integers on a number line, the number on the left is **less than** the number on the right, and the number on the right is **greater than** the number on the left. For example, in Figure 5.16, $^-8 < ^-3$, $^-7 < ^-4$, and $^-5 < 0$.

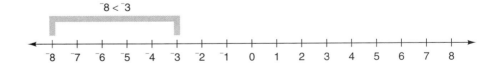

Figure 5.16

This property is stated more precisely in the following definition of inequality of integers. Although this definition is stated for *less than,* a corresponding statement holds for *greater than.*

> **INEQUALITY OF INTEGERS**   For any two integers m and n, m is less than n, written $m < n$, if there is a positive integer k such that $m + k = n$.

In thinking about inequalities of negative numbers, you may find it helpful to recall the applications at the beginning of this section. Temperatures of $^-15°C$ and $^-6°C$ are both cold, but $^-15°C$ is colder than $^-6°C$: $^-15 < ^-6$ because there is a positive integer that can be added to $^-15$ to yield $^-6$ ($^-15 + 9 = ^-6$). Similarly, an altitude of $^-8000$ feet is farther below sea level than an altitude of $^-5000$ feet: $^-8000 < ^-5000$ because there is a positive integer that can be added to $^-8000$ to yield $^-5000$ ($^-8000 + 3000 = ^-5000$).

Example L

Write the appropriate inequality ($<$ or $>$) for each pair of numbers.

1. $^-37, ^-55$ **2.** $^-110, 420$ **3.** $^-76, ^-125$

Solution   1. $^-37 > ^-55$ 2. $^-110 < 420$ 3. $^-76 > ^-125$

Properties of Integers

INVERSES FOR ADDITION   Addition of integers has one property that addition of whole numbers does not have. For any integer, there is a unique integer, called its **opposite** or **inverse**, such that the integer plus its opposite is equal to zero. We refer to this property by saying that each integer has an **inverse for addition.**

Example M

Find the integer that satisfies each equation.

1. $174 + \square = 0$ **2.** $^-351 + \square = 0$ **3.** $0 + \square = 0$

Solution   1. $^-174$ 2. 351 3. 0 (zero is its own inverse)

CLOSURE PROPERTIES   The sum of any two integers is a unique integer, and the product of any two integers is also a unique integer. That is, the set of integers is closed for addition and multiplication.

IDENTITY PROPERTIES   Any integer added to 0 equals the given integer, and any integer multiplied by 1 equals the given integer. That is, 0 is the *identity for addition,* 1 is the *identity for multiplication,* and these are the only identity elements (they are unique) for addition and multiplication of integers.

COMMUTATIVE PROPERTIES   The operations of *addition and multiplication are commutative* for the integers. In particular, these properties hold for negative integers. For example,

$$^-37 + ^-52 = ^-52 + ^-37 \quad \text{and} \quad ^-37 \times ^-52 = ^-52 \times ^-37$$

ASSOCIATIVE PROPERTIES   The operations of *addition and multiplication are associative* for the integers. These properties hold for any combination of three integers. For the integers $^-7$, $^-2$, and $^-6$,

$$(^-7 + ^-2) + ^-6 = ^-7 + (^-2 + ^-6) \quad \text{and} \quad (^-7 \times ^-2) \times ^-6 = ^-7 \times (^-2 \times ^-6)$$

DISTRIBUTIVE PROPERTY   The *distributive property of multiplication over addition* holds in the set of integers. (See Example N.)

Example N

Show that the distributive property holds for the following equation by computing both sides of this equation:

$$^-2 \times (3 + {}^-7) = {}^-2 \times 3 + {}^-2 \times {}^-7$$

Solution   Left side of equation: $^-2 \times (3 + {}^-7) = {}^-2 \times {}^-4 = 8$
Right side of equation: $^-2 \times 3 + {}^-2 \times {}^-7 = {}^-6 + 14 = 8$

Mental Calculations

Acquiring number sense is an important objective for elementary school students. Learning to do mental calculations can help them reach this objective. *Mental math techniques* encourage students to use number properties and discover computational shortcuts rather than perform rote calculations.

COMPATIBLE NUMBERS   Finding combinations of compatible numbers is a technique for mental calculation that works with integers as well as with whole numbers.

Example O

Do these computations in your head.

1. $50 + {}^-23 + {}^-60$

2. $15 + {}^-26 + 10 + {}^-5$

3. $^-5 \times 18 \times {}^-2$

Solution   One approach to each problem is shown below; your selections of compatible numbers may differ from these: 1. $50 + {}^-60 = {}^-10$, and $^-10 + {}^-23 = {}^-33$ 2. $15 + {}^-5 = 10$, $10 + 10 = 20$, and $20 + {}^-26 = {}^-6$ 3. $^-5 \times {}^-2 = 10$ and $10 \times 18 = 180$

SUBSTITUTIONS   Using the technique of substitution involves replacing a number by a sum, difference, product, or quotient that is more convenient to use in the computation.

Example P

Do each computation mentally, using a convenient substitution.

1. $180 + {}^-37$

2. $^-6 \times 19$

3. $^-150 \div 6$

4. $12 \times {}^-54$

Solution   Different substitutions may occur to you.   1. $180 + {}^-37 = 180 + ({}^-30 + {}^-7)$, and by the associative property for addition this equals $150 + {}^-7 = 143$.   2. $^-6 \times 19 = {}^-6 \times (20 + {}^-1)$, and by the distributive property this equals $^-120 + 6 = {}^-114$.   3. Using the equal quotients technique described in Section 3.4, we can divide both 150 and 6 by 2. So $^-150 \div 6 = {}^-75 \div 3 = {}^-25$. Or both $^-150$ and 6 can be divided by 3: $^-150 \div 6 = {}^-50 \div 2 = {}^-25$.   4. Using the equal products technique described in Section 3.3, we can divide 12 by 2 and multiply $^-54$ by 2: $12 \times {}^-54 = 6 \times {}^-108 = {}^-648$.

Estimation

Computing estimations is one of the most powerful means of acquiring number sense. Estimation requires a knowledge of mental mathematics because one must choose approximate numbers that are convenient for mental calculations.

ROUNDING AND COMPATIBLE NUMBERS   The mental calculating techniques of rounding and compatible numbers are often combined to obtain an estimation.

Example Q

Obtain an estimation by rounding and compatible numbers. (*Note:* In **4**, division should be performed before addition.)

1. $81 + {}^-32 + 21 + {}^-47$

2. ${}^-53 \times 142 \times {}^-2$

3. $12 \times 67 \times {}^-5$

4. ${}^-250 + 90 \div 32$

Solution   You may find other estimations.   **1.** $81 + {}^-32 + 21 + {}^-47 \approx (80 + 20) + ({}^-30 + {}^-50) = 100 + {}^-80 = 20$ **2.** ${}^-53 \times 142 \times {}^-2 \approx {}^-50 \times {}^-2 \times 142 = 100 \times 142 = 14{,}200$ **3.** $12 \times 67 \times {}^-5 = 12 \times {}^-5 \times 67 = {}^-60 \times 67 \approx {}^-60 \times 70 = {}^-4200$ **4.** ${}^-250 + 90 \div 32 \approx {}^-250 + 90 \div 30 = {}^-250 + 3 = {}^-247$

Note: The number of negative integers in a product of numbers determines whether the product is positive or negative. Since there are two negative integers in **2**, the product of the three numbers is positive. Similarly, in **3** there is one negative integer, so the answer is negative.

Problem-Solving Application

The following problem involves sums of positive and negative integers. Try to solve this problem before you read the solution. You may find it helpful to use the strategies of *solving a simpler problem* and *making an organized list*.

PROBLEM

Consider the positive integers from 1 to 25 and their opposites.

$$\pm 1, \pm 2, \pm 3, \pm 4, \pm 5, \ldots, \pm 21, \pm 22, \pm 23, \pm 24, \pm 25$$

Describe all the different numbers that can be obtained by using each integer or its opposite exactly once to form sums of 25 integers.

Understanding the Problem   Each sum must have 25 integers. One possibility is to use the opposites of 1, 2, and 3 and the positive integers from 4 to 25.

$${}^-1 + {}^-2 + {}^-3 + 4 + 5 + 6 + \cdots + 22 + 23 + 24 + 25 = 313$$

The greatest possible sum is 325. **Question 1:** What is the least possible sum?

Devising a Plan   Let's solve a simpler problem by using the integers 1, 2, 3, 4, and 5 and their opposites. It is natural to *make an organized list* to consider all the possibilities. This can be done by writing the sum $1 + 2 + 3 + 4 + 5$ and systematically replacing positive integers by their opposites.

$$1 + 2 + 3 + 4 + 5 = 15$$
$$^-1 + 2 + 3 + 4 + 5 = 13$$
$$1 + ^-2 + 3 + 4 + 5 = 11$$
$$^-1 + ^-2 + 3 + 4 + 5 = 9$$

Question 2: Why can't a sum of 0 be obtained from such integers?

Carrying Out the Plan   The list of sums, continued below, reveals a pattern.

$$^-1 + 2 + ^-3 + 4 + 5 = 7$$
$$^-1 + 2 + 3 + ^-4 + 5 = 5$$
$$^-1 + 2 + 3 + 4 + ^-5 = 3$$
$$1 + ^-2 + 3 + 4 + ^-5 = 1$$
$$1 + 2 + ^-3 + 4 + ^-5 = ^-1$$
$$1 + 2 + 3 + ^-4 + ^-5 = ^-3$$
$$^-1 + 2 + 3 + ^-4 + ^-5 = ^-5$$
$$1 + ^-2 + 3 + ^-4 + ^-5 = ^-7$$
$$1 + 2 + ^-3 + ^-4 + ^-5 = ^-9$$
$$^-1 + 2 + ^-3 + ^-4 + ^-5 = ^-11$$
$$1 + ^-2 + ^-3 + ^-4 + ^-5 = ^-13$$
$$^-1 + ^-2 + ^-3 + ^-4 + ^-5 = ^-15$$

We obtained all the odd numbers from 15 to $^-$15. Perhaps you noticed a reason for this. Each time a positive integer is replaced by its opposite, the new sum differs by an even number. For example, if 1 is replaced by $^-$1, the new sum is decreased by 2. Similarly, replacing 2 by $^-$2 decreases the sum by 4; replacing 3 by $^-$3 decreases the sum by 6; etc. Thus we obtain all the odd numbers from $^-$15 to 15. **Question 3:** What does this suggest about the solution to the original problem?

Looking Back   The original problem and the simplified problem considered the positive integers from 1 to 25 and their opposites. Suppose the original problem were changed to consider the integers from 1 to 24 and their opposites. **Question 4:** What sums would be obtained?

Answers to Questions 1–4   **1.** $^-$325   **2.** The sum of integers from 1 to 5 is 15, an odd number. Since replacing any one of the numbers from 1 to 5 by its opposite changes the sum by 2 times the number, which is an even number, such replacements will change the sum of 15 by an even number. Thus the sum of all such integers is an odd number and therefore cannot be 0.   **3.** The solution will include all odd numbers from 325 to $^-$325.   **4.** All even numbers from 300 to $^-$300 would be obtained.

EXERCISES AND PROBLEMS 5.1

Antarctica, the only polar continent, is centered near the South Pole and is covered by a huge ice dome reaching a height between 2 and 3 miles. One of the hazards of exploration is the hidden crevasses in the ice. This photo shows a crevasse detector operating in Antarctica.

1. If five daytime Fahrenheit temperatures recorded during an Antarctic summer are ⁻18, ⁻17, ⁻24, ⁻34, and ⁻28°F, what is the highest (warmest) of these temperatures?

2. Winter temperatures in Antarctica are usually below ⁻100°F. What is the lowest (coldest) of the following temperatures? ⁻119, ⁻98, ⁻110, ⁻114, and ⁻108°F

Find an integer that makes the left side of each equation in exercises 3 and 4 equal to the right side. Then write an inequality using < or > for each pair of numbers below the equations.

3. a. ⁻3 + □ = ⁻2
      ⁻3, ⁻2
   b. ⁻14 + □ = 3
      3, ⁻14
   c. ⁻7 + □ = 1
      ⁻7, 1

4. a. ⁻17 + □ = 31
      ⁻17, 31
   b. ⁻84 + □ = ⁻23
      ⁻84, ⁻23
   c. 140 + □ = ⁻95
      140, ⁻95

Sketch a number line and locate each of the integers in exercises 5 and 6. Draw an arrow from each integer to its opposite.

5. 8, ⁻3, 5, and ⁻1

6. ⁻7, 5, 0, 2, and ⁻4

Answer each question in exercises 7 and 8 with an integer.

7. a. The temperature at 6 a.m. was ⁻15°F, and by noon it had warmed up 8°. What was the noontime temperature?

   b. The nation's trade balance for the first quarter of a year was $⁻23 billion, and for the second quarter it was $9 billion less. What was the second-quarter trade balance in billions of dollars?

8. a. A submarine has an altitude of ⁻5500 feet, and it dives down 1500 feet. What is its new altitude in feet?

   b. At ⁻40 minutes in the countdown for a space shuttle launch, technicians began a 7-minute check of the shuttle's compression system. What was the time in the countdown at the end of this check?

Use the black and red chips model in exercises 9 and 10 to sketch three different sets illustrating each integer.

9. a. ⁻7   b. 0   c. 3

10. a. 4   b. ⁻9   c. ⁻1

Show how to use the given chips or sketch the missing chips to illustrate each operation in exercises 11 and 12. Explain your reasoning and complete each equation.

11. a.

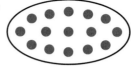

⁻15 ÷ 5 =

   b.

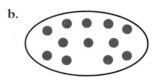

⁻12 ÷ ⁻4 =

c.

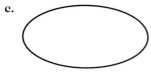

$$3 \times {}^-5 =$$

12. a.

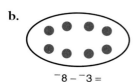

$$3 \quad + \quad {}^-7 \quad =$$

b.

$$^-8 - {}^-3 =$$

c.

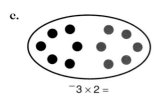

$$^-3 \times 2 =$$

Show a replacement for each set of chips in exercises 13 and 14 so that the difference can be determined by using the *take-away* concept. Then complete the equation.

13.

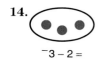

$$2 - 5 =$$

14.

$$^-3 - 2 =$$

Answer each question in exercises 15 and 16, and then write a multiplication fact that the problem illustrates.

15. a. If the temperature is now 30°F, what was it 2 hours ago if it has been decreasing 6°F each hour?

   b. If the temperature is now 12°F, what was it 6 hours ago if it has been increasing 4°F each hour?

16. a. If the temperature is now 0°F, what was it 5 hours ago if it has been increasing 3°F each hour?

   b. If the temperature is now 10°F, what will it be 3 hours from now if it decreases 2°F each hour?

Draw a number line to illustrate each sum in exercises 17 and 18.

17. a. $6 + {}^-5$ **b.** $^-4 + 9$

18. a. $^-3 + {}^-4$ **b.** $^-5 + 5$

Compute each product or quotient in exercises 19 and 20.

19. a. $14 \times {}^-23$
   b. $^-156 \div 13$
   c. $^-278 \times {}^-46$
   d. $^-1431 \div {}^-53$

20. a. $^-6 \times 2$ **b.** $^-8 \times {}^-3$
   c. $24 \div {}^-6$ **d.** $^-20 \div 4$

Find the missing numbers for each equation in exercises 21 and 22.

21. a. $4 + \square = {}^-10$
   b. $6 - \square = 10$
   c. $^-6 \times \square = {}^-12$
   d. $^-3 + \square = 0$

22. a. $^-15 \div \square = {}^-3$
   b. $^-4 - \square = 7$
   c. $^-1 \times \square = 1$
   d. $24 \div \square = {}^-8$

Which number property of the integers is being used in each equality in exercises 23 and 24?

23. a. $({}^-8 + 7) + 2 \times ({}^-6 \times {}^-5) = $
   $({}^-8 + 7) + (2 \times {}^-6) \times {}^-5$

   b. $^-3 \times \dfrac{16 \times {}^-5}{{}^-14 + 2} = {}^-3 \times \dfrac{{}^-5 \times 16}{{}^-14 + 2}$

24. a. $^-4 \times \dfrac{16 + {}^-9}{{}^-6 + 13} = {}^-4 \times \dfrac{16 + {}^-9}{13 + {}^-6}$

   b. $^-4 \times ({}^-3 + 3) + {}^-17 = $
   $({}^-4 \times {}^-3) + ({}^-4 \times 3) + {}^-17$

Determine whether the set is closed for the given operations in exercises 25 and 26.

25. a. The set of integers for subtraction
   b. The set of integers for division

26. a. The set of negative integers for multiplication
   b. The set of negative integers for addition

Use *compatible numbers* or a *substitution* in exercises 27 and 28 to calculate each sum or difference mentally. Explain your method.

27. a. $^-125 + 17 + {}^-25 + 13$
   b. $700 + {}^-298 + 135$

28. a. $70 + 43 + {}^-60$
   b. $260 + {}^-49$

Use *equal products* or *equal quotients* in exercises 29 and 30 to do each computation mentally.

29. a. $24 \times {}^-25$ **b.** ${}^-90 \div 18$
c. ${}^-28 \times 5$ **d.** $400 \div {}^-16$

30. a. $16 \times {}^-35$ **b.** ${}^-900 \div {}^-45$
c. ${}^-1260 \div 140$ **d.** ${}^-28 \times 25$

Round each integer in exercises 31 and 32 to its leading digit and mentally approximate the sum of the numbers.

Example:

118	${}^-235$	${}^-190$	485	Approximate
Think	Think	Think	Think	sum
100	${}^-200$	${}^-200$	500	200

31. a.   78 ${}^-41$ 19 ${}^-38$
b. ${}^-23$ 51 ${}^-48$ ${}^-82$

32. a. ${}^-123$ 207 ${}^-315$ 186
b. ${}^-238$ 175 ${}^-103$ ${}^-214$

Replace numbers in exercises 33 and 34 by *compatible numbers* to obtain estimations. Show how you obtain your estimations.

33. a. ${}^-241 \div 60$ **b.** $64 \times {}^-11$

34. a. $26 + 59 \div {}^-3$ **b.** ${}^-31 \times 19$

In exercises 35 and 36, do not compute the answer, just determine whether it is positive or negative. Explain your reasoning.

35. a. ${}^-34 \times 46 \times 381 \times {}^-13$
b. ${}^-22 \times 17 \times 12 + 50$

36. a. $41 \times {}^-65 + 500$
b. $625 \div {}^-25 + {}^-250$

Extend the patterns in the columns of equations in exercises 37 and 38 by writing the next three equations. What multiplication rule for negative numbers is suggested by the last few equations that you write in each column?

37. a. $5 \times 3 = 15$ **b.** $3 \times 6 = 18$
$5 \times 2 = 10$ $2 \times 6 = 12$
$5 \times 1 = 5$ $1 \times 6 = 6$
$5 \times 0 = 0$ $0 \times 6 = 0$

38. a. ${}^-3 \times 3 = {}^-9$ **b.** $3 \times 3 = 9$
${}^-3 \times 2 = {}^-6$ $3 \times 2 = 6$
${}^-3 \times 1 = {}^-3$ $3 \times 1 = 3$
${}^-3 \times 0 = 0$ $3 \times 0 = 0$

The computations in exercises 39 and 40 involve the change-of-sign key $\boxed{+/-}$ on a calculator. Determine what computation is being performed, and find the answer for each.

39. a. $217 \boxed{+/-} - 366$
b. $483 \boxed{+/-} + 225$
c. $2257 \div 37 \boxed{+/-}$
d. $1974 \boxed{+/-} \div 42$

40. a. $16 \boxed{+/-} + 7 \boxed{+/-}$
b. $25 \boxed{+/-} - 30 \boxed{+/-}$
c. $54 \times 35 \boxed{+/-}$
d. $408 \div 17 \boxed{+/-}$

Suppose you have a calculator that does not have a change-of-sign key. Explain how the rules of signs for operations with integers can be used to compute the expressions in exercises 41 and 42. Find each answer.

41. a. ${}^-487 + {}^-653$ **b.** $360 - {}^-241$
c. $32 \times {}^-14$ **d.** $336 \div {}^-16$

42. a. ${}^-1854 \div {}^-103$ **b.** ${}^-488 - {}^-179$
c. ${}^-133 \times 82$ **d.** $729 \div {}^-27$

Some calculators designed for elementary school students have a constant function which adds, subtracts, multiplies, and divides by constants. For example, pressing $2 \boxed{+} {}^-3$ and repeatedly pressing $\boxed{=}$ or a constant key will produce the arithmetic sequence ${}^-1, {}^-4, {}^-7, {}^-10, {}^-13, \ldots .$ Assume that you have such a calculator, and write the sequences that will be obtained in exercises 43 and 44. (*Recall:* The change-of-sign key $\boxed{+/-}$ is used to obtain opposites, not the key for subtraction $\boxed{-}$.)

43. a. $0 \boxed{+} {}^-17 \boxed{=} \boxed{=} \boxed{=} \boxed{=} \boxed{=}$
b. $2 \boxed{\times} {}^-26 \boxed{=} \boxed{=} \boxed{=} \boxed{=} \boxed{=}$

44. a. $10 \boxed{+} {}^-43 \boxed{=} \boxed{=} \boxed{=} \boxed{=} \boxed{=}$
b. $1 \boxed{\times} {}^-13 \boxed{=} \boxed{=} \boxed{=} \boxed{=} \boxed{=}$

45. Determine the calculator results for each of the following sequences of steps, where $\boxed{+/-}$ is the change-of-sign key. Which sequence computes ${}^-15 - {}^-6$?

a. $\boxed{-} 15 \boxed{-} 6 \boxed{=}$
b. $15 \boxed{+/-} \boxed{-} 6 \boxed{+/-} \boxed{=}$
c. $\boxed{-} 15 \boxed{-} 6 \boxed{+/-} \boxed{=}$

46. Determine the calculator results for the following sequences of steps, where $\boxed{+/-}$ is the change-of-sign key. Which sequence computes ${}^-245 - {}^-182$?

a. $\boxed{-} 245 \boxed{-} 182 \boxed{+/-} \boxed{=}$
b. $\boxed{-} 245 \boxed{-} 182 \boxed{=}$
c. $245 \boxed{+/-} \boxed{-} 182 \boxed{+/-} \boxed{=}$

REASONING AND PROBLEM SOLVING

47. NASA's *Voyager 1* achieved its closest approach to Jupiter (about 280,000 kilometers) on March 5, 1979. In December 1978, ⁻80 days with respect to its time of closest approach, the spacecraft swiveled its narrow-angle television camera to begin its observational phase. The inner squares in the sketch below represent the camera's field of view at four different approach times.

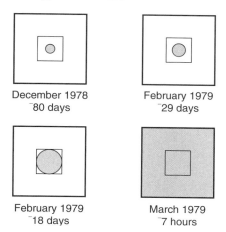

December 1978
⁻80 days

February 1979
⁻29 days

February 1979
⁻18 days

March 1979
⁻7 hours

a. How much time elapsed between the ⁻80-day view and the ⁻29-day view?

b. How much time elapsed between the ⁻18-day view and the ⁻7-hour view?

c. As *Voyager 1* moved away from Jupiter, it examined its moons: Io at ⁺3 hours, Europa at ⁺5 hours, and Ganymede at ⁺14 hours. Thirty-six hours after the ⁻7-hour view, *Voyager 1* examined Callisto. How many hours was this after its closest approach to Jupiter?

48. Featured Strategies: Solving a Simpler Problem and Guessing and Checking How can the integers from ⁻4 to 4 be placed around a circle so that each integer from ⁻10 to 10 can be obtained by adding two or more neighbor numbers (numbers next to each other)?

a. Understanding the Problem The problem requires that the nine integers from ⁻4 to 4 be used and that the sums involve two or more adjacent integers. The following placement of integers will yield some of the numbers from ⁻10 to 10, but not all of them. For example, $0 = {}^{-}3 + 0 + 3$, and $1 = 0 + 3 + {}^{-}4 + 2$. Find some integers from ⁻10 to 10 that cannot be obtained by adding two or more adjacent integers from this circle.

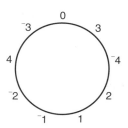

b. Devising a Plan This type of problem can be solved by *guessing and checking* the results. It may also help to *solve a simpler problem.* Consider placing the numbers ⁻2, ⁻1, 0, 1, and 2 around a circle to obtain all the sums from 3 to ⁻3. Show why it doesn't work to place each integer next to its opposite. How should these numbers be placed?

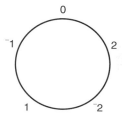

c. Carrying Out the Plan The solution to part b may suggest a solution to the original problem. The requirement that we be able to obtain a sum of 10 and a sum of ⁻10 completely determines the solution. Explain why. How can the integers from ⁻4 to 4 be placed to solve the problem?

d. Looking Back Another observation concerning the original problem is that each of the integers from ⁻4 to 4 can be routinely obtained by adding all the numbers on the circle except the negative of the given number. Explain why.

49. A radio station that keeps records of the low temperature each day obtained the following information. The temperature on Monday was below zero, and on Tuesday it was 8°F colder. Wednesday the temperature reading was twice as low as for Tuesday. Thursday the temperature was 4°F higher than on Wednesday. On Friday the temperature warmed up to ⁻14°F, which was just half of the temperature on Thursday. What was the recorded temperature for Monday?

50. In a city golf tournament each golfer played 18 holes of golf per day for 4 days. If a player **pars** a hole, that is, gets the ball in the hole in the number of strokes designed for the hole, the player receives a score of 0 for the hole. If the player gets the ball in the hole in one stroke under par, it is called a **birdie** and the score for the hole is $^-1$. If the player gets the ball in the hole in one stroke over par, it is called a **bogey** and the score for the hole is $^+1$. The winner of the tournament had a 4-day total score of $^-13$ with 5 bogeys. If the winner had only birdies, pars, and bogeys, how many birdies did the player have?

51. Keeping the single-digit numbers from 1 to 7 in order.

$$1 \quad 2 \quad 3 \quad 4 \quad 5 \quad 6 \quad 7$$

it is possible to insert five plus or minus signs to obtain a sum of 50.

$$^-12 + 3 - 4 + 56 + 7$$

Show how three plus or minus signs can be inserted to obtain a sum of 50.

52. Here are the positive and negative values of the consecutive whole numbers from 1 to 3.

$$\pm1 \quad \pm2 \quad \pm3$$

Consider selecting either the positive or the negative value of each integer. For example, we could select $^-1, 2, ^-3$; or $1, 2, 3$; or $1, 2, ^-3$; etc. By using all such possible selections, the following sums are possible: $^-6, ^-4, ^-2, 0, 2, 4,$ and 6. For example, $^-6$ is obtained by using all the negative values $^-1 + ^-2 + ^-3$; the sum of $^-2$ is obtained from $^-3 + ^-1 + 2$; and the largest possible sum of 6 is obtained by adding all the positive values: $1 + 2 + 3$. What sums can be obtained by using either the positive or the negative value of each integer for these sequences?

a. $\pm1 \quad \pm2 \quad \pm3 \quad \pm4$
b. $\pm1 \quad \pm2 \quad \pm3 \quad \pm4 \quad \pm5$
c. $\pm1 \quad \pm2 \quad \pm3 \quad \pm4 \quad \pm5 \quad \pm6$
d. Look for patterns and state a general conjecture regarding the sums for

$$\pm1 \quad \pm2 \quad \pm3 \quad \pm4 \quad \pm5 \quad \pm6 \quad \ldots \quad \pm n$$

where n is any whole number greater than 1.

· ·

ONLINE LEARNING CENTER   www.mhhe.com/bennett-nelson

 • Math Investigation 5.1   *Integer Differences*
 Section-Related: • Links   • Writing/Discussion Problems   • Bibliography

· ·

PUZZLER

A square array of numbers in which the sum of numbers in any horizontal row, vertical column, or diagonal is always the same is called a **magic square.** Enter the numbers below into the given grid to produce a magic square.

$$^-10 \quad ^-8 \quad ^-6 \quad ^-4 \quad 0 \quad 2 \quad 4 \quad 6$$

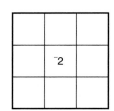

MATH ACTIVITY 5.2

EQUALITY AND INEQUALITY WITH FRACTION BARS

Materials: Fraction Bars in the Manipulative Kit.

1. The fractions for these bars are equal because both bars have the same shaded amount. In the deck of 32 Fraction Bars there are 3 bars whose fractions equal $\frac{2}{3}$. Sort your deck of bars into piles so bars with the same shaded amounts are in the same pile.

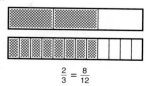

$$\frac{2}{3} = \frac{8}{12}$$

   a. Find all the fractions from the bars which equal the following fractions, and write equalities: $\frac{1}{2}, \frac{4}{6}, \frac{1}{4}, \frac{9}{12},$ and $\frac{1}{3}$.

   b. If a bar is all shaded, it is called a **whole bar** and its fraction is equal to 1. If a bar has no parts shaded, it is called a **zero bar** and its fraction is equal to 0. List all the fractions for the whole bars and zero bars.

2. A fraction is **not in lowest terms** if the numerator and denominator have a common factor greater than 1. List all the fractions from the deck other than those equal to 0 or 1 which are not in lowest terms. Then write each fraction in lowest terms.

*3. A $\frac{3}{4}$ bar has more shading than a $\frac{2}{3}$ bar, so $\frac{3}{4} > \frac{2}{3}$. For each of the following pairs of fractions, find a fraction from the deck which is greater than the smaller fraction and less than the larger fraction.

   a. $\frac{1}{2}, \frac{2}{3}$ b. $\frac{1}{6}, \frac{1}{3}$ c. $\frac{3}{4}, \frac{11}{12}$ d. $\frac{2}{3}, \frac{5}{6}$

4. Each part of this $\frac{3}{4}$ bar has been split into 2 equal parts. There are now 8 equal parts, and 6 of these are shaded. This illustrates the equality $\frac{3}{4} = \frac{6}{8}$.

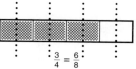

$$\frac{3}{4} = \frac{6}{8}$$

   a. Find bars from the deck for each of the following fractions: $\frac{1}{4}, \frac{2}{3}, \frac{11}{12}, \frac{1}{2}, \frac{5}{6}$. Split each part of the bar into two equal parts to illustrate another fraction, and write equalities for these pairs of fractions.

   b. Use the bars in part a and split each part of each bar into three equal parts to illustrate another fraction. Write equalities for these pairs.

5. The top two bars shown here have different-size parts. Sometimes it is necessary to further subdivide the parts of a bar so that both bars have parts of the same size. If each part of the $\frac{1}{3}$ bar is divided into 4 equal parts and each part of the $\frac{5}{6}$ bar is divided into 2 equal parts, both bars will have 12 equal parts. Divide the parts of the following pairs of bars so that both bars have parts of the same size. What fraction concept is being modeled by this activity?

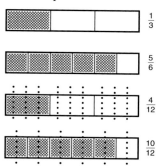

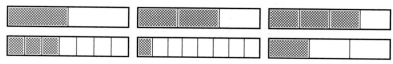

SECTION 5.2

INTRODUCTION TO FRACTIONS

Trading floor of the New York Stock Exchange

Three tired and hungry people had a bag of apples. While the other two were asleep, one of the three awoke, ate one-third of the apples, and went back to sleep. Later a second person awoke, ate one-third of the remaining apples, and went back to sleep. Finally, the third person awoke and ate one-third of the remaining apples, leaving 8 apples in the bag. How many apples were in the bag originally?

The sale of stocks and bonds on the New York Stock Exchange is carried out on the three-story trading floor shown in the photo. Until a recent change to decimals, the prices of stocks were stated in halves, fourths, eighths, and sixteenths of a dollar. Historically, whenever a smaller unit of measure was needed, one-half of the original measure was used. For a still smaller amount, one-half of one-half produced one-fourth. Similarly, eighths, sixteenths, and thirty-seconds resulted from repeatedly halving the original unit. The inch, with its halves, fourths, eighths, sixteenths, etc., is also a familiar example of this halving process. Another example is shutter speeds on a camera, which are calibrated in fractions of a second: $\frac{1}{2}, \frac{1}{4}, \frac{1}{8}, \frac{1}{15}, \frac{1}{30}, \frac{1}{60}$, etc. (see exercises 46 and 47 in Exercises and Problems 5.2).

HISTORICAL HIGHLIGHT

Egyptian leather scroll describing simple relations between fractions (ca. 1700 B.C.)

The Egyptians were using fractions before 2500 B.C. With the exception of $\frac{2}{3}$, all Egyptian fractions were **unit fractions,** that is, fractions with a numerator of 1 ($\frac{1}{3}$, $\frac{1}{4}$, etc.).

In hieratic (sacred) writings like the scroll shown here, the Egyptians placed a dot above a numeral to represent a unit fraction. For example, $\wedge$ represents the number 30, and $\overset{\cdot}{\wedge}$ represents the fraction $\frac{1}{30}$. It is interesting to note that as late as the 18th century, over 3000 years after the ancient Egyptians used such symbols, the symbols $\overset{\cdot}{2}$ and $\overset{\cdot}{4}$ were used in English books for the fractions $\frac{1}{2}$ and $\frac{1}{4}$.

Whereas the Egyptians used fractions with fixed numerators, the Babylonians (ca. 2000 B.C.) used only fractions with denominators of 60 and 60^2. The fraction $\frac{1}{60}$ was referred to as "the first little part" and $\left(\frac{1}{60}\right)^2$ as "the second little part." Our use of the minute, $\frac{1}{60}$ of an hour, and second, $\left(\frac{1}{60}\right)^2$ of an hour, was handed down to us from the Babylonians.

Fraction Terminology

Research Statement

Students with an understanding of the written symbols for fractions are able to connect them to other representations, such as physical objects, pictorial representations, and spoken language.

Wearne and Kouba 2000

The word *fraction* comes from the Latin word *fractio,* a form of the Latin word *frangere,* meaning *to break.* The terms *broken number* and *fragment* frequently were used in the past as synonyms for *fraction.* Historically, fractions were first used for amounts less than a whole unit. This is how children first encounter fractions: one-half of a candy bar, one-third of a pizza, etc. Today fractions also include numbers that are greater than or equal to 1.

The term **fraction** is used to refer both to a number written in the form a/b and to the numeral a/b. You need not be concerned about the distinction between a/b as a number and a/b as a numeral; the meaning will be clear from the context. For example, when we say the top number of a fraction is called the **numerator** and the bottom number is called the **denominator,** we are thinking of the fraction as a symbol or numeral with two parts. On the other hand, when we say, "Add the fractions $\frac{1}{2}$ and $\frac{1}{3}$," we are thinking of fractions as numbers.

Children in the early grades use fractions whose numerators and denominators are whole numbers. In the later grades fractions are encountered whose numerators and denominators are integers. The numerator and denominator can be any numbers as long as the denominator is not zero. (See Sections 6.3 and 6.4 for examples of fractions involving decimals and irrational numbers.)

Models for Fractions

Three concepts of fractions will be illustrated by models in the following paragraphs: the *part-to-whole concept,* the *division concept,* and the *ratio concept.*

PART-TO-WHOLE CONCEPT   The most common use of fractions involves the **part-to-whole concept,** that is, the use of a fraction to denote part of a whole. In the fraction *a/b,* the bottom number *b* indicates the number of equal parts in a whole, and the top number *a* indicates the number of parts being considered.

Example A

Write the fraction for the shaded or lettered part of each figure.

1.   2.   3.    4.

Solution   1. $\frac{3}{8}$ 2. $\frac{7}{16}$ 3. $\frac{1}{6}$ 4. $\frac{5}{9}$

The Fraction Bars* model is a part-to-whole model for fractions in which the denominator of a fraction is represented by the number of equal parts in a bar and the numerator is the number of shaded parts.

Example B

Write the fraction represented by the shaded portion of each bar.

1.   2.   3.

Solution   1. $\frac{1}{2}$ 2. $\frac{2}{3}$ 3. $\frac{3}{4}$

The part-to-whole concept of a fraction also is used in describing part of a set of individual objects.

Example C

1. Write the fraction that shows what part of the following set is circles.

2. Write the fraction that shows what part of the set is squares.

Research Statement

In the 7th national mathematics assessment, fourth-grade students found representing a fraction to be easier if the unit was a region than if it was a set of objects.

Wearne and Kouba 2000

---

*Fraction Bars is a registered trademark of Scott Resources, Inc.

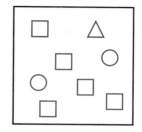

Research Statement

Interpreting fractions and decimals on a number line is more difficult for students than interpreting fractions as part of geometric regions.

Kouba, Zawojewski, and Strutchens 1997

Solution 1. $\frac{2}{8}$ of the objects are circles. 2. $\frac{5}{8}$ of the objects are squares.

Fractions can be located on a number line by using the part-to-whole concept. First select a **unit,** and then divide this interval into equal parts. To locate the fraction r/s, subdivide the unit interval into s equal parts, and beginning at 0, count off r of these parts. Figure 5.17 shows the sixths and tenths between ⁻1 and 1.

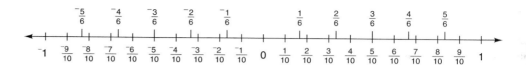

Figure 5.17

Applications of fractions that involve the part-to-whole concept are numerous. Two examples are shown below.

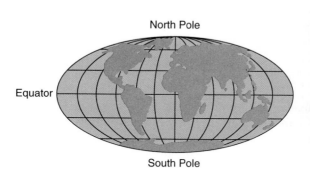

Two-thirds of the earth's surface area is covered by water.

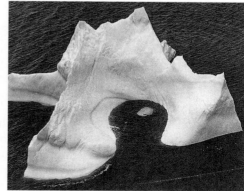

Eight-ninths of the volume of an iceberg is under water.

DIVISION CONCEPT   In the following cartoon Charlie Brown's little sister Sally has a problem. She is trying to divide 25 by 50. Charlie Brown's comment shows that he thinks of division only in terms of the *measurement concept,* that is, "How many 50s are in 25?" However, there is another approach to division. Remember that Section 3.4 discussed two concepts of division: *measurement (subtractive)* and *sharing (partitive).* With the *sharing concept,* dividing by 50 means there will be 50 parts. If we divide 25 objects of equal size, such as sticks of gum, into 50 equal parts, each part will be one-half of a stick: $25 \div 50 = \frac{1}{2}$.

Peanuts © UFS. Reprinted by Permission.

In addition to work with whole numbers, young children should also have some experience with simple fractions through connections to everyday situations.

Standards 2000, p. 82

Here is another illustration of the division concept that involves fractions. Figure 5.18 shows 3 whole bars placed end to end. To compute $3 \div 4$, we use the sharing concept of division and divide the 3 bars into 4 equal parts. This can be done by dividing the 3-bar in half and then dividing each half in half, as shown by the dashed lines. Comparing one of these four parts to a $\frac{3}{4}$ bar shows that $3 \div 4 = \frac{3}{4}$.

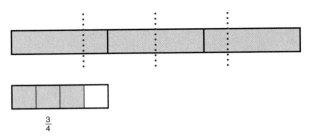

Figure 5.18

Both of the preceding examples show that a fraction results from the division of one whole number by another. This relationship between fractions and division of numbers is sometimes used to define a fraction as a quotient of two numbers.

For any numbers a and b, with $b \neq 0$,

$$\frac{a}{b} = a \div b$$

One of the major influences in the early development of fractions was the need to solve problems involving division of whole numbers. A problem found in Egyptian writings from 1650 B.C. requires that 4 loaves of bread be divided equally among 10 people. According to the previous definition, $4 \div 10 = \frac{4}{10}$, and each person would receive $\frac{4}{10}$ of a loaf of bread. Figure 5.19 shows 4 loaves of bread divided into 10 equal parts.

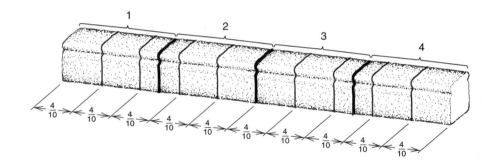

Figure 5.19

Example D

Answer each question with a fraction.

1. Two gallons of cider is poured into 7 containers in equal amounts. How much cider is there in each container?

2. Four acres of land is divided equally into 15 parts. How much land is in each part?

Solution   1. $\frac{2}{7}$ gallon   2. $\frac{4}{15}$ acre

RATIO CONCEPT   Another use of fractions involves the *ratio concept.* In this case, fractions are used to compare one amount to another. For example, we might say that a boy's height is one-third of his mother's height.

The *ratio concept* of fractions can be illustrated with Cuisenaire Rods by comparing the lengths of two rods (see Figure 5.20). It takes 3 red rods to equal the length of 1 dark green rod in part a, so the length of the red rod is $\frac{1}{3}$ the length of the dark green rod. If the length of the dark green rod is chosen as the unit, then the red rod represents $\frac{1}{3}$. If a different unit is selected, the red rod will represent a different fraction. For example, if the yellow rod in part b is the unit length, then the red rod represents $\frac{2}{5}$, because the length of the red rod is $\frac{2}{5}$ the length of the yellow rod. Several different rods can represent the same fraction, depending on the choice of unit. In part a, $\frac{1}{3}$ is represented by a red rod, but if the unit is the length of the blue rod, as in part c, then the green rod represents $\frac{1}{3}$.

Figure 5.21 provides another example of the ratio concept of a fraction. The length of the San Andreas fault is compared to the length of California's coastal region. Ratios are discussed in greater detail in Section 6.3.

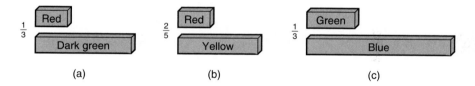

(a)   (b)   (c)

Figure 5.20

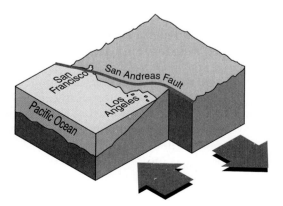

Figure 5.21
The San Andreas fault runs three-fourths of the length of California's coastal region.

Example E

It takes 4 red rods to equal the length of 1 brown rod and 5 white rods to equal the length of 1 yellow rod.

1. If the brown rod is the unit, what is the length of 1 red rod?

2. If the brown rod is the unit, what is the length of 3 red rods?

3. If the yellow rod is the unit, what is the length of 3 white rods?

Solution   1. $\frac{1}{4}$ 2. $\frac{3}{4}$ 3. $\frac{3}{5}$

Equality of Fractions

By using an area model in which part of a region is shaded, students can see how fractions are related to a unit whole, compare fractional parts of a whole, and find equivalent fractions.

Standards 2000, p. 150

Equality of fractions can be illustrated by comparing parts of figures. The charts in Figure 5.22 show that $\frac{1}{3} = \frac{2}{6}$, $\frac{1}{3} = \frac{4}{12}$, $\frac{1}{2} = \frac{2}{4}$, etc.

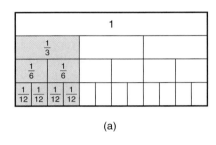

Figure 5.22   (a)   (b)

Example F

Write three more equalities that are illustrated by each of the charts in Figure 5.22.

Solution   Here are some possibilities:

Part a: $\frac{2}{3} = \frac{4}{6}$, $\frac{2}{3} = \frac{8}{12}$, $\frac{3}{6} = \frac{6}{12}$, $1 = \frac{3}{3}$, $1 = \frac{6}{6}$

Part b: $\frac{1}{2} = \frac{4}{8}$, $\frac{1}{4} = \frac{2}{8}$, $\frac{3}{4} = \frac{6}{8}$, $1 = \frac{4}{4}$, $1 = \frac{8}{8}$

Equality of fractions can also be illustrated with sets of objects. For example, 3 out of 12, or $\frac{3}{12}$, of the points shown in Figure 5.23 are circled. Viewed in another way, $\frac{1}{4}$ of the points are circled, because there are 4 rows, each containing the same number of points, and 1 row is circled. So $\frac{3}{12}$ and $\frac{1}{4}$ are equivalent fractions representing the same amount.

For every fraction there are an infinite number of other fractions that represent the same number. The Fraction Bars in Figure 5.24 show one method of obtaining fractions equal to $\frac{3}{4}$. In part b, each part of the $\frac{3}{4}$ bar has been split into 2 equal parts to show that $\frac{3}{4} = \frac{6}{8}$. We see that doubling the number of parts in a bar also doubles the number of shaded parts. This is equivalent to multiplying the numerator and denominator of $\frac{3}{4}$ by 2. Similarly, part c shows that splitting each part of a $\frac{3}{4}$ bar into 3 equal parts triples the number of parts in the bar and triples the number of shaded parts. This has the effect of multiplying the numerator and denominator of $\frac{3}{4}$ by 3 and shows that $\frac{3}{4}$ is equal to $\frac{9}{12}$.

Figure 5.23

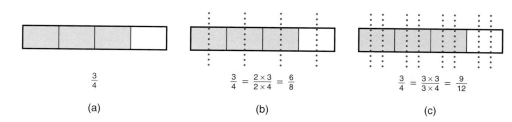

$\dfrac{3}{4}$

(a)

$\dfrac{3}{4} = \dfrac{2 \times 3}{2 \times 4} = \dfrac{6}{8}$

(b)

$\dfrac{3}{4} = \dfrac{3 \times 3}{3 \times 4} = \dfrac{9}{12}$

(c)

Figure 5.24

The examples in Figure 5.24 illustrate the *fundamental rule for equality of fractions:* For any fraction, an **equal fraction** will be obtained by multiplying the numerator and denominator by a nonzero number.

Research Statement

An understanding of equivalence of fractions is important in developing sense of relative size of fractions and helping students connect their intuitive understandings to more general methods.

Wearne and Kouba 2000

FUNDAMENTAL RULE FOR EQUALITY OF FRACTIONS   For any fraction *a/b* and any number $k \neq 0$,

$$\frac{a}{b} = \frac{ka}{kb}$$

The rule for equality of fractions, $\dfrac{a}{b} = \dfrac{ka}{kb}$ when $k \neq 0$, holds because multiplying a number by 1 does not change the identity of the number, and for $k \neq 0, \dfrac{k}{k} = 1$.

$$\frac{a}{b} = 1 \times \frac{a}{b} = \frac{k}{k} \times \frac{a}{b} = \frac{ka}{kb}$$

SIMPLIFYING FRACTIONS   The definition of equality of fractions justifies a process called **simplifying fractions**. For example, since 6 and 15 have a common factor of 3, $\frac{6}{15}$ may be written as a fraction with a smaller numerator and denominator:

$$\frac{6}{15} = \frac{3 \times 2}{3 \times 5} = \frac{2}{5} \qquad \text{or} \qquad \frac{6}{15} = \frac{6 \div 3}{15 \div 3} = \frac{2}{5}$$

Figure 5.25 illustrates these equalities. If the figure is viewed as a bar with 5 equal parts, 2 of which are shaded, it represents $\frac{2}{5}$. Splitting each part into 3 equal parts shows that $\frac{2}{5} = \frac{6}{15}$. If the figure is viewed as a bar with 15 equal parts, 6 of which are shaded, it represents $\frac{6}{15}$. Grouping the 15 parts of the bar into 5 equal groups of 3 parts each produces a bar with 5 equal parts, 2 of which are shaded, to show that $\frac{6}{15} = \frac{2}{5}$.

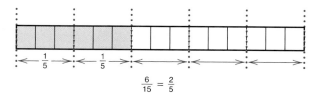

$\dfrac{1}{5}$ $\dfrac{1}{5}$

$\dfrac{6}{15} = \dfrac{2}{5}$

Figure 5.25

Whenever the numerator and denominator of a fraction have a common factor greater than 1, they can be divided by this factor to obtain a fraction with a smaller numerator and denominator. If the numerator and denominator of a fraction are divided by their greatest common factor (GCF), the resulting fraction is called the **simplest form** and the fraction is said to be in **lowest terms**.

Example G

Write each fraction in simplest form.

1. $\dfrac{8}{12}$ 2. $\dfrac{24}{28}$ 3. $\dfrac{8}{16}$

Solution   1. $\dfrac{2}{3}$ 2. $\dfrac{6}{7}$ 3. $\dfrac{1}{2}$

 There are several different brands of calculators which display fractions. The keystrokes and view screens for four of these are shown in Figure 5.26.

18 $\boxed{\tfrac{x}{y}}$ 24

18 $\boxed{/}$ 24

18 $\boxed{b/c}$ 24

18 2nd $\boxed{b/c}$ 24

Figure 5.26

Entering a fraction and pressing $\boxed{=}$ (or Enter) will display the fraction in simplest form in most calculators designed for fractions. However, to help school children learn fraction concepts, some calculators have keys, such as $\boxed{\text{SIMP}}$, for simplifying fractions. The following keystrokes show the use of the key $\boxed{\text{SIMP}}$. Look carefully at the view screens to see how this key simplifies the fraction $\frac{18}{24}$.

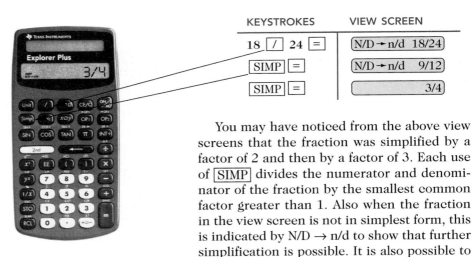

KEYSTROKES	VIEW SCREEN
18 $\boxed{/}$ 24 $\boxed{=}$	N/D → n/d 18/24
$\boxed{\text{SIMP}}$ $\boxed{=}$	N/D → n/d 9/12
$\boxed{\text{SIMP}}$ $\boxed{=}$	3/4

Figure 5.26A

You may have noticed from the above view screens that the fraction was simplified by a factor of 2 and then by a factor of 3. Each use of $\boxed{\text{SIMP}}$ divides the numerator and denominator of the fraction by the smallest common factor greater than 1. Also when the fraction in the view screen is not in simplest form, this is indicated by N/D → n/d to show that further simplification is possible. It is also possible to select a common factor for simplifying a fraction. If $\frac{12}{30}$ is on the calculator view screen, pressing $\boxed{\text{SIMP}}$ $\boxed{3}$ will replace the fraction by $\frac{4}{10}$, or pressing $\boxed{\text{SIMP}}$ $\boxed{6}$ will replace the fraction by $\frac{2}{5}$.

Some calculators with a key for simplifying fractions print common factors of the numerator and denominator on the view screen. The view screens shown on the next page begin with $\frac{18}{24}$. The first time $\boxed{\text{SIMP}}$ is pressed, the common factor 2 of 18 and 24 flashes briefly on the screen, and the fraction $\frac{9}{12}$ is printed. The second time $\boxed{\text{SIMP}}$ is pressed, the common factor 3 of 9 and 12 flashes briefly on the screen and $\frac{3}{4}$ is printed. It is also possible on this calculator to select common factors of the numerator and denominator in order to simplify a fraction.

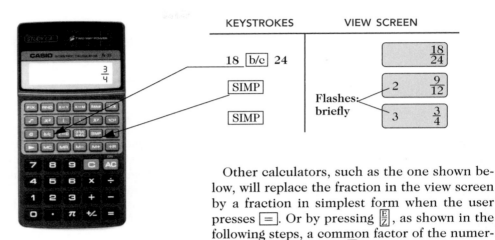

Figure 5.26B

Other calculators, such as the one shown below, will replace the fraction in the view screen by a fraction in simplest form when the user presses $\boxed{=}$. Or by pressing $\boxed{\frac{E}{Z}}$, as shown in the following steps, a common factor of the numerator and denominator can be entered. Notice that when $\boxed{\frac{E}{Z}}$ is pressed, the calculator prints a question mark to ask that a factor be entered.

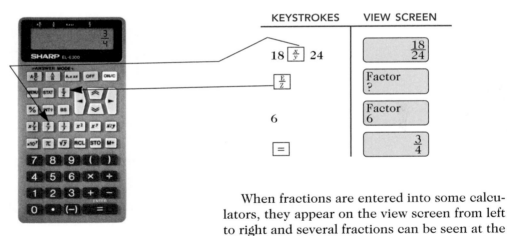

Figure 5.26C

When fractions are entered into some calculators, they appear on the view screen from left to right and several fractions can be seen at the same time (Figure 5.26D). If more fractions are entered than can be displayed on the view screen, previously entered fractions are moved off the screen but are retained internally in the calculator's memory.

Figure 5.26D

Example H

Determine which fractions are in lowest terms. If a fraction is not in lowest terms, write the fraction in simplest form.

1. $\dfrac{4}{15}$ 2. $\dfrac{^{-}8}{24}$ 3. $\dfrac{18}{30}$ 4. $\dfrac{10}{21}$ 5. $\dfrac{10}{^{-}15}$

Solution   1. $\dfrac{4}{15}$ is in lowest terms.   2. GCF(8, 24) = 8, so $\dfrac{^{-}8}{24} = \dfrac{^{-}1}{3}$ 3. GCF(18, 30) = 6, so $\dfrac{18}{30} =$ $\dfrac{3}{5}$ 4. $\dfrac{10}{21}$ is in lowest terms.   5. GCF(10, 15) = 5, so $\dfrac{10}{^{-}15} = \dfrac{2}{^{-}3}$

Common Denominators

Research Statement

One implication for teachers from the 7th national mathematics assessment, is that there is a need to develop more fully the basic notions of rational numbers.

Wearne and Kouba 2000

One of the more important skills in the use of fractions is to replace two fractions with different denominators by two fractions with equal denominators. The fractions $\frac{1}{6}$ and $\frac{1}{4}$ have different denominators, and the Fraction Bars representing these fractions have different numbers of parts (see bars on left in Figure 5.27). If each part of the $\frac{1}{6}$ bar is split into 2 equal parts and each part of the $\frac{1}{4}$ bar is split into 3 equal parts, both bars will have 12 equal parts. The fractions for these new bars, $\frac{2}{12}$ and $\frac{3}{12}$, have a **common denominator** of 12.

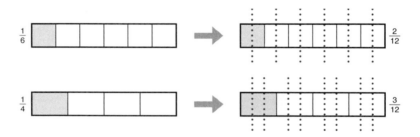

Figure 5.27

Obtaining the same number of equal parts for two bars is a visual way of finding a common denominator. The *Curriculum and Evaluation Standards for School Mathematics* notes the importance of using models to understand the common ideas underlying different types of numbers:

> . . . to compare $\frac{2}{3}$ and $\frac{3}{4}$, students can use concrete materials to represent them as $\frac{8}{12}$ and $\frac{9}{12}$, respectively, and then conclude that $\frac{8}{12}$ is less than $\frac{9}{12}$, since 8 is less than 9. Thus, they learn that comparing fractions is like comparing whole numbers once common denominators have been identified.*

Another method for finding common denominators of two fractions is to list the multiples of their denominators. The arrows in Figure 5.28 point to the common multiples of 6 and 4. The least common multiple (LCM) of 6 and 4 is 12. This is also the smallest common denominator for $\frac{1}{6}$ and $\frac{1}{4}$. In general, the **smallest common denominator** of two fractions is the least common multiple of their denominators.

Curriculum and Evaluation Standards for School Mathematics (Reston, VA: National Council of Teachers of Mathematics, 1989), p. 92.

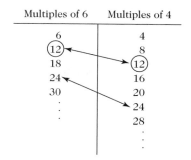

Figure 5.28

Once a common denominator has been found, two fractions can be replaced by fractions having the same denominator.

$$\frac{1}{6} = \frac{2 \times 1}{2 \times 6} = \frac{2}{12} \qquad \frac{1}{4} = \frac{3 \times 1}{3 \times 4} = \frac{3}{12}$$

Example I

Replace the fractions in each pair by equal fractions having the smallest common denominator.

1. $\dfrac{3}{4}, \dfrac{2}{5}$ 2. $\dfrac{7}{12}, \dfrac{^-3}{8}$ 3. $\dfrac{1}{6}, \dfrac{5}{18}$ 4. $\dfrac{1}{-4}, \dfrac{3}{7}$

Solution   1. LCM(4, 5) = 20; $\dfrac{3}{4} = \dfrac{15}{20}$ and $\dfrac{2}{5} = \dfrac{8}{20}$ 2. LCM(12, 8) = 24; $\dfrac{7}{12} = \dfrac{14}{24}$ and $\dfrac{^-3}{8} = \dfrac{^-9}{24}$ 3. LCM(6, 18) = 18; $\dfrac{1}{6} = \dfrac{3}{18}, \dfrac{5}{18}$ does not need to be replaced.   4. First replace $\dfrac{1}{-4}$ by a fraction with a positive denominator $\left(\dfrac{^-1}{4}\right)$. LCM(4, 7) = 28; $\dfrac{^-1}{4} = \dfrac{^-7}{28}$ and $\dfrac{3}{7} = \dfrac{12}{28}$.

Sometimes it is convenient to replace a fraction involving negative signs by equal fractions. In problem 4 of Example I, a fraction with a negative denominator was replaced by a fraction with a positive denominator. The rules for making such substitutions are shown below and follow directly from the *rule of signs for division of integers* on page 263.

RULES OF SIGNS FOR FRACTIONS   For integers *a* and *b* with *b* ≠ 0,

$$\frac{a}{-b} = \frac{^-a}{b} = ^-\left(\frac{a}{b}\right) \quad \text{and} \quad \frac{^-a}{-b} = \frac{a}{b}$$

$$\frac{5}{-12} = \frac{^-5}{12} = ^-\left(\frac{5}{12}\right) \quad \text{and} \quad \frac{^-3}{-10} = \frac{3}{10}$$

We can determine whether two fractions are equal by obtaining their common denominators. Consider the fractions $\frac{19}{62}$ and $\frac{8}{27}$. Using the fundamental rule for equality of fractions, we can multiply the numerator and denominator of $\frac{19}{62}$ by 27 and the numerator and denominator of $\frac{8}{27}$ by 62.

$$\frac{19}{62} = \frac{27 \times 19}{27 \times 62} \quad \text{and} \quad \frac{8}{27} = \frac{62 \times 8}{62 \times 27}$$

These fractions now have a common denominator, and they are equal if and only if their numerators, 27×19 and 8×62, are equal. Are the fractions equal? This approach to determining equality suggests the following test for equality of fractions.

TEST FOR EQUALITY OF FRACTIONS   For any fractions a/b and c/d,

$$\frac{a}{b} = \frac{c}{d} \qquad \text{if and only if} \qquad ad = bc$$

Example J

Use the test for equality of fractions to determine which pairs of fractions are equal.

1. $\dfrac{42}{105}, \dfrac{14}{35}$ 2. $\dfrac{^-2}{3}, \dfrac{2}{^-3}$ 3. $\dfrac{8}{71}, \dfrac{5}{43}$ 4. $\dfrac{3}{^-9}, \dfrac{4}{^-12}$

Solution   1. $42 \times 35 = 105 \times 14 = 1470$, so $\dfrac{42}{105} = \dfrac{14}{35}$ 2. $(^-2)(^-3) = (3)(2) = 6$, so $\dfrac{^-2}{3} = \dfrac{2}{^-3}$
3. $8 \times 43 = 344 \neq 71 \times 5 = 355$, so $\dfrac{8}{71} \neq \dfrac{5}{43}$ 4. $3 \times ^-12 = ^-9 \times 4 = ^-36$, so $\dfrac{3}{^-9} = \dfrac{4}{^-12}$

Inequality

Charts such as the one in Figure 5.29 illustrate many different inequalities of fractions.

In grades 3–5 students should be able to reason about numbers by, for instance, explaining that $\frac{1}{2} + \frac{3}{8}$ must be less than 1 because each addend is less than or equal to $\frac{1}{2}$.

Standards 2000, p. 33

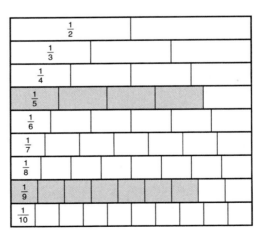

Figure 5.29

Example K

Place the edge of a piece of paper on this chart to determine an inequality, either $<$ or $>$, for each of the following pairs of fractions.

1. $\dfrac{4}{5}, \dfrac{7}{9}$ 2. $\dfrac{5}{8}, \dfrac{2}{3}$ 3. $\dfrac{2}{7}, \dfrac{3}{10}$ 4. $\dfrac{3}{4}, \dfrac{5}{7}$

Solution   1. $\dfrac{4}{5} > \dfrac{7}{9}$ 2. $\dfrac{5}{8} < \dfrac{2}{3}$ 3. $\dfrac{2}{7} < \dfrac{3}{10}$ 4. $\dfrac{3}{4} > \dfrac{5}{7}$

Example L   List a few other inequalities of fractions that are illustrated in Figure 5.29. What patterns of inequalities are there?

Solution   Here are a few of the many inequalities:

$$\frac{1}{4} < \frac{1}{3} \qquad \frac{2}{3} < \frac{3}{4} \qquad \frac{1}{2} < \frac{2}{3} \qquad \frac{5}{8} < \frac{6}{9} \qquad \frac{1}{6} > \frac{1}{7} \qquad \frac{4}{5} > \frac{3}{4}$$

The left edge of Figure 5.29 shows a pattern of decreasing inequalities

$$\frac{1}{2} > \frac{1}{3} > \frac{1}{4} > \frac{1}{5} > \frac{1}{6} > \frac{1}{7} > \frac{1}{8} > \frac{1}{9} > \frac{1}{10}$$

and the right edge shows an increasing pattern

$$\frac{1}{2} < \frac{2}{3} < \frac{3}{4} < \frac{4}{5} < \frac{5}{6} < \frac{6}{7} < \frac{7}{8} < \frac{8}{9} < \frac{9}{10}$$

One of the reasons for finding a common denominator for two fractions is to be able to determine the greater fraction. It is difficult to determine whether $\frac{5}{8}$ or $\frac{3}{5}$ is greater without first replacing them by fractions having a common denominator. The least common multiple of 8 and 5 is 40. Replacing both $\frac{5}{8}$ and $\frac{3}{5}$ by fractions having a denominator of 40, we see that $\frac{5}{8}$ is the greater fraction.

$$\frac{5}{8} = \frac{5 \times 5}{5 \times 8} = \frac{25}{40} \qquad \frac{3}{5} = \frac{8 \times 3}{8 \times 5} = \frac{24}{40}$$

In general, an inequality for two fractions a/b and c/d with positive denominators can be determined by replacing them with fractions having a common denominator

$$\frac{ad}{bd} \qquad \text{and} \qquad \frac{bc}{bd}$$

and comparing their numerators ad and bc.

TEST FOR INEQUALITY OF FRACTIONS   For any fractions a/b and c/d, with b and d positive integers,

$$\frac{a}{b} < \frac{c}{d} \quad \text{if and only if} \quad ad < bc$$

and

$$\frac{a}{b} > \frac{c}{d} \quad \text{if and only if} \quad ad > bc$$

Example M   Determine an inequality for each pair of fractions.

1. $\dfrac{3}{7}, \dfrac{4}{10}$ 2. $\dfrac{3}{4}, \dfrac{7}{9}$ 3. $\dfrac{^-3}{7}, \dfrac{^-2}{5}$ 4. $\dfrac{1}{2}, \dfrac{1}{^-3}$

Solution   1. $3 \times 10 > 7 \times 4$, so $\dfrac{3}{7} > \dfrac{4}{10}$ 2. $3 \times 9 < 4 \times 7$, so $\dfrac{3}{4} < \dfrac{7}{9}$ 3. $^-3 \times 5 < 7 \times ^-2$, so $\dfrac{^-3}{7} < \dfrac{^-2}{5}$ 4. $\dfrac{1}{2} > \dfrac{1}{^-3}$ because $\dfrac{1}{2}$ is positive and $\dfrac{1}{^-3}$ is negative.

Density of Fractions

The integers are evenly spaced on the number line, and for any integer there is a "next" integer, both to its right and to its left. For fractions, however, this is not true.

Example N

There is no single fraction that is the *next one* greater than $\frac{1}{2}$. Find a fraction that is between $\frac{1}{2}$ and $\frac{6}{10}$.

Solution   One method of finding fractions between two given fractions is to express both fractions with a larger common denominator. The following figure shows several sections of a number line with fractions that are equal to $\frac{1}{2}$ and $\frac{6}{10}$. By increasing the denominators, we can easily find fractions between $\frac{1}{2}$ and $\frac{6}{10}$. For example, the third number line shows that the 9 fractions from $\frac{51}{100}$ to $\frac{59}{100}$ are between $\frac{1}{2}$ and $\frac{6}{10}$, and the fourth number line shows that the 99 fractions from $\frac{501}{1000}$ to $\frac{599}{1000}$ are between $\frac{1}{2}$ and $\frac{6}{10}$.

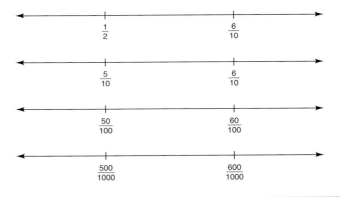

Similarly, there is no fraction next to zero. To state this another way, there is no smallest fraction greater than zero. The following sequence of fractions gets closer and closer to zero, but no matter how far we go in this sequence, these fractions will always be greater than zero.

$$\frac{1}{2}, \ \frac{1}{4}, \ \frac{1}{8}, \ \frac{1}{16}, \ \frac{1}{32}, \ \frac{1}{64}, \ \frac{1}{128}, \ \cdots$$

These examples are special cases of the more general fact that between any two fractions there is always another fraction. We refer to this property by saying that the fractions are **dense**. Because of this property of denseness, there are an infinite number of fractions between any two fractions.

Mixed Numbers and Improper Fractions

Historically, a fraction stood for part of a whole and represented a number less than 1. The idea that there could be fractions such as $\frac{4}{4}$ or $\frac{5}{4}$ with numerators greater than or equal to the denominator was uncommon even as late as the sixteenth century. Such fractions are called **improper fractions,** and as their name indicates, at one time they were not thought of as authentic fractions.

When improper fractions are written as a combination of whole numbers and fractions, they are called **mixed numbers.** The numbers below are examples of mixed numbers:

$$1\frac{1}{5} \qquad 2\frac{3}{4} \qquad 4\frac{2}{3} \qquad 15\frac{1}{8}$$

Placing a whole number and a fraction side by side, as in mixed numbers, indicates the sum of the two numbers. For example, $1\frac{1}{5}$ means $1 + \frac{1}{5}$. This fact is used in converting a mixed number to an improper fraction. For example,

$$1\frac{1}{5} = 1 + \frac{1}{5} = \frac{5}{5} + \frac{1}{5} = \frac{6}{5} \quad \text{and} \quad 2\frac{3}{4} = 2 + \frac{3}{4} = \frac{8}{4} + \frac{3}{4} = \frac{11}{4}$$

Example O

Write a mixed number and an improper fraction to express the shaded amount of each figure. In part 1, each disk represents 1, and in part 2, each bar represents 1.

1. 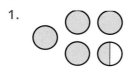   2.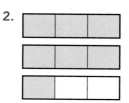

Solution   1. $4\frac{1}{2}$ or $\frac{9}{2}$ (Since each whole disk has 2 halves, a total of 9 halves are shaded.)

$$4\frac{1}{2} = 4 + \frac{1}{2} = \frac{8}{2} + \frac{1}{2} = \frac{9}{2}$$

2. $2\frac{1}{3}$ or $\frac{7}{3}$ (Since each whole bar has 3 thirds, a total of 7 thirds are shaded.)

$$2\frac{1}{3} = 2 + \frac{1}{3} = \frac{6}{3} + \frac{1}{3} = \frac{7}{3}$$

Example P

Write the missing mixed number above each improper fraction on the following number line, and write the missing improper fraction below each mixed number on the number line.

Research Statement

Performance suggests that many students are not proficient at locating points on the number line when mixed numbers are required.

Blume and Heckman 2000

Solution $\frac{^-9}{5} = {^-}1\frac{4}{5}, \ {^-}1\frac{3}{5} = \frac{^-8}{5}, \ {^-}1\frac{1}{5} = \frac{^-6}{5}, \ 1\frac{2}{5} = \frac{7}{5}, \ \frac{8}{5} = 1\frac{3}{5}, \ 1\frac{4}{5} = \frac{9}{5}$

Notice that in a negative mixed number the negative sign is on only the whole number part and yet the fraction is also understood to be negative. For example, ${^-}1\frac{1}{5}$ is equal to ${^-}1 + {^-}\left(\frac{1}{5}\right)$.

The number line in Example P indicates that the improper fractions $\frac{5}{5}$ and $\frac{10}{5}$ are equal to whole numbers. One method of illustrating such equalities is to use the sharing concept of division. For example, $\frac{5}{5}$ can be illustrated by 5 divided into 5 equal parts, as shown in Figure 5.30, and $\frac{10}{5}$ by 10 divided into 5 equal parts.

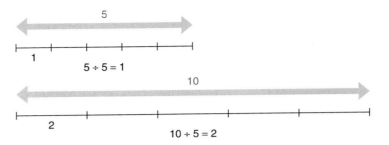

Figure 5.30

 Calculators which display fractions will convert improper fractions to mixed numbers. Some calculators will automatically replace an improper fraction which has been entered by a mixed number whose fraction is in simplified form. For example, the keystrokes shown below yield the fraction $\frac{30}{18}$, and pressing $\boxed{=}$ replaces the improper fraction by $1\frac{2}{3}$.

KEYSTROKES	VIEW SCREEN
30 $\boxed{\frac{x}{y}}$ 18	$\frac{30}{18}$
$\boxed{=}$	$1\frac{2}{3}$

In this next sequence of keystrokes, we see that once an improper fraction is entered, pressing $\boxed{\text{A b/c}}$ will replace the fraction by a mixed number or integer, but it will not necessarily be in simplified form. These keystrokes also show the use of the key $\boxed{\text{SIMP}}$ for simplifying fractions. Notice the u-shaped symbol that separates the whole number from the fraction in these view screens.

KEYSTROKES	VIEW SCREEN
30 $\boxed{/}$ 18 $\boxed{=}$	N/D → n/d 30/18
$\boxed{\text{A b/c}}$	N/D → n/d 1⌴12/18
$\boxed{\text{SIMP}}$ $\boxed{=}$	N/D → n/d 1⌴6/9
$\boxed{\text{SIMP}}$ $\boxed{=}$	1⌴2/3

Some calculators have a key for converting back and forth from an improper fraction to a mixed number, as illustrated below.

KEYSTROKES	VIEW SCREEN
5 $\boxed{\text{b/c}}$ 3	$\frac{5}{3}$
$\boxed{\begin{array}{c}\text{a b/c}\\ \text{↔ d/c}\end{array}}$	$1\frac{2}{3}$
$\boxed{\begin{array}{c}\text{a b/c}\\ \text{↔ d/c}\end{array}}$	$\frac{5}{3}$

Mental Calculations

The *Curriculum and Evaluation Standards for School Mathematics* states, "Fraction symbols, such as $\frac{1}{4}$ and $\frac{2}{3}$, should be introduced only after children have developed the concepts and oral language necessary for symbols to be meaningful and should be carefully connected to both the models and oral language."* One reason for the use of models is to build number sense for mental calculations. Inequalities of fractions can often be determined by appealing to visual models. For example, the chart in Figure 5.31 shows why it is easy to determine an inequality for two unit fractions: *The more parts in a bar, the smaller the parts.*

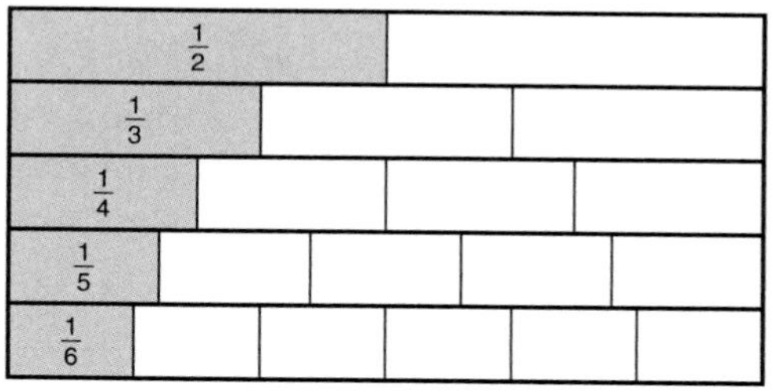

Figure 5.31

Example Q

Use the observation in the paragraph above to mentally determine an inequality for each of the following pairs of fractions.

1. $\dfrac{1}{12}, \dfrac{1}{5}$ 2. $\dfrac{1}{9}, \dfrac{1}{20}$ 3. $\dfrac{1}{11}, \dfrac{1}{3}$

Solution   1. $\dfrac{1}{12} < \dfrac{1}{5}$ because a bar with 12 equal parts has smaller parts than a bar with 5 equal parts.
2. $\dfrac{1}{9} > \dfrac{1}{20}$ because a bar with 9 equal parts has larger parts than a bar with 20 equal parts.   3. $\dfrac{1}{11} < \dfrac{1}{3}$ because a bar with 11 equal parts has smaller parts than a bar with 3 equal parts.

It is also easy to compare two fractions mentally when the numerator of each fraction is 1 less than the denominator of the fraction. For example, to compare $\frac{4}{5}$ and $\frac{2}{3}$ (see Figure 5.32), we note that a $\frac{4}{5}$ bar is within $\frac{1}{5}$ of being a whole bar and a $\frac{2}{3}$ bar is within $\frac{1}{3}$ of being a whole bar. Since $\frac{1}{5} < \frac{1}{3}$, a $\frac{4}{5}$ bar is closer in length to a whole bar than a $\frac{2}{3}$ bar is. So $\frac{4}{5} > \frac{2}{3}$.

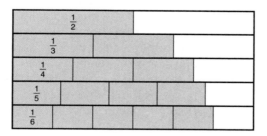

Figure 5.32

Curriculum and Evaluation Standards for School Mathematics (Reston, VA: National Council of Teachers of Mathematics, 1989), p. 58.

Example R

Mentally determine an inequality for each of the following pairs of fractions.

1. $\dfrac{9}{10}, \dfrac{2}{3}$　　　　2. $\dfrac{3}{4}, \dfrac{14}{15}$　　　　3. $\dfrac{19}{20}, \dfrac{5}{6}$

Solution　1. $\dfrac{9}{10} > \dfrac{2}{3}$ because $\dfrac{1}{10} < \dfrac{1}{3}$　2. $\dfrac{3}{4} < \dfrac{14}{15}$ because $\dfrac{1}{4} > \dfrac{1}{15}$　3. $\dfrac{19}{20} > \dfrac{5}{6}$ because $\dfrac{1}{20} < \dfrac{1}{6}$

Comparing fractions to $\frac{1}{2}$ is also a convenient method of determining inequalities for some pairs of fractions. Consider the fractions $\frac{3}{7}$ and $\frac{5}{9}$. Figure 5.33 shows that if the numerator is less than one-half the denominator, the bar for the fraction is less than half shaded and the fraction is less than $\frac{1}{2}$. If the numerator is equal to one-half the denominator, the bar for the fraction is half shaded and the fraction is equal to $\frac{1}{2}$. If the numerator is greater than one-half the denominator, more than half of the bar for the fraction is shaded and the fraction is greater than $\frac{1}{2}$. Since $\frac{3}{7} < \frac{1}{2}$ and $\frac{5}{9} > \frac{1}{2}$, we know that $\frac{3}{7} < \frac{5}{9}$.

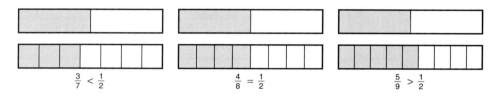

$\dfrac{3}{7} < \dfrac{1}{2}$　　　　$\dfrac{4}{8} = \dfrac{1}{2}$　　　　$\dfrac{5}{9} > \dfrac{1}{2}$

Figure 5.33

Example S

Mentally determine an inequality for each pair of fractions by comparing each fraction to $\frac{1}{2}$.

1. $\dfrac{5}{8}, \dfrac{4}{11}$　　　　2. $\dfrac{7}{15}, \dfrac{5}{9}$　　　　3. $\dfrac{9}{20}, \dfrac{3}{5}$

Solution　1. $\dfrac{5}{8} > \dfrac{1}{2}$ and $\dfrac{4}{11} < \dfrac{1}{2}$, so $\dfrac{5}{8} > \dfrac{4}{11}$　2. $\dfrac{7}{15} < \dfrac{1}{2}$ and $\dfrac{5}{9} > \dfrac{1}{2}$, so $\dfrac{7}{15} < \dfrac{5}{9}$　3. $\dfrac{9}{20} < \dfrac{1}{2}$ and $\dfrac{3}{5} > \dfrac{1}{2}$, so $\dfrac{9}{20} < \dfrac{3}{5}$

Estimation

Estimations involving fractions are often obtained by rounding. Rounding fractions and mixed numbers to the nearest whole number involves comparing fractions to $\frac{1}{2}$. If the fraction is less than $\frac{1}{2}$, it is rounded to 0; and if it is greater than $\frac{1}{2}$, it is rounded to 1. If the fraction is equal to $\frac{1}{2}$, it may be rounded up or down; in this text we will round such fractions up. Similarly, a mixed number is rounded down or up depending on whether the fraction rounds to 0 or to 1.

Rounding can be thought of by considering which whole number on a number line a given number is closest to (see Figure 5.34). For example, $2\frac{5}{8}$ is closer to 3 than to 2, so it rounds to 3; and $\frac{3}{8}$ is closer to 0 than to 1, so it rounds to 0.

Figure 5.34

Example T

Round each fraction or mixed number to the nearest whole number.

1. $\dfrac{2}{5}$ 2. $4\dfrac{3}{7}$ 3. $\dfrac{8}{3}$ 4. $7\dfrac{3}{6}$

Solution   1. 0   2. 4   3. 3   4. 8

Another method of approximating fractions is to replace a fraction by a close approximation that is in simpler form. For example,

$$\frac{7}{22} \approx \frac{7}{21} = \frac{1}{3} \quad and \quad 1\frac{4}{9} \approx 1\frac{3}{9} = 1\frac{1}{3}$$

Example U

Replace each fraction or mixed number by a close approximation that is in simpler form.

1. $4\dfrac{17}{30}$ 2. $12\dfrac{5}{26}$ 3. $\dfrac{4}{13}$ 4. $\dfrac{19}{80}$

Solution   Here are some possible replacements. Others may occur to you.   1. $4\dfrac{17}{30} \approx 4\dfrac{15}{30} = 4\dfrac{1}{2}$
2. $12\dfrac{5}{26} \approx 12\dfrac{5}{25} = 12\dfrac{1}{5}$ 3. $\dfrac{4}{13} \approx \dfrac{4}{12} = \dfrac{1}{3}$ 4. $\dfrac{19}{80} \approx \dfrac{20}{80} = \dfrac{1}{4}$

Problem-Solving Application

The following problem can be solved by *guessing and checking* or by *making a drawing*. Try to solve this problem before you read the solution. If you need assistance, read the paragraph "Understanding the Problem" and then try to find the solution.

PROBLEM

In a certain community two-thirds of the women are married and one-half of the men are married. No one in the community is married to a person outside the community. What fraction of the adults are unmarried?

Understanding the Problem   Let's *guess* at some numbers to obtain a better understanding of the problem. For the number of women, we want to select a number that is divisible by 3 (12, 15, 18, 24, 30, 60, etc.) so that we can find $\frac{2}{3}$ of it. Suppose we choose a total of 24 women. In this case 16 women ($\frac{2}{3}$ of 24) are married. Since for each married woman there is a married man, there are 16 married men and thus 32 men in the community. **Question 1:** For this example, what fraction of the adults are married and what fraction are unmarried?

Devising a Plan   Another approach is to *make a drawing* to see if it leads to a solution. The married women can be represented by shading $\frac{2}{3}$ of a figure and the married men by shading $\frac{1}{2}$ of a figure, as shown on the next page. These two figures represent the total population. **Question 2:** Why are the shaded regions equal?

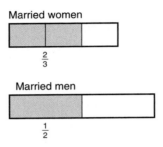

Carrying Out the Plan   Let's continue the visual approach. If we divide in halves both the shaded and unshaded parts of the figure representing the men, each new part is the same size as each part of the figure representing the women. **Question 3:** How does this show that $\frac{4}{7}$ of the people are married and $\frac{3}{7}$ are not married?

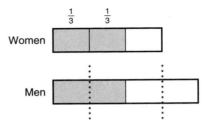

Looking Back   The visual approach suggests that it is not necessary to know the number of women and men in the community; we will obtain the same answer regardless of the number of women used in a numerical approach. Suppose we select 30 as the number of women. Then there will be 20 married women ($\frac{2}{3}$ of 30 is 20) and 20 married men. Since $\frac{1}{2}$ of 40 is 20, there will be 40 men in the community and a total of 70 people. **Question 4:** In this case, how many people are not married, and what fraction of the people are not married?

Answers to Questions 1–4   **1.** $\frac{32}{56} = \frac{4}{7}$ are married and $\frac{24}{56} = \frac{3}{7}$ are unmarried.   **2.** There is the same number of married men as married women in the community.   **3.** There are a total of 7 equal parts: the 4 shaded parts represent the married people, so $\frac{4}{7}$ are married; the 3 unshaded parts represent the unmarried people, so $\frac{3}{7}$ are not married.   **4.** 30 people are not married, so $\frac{30}{70} = \frac{3}{7}$ are not married.

PUZZLER
After a cake has been cut into three equal pieces, as shown here, a hostess discovers that four people each want an equal share of the cake. How can she make one more straight cut so that each of the four people gets the same amount of cake?

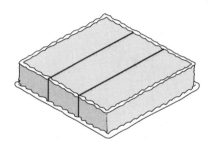

EXERCISES AND PROBLEMS 5.2

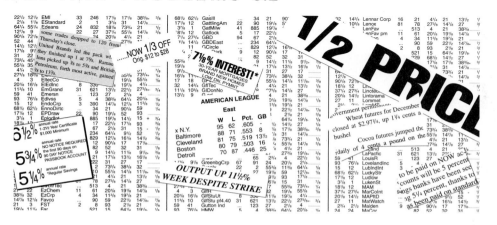

Use the above collage in exercises 1 and 2. Only a few different denominators occur in the fractions that appear frequently in newspapers, magazines, sales ads, etc.

1. **a.** Name four fractions with different denominators from the collage.
    b. The four fractions in part a can be paired in six ways. Write the common denominator for each of these pairs of fractions.

2. **a.** There are many mixed numbers in the collage. Name five of them.
    b. Write the mixed numbers in part a as improper fractions.

For each figure in exercises 3 and 4, write two fractions: one to indicate what part of the figure is shaded and one to indicate what part of the figure is unshaded.

3. **a.**

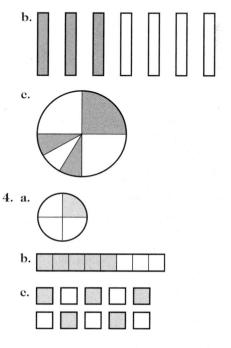

b.

c.

4. **a.**

b.

c.

Using each figure in exercises 5 and 6 and the *sharing (partitive) concept* of division, illustrate the quotient. Complete the equation and describe how the answer is obtained from the figure.

5. a.

$3 \div 2$

b.

$2 \div 4$

6. a.

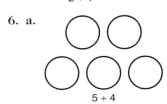

$5 \div 4$

b.

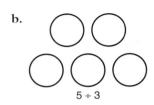

$5 \div 3$

Cuisenaire Rods can represent various fractions, depending on the choice of the unit rod. For example, if the unit rod is brown, then the purple rod represents $\frac{1}{2}$. Use the Cuisenaire Rods in exercises 7 and 8.

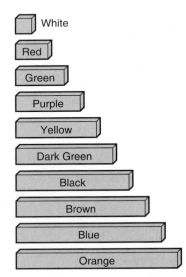

White
Red
Green
Purple
Yellow
Dark Green
Black
Brown
Blue
Orange

7. a. If the dark green rod represents $\frac{3}{4}$, what is the unit rod?
   b. What fraction is represented by the yellow rod if the black rod is the unit rod?

8. a. What is the unit rod if the purple rod represents $\frac{2}{3}$?
   b. If the unit rod is the orange rod, what fraction is represented by the black rod?

9. Use the array of dots to illustrate each equality.

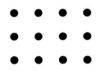

a. $\frac{1}{3} = \frac{4}{12}$ **b.** $\frac{6}{12} = \frac{1}{2}$

c. $\frac{2}{3} = \frac{8}{12}$ **d.** $\frac{9}{12} = \frac{3}{4}$

10. Use the array of dots to illustrate each equality.

a. $\frac{1}{4} = \frac{5}{20}$ **b.** $\frac{3}{5} = \frac{12}{20}$

c. $\frac{4}{5} = \frac{16}{20}$ **d.** $\frac{3}{4} = \frac{15}{20}$

Write the missing numbers for the fractions in exercises 11 and 12.

11. a. $\frac{3}{7} = \frac{12}{\_\_}$ **b.** $\frac{\_\_}{8} = \frac{25}{40}$

  c. $\frac{5}{6} = \frac{\_\_}{30}$ **d.** $\frac{9}{\_\_} = \frac{27}{12}$

12. a. $\frac{7}{8} = \frac{\_\_}{32}$ **b.** $\frac{\_\_}{3} = \frac{40}{24}$

  c. $\frac{2}{3} = \frac{12}{\_\_}$ **d.** $\frac{5}{\_\_} = \frac{20}{24}$

Write each fraction in exercises 13 and 14 in lowest terms.

13. a. $\frac{4}{18}$ **b.** $\frac{12}{27}$

  c. $\frac{4}{12}$ **d.** $\frac{^-16}{24}$

14. a. $\frac{18}{15}$ **b.** $\frac{^-20}{42}$

  c. $\frac{63}{70}$ **d.** $\frac{99}{154}$

Split the parts of the Fraction Bars in exercises 15 and 16 to illustrate the given equalities.

15. a. 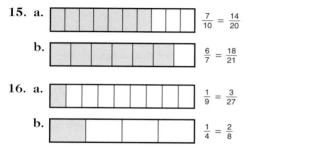 $\frac{7}{10} = \frac{14}{20}$

b. $\frac{6}{7} = \frac{18}{21}$

16. a. $\frac{1}{9} = \frac{3}{27}$

b. $\frac{1}{4} = \frac{2}{8}$

Group the parts of each bar in exercises 17 and 18 to show why the fraction on the left side of the equation equals the fraction on the right side.

17. a. 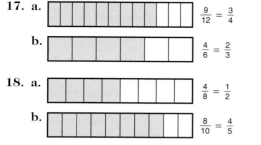 $\frac{9}{12} = \frac{3}{4}$

b. $\frac{4}{6} = \frac{2}{3}$

18. a. $\frac{4}{8} = \frac{1}{2}$

b. $\frac{8}{10} = \frac{4}{5}$

Complete the equations in exercises 19 and 20 so that each pair of fractions has the smallest common denominator.

19. a. $\frac{2}{3} =$ **b.** $\frac{1}{6} =$

$\frac{4}{5} =$ $\frac{^{-}7}{12} =$

20. a. $\frac{3}{15} =$ **b.** $\frac{5}{8} =$

$\frac{5}{6} =$ $\frac{3}{^{-}10} =$

Determine an inequality ($<$ or $>$) for each pair of fractions in exercises 21 and 22.

21. a. $\frac{3}{7}, \frac{5}{9}$ **b.** $\frac{1}{4}, \frac{1}{6}$ **c.** $\frac{^{-}5}{6}, \frac{^{-}7}{8}$

22. a. $\frac{1}{4}, \frac{2}{9}$ **b.** $\frac{3}{8}, \frac{1}{3}$ **c.** $\frac{4}{7}, \frac{^{-}5}{9}$

Between any two fractions there are an infinite number of fractions. Find a fraction that is between the fractions in each pair in 23 and 24.

23. a. $\frac{1}{20}, \frac{1}{10}$ **b.** $\frac{1}{2}, \frac{5}{8}$

24. a. $\frac{1}{3}, \frac{1}{4}$ **b.** $\frac{8}{9}, \frac{9}{10}$

Write each of the fractions in exercises 25 and 26 as a mixed number or a whole number.

25. a. $\frac{5}{3}$ **b.** $\frac{8}{8}$ **c.** $\frac{25}{6}$

26. a. $\frac{^{-}21}{7}$ **b.** $\frac{17}{5}$ **c.** $\frac{18}{2}$

Write each of the mixed numbers in exercises 27 and 28 as a fraction.

27. a. $1\frac{3}{4}$ **b.** $^{-}2\frac{1}{5}$ **c.** $4\frac{2}{3}$

28. a. $2\frac{5}{6}$ **b.** $1\frac{3}{7}$ **c.** $^{-}3\frac{1}{2}$

For each point indicated on the number lines in exercises 29 and 30, write the fraction or improper fraction that identifies it below the line. Then write the mixed number for each improper fraction above the line.

29.

30.

Mentally determine an inequality for each pair of fractions in exercises 31 and 32, and explain your reasoning by using a drawing.

31. a. $\frac{1}{12}, \frac{1}{20}$ **b.** $\frac{7}{8}, \frac{9}{10}$ **c.** $\frac{5}{12}, \frac{6}{11}$

32. a. $\frac{^{-}1}{50}, \frac{^{-}1}{30}$ **b.** $\frac{5}{9}, \frac{3}{7}$ **c.** $\frac{11}{12}, \frac{19}{20}$

Round each fraction or mixed number in exercises 33 and 34 to the nearest whole number.

33. a. $\frac{4}{10}$ **b.** $1\frac{1}{3}$ **c.** $3\frac{1}{2}$

34. a. $\frac{4}{7}$ **b.** $^{-}2\frac{3}{4}$ **c.** $\frac{2}{5}$

Some calculators for middle school students have a key for simplifying fractions. The key $\boxed{\text{SIMP}}$ is used for this purpose in exercises 35 and 36. Determine each fraction for the given steps if the numerator and the denominator of each fraction are divided by their smallest common factor other than 1 in moving from one calculator view screen to the next.

35.

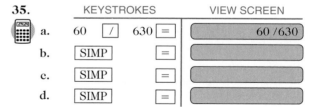

36.

KEYSTROKES	VIEW SCREEN
a. 126 $\boxed{/}$ 210 $\boxed{=}$	126/210
b. $\boxed{\text{SIMP}}$ $\boxed{=}$	
c. $\boxed{\text{SIMP}}$ $\boxed{=}$	
d. $\boxed{\text{SIMP}}$ $\boxed{=}$	

Assume that you have a calculator with the key $\boxed{\text{A b/c}}$ (or $\boxed{x\frac{y}{z}}$) and that pressing this key replaces an improper fraction by a mixed number in lowest terms. Determine the view screens in exercises 37 and 38 for such a calculator.

37.

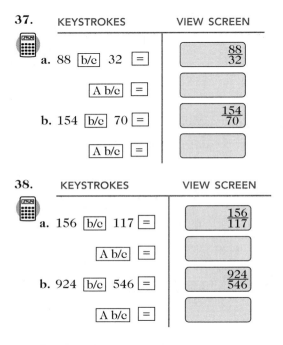

KEYSTROKES	VIEW SCREEN
a. 88 $\boxed{\text{b/c}}$ 32 $\boxed{=}$	$\frac{88}{32}$
$\boxed{\text{A b/c}}$ $\boxed{=}$	
b. 154 $\boxed{\text{b/c}}$ 70 $\boxed{=}$	$\frac{154}{70}$
$\boxed{\text{A b/c}}$ $\boxed{=}$	

38.

KEYSTROKES	VIEW SCREEN
a. 156 $\boxed{\text{b/c}}$ 117 $\boxed{=}$	$\frac{156}{117}$
$\boxed{\text{A b/c}}$ $\boxed{=}$	
b. 924 $\boxed{\text{b/c}}$ 546 $\boxed{=}$	$\frac{924}{546}$
$\boxed{\text{A b/c}}$ $\boxed{=}$	

REASONING AND PROBLEM SOLVING

39. A furlong equals $\frac{1}{8}$ mile, and it is used for measuring distances on horse racetracks. If a horse runs 1 mile in 1 minute 30 seconds, how long will it take the horse to run 6 furlongs at the same rate?

40. A buyer's guide for single-lens reflex cameras gives the following shutter speeds in seconds. Mila needs a shutter speed opening which is less than $\frac{1}{200}$ second. Which of these shutter speeds can she use?

$$\frac{1}{90} \qquad \frac{1}{250} \qquad \frac{1}{60} \qquad \frac{1}{1000} \qquad \frac{1}{100}$$

41. Suppose you need to drill a $\frac{3}{8}$-inch hole, but the set of drill bits is measured in sixteenths of an inch. What size drill bit should you use?

42. To pass inspection in a certain state, a car's tire treads must have a depth of at least $\frac{1}{16}$ inch. If the tires on a car have tread depths in inches of $\frac{1}{2}$, $\frac{1}{8}$, $\frac{1}{32}$, and $\frac{1}{4}$, which tire will not pass inspection?

43. One-fiftieth of the earth's crust is magnesium, and $\frac{1}{20}$ of the earth's crust is iron. Is there more iron or more magnesium in the earth's crust?

44. Pure gold is quite soft. To make it more useful for such items as rings and jewelry, jewelers mix it with other metals, such as copper and zinc. Pure gold is marked 24k (24 karat). What fraction of a ring is pure gold if it is marked 14k?

45. Some health authorities say that we should have 1 gram of protein per day for each kilogram of weight. There are about 40 grams of protein in 1 liter of milk. A liter of fat-free milk weighs about 1040 grams. What fraction of the milk's weight is protein?

Use the following information on the shutter speed knob which is on top of the 35-millimeter camera shown here to answer problems 46 and 47. The numerals on this knob determine the amount of time the camera's shutter stays open. The settings of 4 and 2 following B on the knob cause the shutter to remain open for 4 and 2 seconds, respectively. The remaining numerals 1, 2, 4, 8, etc. represent 1 second and $\frac{1}{2}$, $\frac{1}{4}$, $\frac{1}{8}$, etc. second. The fastest opening on this camera is $\frac{1}{1000}$ second.

46. The less light that is available, the longer the shutter must stay open for the film to be properly exposed. Will a shutter setting of 15 allow more or less light than a setting of 60?

47. If a shutter setting of 250 doesn't allow quite enough light, on what number should the dial be set?

Use the following news clipping, from before year 2000, in problems 48 and 49. The numbers show stock prices in dollars and fractions of a dollar on a given day for the 5 most active stocks and the 20 top stocks. The first column of numbers contains the daily closing prices. The second column shows whether those prices were up (u), down (d), or unchanged (unc.) from the previous day's price. The third column shows the fraction of a dollar by which each price changed.

5 MOST ACTIVE		
Occid. Pt	17 3/8	d	1/8
Dow Ch	44 3/8	d	1/4
Gn Mot	67 1/4	u	5/8
Aetna Lf	31 1/2	unc.	
Brist My	74	u	3/8

20 TOP STOCKS		
Am T&T	59	u	1/4
RCA	27 1/8	u	1/8
Data Genl	47 5/8	u	3/8
Nat Gyp	14 3/8	unc.	
P Sv Eg	20 3/4	u	1/8
Con Foods	25 1/4	d	1/8
Reyn Ind	60	u	1/4
Pub S.N.H.	20 1/2	unc.	
Xerox	63 3/8	u	3/16
U.S. Steel	47 3/4	d	1/2
Exxon	51 7/8	u	1/2
Whel Fry	22 1/8	d	1/4
Gen Elec	52 3/4	u	1/4
Gulf Oil	25 7/8	d	1/4
Polaroid	37 7/8	u	1/4
Unit Tech	33 1/4	u	1/16
Con Edis	18 7/8	d	1/8
Tyco Lb	12 5/8	d	1/4
Ca Pw Pf	27 7/8	unc.	
IBM	271 3/4	u	1/2

48. Find the closing price in dollars and cents for each of the following stocks: Dow Ch, Gen Elec, and Gulf Oil.

49. Find the daily change in cents for RCA, Xerox, and Tyco Lb.

Below is a daily report, from before year 2000, on prices of five stocks showing the lowest and highest prices per share for the day. Use this report in problems 50 and 51.

COMPANY	LOW PRICE ($)	HIGH PRICE ($)
Alaska Airlines	$7\frac{5}{8}$	$8\frac{3}{4}$
Canadian Homestead	$7\frac{15}{16}$	$8\frac{1}{4}$
Mobile Home Indiana	$23\frac{5}{8}$	$24\frac{1}{2}$
Ranger O Can	$19\frac{1}{2}$	$20\frac{3}{8}$
Vintage Enterprise	$28\frac{3}{8}$	$29\frac{3}{4}$

50. a. Which of these five stocks had the lowest price for the day?
b. Which stock had the highest price for the day?

51. a. Alaska Airlines finished the day at $8\frac{3}{16}$ dollars. Is this greater or less than the day's high price for this stock?
b. Vintage Enterprise started the day at $28\frac{5}{16}$. Is this greater or less than its low price for the day?

52. Featured Strategies: Guessing and Checking, Solving a Simpler Problem, and Finding a Pattern
Five jars numbered 1 through 5 contain a total of 92 candy bars. If each jar contains two more candy bars than the previous jar, how much candy is in each jar?

a. Understanding the Problem Sometimes a problem such as this one can be solved by *guessing* and then adjusting the next guess. Even if no solution is found, you may obtain a better understanding of the problem. Try a few numbers, and describe what you learn by guessing.
b. Devising a Plan Your guesses in part a should suggest that the answers are not whole numbers. Let's simplify the problem by changing the number of candy bars. How many bars will there be in each jar if there is a total of 100 bars?
c. Carrying Out the Plan Continue by determining the number of bars in each jar in each of the following cases, assuming there are 100 candy bars.
(1) Each jar has 3 more than the previous jar.
(2) Each jar has 4 more than the previous jar.
(3) Each jar has 5 more than the previous jar.
Look for a pattern in your answers. What general approach to solving this type of problem is suggested? What is the solution to the original problem with 92 candy bars?

d. Looking Back Solve this problem for 7 jars containing 92 candy bars, assuming each jar has 2 more bars than the previous jar.

53. The Fibonacci numbers 1, 1, 2, 3, 5, 8, 13, . . . occur as the numerators and denominators of fractions associated with patterns of leaf arrangements on trees and plants. These numbers are used in problems 53 and 54. This drawing shows the leaf arrangement from a branch of a pear tree.

Pear tree stem

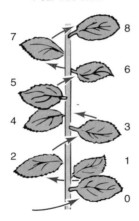

If you begin with a leaf on a pear tree branch and count the number of leaves until you reach a leaf that grows from a point just above the first, the number of leaves, not counting the first (zero leaf), will be the Fibonacci number 8. Furthermore, in passing around the branch from a leaf to the leaf directly above, you will make 3 complete turns. This means that each leaf is $\frac{3}{8}$ of a turn from its adjacent leaves. The pattern described by this fraction is called *phyllotaxis* (or leaf divergence). For any given species of tree, the appropriate fraction can be found by counting the leaves (or branches) and the turns around the stem. Fill in the missing numbers in the fractions for phyllotaxis in the following table by finding a pattern for the numerator and denominator in each of the first three fractions.

TREE	PHYLLOTAXIS
Apple	$\frac{2}{5}$
Pear	$\frac{3}{8}$
Beech	$\frac{1}{3}$
Almond	$\frac{5}{\Box}$
Elm	$\frac{\Box}{2}$
Willow	$\frac{3}{\Box}$

54. The seeds of sunflowers and daisies, the scales of pinecones and pineapples, and the leaves on certain vegetables are arranged in two spirals. In these cases the numerator and denominator of the fraction for phyllotaxis give the number of clockwise and counterclockwise spirals. Find a pattern for the numerator and denominator of each fraction in the table shown here, and given that the fraction is not equal to 1 fill in the missing numbers in the fractions for phyllotaxis.

PLANT	PHYLLOTAXIS
White pinecone	$\frac{5}{8}$
Pineapple	$\frac{8}{13}$
Daisy	$\frac{21}{34}$
Cauliflower	$\frac{\Box}{3}$
Celery	$\frac{1}{\Box}$
Medium sunflower	$\frac{55}{\Box}$
Large sunflower	$\frac{\Box}{144}$

ONLINE LEARNING CENTER   www.mhhe.com/bennett-nelson

• Math Investigation 5.2   *Paper Folding*
Section-Related: • Links   • Writing/Discussion Problems   • Bibliography

MATH ACTIVITY 5.3

OPERATIONS WITH FRACTION BARS

Materials: Fraction Bars in the Manipulative Kit.

1. The sum of two fractions is modeled by placing the shaded amounts of their bars end to end. The bars at the right show that the total shaded amount is $\frac{5}{6}$. Write addition equations for the fractions represented by the following pairs of bars.

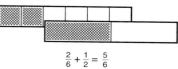

$$\frac{2}{6} + \frac{1}{2} = \frac{5}{6}$$

a.  b.  c.

*2. The difference of two fractions is modeled by lining up their bars and comparing their shaded amounts. Write subtraction equations for the fractions represented by the following pairs of bars.

a.  b. 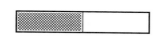 c.

3. Turn the shaded amounts of the Fraction Bars face down and select any two bars. If any fractions equal 0 or 1, place them aside and select others. Write equations for the sum and difference of these fractions. Then repeat this activity for three other pairs of bars.

4. The product $\frac{1}{3} \times \frac{1}{4}$ means $\frac{1}{3}$ of $\frac{1}{4}$ and can be illustrated by splitting each part of a $\frac{1}{4}$ bar into 3 equal parts. One-third of the shaded amount is $\frac{1}{12}$, so $\frac{1}{3} \times \frac{1}{4} = \frac{1}{12}$. Draw sketches to illustrate and compute each of the following products.

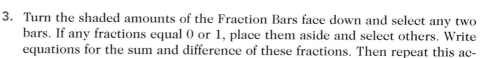

$$\frac{1}{12} \qquad \frac{1}{3} \times \frac{1}{4} = \frac{1}{12}$$

a. $\frac{1}{2} \times \frac{1}{2}$ b. $\frac{1}{3} \times \frac{1}{7}$ c. $\frac{1}{4} \times \frac{1}{2}$ d. $\frac{2}{3} \times \frac{1}{5}$

*5. The quotient of two fractions is modeled by lining up their bars and determining how many times greater the shaded amount of one is than the other. The bars at the right show that $\frac{1}{3}$ can be subtracted from (or "fits into") $\frac{4}{6}$ twice. Write division equations for the fractions represented by the following pairs of bars.

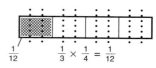

$$\frac{4}{6} \div \frac{1}{3} = 2$$

a.  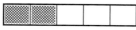 b.  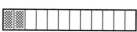 c.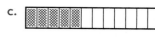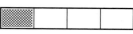

SECTION 5.3

OPERATIONS WITH FRACTIONS

*United States space shuttle
Enterprise.*

Your father gives one-half of the money in his pocket to your mother, one-fourth of what is left to your brother, and one-third of what then remains to your sister. He then splits the rest with you. If you get $2, how much did your father start with?

Fractions are often used to indicate how much smaller a diagram or model is than the life-size object. For example, the dimensions of the model of the space shuttle in Figure 5.35 are one-fiftieth of the dimensions of the space shuttle *Enterprise*. This means that each length on the model can be obtained by multiplying the corresponding length on the *Enterprise* by $\frac{1}{50}$. In this section we will examine the four basic operations with fractions.

Figure 5.35

Italy's Maria Gaetana Agnesi, a brilliant linguist, philosopher, and mathematician, was the first of 21 children of a professor of mathematics at the University of Bologna. By her 13th birthday she was fluent in Latin, Greek, Hebrew, French, Spanish, and German as well as her native Italian. In 1748 she published *Instituzioni Analitiche,* two huge volumes containing a complete and unified treatment of algebra, analysis, and recent advances in calculus. This is the first surviving mathematical work written by a woman. Widely acclaimed as a model of clarity and exposition, it was translated into French (1775) and English (1801). In recognition of her exceptional accomplishments, Pope Benedict XIV appointed Agnesi to the chair of mathematics and natural philosophy at the University of Bologna in 1750. Maria Agnesi is said to have been the first woman professor of mathematics on a university faculty.*

*Maria Gaetana Agnesi
1718–1799*

*D. M. Burton, *The History of Mathematics,* 4th ed. (New York: McGraw-Hill, 1999), pp. 395–396.

Addition

The concept of addition is the same for fractions as for whole numbers. The addition of whole numbers is illustrated by putting together, or combining, two sets of objects. Similarly, the addition of fractions can be illustrated by combining two amounts.

Example A

Suppose that parts of two school days are used for a national testing program: $\frac{1}{3}$ day is required for test A, and $\frac{1}{5}$ day is required for test B. Approximately what part of a whole day is used for testing?

Solution   One approach to solving this problem is to sketch a figure to represent each amount. The following figures represent $\frac{1}{3}$ and $\frac{1}{5}$, and we can see that when the shaded amounts are combined, the total is approximately $\frac{1}{2}$.

The development of rational number concepts is a major goal for grades 3–5, which should lead to informal methods for calculating with fractions.

Standards 2000, p. 33

Finding the sum of two fractions is easy when they have the same denominator. Figure 5.36 shows Fraction Bars for $\frac{4}{6}$ and $\frac{3}{6}$. If the shaded parts of each bar are placed end to end, the total shaded amount is 1 whole bar and $\frac{1}{6}$ bar. So $\frac{4}{6} + \frac{3}{6} = \frac{7}{6}$, or $1\frac{1}{6}$.

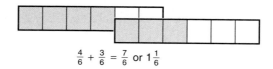

$$\frac{4}{6} + \frac{3}{6} = \frac{7}{6} \text{ or } 1\frac{1}{6}$$

Figure 5.36

Addition of fractions can also be illustrated on a number line (Figure 5.37) by placing arrows for the fractions end to end.

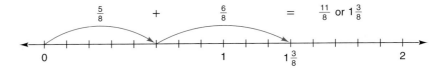

Figure 5.37

Example B

Write each sum as a fraction or a mixed number.

1. $\dfrac{4}{5} + \dfrac{3}{5}$ 2. $\dfrac{2}{9} + \dfrac{6}{9}$ 3. $\dfrac{5}{3} + \dfrac{2}{3}$

Solution   1. $\dfrac{7}{5} = 1\dfrac{2}{5}$ 2. $\dfrac{8}{9}$ 3. $\dfrac{7}{3} = 2\dfrac{1}{3}$

UNLIKE DENOMINATORS   The difficulty in adding fractions occurs when the denominators are unequal. The $\frac{2}{5}$ bar and the $\frac{1}{3}$ bar in part a of Figure 5.38 show that $\frac{2}{5} + \frac{1}{3}$ is greater than $\frac{3}{5}$ but less than $\frac{4}{5}$. To determine this sum exactly, we must replace the two fractions by fractions having the same denominator. Since the smallest common denominator of $\frac{2}{5}$ and $\frac{1}{3}$ is 15, these fractions can be replaced by $\frac{6}{15}$ and $\frac{5}{15}$, as shown in part b of Figure 5.38. The sum of these two fractions is $\frac{11}{15}$, so $\frac{2}{5} + \frac{1}{3} = \frac{11}{15}$.

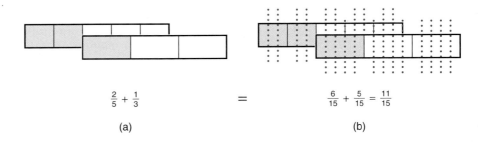

$\dfrac{2}{5} + \dfrac{1}{3}$ $=$ $\dfrac{6}{15} + \dfrac{5}{15} = \dfrac{11}{15}$

Figure 5.38   (a)   (b)

Multiplying the denominators of two fractions by each other will always yield a common denominator (but not necessarily the smallest one). Once two fractions have a common denominator, their sum is computed by adding the numerators and retaining the denominator. This is stated in the following rule for adding fractions.

ADDITION OF FRACTIONS   For any fractions *a/b* and *c/d*,

$$\frac{a}{b} + \frac{c}{d} = \frac{ad}{bd} + \frac{bc}{bd} = \frac{ad + bc}{bd}$$

Objective: Add fractions with like denominators.

Add Fractions

Learn

Math Word

simplest form
a fraction in which the numerator and the denominator have no common factor greater than 1

The Bayview Elementary School is publishing a recipe book. An article is being written about the book for the local newspaper. Which fractional part of their cookbook should the newspaper say has recipes for breakfast and dinner?

All You Need Cookbook

Chapter 1: Quick Breakfasts
Chapter 2: Quick Lunches
Chapter 3: Hot Lunches
Chapter 4: Cold Lunches
Chapter 5: Quick Dinners
Chapter 6: Hot Dinners
Chapter 7: Cold Dinners
Chapter 8: Easy Desserts

Example

Find: $\frac{1}{8} + \frac{3}{8}$

Think: $\frac{1}{8}$ of the chapters are for breakfast, $\frac{3}{8}$ are for dinner.

1

Add the numerators and use the same denominator.

 $\frac{1}{8} + \frac{3}{8} = \frac{4}{8}$

2

Write the sum in **simplest form**.

 $\frac{4}{8} = \frac{1}{2}$

There are breakfast and dinner recipes in $\frac{1}{2}$ of the cookbook.

Another Example

$\frac{4}{10} + \frac{8}{10}$  $\frac{4}{10} + \frac{8}{10} = \frac{12}{10} = 1\frac{1}{5}$

Try It Add. Write each sum in simplest form.

1. $\frac{3}{4} + \frac{2}{4}$ **2.** $\frac{5}{12} + \frac{2}{12}$ **3.** $\frac{2}{3} + \frac{1}{3}$ **4.** $\frac{1}{4} + \frac{2}{4}$ **5.** $\frac{7}{12} + \frac{3}{12}$

Sum it Up **Explain** how you would find $\frac{5}{8} + \frac{5}{8}$.

554 Cluster B

Example C

Find each sum.

1. $\dfrac{1}{4} + \dfrac{3}{7}$ 2. $\dfrac{5}{6} + \dfrac{^-1}{8}$ 3. $\dfrac{7}{10} + \dfrac{9}{20}$

Solution   1. $\dfrac{1}{4} + \dfrac{3}{7} = \dfrac{1 \times 7}{4 \times 7} + \dfrac{3 \times 4}{7 \times 4} = \dfrac{7}{28} + \dfrac{12}{28} = \dfrac{19}{28}$

2. $\dfrac{5}{6} + \dfrac{^-1}{8} = \dfrac{5 \times 4}{6 \times 4} + \dfrac{^-1 \times 3}{8 \times 3} = \dfrac{20}{24} + \dfrac{^-3}{24} = \dfrac{17}{24}$

3. $\dfrac{7}{10} + \dfrac{9}{20} = \dfrac{7 \times 2}{10 \times 2} + \dfrac{9}{20} = \dfrac{14}{20} + \dfrac{9}{20} = \dfrac{23}{20} = 1\dfrac{3}{20}$

MIXED NUMBERS   Mixed numbers are combinations of whole numbers and fractions. The sum of two mixed numbers can be found by adding the whole numbers and fractions separately. If the denominators of the fractions are unequal, as in problem 2 in Example D, a common denominator is found before the fractions are added.

Example D

Compute each sum.

1. $6\dfrac{2}{5}$ 2. $3\dfrac{1}{2}$

$+ 3\dfrac{4}{5}$ $+ 5\dfrac{2}{3}$

Solution   1. $6\dfrac{2}{5}$ 2. $3\dfrac{1}{2} = \quad 3\dfrac{3}{6}$

$+ 3\dfrac{4}{5}$ $5\dfrac{2}{3} = + 5\dfrac{4}{6}$

$9\dfrac{6}{5} = 10\dfrac{1}{5}$ $8\dfrac{7}{6} = 9\dfrac{1}{6}$

Subtraction

The concepts of subtraction are the same for fractions as for whole numbers. That is, the *take-away concept,* the *missing-addends concept,* and the *add-up concept* apply to subtraction of fractions. The bars in part a of Figure 5.39 show that $\frac{1}{2}$ take away $\frac{1}{6}$ is $\frac{2}{6}$, or that $\frac{2}{6}$ must be added to $\frac{1}{6}$ to obtain $\frac{1}{2}$. Part b of the figure illustrates subtraction on a number line and shows that $\frac{11}{12}$ take away $\frac{7}{12}$ equals $\frac{4}{12}$, or that $\frac{4}{12}$ must be added to $\frac{7}{12}$ to obtain $\frac{11}{12}$.

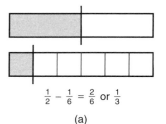

$\frac{1}{2} - \frac{1}{6} = \frac{2}{6}$ or $\frac{1}{3}$

(a)

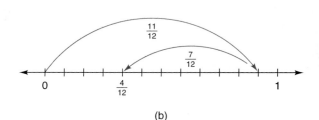

(b)

Figure 5.39

The NCTM K–4 Standard, *Fractions and Decimals,* advises that

Physical materials should be used for exploratory work in adding and subtracting basic fractions, solving simple real-world problems, and partitioning sets of objects to find fractional parts of sets and relating this activity to division. For example, children learn that $\frac{1}{3}$ of 30 is equivalent to "30 divided by 3," which helps them relate operations with fractions to earlier operations with whole numbers.*

Students who have a solid conceptual foundation in fractions should be less prone to committing computational errors than students who do not have such a foundation.

Standards 2000, p. 218

UNLIKE DENOMINATORS   The bars in part a of Figure 5.40 show that the difference between $\frac{5}{6}$ and $\frac{1}{4}$ is greater than $\frac{3}{6}$ and less than $\frac{4}{6}$. To compute this difference, we can replace these fractions by fractions having a common denominator. The smallest common denominator of $\frac{5}{6}$ and $\frac{1}{4}$ is 12, so these fractions can be replaced by $\frac{10}{12}$ and $\frac{3}{12}$, as shown in part b of the figure. The difference between these two fractions is $\frac{7}{12}$, so $\frac{5}{6} - \frac{1}{4} = \frac{7}{12}$.

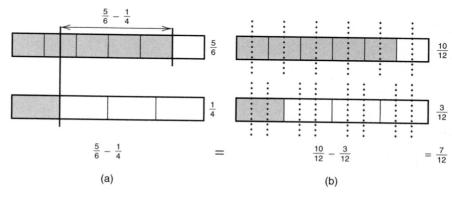

Figure 5.40

$$\frac{5}{6} - \frac{1}{4} \qquad = \qquad \frac{10}{12} - \frac{3}{12} \qquad = \frac{7}{12}$$

(a)   (b)

The general rule for subtracting fractions is usually stated using a common denominator that is the product of the two denominators, even though this may not be the smallest common denominator. Once two fractions have a common denominator, their difference is computed by subtracting the numerators and retaining the denominator. The resulting fraction may sometimes be simplified if its numerator and denominator are found to have a factor in common.

SUBTRACTION OF FRACTIONS   For any fractions a/b and c/d,

$$\frac{a}{b} - \frac{c}{d} = \frac{ad}{bd} - \frac{bc}{bd} = \frac{ad - bc}{bd}$$

Example E

Find each difference.

1. $\dfrac{7}{8} - \dfrac{1}{3}$ 2. $\dfrac{1}{2} - \dfrac{4}{5}$ 3. $\dfrac{2}{3} - \dfrac{^{-}1}{4}$

Solution   1. $\dfrac{7}{8} - \dfrac{1}{3} = \dfrac{7 \times 3}{8 \times 3} - \dfrac{1 \times 8}{3 \times 8} = \dfrac{21}{24} - \dfrac{8}{24} = \dfrac{13}{24}$ 2. $\dfrac{1}{2} - \dfrac{4}{5} = \dfrac{1 \times 5}{2 \times 5} - \dfrac{4 \times 2}{5 \times 2} = \dfrac{5}{10} - \dfrac{8}{10} = \dfrac{^{-}3}{10}$

*Curriculum and Evaluation Standards for School Mathematics (Reston, VA: National Council of Teachers of Mathematics, 1989), p. 59.

3. $\dfrac{2}{3} - \dfrac{^-1}{4} = \dfrac{2 \times 4}{3 \times 4} - \dfrac{^-1 \times 3}{4 \times 3} = \dfrac{8}{12} - \dfrac{^-3}{12} = \dfrac{8}{12} + \dfrac{3}{12} = \dfrac{11}{12}$

MIXED NUMBERS   The difference between two mixed numbers can be found by subtracting the whole-number parts and the fractions separately. Sometimes regrouping (borrowing) is necessary before this can be done, as in problem 1 in Example F. If the denominators of the fractions in the mixed numbers are unequal, the fractions must be replaced by fractions having a common denominator. In some cases, both regrouping (borrowing) and changing denominators will be necessary before mixed numbers can be subtracted, as in problem 2 in Example F.

Example F

Compute each difference.

1. $4\dfrac{1}{5}$

$-1\dfrac{2}{5}$

2. $5\dfrac{1}{6}$

$-2\dfrac{3}{4}$

Solution   1. $4\dfrac{1}{5} = 3\dfrac{6}{5}$

$-1\dfrac{2}{5} = -1\dfrac{2}{5}$

$\phantom{-1\dfrac{2}{5} =\ } 2\dfrac{4}{5}$

2. $5\dfrac{1}{6} = 5\dfrac{2}{12} = 4\dfrac{14}{12}$

$-2\dfrac{3}{4} = -2\dfrac{9}{12} = -2\dfrac{9}{12}$

$\phantom{-2\dfrac{3}{4} = -2\dfrac{9}{12} =\ } 2\dfrac{5}{12}$

Multiplication

$\frac{1}{3} \times 6 = 2$

Figure 5.41

Given a product of two whole numbers $m \times n$, we can think of the first number m as indicating "how many" of the second number. For example, 2×3 means 2 of the 3s. Multiplication of fractions may be viewed in a similar manner. In the product $\frac{1}{3} \times 6$, the first number tells us "how much" of the second; that is, $\frac{1}{3} \times 6$ means $\frac{1}{3}$ of 6 (Figure 5.41).

There is a major difference between the outcome of multiplying by a whole number and the outcome of multiplying by a fraction. When we multiply by a whole number greater than 1, the product is greater than the second number being multiplied. However, when we multiply by a fraction less than 1, the product is less than the second number being multiplied. This is often a problem for school children who have been accustomed to multiplying by whole numbers before encountering products with fractions.[*]

WHOLE NUMBER TIMES A FRACTION   In this case we can interpret multiplication to mean *repeated addition,* just as we did with multiplication of whole numbers in Chapter 3. The whole number indicates the number of times the fraction is to be added to itself. Figure 5.42 illustrates $3 \times \frac{2}{5}$ and shows that this product equals $1\frac{1}{5}$.

[*]According to D. E. Smith, in his *History of Mathematics,* 2d ed. (Lexington, MA: Ginn, 1925), p. 225, as early as the fifteenth and sixteenth centuries, writers on the subject of fractions expressed concern over this problem.

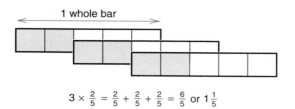

Figure 5.42

$$3 \times \tfrac{2}{5} = \tfrac{2}{5} + \tfrac{2}{5} + \tfrac{2}{5} = \tfrac{6}{5} \text{ or } 1\tfrac{1}{5}$$

FRACTION TIMES A WHOLE NUMBER   The product $\tfrac{1}{3} \times 4$ means $\tfrac{1}{3}$ of 4. This product can be illustrated by using 4 bars and dividing each into 3 equal parts (Figure 5.43). The vertical lines split these bars into three equal parts A, B, and C. Part A, which is one-third of the 4 bars, consists of 4 one-thirds, or 4 thirds.

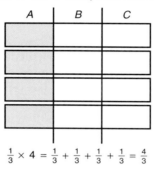

Figure 5.43

$$\tfrac{1}{3} \times 4 = \tfrac{1}{3} + \tfrac{1}{3} + \tfrac{1}{3} + \tfrac{1}{3} = \tfrac{4}{3}$$

The product $\tfrac{1}{3} \times 4$ also can be illustrated by beginning with a 4-bar, as shown in Figure 5.44, and dividing it into 3 equal parts. Each part is $1\tfrac{1}{3}$ whole bars, so $\tfrac{1}{3} \times 4 = 1\tfrac{1}{3}$.

Figure 5.44

These examples suggest the following definition for products involving a whole number and a fraction.

> **WHOLE NUMBER TIMES A FRACTION**   For any whole number **k** and fraction **a/b**,
>
> $$k \times \frac{a}{b} = \frac{ka}{b}$$

Example G

Compute the following products.

1. $3 \times \dfrac{2}{7}$ 2. $\dfrac{2}{5} \times {}^-24$ 3. $6 \times \dfrac{3}{8}$

Solution   1. $\dfrac{6}{7}$ 2. $\dfrac{{}^-48}{5} = {}^-9\dfrac{3}{5}$ 3. $\dfrac{18}{8} = 2\dfrac{2}{8}$

FRACTION TIMES A FRACTION   The product $\frac{1}{3} \times \frac{1}{5}$ means $\frac{1}{3}$ of $\frac{1}{5}$. This can be illustrated by beginning with a figure that has 1 part out of 5 shaded and taking $\frac{1}{3}$ of its shaded amount. To do this, Figure 5.45 has been split into 3 equal parts A, B, and C. The darker part of the figure is $\frac{1}{3}$ of $\frac{1}{5}$. Each of the new small parts is $\frac{1}{15}$ of the whole, so $\frac{1}{3} \times \frac{1}{5} = \frac{1}{15}$.

Figure 5.45

To illustrate $\frac{2}{3} \times \frac{4}{5}$, we will begin with a figure that has 4 parts out of 5 shaded and take $\frac{2}{3}$ of each shaded part. In order to do this, Figure 5.46 has been split into 3 equal parts A, B, and C. Each of the new small parts is $\frac{1}{15}$ of a whole bar. The 8 darker parts of the bar represent $\frac{8}{15}$, so $\frac{2}{3} \times \frac{4}{5} = \frac{8}{15}$.

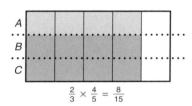

Figure 5.46

The rule for computing the product of two fractions is suggested in the preceding illustrations. In each of these examples, the product can be found by *multiplying numerator by numerator and denominator by denominator.*

> **MULTIPLICATION OF FRACTIONS**   For any fractions *a/b* and *c/d,*
>
> $$\frac{a}{b} \times \frac{c}{d} = \frac{ac}{bd}$$

Notice that since the whole number k is equal to the fraction $\frac{k}{1}$, a product involving a whole number and a fraction is a special case of the definition of multiplication of fractions.

E x a m p l e H

Compute each product.

1. $\dfrac{1}{2} \times \dfrac{8}{9}$ 2. $\dfrac{4}{7} \times \dfrac{^-2}{5}$ 3. $6 \times \dfrac{4}{5}$

Solution   1. $\dfrac{8}{18}$ or $\dfrac{4}{9}$ 2. $\dfrac{^-8}{35}$ 3. $\dfrac{24}{5}$ or $4\dfrac{4}{5}$

Products involving a mixed number can be computed by replacing the mixed number by an improper fraction.

Example 1

Compute each product.

1. $\dfrac{3}{4} \times 6\dfrac{1}{5}$ **2.** $3\dfrac{1}{8} \times {}^-2\dfrac{1}{3}$

Solution **1.** $\dfrac{3}{4} \times 6\dfrac{1}{5} = \dfrac{3}{4} \times \dfrac{31}{5} = \dfrac{93}{20} = 4\dfrac{13}{20}$ **2.** $3\dfrac{1}{8} \times {}^-2\dfrac{1}{3} = \dfrac{25}{8} \times \dfrac{{}^-7}{3} = \dfrac{{}^-175}{24} = {}^-7\dfrac{7}{24}$

Division

Division of fractions can be viewed in much the same way as division of whole numbers. One of the meanings of division of whole numbers is represented by the measurement (subtractive) concept. For example, to explain $15 \div 3$, we often say, "How many times can we subtract 3 from 15?" Similarly, for $\frac{3}{5} \div \frac{1}{10}$ we can ask, "How many times can we subtract $\frac{1}{10}$ from $\frac{3}{5}$?" Figure 5.47 shows that the shaded amount of a $\frac{1}{10}$ bar can be subtracted from the shaded amount of a $\frac{3}{5}$ bar 6 times. Or, viewed in terms of multiplication, the shaded amount of the $\frac{3}{5}$ bar is 6 times the shaded amount of the $\frac{1}{10}$ bar.

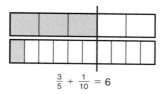

$\frac{3}{5} \div \frac{1}{10} = 6$

Figure 5.47

This interpretation of division of fractions continues to hold even when the quotient is not a whole number. Figure 5.48 shows that the shaded amount of the $\frac{1}{3}$ bar can be subtracted from the shaded amount of the $\frac{5}{6}$ bar 2 times, and there is a remainder. Just as in whole number division, the remainder is then compared to the divisor using a fraction. In this example, the remainder is $\frac{1}{2}$ as big as the divisor, so the quotient is $2\frac{1}{2}$.

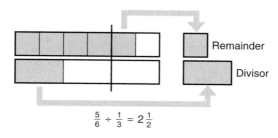

$\frac{5}{6} \div \frac{1}{3} = 2\frac{1}{2}$

Figure 5.48

One of the early methods of dividing one fraction by another was to replace both fractions by fractions having a common denominator. When this is done, the quotient can be obtained by disregarding the denominators and dividing the two numerators. For example,

$$\frac{3}{4} \div \frac{2}{5} = \frac{15}{20} \div \frac{8}{20} = 15 \div 8 = 1\frac{7}{8}$$

One method currently taught to divide one fraction by another is to *invert the divisor and multiply.*

$$\frac{1}{2} \div \frac{1}{3} = \frac{1}{2} \times \frac{3}{1} = \frac{3}{2} = 1\frac{1}{2}$$

Figure 5.49 helps to show why the method of *inverting and multiplying* works. We saw in Section 3.4 the mental calculating technique called *equal quotients,* whereby we recognize that the relative size of two sets does not change if both sets are halved or both sets are tripled. In general, the quotient of two numbers can be replaced by dividing or multiplying both numbers by the same number. The relative size of the shaded amounts of the two bars in part a of Figure 5.49 is unchanged by tripling these amounts to obtain the bars in part b. The new bars in part b show that the total shaded amount of the top two bars is $1\frac{1}{2}$ times the total shaded amount of the lower bar.

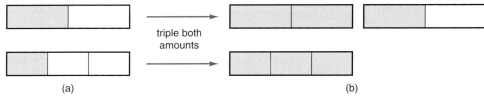

Figure 5.49

(a)   (b)

This illustration of tripling the amounts in Figure 5.49 is recorded in the following equations by multiplying both fractions by 3.

$$\frac{1}{2} \div \frac{1}{3} = \left(\frac{1}{2} \times 3\right) \div \left(\frac{1}{3} \times 3\right) = \frac{3}{2} \div 1 = \frac{3}{2}$$

In a similar manner, to divide a/b by c/d, the *equal-quotients* technique enables us to multiply both numbers by bd.

$$\frac{a}{b} \div \frac{c}{d} = (bd)\frac{a}{b} \div (bd)\frac{c}{d} = (\cancel{b}d)\frac{a}{\cancel{b}} \div (b\cancel{d})\frac{c}{\cancel{d}} = \frac{ad}{bc}$$

This is the result produced by the invert-and-multiply rule for finding the quotient of two fractions.

DIVISION OF FRACTIONS   For any fractions a/b and c/d, with $c/d \neq 0$,

$$\frac{a}{b} \div \frac{c}{d} = \frac{a}{b} \times \frac{d}{c} = \frac{ad}{bc}$$

Example J

Compute each quotient.

1. $\dfrac{1}{2} \div \dfrac{1}{3}$ 2. $\dfrac{7}{8} \div \dfrac{2}{5}$ 3. $\dfrac{2}{3} \div \dfrac{^{-}1}{4}$

Solution   1. $\dfrac{1}{2} \div \dfrac{1}{3} = \dfrac{1}{2} \times \dfrac{3}{1} = \dfrac{3}{2} = 1\dfrac{1}{2}$ 2. $\dfrac{7}{8} \div \dfrac{2}{5} = \dfrac{7}{8} \times \dfrac{5}{2} = \dfrac{35}{16} = 2\dfrac{3}{16}$

3. $\dfrac{2}{3} \div \dfrac{^{-}1}{4} = \dfrac{2}{3} \times \dfrac{^{-}4}{1} = \dfrac{^{-}8}{3} = {}^{-}2\dfrac{2}{3}$

One method of computing the quotient of two mixed numbers is to replace each mixed number by an improper fraction and use the definition of division of fractions.

Example **K**

Compute each quotient.

1. $5\frac{1}{3} \div 1\frac{1}{8}$ **2.** $8\frac{3}{4} \div 2\frac{1}{2}$

Solution   **1.** $5\frac{1}{3} \div 1\frac{1}{8} = \frac{16}{3} \div \frac{9}{8} = \frac{16}{3} \times \frac{8}{9} = \frac{128}{27} = 4\frac{20}{27}$ **2.** $8\frac{3}{4} \div 2\frac{1}{2} = \frac{35}{4} \div \frac{5}{2} = \frac{35}{4} \times \frac{2}{5} = \frac{70}{20} = \frac{7}{2} = 3\frac{1}{2}$

 The four basic operations can be performed on fractions and mixed numbers with calculators which display fractions, and the results will usually be displayed as fractions or mixed numbers in lowest terms. Each of these operations is illustrated in the following examples.

1 b/c 2 + 3 b/c 10 = $\boxed{\dfrac{4}{5}}$

5 b/c 6 − 1 b/c 3 = $\boxed{\dfrac{1}{2}}$

5 b/c 6 × 3 b/c 20 = $\boxed{\dfrac{1}{8}}$

7 b/c 8 ÷ 1 b/c 2 = $\boxed{1\dfrac{3}{4}}$

However, on some calculators designed for school children, the results from fraction operations will not be displayed in simplest form. The purpose is to help students follow the processes involved in computing. Fractions and mixed numbers can then be simplified by calculator keys. With such calculators the view screens in the four preceding examples would appear as follows. Try the operations above to see if you get these results.

$\boxed{\dfrac{8}{10}}$ $\boxed{\dfrac{3}{6}}$ $\boxed{\dfrac{15}{120}}$ $\boxed{\dfrac{14}{8}}$

Number Properties

The inverse property for addition and the closure, identity, commutative, associative, and distributive properties, which hold for addition and multiplication of integers, also hold for addition and multiplication of fractions. Furthermore, multiplication of fractions has an additional property: *inverses for multiplication.* The rules for adding and multiplying fractions will be used to illustrate each of these properties in the following examples.

CLOSURE FOR ADDITION OF FRACTIONS   The sum of any two fractions is another unique fraction. This property results from the closure and uniqueness properties for addition and multiplication of integers. Notice how multiplication and addition of integers are needed to compute the following sum of fractions.

$$\frac{^-2}{3} + \frac{4}{5} = \frac{^-2 \times 5}{3 \times 5} + \frac{4 \times 3}{5 \times 3} = \frac{^-10}{15} + \frac{12}{15} = \frac{2}{15}$$

CLOSURE FOR MULTIPLICATION OF FRACTIONS   The product of any two fractions is another unique fraction. This property is a direct result of the closure and uniqueness properties for multiplication of integers. The equations below show where multiplication of integers is needed.

$$\frac{^-2}{3} \times \frac{4}{5} = \frac{^-2 \times 4}{3 \times 5} = \frac{^-8}{15}$$

IDENTITY FOR ADDITION   The sum of any fraction and 0 is the given fraction. This property follows from the fact that 0 plus any integer is the given integer.

$$\frac{5}{6} + 0 = \frac{5}{6} + \frac{0}{6} = \frac{5+0}{6} = \frac{5}{6}$$

IDENTITY FOR MULTIPLICATION   The product of any fraction and 1 is the given fraction. This property is a result of the corresponding property for integers, which states that 1 times any integer is the given integer.

$$1 \times \frac{^-4}{5} = \frac{1 \times ^-4}{5} = \frac{^-4}{5}$$

ADDITION IS COMMUTATIVE   Two fractions that are being added can be interchanged (commuted) without changing the sum.

$$\frac{7}{8} + \frac{3}{5} = \frac{35}{40} + \frac{24}{40} = \frac{59}{40} = 1\frac{19}{20}$$

$$\frac{3}{5} + \frac{7}{8} = \frac{24}{40} + \frac{35}{40} = \frac{59}{40} = 1\frac{19}{40}$$

This property is illustrated on the number lines in Figure 5.50.

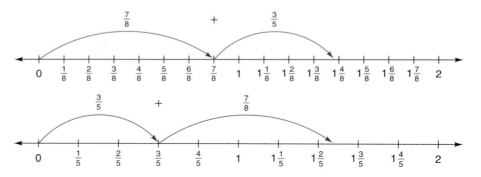

Figure 5.50

ADDITION IS ASSOCIATIVE   In a sum of three fractions, the middle number may be grouped (associated) with either of the other two numbers.

Example L

Compute the sum on each side of the equation. (The sums inside the parentheses should be computed first.)

$$\left(\frac{1}{3} + \frac{1}{4}\right) + \frac{1}{6} = \frac{1}{3} + \left(\frac{1}{4} + \frac{1}{6}\right)$$

Solution   Left side: $\left(\frac{1}{3} + \frac{1}{4}\right) + \frac{1}{6} = \frac{7}{12} + \frac{1}{6} = \frac{9}{12}$

Right side: $\frac{1}{3} + \left(\frac{1}{4} + \frac{1}{6}\right) = \frac{1}{3} + \frac{5}{12} = \frac{9}{12}$

MULTIPLICATION IS COMMUTATIVE   Two fractions that are being multiplied can be interchanged (commuted) without changing the product:

$$\frac{1}{2} \times \frac{1}{3} = \frac{1}{6} \quad \text{and} \quad \frac{1}{3} \times \frac{1}{2} = \frac{1}{6}$$

An illustration of this property is interesting because the processes of taking $\frac{1}{2}$ of something and taking $\frac{1}{3}$ of something are quite different. To take $\frac{1}{2}$ of $\frac{1}{3}$, we begin with a $\frac{1}{3}$ bar, as shown in part a of Figure 5.51; and to take $\frac{1}{3}$ of $\frac{1}{2}$, we use a $\frac{1}{2}$ bar, as shown in part b of Figure 5.51. In each representation the darker part of the bar is $\frac{1}{6}$ of a whole bar, so $\frac{1}{2} \times \frac{1}{3} = \frac{1}{3} \times \frac{1}{2}$.

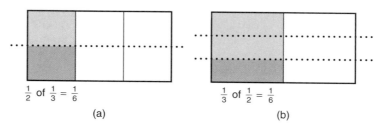

$$\frac{1}{2} \text{ of } \frac{1}{3} = \frac{1}{6} \qquad\qquad \frac{1}{3} \text{ of } \frac{1}{2} = \frac{1}{6}$$

Figure 5.51 (a) (b)

MULTIPLICATION IS ASSOCIATIVE   In a product of three fractions, the middle number may be grouped with either of the other two numbers.

Example M

Compute the product on each side of the equation.

$$\left(\frac{1}{2} \times \frac{3}{4}\right) \times \frac{1}{5} = \frac{1}{2} \times \left(\frac{3}{4} \times \frac{1}{5}\right)$$

Solution   Left side: $\left(\frac{1}{2} \times \frac{3}{4}\right) \times \frac{1}{5} = \frac{3}{8} \times \frac{1}{5} = \frac{3}{40}$

Right side: $\frac{1}{2} \times \left(\frac{3}{4} \times \frac{1}{5}\right) = \frac{1}{2} \times \frac{3}{20} = \frac{3}{40}$

MULTIPLICATION IS DISTRIBUTIVE OVER ADDITION   When a sum (or difference) of two fractions is multiplied by a third number, we can add (or subtract) the two fractions and then multiply, or we can multiply both fractions by the third number and then add (or subtract).

Example N

Perform the calculations on each side of the equation.

$$\frac{1}{2} \times \left(\frac{3}{4} + \frac{7}{10}\right) = \left(\frac{1}{2} \times \frac{3}{4}\right) + \left(\frac{1}{2} \times \frac{7}{10}\right)$$

Solution   Left side: $\frac{1}{2} \times \left(\frac{3}{4} + \frac{7}{10}\right) = \frac{1}{2} \times \left(\frac{15}{20} + \frac{14}{20}\right) = \frac{1}{2} \times \frac{29}{20} = \frac{29}{40}$

Right side: $\left(\frac{1}{2} \times \frac{3}{4}\right) + \left(\frac{1}{2} \times \frac{7}{10}\right) = \frac{3}{8} + \frac{7}{20} = \frac{15}{40} + \frac{14}{40} = \frac{29}{40}$

INVERSES FOR ADDITION   For every fraction there is another fraction, called its **opposite** or **inverse for addition**, such that the sum of the two fractions is 0. The fractions $\frac{3}{4}$ and $\frac{^{-}3}{4}$ are inverses for addition.

$$\frac{3}{4} + \frac{^{-}3}{4} = \frac{3 + {^{-}3}}{4} = \frac{0}{4} = 0$$

INVERSES FOR MULTIPLICATION For every fraction not equal to zero, there is a nonzero fraction, called its **reciprocal** or **inverse for multiplication,** such that the product of the two numbers is 1. The reciprocal of the fraction $\frac{3}{8}$ is $\frac{8}{3}$.

$$\frac{3}{8} \times \frac{8}{3} = \frac{3 \times 8}{8 \times 3} = \frac{24}{24} = 1$$

Mental Calculations

The mental calculating techniques that we have used for computing with whole numbers—*compatible numbers, substitutions, equal differences, add-up,* and *equal quotients*—are also appropriate for fractions. We will look at examples of these techniques and point out some of the number properties that make them possible.

COMPATIBLE NUMBERS Compatible fractions are numbers that can be conveniently combined in a given computation.

Example O

Perform each calculation mentally by finding compatible fractions.

1. $2\frac{1}{5} + \frac{2}{3} + 1\frac{4}{5}$

2. $5\frac{5}{6} - \frac{3}{4} + 2\frac{1}{6} + 4$

3. $\frac{1}{3} \times 14 \times 9 \times \frac{1}{2}$

Solution   1. $2\frac{1}{5} + \frac{2}{3} + 1\frac{4}{5} = 2\frac{1}{5} + 1\frac{4}{5} + \frac{2}{3} = 4 + \frac{2}{3} = 4\frac{2}{3}$ 2. $5\frac{5}{6} - \frac{3}{4} + 2\frac{1}{6} + 4 = 5\frac{5}{6} + 2\frac{1}{6} + 4 - \frac{3}{4} =$ $8 + 4 - \frac{3}{4} = 11\frac{1}{4}$ 3. $\frac{1}{3} \times 14 \times 9 \times \frac{1}{2} = \frac{1}{3} \times 9 \times 14 \times \frac{1}{2} = 3 \times 7 = 21$ *Note:* The rearrangements of numbers in these examples require the use of the commutative and associative properties of addition and multiplication of fractions.

Products involving fractions and whole numbers in which the denominator of the fraction divides the whole number can be calculated mentally by dividing the whole number by the denominator. To compute $\frac{2}{3} \times 24$, we can divide 24 by 3 and multiply the result by 2, as shown in the following equations. We use the fact that $\frac{2}{3} = 2 \times \frac{1}{3}$ in the first equation and the associative property for multiplication in the second equation.

$$\frac{2}{3} \times 24 = \left(2 \times \frac{1}{3}\right) \times 24 = 2 \times \left(\frac{1}{3} \times 24\right) = 2 \times 8 = 16$$

The steps in the preceding equations can be shortened considerably by dividing the denominator of the fraction and the whole number by their greatest common factor.

$$\frac{2}{3} \times 24 = \frac{2}{\overset{}{3}} \times \overset{8}{24} = 16$$

Example P

Calculate each of the following products mentally, using compatible fractions.

1. $\dfrac{5}{8} \times 32$ 2. $^-54 \times \dfrac{5}{9}$ 3. $\dfrac{4}{3} \times 18$

Solution   1. $\dfrac{5}{8} \times 32 = 5 \times \left(\dfrac{1}{8} \times 32\right) = 5 \times 4 = 20 \left(\text{or } \dfrac{5}{8} \times \overset{4}{\cancel{32}} = 20\right)$ 2. $^-54 \times \dfrac{5}{9} = \left(^-54 \times \dfrac{1}{9}\right) \times 5 =$

$^-6 \times 5 = ^-30 \left(\text{or } \overset{^-6}{\cancel{^-54}} \times \dfrac{5}{9} = ^-30\right)$ 3. $\dfrac{4}{3} \times 18 = 4 \times \left(\dfrac{1}{3} \times 18\right) = 4 \times 6 = 24 \left(\text{or } \dfrac{4}{3} \times \overset{6}{\cancel{18}} = 24\right)$

SUBSTITUTIONS   Sometimes it is possible to substitute one form of a number for another to obtain compatible fractions. For example:

$$4 \times 2\dfrac{6}{7} = 4 \times \left(3 - \dfrac{1}{7}\right) = 12 - \dfrac{4}{7} = 11\dfrac{3}{7}$$

Example Q

Find a convenient substitution in order to perform each calculation mentally.

1. $2\dfrac{7}{8} + \dfrac{1}{4}$ 2. $4\dfrac{5}{6} - \dfrac{1}{2}$ 3. $7 \times 2\dfrac{9}{10}$

Solution   1. $2\dfrac{7}{8} + \dfrac{1}{4} = 2\dfrac{7}{8} + \dfrac{1}{8} + \dfrac{1}{8} = 3 + \dfrac{1}{8} = 3\dfrac{1}{8}$ 2. $4\dfrac{5}{6} - \dfrac{1}{2} = 4\dfrac{2}{6} + \dfrac{3}{6} - \dfrac{1}{2} = 4\dfrac{2}{6}$

3. $7 \times 2\dfrac{9}{10} = 7 \times \left(3 - \dfrac{1}{10}\right) = 21 - \dfrac{7}{10} = 20\dfrac{3}{10}$ [Notice the use of the distributive property to multiply 7 times $\left(3 - \dfrac{1}{10}\right)$ in problem 3.]

EQUAL DIFFERENCES AND ADD-UP   Changing two numbers by adding the same amount to both, results in the same difference between the two numbers. This technique is very useful in subtracting fractions because in some cases it avoids the need for regrouping (borrowing). For example, to mentally compute $5 - 2\frac{4}{5}$, we can increase both numbers by $\frac{1}{5}$ to obtain the difference easily.

$$5 - 2\dfrac{4}{5} = 5\dfrac{1}{5} - 3 = 2\dfrac{1}{5}$$

The reason we can add $\frac{1}{5}$ to both numbers is that in so doing we are really adding 0 (using the identity property for addition), as shown in the first of the next few equations.

$$5 - 2\dfrac{4}{5} = (5 + 0) - 2\dfrac{4}{5} = 5 + \left(\dfrac{1}{5} - \dfrac{1}{5}\right) - 2\dfrac{4}{5}$$

$$= \left(5 + \dfrac{1}{5}\right) - \left(2\dfrac{4}{5} + \dfrac{1}{5}\right) = 5\dfrac{1}{5} - 3 = 2\dfrac{1}{5}$$

Or the difference can be obtained by adding up from the smaller number to the larger:

$$2\dfrac{4}{5} + \dfrac{1}{5} = 3 \quad \text{and} \quad 3 + 2 = 5 \quad \text{so} \quad 5 - 2\dfrac{4}{5} = 2\dfrac{1}{5}$$

Example **R**

Calculate each difference mentally, using the *equal-differences* technique.

1. $3\frac{2}{8} - 1\frac{7}{8}$ 2. $5\frac{3}{10} - 3\frac{9}{10}$ 3. $6\frac{1}{5} - 2\frac{3}{5}$

Solution   1. $3\frac{2}{8} - 1\frac{7}{8} = 3\frac{3}{8} - 2 = 1\frac{3}{8}$ $\left(\text{Increase both by }\frac{1}{8}\right)$ 2. $5\frac{3}{10} - 3\frac{9}{10} = 5\frac{4}{10} - 4 = 1\frac{4}{10}$

$\left(\text{Increase both by }\frac{1}{10}\right)$ 3. $6\frac{1}{5} - 2\frac{3}{5} = 6\frac{3}{5} - 3 = 3\frac{3}{5}$ $\left(\text{Increase both by }\frac{2}{5}\right)$ *Note:* The add-up method is also

convenient for computing each of these differences.

EQUAL QUOTIENTS   The mental calculating technique called *equal quotients* is especially convenient when we are dividing by unit fractions—fractions whose denominator is 1.

Example **S**

Calculate each quotient mentally by using the *equal-quotients* technique.

1. $\frac{7}{9} \div \frac{1}{4}$ 2. $\frac{5}{4} \div \frac{1}{3}$ 3. $\frac{6}{7} \div \frac{2}{3}$

Solution   1. $\frac{7}{9} \div \frac{1}{4} = 4\left(\frac{7}{9}\right) \div 4\left(\frac{1}{4}\right) = \frac{28}{9} \div 1 = 3\frac{1}{9}$ 2. $\frac{5}{4} \div \frac{1}{3} = 3\left(\frac{5}{4}\right) \div 3\left(\frac{1}{3}\right) = \frac{15}{4} \div 1 = 3\frac{3}{4}$

3. $\frac{6}{7} \div \frac{2}{3} = 3\left(\frac{6}{7}\right) \div 3\left(\frac{2}{3}\right) = \frac{18}{7} \div 2 = \left(\frac{1}{2}\right)\frac{18}{7} \div \left(\frac{1}{2}\right)2 = \frac{9}{7} \div 1 = 1\frac{2}{7}$

Estimation

Skill at estimating with fractions is especially important, since approximations by whole numbers or compatible fractions are often all that is needed. One of the most common estimating techniques is *rounding*.

Students in grades 3–5 will need to be encouraged to routinely reflect on the size of an anticipated solution. If $\frac{3}{8}$ of a cup of sugar is needed for a recipe and the recipe is doubled, will more or less than one cup of sugar be needed?

Standards 2000, p. 156

ROUNDING   The sum or difference of mixed numbers and fractions can be estimated by rounding each number to the nearest whole number.

$$6\frac{1}{3} + 2\frac{3}{4} + 1\frac{1}{5} \approx 6 + 3 + 1 = 10$$

$$8\frac{1}{3} - 2\frac{3}{5} \approx 8 - 3 = 5$$

Estimating a product by rounding two mixed numbers to the nearest whole number may produce a good estimation, as in the following example.

$$6\frac{3}{4} \times 8\frac{1}{3} \approx 7 \times 8 = 56 \qquad \text{The actual product is } 56\frac{1}{4}.$$

Or it may give a rough estimation, as in the next example.

$$6\frac{1}{2} \times 8\frac{1}{2} \approx 7 \times 9 = 63 \qquad \text{The actual product is } 55\frac{1}{4}.$$

A more reliable estimation for $6\frac{1}{2} \times 8\frac{1}{2}$ can be obtained by multiplying the two whole numbers, 6×8, and then adding the products of each fraction and the opposite whole number: $\frac{1}{2} \times 8$ and $\frac{1}{2} \times 6$.

$$6\frac{1}{2} \times 8\frac{1}{2} \approx (6 \times 8) + \left(\frac{1}{2} \times 8\right) + \left(6 \times \frac{1}{2}\right)$$
$$= 48 + 4 + 3$$
$$= 55$$

Figure 5.52 shows why this method produces a good estimation. The actual product is represented by the region whose dimensions are $6\frac{1}{2}$ by $8\frac{1}{2}$. The estimation is represented by the 6×8 colored region and the $\frac{1}{2} \times 6$ and $\frac{1}{2} \times 8$ colored strips. The $\frac{1}{2} \times \frac{1}{2}$ gray region in the lower right corner represents the difference between the actual product and the estimation, which we obtained in the preceding example. This shows that the difference between the product and the estimation is small.

The distributive property is used below to obtain the four partial products that correspond to the four regions in Figure 5.52. It is used once in going from step 1 to step 2 and twice in going from step 2 to step 3.

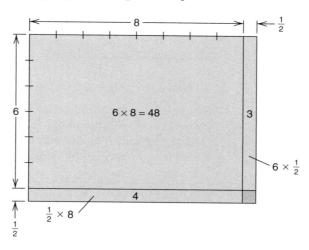

Figure 5.52

Step 1 $6\frac{1}{2} \times 8\frac{1}{2} = \left(6 + \frac{1}{2}\right) \times \left(8 + \frac{1}{2}\right)$

Step 2 $= \left(6 + \frac{1}{2}\right)8 + \left(6 + \frac{1}{2}\right)\frac{1}{2}$

Step 3 $= (6 \times 8) + \left(\frac{1}{2} \times 8\right) + \left(6 \times \frac{1}{2}\right) + \left(\frac{1}{2} \times \frac{1}{2}\right)$

Step 4 $= 48 + 4 + 3 + \frac{1}{4}$

Step 5 $= 55\frac{1}{4}$

Example T

Estimate $10\frac{1}{2} \times 6\frac{1}{5}$ by multiplying the two whole numbers and then adding the products of each fraction and the opposite whole number.

Solution $10\frac{1}{2} \times 6\frac{1}{5} \approx (10 \times 6) + \left(\frac{1}{2} \times 6\right) + \left(10 \times \frac{1}{5}\right) = 60 + 3 + 2 = 65$

COMPATIBLE NUMBERS   Replacing a fraction by a reasonably close and compatible fraction can be very useful in obtaining an estimation. Similarly, if a product involves a whole number and a fraction, we can often obtain an estimation by replacing the whole number with a reasonably close whole number that is divided evenly by the denominator of the fraction.

$$\frac{2}{7} \times 20 \approx \frac{2}{7} \times 21 = \frac{2}{\cancel{7}} \times \cancel{21}^{3} = 6$$

Or in a sum or difference, we can replace a fraction by a compatible fraction.

$$3\frac{5}{8} + 9\frac{1}{7} \approx 3\frac{5}{8} + 9\frac{1}{8} = 12\frac{6}{8}, \text{ or } 12\frac{3}{4}$$

Example U

Use compatible numbers to estimate each computation mentally.

1. $\frac{3}{4} \times 31$ 2. $4\frac{7}{10} + 2\frac{2}{11}$ 3. $6 \times 2\frac{1}{7}$

Solution 1. $\frac{3}{4} \times 31 \approx \frac{3}{4} \times 32 = \frac{3}{\cancel{4}} \times \cancel{32}^{8} = 24$ 2. $4\frac{7}{10} + 2\frac{2}{11} \approx 4\frac{7}{10} + 2\frac{2}{10} = 6\frac{9}{10}$ 3. $6 \times 2\frac{1}{7} \approx 6$ $\times 2\frac{1}{6} = 12 + 1 = 13$ $\Big($Notice in this solution that the distributive property is needed to multiply 6 times $2\frac{1}{6}$, since $2\frac{1}{6} = 2 + \frac{1}{6}.\Big)$

Problem-Solving Application

When two people or machines can accomplish a task at different rates, sometimes we need to determine how much time will be required for them to do the job together. The solutions to such problems often require fractions, and the information can be illustrated by diagrams.

PROBLEM

Mary and Bill have the responsibility of mowing their school's soccer field. Mary can mow it in 4 hours with her lawn mower, and Bill can mow it in 6 hours with his lawn mower. How long will it take them if they work together?

Research Statement

The 6th national mathematics assessment found that only 25% of the eighth-grade students could write a word problem involving division of a whole number and a fraction.

Kouba, Zawojewski, and Strutchens 1997

Understanding the Problem   We know it will require less than 4 hours because Mary can do the job alone in 4 hours. It will require more than 1 hour because Mary can mow $\frac{1}{4}$ of the field in 1 hour and Bill can mow $\frac{1}{6}$ of the field in 1 hour. **Question 1:** What fraction of the field can they mow in 1 hour, working together?

Devising a Plan   One approach is to *make a drawing*. Since Mary and Bill can mow $\frac{1}{4} + \frac{1}{6} = \frac{5}{12}$ of the field in 1 hour, let's consider a figure to illustrate this part of the total field. The following figure has 12 equal parts, and the 5 shaded parts represent the amount they can mow in 1 hour. **Question 2:** According to this diagram, approximately how long (to the nearest hour) will it take them, working together, to mow the field?

1st hour

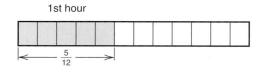

Carrying Out the Plan   The next figure shows that in 2 hours they can mow $\frac{10}{12}$ of the field and that 2 of the 12 parts remain to be mowed. **Question 3:** How long will it take them, working together, to mow the entire field?

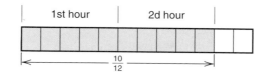

Looking Back   Mary and Bill can mow the entire field in $2\frac{2}{5}$ hours (2 hours 24 minutes). **Question 4:** If Bill gets his mower sharpened and can then mow the field in 5 hours, can Mary and Bill, working together, mow the field in less than 2 hours?

Answers to Questions 1–4   **1.** $\frac{5}{12}$ **2.** 2 hours   **3.** $2\frac{2}{5}$ hours, or 2 hours 24 minutes   **4.** No. Since Mary can mow $\frac{1}{4}$ of the field in 1 hour and Bill can mow $\frac{1}{5}$ in 1 hour, together they can mow $\frac{1}{4} + \frac{1}{5} = \frac{9}{20}$ in 1 hour. Thus, in 2 hours they can only mow $\frac{9}{20} + \frac{9}{20} = \frac{18}{20}$ of the field.

PUZZLER

Diophantus (ca. 250 B.C.) was a great mathematician who brought fame to Alexandria. The brief record we have of his life is related in the following description. His boyhood lasted $\frac{1}{6}$ of his life; his beard grew after $\frac{1}{12}$ more; he married after $\frac{1}{7}$ more; and his son was born 5 years later. The son lived to one-half his father's age, and the father died 4 years after his son. How many years did Diophantus live?

EXERCISES AND PROBLEMS 5.3

Foxhound

$\frac{1}{32}$

Trumpeter

$\frac{1}{12}$

Turkey buzzard

$\frac{1}{15}$

The fraction by each of the animals shown above tells what portion of the life-size object the picture is. Use this information in exercises 1 and 2.

1. **a.** The length of the dog is 1 inch. How long is the corresponding life-size dog?
   b. The height of the trumpeter is $1\frac{1}{2}$ inches. What is the height of the life-size trumpeter?

2. **a.** The claw span of the turkey buzzard is $\frac{1}{3}$ inch. What is the claw span of the life-size turkey buzzard?
   b. The length of a leg of the trumpeter is $\frac{1}{2}$ inch. What is the length of the leg of the life-size trumpeter?

Sketch Fraction Bars in exercises 3 and 4 to illustrate each computation.

3. **a.** $\frac{3}{10} + \frac{2}{5} = \frac{7}{10}$ **b.** $\frac{5}{6} - \frac{1}{3} = \frac{3}{6}$
   c. $\frac{2}{3} \div \frac{1}{6} = 4$ **d.** $\frac{1}{4} \times 3 = \frac{3}{4}$
   e. $\frac{1}{3} \times \frac{1}{4} = \frac{1}{12}$ **f.** $\frac{1}{3} \times \frac{1}{6} = \frac{1}{18}$

4. **a.** $\frac{1}{3} + \frac{1}{2} = \frac{5}{6}$ **b.** $\frac{1}{2} \times \frac{1}{2} = \frac{1}{4}$
   c. $2 \div \frac{1}{3} = 6$ **d.** $\frac{5}{6} - \frac{1}{4} = \frac{7}{12}$
   e. $\frac{1}{3} \times \frac{3}{7} = \frac{1}{7}$ **f.** $\frac{9}{12} \div \frac{1}{3} = 2\frac{1}{4}$

The figure on the next page can be used to show that $\frac{1}{3} \times 15 = 5$, since 15 dots can be divided into 3 equal groups of 5 dots each.

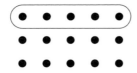

Sketch sets of dots to illustrate and determine the products in exercises 5 and 6.

5. a. $\frac{3}{8} \times 24$ **b.** $\frac{2}{5} \times 30$

6. a. $\frac{5}{6} \times 18$ **b.** $\frac{3}{7} \times 28$

Sums of fractions can be approximated on number lines. For example, place the edge of a piece of paper on the eighths line below, and mark off the length $1\frac{1}{8}$. Then place the beginning of this marked-off length at the $1\frac{1}{5}$ point on the fifths line to approximate the sum $1\frac{1}{5} + 1\frac{1}{8}$. A different approximation can be obtained by marking off the sum on the eighths line.

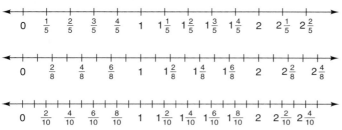

Use the preceding number lines to approximate the sums in exercises 7 and 8. Write the number that the sum is closest to on the given line. Then compute these sums and compare them to your approximations.

7. a. $\frac{4}{5} + 1\frac{3}{8}$ (fifths line)
   b. $\frac{5}{8} + \frac{7}{10}$ (eighths line)

8. a. $\frac{3}{10} + 1\frac{4}{5}$ (tenths line)
   b. $1\frac{1}{5} + 1\frac{1}{8}$ (fifths line)

Differences of fractions can be approximated on number lines. For example, place the edge of a piece of paper on the fifths line above, and mark off the length $\frac{3}{5}$. Then place the end of this marked-off length at the point $1\frac{7}{8}$ on the eighths line above, to approximate the difference $1\frac{7}{8} - \frac{3}{5}$. Use the preceding number lines to approximate the differences in exercises 9 and 10. Write the number that the difference is closest to on the given line. Then compute these differences and compare them with your approximations.

9. a. $1\frac{4}{5} - \frac{5}{8}$ (fifths line)
   b. $1\frac{1}{8} - \frac{7}{10}$ (eighths line)

10. a. $\frac{9}{10} - \frac{3}{5}$ (tenths line)
    b. $1\frac{7}{8} - \frac{3}{5}$ (eighths line)

Perform the operations in exercises 11 and 12. Replace all improper fractions in your answers with whole numbers or mixed numbers, and write all fractions in lowest terms.

11. a. $\frac{2}{3} + \frac{3}{4}$ **b.** $\frac{1}{6} + \frac{3}{8}$ **c.** $\frac{2}{3} \times 6$
    d. $\frac{-3}{4} \times \frac{2}{5}$ **e.** $2\frac{1}{4} + 1\frac{1}{3}$ **f.** $^{-}1\frac{5}{6} + 3\frac{1}{2}$
    g. $2\frac{1}{4} \times 3\frac{1}{2}$ **h.** $14\frac{1}{2} \div 2\frac{1}{4}$ **i.** $\frac{7}{8} - \frac{1}{3}$

12. a. $\frac{3}{4} - \frac{2}{5}$ **b.** $\frac{3}{4} \div \frac{1}{10}$ **c.** $\frac{2}{3} \div \frac{1}{5}$
    d. $3\frac{1}{4} - 1\frac{1}{8}$ **e.** $5\frac{1}{3} - 2\frac{1}{2}$ **f.** $^{-}3 \div \frac{1}{5}$
    g. $4 \times 5\frac{1}{8}$ **h.** $3\frac{1}{4} + 7\frac{5}{6}$ **i.** $2\frac{1}{3} \times 6\frac{1}{4}$

Write the opposite (inverse for addition) and the reciprocal (inverse for multiplication) of each number in the tables in exercises 13 and 14.

13.

	$\frac{7}{8}$	$^{-}4$	$\frac{^{-}1}{2}$	10
Opposite				
Reciprocal				

14.

	$\frac{^{-}12}{5}$	27	$\frac{3}{8}$	$^{-}249$
Opposite				
Reciprocal				

Error analysis In computing with fractions, several types of errors frequently occur. In the following example, $3\frac{2}{5}$ should have been replaced by $2\frac{7}{5}$. Instead, the 1 that was regrouped from the 3 was erroneously placed in the numerator to form $2\frac{12}{5}$.

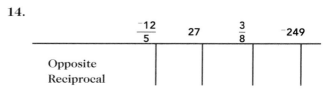

Find plausible reasons for the errors in the computations in exercises 15 and 16.

15. a. $\frac{1}{3} + \frac{1}{4} = \frac{6}{8} + \frac{5}{8} = \frac{11}{8}$ **b.** $5\frac{3}{7} - \frac{1}{4} = 5\frac{2}{3}$
    c. $\frac{1}{2} \times \frac{4}{11} = \frac{8}{11}$ **d.** $\frac{11}{12} \div \frac{1}{3} = \frac{11}{3}$

16. a. $\frac{1}{4} + \frac{5}{6} = \frac{6}{10}$ **b.** $\frac{7}{8} - \frac{2}{3} = \frac{5}{5}$
    c. $\frac{1}{2} \times \frac{3}{8} = \frac{6}{8}$ **d.** $\frac{3}{4} \div \frac{1}{5} = \frac{4}{15}$

State the number property in exercises 17 and 18 that is being used in each of these equalities.

17. a. $\frac{3}{7} + \left(\frac{2}{9} + \frac{1}{3} \right) = \frac{3}{7} + \left(\frac{1}{3} + \frac{2}{9} \right)$

b. $\frac{3}{7} + \left(\frac{2}{9} \times \frac{9}{2}\right) = \frac{3}{7} + 1$

c. $\frac{2}{9} + \left(\frac{3}{7} + \frac{1}{3}\right) = \left(\frac{2}{9} + \frac{3}{7}\right) + \frac{1}{3}$

18. a. $\frac{5}{6} \times \left(\frac{3}{4} + \frac{1}{2}\right) = \left(\frac{3}{4} + \frac{1}{2}\right) \times \frac{5}{6}$

b. $\frac{3}{4} \times \frac{5}{6} + \frac{1}{2} \times \frac{5}{6} = \left(\frac{3}{4} + \frac{1}{2}\right) \times \frac{5}{6}$

c. $\frac{7}{8} + \left(\frac{-2}{3} + \frac{2}{3}\right) = \frac{7}{8} + 0$

Determine whether the set in exercises 19 and 20 is closed for the given operation.

19. a. The set of positive fractions for addition
   b. The set of negative fractions for multiplication

20. a. The set of positive fractions for division
   b. The set of fractions between $^-10$ and 10 for subtraction

Exercises 21 and 22 contain compatible fractions. Use mental calculations to find exact answers, and show or explain your method.

21. a. $^-2\frac{2}{3} + 5\frac{1}{2} + 6\frac{1}{3} + 1\frac{1}{2}$
   b. $5\frac{5}{8} + 2\frac{1}{2} - 1\frac{1}{8}$
   c. $\frac{-1}{3} \times \frac{2}{5} \times 12 \times 20$
   d. $\frac{7}{4} \times 24 + 8$

22. a. $\frac{1}{4} \times 17 \times 120$
   b. $\frac{3}{7} + 2\frac{1}{5} + 1\frac{4}{7}$
   c. $\frac{2}{3} \times 14 \times 18 \times \frac{1}{7}$
   d. $15\frac{1}{2} + 5\frac{1}{3} - 4\frac{1}{2}$

Find convenient substitutions in exercises 23 and 24, and determine exact answers by performing each calculation mentally. Show your substitution.

23. a. $215\frac{1}{5} - 10\frac{4}{5}$
   b. $4 \times 9\frac{6}{7}$
   c. $86\frac{11}{12} + 10\frac{1}{2}$

24. a. $3 \times 3\frac{4}{5}$
   b. $6\frac{7}{10} - 1\frac{1}{2}$
   c. $12\frac{5}{6} + \frac{1}{3}$

Compute each difference or quotient in exercises 25 and 26 by using *equal differences, add-up,* or *equal quotients.* Show your method.

25. a. $8 - 3\frac{6}{7}$
   b. $15\frac{3}{10} - 10\frac{9}{10}$
   c. $\frac{5}{8} \div \frac{1}{3}$

26. a. $\frac{7}{4} \div \frac{1}{6}$
   b. $7\frac{1}{8} - 3\frac{3}{4}$
   c. $\frac{4}{7} \div \frac{1}{5}$

Round each mixed number in exercises 27 and 28 to the nearest whole number, and compute the sum of numbers in each row.

Example:

$7\frac{2}{3}$ $2\frac{3}{4}$ $4\frac{1}{8}$ $5\frac{9}{10}$ Approximate sum
Think 8 Think 3 Think 4 Think 6   21

27. a. $1\frac{2}{3}$ $3\frac{1}{4}$ $1\frac{1}{2}$ $2\frac{1}{10}$
    b. $3\frac{4}{5}$ $2\frac{1}{6}$ $3\frac{2}{5}$ $4\frac{1}{2}$

28. a. $10\frac{1}{3}$ $5\frac{1}{2}$ $2\frac{7}{8}$ $5\frac{1}{6}$
    b. $6\frac{1}{2}$ $2\frac{3}{4}$ $1\frac{1}{4}$ $2\frac{5}{6}$

Approximate the product of each pair of mixed numbers in exercises 29 and 30 by multiplying the whole numbers and adding the products of the fractions and the opposite whole numbers. Show each step in obtaining the answer.

29. a. $4\frac{1}{3} \times 6\frac{1}{2}$
   b. $5\frac{1}{4} \times 8\frac{2}{5}$

30. a. $3\frac{1}{4} \times 4\frac{2}{3}$
   b. $10\frac{1}{3} \times 6\frac{1}{2}$

Estimate each computation in exercises 31 and 32, using *compatible numbers.* Show your compatible-number replacement.

31. a. $\frac{6}{7} \times 34$ **b.** $9\frac{4}{5} + 5\frac{1}{6}$

32. a. $8 \times 4\frac{1}{7}$ **b.** $\frac{3}{4} \times 81$

REASONING AND PROBLEM SOLVING

Draw a diagram to illustrate the given information and the solution for 33 through 38.

33. What fractional amount of the earth's surface is covered by oceans or glaciers if $\frac{2}{3}$ is covered by water and $\frac{1}{10}$ by glaciers? (*Note:* Glaciers occur only over land.)

34. An experiment calls for $8\frac{1}{2}$ ounces of sulfate, but the classroom chemistry kit has only $3\frac{1}{5}$ ounces. How much more sulfate is needed?

35. In 1897, 48 million pounds of blue shad was caught in the ocean between Maine and Florida. The yearly catch is now $\frac{1}{6}$ of the 1897 catch. How many pounds of blue shad are caught yearly now?

36. A school's enrollment decreased by $\frac{1}{4}$ because of a reorganization of districts. The new enrollment is 270. What was the school's enrollment before the change?

37. On Wednesday it rained $1\frac{1}{2}$ inches and on Thursday it rained only $\frac{1}{3}$ as much as it had on Wednesday. What fraction of an inch did it rain on Thursday?

38. Sound travels $\frac{1}{5}$ mile in 1 second. How many seconds will it take a sound wave to travel 2 miles?

The sequences of numbers and keys in exercises 39 and 40 are for a calculator which displays fractions. For example, $\frac{2}{7}$ is entered by the keystrokes 2 $\boxed{\text{b/c}}$ 7. Determine the fraction or mixed number in lowest terms for each computation.

39. a. 2 $\boxed{\text{b/c}}$ 7 $\boxed{+}$ 3 $\boxed{\text{b/c}}$ 4 $\boxed{=}$
   b. 7 $\boxed{\text{b/c}}$ 8 $\boxed{-}$ 2 $\boxed{\text{b/c}}$ 3 $\boxed{=}$
   c. 9 $\boxed{\text{b/c}}$ 14 $\boxed{\times}$ 4 $\boxed{\text{b/c}}$ 9 $\boxed{=}$
   d. 5 $\boxed{\text{b/c}}$ 6 $\boxed{\div}$ 7 $\boxed{\text{b/c}}$ 8 $\boxed{=}$

40. a. 8 $\boxed{\text{b/c}}$ 9 $\boxed{+}$ 5 $\boxed{\text{b/c}}$ 7 $\boxed{=}$
   b. 4 $\boxed{\text{b/c}}$ 11 $\boxed{-}$ 1 $\boxed{\text{b/c}}$ 6 $\boxed{=}$
   c. 3 $\boxed{\text{b/c}}$ 22 $\boxed{\times}$ 4 $\boxed{\text{b/c}}$ 7 $\boxed{=}$
   d. 2 $\boxed{\text{b/c}}$ 3 $\boxed{\div}$ 4 $\boxed{\text{b/c}}$ 9 $\boxed{=}$

41. Jan and Carl were using their calculators to compute $80 \div \frac{3}{5}$. What quotient will be obtained for each sequence of steps if their calculators are designed to follow the *order of operations*? Whose sequence of calculator steps will not produce the correct answer? Explain why.

JAN'S STEPS	CARL'S STEPS
1. 80	1. 80
2. $\boxed{\div}$	2. $\boxed{\div}$
3. (3 $\boxed{\div}$ 5)	3. 3 $\boxed{\div}$ 5
4. $\boxed{=}$	4. $\boxed{=}$

42. Annette and Sharon computed $\frac{3}{5} \div \frac{1}{8}$ on their calculators by using the steps below. What quotient will be obtained for each sequence of steps if their calculators are designed to follow the *order of operations*? Whose sequence of calculator steps will produce the correct quotient?

ANNETTE'S STEPS	SHARON'S STEPS
1. 3 $\boxed{\div}$ 5	1. 3 $\boxed{\div}$ 5
2. $\boxed{\div}$	2. $\boxed{\div}$
3. 1 $\boxed{\div}$ 8	3. (1 $\boxed{\div}$ 8)
4. $\boxed{=}$	4. $\boxed{=}$

43. A taxpayer computes her federal income tax report, using the following method. Some of the amounts are shown. Compute the missing amounts.

(1) $\frac{1}{3}$ of base income of $22,000 _____
(2) $\frac{1}{5}$ of averageable income of $12,000 _____
(3) Line 1 plus line 2 _____
(4) Tax on line 3 $2318
(5) Tax on line 1 $1630
(6) Line 4 minus line 5 _____
(7) Line 6 multiplied by 4 _____
(8) Line 4 plus line 7 (total tax) _____

The following table shows high and low prices for the stocks of six companies during one day. Use this table for exercises 44 and 45.

	HIGH PRICE	LOW PRICE
Canadian Homestead	$8\frac{1}{4}$	$7\frac{15}{16}$
Drew National	$11\frac{1}{8}$	$9\frac{7}{8}$
General Plywood	$3\frac{3}{4}$	
MEM Company	$26\frac{1}{4}$	$25\frac{5}{8}$
Old Town	$7\frac{3}{4}$	$6\frac{3}{8}$
Sea Container		$16\frac{1}{2}$

44. a. General Plywood's low price was $\frac{1}{8}$ of a dollar less than its high price for the day. What was its low price?
   b. The day's high price for Sea Container was $\frac{3}{16}$ of a dollar above its low price. What was the high price?

45. a. Calculate the difference between the high price and low price for each of these stocks: Drew National, MEM Company, and Old Town.
   b. How much money would a person have saved if he or she had purchased 1000 shares of MEM Company stock at the low price for the day rather than at the high price?

46. Featured Strategies: Guessing and Checking, and Drawing Venn Diagrams Mr. Hash bought some plates at a yard sale. After arriving home he found that $\frac{2}{3}$ of the plates were chipped, $\frac{1}{2}$ were cracked, $\frac{1}{4}$ were both chipped and cracked. Only 2 plates were without chips or cracks. How many plates did he buy in all?
   a. Understanding the Problem Let's guess a number to become more familiar with the problem. If Mr. Hash bought 48 plates, how many were cracked and how many were chipped?
   b. Devising a Plan We could continue guessing and checking. Another approach is to *draw a Venn diagram*. The following figure uses circles to represent the chipped plates and the cracked plates. Two plates were neither chipped nor cracked. Since $\frac{2}{3}$ were chipped and $\frac{1}{4}$ were

chipped and cracked, $\frac{2}{3} - \frac{1}{4} = \frac{5}{12}$ were chipped but not cracked. What fraction of the plates were cracked but not chipped?

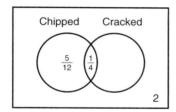

c. **Carrying Out the Plan**   After determining the fraction of the cracked plates that were not chipped, we can add the three fractions to find the fraction of the plates that were chipped and/or cracked. How can this information lead to the solution? How many plates did Mr. Hash buy?

d. **Looking Back**   Suppose that instead of 2 plates, there were 3 plates that were neither chipped nor cracked. In this case what would be the total number of plates purchased?

47. Musical notes produced from two strings of equal diameter and tension will vary according to the lengths of the strings. Different fractions of the length of the unit string (the lowest string in the illustration) can be used to produce the notes C, D, E, F, G, A, B, and c (do, re, mi, fa, so, la, ti, and do). In particular, if a string is one-half as long as another, its tone or note will be an octave higher than the longer string.*

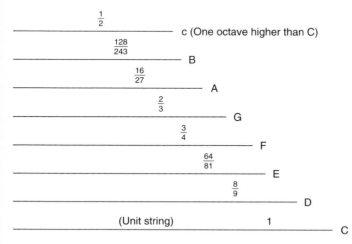

*See C. F. Linn, *The Golden Mean* (New York: Doubleday, 1974), pp. 9–13, for an elementary explanation of the origin of these fractions.

a. With the exception of two strings, each string from the unit string to the top string is $\frac{8}{9}$ the length of the previous string. For example, the G string is $\frac{8}{9}$ the length of the F string since $\frac{8}{9} \times \frac{3}{4} = \frac{2}{3}$. Which other strings are $\frac{8}{9}$ of the length of the preceding strings?

b. The white piano keys pictured below are the notes of the scale from c to C. All but two of these keys are separated by black keys. How is this observation related to the answer for part a?

48. One painter can paint a room in 2 hours; another painter requires 4 hours to paint the same room. How long will it take them to paint the room together?

49. Two-thirds of Mrs. Hoffman's fifth-grade students are boys. To make the number of boys and girls equal, 4 boys go to the other fifth-grade class, and 4 girls come from that class into Mrs. Hoffman's class. Now one-half of her students are boys. How many students are in Mrs. Hoffman's class?

50. You have two candles. One is blue and 8 inches tall and the other is yellow and 12 inches tall. The blue candle burns $\frac{1}{4}$ inch every hour and the yellow candle burns $\frac{1}{2}$ inch every hour. If the yellow candle is lighted 6 hours after the blue candle is lighted and both candles burn continuously, which candle will burn out first? After the first candle has burned out, how much longer will the other candle burn?

51. Paula removed $\frac{4}{5}$ of the disks from a new box of computer disks, and Sam removed $\frac{7}{10}$ of the disks that remained in the box. If Sam removed 28 disks from the box, how many disks did Paula remove?

52. Two antenna cables differ in length by 164 inches. The shorter cable is $\frac{1}{3}$ the length of the other. Samir needs 350 inches of antenna cable. If he splices the two cables together, will he have enough cable?

53. A common mistake of school children in adding fractions is to add numerator to numerator and denominator to denominator. However, one student noticed that for the fractions $\frac{1}{3}$ and $\frac{4}{5}$, the fraction obtained by this method, $(1 + 4)/(3 + 5) = \frac{5}{8}$, is greater than $\frac{1}{3}$ and less than $\frac{4}{5}$. Are there other pairs of fractions for which this process will produce a third fraction that is between the original two fractions? Form a conjecture and show examples to support your reasoning.

ONLINE LEARNING CENTER   www.mhhe.com/bennett-nelson

• Math Investigation 5.3   *Fraction Patterns*
Section-Related: • Links   • Writing/Discussion Problems   • Bibliography

PUZZLER

In his will Farmer Smith bequeathed his 17 horses to his three sons in the following manner: $\frac{1}{2}$ of his horses to the oldest son, Al; $\frac{1}{3}$ of his horses to the middle son, Garry; and $\frac{1}{9}$ of his horses to the youngest son, Greg. Being fairly capable with fractions, the boys computed their shares to be $8\frac{1}{2}$ horses, $5\frac{2}{3}$ horses, and $1\frac{8}{9}$ horses. However, each boy was disappointed at the prospect of getting parts of a horse, and they fell to quarreling about their predicament. At that point Farmer Smith's neighbor rode up and, after being informed of their dilemma, proposed the following solution. First he donated his horse, to make a total of 18 horses. Then he gave $\frac{1}{2}$ of the 18 horses to Al, $\frac{1}{3}$ of the 18 to Garry, and $\frac{1}{9}$ of the 18 to Greg. How many horses did each boy receive? What was the total number of these horses? Seeing their satisfaction with his solution, Farmer Smith's neighbor jumped on his horse and rode away. Why was his solution possible?

CHAPTER REVIEW

1. **Integers**
   a. The negative whole numbers together with the whole numbers are called **integers.**
   b. For each integer, there is another integer, called its **opposite**, such that their sum is zero.
   c. For any two integers m and n, m is **less than** n, written $m < n$, if there is a positive integer k such that $m + k = n$.
   d. The integers less than zero are called **negative integers** ($^-1$, $^-2$, $^-3$, . . .). Often they are denoted by a raised minus sign to avoid confusion with the operation of subtraction.
   e. The integers greater than zero are called **positive integers.** They are sometimes denoted by a raised plus sign to emphasize that they are positive.

2. **Operations on integers**
   a. **Addition**   Positive plus positive equals positive. Negative plus negative equals negative. Negative plus positive may be positive ($^-5 + 8 = 3$), negative ($^-5 + 2 = ^-3$), or zero ($^-5 + 5 = 0$).
   b. **Subtraction**   For any two integers n and s, $n - s$ is the sum of n plus the opposite of s.
   c. **Multiplication**   Positive times positive equals positive. Positive times negative equals negative. Negative times positive equals negative. Negative times negative equals positive.

   d. **Division**   For any integers n and s, with $s \neq 0$, $n \div s = k$ if and only if $n = s \times k$ for some integer k.

3. **Fractions**
   a. A **fraction** is a number in the form a/b, where a and b are any numbers except $b \neq 0$. In this chapter a and b are integers.
   b. In the fraction a/b, a is called the **numerator** and b is called the **denominator.**
   c. There are three concepts of fractions: the **part-to-whole concept**, the **division concept**, and the **ratio concept.**
   d. For any fraction a/b and any number $k \neq 0$, a/b is equal to ka/kb.
   e. To **simplify a fraction** a/b, divide a and b by GCF(a, b).
   f. If GCF(a, b) = 1, then a/b is said to be in **lowest terms** or **simplified.**
   g. The **smallest common denominator** of a/b and c/d is LCM(b, d).
   h. Between any two fractions there is always another fraction. This property is referred to by saying the fractions are **dense.**
   i. If the numerator of a fraction is greater than or equal to the denominator, the fraction is called an **improper fraction.**
   j. A number that is written as a whole number and a fraction is called a **mixed number.**

4. Fraction operations
  a. Addition   For fractions a/b and c/d,

$$\frac{a}{b} + \frac{c}{d} = \frac{ad + bc}{bd}$$

  b. Subtraction   For fractions a/b and c/d,

$$\frac{a}{b} - \frac{c}{d} = \frac{ad - bc}{bd}$$

  c. Multiplication   For fractions a/b and c/d,

$$\frac{a}{b} \times \frac{c}{d} = \frac{ac}{bd}$$

  d. Division   For fractions a/b and c/d, with $c/d \neq 0$,

$$\frac{a}{b} \div \frac{c}{d} = \frac{a}{b} \times \frac{d}{c} = \frac{ad}{bc}$$

5. Models
  a. Black and red chips are used to illustrate integers, with black chips representing positive integers (credits) and red chips representing negative integers (debts).
  b. Number lines illustrate integers, with negative integers below zero and positive integers above zero.
  c. Fraction Bars and **sets of dots** illustrate the part-to-whole concept of fractions.
  d. Cuisenaire Rods illustrate the ratio concept of fractions.
  e. The part-to-whole concept of fractions can be illustrated with **number lines** by dividing unit intervals into equal numbers of parts.

6. Number properties
  Properties a through j are true for addition and multiplication of integers and fractions. Property k holds for multiplication of fractions.
  a. A set is closed for addition if the sum of any two numbers from the set is in the set.
  b. A set is closed for multiplication if the product of any two numbers from the set is in the set.
  c. Identity for addition.
  d. Identity for multiplication.
  e. Addition is commutative.
  f. Multiplication is commutative.
  g. Addition is associative.
  h. Multiplication is associative.
  i. Multiplication distributes over addition and subtraction.
  j. Every number has a unique **inverse for addition** called its **inverse** such that the sum of the two numbers is zero.
  k. Every fraction not equal to zero has a unique **inverse for multiplication** called its **reciprocal** such that the product of the two fractions is 1.

7. Mental calculations
  a. Compatible numbers is the technique of using pairs of numbers that are especially convenient for mental calculation.
  b. Substitution is the technique of breaking a number into a convenient sum, difference, product, or quotient.
  c. Equal differences is the technique of increasing or decreasing both numbers in a difference by the same amount.
  d. Add-up is the technique of finding a difference by adding up from the smaller number to the larger.
  e. Equal quotients is a type of substitution that uses the fact that the quotient of two numbers remains the same when both numbers are divided by the same number.

8. Estimation
  a. Rounding is the technique of replacing one or more numbers in a sum, difference, product, or quotient by an approximate number to obtain an estimation. Often fractions are rounded to the nearest whole number.
  b. Compatible numbers is the technique of computing estimations by replacing one or more numbers with convenient approximate numbers.

CHAPTER TEST

1. Sketch sets of black and red chips to illustrate each operation, and determine each answer.
  a. $8 + {}^-5$ **b.** ${}^-7 - {}^-3$ **c.** $3 \times {}^-4$
  d. ${}^-20 \div {}^-4$ **e.** $6 - 2$ **f.** ${}^-15 \div 3$

2. Sketch a number line to illustrate each sum.
  a. ${}^-8 + 3$ **b.** ${}^-8 + {}^-6$

3. Compute each product or quotient.
  a. ${}^-7 \times {}^-6$ **b.** $30 \div {}^-5$
  c. $8 \times {}^-10$ **d.** ${}^-40 \div {}^-8$

4. Use *equal products* or *equal quotients* to calculate each answer mentally. Explain your method.
  a. ${}^-16 \times 25$ **b.** $800 \div {}^-16$

5. Use *compatible numbers* to obtain an estimation. Show your replacement.
   a. $^-271 \div 30$ **b.** $\frac{1}{8} \times 55$
   c. $4 \times 6\frac{1}{5}$ **d.** $11 \times {}^-34$

6. Use each figure to illustrate the operation or equality. Determine the answer for each operation.
   a. $6 \div 4$ **b.** $\frac{1}{3} \times 15$

   c. $\frac{2}{3} \times \frac{1}{5}$

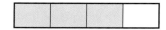

   d. $\frac{3}{4} = \frac{6}{8}$

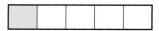

7. Complete each equation so that the pairs of fractions have the smallest common denominator.
   a. $\dfrac{3}{14} =$ **b.** $\dfrac{1}{24} =$

   $\dfrac{5}{16} =$ $\dfrac{^-7}{8} =$

8. Determine an inequality for each pair of fractions.
   a. $\dfrac{6}{11}, \dfrac{5}{9}$ **b.** $\dfrac{3}{5}, \dfrac{6}{11}$ **c.** $\dfrac{^-4}{9}, \dfrac{^-3}{7}$

9. Mentally determine an inequality for each pair of fractions, and explain your reasoning.
   a. $\dfrac{1}{8}, \dfrac{1}{10}$ **b.** $\dfrac{4}{7}, \dfrac{5}{12}$
   c. $\dfrac{1}{2}, \dfrac{7}{12}$ **d.** $\dfrac{5}{6}, \dfrac{7}{8}$

10. Compute these sums and differences.
   a. $\begin{array}{r} 2\frac{1}{6} \\ +\ 4\frac{1}{3} \\ \hline \end{array}$ **b.** $\begin{array}{r} 5\frac{2}{3} \\ -1\frac{1}{5} \\ \hline \end{array}$

   c. $\begin{array}{r} 6\frac{5}{8} \\ +1\frac{2}{3} \\ \hline \end{array}$ **d.** $\begin{array}{r} 10\frac{1}{5} \\ -4\frac{5}{6} \\ \hline \end{array}$

11. Compute these products and quotients.
   a. $2\frac{1}{4} \times 6\frac{1}{3}$ **b.** $8\frac{4}{5} \div 2\frac{1}{8}$
   c. $\frac{2}{3} \times {}^-14$ **d.** $6 \div 1\frac{1}{2}$

12. State the number property that is being used in each of these equations.
   a. $6 + \left(\frac{3}{5} \times \frac{5}{3}\right) = 6 + 1$
   b. $\frac{3}{4} \times \left(7 + \frac{^-1}{2}\right) = \frac{3}{4} \times 7 + \frac{3}{4} \times \frac{^-1}{2}$
   c. $\frac{2}{3} \times \left(\frac{1}{5} + \frac{1}{2}\right) = \left(\frac{1}{5} + \frac{1}{2}\right) \times \frac{2}{3}$
   d. $8 + \left(\frac{4}{5} + \frac{^-4}{5}\right) = 8 + 0$

13. True or false?
   a. Subtraction of integers is commutative.
   b. The set of positive integers is closed for multiplication.
   c. The set of positive fractions is closed for multiplication.
   d. The set of integers is closed for division.
   e. Subtraction of fractions is associative.

14. This picture of a blue shark has a length of $1\frac{3}{4}$ inches. The scale factor from an actual blue shark to this picture is $\frac{1}{120}$.

   a. How many feet long is the actual blue shark?
   b. A right whale has a length of approximately 40 feet. If the scale factor from a life-size whale to a picture of the whale is $\frac{1}{300}$, how many inches long is the whale in the picture?

15. A school's new pump can fill the swimming pool in 5 hours; the old pump takes 10 hours. How long will it take to fill the pool if both pumps are used together?

DECIMALS: RATIONAL AND IRRATIONAL NUMBERS

SPOTLIGHT ON TEACHING

Excerpts from NCTM's Standards for School Mathematics Grades 6–8*

In the middle grades, students should become facile in working with fractions, decimals, and percents. Teachers can help students deepen their understanding of rational numbers by presenting problems, such as those in Figure 6.1 that call for flexible thinking.

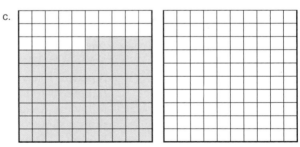

a. If ▭ is 3/4, draw the fraction strip for 1/2, for 2/3, for 4/3, and for 3/2. Be prepared to justify your answers.

b. Using the points you are given on the number line above, locate 1/2, 2 1/2, and 1/4. Be prepared to justify your answers

c. Use the drawing above to justify in as many different ways as you can that 75% of the square is equal to 3/4 of the square. You may reposition the shaded squares if you wish

Figure 6.1

At the heart of flexibility in working with rational numbers is a solid understanding of different representations for fractions, decimals, and percents. In grades 3–5, students should have learned to generate and recognize equivalent forms of fractions, decimals, and percents, at least in some simple cases. In the middle grades, students should build on and extend this experience to become facile in using fractions, decimals, and percents meaningfully. Students can develop a deep understanding of rational numbers through experiences with a variety of models, such as fraction strips, number lines, 10×10 grids, area models, and objects.

Principles and Standards for School Mathematics (Reston, VA: National Council of Teachers of Mathematics, 2000), p. 215.

MATH ACTIVITY 6.1

DECIMAL PLACE VALUE WITH BASE-TEN PIECES

Materials: Base-ten pieces in the Manipulative Kit and Decimal Squares recording paper (three copies from inside cover page of the text or from the website).

*1. When the largest base-ten piece in your kit represents the unit, the other base-ten pieces take on the values shown here. Notice that the hundredths piece is divided into 10 equal parts, and 1 part is shaded to represent 1 thousandth.

   a. List some relationships between these four types of pieces.

   b. Form the collection of 1 unit piece, 4 tenths pieces, and 12 hundredths pieces. By using only your base-ten pieces and exchanging (trading) the pieces, it is possible to represent this collection in many different ways. In a place value table like the one shown here, record some of these different collections, including the collection that requires the least number of pieces.

UNITS	TENTHS	HUNDREDTHS	THOUSANDTHS
1	4	12	

2. Here the decimal .263 is illustrated by both base-ten pieces and the shaded amount of a Decimal Square. Use your base-ten pieces to illustrate the following decimals, and draw a sketch of each collection. Then shade and label a square on the Decimal Squares recording paper for each decimal.

   a. 1   b. .44   c. .73

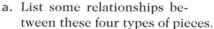

3. Four base-ten pieces for .1 can be traded for 40 of the pieces for .01. That is, .4 = .40. This is illustrated by these Decimal Squares. Shade squares on the Decimal Squares recording paper to illustrate equality for the following pairs of decimals. Connect each pair of squares with a curved line, as shown, and write an equality for the decimals on the line.

   a. .17, .170   b. .1, .10   c. .6, .600

SECTION 6.1

DECIMALS AND RATIONAL NUMBERS

*Circular patterns of atoms in
an iridium crystal, magnified
more than 1 million times by
a field ion microscope.*

A carpenter agrees that during a specified 30-hour period he be paid $15.50
every hour he works and that he pay $16.60 every hour he does not work. At
the end of 30 hours, he finds he has earned $47.70. How many hours did he
work?*

Each dot in the remarkable photograph above is an atom in an iridium crystal.
The circular patterns show the order and symmetry governing atomic structures.
The diameters of atoms, and even the diameters of electrons contained in atoms,
can be measured by decimals. Each atom in this picture has a diameter of
.000000027 centimeter, and the diameter of an electron is .00000000000056354
centimeter.

The use of decimals is not restricted to describing small objects. The gross national product (GNP) and the national income (NI) for selected 5-year periods are
expressed to the nearest tenth of a billion dollars in Figure 6.1.†

Figure 6.1

	1980	1985	1990	1995	1999
GNP (billions)	$2631.7	$4053.1	$5803.2	$7400.5	$9256.1
NI (billions)	$2116.6	$3229.9	$4642.1	$5876.7	$7496.3

In our daily lives we encounter decimals in representations of dollar amounts:
$17.35, $12.09, $24.00, etc. In elementary school, pennies, dimes, and dollars are
commonly used for teaching decimals.

*"Problems of the Month," *Mathematics Teacher* 80, no. 7 (October 1987): 555.

†Adapted from *Statistical Abstract of the United States*, 120th ed. (Washington, DC: Bureau of the Census,
2000), p. 456.

The person most responsible for our use of decimals is Simon Stevin, a Dutchman. In 1585 Stevin wrote *La Disme,* the first book on the use of decimals. He not only stated the rules for computing with decimals but also pointed out their practical applications. Stevin showed that business calculations with decimals can be performed as easily as those involving only whole numbers. He recommended that the government adopt the decimal system and enforce its use.

As decimals gained acceptance in the sixteenth and seventeenth centuries, a variety of notations were used. Many writers used a vertical bar in place of a decimal point. Here are some examples of how 27.847 was written during this period.

27 | 847   27(847)   27|847   27 847

27847 . . . ③   27,8ⁱ4ⁱⁱ7ⁱⁱⁱ   27847   27 ⓪ 8 ① 4 ② 7 ③
                                            ₒ

Decimal Terminology and Notation

The word *decimal* comes from the Latin *decem,* meaning *ten.* Technically, any number written in base-ten positional numeration can be called a decimal. However, **decimal** most often refers only to numbers such as 17.38 and .45, which are expressed with **decimal points.** A combination of a whole number and a decimal, such as 17.38, is also called a **mixed decimal.**

There are currently many variations in decimal notation. In England the decimal point is placed higher above the line than in the United States. In other European countries, a comma is used in place of a decimal point. A comma and a raised numeral denote a decimal in Scandinavian countries.

United States	England	Europe	Scandinavian countries
82.17	82·17	82,17	82,¹⁷

The number of digits to the right of the decimal point is called the **number of decimal places.** There are two decimal places in 7.08 and one decimal place in 104.5. The positions of the digits to the left of the decimal point represent **place values** that are increasing powers of 10 (1, 10, 10^2, 10^3, . . .). The positions to the right of the decimal point represent **place values** that are decreasing powers of 10 (10^{-1}, 10^{-2}, 10^{-3}, . . .), or reciprocals of powers of 10 (1/10, $1/10^2$, $1/10^3$, . . .). In the decimal 5473.286 (Figure 6.2), the 2 represents $\frac{2}{10}$, the 8 represents $\frac{8}{100}$, and the 6 represents $\frac{6}{1000}$. Notice the similarity in pairs of names to the right and left of the units digit, for example, tens and tenths, hundreds and hundredths, etc. The convention in the preceding Historical Highlight of placing a small zero under the units digit helped to focus attention on these pairs of names.

Figure 6.2

Example A

Express the value of the digit marked by the arrow as a fraction whose denominator is a power of 10.

1. 47.3<u>5</u>   2. 6.0<u>8</u>9   3. 14.<u>0</u>7

Solution   1. $\frac{5}{100}$ 2. $\frac{9}{1000}$ 3. $\frac{0}{10}$

Like whole numbers, decimals can be written in expanded form to show the powers of 10 (Figure 6.3).

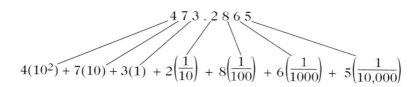

Figure 6.3

$$4(10^2) + 7(10) + 3(1) + 2\left(\frac{1}{10}\right) + 8\left(\frac{1}{100}\right) + 6\left(\frac{1}{1000}\right) + 5\left(\frac{1}{10,000}\right)$$

In grades 3–5, students should have learned to think of decimal numbers as a natural extension of the base-ten place-value system to represent quantities less than 1. In grades 6–8 they should also understand decimals as fractions whose denominators are powers of 10.

Standards 2000, p. 216

READING AND WRITING DECIMALS   The digits to the left of the decimal point are read as a whole number, and the decimal point is read *and.* The digits to the right of the point are also read as a whole number, after which we say the name of the place value of the last digit. For example, 1208.0925 is read "one thousand two hundred eight and nine hundred twenty-five ten-thousandths."

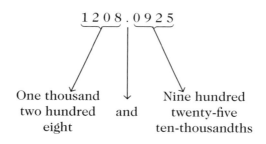

Example B

Write the name of each decimal.

1. 3.472   2. 16.14   3. .3775

Solution   1. Three and four hundred seventy-two thousandths   2. Sixteen and fourteen hundredths   3. Three thousand seven hundred seventy-five ten-thousandths

---

One place where you may see the names of numbers is on bank checks. When writing an amount of money, some people write the decimal part of a dollar in words. Notice that on the bank check in Figure 6.4 it is unnecessary to write *dollars* or *cents.* The amount is in terms of dollars, and this unit is printed at the end of the line on which the amount of money is written. Some people write the decimal part of a dollar as a fraction. For example, the amount of this check might have been written "one hundred seventy-seven and $\frac{24}{100}$."

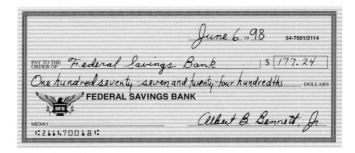

Figure 6.4

Models for Decimals

Models are important for providing conceptual understanding and insight into the use of decimals.

It is important that decimals be thought of as numbers and the ability to relate them to models should assist in this. We should be spending more time having children become familiar with decimals, their meanings and uses, before rushing directly to decimal computation. Think of the time we spend with counting objects and modeling whole numbers before formal operations with whole numbers are introduced.*

DECIMAL SQUARES   The Decimal Squares model illustrates the part-to-whole concept of decimals and place value. Unit squares are divided into 10, 100, and 1000 equal parts (Figure 6.5), and the decimal tells what part of the square is shaded.†

Research Statement

As with fractions, an understanding of the symbolism for representing decimals is essential to developing understanding of operations with decimals.

Resnick et al. 1989

Tenths square

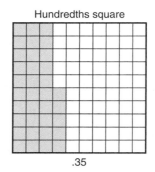

Hundredths square

Thousandths square

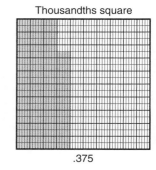

.3   .35   .375

Figure 6.5

Each decimal in Figure 6.5 can be obtained by beginning with the fraction for the shaded amount of the square and obtaining the expanded form of the decimal. For example, the fraction for the square representing 375 parts out of 1000 is $\frac{375}{1000}$.

$$\frac{375}{1000} = \frac{300}{1000} + \frac{70}{1000} + \frac{5}{1000} = \frac{3}{10} + \frac{7}{100} + \frac{5}{1000} = .375$$

	TENTHS	HUNDREDTHS	THOUSANDTHS
Place-value table	3	7	5

Similarly, the decimal for $\frac{3}{10}$ is .3, and the decimal for $\frac{35}{100}$ is .35.

---

*T. P. Carpenter, H. Kepner, M. K. Corbitt, M. M. Lindquist, and R. E. Reys, "Decimals: Results and Implications from National Assessment," *Arithmetic Teacher* 28 (April 1981): 34–37.

†Decimal Squares is a registered trademark of Scott Resources, Inc.

Make Connections

You can use a model and a place-value chart to read and write decimals. The **decimal point** separates the ones from the tenths.

Using Models

Think: $\frac{50}{100}$ of the grid is shaded.

Simplify: $\frac{50}{100} = \frac{5}{10} = \frac{1}{2}$

Using Paper and Pencil

Ones		Tenths	Hundredths
0	.	5	0

0.50 and 0.5 are **equivalent decimals** because they represent the same amount. $\frac{1}{2}$ is equivalent to 0.50.

Think: $\frac{75}{100}$ of the grid is shaded.

Simplify: $\frac{75}{100} = \frac{3}{4}$

Ones		Tenths	Hundredths
0	.	7	5

$\frac{3}{4}$ is equivalent to 0.75.

Try It   Write a fraction and a decimal for each shaded part. Then write the fraction in simplest form.

1.
2.
3.
4.

Sum it Up   How are 0.2 and 0.20 equivalent? 0.2 and $\frac{2}{10}$?

Practice   Write a fraction and a decimal for each shaded part. Then write the fraction in simplest form.

5.
6.
7.
8.

Write each as a decimal.

9. $\frac{1}{10}$ 10. $\frac{1}{4}$ 11. $\frac{30}{100}$ 12. $\frac{3}{5}$ 13. $\frac{5}{100}$ 14. $\frac{65}{100}$

Example C   Describe the square that would represent each fraction, and write the decimal for each fraction.

1. $\dfrac{4728}{10{,}000}$ 2. $\dfrac{6}{100}$

Solution   1. A square with 4728 parts shaded out of 10,000

$$\frac{4728}{10{,}000} = \frac{4000}{10{,}000} + \frac{700}{10{,}000} + \frac{20}{10{,}000} + \frac{8}{10{,}000}$$

$$= \frac{4}{10} + \frac{7}{100} + \frac{2}{1000} + \frac{8}{10{,}000}$$

$$= .4728$$

2. A square with 6 parts shaded out of 100

$$\frac{6}{100} = \frac{0}{10} + \frac{6}{100} = .06$$

     The preceding example shows that it is easy to obtain the decimal for a fraction whose denominator is a power of 10; it is just a matter of locating the decimal point. Try the example on your calculator by dividing 4728 by 10,000 and 6 by 100. It is also instructive to enter 4728 into a calculator and then repeatedly divide by 10. Each time the decimal point moves one digit to the left.

KEYSTROKES	VIEW SCREEN
4728 ÷ 10 =	472.8
÷ 10 =	47.28
÷ 10 =	4.728
÷ 10 =	.4728

In general, to divide an integer by a power of 10, *begin with the units digit and, for each factor of 10, count off a digit to the left to locate the decimal point.*

NUMBER LINE   The number line is a common model for illustrating decimals. One method of marking off a unit from 0 to 1 is to use the edge of a Decimal Square, as shown in Figure 6.6. This approach shows the relationship between a *region model* for a unit (the Decimal Square) and a *linear model* for a unit (the edge of a square). The Decimal Square can be used repeatedly to mark off tenths on the number line from 0 to 1, 1 to 2, etc.

Figure 6.6

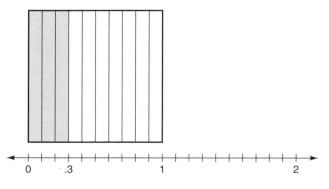

Consider locating the point for .372 on a number line. One approach is to use the expanded form of the decimal

$$.372 = \tfrac{3}{10} + \tfrac{7}{100} + \tfrac{2}{1000}$$

and locate the point in several steps, as shown in Figure 6.7. First, the point for $\tfrac{3}{10}$ (.3) is located at the end of the third interval, as in Figure 6.6. Second, the expanded form shows that we must add $\tfrac{7}{100}$, so the interval from .3 to .4 is divided into 10 equal parts, which are hundredths. To add $\tfrac{7}{100}$ (.07), we begin at .3 and go to the end of the seventh interval. This is the point for .37. Finally, the interval from .37 to .38 is divided into 10 equal parts, which are thousandths. To add $\tfrac{2}{1000}$, we begin at .37 and go to the end of the second interval. This is the point for .372.

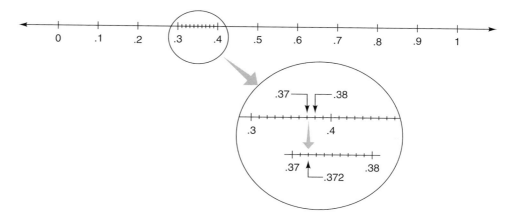

Figure 6.7

Example D

Sketch a number line and mark the approximate location of each decimal.

1. .46   **2.** 1.75   **3.** 2.271

Solution

Students' understanding and ability to reason will grow as they represent fractions and decimals with physical materials and on number lines. . . .

Standards 2000, p. 33.

Decimals are used for negative as well as positive numbers. The graph in Figure 6.8 represents increasing and decreasing changes from year to year in the producer price index for crude materials, in tenths of a percent, from 1985 to 1997.* The producer price index decreased in 1985 and 1986, and increased from 1987 to 1990.

Statistical Abstract of the United States, 118th ed. (Washington, DC: Bureau of the Census, 1998), p. 497.

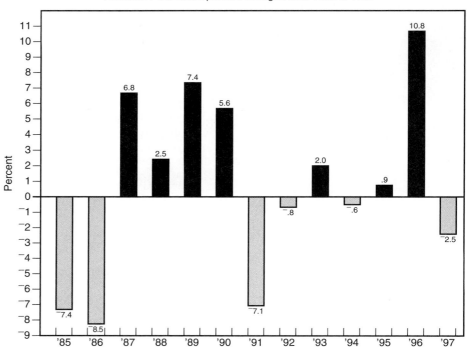

Figure 6.8

The decimals 2.5 and ⁻2.5 for the years of 1988 and 1997 are opposites. For every decimal, whether positive or negative, there is a corresponding decimal called its **opposite** (or **inverse for addition**) such that the sum of the two decimals is zero. Several decimals and their opposites are shown on the number line in Figure 6.9.

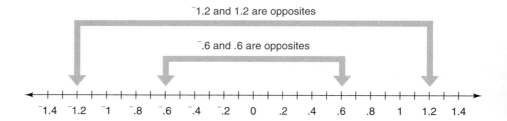

Figure 6.9

Equality of Decimals

Equality of decimals can be illustrated visually by comparing the shaded amounts in their Decimal Squares. Figure 6.10 shows that 4 parts out of 10, 40 parts out of 100, and 400 parts out of 1000 are all represented by the same amount of shading—in each Decimal Square, four columns are shaded. This shows that

$$.4 = .40 = .400$$

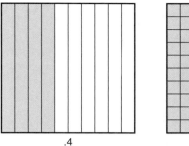 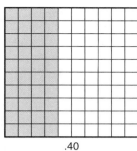 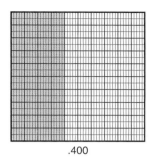

Figure 6.10

.4   .40   .400

Example E

Complete each equation by writing the indicated decimal, and describe the square representing each decimal in the equation.

1. .35 = _____ (thousandths)

2. .670 = _____ (hundredths)

3. .600 = _____ (tenths)

Solution   1. .35 = .350 (35 parts out of 100 and 350 parts out of 1000 are shaded)   2. .670 = .67 (670 parts out of 1000 and 67 parts out of 100 are shaded)   3. .600 = .6 (600 parts out of 1000 and 6 parts out of 10 are shaded)

Students in these grades [3–5] should use models and other strategies to represent and study decimal numbers. For example, they should count by tenths verbally or use a calculator.

Standards 2000, p. 150

Decimal Squares also give us a visual model for place value. Consider the Decimal Square for .475 in Figure 6.11. The 4 full columns that are shaded (400 thousandths) represent $\frac{4}{10}$ or .4 ($\frac{400}{1000} = \frac{4}{10}$); the 7 small squares that are shaded (70 thousandths) represent $\frac{7}{100}$ or .07 ($\frac{70}{1000} = \frac{7}{100}$); and the 5 small parts that are shaded (5 thousandths) represent $\frac{5}{1000}$ or .005. Thus the decimal .475 can be thought of as 4 tenths, 7 hundredths, and 5 thousandths.

$$.475 = .4 + .07 + .005$$

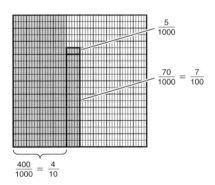

$\frac{5}{1000}$

$\frac{70}{1000} = \frac{7}{100}$

$\frac{400}{1000} = \frac{4}{10}$

Figure 6.11

Inequality of Decimals

Research indicates that students from elementary school through college often have difficulty determining inequalities for decimals. One source of confusion is to think of the digits in the decimal as representing whole numbers (see Example F).

Figure 6.12 shows that .47 < .6. Even though 47 is greater than 6, a smaller amount of the square is shaded for .47 than for .6.

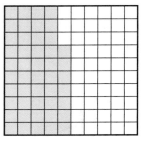
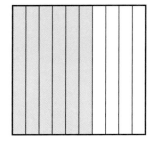

Figure 6.12

We can also see that .47 < .6 by noting that in the Decimal Square for .47, 4 full columns and part of another are shaded, whereas in the Decimal Square for .6, 6 full columns are shaded. In other words, the digit in the tenths place for .47 is less than the digit in the tenths place for .6. In general, the following *place value test* determines inequalities for decimals.

> **PLACE VALUE TEST FOR INEQUALITY OF DECIMALS**   The greater of two positive decimals that are both less than 1 will be the decimal with the greater digit in the tenths place. If these digits are equal, this test is applied to the hundredths digits, and so on.

The question in the next example is from a test given as part of a nationwide testing program in schools every 4 years.* Over one-half of the 13-year-olds who took the test in 1980 selected an incorrect answer.

Example F

Which number is the greatest?

.19   .036   .195   .2

Solution   One approach is to use the place value test for inequality of decimals. Since 2 is the greatest of the digits in the tenths place of these four decimals, .2 is the greatest number. Another approach is to change each decimal to thousandths. This will show that 200 thousandths is the greatest number of thousandths among these four decimals.

.190   .036   .195   .200

A visual approach with Decimal Squares shows that 2 full columns of shading (or 2 parts shaded out of 10) is more than 19 parts shaded out of 100 or 195 parts shaded out of 1000.

Without a solid conceptual foundation, students often think of decimal numbers incorrectly; they may, for example, think that 3.75 is larger than 3.8 because 75 is more than 8 (Resnick et al. 1989).

Standards 2000, p. 216

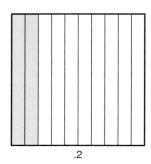
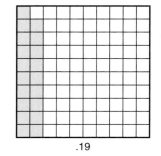
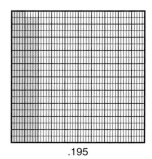

.2   .19   .195

Note: Of the 13-year-olds tested in 1980, 47 percent selected .195 for the answer. This error may be due to the fact that 195 is greater than 19, 36, or 2.

---

*T. P. Carpenter, M. K. Corbitt, H. S. Kepner, M. M. Lindquist, and R. E. Reys, *Results from the Second Mathematics Assessment of the National Assessment of Educational Progress* (Reston, VA: National Council of Teachers of Mathematics, 1981).

Rational Numbers

Up to this point, numbers written in the form a/b, where a and b are integers, have been called *fractions*. This is the terminology commonly used in elementary and middle schools. However, the word *fraction* has a more general meaning and includes the quotient of any two numbers, integers or not, as long as the denominator is not zero. Numbers that are quotients of two integers are called **rational numbers.**

> Any number that can be written in the form a/b, where $b \neq 0$ and a and b are integers, is called a **rational number.**

For example, $\frac{1}{9}, \frac{-3}{7}, \frac{1}{5}, \frac{7}{10}$, and $\frac{-1}{3}$ are rational numbers. When the denominator of a rational number equals 1, the rational number equals an integer: $\frac{6}{1} = 6, \frac{-4}{1} = {}^-4, \frac{12}{1} = 12$, etc. Therefore, integers are also rational numbers.

Rational numbers can be expressed by many different number symbols or numerals. For example, $\frac{3}{10}$ is a rational number and $\frac{3}{10} = .3$, so .3 is also a rational number. In the following paragraphs we will show that all rational numbers a/b can be written as decimals.

We have seen that it is easy to convert a fraction to a decimal if the denominator is a power of 10:

Research Statement

Research has shown that most middle-grades children were unsuccessful with a set of tasks that mixed fraction and decimal notation.

Markovits and Sowder 1991

$$\frac{64}{100} = .64 \qquad \frac{7283}{1000} = 7.283 \qquad \frac{54}{10,000} = .0054$$

Sometimes when the denominator is not a power of 10, the fraction can be replaced by an equal fraction whose denominator is a power of 10. For example, $\frac{1}{4}$ can be replaced by $\frac{25}{100}$ because 100 is a multiple of 4:

$$\frac{1}{4} = \frac{25 \times 1}{25 \times 4} = \frac{25}{100} = .25$$

Since $10 = 2 \times 5$, by the Fundamental Theorem of Arithmetic any power of 10 will have factors of only 2 and 5.

$$10 = 2 \times 5 \qquad 100 = 10^2 = 2^2 \times 5^2 \qquad 1000 = 10^3 = 2^3 \times 5^3 \ldots$$

Consider replacing $\frac{3}{8}$ by a fraction whose denominator is a power of 10. Since $8 = 2^3$, we need to multiply the numerator and denominator of $\frac{3}{8}$ by 5^3.

$$\frac{3}{8} = \frac{3}{2^3} = \frac{3 \times 5^3}{2^3 \times 5^3} = \frac{375}{10^3} = .375$$

Example G

Convert each fraction to a decimal by first writing a fraction whose denominator is a power of 10.

1. $\dfrac{7}{20}$ 2. $\dfrac{3}{25}$ 3. $\dfrac{11}{16}$ 4. $\dfrac{3}{40}$

Solution   1. $\dfrac{7}{20} = \dfrac{35}{100} = .35$ 2. $\dfrac{3}{25} = \dfrac{12}{100} = .12$ 3. $\dfrac{11}{16} = \dfrac{11}{2^4} = \dfrac{11 \times 5^4}{2^4 \times 5^4} = \dfrac{6875}{10^4} = .6875$

4. $\dfrac{3}{40} = \dfrac{3}{2^3 \times 5} = \dfrac{3 \times 5^2}{2^3 \times 5^3} = \dfrac{75}{10^3} = .075$

In the preceding example, all the decimals had a finite number of digits. Such decimals are called **terminating** (or **finite**) **decimals**. However, there are decimals that are not terminating. There is no power of 10 that has 3 as a factor, so $\frac{1}{3}$ cannot be written as a fraction whose denominator is a power of 10. In general, we have the following rule.

> If a rational number a/b is in simplest form, it can be written as a terminating decimal if and only if b has only 2s and 5s in its prime factorization.

Example H

Which of these rational numbers can be written as terminating decimals?

1. $\frac{5}{6}$ 2. $\frac{1}{80}$ 3. $\frac{9}{15}$ 4. $\frac{3}{14}$

Solution   1. 6 has a factor of 3, so $\frac{5}{6}$ cannot be written as a terminating decimal.   2. 80 has only factors of 2 and 5, so $\frac{1}{80}$ can be written as a terminating decimal.   3. $\frac{9}{15} = \frac{3}{5}$, and since the denominator of the fraction in simplest form has only 5 as a factor, $\frac{9}{15}$ can be written as a terminating decimal. 4. 14 has a factor of 7, so $\frac{3}{14}$ cannot be written as a terminating decimal.

Let's consider finding a decimal for $\frac{1}{3}$. We know from Section 5.2 that $\frac{1}{3} = 1 \div 3$. Figure 6.13 illustrates the first few steps in dividing 1 by 3. Part a shows a unit square with 10 tenths and illustrates that $1 \div 3$ is .3 with .1 remaining. In part b, the remaining .1 is replaced by 10 hundredths, and dividing by 3 produces .03 with .01 remaining. In part c, 1 hundredth is replaced by 10 thousandths, and dividing by 3 produces .003 with .001 remaining. The three steps of the division process in Figure 6.13 produce .3, .03, and .003, which give a total shaded amount of .333 with .001 remaining.

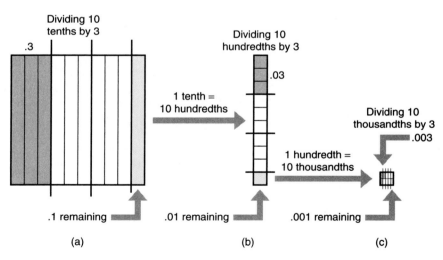

Figure 6.13   (a)   (b)   (c)

Continuing this process of regrouping and dividing by 3 shows that the decimal for $\frac{1}{3}$ has a repeating pattern of 3s. When a decimal does not terminate and contains a repeating pattern of digits, it is called a **repeating decimal.***

The step-by-step visual illustration in Figure 6.13 has a corresponding numerical division algorithm. The first step is to divide 10 tenths by 3. The result is .3

*The computer program Repeating Decimals in the *Mathematics Investigator* software (see website) prints the decimal for positive rational numbers a/b with $a < 10,000$ and $b < 10,000$. If the decimal is repeating, it counts the number of digits in the nonrepeating part (if any) and the number of digits in the repeating part (repetend).

with .1 remaining. The second step is to divide 10 hundredths by 3. The result of the first two steps is .33 with .01 remaining. In the third step, 10 thousandths are divided by 3. The result of the first three steps is a quotient of .333 with .001 remaining. This process can be continued to obtain any number of 3s in the decimal approximation for $\frac{1}{3}$.

The study of rational numbers in the middle grades should build on students' prior knowledge of whole-number concepts and skills and their encounters with fractions, decimals, and percents in lower grades and in everyday life.

Standards 2000, p. 215

Step 1	Step 2	Step 3
.3	.33	.333
3)1.0	3)1.00	3)1.000
9	9	9
One-tenth → 1	10	10
	9	9
	One-hundredth → 1	10
		9
		One-thousandth → 1

The division algorithm can be used to obtain a terminating or repeating decimal for any rational number. For example, when the numerator of $\frac{3}{8}$ is divided by its denominator, the division algorithm shows that the decimal terminates after three digits.

$$
\begin{array}{r}
.375 \\
8)\overline{3.000} \\
\underline{24} \\
60 \\
\underline{56} \\
40 \\
\underline{40}
\end{array}
$$

On the other hand, when the numerator of $\frac{4}{7}$ is divided by its denominator, the quotient does not terminate but repeats the same arrangement of six digits (571428) over and over. In this case the decimal is repeating. The reason for this can be seen by looking at the remainders 5, 1, 3, 2, 6 and 4, which are circled below. These six numbers, plus 0, are all the possible remainders when a number is divided by 7. So after six steps in the process of dividing 4 by 7, the numbers in the decimal quotient repeat. Notice the use of the bar above the six digits in the quotient to indicate the repeating pattern. The block of digits that is repeated over and over is called the **repetend**.

$$
\begin{array}{r}
\overline{.5714285} \\
7)\overline{4.0000000} \\
\underline{35} \\
⑤0 \\
\underline{49} \\
①0 \\
\underline{7} \\
③0 \\
\underline{28} \\
②0 \\
\underline{14} \\
⑥0 \\
\underline{56} \\
④0 \\
\underline{35}
\end{array}
$$

The preceding example illustrates why every rational number r/s can be represented by either a repeating decimal or a terminating decimal. When r is divided by s, the remainders are always less than s (see the Division Theorem, page 188). If a remainder of 0 occurs in the division process, as it does when we divide 3 by 8, then the decimal terminates. If there is no zero remainder, then eventually a remainder will be repeated, in which case the digits in the quotient will also start repeating.

 Calculators are convenient for finding decimal representations of fractions. For fractions represented by repeating decimals, such as $\frac{7}{12} = .5833333333\cdots$, the number in the calculator view screen is an approximation because it shows only a few of the digits. For many applications this is sufficient accuracy.

Most calculators use several more digits than are shown in their view screens. When the number of digits in a decimal exceeds the space in a calculator's view screen, the calculator may keep several hidden digits which are used internally for greater accuracy. To determine if your calculator uses hidden digits, try the following keystrokes to obtain a decimal approximation for $\frac{1}{17}$.

KEYSTROKES	VIEW SCREEN
1 ÷ 17 =	0.0588235
× 100,000 =	5882.3529
− 5882 =	0.3529411

Notice that the final view screen shows five hidden digits 2, 9, 4, 1, and 1 that were not in the first view screen. The purpose of multiplying by a power of 10 and subtracting the whole number part of the product is to move the digits in the view screen to the left to make room for digits that may be hidden. Did you "uncover" hidden digits beyond the last digit that was initially printed for $\frac{1}{17}$ by your calculator?

Example I

Write the decimal for each rational number. Use a bar to show the repetend (repeating digits).

1. $\dfrac{3}{11}$ 2. $\dfrac{5}{6}$ 3. $\dfrac{5}{12}$

Solution 1. $.\overline{27}$ 2. $.8\overline{3}$ 3. $.41\overline{6}$

Notice in the solutions to Example I that the repeating pattern in $.8\overline{3}$ does not begin until the hundredths digit and the repeating pattern in $.41\overline{6}$ does not begin until the thousandths digit.

Every rational number is the quotient of two integers, and we have seen that such numbers can be written as a terminating or repeating decimal. Conversely, every terminating or repeating decimal can be written as the quotient of two integers. An example of a terminating decimal written as a quotient of two integers is shown below. A method for writing repeating decimals as the quotient of two integers will be shown in Section 6.2.

Terminating decimals can be written as fractions whose denominators are powers of 10. The following equations show why $.378$ equals $\frac{378}{1000}$. In the first equation, $.378$ is written in expanded form. The least common denominator for the fractions is 1000, and their sum is $\frac{378}{1000}$.

$$.378 = \frac{3}{10} + \frac{7}{100} + \frac{8}{1000}$$
$$= \frac{300}{1000} + \frac{70}{1000} + \frac{8}{1000} = \frac{378}{1000}$$

Density of Rational Numbers

In Chapter 5 we saw examples of the fact that the rational numbers, when written as fractions, are *dense*. That is, between any two such numbers there is always another. To show this, we looked at a method for finding a fraction between two given fractions. In the following example, we will consider ways of finding a decimal between any two given decimals.

Example J

Sketch a number line and mark the location of each pair of decimals. Then find another decimal between them.

1. .124 and .125   **2.** .47 and .621   **3.** 1.1 and 1.2

Solution   **1.** One method of finding decimals between two given decimals is to express both decimals with a greater number of decimal places. For example, .124 = .1240 and .125 = .1250, and the 9 four-place decimals .1241, .1242, . . . , .1249 are between .124 and .125. Also, .124 = .12400 and .125 = .12500 and the 99 five-place decimals .12401, .12402, . . . , .12499 are between .124 and .125. Similarly, the process can be continued as there are 999 six-place decimals between .124000 and .125000, etc.   **2.** Since .47 = .470, any of the three-place decimals between .47 and .621 may be selected, and by increasing the number of decimal places for .47 and .621, more decimals can be found between these numbers.   **3.** 1.1 = 1.10 and 1.2 = 1.20, so the 9 decimals 1.11, 1.12, . . . , 1.19 are between 1.1 and 1.2. Also, 1.1 = 1.100 and 1.2 = 1.200, so the 99 decimals 1.101, 1.102, . . . , 1.199 are between 1.1 and 1.2, etc.

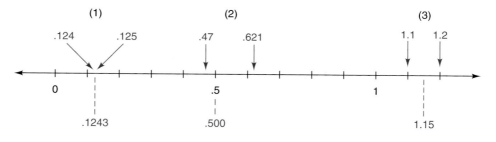

Estimation

Often a calculator view screen will be filled with the digits of a decimal, when some approximate value is all that is necessary. Rounding to a given place value is the most common method of obtaining decimal estimations.

ROUNDING   Decimals can be rounded to the nearest whole number, nearest tenth, nearest hundredth, etc. Before we look at a rule for rounding decimals, let's consider some visual illustrations.

Squares for three decimals are shown in Figure 6.14. Consider rounding these decimals to the nearest tenth. The decimal .648 rounds to .6 because 6 full columns and *less than one-half* of the next column are shaded; .863 rounds to .9 because 8 full columns and *more than one-half* of the next column are shaded; .35 can be either *rounded up* to .4 or *rounded down* to .3, because 3 full columns and *one-half* of the next column are shaded. In this text we adopt the policy of *rounding up*.

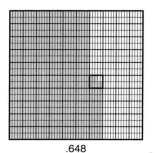

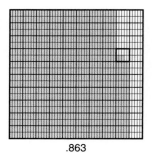

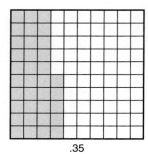

Figure 6.14   .648   .863   .35

Next consider rounding the decimals in Figure 6.14 to the nearest hundredth. The square for .648 shows that 64 hundredths are shaded (6 full columns and 4 hundredths in the next column); the remaining 8 thousandths are more than one-half of the next hundredth, so .648 rounds to .65. The Decimal Square for .863 shows that 86 hundredths are shaded (8 full columns and 6 hundredths in the next column); the remaining 3 thousandths are less than one-half of the next hundredth, so .863 rounds to .86.

Example K

Round each decimal to the nearest tenth and to the nearest hundredth.

1. .283   **2.** .068   **3.** 14.649

Solution   **1.** .283 rounded to the nearest tenth is .3 and to the nearest hundredth is .28.   **2.** .068 rounded to the nearest tenth is .1 and to the nearest hundredth is .07.   **3.** 14.649 rounded to the nearest tenth is 14.6 and to the nearest hundredth is 14.65.

Notice in Example K that 14.649 rounded to the nearest tenth is not 14.7. You can confirm this by visualizing a Decimal Square for .649: 6 full columns are shaded and less than one-half of the next column—49 thousandths—is shaded.

The preceding examples are special cases of the following general rule for rounding decimals. Notice that this is similar to the rule that was stated for rounding whole numbers on page 129 of Chapter 3.

RULE FOR ROUNDING DECIMALS
1. Locate the place value to which the number is to be rounded, and check the digit to its right.
2. If the digit to the right is 5 or greater, then all digits to the right are dropped and the digit with the given place value is increased by 1.
3. If the digit to the right is 4 or less, then all digits to the right of the digit with the given place value are dropped.

Example L

Round 1.6825 to the given number of decimal places.

1. Two decimal places (round to hundredths)

2. One decimal place (round to tenths)

3. Three decimal places (round to thousandths)

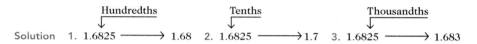

Solution   1. $1.6825 \longrightarrow 1.68$ 2. $1.6825 \longrightarrow 1.7$ 3. $1.6825 \longrightarrow 1.683$

Some calculators automatically round decimals that exceed the space in the view screen. On such calculators, if 2 is divided by 3, the decimal $0.66 \cdots 667$ will be displayed, where the last digit in the view screen is rounded from 6 to 7. Almost all calculators that round off at a digit that is followed by 5 will increase this digit, as described in the preceding rule for rounding numbers. For example, $\frac{55}{99}$ is equal to the repeating decimal $.5555 \cdots$. If 55 is divided by 99 on a calculator that rounds, $0.55 \cdots 556$ will show in the display. Try this on your calculator.

Some calculators have a key for obtaining a fixed decimal point display. With this key a calculator can be set to round decimals to zero places (nearest integer), one place, two places, etc. The use of one such key, $\boxed{\text{Fix}}$, is illustrated by the following keystrokes and view screens:

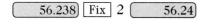

Once the number of decimal places is fixed, the calculator will round all decimals obtained from calculations to this number of decimal places. However, even though a calculator with a fixed decimal point display may show only two decimal places in the view screen, internally the calculator maintains the value of the decimal to more decimal places. Consider the following keystrokes for a calculator that has been set for two decimal places. Why do these keystrokes and view screens show that internally this calculator is using more than the two digits displayed as the decimal for $2 \div 3$? (*Hint:* Try to compute $.67 \times \frac{3}{2}$ to see if you obtain 1.)

Problem-Solving Application

The price of a single pen is 39 cents. This price is reduced if pens are purchased in quantity. The price per pen is always a whole number of cents and never less than 2 cents. If we know that a person bought all the pens in a box for $22.91, we can determine the number of pens. What is this number?

Understanding the Problem   Assume the cost per pen is less than 39 cents and it must be a whole number of cents. Question 1: What are the possibilities for the reduced price?

Devising a Plan   Since there is a reasonably small number of possible prices, one approach, if a calculator is available, is to *guess and check*. This can be done by replacing $22.91 by 2291 and dividing by the whole numbers 38, 37, 36, etc. until a whole number quotient is obtained; or we can divide $22.91 by the decimals .38, .37, .36, etc. If we view this problem as a matter of whole numbers (whole numbers of pennies) and divisibility, we arrive at another approach: finding the prime factorization of 2291. Question 2: How does the fact that there is only one solution tell us that the reduced price in cents is a prime number?

Carrying Out the Plan A quick use of the divisibility tests for 2, 3, and 5 shows that these numbers are not factors of 2291. Since the prime is less than 39, we need only check the primes 7, 11, 13, 17, 19, 23, 29, 31, and 37. **Question 3:** Which prime divides 2291, and what is the number of pens in the box?

Looking Back Suppose we kept the conditions of the problem the same but changed the reduced price for the entire box to $15.17. **Question 4:** How many pens would be in the box?

Answers to Questions 1–4   1. Whole numbers of cents from 2 to 38   2. If a composite number less than 39 divides 2291, then the factors of the composite number will divide 2291 and there will be more than one possibility for the cost of each pen.   3. 29 is a factor of 2291, so the cost of each pen is 29 cents and there are 79 pens in the box.   4. The first prime less than 39 that divides 1517 is 37. Since 37 × 41 = 1517, the number of pens in the box is 41.

EXERCISES AND PROBLEMS 6.1

Intervals of time can be measured by this cesium-beam atomic clock to an accuracy of .0000000000001 second. This is equivalent to an accuracy of within 1 second every 300,000 years. This strange clock, which is over 19 feet long, is located in Boulder, Colorado, and is operated by the National Bureau of Standards.

The clock shown above can be adjusted for time intervals as short as one-billionth second. What is the decimal for each time in exercises 1 and 2?

1. a. 1 thousandth of a second
   b. 1 millionth of a second

2. a. 1 billionth of a second
   b. 1 hundredth of a second

The first book about decimals was written by Simon Stevin in 1585. He used small circled numerals between the digits to indicate decimal places. Among his examples he wrote $27 + \frac{847}{1000}$ as 27⓪8①4②7③ Use Stevin's method of notation in exercises 3 and 4.

3. a. How would the number 7.46 be written, using this system?
   b. Explain how the decimal point could have evolved from this system.

4. a. How would the number 245.639 be written, using this system?
   b. Consider the number in Stevin's example. In England this decimal is written as 27·847 and in the United States as 27.847. What advantage is there in the English location of the decimal point?

For each indicated digit in exercises 5 and 6, write a fraction whose denominator is a power of 10.

5. a. 23.1↓78   **b.** 7.2↓016
   c. .00↓33   **d.** .99↓99

6. a. .0↓38   **b.** 47.29↓3
   c. .5↓556   **d.** .65↓5

Find the decimal for each fraction in exercises 7 and 8, and write the name of the decimal.

7. a. $\dfrac{33}{100}$ **b.** $\dfrac{392}{10,000}$

c. $\dfrac{54}{1000}$ **d.** $\dfrac{7481}{10}$

8. a. $\dfrac{42}{100}$ **b.** $\dfrac{64,193}{10,000}$

c. $\dfrac{9}{1000}$ **d.** $\dfrac{436}{10}$

Write the name of each dollar amount in exercises 9 and 10.

9. a. $347.96
  b. $23.50
  c. $1144.03

10. a. $502.85
  b. $1,372,500
  c. $6035.25

Draw an arrow from each number to its approximate location on the number line in exercises 11 and 12. Also, write the number that corresponds to each point on the line that is labeled with a letter.

11.

12.

Write an equal decimal having the given number of decimal places in exercises 13 and 14. Briefly describe the Decimal Squares for both decimals in the equation.

13. a. .4 = _____ (hundredths)
   b. .47 = _____ (thousandths)

14. a. .300 = _____ (tenths)
   b. .270 = _____ (hundredths)

Describe Decimal Squares for each side of the equality or inequality in exercises 15 and 16 to explain why each statement is true.

15. a. .7 = .70
   b. .43 = .430
   c. .45 < .6

16. a. .3 > .295
   b. .085 < .13
   c. .19 = .190

In exercises 17 and 18, what number is represented by the following figures for each of the given units?

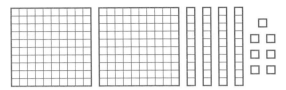

17. a. Each small square represents 1 unit.
   b. Each large square represents 1 unit.

18. a. Each 1 × 10 strip represents 1 unit.
   b. Each small square represents 10 units.

Sketch Decimal Squares for each fraction in exercises 19 and 20, and describe how to find the decimal for the fraction. (Copy Decimal Squares from the inside cover of the book or from the website.)

19. a. $\frac{1}{4}$
   b. $\frac{1}{5}$

20. a. $\frac{1}{8}$
   b. $\frac{1}{6}$ (to three decimal places)

Write each fraction in exercises 21 and 22 as a decimal. If the decimal is repeating, use a bar to show the repeating digits.

21. a. $\dfrac{3}{8}$ **b.** $\dfrac{2}{11}$

   c. $\dfrac{345}{990}$ **d.** $\dfrac{15}{4}$

22. a. $\dfrac{5}{9}$ **b.** $\dfrac{13}{5}$

   c. $\dfrac{439}{900}$ **d.** $\dfrac{6}{37}$

Match each rational number in the first column with an equal rational number in the second column in exercises 23 and 24.

23. $\frac{1}{3}$ $.8\overline{3}$

.25   .34

$\frac{5}{6}$ $\frac{7}{8}$

$.41\overline{6}$ $.\overline{3}$

.875 $\frac{1}{15}$

$.0\overline{6}$ $\frac{1}{4}$

$\frac{3}{10}$ $\frac{5}{12}$

$\frac{34}{99}$ .3

24. $\frac{3}{16}$ $\frac{34}{90}$

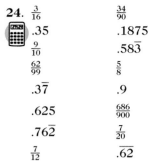 .35   .1875

$\frac{9}{10}$ .58$\overline{3}$

$\frac{62}{99}$ $\frac{5}{8}$

.3$\overline{7}$ .9

.625 $\frac{686}{900}$

.76$\overline{2}$ $\frac{7}{20}$

$\frac{7}{12}$.$\overline{62}$

Which of the fractions in exercises 25 and 26 have terminating decimals, and which have repeating decimals?

25. **a.** $\frac{7}{17}$ **26.** **a.** $\frac{1}{50}$
 b. $\frac{2}{9}$ **b.** $\frac{3}{18}$
       c. $\frac{6}{15}$ **c.** $\frac{5}{13}$

For each fraction in exercises 27 and 28, use a Decimal Square with 100 equal parts and explain how the first two digits in the decimal for the fraction can be represented by shading. Then explain how the decimal can be rounded to two decimal places. (Copy Decimal Squares from the inside cover of the book or from the website.)

27. **a.** $\frac{1}{3}$ **b.** $\frac{1}{9}$ **c.** $\frac{1}{8}$

28. **a.** $\frac{1}{6}$ **b.** $\frac{1}{7}$ **c.** $\frac{1}{12}$

Replace each decimal in exercises 29 and 30 with an approximation that is obtained from the leading nonzero digit. Then determine the approximation if the decimal is *rounded* to the leading nonzero digit.

29. **a.** .0045   **30.** **a.** .062
       b. .408   **b.** .0027
       c. .074   **c.** .165
       d. .00263   **d.** .228

One method of comparing two fractions for inequalities is to find their decimal representations. Use this method in exercises 31 and 32 to rearrange the fractions in increasing order from left to right.

31. $\frac{16}{20}, \frac{19}{34}, \frac{38}{52}, \frac{21}{25}, \frac{11}{17}$

32. $\frac{5}{7}, \frac{26}{30}, \frac{32}{51}, \frac{10}{13}, \frac{5}{6}$

Find the decimal for each fraction in exercises 33 and 34, and round it to the nearest ten-thousandth (four decimal places).

33. **a.** $\frac{1}{16}$ **b.** $\frac{3}{32}$
       c. $\frac{7}{64}$ **d.** $\frac{35}{64}$

34. **a.** $\frac{1}{13}$ **b.** $\frac{5}{7}$
       c. $\frac{2}{3}$ **d.** $\frac{7}{9}$

Round each decimal in exercises 35 and 36 to the given place value.

35. **a.** .3728 (hundredths)
       b. .084 (tenths)
       c. 14.3716 (thousandths)
       d. .349 (tenths)

36. **a.** .384615 (thousandths)
       b. .35294 (tenths)
       c. 2.8 (hundredths)
       d. 6.043478 (ten-thousandths)

37. **a.** Which of the following decimals is the smallest? Sketch or describe Decimal Squares to support your answer.

.07   1.003   .08   .075   .3

   b. The preceding question was part of a test on decimals that was given to over 7000 students entering college.* Approximately $\frac{2}{5}$ of these students chose the incorrect answer of .075. What confusion about decimals might have motivated this choice?

38. **a.** Which of the following decimals is the greatest? Sketch or describe Decimal Squares to support your answer.

.19   .036   .195   .2

   b. The preceding question was given to students aged 13 as part of the Second Math Assessment of the National Assessment of Educational Progress.† More students chose the incorrect answer .195 than the correct answer. What confusion about decimals might have led to this choice?

39. Match each rational number in the first column with an equal rational number from the second column.

.05 $\frac{532}{999}$

$\frac{2}{3}$ .3$\overline{8}$

.125   .$\overline{6}$

.4 $\frac{1}{8}$

.58$\overline{3}$ $\frac{1}{20}$

$\frac{7}{18}$ $\frac{2}{5}$

.$\overline{532}$ $\frac{4}{15}$

.2$\overline{6}$ $\frac{7}{12}$

*A. S. Grossman, "Decimal Notation: An Important Research Finding," *The Arithmetic Teacher* 30 (May 1983): 32–33.

†T. P. Carpenter, H. Kepner, M. K. Corbitt, M. M. Lindquist, and R. E. Reys, "Decimals: Results and Implications from National Assessment," *Arithmetic Teacher* 28 (April 1981): 34–37.

Assume that a calculator which operates with three hidden digits (three more digits than are shown on the view screen) is used in exercises 40 and 41. Determine the next three hidden digits for the decimals in each of the view screens.

40. a. $1 \div 31 = \boxed{0.0322580}$

b. $8 \div 23 = \boxed{0.3478260}$

41. a. $2 \div 19 = \boxed{0.1052631}$

b. $14 \div 29 = \boxed{0.4827586}$

REASONING AND PROBLEM SOLVING

42. Money amounts are often rounded to values that can be paid in standard currency. Use the following values in parts a to c: $45.789, $45.443, $45.375, $45.4650, $45.6749.
    a. Round each amount to the nearest hundredth of a dollar (nearest cent).
    b. Some mortgage lenders round up any fraction of a cent. Using this method, round these amounts up to the nearest one-hundredth of a dollar.
    c. Some lenders even round up to the nearest dime. Using this method, what are these amounts rounded to the nearest tenth of a dollar?

43. a. A catalog lists the following camera weights in ounces: 17.31, 16.25, 15.90, 28.06, and 22.55. What is each weight rounded to the nearest tenth of an ounce?
    b. In one year .20 of the injuries to players of the National Football League were to the knees and .025 were to the arms. Were there more injuries to the knees or to the arms?
    c. A pointer on a water meter is halfway between .8 and .9. What is the decimal position of the pointer?

44. a. A sewing machine has attachments called *throat plates* for making eyelets. If the holes on a certain throat plate are .218, .14, .2, and .196 inch in diameter, which is the largest hole?
    b. Physicists have calculated that one cubic foot of air weighs 1.29152 ounces. What is this weight rounded to the nearest tenth of an ounce?
    c. One kilometer is 1000 meters. The length of a soccer field for international matches is 110 meters. What decimal part of a kilometer equals 110 meters?

45. Fiona has a set of drill bits which are printed in fractions of an inch with the following sizes:

$$\frac{5}{32} \quad \frac{1}{8} \quad \frac{3}{16} \quad \frac{1}{4} \quad \frac{1}{16} \quad \frac{3}{32}$$

a. If the blueprints for her cabinet call for drilling holes of .13 inch, which drill bit is the closest size?
b. Her plans call for drilling holes of .32. Does she have a drill bit large enough?
c. She needs to drill 20 very small holes in the cabinet for inserting finishing nails. What is her smallest drill bit?

The *Guinness Book of Records* documents the evolution of sports records in the twentieth century. Four records for the high jump are shown in exercises 46 and 47. Convert the feet and inches to feet, rounding to two decimal places.

46. a. M. Sweeney, 6 feet $5\frac{5}{8}$ inches, United States, 1895
    b. Zhu Jianhua, 7 feet $9\frac{1}{4}$ inches, China, 1983

47. a. Lester Steers, 6 feet 11 inches, United States, 1941
    b. Heike Henkel, 6 feet $9\frac{1}{2}$ inches, Germany, 1982

48. **Featured Strategies: Solving a Simpler Problem and Making a Table**   A piece of paper is cut in half, and one piece is placed on top of the other. Then the two pieces are cut in half, and one half is placed on top of the other, forming a stack with four pieces. If this process is carried out a total of 25 times and the original piece of paper is .003 inch thick, what is the height of the stack to the nearest foot?
    a. **Understanding the Problem**   Simplifying the problem may suggest what needs to be done to obtain a solution. Suppose each piece of paper were $\frac{1}{2}$ inch thick. How thick would the stack be after three cuts?
    b. **Devising a Plan**   Forming a table will help you see a pattern between the number of cuts and the number of pieces of paper. What numbers should appear in the blank lines of the table below? What is the number of pieces of paper after 25 cuts, expressed as a power of 2?

NUMBER OF CUTS	NUMBER OF PIECES
1	2
2	4
3	8
4	—
5	—
⋮	⋮
25	—

c. **Carrying Out the Plan**   Our simplification in part a suggests that we must multiply the thickness of the paper (.003, or $\frac{3}{1000}$ inch) by the total number of pieces of paper. What is the final height of the stack to the nearest foot?

d. **Looking Back** Another way to think of the height of the final stack is to divide the number of feet by 5280, the number of feet in 1 mile. How high is the stack to the nearest tenth of a mile?

Describe some of the patterns among the equations in 49 and 50, and determine if the patterns continue to hold when the equations are extended. Are new patterns formed as the equations are extended?

49. $\frac{1}{9} = .111111\cdots$
PS $\frac{2}{9} = .222222\cdots$
$\frac{3}{9} = .333333\cdots$

50. $\frac{1}{11} = .090909\cdots$
PS $\frac{2}{11} = .181818\cdots$
$\frac{3}{11} = .272727\cdots$

- -

ONLINE LEARNING CENTER   www.mhhe.com/bennett-nelson

• Math Investigation 6.1   *Repeating Decimals*
Section-Related: • Links   • Writing/Discussion Problems   • Bibliography

- -

PUZZLER

A truck driver noticed that the mileage on the truck odometer was 72,927. A number that reads the same from left to right as from right to left is called a **palindromic number.** Four hours later the driver was surprised to find that the odometer showed another palindromic number. What was the truck's average speed during this 4-hour period?

MATH ACTIVITY 6.2

DECIMAL OPERATIONS WITH BASE-TEN PIECES AND DECIMAL SQUARES

Materials: Base-ten pieces in the Manipulative Kit and Decimal Squares recording paper (three copies from inside cover page of the text or the website).

*1. The base-ten pieces for decimals (see Math Activity 6.1) represent units, tenths, hundredths, and thousandths. Use your base-ten pieces and the concepts of addition (*put together*) and subtraction (*take-away, comparison,* or *add-up*) to determine the following sums and differences. Sketch these pieces and explain your reasoning. Then shade squares on the Decimal Squares recording paper to illustrate each sum and difference (see examples).

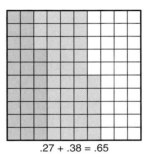

.27 + .38 = .65

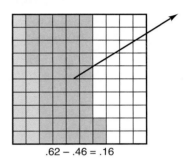

.62 − .46 = .16

    a. .46 + .3   **b.** .235 + .41   **c.** .53 − .29   **d.** .66 − .4

2. Use your base-ten pieces and the *sharing (partitive) concept* of division to compute the following quotients. For example, to compute .75 ÷ 5, represent .75 with base-ten pieces and divide the pieces into 5 equal groups. Then shade squares on the Decimal Squares recording paper to illustrate each quotient. Label each square by writing a division equation for the quotient.

    a. .8 ÷ 4   **b.** .72 ÷ 8   **c.** .168 ÷ 7

3. Use your base-ten pieces and the *measurement (subtractive) concept* of division to compute the following quotients. For example, to compute .28 ÷ .04, represent .28 by base-ten pieces, regroup as necessary, and subtract groups of 4 hundredths. Shade and mark off squares on the Decimal Squares recording paper to illustrate each quotient. Label each with a division equation.

    a. .8 ÷ .2   **b.** .90 ÷ .05   **c.** .275 ÷ .025

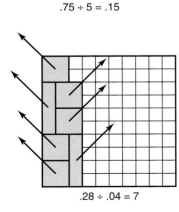

.75 ÷ 5 = .15

.28 ÷ .04 = 7

SECTION 6.2

OPERATIONS WITH DECIMALS

A phototimer finish of a 1-mile race between Marty Liquori and Jim Ryun

Helen Chen wants to seed her front lawn. Grass seed can be bought in 3-pound boxes that cost $4.50 or in 5-pound boxes that cost $6.58. She needs 17 pounds of seed. How many boxes of each size should she purchase to get the best buy?*

Electronic timers for athletic competition measure time to hundredths and thousandths of a second. The above picture shows a phototimer finish of a 1-mile race in which Marty Liquori of Villanova beat Jim Ryun of the Oregon Track Club. Both runners were clocked at 3 minutes 54.6 seconds by officials using hand-operated stopwatches. However, the phototimer clocked Liquori at 3 minutes 54.54 seconds and Ryun at 3 minutes 54.75 seconds, a difference of .21 second. What you see in the preceding photo is not a simultaneous photograph of the two runners (in which it would appear that they were crossing the finish line together) but a continuous photograph of the finish line. This shows the runners as they crossed the finish line in the span of .21 second, which is represented in the photograph by the space of approximately 2 inches between the men.

Addition

The concept of addition of decimals is the same as the concept of addition of whole numbers and fractions: It involves putting together, or combining, two amounts. Figure 6.15 shows a Decimal Square with 47 parts shaded out of 100, representing .47, and a Decimal Square with 36 parts shaded out of 100, representing .36. The total number of shaded parts is 47 + 36 = 83, and since each of these parts is one-hundredth of a whole square, the total shaded amount represents .83.

This example with Decimal Squares indicates why addition of decimals is very similar to addition of whole numbers. We added whole numbers (47 + 36) of

*C. R. Hirsch, ed., *Activities for Implementing Curricular Themes from the Agenda for Action* (Reston, VA: National Council of Teachers of Mathematics, 1986), p. 17.

parts, and then, taking into account that the small parts were hundredths, we located the decimal point.

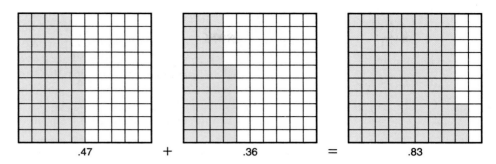

Figure 6.15

The following equations compute this sum by using fractions. Notice that in going from the third to the fourth expression we compute the whole number sum $47 + 36$.

$$.47 + .36 = \frac{47}{100} + \frac{36}{100} = \frac{47 + 36}{100} = \frac{83}{100} = .83$$

PENCIL-AND-PAPER ALGORITHM In one pencil-and-paper algorithm for addition of decimals, the digits are aligned, tenths under tenths, hundredths under hundredths, etc., as shown in the following example. When the sum of the digits in any column is 10 or greater, regrouping is necessary. Since .47 can be thought of as 4 tenths and 7 hundredths and .36 as 3 tenths and 6 hundredths, the sum of 7 and 6 in the hundredths column is 13 hundredths.

$$\begin{array}{r} {\scriptstyle 1} \\ .47 \\ + \ .36 \\ \hline .83 \end{array}$$

Ten of the hundredths can be visualized as 1 tenth by recalling that in a decimal square, 10 hundredths fill one column ($\frac{1}{10}$ of a square). Also, we know that the fraction $\frac{10}{100}$ in lowest terms is $\frac{1}{10}$. So 1 tenth is regrouped to the tenths column, and 3 is recorded in the hundredths column, as shown above.

Example A

Use the preceding pencil-and-paper algorithm to compute each sum, and show the numbers that are regrouped.

1. $62.47 + 114.86$ 2. $4.039 + 17.18$ 3. $.267 + .5163$

Solution

$$\begin{array}{r} {\scriptstyle 1\ 1} \\ 62.47 \\ 1. \ + 114.86 \\ \hline 177.33 \end{array} \qquad \begin{array}{r} {\scriptstyle 1\ 1} \\ 4.039 \\ 2. \ + 17.180 \\ \hline 21.219 \end{array} \qquad \begin{array}{r} {\scriptstyle 1} \\ .2670 \\ 3. \ + .5163 \\ \hline .7833 \end{array}$$

Notice in solution 2 of Example A that 17.18 was replaced by 17.180. This can be done because 18 hundredths is equal to 180 thousandths. Similarly, in solution 3, .267 was replaced by .2670.

Subtraction

Subtraction of decimals, like subtraction of whole numbers and fractions, can be illustrated with the take-away concept, as shown in part a of Figure 6.16, or with the comparison concept, as shown in part b. The shaded area in part a plus the area to its left represents .625, and the arrow shows 238 parts out of 1000 being taken away from 625 parts out of 1000. This leaves 387 parts out of 1000, which represents .387. In part b, we can compare the shaded amounts of the squares for .75 and .40 to see that the difference is 35 parts out of 100, or .35. The third concept of subtraction, *add-up,* can be illustrated for .75 − .40 by beginning with the square for .40 in part b and counting up from 40 to 75 parts.

Research Statement

Students who do not understand decimal notation frequently resort to memorizing procedural rules.

Bell, Swain, and Taylor 1981; Sackur-Grisvard and Leonard 1985

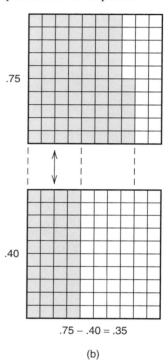

.75

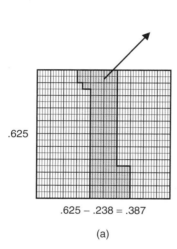

.625

.40

.625 − .238 = .387

.75 − .40 = .35

Figure 6.16

(a)

(b)

PENCIL-AND-PAPER ALGORITHM   The Decimal Squares provide a visual model for computing the difference of whole numbers of small parts. This provides a method of viewing subtraction of decimals as subtraction of whole numbers and helps to show the similarity of these operations.

In one pencil-and-paper algorithm for subtraction of decimals, the digits are aligned as they are for addition of decimals. Subtraction then takes place from right to left, with thousandths subtracted from thousandths, hundredths from hundredths, etc. When regrouping (borrowing) is necessary, it is done just as it is in subtracting whole numbers.

In the following example, .625 can be thought of as 6 tenths, 2 hundredths, and 5 thousandths and .238 as 2 tenths, 3 hundredths, and 8 thousandths. To subtract 8 thousandths from 5 thousandths, regrouping is needed. Since 1 hundredth equals 10 thousandths ($\frac{1}{100} = \frac{10}{1000}$), 1 hundredth can be regrouped from the hundredths column to increase 5 thousandths to 15 thousandths. Then we can subtract 8 from 15 to obtain 7 in the thousandths column. A slash through the 2 indicates that it has been decreased by 1. Similarly, 6 in the tenths column is decreased by 1 to obtain 10 more hundredths for the hundredths column ($\frac{1}{10} = \frac{10}{100}$). Then 3 is subtracted from 11 to obtain 8 in the hundredths column. Finally, 2 is subtracted from 5 to obtain 3 in the tenths column.

$$
\begin{array}{r}
\overset{5\ 1}{.\cancel{6}2\cancel{5}} \\
-\ .238 \\
\hline
.387
\end{array}
$$

The following equations show how this difference can be computed by using fractions. Notice that we subtract whole numbers in going from the third to the fourth expression.

$$.625 - .238 = \frac{625}{1000} - \frac{238}{1000} = \frac{625 - 238}{1000} = \frac{387}{1000} = .387$$

Example B

Use the preceding pencil-and-paper algorithm to compute each difference, and show where regrouping is needed.

1. $46.32 - 18.47$ 2. $.4074 - .356$ 3. $15.06 - 2.743$

Solution

$$
\begin{array}{r}
\overset{3\ 5\ 2}{4\cancel{6}.\cancel{3}2} \\
1.\quad -\ 18.47 \\
\hline
27.85
\end{array}
\qquad
\begin{array}{r}
\overset{3}{.\cancel{4}074} \\
2.\quad -\ .3560 \\
\hline
.0514
\end{array}
\qquad
\begin{array}{r}
\overset{4\quad 5}{1\cancel{5}.0\cancel{6}0} \\
3.\quad -\ 2.743 \\
\hline
12.317
\end{array}
$$

Notice that extra zeros were appended to some of the numbers in solutions 2 and 3 of Example B in order to perform the subtraction.

Multiplication

The product of a whole number and a decimal can be illustrated by repeated addition. Each of the Decimal Squares in Figure 6.17 has seven shaded parts. In all there are a total of $2 \times 7 = 14$ shaded parts. This is four more shaded parts than would be contained in a whole square, so $2 \times .7 = 1.4$.

1 whole square

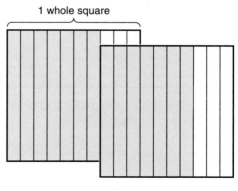

$2 \times .7 = 1.4$

Figure 6.17

The product of a decimal and a decimal, such as $.2 \times .3$, can be interpreted as $.2$ of $.3$. This is illustrated in Figure 6.18 by using a Decimal Square for $.3$ and taking $.2$ of its shaded part. To do this, we split the shaded part of the Decimal Square for .3 into 10 equal parts. The 6 darker parts of the square represent .2 of .3. Since each of the darker parts is 1 hundredth of a whole square, .2 × .3 = .06.

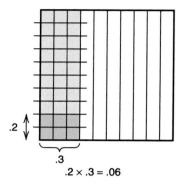

.2 × .3 = .06

Figure 6.18

PENCIL-AND-PAPER ALGORITHM   The illustrations in Figures 6.17 and 6.18 show that computing products of decimals is closely related to computing products of whole numbers. To compute products involving decimals, we multiply the numbers as though they were whole numbers and then locate the decimal point in the product. The next example shows the product of a one-place decimal and a two-place decimal. The digits do not have to be positioned so that units are above units, tenths above tenths, etc., as they are for addition and subtraction of decimals. The number of decimal places in the answer is the total number of decimal places in the original two numbers.

$$
\begin{array}{r}
27.48 \\
\times \quad 9.2 \\
\hline
5\,4\,9\,6 \\
2\,4\,7\,3\,2 \\
\hline
2\,5\,2.8\,1\,6
\end{array}
$$

The following equations show why 9.2 × 27.48 can be computed by first computing 92 × 2748.

$$
9.2 \times 27.48 = \frac{92}{10} \times \frac{2748}{100} = \frac{92 \times 2748}{10 \times 100} = \frac{252{,}816}{1000} = 252.816
$$

Example C

Use the pencil-and-paper algorithm for the multiplication of decimals to compute each product.

1. 3.7 × 2.5   2. 4.6 × .35   3. 1.8 × .473

Solution   1.
$$
\begin{array}{r}
2.5 \\
\times \ 3.7 \\
\hline
175 \\
75 \\
\hline
9.25
\end{array}
$$
2.
$$
\begin{array}{r}
.35 \\
\times \ 4.6 \\
\hline
210 \\
140 \\
\hline
1.610
\end{array}
$$
3.
$$
\begin{array}{r}
.473 \\
\times \ 1.8 \\
\hline
3784 \\
473 \\
\hline
.8514
\end{array}
$$

The base-ten grid that was used for multiplying whole numbers in Chapter 3 can be used to model the products of decimals. The product 2.3×1.7 is illustrated in Figure 6.19. The two regions of this rectangle correspond to the two partial products 2×1.7 and $.3 \times 1.7$. The colored region has the equivalent of 3 unit squares and 4 tenths of a unit square; the gray region has 51 hundredths of a unit square.

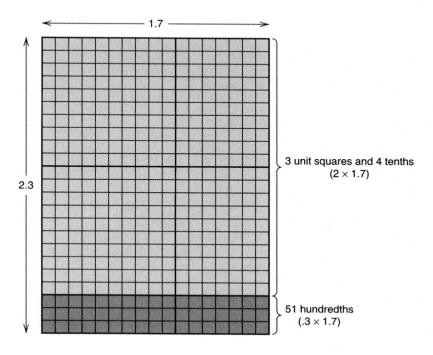

Figure 6.19

$$2.3 \times 1.7 = (2 + .3) \times 1.7$$
$$= (2 \times 1.7) + (.3 \times 1.7)$$
$$= 3.4 + .51$$
$$= 3.91$$

NCTM's 5–8 Standard, *Number and Number Relationships,* recommends the use of area models:

Area models are especially helpful in visualizing numerical ideas from a geometric point of view. For example, area models can be used to show that $\frac{8}{12}$ is equivalent to $\frac{2}{3}$, that $1.2 \times 1.3 = 1.56$, and that 80% of 20 is 16. Later, students can extend area models to the study of algebra, probability, dimension analysis in measurement situations, and other more advanced subjects.*

Curriculum and Evaluation Standards for School Mathematics (Reston, VA: National Council of Teachers of Mathematics, 1989), p. 88.

One style of notation used in the sixteenth century called for the number of decimal places to be specified by a circled index to the right of the numeral. For example, 27.487 was represented as 27487 . . .③, and 9.21 was 921 . . .②. This notation is especially convenient for computing the product of two decimals. The whole numbers are multiplied, and then the numbers in circles are added to determine the location of the decimal point. Using our present notation, we would place the decimal point between the 3 and the 1 in this product.

$$
\begin{array}{r}
27487 \quad \ldots ③ \\
\times\,921 \quad \ldots ② \\
\hline
27487 \\
54974 \\
247383 \\
\hline
25315527 \quad \ldots ⑤
\end{array}
$$

MULTIPLYING BY POWERS OF 10   One way to illustrate multiplication of decimals by powers of 10 is to use Decimal Squares and repeated addition. Figure 6.20 shows squares for .1, .01, and .001 and corresponding squares whose shaded amounts are 10 times greater. Multiplying by higher powers of 10 can be similarly represented, for example, $100 \times .1 = 10$ and $100 \times .01 = 1$.

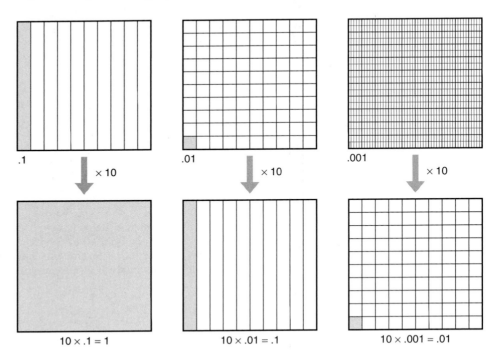

Figure 6.20

$10 \times .1 = 1$ $10 \times .01 = .1$ $10 \times .001 = .01$

To illustrate $10 \times .165$ with Decimal Squares, we can replace each tenth by 1 whole square, each hundredth by 1 tenth of a square, and each thousandth by 1 hundredth of a square (Figure 6.21).

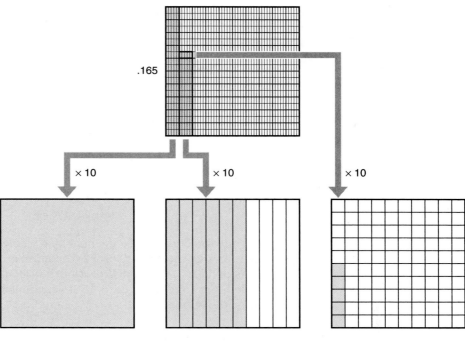

Figure 6.21

$10 \times .165 = 1.65$

Another way to show the results of multiplying by powers of 10 is to replace the decimal by a sum of fractions and use the distributive property.

$$10 \times .165 = 10 \times \left(\tfrac{1}{10} + \tfrac{6}{100} + \tfrac{5}{1000} \right) = \tfrac{10}{10} + \tfrac{60}{100} + \tfrac{50}{1000}$$

$$= 1 + \tfrac{6}{10} + \tfrac{5}{100}$$
$$= 1.65$$

These examples suggest the following algorithm.

> To multiply a decimal by a power of 10, move the decimal point one place to the right for each power of 10.

Example D

Compute each product mentally.

1. $100 \times .45$ **2.** 10×14.08 **3.** $1000 \times .32714$

Solution   1. 45   2. 140.8   3. 327.14

Division

The two concepts of division—*the measurement (subtractive) concept* and the *sharing (partitive) concept*—are both useful for illustrating division with decimals. The measurement concept involves repeatedly measuring off or subtracting one amount from another. For example, to compute .90 ÷ .15, determine how many times .15 can be subtracted from .90. The Decimal Square in Figure 6.22 has been marked off to show that the quotient is 6.

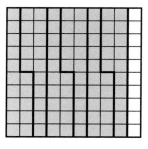

.90 ÷ .15 = 6

Figure 6.22

To illustrate the division of a decimal by a whole number, we can use the sharing concept. In this case, the divisor is the number of equal parts into which a set or region is divided. The shaded part of the Decimal Square in Figure 6.23 has been divided into four equal parts to illustrate .80 ÷ 4. Since each part has 20 hundredths, the quotient is .20.

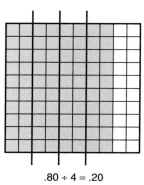

.80 ÷ 4 = .20

Figure 6.23

PENCIL-AND-PAPER ALGORITHM　The preceding examples illustrate the close relationship between division of whole numbers and division of decimals. Consider the illustration of dividing .80 by 4 in Figure 6.23. Since the Decimal Square has 80 parts shaded out of 100, we were able to think in terms of whole numbers and divide 80 by 4. Then since the quotient has 20 small squares, each one-hundredth of a whole square, the quotient .80 ÷ 4 is equal to .20. Similar steps are carried out to divide any decimal by a whole number: first divide, using the long division algorithm for whole numbers, and then place the decimal point in the quotient directly above its location in the dividend. These steps are shown here for dividing .80 by 4.

$$
\begin{array}{r}
.20 \\
4\overline{)\,.80} \\
\underline{8} \\
0 \\
\underline{0} \\
\end{array}
$$

In the long division algorithm for dividing with decimals, we never actually divide by a decimal. Before we divide, an adjustment is made so that the divisor is always a whole number. For example, the algorithm shown below indicates that we are to divide 1.504 by .32. Before dividing, however, we move the decimal points in .32 and 1.504 both two places to the right. This has the effect of changing the divisor and the dividend so that we are dividing 150.4 by 32.

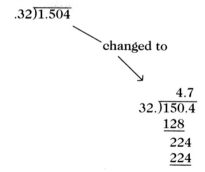

The rule for dividing by a decimal is to count the number of decimal places in the divisor and then move the decimal points in the divisor and the dividend that many places to the right. In the previous example the decimal points in .32 and 1.504 were moved two places to the right because .32 has two decimal places. The justification for this process of shifting decimal points is illustrated in the following equations. In the second expression, we use the fact that the numerator and denominator of a fraction can be multiplied by the same nonzero number to produce an equal fraction.

$$\frac{1.504}{.32} = \frac{1.504 \times 10^2}{.32 \times 10^2} = \frac{150.4}{32}$$

These equations show that the answer to $1.504 \div .32$ is the same as that for $150.4 \div 32$. No further adjustment is needed as long as we shift the decimal points in both the divisor and the dividend by the same amount. Thus division of a decimal by a decimal can always be carried out by dividing a decimal (or whole number) by a whole number.

Example E

Use the long division algorithm to compute each quotient.

1. $106.82 \div 7$ 2. $.498 \div .6 = 4.98 \div 6$ 3. $34.44 \div 1.4 = 344.4 \div 14$

Solution

1.
```
        15.26
    7)106.82
        7
        36
        35
        18
        14
        42
        42
```

2.
```
        .83
   .6).498
        48
        18
        18
```

3.
```
        24.6
  1.4)34.44
        28
        64
        56
        84
        84
```

DIVIDING BY POWERS OF 10   In Section 6.1 we saw that a whole number can be divided by a power of 10 by relocating a decimal point. This is also true for dividing decimals by powers of 10, as Figure 6.24 shows for $.37 \div 10$. Since 3 full columns (see first square) represent .3 or 300 thousandths, dividing by 10 results in 30 thousandths (see second square). Since 7 small hundredths squares (see first square) represent 70 thousandths, dividing by 10 results in 7 thousandths (see second square).

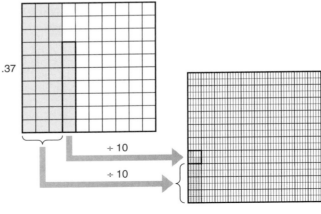

Figure 6.24

.37 ÷ 10 = .037

The effects of dividing by powers of 10 can be shown by writing the decimals in expanded form. Consider dividing .37 by 10 and 100.

$$.37 \div 10 = \left(\tfrac{3}{10} + \tfrac{7}{100}\right) \times \tfrac{1}{10} = \tfrac{3}{100} + \tfrac{7}{1000} = .037$$

$$.37 \div 100 = \left(\tfrac{3}{10} + \tfrac{7}{100}\right) \times \tfrac{1}{100} = \tfrac{3}{1000} + \tfrac{7}{10,000} = .0037$$

These examples are special cases of the following algorithm.

> **DIVIDING BY POWERS OF 10**   To divide a decimal by a power of 10, move the decimal point one place to the left for each power of 10.

Example F

Compute each quotient mentally.

1. .35 ÷ 10   **2.** 4.6 ÷ 100   **3.** .8 ÷ 1000

Solution   1. .035   2. .046   3. .0008

Order of Operations

When addition and subtraction are combined with multiplication and division, care must be taken regarding the order of operations on decimals. As in the case of whole numbers, multiplication and division are performed before addition and subtraction. Consider the following example of computing income tax. In 2002, according to Schedule X in the Internal Revenue Service forms, the tax on earnings greater than $27,950 and less than $67,700 was $3892.50 plus .27 times the amount over $27,950. Therefore, the tax on $34,600 would be

$$\$3892.50 + .27 \times \$6650$$

   On calculators that are designed to follow the *order of operations*, this tax can be computed by entering the numbers and operations into the calculator as they appear from left to right. On calculators without the *order of operations,* this tax can be obtained by computing .27 × 6650 and then adding 3892.50.

Example G

Determine the tax on the following amounts according to the 2002 Schedule X instructions from the previous paragraphs.

1. $42,672   **2.** $51,320

Solution   1. $3892.50 + .27 × $14,722 = $3892.50 + $3974.94 = $7867.44   **2.** $3892.50 + .27 × $23,370 = $3892.50 + $6309.90 = $10,202.40

Repeating Decimals

In Section 6.1 we saw that terminating decimals can be written as fractions whose numerators are integers and whose denominators are powers of 10.

$$.47 = \frac{47}{100} \qquad 3.802 = \frac{3802}{1000} \qquad 64.3 = \frac{643}{10}$$

A repeating decimal can also be written as a fraction whose numerator and denominator are integers. To show this, first we look at the repeating decimals for the fractions $\frac{1}{9}$, $\frac{1}{99}$, and $\frac{1}{999}$. Figure 6.25 shows the first three steps of a demonstration for finding the decimal for $\frac{1}{9}$. In step 1, we begin dividing 1 by 9 by dividing 10 tenths into 9 equal parts. There is a remainder of 1 tenth, which is regrouped to 10 hundredths so that the process of dividing by 9 can continue in step 2. Figure 6.25 shows that $\frac{1}{9} = .111$ with .001 remaining. This process can be continued to show that $\frac{1}{9} = .111 \cdots$.

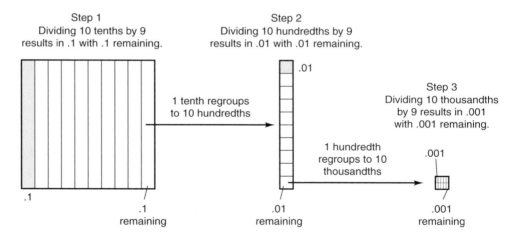

Figure 6.25

The demonstration in Figure 6.26 shows how to obtain the first few decimal places for $\frac{1}{99}$. In step 1, we begin dividing 1 by 99 by dividing 100 hundredths into 99 equal parts. There is a remainder of one hundredth, and this is regrouped to 100 ten-thousandths so that the process of dividing by 99 can continue in step 2. The first two steps show that $\frac{1}{99} = .0101$ (.01 + .0001) with .0001 remaining. Continuing this process will show that $\frac{1}{99} = .010101 \cdots$.

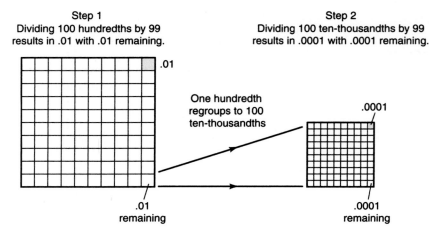

Figure 6.26

Similarly, by beginning with a Decimal Square for thousandths and dividing it into 999 parts, it can be shown that $\frac{1}{999} = .001$ with a remainder of .001; and if the process of regrouping and dividing by 999 were to be continued, we would see that $\frac{1}{999} = .001001 \cdots$.

Now let's consider writing a repeating decimal as the quotient of two integers. The following equations show that the infinite repeating decimal $.888 \cdots$ is equal to $\frac{8}{9}$.

$$.888 \cdots = 8 \times .111 \cdots$$
$$= 8 \times \tfrac{1}{9}$$
$$= \tfrac{8}{9}$$

A similar process is used when the repetend has two digits, as here:

$$.373737 \cdots = 37 \times .010101 \cdots$$
$$= 37 \times \tfrac{1}{99}$$
$$= \tfrac{37}{99}$$

Any digits in the decimal which precede the repetend can be separated by multiplying by powers of 10. For example,

$$.2373737 \cdots = \tfrac{1}{10} \times 2.373737 \cdots$$
$$= \tfrac{1}{10} \times (2 + \tfrac{37}{99})$$
$$= \tfrac{2}{10} + \tfrac{37}{990} = \tfrac{235}{990}$$

 Check the preceding examples by using a calculator to divide the numerators of the fractions by their denominators. Will you obtain the original decimal in each case? (*Note:* Some calculators that are designed for fractions will convert fractions to decimals, and terminating decimals of three or fewer digits to fractions.*)

Example H

Replace each repeating decimal with a quotient of two integers. Check the results with a calculator.

1. $.\overline{17}$ 2. $.\overline{7}$ 3. $.\overline{238}$ 4. $.1\overline{8}$

Solution   1. $\frac{17}{99}$ 2. $\frac{7}{9}$ 3. $\frac{238}{999}$ 4. $\frac{2}{11}$

---

*CASIO fx-55, SHARP EL-E300, and Texas Instruments' Explorer Plus are examples of such calculators.

Properties of Rational Numbers

We have seen that a rational number can always be represented as the quotient of two integers a/b or as a decimal. That is, there are two different types of numerals that represent rational numbers. In Section 5.3 we used the definitions of addition and multiplication of fractions to show that these operations satisfy certain number properties. These properties are restated below for the rational numbers.

CLOSURE PROPERTIES   The set of rational numbers is closed under addition and multiplication. For any rational numbers a and b, $a + b$ and $a \times b$ are unique rational numbers.

COMMUTATIVE PROPERTIES   Addition and multiplication are commutative. For any rational numbers a and b, $a + b = b + a$ and $a \times b = b \times a$.

ASSOCIATIVE PROPERTIES   Addition and multiplication are associative. For any rational numbers a, b, and c, $(a + b) + c = a + (b + c)$ and $(a \times b) \times c = a \times (b \times c)$.

IDENTITY PROPERTIES   The identity for addition is 0, and the identity for multiplication is 1. For any rational number b, there are unique identity elements 0 and 1 such that $0 + b = b$ and $1 \times b = b$.

INVERSE PROPERTIES   For every rational number, there is a unique inverse for addition; and for every nonzero rational number, there is a unique inverse for multiplication. In other words, for any rational number b, there is a unique rational number ^-b such that $b + {}^-b = 0$; and for any rational number $c \neq 0$, there is a unique rational number $1/c$ such that $c \times 1/c = 1$.

DISTRIBUTIVE PROPERTY   Multiplication is distributive over addition. For any rational numbers a, b, and c, $a \times (b + c) = a \times b + a \times c$.

Mental Computation

We have seen that computations with decimals can be carried out by first computing with whole numbers and then placing decimal points. This fact can be used to compute decimals mentally.

> Students should also develop and adapt procedures for mental calculation and computational estimation with fractions, decimals, and integers.
>
> Standards 2000, p. 220

E x a m p l e I

Calculate each answer mentally by first computing with whole numbers and then placing decimal points.

  1. $.4 \times .22$ **2.** $.35 + .55$ **3.** $5 \times .003$

  4. $.345 - .2$ **5.** $.001 \times 62$ **6.** $.24 \div .04$

Solution   **1.** $4 \times 22 = 88$, and since there is a total of three decimal places, $.4 \times .22 = .088$.   **2.** $35 + 55 = 90$, so $.35 + .55 = .90$.   **3.** $5 \times 3 = 15$, and since there is a total of three decimal places, $5 \times .003 = .015$.   **4.** $345 - 200 = 145$, so $.345 - .2 = .145$.   **5.** $1 \times 62 = 62$, and since there is a total of three decimal places, $.001 \times 62 = .062$.   **6.** $24 \div 4 = 6$, and since both numbers have the same number of decimal places, $.24 \div .04 = 6$.

SUBSTITUTIONS AND ADD-UP   The mental calculating techniques for whole numbers can also be used for mental calculations with decimals. For example, to compute $.54 - .38$, we can use the add-up method:

$$.38 + .02 = .40 \qquad \text{and} \qquad .40 + .14 = .54 \qquad \text{so} \qquad .38 + .16 = .54$$

Thus $.54 - .38 = .16$.

Example J

Calculate each answer mentally, using either the substitutions or add-up techniques.

1. $.37 + .28$ **2.** $.76 - .29$ **3.** $3 \times .98$ **4.** 4.3×102

Solution **1.** Substitution: $.37 + .28 = .37 + (.20 + .08) = .57 + .08 = .65$ **2.** Add up: $.29 + .01 = .30$ and $.30 + .46 = .76$, so $.29 + .47 = .76$, and $.76 - .29 = .47$ **3.** Substitution: $3 \times .98 = 3 \times (1 - .02) = 3 - .06 = 2.94$ **4.** Substitution: $4.3 \times 102 = 4.3 \times (100 + 2) = 430 + 8.6 = 438.6$

EQUAL QUOTIENTS   Multiplying both numbers in a quotient of two decimals by the same number is sometimes a convenient method of obtaining a mental calculation, especially if the divisor is replaced by a power of 10.

Example K

Compute each quotient by using the equal-quotients technique to replace the divisor by a power of 10.

1. $.21 \div 2.5$ **2.** $.34 \div 50$ **3.** $.16 \div 200$

Solution **1.** $.21 \div 2.5 = 4(.21) \div 4(2.5) = .84 \div 10 = .084$ **2.** $.34 \div 50 = 2(.34) \div 2(50) = .68 \div 100 = .0068$ **3.** $.16 \div 200 = \frac{1}{2}(.16) \div \frac{1}{2}(200) = .08 \div 100 = .0008$

COMPATIBLE NUMBERS   Sometimes in computing products mentally it helps to recognize the decimal equivalents of a few simple fractions. Here are some that are useful:

$$.25 = \tfrac{1}{4} \quad .5 = \tfrac{1}{2} \quad .75 = \tfrac{3}{4} \quad .2 = \tfrac{1}{5} \quad .4 = \tfrac{2}{5} \quad .6 = \tfrac{3}{5} \quad .8 = \tfrac{4}{5} \quad .125 = \tfrac{1}{8}$$

Example L

Compute each product by replacing the decimal by an equivalent fraction.

1. $.25 \times 800$ **2.** $.5 \times .6$ **3.** $.2 \times 30$

4. $.125 \times 24$ **5.** $.6 \times 45$ **6.** $.75 \times 12$

Solution **1.** $\frac{1}{4} \times 800 = 200$ **2.** $\frac{1}{2} \times .6 = .3$ **3.** $\frac{1}{5} \times 30 = 6$ **4.** $\frac{1}{8} \times 24 = 3$ **5.** $\frac{3}{5} \times \overset{9}{\cancel{45}} = 3 \times 9 = 27$ **6.** $\frac{3}{\cancel{4}} \times \overset{3}{\cancel{12}} = 3 \times 3 = 9$

Estimation

There are times when estimations are as helpful as exact computations. The techniques of rounding, front-end estimation, and compatible numbers are illustrated in the following examples.

ROUNDING   Rounding to obtain an estimation mentally will often save time. For example, to make a decision regarding a purchase, all we may need is a rough idea of the cost.

Example M

Estimation serves as an important companion to computation. It provides a tool for judging the reasonableness of calculator, mental, and paper-and-pencil computations.

Standards 2000, p. 155

Suppose you are interested in the total cost of a stereo system whose components are priced as follows: tape deck, $219.50; turntable with cartridge, $179; pair of speakers, $284; and receiver, $335.89. Estimate the cost by rounding each amount to the nearest hundred dollars.

Solution   The exact sum and the estimation obtained by using numbers rounded to the hundreds place are shown below.

EXACT SUM	ESTIMATION
$ 219.50	$ 200
179.00	200
284.00	300
335.89	300
$1018.39	$1000

Notice that the estimation in Example M can be obtained quickly by adding the leading digits if the leading digit in $179 is rounded to 2 and the leading digit in $284 is rounded to 3.

The rectangular grid in Figure 6.27 shows the reasonableness of estimating 1.7 × 3.2 by rounding each number to the nearest whole number. The gray region shows the increase due to rounding 1.7 to 2, and the colored region shows the decrease caused by rounding 3.2 to 3. Notice the 6 unit squares in the grid that illustrate the estimated product. The fact that the gray region (the increase) is larger than the colored region (the decrease) shows that the estimated product is larger than the actual product.

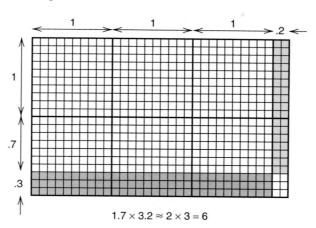

Figure 6.27

$1.7 \times 3.2 \approx 2 \times 3 = 6$

Example N

Estimate each product mentally by rounding the decimals to the nearest whole numbers.

1. 4.6 × 8.21   2. 10.263 × 5.9

Solution   1. 4.6 × 8.21 ≈ 5 × 8 = 40   2. 10.263 × 5.9 ≈ 10 × 6 = 60

FRONT-END ESTIMATION   A quick and easy method of obtaining a rough estimation is to use only the leading nonzero digit. For example,

$$762 \times .26 \approx 700 \times .2 = 140$$

Example O

Estimate each computation mentally by using the leading nonzero digit in each number.

1. .328 + .511   2. .361 − .14   3. 2.6 ÷ .53   4. 3.8 × .023

Solution   1. .328 + .511 ≈ .3 + .5 = .8   2. .361 − .14 ≈ .3 − .1 = .2   3. 2.6 ÷ .53 ≈ 2 ÷ .5 = 4
4. 3.8 × .023 ≈ 3 × .02 = .06

COMPATIBLE NUMBERS   Decimals can be replaced by compatible decimals or compatible fractions—numbers that are more convenient for the given computation. For example, in the sum 3.71 + .24, it is more convenient to use 3.7 in place of 3.71 and .3 in place of .24.

$$3.71 + .24 \approx 3.7 + .3 = 4$$

Example P

Estimate each computation by replacing a decimal by a more compatible decimal or fraction.

1. 6 ÷ .26   2. 1.43 − .5   3. .35 × 268

4. 2.87 + 5.15   5. .19 × 45   6. 27.7 − 1.8

Solution   1. $6 \div .26 \approx 6 \div \frac{1}{4} = 24$ 2. $1.43 - .5 \approx 1.5 - .5 = 1$ 3. $.35 \times 268 \approx \frac{1}{3} \times 270 = 90$
4. $2.87 + 5.15 \approx 2.85 + 5.15 = 8$ 5. $.19 \times 45 \approx \frac{1}{5} \times 45 = 9$ 6. $27.7 - 1.8 \approx 27.7 - 1.7 = 26$

Whenever an exact answer is required, an estimation can serve as a guide for detecting large errors. One source of error is caused by misplacing a decimal point when a number is entered into a calculator. Suppose, in computing .46 × 34.28, that you mistakenly enter 342.8. Then the calculator will show a product of

$$.46 \times 342.8 = 157.688$$

This error can be discovered by mental estimation: Replace .46 by $\frac{1}{2}$ and take one-half of 34.

$$.46 \times 34.28 \approx \frac{1}{2} \times 34 = 17$$

Since 17 is much smaller than 157.688, there is an indication of an error in the original computation.

Problem-Solving Application

Occasionally a number is written using both decimal and fraction notation together, as in the next problem. Try to solve this problem. If you need help, read as much of the following information as you need.

PROBLEM

Unleaded gas sells for 1.18\frac{9}{10}$ per gallon if you use a credit card. The gas pump meter is calibrated for this amount. A discount that lowers the price to 1.14\frac{9}{10}$ per gallon is offered if you choose to pay cash. If you hand the attendant a $10 bill and ask for $10 worth of gas, what should the dollar amount on the gas pump read after the attendant has finished?*

Understanding the Problem   These prices use hundredths of a dollar, $1.18 and $1.14, plus the fraction $\frac{9}{10}$ to indicate $\frac{9}{10}$ of a hundredth; $\frac{9}{10}$ of a hundredth is $\frac{9}{10} \times$ .01, which is equal to .009. Question 1: What are the two prices per gallon, written as decimals?

Devising a Plan   Sometimes *forming a table* with a few calculations will suggest a plan for solving the problem. The following table shows the cost of the first few gallons of gas with cash payment or with credit card payment. For example, 3 gallons of gas will cost 3 × $1.149 = $3.447 with cash and 3 × $1.189 = $3.567 with a credit card.

NUMBER OF GALLONS	CASH COST	CREDIT CARD COST
1	$1.149	$1.189
2	2.298	2.378
3	3.447	3.567

Question 2:   Since a cash payment of $3.447 will buy 3 gallons of gas (3.447 ÷ 1.149 = 3), how many gallons will a cash payment of $10 buy?

Carrying Out the Plan   Dividing 10 by 1.149 shows that you should receive approximately 8.703 gallons of gas.

$$10 \div 1.149 \approx 8.703$$

The cost of purchasing 8.703 gallons of gas with a credit card is 8.703 × $1.189, which is the cost that will show on the gas pump. Question 3: What is this amount rounded to the nearest hundredth of a dollar?

Looking Back   Another way to determine the total cost on the gas pump is to determine the extra cost for each gallon when a credit card is used ($1.189 − $1.149 = $.04, or 4 cents) and multiply this difference by the number of gallons, 8.703. This yields on extra cost that, when added to $10, will be the dollar amount on the gas pump. Question 4: What is this extra cost, rounded to the nearest cent?

Answers to Questions 1–4   1. $1.189 and $1.149   2. Approximately 8.703 gallons   3. $10.35
4. $.35 (35 cents)

PUZZLER

Ken bought some items at the Five and Ten store. All the items cost the same, and the total number of items was the same as the number of cents in the cost of each item. His bill was $6.25. How many items did he buy?

*"Problems of the Month," *Mathematics Teacher* 81 (December 1988): 738.

EXERCISES AND PROBLEMS 6.2

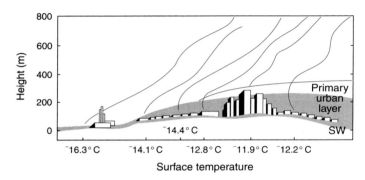

The preceding sketch is from a study showing the influence of surface temperature on air currents. Use these Celsius temperatures in exercises 1 and 2.

1. a. What is the highest surface temperature on this graph?
   b. What is the difference between the highest and lowest surface temperatures?

2. a. What is the lowest surface temperature on this graph?
   b. What is the difference between the two lowest surface temperatures?

Use Decimal Squares to illustrate each of the following computations in exercises 3 and 4. (Copy Decimal Squares from the inside cover of the book or from the website.)

3. a. $.3 + .45 = .75$
   b. $.350 - .2 = .15$
   c. $3 \times .65 = 1.95$
   d. $10 \times .37 = 3.7$

4. a. $.1 \times .2 = .02$
   b. $.3 \times .4 = .12$
   c. $.75 \div .05 = 15$
   d. $.60 \div 10 = .06$

In the example shown here, a 1 is regrouped from the hundredths column to the tenths column. This can be explained by adding the fractions for 4 hundredths and 9 hundredths to get 13 hundredths.

$$58.347$$
$$+ 1.091$$
$$59.438$$

$$\frac{4}{100}$$
$$+ \frac{9}{100}$$
$$\frac{13}{100} = \frac{10}{100} + \frac{3}{100} = \frac{1}{10} + \frac{3}{100}$$

In exercises 5 and 6, there is one column for which regrouping is needed. Mark this column and use equations to explain how the regrouping takes place.

5. a. 4.821
             $+ 61.73$

   b. $.367$
              $.015$
            $+ .509$

6. a. 66.43
             $- 41.72$

   b. $.046$
             $- .018$

Use a grid or a sketch to illustrate the products in exercises 7 and 8. Label the unit squares and parts of unit squares in the grid. (Copy the base-ten grid from the inside cover of the book or from the website.)

7. a. $1.7 \times 2.2 = 3.74$
   b. $4.1 \times 2.7 = 11.07$

8. a. $2.5 \times 3.7 = 9.25$
   b. $1.8 \times 4.6 = 8.28$

Use the pencil-and-paper algorithm in exercises 9 and 10 to compute each product or quotient. Indicate how the location of the decimal point in the product or quotient was found.

9. a. 3.2×7.8
   b. $1.4146 \div .22$

10. a. $1.44 \div .3$
    b. $.012 \times 9.3$

Calculate each product or quotient in exercises 11 and 12 mentally. Explain your method.

11. a. $.01 \times 7.6$
     b. $.001 \times 34$
     c. $.03 \div 100$
     d. $.04 \div 10$

12. a. $100 \times .65$
  b. $.01 \times 362$
  c. $.7 \div 10$
  d. $7.2 \div 100$

Write each repeating decimal in exercises 13 and 14 as a fraction.

13. a. $.\overline{5}$ **b.** $.\overline{14}$ **c.** $.1\overline{5}$

14. a. $.\overline{217}$ **b.** $.4\overline{19}$ **c.** $.\overline{7}$

Find a decimal that is between each pair of decimals in exercises 15 and 16.

15. a. $.6$ and $.7$ **b.** $.005$ and $.006$

16. a. 5.16 and 5.17 **b.** 13.99 and 14

Calculate each answer in exercises 17 and 18 mentally. Explain your method.

17. a. $.337 - .294$
  b. $4.3 + .8$
  c. 2.6×101
  d. $12.9 \div 300$

18. a. $9 \times .6$
  b. $.81 - .35$
  c. $3.2 \div 25$
  d. $17.3 + 8.9$

Calculate each product in exercises 19 and 20 mentally by replacing a decimal by an equivalent fraction. Show your replacement.

19. a. $.25 \times 48$ **20. a.** $8 \times .125$
  b. $.5 \times 40.8$ **b.** $.6 \times 555$
  c. $5.5 \times .2$ **c.** $.75 \times 40$

Obtain a front-end estimation for each sum or difference in exercises 21 and 22. Then obtain a second estimation by rounding to the leading digit.

21. a. $\$26.31$ **22. a.** $\$346.32$
         47.66 260.40
         21.18 118.63
      $+ 14.92$ $+ 752.01$

  b. $\$471.32$ **b.** $\$58.14$
      $- 113.81$ $- 16.71$

Estimate each product in exercises 23 and 24 by rounding the decimals to the nearest whole number. Sketch a rectangular grid that illustrates the actual product. Then sketch and shade the regions that represent the increase due to rounding up and the decrease due to rounding down. Use these regions to predict whether the estimated product is less than or greater than the actual product. (Copy the base-ten grid from the inside cover of the book or from the website.)

23. a. 3.1×4.9 **b.** 5.3×1.6
24. a. 3.4×5.8 **b.** 6.5×2.1

Estimate each computation in exercises 25 and 26 by replacing a decimal by a compatible decimal or fraction.

25. a. $8 \div .48$
  b. $11.63 + .4$
  c. $.34 \times 120$
  d. $.23 \times 81.6$

26. a. $.19 \times 80$
  b. $.34 - .101$
  c. $2 \div .49$
  d. $6.85 + 10.17$

The following decimal estimation exercise was given to 13-year-olds as a part of the National Assessment of Educational Progress.* The numbers at the right in the table below show the percentages of students who selected each response on the left. Use this table in exercises 27 and 28.

ESTIMATE THE ANSWER TO 3.04×5.3	PERCENTAGES
1.6	28
16	21
160	18
1600	23
I don't know	9

27. a. What percentage of the students selected either the incorrect response or "I don't know"?
  b. What misunderstandings about decimal concepts might have caused students to select 1600?

28. a. What percentage of the students selected the correct response?
  b. What misunderstandings of decimal concepts might have caused students to select 1.6?

Many types of errors can occur in computation, even when a student knows the basic operations with single-digit numbers. Determine which common types of errors were committed in exercises 29 and 30.

29. a. $.4$ **b.** 99.4
         $+ .8$ $- 27.86$
         $.12$ 71.66

*M. M. Lindquist, T. P. Carpenter, E. A. Silver, and W. Matthews, "The Third National Mathematics Assessment: Results and Implications for Elementary and Middle Schools," *The Arithmetic Teacher* 31, no. 4 (December 1983): 14–19.

c.   21.8
    ×   .4
    ─────
    87.2

d.   9.62
    4)38.6
    36
    ──
    26
    24
    ──
    2

30. a.   2.34
        × .75
        ─────
        1 1 70

        163 8
        ──────
        175.50

b.   2.7
    + .8
    ─────
    2.15

c.   30.08
    − 7.32
    ───────
    22.36

d.   .62
    7)4.214
    4 2
    ──
    14
    14
    ──

Enter 273.5186 into a calculator. What single addition or subtraction can be performed on a calculator to change this number to each number in exercises 31 and 32?

31. a. 273.5193
b. 203.5180
    c. 273.0156

32. a. 273.5086
    b. 273.5196
    c. 273.5786

Every decimal except 0 has a reciprocal. The product of a decimal and its reciprocal is 1. The reciprocal of 2.318 is $\frac{1}{2.318}$, which in decimal form to seven places is .4314064. Use a calculator to compute the reciprocals of the decimals in exercises 33 and 34, and multiply each number by its reciprocal. Record each reciprocal by rounding it to five decimal places

33. a. 2.4   b. .48   c. .0046

34. a. 46.3   b. .087   c. 3.41

Assume in exercises 35 and 36 that a calculator is being used which has a constant function that repeatedly carries out the operation in step 2 by pressing $=$. Determine the numbers for the view screens in steps 4 and 5.

35. a.   KEYSTROKES   VIEW SCREEN

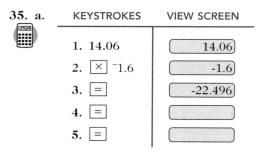

	KEYSTROKES	VIEW SCREEN
1.	14.06	14.06
2.	× ⁻1.6	-1.6
3.	=	-22.496
4.	=	
5.	=	

b.

	KEYSTROKES	VIEW SCREEN
1.	472.8	472.8
2.	− 16.3	16.3
3.	=	456.5
4.	=	
5.	=	

36. a.

	KEYSTROKES	VIEW SCREEN
1.	192.38	192.38
2.	+ ⁻6.55	-6.55
3.	=	185.83
4.	=	
5.	=	

b.

	KEYSTROKES	VIEW SCREEN
1.	160	160
2.	÷ 2.5	2.5
3.	=	64
4.	=	
5.	=	

Determine whether each sequence in exercises 37 and 38 is arithmetic or geometric. Then find each common difference or common ratio, and write the next number for each sequence.

37. a. 4.2,   7.56,   13.608,   24.4944
    b. 16.3,   15.6,   14.9,   14.2

38. a. 3.22,   8.82,   14.42,   20.02
    b. 44.3,   13.29,   3.987,   1.1961

REASONING AND PROBLEM SOLVING

39. Michelle pays a FICA/OASI (Federal Insurance Contributions Act/Old Age Survivors and Disability Insurance) tax of .062 and a FICA/Medicare tax of .0145 on her annual salary of $61,150. What is the total amount she pays for these two taxes?

40. Brian's annual salary is $25,600 before any deductions. After setting aside some of his salary in a tax-deferred retirement plan and subtracting certain deductions, he pays taxes on an adjusted gross salary of $18,400.

a. Find his federal tax by multiplying .15 and $18,400.

b. Find his state tax by multiplying .029 by $18,400.

c. Find his FICA tax by multiplying .0765 by $18,400.

d. Subtract the sum of the taxes in parts a to c from $18,400 to determine Brian's "after-tax" amount.

41. Credit card companies have different policies and rates. One company's policies are as follows.

a. The monthly finance charge on the amount due is determined by the following rule: .0125 times the first $500; .0095 times the next $500; and .0083 times the amount over $1000. What is the finance charge on $1200?

b. The late charges are .05 times the amount past due. Compute the late charge on $75.25, rounding the answer to the nearest hundredth of a dollar.

Use the following table to answer exercises 42 and 43. This table shows the annual percentage changes in energy consumption from 1988 to 1998, where positive numbers represent increases and negative numbers represent decreases.*

Annual percentage change in energy consumption

YEAR	COAL	NATURAL GAS	PETROLEUM
1988	4.7	4.6	4.1
1989	.4	4.5	.0
1990	.9	⁻.4	⁻1.9
1991	⁻1.7	1.6	⁻2.1
1992	.5	2.6	2.1
1993	2.9	3.4	.9
1994	.6	2.4	2.6
1995	.4	4.0	⁻.3
1996	6.8	1.7	3.1
1997	2.9	.1	1.3
1998	.9	⁻3.1	.5

42. a. Find a year in which the consumption of both coal and petroleum decreased. What happened to the demand for natural gas during this year?

*Statistical Abstract of the United States, 118th ed. (Washington, DC: Bureau of the Census, 1998), p. 589; and Monthly Energy Review, March 1999 (Washington, DC: Energy Information Administration), p. 1.

b. Find 7 consecutive years in which there was an increase in the demand for natural gas. What is the total of these increases?

c. Find 2 consecutive years during which the demand for petroleum decreased. What is the total of these decreases?

43. a. Over the 11-year period covered by this table there was 1 year in which the energy consumption of petroleum and coal decreased and the consumption of natural gas increased. What year was this?

b. Find 7 consecutive years in which there was an increase in the demand for coal. What is the total of these increases?

c. In which year did the consumption of natural gas decrease the most and what happened to the consumption of coal and petroleum during this time?

The basic unit for measuring electricity is the kilowatt-hour. This is the amount of electric energy required to operate a 1000-watt appliance for 1 hour. For example, it takes 1 kilowatt-hour of electricity to light ten 100-watt bulbs for 1 hour. The following table lists the average number of kilowatt-hours required to operate each appliance for 1 month. If it costs $.04 for each kilowatt-hour, use this information to answer the questions in exercises 44 and 45.

APPLIANCE	KILOWATT-HOURS PER MONTH	COST PER MONTH
Microwave oven	15.8	_____
Range with oven	97.6	_____
Refrigerator	94.7	_____
Frost-free refrigerator	152.4	_____
Water heater	400.0	_____
Radio	7.5	_____
Television (black and white)	29.6	_____
Television (color)	55.0	_____

44. a. What is the sum of the kilowatt-hours required for operating these eight appliances for 1 month?

b. What is the monthly cost of operating each of these appliances? Round your answers to the nearest penny.

c. Compute the sum of the monthly costs in part b for the eight appliances.

45. a. Compute the difference in the monthly costs of electricity for a black-and-white television and a color television.

b. How much could a person save in 1 year by operating a regular refrigerator rather than a frost-free refrigerator?

c. How much more expensive would it be to operate a range with an oven for 1 year than to operate a microwave oven for 1 year?

The greatest record-breaking spree occurred in the 1976 Olympic swimming competition when world records were set in 22 out of 26 events. In one of these events, an East German, Petra Thumer, set a world record in the 400-meter freestyle, winning in 4:09.89 (4 minutes 9.89 seconds). Use this information in exercises 46 and 47.

46. a. Thumer's time was 1.87 seconds faster than the old record. What was the old record?
   b. A world record in the 200-meter freestyle was set by another East German, Kornelia Ender, whose time was 1:59.26. If this rate of speed could be maintained, how long would it take to swim the 400-meter event? Compare this time with Thumer's time for the 400-meter event.
   c. In the 1964 Olympics in Tokyo, Don Schollander, of the United States, had a winning time of 4:12.2 in the 400-meter freestyle. How many seconds faster was Thumer's time for the 400-meter event?

47. a. In 1988, Janet Evans of the United States set an Olympic swimming record in the 400-meter freestyle with a time of 4:03.85. How much faster was her time than Petra Thumer's Olympic time for this event in 1976?
   b. In the 1992 summer Olympics in Barcelona, Spain, Dagmar Hase of Germany won the 400-meter swimming freestyle with a time of 4:07.18. How much faster was Janet Evan's time for this event in 1988?

48. **Featured Strategy: Making a Table**   During their summer vacation, Holly and Kathy traveled to Canada. Holly exchanged her U.S. money for Canadian money before leaving. For each 82 cents she received $1 in Canadian money. Kathy exchanged her money in Canada. For each U.S. dollar she received $1.20 in Canadian money. Who had the better rate of exchange?
   a. **Understanding the Problem**   Let's answer a few easy questions to become more familiar with the problem. If Holly received $100 in Canadian money, what did it cost her in U.S. money? If Kathy exchanged $50 in U.S. money, how much did she receive in Canadian money?
   b. **Devising a Plan**   It is tempting to conclude that Kathy had the better rate of exchange because it looks as if she "gained" 20 cents while Holly only "gained" 18 cents. Let's form a table to look at the cost of the first few dollars. Complete the next line of the table.

HOLLY		KATHY	
U.S.	CANADA	U.S.	CANADA
$ .82	$1	$1	$1.20
$1.64	$2	$2	$2.40

   c. **Carrying Out the Plan**   Extend the table to determine how much it will cost each person in U.S. dollars to buy a gift in Canada for 6 Canadian dollars? Who had the better rate of exchange, Holly or Kathy?
   d. **Looking Back**   The results in the table can be used to answer questions involving larger amounts of money. For example, how much less in U.S. money would it cost Holly than Kathy to buy an item for 48 Canadian dollars?

49. Misplacing a decimal point can result in a costly mistake, as described in this newspaper article.

Subtraction error to cost Rochester schools $3,000

By MARK C. BUDRIS
Rochester Bureau Chief

ROCHESTER- An arithmetic error may end up costing the School Department almost $3,000 next year.

School Board Chairman Roland Roberge said Thursday night the subtraction error during a comparison of milk bids led the board to accept a bid it thought was only $298 higher than a second. It was actually $2,986 higher.

"Well, the decimal point was put in the wrong place," Roberge told the board.

He said the error was in turning a half-cent difference in milk prices into a .05-cent difference, which was then multiplied out over the more than 650,000 cartons of milk used in a year by the School Department.

---

a. This article says that a .05-cent difference was used rather than a half-cent difference. What is the decimal for one-half cent?
b. If a bid for 650,000 cartons is .05 cent per carton higher than another bid, how many dollars greater is it?

c. If a bid for 650,000 cartons of milk is .5 cent per carton higher than another bid, how many dollars greater is it?

d. How much money did the school lose by misplacing the decimal point? (*Hint:* Use the answers from parts b and c.)

50. A pharmacist filled a prescription for a patient which called for an injection of .10 milliliter of insulin before the first meal of each day. The nurse's assistant at the hospital called the pharmacy to question the .10 amount of the injection, explaining that on several preceding occasions the prescription had called for .1 milliliter of insulin.

a. Is .1 equal to .10?

b. Explain how these two decimals could have different meanings.

- -

ONLINE LEARNING CENTER   www.mhhe.com/bennett-nelson

• Math Investigation 6.2   *Digit Draw*
Section-Related: • Links   • Writing/Discussion Problems   • Bibliography

- -

PUZZLER

How can the decimals .1, .2, .3, .4, .5, and .6 be placed in the circles so that the sum of the three numbers on each side of the triangle is .9?

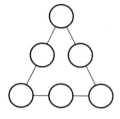

MATH ACTIVITY 6.3

PERCENTS WITH DECIMAL SQUARES

Materials: Decimal Square recording paper (three copies from inside cover page of the text or from the website)

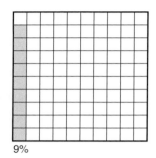

9%

1. The 10 × 10 Decimal Square represents 1 unit, or 100 percent. By shading 9 out of 100 parts of the unit, 9 percent is represented. Percents greater than 100 are illustrated by shading more than one 10 × 10 square. Shade and label squares on the Decimal Squares recording paper to illustrate the following decimals.

   a. 37 percent   **b.** 2 percent   **c.** $\frac{1}{2}$ percent   **d.** 126 percent

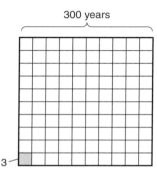

300 years

3

*2. If the square at the left represents 300 years and this amount is evenly divided among the 100 smaller squares, then each small square represents 3 years. How many years are represented by 14 small squares (14 percent)? How many small squares are required to represent 24 years?

*3. Shade a portion of a square on the Decimal Squares recording paper to represent 45 percent. If a 10 × 10 square represents 180 skateboards, how many skateboards are represented by 45 small squares? Write the letter S in as many small squares as necessary to represent 27 skateboards. How many small squares should be labeled with the letter S?

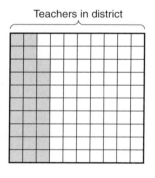

Teachers in district

4. The 10 × 10 square at the left represents the number of teachers in a school district, and the 28 shaded squares represent 70 of the teachers. Label a square on the Decimal Squares recording paper with this information. How many teachers are represented by 1 small square (1 percent)? How many teachers are in the school district?

5. One year a car dealer sold 1584 cars, which was 132 percent of the number sold the previous year. The shaded region of the squares shown below represents 1584 cars, which is 132 percent. Shade and label squares on the Decimal Squares recording paper with this information, and determine the value of 1 small square (1 percent), 15 small squares (15 percent), and 100 small squares (100 percent).

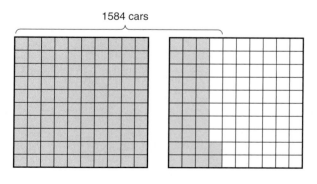

1584 cars

SECTION 6.3

RATIO, PERCENT, AND SCIENTIFIC NOTATION

Juxtaposition of photographs of planets, each taken by a different spaceship

A jar containing 140 marbles weighs 20 ounces, and the same jar containing only 100 marbles weighs 16 ounces. What is the weight of the jar?

One method of measuring large distances in our solar system is to compare each distance to the distance from Earth to the Sun. The distance from Earth to the Sun is called an **astronomical unit.** The distance from Jupiter to the Sun is 5.2 astronomical units, which means that Jupiter's distance from the Sun is 5.2 times Earth's distance from the Sun. Measuring with astronomical units involves the idea of *ratios,* which is introduced in this section.

HISTORICAL HIGHLIGHT

Isaac Newton, 1642–1727

England's Isaac Newton was born on Christmas in the year in which Galileo died. He was born prematurely and was so small and frail that his mother said he could have fit into a quart pot. Newton once told of how he performed his first scientific experiment as a young man. To determine the strength of the wind, he first broad-jumped with the wind and then broad-jumped against the wind. Comparing these distances with the extent of his broad jump on a calm day, he obtained the strength of the wind, expressed as so many feet strong. Newton is ranked by many as the greatest mathematician the world has produced. His *Principia,* which contains his laws of motion and describes the motions of the planets, is regarded as the greatest scientific work of all time. There are many testimonials to Newton's accomplishments, including the following lines by Alexander Pope:

> Nature and Nature's laws lay hid in night:
> God said, "Let Newton be," and all was light.*

*H. W. Eves, *In Mathematical Circles* (Boston: Prindle, Weber, and Schmidt, 1969), 7–11.

Ratios

In the middle grades students should encounter problems involving ratios (e.g., 3 adult chaperons for every 8 students) and rates (e.g., scoring a soccer goal on 3 of every 8 penalty kicks).

Standards 2000, p. 216

Ratio is one of the most useful ideas in everyday mathematics. A **ratio** is a pair of positive numbers that is used to compare two sets. The idea of ratio is illustrated in Figure 6.28, which shows that for every 3 chips there are 4 tiles. This ratio is written as 3:4 (read "3 to 4") or as the fraction $\frac{3}{4}$.

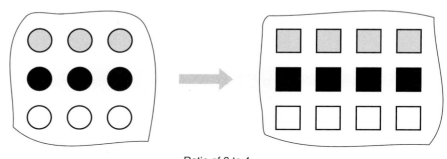

Figure 6.28

Ratio of 3 to 4

A ratio gives the relative sizes of two sets but not the actual numbers of objects in those sets. For example, the fact that the ratio of boys to girls in a certain class-room is 1 to 3 tells us that for every boy there are 3 girls, or that the number of boys is one-third the number of girls, but it does not tell us the number of boys or girls.

> For any two positive numbers *a* and *b*, the **ratio** of *a* to *b* is the fraction *a/b*. This ratio is also written as *a:b*.

Example A

In 1997, for every woman inmate in the United States, there were 9 men inmates.*

1. What is the ratio of the number of men inmates to the number of women in-mates?

2. What is the ratio of the number of women inmates to the number of men in-mates?

Research Statement

There is ample evidence that students experience difficulty solving problems involving fractions and proportions, even simple ones.

Behr et al. 1984; Noelting 1980; Vergnaud 1983

Solution 1. 9 to 1 or $\frac{9}{1}$ 2. 1 to 9 or $\frac{1}{9}$

Proportions

Comparing the relative sizes of large sets through the use of small numbers is a common use of ratios. In Figure 6.29 there are 8 teeth on the small gear and 40 teeth on the large gear. This is a ratio of 8 to 40 and, since $\frac{8}{40} = \frac{1}{5}$ in lowest terms, the ratio of teeth on the small gear to teeth on the large gear is 1 to 5 (1:5).

*Statistical Abstract of the United States, 120th ed. (Washington, DC: Bureau of the Census, 2000), p. 220.

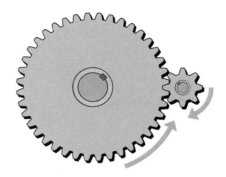

Figure 6.29

An equality of ratios is called a *proportion*. Each ratio gives rise to many pairs of equal ratios. For example, in 1998 the ratio of trucks to cars involved in fatal crashes was 2 to 21. This means that for every 2 trucks there were 21 cars, for every 4 trucks there were 42 cars, etc., as shown in the following table. These are all equal ratios.*

Proportionality is an important integrative thread that connects many of the mathematics topics studied in grades 6–8.

Standards 2000, p. 217

TRUCK ACCIDENTS	CAR ACCIDENTS
2	21
4	42
6	63
8	84
.	.
.	.
.	.

For any two ratios *a/b* and *c/d,*

$$\frac{a}{b} = \frac{c}{d}$$

is called a **proportion.**

Proportions are useful in problem solving. Typically, three of the four numbers in a proportion are given and the fourth is to be found.

Example B

If the ratio of teachers to students in a school is 1 to 18 and there are 360 students, how many teachers are there?

Solution   One method for obtaining the solution is to form a table showing equal ratios and continue this list until you reach 360 students.

NUMBER OF TEACHERS	NUMBER OF STUDENTS
1	18
2	36
3	54
4	72
.	.
.	.
.	.

Statistical Abstract of the United States, 120th ed. (Washington, DC: Bureau of the Census, 2000), p. 635.

Another method is to write a proportion as two equal fractions, with x representing the number of teachers.

$$\frac{1}{18} = \frac{x}{360}$$

We know that the numerator and denominator of $\frac{1}{18}$ must be multiplied by the same number to result in an equal fraction. Since the denominator of $\frac{1}{18}$ must be multiplied by 20 to get 360 ($360 \div 18 = 20$),

$$\frac{1 \times 20}{18 \times 20} = \frac{20}{360}$$

So the number of teachers is 20.

Historically, the rule of proportions was so valuable to merchants that it was called the *golden rule*. Often we know the price of some quantity of a given item and want to determine the price of a different amount.

Example C

If 4.8 pounds of flour costs \$1.20, how much will 6 pounds cost?

Solution   Using the ratio of pounds to cost produces the following proportion, with x representing the cost for 6 pounds.

$$\frac{4.8}{1.20} = \frac{6}{x}$$

By the rule for equality of fractions, we obtain

$$4.8 \times x = 1.20 \times 6$$
$$x = \frac{1.20 \times 6}{4.8}$$
$$x = 1.5$$

Thus the cost of 6 pounds is \$1.50.

Percent

The word **percent** comes from the Latin *per centum,* meaning *out of 100.* Percent was first used in the fifteenth century for computing interest, profits, and losses. Currently it has much broader applications, as illustrated by the news clippings in Figure 6.30.

Figure 6.30

Research Statement

One reason percents may be difficult is concise linguistic form which leads students to manipulate numbers based on learned procedures rather than on underlying relationships.

Parker and Leinhardt 1995

Percents are ways of representing fractions with denominators of 100. For example, 15 percent means $\frac{15}{100}$ and is written as 15%. Diagrams are one method of gaining an understanding of percents. A 10 × 10 grid with 100 equal parts is a common model in elementary school texts for illustrating percents (see Figure 6.31). Decimal Squares for tenths, hundredths, and thousandths will be used in this section to describe percents.

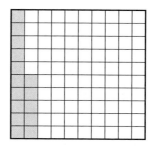

15%

Figure 6.31

Example D

Describe a Decimal Square to represent each percent.

1. 90%   **2.** 9%   **3.** 35.5%

Solution   **1.** 90 parts shaded out of 100, or 9 parts shaded out of 10   **2.** 9 parts shaded out of 100
3. 35.5 parts shaded out of 100, or 355 parts shaded out of 1000

Notice the similarity between the percent symbol % and the numeral 100. This is helpful in remembering how to replace a percent by a fraction or a decimal. First, drop the percent symbol and write the percent as a fraction with a denominator of 100. Then, to obtain a decimal, divide the numerator by the denominator.

Example E

Write each percentage as a decimal. Then describe a Decimal Square that represents or approximately represents the decimal.

1. 42%   **2.** 6.8%   **3.** $21\frac{3}{4}$%   **4.** 100%

Solution   **1.** $42\% = \frac{42}{100} = .42$ (42 parts shaded out of 100)   **2.** $6.8\% = \frac{6.8}{100} = .068$ (between 6 and 7 parts shaded out of 100, or 68 parts shaded out of 1000)   **3.** $21\frac{3}{4}\% = \frac{21\frac{3}{4}}{100} = \frac{21.75}{100} = .2175$ (between 21 and 22 parts shaded out of 100, or between 217 and 218 parts shaded out of 1000)   **4.** $100\% = \frac{100}{100} = 1$ (100 parts shaded out of 100)

Example E suggests a shortcut for writing a percent as a decimal: *drop the percent symbol and divide by 100*. Some calculators with percent keys operate in this manner. That is, if 4, 2, and the % key are pressed, .42 will show in the display. To write a decimal as a percentage, reverse the process: Write the decimal first as a fraction with a denominator of 100 and then as a percent.

Example F

Describe the Decimal Square for each decimal, and then write the decimal as a percent.

1. .07   **2.** .647   **3.** 3.25   **4.** .008

Solution 1. 7 parts shaded out of 100: $.07 = \frac{7}{100} = 7\%$

2. 647 parts shaded out of 1000: $.647 = \frac{647}{1000} = \frac{64.7}{100} = 64.7\%$

3. 3 whole squares and 25 parts shaded out of 100: $3.25 = \frac{325}{100} = 325\%$

4. 8 parts shaded out of 1000: $.008 = \frac{8}{1000} = \frac{.8}{100} = .8\%$

To write a fraction as a percent, first write it as a decimal and then write the decimal as a fraction with a denominator of 100. For example, to write $\frac{1}{6}$ as a percent,

$$\frac{1}{6} = .1\overline{6} = \frac{16.\overline{6}}{100} = 16.\overline{6}\% \quad \text{or} \quad 16\frac{2}{3}\%$$

Example G

Write each fraction as a percent,

1. $\frac{1}{5}$ **2.** $\frac{1}{8}$ **3.** $\frac{1}{3}$

Solution **1.** $\frac{1}{5} = \frac{20}{100} = 20\%$ **2.** $\frac{1}{8} = \frac{12\frac{1}{2}}{100} = 12\frac{1}{2}\%$ **3.** $\frac{1}{3} = \frac{33\frac{1}{3}}{100} = 33\frac{1}{3}\%$

The importance of recognizing equivalent forms of numbers is noted in the *Curriculum and Evaluation Standards for School Mathematics:*

. . . the development of concepts for fractions, ratios, decimals, and percents and the ideas of multiple representations of these numbers need special attention and emphasis. The ability to generate, read, use, and appreciate multiple representations of the same quantity is a critical step in learning to understand and do mathematics.*

Calculations with Percents

Calculations with percents fall into three categories:

1. Given the *whole* and the *percent,* find the *part.*

2. Given the *whole* and the *part,* find the *percent.*

3. Given the *percent* and the *part,* find the *whole.*

WHOLE AND PERCENT When the whole and the percent are given, the part can be found by multiplying the percent by the whole. For example, suppose 12 percent of the 250 teachers in a school have master's degrees. The word *of* is a clue that the percent is acting as a multiplier and that the number of teachers with master's degrees is found by multiplying .12 × 250.

$$12\% \text{ of } 250 = .12 \times 250 = 30$$

Figure 6.32 illustrates the information in the preceding problem. The Decimal Square is 12 percent shaded, and the whole square represents 250 teachers. This suggests another way to solve the problem. If the whole square represents 250

Curriculum and Evaluation Standards for School Mathematics (Reston, VA: National Council of Teachers of Mathematics, 1989), p. 87.

teachers, then each small hundredths square represents $\frac{250}{100} = 2.5$ teachers. So the number of teachers represented by 12 small squares is $12 \times 2.5 = 30$.

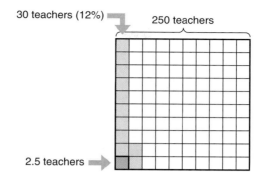

30 teachers (12%)   250 teachers

2.5 teachers

Figure 6.32

Example **H**

A survey of football players revealed that 20 percent of 1180 players had knee injuries. How many players had knee injuries?

Solution   20% of 1180 = .20 × 1180 = 236. So 236 players had knee injuries.

PART AND WHOLE   When the part and the whole are given, the percent can be found by writing the fraction for the part of the whole and then writing this fraction as a percent. For example, if 8 of a radio station's top 40 songs for a given week are new songs, then $\frac{8}{40}$ of the songs are new. To represent $\frac{8}{40}$ as a percent, we can divide 8 by 40 to obtain a decimal and then replace the decimal by a percent.

$$8 \div 40 = .2 \quad \text{and} \quad .2 = \frac{20}{100} = 20\%$$

Figure 6.33 provides a visual approach to solving the preceding problem: 8 is what percent of 40? If we let the total square represent 40, then since the square has 100 equal parts, each part represents $40 \div 100 = .4$. Thus, 2 small squares represent .8, 10 small squares represent 4, and 20 small squares represent 8. Since 20 squares out of 100 is 20 percent, 8 is 20 percent of 40.

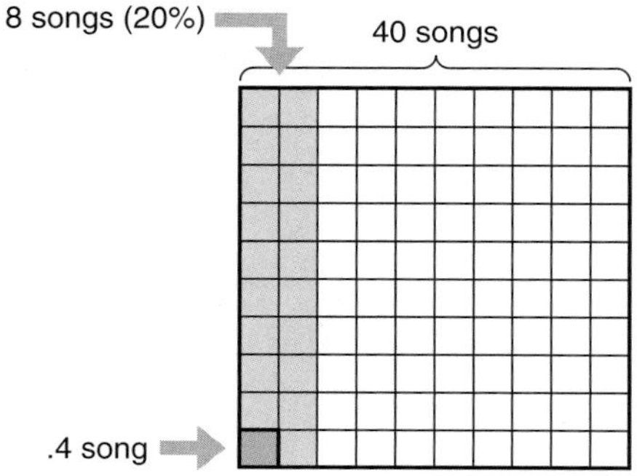

Research Statement

Several research studies have found that students have trouble solving problems involving percents.

Kouba et al. 1988; Kouba, Zawojewski, and Strutchens 1997; Risacher 1993

8 songs (20%)   40 songs

.4 song

Figure 6.33

In some cases it is necessary to compare one number to a smaller one. For example, since 90 is 2 times 45, it is 200 percent of 45.

$$\frac{90}{45} = 2 = \frac{200}{100} = 200\%$$

Example I

Determine the following percents.

1. 120 is what percentage of 80?

2. 33 is what percentage of 11?

3. 60 is what percentage of 50?

Solution   1. 120 is 150 percent of 80: $\frac{120}{80} = 1.5 = \frac{150}{100} = 150\%$ **2.** 33 is 300 percent of 11: $\frac{33}{11} = 3 = \frac{300}{100} = 300\%$ **3.** 60 is 120 percent of 50: $\frac{60}{50} = 1.2 = \frac{120}{100} = 120\%$

Example J

1. If $880 of a $2000 loan has been paid off, what percentage is this?

2. If a company's profits were 1.4 billion dollars in the year 2000 and 1.8 billion dollars in 2001, the 2001 profits were what percent of the 2000 profits?

Solution   1. The fraction of the loan that has been paid off is $\frac{880}{2000}$, which equals .44. So 44 percent of the loan has been paid off.   **2.** 1.8 is approximately 1.29 times 1.4: $\frac{1.8}{1.4} \approx 1.29 = \frac{129}{100} = 129\%$

PERCENT AND PART   When the percent and the part are given, the whole can be found by using a proportion. Suppose a down payment of $14,400 is required for a home loan and this down payment is 18 percent of the loan. Then the amount of the loan is the denominator x in the following proportion.

$$\frac{\text{Part}}{\text{Whole}} = \frac{18}{100} = \frac{14,400}{x}$$

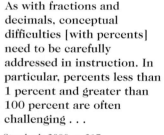

As with fractions and decimals, conceptual difficulties [with percents] need to be carefully addressed in instruction. In particular, percents less than 1 percent and greater than 100 percent are often challenging . . .

Standards 2000, p. 217

Using the rule for equality of fractions, we can write this equation as

$$18 \times x = 14,400 \times 100$$
$$x = \frac{1,440,000}{18}$$
$$x = 80,000$$

So the amount of the loan is $80,000.

Another method of solution for the preceding problem is illustrated in Figure 6.34. The Decimal Square is 18 percent shaded, and the shaded amount represents the $14,400 down payment. If 18 of the small hundredths squares represent $14,400, then each small square represents $14,400 ÷ 18 = $800. So the total of 100 squares represents 100 × $800 = $80,000.

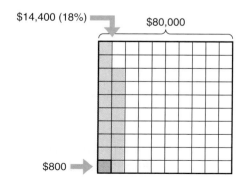

$14,400 (18%) — $80,000

$800

Figure 6.34

Example K

In 1997 Nebraska had 112 one-teacher schoolhouses. To the nearest percent, this number was 23 percent of the total number of one-teacher schoolhouses in the United States. How many one-teacher schoolhouses were there in the United States in 1997?

Solution The ratio of 23 percent ($\frac{23}{100}$) is equal to the ratio of 112 to the total number of one-teacher schoolhouses. If x equals the number of one-teacher schoolhouses,

$$\frac{23}{100} = \frac{112}{x}$$

Using the rule for equality of fractions, we can rewrite the above equation as

$$23 \times x = 112 \times 100$$
$$x = \frac{11,200}{23}$$
$$x = 486.9$$

So there were 487 one-teacher schoolhouses in the United States in 1997.*

The same procedure can be used for setting up a proportion when the percent is greater than 100. Suppose we know that after a physical exertion test a person's pulse rate is 144 beats per minute, and this is 180 percent of the person's resting pulse rate. The ratio of 180 percent (180/100) is equal to the ratio of 144 to the resting pulse rate. If x equals the person's resting pulse rate,

$$\frac{180}{100} = \frac{144}{x}$$

Using the rule for equality of fractions, we find that

$$180 \times x = 144 \times 100$$
$$x = \frac{14,400}{180}$$
$$x = 80$$

So the person's resting pulse rate is 80 beats per minute.

Example L

The school population for the new year in a certain town is 135 percent of the school population for the previous year. If the new population is 378, how many students did the school have the previous year?

Solution The ratio of 135 percent (135/100) is equal to the ratio of the new population to the previous year's population. If x equals the previous year's population,

$$\frac{135}{100} = \frac{378}{x}$$
$$135 \times x = 378 \times 100$$
$$x = \frac{37,800}{135}$$
$$x = 280$$

Thus there were 280 students the previous year.

 A common occurrence of percents is found in computing discounts and sales taxes. In the case of discounts we want to subtract a certain percentage of the

Digest of Educational Statistics (Washington, DC: U.S. Department of Education, 1998), p. 97.

original cost. For example, what is the cost of an object that is listed for $36.40 with a 15 percent discount? Some calculators with percent keys are designed to compute this cost by using the keystrokes below. When 15 percent is entered in step 3, the view screen shows the amount to be subtracted from $36.40. Pressing ⌸=⌸ in step 4 shows the discounted price. You may wish to try these keystrokes if you have a calculator with a percent key.

KEYSTROKES	VIEW SCREEN
1. Enter 36.40	36.40
2. ⌸−⌸	36.40
3. Enter 15 ⌸%⌸	5.46
4. ⌸=⌸	30.94

The cost of an object plus the sales tax is computed in a similar way with the minus sign in step 2 of the above example replaced by a plus sign. The cost of a $30.94 item plus 6 percent sales tax is obtained by the following steps.

KEYSTROKES	VIEW SCREEN
1. Enter 30.94	30.94
2. ⌸+⌸	30.94
3. Enter 6 ⌸%⌸	1.8564
4. ⌸=⌸	32.7964

 Calculators with a percent key that add a given percentage, as in the preceding example, make it easy to compute interest on saving accounts, credit cards, etc. Suppose that you owe $500 on a credit card that charges 1 percent interest compounded monthly. This means that at the end of each month you own 1 percent of the unpaid balance. After the first month you will have a debt of $500 plus 1 percent of $500, which according to step 2 in the following example is $505. Step 3 shows the amount owed at the end of the second month, and each succeeding step shows the amount owed at the end of each month, if no payments or further charges are made to the account. This is an example of **compound interest** because interest is charged on unpaid interest.

KEYSTROKES	VIEW SCREEN
1. Enter 500	500.
2. ⌸+⌸ 1 ⌸%⌸ ⌸=⌸	505. (end of first month)
3. ⌸+⌸ 1 ⌸%⌸ ⌸=⌸	510.05 (end of second month)
4. ⌸+⌸ 1 ⌸%⌸ ⌸=⌸	515.1505 (end of third month)

Notice that the balance of $505 at the end of the first month also can be computed by multiplying 1.01×500, as shown by the distributive property.

$$500 + .01 \times 500 = (1 + .01) \times 500$$
$$= 1.01 \times 500$$

This gives us another approach to determine each balance in the preceding example: Simply multiply each monthly balance by 1.01 (100% + 1%). This method can be used on any calculator. The following keystrokes produce the credit card balance at the end of 3 months.

$$500 \boxed{\times} \ 1.01 \ \boxed{\times} \ 1.01 \ \boxed{\times} \ 1.01 \ \boxed{=} \ \boxed{515.1505}$$

 Another expression for the left side of the preceding equation is $500 \times (1.01)^3$. Using a calculator key for raising numbers to powers, such as $\boxed{y^x}$ or $\boxed{\wedge}$, the credit card balance after 3 months is

$$500 \boxed{\times} \ 1.01 \ \boxed{\wedge} \ 3 \ \boxed{=} \ \boxed{515.1505}$$

Mental Calculations with Percents

The frequent occurrence of percents in everyday life has led people to adopt certain techniques for mental calculations. Two of these—*compatible numbers* and *substitutions*—are introduced here.

Mental computation and estimation are also useful in many calculations involving percents. Because these methods often require flexibility in moving from one representation to another, they are useful in deepening students' understanding of rational numbers.

Standards 2000, p. 220

COMPATIBLE NUMBERS   Certain percents are convenient for calculations. One of these is 10 percent, because multiplying by .10 is just a matter of moving a decimal point. For example, 10 percent of 16.50 = .10 × 16.50 = 1.65. Once we know 10 percent of a number, we can use that amount to determine other percents such as 5, 15, 20, 25, and 40 percent. The relationship of these percents to 10 percent is illustrated in Figure 6.35.

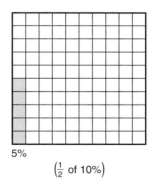

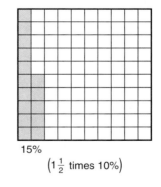

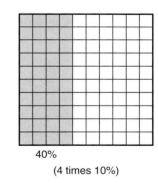

5%
$\left(\frac{1}{2} \text{ of } 10\%\right)$

15%
$\left(1\frac{1}{2} \text{ times } 10\%\right)$

40%
(4 times 10%)

Figure 6.35

Example M

A store is having a sale, and prices are being discounted 15, 20, and 25 percent. Calculate the amount of each discount mentally.

1. 15 percent of $82   **2.** 20 percent of $31.40   **3.** 25 percent of $30

Solution   1. Since 10% of $82 = $8.20 and 5% is one-half as much, 15% of $82 = $8.20 + $4.10 = $12.30.   **2.** Since 10% of $31.40 = $3.14 and 20% is twice as much, 20% of $31.40 = $6.28. **3.** Since 10% of $30 = $3 and 25% = 10% + 10% + 5%, 25% of $30 = $3 + $3 + $1.50 = $7.50.

For some computations it is convenient to replace a percent by a fraction. A few percents and their fractions are shown in Figures 6.35 and 6.36.

By middle grades children should understand that numbers can be represented in various ways, so that they can see that $\frac{1}{4}$, 25%, and 0.25 are all different names for the same number.

Standards 2000, p. 33

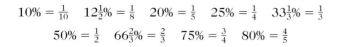

$$10\% = \tfrac{1}{10} \quad 12\tfrac{1}{2}\% = \tfrac{1}{8} \quad 20\% = \tfrac{1}{5} \quad 25\% = \tfrac{1}{4} \quad 33\tfrac{1}{3}\% = \tfrac{1}{3}$$

$$50\% = \tfrac{1}{2} \quad 66\tfrac{2}{3}\% = \tfrac{2}{3} \quad 75\% = \tfrac{3}{4} \quad 80\% = \tfrac{4}{5}$$

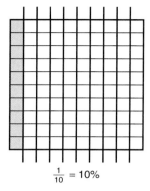
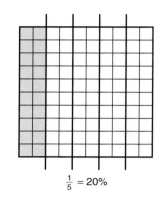
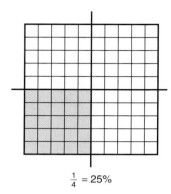

Figure 6.36

$$\tfrac{1}{10} = 10\% \qquad \tfrac{1}{5} = 20\% \qquad \tfrac{1}{4} = 25\%$$

Example N

Calculate each percentage mentally by first replacing the percent by a fraction.

1. 25 percent of 88   2. 20 percent of 55   3. $33\tfrac{1}{3}$ percent of 45

4. 75 percent of 24

Solution   1. 25 percent of 88 = $\tfrac{1}{4} \times 88 = 22$ 2. 20 percent of 55 = $\tfrac{1}{5} \times 55 = 11$ 3. $33\tfrac{1}{3}$ percent of 45 = $\tfrac{1}{3} \times 45 = 15$ 4. 75 percent of 24 = $\tfrac{3}{4} \times 24 = 18$

SUBSTITUTIONS   The solution to a problem is sometimes easily obtained by replacing a percent by a sum or difference of two percents. For example, to find 90 percent of 140, we can use the fact that 90% = 100% − 10%.

$$90\% \text{ of } 140 = 100\% \text{ of } 140 - 10\% \text{ of } 140 = 140 - 14 = 126$$

Example O

Calculate each percentage mentally by replacing the percent by a sum or difference of two convenient percents.

1. 95 percent of 200   2. 110 percent of 430   3. 45 percent of 18

Solution   1. 95% of 200 = 100% of 200 − 5% of 200 = 200 − 10 = 190 (*Note:* 10% of 200 = 20 so 5 percent of 200 is one-half of 20.)   2. 110% of 430 = 100% of 430 + 10% of 430 = 430 + 43 = 473   3. 45% of 18 = 50% of 18 − 5% of 18 = 9 − .9 = 8.1 (*Note:* 10% of 18 = 1.8 so 5% of 18 = .9.)

Estimation

COMPATIBLE NUMBERS   Sometimes it is convenient to replace a given percent by an approximation, which may be either another percent or a fraction. For example, percentages such as 47, 52, and 48 percent, which are close to 50 percent, may be replaced by $\tfrac{1}{2}$; percentages such as 34, 35, and 33 percent, which are close to $33\tfrac{1}{3}$ percent, are sometimes replaced by $\tfrac{1}{3}$; etc. At times both numbers in a calculation are replaced by approximations to obtain compatible numbers. For example, 24 percent of $18.75 may be replaced by $\frac{1}{4}$ of $20, because $\frac{1}{4}$ and $20 are compatible numbers that are approximately equal to the original numbers.

Example P

Estimate each percentage mentally by replacing one or both numbers by compatible numbers.

1. 34 percent of 62.4   **2.** 47 percent of $87.62   **3.** 8 percent of 65

Solution Here are some possible solutions: **1.** $\frac{1}{3} \times 60 = 20$, or $\frac{1}{3} \times 63 = 21$ **2.** $\frac{1}{2}$ of $88 = $44, or $\frac{1}{2}$ of $80 = $40 (*Note:* Since 47 percent is increased to $\frac{1}{2}$, $87.62 is decreased to $80 for the second estimation.)   **3.** 10% of 65 = 6.5 or 10% of 60 = 6

When a percentage is written as a fraction, replacing the numerator and denominator by compatible numbers often provides a close estimation. For example, when answers to 47 out of 60 questions on a test are correct, $\frac{47}{60}$ is the fraction of correct answers. Here are two possibilities for expressing this fraction as a percentage:

$$\frac{47}{60} \approx \frac{48}{60} = \frac{8}{10} = 80\%$$

$$\frac{47}{60} \approx \frac{49}{63} = \frac{7}{9} = \frac{77}{99} \approx \frac{77}{100} = 77\%$$

Example Q

Determine approximate percents by replacing the numerators and/or denominators by compatible numbers.

1. $\dfrac{16}{62}$ **2.** $\dfrac{300}{2490}$ **3.** $\dfrac{42}{87}$

Solution   **1.** $\frac{16}{62} \approx \frac{15}{60} = \frac{1}{4} = 25\%$ or $\frac{16}{62} \approx \frac{16}{64} = \frac{2}{8} = \frac{1}{4} = 25\%$ **2.** $\frac{300}{2490} \approx \frac{300}{2500} = \frac{3}{25} = \frac{12}{100} = 12\%$ **3.** $\frac{42}{87} \approx \frac{1}{2} = 50\%$

Scientific Notation

In the middle grades, students should . . . develop a sense of magnitude of very large numbers. For example, they should recognize and represent 2 300 000 000 as 2.3×10^9 in scientific notation and also as 2.3 billion.

Standards 2000, p. 217

Large and small numbers can be written conveniently by using powers of 10. Consider the following example: Some computers can perform 400,000,000 calculations per second. Using a power of 10, we can write

$$400,000,000 = 4 \times 10^8$$

Decimals that are less than 1 can be written by using negative powers of 10. For example, the average human hair, which is approximately .003 inch thick, can be written as

$$.003 = \frac{3}{1000} = \frac{3}{10^3} = 3 \times 10^{-3}$$

where $\frac{1}{10^3} = 10^{-3}$. In general, for any number $x \neq 0$ and any integer n,

$$\frac{1}{x^n} = x^{-n}$$

Any positive number can be written as the product of a number from 1 to 10 and a power of 10. For example, 2,770,000,000 can be written as 2.77×10^9. This method of writing numbers is called **scientific notation**. The number between 1 and 10 is called the **mantissa**, and the exponent of 10 is called the **characteristic**. In the preceding example, the mantissa is 2.77 and the characteristic is 9.

Example R

The following table contains examples of numbers written in scientific notation. Fill in the missing numbers in the last two rows.

	POSITIONAL NUMERATION	SCIENTIFIC NOTATION
Years since age of dinosaurs	150,000,000	1.5×10^8
Seconds of half-life of U-238	142,000,000,000,000,000	1.42×10^{17}
Wavelength of gamma ray (meters)	.0000000000003048	3.048×10^{-13}
Size of viruses (centimeters)	.000000914	_____
Orbital velocity of Earth (kilometers per hour)	_____	4.129×10^4

Solution $.000000914 = 9.14 \times 10^{-7}$; $4.129 \times 10^4 = 41,290$

Numbers written in scientific notation are especially convenient for computing. The graph in Figure 6.37 shows increases in the world's population. It wasn't until 1825 that the population reached 1 billion (1×10^9); by 1999 it was 6.1 billion (6.1×10^9). Since there is about 2.26×10^3 square yards of cultivated land per person, the total amount of cultivated land worldwide, in square yards, is

$$(6.1 \times 10^9) \times (2.26 \times 10^3)$$

Rearranging these numbers and using the rule for adding exponents, we can rewrite this product as

$$(6.1 \times 2.26) \times 10^{12}$$

Finally, we compute the product of the mantissas (6.1×2.26) and write the answer in scientific notation:

$$(6.1 \times 2.26) \times 10^{12} = 13.786 \times 10^{12} = 1.3786 \times 10^{13}$$

So there is approximately 1.3786×10^{13}, or 13,786,000,000,000 square yards of cultivated land in the world. Notice in the preceding equation that 13.786 is not between 1 and 10, so we divide by 10 to obtain the mantissa of 1.3786 and then increase the characteristic (the power of 10) from 12 to 13 to obtain an answer in scientific notation.

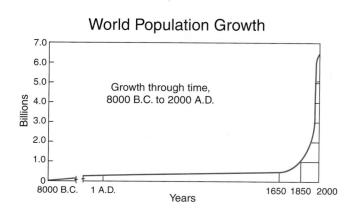

Figure 6.37

The preceding example illustrates the method of computing products of numbers in scientific notation: (1) Multiply the mantissas (numbers from 1 to 10); and (2) add the characteristics to obtain a new power of 10.

Example S

Compute each product and write the answer in scientific notation.

1. $(6.3 \times 10^4) \times (5.21 \times 10^3)$

2. $(1.55 \times 10^4) \times (8.7 \times 10^{-6})$

Solution   **1.** $(6.3 \times 5.21) \times (10^4 \times 10^3) = 32.823 \times 10^7$, but since 32.823 is not between 1 and 10, a requirement for scientific notation, we replace it by 3.2823×10.

$$32.823 \times 10^7 = 3.2823 \times 10 \times 10^7 = 3.2823 \times 10^8$$

2. $(1.55 \times 8.7) \times (10^4 \times 10^{-6}) = 13.485 \times 10^{-2}$, but since 13.485 is not between 1 and 10, we replace it by 1.3485×10.

$$13.485 \times 10^{-2} = 1.3485 \times 10 \times 10^{-2} = 1.3485 \times 10^{-1}$$

 Calculators that operate with scientific notation will print the mantissa and the characteristic when ever a computation produces a number that is too large for the screen. The keystrokes for entering 4.87×10^{17} and the view screen are shown below.

KEYSTROKES	VIEW SCREEN
4.87	4.87
$\times$	4.87
10 $\wedge$ 17	1. 17
$=$	4.87 17

To compute with numbers in scientific notation, the numbers and operations can be entered as they are written from left to right. The following keystrokes compute $(4.87 \boxed{\times} 10^{17}) \boxed{\times} (9.2 \boxed{\times} 10^5)$ and display the answer in scientific notation. Notice that parentheses are not needed as long as the calculator is programmed to follow thae order of operations.

KEYSTROKES	VIEW SCREEN
4.87 $\boxed{\times}$ 17 $\boxed{10^x}$ $\boxed{\times}$ 9.2 $\boxed{\times}$ 5 $\boxed{10^x}$ $\boxed{=}$	4.4804 23

 Try the following product to see if your calculator uses scientific notation: $2{,}390{,}000 \times 1{,}000{,}000$. This product equals 2.39×10^{12}, where the mantissa is 2.39 and the characteristic is 12. Notice that the base of 10 does not appear in the calculator view screens of the first two displays in Figure 6.38. Most calculators that display numbers in scientific notation show the mantissa and the characteristic but not the base 10.

Figure 6.38

 If a number is too small for the view screen, it will be represented by a mantissa and a negative power of 10. Use your calculator to compute .0004 × .000006, which is .0000000024, or 2.4×10^{-9} in scientific notation. If this is computed on a calculator whose view screen has only eight places for digits and no scientific notation, it may show a product of 0, or the error message E or Error. On a calculator with scientific notation, a mantissa of 2.4 and a characteristic of ⁻9 will appear in the view screen as shown in Figure 6.39.

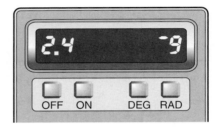

Figure 6.39

Problem-Solving Application

PROBLEM

Two elementary school classes have equal numbers of students. The ratio of girls to boys is 3 to 1 in one class and 2 to 1 in the other. If the two classes are combined into one large class, what is the new ratio of girls to boys?

Understanding the Problem   To obtain a better understanding of the ratios, let's select a particular number of students and compute the number of girls and boys. Suppose there are 24 students in each class. The class with the 3-to-1 ratio has 18 girls and 6 boys. **Question 1:** How many girls and how many boys are in the class with the 2-to-1 ratio?

Devising a Plan   One approach is to *make a drawing* representing the two classes and indicate their ratios. The following figures illustrate the girl-to-boy ratios in the two classes and show that each class is the same size. **Question 2:** Why can't we conclude from these figures that the ratio of girls to boys in the combined class is 5 to 2?

2 : 1 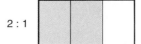   3 : 1

Carrying Out the Plan   To obtain information from the sketches of the classes, we need to subdivide the parts so that each figure has parts of the same size. The smallest number of such parts is 12, as shown in the following figure. The combined class will have 24 equal parts. **Question 3:** What is the ratio of girls to boys in the combined class?

2 : 1 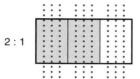   3 : 1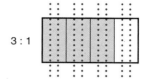

Looking Back   Above we chose 24 students per class as a numerical example and from this established girl-to-boy ratios of 18 to 6 and 16 to 8. **Question 4:** Do these numbers produce the same ratio for the combined class as that obtained from the sketches?

Answers to Questions 1–4   **1.** 16 girls and 8 boys   **2.** Because the parts of the sketches are different sizes   **3.** 17 to 7   **4.** Yes; the ratio of 34 to 14 is equal to the ratio of 17 to 7.

EXERCISES AND PROBLEMS 6.3

In this morning's rush hour, empty seats outnumbered full seats 4 to 1.

In a city the size of Los Angeles, that's 9,000,000 empty seats in cars jammed up on the freeways.
Think about that while you're sitting in traffic.

Share the ride with a friend. It sure beats driving alone.

Presented as a public service by
Eugene Register-Guard
Daily and Sunday

1. The public service advertisement to the left points out the need for carpooling to reduce traffic.
   a. According to this advertisement, what fraction of the car seats are empty during rush hour?
   b. In a city the size of Los Angeles, there would be 9,000,000 empty seats during rush hour. How many seats would be filled?

Use a sketch to illustrate the given information and the solutions in exercises 2 and 3.

2. **a.** The ratio of apples to oranges in a gift box is 3 to 2, and there are 18 apples. How many oranges are there?
   b. If the ratio of cars to trucks in a parking lot is 7 to 2 and there are 26 trucks, how many cars are there?

3. **a.** The ratio of U.S. citizens to noncitizens among patent applicants during a given period was 11 to 3. If 407 patent applications were received from U.S. citizens, how many were received from noncitizens?
   b. Erik is twice as fast at typing as Trenton. If Trenton types 25 words every minute, how many words will Erik type in 3 minutes?

Answer each question in exercises 4 and 5 by assuming that the rate for the smaller quantity and the rate for the larger quantity remain the same.

4. **a.** Jessica purchased 2.3 pounds of chicken for $1.36. If Glen purchased 3.8 pounds of chicken, how much should he pay to the nearest cent for his purchase?
   b. Jason has $6.50, and sliced ham is $2.79 for 1.2 pounds. How many pounds of ham to the nearest tenth can he buy for $6.50?
   c. If Lakeside Farm cheese costs $1.19 for each $\frac{1}{4}$ pound, how many pounds of cheese to the nearest tenth can be purchased for $5?

5. **a.** If 1.5 pounds of fish cost $3.12, how much does 3.5 pounds cost?
   b. If 8 ounces of yarn cost $2.66, what is the cost for 20 ounces?
   c. If 10 pounds of nails cost $4.38, what is the cost to the nearest cent of 3.2 pounds of the same type of nail?

Write each percent as a decimal in exercises 6 and 7, and shade or describe a 10 × 10 Decimal Square to illustrate the percent. (Copy Decimal Squares from the inside cover of the book or from the website.)

6. **a.** 7%   **b.** 18.2%   **c.** $34\frac{1}{4}$%
7. **a.** $37\frac{1}{2}$%   **b.** 6.5%   **c.** $28\frac{1}{3}$%

Use or describe a Decimal Square for each decimal in exercises 8 and 9, and write the decimal as a percent. (Copy Decimal Squares from the inside cover of the book or from the website.)

8. **a.** .426   **b.** .003   **c.** .09
9. **a.** .60   **b.** .06   **c.** .256

Write each fraction in exercises 10 and 11 as a percent, rounded to the nearest tenth of a percent.

10. **a.** $\frac{7}{25}$ **b.** $\frac{1}{8}$ **c.** $\frac{5}{12}$
11. **a.** $\frac{4}{5}$ **b.** $\frac{5}{6}$ **c.** $\frac{7}{4}$

Determine each answer in exercises 12 and 13 to the nearest tenth. Use Decimal Squares and the visual methods outlined in Figures 6.32 to 6.34 for parts a and b. Label each diagram and explain your reasoning. (Copy Decimal Squares from the inside cover of the book or from the website.)

12. **a.** What percentage of 20 is 14?
    b. What is 12 percent of 60?
    c. If 12 is 8 percent of some number, what is the number?
    d. 36.25 is what percentage of 14.5?

13. **a.** What is 27 percent of 160?
    b. 40 is what percentage of 200?

c. If 10 percent of a number is 4, what is the number?
d. What is 140 percent of 65?
e. 75 is what percentage of 50?

Calculate each percent in exercises 14 and 15 mentally, and explain your method.

14. **a.** 15 percent of $42   **b.** 25 percent of 28
    c. $33\frac{1}{3}$ percent of 15   **d.** 5 percent of $42.60

15. **a.** 10 percent of $128.50   **b.** 75 percent of 32
    c. 90 percent of $60   **d.** 110 percent of 80

Estimate each percentage in exercises 16 and 17 mentally by replacing one or both numbers by compatible numbers. Show your replacements.

16. **a.** 51 percent of 78.3   **b.** 23 percent of 1182
    c. 11 percent of $19.99   **d.** 32 percent of $612.40

17. **a.** 9 percent of $30.75   **b.** 19 percent of 60
    c. 4.9 percent of 128   **d.** 15 percent of 241

Calculate approximate percentages for the fractions in exercises 18 and 19 mentally by replacing the numerators or denominators by compatible numbers. Show your replacements.

18. **a.** $\frac{14}{27}$ **b.** $\frac{9}{38}$ **c.** $\frac{7}{32}$
19. **a.** $\frac{2}{19}$ **b.** $\frac{408}{1210}$ **c.** $\frac{100}{982}$

Write the numbers in exercises 20 and 21 in scientific notation.

20. **a.** Size of a minute insect in inches is .013
    b. Length of a day in seconds is 86,400

21. **a.** Number of years since Earth's formation is 4,600,000,000
    b. Diameter of an atom in centimeters is .000000027

Write the numbers in exercises 22 and 23 in positional numeration.

22. **a.** Total number of possible bridge hands is 6.35×10^{11}
    b. U.S. trade balance in 1997 was -1.814882×10^{11}

23. **a.** Wavelength of X rays in inches is 1.2×10^{-9}
    b. Approximate length of solar year in seconds is 3.15569×10^7

Write the answers for exercises 24 and 25 in scientific notation.

24. **a.** The velocity of a jet plane is 1.1×10^3 miles per hour, and the escape velocity of a rocket from earth is 22.7 times the plane's velocity. Find the rocket's velocity by computing $1.1 \times 10^3 \times 22.7$.

b. Earth travels 6.21×10^8 miles around the sun each year in approximately 9×10^3 hours. Compute $(6.21 \times 10^8) \div (9 \times 10^3)$ to determine Earth's speed in miles per hour.

25. a. A light-year, the distance that light travels in 1 year, is 5.868×10^{13} miles. The sun is 2.7×10^4 light-years from the center of our galaxy. Find this distance in miles by computing $5.868 \times 10^{13} \times 2.7 \times 10^4$.

b. At one point in *Voyager I*'s journey to Jupiter, its radio waves traveled 4.62×10^8 miles to reach Earth. These waves travel at a speed of 3.1×10^5 miles per second. Compute $(4.62 \times 10^8) \div (3.1 \times 10^5)$ to determine the number of seconds it took these signals to reach Earth.

The following figure shows the percentages of injuries to different parts of the body, as revealed in a study of 1180 injured professional football players. Determine the number of players with each of the types of injuries in exercises 26 and 27 rounded to the nearest whole number.

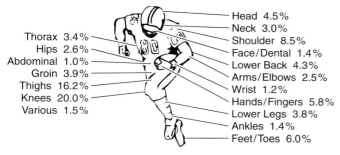

Thorax 3.4%
Hips 2.6%
Abdominal 1.0%
Groin 3.9%
Thighs 16.2%
Knees 20.0%
Various 1.5%

Head 4.5%
Neck 3.0%
Shoulder 8.5%
Face/Dental 1.4%
Lower Back 4.3%
Arms/Elbows 2.5%
Wrist 1.2%
Hands/Fingers 5.8%
Lower Legs 3.8%
Ankles 1.4%
Feet/Toes 6.0%

Professional Football Players' Injuries

26. a. Head injuries   **b.** Shoulder injuries

27. a. Lower back injuries
   b. Injuries to the feet and toes

The table below shows the numbers of students and teachers (to the nearest thousand) in grades K–12 in public schools in several states.* The student/teacher ratio for each state is the number of students divided by the number of teachers. Use this table in exercises 28 and 29.

STATE	NUMBER OF TEACHERS	NUMBER OF STUDENTS	STUDENT/ TEACHER RATIO
Alabama	45,000	746,000	_____
Florida	120,000	2,177,000	_____
Hawaii	11,000	188,000	_____
Iowa	33,000	502,000	_____
Maine	16,000	214,000	_____
Missouri	59,000	890,000	_____
Oregon	27,000	528,000	_____
Wyoming	7,000	100,000	_____

Statistical Abstract of the United States, 118th ed. (Washington, DC: Bureau of the Census, 1998), p. 173.

28. a. Compute the ratios to the nearest tenth for the first four states in the table.
   b. Which of these states has the best (lowest) student/ teacher ratio?
   c. Which has the poorest (highest) student/teacher ratio?

29. a. Compute the ratios to the nearest tenth for the last four states in the table.
   b. Which of these states has the best (lowest) student/ teacher ratio?
   c. Which has the poorest (highest) student/teacher ratio?

REASONING AND PROBLEM SOLVING

30. Compute each percent to the nearest tenth of a percent.
   a. A down payment of $200 is what percentage of the cost of $1460?
   b. A cost of $3.63 in the year 2000 is what percentage of a 1998 cost of $2.75?
   c. The school has collected $744, which is 62 percent of its goal. What is the total amount of the school's goal?
   d. During a flu epidemic, 17 percent of a school's 283 students were absent on a particular day. How many students were absent?

31. Compute each percent to the nearest tenth of a percent and each dollar amount to the nearest hundredth of a dollar.
   a. With a discount of 70 percent, the cost of a bracelet is $17.99. What is the price before the discount?
   b. A cordless intercom system is marked down from $99.99 to $79.99. By what percent is the intercom discounted?
   c. A teacher's salary in the year 2001 is 107.5 percent of her salary in 2000. If the salary in 2000 is $32,000, what is the salary in 2001?
   d. If 6 of the 28 students in a class did not enroll in the school's insurance plan, what percentage did enroll in the plan?

32. Which package in each of the following pairs is the better buy?
   a. Betty Crocker Complete Buttermilk: small size, 40 ounces at $2.35, or large size, 56 ounces at $3.14
   b. Bisquick Variety Baking Mix: small size, 20 ounces at $1.17, or large size, 32 ounces at $1.99

c. Plastic tape: small roll, 15.2 yards for 69 cents, or large roll, 23.6 yards for $1.60

33. One method of determining which of two packages is the better buy is to compute the price per unit of both packages. For example, each ounce of mix in the large box costs 264¢ ÷ 48 = 5.5¢.

48 ounces for $2.64   32 ounces for $1.89

a. What is the cost per ounce for the small package?
b. Which is the better buy?
c. If the large box has enough mix for 115 four-inch pancakes, how many four-inch pancakes can be made from the small box?

34. Todd sells 3 newspapers every 10 minutes at his newsstand, and Shauna sells 4 newspapers every 12 minutes at her newsstand. If they work at these rates and combine their sales, how many newspapers will they sell in 30 minutes?

35. The cost of a $9.85 item that is being discounted 12 percent can be determined by subtracting 12 percent of $9.85 from $9.85. The following equations show that the cost of this item can also be found by taking 88 percent of $9.85. What number properties are used in the first two of these equations?

$$9.85 - (.12 \times 9.85) = (1 \times 9.85) - (.12 \times 9.85)$$
$$= (1 - .12) \times 9.85$$
$$= .88 \times 9.85$$

Use one of these two methods to compute the discounted cost of each of the following items.
a. Portable typewriter, $209.50 (15 percent off)
b. Backpacker sleeping bag, $153.95 (20 percent off)
c. Snowshoes, $86 (28 percent off)

36. The total cost of a $15.70 item plus a 6 percent sales tax can be determined by adding 6 percent of $15.70 to $15.70. The total cost can also be found by multiplying 1.06 times $15.70, as shown by the following equations. What number properties are used in the first two equations?

$$15.70 + (.06 \times 15.70) = (1 \times 15.70) + (.06 \times 15.70)$$
$$= (1 + .06) \times 15.70$$
$$= 1.06 \times 15.70$$

Use one of these two methods to compute the cost plus the sales tax for each of the following items. Round each answer to the nearest hundredth of a dollar.
a. Fishing tackle outfit, $48.60 (4 percent tax)
b. Ten-speed bike, $189 (5 percent tax)
c. Cassette tape recorder, $69.96 (6 percent tax)

37. Costs due to an annual inflation rate of 4 percent can be determined by repeatedly multiplying the cost of an item by 1.04. For example, if the cost of a $50 item increases 4 percent, the new cost is 1.04 × 50 = 52. Use this rate of inflation to determine the following amounts to the nearest hundredth.
a. How much will the cost of a $545 washing machine increase in 1 year due to inflation?
b. How much will the cost of a $545 washing machine increase in 5 years if the rate of inflation remains at 4 percent?
c. Approximately how many years will pass before the cost of the washing machine in part a increases $200 if the rate of inflation remains at 4 percent?
d. If a $28,500 salary is increased 5 percent each year to keep ahead of inflation, what will this salary be after 3 years?

38. A consumer will be charged monthly interest at the rate of 1.5 percent (compounded monthly) on a loan of $8000.
a. What is the interest on this loan for the first month?
b. If none of the loan is paid by the consumer, how much will be owed at the end of the first month?
c. How much will be owed by the consumer at the end of 3 months if no payments are made on the loan?
d. How much money will the consumer save if the loan of $8000 for 3 months is obtained for a monthly interest rate of 1 percent rather than 1.5 percent?

39. In his will dated July 17, 1788, Benjamin Franklin stated that he wished "to be useful even after my death if possible," and to this end Franklin left 1000 pounds sterling (about $4570) to be used to make loans to the inhabitants of Boston.
a. Franklin's will stipulated that not more than 60 pounds, about $274, was to be loaned to apprentices at a 5 percent annual interest rate. What is the interest on this amount for 1 year?

b. The will also required that at the end of each year the borrower pay off 10 percent of the total amount owed. Add the interest from part a to $274 to determine the total amount owed at the end of the first year. What is 10 percent of this amount?

c. Franklin predicted that the 1000 pounds he was leaving would grow to 131,000 pounds in 100 years if loaned at 5 percent interest and compounded yearly. This means that each year the 5 percent is computed on the total amount in the account, including the past interest. What will 1000 pounds grow to if interest is compounded yearly at 5 percent for 5 years?

40. Population density is a ratio. The ratio for each state is determined by dividing the state's population by its land area in square miles.

a. Calculate the 1997 population densities, using the information in the following table. Round each ratio to the nearest tenth.

b. Which of the four states had the greatest increase in population density from 1988 to 1997?

	CALIFORNIA	NEW JERSEY	TEXAS	ARKANSAS
1997 population*	32,268,000	8,530,000	19,439,000	2,520,000
Square miles	156,361	7,521	262,134	53,182
1988 density	181.1	1026.6	64.2	45.0
1997 density	———	———	———	———

41. One astronomical unit is 93,003,000 miles, Earth's average distance from the sun. The distance of the other planets from the sun in astronomical units is their distance divided by 93,003,000. Determine the missing numbers in the following table. Compute each astronomical unit to the nearest tenth.

PLANET	SCIENTIFIC NOTATION	POSITIONAL NUMERATION	ASTRONOMICAL UNITS
Mercury	3.6002×10^7	———	———
Venus	———	67,273,000	———
Earth	9.3003×10^7	———	1
Mars	———	141,709,000	———
Jupiter	4.83881×10^8	———	———
Saturn	———	887,151,000	———
Uranus	1.784838×10^9	———	———
Neptune	———	2,796,693,000	———
Pluto	3.669699×10^9	———	———

42. Featured Strategy: Guessing and Checking Suppose an item is on sale at a 20 percent discount but there is a 5 percent sales tax. Is the consumer better off if the discount is computed before the tax or if the tax is computed before the discount?

a. Understanding the Problem If the discount is taken first, then the sales tax will be computed on an amount that is less than the original price. If the sales tax is computed first, then the discount will be taken on an amount that is more than the original price. Is one method better for the consumer than the other? Make an intuitive guess.

b. Devising a Plan One approach to this problem is to *guess and check* by trying a few different prices, comparing the results, and using inductive reasoning. What happens when the two methods are used for an item that costs $25?

c. Carrying Out the Plan Use the plan suggested in part b or your own plan to solve this problem.

d. Looking Back It may have occurred to you to compute the final cost of the item by taking a discount of 15 percent (20 percent discount minus 5 percent tax). Will this method produce the correct result?

e. Looking Back Again The methods described in the original problem result in the payment of different amounts of sales tax to the state. Which method would the owner of the business prefer, discount and then tax or tax and then discount?

43. After the first term, the top sequence shown below is a geometric sequence. Write the next two numbers in this sequence. Add 4 to each number in the top sequence, and divide the results by 10 to complete the lower sequence.

0   3   6   12   24   __   __

.4   .7   __   __   __   __   __

a. This famous sequence of numbers is the basis of Bode's law, which gives an amazingly close approximation of the distances from the first seven planets to the sun in astronomical units. Using this sequence of numbers and inductive reasoning, astronomers predicted that there would be a planet between Mars and Jupiter (see the following table). What was the predicted distance in astronomical units of this planet from the sun? (Asteroids were eventually found between Mars and Jupiter, the biggest of which is Ceres, about 500 miles in diameter.)

Statistical Abstract of the United States, 118th ed. (Washington, DC: Bureau of the Census, 1998), p. 28.

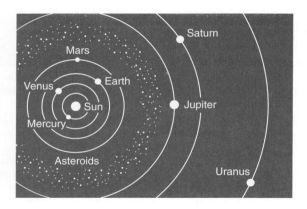

b. In the 1770s when Bode's law was discovered, only the first five planets in the following table had been discovered. Using Bode's law, astronomers found Uranus. What would its distance from the sun have been in astronomical units if it had conformed to Bode's law?

PLANET	DISTANCE FROM SUN IN ASTRONOMICAL UNITS	DISTANCE PREDICTED BY BODE'S LAW
Mercury	0.4	0.4
Venus	0.7	0.7
Earth	1.0	1.0
Mars	1.52	1.6
Ceres	2.77	—
Jupiter	5.2	5.2
Saturn	9.5	10.0
Uranus	19.2	—
Neptune	30.1	38.8
Pluto	39.5	77.2

44. In Lord Tennyson's poem "The Vision of Sin," there **PS** is a verse which reads

Every minute dies a man,
Every minute one is born.

In response to these lines, the English engineer Charles Babbage wrote a letter to Tennyson in which he noted that if this were true, the population of the world would be at a standstill. He suggested that the next edition of the poem should read

Every minute dies a man,
Every minute $1\frac{1}{16}$ is born.

a. Using Babbage's mixed number, what is the ratio of the number of people who are born to the number of people who die?
b. In recent years there has been a birth every 10 seconds and a death every 16 seconds. At these rates, what is the ratio of births to deaths?
c. What mixed number should be used in recent years in place of the mixed number suggested by Babbage?

· ·

ONLINE LEARNING CENTER   www.mhhe.com/bennett-nelson

• Math Investigation 6.3   *Palindromic Decimals*
Section-Related: • Links   • Writing/Discussion Problems   • Bibliography

· ·

PUZZLER

Two engineering students were discussing the need for engines that conserve energy. One student told of three new devices that could be installed in an engine: one saved 20 percent on fuel, another saved 30 percent, and the third saved 50 percent. "But that's not possible," said the other student, "that's a savings of 100 percent—the engine wouldn't require any fuel!" What is the total percent of fuel that could be saved if all three devices were used?

MATH ACTIVITY 6.4

IRRATIONAL NUMBERS ON GEOBOARDS

Materials: Geoboard paper (copy Dot Grid from inside cover pages of the text or from the website to form geoboard paper)

1. The small shaded square on this geoboard has an area of **1 square unit.** Find the area of the second figure on the geoboard.

2. Form figures on geoboard paper which have the following areas. Use a geoboard square as in the above figure for the unit square. Label each figure with its area.

   a. Area of $3\frac{1}{2}$ **b.** Area of 10   **c.** Area of 7   **d.** Area of $14\frac{1}{2}$

3. The triangle on the geoboard at the left has an area of 6 square units. One way to determine this area is to enclose the triangle in a rectangle and take one-half of the area of the rectangle. Form triangles on geoboard paper with areas of $\frac{1}{2}$, 1, $1\frac{1}{2}$, 2, $2\frac{1}{2}$, and 3. Label each triangle with its area.

* 4. Squares can be formed on the geoboard having areas of 1, 2, 4, 5, 8, 9, 10, and 16. The square shown here has an area of 5. Sketch the remaining seven squares on geoboard paper and label each with its area. (*Hint:* Areas of some figures can be easily found by enclosing the figure in a rectangle or square and subtracting the area of the region outside the figure, as shown here.)

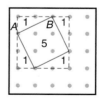

* 5. The area of a square is the product of the length of one side and the length of the other. The square in the preceding figure has an area of 5, so we need a number which, when multiplied by itself, yields 5. We call this number the **positive square root** of 5, written $\sqrt{5}$. Thus, line segment $\overline{AB}$ on the above geoboard has a length of $\sqrt{5}$. The positive square roots of all whole numbers which are not perfect squares are **irrational numbers.** This type of number is studied in Section 6.4. Label the side of each square in activity 4 with its length. Use your squares to show that $\sqrt{8} = 2\sqrt{2}$.

SECTION 6.4

IRRATIONAL AND REAL NUMBERS

An Egyptian painting, dating from about the fifteenth century B.C., depicting the needs of an advanced society. The upper part shows surveyors with rope.

PROBLEM OPENER

If the digits in the decimal .07007000700007 · · · continue, this pattern of increasing numbers of 0s followed by 7s (five 0s and a 7, six 0s and a 7, etc.), what will the 100th digit be?

The number line in Figure 6.40 shows the locations of a few positive rational numbers. Each rational number corresponds to a point on the number line, and between any two such numbers, no matter how close, there is always another rational number. It would seem that there is no room left for any new types of numbers.

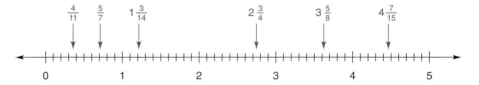

Figure 6.40

There are, however, points on the number line that correspond to numbers that are not rational. For example, there is no rational number which, when multiplied by itself, yields 2. The following equations show that such a number is close to, but greater than, 1.4. Try these products on a calculator. Find a rational number that, when multiplied by itself, yields a value that is closer to 2 than the numbers shown below.

$$1.4 \times 1.4 = 1.96$$
$$1.41 \times 1.41 = 1.9881$$
$$1.414 \times 1.414 = 1.999396$$
$$1.4142 \times 1.4142 = 1.99996164$$

The purpose of this section is to introduce new types of numbers whose decimals are nonrepeating. In the preceding equation, 1.4142 contains the first few digits of a **nonrepeating decimal.** In such a number, there is no repeating pattern of digits as there is for a rational number. Such nonrepeating decimals are called **irrational numbers.** It is easy to create examples of this type of decimal. In the following numeral, each 7 is preceded by one more 0 than the previous 7: .07007000700007 ⋯. Although there is a pattern here, there is no block of digits (repetend) that is repeated over and over, as in the case of a rational number. Therefore this is an irrational number.

Example A

Which of the following numbers are irrational?

1. .006006006 ⋯   **2.** .060060006 ⋯   **3.** .01001

4. .731731173111731111 ⋯   **5.** .73737373 ⋯   **6.** .21060606 ⋯

Solution   There is no block of repeating digits in either 2 or 4, so these are irrational numbers. The numbers in 1, 5, and 6 are repeating decimals, and 3 has a terminating decimal, so these are all rational numbers.

Pythagorean Theorem

Numbers that are not rational were first recognized by the Pythagoreans, followers of the Greek mathematician Pythagoras who lived in the fifth century B.C. It is possible that the discovery of such numbers arose in connection with the Pythagorean theorem. This theorem concerns triangles with a right angle, that is, a 90° angle (see Figure 6.41). The two shorter sides of such a triangle are called **legs,** and the longest side, which is opposite the right angle, is called the **hypotenuse.** The theorem states that for any right triangle, the sum of the areas of the squares on the legs (square A and square B) is equal to the area of the square on the hypotenuse (square C).

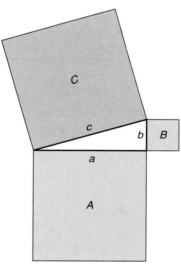

Figure 6.41

Area A + area B = area C

Since the area of a square is the square of the length of its side, the area of square A is a^2, the area of square B is b^2, and the area of square C is c^2. So the theorem can be stated as

$$a^2 + b^2 = c^2$$

Figure 6.42 shows a right triangle with legs of lengths 3 and 4 and a hypotenuse of length 5. Notice that the sum of the squares of the lengths of the two legs equals the square of the length of the hypotenuse.

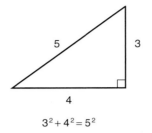

Figure 6.42

$$3^2 + 4^2 = 5^2$$

Numbers that are not rational may have been discovered by using a right triangle whose legs both have a length of 1, as shown in Figure 6.43. In this case the sum of the squares of the lengths of the two legs is $1^2 + 1^2 = 2$, and the length of the hypotenuse is the number which, when multiplied by itself, yields 2. As we have noted, this number is $\sqrt{2}$, which is irrational. Thus the hypotenuse of this triangle has a length that is an irrational number.

Figure 6.43

$$1^2 + 1^2 = (\sqrt{2})^2$$

The Pythagorean theorem is one of the most familiar statements in all mathematics.

PYTHAGOREAN THEOREM   For any right triangle with legs of lengths *a* and *b* and hypotenuse of length *c*,

$$a^2 + b^2 = c^2$$

E x a m p l e B

Use the Pythagorean theorem to find the missing length in each triangle.

1.

$$6^2 + 8^2 = \square^2$$

2.

$$\square^2 + 12^2 = 13^2$$

3.

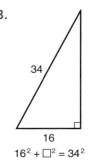

$$16^2 + \square^2 = 34^2$$

Solution   **1.** $6^2 + 8^2 = 100$. Since $10^2 = 100$, the missing length is 10.   **2.** $13^2 - 12^2 = 169 - 144 = 25$. Since $5^2 = 25$, the missing length is 5.   **3.** $34^2 - 16^2 = 1156 - 256 = 900$. Since $30^2 = 900$, the missing length is 30.

Before the Pythagoreans discovered that some numbers were not rational, they believed that all practical and theoretical affairs of life could be explained by ratios of whole numbers, that is, positive rational numbers. The discovery of line segments whose lengths were not rational numbers caused a logical scandal which threatened to destroy the Pythagorean philosophy. According to one legend, the Pythagoreans attempted to keep the matter secret by taking the discoverer of such numbers, Hippacus, on a sea voyage from which he never returned.

There are many proofs of the Pythagorean theorem. *The Pythagorean Proposition* is a book that describes 370 proofs of this theorem.* The proof suggested in Figure 6.44 was known by the Greeks and may have been the one given by Pythagoras. Part a has a small square of area a^2, a larger square of area b^2, and four right triangles. The total area of the figure in part a is $a^2 + b^2 + 4T$, where T is the area of each triangle. Part b has a square of area c^2 and four right triangles that are each the same size as those in part a. The total area of the figure in part b is $c^2 + 4T$. Since the large square in part a and the large square in part b both have sides of length $a + b$, they have the same area. Setting these areas equal to each other, we have

$$a^2 + b^2 + 4T = c^2 + 4T$$

and subtracting $4T$ from both sides leaves

$$a^2 + b^2 = c^2$$

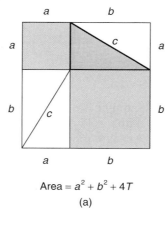

Area = $a^2 + b^2 + 4T$

(a)

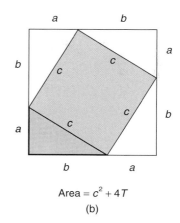

Area = $c^2 + 4T$

(b)

Figure 6.44

The converse of the Pythagorean theorem also holds. *If the sum of the squares of two sides of a triangle equals the square of the third side, then the triangle is a right triangle.* This means that if you used a rope with 30 knotted intervals of equal length and formed a triangle of sides 5, 12, and 13, as shown in Figure 6.45, it would be a right triangle. This fact was undoubtedly known by the ancient

*E. S. Loomis, *The Pythagorean Proposition* (Washington, DC: National Council of Teachers of Mathematics, 1968).

Egyptians and used by their surveyors to form right triangles (see the photograph on page 402).

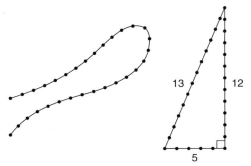

13   12

5

Figure 6.45

The first proof of the Pythagorean theorem is thought to have been given by Pythagoras (ca. 540 B.C.). According to legend, when Pythagoras discovered this theorem, he was so overjoyed that he offered a sacrifice of oxen to the gods. The theorem had been used for centuries, however, by the Babylonians and Egyptians. It is illustrated on this 4000-year-old Babylonian tablet, which shows a square and its diagonals. The numbers on this tablet are in base-sixty numeration and show that the Babylonians had computed the value of $\sqrt{2}$ to 6 decimal places: 1.414213.

Babylonian stone tablet with approximation of $\sqrt{2}$

Square Roots and Other Roots

In the middle grades, students should also add another pair to their repertoire of inverse operations—squaring and taking square roots. In grades 6–8, students frequently encounter squares and square roots when they use the Pythagorean relationship.

Standards 2000, p. 220

A **square root** of a number is defined as a number that, when multiplied by itself, yields the original number. For example, 3 is a square root of 9, since $3 \times 3 = 9$. However, $^-3$ is also a square root of 9, because $^-3 \times {}^-3 = 9$. Often we are concerned with only the positive square root of a number. For example, suppose the area of the square in Figure 6.46 is 64 square units. Since the area of a square is the product of the lengths of two of its sides, the length of one side of the square is the positive square root of 64, which is 8. In this example the negative square root $^-8$ has no meaning. The positive square root of a number is called the **principal square root.**

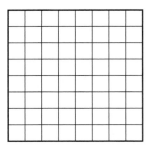

Figure 6.46

Example C

Find the principal square root and the negative square root of each number.

1. 49   **2.** 20.25   **3.** .64   **4.** $\frac{1}{4}$

Solution   **1.** 7, $^-$7   **2.** 4.5, $^-$4.5   **3.** .8, $^-$.8   **4.** $\frac{1}{2}, \frac{-1}{2}$

The symbol for the principal square root of a number b is $\sqrt{b}$. The symbol $\sqrt{\ }$ is called the **radical sign** and was represented first by the letter r, then by $\sqrt{\ }$, and finally by $\sqrt{\ }$. The negative square root of b is written as $^-\sqrt{b}$.

> For any positive number **b**,
> $$\sqrt{b} \times \sqrt{b} = b$$

Example D

Evaluate the following expressions.

1. $\sqrt{14} \times \sqrt{14}$ **2.** $(\sqrt{6})^2$ **3.** $\sqrt{9} \times \sqrt{9}$

Solution   **1.** 14   **2.** 6   **3.** 9

The square roots of square numbers (1, 4, 9, 16, 25, etc.) are whole numbers. The square roots of all other whole numbers greater than zero ($\sqrt{2}$, $\sqrt{3}$, $\sqrt{5}$, $\sqrt{6}$, $\sqrt{7}$, $\sqrt{8}$, etc.) are irrational. These numbers all have nonrepeating decimals. If a number is entered into a calculator and the square root key $\boxed{\sqrt{x}}$ is pressed, the display will show the principal square root of the number. If the square root of the number is irrational, the decimal that appears in the display will be an approximation.

Example E

Classify each number as either rational or irrational. If it is rational, evaluate the square root; if it is irrational, find an approximation to the nearest tenth.

1. $\sqrt{81}$ **2.** $\sqrt{10}$ **3.** $\sqrt{30}$

4. $\sqrt{\frac{4}{9}}$ **5.** $\sqrt{18}$ **6.** $\sqrt{.16}$

Solution   **1.** Rational, 9   **2.** Irrational, approximately 3.2   **3.** Irrational, approximately 5.5   **4.** Rational, $\frac{2}{3}$ **5.** Irrational, approximately 4.2   **6.** Rational, .4

Even though we cannot write the complete decimals for irrational numbers, these numbers should not be thought of as mysterious or illusive. They are the lengths of line segments, as illustrated by the triangles in Figure 6.47. The legs of the triangle on the left each have a length of 1, so, by the Pythagorean theorem, the hypotenuse is $\sqrt{2}$. The legs of the middle triangle have lengths of 1 and $\sqrt{2}$, and the hypotenuse is $\sqrt{3}$. In the triangle on the right, legs of length $\sqrt{2}$ and $\sqrt{3}$ are used to obtain a hypotenuse of $\sqrt{5}$. Line segments of lengths $\sqrt{6}$, $\sqrt{7}$, $\sqrt{8}$, etc., can be constructed in a similar manner. The lengths of the hypotenuses of these triangles, $\sqrt{2}$, $\sqrt{3}$, and $\sqrt{5}$, are indicated on the number line below the triangles in Figure 6.47. Check the locations of these numbers on the number line by using the edge of a piece of paper to mark off the lengths $\sqrt{2}$, $\sqrt{3}$, and $\sqrt{5}$ from the triangles.

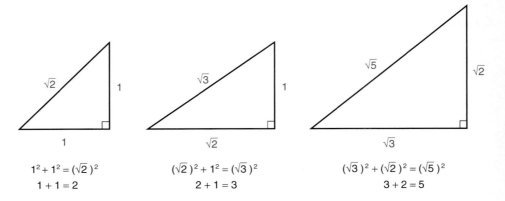

$$1^2 + 1^2 = (\sqrt{2})^2 \qquad (\sqrt{2})^2 + 1^2 = (\sqrt{3})^2 \qquad (\sqrt{3})^2 + (\sqrt{2})^2 = (\sqrt{5})^2$$
$$1 + 1 = 2 \qquad\qquad 2 + 1 = 3 \qquad\qquad 3 + 2 = 5$$

Figure 6.47

Example F

Find the length of each hypotenuse.

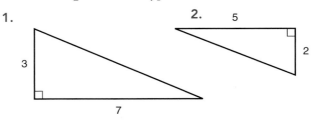

Solution   1. $\sqrt{58}$ 2. $\sqrt{29}$

Example G

Mark the approximate location of the length of each hypotenuse from Example F on the following number line.

Solution   1. To the nearest tenth, $\sqrt{58}$ is 7.6, which is 1 tenth beyond 7.5 on the number line.
2. To the nearest tenth, $\sqrt{29}$ is 5.4, which is 1 tenth before 5.5 on the number line.

The **cube root** of a number n is written as $\sqrt[3]{n}$. This is the number s such that $s \times s \times s$ equals n. The cube roots of **perfect cubes**, 1, 8, 27, 64, etc. are whole numbers. The cube roots of all other whole numbers are irrational numbers. For example, the cube roots of 4, 10, and 35 are nonrepeating decimals. Their approximate locations are shown on the number line in Figure 6.48. Try to cube these decimals to see how close you get to 4, 10, and 35.

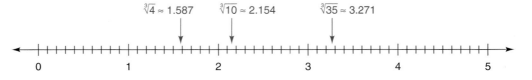

Figure 6.48

Example H

Classify each number as either rational or irrational. If it is rational, find the cube root; if it is irrational, find an approximation to the nearest tenth.

1. $\sqrt[3]{30}$ **2.** $\sqrt[3]{125}$ **3.** $\sqrt[3]{100}$

Solution **1.** Irrational, approximately 3.1   **2.** Rational, 5   **3.** Irrational, approximately 4.6

In addition to square roots and cube roots, for positive numbers b, the fourth root of b is $\sqrt[4]{b}$ and $(\sqrt[4]{b})^4 = b$; the fifth root of b is $\sqrt[5]{b}$ and $(\sqrt[5]{b})^5 = b$; etc. In general, the **nth root** of a positive number b is written as $\sqrt[n]{b}$, or expressed in exponential form as $b^{1/n}$, and n is called the **index**. Notice that for square roots ($\sqrt{10}$, $\sqrt{3}$, etc.) the index 2 is not written. Furthermore, since it is possible to have odd roots of negative numbers, for example $\sqrt[3]{-8} = {}^-2$ because $({}^-2)^3 = {}^-8$, the following definition is stated in two parts.

> **nth ROOTS**   (1) For $b \geq 0$ and positive integer n, or (2) for $b < 0$ and odd positive integer n,
>
> $$(\sqrt[n]{b})^n = b \qquad \text{and} \qquad \sqrt[n]{b} = b^{1/n}$$

Some calculators have a key for finding roots (cube root, fourth root, etc.). One common notation for this key is $\boxed{\sqrt[x]{y}}$. Here are the keystrokes for finding the cube root of 12 using such a calculator. The number in the view screen in step 4 is only an approximation because $\sqrt[3]{12}$ is an irrational number.

KEYSTROKES	VIEW SCREEN
1. Enter 12	12.
2. Press $\boxed{\sqrt[x]{y}}$	12.
3. Enter 3	3.
4. $\boxed{=}$	2.289428485

Your calculator may not have a key for roots ($\boxed{\sqrt[x]{y}}$), but it may have a key for raising numbers to powers, such as $\boxed{y^x}$, $\boxed{x^y}$, or $\boxed{\wedge}$. The preceding definition enables us to find the roots of numbers by using exponents. For example, since $\sqrt[3]{20} = 20^{1/3}$, the first few digits in the cube root of 20 are obtained by the next keystrokes.

$$20 \; \boxed{x^y} \; (1/3) \; \boxed{=} \; \boxed{2.714417617}$$

Similarly, square roots can be obtained by raising numbers to the $\frac{1}{2}$ power. The following keystrokes make use of the fact that $\sqrt{60} = 60^{1/2}$. Note that $\frac{1}{2}$ can be replaced by .5.

$$60 \; \boxed{x^y} \; (1/2) \; \boxed{=} \; \boxed{7.745966692}$$

Real Numbers

The irrational numbers and the rational numbers together form the set of **real numbers**. Figure 6.49 shows the relationships among the familiar sets of numbers. The set of rational numbers and the set of irrational numbers are disjoint, and their union is the set of real numbers R. The rational numbers Q contain the integers $Z = \{0, \pm1, \pm2, \pm3, \ldots\}$, and the integers contain the whole numbers $W = \{0, 1, 2, 3, \ldots\}$. Viewed in another way, the sets W, Z, and Q form an increasing sequence of subsets of R. The set of whole numbers is contained in the set of integers, $W \subset Z$; the set of integers is contained in the set of rational numbers, $Z \subset Q$; and the set of rational numbers is contained in the set of real numbers, $Q \subset R$.

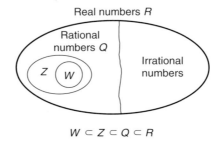

Figure 6.49

$$W \subset Z \subset Q \subset R$$

Each whole number is in all the sets W, Z, Q, and R. Other numbers are in only one, two, or three of these sets. For example, $\frac{1}{7}$ is in the set of rational numbers Q and the set of real numbers R, but not in the set of whole numbers W or integers Z.

Example ▌ Use the letters W, Z, Q, and R to indicate to which set(s) each number belongs.

1. $^{-}12$ **2.** $\sqrt{15}$ **3.** $.23$ **4.** 130

5. $\frac{3}{5}$ **6.** $.\overline{27}$ **7.** $\sqrt{10}$ **8.** $\sqrt{25}$

Solution   1. Z, Q, R 2. R 3. Q, R 4. W, Z, Q, R 5. Q, R 6. Q, R 7. R 8. W, Z, Q, R

Properties of Real Numbers

We have seen that the whole numbers, integers, rational numbers, and real numbers form an increasing sequence, with each set of numbers contained in the next. Although these number systems have several properties in common (the commutative, associative, and distributive properties), each number system was developed because it had number properties that the existing number systems did not have. For example, the whole numbers do not have inverses for addition (negative numbers), so the integers were developed; the integers do not have inverses for multiplication (reciprocals), so the rational numbers were developed. Similarly, the rational numbers lack a number property that the real numbers have.

The real numbers have the property of *completeness*. Intuitively, we can interpret **completeness** as meaning that all line segments can be measured. If we limit ourselves to the rational numbers, this is not true. For example, we have seen that there is no rational number corresponding to the length of the hypotenuse of a right triangle whose legs have lengths of 1 unit.

Expressed in a slightly different way, completeness of the real numbers means that there is a one-to-one correspondence between the real numbers and the points on a line. Because of this relationship, a line called the **real number line** is used as a model for the real numbers. Once a zero point has been labeled and a unit has been selected, each real number can be assigned to a point on the line. Each positive real number is assigned a point to the right of zero such that the real number is the distance from this point to the zero point. The negative of this number corresponds to a point that is the same distance to the left of zero. A few examples are shown in Figure 6.50.

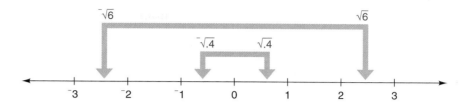

Figure 6.50

The following list contains 12 properties of the real number system.

CLOSURE UNDER ADDITION   The sum of any two real numbers is another unique real number. That is, the set of real numbers is closed under addition.

CLOSURE UNDER MULTIPLICATION   The product of any two real numbers is another unique real number. That is, the set of real numbers is closed under multiplication.

ADDITION IS COMMUTATIVE   For any real numbers r and s, $r + s = s + r$.

MULTIPLICATION IS COMMUTATIVE   For any real numbers r and s, $r \times s = s \times r$.

ADDITION IS ASSOCIATIVE   For any real numbers r, s, and t, $(r + s) + t = r + (s + t)$.

MULTIPLICATION IS ASSOCIATIVE   For any real numbers r, s, and t, $(r \times s) \times t = r \times (s \times t)$.

IDENTITY FOR ADDITION   For any real number r, $0 + r = r$. Zero is called the **identity for addition**, and it is the only number with this property.

IDENTITY FOR MULTIPLICATION   For any real number r, $1 \times r = r$. The number 1 is called the **identity for multiplication**, and it is the only number with this property.

INVERSES FOR ADDITION   For any real number r, there is a unique real number ^-r, called its **opposite** or **inverse for addition**, such that $r + {}^-r = 0$.

INVERSES FOR MULTIPLICATION   For any nonzero real number r, there is a unique real number $\frac{1}{r}$, called its **reciprocal** or **inverse for multiplication**, such that $r \times \frac{1}{r} = 1$.

MULTIPLICATION IS DISTRIBUTIVE OVER ADDITION   For any real numbers r, s, and t, $r \times (s + t) = r \times s + r \times t$.

COMPLETENESS PROPERTY   All line segments can be measured with real numbers.

Operations with Irrational Numbers

At first it is difficult to imagine how to perform arithmetic operations with numbers that cannot be expressed exactly in decimal notation. One solution is to replace irrational numbers by rational approximations. The square in Figure 6.51 has sides of length $\sqrt{2}$ units. Since $\sqrt{2} \approx 1.4$, the total length of the four sides, that is, the perimeter of the square, is approximately 4×1.4, or 5.6 units. For many purposes this is sufficient accuracy.

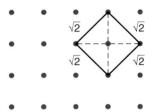

Figure 6.51

Another solution is to write products and sums by using irrational numbers. The total length of the sides of the square in Figure 6.51 can be written as $4\sqrt{2}$, which means 4 times $\sqrt{2}$.

Is $4\sqrt{2}$ a rational or an irrational number? We know by the property of closure for real numbers under multiplication that $4\sqrt{2}$ is a real number, so it is either rational or irrational. Let's suppose it is a rational number and denote it by r. That is,

$$r = 4\sqrt{2}$$

Multiplying both sides of this equation by $\frac{1}{4}$, we get

$$r \times \tfrac{1}{4} = \sqrt{2}$$

Now by the property of closure for rational numbers under multiplication, $r \times \frac{1}{4}$ is a rational number. However, this cannot be true because $\sqrt{2}$ is an irrational number and the preceding equation would then have an irrational number equal to a rational number. Since the assumption that $4\sqrt{2}$ is rational leads to a contradiction, $4\sqrt{2}$ must be irrational. A similar argument can be used to prove that *the product of any nonzero rational number and an irrational number is an irrational number.* Thus we can obtain an infinite number of irrational numbers by multiplying each nonzero rational number by $\sqrt{2}$. Let's consider another example of computing with irrational numbers. The total length of the sides of the triangle in Figure 6.52 can be written as $3 + \sqrt{5}$.

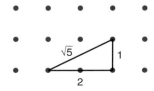

Figure 6.52

This is also an irrational number, as can be proved by an argument similar to the previous one. For if we assume that $3 + \sqrt{5}$ is a rational number and denote it by s, then

$$s = 3 + \sqrt{5} \quad \text{and} \quad s - 3 = \sqrt{5}$$

But this equation contains a contradiction. Since s and $^-3$ are rational numbers, by the closure property for rational numbers under addition, their sum is also a rational number. But $\sqrt{5}$ is an irrational number. So the assumption that $3 + \sqrt{5}$ is rational is false. In general, the sum of any rational number and irrational number is an irrational number. So once again, an infinite number of irrational numbers can be obtained by adding rational numbers to an irrational number.

Example J	Classify each sum or product as rational or irrational, and if it is rational, evaluate the expression. **1.** $3\sqrt{24}$ **2.** $5\sqrt{36}$ **3.** $14 + \sqrt{14}$ **4.** $\sqrt{81} + 18$ **Solution** **1.** Irrational **2.** Rational, 30 **3.** Irrational **4.** Rational, 27

The total length of the sides of the square in Figure 6.51 and the triangle in Figure 6.52 can be approximated by using rational number approximations for $\sqrt{2}$ and $\sqrt{5}$. However, there are cases in which we can compute with irrational numbers and obtain rational numbers without replacing them by decimal approximations. For example, we know that $\sqrt{2} \times \sqrt{2} = 2$. This can also be seen by looking at the square in Figure 6.51. The area of the square is $\sqrt{2} \times \sqrt{2}$, and we can see that the area is 2 by dividing it into four smaller half-squares, or triangles. Thus in this example the product of two irrational numbers is a rational number.

Let's consider another example of a product of two irrational numbers. The rectangle in Figure 6.53 has a length of $\sqrt{18}$ because it is the hypotenuse of a right triangle whose legs each have a length of 3. The width of this rectangle is $\sqrt{2}$. Its area, according to the formula for the area of a rectangle, length times width, is $\sqrt{18} \times \sqrt{2}$. Using a second method, we can show this area to be 6 square units by dividing the rectangle into two squares and eight half-squares, or triangles. These two methods of finding area show that $\sqrt{18} \times \sqrt{2} = 6$. This example illustrates a case in which the product of two different irrational numbers is a rational number.

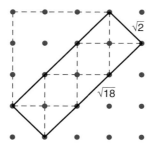

Figure 6.53

In the preceding example we saw that $\sqrt{18} \times \sqrt{2} = 6$. But since $6 = \sqrt{36} = \sqrt{18 \times 2}$, we see that $\sqrt{18} \times \sqrt{2} = \sqrt{18 \times 2}$. This suggests that *the product of the square roots of two numbers is equal to the square root of the product of the two numbers.* This result is stated in the following theorem.

For any positive numbers **a** and **b,**

$$\sqrt{a} \times \sqrt{b} = \sqrt{a \times b}$$

Example K

Compute each product and determine if it is rational or irrational.

1. $\sqrt{8} \times \sqrt{6}$ 2. $\sqrt{12} \times \sqrt{3}$ 3. $\sqrt{5} \times \sqrt{20}$ 4. $\sqrt{6} \times \sqrt{10}$

Solution   1. $\sqrt{48}$, irrational   2. $\sqrt{36} = 6$, rational   3. $\sqrt{100} = 10$, rational   4. $\sqrt{60}$, irrational

In addition to allowing us to compute the products of square roots, the preceding theorem is useful for simplifying square roots. For example, $\sqrt{18} = \sqrt{9 \times 2} = \sqrt{9} \times \sqrt{2} = 3\sqrt{2}$. A square root is in **simplified form** if the number under the radical sign has no factor other than 1 that is a square number.

Example L

Write each square root in simplified form.

1. $\sqrt{50}$ 2. $\sqrt{54}$ 3. $\sqrt{80}$

Solution   1. $\sqrt{50} = \sqrt{25 \times 2} = \sqrt{25} \times \sqrt{2} = 5\sqrt{2}$ 2. $\sqrt{54} = \sqrt{9 \times 6} = \sqrt{9} \times \sqrt{6} = 3\sqrt{6}$
3. $\sqrt{80} = \sqrt{16 \times 5} = \sqrt{16} \times \sqrt{5} = 4\sqrt{5}$

Quotients of real numbers, such as $2 \div \sqrt{3}$, are often written as fractions, such as $\frac{2}{\sqrt{3}}$. When the denominator of a fraction contains a square root, cube root, etc., it is sometimes necessary to find an equal fraction that has a rational number for its denominator. The process of replacing a denominator that is irrational by a denominator that is rational is called **rationalizing the denominator.** The denominator of $\frac{2}{\sqrt{3}}$ can be rationalized by using the fundamental rule for equality of fractions to multiply the numerator and denominator by $\sqrt{3}$.

$$\frac{2}{\sqrt{3}} = \frac{2 \times \sqrt{3}}{\sqrt{3} \times \sqrt{3}} = \frac{2\sqrt{3}}{3}$$

Example M

Rationalize the denominator of each fraction.

1. $\dfrac{1}{\sqrt{2}}$ 2. $\dfrac{^-6}{\sqrt{5}}$ 3. $\dfrac{7}{\sqrt{7}}$

Solution   1. $\dfrac{1}{\sqrt{2}} = \dfrac{1 \times \sqrt{2}}{\sqrt{2} \times \sqrt{2}} = \dfrac{\sqrt{2}}{2}$ 2. $\dfrac{^-6}{\sqrt{5}} = \dfrac{^-6 \times \sqrt{5}}{\sqrt{5} \times \sqrt{5}} = \dfrac{^-6\sqrt{5}}{5}$

3. $\dfrac{7}{\sqrt{7}} = \dfrac{7 \times \sqrt{7}}{\sqrt{7} \times \sqrt{7}} = \dfrac{7\sqrt{7}}{7} = \sqrt{7}$

Problem-Solving Application

To solve the following problem, we use the Pythagorean theorem and the fact that the length of the sides of a square is the square root of its area. Try to solve this problem before you read the solution. You may find the strategies of *making a table* and *finding a pattern* to be useful in obtaining the solution.

PROBLEM

The inner square in the following sketch was obtained by connecting the midpoints of the sides of the outer square. If this process of forming smaller inner squares by connecting the midpoints of the sides of the preceding square is continued, what will be the dimensions of the ninth square?

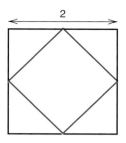

Understanding the Problem   The outer square is 2 units by 2 units and has an area of 4. The second square is contained inside the first square and is smaller. **Question 1:** What is the length of the side of the second square, and what is the area of this square?

Devising a Plan   One approach to solving the problem is to *form a table* listing the lengths of the sides and the areas of the first few squares. The second square has sides of length $\sqrt{2}$ and an area of 2 (see the figure below). **Question 2:** What is the length of the side of the third square, and what is its area?

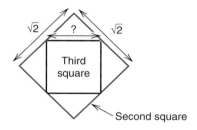

Carrying Out the Plan   The following table lists the lengths of the sides and areas of the first four squares. Find a pattern and predict the area of the ninth square. **Question 3:** What is the length of the side of the ninth square?

	SQUARE 1	SQUARE 2	SQUARE 3	SQUARE 4	SQUARE 5	SQUARE 6
Length of side	2 by 2	$\sqrt{2}$ by $\sqrt{2}$	1 by 1	$\dfrac{1}{\sqrt{2}}$ by $\dfrac{1}{\sqrt{2}}$		
Area	4	2	1	$\dfrac{1}{2}$		

Looking Back   You may have noticed that the area of each square is one-half the area of the preceding square. Based on this pattern, the area of the ninth square is $\frac{1}{64}$. Thus the length of the side of the ninth square is $\sqrt{\frac{1}{64}} = \frac{1}{8}$. The fact that the area of each succeeding square decreases by one-half is suggested by the following figure. **Question 4:** How can the dashed lines be used to show that the inner square has one-half the area of the outer square?

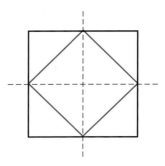

Answers to Questions 1–4   1. The length h of the side of the second square is the hypotenuse of a triangle whose sides have length 1. The length of the hypotenuse is $\sqrt{2}$, and the area of the second square is $\sqrt{2} \times \sqrt{2} = 2$.

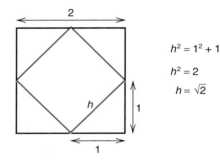

$$h^2 = 1^2 + 1^2$$
$$h^2 = 2$$
$$h = \sqrt{2}$$

2. The length k of the sides of the third square is the hypotenuse of a triangle whose sides have length $\frac{\sqrt{2}}{2}$. The length of the hypotenuse is 1, and the area of the third square is 1.   **3.** The area of the ninth square is $\frac{1}{64}$, and the length of its side is $\sqrt{\frac{1}{64}} = \frac{1}{8}$.   **4.** The outer square region is formed by eight triangular regions of equal size, and the inner square region is formed by four of these triangular regions.

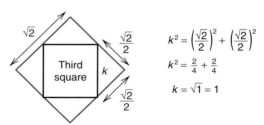

$$k^2 = \left(\frac{\sqrt{2}}{2}\right)^2 + \left(\frac{\sqrt{2}}{2}\right)^2$$
$$k^2 = \frac{2}{4} + \frac{2}{4}$$
$$k = \sqrt{1} = 1$$

EXERCISES AND PROBLEMS 6.4

There once was a student named Lew,
Who computed the square root of 2.
    When no pattern repeated
    He gave up defeated,
Two million digits is all he would do.

$\sqrt{2}=$ 1.41421356241933916628197598
87130795986834890650961931897
43242352661427981910045554661
66704325437650546094505594570
28253271931476474128854 6 · · ·

Determine which of the numbers in exercises 1 and 2 are irrational.

1. a. $\sqrt{49}$ **b.** .131131113 · · ·
    c. .113113113 · · ·   **d.** $\sqrt{14}$

2. a. $\sqrt{50}$ **b.** $6.404004000\cdots$
c. $2\sqrt{25}$ **d.** 151551555

Use the Pythagorean theorem to find the missing length for each of the right triangles in exercises 3 and 4. Write both the exact answer and the decimal approximation to one decimal place.

3. a. **b.**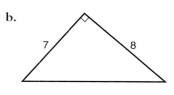

4. a. **b.**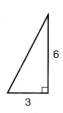

Find the indicated root of each number in exercises 5 and 6.

5. a. $\sqrt{\frac{1}{16}}$ **b.** $\sqrt[3]{64}$ **c.** $\sqrt{9.61}$ **d.** $\sqrt[3]{-125}$

6. a. $\sqrt[3]{8000}$ **b.** $\sqrt{625}$ **c.** $\sqrt[3]{\frac{8}{27}}$ **d.** $\sqrt[3]{-64}$

Classify each number in exercises 7 and 8 as rational or irrational. If it is rational, find its root; if it is irrational, find an approximation to the nearest tenth.

7. a. $\sqrt{18}$ **b.** $\sqrt[3]{216}$ **c.** $\sqrt{\frac{1}{9}}$

8. a. $\sqrt[3]{30}$ **b.** $\sqrt{80}$ **c.** $\sqrt{121}$

Write each number in exercises 9 and 10 as a decimal to the nearest tenth, and mark its approximate location on a number line.

9. a. $\sqrt{7}$ **b.** $\sqrt[3]{30}$ **c.** $\sqrt{3}$

10. a. $\sqrt{15}$ **b.** $\sqrt{8}$ **c.** $\sqrt[3]{3.5}$

Any three whole numbers a, b, and c such that $a^2 + b^2 = c^2$ are called **Pythagorean triples.** We can find such numbers by substituting whole numbers for u and v in the following equations:

$$a = 2uv \qquad b = u^2 - v^2 \qquad c = u^2 + v^2$$

Determine the Pythagorean triple for the values of u and v in exercises 11 and 12. Check your answers by showing that $a^2 + b^2 = c^2$.

11. a. $u = 2, v = 1$
b. $u = 3, v = 2$
c. $u = 6, v = 5$

12. a. $u = 4, v = 3$
b. $u = 4, v = 2$
c. $u = 5, v = 3$

13. Form a table like the one shown below, and put checks in the appropriate columns to indicate the relevant set membership(s) for each number at the left. For example, $^-3$ is an integer, a rational number, and a real number.

	WHOLE NUMBERS	INTEGERS	RATIONAL NUMBERS	REAL NUMBERS
$^-3$		✔	✔	✔
$\frac{1}{8}$				
$\sqrt{3}$				
π				
14				
$\frac{1.6}{4}$				
$.82$				

14. Form a table like the one in exercise 13, and write the following numbers in the leftmost column. Then put checks in the columns for each number to indicate relevant set membership(s). For example, see the checkmarks for $^-3$ in exercise 13.

$$\frac{^-1}{2} \quad \frac{1}{1.2} \quad \sqrt{1000} \quad .42\overline{7} \quad \sqrt{24} \quad 365 \quad \frac{17}{6}$$

Which of the sets in exercises 15 and 16 are closed with respect to the given operations? If a set is not closed under a given operation, provide an example to show this.

15. a. The set of whole numbers under subtraction
b. The set of nonzero rational numbers under division

16. a. The set of irrational numbers under multiplication
b. The set of integers under addition

State the property of the real numbers that is being used in each equality in exercises 17 and 18.

17. a. $\sqrt{3} \times \sqrt{6} = \sqrt{6} \times \sqrt{3}$
b. $(3 + \sqrt{2}) \times \sqrt{7} = 3\sqrt{7} + \sqrt{2} \times \sqrt{7}$
c. $(4 + \sqrt{8}) + 2\sqrt{5} = 2\sqrt{5} + (4 + \sqrt{8})$

18. a. $^-\sqrt{10} + (\sqrt{10} + 6) = (^-\sqrt{10} + \sqrt{10}) + 6$
b. $\sqrt{3} \times \left(\frac{1}{\sqrt{3}} \times \sqrt{3}\right) = \sqrt{3} \times 1$
c. $^-18 + (\sqrt{12} + {}^-\sqrt{12}) + 471 = {}^-18 + 0 + 471$

Classify each sum or product in exercises 19 and 20 as rational or irrational. If the expression is rational, evaluate it.

19. a. $\sqrt{2} \times \sqrt{20}$ **b.** $10 + \sqrt{8}$ **c.** $\sqrt{6} \times \sqrt{24}$

20. a. $4\sqrt{15}$ **b.** $\sqrt{25} + 11$ **c.** $\sqrt{7} \times \sqrt{28}$

Simplify the square roots in exercises 21 and 22 so that the smallest possible whole number is left under the square root symbol.

21. a. $\sqrt{45}$ **b.** $\sqrt{48}$ **c.** $\sqrt{60}$

22. a. $\sqrt{150}$ **b.** $\sqrt{1000}$ **c.** $\sqrt{288}$

Determine whether the equations in exercises 23 and 24 are true or false for positive numbers a and b; and if an equation is false, show a counterexample.

23. a. $\sqrt{a} \times \sqrt{b} = \sqrt{ab}$
  b. $\sqrt{a} - \sqrt{b} = \sqrt{a - b}$

24. a. $\sqrt{a} + \sqrt{b} = \sqrt{a + b}$
  b. $\sqrt{a} / \sqrt{b} = \sqrt{a/b}$

Rationalize the denominator of each fraction in exercises 25 and 26.

25. a. $\dfrac{4}{\sqrt{7}}$ **b.** $\dfrac{3}{2\sqrt{6}}$

26. a. $\dfrac{5}{\sqrt{5}}$ **b.** $\dfrac{^{-}1}{\sqrt{2}}$

Suppose a calculator determines square roots when a number is entered and $\boxed{\sqrt{x}}$ is pressed. Write the number in exercises 27 and 28 that is displayed for step 4. If you continue to press the square root key in these examples, eventually you will see the same number in every view screen. What is this number?

27.   KEYSTROKES   VIEW SCREEN

1. Enter 2 $\boxed{2}$

2. $\boxed{\sqrt{x}}$ $\boxed{1.4142136}$

3. $\boxed{\sqrt{x}}$ $\boxed{1.1892071}$

4. $\boxed{\sqrt{x}}$ $\boxed{}$

28.   KEYSTROKES   VIEW SCREEN

1. Enter .5 $\boxed{.5}$

2. $\boxed{\sqrt{x}}$ $\boxed{.70710678}$

3. $\boxed{\sqrt{x}}$ $\boxed{.84089642}$

4. $\boxed{\sqrt{x}}$ $\boxed{}$

If you use a calculator with a square root key, what number will eventually show in the view screen if you enter the types of numbers in exercises 29 and 30 and repeatedly press this key?

29. Enter a positive number less than 1.

30. Enter a positive number greater than 1.

A calculator with the key $\boxed{y^x}$ (or $\boxed{\wedge}$) for raising numbers to powers is used in exercises 31 and 32 to evaluate the roots of numbers. Write each root which is being evaluated in the form $\sqrt[x]{y}$, and determine the number which will be displayed in a view screen with eight places for digits.

31. a. $81 \boxed{y^x} .25 \boxed{=}$
  b. $2.25 \boxed{y^x} (1 \div 2) \boxed{=}$
  c. $3.0625 \boxed{y^x} .5 \boxed{=}$
  d. $^{-}2.197 \boxed{y^x} (1 \div 3) \boxed{=}$

32. a. $2116 \boxed{y^x} .5 \boxed{=}$
  b. $2744 \boxed{y^x} (1 \div 3) \boxed{=}$
  c. $10.5625 \boxed{y^x} (1 \div 2) \boxed{=}$
  d. $^{-}4.096 \boxed{y^x} (1 \div 3) \boxed{=}$

REASONING AND PROBLEM SOLVING

33. Each day Ed walks past a rectangular athletic field on his way home from school. If the field is being used, Ed walks along two sides of the field. If the field is not being used, he cuts across from corner to corner. If he takes 300 steps along one edge of the field and 500 steps along the other edge, approximately how many steps can Ed save by walking from corner to corner?

34. In a game for three students, one opens a book and multiplies the numbers of the facing pages. This student states the product, and the other two students race to see who can determine the page numbers. What page numbers yield the product 18,090?

35. A school's basketball hoop is mounted on a pipe that is cemented into the ground. The hoop is 10 feet above the ground. To stop it from swaying, some students put a brace from behind the hoop to a point on the ground that is 8 feet from the cement base. What is the length of the brace from the hoop to the ground (to the nearest foot)?

36. The infield of a baseball field is a 90×90 foot
square. The pitching mound is 60.5 feet from home-
plate. How far is the mound from second base (to
the nearest foot)?

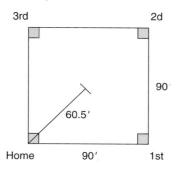

37. A home plate for a baseball field can be formed by
making two 12-inch cuts from a square region, as
shown in the following figure. What are the dimensions of the original square, to the nearest tenth of
an inch?

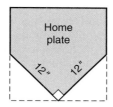

38. A 30-foot ladder is leaning against a house, with the
foot of the ladder 8 feet from the house. If the foot
of the ladder is pulled 7 more feet from the house,
how far down the side of the house will the ladder
move (to the nearest foot)?

39. The time it takes a satellite to orbit the earth depends on its apogee and perigee. The **apogee** A of a
satellite is its greatest distance from the center of
the earth and the **perigee** P is its smallest distance.
The formula for the time in hours T required for
one orbit is

$$T = \frac{(A + P)\sqrt{A + P}}{501,186}$$

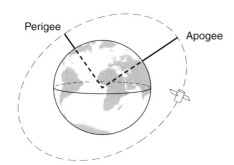

a. Suppose a satellite orbiting the earth has an
apogee of 4300 miles and a perigee of 4100
miles. How long does it take to complete one orbit (to the nearest tenth of an hour)?

b. Satellites are often placed in circular orbits with
apogees and perigees of approximately 26,300
miles. Why is this distance chosen?

40. **Featured Strategy: Making a Drawing**   Suppose a
1-mile-long metal bridge that was not built to allow
for expansion nevertheless expands 2 feet and
buckles upward at the center. How high will the
center be pushed up?

a. **Understanding the Problem**   The first step in
understanding the problem is to *make a drawing*. The distance along the line from A to B represents the bridge and the curve represents the
expanded bridge. Since there is 5280 feet in a
mile, what is the distance along the curve from A
to B?

b. **Devising a Plan**   Let's approximate the shape of
the buckled bridge by two right triangles, as
shown in the next figure. The length from C to B
is $5280 \div 2 = 2640$. Explain why the length from
D to B is approximately 2641 feet.

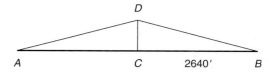

c. **Carrying Out the Plan**   What is the distance
from C to D?

d. **Looking Back**   If the bridge had been 2 miles
long and had expanded 2 feet, how high would
the bridge have buckled?

41. For over 2000 years, architects and artists have
been fond of using a rectangle called the *golden rectangle*. The length of a golden rectangle divided by
its width is an irrational number that, when
rounded to six decimal places, is 1.618033. This irrational number is called the *golden ratio*.

Golden rectangle

Fibonacci numbers are related to the golden ratio. The first 10 Fibonacci numbers are listed here.

1   1   2   3   5   8   13   21   34   55

a. Compute the ratios formed by dividing each Fibonacci number by the previous Fibonacci number.

b. Extend the sequence and find two consecutive Fibonacci numbers whose ratio to four decimal places equals the golden ratio to four decimal places.

42. The spiral of right triangles shown here somewhat resembles a cross section of the seashell of the chambered nautilus. It represents the square roots of consecutive whole numbers. The first triangle has two legs of unit length and a hypotenuse of $\sqrt{2}$. This hypotenuse becomes a leg of the next triangle, which has a hypotenuse of $\sqrt{3}$. Each triangle uses the hypotenuse of the preceding triangle as a leg.

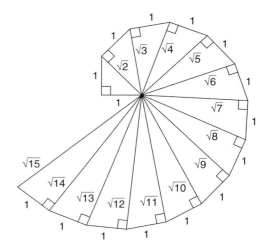

a. Copy the rectangular grid from the inside cover of the book or from the website. Identify two grid lines to be horizontal and vertical axes, respectively. For each whole number n on the horizontal axis of the grid, plot a point approximately $\sqrt{n}$ units above the axis.

b. Connect the points on the grid. Use the graph to approximate $\sqrt{7.5}$. Could this graph be used to approximate the square root of any number greater than 1 and less than 12?

....

ONLINE LEARNING CENTER   www.mhhe.com/bennett-nelson

• Math Investigation 6.4   *Pythagorean Theorem*
Section-Related: • Links   • Writing/Discussion Problems   • Bibliography

....

PUZZLER

A moat filled with crocodiles surrounds an old abandoned castle. The outer and inner edges of the moat form two squares with the same center. The width of the moat is 20 feet. How can a person with no objects other than two 19-foot planks cross the moat to the castle?

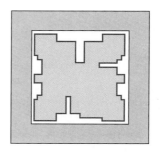

CHAPTER REVIEW

1. **Decimals**
   a. The word *decimal* comes from the Latin *decem,* meaning 10.
   b. The number of digits to the right of the decimal point is called the **number of decimal places.**
   c. The **place values** to the right of the decimal point are decreasing powers of 10.
   d. **Decimal Squares** and **number lines** are visual models for decimals.
   e. An **inequality** for decimals less than 1 can be determined by comparing their tenths digits. If these are equal, compare their hundredths digits, etc.

2. **Rational numbers**
   a. Any number that can be written in the form a/b, where $b \neq 0$ and a and b are integers, is called a **rational number.**
   b. Every rational number can be represented as either a **terminating** or a **repeating decimal.**
   c. Every terminating or repeating decimal can be written as a rational number in the form a/b.
   d. A rational number a/b in lowest terms can be written as a terminating decimal if and only if b has only 2s or 5s in its prime factorization.
   e. The block of repeating digits in a repeating decimal is called the **repetend.**
   f. The rational numbers are **dense.** That is, between any two such numbers there is always another rational number.
   g. The operations of addition and multiplication on the set of rational numbers satisfy the 11 **number properties** stated in Section 6.2.

3. **Operations with decimals**
   a. **Decimal Squares** provide a visual model for decimal operations and can be used to show the similarity between these operations and the operations on whole numbers.
   b. The **pencil-and-paper algorithms** for decimals can be illustrated by computing with fractions.
   c. To compute the product of a decimal and a positive power of 10, move the decimal point one place to the right for each factor of 10.
   d. To divide a decimal by a positive power of 10, move the decimal point one place to the left for each power of 10.

4. **Mental calculations**
   a. Products and quotients of decimals can be calculated mentally by computing with whole numbers and then locating decimal points.

   b. **Compatible numbers** is the technique of using pairs of numbers that are especially convenient for mental calculation. In computing with decimals it is sometimes convenient to use equivalent fractions in place of the decimals.
   c. **Substitution** is the technique of replacing a decimal or a percent by a sum or difference of two decimals or percents.
   d. **Add-up** is the technique of obtaining the difference of two decimals by adding up from the smaller to the larger decimal.

5. **Estimation**
   a. **Compatible numbers** is the technique of computing estimations by replacing one or more numbers with approximate compatible numbers.
   b. **Rounding** is the technique of replacing one or both numbers in a computation with approximate numbers.
   c. **Front-end estimation** is the technique of using the leading nonzero digit to obtain a rough estimation.

6. **Ratio and percent**
   a. For any two positive numbers a and b, the **ratio** of a to b ($a{:}b$) is the fraction a/b.
   b. For two equal ratios a/b and c/d, $a/b = c/d$ is called a **proportion.**
   c. The word *percent* is from the Latin *per centum,* meaning *out of 100.*
   d. There are three types of computations involving percents: computations using **whole and percent,** computations using **part and whole,** and computations using **percent and part.**

7. **Scientific notation**
   a. The method of writing a number as a product of a number from 1 to 10 and a power of 10 is called **scientific notation.**
   b. When a number is written in scientific notation, the part from 1 to 10 is called the **mantissa** and the exponent of 10 is called the **characteristic.**

8. **Real numbers**
   a. An infinite nonrepeating decimal is called an **irrational number.**
   b. The **principal square root** of a positive number b is denoted by $\sqrt{b}$ and is defined to be the positive number that, when multiplied by itself, yields b.
   c. For any positive number b and any positive whole number n, $\sqrt[n]{b}$ is called the **nth root** of b and defined by $(\sqrt[n]{b})^n = b$.

d. The rational numbers together with the irrational numbers form the set of **real numbers.**

e. In addition to the eleven **number properties** stated for the rational numbers, the real numbers have the property of **completeness:** all line segments can be measured with real numbers.

f. The sum or product of a nonzero rational number and an irrational number is an irrational number.

g. For any positive numbers a and b, $\sqrt{a} \times \sqrt{b} = \sqrt{a \times b}$.

h. The process of replacing a denominator that is irrational by a denominator that is rational is called **rationalizing the denominator.**

CHAPTER TEST

1. Describe Decimal Squares to explain each of the following:
   a. $.4 > .27$ **b.** $.7 = .70$
   c. $.225 < .35$ **d.** $.09 < .1$

2. Write each fraction as a decimal.
   a. $\frac{3}{4}$ **b.** $\frac{7}{100}$ **c.** $\frac{2}{3}$
   d. $\frac{7}{8}$ **e.** $\frac{4}{9}$ **f.** $\frac{6}{25}$

3. Write each decimal as a fraction.
   a. $.278$ **b** $.\overline{35}$ **c.** $.03$ **d.** $.7\overline{326}$

4. Round each decimal to the given place value.
   a. $.878$ (hundredths)   **b.** $.449$ (tenths)
   c. $.5096$ (thousandths)   **d.** $.\overline{6}$ (ten thousandths)

5. Perform each operation and describe Decimal Squares to illustrate each answer.
   a. $.7 + .6 =$ **b.** $3 \times .4 =$
   c. $.62 - .48 =$ **d.** $.80 \div .05 =$

6. Perform the following operations.
   a. $.006 + .38 - .2$ **b.** $.62 \times .08$
   c. $.14763 \div .21$ **d.** $47 + .8 \times 340$

7. Calculate each answer mentally and explain your method.
   a. $100 \times .073$ **b.** $7 \times .6$
   c. $4.9 \div 1000$ **d.** $.01 \times 372$
   e. 15 percent of 260   **f.** 25 percent of 36

8. Estimate each answer by replacing the decimal or percent by a compatible fraction. Show your replacement.
   a. $.49 \times 310$ **b.** $.24 \times 416$
   c. 33 percent of 60   **d.** 76 percent of 40

9. Determine each answer to the nearest tenth.
   a. What is 36 percent of 46?
   b. 30 is what percentage of 80?
   c. 15 is 24 percent of what number?
   d. What is 118 percent of 125?
   e. 322 is what percentage of 230?

10. Write each number in scientific notation.
    a. 437.8 **b.** $.000106$

11. Classify each number as rational or irrational.
    a. $\sqrt{60}$ **b.** $\sqrt[3]{27}$ **c.** $6\sqrt{8}$
    d. $\sqrt{10} + 5$ **e.** $\sqrt{\frac{1}{4}}$ **f.** $\sqrt[3]{60}$

12. Approximate each number below to one decimal place.
    a. $\sqrt{34}$ **b.** $\sqrt[3]{18}$

13. Determine whether each set is closed or not closed with respect to the given operation, and give a reason or show a counterexample.
    a. The set of rational numbers under addition
    b. The set of irrational numbers under multiplication
    c. The set of irrational numbers under addition

14. Simplify each square root.
    a. $\sqrt{405}$ **b.** $\sqrt{24}$

15. Find the missing length for each triangle.

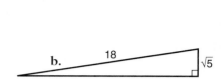

16. Jon paid $187 for a coat that was on sale at 15 percent off. What was the original price of the coat?

17. A restaurant sells a 20-ounce glass of orange juice for $1.50 and a 16-ounce glass for $1.10. What size glass is the better buy?

18. A rectangular swimming pool has a length of 60 feet and a width of 30 feet. What is the distance from one corner of the pool to the opposite corner, to the nearest one-tenth foot?

19. A fuel company charges monthly finance fees of 1.2 percent for the first $500 due and .8 percent for any amount over $500. What is the monthly finance fee for an account with a balance of $650?

20. If the ratio of private school students to public school students in a city is 3 to 16 and there is a total of 18,601 students, how many students are in public schools?

STATISTICS

SPOTLIGHT ON TEACHING

Excerpts from NCTM's Standards for School Mathematics Prekindergarten through Grade 2*

Methods used by students in different grades to investigate the number of pockets in their clothing provide an example of students' growth in data investigations during the period through grade 2. Younger students might count pockets (Burns 1996). They could survey their classmates and gather data by listing names, asking how many pockets, and noting the number beside each name. Together the class could create one large graph to show the data about all the students by coloring a bar on the graph to represent the number of pockets for each student (see Fig. 4.21). In the second grade, however, students might decide to count the number of classmates who have various numbers of pockets (see Fig. 4.22).

Fig. 4.21
A bar graph illustrating the number of pockets in kindergarten students' clothes

Fig. 4.22
A line plot graph of the number of students in a second-grade class who have from one to ten pockets.

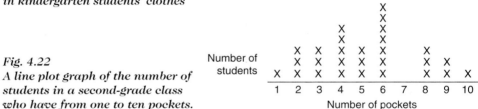

*Principles and Standards for School Mathematics (Reston, VA: National Council of Teachers of Mathematics 2000), pp. 110–111.

MATH ACTIVITY 7.1

AVERAGES WITH COLUMNS OF TILES

Materials: Color tiles in the Manipulative Kit.

When two or more columns of tiles like those at the left are "leveled off" so they have the same height but the number of columns does not change, the common height is called the **average** of the original heights.*

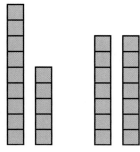

The average of 9 and 5 is 7

* **1.** Use the color tiles to build a column of height 9 and another of height 15. Other than moving one tile at a time, find at least two methods for leveling the tiles so that there are two columns of the same height.

   a. Using the heights of the columns, 9 and 15, and the operations of arithmetic, express each of your leveling-off methods with a number expression.

   b. Using the results from part a, write two rules for determining the average of two whole numbers x and y, where x is greater than or equal to y.

   c. Express your two rules in part b as algebraic expressions and show these expressions are equal.

2. Use the color tiles to solve each of the following problems. Draw a diagram and explain your reasoning.

   a. The average height of two columns is 10 and the difference of their heights is 3 times the height of the smaller. What are their heights?

   b. There are a total of 16 tiles in two columns and one of the columns is $1\frac{2}{3}$ times the height of the other. What is the height of each column?

3. The six columns at the right represent the average score for a student on six 20-point quizzes. The average is 14, but to obtain a satisfactory grade, an average of 15 is needed. The teacher gives two options to raise the average: (1) Throw out the lowest quiz score and base the average on the five remaining quiz scores or (2) take a seventh 25-point quiz to raise the average. Which of these options should the students choose if the lowest score on the six quizzes was 10 points?

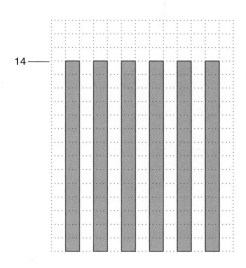

14 —

*A. B. Bennett, E. Maier, and L. T. Nelson, "Visualizing Number Concepts," *Math and the Mind's Eye* (Salem, OR: Math Learning Center, 1988).

SECTION 7.1

COLLECTING AND GRAPHING DATA

Statistics had its beginning in the seventeenth century in the work of Englishman John Graunt. Graunt used a publication called *Bills of Mortality,* which listed births, christenings, and deaths. Here are some of his conclusions: The number of male births exceeds the number of female births; there is a higher death rate in urban areas than in rural areas; and more men than women die violent deaths. Graunt used these statistics in his book *Natural and Political Observations of Mortality.* In his work he summarized great amounts of information to make it understandable (descriptive statistics) and made conjectures about large populations based on small samples (inferential statistics).

PROBLEM OPENER

Two line plots are shown below with each x representing a fourth-grade student. One line plot shows the number of students having a given number of cavities, and the other shows the number of students having a given number of people in their families. Which plot contains the data on cavities?*

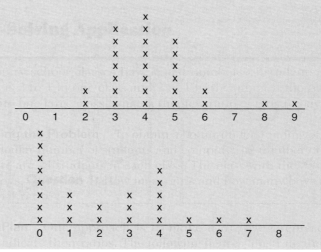

Graphs provide quick visual summaries of information and methods of making predictions. Some of the more common graphs are introduced in this section.

*J. Zawojewski, "Polishing a Data Task: Seeking Better Assessment," *Teaching Children Mathematics* 2 (February, 1996): 372–378.

Bar Graphs

The table in Figure 7.1 lists the responses of 40 teachers to a proposal to begin and end the school day one-half hour earlier. Teachers' responses are classified into one of three categories: favor (F); oppose (O); or no opinion (N).

By the end of the second grade, students should be able to organize and display their data through both graphical displays and numerical summaries. They should use counts, tallies, tables, bar graphs, and line plots

Standards, 2000, p. 109

TEACHER	CATEGORY	TEACHER	CATEGORY	TEACHER	CATEGORY
1	F	14	F	27	N
2	F	15	O	28	O
3	O	16	F	29	F
4	N	17	N	30	O
5	F	18	O	31	F
6	O	19	F	32	F
7	O	20	N	33	N
8	F	21	F	34	F
9	F	22	F	35	O
10	F	23	O	36	F
11	O	24	F	37	N
12	O	25	N	38	F
13	N	26	O	39	O
				40	O

Figure 7.1

Research Statement

Fourth-grade students were successful at literal reading of bar graphs (over 95% success rate), they were less successful at interpreting (52% success rate) and predicting (less than 20% success rate).

Pereira-Mendoza and Mellor 1991

The data from the preceding table are summarized by the **bar graph** in Figure 7.2. The intervals on the horizontal axis represent the three categories, and the vertical axis indicates the number of teachers for each category. Compare the graph to the table and notice that this graph provides a quick summary of the data.

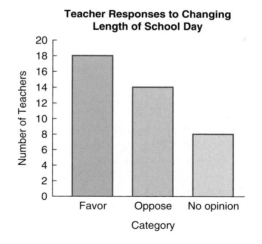

Figure 7.2

Some types of bar graph have two bars for each category and are called a **double-bar graph,** while others have three bars for each category and are called a **triple-bar graph.** Figure 7.3 is a triple-bar graph which has four categories of age groups and compares the percentages of black children, Hispanic children, and white children who have not seen a physician in the past year.*

*U.S. Department of Health and Human Services, *Child Health USA 1998* (Washington, DC: U.S. Government Printing Office, 1998), p. 53.

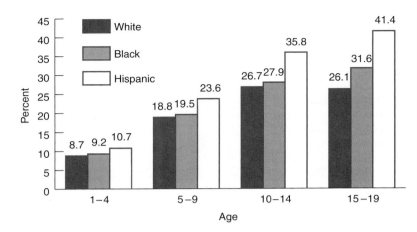

Percentage of Children with No Physician Visit in Past Year

Figure 7.3

Example **A**

Use the information in the graph in Figure 7.3.

1. What is the difference between the percentage of Hispanic children and the percentage of white children aged 15 to 19 who have not seen a physician in the past year?

2. What percentage of black children aged 10 to 14 years visited a physician in the past year?

3. Was there a greater difference in the percentages of black children and white children who did not visit a physician during the past year in the age group of 5 to 9 or the age group of 10 to 14?

Solution   1. 15.3 percent   2. 72.1 percent   3. Age group of 10 to 14

Pie Graphs

A **pie graph** (circle graph) is another way to summarize data visually. A disk (pie) is used to represent the whole, and its pie-shaped sectors represent the parts in proportion to the whole. Consider, for example, the data from Figure 7.1. A total of 40 responses are classified into three categories: 18 in favor, 14 opposed, and 8 with no opinion. These categories represent $\frac{18}{40}$, $\frac{14}{40}$, and $\frac{8}{40}$ of the total responses, respectively. To determine the central angles for the sectors of a pie graph, we multiply these fractions by 360°.

$$\tfrac{18}{40} \times 360° = 162° \qquad \tfrac{14}{40} \times 360° = 126° \qquad \tfrac{8}{40} \times 360° = 72°$$

The pie graph for this data is constructed by first drawing a circle and making three sectors, using the central angles, as in part a of Figure 7.4. Then each sector is labeled so that the viewer can easily interpret the results, as in part b.

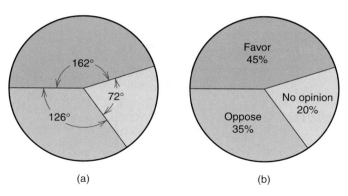

Pie Graph of Teacher Responses to Changing Hours of School Day

Figure 7.4

(a)   (b)

Pictographs

A **pictograph** (see Figure 7.5) is similar to a bar graph. The individual figures or icons that are used each represent the same value. For example, each stick figure in the following pictograph represents 10,000 juveniles (ages 10 to 17).* Notice how easily you can see increases and decreases in the numbers of juveniles for the given years.

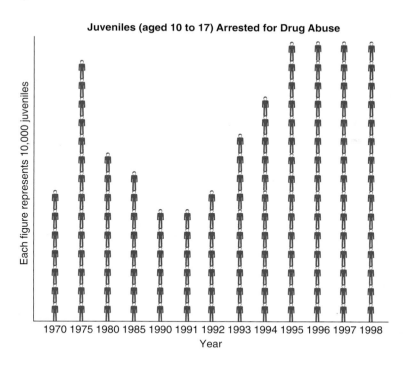

Figure 7.5

_____

Statistical Abstracts of the United States, 120th ed. (Washington, DC: Bureau of the Census, 2000), p. 211.

Objective: Collect, organize, and display data. Make and interpret frequency tables, line plots, and pictographs.

Collect, Organize, and Display Data

Learn

Math Words

data
survey
frequency table
frequency
line plot
gap
cluster
pictograph
key

Do you watch TV on the weekends? On Monday, Carmen asked everyone in her class, "How many hours did you watch TV yesterday?" She recorded their answers in the table.

Carmen collected her data by conducting a survey. **Data** is collected information. A **survey** is a way to gather information by asking questions or observing events. Carmen used a frequency table to organize her data. A **frequency table** shows the number of times each item or number appears. In Carmen's survey, the **frequency** is the number of students who gave each answer.

Hours Spent Watching TV on November 11		
Number of Hours	Tally	Number of Students
0	|||	3
1	||||	4
2	ⅢⅢ |||	8
3	ⅢⅢ	5
4		0
5 or more	|||	3

Example 1

You can organize Carmen's data in a line plot. A **line plot** is a vertical graph that shows data in columns of Xs above a number line.

1

Draw a number line.

Under the number line, write the numbers for the number of hours.

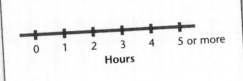

2

Use an X to represent one student. Give the line plot a title.

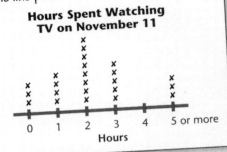

The **gap**, or empty space, at 4 means none of the students in Carmen's class watched TV for 4 hours. The data form a cluster around 2 hours. A **cluster** is data that are close together in value.

Example B

The number of juveniles arrested for drug abuse in each of the years given in Figure 7.5 is rounded to the nearest 10,000.

1. How many fewer juveniles, to the nearest 10,000, were arrested for drug abuse in 1980 than in 1975?

2. To the nearest 10,000, what was the total number of juveniles arrested for drug abuse in 1990 through 1995?

3. Were there more juveniles arrested in the 5-year period from 1990 through 1994 or the 4-year period from 1995 through 1998?

Solution   1. 50,000   **2.** 560,000   **3.** More in the period from 1995 through 1998

Line Plots

The following table shows the countries that won one or more gold medals at the 2000 Summer Olympics in Sydney, Australia. Some information can be spotted quickly from the table, such as determining the countries that won large numbers of gold medals, but details such as comparing the numbers of countries that won one, two, or three gold medals are more time-consuming.

Countries that won at least one gold medal in the 2000 Summer Olympics

Algeria	1	Ethiopia	4	New Zealand	1
Australia	16	Finland	2	Norway	4
Austria	2	France	13	Poland	6
Azerbaijan	2	Germany	14	Romania	11
Bahamas	1	Greece	4	Russia	32
Belarus	3	Hungary	8	Slovakia	1
Britain	11	Indonesia	1	Slovenia	2
Bulgaria	5	Iran	3	South Korea	8
Cameroon	1	Italy	13	Spain	3
Canada	3	Japan	5	Sweden	4
China	28	Kazakhstan	3	Switzerland	1
Columbia	1	Kenya	2	Thailand	1
Croatia	2	Latvia	1	Turkey	3
Cuba	11	Lithuania	2	Ukraine	3
Czech Republic	2	Mexico	1	United States	40
Denmark	2	Mozambique	1	Uzbekistan	1
Estonia	1	Netherlands	12	Yugoslavia	1

To assist in analyzing and viewing the data in the table, a line plot has been drawn in Figure 7.6. A **line plot** is formed by drawing a line, marking categories and recording data by placing a mark such as a dot or an X above the line for each value of the data.

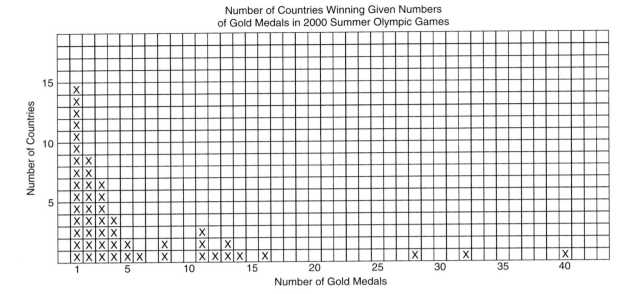

Figure 7.6

A line plot is easy to construct and interpret, and it gives a clear graphical picture of the data. Also certain features of the data become more apparent from a line plot than from a table. Such features include **gaps** (large spaces in the data) and **clusters** (isolated groups of data).

Example C

Use the line plot in Figure 7.6 to answer these questions.

1. There is one large cluster of data for the countries that won six or fewer gold medals. How many countries are represented in this cluster?

2. The largest gap in the data occurs between which two numbers? How large is this gap?

Solution   1. 38   2. Between 16 and 28. The size of the gap is 11.

Stem-and-Leaf Plots

A **stem-and-leaf plot** is a quick numerical method of providing a visual summary of data. As the name indicates, this method suggests the stems of plants and their leaves. Consider the following test scores for a class of 26 students:

82	66	70	77	94	67	73	78	82	74	90	45	62
85	57	72	94	83	85	70	95	71	89	87	75	74

Since the scores in the preceding list range from the 40s to the 90s, the tens digits of 4, 5, 6, 7, 8, and 9 are chosen as the stems, and the unit digits of the numbers will represent the leaves (Figure 7.7). The first step in forming a stem-and-leaf plot is to list the stem values in increasing order in a column (see part a). Next, each leaf value is written in the row corresponding to that number's stem (part b). Here the leaf values have been recorded in the order in which they appear, but they could be listed in increasing order. For example, the leaves for stem 6 can be recorded as 2, 6, 7 rather than 6, 7, 2, as shown in Figure 7.7b. The stem-and-leaf plot shows at a glance the lowest and highest test scores and that the 70s interval has the greatest number of scores.

Stem	Leaf
4	
5	
6	
7	
8	
9	

(a)

Stem	Leaf
4	5
5	7
6	6 7 2
7	0 7 3 8 4 2 0 1 5 4
8	2 2 5 3 5 9 7
9	4 0 4 5

(b)

Figure 7.7

A stem-and-leaf plot shows where the data are concentrated and the extreme values. You may have noticed that this method of portraying data is like a bar graph turned on its side (rotate this page 90° counterclockwise). Although a stem-and-leaf plot is not as attractive as a bar graph, it has the advantage of showing all the original data. Furthermore, unlike a bar graph, it shows any gaps, clusters, or outliers in the data.

A stem-and-leaf plot that compares two sets of data can be created by forming a central stem and plotting the leaves for the first set of data on one side of the stem and the leaves for the second set on the other side (Figure 7.8). This is called a **back-to-back stem-and-leaf plot.** Suppose the same class of students whose test scores are shown on previous page obtains the following scores on a second test:

$$85 \quad 89 \quad 70 \quad 76 \quad 49 \quad 66 \quad 71 \quad 71 \quad 75 \quad 82 \quad 73 \quad 77 \quad 68$$
$$79 \quad 55 \quad 91 \quad 52 \quad 63 \quad 64 \quad 84 \quad 81 \quad 68 \quad 73 \quad 67 \quad 66 \quad 72$$

A stem-and-leaf plot of the scores on both tests is shown in Figure 7.8. In this plot the leaves for both sets of scores have been arranged in order to aid in comparing the test scores. It appears that overall performance was better on the first test. For example, the first test has almost twice as many scores above 80 and one-half as many scores below 70 as the second test.

Second test Leaf	Stem	First test Leaf
9	4	5
5 2	5	7
8 8 7 6 6 4 3	6	2 6 7
9 7 6 5 3 3 2 1 1 0	7	0 0 1 2 3 4 4 5 7 8
9 5 4 2 1	8	2 2 3 5 5 7 9
1	9	0 4 4 5

Figure 7.8

Histograms

When data fall naturally into a few categories, as in Figure 7.1 on page 427, they can be illustrated by bar graphs or pie graphs. However, data are often spread over a wide range with many different values. In this case it is convenient to group the data in intervals.

The following list shows the gestation periods in days for 42 species of animals.

Ass 365	Deer 201	Moose 240
Baboon 187	Dog 61	Mouse 21
Badger 60	Elk 250	Opossum 15
Bat 50	Fox 52	Pig 112
Black bear 219	Giraffe 425	Puma 90
Grizzly bear 225	Goat, domestic 151	Rabbit 37
Polar bear 240	Goat, mountain 184	Rhinoceros 498
Beaver 122	Gorilla 257	Sea lion 350
Buffalo 278	Guinea pig 68	Sheep 154
Camel 406	Horse 330	Squirrel 44
Cat 63	Kangaroo 42	Tiger 105
Chimpanzee 231	Leopard 98	Whale 365
Chipmunk 31	Lion 100	Wolf 63
Cow 284	Monkey 165	Zebra 365

Since there are many different gestation periods, we group them in intervals. The intervals should be nonoverlapping, and their number is arbitrary but usually a number from 5 to 15. One method of determining the length of each interval is to first compute the difference between the highest and lowest values, which is $498 - 15 = 483$. Then select the desired number of intervals and determine the length of the interval. If we select 10 as the number of intervals, then

$$483 \div 10 = 48.3$$

and we may choose 49 (because of its convenience) as the width of each interval. Figure 7.9 lists the number of animals in each interval and is called a **frequency table.**

Frequency table

Interval	0–49	50–99	100–149	150–199	200–249	250–299	300–349	350–399	400–449	450–499
Frequency	6	9	4	5	6	4	1	4	2	1

Figure 7.9

The graph for the grouped data in the frequency table is shown in Figure 7.10. This graph, which is similar to a bar graph, is called a **histogram.** A histogram is made up of adjoining bars which have the same width, and the bars are centered above the midpoints of the intervals or categories. The vertical axis shows the frequency of the data for each interval or category on the horizontal axis. We can see from this histogram that the greatest number of gestation periods occurs in the interval from 50 to 99 days, and there are only a few animals with gestation periods over 400 days.

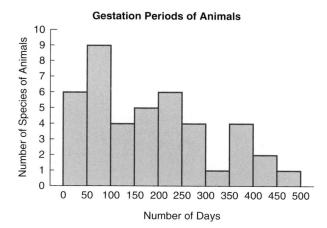

Figure 7.10

Line Graphs

Another method of presenting data visually is the **line graph.** This type of graph is often used to show changes over a period of time. For example, the line graph in Figure 7.11 shows the increase in population from 1800 to 2000 at 20-year intervals.

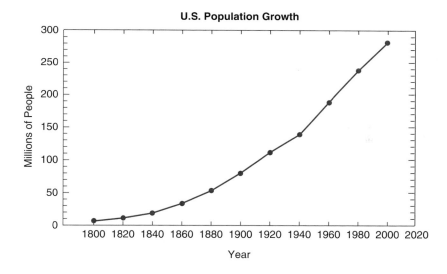

Figure 7.11

Example D

Use the line graph in Figure 7.11 to answer these questions.

1. What was the approximate population increase from 1880 to 1920?

2. Compare the population change for the period from 1800 to 1900 to the population change from 1960 to 2000. Which period had the greater increase in population?

Solution   1. 55 million   2. 1960 to 2000

Scatter Plots

Consider the following table which records the heights and corresponding shoe sizes of 30 fourth-grade to eighth-grade boys. It is difficult to see any patterns or relationships between the heights and shoe sizes from this information.

Height (inches)	59	71	57	72	64	60	64	62	66	63	74	60	67
Shoe size	6.5	11.5	4	10.5	9.5	5	7.5	8.5	9	7	11.5	4.5	8

64	65	62	56	69	61	58	62	63	67	69	64	68	60	58	66	57
6.5	12	6	4.5	9	7	4	5	5.5	10	9	6	10.5	6.5	3.5	8.5	5

The pairs of numbers in the table have been graphed in Figure 7.12, where the first coordinate of each point on the graph is a height and the second coordinate of the point is the corresponding shoe size. Such a graph is called a **scatter plot.** The scatter plot enables us to see if there are any patterns or trends in the data. Although there are boys who have larger shoe sizes than some of the boys who are taller, in general it appears that taller boys have larger shoe sizes.

Students should see a range of examples in which plotting data suggests linear relationships, nonlinear relationships, and no apparent relationship at all. When a scatter plot suggests that a relationship exists, teachers should help students determine the nature of the relationship from the shape and direction of the plot.

Standards 2000, p. 253

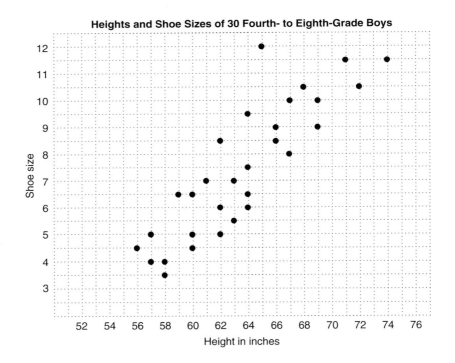

Figure 7.12

TREND LINES   A straight line can be drawn from the lower left to the upper right which approximates the points of the graph in Figure 7.12. Such a line is called a **trend line.** One method of locating a trend line is to place a line so that it approximates the location of the points and there are about the same number of points of the graph above the line as below.

E x a m p l e E

1. Draw a trend line for the scatter plot in Figure 7.12.

2. Use your trend line to predict the shoe size for a boy of height 68 inches and the height of a boy with a shoe size of 8.

Solution   1. While different people may select different locations for a trend line, these lines will be fairly close to the line shown on the scatter plot below.   2. Approximately 9.5; approximately 65 inches.

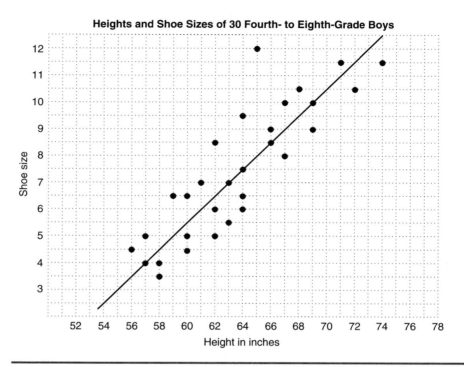

Heights and Shoe Sizes of 30 Fourth- to Eighth-Grade Boys

Some scatter plots, such as the one in Figure 7.13a, may show *no association* between the data. Or, if the trend line goes from lower left to upper right, as for Figure 7.13b, there is a positive association (slope of line is positive), and if the trend line goes from upper left to lower right, as for Figure 7.13c, there is a negative association (slope of line is negative). When data are entered into a graphing calculator or computer, the value of a variable r will be computed which indicates the strength of the association between the data. This number is called a **correlation coefficient** and it varies from $^-1$ to 1 ($^-1 \leq r \leq 1$). If r is close to 0, there is little or no association. If r is close to 1, there is a strong positive association; and if r is close to $^-1$, there is a strong negative association.

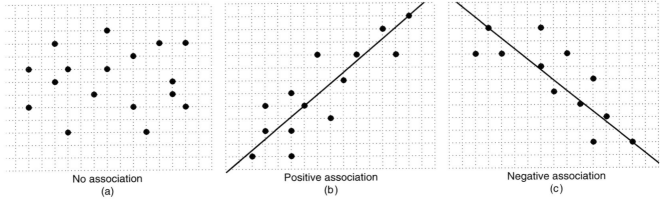

No association
(a)

Positive association
(b)

Negative association
(c)

Figure 7.13

The scatter plot in Example E shows a positive association between the heights of the boys and their shoe sizes: as heights increase, shoe sizes increase. In Example F, there is a negative association between the two types of data.

Example F

The table below contains data on one aspect of child development—the time required to hop a given distance.* The age of each child is rounded to the nearest half-year.

Age (years)	5	5	5.5	5.5	6	6	6.5	7	7	8	8	8.5	8.5	9	9	9.5	10	11
Time (seconds) to hop 50 feet	10.8	10.8	10.5	9.0	8.4	7.5	9.0	7.1	6.7	7.5	6.3	7.5	6.8	6.7	6.3	6.3	4.8	4.4

1. Form a scatter plot of these data. Mark intervals for ages of the horizontal axis and intervals for time on the vertical axis.

2. Locate a trend line.

3. Use your line to predict the time for a $7\frac{1}{2}$-year-old girl to hop 50 feet.

4. The negative (downward) slope of your line shows an association between the age of the girl and the time required to hop 50 feet. Describe this association.

Solution   1. The 2 in the following scatter plot indicates that two children of the same age required the same time to hop 50 feet.   2. The trend line sketched below has 2 points on the line and both 8 points above and below the line.   3. Approximately 8 seconds   4. The older a 5- to 11-year-old girl becomes, the less time is required to hop 50 feet.

Times of 18 Girls to Hop 50 Feet

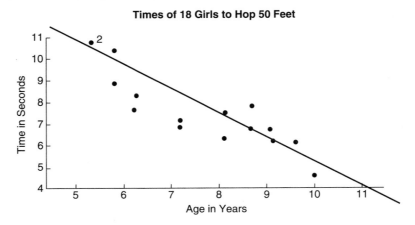

*Adapted from Kenneth S. Holt, *Child Development* (Boston: Butterworth-Heinmann, 1991), p. 143.

Curves of Best Fit

Most graphing calculators and some computer software such as Excel and Minitab have graphing features that include scatter plots and trend lines or curves of best fit. A graphing calculator screen is shown in Figure 7.14 with the scatter plot and trend line for the data in Example F.

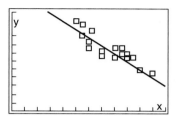

Figure 7.14

If you have a graphing calculator or a computer with suitable software, you may wish to enter the data from some of the preceding examples and obtain the trend lines. The calculator or computer will print the equation of a trend line $y = ax + b$, where a is the slope of the line and b is the y intercept. You may find it interesting to use such equations to obtain new predictions. For example, the equation of the trend line in Figure 7.14 with the slope and y intercept rounded to the nearest hundredth is $y = {}^-.92x + 14.45$. Using this equation with $x = 7.5$, approximately how much time is required for a $7\frac{1}{2}$-year-old girl to hop 50 feet? Calculate this time and compare it to the time of 8 seconds obtained from the trend line in Example F.

Sometimes the *curve of best fit* for a scatter plot is not a straight line. Graphing calculators and some computer software have several types of curves of best fit. The equations for curves and trend lines are called **regression equations**, and such equations are algebraic models for approximating the location of points in a scatter plot. In addition to a straight line, the three types of curves shown in Figure 7.15 are common curves of best fit.

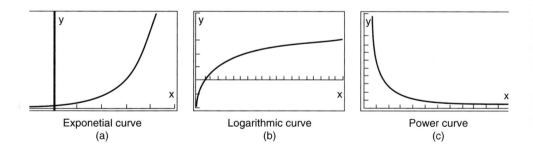

Figure 7.15

A curve of best fit often can be obtained by visualizing a curve that approximates the location of points on a graph, as in the next example.

Example G

The scatter plot shows the earnings of the top 32 women tennis players. Notice the notation which indicates that the earnings for the number 1 player ($652,000) and the number 2 player ($994,000) are off the graph.

1. Which type of curve from Figure 7.15 best fits the points of this graph?

2. Visualize this curve and use it to predict the earnings for the woman tennis player who ranks 35th.

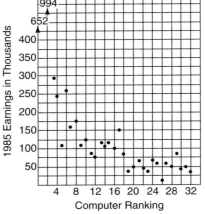

Earnings of Top 32 Women Tennis Players

Solution   1. The power curve   2. Between $20,000 and $40,000

Problem-Solving Application

A strong association between data does not necessarily imply that one type of measurement causes the other. Cigarette consumption and coronary heart disease mortality rates (see the problem-solving application below) are an example of a strong association between data that has generated debate over cause and effect between these measurements.

PROBLEM

The table on the next page lists the number of deaths for each 100,000 people aged 35 to 64 due to coronary heart disease and the average number of cigarettes consumed per adult per year for 21 countries.* Given this information, what is the number of deaths per 100,000 people due to coronary heart disease for the country that consumes 2000 cigarettes per adult per year?

*R. Mulcahy, J. W. McGiluary, and N. Hickey, "Cigarette Smoking Related to Geographic Variations in Coronary Heart Disease Mortality and to Expectation of Life in the Two Sexes," *American Journal of Public Health,* vol. 60, 1970.

Understanding the Problem   The cigarette consumption and mortality rates on the next page are given for 21 countries. The problem requires predicting the mortality rate due to coronary heart disease for a country with a consumption of 2000 cigarettes per adult per year. **Question 1:** Which country in the table has a cigarette consumption that is closest to 2000?

Devising a Plan   One approach is to use the data in the table for West Germany and Finland, the two countries whose cigarette consumption is closest to 2000. **Question 2:** How can the data for these countries be used, and what approximation do you obtain by your method? Another approach is to use a scatter plot of the data in the table and a trend line to make a prediction.

Carrying Out the Plan   The scatter plot and trend line on the next page are for the data in the table. **Question 3:** Given this trend line, what is the coronary heart disease mortality rate for a country that consumes an average of 2000 cigarettes per adult per year?

COUNTRY	CIGARETTE CONSUMPTION PER ADULT PER YEAR	MORTALITY RATE PER 100,000 PEOPLE
Australia	3220	238
Austria	1770	182
Belgium	1700	118
Canada	3350	212
Denmark	1500	145
Finland	2160	233
France	1410	60
Greece	1800	41
Iceland	2770	111
Ireland	2770	187
Italy	1510	114
Mexico	1680	32
Netherlands	1810	125
New Zealand	3220	212
Norway	1090	136
Spain	1200	44
Sweden	1270	127
Switzerland	2780	125
United Kingdom	2790	194
United States	3900	257
West Germany	1890	150

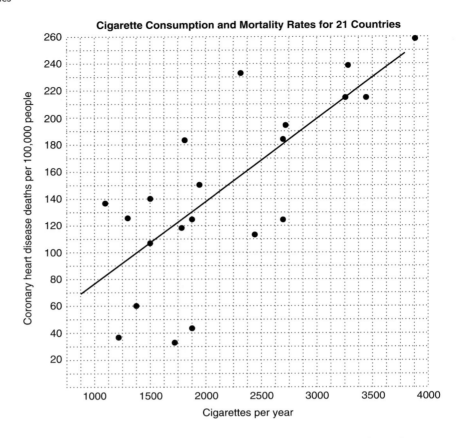

Cigarette Consumption and Mortality Rates for 21 Countries

(Scatter plot: vertical axis "Coronary heart disease deaths per 100,000 people" from 20 to 260; horizontal axis "Cigarettes per year" from 1000 to 4000.)

Looking Back   The trend line also enables predictions regarding the cigarette consumption for a country, if the coronary heart disease mortality rate is known. **Question 4:** What is the average number of cigarettes consumed per adult per year by a given country whose coronary heart disease mortality rate is 240 for every 100,000 people?

Answers to Questions 1–4   **1.** West Germany   **2.** One possibility is 191.5, the mean of 150 and 233. Another possibility is 184, since 2000 is approximately 41 percent of the distance between 1890 and 2160 and 184 is approximately 41 percent of the distance between 150 and 233.   **3.** Approximately 140   **4.** Approximately 3600*

Sometimes the *looking-back* part of solving a problem involves using a different approach. Figure 7.16 shows a computer printout of the scatter plot for the data in the preceding table using the software Minitab.* Notice that the trend line is in about the same position as the one shown in the above scatter plot. The equation for this line, $y = .06x + 15.64$, is printed on the screen by the computer. Using this equation, we can obtain another prediction of the number of coronary heart disease mortalities for a country that consumes an average of 2000 cigaretetes per adult per year:

$$y = .06(2000) + 15.64 = 135.64$$

Note: Entering the data from the table on cigarette consumption into a graphing calculator shows there is a positive correlation with $r \approx .71$ and the equation of the trend line is approximately $y = .06x + 20.4$.
*Minitab Release 11 (State College, Pennsylvania: Minitab Incorporated, 1996).

To the nearest whole number, this is 136 deaths for each 100,000 people. Compare this to the prediction we obtained from drawing the trend line in the preceding scatter plot.

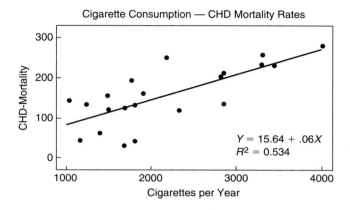

Figure 7.16

SUMMARY   Bar and pie graphs, pictographs, line plots, stem-and-leaf plots, and histograms provide visual descriptions for interpreting data that involve **one variable,** that is, data with one type of measurement. For example, the pictograph in Figure 7.5 records the number of juveniles arrested for drug abuse, and there is one variable—*number of arrests.* Often we wish to compare two or more sets of data that involve one type of measurement (one variable) and double-bar or triple-bar graphs, and back-to-back stem-and-leaf plots are used for this purpose. As examples, in Figure 7.3 a triple-bar graph compares data on three sets of children, and in Figure 7.8 a back-to-back stem-and-leaf plot compares two sets of test scores.

A line graph and a scatter plot, on the other hand, provide a visual description of data that involve **two variables,** that is, data with two different types of measurement. As examples, the line graph in Figure 7.11 plots population for given years and the two variables are *numbers of people* and *years,* and in Figure 7.12 the heights and shoe sizes of boys were graphed on a scatter plot, and the two variables are *height* and *shoe size.*

Usually any one of several graphical methods can be chosen for one-variable sets of data, but there are some general guidelines. Bar graphs, pie graphs, and pictographs are best chosen when there are relatively small numbers of categories, such as 3 to 10. A histogram is often used for grouped data and 10 to 12 is a convenient number of groups. A line plot is used for plotting intermediate numbers of data, such as 25 to 50. Stem-and-leaf plots accommodate a greater number of data, such as 20 to 100. To compare two sets of data with a back-to-back stem-and-leaf plot, there should be approximately the same number of values on both sides of the stem. Line plots and stem-and-leaf plots have an advantage over bar graphs and histograms in showing individual values of data, gaps, clusters, and outliers.

EXERCISES AND PROBLEMS 7.1

"We understand you tore the little tag off your mattress."

The numbers of troops (to the nearest 100,000) in active service in 1997 in the four major branches of the service are as follows: Army, 5; Navy, 4; Air Force, 4; and Marine Corps, 2.* Use this information in exercises 1 and 2.

1. Draw a bar graph for the data.†
   a. The number of people in the Army is how many times the number of people in the Marine Corps?
   b. How many more people are in the Navy than in the Marine Corps?

2. Draw a pie graph for the data.
   a. What is the measure of the central angle for each of the four regions of the pie graph?
   b. What is the total number of people in the four branches of the service?

The following graph shows the average annual prime rate of interest (to the nearest whole percent) charged by banks for each of the years from 1987 to 1999.** Use this graph in exercises 3 and 4.

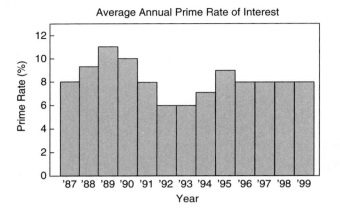

3. a. In which year was the prime rate the highest, and what was the rate?
   b. In which years did the prime rate increase, and how much was the increase?

4. a. In which year was the prime rate the lowest, and what was the rate?
   b. In which years did the prime rate decrease, and how much was the decrease?

5. A family's monthly budget is divided as follows: rent, 32 percent; food, 30 percent; utilities, 15 percent; insurance, 4 percent, medical, 5 percent; entertainment, 8 percent; other, 6 percent.
   a. Draw a pie graph of the data.
   b. What is the measure of the central angle (to the nearest degree) in each of the seven regions of the graph?

The graphs on the next page show the average monthly amounts of precipitation for Kansas City, Missouri, and Portland, Oregon.* Use these graphs in exercises 6 and 7.

*Statistical Abstract of the United States, 120th ed. (Washington, DC: U.S. Department of Defense, 2000), p. 366.
†Copy the rectangular grid from the inside cover of the book or from the website for the bar graphs and histograms on these pages.
**Statistical Abstract of the United States, 118th ed. (Washington, DC: Bureau of the Census, 1998), p. 526.

*Statistical Abstract of the United States, 118th ed. (Washington, DC: Bureau of the Census, 1998), p. 253.

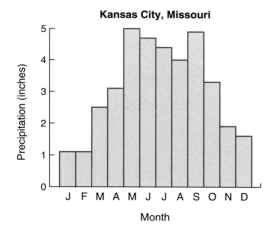

Kansas City, Missouri

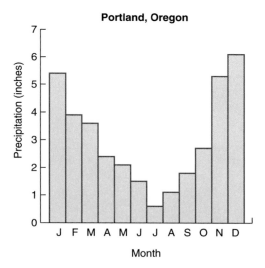

Portland, Oregon

6. a. In Portland, which two months have the greatest amounts of precipitation?
   b. In Kansas City, which month has the least amount of precipitation?

7. a. Compare the amounts of precipitation during the summer months (June, July, and August). Which city has the most precipitation during the summer?
   b. Rounding the amount of precipitaion for each month to the nearest whole number, determine the approximate amount of precipitation for each city for the year.

Sometimes the bars on a graph are placed horizontally rather than vertically. The double-bar graph on the next page compares the percentages of participation of males and females over 7 years of age in the 10 most popular sports activities.* Use this graph in exercises 8 and 9.

*Statistical Abstract of the United States, 120th ed. (Washington, DC: Bureau of the Census, 2000), p. 262.

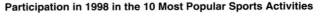

Participation in 1998 in the 10 Most Popular Sports Activities

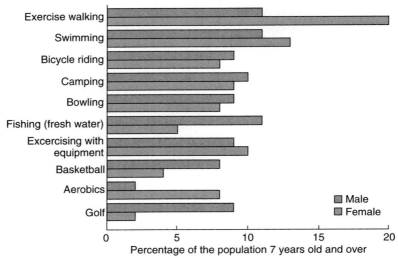

Percentage of the population 7 years old and over

8. **a.** In which sports activities do the females have the greater percentage of participation?
   b. In which sports activities is the percentage of participation by females 4 times the percentage of participation by males?
   c. In which sports activities is the participation by males about 1 percent greater than the participation by females?

9. **a.** In which sports activities do the males have the greater percentage of participation?
   b. In which sports activities is the percentage of participation by males more than 4 times the percentage of participation by females?
   c. In which sports activity is the percentage of participation by females almost twice the percentage of participation by males?

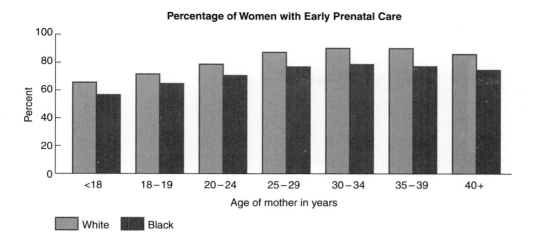

Percentage of Women with Early Prenatal Care

This double-bar graph shows the percentage of women with early prenatal care by age and race for 1998.* Use this information in exercises 10 and 11.

10. a. Which age groups have a difference of over 10 percent between black women with prenatal care and white women with prenatal care?
   b. What percentage of white women of ages 18 to 19 does not have early prenatal care?
   c. The percentage of black women with prenatal care increases for the first few age groups and then decreases. For which age groups was this percentage decreased from the previous age group?

11. a. Which age group has the least difference between the percentage of black women with early prenatal care and the percentage of white women with early prenatal care?
   b. What percentage of the black women aged 18 to 19 does not have early prenatal care?
   c. The percentage of white women with early prenatal care increases for the first few age groups and then decreases. For which age groups was this percentage increased from the previous age group?

The following table shows the percentage of health care coverage for children under 18 years of age and for children in poverty under 18 years of age.† Use this information in exercises 12 and 13.

	CHILDREN UNDER AGE 18	CHILDREN IN POVERTY UNDER AGE 18
No coverage	14.8%	24.0%
Public assistance	24.9%	63.4%
Private insurance	66.3%	18.8%

Note: Percentages add to more than 100 because some individuals receive coverage from more than one source.

12. a. Form a double-bar graph for the following three categories: no coverage, public assistance, and private insurance on the horizontal axis.
   b. What is the difference between the percentage of private insurance for all children under age 18 and the percentage of private insurance for children in poverty under age 18?

13. a. Form a double-bar graph for the following three categories: coverage, no public assistance, and no private insurance on the horizontal axis.
   b. What is the difference between the percentage of no public assistance for children in poverty under 18 years of age and the percentage of no public assistance for all children under age 18?

*U.S. Department of Health and Human Services, *Child Health USA, 1998* (Washington, DC: U.S. Government Printing Office, 1998), p. 58.
†U.S. Department of Health and Human Services, *Child Health USA, 1998* (Washington, DC: U.S. Government Printing Office, 1998), p. 49.

The pie graph below represents the percentages of federal funds spent on programs for the handicapped in public schools. Use this graph in exercises 14 and 15.

(Region *A*, hearing-impaired, 1.3 percent; region *B*, orthopedically handicapped, 1.1 percent; region *C*, other health impaired, 1.3 percent; region *D*, visually handicapped, .7 percent; and region *E*, multihandicapped, 2.2 percent.)

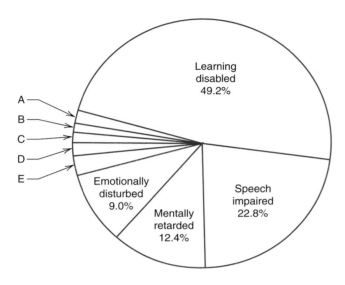

14. a. What was the total percentage spent on the learning-disabled and speech-impaired?
  b. The amount of money spent on programs for the speech-impaired was how many times to the nearest .1 the amount spent on programs for the emotionally disturbed?

15. a. What was the total percentage spent on the hearing-impaired and visually handicapped?
  b. The amount of money spent on programs for the mentally retarded was how many times to the nearest .1 the amount spent on programs for the hearing-impaired?

The following table shows the percentage to the nearest whole number of elementary schools, in the United States in 1997–1998 for various size categories.* Use this table in exercises 16 and 17.

SIZE OF SCHOOL (NO. OF STUDENTS)	PERCENTAGE OF SCHOOLS
Under 100	6
100 to 199	9
200 to 299	12
300 to 399	15
400 to 499	16
500 to 599	14
600 to 699	10
700 to 799	7
800 to 899	3
900 to 999	3
1000 or more	4

16. a. Draw a pie graph of these data. Label the measure to the nearest degree of the central angle for each region of the graph.
  b. What percentage of elementary schools has 500 or more students?

17. a. Draw a bar graph of these data.
  b. What percentage of elementary schools has from 200 to less than 500 students?

18. The number of microcomputers in public schools for student instruction in 1999–2000 is contained in the following table.*

SCHOOL LEVEL	NUMBER OF COMPUTERS
Elementary	4,384,000
Middle/Junior High	1,783,000
Senior High	3,047,000
K–12 other	582,000

  a. Form a pictograph of the data in the table by choosing an icon and selecting the number of computers that the icon represents. Label the categories on the horizontal axis, and select an informative title for the graph.
  b. Discuss the reasons for your choice of value for the icon. In general, what disadvantages result if the value of the icon is too large or too small?

*Statistical Abstract of the United States, 118th ed. (Washington, DC: Bureau of the Census, 1998), p. 172.

*Statistical Abstract of the United States, 120th ed. (Washington, DC: Bureau of the Census, 2000), p. 173.

19. The following table shows the number of people to the nearest 1000 in different age categories who were involved in automobile crashes, as reported by the police in 1998.*

AGE LEVELS	NUMBER OF PEOPLE
16 to 20	13,001,000
21 to 24	12,481,000
25 to 34	37,265,000
35 to 44	41,857,000
45 to 54	33,662,000
55 to 64	21,337,000
65 and older	25,814,000

a. Form a pictograph of the data in the table by choosing an icon and selecting the number of people that the icon represents. Label the categories on the horizontal axis, and select an informative title for the graph.

b. What does the pictograph show about the total number of people aged 16 to 24 years who had crashes compared to the number of people aged 25 to 34 years?

20. The numbers of students in thousands in public schools in grades K–8 are shown by states in the following table.†

STATE	STUDENTS (1000)	STATE	STUDENTS (1000)
Alabama	542	Missouri	651
Alaska	97	Montana	110
Arizona	623	Nebraska	200
Arkansas	319	Nevada	229
California	4270	New Hampshire	147
Colorado	501	New Jersey	936
Connecticut	399	New Mexico	232
Delaware	80	New York	2028
District of		North Carolina	921
Columbia	57	North Dakota	77
Florida	1704	Ohio	1301
Georgia	1029	Oklahoma	448
Hawaii	135	Oregon	380
Idaho	169	Pennsylvania	1267
Illinois	1452	Rhode Island	112
Indiana	693	South Carolina	478
Iowa	337	South Dakota	91
Kansas	327	Tennessee	665
Kentucky	465	Texas	2868
Louisiana	558	Utah	329
Maine	151	Vermont	73
Maryland	602	Virginia	815
Massachusetts	705	Washington	696
Michigan	245	West Virginia	206
Minnesota	586	Wisconsin	601
Mississippi	365	Wyoming	64

a. Form a line plot for the numbers of students in each state by marking off the horizontal axis in intervals of 100 students. (*Note:* To accommodate all the intervals, you may find it convenient to place breaks in the axis.)

b. What is the interval that contains the median of the numbers represented in the line plot?

c. What percentage of the states to the nearest whole percent have less than 700,000 students?

d. What percentage of the states to the nearest whole percent have more than 2,000,000 students?

Statistical Abstract of the United States, 120th ed. (Washington, DC: Bureau of the Census, 2000), p. 638.

†*Statistical Abstract of the United States,* 120th ed. (Washington, DC: Bureau of the Census, 2000), p. 167.

21. The following table shows the average salaries of classroom teachers in 1999–2000.*

Salaries (in thousands) of K–12 classroom teachers, 1999–2000

STATE	AVERAGE SALARY	STATE	AVERAGE SALARY
Alabama	$35.8	Montana	$31.4
Alaska	46.8	Nebraska	32.9
Arizona	35.0	Nevada	38.9
Arkansas	32.4	New Hampshire	37.4
California	45.4	New Jersey	51.2
Colorado	38.0	New Mexico	32.4
Connecticut	51.6	New York	49.4
Delaware	43.2	North Carolina	36.1
District of Columbia	47.2	North Dakota	29.0
Florida	35.9	Ohio	40.6
Georgia	39.7	Oklahoma	31.1
Hawaii	40.4	Oregon	42.8
Idaho	34.1	Pennsylvania	48.5
Illinois	45.6	Rhode Island	45.7
Indiana	41.2	South Carolina	34.5
Iowa	34.9	South Dakota	28.6
Kansas	37.4	Tennessee	36.5
Kentucky	35.5	Texas	35.0
Louisiana	32.5	Utah	33.0
Maine	34.9	Vermont	36.8
Maryland	42.5	Virginia	37.5
Massachusetts	45.1	Washington	38.7
Michigan	48.2	West Virginia	34.2
Minnesota	39.5	Wisconsin	40.7
Mississippi	29.5	Wyoming	33.5
Missouri	34.7		

a. Form a line plot for the 51 teachers' salaries by using intervals of $1000 on the horizontal axis. (Round up each tenth which is greater than or equal to .5)
b. What is the interval with the most salaries represented in the line plot?
c. The average U.S. salary of the K–12 teachers is $40,600. What percentage of the salaries, to the nearest .1 percent, represented in the line plot is less than $41,000?

22. The following 40 scores are from a college mathematics test for elementary school teachers.

92, 75, 78, 90, 73, 67, 85, 80, 58, 87, 62, 74, 74, 76, 89, 95, 72, 86, 80, 57, 89, 97, 65, 77, 91, 83, 71, 75, 67, 68, 57, 86, 62, 65, 72, 75, 81, 72, 76, 69

a. Form a stem-and-leaf plot for these test scores.
b. How many scores are below 70?
c. What percentage of the scores is greater than or equal to 80?

23. The life spans in years of the 36 U.S. Presidents from George Washington to Richard Nixon are listed below.

67, 90, 83, 85, 73, 80, 78, 79, 68, 71, 53, 65, 74, 64, 77, 56, 66, 63, 70, 49, 57, 71, 67, 58, 60, 72, 67, 57, 60, 90, 63, 88, 78, 46, 64, 81

a. Form a stem-and-leaf plot of these data.
b. What percentage, to the nearest .1 percent, of the 36 Presidents lived 80 years or more?
c. What percentage, to the nearest .1 percent, of the 36 Presidents did not live 60 years?

24. The following test scores are for two classes that took the same test. (The highest possible score on the test was 60.)

Class 1 (24 scores): 34, 44, 53, 57, 19, 50, 41, 56, 38, 27, 56, 49, 39, 24, 41, 50, 45, 47, 35, 51, 40, 44, 48, 43

Class 2 (25 scores): 51, 40, 45, 28, 44, 56, 31, 33, 41, 34, 34, 39, 50, 36, 37, 32, 50, 22, 35, 43, 40, 50, 45, 33, 48

a. Form a stem-and-leaf plot with one stem. Put the leaves for one class on the right side of the stem and the leaves for the other class on the left side. Record the leaves in increasing order.
b. Which class appears to have better performance? Support your answer.

25. The following data are the weights in kilograms of 53 third-graders.

19.3, 20.2, 22.3, 17.0, 23.8, 24.6, 20.5, 20.3, 21.8, 16.6, 23.4, 25.1, 20.1, 21.6, 22.5, 19.7, 19.0, 18.2, 20.6, 21.5, 27.7, 21.6, 21.0, 20.4, 18.2, 17.2, 20.0, 22.7, 23.1, 24.6, 18.1, 20.8, 24.6, 17.3, 19.9, 20.1, 22.0, 23.2, 18.6, 25.3, 19.7, 20.6, 21.4, 21.2, 23.0, 21.2, 19.8, 22.1, 23.0, 19.1, 25.0, 22.0, 24.2

a. Form a stem-and-leaf plot of these data, using 16 through 27 as stems and the tenths digits as the leaves. (*Note:* It is not necessary to write decimal points.)
b. Which stem value has the greatest number of leaves?
c. What are the highest and lowest weights?

26. The average annual per capita incomes by states for 1999 are shown in the following table.*

*Statistical Abstract of the United States, 120th ed. (Washington, DC: Bureau of the Census, 2000), p.169.

*Statistical Abstract of the United States, 120th ed. (Washington, DC: Bureau of the Census, 2000), p. 460.

Average annual per capita income by states for 1999

STATE	INCOME	STATE	INCOME
AL	$22,946	MT	$22,314
AK	28,523	NE	27,437
AZ	25,307	NV	30,351
AR	22,114	NH	30,905
CA	29,819	NJ	36,106
CO	31,678	NM	22,063
CT	39,167	NY	33,946
DE	30,685	NC	26,220
DC	28,228	ND	23,518
FL	28,023	OH	27,081
GA	27,198	OK	22,801
HI	27,842	OR	27,135
ID	23,445	PA	28,676
IL	31,278	RI	29,720
IN	26,092	SC	23,496
IA	25,727	SD	25,107
KS	26,633	TN	25,581
KY	23,161	TX	26,525
LA	22,792	UT	23,356
ME	24,960	VT	25,892
MD	32,166	VA	29,484
MA	35,733	WA	30,295
MI	27,844	WV	20,888
MN	30,622	WI	27,412
MS	20,506	WY	26,003
MO	26,187		

a. Complete the frequency table by recording a tally mark for each income.

INTERVAL ($)	TALLIES
20,000–20,999	_____
21,000–21,999	_____
22,000–22,999	_____
23,000–23,999	_____
24,000–24,999	_____
25,000–25,999	_____
26,000–26,999	_____
27,000–27,999	_____
28,000–28,999	_____
29,000–29,999	_____
30,000–30,999	_____
31,000–31,999	_____
32,000–32,999	_____
33,000–33,999	_____
34,000–34,999	_____
35,000–35,999	_____
36,000–36,999	_____
37,000–37,999	_____
38,000–38,999	_____
39,000–39,999	_____

b. Construct a histogram for the given intervals.

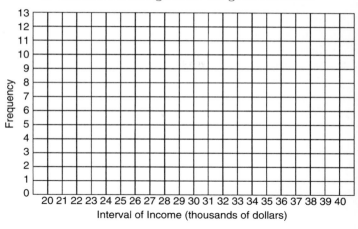

c. Which interval has the greatest frequency of incomes?

d. In how many states was the per capital income greater than $32,000?

e. In how many states was the per capita income less than $22,000?

27. The following table records the amounts of snowfall (to the nearest inch) for 1998 for selected cities.*

*Statistical Abstract of the United States, 120th ed. (Washington, DC: Bureau of the Census, 2000), p. 249.

CITY	SNOWFALL	CITY	SNOWFALL
Juneau	99	St. Louis	20
Denver	60	Great Falls	58
Hartford	49	Omaha	30
Wilmington	21	Reno	24
Washington	17	Concord	64
Boise	21	Atlantic City	16
Chicago	38	Albany	64
Peoria	25	Buffalo	91
Indianapolis	23	New York	28
Des Moines	33	Bismarck	44
Wichita	16	Cincinnati	24
Louisville	17	Cleveland	56
Portland, ME	71	Pittsburgh	44
Baltimore	21	Providence	36
Boston	42	Salt Lake City	59
Detroit	41	Burlington	78
Sault Ste. Marie	118	Seattle-Tacoma	11
Duluth	81	Spokane	49
Minneapolis	50	Charleston	34

a. Form a frequency table for the snowfall data, using the following intervals: 0–15; 16–30; 31–45; 46–60; 61–75; 76–90; 91–105; 106–120.

b. Draw a histogram for the snowfall data for the intervals in part a.

c. Which interval contains the greatest number of cities?

d. How many cities had snowfalls of more than 60 inches?

Vaccines for measles became available for use in 1963. The line graph below shows the approximate number of children with measles from 1984 to 1998.* Use this information in exercises 28 and 29.

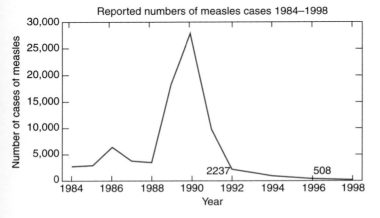

Reported numbers of measles cases 1984–1998

28. a. Was the number of cases of measles increasing or decreasing from 1984 to 1985?

b. To the nearest 1000, how many more cases of measles were reported in 1988 than in 1998?

c. In which year were the fewest cases of measles reported?

d. There was a 2-year period in which the number of cases of measles reported rose sharply, due in part to the failure to immunize children at the recommended ages of 12 to 15 months. What were these two years, and what was the increase to the nearest 1000?

29. a. Was the number of cases of measles increasing or decreasing from 1986 to 1988?

b. To the nearest 1000 how many more cases of measles were reported in 1991 than in 1992?

c. In which year was the greatest number of cases of measles reported?

d. In which 2-year period was the greatest decrease in the number of measles cases reported? What was this decrease to the nearest 1000?

The red line in the next figure shows the average annual mortgage rates for new homes from 1970 to 1999, and the black line shows the average annual interest rates on Treasury bills during the same period.* Use these line graphs to determine approximate answers in exercises 30 and 31.

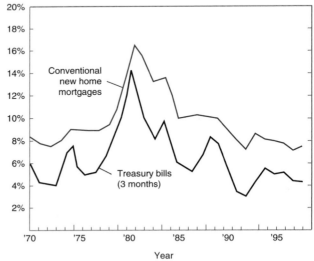

*U.S. Department of Health and Human Services, *Child Health USA 1998* (Washington, DC: U.S. Government Printing Office, 1998), p. 50.

Statistical Abstract of the United States, 120th ed. (Washington, DC: Bureau of the Census, 2000), p. 521.

30. a. What was the highest annual mortgage rate between 1970 and 1999 and in what year did it occur?
  b. What was the annual mortgage rate for 1999?
  c. What was the lowest annual interest rate for Treasury bills between 1970 and 1999?
  d. What was the greatest difference between the annual mortgage rate and the Treasury bill interest rate from 1970 to 1999, and what was the year?

31. a. What was the lowest annual mortgage rate between 1970 and 1999, and in what years did it occur?
  b. What was the annual mortgage rate for 1980?
  c. What was the highest annual interest rate for Treasury bills between 1970 and 1999?
  d. What was the smallest difference between the annual mortgage rate and the Treasury bill interest rate from 1970 to 1999, and what was the year?

32. This line graph shows the average salaries for public school teachers between 1985 and 1999.*

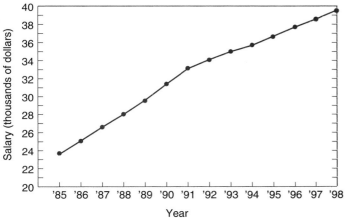

  a. What is the approximate average salary for public school teachers in 1999 if the increase from 1998 to 1999 is the same as in the preceding year?
  b. Which 5-year period had the greater increase in salaries, 1985–1990 or 1993–1998?
  c. What is the total increase in salaries from 1985 to 1998?

The percentages of public elementary schools with Internet access for instruction from 1994 to 1998 are as follows: 1994, 30 percent; 1995, 46 percent; 1996, 61 percent; 1997, 75 percent; and 1998, 88 percent.* Use this information in exercises 33 and 34.

33. a. Draw a line graph with the years from 1994 to 1998 represented on the horizontal axis.
  b. During which two-year period did the percentage of elementary schools with Internet access approximately double?

34. a. Draw a bar graph with the years from 1994 to 1998 represented on the horizontal axis.
  b. During which group of years did the percentage of elementary schools with Internet access approximately triple?

Inheritance factors in physical growth have been studied to compare the mother's height to the daughter's and son's heights and the father's height to the daughter's and son's heights. Some researchers have found that the **midparent height,** which is the number halfway between the height of each parent, is more closely related to the heights of their children. The scatter plots in exercises 35 and 36 compare midparent heights to the daughters' heights and midparent heights to the sons' heights.†

35. a. Locate a trend line for the following scatter plot. Briefly explain your method of determining this line.
  b. Use your line to predict the heights of daughters for midparent heights of 160 and 174 centimeters.
  c. Use your line to predict the midparent heights for daughters' heights of 163 and 170 centimeters.

*Statistical Abstract of the United States, 120th ed. (Washington, DC: Bureau of the Census, 2000), p. 169.

*Statistical Abstract of the United States, 118th ed. (Washington, DC: Bureau of the Census, 1998), p. 179.
†W. M. Krogman, Child Growth (Ann Arbor: The University of Michigan Press, 1972), p. 157.

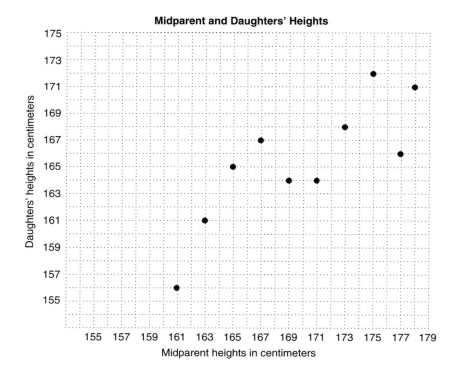

Midparent and Daughters' Heights

36. **a.** Locate a trend line for the scatter plot at the right. Briefly explain your method of determining this line.
   b. Use your line to predict the sons' heights for the midparent heights of 170 and 180 centimeters.
   c. Use your line to predict the midparent heights for the sons' heights of 179 and 182 centimeters.

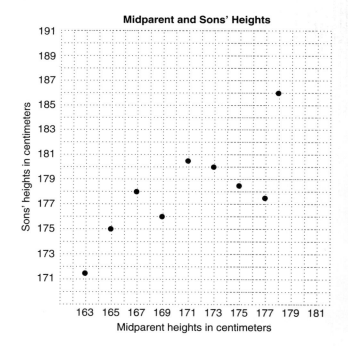

Midparent and Sons' Heights

As of October 1998, approximately 479,000 youths ages 16–24 had dropped out of high school in the previous 12 months. Those most likely to drop out of school in 1998 were those living in western states, boys, students aged 19 and older, and students living in low-income families. The table below contains the percentages of adolescents (aged 16 to 24) who were high school dropouts for the odd-numbered years 1971 to 1999.* Use this information in exercises 37 and 38.

Percentages of adolescent high school dropouts

YEAR	WHITE, NON-HISPANIC	BLACK, NON-HISPANIC	HISPANIC ORIGIN
1971	13.4	23.7	34.1
1973	11.6	22.2	33.5
1975	11.4	22.9	29.2
1977	11.9	19.8	33.0
1979	12.0	21.1	33.8
1981	11.4	18.4	33.2
1983	11.2	18.0	31.6
1985	10.4	15.2	27.6
1987	10.4	14.1	28.6
1989	9.4	13.9	33.0
1991	8.9	13.6	35.3
1993	7.9	13.6	27.5
1995	8.6	12.1	30.3
1997	7.1	13.0	29.1
1999	7.9	14.0	30.1

37. **a.** What was the percentage decrease in black non-Hispanic school dropouts from 1971 to 1997?
   b. The percentage decrease of black non-Hispanic dropouts from 1971 to 1997 was how many times the percentage decrease of Hispanic dropouts (to the nearest whole number)?
   c. Form a scatter plot to compare the white non-Hispanic dropouts to the black non-Hispanic dropouts by forming intervals from 6 to 14 percent on the horizontal axis for white non-Hispanic and from 12 to 24 percent on the vertical axis for black non-Hispanic. Is there a positive or negative association?
   d. Locate a trend line for your scatter plot, and use it to predict the black non-Hispanic dropout percentage for a white non-Hispanic dropout rate of 12 percent.

38. **a.** What was the percentage decrease in white non-Hispanic dropouts from 1971 to 1997?
   b. The percentage decrease of black non-Hispanic dropouts from 1971 to 1977 was how many times the percentage decrease of white non-Hispanic dropouts (to the nearest whole number)?
   c. Form a scatter plot to compare the black non-Hispanic dropouts to the Hispanic dropouts by forming intervals from 12 to 24 percent on the horizontal axis for black non-Hispanic dropouts and from 26 to 36 percent on the vertical axis for Hispanic dropouts. Is there a positive or negative association?
   d. Locate a trend line for your scatter plot, and use it to predict the Hispanic dropout percentage to the nearest percent for a black non-Hispanic dropout rate of 17 percent.

*U.S. Department of Health and Human Services, *Child Health USA 2000* (Washington, DC: U.S. Government Printing Office, 2000).

39. This scatter plot shows the ages of 27 trees and their corresponding diameters.*

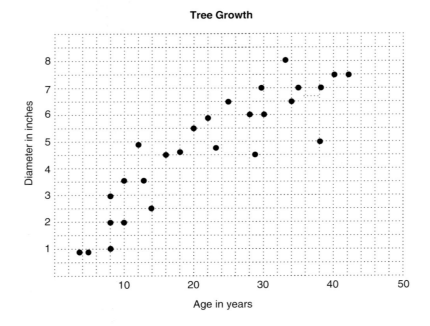

Tree Growth

a. What are the greatest diameter and the oldest age of the trees represented in this graph?

b. Is there a positive or negative association?

c. Locate a trend line and use it to predict the diameters of a 26-year-old tree and a 32-year-old tree.

d. Use your trend line to predict the approximate age of a tree, if its diameter is 9 inches.

REASONING AND PROBLEM SOLVING

40. Featured Strategy: Drawing a Graph Two ardent baseball fans were comparing the numbers of home runs hit by the American and National Leagues' home run leaders and posed the following question: Is there an association from year to year between the numbers of these runs? That is, in general, if the number of home runs hit by one league's home run leader for a given year is low (or high), will the number of home runs hit by the other league's home run leader be low (or high)? Use the tables on pages 474 and 475.

a. **Understanding the Problem** Consider the two years with the smallest numbers of home runs by the leaders and the two years with the largest numbers of home runs by the leaders. What were these years and numbers?

*Data Analysis and Statistics across the Curriculum (Reston, VA: National Council of Teachers of Mathematics, 1992), p. 43.

b. **Devising a Plan** One possibility for considering an association between the data is to form a scatter plot. To form a scatter plot, first mark off axes for numbers of home runs by each league's home run leaders. For each league, what is the difference between the smallest number of home runs by the leaders and the greatest number?

c. **Carrying Out the Plan** Form a scatter plot by plotting the number of home runs hit by each pair of leaders for each year to see if there appears to be an association between the data. If so, is the association positive or negative? Are there points of the plot that might be considered outliers? Use your graph to determine the year with the greatest difference in the number of home runs hit by each league's home run leaders.

d. **Looking Back** Draw a trend line and use your line to predict the number of home runs by the National League's home run leader for a given year if the number of home runs by the American League's leader is 47.

41. A company's record of amounts invested in advertisements and the corresponding amounts of sales produced are listed by the following pairs of numbers. The first number is the amount for advertisements to the nearest tenth of a million dollars, and the second number is the amount of sales to the nearest million dollars. (3.8, 17), (1.4, 3), (2.8, 7), (4.9, 26), (2.3, 5), (1.8, 3), (3.3, 10), (5.3, 39), (4.4, 23), (5.1, 31), (2.6, 6), (1.2, 2)

a. Form a scatter plot with the amounts for advertisements on the horizontal axis and the corresponding amounts for sales on the vertical axis.

b. Which type of curve from Figure 7.15 best fits the points of the scatter plot?

c. Sketch the curve of best fits from part b and use your curve to predict the amount of sales for $3.6 million in advertisements.

d. Use your sketch in part c to predict the amount invested in advertisements, if the total resulting sales was $20 million.

42. For a math project one middle school student recorded the number of names that her friend Amy was able to memorize in different amounts of time. In the following pairs of numbers, the first number is the amount of time, and the second is the number of words memorized for the given time: (.5, 5), (1, 9), (1.5, 11), (2, 12), (2.5, 13), (3, 14), (3.5, 15), (4, 15), (4.5, 13), (5.5, 16), (5.5, 18), (6, 17), (7, 18), (8, 18)

a. Form a scatter plot for this data with the times on the horizontal axis and the corresponding numbers of words on the vertical axis.

b. Which type of curve from Figure 7.15 best fits the points of the scatter plot?

c. Sketch the type of curve from part b to approximate the location of points on the scatter plot and use your curve to predict the number of words that Amy could memorize in 9 minutes.

d. Use your curve in part c to predict the time period, if Amy memorized 10 words.

- -

ONLINE LEARNING CENTER   www.mhhe.com/bennett-nelson

- Math Investigation 7.1   *Trend Lines*
  Section-Related: • Links   • Writing/Discussion Problems   • Bibliography

MATH ACTIVITY 7.2

SIMULATIONS IN STATISTICS

Materials: Spinners in the Manipulative Kit. Bend a paper clip and hold a pencil at the center of the spinner, as shown below.

1. A certain brand of nonfat yogurt contains one of the letters A, B, C, or D on the inside of the cover. A person collecting one of each type of cover can return them to the store and receive one free container of yogurt. Assuming that each letter has the same chance of being selected, how many yogurts might a person expect to buy on average before getting one of each type of cover? Make a guess.

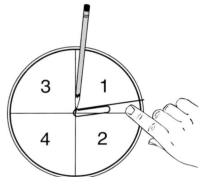

   Rather than buy yogurts, we can devise an experiment (called a **simulation**) to model the situation. Since there are four types of covers, we can use the 1-to-4 spinner, letting 1, 2, 3, and 4 represent the A, B, C, and D covers, respectively. Spin the 1-to-4 spinner, and record the total number of spins needed to get each of the numbers at least once. Repeat this experiment 20 times, and record the number of spins for each experiment.

   a. What is the smallest number of your spins needed to get all four numbers?

   b. What is the greatest number of your spins to get all four numbers?

   c. What is the average of the numbers of spins for your 20 experiments?

   d. On the basis of your experiments, write a statement about the number of yogurts a person might normally be expected to buy before getting all four types of covers.

   *e. Results tend to be more accurate for larger numbers of experiments. Compute the averages of the answers in part c by pooling data with several other students.

2. Approximately two out of every five people have type A blood. How many people on average will need to be randomly selected to obtain three people with type A blood?

   (*Hint:* Model the situation by using the 1-to-6 spinner. Cross off one number (for example, the number 6) and designate two of the remaining five numbers as representing people with type A blood.

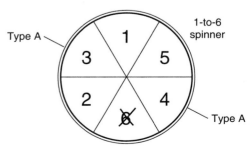

SECTION 7.2

DESCRIBING AND ANALYZING DATA

"Hello? Beasts of the Field? This is Lou, over in Birds of the Air. Anything funny going on at your end?"

Drawing by
Ziegler; © 1974
*The New Yorker
Magazine, Inc.*

PROBLEM OPENER

A large metropolitan police department made a check of the clothing worn by pedestrians killed in traffic at night. About $\frac{4}{5}$ of the victims were wearing dark clothes, and $\frac{1}{5}$ were wearing light-color garments. Explain why this study does not necessarily show that pedestrians are less likely to encounter traffic mishaps at night if they wear something white.

The employees of Animated Animal Company keep records of the number of toys each machine produces and the number of breakdowns of each machine. Figure 7.17 shows that machine III outproduced machines I and II, and machine II had the most problems. Such numerical information is called **statistics.**

Weekly record of birds produced

	M	T	W	TH	F	BREAKDOWNS
Machine I	165	158	98	125	260	13
Machine II	117	82	46	6	30	24
Machine III	182	243	196	305	261	4

Figure 7.17

The word *statistics* also means the science of collecting and interpreting data. There are two broad areas of this science: *descriptive statistics* and *inferential statistics*. **Descriptive statistics** is the science of describing data. The average number of birds produced each day by machine I is an example of a descriptive statistic. **Inferential statistics** is the science of interpreting data in order to make predictions. Sampling is an important part of inferential statistics. For example, if the manager of Birds of the Air randomly selects 100 birds from the assembly line and finds that 3 are defective, he can estimate that the number of bad birds in a batch of 5000 will be 150. How? Methods of describing and analyzing data will be introduced in this section.

Measures of Central Tendency

An important source of data, especially for children, comes from conducting **surveys,** and this should begin in the early grades. Questions of interest to children, such as the amount of time spent watching television or the most popular soda pop, can lead to the design of a survey of their class, families, friends, etc. for gathering data.

Once data have been collected, they need to be organized and described so that the results can be understood and communicated. For example, if a student records the amount of time spent watching television each day for a 10-day period, these 10 numbers can be replaced by a "typical number" or "central number" to describe the amount of time in general that students watched television. There are three types of such numbers: the *mean* (also called the *average*), the *median,* and the *mode.* Each of these three numbers is called a **measure of central tendency.**

Students need to understand that the mean "evens out" or "balances" a set of data and that the median identifies the "middle" of the data set. They should compare the utility of the mean and median as measures of center for different data sets.

Standards, 2000, p. 251

MEAN   Figure 7.18a represents the heights of seven children. One way to represent all the heights by a single number is to "level off" the heights. If 3 centimeters is taken from each of the three tallest heights and is distributed among the four shortest, as shown in part b, the heights level off at 126 centimeters.

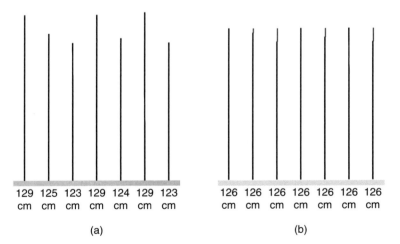

129 125 123 129 124 129 123
cm   cm   cm   cm   cm   cm   cm

(a)

126 126 126 126 126 126 126
cm   cm   cm   cm   cm   cm   cm

(b)

Figure 7.18

Perhaps you can see by looking at Figure 7.18 why the same result is obtained by adding the seven numbers

$$123 + 123 + 124 + 125 + 129 + 129 + 129 = 882$$

and dividing the sum by 7

$$882 \div 7 = 126$$

This type of "center" number is called the **mean** and is the number we often refer to as the *numerical average* or, simply, the *average.*

Selected major earthquakes from 1976 to 2001*

DATE	PLACE	DEATHS	MAGNITUDE
1976 July 28	Tangshan, China	800,000	8.2
1977 Mar. 4	Romania, Bucharest, etc.	1,542	7.5
1977 Aug. 19	Indonesia	200	8.0
1977 Nov. 23	Northwestern Argentina	100	8.2
1978 June 19	Sendai, Japan	21	7.5
1978 Sept. 16	Northeast Iran	25,000	7.7
1979 Sept. 12	Indonesia	100	8.1
1979 Dec. 12	Colombia, Ecuador	800	7.9
1980 Oct. 10	Northwest Algeria	4,500	7.3
1980 Nov. 23	Southern Italy	4,800	7.2
1982 Dec. 13	Northern Yemen	2,800	6.0
1983 Mar. 31	Southern Colombia	250	5.5
1983 May 26	Honshu, Japan	81	7.7
1983 Oct. 30	Eastern Turkey	1,300	7.1
1985 Mar. 3	Chile	146	7.8
1985 Sept. 19–21	Mexico City	4,200	8.1
1987 Mar. 5–6	Ecuador	4,000	7.3
1988 Dec. 7	Northwestern Armenia	55,000	6.8
1990 June 21	Northwestern Iran	40,000	7.7
1992 Mar. 13	Eastern Turkey	4,000	6.2
1992 Dec. 12	Flores, Indonesia	2,500	7.5
1993 July 12	Hokkaido, Japan	200	7.8
1993 Sept. 29	Latur, India	9,784	6.3
1994 Feb. 15	So. Sumatra, Indonesia	207	7.0
1994 June 2	Jawa, Indonesia	250	7.2
1994 June 6	Colombia	295	6.4
1995 Jan. 16	Kobe, Japan	5,542	6.8
1995 May 27	Sakhalin Island	1,989	7.5
1995 Oct. 1	Turkey	100	6.2
1996 Feb. 3	Yunnan, China	322	6.5
1996 Feb. 17	Irian Jaya	108	8.1
1997 Feb. 28	Armenia-Azerbaijan	1,100	6.1
1997 May 10	Northern Iran	1,567	7.3
1998 Feb. 4	Afghanistan	2,323	6.1
1998 May 22	Central Bolivia	105	6.6
1998 May 30	Afghanistan	5,000	6.9
1999 Jan. 25	Colombia	1,883	6.0
1999 Aug. 17	Turkey	17,000	7.6
1999 Sept. 20	Taiwan	2,400	7.7
2000 May 4	Sulawesi, Indonesia	46	7.6
2000 June 4	Sumatera, Indonesia	103	8.0
2001 Jan. 13	El Salvador	852	7.7
2001 Jan. 26	Gujarat, India	20,103	7.7
2001 Feb. 13	El Salvador	315	6.6

Figure 7.19

*National Earthquake Information Center of the United States Geological Survey.

The **mean** of a set of data is the sum of all measurements divided by the total number of measurements.

$$\bar{x} = \frac{x_1 + x_2 + x_3 + \cdots + x_n}{n}$$

where x_1, x_2, etc. are n measurements and $\bar{x}$ (read "x bar") denotes the mean.

The table in Figure 7.19 lists magnitudes of selected major earthquakes from 1976 to 2001 and the number of deaths caused by each quake. The death tolls vary from a low of 21 to a high of 800,000. Let's calculate the mean for these data. The sum of the number of deaths from the 44 earthquakes is 1,022,934. The mean to the nearest whole number is 1,022,934/44, which equals 23,249 deaths per earthquake. Notice that this *central number* is higher than all but four of the numbers in the list, which indicates that the mean may not be the best number for describing the "typical" number of deaths for these earthquakes.

MEDIAN   We have seen from the earthquake data that the mean is not always a *representative* central number. The next type of central number can be more informative. Consider the heights of the seven children shown in Figure 7.20a. In part b these heights have been placed in increasing order. There are three heights less than and three heights greater than the measurement in the fourth position of part b. Thus it seems reasonable to select the measurement in the fourth position (125 centimeters) as the representative height. This type of central number is called the *median*. Notice that this number is different from the mean, which is 126 centimeters.

Research Statement

The 7th national mathematics assessment found that when given a choice about which statistic to use, students tended to select the mean over the median regardless of the distribution of data.

Zawojewski and Shaughnessy 2000

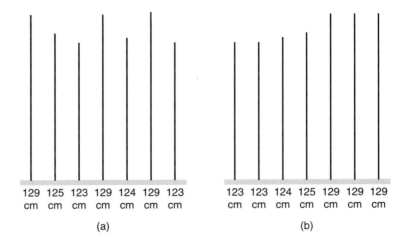

| 129 cm | 125 cm | 123 cm | 129 cm | 124 cm | 129 cm | 123 cm |

(a)

| 123 cm | 123 cm | 124 cm | 125 cm | 129 cm | 129 cm | 129 cm |

(b)

Figure 7.20

1. The **median** of a set of data with an odd number of measurements is the middle number when the measurements are listed from smallest to largest (or largest to smallest).
2. The **median** of a set of data with an even number of measurements is the mean of the two middle numbers when the measurements are listed from smallest to largest (or largest to smallest).

The numbers of earthquake deaths from Figure 7.19 are listed below from smallest to largest. Since the number of measurements is even, we must compute the mean of the two middle numbers. The median for this set of data is 1421, the mean of the two circled numbers. Twenty-two of the numbers are less than 1421, and 22 of the numbers are greater than 1421.

21, 46, 81, 100, 100, 100, 103, 105, 108, 146, 200, 200, 207, 250, 250, 295, 315, 332, 800, 852, 1,100, (1,300), (1,542), 1,567, 1,883, 1,989, 2,323, 2,400, 2,500, 2,800, 4,000, 4,000, 4,200, 4,500, 4,800, 5,000, 5,542, 9,784, 17,000, 20,103, 25,000, 40,000, 55,000, 800,000

MODE   The median seems to be a more representative central number for the earthquake data than the mean, but there are no death tolls that actually equal the median. Let's consider the third type of central measure. Observe that three of the children whose heights are represented in Figure 7.21 are 129 centimeters tall. This height might be considered the most representative as a central measure because it occurs most frequently. This type of central measure is called the *mode*. Notice that this height is different from the mean (126 centimeters) and the median (125 centimeters).

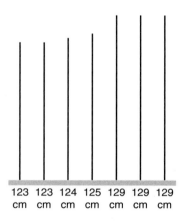

Figure 7.21

123 123 124 125 129 129 129
cm   cm   cm   cm   cm   cm   cm

MODE   The **mode** of a set of data is the measurement that occurs most often.

The mode for the earthquake deaths is 100, the measurement that occurs three times. When a set of data has two different measurements that each occurs the most often, then the data have two modes and the set is called **bimodal.**

Example A

Determine the mean, median, and mode of the earthquake magnitudes in Figure 7.19.

Solution   The mean is approximately 7.2 (317/44). To determine the median, we must first list the earthquake magnitudes in increasing order.

5.5, 6.0, 6.0, 6.1, 6.1, 6.2, 6.2, 6.3, 6.4, 6.5, 6.6, 6.6, 6.8, 6.8, 6.9, 7.0, 7.1, 7.2, 7.2, 7.3, 7.3, (7.3), (7.5), 7.5, 7.5, 7.5, 7.6, 7.6, 7.7, 7.7, 7.7, 7.7, 7.7, 7.7, 7.8, 7.8, 7.9, 8.0, 8.0, 8.1, 8.1, 8.1, 8.2, 8.2

The median is 7.4, the mean of the two circled numbers. The mode is 7.7, a measure that occurs 6 times.

The mean, median, and mode each have their advantages, depending on the data and type of information desired. In some cases one of these central numbers is clearly more representative of a set of data than another.

Values of data that are substantially larger or smaller than the other values are called **outliers.** The number 800,000 in the list of earthquake deaths is an example of an outlier (see pages 467 and 468 for determining outliers). The median often has an advantage over the mean in describing data because outliers usually have less effect on the median.

Example B

Determine the mean, median, and mode of the following salaries for people in a small company. Which salaries might be considered outliers? What is the best measure of central tendency?

One president	$210,000
One vice-president	120,000
One salesperson	40,000
One supervisor	22,000
One machine operator	20,000
Five mill workers (each earning)	15,000
Six apprentice workers (each earning)	13,000

Solution   The sum of the 16 salaries is

$$\$210{,}000 + \$120{,}000 + \$40{,}000 + \$22{,}000 + \$20{,}000 + 5(\$15{,}000) + 6(\$13{,}000) = \$565{,}000$$

So the mean is $565,000/16 = $35,312.50. The median is the mean of the eighth and ninth salaries when the salaries are considered in increasing order. Since the eighth and ninth salaries are both 15,000, the median is

$$\frac{\$15{,}000 + \$15{,}000}{2} = \$15{,}000$$

The mode is $13,000, since this salary occurs most frequently. Both the median and the mode are more representative of the majority of salaries than the mean. The mean of $35,312.50 is greater than 13 of the 16 salaries.

Problem-Solving Application

PROBLEM

An elementary school principal was interested in computing the mean of the verbal reasoning scores on a differential aptitude test taken by all the students in the school. The mean test score for the 62 students in the Talented and Gifted (TAG) program was 96, and the mean of the scores for the remaining 418 students was 72. What was the mean of the test scores for all the students?

Understanding the Problem   *Drawing a graph* is one way of visualizing the given information. We can think of each of the 418 students as having a score of 72 and each of the 62 TAG students as having a score of 96. The mean for the total group of 480 students can be visualized by "evening off" both columns. **Question 1:** Will the mean be closer to 72 or to 96?

Average Grades of TAG and non-TAG Students

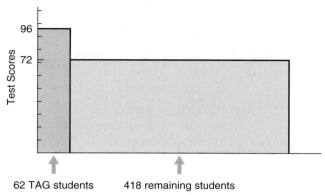

Devising a Plan   The graph above suggests a plan. The difference between the height of the region representing the TAG students and the height of the region for the remaining students is $96 - 72 = 24$. Thus, if the column for the TAG students is cut down to a height of 72, the 62×24 additional test score points can be "spread" across the entire top of the new graph. To determine the increase in the mean of 72, we can divide the 1488 extra points by the total number of students (480). **Question 2:** What is this increase?

Carrying Out the Plan   The increase in the mean is $1488 \div 480 = 3.1$. So if the extra points for the TAG students' scores are evenly spread across the top of the graph, the new mean will be $72 + 3.1 = 75.1$. You might have been tempted to obtain the new mean by finding the mean of 96 and 72: $(96 + 72)/2 = 84$. **Question 3:** How does the graph help to show that this is not reasonable for the new mean?

Looking Back   Another approach to solving the original problem is to find the total of all the scores for the 480 students and then divide by 480. **Question 4:** How can the sum of the scores for all 480 students be obtained if we know that the mean for 62 students is 96 and the mean for 418 students is 72?

Answers to Questions 1–4   1. Closer to 72   **2.** 3.1   **3.** A horizontal line drawn on the graph at a height of 84 (halfway between 72 and 96) makes it evident that the part of the TAG students' bar above 84 does not have enough area to increase the total graph to a height of 84.   **4.** The sum of the scores for the total 480 students is $62(96) + 418(72) = 36{,}048$. So the new mean of the test scores for all the students is $36{,}048/480 = 75.1$.

Box-and-Whisker Plots

An application of the median is found in the formation of a visual diagram called a **box-and-whisker plot,** or more briefly, a **box plot.** For this type of plot, the data are divided into four parts with approximately the same amount of data in each part. First, the median is used to divide the data into a lower part and an upper part, and then each of these parts is separated into two parts by their medians.

Let's illustrate this process with a set of data. First order the data from the smallest value to largest, and mark the location of the median, as shown on the following page. The "lower half" has the numbers 1, 3, 3, 7, 8, 8, 11, and its median is 7. The median of the "lower half" is called the **lower quartile.** The "upper half" has the numbers 15, 19, 21, 21, 21, 26, 29, and its median is 21. The median of the "upper half" is called the **upper quartile.**

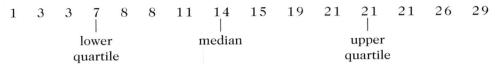

1   3   3   7   8   8   11   14   15   19   21   21   21   26   29
               | | |
       lower   median   upper
      quartile   quartile

The next sample shows 20 scores from a science test which have been listed in increasing order. The median test score is 70 and the lower and upper quartiles are 66 and 80, respectively.

57 58 62 63 66 66 67 67 68 70 70 72 73 75 80 80 81 83 85 99
              | | |
      lower   median   upper
    quartile   quartile

The box-and-whisker plot for this set of data is shown in Figure 7.22. The median is marked by the vertical line in the rectangle, and the lower quartile Q_1 and upper quartile Q_3 are marked by the left edge and right edge of the rectangle. Each of the four parts of the box-and-whisker plot represent approximately 25 percent of the data. The rectangle is the **box** of the plot and illustrates the middle 50 percent of the data. The lines extending from the ends of the rectangle to the smallest number (57) and the largest number (99) are the **whiskers** and they illustrate the lower 25 percent and upper 25 percent of the data. The box plot shows that the 25 percent of the test scores in the interval from 70 to 80 are more than twice as widely spread as the 25 percent of the scores in the interval from 66 to 70. Also the length of the whiskers provides information about how close the smallest and greatest measurements are to the quartiles: The smallest test score (57) is much closer to the lower quartile (66) than the greatest score (99) is to the upper quartile (80), so the upper 25 percent of the test scores are more widely spread than the lower 25 percent.

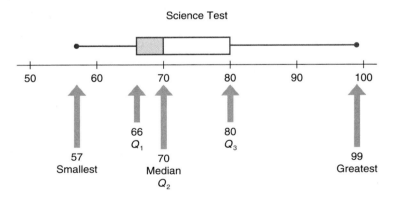

Figure 7.22

Example C

Form a box-and-whisker plot for the following 20 scores on a history test:

55 59 64 64 68 70 73 75 76 79 81 81 82 84 85 85 87 92 95 98

1. Make a few observations about this plot.

2. Compare the box-and-whisker plot of scores on the history test to the plot of scores on the science test (Figure 7.22) by sketching the science test box plot above the history test box plot. Write a few observations.

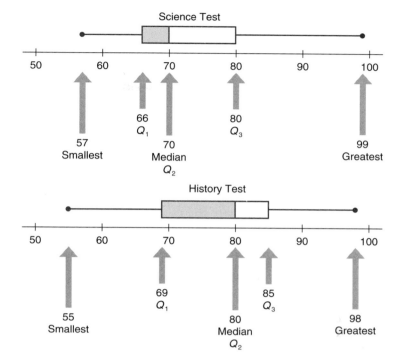

Box plots do not convey as much specific information about the data set, such as where clusters occur, as histograms do. But box plots can provide effective comparisons between two data sets because they make descriptive characteristics such as median and interquartile range readily apparent.

Standards 2000, p. 251

Solution   **1.** The rectangle in the box-and-whisker plot for the history test shows that 25 percent of the scores are in the interval from 69 to 80 and 25 percent are in the interval from 80 to 85, which is approximately one-half as long. Also, 50 percent of the scores are above 80, and 25 percent are above 85.   **2.** A comparison of the box-and-whisker plots for the history and science tests shows that, overall, performance on the history test was better. Although the ranges of both tests are approximately the same ($98 - 55 = 43$ compared to $99 - 57 = 42$), the median and quartiles for the history test are greater than the median and corresponding quartiles for the science test. For example, the median for the history test (80) equals the upper quartile for the science test. That is, 50 percent of the scores on the history test are above 80, whereas only 25 percent of the scores on the science test are above 80. Also, the lower quartile (69) for the history test is approximately equal to the median (70) for the science test, which means that there are approximately twice as many scores below 70 on the science test as on the history test.

INTERQUARTILE RANGE   We have seen that the box in the box-and-whisker plot has special significance, as it represents approximately 50 percent of the data. The length of the box which is the difference between the upper quartile and the lower quartile is called the **interquartile range.** For example, the box plot in Example C shows that the interquartile range for the history test scores is $85 - 69 = 16$.

The interquartile range is used for determining which values of the data, if any, are outliers. If a value of the data is more than 1.5 times the interquartile range above the upper quartile or below the lower quartile, the value is considered to be an **outlier.**

Let's consider Example B once again from page 464. The salaries from this example are shown below in thousands of dollars (that is, 13 represents 13,000, etc.), and the median and quartiles have been marked.

13   13   13   13   13   13   15   15   15   15   15   20   22   40   120   210

lower quartile   median   upper quartile

When doing Example B, you may have felt that $210,000 was an outlier, but you may have been uncertain about $120,000 or $40,000. Let's use the previous test to determine if these numbers are outliers.

Interquartile range: $21,000 - 13,000 = 8000$
1.5 × interquartile range: $1.5 \times 8000 = 12,000$
Upper quartile + 12,000: $21,000 + 12,000 = 33,000$
Lower quartile - 12,000: $13,000 - 12,000 = 1000$

Since $40,000, $120,000, and $210,000 are greater than $33,000, these salaries are outliers. However, there are no salaries less than $1000, so there are no outliers at the lower end of the data.

Example D

What are the outliers, if any, for the science test scores that are represented by the box plot in Figure 7.22?

Solution   The interquartile range is $80 - 66 = 14$. Since there are no scores above $80 + 1.5(14) = 101$ and no test scores below $66 - 1.5(14) = 45$, there are no outliers.

Measures of Variability

The mean, median, mode, and quartiles are single numbers used to describe a set of data; yet, even when they are all used, they do not present the whole picture. You will find something quite interesting about the sets of data in the next example which will indicate the need for further methods of describing data.

Example E

1. Compute the mean, median, mode, and quartiles for sets A and B.

2. In which set are the data more spread out about the mean?

Set A:	13	14	15	19	20	20	28	29	30	32	33
Set B:	1	4	15	16	17	20	20	21	30	31	78

Solution   1. Both sets have the same mean, median, mode, and quartiles: mean, 23; median, 20; mode, 20; lower quartile, 15; and upper quartile, 30.   2. The data in set B are more spread out about the mean.

Example E shows that it is possible for the mean, median, mode, and quartiles of one set of data to equal those of another, while the data in one of these sets are more spread out than the data in the other. To help describe a set of data, we need to measure the amount of spread among the data. A **measure of variability** is a number that describes the spread or dispersion in a set of data. We have seen that the interquartile range is one indicator of the spread in the middle 50 percent of the data. Another common method of measuring variation uses the *range*.

RANGE   The **range** is the difference between the greatest and least values in a set of data.

The range of set A in Example E is 20 and the range of set B is 77. Even when two sets of data have the same range, there may be differences in the way the data are centered or spread about the mean. Consider the data and graphs in Figure 7.23. The range of the data in both part a and part b is 4 (the greatest value is 5, and the least value is 1). However, the data represented in part a are more concentrated about the mean than the data represented in part b.

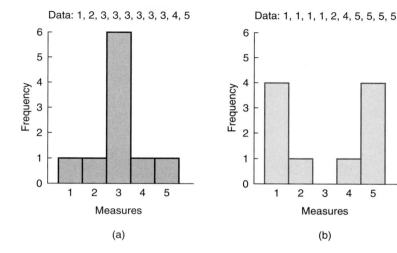

Data: 1, 2, 3, 3, 3, 3, 3, 3, 4, 5

Data: 1, 1, 1, 1, 2, 4, 5, 5, 5, 5

(a)   (b)

Figure 7.23

The two sets of data in Figure 7.23 show the need for a measure of variability that is more sensitive than the range. The next measure of variability is called the *standard deviation*.

STANDARD DEVIATION   The following are steps in determining the **standard deviation** of a set of data.

1. Determine the mean.
2. Find the difference between each value of data and the mean.
3. Square the differences.
4. Determine the mean of the squared differences.
5. Compute the square root of this mean to find the standard deviation.

$$\text{Standard deviation } \sqrt{\frac{(x_1 - \bar{x})^2 + (x_2 - \bar{x})^2 + \cdots + (x_n - \bar{x})^2}{n}}$$

where x_1, x_2, etc. are n values of data and $\bar{x}$ is the mean.

The tables in Figure 7.24 illustrate the steps for computing the standard deviation for each of the sets of data in Figure 7.23.

Set A (mean = 3)
1, 2, 3, 3, 3, 3, 3, 3, 4, 5

MEASURE x	DIFFERENCE FROM MEAN $x - \bar{x}$	SQUARE OF DIFFERENCE $(x - \bar{x})^2$
1	$1 - 3 = {}^-2$	4
2	$2 - 3 = {}^-1$	1
3	$3 - 3 = 0$	0
3	$3 - 3 = 0$	0
3	$3 - 3 = 0$	0
3	$3 - 3 = 0$	0
3	$3 - 3 = 0$	0
3	$3 - 3 = 0$	0
4	$4 - 3 = 1$	1
5	$5 - 3 = 2$	4
		Total 10

Set B (mean = 3)
1, 1, 1, 1, 2, 4, 5, 5, 5, 5

MEASURE x	DIFFERENCE FROM MEAN $x - \bar{x}$	SQUARE OF DIFFERENCE $(x - \bar{x})^2$
1	$1 - 3 = {}^-2$	4
1	$1 - 3 = {}^-2$	4
1	$1 - 3 = {}^-2$	4
1	$1 - 3 = {}^-2$	4
2	$2 - 3 = {}^-1$	1
4	$4 - 3 = 1$	1
5	$5 - 3 = 2$	4
5	$5 - 3 = 2$	4
5	$5 - 3 = 2$	4
5	$5 - 3 = 2$	4
		Total 34

Figure 7.24

Mean of squared differences $= \dfrac{10}{10} = 1$

Standard deviation $= \sqrt{1} = 1$

Mean of squared differences $= \dfrac{34}{10} = 3.4$

Standard deviation $= \sqrt{3.4} \approx 1.8$

The standard deviation for set A is 1, and the standard deviation for set B is approximately 1.8 (about twice as large). The larger standard deviation for set B confirms our visual interpretation of the graphs in Figure 7.23. The data graphed in part b are more widely spread about the mean than the data in part a. In general, the more varied (spread out) the data, the greater the standard deviation; and the less varied the data, the smaller the standard deviation (closer to zero).

Example F

Two sets of data and their means are given below. Inspect the sets of data and predict which set has the smaller standard deviation. Compute the standard deviation for both sets of data.

$$\text{Set A:} \quad 18 \quad 19 \quad 20 \quad 20 \quad 26 \quad 28 \quad 30 \qquad \text{mean} = 23$$
$$\text{Set B:} \quad 0 \quad 1 \quad 10 \quad 20 \quad 20 \quad 50 \quad 60 \qquad \text{mean} = 23$$

Solution The numbers in set A are fairly close together and less spread out than the numbers in set B. So the numbers in set A should have the smaller standard deviation.

MEASURE x	DIFFERENCE FROM MEAN $x - \bar{x}$	SQUARE OF DIFFERENCE $(x - \bar{x})^2$
30	7	49
28	5	25
26	3	9
20	${}^-3$	9
20	${}^-3$	9
19	${}^-4$	16
18	${}^-5$	25
		Total 142

MEASURE x	DIFFERENCE FROM MEAN $x - \bar{x}$	SQUARE OF DIFFERENCE $(x - \bar{x})^2$
60	37	1369
50	27	729
20	${}^-3$	9
20	${}^-3$	9
10	${}^-13$	169
1	${}^-22$	484
0	${}^-23$	529
		Total 3298

Mean of squared differences $= \dfrac{142}{7} \approx 20.3$

Standard deviation $\approx \sqrt{20.3} \approx 4.5$

Mean of squared differences $= \dfrac{3298}{7} \approx 471.1$

Standard deviation $\approx \sqrt{471.1} \approx 21.7$

These standard deviations (4.5 compared to 21.7) show that the measures in set *A* are less spread out than the measures in set *B*.

Standard deviations determine intervals about the mean. For set *A* in Example F, 1 standard deviation above the mean is 23 + 4.5, or 27.5, and 1 standard deviation below the mean is 23 − 4.5, or 18.5 (Figure 7.25). The interval within ±1 standard deviation of the mean is the interval from 18.5 to 27.5. The interval within ±2 standard deviations of the mean is from 14 to 32. Notice the use of the lowercase Greek letter sigma (σ) in Figure 7.25 to represent the standard deviation.

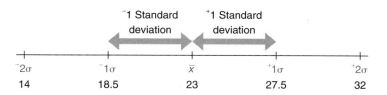

Figure 7.25

> **DISTRIBUTION OF DATA**   At least 75 percent of the measurements in any set of data will lie within 2 standard deviations of the mean (see Figure 7.26).

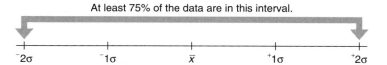

Figure 7.26

The percentage of data within 2 standard deviations of the mean is usually much higher than 75. In fact, if only 75 percent of the data in a given set are within 2 standard deviations of the mean, the data have a rather unique distribution (see Computer Investigation 7.2 on the website). For sets of data that reflect real-life situations, 90 percent or more of the data are usually within 2 standard deviations of the mean (see the section on *normal distributions,* page 486).

CALCULATORS   Calculators and computers that are programmed with statistics functions compute the mean, standard deviation, and other statistical measures for data that are entered. Figure 7.27 shows a calculator's view screen for the data in set *A* of Example F.* The variable *n* on this screen shows that seven numbers were entered, and the first line has the mean of these numbers. Also Σx and Σx^2 are the sum of the seven numbers and the sum of the squares of the numbers, respectively. Notice that the median, lower quartile Q_1, and upper quartile Q_3 are also given. The standard deviation computed in Example F was approximately 4.5, and this is denoted on the view screen by σx. The symbol Sx also represents a standard deviation, but for a sample. This standard deviation is larger than σx because in the formula for standard deviation on page 469, $n − 1$ is used for the

---

*This view screen is from Texas Instrument's TI-83 calculator.

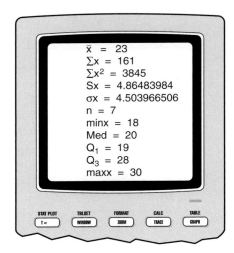

$\bar{x}$ = 23
Σx = 161
Σx^2 = 3845
Sx = 4.86483984
σx = 4.503966506
n = 7
minx = 18
Med = 20
Q_1 = 19
Q_3 = 28
maxx = 30

Figure 7.27

denominator rather than n. Using the smaller denominator $n - 1$, rather than n, produces a larger standard deviation which is better suited for making inferences from samples.

SUMMARY   The mean, median, and mode are single numbers that describe the central tendency of a set of data. Often the median is a more reliable measure than the mean because a few extremely large or small values of data will have less effect on the median than on the mean. The median is used in forming box-and-whisker plots for visual illustrations of data. This type of plot makes it easy to focus attention on the median, quartiles, and the largest and smallest values of data. In particular, the box illustrates the "middle" 50 percent of the data, and the length of the box is the interquartile range, which is one measure of the spread of the data. The interquartile range provides a method of determining if there are outliers in the data. The standard deviation and the range are also methods of measuring the amount of spread of the data.

One major advantage of a box plot is that it does not become more cluttered with large amounts of data, as illustrated in the next example.

Example G

The ages of the women and men who have won Oscars for best actress and actor from 1928 to 2000 are shown here. The ages have been listed in increasing order.

Women: 21 22 24 24 24 24 24 25 25 25 26 26 26 26
        26 26 26 27 27 27 28 28 29 29 29 29 30 30
        30 30 31 31 32 33 33 33 33 33 34 34 34 34
        34 34 35 35 35 36 37 37 38 38 38 39 40 41
        41 41 41 41 42 43 45 45 48 49 49 60 61 61
        62 74 80

Men: 30 31 32 32 32 33 33 34 34 35 35 35 35 36
        36 36 37 37 38 38 38 38 38 38 38 39 39 39
        40 40 40 40 41 41 41 41 42 42 42 43 43 43
        43 44 44 45 45 46 46 46 47 47 48 48 48 49
        49 49 51 51 52 52 53 54 55 56 56 56 60 60
        61 62 76

1. What are the quartiles and median for each set of data?

2. Form a box-and-whisker plot to compare these sets of data. List some observations.

3. Use the interquartile range to determine if there are any outliers. If so, what are they?

Solution   1. Women: quartiles, 27 and 40.5; median, 33. Men: quartiles, 37.5 and 48.5; median, 42.

2.

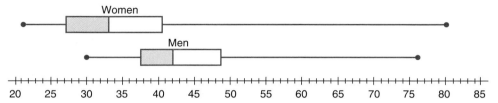

Observations: The median of the men's ages is greater than the upper quartile of the women's ages, which means that more than 75% of the women were younger than the median age of the men; and the median of the women's ages is below the lower quartile of the men's ages, which means that more than 50% of the women were younger than the lower quartile age of the men. In general, the men have higher ages, although the women have the greatest age. The boxes show that the middle 50 percent of each set of data is slightly more variable (spread out) for the women than for the men.

3.   The interquartile range for the women is $40.5 - 27 = 13.5$, and $1.5(13.5) + 40.5 = 60.75$. So 61, 62, 74 and 80 are outliers for the women's data. The interquartile range for the men is $48.5 - 37.5 = 11$, and $1.5 (11) + 48.5 = 65$. So 76 is an outlier for the men's data.

The box plot in Example G shows that the range (greatest value minus the smallest value) is greater for the women's data than for the men's. The boxes also indicate that the women's data are more variable. The standard deviation will provide another measure of this variability. A calculator with a statistics mode is convenient for finding the standard deviation.* After the appropriate keys are pressed to obtain the statistics mode and clear the statistical register, the data can be entered by pressing a key such as $\boxed{\Sigma+}$. Here is the sequence of steps for entering four numbers using this key.

$$16.8 \quad \boxed{\Sigma+} \quad 48.3 \quad \boxed{\Sigma+} \quad 77.1 \quad \boxed{\Sigma+} \quad 49.2$$

Once the data are entered, a number of calculations can be performed, including finding the mean by pressing $\bar{x}$ and the standard deviation by pressing σ_n or σ_{n-1}. To the nearest .1, the means for the women's and men's data are 35.8 and 43.3 and the standard deviations (using σ_n) are 11.9 and 8.7, respectively. The greater standard deviation for the women's data shows that these data are more spread out than the data for the men. Notice that the means for these sets of data are both greater than the medians.

*The computer program Standard Deviations on the *Mathematics Investigator* software (see website) computes the mean, median, mode, quartiles, and standard deviation for any data entered. It also prints the percentage of data within ± 1, ± 2, and ± 3 standard deviations of the mean.

EXERCISES AND PROBLEMS 7.2

Calculate the mean, median, and mode for each set of data in exercises 1 and 2.

1. a. 4, 7, 6, 2, 4, 5   **b.** 0, 1, 5, 0, 2, 0, 3, 1

2. a. 4, $^-$3, 2, 8, $^-$2, 0   **b.** 78, 85, 83, 71, 62, 83, 77

Which measure of central tendency—mean, median, or mode—is best for describing the instances in exercises 3 and 4?

3. a. The typical size of bicycles (by tire size) sold by a bicycle shop
   b. The typical size of dresses sold in a store
   c. The typical cost of homes in a community

4. a. The typical size of hats sold in a store
   b. The typical heights of players on a basketball team
   c. The typical age of seven people in a family if six of them are under 40 and one is 96 years old

The table below lists the number of nuclear power reactors operating in 21 countries in 1997 and their gross capacity in megawatts (1 million watts).* Use this table in exercises 5 and 6.

COUNTRY	NUMBER OF REACTORS	MEGAWATT CAPACITY
Argentina	2	1,005
Belgium	7	5,995
Bulgaria	6	3,760
Canada	21	15,795
China: Taiwan	6	5,144
Finland	4	2,605
France	56	60,674
Germany	20	23,496
Great Britain	35	15,272
Hungary	4	1,840
India	10	2,270
Japan	53	45,248
Mexico	2	1,350
Netherlands	2	540
Russia	29	21,266
South Africa	2	1,930
South Korea	12	10,315
Spain	9	7,572
Sweden	12	10,445
Switzerland	5	3,229
United States	109	106,541

Statistical Abstract of the United States, 120th ed. (Washington, DC: Bureau of the Census, 2000) p. 845.

5. a. What is the mean capacity in megawatts (to the nearest tenth) of the reactors in the United States, France, Japan, and Great Britain?
   b. Which of the four countries in part a has the smallest average megawatt capacity per reactor?

6. a. What is the mean number of reactors (to the nearest whole number) in these 21 countries? Explain why the mean is a misleading measure of central tendency in this example.
   b. What is the median for the numbers of reactors in these 21 countries?

The home run leaders in the National and American Leagues from 1982 to 2001 are listed below. Use these data in exercises 7 and 8.

Home run leaders

YEAR	AMERICAN LEAGUE	HOME RUNS
1982	Gorman Thomas, Milwaukee	
	Reggie Jackson, California	39
1983	Jim Rice, Boston	39
1984	Tony Armas, Boston	43
1985	Darrell Evans, Detroit	40
1986	Jesse Barfield, Toronto	40
1987	Mark McGwire, Oakland	49
1988	Jose Canseco, Oakland	42
1989	Fred McGriff, Toronto	36
1990	Cecil Fielder, Detroit	51
1991	Cecil Fielder, Detroit	
	Jose Canseco, Oakland	44
1992	Juan Gonzalez, Texas	43
1993	Juan Gonzalez, Texas	46
1994	Ken Griffey, Jr., Seattle	40
1995	Albert Belle, Cleveland	50
1996	Mark McGuire, Oakland	52
1997	Ken Griffey, Seattle	56
1998	Ken Griffey, Seattle	56
1999	Ken Griffey, Seattle	48
2000	Troy Glaus, Anaheim	47
2001	Alex Rodriquez, Texas	52

Home run leaders

YEAR	NATIONAL LEAGUE	HOME RUNS
1982	Dave Kingman, New York	37
1983	Mike Schmidt, Philadelphia	40
1984	Mike Schmidt, Philadelphia Dale Murphy, Atlanta	36
1985	Dale Murphy, Atlanta	37
1986	Mike Schmidt, Philadelphia	37
1987	Andre Dawson, Chicago	49
1988	Darryl Strawberry, New York	39
1989	Kevin Mitchell, San Francisco	47
1990	Ryne Sandberg, Chicago	40
1991	Howard Johnson, New York	38
1992	Fred McGriff, San Diego	35
1993	Barry Bonds, San Francisco	46
1994	Matt Williams, San Francisco	43
1995	Dante Bichette, Colorado	40
1996	Andres Galarraga, Colorado	47
1997	Larry Walker, Colorado	49
1998	Mark McGuire, St. Louis	70
1999	Mark McGuire, St. Louis	65
2000	Sammy Sosa, Chicago	50
2001	Barry Bonds, San Francisco	73

7. a. Compute the mean, median, and mode for the numbers of home runs in the National League.
  b. Compute the mean, median, and mode for the numbers of home runs in the American League.
  c. In how many different years did the American League home run leaders hit at least as many home runs as those of the National League?
  d. Which league's home run leaders have the better record? Support your conclusion.

8. Form a box-and-whisker plot for the numbers of home runs hit by the American and National League home run leaders from 1982 to 2001. Based on observations of the plot, which league's home run leaders, if either, have the better record? Support your conclusion.

The following box-and-whisker plot is for 40 test scores. Use this plot in exercises 9 and 10.

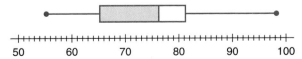

9. a. What is the lower quartile?
  b. Approximately how many test scores are between 65 and 76?
  c. Approximately how many test scores are above 65?
  d. What is the interquartile range?

10. a. What are the lowest and highest scores?
  b. What is the median score?
  c. What is the upper quartile?
  d. Approximately how many of the test scores are below 65?

Draw a box-and-whisker plot for the data in exercises 11 and 12.

11. 52, 61, 67, 75, 79, 81, 82, 83, 90, 93, 96
  a. What is the range of these data?
  b. What observations can you make from the plot?

12. 30, 162, 201, 149, 157, 214, 227, 154, 153, 179, 147, 226, 188, 230, 174, 223
  a. What is the range of these data?
  b. What observations can you make from the plot?

13. This list of the 25 largest states by population shows the percentage (to the nearest .1) of students completing high school according to the 1999 census.*

Alabama	81.1	Missouri	85.0
Arizona	83.1	New Jersey	87.4
California	80.4	New York	81.9
Florida	82.7	N. Carolina	79.8
Georgia	80.7	Ohio	86.1
Illinois	85.4	South Carolina	78.6
Indiana	82.9	Tennessee	79.1
Kentucky	78.2	Pennsylvania	86.1
Louisiana	78.3	Texas	78.2
Maryland	84.7	Virginia	87.3
Massachusetts	85.1	Washington	91.2
Michigan	85.5	Wisconsin	86.8
Minnesota	91.1		

  a. Draw a box-and-whisker plot of these data.
  b. What is the median and what information does it provide?
  c. What is the upper quartile, and what information does it provide?
  d. What is the lower quartile, and what information does it provide?

14. The box-and-whisker plots below illustrate the test scores of three classes that took the same test. Which class performed the best and which performed the worst? Support your conclusion.

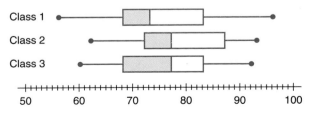

*Statistical Abstract of the United States, 120th ed. (Washington, DC: Bureau of the Census, 2000) p. 159.

The box plots below are the results of the ratings of eight different kinds of cars.* Each car was rated in 11 categories and received a number from 1 to 40 for each category. The 11 numbers for each car are the data for the box plots. Use these plots in exercises 15 and 16.

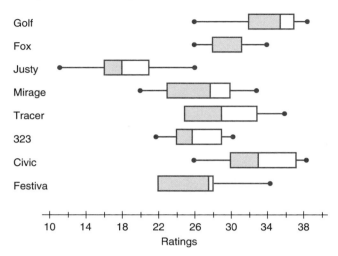

15. **a.** One measure of variability within the rating of each car is the size of the interquartile range, with greater size implying greater variability. Which car has the most variability in its ratings?
    b. Which car's ratings have the highest upper quartile?
    c. Which car's ratings have the lowest median?
    d. Which car has the best ratings? Support your choice.

16. **a.** If the smallest interquartile range indicates the least variability, which car's ratings are the least variable?
    b. Which car's ratings have the highest lower quartile?
    c. Which car's ratings have the highest median?
    d. The Justy has the poorest ratings. Which car has the second-poorest ratings? Support your conclusion.

17. The following table contains the percentage ratings of the top all-time television programs from 1977 to 2000.†

CBS	42.8	42.9	43.8	44.0	44.1	44.1	44.2
	45.3	45.8	46.3	46.4	47.2	48.5	48.5
	49.1	53.3	60.2				
ABC	42.5	43.1	43.2	43.3	43.4	43.8	44.1
	44.8	45.7	45.9	45.9	46.0	46.4	51.1
NBC	42.7	43.5	44.4	44.4	44.5	45.0	45.1
	45.5	45.5	45.5	46.5	46.6	47.1	47.4
	47.7	48.3	48.6				

   a. Form a box plot for each set of data, and use the plot to determine the network with the best ratings and the network with the worst ratings.
   b. Use the interquartile range to determine if there are any ratings which are outliers. If there are any outliers, write a statement about their meaning.

18. The grades of eight students on a 10-point test were 1, 3, 5, 5, 7, 8, 9, and 10.
    a. Compute the mean of these test scores.
    b. Compute the standard deviation of these scores to the nearest .01.
    c. Another class took the same test and had the same mean. What can be said about the two sets of test scores if the second class had a standard deviation of 2?

19. The following two sets of data both have a mean of 6.

   Set *A*: 0, 2, 4, 6, 8, 10, 12
   Set *B*: 3, 4, 5, 6, 7, 8, 9

    a. Predict which set of data will have the smaller standard deviation.
    b. Calculate the standard deviation for both sets of data.
    c. Do the standard deviations in part b support your prediction in part a? Explain.

Use the following list of resting pulse rates of 55 people in exercises 20 and 21. The mean of these rates is 72, and the standard deviation is approximately 9.2.

51	56	56	57	57	61	62	62	62	63	64	65
65	65	66	67	67	68	68	69	69	70	70	70
70	70	70	72	73	73	74	74	74	74	75	75
76	76	76	77	78	79	79	80	80	80		
81	82	84	84	86	86	89	91	92			

20. **a.** Determine the pulse rates that are within 1 standard deviation of the mean. What percentage of the total to the nearest .1 percent do these rates represent?
    b. What percentage of the pulse rates to the nearest .1 percent are within 2 standard deviations of the mean?

21. **a.** What percentage of the pulse rates to the nearest .1 percent are more than 2 standard deviations above the mean?

b. What percentage of the pulse rates to the nearest .1 percent are more than 2 standard deviations above or 2 standard deviations below the mean?

22. People often talk about "the good old days," but how good were they? The following table contains the amounts of time a person had to work in 1925 compared to the amount of time in 2000 to buy the items listed.

The Good Old Days

| To Buy | You Would Work in | |
	1925	2000
New car	41½ wks	30 wks
Year in college	31 wks	20 wks
Gas range	138 hrs	54 hrs
Washing machine	120½ hrs	50 hrs
Sewing machine	101½ hrs	38 hrs
Woman's skirt	6½ hrs	2 hrs
Dozen oranges	3/4 hrs	1/4 hrs
Dozen eggs	53 min	12 min
Pound of coffee	48 min	10 min
Pound of butter	1 min	8 min

a. Divide each amount of work time in 1925 by the corresponding amount of work time in 2000. Each 1925 work time is how many times the corresponding 2000 value? Compute your answer to the nearest .1.

b. Compute the mean of your answers in part a. On the average, the work time needed in 1925 to buy the items listed is how many times the work time needed in 2000 to the nearest tenth?

The 50 states of the United States and the District of Columbia are classified in four regions in the table on page 478.* The data in this table are used in subsequent exercises.

Use the data from the table on page 478 involving the average amount of money spent by state per student in exercises 23 and 24.

23. a. What are the quartiles and medians of the data for the states of the south and west?

b. Form box plots for the data for these two regions, and list some observations.

c. Compare the upper quartile for the south and the median for the west. Which is greater, and what does this mean?

d. Which of these two regions has the greater interquartile range? What does this show?

24. a. What are the quartiles and medians of the data for the states of the midwest and northeast–mid-Atlantic?

b. Form box plots for the data for these two regions, and list some observations.

c. Compare the median for the northeast–mid-Atlantic region to the greatest value of data for the midwest. What does this show?

d. Compare the upper quartile of the midwest to the lowest value of data for the northeast–mid-Atlantic region. What does this show, and what is its meaning?

Use the data from the table on page 478 involving the percentage of the population that is not composed of high school graduates in exercises 25 and 26.

25. a. What are the quartiles and medians of the data for the states of the west and midwest?

b. Form box plots for the data for these two regions.

c. Compare the box plots and state some observations.

d. Use the interquartile range for both sets of data to determine if there are any outliers.

26. a. What are the quartiles and medians of the data for the states of the south and northeast–mid-Atlantic?

b. Form box plots for the data for these two regions.

c. Compare the box plots and state some observations.

d. Use the interquartile range for both sets of data to determine if there are any outliers.

The data from the table on page 478 on the average (mean) personal income per capita by states are in thousands of dollars. For example, 19.5 represents $19,500. These incomes are rounded to the nearest $100. Use these data in exercises 27, 28, and 29.

27. a. Form box plots for the data for the states of the west and south.

b. What are the interquartile ranges for these sets of data. What do they show?

c. Compare the upper 50 percent of the incomes from the west to the upper 50 percent of the incomes from the south. What do the box plots show?

d. Which is greater, the median income for the south or the lower quartile income for the west?

e. Draw some conclusions from the box plots.

*From *Statistical Abstract of the United States,* 115th ed. (Washington, DC: Bureau of the Census, 1995), pp. 159, 168, 461, 482.

Four regions of U.S. data

	PERSONAL INCOME PER CAPITA (1994, IN THOUSANDS OF DOLLARS)	PERCENTAGE OF POPULATION NOT HIGH SCHOOL GRADUATES (1994, TO NEAREST PERCENT)	AVERAGE AMOUNT OF MONEY SPENT FOR EDUCATION PER STUDENT (1993, IN THOUSANDS OF DOLLARS)	PERCENTAGE OF POPULATION BELOW POVERTY LEVEL (1993, TO TENTH OF A PERCENT)
Northeast, Mid-Atlantic				
Maine	19.7	21	6.1	15.4
New Hampshire	23.4	18	5.6	9.9
Vermont	20.2	19	6.7	10.0
Massachusetts	25.6	20	6.6	10.7
Rhode Island	22.3	28	6.6	11.2
Connecticut	29.4	21	8.2	8.5
New York	30.0	25	8.8	16.4
New Jersey	28.0	23	9.5	10.9
Pennsylvania	22.3	25	6.9	13.2
Delaware	22.8	23	6.4	10.2
Maryland	24.9	22	6.4	9.7
District of Columbia	31.1	27	8.0	26.4
West Virginia	17.2	34	5.7	22.2
Midwest				
Ohio	20.9	24	5.3	13.3
Indiana	20.4	24	5.4	12.2
Illinois	23.8	24	5.4	13.6
Michigan	22.3	23	6.4	15.4
Wisconsin	21.0	21	6.5	12.6
Minnesota	22.5	18	5.6	11.6
Iowa	20.3	20	5.2	10.3
Missouri	20.7	26	4.5	16.1
North Dakota	18.5	23	4.9	11.2
South Dakota	19.6	23	4.4	14.2
Nebraska	20.5	18	4.9	10.3
Kansas	20.9	19	5.5	13.1
South				
Virginia	22.6	25	5.3	9.7
North Carolina	19.7	30	4.9	14.4
South Carolina	17.7	32	4.7	18.7
Georgia	20.3	29	4.7	13.5
Florida	21.7	26	5.3	17.8
Kentucky	17.8	35	4.9	20.4
Tennessee	19.5	33	4.0	19.6
Alabama	18.0	33	3.8	17.4
Mississippi	15.8	36	3.4	24.7
Arkansas	16.9	34	3.8	20.0
Louisiana	17.7	32	4.3	26.4
Oklahoma	17.7	25	4.1	19.9
Texas	19.9	28	4.9	17.4
West				
Montana	17.9	19	5.5	14.9
Idaho	18.2	20	4.0	13.1
Wyoming	20.4	17	5.8	13.3
Colorado	22.3	16	5.1	9.9
New Mexico	17.1	25	4.6	17.4
Arizona	19.0	21	4.1	15.4
Utah	17.0	15	3.2	10.7
Nevada	24.0	21	4.9	9.8
Washington	22.6	16	5.5	12.1
Oregon	20.4	19	6.1	11.8
California	22.5	24	4.6	18.2
Alaska	23.8	13	9.3	9.1
Hawaii	24.0	20	5.8	8.0

28. **a.** Form box plots for the data for the states of the midwest and northeast–mid-Atlantic.
   b. What are the interquartile ranges for these sets of data. What do they show?
   c. Compare the greatest income for the midwest with that for the northeast–mid-Atlantic. What do the box plots show?
   d. What do the upper quartile of the incomes of the midwest and the lower quartile of the incomes of the northeast–mid-Atlantic show about the average personal income in these two regions?
   e. The smallest data value for the northeast–mid-Atlantic is less than the smallest data value for the midwest. Is the data value for the northeast–mid-Atlantic an outlier?

29. **a.** Form box plots for the data for the states of the west and midwest.
   b. The interquartile range of incomes for the states of the west is about how many times the interquartile range of incomes for the states of the midwest?
   c. Compare the lower 25 percent of the incomes for the west to the lower 25 percent of the incomes of the midwest. What do the box plots show?
   d. State some conclusions from the box plots.

REASONING AND PROBLEM SOLVING

30. **Featured Strategy: Drawing a Graph** Richard bowled 25 games, and the mean of his scores was 195. His four lowest scores were 126, 130, 134, and 138. If he throws out these four low scores, what is the new mean?
   a. **Understanding the Problem** Throwing out four scores that are below the mean of 195 will result in a greater mean. How many games will be used to determine the new mean?
   b. **Devising a Plan** Sometimes *drawing a graph* of the given information will suggest a plan. A mean of 195 for 25 games can be pictured as 25 games, each with a score of 195. This is shown in the graph, in the next column, where the dashed lines represent the four low scores. What amounts would need to be added to the low scores to bring them up to 195? Devise a plan to determine the new mean when these low scores are thrown out.

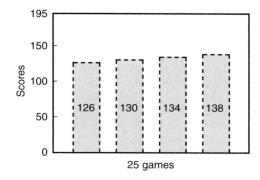

25 games

c. **Carrying Out the Plan** Use your plan to determine the new mean for the 21 games.
d. **Looking Back** You may have used the approach of determining the total score for the 25 games. What is the total? Then the four low scores can be subtracted to obtain a new total. Show how to determine the new mean by using this approach.

31. An ice cream shop owner hires a clerk and informs him that the mean weight of scoops of ice cream should be 45 grams. The clerk weighs out seven ice cream scoops with the following weights in grams: 43, 46, 44, 41, 44, 45, and 39. How many grams of ice cream should be added to the smallest of these scoops to obtain an average weight of 45 grams for the seven scoops?

32. The mean for the numbers of earthquake deaths (see Figure 7.19) is 23,249. This mean is high because of the unusually high number of deaths from the 1976 earthquake in China. A number from a set of data which is far removed from the other numbers is called an **outlier.** What would be the mean to the nearest whole number of the 44 numbers of earthquake deaths if the 800,000 deaths were replaced by the mean of the remaining 43 numbers?

33. In the Lee Middle School, the ratio of the number of fifth-graders to the number of sixth-graders is 4 to 3, and there are 18 more fifth-graders. If the ratio of the number of sixth-graders to the number of seventh-graders is 2 to 3, what is the mean number of students in the three grades?

34. Demetra has taken nine quizzes in an environmental conservation course, and the mean of her scores is 81. The course syllabus states that two of the lowest quiz scores will be thrown out. If her lowest scores are 57 and 62, what is the mean to the nearest whole number of her seven remaining scores?

35. A scientist is testing a new sweetener on 10 mice. In a period of 3 days the mice gain the following weights in grams: 4.9, 6.3, 5.1, 6.1, 5.8, 6.2, 5.7, 6.3, 6.0, and 5.6. To compare this experiment to the results of previous tests, the scientist needs to determine the percentage of these gains in weight that is within ±1 standard deviation of the mean of the 10 weights.

   a. What is the mean of these weights?

   b. What is the standard deviation to the nearest .01 of these weights?

   c. What percentage of these weights is within ±1 standard deviation of the mean?

36. Ian and Meredith each took eight quizzes in a biology course, one quiz for each of eight chapters of a text. If they both had a mean of 71 for their eight scores and Ian's standard deviation was 11 while Meredith's standard deviation was 4, what conclusion can you draw regarding their knowledge of the material of the eight chapters?

37. Peter and Sally each shoot 12 arrows at a target which is circular with a diameter of 72 inches. The mean of the distances that Peter's arrows strike from the center of the target is 20 inches, and the standard deviation of his distances is 3 inches. The mean of the distances that Sally's arrows strike from the center of the target is 16 inches, and the standard deviation of her distances is 4 inches. What statements can be made about the region of the target that at least 75 percent of Peter's arrows strike and the region of the target that at least 75 percent of Sally's arrows strike?

ONLINE LEARNING CENTER   www.mhhe.com/bennett-nelson

   • Math Investigation 7.2   *Standard Deviation*
   Section-Related: • Links   • Writing/Discussion Problems   • Bibliography

---

PUZZLER

The school ski team drove 120 miles into the mountains at an average speed of 40 miles per hour. The return trip was completed at an average speed of 60 miles per hour. When the coach computed the average speed for the entire trip, she was surprised to find that it was not 50 miles per hour (the average of 40 and 60). What was the average speed for the trip?

MATH ACTIVITY 7.3

GRAPHING BELL-SHAPED DISTRIBUTIONS

Materials: Spinners and color tiles in the Manipulative Kit. Copy the 2-centimeter grid from the inside cover of the text or the website. (Use a paper clip for the spinner, as shown on page 458.)

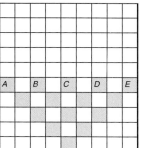

Start

1. Use a 2-centimeter grid to make a copy of the grid shown at the left. Place a tile on the square marked *Start*. Spin the 1-to-4 spinner to obtain a color. Move the tile right to the shaded square in the second row if the color is red and left to the shaded square if the color is green. Continue spinning and moving the tile forward (right for red and left for green) until it is at one of the shaded squares marked *A, B, C, D,* or *E*. Place the tile above the lettered square.

   a. Do you think that each lettered square has the same chance of receiving a tile? Assuming this process was carried out 32 times with 32 tiles, make a prediction as to how many tiles would land on each lettered square and write the predictions next to the letters.

   b. Place a different tile at the Start square and carry out this process a total of 32 times. Place each of the tiles above the shaded square on which it lands to form a bar graph.

   c. From your results, which squares are most likely to have a tile land on them and which are least likely?

2. The diagram at the left shows that there is only one path from the Start square to the square lettered *A*.

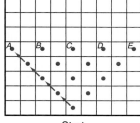

Start

   * a. Trace out and count the number of different paths to each lettered square.

   b. Determine what percentage of the paths leads to each lettered square.

   c. If you completed the process of spinning and moving 128 tiles to the lettered squares, what is the theoretical number of tiles that might be expected to land on each lettered square of the graph?

   d. Distributions like the one in part c are called **bell-shaped.** Is your bar graph from activity 1 approximately bell-shaped? Combine your data with a classmate's to see if the total data are approximately bell-shaped.

SECTION 7.3

SAMPLING, PREDICTIONS, AND SIMULATIONS

"That's the worst set of opinions I've heard in my entire life

Drawing by Robert Weber; © 1995 The New Yorker Magazine, Inc.

In one survey of trout populations, biologists caught and marked 232 trout from a lake. Three months later the biologists selected a second sample of 329 trout from the lake, and 16 were found to be marked. Assuming that the 232 marked trout intermingled freely with unmarked trout during the 3-month period, estimate the number of trout in the lake.

Making predictions from samples is an important part of *inferential statistics.* Because of the many possibilities for errors, strict procedures must be followed in gathering data. The sample must be large enough, and it must be a representative cross section of the whole.

The need for scientific sampling techniques was dramatically illustrated in the 1936 Presidential election. *Literary Digest,* which had been conducting surveys of elections since 1920, sent questionnaires to 10 million voters (Figure 7.28). Its sample was obtained from telephone directories and lists of automobile owners. By choosing the sample this way, the magazine's editors selected people with above-average incomes (that is, voters who could afford what were relative luxuries at that time: phones and cars) rather than voters from a range of income levels. Based on its sample, the *Digest* predicted that Alfred Landon would win. Instead, the election was a landslide victory for Franklin D. Roosevelt, who had much popular support among middle- and low-income voters.

Topics of the day

LANDON, 1,293,669; ROOSEVELT, 972,897

Final returns in The Digest's Poll of Ten Million Voters

Well, the great battle of the ballots in the Polls of ten million voters, scattered throughout the forty eight capital states of the Union, is now finished, and in the table below we record the figures received up to the hour of going to press.

These figures are exactly from more than opp polled in our c

tran National Committee purchased *THE LITERARY DIGEST* ?" And all types and variables including: "Have

Figure 7.28

The concept of sample is difficult for young students. Most of their data gathering is for full populations such as their own class.

Standards 2000, p. 113

Sampling

A **sample** is a collection of people or objects chosen to represent a larger collection of people or objects, called the **population.** For example, when a national poll of 1873 people is used to determine the popularity of a television program, the 1873 people form the sample and all television watchers in the country are the population.

RANDOM SAMPLING If a sample is obtained in such a way that every element in the population has the same chance of being selected, it is called a **random sample** and the process is called **random sampling.**

Randomness is difficult to achieve. Repeatedly tossing a coin may appear to be a random method of making yes-or-no decisions, but imbalances in the coin's weight and tossing it to approximately the same height each time are two factors that could cause a biased result. Similarly, dice and spinners produce fairly random sequences of numbers, but these also have slight biases due to their physical imperfections.

One method of obtaining a random sample is to use a table of **random digits.** Many types of calculators are programmed to generate random digits.* The list of random digits in Figure 7.29 is from a computer printout. The digits are printed in pairs and groups of 10 for ease of reading and counting.

```
40 09 18 94 06   62 89 97 10 02   58 63 02 91 44   79 03 55 47 69   14 11 42 33 99
33 19 98 40 42   13 73 63 72 59   26 06 08 92 65   63 08 82 45 85   14 45 81 65 21
69 49 02 58 44   45 45 19 69 33   51 68 97 99 05   77 54 22 70 97   59 06 64 21 68
17 49 43 65 45   04 95 82 76 31   85 53 15 21 70   59 17 27 54 67   07 76 13 95 00
43 13 78 80 55   90 80 88 19 13   13 89 11 00 60   41 86 23 07 60   22 77 93 30 83
```

Figure 7.29

The following example illustrates the use of random digits for obtaining a random sample. First a number is assigned to each element of the population. Then, to ensure randomness, an arbitrary starting place is selected in a table of random digits.

*The TI-81, SHARP EL-520 G, and CASIO fx-250 D calculators have function keys for producing lists of random digits.

Example A

How can a table of random digits be used to select 10 questions randomly from a list of 50 questions?

Solution   Number the questions from 1 to 50. Then arbitrarily select a pair of numbers from the table in Figure 7.25, say 26, the 11th pair in the second row. Beginning with this number and moving to the right along the row, list the first 10 different numbers that are less than or equal to 50. The numbers of the 10 questions to be selected are 26, 6, 8, 45, 14, 21, 49, 2, 44, and 19.

The list of digits in Figure 7.29 may also be used to obtain random single-digit numbers or numbers with three or more digits.

Example B

How can a list of random digits be used to select a random sample of 65 items from a list of items numbered 1 to 650?

Solution   One way is to start with any digit in a table of random digits and list consecutive groups of three digits until you have found 65 numbers between 1 and 650. The numerals 001, 002, etc., represent 1, 2, etc., and any triples of numbers from the table that are greater than 650 are discarded. If we use this method with the table of random digits in Figure 7.29 and begin with the first line, 400 is the first number. Then 918, 940, 662, 899, and 710 are discarded because they are greater than 650. The next acceptable number is 025, which represents 25. Using this process with a sufficiently large table of random digits will produce a random sample of 65 items.

STRATIFIED SAMPLING   In **stratified sampling,** a population is divided into groups. The number sampled from each group is then determined by the ratio of the size of the group to the size of the total population.

Example C

Research Statement

The 7th national mathematics assessment found that proportional reasoning was a source of difficulty for students in reasoning about data, graphs, and chance.

Zawojewski and Shaughnessy 2000

A city council wants to sample the opinion of the city's adult population of 80,000 people on a plan to build a public swimming pool. The population is divided into three groups—high-income, middle-income, and low-income—and 1500 people are to be sampled. If 16,000 people are low-income, 56,000 are middle-income, and 8000 are high-income, determine the size of the sample for each income group.

Solution   Since 16,000/80,000 = .2 and .2 × 1500 = 300, 300 people will be sampled from the low-income group. Since 56,000/80,000 = .7 and .7 × 1500 = 1050, 1050 people will be sampled from the middle-income group. Finally, since 8000/80,000 = .1 and .1 × 1500 = 150, 150 people will be sampled from the high-income group.

Skewed and Symmetric Distributions

The graph of a set of data provides a visual way of illustrating the **distribution** of the data, that is, how the data are clustered together, isolated from each other, or spread out.

For example, the bar graph in Figure 7.30 shows that about 97 families have no children, about 105 families have 1 child, etc. The most common number of children per family (the mode) is 2. Graphs that show the data piled up at one end of the scale and tapering off toward the other end are called **skewed.** The direction of skewness is determined by the longer "tail" of the distribution. The graph in Figure 7.30 is said to be **skewed to the right** (positively skewed).

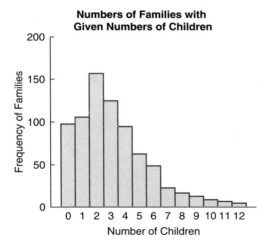

Figure 7.30

Similarly, a graph may have data piled up at the right with the "tail" extending to the left. This type of graph is said to be **skewed to the left** (negatively skewed). Such a graph is illustrated in Figure 7.31. It shows the numbers of teachers in a school system who drive cars built in the years from 1985 to 2000; the greatest number of teachers have cars that were built in recent years. The mode in this example is the year 1996.

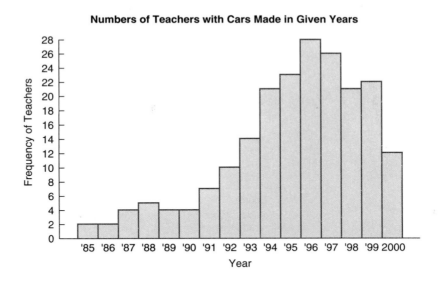

Figure 7.31

A distribution of data in which measurements at equal distances from the center of the distribution occur with the same frequency is said to be **symmetric.** A symmetric distribution and two skewed distributions are shown in Figure 7.32. The graph shows the relative positions of the mean, median, and mode for these distributions. Notice that in a symmetric distribution the mean, median, and mode are all equal.

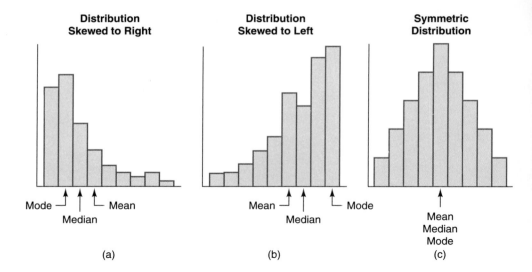

Figure 7.32

(a)   (b)   (c)

Example D

School test results sometimes produce skewed graphs, especially if the test is too difficult or too easy for the students. Determine the types of distributions of test scores that will occur in each of the following cases.

1. A test designed for fifth-graders is given to second-graders.

2. A test designed for fifth-graders is given to fifth-graders.

3. A test designed for fifth-graders is given to eighth-graders.

Solution   1. The majority of scores will be low, and the distribution will be skewed to the right, as shown in (*a*) below.   2. The distribution of scores will be more or less symmetric, as illustrated in (*b*).   3. The majority of scores will be high, and the distribution will be skewed to the left, as in (*c*).

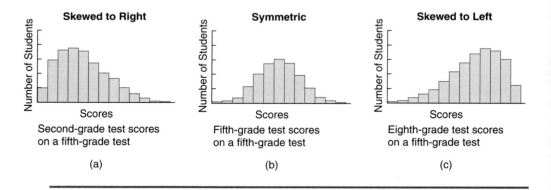

(a)   (b)   (c)

Normal Distributions

As the number of values in a set of data increases and the width of the intervals for the grouped data (width of bars) on the histogram becomes smaller, the shape of the top of the histogram approaches a smooth curve. Thus in graphing large sets of data, it is customary to approximate the histogram (see Figure 7.33a) by a smooth curve (see Figure 7.33b).

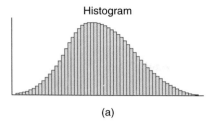

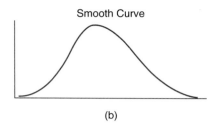

Figure 7.33 (a)   (b)

A smooth symmetric bell-shaped curve, such as the curve shown in Figure 7.34, is called a **normal curve,** and the distribution of its data is called a **normal distribution.** Normal distributions have certain important properties. About 68 percent of the values are within 1 standard deviation of the mean; about 95 percent are within 2 standard deviations of the mean; and about 99.7 percent fall within 3 standard deviations of the mean. The remaining percentage is evenly divided above and below 3 standard deviations. These approximate percentages hold for any normal distribution, regardless of the mean or the size of the standard deviation.

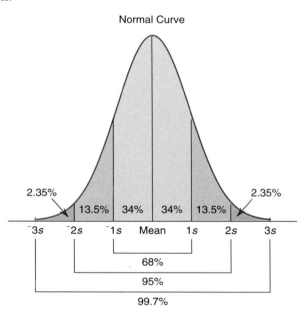

Figure 7.34

The shapes of normal curves vary, as shown in Figure 7.35. The standard deviation of the data determines the shape of the curve. The smaller the standard deviation is, the less spread out the data and the taller and thinner the curve, as in Figure 7.35a. The larger the standard deviation is, the more spread out the data and the lower and flatter the curve, as in Figure 7.35c. The standard deviations of the three sets of data for the normal curves in Figure 7.35 increase from part a to part c.

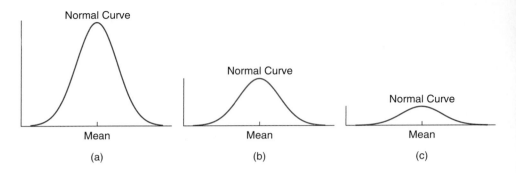

Figure 7.35

The mean and standard deviation of a normal distribution are used to provide information about the distribution of data, as shown in the next two examples.

Example E

The following graph, showing the distribution of the heights of 8585 men, is an approximation to a nearly normal distribution. The mean is approximately 68 inches (5 feet 8 inches), and the standard deviation is approximately 3 inches.

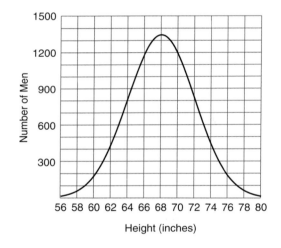

1. How many of these men are between 5 feet 5 inches and 5 feet 11 inches tall?

2. How many men are between 5 feet 2 inches and 6 feet 2 inches tall?

3. How many men are less than 5 feet 2 inches tall?

Solution   1. One standard deviation above and below the mean includes the heights from 5 feet 5 inches to 5 feet 11 inches, and this interval contains 68 percent of the data. Since .68 × 8585 ≈ 5838, there are approximately 5838 men with heights in this interval.   2. Two standard deviations above and below the mean includes the heights from 5 feet 2 inches to 6 feet 2 inches, and this interval contains 95 percent of the data. Since .95 × 8585 ≈ 8156, there are approximately 8156 men in this interval.   3. More than 2 standard deviations above and below the mean corresponds to heights of less than 5 feet 2 inches and more than 6 feet 2 inches; these intervals together contain 5 percent of the data, so each contains approximately 2.5 percent of the data. Since .025 × 8585 ≈ 215, there are approximately 215 men who are less than 5 feet 2 inches tall.

Example F

The National Academy of Sciences has suggested a standard for public water that allows no more than 100 milligrams of sodium per liter of water. The records of a certain city's water treatment plant for a 200-day period are normally distributed and show that the mean number of milligrams per liter is 94.0 with a standard deviation of 3.0. For how many days of this period were the sodium levels above 100 milligrams?

Solution Two standard deviations above the mean of 94 is 100. Since approximately 2.5 percent of the measurements of a normal distribution is above 2 standard deviations, and $.025 \times 200 = 5$, the sodium level was above 100 milligrams per liter on five days.

HISTORICAL HIGHLIGHT

The word *normal* is used to indicate that a normal distribution is very common in nature. About 1833, Belgian scientist L. A. J. Quetelet collected large amounts of data on human measurements: height, weight, length of limbs, intelligence, etc. He found that all measurements of mental and physical characteristics of humans tended to be normally distributed. That is, the majority of people have measurements that are close to the mean (average), and measurements farther from the mean occur less frequently. Quetelet was convinced that nature aims at creating the perfect person but misses the mark and thus creates deviations on both sides of the ideal.

Measures of Relative Standing

We often wish to determine the relative standing of one measurement in a given set of data, that is, to compare one value with the distribution of all values. This is especially important in analyzing test results. The mean is one common **measure of relative standing.** If the mean of some test scores is 70 and a student has a score of 85, then we know the student has done better than average. However, this information does not tell us how many students scored higher than 70 or whether 85 was the highest score on the test.

PERCENTILES One popular method of stating a person's relative performance on a test is to give the percentage of people who did not score as high. For example, a person who scores higher than 80 percent of the people taking a test is said to be in the *80th percentile.*

> *p*TH PERCENTILE The **pth percentile** of a set of data is a number that is greater than **p** percent of the data and less than $(100 - p)$ percent of the data.

Percentiles range from a low of 1 to a high of 99 percent; the 50th percentile is the median. It is customary on standardized tests to establish percentiles for large samples of people. When you take such a test, your score is compared to those of the sample. A percentile score of 65 means that you did better than 65 percent of the sample group. The table and bar graph in Figure 7.36 show a student's performance on a differential aptitude test. Nine categories are listed in the table at the top of this form: verbal reasoning, numerical ability, VR + NA (verbal reasoning and numerical ability together), abstract reasoning, etc. The raw score in each category represents the number of questions that the student answered correctly. The student's percentile score is obtained by comparing these raw scores with the scores from a sample of thousands of other students. The bar graph is a visual representation of the percentile scores. A horizontal line at the 50th percentile makes it easier to spot scores above and below the median.

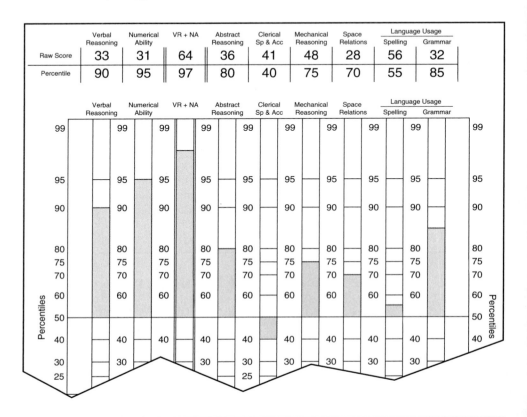

| | Verbal Reasoning | Numerical Ability | VR + NA | Abstract Reasoning | Clerical Sp & Acc | Mechanical Reasoning | Space Relations | Language Usage | |
								Spelling	Grammar
Raw Score	33	31	64	36	41	48	28	56	32
Percentile	90	95	97	80	40	75	70	55	85

Figure 7.36

The 50th percentile (median) splits any set of data into two parts: the lower part and the upper part. The median of the lower part is the 25th percentile or **lower quartile** (see Figure 7.37), and the median of the upper part is the 75th percentile or **upper quartile**.

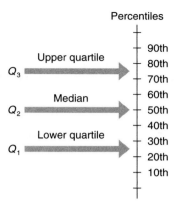

Figure 7.37

Z SCORES Percentiles are a method of stating a person's relative standing on a test compared to that of others on the same test. But suppose you wish to compare performances on two different tests. One popular method of determining relative standing is to compute the number of standard deviations that a person's test score is from the mean.

Example H

John scored 572 on the mathematics part of the Scholastic Aptitude Test (SAT). The mean score for this test was 460, and the standard deviation was 112. Bev scored 28 on the American College Test (ACT), and this test had a mean of 18 and a standard deviation of 5. Who had the better performance?

Solution   John's score of 572 is 1 standard deviation above the mean ($460 + 112 = 572$). Bev's score of 28 is 2 standard deviations above the mean. Even though Bev's score of 28 on the ACT appears much lower than John's score of 572 on the SAT, Bev's performance was better.

The number of standard deviations that a measurement is from the mean is called the *z* **score.** A *z* score can be defined for every measure in a set of data.

The *z* **score** for a measurement *x* is denoted by

$$z = \frac{x - \bar{x}}{\sigma}$$

where $\bar{x}$ is the mean and σ is the standard deviation for the set of data.

Notice that in Example H, John has a *z* score of 1, since

$$z = \frac{572 - 460}{112} = 1$$

and Bev has a *z* score of 2, since

$$z = \frac{28 - 18}{5} = 2$$

Figure 7.38 shows a few *z* scores and their relationship to the standard deviation and mean. Notice that if a measurement has a *z* score of 0, the measurement equals the mean.

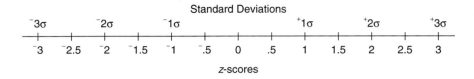

Figure 7.38

Example I

Three students each took a different test, and these three tests had different means and standard deviations. The results are listed below. Which student had the best relative performance and which had the worst?

Student 1 scored 82 on test 1. The mean on this test was 78.5, and the standard deviation was 2.3.

Student 2 scored 55 on test 2. The mean on this test was 48.2, and the standard deviation was 4.3.

Student 3 scored 392 on test 3. The mean on this test was 460, and the standard deviation was 85.

Solution   Student 1:
$$z = \frac{82 - 78.5}{2.3} \approx 1.52$$

Student 2:
$$z = \frac{55 - 48.2}{4.3} \approx 1.58$$

Student 3:
$$z = \frac{392 - 460}{85} = {}^{-}.8$$

Student 2 had the best relative performance with a z score of 1.58, and student 3 had the worst performance. Notice that student 3 scored below the mean, so the z score is a negative number.

USING Z SCORES FOR PREDICTIONS   Almost all z scores are between $^{-}3$ and $^{+}3$, and most z scores are between $^{-}2$ and $^{+}2$. Thus, since few measurements are more than 2 standard deviations from the mean, we will define such measurements to be *rare events.*

> RARE EVENT   If a measurement for a set of data is more than 2 standard deviations from the mean, it is considered to be a **rare event.** That is, if its z score is less than $^{-}2$ or more than $^{+}2$, it is considered to be a rare event.

This definition can be applied to make predictions.

Example J

In a certain school system, the mean annual salary for male teachers with more than 20 years of teaching experience was $47,320 with a standard deviation of $2540. A female teacher with more than 20 years of teaching experience and an annual salary of $42,000 filed a grievance procedure, claiming that her salary was low due to sex discrimination. Is there evidence to support her claim?

Solution   The z score for the female teacher's salary is

$$\frac{42,000 - 47,320}{2540} \approx {}^{-}2.1$$

Since the z score is below $^{-}2$, the female teacher's salary is considered a rare event; that is, it is evidence of discrimination.

Simulations

There are many statistical problems that are of interest to children but are beyond their abilities to solve theoretically. The next example contains a type of problem that might appeal to elementary school children. Such problems are related to sampling and can be solved by conducting experiments.

Example K

Each package of a certain brand of cereal contains one of seven cards about superheroes. The students in an elementary school class wanted to know how many boxes of cereal they could expect to buy before getting the entire set.*

Solution   The elementary school class solved this problem by writing the names of the seven superheroes on slips of paper and then performing the following experiment: (1) The seven slips of paper were put in a bag.   (2) A slip was drawn at random from the bag, the superhero's name was tallied, and the slip of paper was returned to the bag.   (3) Step 2 was repeated until the name of each superhero had been drawn at least once.   (4) The total number of draws was recorded. This total represents the number of boxes needed in this experiment to obtain an entire set of superhero cards.

This experiment was repeated 20 times. Here are the numbers of boxes obtained in the 20 experiments:

20, 14, 27, 18, 17, 15, 19, 19, 19, 20, 16, 11, 15, 21, 15, 22, 20, 28, 12, 26

The average (mean) number of "boxes" for this experiment before one gets the entire set of cards is the sum of these numbers divided by 20:

$$\frac{374}{20} = 18.7 \approx 19$$

> If simulations are used, teachers need to help students understand what the simulation data represent and how they relate to the problem situation, . . .
>
> Standards 2000, p. 254

The students could see that they might have to go through more than 19 boxes to get all seven cards if they were unlucky; or they might collect all seven cards after buying fewer than 19 boxes, if they were lucky.

Finding an answer to the question in Example K by purchasing boxes of cereal would be expensive. Representing cereal box prizes by writing names on slips of paper and performing experiments is an example of a *simulation*. In general, a **simulation** is a procedure in which experiments that closely resemble the given situation are conducted repeatedly. This method relies on identifying a model, such as rolling dice, tossing a coin, or using a table of random digits, that can be used to *simulate* an event and then performing experiments using the model.

Problem-Solving Application

Using a simulation is a powerful problem-solving technique.

PROBLEM

If people are selected randomly, how many must be selected (on average) to find two who have a birthday in the same month?

Understanding the Problem   It might be necessary to select several people to find two with a birthday in the same month. **Question 1:** What is the minimum number that must be chosen before this will happen?

---

*Ann E. Watkins, "Monte Carlo Simulations: Probability the Easy Way," in *Teaching Statistics and Probability*, 1981 Yearbook (Reston, VA: National Council of Teachers of Mathematics, 1981), pp. 203–209.

Devising a Plan   Conducting a simulation will be more convenient than interviewing large numbers of people. One method of simulation involves writing the whole numbers from 1 to 12 on 12 slips of paper to represent each of the 12 months and placing them in a box. A slip is then randomly selected, its number is recorded, and the slip is returned to the box. An experiment consists of selecting numbers one at a time until the same number is obtained twice. After this experiment has been carried out several times, we can determine the mean of the numbers of selections. **Question 2:** Why must each slip of paper be returned to the box after it is selected?

Carrying Out the Plan   The following 19 groups of numbers were obtained by selecting slips of paper from a box until the same number was chosen twice for each group. Determine the mean (average) size of these groups of numbers. **Question 3:** According to this experiment, how many people must be interviewed (on average) to find two with a birthday in the same month?

7, 2, 2   1, 9, 10, 3, 5, 6, 9   7, 2, 2   10, 11, 8, 10   11, 9, 2, 3, 7, 9
9, 4, 9   7, 11, 9, 6, 4, 6   5, 9, 9   7, 12, 6, 11, 12   9, 12, 3, 11, 1, 4, 1
12, 2, 8, 6, 6   7, 2, 3, 9, 11, 9   12, 9, 3, 7, 5, 3   7, 2, 11, 4, 10, 5, 12, 9, 7
1, 4, 12, 2, 12   5, 9, 8, 3, 8   11, 11   6, 2, 12, 7, 1, 1   5, 2, 12, 10, 12

Looking Back   Another solution to this problem can be found by using a table of random numbers for the simulation (see below). One way to use such a table is to select one of the numbers arbitrarily as a beginning point and then, moving from left to right, to record pairs of numbers that are greater than 0 and less than or equal to 12, with 01, 02, etc., being counted as 1, 2, etc. Solve the original problem by carrying out a simulation, using the following list of random digits. **Question 4:** What number do you obtain as a solution to the problem by using this simulation?

89 81 80 69 77 09 86 76 77 71 21 52 23 86 53 95 20 94 29 48 33 37 58 33 93
24 30 87 37 31 80 37 25 47 06 72 78 11 30 08 88 84 78 78 46 51 14 96 58 12
77 02 18 48 54 50 76 36 05 12 33 77 59 58 76 17 68 58 89 84 38 35 42 17 55
58 01 63 92 45 47 24 54 42 80 55 53 09 95 46 98 94 67 27 15 52 56 08 82 56
24 39 68 08 01 15 72 23 88 37 38 00 36 94 14 47 88 90 44 74 28 27 01 71 16
05 61 62 60 18 72 01 75 51 88 52 95 13 39 81 75 76 66 02 76 29 69 77 96 77
62 23 95 43 71 34 38 09 45 82 85 62 72 58 62 74 51 95 87 44 45 01 77 67 26
43 07 96 21 98 68 25 01 17 11 59 32 39 70 13 21 43 81 57 55 86 59 28 45 34
95 78 66 81 10 85 54 62 86 27 44 89 51 18 75 48 62 29 43 54 44 46 13 32 13
55 00 90 00 42 27 01 23 24 10 49 21 46 26 14 82 31 94 54 39 55 07 81 32 57
81 57 86 88 83 81 54 91 42 82 82 14 44 13 30 27 84 31 77 21 88 67 72 04 36
99 94 94 09 62 81 41 09 62 30 95 13 69 92 15 18 76 02 78 22 15 86 90 86 72

Answers to Questions 1–4   1. Two   **2.** There should be an equal chance of any number's being chosen in any selection from the box   **3.** The following numbers represent the sizes of the groups: 3, 7, 3, 4, 6, 3, 6, 3, 5, 7, 5, 6, 6, 9, 5, 5, 2, 6, 5. The mean of these numbers is 96/19 ≈ 5.05. Thus on average approximately five people must be chosen before two are found with a birthday in the same month.   **4.** Starting at the beginning of the list at 89, we obtain the following groups: [09, 06, 11, 08, 12, 02, 05, 12], [01, 09, 08, 08], [01, 01], [05, 01, 02, 09, 01], [07, 01, 11, 10, 01], [10, 07, 04, 09, 09]. The mean size of these six groups is approximately 4.8.

EXERCISES AND PROBLEMS 7.3

> ### Student Flips, Finds Penny Is Tail Heavy
>
> by Martin Weil
>
> Washington Post Staff Writer
>
> Edward J. Kelsey, 16, turned his dining room into a penny pitching parlor one day last spring, all in the name of science and statistics.
>
> In ten hours the Northwestern High School senior registered 17,950 coin flips and showed the world that you didn't get as many heads as tails. You get more.
>
> Edward got 464 more, enough to make him study the coin's balance and so discover that the United States Mint produces tail-heavy pennies.

As the above article from the *Washington Post* reports, a student recorded 17,950 coin flips and got 464 more heads than tails. He concluded that the U.S. Mint produces tail-heavy coins. For many repeated experiments of 17,950 tosses of a fair coin, we can expect an approximately normal distribution with a mean of 8975 heads and a standard deviation of 67. Use this information in exercises 1 and 2.

1. a. The area under a normal curve within ± 1 standard deviation of the mean is 68 percent of the total area under the curve. Therefore, 68 percent of the time, the number of heads should be between what two numbers?

    b. The area under a normal curve within ± 2 standard deviations of the mean is approximately 95 percent of the total area under the curve. Therefore, approximately 95 percent of the time, the number of heads should be between what two numbers?

2. a. The area under a normal curve which is less than $^+3$ standard deviations is approximately 99.85 percent of the total area under the curve. Therefore, 99.85 percent of the time, the number of heads should be less than what number?

    b. Edward Kelsey got 9207 heads. Was he justified in concluding that the coins are tail-heavy?

Describe a method for using a table of random digits in exercises 3 and 4 to obtain the random samples. Then use the table of random digits on page 494 to obtain the sample.

3. a. The names of 2 people from a list of 9
    b. Ten test questions from a total of 60

4. a. Five people from a group of 30
    b. The health records of 8 children from a class of 25

5. An elementary school has the following numbers of students in grades K to 4: grade K, 50; grade 1, 80; grade 2, 90; grade 3, 80; and grade 4, 100. If a stratified sample of 80 children is to be chosen, how many will be chosen from each grade?

6. There are 18 girls and 12 boys in a class. If stratified sampling is used to select 10 students, how many girls will be selected?

Describe the distribution of scores (skewed to the right, symmetric, skewed to the left) for the tests in exercises 7 and 8.

7. a. A test designed for third-graders and given to first-graders
    b. A test designed for sixth-graders and given to eighth-graders

8. a. A test designed for fourth-graders and given to second-graders
    b. A test designed for second-graders and given to second-graders

Would you expect the distribution of the sets of data in exercises 9 and 10 to be skewed to the right, symmetric, or skewed to the left? (*Hint:* Sketch a graph with some typical values.)

9. a. Amounts of time students study in a 24-hour period before an exam
    b. Widths of the hand spans of fifth-graders
    c. Sneaker sizes of professional basketball players

10. a. Heights of college students
    b. Test scores of third-graders on a pretest on fractions at the beginning of the school year
    c. Weights of newborn babies

The normal curve below shows a distribution of college entrance exam scores that has a mean of 500 and a standard deviation of 100. Use this curve in exercises 11 and 12.

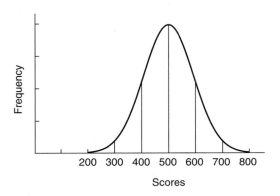

Scores

11. a. What percentage of students scored between 400 and 600?
  b. What percentage of students scored above 600?
  c. What percentage of students scored below 300?

12. a. What percentage of students scored between 300 and 600?
  b. What percentage of students scored above 700?
  c. What percentage of students scored above 800?

One method of grading tests that uses a normal curve gives students letter grades depending on the standard-deviation interval above or below the mean that contains their score: a grade of F for below $^-2$ standard deviations; D for $^-2$ to $^-1$ standard deviation; C for $^-1$ to 1; B for 1 to 2; and A for above 2 standard deviations. In exercises 13 and 14, use this grading system and the fact that on a test given to 50 students the mean score was 78 and the standard deviation was 6.

13. a. How many students failed the course?
  b. How many students received a grade of B?
  c. How many students received a D?

14. a. How many students received a C?
  b. How many students received a grade below C?
  c. How many students received an A?

This bar graph shows the measures of the diameters (to the nearest inch) of 100 trees of the same species. The mean diameter is 12 inches, and the standard deviation is approximately 2 inches. Use this information in exercises 15 and 16.

Diameters of Trees

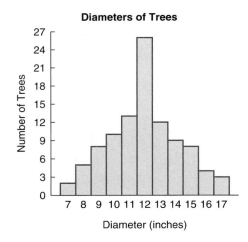

Diameter (inches)

15. a. What type of distribution does this graph illustrate?
  b. Make a frequency table showing the numbers of trees of each diameter.
  c. What percentage of the diameters are within 1 standard deviation of the mean?

16. a. What percentage of the trees have diameters within 2 standard deviations of the mean?
  b. What percentage of the trees have diameters greater than $^+2$ standard deviations?
  c. What can be said about the difference between the mean diameter of the trees and the diameter of a tree which is more than 2 standard deviations below the mean?

Trace the graph below on a sheet of paper, and mark the approximate locations of the 10th, 25th, 50th, 75th, and 99th percentiles on the horizontal axis. Use this graph in exercises 17 and 18.

Measurements

17. a. What percentage of the measurements is less than or equal to the 30th percentile?
  b. What percentage of the measurements is greater than or equal to the 90th percentile?

18. a. What percentage of the measurements is between the 30th and 90th percentiles?
  b. What percentage of the measurements is between the median and the 80th percentile?

The score form below shows a fourth-grade student's scores on six of the subtests of the Stanford Achievement Test. The top row of numbers listed for each subtest shows the number of questions answered correctly out of the total number of questions for that subtest. The first number in the second row of each column shows the national percentile; and the first number in the third row of each column shows the local percentile. For example, this student was in the 90th percentile nationally on the vocabulary test and in the 69th percentile locally on the vocabulary test. Use this score form in exercises 19, 20, and 21.

Stanford ACHIEVEMENT TEST

		SCORE TYPE	MATH COMP
ψ	GR 4 NORMS GR 4.8	RS/NO POSS	29/44
	LEVEL INTER 1 FORM E	NAT'L PR-S	54 - 5
	STUDENT NO 400000044	LOCAL PR-S	68 - 6
	OTHER INFO	GRADE EQUIV	5.5
AGE 9-6	TEST DATE 5/10/99		

READING COMP	VOCAB-ULARY	MATH APPL	SPELLING	LANGUAGE
57/60	32/36	32/40	37/40	40/53
96 - 9	90 -	77 -	86 -	63 -
78 - 7	69 -	62 -	83 -	45 -
	8.4	6.4	8.9	5.4

19. a. Nationally, what percentage of the students scored below this student in mathematics comprehension?
  b. Locally, what percentage of the students scored below this student in mathematics comprehension?
  c. This student scored higher in reading comprehension than what percentage of the national group?
  d. Which of the local percentile scores is not lower than the corresponding national percentile score?
  e. If a local percentile is lower than a national percentile, it means that the local level of achievement is higher than the national level of achievement. Explain why.

20. a. Nationally, what percentage of the students scored below this student in mathematics application?
  b. Locally, what percentage of the students scored below this student in language?
  c. This student scored higher in spelling than what percentage of the national group?
  d. The last row of each column shows the *grade equivalent*—the grade level of the student's achievement. What is the grade level of this student's achievement in vocabulary?
  e. If a local percentile is higher than a national percentile, it means that the local level of achieve-

ment is lower than the national level of achievement. Explain why.

21. a. Nationally, what percentage of the students scored below this student in spelling?
  b. Locally, what percentage of the students scored below this student in reading comprehension?
  c. This student scored higher in vocabulary than what percentage of the national group?
  d. What percentage of the questions on the mathematics application subtest did the student answer correctly?

Rather than being divided into 100 parts, as in the case of percentiles, a distribution is sometimes divided into 9 parts called **stanines,** a contraction of the term *standard nine.* Stanines are numbered from a low of 1 to a high of 9, with 5 representing average performance. The stanines that correspond to percentile intervals are shown in the following graph. Use this graph in exercises 22 and 23.

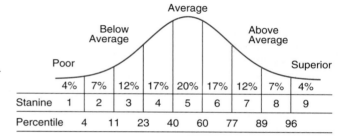

4%	7%	12%	17%	20%	17%	12%	7%	4%

Stanine	1	2	3	4	5	6	7	8	9
Percentile	4	11	23	40	60	77	89	96	

22. a. Determine the stanine for the 70th percentile.
  b. The Stanford Achievement Test chart in exercises 19 through 21 records a stanine score beside each percentile. For example, under Math Comp, the 54th percentile corresponds to a stanine score of 5. Determine the student's four national stanine scores missing from that chart.

23. a. Determine the stanine for the 44th percentile.
  b. The Stanford Achievement Test chart in exercises 19 through 21 records a stanine score beside each percentile. For example, the chart shows a stanine score of 7 for the local percentile of 78 under Reading Comp. Determine the student's four local stanine scores which are missing from the chart.

Determine a z score to the nearest .01 for each of the test scores in exercises 24 and 25 and determine the better score.

24. Test A: mean, 74.3; standard deviation, 3.6; test score 81. Test B: mean 720; standard deviation 146; test score 840.

25. Test A: mean, 3.1; standard deviation 2.1; test score 2.8. Test B: mean 6.2; standard deviation 1.7; test score 5.3.

Use the computer-generated set of random numbers below in exercises 26 and 27.

$$\begin{array}{ccccc} 61 & 44 & 34 & 03 & 09 \\ 41 & 17 & 26 & 81 & 06 \\ 73 & 73 & 97 & 24 & 18 \end{array} \qquad \begin{array}{ccccc} 05 & 64 & 20 & 54 & 24 \\ 85 & 19 & 76 & 44 & 59 \\ 38 & 25 & 89 & 37 & 20 \end{array}$$

$$\begin{array}{ccccc} 65 & 69 & 66 & 39 & 80 \\ 08 & 60 & 20 & 66 & 68 \\ 72 & 47 & 40 & 14 & 34 \end{array} \qquad \begin{array}{ccccc} 13 & 97 & 76 & 63 & 34 \\ 42 & 99 & 28 & 71 & 47 \\ 38 & 57 & 30 & 80 & 89 \end{array}$$

26. Explain how to simulate the flipping of a coin by using the table of random numbers. Use your method and record the first 10 "coin tosses."

27. Devise a way to use these random numbers to simulate the rolling of a die. Use your method and record the first 10 "rolls" of the die.

REASONING AND PROBLEM SOLVING

28. A student scored 650 on the mathematics part of the Scholastic Aptitude Test in a year in which the mean for that subtest was 455 and the standard deviation was 112. When the same student took a university entrance exam for engineers, he scored 140 on a mathematics test that had a mean of 128 and a standard deviation of 9.5.
   a. What was his z score for each test?
   b. On which of the two tests was his performance stronger, relative to the performance of the other students taking the test?

29. A student scored 31 on the mathematics section of the American College Test. The mean score for the ACT was 17.4, and the standard deviation was 7.8. The same student scored 582 on the Scholastic Aptitude Test. The SAT had a mean of 458 and a standard deviation of 117.
   a. What was her z score for each test?
   b. On which of the two tests was her performance stronger relative to the performance of the other students taking the tests?

Objects that are manufactured to certain specifications tend to vary slightly from their specified measurements. In answering the questions in exercises 30 and 31, assume the measurements are normally distributed.

30. A certain type of bulb has a mean life of 2400 hours with a standard deviation of 200 hours. What percentage of these bulbs can be expected to burn longer than 2600 hours?

31. A brand of crockpots has a mean high temperature of 260°F and a standard deviation of 3°F. If a crockpot's highest temperature is below 254°F or above 266°F, it is considered defective. What percentage of these pots can be expected to be defective?

32. A DC-10 shuttle flight between two cities has a total seating of 312, a mean of 286 passengers, and a standard deviation of 13. What percentage of the time is this flight able to meet the demand for seats? (Assume that the numbers of passengers for this flight are normally distributed.)

33. A certain university's WATS line can handle as many as 20 calls per minute. The average number of calls per minute during peak periods is 16 with a standard deviation of 4. What percentage of the time will the WATS line be overloaded during peak periods? (Assume that the numbers of phone calls are normally distributed during the peak period.)

Determine a z score in exercises 34 to 36 and use the definition of *rare event* to support your conclusions.

34. The guarantee on the box of a product called Rechargeable Lamp Light states that in case of power failure, the lamp automatically provides light for an average of 90 minutes. If the standard deviation of the times that these lamps burn is 9.5 minutes, what might you suspect about the guarantee if you purchased one of these lamps and it burned for only 70 minutes?

35. A company that manufactures an exercise belt claims that at least 15 minutes' use of the machine per day for 60 days will result in an average loss of 3.3 inches in the distance around the abdomen. Assume that the standard deviation of these measurements is 1.4 inches. Suppose that a person is randomly selected from those who used this machine for 15 minutes per day for a 60-day period, and this person lost only .3 inch in distance around the abdomen. What might be predicted about the company's claim?

36. An automobile manufacturer claims that its midsize car will accelerate from 0 to 60 miles per hour in 8 seconds, and it is known that the standard deviation is 1.3 seconds. If you randomly select one of these cars from a dealer's lot and find that it requires 10 seconds to accelerate from 0 to 60 miles per hour, are you justified in being suspicious of the manufacturer's claim?

Use a simulation to solve exercises 37 to 39. Describe your use of this method.

37. A manufacturer puts one of five different randomly selected colored markers in each box of crackerjacks. What is the average number of boxes that must be purchased to obtain all five different markers?

38. Pepe and Anna are playing a penny-tossing game. The player who can toss 10 heads in the fewest tosses wins the game. How many tosses of a fair coin on average are required to obtain 10 heads?

39. A newly married couple would like to have a child of each sex. Assuming that the chances of having a boy and a girl are equally likely, what is the average number of children the couple must have in order to have at least 1 boy and 1 girl?

40. Featured Strategy: Using a Simulation   A cloak-room attendant receives 9 hats from 9 men and gets the hats mixed up. If the hats are returned at random and simultaneously, what is the average number of hats that will go to the correct owners?
   a. Understanding the Problem   There are 9 men, and each man has exactly 1 hat. Is it possible that each hat might be returned to its owner?
   b. Devising a Plan   One way to approach the problem is to conduct experiments with 9 men and 9 hats, using some random method of returning the hats. Another plan is to design a simulation. How might such a simulation be designed?
   c. Carrying Out the Plan   The simulation must be carried out several times to determine the number of "hats" (on average) that will be returned correctly. What is this number?
   d. Looking Back   Suppose that instead of 9 hats and 9 men, there are fewer men, each having 1 hat. Will the average number of hats that are returned correctly increase?

41. Graphs of distributions are sometimes intended to be misleading. The scale used on the vertical axis will determine whether the graph of the distribution of sales shown in the table below will be skewed. Plot bar graphs of these sales on each of the following grids. What impression do these two graphs give to the reader? Which graph better illustrates the true increase in sales? Explain why. (Copy the rectangular grid from the inside cover of the book or from the website.)

YEAR	SALES
1993	$191,000,000
1994	191,500,000
1995	193,000,000
1996	195,000,000
1997	198,000,000
1998	200,500,000

(i)
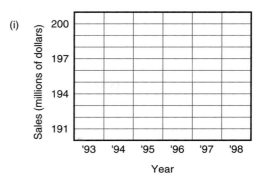

(ii)
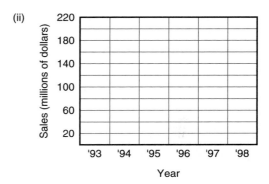

42. The Montagnais-Naskapi, a northeastern Native American tribe, bake the shoulder blade of the caribou to get guidance on decisions concerning the well-being of their tribe. They determine the direction of the next hunt from the direction of the cracks that appear in the animal's shoulder blade as it is baked. This method of determining direction is a fairly random device that avoids human bias. It suggests that some practices in magic need to be reassessed.*
   a. Explain how a table of random numbers can be used to randomly determine directions of 0° to 360° for hunting.
   b. How can a table of random numbers can be used to randomly determine both directions and distances in miles to be traveled for the hunt?
   c. Use your method in part b and the table of random digits on page 494 to determine the direction and distance of your first hunt.

*O. K. Moore, "Divination—A New Perspective," *American Anthropologist,* 59 (1965): 121–128.

ONLINE LEARNING CENTER   www.mhhe.com/bennett-nelson

• Math Investigation 7.3   *Dice Roll Simulation*
Section-Related: • Links   • Writing/Discussion Problems   • Bibliography

PUZZLER

Cryptology is the science of coding and decoding secret messages. Try to break the following code. It is a statement by the nineteenth-century mathematician Pierre Laplace.

CA CW GZJHGBHYRZ AOHA H
WVCZQVZ MOCVO YZFHQ MCAO
AOZ VLQWCXZGHACLQ LK
FHJZW LK VOHQVZ WOLERX YZ
ZRZSHAZX AL AOZ GHQB LK AOZ
JLWA CJILGAHQA WEYPZVAW LK
OEJHO BQLMRZXFZ.

Hint: Make a frequency distribution showing the number of times each letter occurs. The four most often used letters in English are e, t, a, and o, in that order. Substitute these letters in that order for the first, second, third, and fourth most frequently used letters in the code. The letters h, n, i, and s also occur with high frequency in our language. Substitute these letters for the fifth, sixth, seventh, and eighth most frequently used letters in the code.

"I forgot the message!"

CHAPTER REVIEW

1. **Statistics**
   a. **Statistics** can refer to numerical information, called **data,** or to the science of collecting data and making inferences.
   b. **Descriptive statistics** is the science of collecting, describing, and analyzing data.
   c. **Inferential statistics** is the science of interpreting data in order to make predictions.

2. **Measures of central tendency**
   a. A **measure of central tendency** is a number that approximates the center of a set of data.
   b. There are three measures of central tendency: **mean** (numerical average), **mode,** and **median.**
   c. The **mean** of n numbers is the sum of the numbers divided by n.
   d. The **median** of a set of numbers is the middle number when the numbers are placed in increasing order, or if no middle number exists, the mean of the two middle numbers.

   e. The **mode** of a set of numbers is the frequency of the number which occurs most often.

3. **Charts and graphs**
   a. A **bar graph** provides an illustration of data and is used when there are a small number of distinct categories. A **double-bar graph** compares two sets of data and a **triple-bar graph** compares three sets of data.
   b. A **pictograph** is similar to a bar graph, but copies of an icon (figure) that has a given numerical value are used to show the amount of data in each of several categories.
   c. A **pie graph** is used for illustrating essentially the same information as bar graphs. Pie graphs, bar graphs, and pictographs are best chosen when there are relatively few categories, such as 3 to 10.
   d. A **line plot** is similar to a bar graph, but tally marks are used for each value of data, and the

graph is best used for plotting intermediate numbers of data, such as 25 to 50.

e. A **stem-and-leaf plot** is a visual method of listing up to 100 or so values of data. When it is used to compare two sets of data, there should be approximately the same number of values on both sides of the stem.

f. A **box-and-whisker plot** (or simply **box plot**) shows the data divided into four parts by the median and quartiles. Several sets of data can be compared with each having its own box plot, and the sizes of the sets of data may vary.

g. A **histogram** is similar to a bar graph. It has adjoining bars of equal width along one axis and the other axis contains the frequency of the data for each interval or category.

h. A **scatter plot** is a graph for comparing two sets of data by graphing coordinates.

i. A **line graph** is a special case of a scatter plot that is often used to show changes over a period of time.

j. A **trend line** approximates the location of the points of a scatter plot. Such a line is used for making predictions about a value in one set of data when given the corresponding value in the other set of data.

k. A **curve of best fit** may be a line or a curve that approximates the location of the points of a scatter plot. Such curves can be visually drawn, or they can be obtained from graphing calculators or computers.

l. A **correlation coefficient** is a measure from $^-1$ to $^+1$ that indicates how well the curve of best fit approximates the points of the scatter plot. The closer the measure is to $^-1$ or $^+1$, the better the fit.

m. If the correlation coefficient is close to zero, there is little or **no association** between the two sets of data; if it is close to 1, there is a strong **positive correlation**; and if it is close to $^-1$, there is a strong **negative correlation**.

4. **Measures of variability**

a. A **measure of variability** is a number which describes the spread or variation in a set of data.

b. The **range** is the difference between the greatest and least measures in a set of data.

c. The **interquartile range** is the difference between the upper quartile and the lower quartile.

d. The **standard deviation** is computed by subtracting the mean from each measurement, squaring each difference, finding the mean of the squared differences, and obtaining the square root of this mean.

e. For any set of data, at least 75 percent of the measurements will lie within 2 standard deviations of the mean.

5. **Measures of relative standing**

a. A **measure of relative standing** is a number that determines the relative position of a measurement in a set of data.

b. The **pth percentile** of a set of data is a number which is greater than p percent of the data and less than $(1 - p)$ percent of the data.

c. The 25th percentile is the **lower quartile**, the 50th percentile is the **median**, and the 75th percentile is the **upper quartile**.

d. A **z score** is a number that can be calculated for any measurement in a set of data. It determines the number of standard deviations that a measurement is above or below the mean.

e. If the z score of a value from a set of data is less than $^-2$ or greater than $^+2$, the value is called a **rare event**.

6. **Sampling**

a. A **sample** refers to a subset taken from a population.

b. A **random sample** is a sample for which every element of the population has the same chance of being selected.

c. In **stratified sampling** the population is divided into groups, and the number sampled from each group is proportional to the size of the group.

7. **Distributions**

a. **Distribution** refers to how the measurements of a set of data are clustered together, isolated from each other, or spread out.

b. If the data are concentrated at the right side of a graph with the "tail" extending to the left, the direction is **skewed to the left**.

c. If the data are concentrated at the left side of the graph with the "tail" extending to the right, the distribution is **skewed to the right**.

d. A distribution in which measurements at equal distances from the center of the distribution occur with the same frequency is called **symmetric**.

e. A smooth symmetric bell-shaped curve is called a **normal curve**, and the distribution of its data is called a **normal distribution**.

CHAPTER TEST

The following table shows sources of public school revenues in percent for each state for 1997.* Use these data to answer questions 1 through 6.

Public school revenues, by source, by state, 1997 (in percent)

	STATE	LOCAL	FEDERAL		STATE	LOCAL	FEDERAL
Hawaii	90.4	2.3	7.3	Louisiana	50.8	37.4	11.8
Washington	68.6	25.4	6.0	Tennessee	50.8	40.8	8.4
Michigan	67.8	25.6	6.6	Florida	48.8	43.8	7.4
Kentucky	66.5	25.5	8.0	Arizona	48.7	44.1	9.2
Arkansas	66.0	25.7	8.3	Montana	48.6	41.6	9.8
Maine	66.0	47.5	6.5	Wyoming	48.4	45.1	6.5
Delaware	66.0	26.4	7.6	Colorado	44.1	50.3	5.6
North Carolina	65.6	27.0	7.4	Texas	42.8	49.4	7.8
New Mexico	65.6	24.7	9.7	Ohio	42.3	51.4	6.3
Alabama	64.8	25.0	10.2	North Dakota	42.1	46.2	11.7
Idaho	63.9	29.3	6.8	Pennsylvania	41.4	53.0	5.6
Alaska	63.5	23.9	12.6	Maryland	40.0	54.4	5.6
West Virginia	62.8	28.6	8.6	Rhode Island	39.7	54.4	5.9
Utah	62.7	31.0	6.3	Missouri	39.6	54.5	5.9
Oklahoma	62.5	28.5	9.0	Connecticut	39.3	56.5	4.2
California	59.9	31.7	8.4	New Jersey	39.2	57.4	3.4
Kansas	57.6	36.9	5.5	New York	39.1	54.8	6.1
Oregon	55.4	37.5	7.1	Nebraska	37.6	58.3	4.1
Mississippi	55.0	30.9	14.1	Virginia	36.8	57.8	5.4
Minnesota	54.9	41.1	4.0	Massachusetts	36.0	58.6	5.4
Wisconsin	54.5	41.1	4.4	Nevada	33.6	62.0	4.4
Iowa	53.6	42.6	3.8	South Dakota	32.0	58.2	9.9
South Carolina	52.7	39.4	7.9	Vermont	28.9	66.1	5.0
Georgia	52.6	40.8	6.6	Illinois	27.0	65.5	7.5
Indiana	52.6	42.4	5.0	New Hampshire	6.7	90.3	3.0

1. a. In which state was the greatest percentage of revenue from the state?
   b. In which state was the smallest percentage of revenue from the state?
   c. What is the range of percentages of revenue supplied by the states?
   d. The states are listed in decreasing order by percentage of revenue from state sources. What is the median of these percentages?

2. a. Draw a pie graph showing the three sources of revenue for California. Label the size of the central angle, to the nearest degree, for each part of the graph.
   b. Draw a bar graph showing the three sources of revenue to the nearest percent for Iowa. Label the axes of the graph.

3. Form a stem-and-leaf plot of the percentages of revenue from the federal government. Use the tens and units digits for the stems and the tenths for the leaves.

4. Form a histogram for the percentages of local revenue, using intervals on the horizontal axis of 0 to 9.95 percent, 10 to 19.95 percent, 20 to 29.95 percent, . . . , 90 to 99.95 percent.

*Statistical Abstract of the United States, 118th ed. (Washington, DC: Bureau of the Census, 1998), p. 178.

a. What is the frequency of states in the interval from 20 to 29.95 percent?

b. What is the frequency of states in the interval from 90 to 99.95 percent?

c. What interval contains the most measurements?

5. a. What is the mean of the percentages of local revenue for the five states with the greatest percentages of local revenue?

b. What is the mean of the percentages of local revenue for the five states with the smallest percentages of local revenue?

6. Form a scatter plot for the 25 states in the first column of the table by plotting the percentage of revenue from each state compared to the percentage of revenue from local sources. Draw a trend line and use this line to predict the amount of revenue from the state if the percentage of revenue from local sources is 35.

7. a. Which of the following sets of data has the greatest mean?

b. Which has the greatest range?

c. Which has the greatest standard deviation?

$$Set\ A: \quad 1, 5, 10, 15, 20$$
$$Set\ B: \quad 21, 22, 23, 24, 25$$

8. Draw a box-and-whisker plot for the following data. Label the three quartiles and the smallest and largest values. Compute the interquartile range and determine if it is less than or greater than one-half the range of the data.

62, 63, 66, 66, 70, 72, 73, 77, 84, 86, 92, 95, 97

9. Mary obtained a mathematics score of 520 on the SAT; the SAT scores had a mean of 435 and a standard deviation of 105. Her mathematics score on the PSAT (Preliminary Scholastic Aptitude Test) was 56; the PSAT scores had a mean of 44 and a standard deviation of 9.5

a. Determine Mary's z score for the SAT (to the nearest .1).

b. Determine Mary's z score for the PSAT (to the nearest .1).

c. On which test was her mathematics performance stronger?

10. A fourth-grade class is given a mathematics pretest at the beginning of the school year and a posttest at the end of the school year.

a. Is the distribution of scores on the pretest most likely to be skewed to the left, skewed to the right, or normal?

b. Describe the most likely distribution for the posttest.

11. A few of the results from a Stanford Achievement Test taken by a fourth-grader are shown below.

Total Reading	Total Listening	Total Language	Total Math	Basic Bat Tot
107/120	68/76	77/93	81/118	333/407
93 - 8	93 - 8	76 - 6	64 - 6	77 - 7
90 - 8	77 - 7	65 - 6	60 - 6	69 - 6
10.0	9.2	6.5	5.5	8.0

a. The first row of numbers under each subtest shows the number of questions answered correctly out of the total number of questions on that subtest. What percentage to the nearest .1 of the questions on Total Language did this student answer correctly?

b. The first number in the second row of each column is the student's percentile score relative to the national group. What percentage of the national group of students scored below this student in Total Reading?

c. The first number in the third row of each column is the student's percentile score relative to the local group. This student is at the 60th percentile in Total Math. What does this mean?

d. The numbers in the fourth row are the grade equivalents indicated by the test results. What do these numbers indicate about this fourth-grader?

12. A district mathematics test for all third-graders had a normal distribution with a mean of 74 and a standard deviation of 11.

a. What percentage of the third-graders tested scored within ±1 standard deviation of the mean?

b. What percentage of the students scored between 52 and 96?

13. Students in two fifth grades were given the same English test. One class of 26 students had a mean of 68, and the second class of 22 students had a mean of 73. What is the mean for the total number of students in both classes to the nearest .1?

14. The mean of three test scores is 74. What must the score on a fourth test be to raise the mean of the four tests to 78?

PROBABILITY

SPOTLIGHT ON TEACHING

Excerpts from NCTM's Standards for School Mathematics Grades 6–8*

Teachers should give middle-grade students numerous opportunities to engage in probabilistic thinking about simple situations from which students can develop notions of chance. They should use appropriate terminology in their discussions of chance and use probability to make predictions and test conjectures. For example, a teacher might give students the following problem:

Suppose you have a box containing 100 slips of paper numbered from 1 through 100. If you select one slip of paper at random, what is the probability that the number is a multiple of 5? A multiple of 8? Is not a multiple of 5? Is a multiple of both 5 and 8?

Teachers can help students relate probability to their work with data analysis and to proportionality as they reason from relative-frequency histograms. For example, referring to the data displayed in Figure 6.27, a teacher might pose a question like, How likely is it that the next time you throw a one-clip paper airplane, it goes at least 27 feet? No more than 21 feet?

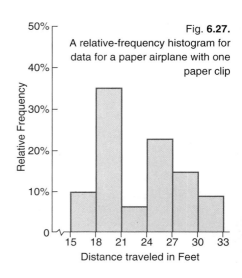

Fig. **6.27.**
A relative-frequency histogram for data for a paper airplane with one paper clip

*Principles and Standards for School Mathematics (Reston, VA: National Council of Teachers of Mathematics 2000), pp. 250, 253.

MATH ACTIVITY 8.1

EXPERIMENTAL PROBABILITIES FROM SIMULATIONS

Materials: Spinners in the Manipulative Kit. Bend a paper clip and hold a pencil at the center of the spinner, as shown below.

1. A school will send two fourth-graders, three fifth-graders, and three sixth-graders to attend a one-day session of the state's House of Representatives. Two students will be picked at random to have lunch with the governor, and the others will have lunch with the legislators. Do you think it is likely or not so likely that at least one sixth-grader will be picked to have lunch with the governor?

    a. One approach to answering this question is to represent the eight students and their grade levels as numbers on the 1-to-8 spinner. The first spin determines one student. Then spinning again until a different number is obtained determines a second student. Repeat this experiment of randomly selecting two students 20 times, recording the grade level of each student.

    * b. Based on your data, how would you rate the chances that at least one sixth-grader will be selected? Write a sentence or two to support your conclusion.

    c. Describe what could be done to increase your confidence about your conclusion.

2. Repeatedly carrying out experiments which closely resemble a given situation is called a **simulation.** The next problem can also be solved by a simulation:

    In New Hampshire, cars have inspection stickers indicating the month of the inspection on their windshields, as shown. If there are approximately the same number of cars due for inspection each month, what is the likelihood that out of six randomly selected cars, all six will have different inspection months?

    a. Use the 1-to-12 spinner, and let each number represent a different month. Spin the spinner 6 times to simulate selecting cars at random and record the numbers. Repeat this experiment 15 times, and determine the percentage of experiments with six different inspection months. This percentage is called an **experimental probability.**

    b. On the basis of your experimental probability, what is the likelihood (unlikely, about 50:50, or likely) that when six cars are selected, they will all have different inspection months?

    c. Explain how the accuracy of your experimental probability can be improved.

SECTION 8.1

SINGLE-STAGE EXPERIMENTS

"Looks like it might be a nice day
tomorrow!"

PROBLEM OPENER

The numbers 3, 4, 5, and 6 are written on four cards. If one number is randomly chosen as the numerator of a fraction and another is randomly chosen as the denominator of the fraction, what is the probability that the fraction is greater than 1 and less than $1\frac{1}{2}$?

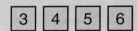

Probability, a relatively new branch of mathematics, emerged in Italy and France during the sixteenth and seventeenth centuries from studies of strategies for gambling games. From these beginnings probability evolved to have applications in many areas of life. Life insurance companies use probability to estimate how long a person is likely to live, doctors use probability to predict the success of a treatment, and meteorologists use probability to forecast weather conditions.

One trend in education in recent years has been to increase emphasis on probability and statistics in the elementary grades. NCTM's *Curriculum and Evaluation Standards for School Mathematics* supports this trend by including statistics and probability as a major strand in the standards for grades K to 4. "Collecting, organizing, describing, displaying, and interpreting data, as well as making decisions and predictions on the basis of that information, are skills that are increasingly important in a society based on technology and communication."*

*National Council of Teachers of Mathematics, *Curriculum and Evaluation Standards for School Mathematics* (Reston, VA: NCTM, 1989), p. 54.

The founders of the mathematical theory of probability were Blaise Pascal and Pierre Fermat (1601–1665), who developed the principles of this subject in letters to each other during 1654. The initial problem that started their investigation was posed by Chevalier de Mere, a professional gambler. The problem was to determine how the stakes should be divided between two gamblers if they quit before the game was finished. The problem amounts to determining the probability each player has of winning the game at any given stage. The theory that originated in a gambler's dispute is now an essential tool in many disciplines.*

*E. T. Bell, Men of Mathematics (New York: Simon and Schuster, 1965), pp. 73–89.

Probabilities of Outcomes

Just as probability had its beginning in games of chance, it is often introduced in the early grades through simple games such as those involving spinners. Consider the experiment of spinning the spinner in Figure 8.1. There are four possible outcomes: blue, red, green, and yellow. We would expect the color blue to come up about $\frac{1}{4}$ of the time if we spin many times. That is, the probability of obtaining blue is $\frac{1}{4}$. This probability is indicated by writing, $P(\text{blue}) = 1/4$

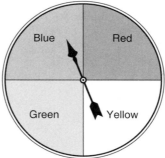

Figure 8.1

In general, an activity such as spinning a spinner, tossing a coin, or rolling a die is called an **experiment,** and the different results that can occur are called **outcomes.** The set of all outcomes of an experiment is called the **sample space.** For the above spinner, the sample space is the set of four outcomes blue, red, green, and yellow.

Example A

For each experiment, determine the sample space and the probability of the given outcome.

1. Rolling a regular six-sided die (faces are numbered from 1 to 6) once and obtaining a 2

2. Tossing a coin once and obtaining a head

3. Selecting a green marble on one draw from a box containing five green marbles and seven blue marbles.

Solution   **1.** The sample space contains the numbers 1 to 6, and $P(2) = \frac{1}{6}$.   **2.** The sample space has two outcomes, heads (H) and tails (T), and $P(H) = \frac{1}{2}$.   **3.** The sample space contains 12 outcomes, five which can be denoted by G_1, G_2, G_3, G_4, and G_5 for the five green marbles, and seven which can be denoted by B_1, B_2, B_3, B_4, B_5, B_6, and B_7 for the seven blue marbles. $P(G) = \frac{5}{12}$.

Research Statement

Recent research has concluded that a substantial number of students in grades 1 through 3 are not able to list the outcomes of a one-dimensional experiment (such as rolling a single die) even after instruction.

National Research Council 2001

There are two methods of determining probabilities. One is to conduct experiments and observe the results. A probability derived in this fashion is called an **experimental probability.** For example, if a coin is tossed 500 times and 300 heads occur, the experimental probability of obtaining a head for this experiment is $\frac{300}{500}$, or $\frac{3}{5}$. The second method of determining probabilities is based on theoretical considerations. Since spinners, dice, coins, and other physical devices for determining random outcomes all have imperfections that lead to biased results, we assign **theoretical probabilities** to the outcomes of ideal experiments. Ideally, for example, the spinner shown in Figure 8.1 will be equally likely to stop on any of the four colors. So the theoretical probability of obtaining blue is $\frac{1}{4}$. From here on, the word *probability* will mean *theoretical probability,* unless otherwise stated.

The probability of obtaining one of a group of equally likely outcomes is defined as follows.

> **PROBABILITY OF AN OUTCOME**   If there are n equally likely outcomes, then the **probability** of any given outcome is $\frac{1}{n}$.

Outcomes are not always equally likely, as shown in the next example.

Example B

Spinning this spinner will result in one of four outcomes: blue (B), red (R), green (G), or yellow (Y). Determine the following probabilities.

1. $P(B)$ **2.** $P(G)$ **3.** $P(Y)$

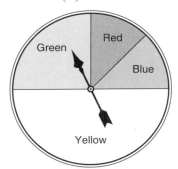

Solution   **1.** $P(B) = \frac{1}{8}$.   **2.** $P(G) = \frac{1}{4}$.   **3.** $P(Y) = \frac{1}{2}$

Probabilities of Events

Consider the experiment of rolling two ordinary dice. The 36 possible outcomes of the sample space are shown in Figure 8.2, and since each outcome is equally likely, the probability of obtaining any given pair of numbers is $\frac{1}{36}$. Notice that there are two different outcomes for rolling a 1 and a 2: a red 1 and a white 2 is a different outcome than a white 1 and a red 2. So, the probability of rolling a sum of 3 is $\frac{2}{36}$. Similarly, there is a $\frac{2}{36}$ probability of rolling a sum of 11.

11.9

Explore Probability

Learn

Math Words

favorable outcomes
desired results in a probability experiment

possible outcomes any of the results that could occur in a probability experiment

You can use a number cube to explore probability. What is the probability of tossing a 6 on a number cube? How many times will you toss it in 50 tries?

Work Together

You Will Need
• **number cube**

► Use a number cube to find how many times you toss a 6 in 50 tries.

- Make a line plot to show your results. Put an X above each number to show how many times that number was rolled.

1	2	3	4	5	6

► How many times did you toss a 6? Compare your results with those of others.

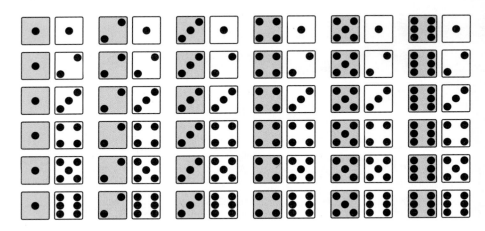

Figure 8.2
Thirty-six possible outcomes
of rolling two dice

Once we know the complete sample space, as in Figure 8.2, it is possible to answer more difficult questions concerning tosses of two dice.

Example C

Determine the probabilities of the following outcomes for the toss of two dice, using Figure 8.2.

1. Obtaining a sum less than 4

2. Obtaining a sum of 5

3. Obtaining a sum greater than or equal to 9

Solution   **1.** There are 3 outcomes whose sum is less than 4, (1, 1), (2, 1), and (1, 2), so $P(\text{sum} < 4)$ $= \frac{3}{36} = \frac{1}{12}$.   **2.** There are 4 outcomes whose sum is 5, so $P(\text{sum} = 5) = \frac{4}{36} = \frac{1}{9}$.   **3.** There are 10 outcomes whose sum is greater than or equal to 9, so $P(\text{sum} \geq 9) = \frac{10}{36} = \frac{5}{18}$.

Notice that in part 1 of Example C the probability of obtaining a sum less than 4 involves more than one outcome: The pairs (1,1), (1,2), and (2,1) all have a sum less than 4. A subset of outcomes in a sample space is called an **event**. For example, the event with sums of 5 has 4 of the 36 outcomes, and the event with sums greater than or equal to 9 has 10 of the 36 outcomes.

Example C suggests the following rule for obtaining the probability of an event.

> **PROBABILITY OF AN EVENT**   If all the outcomes of a sample space **S** are equally likely, the **probability of an event E** is
>
> $$P(E) = \frac{\text{number of outcomes in } E}{\text{number of outcomes in } S}$$

Let's use this rule to determine the probability of the event, obtaining a sum of 7 on a toss of two dice. Figure 8.2 shows that there are 6 ways of rolling a 7 (6 favorable outcomes), so

$$P(\text{sum} = 7) = \frac{6}{36} = \frac{1}{6}$$

Listing all the outcomes of a sample space (as in Figure 8.2) and counting the favorable outcomes is a common method of determining the probability of an event when there are relatively few outcomes. This approach is used in Examples D and E.

Example D

List the sample space for the experiment of tossing 3 coins and observing heads or tails for each coin. Then determine the probabilities of the following events.

1. Obtaining exactly 2 heads

2. Obtaining at least 2 heads

Solution   There are 8 outcomes:

$$HHH \quad HHT \quad HTH \quad THH \quad TTT \quad TTH \quad THT \quad HTT$$

1. There are 3 outcomes with exactly 2 heads (HHT, HTH, and THH), so

$$P(\text{exactly 2 heads}) = \tfrac{3}{8}$$

2. There are 4 outcomes with at least 2 heads (HHT, HTH, THH, and HHH), so

$$P(\text{at least 2 heads}) = \tfrac{4}{8} = \tfrac{1}{2}$$

Example E

Five tickets numbered 1, 2, 3, 4, and 5 are placed in a box, and two are selected at random. List the sample space and determine the following probabilities:

1. Obtaining a 1 or a 2 or both

2. Obtaining two odd numbers

3. Obtaining the number 6

4. Obtaining a number less than 6

Solution   There are 10 outcomes in the sample space:

$$1,2 \quad 1,3 \quad 1,4 \quad 1,5 \quad 2,3 \quad 2,4 \quad 2,5 \quad 3,4 \quad 3,5 \quad 4,5$$

1. There are 7 outcomes containing either a 1 or a 2 or both, so

$$P(1 \text{ or } 2 \text{ or both}) = \tfrac{7}{10}$$

2. There are 3 outcomes in which both numbers are odd, so

$$P(\text{both odd}) = \tfrac{3}{10}$$

3. There are no outcomes that include the number 6, so

$$P(6) = 0$$

4. All 10 outcomes include numbers less than 6, so

$$P(\text{number} < 6) = \tfrac{10}{10} = 1$$

Students should come to understand and use 0 to represent the probability of an impossible event and 1 to represent the probability of a certain event, and they should use common fractions to represent the probability of events that are neither certain nor impossible.

Standards 2000, p. 181

In part 3 of Example E the event of obtaining the number 6 is the empty set. In this case the event is called an **impossible event,** and it has a probability of 0. At the opposite extreme, the event in part 4 of Example E contains all possible outcomes. Such an event is called a **certain event** and has a probability of 1. Since the number of favorable outcomes is always less than or equal to the total number of outcomes, the *probability of an event is always less than or equal to 1.* These observations are summarized in the following inequalities, which hold for any event E.

$$0 \leq P(E) \leq 1$$

We have been computing the probabilities of events by dividing the number of favorable outcomes by the total number of outcomes. Perhaps you have noticed that the probability of an event can also be found by adding the probabilities of the various outcomes in the event. In part 2 of Example E, there are 3 outcomes in which both numbers are odd, so the probability of selecting a pair of odd numbers is $\frac{3}{10}$. The probability of this event can also be found by adding the probabilities of each outcome:

$$\frac{1}{10} + \frac{1}{10} + \frac{1}{10} = \frac{3}{10}$$

This is a special case of the following property.

PROBABILITY OF EVENTS   The **probability of an event E**, which has outcomes $e_1, e_2, \ldots, e_n$, is the sum of the probabilities of the outcomes.

$$P(E) = P(e_1) + P(e_2) + \cdots + P(e_n)$$

This property holds for events with equally likely outcomes as well as for those whose outcomes are not equally likely, as in Example F.

Example F

The outcomes of spinning the spinner shown below have these probabilities:

$$P(\text{purple}) = \frac{1}{12} \qquad P(\text{blue}) = \frac{1}{6} \qquad P(\text{red}) = \frac{1}{6}$$
$$P(\text{yellow}) = \frac{1}{6} \qquad P(\text{green}) = \frac{1}{12} \qquad P(\text{orange}) = \frac{1}{3}$$

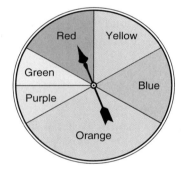

Determine the probabilities of the following events.

1. *E*: Obtaining a primary color (red, blue, or yellow)

2. *T*: Obtaining a color with six letters in its name

Solution   1. $P(E) = P(\text{red}) + P(\text{blue}) + P(\text{yellow}) = \frac{1}{6} + \frac{1}{6} + \frac{1}{6} = \frac{3}{6} = \frac{1}{2}$ 2. $P(T) = P(\text{purple}) + P(\text{orange}) + P(\text{yellow}) = \frac{1}{12} + \frac{1}{3} + \frac{1}{6} = \frac{7}{12}$

Middle-grade students should learn and use appropriate terminology and should be able to compute probabilities for simple compound events, such as the number of expected occurrences of two heads when two coins are tossed 100 times.

Standards 2000, p. 51

Probabilities of Compound Events

An event that can be described in terms of the union, intersection, or complement of other sets is called a **compound event**. For the events E and T in Example F, $E \cup T$ (the event that E, or T, or both occur) and $E \cap T$ (the event that both E and T occur) are examples of compound events. Since E and T in Example F are not disjoint (they have the outcome *yellow* in common), the probability of $E \cup T$ cannot be obtained by adding $P(E)$ and $P(T)$ because $P(\text{yellow})$ would be counted twice. The following equation confirms that $P(E \cup T)$ cannot be computed in this way because it gives $P(E) + P(T) > 1$.

$$P(E) + P(T) = P(\text{red}) + P(\text{blue}) + P(\text{yellow}) + P(\text{purple}) + P(\text{orange}) + P(\text{yellow})$$
$$= 1\tfrac{1}{12}$$

However, $P(E \cup T)$ is equal to $P(E) + P(T) - P(\text{yellow})$. In general, we have the following property.

ADDITION PROPERTY   If events A and B are not disjoint, then

$$P(A \cup B) = P(A) + P(B) - P(A \cap B)$$

If events A and B are disjoint, then

$$P(A \cup B) = P(A) + P(B)$$

When A and B are disjoint, they are called **mutually exclusive**. In this case $A \cap B = \varnothing$, and so $P(A \cap B) = 0$. This explains why the second equation of the *addition property* is a simple variation of the first equation.

Example G

Several events containing the outcomes of spinning the spinner in Example F are defined as follows.

> E: Obtaining a primary color (red, blue, or yellow)
> T: Obtaining a color with six letters in its name
> H: Obtaining a color with five letters in its name
> K: Obtaining a color with four letters in its name
> N: Obtaining a color with fewer than six letters in its name

Use these events to determine the following probabilities.

1. $P(E \cup H)$ **2.** $P(T)$ **3.** $P(T \cup K)$ **4.** $P(N)$ **5.** $P(E \cup K)$ **6.** $P(E \cap K)$

Solution   **1.** $P(E \cup H) = P(E) + P(H) = \frac{1}{2} + \frac{1}{12} = \frac{7}{12}$ **2.** $P(T) = \frac{7}{12}$ **3.** $P(T \cup K) = P(T) + P(K) = \frac{7}{12} + \frac{1}{6} = \frac{9}{12} = \frac{3}{4}$ **4.** $P(N) = P(\text{red}) + P(\text{blue}) + P(\text{green}) = \frac{1}{6} + \frac{1}{6} + \frac{1}{12} = \frac{5}{12}$ **5.** $P(E \cup K) = \frac{1}{2} + \frac{1}{6} - \frac{1}{6} = \frac{1}{2}$ **6.** $P(E \cup K) = \frac{1}{6}$

Did you notice that events T and N in Example G are complementary sets? That is, they have no outcomes in common, and their union contains all the outcomes of the sample space. Such events are called **complementary events**. Notice also that $P(T) + P(N) = \frac{7}{12} + \frac{5}{12} = 1$. In general, if A and B are complementary events, then we can determine the probability of one by knowing the probability of the other:

$$P(A) + P(B) = 1$$

For example, if a regular six-sided die is rolled, the event D of obtaining a number divisible by 3 and the event N of obtaining a number not divisible by 3 are complementary events. Since 3 and 6 are the only numbers divisible by 3, $P(D) = \frac{2}{6}$, and so $P(N) = 1 - P(D) = \frac{4}{6}$.

The *addition property* is sometimes used in analyzing data in tables.

Projected school enrollments in 2000* (in millions of students)

	PUBLIC	PRIVATE	TOTAL
K through grade 8	34	5	39
Secondary	14	1	15
College	12	3	15
Total	60	9	69

Let S be the event "a student is in secondary school" and C be the event "a student is in college." If a student is chosen at random from the 69 million students, what is the probability that he or she is in secondary school or college? Using the addition property and the fact that the intersection of S and C is the empty set, we have

$$P(S \cup C) = P(S) + P(C) - P(S \cap C)$$
$$= \tfrac{15}{69} + \tfrac{15}{69} - 0$$
$$= \tfrac{30}{69} \approx .43$$

Let's consider another example, using the data in the above table. Let E be the event that a student is in a private educational institution. For a randomly chosen student, what is the probability that she or he is a college student or in a private educational institution?

$$P(C \cup E) = P(C) + P(E) - P(C \cap E)$$
$$= \tfrac{15}{69} + \tfrac{9}{69} - \tfrac{3}{69}$$
$$= \tfrac{21}{69} \approx .30$$

If three of the four parts in the equation for the addition property are known, the equation can be solved for the missing part, as in the next example. Two symptoms of a common disease are a fever (F) and a rash (R). For people who have this disease, 20 percent will have the fever alone, 30 percent will have the rash alone, and 40 percent will have a fever or a rash or both. What is the probability that a randomly selected person with the disease will have both a fever and a rash?

$$P(F \cup R) = P(F) + P(R) - P(F \cap R)$$
$$.40 = .20 + .30 - P(F \cap R)$$
$$P(F \cap R) = .10$$

So, 10 percent will have both a fever and a rash.

"Blue Boy seems to be holding back a bit."

Odds

Racetracks state probabilities in terms of odds. Suppose that the odds against Blue Boy's winning are 4 to 1. This means that the racetrack management will match every $1 you bet on Blue Boy with $4. Each time you win, you receive the money you bet plus the money put up by the racetrack. That is, for $1 you receive $5, for $2 you receive $10, etc. The 4-to-1 odds indicate that the racetrack management

*Statistical Abstract of the United States, 118th ed. (Washington, DC: Bureau of the Census, 1998), p. 164.

expects Blue Boy to lose 4 out of every 5 races he runs. Thus the probability of Blue Boy's losing the race is $\frac{4}{5}$, and the probability of his winning is $\frac{1}{5}$.

This example shows the close relationship between odds and probability: They are different ways of presenting the same information. This relationship is illustrated in Figure 8.3. The bar has 5 equal parts, 4 to represent the unfavorable outcomes (Blue Boy's losing) and 1 to represent the favorable outcome (Blue Boy's winning). The odds of 4 to 1 are shown by the ratio of the 4 unshaded parts to the 1 shaded part. The probability of $\frac{4}{5}$ is the ratio of the 4 unshaded parts to the whole (5 parts).

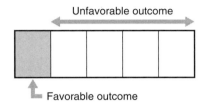

Figure 8.3

In general, **odds** are ratios. If the **odds in favor** of an event are **n to m,** then the probability of the event's occurring is **n/(n + m)** (Figure 8.4). In this case the **odds against** the event are **m to n,** and the probability of the event's not occurring is **m/(n + m).**

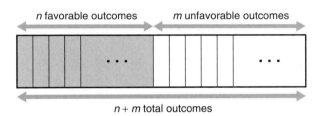

Figure 8.4

Example H

One card is selected at random from an ordinary deck of 52 cards, which contains four aces. Determine the following odds and probabilities.

1. Odds of obtaining 1 ace

2. Probability of obtaining 1 ace

3. Odds of not obtaining 1 ace

4. Probability of not obtaining 1 ace

Solution   **1.** Ratio of the number of favorable outcomes to the number of unfavorable outcomes = 4 to 48 = 1 to 12   **2.** $\frac{\text{Number of favorable outcomes}}{\text{Total number of outcomes}} = \frac{4}{52} = \frac{1}{13}$ **3.** Ratio of the number of unfavorable outcomes to the number of favorable outcomes = 48 to 4 = 12 to 1.   **4.** $\frac{\text{Number of unfavorable outcomes}}{\text{Total number of outcomes}} = \frac{48}{52} = \frac{12}{13}$

Example H helps us to see that if the odds of an event's happening are low, the probability is close to 0; and if the odds are high, the probability is close to 1. The odds of selecting an ace are low, 4 to 48, and the probability is $\frac{1}{13}$. Similarly, the odds of selecting a card that is not an ace are high, 48 to 4, and the probability is $\frac{12}{13}$.

Experimental Probability

It is often more difficult to determine a theoretical probability than to determine an experimental probability. Moreover, experimental probabilities involve conducting repeated trials and observing and recording data, activities that are appropriate for students at all levels.

Example 1

Consider tossing a bottle cap to determine the experimental probability that it will land with its edge down (see figure). What is this probability for the 50 tosses shown below?

Edge up   Edge down

D U U U D D U D U D
U U U U D U U D U U
U D U U U U U U D U
U U U D U U U D U U
D U U D U D U D U U

Although simulations can be useful, students also need to develop their probabilistic thinking by frequent experience with actual experiments.

Standards 2000, p. 254

Solution   The bottle cap landed with its edge down 15 times out of 50, so the experimental probability for this experiment is $\frac{15}{50} = \frac{3}{10}$. If many repeated experiments yield approximately the same result, we can conclude that the experimental probability is approximately $\frac{3}{10}$.

In many fields the empirical approach is the only means of determining probability. Insurance companies measure the risks against which people are buying insurance in order to set premiums. A person's age and life expectancy are important factors. To compute the probability that a person 20 years old will live to be 65 years old, insurance companies gather birth and death records of large numbers of people and compile mortality tables. One such table appears in Figure 8.5; it shows that out of every 10 million people born in the United States, 6,800,531 will live to age 65.* Thus the probability that a newborn baby will live to age 65 is 6,800,531/10,000,000, or about .68 (68 percent). According to the table, 9,664,994 people will live to age 20. Therefore, the probability of a newborn baby living to age 20 is about .966, or 96.6 percent.

---

*Robert Mehr and Emerson Commack, *Principles of Insurance,* 8th ed. (New York: McGraw-Hill, 1985).

AGE	NUMBER LIVING	NUMBER DYING	AGE	NUMBER LIVING	NUMBER DYING
0	10,000,000	70,800	35	9,373,807	23,528
1	9,929,200	17,475	36	9,350,279	24,685
2	9,911,725	15,066	37	9,325,594	26,112
3	9,896,659	14,449	38	9,299,482	27,991
4	9,882,210	13,835	39	9,271,491	30,132
5	9,868,375	13,322	40	9,241,359	32,622
6	9,855,053	12,812	41	9,208,737	35,362
7	9,842,241	12,401	42	9,173,375	38,253
8	9,829,840	12,091	43	9,135,122	41,382
9	9,817,749	11,879	44	9,093,740	44,741
10	9,805,870	11,865	45	9,048,999	48,412
11	9,794,005	12,047	46	9,000,587	52,473
12	9,781,958	12,325	47	8,948,114	56,910
13	9,769,633	12,896	48	8,891,204	61,794
14	9,756,737	13,562	49	8,829,410	67,104
15	9,743,175	14,225	50	8,762,306	72,902
16	9,728,950	14,983	51	8,689,404	79,160
17	9,713,967	15,737	52	8,610,244	85,758
18	9,698,230	16,390	53	8,524,486	92,832
19	9,681,840	16,846	54	8,431,654	100,337
20	9,664,994	17,300	55	8,331,317	108,307
21	9,647,694	17,655	56	8,223,010	116,849
22	9,630,039	17,912	57	8,106,161	125,970
23	9,612,127	18,167	58	7,980,191	135,663
24	9,593,960	18,324	59	7,844,528	145,830
25	9,575,636	18,481	60	7,698,698	156,592
26	9,557,155	18,732	61	7,542,106	167,736
27	9,538,423	18,981	62	7,374,370	179,271
28	9,519,442	19,324	63	7,195,099	191,174
29	9,500,118	19,760	64	7,003,925	203,394
30	9,480,358	20,193	65	6,800,531	215,917
31	9,460,165	20,718	66	6,584,614	228,749
32	9,439,447	21,239	67	6,355,865	241,777
33	9,418,208	21,850	68	6,114,088	254,835
34	9,396,358	22,551	69	5,859,253	267,241

Figure 8.5

Example J

Determine the experimental probabilities of the following events, using the table in Figure 8.5.

1. A newborn baby will live to age 60.

2. A person aged 20 will live to be 60 years old.

3. A person aged 50 will live to be 60 years old.

Solution   **1.** Approximately .77   **2.** Out of 10 million births, there are 9,664,994 people living at age 20 and 7,698,698 living at age 60, so the probability of a person's surviving from age 20 to age 60 is 7,698,698/9,664,994 ≈ .797, or approximately 80 percent.   **3.** Out of 10 million births, there are 8,762,306 people living at age 50 and 7,698,698 living at age 60, so the probability of a person's surviving from age 50 to 60 is 7,698,698/8,762,306 ≈ .879, or approximately 88 percent.

Simulations

You may remember from Chapter 7 that a simulation is a procedure in which experiments that closely resemble a real situation are conducted repeatedly. In that chapter, simulations provided answers to questions in statistics. Simulations are also used to obtain approximations to theoretical probabilities.

Example K

What is the probability that in a group of 5 people chosen at random at least 2 will have a birthday in the same month?

Solution   One approach to this problem is to conduct experiments. Since polling a large number of people to determine their birth months is time-consuming, we will use a simulation. The following 20 groups of 5 numbers each were obtained by spinning a spinner labeled with whole numbers from 1 to 12. Since in 12 of the 20 groups the same number occurs 2 or more times, the probability for this simulation is $\frac{12}{20} = \frac{3}{5}$.

Simulations afford students access to relatively large samples that can be generated quickly and modified easily.

Standards 2000, p. 254

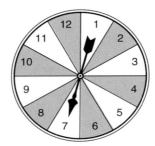

9	3	9	9	11		7	2	5	4	4		6	9	9	11	12		1	1	10	8	5
1	2	6	12	10		3	9	10	9	1		9	5	9	11	11		7	11	12	2	6
2	7	5	9	2		5	11	4	9	7		11	12	5	8	6		12	3	2	12	8
2	6	3	11	2		7	10	11	7	9		7	2	6	3	12		2	12	5	1	7
7	6	10	9	7		3	8	2	3	12		9	12	4	8	7		6	9	1	4	12

The theoretical basis for approximating probabilities with simulations is called the **law of large numbers.** This law states that the more times a simulation is carried out, the closer the probability

$$\frac{\text{Number of favorable outcomes}}{\text{Total number of outcomes}}$$

is to the theoretical probability.

The *Curriculum and Evaluation Standards for School Mathematics* suggest the use of a computer to carry out simulations:

Once students have experimented with a problem, a computer can generate hundreds or thousands of simulated results. It is important that the computer simulation follow active student exploration. This follow-up broadens students' understanding and provides them with an opportunity to observe how a greater number of trials can refine the probability model.*

Tables of random digits are also commonly used for simulations. A portion of such a table is shown in Figure 8.6.

Curriculum and Evaluation Standards for School Mathematics (Reston, VA: National Council of Teachers of Mathematics, 1989), p. 111.

57455	72455	93949	03017	33463	50612	65976	18630	26080	99135
01177	18110	31846	33144	99175	43471	29341	07096	69643	85566
25107	69058	16098	53085	88020	30108	81469	33487	55936	34594
73312	70522	45206	00165	06447	65724	29908	96532	14636	25790
72526	06721	23176	95705	10722	72474	01434	38573	08089	09806
68868	49240	16140	11046	38620	49148	80338	45266	39020	06304
45101	17710	54682	31812	76734	87045	96291	67557	18680	18886
12672	99918	24766	14132	63739	18576	80955	67381	60403	09892
12201	94684	41296	86044	83170	95446	14032	86602	34998	49065
46062	88535	71445	10422	72088	50200	55509	03741	73748	38899
12483	92564	43692	60562	93982	44567	62843	51987	11525	02695
33791	32729	88363	65524	45698	02573	97181	30352	10505	02352
78160	17311	24688	87381	00257	76315	69875	34128	01483	21765
43595	78341	07757	76471	37801	90306	20915	38132	91714	44436
92750	50923	26074	03327	57400	79251	04823	74914	11445	93818
96564	04624	46940	79735	27074	99264	32920	51271	57583	82685
55645	86878	27211	89358	30594	70161	26045	33370	19425	25961
32582	88628	11166	47654	62462	05080	51664	39828	01770	01607
07866	68988	70054	83887	31538	66864	58710	70349	65126	02265
97092	11334	78242	15410	99001	65756	23979	63446	84808	06072

Figure 8.6

Example L

Misconceptions about probability have been held not only by many students but also by many adults (Konold 1989). To correct misconceptions, it is useful for students to make predictions and then compare the predictions with actual outcomes.

Standards 2000, p. 254

Try to answer the following question by using the table of random digits to carry out a simulation. What is the probability that in a family of 5 children there are 3 boys and 2 girls?

Solution   Let each odd digit from the table in Figure 8.6 represent a boy and each even digit represent a girl. Then examine groups of 5 digits, and circle those with 3 odd digits and 2 even digits. Starting at the beginning of the list, we find that the first group with 3 odd and 2 even digits is 72455. There are 30 groups out of the first 100 groups with 3 odd and 2 even digits. These are listed below. Thus the probability based on this simulation is $\frac{30}{100} = .3$. This ratio is an approximation to the theoretical probability of a family's having 3 boys and 2 girls among 5 children.

72455	03017	33463	65976	18110	33144	43471	29341	25107	53085
33487	34594	96532	25790	23176	45101	31812	76734	96291	14132
18576	80955	67381	83170	34998	88535	71445	03741	73748	38899

Problem-Solving Application

Solutions to problems in probability quite often conflict with our intuition. For example, if 2 coins are tossed, the probability of obtaining exactly 1 head is 50 percent; however, if 4 coins are tossed, the probability of obtaining exactly 2 heads is not 50 percent.

PROBLEM

To create interest in probability, a teacher asks for a volunteer to play the following game: Four coins will be tossed, and if exactly 2 heads are obtained, the student wins the coins; otherwise, the student loses. What is the probability that the student will win?

Understanding the Problem   In order to win, the student must obtain exactly 2 heads. **Question 1:** What happens if the student obtains 3 heads or 4 heads?

Devising a Plan   One plan is to toss 4 coins, record the number of heads, and repeat this experiment many times. An experimental probability can then be determined by dividing the number of times exactly 2 heads appear by the total number of experiments. A second plan is to *use a simulation.* In a list of random digits, each even digit can be designated as a head (H) and each odd digit as a tail (T). **Question 2:** If the digits from 0 to 9 are used, are there equal numbers of heads and tails?

Carrying Out the Plan   Use the list of random digits in Figure 8.6 to carry out a simulation. One way to do this is to consider only the first 4 digits in each group of 5 digits. For example, in the first row of the table, 5 of the 10 groups have exactly 2 "heads" (see the following list). Continue the simulation, using the first 10 rows of the table. **Question 3:** For this simulation what is the probability of obtaining exactly 2 heads in a toss of 4 coins?

   2H   2H   2H   2H   2H

57455 72455 93949 03017 33463 50612 65976 18630 26080 99135

Looking Back   The theoretical probability of obtaining exactly 2 heads can be found by listing the 16 different outcomes of tossing 4 coins and counting those with exactly 2 heads (see below). **Question 4:** What is this probability? How does it compare to the probability obtained from the simulation?

HTHT   HHHH   HHHT   HHTH   HTHH   THHH   HHTT   HTTH
TTHH   THTH   TTTT   TTTH   TTHT   THTT   HTTT   THHT

Answers to Questions 1–4   **1.** The student loses.   **2.** Yes (remember, zero is an even number)   **3.** Since 42 groups have exactly 2 even digits and 2 odd digits among the first 4 digits, the approximation to the theoretical probability of obtaining exactly 2 heads in tossing 4 coins is 42/100 = .42.   **4.** Six of the 16 outcomes have exactly 2 heads, so the theoretical probability is $\frac{6}{16}$ = .375. This is reasonably close to the probability of .42, which was obtained from the simulation.

EXERCISES AND PROBLEMS 8.1

1. Out of 36 possible outcomes of tossing two dice, 6 produce a sum of 7. Complete the following table by computing the probability of rolling each of the other sums. (You may want to use the array of dice shown in Figure 8.2 at the beginning of this section.)

Sum	2	3	4	5	6	7	8	9	10	11	12
Probability						$\frac{6}{36}$					

a. What is the probability of obtaining a sum greater than or equal to 8?

b. What is the probability of obtaining a sum greater than 4 and less than 8?

The dice game called *craps* has the following rules. If the player rolling the dice gets a sum of 7 or 11, he or she wins. If the player rolls a sum of 2, 3, or 12, she or he loses. If the first sum rolled is a 4, 5, 6, 8, 9, or 10, the player continues to roll the dice. After the first roll, the player wins if she or he can obtain the first sum rolled before rolling a 7. Use this information in exercises 2 and 3.

2. a. What is the probability of rolling a 7 or an 11? (See the table in exercise 1.)

b. What is the probability of losing on the first roll?

3. a. What is the probability of rolling a 4, 5, 6, 8, 9, or 10 on the first roll?

b. Suppose a player rolls an 8 on the first roll. Which has the greater probability, rolling a 7 on the second roll or rolling another 8?

A box contains seven tickets numbered 1 through 7. One ticket will be selected at random from the box. Use this information in exercises 4 and 5.

4. a. What are the elements of the sample space for this experiment?

b. What is the probability of obtaining an even number?

c. What is the probability of obtaining a number greater than 3?

5. a. What is the probability of obtaining a prime number?

b. What is the probability of obtaining a number less than 5?

c. What is the probability of obtaining an odd number?

A chip is to be drawn from a box containing the following color chips: 8 orange, 5 green, 3 purple, and 2 red chips. Describe the sample space and determine the probabilities of selecting the types of chips in exercises 6 and 7.

6. a. A purple chip

b. A green or purple chip

c. A chip that is not orange

7. a. A red chip

b. A red or green chip

c. A chip that is not red

The five regular polyhedra, called *Platonic solids,* are pictured below. These are the only polyhedra that can be used for fair dice. The regular polyhedron with 20 faces (icosahedron) was used as a die by the Egyptians more than 2000 years ago. The faces of these five polyhedra are labeled with consecutive whole numbers beginning with 1. For example, the tetrahedron has numbers 1, 2, 3, 4; and the icosahedron has numbers from 1 to 20.

Tetrahedron	Cube	Octahedron	Dodecahedron	Icosahedron
(4 faces)	(6 faces)	(8 faces)	(12 faces)	(20 faces)

Determine the probabilities of rolling the numbers in exercises 8 and 9 with each type of die, and record the probabilities in a copy of the table below.

8. a. A number less than 3

b. An even number

9. a. The number 2

b. A number greater than 3

	TETRA-HEDRON	CUBE	OCTA-HEDRON	DODECA-HEDRON	ICOSA-HEDRON
8. a.					
b.					
9. a.					
b.					

For an experiment consisting of spinning the spinner shown here, determine the probabilities in exercises 10 and 11.

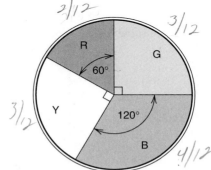

10. a. $P(B)$ **b.** $P(Y)$
    c. $P(R)$ **d.** $P(R \text{ or } B)$

11. a. $P(R \text{ or } G)$ **b.** $P(R \text{ or } G \text{ or } B)$
    c. $P(G)$ **d.** $P(Y \text{ or } G)$

12. A purse contains three identical-looking keys, but only two of the three keys will unlock the side door of a house. Answer the following questions if two of the three keys are randomly selected.
    a. List all the outcomes of the sample space
    b. What is the probability of selecting one key that will open the door and one key that will not?
    c. What is the probability of selecting both keys that will open the door?

13. Four identical chips lettered A, B, C, and D are placed in a box. An experiment consists of selecting two chips at random.
    a. List all the outcomes of the sample space.
    b. What is the probability that one of the two chips will be lettered B?
    c. What is the probability that one chip will be lettered C and the other D?

14. A box contains 3 red marbles and 2 green marbles. An experiment consists of selecting 2 marbles at random from the box.
    a. List all the outcomes of the sample space.
    b. What is the probability of obtaining 1 red and 1 green marble?
    c. What is the probability that both marbles will be red?

15. An electric blender comes in blue, red, yellow, green, white, and pink. Two are ordered, and the customer does not specify the color. Assume that there is approximately the same number of blenders of each color and that the company randomly selects the blenders without regard to color for shipment.
    a. List all the outcomes of the sample space.
    b. What is the probability of receiving two blue blenders?
    c. What is the probability of receiving at least one green blender?
    d. What is the probability of not receiving a red blender?

An experiment consists of tossing a regular die with faces numbered 1 through 6. Use the following events to determine the probabilities in exercises 16 and 17.

> E: Obtaining an even number
> F: Obtaining a prime number
> G: Obtaining an odd number
> H: Obtaining a number greater than 4

16. a. $P(E \cup G)$ and $P(E) + P(G)$
    b. $P(F \cup G)$ and $P(F) + P(G)$
    c. Which pairs of probabilities in parts a and b are equal? Explain why.

17. a. $P(F \cup H)$ and $P(F) + P(H)$
    b. $P(E \cup F)$ and $P(E) + P(F)$

c. Which pairs, if any, of the probabilities in parts a and b are equal? What conditions must exist in order for the probability of the union of two events to equal the sum of the probabilities of the two events?

Consider a regular deck of 52 cards with 13 cards (including 3 face cards) in each of 4 suits. Use the following events to determine the probabilities in exercises 18 and 19.

> E: Selecting a face card (jack, queen, king)
> F: Selecting an ace
> G: Selecting a spade
> H: Selecting a heart

18. a. $P(E)$ b. $P(G)$
    c. $P(E \cup F)$ d. $P(F \cup H)$
    e. $P(E \cap H)$

19. a. $P(F)$ b. $P(H)$
    c. $P(G \cup H)$ d. $P(E \cup H)$
    e. $P(G \cap E)$

The sum of the probability that an event will happen and the probability that the event will not happen is 1. Consider the experiment of selecting 1 card at random from a complete deck of 52 cards. Compute the probabilities of the events in exercises 20 and 21.

20. a. Not drawing a diamond
    b. Not drawing a red card
    c. Drawing a face card or an ace or a number less than 8
    d. Not drawing a 6

21. a. Not drawing an ace
    b. Not drawing a face card
    c. Drawing a club, heart, or diamond
    d. Not drawing a black face card

Compute the probability and odds of selecting each of the cards in exercises 22 and 23 at random from a complete deck of 52 cards.

22. a. An ace
   b. A face card
   c. A diamond
   d. A black face card

23. a. A club
   b. An 8 or a 9
   c. A red card
   d. A spade or a heart

Given the probabilities in exercises 24 and 25, determine the odds in favor of each event.

24. a. The probability of winning the lottery is $\frac{1}{1,000,000}$.
   b. The probability of selecting a defective part is 4 percent.
   c. The probability that interest rates will increase is $\frac{1}{5}$.
   d. There is a 90 percent chance that the operation will be successful.

25. a. The probability of living to age 65 is $\frac{7}{10}$.
   b. The probability of selecting a person with type O blood is $\frac{3}{5}$.
   c. The probability of winning a certain raffle is $\frac{1}{500}$.
   d. The probability of rain on Monday is 80 percent.

Gambling syndicates predict the outcomes of sporting events in terms of odds. Convert each of the odds in exercises 26 and 27 to a probability.

26. a. The odds that the Packers will beat the Rams are 4 to 3.
   b. The odds that the University of Michigan will defeat Ohio State are 7 to 5.

27. a. The odds that the Yankees will win the pennant are 10 to 3.
   b. The odds of recovering the missing space capsule are 1 to 4.

Determine the experimental probabilities of the events in exercises 28 and 29 to the nearest .01.

28. a. Tossing a paper cup and having it land with its bottom down if it landed in this position 18 times in 150 tosses
   b. Spinning a spinner and obtaining the color green if this color was obtained in 46 out of 130 spins

29. a. Tossing a tack and having it land with its point up if it landed in this position for 19 out of 90 tosses
   b. Selecting a nondefective part from an assembly line if 194 out of 200 of the previous selections have been nondefective

The mortality table in Figure 8.5 was computed on the basis of births and deaths among policyholders of several large insurance companies. Use the information in that table to answer exercises 30 and 31.

30. a. What is the experimental probability that a child will live to be 1 year old?
   b. What is the experimental probability that a person will live to age 50?
   c. What is the experimental probability that a person aged 34 will live to age 65?
   d. If an insurance company has 2356 policyholders at age 60, how many death claims is the company likely to have to pay on behalf of those who do not reach age 61?

31. a. What is the experimental probability that a 60-year-old person will live to age 65?
   b. What is the experimental probability that a child will live to be 12 years old?
   c. What is the experimental probability that a person will live to be 70 years old?
   d. If an insurance company has 7000 policyholders aged 28, how many death claims is the company likely to have to pay on behalf of those who do not reach age 29?

32. Use the table of random digits in Figure 8.6 to carry out a simulation that approximates the probability of obtaining at least one 6 in five rolls of a die. Describe your simulation.

33. Use the table of random digits in Figure 8.6 to carry out a simulation that approximates the probability of obtaining at least 5 heads in a toss of 10 fair coins. Describe your simulation.

REASONING AND PROBLEM SOLVING

34. Featured Strategy: Using a Simulation   A machine that sells gumballs for a nickel apiece contains 5 white gumballs and 2 red gumballs. If 2 nickels are put into the machine, what is the probability of obtaining a red gumball if each gumball has an equal chance of being chosen?

a. **Understanding the Problem**   The problem is to determine the probability of obtaining at least 1 red gumball. If only 1 nickel is put into the machine, what is the probability of obtaining 1 red gumball?

b. **Devising a Plan**   One approach is to use a simulation to approximate the probability. Describe such a simulation.

c. **Carrying Out the Plan**   What probability do you obtain by using your simulation?

d. **Looking Back**   It is also possible to determine the theoretical probability by designating the gumballs as R_1, R_2, W_1, W_2, W_3, W_4, and W_5, listing outcomes of the sample space, and counting those that contain at least 1 red. What is the theoretical probability obtained with this approach?

Use simulations to approximate the probabilities in exercises 35 to 38. Describe your method.

35. What is the probability that in a family of 3 boys and 2 girls the 3 boys were born in succession?

36. On a certain quiz show, people are required to guess which of 3 identical envelopes contains a $1000 bill. What is the probability that exactly 4 out of 8 people will guess the correct envelope?

37. A baseball player has a batting average of .300, which means that on average the player gets 3 hits in 10 times at bat. What is the probability this player will get at least 3 hits in the next 5 times at bat?

38. At a certain university it is required by state law that 3 out of 4 students be from the state. If 10 students are selected at random from this university, what is the probability that 4 or more will be from outside the state?

39. The problem-solving application on pages 519–520 shows that the probability of obtaining exactly 2 heads in a toss of 4 fair coins is .375.

a. Use a simulation to approximate the probability of obtaining exactly 3 heads in a toss of 6 fair coins. Describe your simulation.

b. Make a conjecture about the probability of obtaining exactly 10 heads in a toss of 20 fair coins. Will it be less than .5, equal to .5, or greater than .5?

40. Kyle made a spinner from the cover of a cardboard box by placing the pointer off the center, as shown in the following figure. One of his classmates claimed that this was not a fair spinner because the blue region and the purple region were both 3 times the size of the green and the red regions. Do you agree with your classmate? Explain your reasoning.

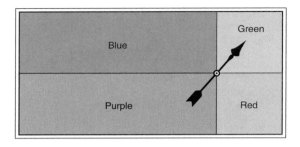

41. Maura is designing spinners for a middle school mathematics and science fair. Each spinner will have four regions, and each region will have one of the colors blue, green, purple, or red. Show with a detailed sketch a design for each of the following spinners.

a. A spinner such that the probability of obtaining the blue (or purple) region is 3 times the probability of obtaining the green (or red) region

b. A spinner such that the probability of obtaining the blue (or purple) region is 4 times the probability of obtaining the green (or red) region

c. A spinner such that the probability of obtaining the blue (or purple) region is 5 times the probability of obtaining the green (or red) region

42. Five students will be randomly selected from the seven top students in mathematics to represent their school in a regional competition. Angela and Brian are among the seven students, and they wish to determine the probability that they will be chosen. Describe a sample space for determining this probability. What is the probability they will both be chosen?

43. Amanda and Dirk are renting roller blades for a day in the park. They both take the same size shoe, and there are 6 pairs remaining in their size. Unbeknownst to them, 3 of the pairs of roller blades have defective bearings. If they randomly choose 2 pairs from the 6 pairs, what is the probability they will both get a pair of roller blades that are not defective? (*Hint:* List the elements of the sample space.)

44. A survey of the 400 students at Bishop Hill Middle School showed that 130 had their own computers, 174 owned graphing calculators, and 80 had both a computer and a graphing calculator. If a student is randomly selected from this school, what is the probability the student will own a computer or a graphing calculator?

45. To gather data involving their classmates, 24 fourth-graders each filled out a personal information survey sheet. In the category of pets, 5 students had a dog, 7 students had a cat, and 4 students had both a dog and a cat. If a student is randomly selected from this class, what is the probability the student will have a dog or a cat?

46. A hospital laboratory uses two tests to classify each sample of blood. The first test correctly identifies the blood type 65 percent of the time, and the second test correctly identifies the blood type 72 percent of the time. If the probability is .80 that at least one of the tests correctly identifies the blood type, what is the probability that both tests correctly identify the blood type?

47. The sales manager of a company believes there is a good chance she will be chosen as vice president of a new division, if the company opens a new division and if this year's sales are higher than last year's sales. She estimates the probability that the company will open a new division is .90, the probability that sales will be higher is .70, and the probability that at least one of these will happen is .75. Based on her estimates, what is the probability she will become vice president of the new division?

The table below shows the numbers to the nearest 100 boys and girls in school districts 1, 2, and 3. Determine the probability of each event in exercises 48 and 49, assuming that a student is selected at random from the three districts.

	DISTRICT 1	DISTRICT 2	DISTRICT 3
Girls	1300	2300	1500
Boys	1400	2200	1300

48. a. Student is a girl.
   b. Student is a boy from district 3.
   c. Student is from district 1 or a girl.

49. a. Student is a boy.
   b. Student is from district 2 and a girl.
   c. Student is a boy or from district 3.

A survey of the teachers in a large school system yielded the information on gender and marital status in the table below. Determine the probability of each event in exercises 50 and 51 for a randomly chosen teacher from the school system.

	MARRIED	SINGLE	DIVORCED	WIDOWED
Male	12%	3%	8%	2%
Female	55%	12%	8%	0%

Events: *M:* teacher is a male; *F:* teacher is a female; *S:* teacher is a single person; *D:* teacher is a divorced person; and *W:* teacher is a widowed person.

50. a. $M \cap D$ **b.** $F \cup D$ **c.** $S \cup D$
51. a. $F \cap S$ **b.** $S \cup W$ **c.** $M \cup S$

ONLINE LEARNING CENTER   www.mhhe.com/bennett-nelson

• Math Investigation 8.1   *Coin Toss Simulation*
Section-Related: • Links   • Writing/Discussion Problems   • Bibliography

PUZZLER

How can the faces of two cubes be numbered so that when they are rolled, the resulting sum is any whole number from 1 to 12 and each sum has the same probability of occurring?

MATH ACTIVITY 8.2

DETERMINING THE FAIRNESS OF GAMES

Materials: Spinners in the Manipulative Kit. Bend a paper clip and hold a pencil at the center of the spinner, as shown below.

1. **Racing Game**   Each player in turn spins the 1-to-4 spinner twice and computes the product of the 2 numbers. If the product is 1, 2, 3, or 4, player A puts an X on the square above that number. In a similar manner Player B records the products 6, 8, 9, 12, and 16. The game ends when one of the players has built a column of X's up to the finish line. Each player receives 1 point for each of his or her X's, and the winner is the player with the greater score. Play this game to form an opinion about whether player A or player B has an advantage.

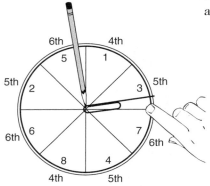

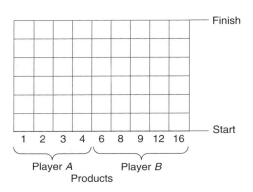

a. Based on playing this game, does it seem fair? That is, do both players seem to have an equal chance of winning?

b. The multiplication table at the left shows the ways that products can occur. For example, the product 12 can occur in two ways: 3 on the first spin and 4 on the second spin; or 4 on the first spin and 3 on the second spin. Complete the table to determine the 16 possible products.

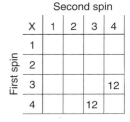

c. Using the table and assuming that each product is equally likely to occur, can you make a case that any one of the numbers is more likely to reach the finish line first? Less likely to reach the finish line first?

* d. Based on the table, is this a fair game? Write an explanation to support your conclusion.

2. **Racing Game**   This game is similar to the above game, but the 1-to-4 spinner is used to obtain one number and the 1-to-6 spinner is used to obtain the second number for each product. Design a game board, and decide which products each player should use so that it is a fair game. Write a convincing argument as to why your game is fair.

SECTION 8.2

MULTISTAGE EXPERIMENTS

Photo from NASA's Synchronous Meteorological Satellite 1.

Make three cards of equal size. Label both sides of one card with the letter A, both sides of the second with the letter B, and one side of the third with the letter A and the other side with the letter B. Select a card at random, and place it on a table. There will be either an A or a B facing up. What is the probability that the letter facing down on this card is different from the letter facing up?

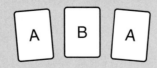

Meteorologists use computers and probability to analyze weather patterns. In recent years meteorological satellites have improved the accuracy of weather forecasting. NASA's Synchronous Meteorological Satellite 1 sent back the above photograph of North and South America showing four storms stretching across the top of the picture from western Canada to the Atlantic Ocean. The structure of cumulus clouds over Florida and the Caribbean Sea enables meteorologists to predict wind speed and direction. Weather forecasts are usually stated in terms of probability, and each probability may be determined from several others. For example, there may be one probability for a cold front and another probability for a change in wind direction. In this section, we will see how to use the probabilities of two or more events to determine the probability of a combination of events.

Probabilities of Outcomes

In Section 8.1 we studied **single-stage** experiments such as spinning a spinner, rolling a die, and tossing a coin. These experiments are over after one step. Now we will study combinations of experiments, called **multistage experiments.**

Suppose we spin spinner A and then spinner B in Figure 8.7. This is an example of a *two-stage experiment.*

Students should also explore probability through experiments that have only a few outcomes, such as using game spinners with certain portions shaded and considering how likely it is that the spinner will land on a particular color.

Standards 2000, p. 181

Figure 8.7

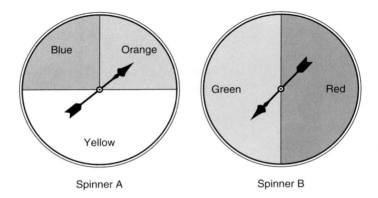

Spinner A   Spinner B

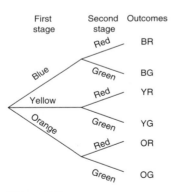

First stage   Second stage   Outcomes

Figure 8.8

The different outcomes for multistage experiments can be determined by constructing *tree diagrams,* which were used in Chapter 3 as a model for the multiplication of whole numbers. Since there are 3 different outcomes from spinner A and 2 different outcomes from spinner B, the experiment of spinning first spinner A and then spinner B has $3 \times 2 = 6$ outcomes (Figure 8.8).

Figure 8.9 shows the probabilities of obtaining each color and each outcome. Such a diagram is called a **probability tree.** The probability of each of the 6 outcomes can be determined from this probability tree. For example, consider the probability of obtaining BR (blue on spinner A followed by red on spinner B). Since blue occurs $\frac{1}{4}$ of the time and red occurs $\frac{1}{2}$ of the times that blue occurs, the probability of BR is $\frac{1}{4} \times \frac{1}{2}$, or $\frac{1}{8}$. This probability is the product of the two probabilities along the path that leads to BR. Similarly, the probability of YG (yellow followed by green) is $\frac{1}{2} \times \frac{1}{2} = \frac{1}{4}$. Notice that the sum of the probabilities for all 6 outcomes is 1.

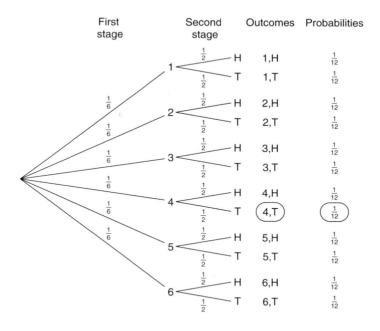

Figure 8.9

The principle of multiplying along the paths of a probability tree can be gener-alized as follows. *If the outcomes of an experiment can be represented as the paths of a tree diagram, then the probability of any outcome is the product of the probabilities on its path.*

Example A

A die is rolled and a coin is tossed. Sketch the probability tree for this experiment, and determine the probability of rolling a 4 on the die and getting a tail on the coin toss.

Solution

The probability of rolling a 4 and getting a tail is $\frac{1}{12}$. In this two-stage experiment there are $6 \times 2 = 12$ outcomes, and each outcome is equally likely.

An experiment may consist of several stages, as in the next example.

Example B

What is the probability that the children in a family of 4 children will be born in the order girl, boy, girl, boy?

Solution   It is customary to assume that the probability of a baby's being a girl is $\frac{1}{2}$ and the probability of a baby's being a boy is also $\frac{1}{2}$.

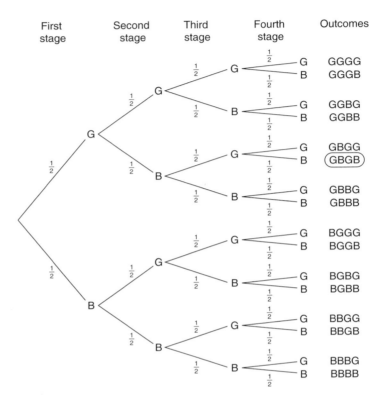

The probability tree shows that all the outcomes are equally likely and that each has a probability of $\frac{1}{16}$ ($\frac{1}{2} \times \frac{1}{2} \times \frac{1}{2} \times \frac{1}{2}$). Since there is only one outcome with the order GBGB, the probability of a family's having a girl, a boy, a girl, and a boy in this order is $\frac{1}{16}$.

Probabilities of Events

Once probabilities have been assigned to the outcomes of a multistage experiment, the probabilities of specific events can be determined. Using the probability tree in Example B, we can determine the probabilities of several events. For example, let E be the event of a family's having 3 girls and 1 boy. Since there are 4 such outcomes,

$$P(E) = \tfrac{1}{16} + \tfrac{1}{16} + \tfrac{1}{16} + \tfrac{1}{16} = \tfrac{4}{16} = \tfrac{1}{4}$$

Or if F is the event of a family's having 2 girls and 2 boys,

$$P(F) = \tfrac{6}{16} = \tfrac{3}{8}$$

since there are 6 outcomes with 2 girls and 2 boys.

Example C

A box contains 2 red marbles and 1 white marble. A marble is randomly selected and returned to the box, and a second marble is randomly selected. What is the probability of selecting 2 red marbles?

Solution

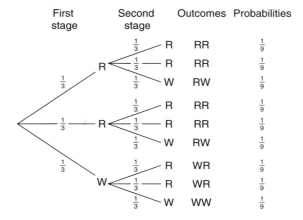

The probability tree shows that there are 9 equally likely outcomes, each with a probability of $\frac{1}{9}$. Since there are 4 outcomes with 2 red marbles, the probability of this event is $\frac{4}{9}$.

The probability tree in Example C can be simplified by combining branches. Since we are interested in only whether the first marble is red or white, the first stage of the experiment can be represented by two branches, one with a probability of $\frac{2}{3}$ (selecting a red marble) and one with a probability of $\frac{1}{3}$ (selecting a white marble). Similarly, in the second stage we simply wish to distinguish between selecting red and white (Figure 8.10). Notice that the probability of obtaining 2 red marbles is the product of the probabilities along the top branch: $\frac{2}{3} \times \frac{2}{3} = \frac{4}{9}$.

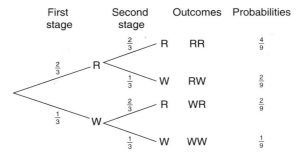

Figure 8.10

Independent and Dependent Events

In the experiment of rolling a die and tossing a coin (see Example A), the outcome from the die does not affect the outcome from the coin. In other words, rolling a die and tossing a coin are independent of each other. If neither of two events affects the probability of the occurrence of the other, we say the two events are **independent.** The stages of the multistage experiments in Examples A through C consist of independent events. The tree diagrams for these experiments show that the probability of an outcome is the product of the probabilities on its path. These examples suggest the following property for finding the probability of events A and B:

> **MULTIPLICATION PROPERTY**   If A and B are independent events, then
>
> $$P(A \cap B) = P(A) \times P(B)$$

Example D

What is the probability of rolling a die and obtaining a 4 and then rolling it a second time and obtaining an even number?

Solution   Since the outcome from the first roll does not affect the outcome on the second roll, these events are independent. The probability of obtaining a 4 on one roll of a die is $\frac{1}{6}$, and the probability of obtaining an even number is $\frac{1}{2}$. By the *multiplication property,* the probability of rolling a 4 and then rolling an even number is $\frac{1}{6} \times \frac{1}{2} = \frac{1}{12}$.

The multiplication property enables us to compute the probability of independent events without sketching a probability tree. For example, the top two branches of the probability tree in Figure 8.10 show the probability of selecting 2 red marbles from a box that contains 2 red marbles and 1 white marble. In this experiment, event A, "obtaining a red marble on the first selection," and event B, "obtaining a red marble on the second selection," are independent events. Thus, the probability of A and B is

$$P(A) \times P(B) = \tfrac{2}{3} \times \tfrac{2}{3} = \tfrac{4}{9}$$

Sometimes events are not independent. In the next example, the first marble selected from the box is *not replaced* for the second draw. In this case the event "obtaining a red marble on the first selection" and the event "obtaining a red marble on the second selection" are not independent. When one event affects the probability of the occurrence of the other, the two events are **dependent.**

Example E

A box contains 2 red (R) marbles and 1 white (W) marble. A marble is selected at random but not returned to the box, and then a second marble is selected. What is the probability of selecting 2 red marbles?

Solution   The probability of selecting a red marble on the first draw is $\frac{2}{3}$. So the first stage of the probability tree is the same as that in Figure 8.10. However, because the first marble is not replaced, the probabilities for the second stage are affected. If a red marble is selected on the first draw, then 1 red marble and 1 white marble are left, so the probability of choosing a red marble on the second draw is $\frac{1}{2}$. The top branches of the following probability tree show that the probability of selecting 2 red marbles in this case is $\frac{2}{3} \times \frac{1}{2} = \frac{1}{3}$.

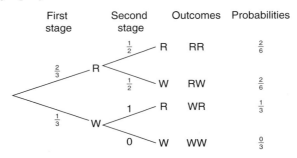

Notice in this example that there is one path leading to RW and one path leading to WR, so the probability of choosing 1 red marble and 1 white marble is $\frac{1}{3} + \frac{1}{3} = \frac{2}{3}$ when the order in which they are selected is not important. Also, the bottom branch of the tree shows that the probability of selecting 2 white marbles is 0 (there is only 1 white marble in the box).

The probability of dependent events also can be computed by using the *multiplication property,* as suggested by the probability tree in Example E. However, care must be taken in determining the probability of an event which is affected by the outcome of the other. The next two examples involve dependent events.

Example F

What is the probability of randomly selecting 2 hearts from the 5 cards shown here?

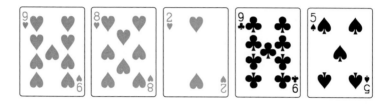

Solution The probability of obtaining a heart on the first draw is $\frac{3}{5}$, and if the first card is a heart, the probability of obtaining a heart on the second draw is $\frac{2}{4}$. The probability of obtaining 2 hearts is $\frac{3}{5} \times \frac{2}{4} = \frac{6}{20} = \frac{3}{10}$.

Example G

Consider the events of selecting 1 card from an ordinary deck of 52 cards and then selecting another card without replacing the first. Determine the probabilities of the following events.

1. Selecting 2 clubs

2. Selecting 2 face cards

3. Selecting 2 aces

4. Selecting 2 red cards

Research Statement

Research has shown that when sixth and seventh graders were asked to determine conditional probabilities, the performance was dramatically lower when the task involved selection without replacement as compared to selection with replacement.

National Research Council 2001

Solution 1. There are 13 clubs: $\frac{13}{52} \times \frac{12}{51} = \frac{156}{2652} \approx .059$ 2. There are 12 face cards: $\frac{12}{52} \times \frac{11}{51} = \frac{132}{2652} \approx .050$ 3. There are 4 aces: $\frac{4}{52} \times \frac{3}{51} = \frac{12}{2652} \approx .005$ 4. There are 26 red cards: $\frac{26}{52} \times \frac{25}{51} = \frac{650}{2652} \approx .245$

The multiplication property can now be combined with the addition property that was introduced in Section 8.1. If A and B are independent events, then the probability of A or B or both becomes

$$P(A \cup B) = P(A) + P(B) - P(A) \times P(B)$$

This property is used in the following example. A certain city's smog will be above acceptable levels 25 percent of the days, and its pollen will be above acceptable levels 20 percent of the days. If S is the event "smog above acceptable levels" and R is the event "pollen above acceptable levels" and if these events are independent, the probability that either the smog or the pollen (or both) will be above acceptable levels on any randomly selected day is

$$P(S \cup R) = P(S) + P(R) - P(S) \times P(R)$$
$$= .25 + .20 - .05$$
$$= .40$$

We can also use the multiplication property to determine if two events are independent. In some cases, such as rolling a die and tossing a coin, it is easy to see that the events are independent. However, in other cases the independence of two events is not as apparent. Consider event S, "smog above acceptable levels," and event R, "pollen above acceptable levels," from the above example. Suppose records show that the probability of a day occurring with both smog and pollen above acceptable levels is .08. Then we have two equations:

$$P(S \cap R) = .08 \qquad \text{and} \qquad P(S) \times P(R) = .25 \times .20 = .05$$

Since $.08 \neq .05$, the events "smog above acceptable levels" and "pollen above acceptable levels" are not independent events. That is, they are dependent events. In general, if

$$P(A \cap B) = P(A) \times P(B)$$

for events A and B, then these events are independent.

Problem-Solving Application

Many probability problems involve fractions, and partitioning regions into parts is a common model for illustrating fractions. These observations suggest a geometric approach to solving probability problems. The following two-stage probability problem will be solved by using a tree diagram and geometric regions.

PROBLEM

The figure shows paths leading to three rooms. If you begin at point S and choose a path at random whenever you reach a branch point, what is the probability of entering room A?

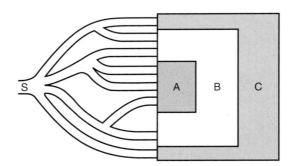

Understanding the Problem   The probability of taking any one of the first four paths is $\frac{1}{4}$. The probability of taking the top path of the first four paths and then at the next branch point taking the top path (that leads to room C) is $\frac{1}{4} \times \frac{1}{2} = \frac{1}{8}$. **Question 1:** What is the probability of taking the top path of the first four paths and entering room B?

Devising a Plan   One approach is to sketch a tree diagram and compute the probability of each outcome.

Carrying Out the Plan   The following tree diagram shows the probabilities for each branch of the tree. Room B can be entered by three paths having probabilities of $\frac{1}{4} \times \frac{1}{2}$, $\frac{1}{4} \times \frac{1}{3}$, and $\frac{1}{4} \times \frac{1}{2}$. The probability of entering room B is the sum of these probabilities. **Question 2:** What is the probability of entering room A?

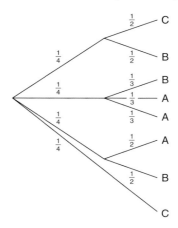

Looking Back   A geometric solution to the problem can be found by subdividing a unit rectangle into parts. Since there are four paths at point S and each is equally likely to be chosen, the rectangle is divided into four congruent regions, as shown in figure (*i*). Next, since the upper path leads to two equally likely paths, the upper region of the rectangle is partitioned into two congruent parts, which are labeled C and B [figure (*ii*)]. Similarly, the other three regions of the rectangle can be partitioned as shown in figure (*iii*).

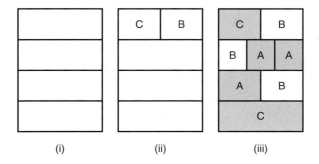

(i)   (ii)   (iii)

Some observations can be made from figure (*iii*). For example, does room A or room B have the greater probability of being entered? **Question 3:** Which of the three rooms has the greatest probability of being entered? To determine the probability of entering each room, we can subdivide the parts of figure (*iii*) into parts of the same size, as shown on the next page in figure (*iv*). **Question 4:** What fractional part of the whole figure represents the total probability of entering room A?

536   CHAPTER 8 • Probability

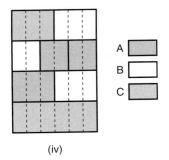

(iv)

Answers to Questions 1–4   1. $\frac{1}{8}$ **2.** $\frac{1}{4} \times \frac{1}{3} + \frac{1}{4} \times \frac{1}{3} + \frac{1}{4} \times \frac{1}{2} = \frac{1}{12} + \frac{1}{12} + \frac{1}{8} = \frac{7}{24}$.   **3.** Room B has a greater probability of being entered than room A; room C has the greatest probability of being entered.   **4.** $\frac{7}{24}$

Complementary Events

There are some problems in which the probability of an event can be most easily found by first computing the probability of its complement.

Example H

If a die is tossed 4 times, what is the probability of obtaining *at least* one 6?

Solution   Let E be the event of obtaining at least one 6 (this includes the possibility of obtaining one, two, three, or four 6s), and let F be the event of not obtaining any 6s. Then E and F are complementary events, and $P(E) + P(F) = 1$. The probability of not obtaining a 6 on 1 roll of a die is $\frac{5}{6}$. So the probability of obtaining no 6s on 4 rolls is

$$P(F) = \frac{5}{6} \times \frac{5}{6} \times \frac{5}{6} \times \frac{5}{6} = \frac{625}{1296} \approx .48$$

and the probability of obtaining at least one 6 is

$$P(E) \approx 1 - .48$$
$$= .52$$

That is, slightly more than half of the time you can expect to obtain at least one 6 in 4 tosses of a die.

Since in Example H obtaining at least one 6 includes several different possibilities (obtaining one 6, two 6s, three 6s, or four 6s), it is easier to consider the probability that this will not happen. The words *at least* are sometimes a clue to the fact that the probability of an event may be more easily found by first computing the probability of its complement.

Example I

Of the ten teachers who have volunteered for a school committee, 7 are women and 3 are men. If 3 of these people are chosen randomly, what is the probability that *at least* 1 person will be a man?

Solution   The probability that a man will not be chosen (that is, that all 3 people will be women) is $\frac{7}{10} \times \frac{6}{9} \times \frac{5}{8} \approx .29$. Thus the probability of at least 1 man being chosen is approximately $1 - .29 = .71$.

There is a well-known problem in probability whose solution often surprises people.

What is the smallest randomly chosen group of people for which there is better than a 50 percent chance that at least 2 of them will have a birthday on the same day of the year?

Surprisingly, the answer is only 23 people. In fact, there is a 70 percent probability that among 30 randomly chosen people, 2 will have birthdays on the same day. With 50 randomly chosen people the probability is about 97 percent. The graph in Figure 8.11 shows that in a group of more than 50 randomly chosen people we can be almost certain of finding 2 with birthdays on the same day.

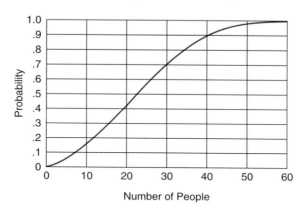

Figure 8.11

The probability that at least 2 out of 23 people have the same birthday can be found by computing the probability of a complementary event. That is, we can determine the probability that all 23 people have birthdays on different days and then subtract this probability from 1. To begin with, consider the problem for just 2 people. No matter when the first person was born, there is a probability of $\frac{364}{365}$ that the second person's birthday will not be on the same day. When a third person joins this group, the probability that his or her birth date will differ from those of the other 2 people is $\frac{363}{365}$. Therefore, the probability that each of 3 people has a different birth date is $\frac{364}{365} \times \frac{363}{365}$. Similarly, the probability that 23 people will have different birthdays is the following product of 22 numbers:

$$\frac{364}{365} \times \frac{363}{365} \times \frac{362}{365} \times \cdots \times \frac{344}{365} \times \frac{343}{365} \approx .49$$

Therefore, the probability that there will be 2 or more people with birthdays on the same day in a group of 23 people is approximately $1 - .49 = .51$. Make a prediction next time you're in a group of 23 or more people. The odds are in your favor that there will be at least 2 people with birthdays on the same day.

Problem-Solving Application

For cases in which it is difficult to find the probability of a multistage experiment, the probability may be approximated by *carrying out a simulation*. At other times a simulation may be used to check on the reasonableness of a calculation that produces a theoretical probability.

PROBLEM

A state lottery has a daily drawing in which 4 ping-pong balls are selected at random from among 10 balls numbered 0, 1, 2, . . . , 9. After a ball is selected, it is returned for the next selection. An elementary school student noticed that quite often two of the four digits drawn are equal. What is the probability that at least two out of four digits will be equal?

Understanding the Problem   The condition *at least two* includes the possibilities that there may be two equal digits, three equal digits, or four equal digits.

Devising a Plan   One way of determining the probability is to carry out a simulation using the table of random digits in Figure 8.6 (page 519). **Question 1:** How can this be done?

Carrying Out the Plan   The first 12 groups of 4 digits (using consecutive digits) from the sixth row of the table in Figure 8.6 are shown below. Notice that six of these groups have two or more equal digits. Continue this simulation through five complete rows of the table. **Question 2:** What is the probability for this simulation?

6886 8492 4016 1401 1046 3862 0491 4880 3384 5266 3902 0063

Looking Back   The theoretical probability for this problem can be found by first computing the probability for the complementary event, that is, the probability that all four digits are different. After the first digit is drawn, the probability that the second digit will not equal the first digit is $\frac{9}{10}$; the probability that the third digit will be different from the first two is $\frac{8}{10}$; and the probability that the fourth will be different from the first three is $\frac{7}{10}$. So the probability of selecting four different digits is

$$\tfrac{9}{10} \times \tfrac{8}{10} \times \tfrac{7}{10} = \tfrac{504}{1000} = .504$$

Question 3: What is the theoretical probability that at least two of the four digits drawn will be equal?

Answers to Questions 1–3   **1.** Start with any digit in the table and consider groups of four digits at a time. The number of groups with two or more equal digits divided by the total number of groups is the probability for this simulation.   **2.** Since 31 out of 62 groups of four digits have two or more equal digits, the experimental probability for this simulation is $\frac{31}{62} = .5$.   **3.** The theoretical probability that at least two of the four digits drawn will be equal is $1 - .504 = .496$, or approximately .5.

Expected Value

To evaluate the fairness of a game, we must consider the prize we can expect to gain as well as the probability of winning. The probability of winning may be fairly small, but if the prize is large enough, the game may be a good risk. Consider the following game.

E x a m p l e J

A game involves rolling two dice. If the player obtains a sum of 7, she or he is paid $5. Otherwise, the player pays $1. Over time, can the player expect to gain money, lose money, or break even?

Solution   The probability of rolling a sum of 7 is $\frac{1}{6}$. Thus for 1 out of every 6 rolls, on average, the player can expect to receive $5. However, for 5 out of 6 rolls, on average, the player can expect to pay $1 per roll. Thus over time the player can expect to break even.

The amounts to be won and lost in Example J can be expressed in an equation. Because there is a $\frac{1}{6}$ chance of winning $5 and a $\frac{5}{6}$ chance of losing $1, the net winnings from the game can be computed as follows:

$$\tfrac{1}{6}(5) + \tfrac{5}{6}(^-1) = \tfrac{5}{6} + \tfrac{^-5}{6} = 0$$

This equation expresses the **expected value** of the game; it is generalized in the following definition.

If the outcomes of an experiment have values v_1, v_2, . . . , v_n and the outcomes have probabilities p_1, p_2, . . . , p_n, respectively, then the **expected value** is

$$p_1 v_1 + p_2 v_2 + \cdots + p_n v_n$$

Sometimes the expected value involves several prizes, and each prize has its own probability of occurring.

Example K

The sweepstakes ticket shown below has two five-digit numbers (one number is hidden on the left of the ticket, and the digits of the other number are hidden by the five dollar signs). The amount you win depends on which digits of the two numbers match. If the two digits in the ten thousands place are equal, you win $2000; if the two digits in the thousands place are equal, you win $20; etc. (as shown on the lottery ticket). Anyone who wins the $5, $2, or $1 ticket prize is eligible for the $100,000 grand prize. Suppose the probabilities of winning $100,000, $2,000, $20, $5, $2, and the $1-ticket prize are $\frac{1}{1,000,000}$, $\frac{1}{20,000}$, $\frac{1}{200}$, $\frac{1}{25}$, $\frac{1}{10}$, and $\frac{1}{5}$, respectively.

1. What is the expected value of this lottery ticket?

2. If each ticket costs $1, will the player who regularly buys them gain or lose money over time?

Solution 1. The expected value is computed by multiplying the amount of each prize by its probability of occurring and adding these products:

$$\frac{1}{1,000,000}(\$100,000) + \frac{1}{20,000}(\$2,000) + \frac{1}{200}(\$20) + \frac{1}{25}(\$5) + \frac{1}{10}(\$2) + \frac{1}{5}(\$1) = \$.90$$

2. Since the expected value is $.90 and each ticket costs $1, the player will lose money. On average, there is a $.10 loss for each ticket that is purchased.

A game is called a **fair game** if the expected value is zero. For example, the game in Example J is a fair game; however, the game in Example K is not a fair game. Most gambling games are not fair games.

Example **L**   A roulette wheel has 38 compartments. Two are numbered 0 and 00 and are colored green. The remaining compartments are numbered 1 through 36; one-half of these are red, and one-half are black. With each spin of the wheel, a ball falls into one of the compartments. One way of playing this game is to bet on the red or black color.

1. What is the probability of obtaining a red number on one spin?

2. If a player bets $1 on red and wins, the player is paid $1 plus the $1 the player bet. What is the expected value of this game?

3. Is this a fair game?

Solution   1. The probability of obtaining a red number is $\frac{18}{38} = \frac{9}{19}$.   2. The expected value of this bet is $\frac{18}{38}(\$1) + \frac{20}{38}(\$^-1) \approx \$^-.05$(or $^-$5 cents).   3. This game is not fair. On average, a player will lose 5 cents on each spin.

EXERCISES AND PROBLEMS 8.2

For a test of 10 true–false questions, determine the probabilities of the events in 1 and 2 if every question is answered by guessing.

1. a. Getting the first two questions correct
   b. Getting the first five questions correct
   c. Getting all 10 questions correct

2. a. Getting the first three questions correct
   b. Answering the first two questions incorrectly

   c. Answering all the even-numbered questions correctly and all the odd-numbered questions incorrectly

Consider the two-stage experiment with the spinners on the following page, spinning first the spinner on the left and then the spinner on the right for exercises 3 and 4.

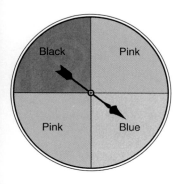 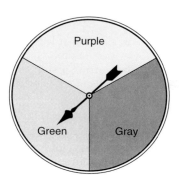

3. a. What is the probability of obtaining pink followed by gray?
   b. What is the probability of obtaining pink or blue followed by gray?
   c. What is the probability of obtaining black followed by purple or green?

4. a. What is the probability of obtaining blue followed by green?
   b. What is the probability of obtaining pink followed by purple?
   c. Sketch a probability tree showing all possible outcomes and their probabilities.

Consider the two-stage experiment of randomly selecting a marble from the bowl on the left and then a marble from the bowl on the right. Use this experiment in exercises 5 and 6.

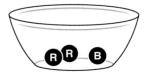 

5. a. What is the probability of selecting 2 red marbles?
   b. What is the probability of selecting at least 1 red marble?
   c. What is the probability of selecting 1 yellow marble?
   d. Sketch a probability tree showing all possible outcomes and their probabilities.

6. a. What is the probability of selecting 1 green marble?
   b. What is the probability of selecting 1 blue marble?
   c. What is the probability of not selecting a red marble?
   d. What is the probability of selecting 1 red marble and 1 green marble?

A family has 3 children. Assume that the chances of having a boy or a girl are equally likely in exercises 7 and 8.

7. a. What is the probability that the family has 3 girls?
   b. What is the probability that the family has at least 1 boy?
   c. What is the probability that the family has at least 2 girls?

8. a. What is the probability that the family has 2 boys and 1 girl?
   b. What is the probability that the family has at least 1 girl?
   c. Draw a probability tree showing all possible combinations of boys and girls.

Exercises 9 and 10 use the fact that a fair coin is tossed 4 times.

9. a. What is the probability of obtaining 3 tails and 1 head?
   b. What is the probability of obtaining at least 2 tails?
   c. Draw a probability tree showing all possible outcomes of heads and tails.

10. a. What is the probability of obtaining 3 heads and 1 tail?
   b. What is the probability of obtaining at least 2 heads?
   c. What is the probability of obtaining 2 heads and 2 tails?

A box contains 7 black, 3 red, and 5 purple marbles. Consider the two-stage experiment of randomly selecting a marble from the box, replacing it, and then selecting a second marble. Determine the probabilities of the events in exercises 11 and 12.

11. a. Selecting 2 red marbles
   b. Selecting 1 red then 1 black marble
   c. Selecting 1 red then 1 purple marble

12. a. Selecting 2 black marbles
   b. Selecting 1 black then 1 purple marble
   c. Selecting 2 purple marbles

13. Suppose that in exercise 11, the first marble selected is not replaced before the second marble is chosen. Determine the probabilities of the events in 11a, b, and c.

14. Suppose that in exercise 12 the first marble is not replaced before the second marble is chosen. Determine the probabilities of the events in 12a, b, and c.

15. a. If you flipped a fair coin 9 times and got 9 heads, what would be the probability of getting a head on the next toss?
   b. If you rolled a fair die 5 times and got the numbers 1, 2, 3, 4, and 5, what would be the probability of rolling a 6 on the next turn?

Classify the events in exercises 16 and 17 as dependent or independent and compute their probabilities.

16. **a.** Tossing a coin 3 times and getting 3 heads in a row
    b. Drawing 2 aces from a complete deck of 52 playing cards if the first card selected is not replaced

17. **a.** Rolling 2 dice and getting a sum of 7 twice in succession
    b. Selecting 2 green balls from a bag of 5 green and 3 red balls if the first ball selected is not replaced

Alice and Bill make one payment each week, and it is determined by the "debits spinner." Assume each outcome on the spinner is equally likely for determining the probabilities in exercises 18 and 19.

"O.K., Alice, spin the wheel and let's see who gets paid this week."

18. **a.** What is the probability of making a fuel payment 2 weeks in a row?
    b. What is the probability they will not make an electricity payment this week?
    c. If they don't make an electricity payment within the next 3 weeks, their lights will be shut off. What is the probability they will lose their lights?

19. **a.** What is the probability of not making a fuel payment this week?
    b. What is the probability of not making a fuel payment and not making an electricity payment this week?
    c. If they don't make a fuel payment within the next 2 weeks, they will be charged interest on the outstanding balance of their bill. What is the probability that a payment will not be made within the next 2 weeks?

Determine the probabilities of the events in exercises 20 and 21. (*Hint:* Use complementary events.)

20. **a.** Getting a sum of 7 at least once on 4 rolls of a pair of dice

b. Getting at least one 6 on 4 rolls of a die

21. **a.** Getting at least one sum of 7 or 11 on 3 rolls of a pair of dice
    b. Getting a sum of 9 or greater at least once in 5 rolls of a pair of dice

The typical slot machine has three wheels that operate independently of one another. Each wheel has six different kinds of symbols that occur various numbers of times, as shown in the chart below. If any one of the winning combinations appears, the player wins money according to the payoff assigned to each combination. Find the probabilities of the events in exercises 22 and 23.

	WHEEL 1	WHEEL 2	WHEEL 3
Cherries	7	7	0
Oranges	3	6	7
Lemons	3	0	4
Plums	5	1	5
Bells	1	3	3
Bars	1	3	1
Totals	20	20	20

22. **a.** A bar on wheel 1
    b. A bar on all three wheels

23. **a.** Bells on wheels 1 and 2 and a bar on wheel 3
    b. Plums on wheels 1 and 2 and a bar on wheel 3

24. Assuming that at each branch point in the maze below any branch is equally likely to be chosen, determine the probability of entering room A.

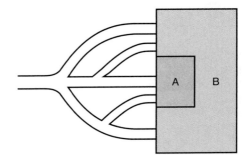

25. Assuming that at each branch point in the maze below any branch is equally likely to be chosen, determine the probability of entering room B.

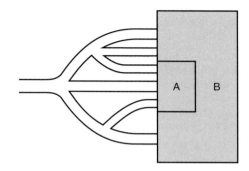

REASONING AND PROBLEM SOLVING

26. A college student is considering 6 elective courses taught by 6 different professors. She must select 2 of the courses. The student is unaware that 2 of the 6 courses will be taught by professors who have received distinguished teaching awards. List the elements of the sample space, and then determine the probabilities of the following events, assuming the student chooses her 2 courses randomly.
  a. Not selecting any courses taught by the award-winning professors
  b. Selecting exactly 1 course taught by an award-winning professor
  c. Selecting at least 1 course taught by an award-winning professor

27. A consumer buys a package of 5 flashbulbs, not knowing that 1 of the bulbs is bad. List the outcomes in the sample space if 2 bulbs are selected randomly, and then find the probabilities of the following events.
  a. Both bulbs are good.
  b. One of the bulbs is bad.

28. A bureau drawer contains 10 black socks and 10 brown socks. Their wearer is a very early riser who selects the socks in the dark. Find the probabilities of the following events:
  a. Selecting 2 socks and having both black
  b. Selecting 2 socks and obtaining 1 black and 1 brown
  c. Selecting 3 socks and obtaining 2 of the same color

29. Mr. and Mrs. Petritz of Butte, Montana, have 5 children who were all born on April 15. Answer the following questions, assuming that it is equally likely that a child will be born on any of the 365 days of the year.

a. After the first Petritz child was born, what was the probability the second child would be born on April 15 if the child was not a twin?
b. If a couple has 1 child on April 15, what is the probability that their next 4 children will be born on April 15 if there are no multiple births?

Use a simulation and complementary events to solve problems 30 and 31. Describe your simulations.

30. A system with three components fails if one or more components fail. The probability that any given component will fail is $\frac{1}{10}$. What is the probability that the system will fail?

31. A manufacturer of bubble gum puts a 5 cent coupon in 1 out of every 5 packages of gum. What is the probability of obtaining at least 1 of these coupons in 4 packages of gum?

32. Suppose there are 3 red, 4 blue, and 5 green chips in a bag and you win by selecting either a red or a green chip. If you get a red chip, you win \$3; a green chip pays \$2; and a blue chip pays \$0.
  a. What is the expected value of this game?
  b. If it costs \$1.50 to play this game, is it a fair game?

33. A game consists of rolling a die; the number of dollars you receive is the number that shows on the die. For example, if you roll a 3, you receive \$3.
  a. What is the expected value of this game?
  b. What should a person pay when playing in order for this to be a fair game?

34. Featured Strategy: Solving a Simpler Problem and Using a Simulation Two players have invented a game. A bowl is filled with an equal number of white and red marbles. One player, called the *holder,* holds the bowl while the other player, called the *drawer,* is blindfolded and selects two marbles. The drawer wins if both marbles are the same color; otherwise, she loses. Which player has the better chance of winning?

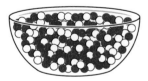

a. Understanding the Problem Either the two marbles selected will both be white or both be red, or the colors will be different. The drawer feels that she has a $\frac{2}{3}$ chance of winning since there are 3 outcomes and 2 are favorable. Is this true?

b. **Devising a Plan** One approach is to simplify the problem and try to solve it for smaller numbers. What is the probability that the drawer will win if there are 3 red and 3 white marbles in the bowl? Another approach is to use a simulation by placing slips of paper representing marbles in a box and drawing them out 1 at a time.

c. **Carrying Out the Plan** Who has the better chance of winning this game? What happens to the probability if greater numbers of marbles are used?

d. **Looking Back** Suppose the game continues with the drawer selecting 2 marbles at a time until there are no marbles left. The drawer wins a point each time the marbles are the same color and otherwise loses a point. Does this game favor the drawer or the holder? (*Hint:* Try some experiments and determine an empirical probability.)

35. Four prize amounts are hidden under the six rectangles on the lottery ticket shown below. If the same prize amount appears in three separate rectangles, the ticket owner wins that prize. The four prizes are $5000, $25, $2, and one ticket (worth $1); and the probabilities of winning these prizes on a given ticket are $\frac{1}{10,000}$, $\frac{1}{100}$, $\frac{1}{20}$, and $\frac{1}{10}$, respectively.

a. What is the expected value for one ticket?
b. If each ticket costs $1, is this a fair game?

One way you can bet in roulette is to place a chip on a single number (see page 540). If the ball lands in the compartment with your number, the house pays you 35 chips plus the chip you bet. Use this information in problems 36 and 37.

36. a. What is the probability that the ball will land on 13?
b. If each chip is worth $1, what is the expected value in this game?

37. a. What is the probability that the ball will not land on 17?
b. Is the expected value for playing a color (as computed on page 540) greater than, less than, or equal to that of playing a particular number?

In an experiment designed to test estimates of probability, people were asked to select one of two outcomes that would be more likely to occur. Determine which out-

come in problems 38 and 39 is more likely to occur. *Note:* Each box has only one winning ticket.

38. a. Obtaining a winning ticket by drawing once from a box of 10 tickets
b. Obtaining a winning ticket both times by drawing twice with replacement from a box of 5 tickets

39. a. Obtaining a winning ticket by drawing once from a box of 10 tickets
b. Obtaining a winning ticket at least once by drawing twice with replacement from a box of 20 tickets (*Hint:* Use complementary events.)

40. An environmental task force estimates that 6 percent of the streams suffer both chemical and thermal pollution, 40 percent suffer chemical pollution, and 30 percent suffer thermal pollution. Are chemical and thermal pollution of the streams independent events?

41. An experimental plane has two engines. The probability that the left one fails is .02, the probability the right one fails is .01, and the probability that neither fails is .98. Are the events "failure of the left engine" and "failure of the right engine" independent events?

42. A deep-sea diver has two independent oxygen systems. Suppose the probability that system A works is .9 and the probability that system B works is .8. What is the probability that either system A or system B will work?

43. A fire alarm in a school has two independent circuits. The alarm will function if one or both of the circuits are working. If the probability that the first circuit is working is .95 and the probability that the second circuit is working is .92, what is the probability that the fire alarm will function?

The following table shows the number of students at a college who were offered teaching positions before graduation. Determine the probability of each event in problems 44 and 45, assuming that one of the students represented in the table is randomly selected.

	OFFER	NO OFFER
Female	104	54
Male	56	36

44. a. Student is a female who received a teaching position offer.
b. Student is a male, and he did not receive a teaching position offer.
c. Student received a teaching position offer or is a male.

45. **a.** Student is a male who received a teaching position offer.
  b. Student is a female, and she did not receive a teaching position offer.
  c. Student received a teaching position offer or is a female.

In Sweden a motorist was accused of overparking in a restricted-time zone. A police officer testified that this particular parked car was seen with the tire valves pointing to 1 o'clock and to 6 o'clock. When the officer returned later (after the allowed parking time had expired), this same car was there with its valves pointing in the same directions—so a ticket was written. The motorist claimed that he had driven the car away from that spot during the elapsed time, and when he returned later, the tire values coincidentally came to rest in the same positions as before. The driver was acquitted, but the judge remarked that if the positions of the tire valves of all four wheels had been recorded and found to point in the same direction, the coincidence claim would be rejected as too improbable. Assume in problems 46 and 47 that because of variations in tire sizes the tires will not turn the same amounts.

46. Using the 12-hour positions, determine the probability that two given tire valves of a car will return to their respective earlier positions when the car is reparked.

47. What is the probability that all four tire valves will return to the same positions as before?

ONLINE LEARNING CENTER   www.mhhe.com/bennett-nelson

• Math Investigation 8.2   *Probability Machines*
Section-Related: • Links   • Writing/Discussion Problems   • Bibliography

---

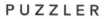

PUZZLER

Suppose you have three containers for marbles. Container I holds 1 black marble and 1 white marble; container II holds 1 black and 2 white; and container III holds 1 black and 1 white. If a marble is selected at random from container I and put into container II and a marble is selected at random from container II and put into container III, what is the probability of drawing a black marble from container III?

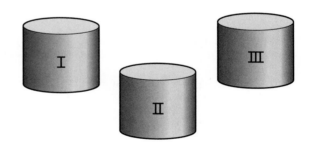

CHAPTER REVIEW

1. **Probability**
   a. Any activity such as spinning a spinner, tossing a coin, or rolling a die is called an **experiment.**
   b. The different results that can occur from an experiment are called **outcomes.**
   c. The set of all outcomes is called the **sample space.**
   d. Probabilities determined from conducting experiments are called **experimental probabilities.**
   e. Probabilities determined from ideal experiments are called **theoretical probabilities.**
   f. If there are n equally likely outcomes, then the **probability of an outcome** is $1/n$.

g. If the outcomes of an experiment have values v_1, $v_2, \cdots, v_n$ and the outcomes have probabilities $p_1, p_2, \cdots p_n$, respectively, then the **expected value** of the experiment is

$$p_1 v_1 + p_2 v_2 + \cdots + p_n v_n$$

h. A game is called a **fair game** if the net earnings are zero.

2. Events
  a. Any subset of an outcome is called an **event.**
  b. If an event is the empty set, it is called an **impossible event** and its probability is 0.
  c. If an event contains all possible outcomes, it is called a **certain event** and its probability is 1.
  d. The **probability of an event** is the sum of the probabilities of its outcomes.
  e. Addition property If events A and B are not disjoint, then $P(A \cup B) = P(A) + P(B) - P(A \cap B)$. If events A and B are disjoint, they are called **mutually exclusive events.** In this case $P(A \cup B) = P(A) + P(B)$.
  f. If events A and B are complementary sets, they are called **complementary events.** In this case $P(A) + P(B) = 1$.

3. Odds and simulations
  a. The **odds in favor** of an event are the ratio of the number of favorable outcomes n to the number of unfavorable outcomes m. The probability of this event's occurring is $n/(n + m)$.
  b. The **odds against** an event are the ratio of the number of unfavorable outcomes m to the number of favorable outcomes n. The probability of this event's not occurring is $m/(n + m)$.
  c. A **simulation** is a representation of an experiment that uses random numbers or some other device such as spinners or coins.

4. Multistage experiments
  a. A tree diagram showing the outcomes of an experiment and their probabilities is called a **probability tree.**
  b. If A and B are two events and the probability of B is not affected by the occurrence of event A, then these events are called **independent events**: otherwise, they are called **dependent events.**
  c. Multiplication property If A and B are independent events, then $P(A \cap B) = P(A) \times P(B)$.
  d. If $P(A \cap B) = P(A) \times P(B)$, then A and B are independent events.

CHAPTER TEST

1. A box contains six tickets lettered A, B, C, D, E, and F. Two tickets will be randomly selected from the box (without replacement).
  a. List all the outcomes of the sample space.
  b. What is the probability of selecting tickets A and B?
  c. What is the probability that one of the tickets will be ticket A?

2. A chip is selected at random from a box that contains 3 blue chips, 4 red chips, and 5 yellow chips. Determine the probabilities of selecting each of the following.
  a. A red chip
  b. A red chip or a yellow chip
  c. A chip that is not red

3. A box contains 3 green marbles and 2 orange marbles. An experiment consists of randomly selecting 2 marbles from the box (without replacement).
  a. List all the outcomes of the sample space.
  b. What is the probability of obtaining 2 green marbles?
  c. What is the probability of obtaining 2 orange marbles?

d. What is the probability of obtaining 1 green and 1 orange marble?

4. The odds of a certain bill's passing through a state senate are 7 to 5.
  a. What are the odds of the bill's not passing?
  b. What is the probability that the bill will be passed?

5. The names *Eben, Evelyn, Eunice, Frieda,* and *Frank* are to be randomly chosen, and each has the same probability of being selected. Use events *E, F, G,* and *H* to determine the probabilities in parts a to d.

  E: Selecting a name with first letter E
  F: Selecting a name with first letter F
  G: Selecting a name with fewer than six letters
  H: Selecting a name with six letters

  a. $P(E \cup F)$ **b.** $P(E \cap H)$
  c. $P(E \cup G)$ **d.** $P(F \cap G)$

6. A box contains 4 red marbles and 2 yellow marbles. Consider the two-stage experiment of randomly selecting a marble from a box, replacing it, and then selecting a second marble. Determine the probabilities of the following events.

a. Selecting 2 red marbles

b. Selecting a red marble on the first draw and a yellow marble on the second

c. Selecting at least 1 yellow marble

7. Suppose that in exercise 6 the first marble that is selected is not replaced. Determine the probabilities of the events in 6a, b, and c.

8. A family has 4 children.

a. Draw a probability tree showing all possible combinations of boys and girls.

b. What is the probability of the family's having 2 boys and 2 girls?

c. What is the probability of the family's having at least 2 girls?

9. A contestant on a quiz show will choose 2 out of 7 envelopes (without replacement). If 2 of the 7 envelopes each contain $10,000, what is the probability the contestant will win at least $10,000?

10. The manufacturer of a certain brand of cereal puts a coupon for a free box of cereal in 20 percent of its boxes. If 3 boxes are purchased, what is the probability of obtaining at least 1 coupon?

11. Players in a die-toss game using a regular die with numbers 1 through 6 can win the following amounts: $2 for an even number; $1 for a 1; $3 for a 3; and $5 for a 5.

a. What is the expected value of the game?

b. In order for this to be a fair game, what should it cost to play?

12. A certain system fails to operate if any one of four relays overloads. The probability of a relay's overloading is .01. What is the probability that the system will fail?

13. An athlete enters three track and field events. She has a .9 probability of winning the 100-meter dash, a .9 probability of winning the low hurdles, and a .8 probability of winning the long jump.

a. What is the probability that the athlete will win the hurdles and the long jump?

b. What is the probability that she will win all three events?

c. What is the probability that she will win at least 1 of the 3 events?

14. A school's computer cluster has access to two mainframe computers. The probability that the first mainframe can be accessed is .9 and the probability that the second mainframe can be accessed is .8. If the probability of accessing at least one of the mainframe computers is .98, do the mainframe computers operate independently of each other?

15. Use the information in this table to answer the questions below.

Years of school completed for persons over 24 years old, 1994 (in millions)*

	FEMALE	MALE
Not a high school graduate	17	15
High school graduate without college	31	25
High school graduate with some college	38	38

a. If a person over 24 years old is chosen at random, what is the probability to the nearest .01 that the person is a high school graduate without college education or not a high school graduate?

b. What is the probability to the nearest .01 that a randomly chosen person over 24 years of age is a female or a high school graduate with some college education?

Statistical Abstract of the United States: 1995, 115th ed. (Washington: Bureau of the Census, 1995), p. 158.

CHAPTER 9

GEOMETRIC FIGURES

SPOTLIGHT ON TEACHING

Excerpts from NCTM's Standard for School Mathematics Grades 3–5*

Students in grades 3–5 can explore shapes with more than one line of symmetry. For example:

> In how many ways can you place a mirror on a square so that what you see in the mirror looks exactly like the original square? Is this true for all squares?
>
> Can you make a quadrilateral with exactly two lines of symmetry? One line of symmetry? No lines of symmetry? If so, in each case, what kind of quadrilateral is it?

Although younger students often create figures with rotational symmetry with, for example, pattern blocks, they have difficulty describing the regularity they see. In grades 3–5, they should be using language about turns and angles to describe designs such as the one in Figure 5.14: "If you turn it 180 degrees about the center, it's exactly the same" or "It would take six equal small turns to get back to where you started, but you can't tell where you started unless you mark it because it looks the same after each small turn."

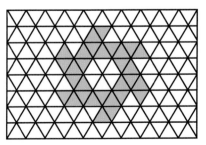

Figure 5.14
Pattern with rotational symmetry.

**Principles and Standards for School Mathematics* (Reston, VA: National Council of Teachers of Mathematics 2000), p. 168.

MATH ACTIVITY 9.1

ANGLES IN PATTERN BLOCK FIGURES

Materials: Pattern block pieces in the Manipulative Kit.

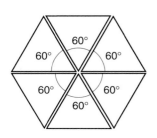

*1. Each of the three angles of a pattern block triangle has a measure of 60°. The **measure** of these angles can be illustrated by placing the **vertices** (corners) of six triangles at a point and using the fact that there are 360° in a circle. Determine the measures of the different interior angles of the pattern blocks, and draw sketches or trace pattern blocks to explain your reasoning.

2. Each of the following pattern block figures has six sides (**hexagon**) and six interior angles.

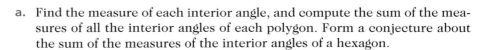

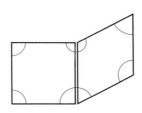 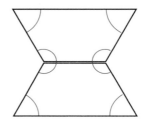 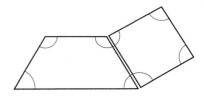

a. Find the measure of each interior angle, and compute the sum of the measures of all the interior angles of each polygon. Form a conjecture about the sum of the measures of the interior angles of a hexagon.

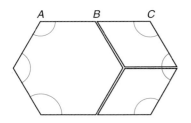

b. The figure shown here also has six sides. These sides meet in six interior angles which have been marked. Notice that the edges of the pattern blocks from *A* to *C* lie on a straight line, so these edges are counted as only one side. Also, the point *B* is not the vertex of an interior angle of the hexagon, because it is not the intersection of two sides. Find the measures of the interior angles of this figure. Does the sum of the measures of these angles support your conclusion in part a?

3. This pattern block figure has five sides (**pentagon**) and five interior angles. Find the sum of the measures of the interior angles.

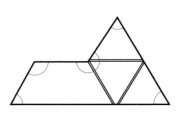

a. Use your pattern blocks to form other figures with five sides, and determine the sums of the measures of their interior angles. (*Suggestion:* It may help you to outline the five sides with bold lines as was done for the figure.)

b. Form a conjecture about the sum of the measures of the interior angles of a pentagon.

4. This pattern block figure has eight sides and eight interior angles. What is the sum of the measures of these interior angles? Use your pattern blocks to form other figures with various numbers of sides. Find a way to predict the sum of the measures of the interior angles, given the number of sides of the figure.

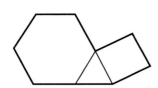

SECTION 9.1

PLANE FIGURES

Cross section of cadmium sulfide crystals

Find a pattern in the three figures, and draw the next two figures according to the pattern.*

Geometry is more than definitions; it is about describing relationships and reasoning.

Standards 2000, p. 40

We have become so accustomed to hearing about the regularity of patterns in nature that we often take it for granted. Still, it is a source of wonder to see figures with straight edges and uniform angles, such as those in the photograph above, occurring in nature.

The study of relationships among lines, angles, surfaces, and solids is a major part of geometry, one of the earliest branches of mathematics. The word **geometry** is from the Latin *geometria,* which means *earth-measure.*

*"Problems of the Month," *Mathematics Teacher* 80 (October 1987): 550.

Mathematical Systems

More than 5000 years ago, the Egyptians and Babylonians were using geometry in surveying and architecture. These ancient mathematicians discovered geometric facts and relationships through experimentation and inductive reasoning. Because of their approach, they could never be sure of their conclusions, and in some cases their formulas were incorrect. The ancient Greeks, on the other hand, viewed points, lines, and figures as abstract concepts about which they could reason deductively. They were willing to experiment in order to formulate ideas, but final acceptance of a mathematical statement depended on proof by deductive reasoning. The Greeks' approach was the beginning of mathematical systems.

A **mathematical system** consists of *undefined terms, definitions, axioms,* and *theorems.* There must always be some words that are undefined. *Line* is an example of an undefined term in geometry. We all have an intuitive idea of what a line is, but trying to define it involves more words, such as *straight, extends indefinitely,* and *has no thickness.* These words would also have to be defined. To avoid this problem of *circularity,* certain basic words such as *point* and *line* are **undefined terms.** These words are then used in **definitions** to define other words. Similarly, there must always be some statements, called **axioms,** that we assume to be true and do not try to prove. Finally, the axioms, definitions, and undefined terms are used together with deductive reasoning to prove statements called **theorems.**

Theorems

↑

Undefined terms
Definitions
Axioms

HISTORICAL HIGHLIGHT

Euclid, ca. 350 B.C.

The crowning achievement of Greek mathematical reasoning was Euclid's *Elements,* a series of 13 books written about 300 B.C. These books contain over 600 theorems, which were obtained by deductive reasoning from 10 basic assumptions called axioms. Although much of the material was drawn from earlier sources, the superbly logical arrangement of the theorems displays the genius of the author. Euclid's *Elements* stood as a model of deductive reasoning for over 2000 years, and few books have been more important to the thought and education of the western world.*

*D. M. Burton, *The History of Mathematics,* 4th ed. (New York: McGraw-Hill, 1999), pp. 138–161.

Points, Lines, and Planes

One fundamental notion in geometry is that of a *point.* All geometric figures are sets of points. **Points** are abstract ideas, which we illustrate by dots, corners of boxes, and tips of pointed objects. These concrete illustrations have width and thickness, but points have no dimensions. The following description of a point, from *Mr. Fortune's Maggot,* by Sylvia Townsend Warner, indicates some of the problems associated with teaching elementary school children the concept of a point.*

Calm, methodical, with a mind prepared for the onset, he guided Lueli down to the beach and with a stick prodded a small hole in it.
    "What is this?"
    "A hole."
    "No, Leuli, it may seem like a hole, but it is a point."
    Perhaps he had prodded a little too emphatically. Lueli's mistake was quite natural. Anyhow, there were bound to be a few misunderstandings at the start. He took out his pocket knife and whittled the end of the stick. Then he tried again.
    "What is this?"
    "A smaller hole."
    "Point," said Mr. Fortune suggestively.
    "Yes, I mean a smaller point."
    "No, not quite. It is a point, but it is not smaller. Holes may be of different sizes, but no point is larger or smaller than another point."

A **line** is a set of points that we describe intuitively as being "straight" and extending indefinitely in both directions. The edges of boxes and taut pieces of string or wire are models of lines. The line in Figure 9.1 passes through points A and B and is denoted by $\overleftrightarrow{AB}$. The arrows indicate that the line continues indefinitely in both directions. If two or more points are on the same line, they are called **collinear.**

Figure 9.1

A plane is another set of points that is undefined. We describe a **plane** as being "flat" like the top of a table, but extending indefinitely. The surfaces of floors and walls are other common models for portions of planes. A plane can be illustrated by a drawing which uses arrows, as in Figure 9.2, to indicate that it extends and is not bounded.

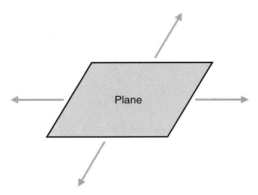

Figure 9.2

*Quoted in J. R. Newman, *The World of Mathematics,* 4th ed. (New York: Simon and Schuster, 1956) p. 2254.

Example A

A standard sheet of paper is a model for part of a plane.

1. What part of a sheet of paper might be used as a model for a line?

2. What part of a sheet of paper might be used as a model for a point?

3. How can models of lines and points be obtained by folding a sheet of paper?

Solution   **1.** Each edge of the paper is a model for part of a line.   **2.** Each corner of the paper is a model for a point.   **3.** The crease made by folding a sheet of paper is a model for part of a line. Two folds can produce parts of two lines that intersect in a point.

Points, lines, and *planes* are undefined terms in geometry that are used to define other terms and geometric figures. The following paragraphs contain some of the more common definitions and examples of figures that occur in planes.

Half-Planes, Segments, Rays, and Angles

HALF-PLANES   A line in a plane partitions the plane into three disjoint sets: the points on the line and **two half-planes.** Line ℓ in Figure 9.3 partitions the plane into half-planes with point A in one half and point B in the other.

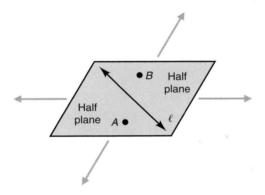

Figure 9.3

LINE SEGMENTS   A **line segment** consists of two points on a line and all the points between them (Figure 9.4). The line segment with **endpoints** A and B is denoted by $\overline{AB}$. To **bisect** a line segment means to divide it into two parts of equal length. The **midpoint** C bisects $\overline{AB}$.

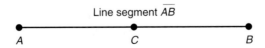
Line segment $\overline{AB}$

Figure 9.4

HALF-LINES AND RAYS   A point on a line partitions the line into three disjoint sets: the point and two **half-lines.** Figure 9.5a shows two half-lines that are determined by point P. A **ray** consists of a point on a line and all the points in one of the half-lines determined by the point. The ray in part b, which has D as an *endpoint* and contains point E, is denoted by $\overrightarrow{DE}$.

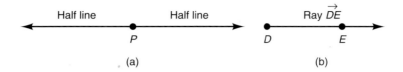

Figure 9.5
(a)   (b)

ANGLES   An **angle** is formed by the union of two rays, as shown in Figure 9.6a, or by two line segments that have a common endpoint, as in part b. This endpoint is called the **vertex,** and the rays or line segments are called the **sides of the angle.** The angle with vertex G, whose sides contain points F and H, is denoted by $\angle FGH$. Sometimes it is convenient to identify an angle by the letter of its vertex, such as $\angle G$ in part a, or by a numeral, such as $\angle 1$ in part b.

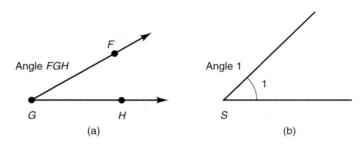

Figure 9.6
(a)   (b)

Example B

Fold a standard sheet of paper to create models of the following terms.

1. Parts of two opposite half-planes   **2.** A bisected line segment

3. Part of a ray   **4.** An angle

Solution   1. Any crease creates two half-planes.   **2.** Fold the paper to obtain a crease and draw a line in the crease, as shown in figure (*a*). Select two points A and B on the line, and fold the line onto itself so that point A coincides with point B. The point where the new crease intersects segment $\overline{AB}$ is the midpoint that bisects $\overline{AB}$ into two segments.   **3.** Any crease creates a line, and selecting a point on the line determines two rays.   **4.** Any two folds that form creases that intersect in a point create four angles having the point as a vertex. Figure (*b*) shows angles 1, 2, 3, and 4.

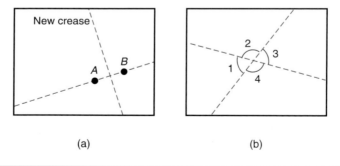

(a)   (b)

Problem-Solving Application

The ability to determine the number of line segments whose endpoints are a given number of points has many practical applications. One of these became evident in the early days of the development of the telephone system. The fundamental problem was how to connect two people who wanted to talk. This was done by

connecting cords and plugs for each pair of people. In 1884, Ezra T. Gilliland devised a mechanical system that would allow 15 subscribers to reach one another
without the aid of an operator.

PROBLEM

How many line segments are needed to connect 15 points in a plane so that each
pair of points are the endpoints of a line segment?

Understanding the Problem   One line segment connects 2 points, and 3 line
segments connect 3 points. **Question 1:** How many line segments are needed to
connect 4 points?

Devising a Plan   Let's examine a few more special cases. Perhaps the strategies
of *solving a simpler problem* and *finding a pattern* will lead to a solution. In the
following figure, 6 line segments have the points *A*, *B*, *C*, and *D* as endpoints.
Question 2: How many new line segments are needed to connect *E* to each of
these 4 points, and what is the total number of line segments connecting the 5
points?

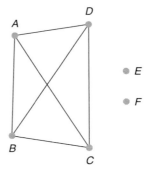

Carrying Out the Plan   Placing a sixth point, *F*, in the diagram, we can see that
there will be 5 new line segments from *F* to the other points and a total of 15 line
segments for the 6 points. Find a pattern and complete the following table. **Question 3:** How many line segments are required to connect 15 points?

No. of points	2	3	4	5	6	7	8	9	10	15
No. of segments	1	3	6	10	15					

Looking Back   You probably recognize the numbers 1, 3, 6, 10, 15, etc., in the
table as triangular numbers (Chapter 1). Note that the first triangular number is
associated with 2 points, the second with 3 points, etc. The formula for the nth
triangular number is $n(n + 1)/2$. Using this formula, you can determine the number of line segments needed to connect 20 points so that the points in each pair
are the endpoints of a line segment. **Question 4:** What is the number?

Answers to Questions 1–4   **1.** 6   **2.** There will be 4 new line segments and a total of 10 line segments for the 5 points.   **3.** 105   **4.** The number of line segments needed to connect 20 points is the
19th triangular number: $(19 \times 20)/2 = 190$.

Angle Measurements

The ancient Babylonians devised a method for measuring angles by dividing a circle into 360 equal parts, called **degrees.** One degree (1°) is $\frac{1}{360}$ of a complete turn about a circle, as shown in Figure 9.7. Each degree can be divided into 60 equal parts, called **minutes,** and each minute can be divided into 60 equal parts, called **seconds.** This is the origin of the modern practice of dividing hours into minutes and seconds.

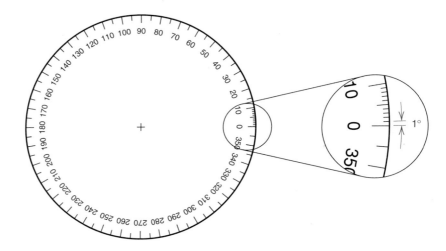

Figure 9.7

A **protractor** is a device for measuring angles (Figure 9.8). To **measure** an angle, place the center of the protractor on the vertex of the angle (B in this example), and line up one side of the angle ($\overline{BC}$) with the baseline of the protractor. The protractor in Figure 9.8 shows that $\angle ABC$ has a measure of approximately 60°.

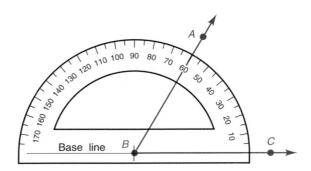

Figure 9.8

If an angle has a measure of 90°, as in Figure 9.9a, it is called a **right angle;** if it is less than 90°, as in part b, it is called an **acute angle;** if it is greater than 90° and less than 180°, as in part c, it is called an **obtuse angle;** and if it has a measure of 180° it is called a **straight angle.** It is customary to draw ⌐ at the vertex of a right angle. Occasionally we use angles with measures of more than 180°, as shown in Figure 9.9d. Such an angle is called a **reflex angle.** To indicate an angle with a measure that is greater than 180°, we draw a circular arc to connect the two sides of the angle.

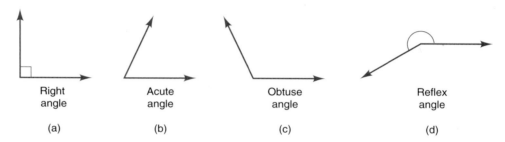

Figure 9.9

(a)   (b)   (c)   (d)

If the sum of two angles is 90°, the angles are called **complementary**; if their sum is 180°, they are called **supplementary**. Figure 9.10 shows special cases of complementary and supplementary angles in which the pairs of angles share a common side. If two angles have the same vertex, share a common side, and do not overlap, they are called **adjacent angles**. Angles 1 and 2 are adjacent complementary angles, and angles 3 and 4 are adjacent supplementary angles.

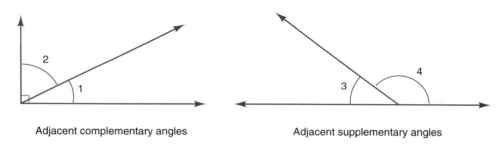

Figure 9.10

Adjacent complementary angles   Adjacent supplementary angles

---

Example C

Fold a standard sheet of paper to create models for the following terms.

1. Acute angle   2. Obtuse angle

3. Supplementary angles   4. Complementary angles

5. Adjacent angles

Research Statement

Findings from research studies suggest that students often have misconceived notions about angles and other geometric figures that are based solely on how these figures are oriented in textbooks.

Clements and Battista 1992

Solution   1, 2, 3, 5. Any crease that intersects an edge of the paper forms supplementary angles with the edges. For example, the crease in figure (a) intersects $\overline{BC}$, forming supplementary angles 1 and 2. These angles are also adjacent angles. The same crease intersects $\overline{AB}$ and forms adjacent supplementary angles 3 and 4. Angles 1 and 4 are acute, and angles 2 and 3 are obtuse.   4, 5. Any crease through a corner of the paper forms adjacent complementary angles with the edges. Angles 5 and 6 in figure (b) are adjacent complementary angles.

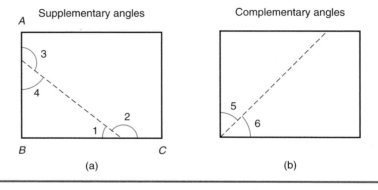

(a)   (b)

Two intersecting lines form four pairs of adjacent supplementary angles. For example, ∡1 and ∡4 in Figure 9.11 are supplementary angles. Nonadjacent angles formed by two intersecting lines, such as ∡2 and ∡4 in Figure 9.11, are called **vertical angles.**

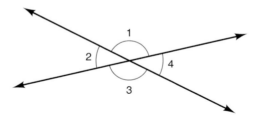

Figure 9.11

Example D

1. Name four pairs of supplementary angles in Figure 9.11.

2. Name two pairs of vertical angles in Figure 9.11.

3. Fold a sheet of paper to create a model of two intersecting lines. Compare the measures of the vertical angles and make a conjecture.

Solution   1. The following pairs of angles are supplementary angles: ∡1 and ∡4; ∡1 and ∡2; ∡2 and ∡3; ∡3 and ∡4.   **2.** The following pairs of angles are vertical angles: ∡2 and ∡4; ∡1 and ∡3. **3.** Two intersecting creases produce vertical angles. Angles 1 and 2 in the figure below are vertical angles. Vertical angles are congruent. This can be illustrated by folding the angles onto each other.

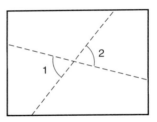

. . . students in grades 3–5 should be expanding their mathematical vocabulary. . . . As they describe shapes, they should hear, understand, and use mathematical terms such as parallel, perpendicular, face, edge, vertex, angle, trapezoid, prism, and so forth, to communicate geometric ideas with greater precision.

Standards 2000, p. 166

Perpendicular and Parallel Lines

If two lines intersect to form right angles, they are **perpendicular.** Lines m and n in Figure 9.12 are perpendicular; this is indicated by writing $m \perp n$. Two line segments, such as $\overline{AB}$ and $\overline{CD}$ in Figure 9.12 are perpendicular if they lie on perpendicular lines. In this case, we write $\overline{AB} \perp \overline{CD}$ or $\overleftrightarrow{AB} \perp \overleftrightarrow{CD}$.

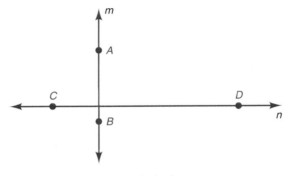

Perpendicular lines

Figure 9.12

If two lines are in a plane and they do not intersect, they are **parallel.** Lines m and n in Figure 9.13 are parallel; this is indicated by writing $m \parallel n$. Similarly, two segments are parallel if they lie in parallel lines. Segments $\overline{EF}$ and $\overline{GH}$ in Figure 9.13 are parallel, and we write $\overline{EF} \parallel \overline{GH}$.

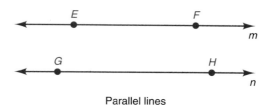

Parallel lines

Figure 9.13

If two lines ℓ and m are intersected by a third line t (see Figure 9.14), we call line t a **transversal.** Two very special angles are created on the alternate sides of the transversal and interior to lines ℓ and m (angles 1 and 2 in Figure 9.14). These angles are called **alternate interior angles.** If the two lines ℓ and m are parallel (as in Figure 9.14), *the alternate interior angles have the same measure.* The converse of this statement is also true: *If the alternate interior angles have the same measure,* lines ℓ and m are parallel. These statements are combined in the following property.

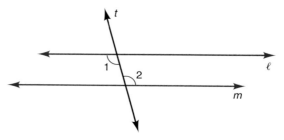

Figure 9.14

ALTERNATE INTERIOR ANGLES   If two lines are intersected by a transversal, the lines are parallel if and only if the alternate interior angles created by the transversal have the same measure.

Example E

Use a standard sheet of paper to model the following geometric terms: parallel lines, perpendicular lines, lines intersected by a transversal, and alternate interior angles having the same measure. Draw and label these on the paper.

Solution   The opposite edges of the paper are parallel line segments, and any two edges that meet at a corner are perpendicular line segments. Any fold of the paper that intersects the opposite parallel edges of the paper will create alternate interior angles with the same measure.

There are other ways of obtaining parallel and perpendicular lines by folding paper. Two perpendicular lines can be obtained by folding the paper in half along one edge and then folding it in half along the other edge. Two parallel lines can be obtained by folding the paper in half along one edge and then folding it in half again along the same edge.

Problem-Solving Application

What is the maximum number of regions into which a plane can be partitioned by 12 lines?

Understanding the Problem   One line partitions a plane into 2 regions, and 2 intersecting lines partition a plane into 4 regions. **Question 1:** What is the maximum number of regions created by 3 lines in a plane?

Devising a Plan   It would be difficult to draw 12 lines and count the resulting regions. Let's *make a table* to record the numbers of regions for the first few lines. This approach may suggest a solution. Three lines divide the plane into 7 regions. **Question 2:** What is the maximum number of regions created by 4 lines?

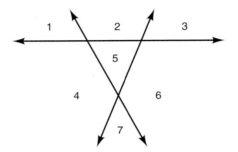

Carrying Out the Plan   The following table lists the maximum number of regions for 1, 2, 3, and 4 lines. Find a pattern and use inductive reasoning to predict the numbers of regions for the next few lines. **Question 3:** How many regions will there be for 12 lines?

No of lines	1	2	3	4	5	6	7	8	9	10	11	12
No. of regions	2	4	7	11								

Looking Back   When a fourth line that is not parallel to any of the first 3 lines is drawn on the plane, by definition it will intersect each of the 3 given lines. Also, it will cut across 4 regions, as shown in the figure below. This accounts for 4 new regions. **Question 4:** How many lines and how many regions will a fifth nonparallel line intersect?

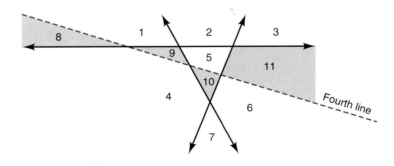

Answers to Questions 1–4   1. 7   2. 11

3.

No. of lines	5	6	7	8	9	10	11	12
No. of regions	16	22	29	37	46	56	67	79

4. The fifth line will intersect 4 lines and 5 regions to create 5 new regions.

Curves and Convex Sets

We can draw a curve through a set of points by using a single continuous motion (Figure 9.15).

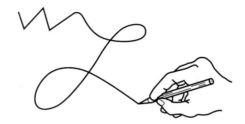

Figure 9.15

Several types of curves are shown in Figure 9.16. Curve *A* is called a **simple curve** because it starts and stops without intersecting itself. Curve *B* is a **simple closed curve** because it is a simple curve that starts and stops at the same point. Curve *C* is a **closed curve,** but since it intersects itself, it is not a simple closed curve.

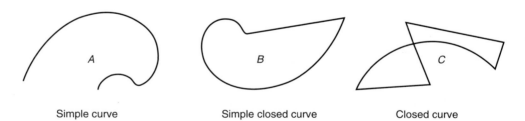

| Simple curve | Simple closed curve | Closed curve |

Figure 9.16

Example F

Classify each curve as simple, simple closed, or closed.

Solution   1. Closed   2. Simple   3. Simple closed   4. Simple closed

A well-known theorem in mathematics, called the **Jordan curve theorem,** states that every simple closed curve partitions a plane into three disjoint sets: the points on the curve, the points in the interior, and the points in the exterior. This means that if K is in the interior and M is in the exterior, then $\overline{KM}$ will intersect the curve (Figure 9.17).

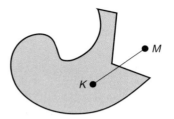

Figure 9.17

CONVEX SETS   The union of a simple closed curve and its interior is called a **plane region.** Plane regions can be classified as *nonconvex* and *convex.* You may have heard the word *concave* rather than *nonconvex.* A plane region is concave if it is "caved in," as in Figure 9.18a, and convex if it is not, as in Figure 9.18b. To be more mathematically precise, we say that a set is **convex** if the line segment joining any two points of the set lies completely in the set. The set in Figure 9.18a is **nonconvex** because $\overline{XY}$ is not completely in the set. An intuitive way of thinking about convexity of plane regions is to imagine enclosing the boundary of a figure with an elastic band. If the elastic touches all points on the boundary (as it will for the set in Figure 9.18b), the set is convex; and if not (as in Figure 9.18a), the set is nonconvex.

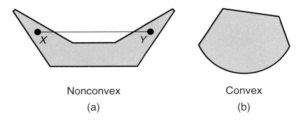

Nonconvex   Convex

(a)   (b)

Figure 9.18

Example G

Classify each region as convex or nonconvex.

1.   2.   3.

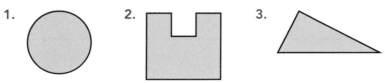

Solution   1. Convex   2. Nonconvex   3. Convex

CIRCLES   A **circle** is a special case of a simple closed curve whose interior is a convex set (Figure 9.19). Each point on a circle is the same distance from a fixed point, called the **center.** A line segment from a point on the circle to its center is a **radius,** and a line segment whose endpoints are both on the circle is a **chord.** A chord that passes through the center is a **diameter.** The words *radius* and *diameter* are also used to refer to the lengths of these line segments. A line that intersects the circle in exactly one point is a **tangent.** The distance around the circle is the **circumference.** The union of a circle and its interior is called a **disk.**

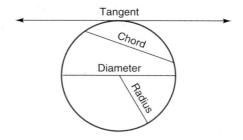

Figure 9.19

Polygons

A **polygon** is a simple closed curve that is the union of line segments. The union of a polygon and its interior is called a **polygonal region.** Polygons are classified according to their number of line segments. A few examples are shown in Figure 9.20. The line segments of a polygon are called **sides,** and the endpoints of these segments are **vertices.** Two sides of a polygon are **adjacent sides** if they share a common vertex, and two vertices are **adjacent vertices** if they share a common side.

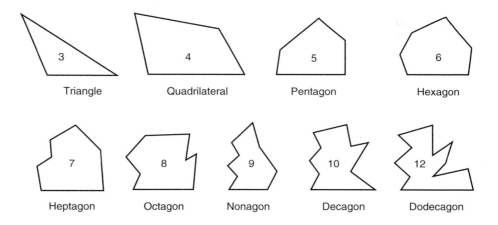

Figure 9.20

Triangle	Quadrilateral	Pentagon	Hexagon
Heptagon	Octagon	Nonagon	Decagon	Dodecagon

Example H

Which of the following figures are polygons?

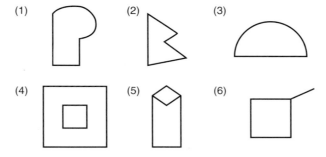

Solution   Figure (*2*) is the only polygon. Figures (*1*) and (*3*) are simple closed curves, but not polygons. Figures (*4*), (*5*), and (*6*) are not simple closed curves.

Any line segment connecting one vertex of a polygon to a nonadjacent vertex is a **diagonal.** Figure 9.21 shows a pentagon with its five diagonals.

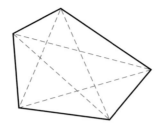

Figure 9.21

Example I

How many diagonals are there in each of the following polygons?

1. Quadrilateral   **2.** Triangle   **3.** Hexagon

Solution   1. Two   2. Zero   3. Nine

In the early grades, students will have classified and sorted geometric objects such as triangles or cylinders by noting general characteristics. In grades 3–5, they should develop more precise ways to describe shapes, focusing on identifying and describing the shape's properties and learning specialized vocabulary associated with these shapes and properties.

Standards 2000, p. 165

Certain triangles and quadrilaterals occur often enough to be given special names. Several of these are shown in Figure 9.22.

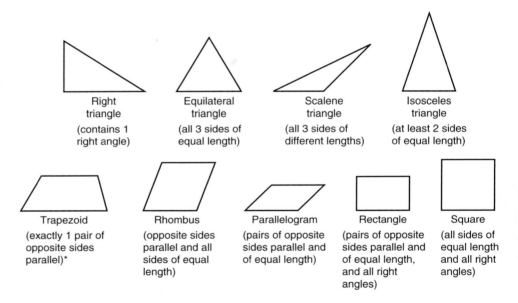

Figure 9.22

Example J

Determine whether each statement is true or false, and state a reason.

1. Every square is a rectangle.

2. Every equilateral triangle is an isosceles triangle.

3. Some right triangles are isosceles triangles.

---

*Some books define a trapezoid as having *at least* one pair of opposite sides parallel. In this case, a parallelogram is also a trapezoid because it has at least one pair of parallel sides.

4. Some trapezoids are parallelograms.

5. Some isosceles triangles are scalene triangles.

Solution   **1.** True. The opposite sides of a square are parallel and of equal length.   **2.** True. An equilateral triangle has three sides of equal length, so it has *at least* two sides of equal length.   **3.** True. A right triangle could have two legs of length 1 and a hypotenuse of length $\sqrt{2}$; the two equal sides would make it an isosceles triangle.   **4.** False. Trapezoids have only one pair of opposite parallel sides; a parallelogram must have two pairs of opposite parallel sides.   **5.** False. All three sides are of different lengths in a scalene triangle.

Example K

Fold a standard sheet of paper to obtain a model of each geometric figure.

1. Isosceles triangle   **2.** Square   **3.** Parallelogram

Solution   Here are some possibilities. There are other ways to obtain these figures.   **1.** Fold the paper in half to obtain point A, as shown in figure (a). Then fold to obtain the crease $\overline{AB}$ and fold again to obtain the crease $\overline{AC}$. Line segment $\overline{AB}$ can be folded onto $\overline{AC}$ to show that triangle ABC is isosceles.   **2.** Fold corner D [figure (b)] down to point S so that $\overline{DF}$ coincides with $\overline{FS}$. With the paper in this folded position, use edge $\overline{DR}$ to draw line $\overline{RS}$. Then figure $DRSF$ is a square.   **3.** Fold the paper in half to obtain points X and Y, as shown in figure (c). Then fold to obtain the creases $\overline{GX}$ and $\overline{IY}$; $GYIX$ is a parallelogram.

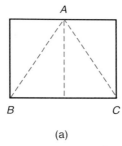

(a)

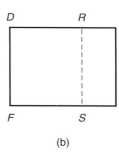

(b)

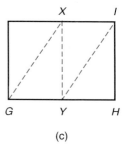

(c)

NCTM's 5–8 Standard, *Geometry,* observes that geometry has a vocabulary of its own and students need ample time to gain confidence with new terms:

Definitions should evolve from experiences in constructing, visualizing, drawing, and measuring two- and three-dimensional figures, relating properties to figures, and contrasting and classifying figures according to their properties.*

Problem-Solving Application

PROBLEM

How many diagonals does a 15-sided polygon have?

Understanding the Problem   A diagonal is a line segment connecting any two nonadjacent vertices of a polygon. Quadrilateral *ABCD*, shown on the following page, has diagonals *AC* and *BD*. Sketch a nonconvex quadrilateral. **Question 1:** Does such a quadrilateral have two diagonals?

Curriculum and Evaluation Standards for School Mathematics (Reston, VA: National Council of Teachers of Mathematics, 1989), p. 113.

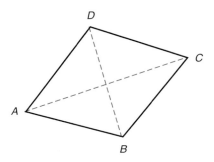

Devising a Plan   One approach is to *simplify the problem* by drawing a few polygons and counting the number of diagonals. By listing these in a table, we may be able to find a pattern. **Question 2:** How many diagonals are there in each of the following polygons?

Pentagon   Hexagon   Heptagon

Carrying Out the Plan   Fill in a few blanks of the table below and *look for a pattern.* Use your pattern and inductive reasoning to complete the table. **Question 3:** How many diagonals are there in a 15-sided polygon?

No. of sides	3	4	5	6	7	8	9	10	11	12
No. of diagonals	0	2	5	9						

Looking Back   Another approach to this problem is to use the result from the problem-solving application on page 555, in which we found the number of line segments connecting 15 points. Since there are 105 line segments connecting 15 points, the number of diagonals in a 15-sided polygon can be found by subtracting 15 (the number of sides in the polygon) from 105. Thus there are 90 diagonals. **Question 4:** How many diagonals are there in a 25-sided polygon?

Answers to Questions 1–4   **1.** Yes   **2.** Pentagon, 5 diagonals; hexagon, 9 diagonals; heptagon, 14 diagonals   **3.** 90   **4.** The number of line segments connecting 25 points is the 24th triangular number: $(24 \times 25)/2 = 300$. Subtracting 25, the number of sides in the polygon, from 300 yields 275 diagonals.

PUZZLER

Cross out eight line segments and leave two squares.

EXERCISES AND PROBLEMS 9.1

1. The sculpture in the photograph has angles formed by steel rods.
   a. What is the approximate measure of these angles? (This can be determined by tracing one angle and measuring it with a protractor.)

   b. Does the measure of the angles decrease, remain the same, or increase as you move from the bottom to the top of the figure? Check your conjecture by tracing.

2. This picture of a cross section of natural sapphire shows angles that each have the same number of degrees.
   a. Are these angles acute or obtuse?
   b. Measure these angles. Approximately how many degrees are there in each of these angles?

3. List the four components of every mathematical system and briefly describe each.

4. a. List three undefined geometric terms.
   b. List three defined geometric terms whose definitions use one or more of the undefined terms.
   c. Explain why it is necessary to have undefined terms in geometry.

Give two examples of physical models that illustrate each term in exercises 5 and 6.

5. a. Line segment
   b. Triangle
   c. Plane

6. a. Angle
   b. Point
   c. Square

7. a. Which angles, if any, are acute?
b. Which angles, if any, are obtuse?
c. Which angles, if any, are right angles?

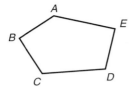

8. a. Which angles, if any, are acute?
b. Which angles, if any, are obtuse?
c. Which angles, if any, are reflex angles?

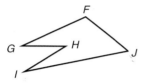

Use the angles in the figures in exercises 9 and 10 to identify the pairs of angles.

9. a. Three pairs of adjacent supplementary angles
b. Two pairs of vertical angles
c. Two pairs of angles with the same measure

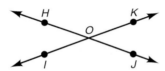

10. a. Three pairs of adjacent supplementary angles
b. Three pairs of vertical angles
c. Two pairs of adjacent complementary angles

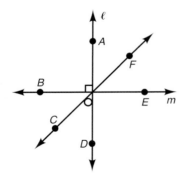

11. Draw a circle that illustrates each of the following geometric situations.
a. A diameter that is perpendicular to a chord
b. A line tangent to the circle at one end of a radius
c. Two chords that bisect each other

12. If ℓ and m are parallel lines, explain why the angles in each pair in parts a through d have the same measure.

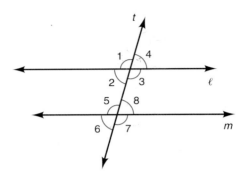

a. $\angle 2$ and $\angle 8$
b. $\angle 2$ and $\angle 4$
c. $\angle 4$ and $\angle 8$ (These angles are called **corresponding angles**.)
d. $\angle 1$ and $\angle 7$
e. Explain why $\angle 3$ and $\angle 8$ are supplementary angles.

13. If r and s are parallel lines and the measure of $\angle a$ is $34.5°$, what is the measure of each of the following angles?
a. $\angle e$
b. $\angle h$
c. $\angle c$
d. $\angle f$

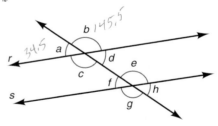

14. If s and t are parallel lines and the measure of $\angle f$ is $32°$ and the measure of $\angle a$ is $40°$, determine the measure of each of the following angles.
a. $\angle b$ **b.** $\angle c$ **c.** $\angle d$ **d.** $\angle e$ **e.** $\angle g$

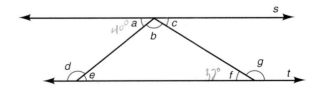

Use the type of clock shown on the following page to answer the questions in exercises 15 and 16.

15. a. What is the measure of the obtuse angle formed by the hour and minute hands of a clock if the time is 8 o'clock?

b. How many degrees will the hour hand of the clock move through when the time changes from 8 o'clock to 10 o'clock?

c. How many minutes have passed when the minute hand has moved through 42°?

16. a. How many degrees will the minute hand of the clock move through when the time changes from 8 o'clock to 8:25?

b. How many hours will have passed when the hour hand has moved through 120°?

c. What is the measure of the obtuse angle formed by the hour hand and the minute hand if the time is 2:30?

Classify each curve in exercises 17 and 18 as simple, simple closed, closed, or none of these.

17. a.   **b.**   **c.**

18. a.   **b.**   **c.**

Classify each region in exercises 19 and 20 as convex or nonconvex.

19. a.   **b.**   **c.**

20.
a.   **b.**   **c.**

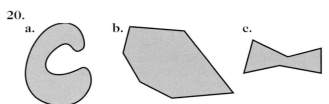

21. The following photograph shows three crystals of the mineral staurolite. These crystals are found in all parts of the world. They are especially common in the Shenandoah Valley. The crystal on the far right is known as the *Fairy Stone* of the Appalachian Mountains. This form and the one on the left are often imitated by jewelers.

a. The ridges on the top of the Fairy Stone form two lines that intersect to form four angles of equal measure. What is the measure of each of these angles?

b. The ridges on the top of the crystal on the left form three lines that intersect to form six angles of equal measure. What is the measure of each of these angles?

Three lines in a plane may intersect in 0, 1, 2, or 3 points. In exercises 22 and 23, draw lines to support your reasoning.

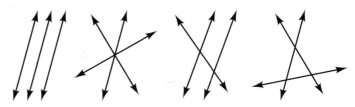

22. Determine all the different numbers of points of intersection that are possible with four lines in a plane.

23. Determine all the different numbers of points of intersection that are possible with five lines in a plane.

Draw some figures in exercises 24 and 25 to determine whether the following statements are true or false. For each false statement show a counterexample.

24. a. The two diagonals of a parallelogram have the same length.
    b. Any two angles in a parallelogram that share a common side are supplementary.
    c. The two diagonals of a rectangle have the same length.

25. a. If the two diagonals in a parallelogram have the same length, the parallelogram is a rectangle.
    b. If the midpoints of the sides of a rectangle are connected, another rectangle is formed.
    c. If the midpoints of the adjacent sides of a quadrilateral are connected, a parallelogram is formed.

REASONING AND PROBLEM SOLVING

26. To prepare for their annual volleyball party, the Chase family has laid out a four-sided volleyball court in which two opposite sides have a length of 30 feet and the other two opposite sides have a length of 60 feet.
    a. Explain why the court may not be rectangular. What shape might it have?
    b. Which statement in exercises 24 or 25 can be used to determine if the court is rectangular?

27. A 70-inch piece of pipe is to be cut at two points A and B such that A and B are not on the ends of the pipe and the length from A to B is 42 inches. How many possibilities are there for obtaining three pieces of pipe of different lengths if the lengths are whole numbers?

28. Featured Strategies: Solving a Simpler Problem and Making a Table What is the maximum number of points of intersection for 12 lines?
    a. Understanding the Problem The problem asks for the greatest possible number of points of intersection. What is the minimum number of points of intersection for 12 lines?
    b. Devising a Plan The following figure shows that the maximum number of points of intersection for four lines is 6. Considering a few other cases for small numbers of lines may reveal a pattern. What is the maximum number of points of intersection for three lines?

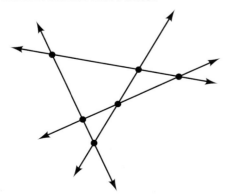

c. Carrying Out the Plan Look for a pattern and complete the table below. What is the maximum number of points of intersection for 12 lines?

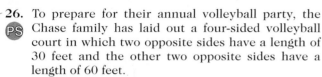

No. of lines	2	3	4	5	6	7	8	9	10	11	12
No. of intersections	1	3	6	10	15	21	28	36	45	55	66

d. Looking Back Use the pattern in part c to determine the maximum number of points of intersection for 50 lines.

29. In 1891, Almon B. Strowger patented a phone-dialing machine that could connect up to 99 subscribers. How many different two-party calls would such a machine permit?

30. Suppose squares A, B, and C are houses and E, G, and W represent sources of electricity, gas, and water, respectively. Try to connect the houses with each utility by drawing lines or curves so that they do not cross one another. It is possible to make only eight of the nine connections. Draw these eight connections.

$$\boxed{A} \qquad \boxed{B} \qquad \boxed{C}$$
$$\boxed{E} \qquad \boxed{G} \qquad \boxed{W}$$

    a. Some of your connections will form a simple closed curve with the remaining unconnected house and utility on opposite sides of this curve. Find this curve and mark it with dark lines.
    b. How does the Jordan curve theorem show that nine connections cannot be completed with the given conditions?

31. The white path in this ornament from the Middle Ages is a curve.

    a. Is it a simple curve?
    b. Is it a closed curve?

32. The curves shown below are simple closed curves. The Jordan curve theorem states that if a point inside a simple closed curve is connected to a point outside the curve, the connecting arc will intersect the curve. Use the fact that points B and D are outside the two curves in (i) and (ii) to answer the questions.

(i)

(ii)

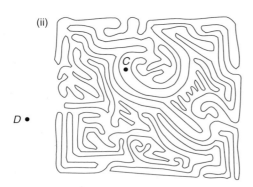

a. Can an arc be drawn from A to B that does not intersect the curve in (i)? Is A inside or outside the curve?

b. Can an arc be drawn from C to D that does not intersect the curve in (ii)? Is C inside or outside the curve in (ii)?

c. Draw line segment $\overline{AB}$. Count the number of times that $\overline{AB}$ intersects the curve in (i). How can this number be used to tell when a point is inside or outside a simple closed curve? (*Hint:* Draw a few simple closed curves.) Check your answer by drawing $\overline{CB}$ for the curve in (ii).

33. The following simple closed curve is from *Puzzles and Graphs* by John Fujii.* Determine whether the points in each pair below are on the same side of the curve.

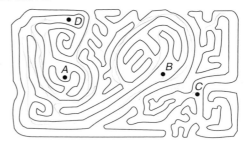

a. A, B   **b.** B, C
c. D, C   **d.** B, D

34. An equilateral triangle has three sides of equal length. Fold a sheet of paper to form an equilateral triangle, using the creases or edges of the paper. (*Hint:* Obtain a centerline by folding the paper in half.)

*John Fujii, *Puzzles and Graphs* (Reston, VA. National Council of Teachers of Mathematics, 1966).

ONLINE LEARNING CENTER   www.mhhe.com/bennett-nelson

• Math Investigation 9.1   *Properties of Triangles*
Section-Related: • Links   • Writing/Discussion Problems   • Bibliography

---

PUZZLER

It is possible to connect A to A', B to B', and C to C' so that no curves intersect and the curves are drawn in the interior of the rectangle. How can this be done?

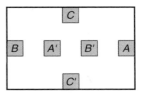

MATH ACTIVITY 9.2

TESSELLATIONS WITH POLYGONS

Materials: Polygons for tessellations in the Manipulative Kit.

1. An arrangement of nonoverlapping figures which are placed together to entirely cover a region is called a **tessellation.** A portion of a tessellation that uses triangles and hexagons is shown here. Form and sketch a tessellation that uses at least two different types of polygons from your set.

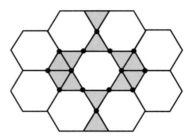

2. Each polygon in your set is called **regular** because all its sides and angles are congruent. If a tessellation can be formed with just one type of regular polygon, it is called a **regular tessellation.** Experiment with your polygons to find those that can be used to form a regular tessellation.

*3. The tessellation shown below is **semiregular** because it uses more than one type of regular polygon and each **vertex of the tessellation** (bold point) is surrounded by the same arrangement of polygons. This tessellation is denoted by the **code** 3,3,3,4,4 because a triangle has three sides and a square has four sides and each vertex is surrounded by three triangles and two squares in clockwise order. Explain why the tessellation in activity 1 is not semiregular.

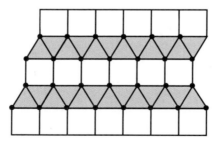

4. There are other semiregular tessellations that can be formed by using two different types of regular polygons. Experiment with your polygons to find some of these. Sketch a portion of each tessellation, and write the numbers for its code.

5. There are two semiregular tessellations which use three different types of polygons. Find one of these and sketch a portion of its tessellation.

6. Is there a semiregular tessellation which uses four different types of polygons from your set? Explain your reasoning.

SECTION 9.2

POLYGONS AND TESSELLATIONS

*Cross section of the gem
tourmaline*

This rectangular region is cut into eight congruent pieces. In how many ways
can a rectangular region be cut into eight congruent pieces?

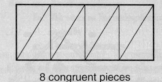

8 congruent pieces

The triangles in the photograph above are another amazing example of geometric
figures that occur in nature. In each triangle, the sides have the same length, and
the angles have the same measure. Such special types of polygons are discussed
in this section.

Angles in Polygons

The vertex angles of a polygon with four or more sides can be any size between $0°$
and $360°$. In the hexagon in Figure 9.23, $\angle B$ is less than $20°$ and $\angle D$ and $\angle A$ are
both greater than $180°$. In spite of this range of possible sizes, there is a relationship between the sum of all the angles in a polygon and its number of sides.

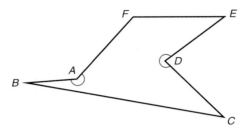

Figure 9.23

In any triangle, the sum of the three angle measures is 180°. This fact was proved by Greek mathematicians in the fourth century B.C. One way of demonstrating this theorem is to draw an arbitrary triangle and cut off its angles, as shown in Figure 9.24. When these angles are placed side by side with their vertices at a point, they form one-half of a revolution (180°) about the point.

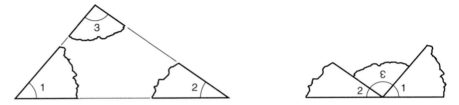

Figure 9.24

The sum of the angles in a polygon of four or more sides can be found by subdividing the polygon into triangles so that the vertices of the triangles are the vertices of the polygon. The quadrilateral in Figure 9.25 is partitioned into two triangles whose angles are numbered from 1 through 6. The sum of all six angles is 2 × 180°, or 360°. Therefore the sum of the four angles of the quadrilateral is 360°.

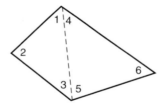

Figure 9.25

An infinite variety of quadrilaterals can be formed, some convex and others nonconvex. However, since each quadrilateral can be partitioned into two triangles such that the vertices of the triangles are also the vertices of the quadrilateral, the sum of the angles of a quadrilateral will always be 360°. A similar approach can be used to find the sum of the angles in any polygon.

E x a m p l e A

Find the sum of all the angles in each polygon.

1. Pentagon   **2.** Octagon

Solution   1. A pentagon can be subdivided into three triangles, as shown in figure (*a*). So the total number of degrees in its angles is 3 × 180° = 540°.   **2.** An octagon can be subdivided into six triangles, as shown in figure (*b*). So the total number of degrees in its angles is 6 × 180° = 1080°.

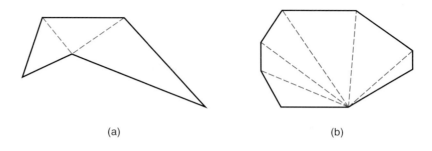

(a)   (b)

Research Statement

The 7th national mathematics assessment found that eighth grade students did not do well when asked to find the missing angle of a triangle, given the measures of the other two angles.

Martin and Strutchens 2000

Congruence

The idea of congruence is quite simple to understand intuitively: Two plane figures, such as those in Figure 9.26, are **congruent** if one can be placed on the other so that they coincide. Another way to describe congruent plane figures is to say that they have the same size and shape. (Congruence is presented in greater detail in Sections 11.1 and 11.2.)

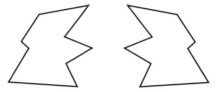

Figure 9.26

We can be more precise at this point about congruence of line segments and angles. Two **line segments are congruent** if they have the same length, and two **angles are congruent** if they have the same measure (Figure 9.27).

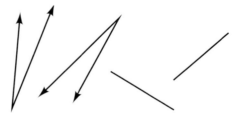

Figure 9.27

Example B   Fold a standard sheet of paper so that it is partitioned into the following figures.

1. Four congruent rectangles
2. Two congruent right triangles and a rectangle
3. Four congruent right triangles
4. Sixteen congruent rectangles

Solution   Here are some methods. There are others.   **1.** Fold the paper twice: once in half perpendicular to one edge and again in half perpendicular to an adjacent edge.   **2.** Fold a corner of the paper down to obtain a rectangle and the largest possible square. The fold forms the diagonal of the square and bisects it into two right triangles.   **3.** Fold the paper in half to obtain a rectangle, and then fold along the diagonal of the rectangle.   **4.** Fold the paper in half perpendicular to the edges a total of 4 times.

Regular Polygons

Sections 9.1 and 9.2 opened with photographs of hexagons and triangles that grow naturally with congruent line segments and congruent angles. The figures in those photographs are examples of regular polygons. A polygon is called a **regular polygon** if it satisfies both of the following conditions:

1. All angles are congruent.

2. All sides are congruent.

A few regular polygons are shown in Figure 9.28.

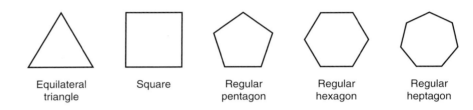

| Equilateral triangle | Square | Regular pentagon | Regular hexagon | Regular heptagon |

Figure 9.28

Example C

The following figures satisfy only one of the two conditions for regular polygons. For each polygon determine which condition is satisfied and which condition is not satisfied.

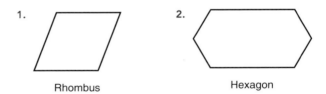

1.   Rhombus   2.   Hexagon

Solution   **1.** The four sides are congruent, but the four angles are not congruent.   **2.** The six angles are congruent, but the six sides are not congruent.

Drawing Regular Polygons

There are three special angles in regular polygons (see Figure 9.29). A **vertex angle** is formed by two adjacent sides of the polygon; a **central angle** is formed by connecting the center of the polygon to two adjacent vertices of the polygon; and an **exterior angle** is formed by one side of the polygon and the extension of an adjacent side.

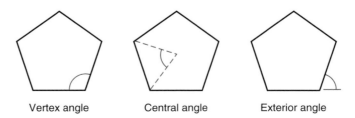

Vertex angle   Central angle   Exterior angle

Figure 9.29

The sum of the measures of the angles in a polygon can be used to compute the number of degrees in each vertex angle of a regular polygon: Simply divide the sum of all the measures of the angles by the number of angles. For example, Figure 9.30a shows a regular pentagon that is subdivided into three triangles. Since each vertex of each triangle is a vertex of the pentagon, the sum of the nine angles in the triangles equals the sum of the five angles in the pentagon. So the sum of the angles in the pentagon is $3 \times 180°$, or $540°$. Therefore, each angle in a regular pentagon is $540° \div 5$, or $108°$, as shown in Figure 9.30b.

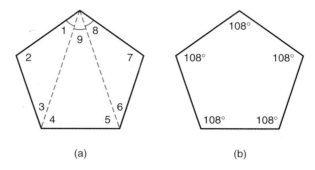

Figure 9.30   (a)   (b)

Figure 9.31 shows the first four steps for drawing a regular pentagon. The process begins in step 1, where a line segment is drawn and a point for the vertex of the angle is marked. Then in step 2 the baseline of a protractor is placed on the line segment so that the center of the protractor's baseline is at the vertex point, and a $108°$ angle is drawn. In step 3 two sides of the pentagon are marked off, and in step 4 the protractor is used to draw another $108°$ angle. This process can be continued to obtain a regular pentagon.

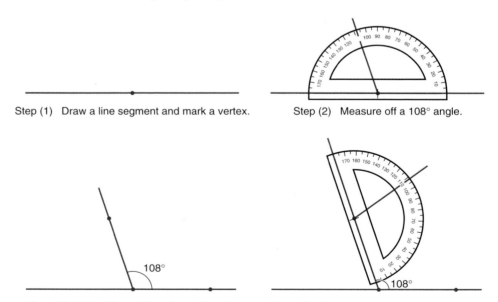

Figure 9.31

Step (1) Draw a line segment and mark a vertex.   Step (2) Measure off a 108° angle.

Step (3) Mark off two sides of equal length.   Step (4) Measure off a second angle of 108°.

Another approach to drawing regular polygons begins with a circle and uses central angles. The number of degrees in the central angle of a regular polygon is 360 divided by the number of sides in the polygon. A decagon has 10 sides, so each central angle is $360° \div 10$, or $36°$ (Figure 9.32).

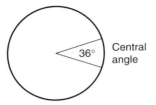

Figure 9.32

A four-step sequence for drawing a regular decagon is illustrated in Figure 9.33. The first and third steps use a **compass,** a device for drawing circles and arcs and marking off equal lengths. The decagon that is obtained is said to be *inscribed in the circle.* Any polygon whose vertices are points of a circle is called an **inscribed polygon.**

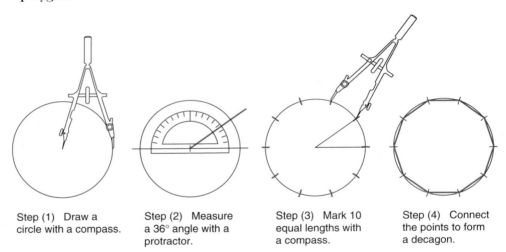

Step (1) Draw a circle with a compass.

Step (2) Measure a 36° angle with a protractor.

Step (3) Mark 10 equal lengths with a compass.

Step (4) Connect the points to form a decagon.

Figure 9.33

Tessellations with Polygons

The hexagonal cells of a honeycomb provide another example of regular polygons in nature (Figure 9.34). The cells in this photograph show that regular hexagons can be placed side by side with no uncovered gaps between them. Any arrangement in which nonoverlapping figures are placed together to entirely cover a region is called a **tessellation.** Floors and ceilings are often *tessellated,* or *tiled,* with square-shaped material, because squares can be joined together without gaps or overlaps. Equilateral triangles are also commonly used for tessellations. These three types of polygons—regular hexagons, squares, and equilateral triangles—are the only regular polygons that will tessellate.

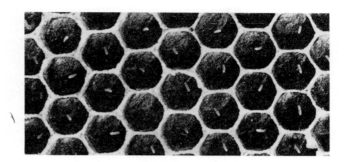

Figure 9.34
Honeycomb with eggs
Courtesy of the American Museum
of National History

*Mary Fairfax Somerville
1780–1872*

Mary Fairfax Somerville has been called "one of the greatest women scientists England ever produced." In spite of her parent's attempts to prevent her from studying mathematics, she acquired Euclid's *Elements of Geometry* and memorized much of the first six books. When she solved a prize problem on Diophantine equations in a mathematical journal, the editor advised her of the classics that would give her a sound background in mathematics. Thus at age 32 she finally acquired a small library of mathematics books to pursue her studies. Somerville published many papers including two on solar rays which appeared in the *Philosophical Transactions of the Royal Society of London* and the *Edinburgh Philosophical Journal.* Her books *Mechanics of the Heavens* and *The Connections of the Physical Sciences* brought her the greatest fame of all her works. Critics called the latter of these two books the best general survey of physical sciences published in England. Somerville belonged to a group of scientists who pioneered the efforts to arouse England's interest in mathematics and scientific progress. At the time of her death at age 92, she was engaged in several mathematical writing projects.*

*L. M. Osen, *Women in Mathematics* (Cambridge, MA: The MIT Press, 1974), pp. 95–116.

From ancient times tessellations have been used as patterns for rugs, fabrics, pottery, and architecture. The Moors, who settled in Spain in the eighth century, were masters of tessellating walls and floors with colored geometric tiles. Some of their work is shown in Figure 9.35, a photograph of a room and bath in the Alhambra, a fortress palace built in the middle of the thirteenth century for Moorish kings.

Figure 9.35
The Sala de Camas, a room
in the Alhambra in Granada,
Spain

When teachers point out
geometric shapes in nature
or in architecture, students'
awareness of geometry in the
environment is increased.

Standards 2000, p. 101

The two tessellations in the center of the above photograph are made up of nonpolygonal (curved) figures. In the following paragraphs, however, we will concern ourselves only with polygons that tessellate. The triangle is an easy case to consider first. You can see that any triangle will tessellate by simply putting two copies of the triangle together to form a parallelogram (see the shaded region of Figure 9.36). Copies of the parallelogram can then be moved horizontally and vertically. The points at which the vertices of the triangle meet are called the **vertex points** of the tessellation. Since the sum of the angles in a triangle is 180°, the 360° about each vertex point of the tessellation will be covered by using each angle of the triangle twice. In the tessellation shown in Figure 9.36, angles 1, 2, and 3 occur twice about each vertex point.

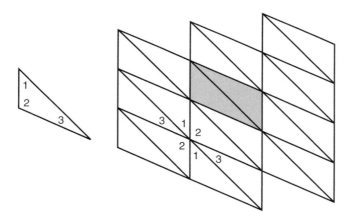

Figure 9.36

The sizes of the angles in a polygon and the sums of these angles will determine whether the polygon will tessellate. The fact that the sum of the angles in a quadrilateral is 360° suggests that a quadrilateral has the right combination of angles to fit around each vertex point of a tessellation. In the tessellation in Figure 9.37, each angle of the quadrilateral (angles 1, 2, 3, and 4) occurs once about each vertex point of the tessellation.

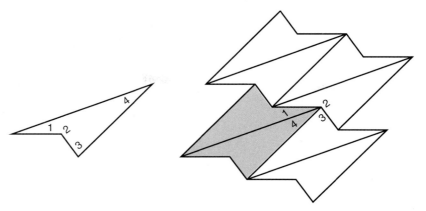

Figure 9.37

The only regular polygons that will tessellate by themselves are the equilateral triangle, the square, and the regular hexagon. However, if we allow two or more regular polygons in a tessellation, there are other possibilities. Two such tessellations are shown in Figure 9.38. The tessellation in part a uses three different regular polygons. Notice that each vertex is surrounded by the same arrangement of polygons: hexagon, square, triangle, and square. A tessellation of two or more noncongruent regular polygons in which each vertex is surrounded by the same arrangement of polygons is called **semiregular.** Part b of Figure 9.38 is a tessellation of regular polygons, but it is *not* semiregular, because some vertices are surrounded by two dodecagons and a triangle (see vertex *A*) and others by a dodecagon, two triangles, and a square (see vertex *B*).

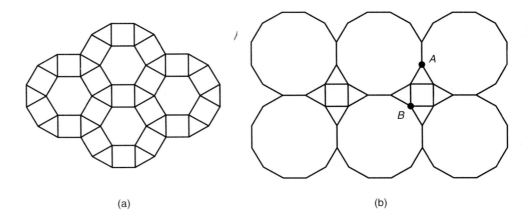

Figure 9.38   (a)   (b)

The quadrilateral in the tessellation in Figure 9.37 is nonconvex. It is quite surprising that every quadrilateral, convex or nonconvex, will tessellate. This is not true for polygons with more than four sides. Although there are some pentagons that will tessellate, there are others that will not tessellate. Similarly, some hexagons will tessellate (for example, a regular hexagon), but not all hexagons will.

If we consider only convex polygons, we can prove that *no polygon with more than six sides* will tessellate. However, there are countless possibilities for tessellations of nonconvex polygons of more than six sides. The tessellation in Figure 9.39 was made using a 12-sided nonconvex polygon.

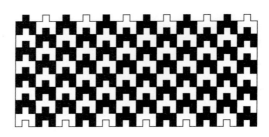

Figure 9.39

Problem-Solving Application

What is the measure of each vertex angle in a regular 50-sided polygon?

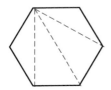

Understanding the Problem   Consider a regular polygon with fewer sides. A regular hexagon has six congruent vertex angles, and since it can be partitioned into four triangles (see figure at left), the sum of all its angles is $4 \times 180° = 720°$. **Question 1:** What is the number of degrees in one of its vertex angles?

Devising a Plan   The number of degrees in each vertex angle of a regular polygon can be determined once we know the sum of the degrees of all its angles. The total number of degrees in the angles of any polygon can be found by first partitioning the polygon into triangles so that the vertices of the triangles are the same as the vertices of the polygon. Let's make a *table* to determine the number of such triangles for the first few polygons. **Question 2:** What is the number of triangles for a heptagon?

No. of sides	3	4	5	6	7	8	9
No. of triangles	1	2	3				
Total no. of degrees	180	2(180)	3(180)				

Carrying Out the Plan   Pentagons, hexagons, and heptagons can be subdivided into three, four, and five triangles, respectively, as shown below. Notice that connecting one vertex of a polygon to each of the other nonadjacent vertices produces exactly one triangle for each of the nonadjacent vertices. This suggests that the number of triangles is 2 less than the number of vertices. Using this observation, we can calculate that the sum of the measures of the angles in a 50-sided polygon is $48 \times 180° = 8640°$. **Question 3:** What is the size of each vertex angle in a regular 50-sided polygon?

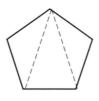

Pentagon

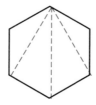

Hexagon

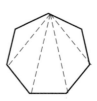

Heptagon

Looking Back   As the number of sides in a regular polygon increases, the shape of the polygon gets closer to a circle and the size of each vertex angle gets closer to 180°. One of the vertex angles for a 50-sided regular polygon is shown in the next figure. **Question 4:** What is the number of degrees in each vertex angle of a regular 100-sided polygon?

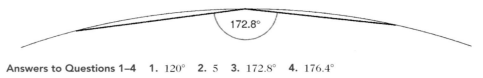

172.8°

Answers to Questions 1–4   1. 120°   **2.** 5   **3.** 172.8°   **4.** 176.4°

PUZZLER

Using only four more matchsticks, divide this region into four congruent regions. (*Hint:* Some of the matchsticks may be broken.)

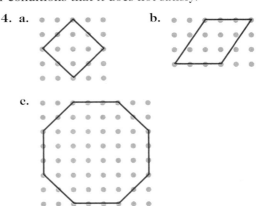

EXERCISES AND PROBLEMS 9.2

Drawing of algae (sea life) by the German biologist Ernst Haeckel (1834–1919)

1. The polygons in the drawing of algae above form the beginning of a tessellation.
   a. There is a regular pentagon at the center. What polygons are adjacent to this pentagon? Are they regular?
   b. There is a second ring of polygons surrounding the inner six. What kind of polygons are these?

Find the sum of all the vertex angles for each polygon in exercises 2 and 3.

2. **a.** Hexagon
   b. Octagon

3. **a.** Decagon
   b. A 15-sided polygon

The figures in exercises 4 and 5 have been drawn on a square lattice of dot paper. Determine whether each figure is a regular polygon. If it is not, write the condition or conditions that it does not satisfy.

4. **a.**   **b.**

   c.

5. a.

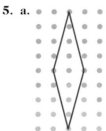

b.

c.

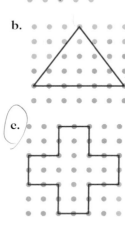

6. The following figure is a regular pentagon, and ∡1 is a central angle. Determine the number of degrees in each of the following angles.

    a. ∡1   **b.** ∡2   **c.** ∡3

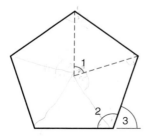

7. Write the number of degrees in the central angles of the regular polygons in the following table.

	TRIANGLE	QUADRILATERAL	PENTAGON	HEXAGON	HEPTAGON	OCTAGON	NONAGON	DECAGON		
No. of sides	3	4	5	6	7	8	9	10	20	100
Central angle	120°	90°								

What regular polygons will be formed by the methods in exercises 8 and 9?

8. a. Tie a long rectangular strip of paper into a knot and smooth it down. (See drawing.)

    b. Cut out an equilateral triangle and fold each vertex into the center.

9. a. Draw a circle with a compass. Open the compass an amount equal to the radius of the circle, use this distance to mark off points on the circumference, and connect adjacent points to form a polygon.

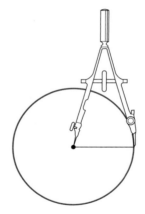

    b. Connect each pair of nonadjacent points in part a to form a polygon.

The numbers of degrees in exercises 10 and 11 are the measures of the central angles of regular polygons. Determine the number of sides for each polygon.

10. a. 18°   **b.** 10°   **c.** 5°

11. a. 24°   **b.** 20°   **c.** 72°

Draw some figures to determine whether the statements in exercises 12 and 13 are true or false. For each false statement, show a counterexample.

12. a. In any quadrilateral the sum of the opposite angles is 180°.

    b. A line segment from a vertex of a triangle to the midpoint of the opposite side is called a **median.** The three medians of a triangle meet in a point.

    c. The diagonals of a regular hexagon are congruent.

13. **a.** If the midpoints of the sides of any regular hexagon are connected to form a simple closed curve, this curve is a regular hexagon.
  b. A line segment from a vertex of a triangle that is perpendicular to the opposite side is called an **altitude.** The lines containing the three altitudes of a triangle meet in a point.
  c. If the midpoints of the sides of any triangle are connected, an equilateral triangle is formed.

Which of the regular polygons in exercises 14 and 15 will tessellate by themselves?

14. **a.** Equilateral triangle
  b. Square
  c. Regular pentagon

15. **a.** Regular hexagon
  b. Regular heptagon
  c. Regular octagon

16. What condition must be satisfied by the vertex angles of a regular polygon in order for the polygon to tessellate?

17. Form as large a tessellation as possible on the following grid, using the triangle. Explain why every triangle will tessellate. (The dot grid can be copied from the inside cover or from the website.)

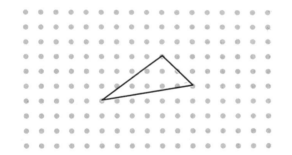

18. Form as large a tessellation as possible on the following grid, using the quadrilateral. Explain why every quadrilateral will tessellate. (The dot grid can be copied from the inside cover or from the website.)

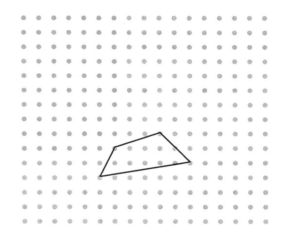

19. Draw a portion of a tessellation that can be made by using each of the following letters.

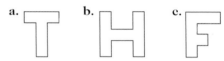

a.   **b.**   **c.**

20. Find an uppercase block letter from the first half of the alphabet which will tessellate and which is different from those in exercise 19. Sketch a portion of your tessellation.

21. Find an uppercase block letter from the second half of the alphabet which will tessellate and which is different from those in exercise 19. Sketch a portion of your tessellation.

22. A polygon with more than six sides will not tessellate if it is convex. The following polygons have more than six sides, but they are nonconvex. Sketch a portion of a tessellation for each of these polygons. (*Hint:* Trace and cut out one copy of the figure.)

a.   **b.**   **c.**

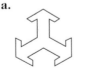   

23. Which of the following tessellations is semiregular? Explain why.

a.

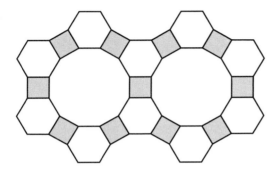

b.

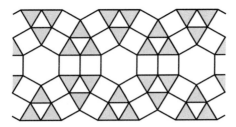

(iii)

(iv)

c. Carrying Out the Plan   The square arrangement of four pictures in figure (*iv*) suggests that we want as many "clusters" like this as possible so that one tack can be used for the corners of four pictures. Thus, we might conjecture that placing the 36 pictures in a square array as shown in figure (*v*) will minimize the number of tacks. How many tacks does this arrangement require?

(v)

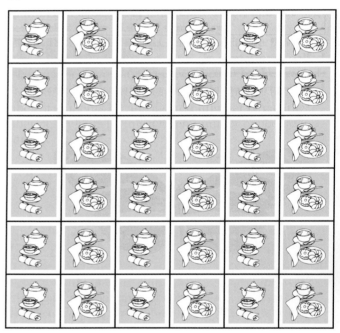

REASONING AND PROBLEM SOLVING

24. Featured Strategies: Solving a Simpler Problem and Making a Drawing   What is the smallest number of tacks needed to hold up 36 pictures of the same size, so that each picture can be seen and each corner is tacked?

a. Understanding the Problem   If two pictures are tacked up separately, as shown in figure (*i*), eight tacks will be required. How many tacks will be needed if the two pictures are placed side by side and slightly overlapping, as in figure (*ii*)?

(i)

(ii)

b. Devising a Plan   Simplifying the problem and making a few drawings may provide some ideas. Consider only four pictures. How many tacks are needed for each of the following arrangements?

d. Looking Back   The grid in figure (*v*) suggests a method for finding the number of tacks for any square number of pictures. What is the smallest number of tacks needed for an 8 × 8 array of pictures?

25. The Canadian nickel on the next page is a regular dodecagon (12 sides). Assume that you have been asked to design a large posterboard model of this coin such that each side of the dodecagon has a length of 1 inch. Describe a method for constructing such a polygon.

26. The seven-pointed star below has a regular heptagon at its center. What is the measure of each angle
at the tips of the star to the nearest .1°?

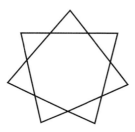

27. Semiregular tessellations can be made by using two
or more of the following regular polygons. Sketch a
portion of a semiregular tessellation which is different from the one shown in Figure 9.38a. (*Hint:* Use
the given measures of the vertex angles.)

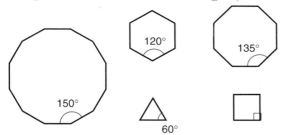

28. The following square figures are made of toothpicks.
  a. How many toothpicks are needed to build the
  fourth figure?
  b. How many toothpicks are needed to build the
  20th figure?

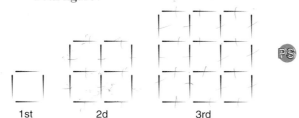

1st   2d   3rd

29. The first three figures in the following pattern contain pentagons formed by toothpicks. How many
toothpicks will be needed to build the 30th figure in
this pattern?

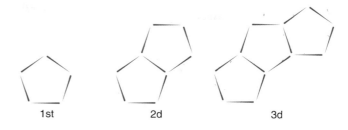

1st   2d   3d

30. The first three figures in the following pattern contain hexagons formed by toothpicks. How many
toothpicks will be needed to build the 10th figure?

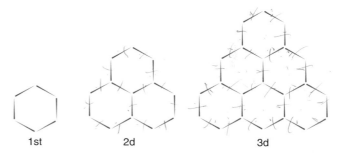

1st   2d   3d

31. Gestalt psychology, developed in Germany in the
1930s, is concerned primarily with the laws of perception. What is represented by the following polygons and their background?

Fold a piece of paper to obtain angles with the degree
measurements in exercises 32 and 33. Label each angle,
and explain how it was obtained.

32. **a.** 60°   **b.** 45°   **c.** 30°

33. **a.** 15°   **b.** 150°   **c.** 120°

ONLINE LEARNING CENTER   www.mhhe.com/bennett-nelson

  • Math Investigation 9.2   *Inscribed Angles in Circles*
  Section-Related: • Links   • Writing/Discussion Problems   • Bibliography

MATH ACTIVITY 9.3

NETS FOR THREE-DIMENSIONAL FIGURES

Materials: Some 2-centimeter grid paper (copy from inside cover of the text or from the website) and scissors. The 2-centimeter cubes for building figures are optional.

*1. A cube can be formed by creasing and folding along the lines of the pattern shown here. Use your grid paper to form and cut out several different types of patterns that will fold into a cube with no overlaps. Show sketches of your patterns. Patterns for three-dimensional figures are called **nets.**

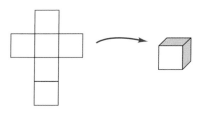

By representing three-dimensional shapes in two dimensions and constructing three-dimensional shapes from two-dimensional representations, students learn about the characteristics of shapes.

Standards 2000, p. 168

2. Form and cut out a net that will fold into the two-cube stack shown here. (*Hint:* One way is to imagine this stack sitting on a square of the grid and visualize the squares that would need to be folded up to cover the stack.) Sketch your net.

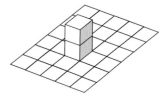

3. Visualize a stack of *n* cubes, and describe a net of squares that will fold and cover this stack. Write an algebraic expression for the number of squares in this net.

4. Select two of the following figures, and form their nets on grid paper. Show sketches of your nets. The number of cubes in the figure is the **volume** of the figure, and the number of squares in the net is the **surface area** of the figure. Determine the volume and surface area of each figure you select.

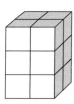

SECTION 9.3

SPACE FIGURES

M. C. Escher's "Cubic Space Division"

PROBLEM OPENER

This is a sketch of a three-dimensional figure that contains 54 small cubes. If the outside of the figure is painted and then the figure is disassembled into 54 individual cubes, how many cubes will have paint on one face, two faces, three faces, and no faces?

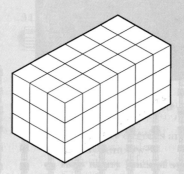

9 × 6

In the above lithograph by the Dutch artist Maurits C. Escher (1898–1970), the girders intersect at right angles to form the edges of large cubes. The Canadian mathematician H. S. M. Coxeter calls it the *cubic honeycomb.* By representing space as being filled with cubes of the same size, Escher gives a wonderful sense of infinite space.

The notion of **space** in geometry is an undefined term, just as the ideas of point, line, and plane are undefined. We intuitively think of space as three-dimensional and of a plane as only two-dimensional. In his theory of relativity, Einstein tied together the three dimensions of space and the fourth dimension of time. He showed that space and time affect each other and give us a four-dimensional universe.

In NCTM's K–4 Standard, *Geometry and Spatial Sense,* the importance of spatial understanding is discussed:

Insights and intuitions about two- and three-dimensional shapes and their characteristics, the interrelationships of shapes, and the effects of changes to shapes are important aspects of spatial sense. Children who develop a strong sense of spatial relationships and who master the concepts and language of geometry are better prepared to learn number and measurement ideas, as well as other advanced mathematical topics.†

HISTORICAL HIGHLIGHT

Sonya Kovalevsky
1850–1891

The Russian mathematician Sonya Kovalevsky is regarded as the greatest woman mathematician to have lived before 1900. Since women were barred by law from institutions of higher learning in Russia, Kovalevsky attended Heidelberg University in Germany. Later she was refused admission to the University of Berlin, which also barred women. Even the famous mathematician Karl Weierstrass, who claimed she had "the gift of intuitive genius," was unable to obtain permission for Kovalevsky to attend his lectures. She obtained her doctorate from the University of Göttingen but was without a teaching position for nine years, until the newly formed University of Stockholm broke tradition and appointed her to an academic position. Kovalevsky's prominence as a mathematician reached its peak in 1888, when she received the famous Prix Bordin from the French Académie des Sciences for her research paper "On the Rotation of a Solid about a Fixed Point." The selection committee "recognized in this work not only the power of an expansive and profound mind, but also a great spirit of invention."*

*D. M. Burton, *The History of Mathematics,* 4th ed. (New York: McGraw-Hill, 1999) pp. 557–560.

Planes

In two dimensions, the figures (lines, angles, polygons, etc.) all occur in a plane. In three dimensions, there are an infinite number of planes. Each plane partitions space into three disjoint sets: the points on the plane and two **half-spaces.** Portions of a few planes are shown in Figure 9.40. Any two planes either are **parallel,** as in part a, or **intersect** in a line, as in part b.

†*Curriculum and Evaluation Standards for School Mathematics* (Reston, VA: National Council of Teachers of Mathematics 1989), p. 48.

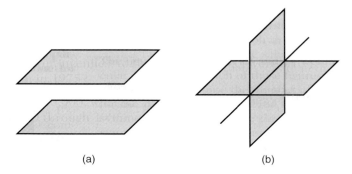

Figure 9.40   (a)   (b)

When two planes intersect, we call the angle between the planes a **dihedral angle.** Figure 9.41 shows three dihedral angles and their measures. A dihedral angle is measured by measuring the angle whose sides lie in the planes and are perpendicular to the line of intersection of the two planes. Parts a, b, and c of Figure 9.41 show examples of obtuse, right, and acute dihedral angles, respectively.

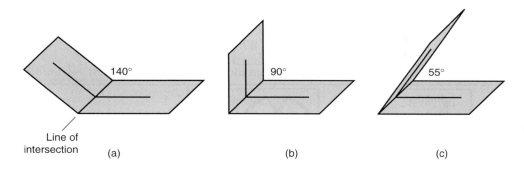

Figure 9.41   (a)   (b)   (c)

When a line m in three-dimensional space does not intersect a plane P, it is **parallel to the plane,** as in Figure 9.42a. A line n is **perpendicular to a plane** Q at a point k if the line is perpendicular to every line in the plane that contains k, as in Figure 9.42b.

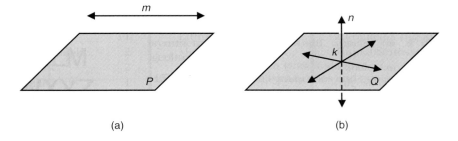

Figure 9.42   (a)   (b)

Polyhedra

The three-dimensional object with flat sides in Figure 9.43 is a crystal that is partially embedded in rock. Its flat pentagonal sides with their straight edges were not cut by people but were shaped by nature.

Figure 9.43

The surface of a figure in space whose sides are polygonal regions, such as the one in Figure 9.43, is called a **polyhedron** (*polyhedra* is the plural). The polygonal regions are called **faces**, and they intersect in the **edges** and **vertices** of the polyhedron. The union of a polyhedron and its interior is called a **solid.** Figure 9.44 shows examples of a polyhedron and two figures that are not polyhedra. The figure in part a is a polyhedron because its faces are polygonal regions. The figures in parts b and c are not polyhedra because one has a curved surface and the other has two faces that are not polygons.

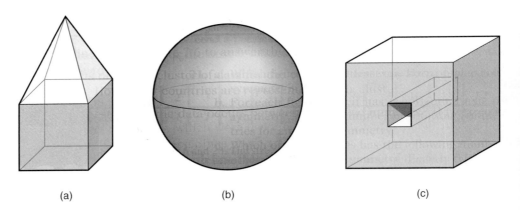

| (a) | (b) | (c) |

Figure 9.44

A polyhedron is **convex** if the line segment connecting any two of its points is contained inside the polyhedron or on its surface.

Example A

Classify the following polyhedra as convex or nonconvex.

1.   2.   3.

 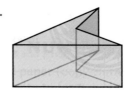 

Research Statement

The 6th national mathematics assessment concluded that students need more experiences with concrete models to enhance their visualization skills and more opportunities to see how geometric concepts relate to real-live situations and other mathematical aspects.

Strutchens and Blume 1997

Solution   Polyhedra 1 and 3 are convex; 2 is nonconvex.

Regular Polyhedra

The best known of all the polyhedra are the *regular polyhedra,* or *Platonic solids.* A **regular polyhedron** is a convex polyhedron whose faces are *congruent regular polygons,* the same number of which meet at each vertex. The ancient Greeks proved that there are only five regular polyhedra. Models of these polyhedra are shown in Figure 9.45. The **tetrahedron** has 4 triangles for faces; the **cube** has 6 square faces; the **octahedron** has 8 triangular faces; the **dodecahedron** has 12 pentagons for faces; and the **icosahedron** has 20 triangular faces.

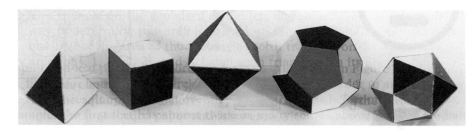

Figure 9.45
From left to right: tetrahedron, cube (hexahedron), octahedron; dodecahedron, icosahedron

The first three of the regular polyhedra shown in Figure 9.45 are found in nature as crystals. The cube and the octahedron occur in the common mineral pyrite, shown in Figure 9.46. The cube, which is embedded in rock, was found in Vermont, and the octahedron is from Peru. The other regular polyhedra, the dodecahedron and the icosahedron, do not occur as crystals but have been found in the skeletons of microscopic sea animals called *radiolarians.*

Figure 9.46
Crystals of pyrite

SEMIREGULAR POLYHEDRA   Some polyhedra have two or more different types of regular polygons for faces. The faces of the boracite crystal in Figure 9.47 are squares and equilateral triangles. This crystal, too, developed its flat, regularly shaped faces naturally, without the help of machines or people. Polyhedra whose faces are two or more regular polygons with the same arrangement of polygons around each vertex are called **semiregular polyhedra.** The boracite crystal is one of these. Each of its vertices is surrounded by three squares and one equilateral triangle.

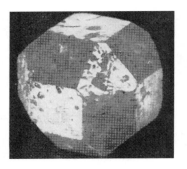

Figure 9.47
Crystal of boracite

Several other semiregular polyhedra are shown in Figure 9.48. You may recognize the combination of hexagons and pentagons in part a as the pattern used on the surface of soccer balls.

 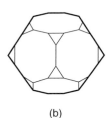  

Figure 9.48   (a)   (b)   (c)   (d)

Example B

For each semiregular polyhedron in Figure 9.48, list the polygons in the order in which they occur about any vertex.

Solution   Part a: hexagon, hexagon, pentagon; part b: dodecagon, dodecagon, triangle; part c: triangle, triangle, triangle, triangle, square; part d: octagon, octagon, triangle

Pyramids and Prisms

Chances are that when you hear the word *pyramid,* you think of the monuments built by the ancient Egyptians. Each of the Egyptian pyramids has a square base and triangular sides rising up to the vertex. This is just one type of pyramid. In general, the **base of a pyramid** can be any polygon, but its sides are always triangular. Pyramids are named according to the shape of their bases. Church spires are familiar examples of pyramids. They are usually square, hexagonal, or octagonal pyramids. The spire in the photograph in Figure 9.49 is an octagonal pyramid.

Figure 9.49
The Bruton Steeple,
Williamsburg, Virginia

Several pyramids with different bases are shown in the following example. Pyramids whose sides are isosceles triangles, as in Figures (1), (3), and (4) of Example C, are called **right pyramids**. Otherwise, as in Figure (2) of Example C, the pyramid is called an **oblique pyramid**. The vertex that is not contained in the pyramid's base is called the **apex**.

Example C

Determine the name of each pyramid.

1.

2.

3.

4.

Solution   **1.** Triangular pyramid (also called a tetrahedron)   **2.** Oblique square pyramid   **3.** Pentagonal pyramid   **4.** Hexagonal pyramid

PRISMS   Prisms are another common type of polyhedron. You probably remember from your science classes that a prism is used to produce the spectrum of colors ranging from violet to red. Because of the angle between the vertical faces of a prism, light directed into one face will be bent when it passes out through the other face (Figure 9.50).

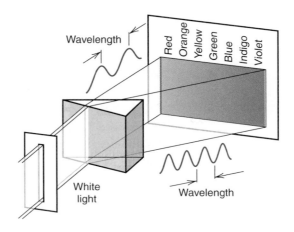

Figure 9.50

A **prism** has two parallel **bases,** upper and lower, which are congruent polygons. Like pyramids, prisms get their names from the shape of their bases. If the lateral sides of a prism are perpendicular to the bases, as in the case of the triangular, quadrilateral, hexagonal, and rectangular prisms in Figure 9.51, they are rectangles. Such a prism is called a **right prism.** A rectangular prism, which is modeled by a box, is the most common type of prism. If some of the lateral faces of a prism are parallelograms that are not rectangles, as in the pentagonal prism, the prism is called an **oblique prism.** The union of a prism and its interior is called a **solid prism.** A rectangular prism that is a solid is sometimes called a **rectangular solid.**

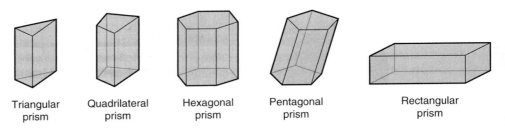

| Triangular prism | Quadrilateral prism | Hexagonal prism | Pentagonal prism | Rectangular prism |

Figure 9.51

Example D

The following figure is a right prism with bases that are regular pentagons.

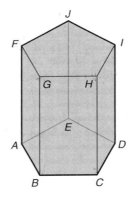

Research Statement

In order to develop a conceptual understanding of geometry, students need to be placed in situations that allow them to apply deductive, inductive, and spatial reasoning.

Geddes and Fortunato 1993

1. What is the measure of the dihedral angle between face *ABGF* and face *BCHG*?

2. What is the measure of the dihedral angle between face *GHIJF* and face *CDIH*?

3. Name two faces that are in parallel planes.

Solution   **1.** It is the same as the measure of ∡*FGH*, which is 108°.   **2.** 90°. Since this is a right prism, the top base is perpendicular to each of the vertical sides.   **3.** *ABCDE* and *FGHIJ*

The two oblique hexagonal prisms in Figure 9.52 are crystals that grew with these flat, smooth faces and straight edges. Their lateral faces are parallelograms.

Figure 9.52
Prisms of the crystal
orthoclase feldspar

Cones and Cylinders

Cones and cylinders are the circular counterparts of pyramids and prisms. Ice cream cones, paper cups, and party hats are common examples of cones. A cone has a circular region (disk) for a **base** and a lateral surface that slopes to the **vertex (apex).** If the vertex lies directly above the center of the base, the cone is called a **right cone** or usually just a cone; otherwise, it is an **oblique cone** (Figure 9.53).

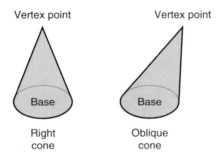

Figure 9.53

Ordinary cans are models of cylinders. A **cylinder** has two parallel circular **bases** (disks) of the same size and a lateral surface that rises from one base to the other. If the centers of the upper base and lower base lie on a line that is perpendicular to each base, the cylinder is called a **right cylinder** or simply a cylinder; otherwise, it is an **oblique cylinder** (Figure 9.54). Almost without exception, the cones and cylinders we use are right cones and right cylinders.

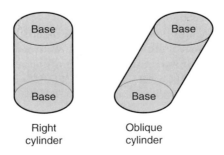

Figure 9.54

12·1

3-Dimensional Figures

Learn

Graham and Naomi built this model of a house for their social studies project. Which 3-dimensional figures did they use?

Math Words

3-dimensional figure a figure in space

rectangular prism

cylinder

cube

cone

pyramid

sphere

base the flat face on which a 3-dimensional figure can rest

vertex the common point of the three or more edges of a 3-dimensional figure; plural form is **vertices**

face a flat side of a 3-dimensional figure

edge a line segment where two faces of a 3-dimensional figure meet

net a flat pattern that can be folded to make a 3-dimensional figure

Example 1

You can compare the blocks used in the house with these **3-dimensional figures** .

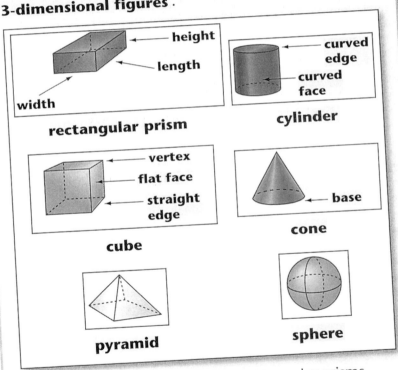

Graham and Naomi used cubes, rectangular prisms, pyramids, and cylinders to build their model house.

 480 Cluster A

Spheres and Maps

The photograph in Figure 9.55 is a view of earth showing its almost perfect spherical shape. It was photographed from the *Apollo 17* spacecraft during its 1972 lunar mission. The dark regions are water. The Red Sea and the Gulf of Aden are near the top center, and the Arabian Sea and Indian Ocean are on the right.

Figure 9.55
Earth, as seen from Apollo 17 *during its 1972 lunar mission*

SPHERE   A **sphere** is the set of points in space that are the same distance from a fixed point, called the **center.** The union of a sphere and its interior is called a **solid sphere.**

A line segment joining the center of a sphere to a point on the sphere is called a **radius.** The length of such a line segment is also called the **radius of the sphere.** A line segment containing the center of the sphere and whose endpoints are on the sphere is called a **diameter,** and the length of such a line segment is called the **diameter of the sphere.**

The geometry of the sphere is especially important for navigating on the surface of the earth. You may have noticed that airline maps show curved paths between distant cities. This is because the shortest distance between two points on a sphere is along an arc of a **great circle.** In the drawing of the sphere in Figure 9.56, *G* (the color arc) is the arc of a great circle, because its center is also the center of the sphere, and arc *B* is not the arc of a great circle. The distance between points *X* and *Y* along arc *G* on a sphere is less than the distance between these points along arc *B*.

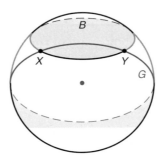

Figure 9.56

Locations on the earth's surface are often given by naming cities, streets, and buildings. A more general method of describing location uses two systems of circles (Figure 9.57). The circles that are parallel to the equator are called **parallels of latitude** and are shown in part a. Except for the equator, these circles are not great circles. Each parallel of latitude is specified by an angle from 0° to 90°, both north and south of the equator. For example, New York City is at a northern latitude of 41°, and Sydney, Australia, is at a southern latitude of 34°. The second system of circles is shown in part b. These circles pass through the north and south poles and are called **meridians of longitude.** These are great circles, and each is perpendicular to the equator. Since there is no natural point at which to begin numbering the meridians of longitude, the meridian that passes through Greenwich, England, was chosen as the zero meridian. Each meridian of longitude is given by an angle from 0° to 180°, both east and west of the zero meridian. The longitude of New York City is 74° west, and that of Sydney, Australia, is 151° east. These parallels of latitude and meridians of longitude shown together in part c, form a grid or coordinate system for locating any point on the earth.

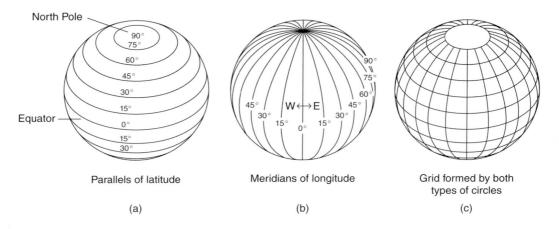

Parallels of latitude	Meridians of longitude	Grid formed by both types of circles
(a)	(b)	(c)

Figure 9.57

MAP PROJECTIONS   The globe is a spherical map of the earth. While such a map accurately represents the earth's shape and relative distances, we cannot see the whole globe at one time, nor can distances be measured easily. Maps on a flat surface are much more convenient. However, since a sphere cannot be placed flat on a plane without separating or overlapping some of its surface, making flat maps of the earth is a problem. There are three basic solutions: copying the earth's surface onto a cylinder, a cone, or a plane (Figure 9.58). These methods of copying are called **map projections**. In each case, some distortions of shapes and distances occur.

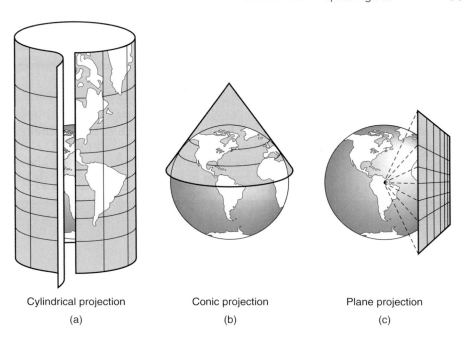

Cylindrical projection
(a)

Conic projection
(b)

Plane projection
(c)

Figure 9.58

A **cylindrical projection** (part a), also called a **mercator projection,** is obtained by placing a cylinder around a sphere and copying the surface of the sphere onto the cylinder. The cylinder is then cut to produce a flat map. Regions close to the equator are reproduced most accurately. The closer we get to the poles, the more the map is distorted.

A **conic projection** (part b) is produced by placing a cone with its apex over one of the poles and copying a portion of the surface of a sphere onto the cone. The cone is then cut and laid flat. This type of map construction is commonly used for countries that lie in an east-west direction and are middle latitude countries, as opposed to those near the poles or equator. The maps of the United States that are issued by the American Automobile Association are conical projections.

A **plane projection** (part c), also called an **azimuthal projection,** is made by placing a plane next to any point on a sphere and projecting the surface onto the plane. To visualize this process, imagine a light at the center of the sphere, and think of the boundary of a country as being pierced with small holes. The light shining through these holes, as shown by the dashed lines in part c, forms an image of the country on the plane. Less than one-half of the sphere's surface can be copied onto a plane projection, with the greatest distortion taking place at the outer edges of the plane. A plane projection, unlike cylindrical and conical projections, has the advantage that the distortion is uniform from the center of the map to its edges. Plane projections are used for hemispheres and maps of the Arctic and Antarctic. To map the polar regions, a plane is placed perpendicular to the earth's axis in contact with the north or south pole.

Problem-Solving Application

There is a remarkable formula that relates the numbers of vertices, edges, and faces of a polyhedron. This formula was first stated by René Descartes about 1635. In 1752 it was discovered again by Leonhard Euler and is now referred to as **Euler's formula.** See if you can discover this formula, either before or as you read the parts of the solution presented below.

PROBLEM

What is the relationship among the numbers of faces, vertices, and edges of a polyhedron?

Understanding the Problem   Euler's formula holds for all polyhedra. Let's look at a specific example. A die is a cube which has six faces. **Question 1:** How many vertices and edges does it have?

Devising a Plan   Let's *make a table;* list the numbers of faces, vertices, and edges for several polyhedra; and look for a relationship. **Question 2:** What are the numbers of faces, vertices, and edges for the polyhedra in figures (a), (b), and (c)?

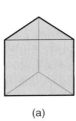  

(a)   (b)   (c)

Carrying Out the Plan   The following table contains the numbers of faces, vertices, and edges for the cube above and the polyhedra in figures (a) through (c). Using F for the number of faces, V for the number of vertices, and E for the number of edges, we can construct Euler's formula from these data. **Question 3:** What is Euler's formula?

	F	V	E
Cube	6	8	12
Figure (a)	5	6	9
Figure (b)	6	6	10
Figure (c)	9	9	16

Looking Back   You may remember that an icosahedron has 20 triangular faces, but may not remember the number of edges or vertices. Altogether, 20 triangles have a total of 60 edges. Since every two edges of a triangle form one edge of an icosahedron, this polyhedron has $60 \div 2 = 30$ edges. Given the numbers of faces and edges for the icosahedron and Euler's formula $F + V - 2 = E$, we can determine the number of vertices. **Question 4:** How many vertices are there?

Answers to Questions 1–4   1. 8 vertices and 12 edges   **2.** Figure (a): 5 faces, 6 vertices, 9 edges; figure (b): 6 faces, 6 vertices, 10 edges; figure (c): 9 faces, 9 vertices, 16 edges   **3.** $F + V - 2 = E$
4. 12; $20 + V - 2 = 30$

HISTORICAL HIGHLIGHT

Switzerland's Leonhard Euler is considered to be the most prolific writer in the history of mathematics. He published over 850 books and papers, and most branches of mathematics contain his theorems. After he became totally blind at the age of 60, he continued his amazing productivity for 17 years by dictating to a secretary and writing formulas in chalk on a large slate. On the 200th anniversary of his birthday in 1907, a Swiss publisher began reissuing Euler's entire collected works; the collection is expected to run to 75 volumes of about 60 pages each.*

Leonhard Euler
1707–1783

*H. W. Eves, *In Mathematical* Circles (Boston: Prindle, Weber, and Schmidt, 1969), pp. 46–49.

PUZZLER

How can four triangles be formed by using six matchsticks that touch only at their endpoints (do not cross)?

EXERCISES AND PROBLEMS 9.3

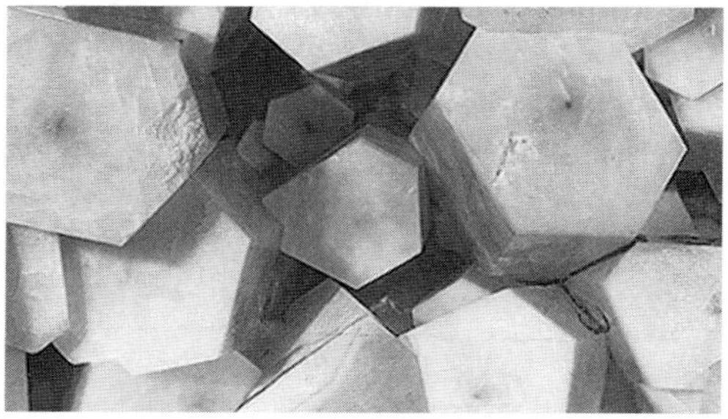

Crystals of calcite

1. The crystals crowded together in the above photograph are growing with flat polygonal faces.
   a. What type of polygon is the top face of these crystals?
   b. What type of polyhedron is formed by these crystals?

Which of the figures in exercises 2 and 3 are polyhedra?

2.

a.

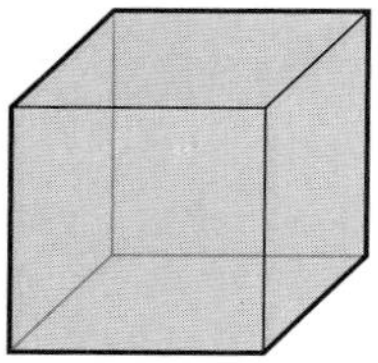

b.

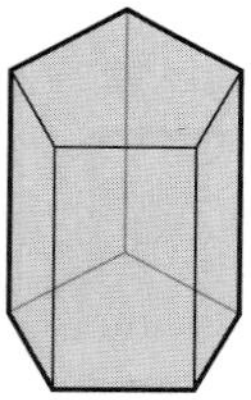

c.

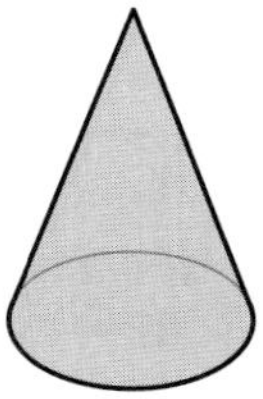

3.

a.

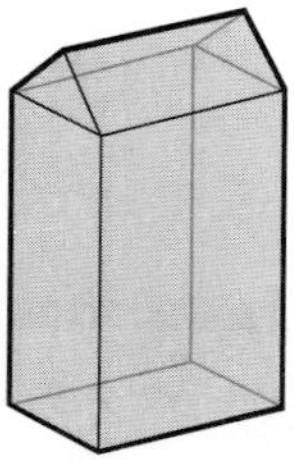

b.

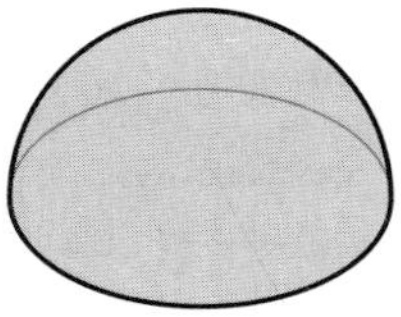

c.

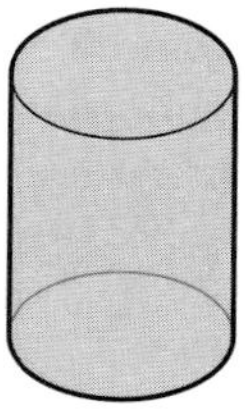

Classify the polyhedra in exercises 4 and 5 as convex or nonconvex.

4.

a.

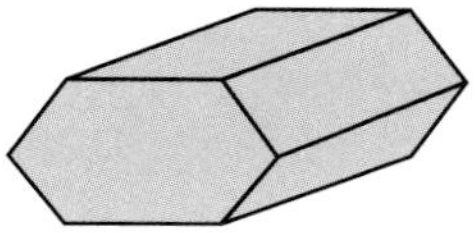

b.

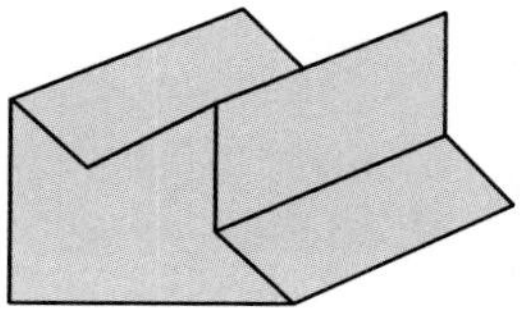

c.

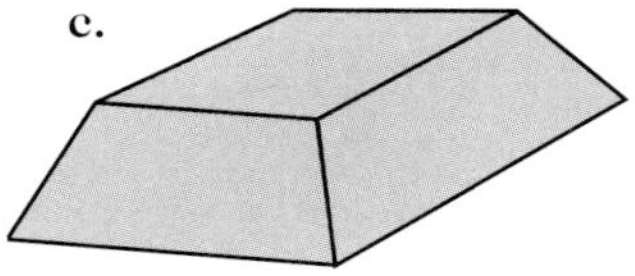

5. a.

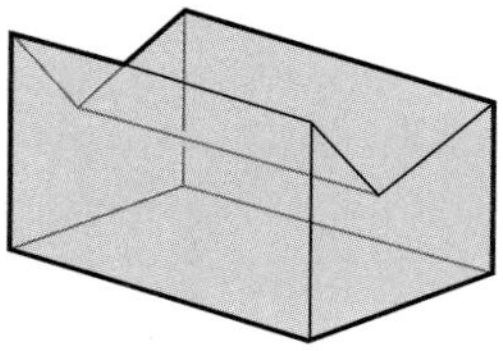

b.

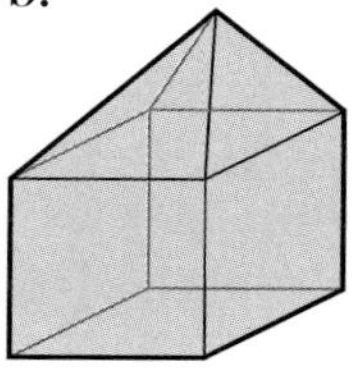

c.

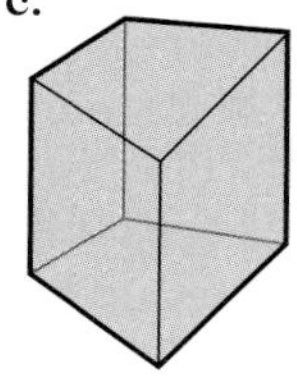

The semiregular polyhedra are classified according to the arrangement of regular polygons around each vertex. Proceeding counterclockwise, list the polygons about a vertex of each polyhedron in exercises 6 and 7.

6. a.

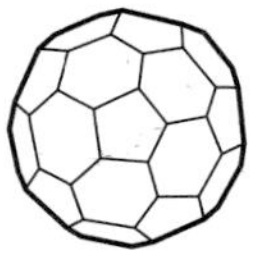

20 hexagons
12 pentagons

b.

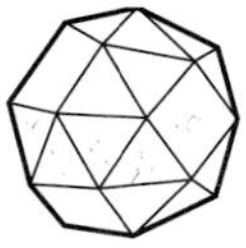

32 triangles
6 squares

7 a.

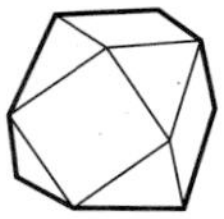

8 triangles
6 squares

b.

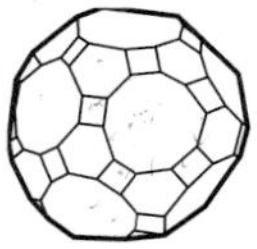

20 hexagons
30 squares
12 decagons

Name each of the figures in exercises 8 and 9.

8. a.   **b.** 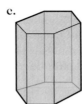   **c.**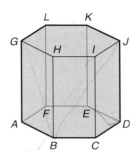

9.
a.   **b.**   **c.**

Name the figures in exercises 10 and 11, and state whether they are right or oblique.

10.
a.    **b.** 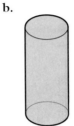   **c.**

11.
a.   **b.** 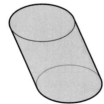   **c.**

12. The polyhedron below is a right pentagonal prism whose bases are regular polygons.

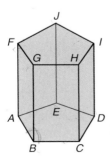

a. What face is parallel to face *ABCDE*?
b. What is the measure of the dihedral angle between face *ABGF* and face *BCHG*?
c. What is the measure of the dihedral angle between face *FGHIJ* and face *EDIJ*?

13. The polyhedron below is a right prism, and its bases are regular hexagons.

a. What face is parallel to face *GHIJKL*?
b. What face is parallel to face *IJDC*?
c. What is the measure of the dihedral angle between face *ABHG* and face *ABCDEF*?
d. What is the measure of the dihedral angle between face *ABHG* and face *BCIH*?

Which of the three types of projections is best suited for making flat maps of the regions in exercises 14 and 15?

14. a. Australia
   b. North, Central, and South America
   c. The entire equatorial region between 30° north latitude and 30° south latitude

15. a. Arctic region
   b. Western hemisphere between 20° north and 20° south
   c. United States

Each of the geometric shapes listed in exercises 16 and 17 can be seen in the following photograph. Locate these objects.

Thompson Hall, University of New Hampshire

16. a. Cone   **b.** Pyramid   **c.** Cylinder
    d. Sphere   **e.** Circle

17. a. 30° angle   **b.** Rectangle   **c.** Semicircle
    d. Square   **e.** 45° angle

18. Use your knowledge of the spherical coordinate system to match each of the following cities with its approximate longitude and latitude.

     Tokyo   38°N and 120°W
     San Francisco   56°N and 4°W
     Melbourne   35°N and 140°E
     Glasgow   35°S and 20°E
     Capetown   38°S and 145°E

19. Two points on the earth's surface that are on opposite ends of a line segment through the center of the earth are called **antipodal points.** The coordinates of such points are nicely related. The latitude of one point is as far above the equator as that of the other is below, and the longitudes are supplementary angles (in opposite hemispheres). For example, (30°N, 15°W) is off the west coast of Africa near the Canary Islands, and its antipodal point (30°S, 165°E) is off the eastern coast of Australia.

Babson College globe:
diameter 28 feet, weight 21 tons

    a. The globe in the accompanying photograph shows that (20°N, 120°W) is a point in the Pacific Ocean just west of Mexico. Its antipodal point is just east of Madagascar. What are the coordinates of this antipodal point?
    b. The point (30°S, 80°E) is in the Indian Ocean. What are the coordinates of its antipodal point? In what country is it located?

20. China is bounded by latitudes of 20°N and 55°N and by longitudes of 75°E and 135°E. It is playfully assumed that if you could dig a hole straight through the center of the earth, you would come out in China. For which of the following starting points is this true?
    a. Panama (9°N, 80°W)
    b. Buenos Aires (35°S, 58°W)
    c. New York (41°N, 74°W)

The intersection of a plane and a three-dimensional figure is called a **cross section.** The cross section produced by the intersection of a plane and a right cylinder, where the plane is parallel to the base of the cylinder (see figure), is a circle. Determine the cross sections of the figures in exercises 21 and 22.

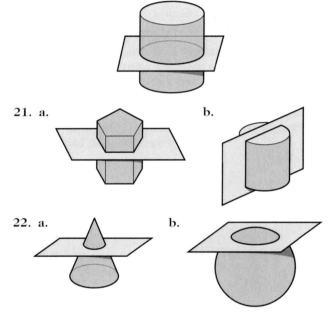

21. a.   **b.**

22. a.   **b.**

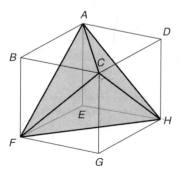

23. A cube can be divided into triangular pyramids in several ways. Pyramid *FHCA* divides this cube into five triangular pyramids. Name the four vertices of each of the other four pyramids.

24. *E*, *F*, *G*, *H*, and *C* are the vertices of a square pyramid inside this cube. Name the five vertices of two more square pyramids that, together with the given pyramid, divide the cube into three pyramids.

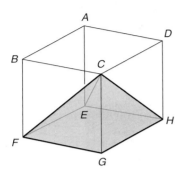

One method of describing a three-dimensional figure is to make a drawing of its different views. There are nine cubes in the following figure (two are hidden), and the top, right, and front views are shown.

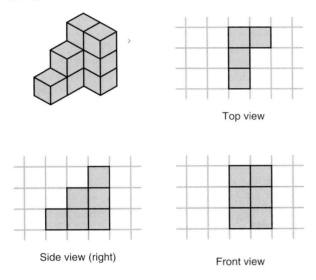

Top view

Side view (right)

Front view

Sketch the top, front, and side views of each of the figures in exercises 25 and 26. (*Note:* Figure 25b has one hidden cube beneath a cube that can be seen, and the color faces of the cubes are part of the front views of the figures.)

25. **a.**   **b.**

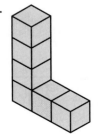

26. **a.**   **b.**

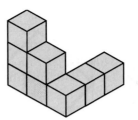
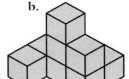

The table of polyhedra below illustrates some of the forms which crystals may take in nature. The polygons at the tops of the columns are the horizontal cross sections of the polyhedra in the columns. Use this table in exercises 27 and 28.

27. a. List the numbers of the polyhedra that are pyramids.
  b. Which of the polyhedra is most like a dodecahedron?

28. a. List the numbers of the polyhedra that are prisms.
  b. Which of the polyhedra is most like an octahedron?

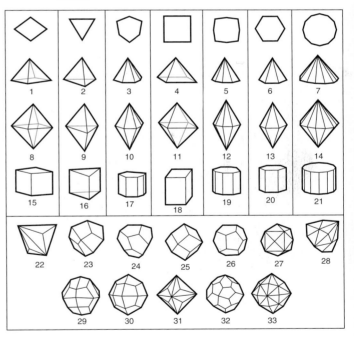

Use Euler's formula in exercises 29 and 30 to determine the missing numbers for each polyhedron. For each set of conditions, find a polyhedron from those numbered from 1 to 21 in the table for exercises 27 and 28 which has the given number of faces, vertices, and edges.

29. a. 7 faces, 7 vertices, _____ edges
  b. 16 faces, _____ vertices, 24 edges
  c. _____ faces, 5 vertices, 8 edges

30. a. 6 faces, _____ vertices, 9 edges
   b. _____ faces, 8 vertices, 12 edges
   c. 14 faces, 24 vertices, _____ edges

Hurricane Ginger was christened on September 10, 1971, and became the longest-lived Atlantic hurricane on record. This tropical storm formed approximately 275 miles south of Bermuda and reached the U.S. mainland 20 days later. Use this map in exercises 31 and 32.

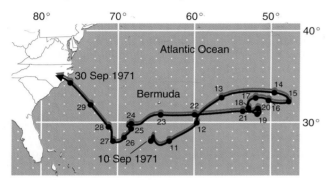

Erratic path of Hurricane Ginger

31. The storm's coordinates on September 10 were (28°N, 66°W). What were its coordinates on September 15, September 23, and September 30?

32. At this latitude on the earth's surface, each degree of longitude spans a distance of approximately 60 miles. About how many miles did this hurricane travel between September 10 and September 30? (*Hint:* Use a piece of string.)

REASONING AND PROBLEM SOLVING

33. Erica is designing a science experiment that requires two different three-dimensional figures such that one fits inside the other and both figures have at least one cross section that is the same for both figures (see exercises 21 and 22). Find such a pair of figures.

34. Here are the first three figures in a staircase pattern. These staircases are polyhedra.

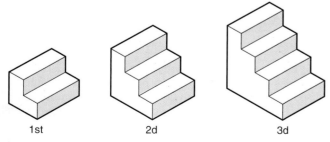

1st   2d   3d

   a. The number of faces for the polyhedron in the first figure is 8. How many faces are there for the polyhedron in the 35th figure?

   b. The number of edges for the polyhedron in the first figure is 18. How many edges are there for the polyhedron in the 35th figure?

   c. The number of vertices for the polyhedron in the first figure is 12. How many vertices are there for the polyhedron in the 35th figure?

35. Sketch and describe how to form a piece of paper into the following figures (without bases).

a.    **b.**    **c.**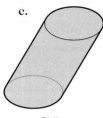

Right circular cylinder   Right circular cone   Oblique circular cylinder

36. Featured Strategies: Making a Drawing and Using a Model   The five regular polyhedra and the numbers and shapes of their faces are shown in the following table. Determine the missing numbers of vertices and edges.

POLYHEDRON	VERTICES	FACES	EDGES
Tetrahedron		4 triangles	
Cube	8	6 squares	12
Octahedron		8 triangles	
Dodecahedron		12 pentagons	
Icosahedron		20 triangles	

   a. Understanding the Problem   The cube is the most familiar of the regular polyhedra. Its 6 faces meet in 12 edges, and its edges meet in 8 vertices (see figure i). How many vertices and edges does a tetrahedron have?

   i.   ii.

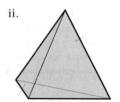

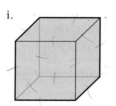

   b. Devising a Plan   One approach is to use a model or a sketch of the polyhedra and to count the numbers of vertices and edges. Or once we determine either the number of vertices or the number of edges, the missing number can be obtained by using Euler's formula $F + V - 2 = E$.
      Another approach that avoids counting is to use the fact that each pair of faces meets in exactly one edge. For example, since a dodecahedron has 12 pentagons for faces and each pair of

pentagons shares an edge, the number of edges is $(12 \times 5)/2 = 30$. Using Euler's formula, determine the number of vertices in a dodecahedron.

c. **Carrying Out the Plan**   Continue to find the numbers of edges by multiplying the number of faces by the number of sides on the face and dividing by 2. For example, what is the number of edges in an icosahedron? Fill in the rest of the table on the preceding page.

d. **Looking Back**   The number of vertices for each regular polyhedron can also be found directly from the number of edges that meet at each vertex. For example, three edges meet at each vertex of the dodecahedron, as shown in Figure iii below. Since there are 12 faces and each face has 5 vertex points, the dodecahedron has $(12 \times 5)/3 = 20$ vertex points. Use this approach to determine the number of vertices for the icosahedron in *iv*.

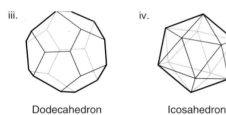

iii.   Dodecahedron

iv.   Icosahedron

37. Each of the following polygons contains five squares. There are only 12 such polygons that can be formed in the plane by joining five squares along their edges, and they are called **pentominoes.**

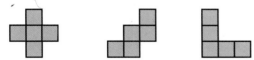

a. Which two of these pentominoes will fold into an open-top box, so that each face of the box is one of the squares?

b. Eight of the 12 pentominoes will fold into an open-top box. Find another one of these.

38. The polygons were formed by joining six squares along their edges. There are 35 such polygons, and they are called **hexominoes.**

a. Which two of these hexominoes will fold into a cube so that each face of the cube is one of the squares?

b. Eleven of the 35 hexominoes will fold into a cube. Find another such hexomino.

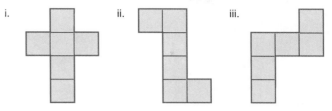

i.   ii.   iii.

39. The centers of the faces of a cube can be connected to form a regular octahedron. Also, the centers of the faces of an octahedron can be connected to form a cube. Such pairs of polyhedra are called **duals.**

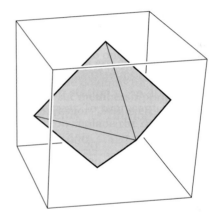

a. How is this dual relationship suggested by the table in exercises 36?

b. Find two other regular polyhedra that are duals of each other.

c. Which regular polyhedron is its own dual?

40. There are six categories of illusions.* One category, called *impossible objects,* is produced by drawing three-dimensional figures on two-dimensional surfaces. Find the impossible feature in each of these figures.

*P. A. Rainey, *Illusions* (Hamden, CT: The Shoe String Press, 1973), pp. 18–43.

a.

M. C. Escher's "Waterfall"

b.

c.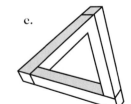

41. A second type of illusion involves depth perception. We have accustomed our eyes to see depth when three-dimensional objects are drawn on two-dimensional surfaces. Answer questions a and b by disregarding the depth illusions.

a. Is one of these cylinders larger than the others?

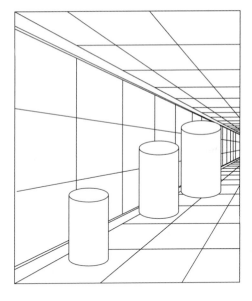

b. Which of the four numbered angles below is the largest? Which are right angles? (*Hint:* Use a corner of a piece of paper.)

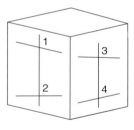

ONLINE LEARNING CENTER   www.mhhe.com/bennett-nelson

   • Math Investigation 9.3   *Pyramid Patterns*
   Section-Related: • Links   • Writing/Discussion Problems   • Bibliography

---

PUZZLER

 Some wildlife researchers, having pitched camp, set out on an exploratory trip. They walked 15 miles due south, then 15 miles due east, where they saw a bear. Walking 15 miles due north, they returned to their camp. What was the color of the bear?

MATH ACTIVITY 9.4

SYMMETRIES OF PATTERN BLOCK FIGURES

Materials: Pattern block pieces in the Manipulative Kit.

Teachers should guide students to recognize, describe, and informally prove the symmetric characteristics of designs through the materials they supply and the questions they ask. Students can use pattern blocks to create designs with line and rotational symmetry or use paper cutouts, paper folding, and mirrors to investigate lines of symmetry.

Standards 2000, p. 100

1. The first pattern block figure shown below has three **lines of symmetry** (dotted lines), because when the figure is folded about any of these lines, it will coincide with itself. The second figure has no lines of symmetry, as can be shown by tracing pattern blocks and paper folding the resulting figure.

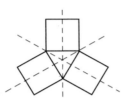 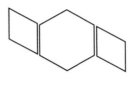

Construct pattern block figures which have exactly one, two, three, and four lines of symmetry. Record your figures and lines of symmetry.

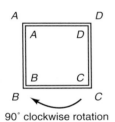

90° clockwise rotation

*2. A frame has been traced about the square pattern block at the left, and each corner of the frame and the corresponding corner of the square have the same letter. If the square is rotated 90° clockwise, it will fit back into the frame with A moving to corner D of the frame, and D, C, and B moving to corners C, B, and A, respectively, of the frame. The square is said to have 90° **rotation symmetry.** It also has 180°, 270°, and 360° rotation symmetries.

Determine all the rotation symmetries less than or equal to 360° for each of the following pattern block figures and the number of degrees for each rotation. (*Suggestion:* Trace each figure to form its frame.)

a. 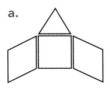   b.    c.   d.

3. Build figures with two or more pattern blocks to satisfy each of the following conditions.
   a. Two lines of symmetry, two rotation symmetries
   b. Three rotation symmetries, no lines of symmetry
   c. Six lines of symmetry, six rotation symmetries

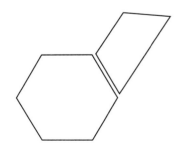

4. A trapezoid has been attached to a hexagon in the figure at the left.
   a. In how many different ways can another trapezoid be attached to this figure to form a figure that has a line of symmetry? Show sketches and lines of symmetry.
   b. In how many different ways can one or more trapezoids be attached to this figure to form a figure that has more than one rotation symmetry?

SECTION 9.4

SYMMETRIC FIGURES

The Taj Mahal, built between 1630 and 1652 on the banks of the Jumna River in Agra, India

PROBLEM OPENER

A vertical line can be drawn through the word MOM so that the left and right sides are mirror images of each other.

Find a word that can be cut by a horizontal line so that the bottom and top halves are mirror images of each other.

The Taj Mahal is considered by many to be the most beautiful building in the world. It is made entirely of white marble and is surrounded by a landscaped walled garden on the banks of the Jumna River in Agra, India. It is an octagonal building, and four of its eight faces contain massive arches rising to a height of 33 meters (108 feet). The form and balance of the Taj Mahal can be described by saying it is *symmetric.* The human race has always found order and harmony in symmetry. Perhaps the most influential factor in our desire for symmetry is the shape of the human body. Even children in their earliest drawings show an awareness of body symmetry.

Reflection Symmetry for Plane Figures

Many years before it became popular to teach geometric ideas in elementary school, cutting out symmetric figures was a common classroom activity. The procedure is to fold a piece of paper and draw a figure that encloses part of or all the crease, as shown in Figure 9.59a. When the figure is cut out and unfolded, it is symmetric (see part b). The crease is called a **line of symmetry,** and the figure is said to have **reflection symmetry.**

 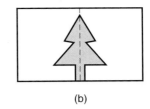

(a)   (b)

Figure 9.59

Intuitively we understand the idea of reflection symmetry to mean that the two halves of the figure will coincide if one is folded onto the other. The word *reflection* is a natural one to use because of the mirror test for symmetry. If the edge of a mirror is placed along a line of symmetry, the half-figure and its image from the mirror will look like the whole figure. You can verify the line of symmetry for the photograph of the building in Figure 9.60 by placing the edge of a mirror along the vertical centerline of the photograph. With the mirror in this position, one-half of the building and its reflection will look like the whole building. Since this is the only way the mirror can be placed so that this will happen, the photograph of the building has only one line of symmetry.

Young children come to school with intuitions about how shapes can be moved. Students can explore motions such as slides, flips, and turns by using mirrors, paper folding, and tracing.

Standards 2000, p. 43

Figure 9.60
Putnam Hall, University of
New Hampshire

The Mira is a convenient device for locating lines of symmetry for plane figures. It is made of Plexiglas so that the user can see through it and at the same time see reflections. If a figure has a line of symmetry, as does the hexagon in Figure 9.61, and the Mira is placed so that the reflection of the figure coincides with the part of the figure behind the Mira, then the edge of the Mira lies on a line of symmetry.

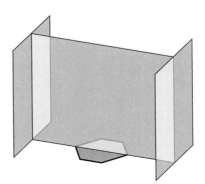

Figure 9.61

Some figures have more than one line of symmetry. To produce a figure with two such lines, fold a sheet of paper in half and then in half again, as shown in Figure 9.62a. Then draw a figure whose endpoints touch the creases, and cut it out. When the paper is opened, the two perpendicular creases will be lines of symmetry for the figure, as shown in Figure 9.62b.

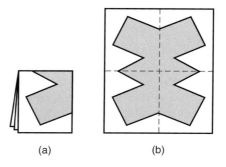

Figure 9.62

(a)   (b)

Example A

Each of the following polygons has two or more lines of symmetry. Determine these lines for each figure.

1.    2.    3.

Solution   **1.** An equilateral triangle has three lines of symmetry: one line through each vertex perpendicular to the opposite side.   **2.** A square has four lines of symmetry: one horizontal line and one vertical line through the midpoints of opposite sides and two lines containing the diagonals.   **3.** This figure has two lines of symmetry: one horizontal line through opposite vertices and one vertical line through the midpoints of opposite sides.

The idea of symmetry can be made more precise by adopting the term *image,* which is suggested by mirrors. If a line can be drawn through a figure so that each point on one side of the line has a matching point on the other side at the same perpendicular distance from the line, it is a **line of symmetry.** If two points on opposite sides of this line match up, one is called the **image** of the other. A few points and their images have been labeled in Figure 9.63, where A corresponds to A', B to B', C to C', and D to D'. Each line segment connecting a point and its image is perpendicular to the line of symmetry.

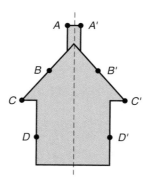

Figure 9.63

Example B

For each of the following figures, show that the dashed line is not a line of symmetry by finding the images of the lettered points.

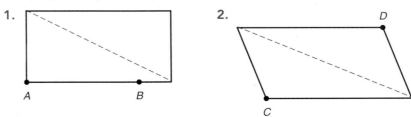

Solution 1, 2. The images of points *A*, *B*, *C*, and *D* do not lie on the given figures. Notice that while each dotted line divides the figure into two parts that are congruent, these lines are not lines of symmetry.

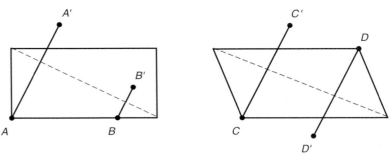

Rotation Symmetry for Plane Figures

Figure 9.64 may look like a drawing of a plant, but it is a drawing of a type of jellyfish called *Aurelia.* It seems to have the form and balance of a symmetric figure, but it has no lines of reflection. It does, however, have **rotation symmetry,** because it can be turned about its center so that it coincides with itself. For example, if it is rotated 90° clockwise, the top "arm" will move to the 3 o'clock position, the bottom "arm" will move to the 9 o'clock position, etc.

Figure 9.64
Aurelia, *the common coastal jellyfish*

Let's consider another example of rotation symmetry. Trace Figure 9.65 and mark the center *X* and the arms *A*, *B*, and *C*. Cut it out and place it on the page so that both figures coincide. If it is held down by a pencil at point *X*, the top figure can be rotated clockwise so that *A* goes to *B*, *B* to *C*, and *C* to *A*. This is an example of rotation symmetry, and X is called the **center of rotation.** Since the figure is rotated 120° (one-third of a full turn), it has a *120° rotation symmetry.* From its original position, this figure can also be made to coincide with itself after a 240° clockwise rotation, with A going to C, B to A, and C to B. This is a 240° rotation symmetry. Since the figure can be rotated back onto itself after a 360° rotation, the figure also has a *360° rotation symmetry. Note:* Any figure can be rotated 360° by using any point as the center of rotation. Thus we will be interested in a 360° rotation symmetry only when a figure has other rotation symmetries.

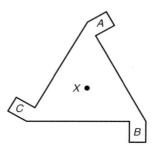

Figure 9.65

Some figures have both reflection symmetry and rotation symmetry. The regular polygons have both types. The central angles of these polygons determine the angles for the rotation symmetries.

Example C

Find all the reflection and rotation symmetries for a regular hexagon.

Solution   Every regular hexagon has six reflection symmetries. Figure (*1*) shows three lines of symmetry passing through opposite pairs of parallel sides, and figure (*2*) shows three lines of symmetry passing through opposite pairs of vertices. Since the central angle in figure (*3*) has a measure of 360° ÷ 6 = 60°, the figure has rotation symmetries of 60°, 120°, 180°, 240°, 300°, and 360°.

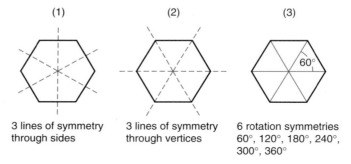

Snowflakes have the reflection and rotation symmetries of the hexagon. Notice the six congruent central angles in the snow crystal in Figure 9.66.* Despite the similarity that results from the six reflection and six rotation symmetries of the hexagon, there is a myriad of various details in snowflakes.

*This photograph is one of more than 2200 in W. A. Bentley and W. J. Humphreys, *Snow Crystals* (New York: McGraw-Hill, 1931).

Figure 9.66

Reflection Symmetry for Space Figures

Some of the ways in which symmetry occurs around us are listed in NCTM's 5–8 Standard, *Geometry:*

Symmetry in two and three dimensions provides rich opportunities for students to see geometry in the world of art, nature, construction, and so on. Butterflies, faces, flowers, arrangements of windows, reflections in water, and some pottery designs involve symmetry. Turning symmetry is illustrated by bicycle gears. Pattern symmetry can be observed in the multiplication table, in numbers arrayed in charts, and in Pascal's triangle.*

The idea of reflection symmetry for three-dimensional objects is similar to that for plane figures. With plane figures we found lines such that one-half of the figure was the reflection of the other. With figures in space there are *planes of symmetry* such that the points on one side of a plane are the reflection of the points on the other side. Consider, for example, the antique chair in Figure 9.67. The plane running down the center of the back and across the seat to the front of the chair divides it into left and right halves, which are mirror images of each other. Such a plane is called a **plane of symmetry.** The chair is said to have reflection symmetry.

*Curriculum and Evaluation Standards for School Mathematics (Reston, VA: National Council of Teachers of Mathematics, 1989), p. 115.

Figure 9.67
*Ebonized walnut armchair,
dating from between 1865
and 1875*

Reflection symmetry for figures in space can be mathematically defined by requiring that for each point on the left side of the chair, there is a corresponding point on the right side such that both points are the same perpendicular distance from the plane of symmetry. For the antique chair, point *A* corresponds to *A'* and *B* corresponds to *B'*. These points are called **images** of each other, and the segments $\overline{AA'}$ and $\overline{BB'}$ are perpendicular to the plane of symmetry.

Two-sided symmetry, such as that of the antique chair in Figure 9.67 and the long-horn beetle and zebra butterfly in Figure 9.68, is sometimes called **vertical symmetry** because the plane of symmetry is perpendicular to the ground. Look around and you may be surprised at the number of things that have vertical symmetry.

Figure 9.68
Long-horn beetle (left) *and
zebra butterfly* (right)

Example D   Determine the planes of symmetry for each of the following objects.

Solution   The square-top table has four vertical planes of symmetry: one from front to back, one from side to side, and one through each diagonal of the top surface. The lamp has six vertical planes of symmetry because its shade has six congruent sections: three planes bisect opposite pairs of sections of the lampshade, and three planes pass through opposite pairs of seams of the shade. The wastebasket has eight vertical planes of symmetry, since its base has the shape of a regular octagon.

Rotation Symmetry for Space Figures

Some three-dimensional objects, such as the table shown in Figure 9.69, have rotation symmetry. If the table is rotated 120°, the legs will change places and the table will be back in the same location or position. That is, leg A will go to the position of leg B, B to C, and C to A. In this example, the table can be rotated about line ℓ, which passes through the center of the table's top and its base. Line ℓ is called the **axis of symmetry,** and the table is said to have rotation symmetry. Since the dihedral angles formed by adjacent legs of this table have measures of 120°, the table has 120°, 240°, and 360° rotation symmetries.

Figure 9.69

The three-legged table in Figure 9.69 also has three vertical planes of symmetry, one passing through each leg. It is not difficult to find objects with both planes of symmetry and axes of symmetry. The small table, the lamp, and the wastebasket in Example D all have both types of symmetry. Occasionally, however, you will see space figures that have rotation symmetry but no plane of symmetry.

Example E

Determine all the rotation symmetries for the paper windmill.

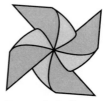

Paper windmill

Solution   The paper windmill has rotation symmetries of 90°, 180°, 270°, and 360° about its axis, which is the line through the center of the windmill and perpendicular to its surface.

Problem-Solving Application

PROBLEM

For every plane figure with two or more reflection symmetries, there is a relationship between the number of these symmetries and the number of rotation symmetries. What is this relationship?

Understanding the Problem   There are plane figures with both rotation and reflection symmetries. For example, a rectangle has two lines of symmetry. **Question 1:** How many rotation symmetries does a rectangle have?

Devising a Plan   *Making a table* and comparing the numbers of reflection and rotation symmetries may reveal a pattern. A square has four reflection symmetries. **Question 2:** How many rotation symmetries does a square have?

Carrying Out the Plan   The numbers of lines of symmetry for several figures are shown below. Determine the numbers of rotation symmetries for these figures and record them in the table. **Question 3:** What does this result suggest?

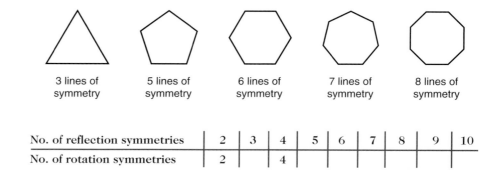

| 3 lines of symmetry | 5 lines of symmetry | 6 lines of symmetry | 7 lines of symmetry | 8 lines of symmetry |

No. of reflection symmetries	2	3	4	5	6	7	8	9	10
No. of rotation symmetries	2		4						

Looking Back   As the results in the table suggest, if a figure has two or more reflection symmetries, it will have the same number of rotation symmetries. The converse, however, is not true. **Question 4:** What symmetries does the following figure have?

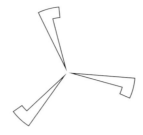

Answers to Questions 1–4   **1.** 2 **2.** 4 **3.** If a figure has two or more reflection symmetries, it will have the same number of rotation symmetries.   **4.** The figure has rotation symmetries of 120°, 240°, and 360°. It has no reflection symmetries.

EXERCISES AND PROBLEMS 9.4

The Alhambra, built in the thirteenth century for Moorish kings, Granada, Spain

1. The pool, building, and fortress in the section of the Alhambra shown in the photograph have a vertical plane of symmetry, about which their left sides are the reflections of their right sides.

　a. List five objects in this photograph that have images about the plane of symmetry.

　b. Physical objects can never be perfectly symmetric. In this scene, for example, there are several objects that deviate from perfect symmetry. List three objects that do not have an image for the vertical plane of symmetry.

　c. Several individual items in this photograph have vertical lines of symmetry. Name an object in this photograph that has a horizontal line of symmetry.

2. In 1850 gold was so plentiful in the United States that dozens of different banks and business firms minted their own coins. Some were square, and others had eight sides, such as this octagonal $50 gold piece.

　a. How many rotation symmetries does a regular octagon have?

　b. How many degrees are there in the smallest rotation symmetry?

　c. How many lines of symmetry does a regular octagon have?

The following sketches of organisms have reflection and rotation symmetries. Determine the number of lines of symmetry and the number of rotation symmetries for each figure in exercises 3 and 4.

3. a.

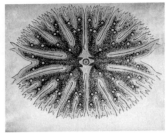

b.

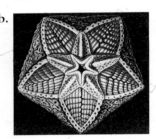

4. a.

b.

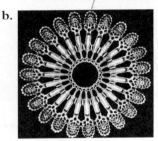

Draw all possible lines of symmetry and find the number of rotation symmetries for each polygon in exercises 5 and 6.

The subject of beauty has been discussed for thousands of years. Aristotle felt that the main elements of beauty are order and symmetry. The U.S. mathematician George Birkhoff (1884–1944) developed a formula for rating the beauty of objects.* Part of his formula involves counting symmetries. If only symmetry is used to rate the beauty of polygons, which polygon in exercise 5 (or exercise 6) has the highest rating (counting all lines

of reflection and rotation symmetries) and which has the lowest rating?

5. a.   **b.**

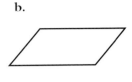

c.   **d.**

6.   a.   **b.**

c.   **d.**

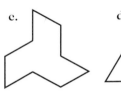

Show that the dashed lines in the figures in exercises 7 and 8 are not lines of symmetry by finding the images of the lettered points.

7.

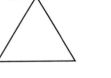

8.

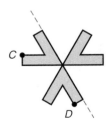

*G. D. Birkhoff, *Aesthetic Measure* (Cambridge, MA: Harvard University Press, 1933), pp. 33–46.

The mirror test for lines of symmetry is very effective when the reflecting is done with a Mira.* To find a line of symmetry, it is necessary only to move the Mira until the image reflected on the Plexiglas coincides with the portion of the figure behind it. This cannot be done for some of the figures in exercises 9 and 10. Which ones?

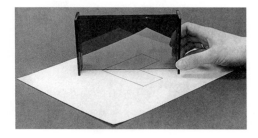

9.

a.   b.   c.

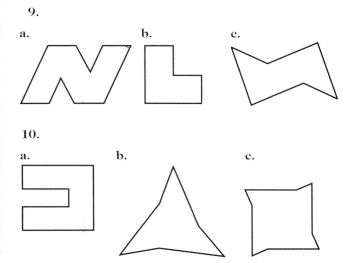

10.

a.   b.   c.

11. a. Which uppercase letters have two lines of symmetry?
  b. Which letters have two rotation symmetries but no lines of symmetry?

ABCDEFGHIJKLM
NOPQRSTUVWXYZ

12. If you write the letter P on a piece of paper and hold it in front of a mirror, it will look reversed.
  a. Which uppercase letters will not appear reversed when they are held in front of a mirror?

*E. Woodward, "Geometry with a Mira," *The Arithmetic Teacher* 25, no. 2 (November 1977): 117–118. The Mira is distributed by several companies that produce educational materials.

  b. What type of symmetry do these letters have?
  c. Use some of the letters from part a to write a word whose reflection in a mirror is also a word.

The figures in exercises 13 and 14 were formed on circular geoboards. Which of these figures have no lines of symmetry? Determine the number of lines of symmetry for the remaining figures. Find the number of rotation symmetries for each figure that has two or more such symmetries, and give the number of degrees for each.

13. a.   b.

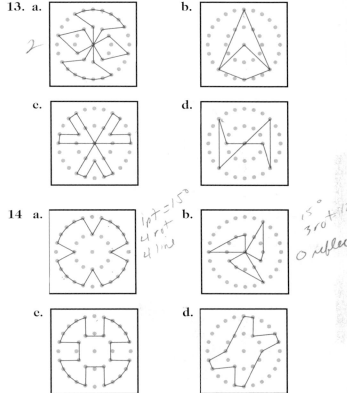

  c.   d.

14 a.   b.

  c.   d.

Sketch figures in exercises 15 and 16 with the given symmetries, as they would appear on a circular geoboard.

15. a. Two rotation symmetries and two reflection symmetries
  b. Three rotation symmetries and no reflection symmetries
  c. 12 rotation symmetries and 12 reflection symmetries

16. a. One rotation symmetry and one reflection symmetry
  b. Eight rotation symmetries and no reflection symmetries
  c. Six rotation symmetries and six reflection symmetries

17. Trace the sketches below and complete the figures so that they are symmetric about the dashed line. You might want to first find the image with a mirror or Mira.

a. 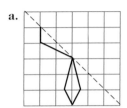 **b.**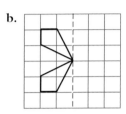

18. Trace the sketches below and complete the figures so that they are symmetric about the two perpendicular dashed lines.

a. 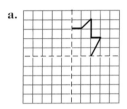 **b.**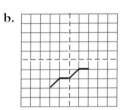

Determine the number of rotation symmetries, if there are two or more, and the number of planes of symmetry for each of the objects in exercises 19 and 20. (The lampshade has 16 panels.)

19. a.

b.

20. a.

b.

The figures below are highly symmetric. Use these figures in exercises 21 and 22.

| Right cone | Right cylinder | Equilateral prism | Sphere | Cube | Rectangular pyramid |

21. a. Which figures have at least one horizontal axis of symmetry?
   b. For each figure which has a horizontal axis of symmetry, give the number of rotation symmetries for an axis of symmetry.
   c. Which of these figures has the following number of planes of vertical symmetry: Exactly two? Exactly three? Exactly four?

22. a. Which figures have a horizontal plane of symmetry?
   b. Does each of these solids have at least one vertical plane of symmetry?
   c. Give the number of rotation symmetries for each vertical axis of symmetry.

23. List all the symmetries for the following figure, which is a sphere mounted on a pentagonal base. (Disregard the design on the sphere.)

M. C. Escher's "Sphere with Fish"

The metalwork designs in exercises 24 and 25 have many pleasing symmetries. How many rotation symmetries and lines of symmetry are there for each figure?

24.

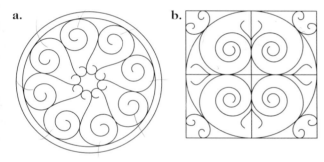

a.

b.

25.

a.

b.

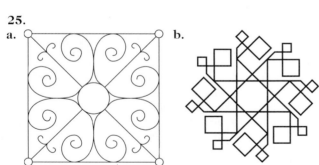

How many rotation symmetries are there for each of the Japanese crests in exercises 26 and 27?

26. a.   b.

27. a.   b.

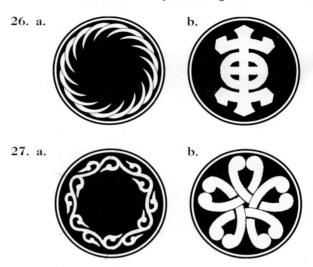

Find the number of rotation symmetries, if there are two or more, and the number of lines of symmetry for the commercial logos in exercises 28 and 29. How many of these logos can you identify?

28. a.   b.

c.

d.

e.

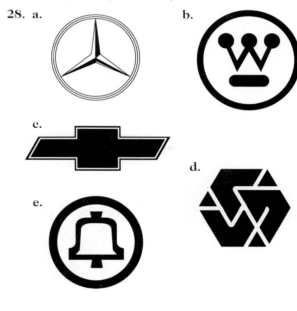

29.

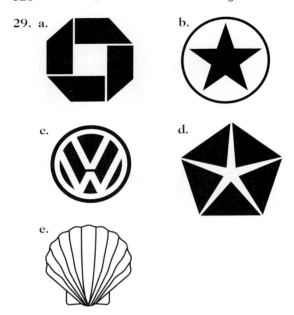

a.
b.
c.
d.
e.

31.

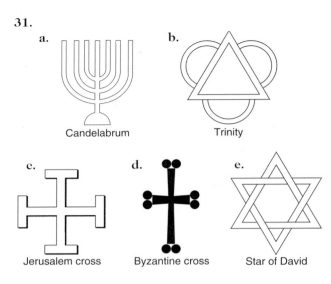

a.   Candelabrum
b.   Trinity
c.   Jerusalem cross
d.   Byzantine cross
e.   Star of David

Determine the number of rotation symmetries, if there are two or more, and the number of lines of symmetry for the symbols in exercises 30 and 31.

30.

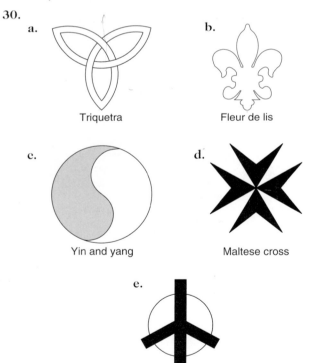

a.   Triquetra
b.   Fleur de lis
c.   Yin and yang
d.   Maltese cross
e.   Peace symbol

REASONING AND PROBLEM SOLVING

32. Featured Strategy: Using a Model   Crystals are classified into different types according to the number of axes of rotation they have. This photograph shows several cubes of a galena crystal. How many axes of symmetry does a cube have?

Intersecting cubes of galena crystals

a. Understanding the Problem   One axis of symmetry in the cube on the next page runs through the centers of faces *EFGH* and *ABCD*. What is the total number of axes of symmetry through the faces of the cube? Describe each by listing the pairs of faces.

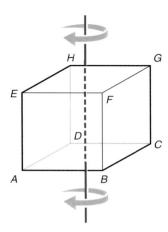

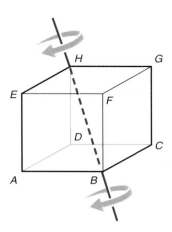

b. Devising a Plan   A posterboard or paper model of a cube that can be pierced by a wire is a helpful device for determining rotations that take the cube back onto itself. The following figure suggests some other possibilities for axes of symmetry. One axis passes through the edges $\overline{FG}$ and $\overline{AD}$. How many axes of symmetry pass through the edges of a cube? Describe each by listing pairs of edges.

d. Looking Back   A cube also has many planes of symmetry. The figure below shows a plane that bisects four edges of the cube: $\overline{AB}$, $\overline{DC}$, $\overline{HG}$, and $\overline{EF}$. How many planes of symmetry bisect edges of the cube? Describe each by listing the four edges.

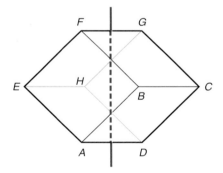

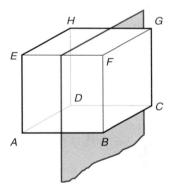

c. Carrying Out the Plan   A model will help to show that a cube has three types of axes of symmetry: through the faces, through the edges, and through the vertices. The following figure shows the axis through the pair of vertices H and B. How many axes of symmetry are there through pairs of vertices, and what is the total number of axes of symmetry for the cube?

33. Two adjacent apartments which are the same size and on the same level are separated by a dividing wall. A water inlet pipe to the apartments is centered at the base of the dividing wall and branches into each apartment, as shown in the following figure. The plans for one apartment show the path of the pipe and its length. If this path is symmetric about the dividing wall to the path of the piping in the adjacent apartment, how far apart are the two terminal points of the pipes in these apartments?

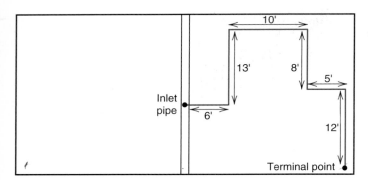

34. Nikita lives in a city where the avenues run north and south and the streets run east and west. She lives on Washington Avenue and has a jogging route which takes her two blocks east, three blocks north, four blocks east, five blocks south, and four blocks west. At this point she stops jogging and walks back to her apartment. One day she decides to jog a new route in such a way that the old and new routes form a path which has a 180° rotation symmetry about the place where she lives. How many blocks (edges of blocks) must she walk to get from the end of her new jogging route to the end of her old jogging route, if she does not cut diagonally?

35. Ms. Harris designed a beanbag game so her fourth-grade students could become familiar with symmetry. Here are the rules: On each player's turn, five beanbags are tossed at eight cups which are placed about a circle (see figure). Only one beanbag will fit in a cup. If one or more beanbags land in cups, the player receives the sum of the numbers on the cups plus the following points: 5 points if two beanbags land in cups which are symmetric about the vertical line through the centers of cups 1 and 5; 5 points if beanbags land in cups which are symmetric about the horizontal line through the centers of cups 7 and 3. What is the greatest score a player can receive on one turn? (*Note:* There are some pairs of cups which are symmetric about both lines of symmetry.)

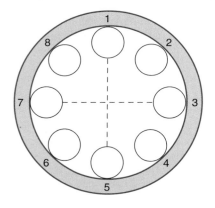

36. Sharon and Justin belong to an outdoor orienteering club. Sharon uses her compass to walk over the trail given by the following directions from her orienteering assignment sheet: Start at the Wilderness Club House; go north 1 mile; go east 2 miles; go southeast 1 mile; go south 1 mile; go northeast 1.5 miles; and go southwest 2 miles. If Justin's route is symmetric to Sharon's route about the east-west line through the clubhouse, will Justin's route end north or south of the clubhouse?

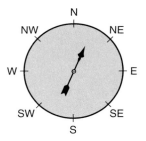

37. Louis Braille, a Frenchman living in the nineteenth century, invented an alphabet for use by blind people. Each letter of this alphabet consisted of a 2 × 3 grid having from one to six raised dots which were placed in the six positions shown in figure (*a*). Figures (*b*) through (*e*) show the letters for T, G, Y, and X. Note that the symbol for T has a 180° rotation symmetry; the symbol for G has a vertical line of symmetry; the symbol for Y has a horizontal line of symmetry; and the symbol for X has both horizontal and vertical lines of symmetry. There is a total of 64 different possible Braille symbols using from zero to six dots of two different sizes in the positions shown in figure (*a*). Find at least two more Braille-type symbols having each of the following types of symmetry.
a. A vertical line of symmetry
b. A horizontal line of symmetry
c. A 180° rotation symmetry, but no lines of symmetry

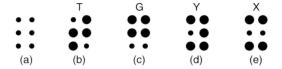

ONLINE LEARNING CENTER   www.mhhe.com/bennett-nelson

• Math Investigation 9.4   *Mirror Cards*
Section-Related: • Links   • Writing/Discussion Problems   • Bibliography

PUZZLER

Subtracting 80 from a certain twentieth-century year (date) with a 180° rotation symmetry yields a nineteenth-century year with both horizontal and vertical lines of symmetry. What are these two years?

CHAPTER REVIEW

1. **Mathematical systems**
   a. A **mathematical system** consists of undefined terms, definitions, axioms, and theorems.
   b. In every mathematical system there must be **undefined words**.
   c. **Definitions** are stated in terms of undefined words or previously defined words.
   d. **Axioms** are statements that are assumed to be true.
   e. **Theorems** are statements that are proved by using definitions and axioms together with deductive reasoning.

2. **Plane figures**
   a. The terms **point, line,** and **plane** are undefined.
   b. **Half-planes, line segments, rays, angles, parallel lines, perpendicular lines,** and **collinear points** are defined.
   c. Each **angle** is measured in degrees. A **degree** is $\frac{1}{360}$ of a complete turn about a circle.
   d. A **protractor** is a device for measuring angles.
   e. Angles are classified as **right, obtuse, acute, straight,** or **reflex.**
   f. Two angles are **complementary** if the sum of their measures is 90° and **supplementary** if the sum of their measures is 180°.
   g. Two intersecting lines form pairs of congruent **vertical angles.**
   h. If two lines are intersected by a third line called a **transversal,** the two lines are parallel if and only if the **alternate interior angles** are congruent.
   i. Curves are classified as **simple, simple closed,** or **closed.**
   j. The union of a simple closed curve and its interior is called a **plane region.**

   k. Plane regions are classified as **convex** or **nonconvex.**
   l. A **circle** is a special type of simple closed curve. **Radius, diameter, circumference, chord, tangent,** and **disk** are defined terms associated with circles.

3. **Polygons**
   a. A **polygon** is a simple closed curve that is the union of line segments.
   b. Two **sides of a polygon are adjacent** if they share a common vertex, and two **vertices of a polygon are adjacent** if they share a common side.
   c. Polygons are classified according to the number of sides: **triangle, quadrilateral, pentagon,** etc.
   d. A polygon is called a **regular polygon** if all its angles are congruent and all its sides are congruent.
   e. The first three regular polygons are the **equilateral triangle,** the **square,** and the **regular pentagon.**
   f. The number of degrees in the **central angle** of a regular polygon is 360 divided by the number of sides in the polygon.
   g. An arrangement of nonoverlapping figures that can be placed together to entirely cover a region is called a **tessellation.**
   h. The **equilateral triangle, square,** and **regular hexagon** are the only regular polygons that will tessellate.
   i. A tessellation with two or more noncongruent regular polygons in which each vertex is surrounded by the same arrangement of polygons is called a **semiregular tessellation.**

4. **Space figures**
   a. The angle between two intersecting planes is called a **dihedral angle.**

b. The surface of a three-dimensional figure whose sides are polygonal regions is called a **polyhedron.**

c. Polyhedra are classified as **convex** or **nonconvex.**

d. A convex polyhedron whose faces are congruent regular polygons and that has the same arrangement of polygons at each vertex is called a **regular polyhedron** or a **platonic solid.**

e. A polyhedron whose faces are two or more noncongruent regular polygons and that has the same arrangement of polygons at each vertex is called a **semiregular polyhedron.**

f. **Pyramids, prisms, cones, cylinders,** and **spheres** are common types of figures in space.

g. Points on the earth's surface are located by two systems of circles: **parallels of latitude** and **meridians of longitude.**

h. **Cylindrical, conic,** and **plane projections** are three types of maps of the earth's surface.

5. Symmetry

a. Plane figures can have **reflection symmetries** about lines and **rotation symmetries** about points.

b. A regular polygon with n sides has n reflection symmetries and n rotation symmetries.

c. Every plane figure with reflection symmetries also has rotation symmetries.

d. A plane figure may have rotation symmetries but no reflection symmetries.

e. Space figures have reflection symmetries about planes and rotation symmetries about axes.

CHAPTER TEST

1. These figures were obtained by folding rectangular sheets of paper.

(i)   (ii)  (iii)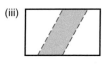

(iv)  (v)   (vi)

Write the numbers of the sheet(s) whose shaded region illustrates the polygon.

a. Hexagon **b.** Parallelogram
c. Trapezoid **d.** Equilateral triangle
e. Pentagon **f.** Isosceles triangle

2. Sketch an example of each of the following figures.
a. Nonconvex pentagon
b. Simple closed curve
c. Convex decagon
d. A closed curve that is not simple

3. Identify the following kinds of angles in the following figure.
a. Acute **b.** Reflex
c. Right **d.** Obtuse

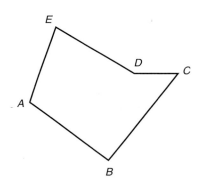

4. Determine whether the statements below are true or false.
a. Every square is a rectangle.
b. Some scalene triangles are right triangles.
c. Every parallelogram is a rectangle.
d. Every rectangle is a parallelogram.
e. Some right triangles are equilateral triangles.

5. Determine the number of degrees in each angle.
a. The central angle of a regular octagon
b. A vertex angle of a regular hexagon
c. An exterior angle of a regular pentagon

6. Determine whether each figure is a regular polygon. If it is not, state the condition it does not satisfy.

a.

b.

c.

d.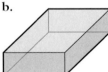

7. State whether each of the following polygons will tessellate.

   a. Regular octagon   **b.** Isosceles triangle
   c. Regular hexagon   **d.** Nonconvex quadrilateral
   e. Regular pentagon

8. Can an equilateral triangle, a square, and a regular octagon, all of whose sides have the same length, be used together for a semiregular tessellation? Explain your answer.

9. Name each of the following figures, and classify each as right or oblique.

a.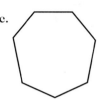

b.

c.

d.

e.

f.

10. Classify each figure as a polyhedron or a nonpolyhedron.

   a. Sphere   **b.** Prism
   c. Pyramid   **d.** Cone
   e. Cube   **f.** Dodecahedron

11. Determine the number of vertices in each of the following polyhedra.

   a. An icosahedron (it has 30 edges) *20 lines*
   b. A semiregular polyhedron with 14 faces and 36 edges

12. Sketch or describe each of the following plane figures.

   a. A figure with three lines of symmetry
   b. A figure with two rotation symmetries but no lines of symmetry
   c. A figure with five rotation symmetries and five reflection symmetries

13. Determine the number of planes of symmetry for each figure.

   a. A right prism whose base is a regular octagon
   b. A right cone
   c. A pyramid whose base is a regular pentagon

14. Finish sketching this figure so that it is symmetric about lines m and n.

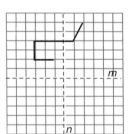

15. Determine the number of lines of symmetry and the number of rotation symmetries for each figure.

   a. A rectangle
   b. A regular heptagon
   c. An equilateral triangle
   d. A parallelogram

16. Seven points in a plane can be endpoints for a total of how many line segments?

17. What is the number of degrees in one vertex angle of a regular polygon with 40 sides?

18. Suppose the interior of a circle is to be partitioned into the maximum number of regions by line segments. One line will divide it into two regions; two lines will divide it into four regions; and three lines will divide it into seven regions.

1 line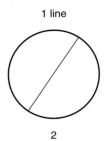

2 lines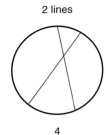

3 lines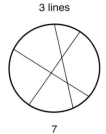

2   4   7

a. What is the maximum number of regions that can be created by four lines?
b. Find a pattern and use inductive reasoning to predict the maximum number of regions that can be created by 10 lines.

CHAPTER 10

MEASUREMENT

SPOTLIGHT ON TEACHING

Excerpts from NCTM's Standards for School Mathematics Grades 3–5*

As they study ways to measure geometric objects, students will have opportunities to make generalizations based on patterns. For example, consider the problem in Figure 5.5. Fourth graders might make a table (see Fig. 5.6) and note the iterative nature of the pattern. That is, there is a consistent relationship between the surface area of one tower and the next-bigger tower: "You add four to the previous number." Fifth graders could be challenged to justify a general rule with reference to the geometric model, for example, "The surface area is always four times the number of cubes plus two more because there are always four square units around each cube and one extra on each end of the tower." Once a relationship is established, students should be able to use it to answer questions like, "What is the surface area of a tower with fifty cubes?" or "How many cubes would there be in a tower with a surface area of 242 square units?"

Fig. **5.5.**
Finding surface areas of towers of cubes

Fig. **5.6.**
a table used in the "tower of cubes" problem

What is the surface area of each tower of cubes (include the bottom)? As the towers get taller, how does the surface area change?

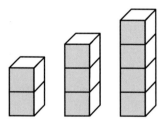

Number of cubes (N)	Surface area in square units. (S)
1	6
2	10
3	14
4	18

**Principles and Standards for School Mathematics* (Reston, VA: National Council of Teachers of Mathematics, 2000), p. 160.

633

MATH ACTIVITY 10.1

1 linear unit

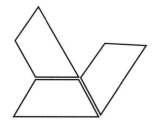

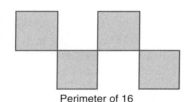

Perimeter of 16

PERIMETERS OF PATTERN BLOCK FIGURES

Materials: Pattern block pieces in the Manipulative Kit

1. If the edge of the pattern block square is 1 linear unit, then its perimeter is 4 linear units. Determine the perimeter of each of the other pattern blocks.

2. The pattern block figure at the left uses three trapezoids and has a perimeter of 11. Build pattern block figures that satisfy the following conditions. Show a sketch of each figure and label its perimeter.

   a. Four triangles, perimeter of 6

   b. Two hexagons, four triangles, perimeter of 10

   c. Four white and four blue parallelograms, perimeter of 10

3. The greatest perimeter of a figure with four pattern block squares is 16, and the least perimeter is 8. By using four pattern block squares, it is possible to build figures with perimeters for all the whole numbers from 8 to 16. Use your pattern block squares to build these figures. Sketch each figure and label its perimeter.

4. Use your pattern blocks to build a figure that has 14 triangles. What are the greatest and least possible perimeters for such figures? Repeat this activity for eight white parallelograms to determine the greatest and least possible perimeters and for six hexagons to determine the greatest and least possible perimeters.

5. What generalization do activities 3 and 4 suggest about the shape of figures for obtaining the greatest perimeter as compared to the least perimeter?

6. The following pattern block figures are the first four in a sequence. The perimeter of the second figure is 5. Find a pattern and predict the perimeter for the fifth figure in this sequence. Then build the fifth figure and check your prediction.

      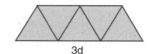   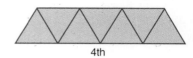

1st   2d   3d   4th

   a. What is the perimeter of the 30th figure in this sequence?

   b. Write an algebraic expression for the number of triangles in the nth figure of this sequence.

   c. Write an algebraic expression for the perimeter of the nth figure in this sequence.

SECTION 10.1

SYSTEMS OF MEASUREMENT

Stonehenge, Salisbury Plain, England, believed to have been constructed between 1900 and 1700 B.C.

Train A and train B are on the same track, headed toward each other. Both trains are traveling at 75 miles per hour. When the trains are 300 miles apart, a flea flies from the front of train A to the front of train B, then back to the front of train A, etc., returning back and forth until it is finally crushed by the colliding trains. How long is the flea in flight between the two trains?

Measurement is one of the most widely used applications of mathematics. It bridges two main areas of school mathematics—geometry and number.

Standards 2000, p. 103

The daily rotations of the earth, the monthly changes of the moon, and our planet's yearly orbits about the sun provided some of the first units of measure. The day was divided into parts by sunrise, midday, and sunset; the year was divided into seasons. Some believe that the construction of the prehistoric monument known as Stonehenge (Figure 10.1) in southern England, was an early attempt to measure the length of a year and its seasons. By studying the shadows of the stones, druid priests may have been able to predict the arrival of the summer solstice and the occurrence of eclipses. Eventually, the sundial was invented to measure smaller periods of time, and it remained the principal method of measuring time until the fifteenth century. Modern atomic clocks measure time to within 1 ten-millionth of a second.

Figure 10.1
Stonehenge as it might have looked 4000 years ago

In today's schools, children first learn about concepts of measure with nonstandard units. The *Curriculum and Evaluation Standards for School Mathematics* supports this practice:

If students' initial explorations use nonstandard units, they will develop some understandings about units and come to recognize the necessity of standard units in order to communicate.*

Later, students should be taught both the English and metric units because both types of units are used in the United States. In this section we will look at examples of nonstandard units of measure as well as units of measure in the *English system* and the *metric system*.

Nonstandard Units of Length

The process of **measuring** consists of three steps:

1. Select an object and an attribute to be measured (length, weight, temperature, etc.).

2. Choose a **unit of measure.**

3. Compare the unit to the object to determine the number of units, called the **measurement.**

Many of the first units of measure were parts of the body. The early Babylonian and Egyptian records indicate that the **span,** the **foot,** the **hand,** and the **cubit** were all units of measure (see Figure 10.2). The hand was used as a basic unit of measure by nearly all ancient civilizations and is the basis of the unit used today to measure the heights of horses. The height of a horse is measured by the number of hands from the ground to the horse's shoulders, and the hand has been standardized as 4 inches. Use the ruler on page 639 to compare the width of your hand to 4 inches.

| Span | Foot | Hand | Cubit |

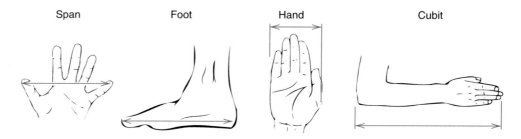

Figure 10.2

Elementary school experiences with measuring should provide the chance to relive our early measurement history through measuring activities with body parts.

Curriculum and Evaluation Standards for School Mathematics (Reston, VA: National Council of Teachers of Mathematics, 1989), p. 52.

Example A

In preschool through grade 2, students should begin their study of measurement by using nonstandard units. They should be encouraged to use a wide variety of objects, such as paper clips to measure length, square tiles to measure area, and paper cups to measure volume.

Standards 2000, p. 45

Choose two units of measure from Figure 10.2 with which to measure one of the following items: the length of a table (or desk), the height of a table, the length or width of a room, or the length of this book. List a few observations from this activity.

Solution   The measurements will vary depending on the units chosen. The smaller the unit, the larger the measure; and the larger the unit, the smaller the measure. The measurement may not be a whole number. Two people may both choose the same unit, such as their hands, and obtain different measurements.

Evidence of other early units of measure still exists today. Seeds and stones were common units for measuring weight. The word **carat,** which is the name of a unit of weight for precious stones, was derived from the word for the carob seeds of Mediterranean evergreen trees. *Carat* also expresses the fineness of a gold alloy. "Fourteen carat" means 14 parts of gold to 10 parts of alloy, or that 14 out of 24 parts are pure gold. The **grain,** a unit based on the average weight of grains of wheat, is another unit of weight used by jewelers. Until recently the **stone** (14 pounds) was a common unit of weight in England and Canada. A newborn baby would weigh about one-half stone.

Such historical examples of units are helpful in understanding the concept of measure and suggest that nonstandard units of measure can be readily invented.

Example B

1. Select an object to be used as a nonstandard unit of measure (paper clip, pencil, pen, handspan, etc.) to measure the length or width of a table, desk, chair, or other object near you. First guess, then check your answer.

2. Use the length of the following safety pin to measure the pencil.

Solution   2. The pencil is approximately $5\frac{1}{2}$ safety pin units long.

It is possible to find the **length** of an object by counting the number of times a chosen unit can be marked off on the object. Once a unit has been chosen, we assign it a length of 1.

Since it is unlikely that the chosen unit will be marked off a whole number of times, three choices are possible for dealing with the part that is left over: (1) Estimate what fraction of the unit is left over, (2) create a smaller unit, or (3) subdivide the unit into an equal number of smaller parts to measure the part that is left over.

Example C

Measure the length of the pen on the next page, using each of the following units.

1. The length of the large paper clip

2. The length of the small paper clip

3. The length of the plastic twist-tie. The twist-tie has been bent into four equal parts.

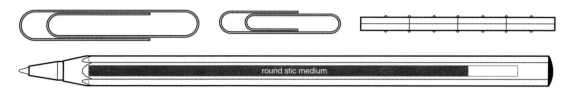

Solution   1. The pen is approximately 3 large paper-clip units long.   **2.** The pen is approximately $4\frac{1}{2}$ small paper clip units long.   **3.** The pen is approximately $2\frac{3}{4}$ twist-tie units long.

English Units

LENGTH   As societies evolved, measures became more complex. Since most units of measure had developed independently of one another, it was difficult to change from one unit to another. The English system, for example, arose from a hodgepodge of nonstandard units: The **inch** was the length of 3 barleycorns placed end to end, the **foot** was the length of a human foot, and the **yard** was the distance from the nose to the end of an outstretched arm. In the twelfth century, the yard was established by royal decree of King Henry I of England as the distance from his nose to his thumb (Figure 10.3). Gradually, the English system of measurements was standardized. The common units for length are shown in Figure 10.4.

Figure 10.3

ENGLISH UNITS FOR LENGTH

Inch	in	$\frac{1}{12}$ foot
Foot	ft	12 inches
Yard	yd	3 feet
Mile	mi	5280 feet

Figure 10.4

Example D

Use the ruler pictured on the next page to answer these questions.

1. What is the length from the tip of your index finger (or thumb) to the first joint?

2. What is the measure of the pencil in Example B?

3. What is the measure of the pen in Example C?

4. Write the number indicated by each arrow above the ruler.

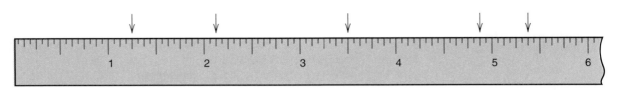

Solution   **1.** On the average adult hand, this length is approximately 1 inch.   **2.** Approximately $5\frac{7}{8}$ inches   **3.** Approximately $5\frac{9}{16}$ inches   **4.** $1\frac{1}{4}$; $2\frac{1}{8}$; $3\frac{1}{2}$; $4\frac{7}{8}$; $5\frac{3}{8}$

Research Statement

The 7th national mathematics assessment found that fourth-grade students have difficulty with all items that asked them to use a ruler to measure an object or to draw a shape with particular dimensions.

Martin and Strutchens 2000

VOLUME   There are two methods of measuring volume in the English system. One uses cubes whose edges have lengths of 1 inch, 1 foot, or 1 yard. For example, a cubic inch is the volume of a cube whose edges are each 1 inch long (Figure 10.5).

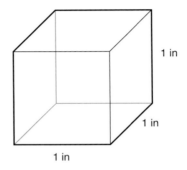

Figure 10.5

The other method of measuring volume uses measures that evolved from an ancient doubling system. Five of these measures are listed in Figure 10.6.

ENGLISH UNITS FOR VOLUME

Ounce	oz	$\frac{1}{8}$ cup
Cup	c	8 ounces
Pint	pt	2 cups
Quart	qt	2 pints
Gallon	gal	4 quarts

Figure 10.6

One inconvenience of the English system is that it is difficult to convert from one unit to another.

Example E

One gallon is equal to 231 cubic inches. Determine the number of cubic inches in each of the following measures.

1. 1 quart   **2.** 1 cup

Solution   **1.** Since 4 quarts = 1 gallon and $231 \div 4 = 57.75$, there are 57.75 cubic inches in 1 quart. **2.** Since 4 cups = 1 quart and $57.75 \div 4 = 14.4375$, there are 14.4375 cubic inches in 1 cup.

UNITS OF VOLUME

2 mouthfuls	= 1 jigger
2 jiggers	= 1 jack (jackpot)
2 jacks	= 1 jill
2 jills	= 1 cup
2 cups	= 1 pint
2 pints	= 1 quart
2 quarts	= 1 pottle
2 pottles	= 1 gallon
2 gallons	= 1 pail

The *mouthful* is a unit of measure for volume used by the ancient Egyptians. It was also part of an English doubling system: 2 mouthfuls equal 1 jigger; 2 jiggers equal 1 jack; 2 jacks equal 1 jill; etc. The familiar nursery rhyme that begins "Jack and Jill went up the hill" mentions three units of volume: the *jack,* the *jill,* and the *pail.* The rhyme was composed as a protest against King Charles I of England for his taxation of the jacks, or jackpots, of liquor sold in taverns. Charles's success at accumulating revenue from the taxes on liquor is the origin of the expression *to hit the jackpot.* The phrase *broke his crown* in the nursery rhyme refers to Charles I. Not only did he lose his crown, but also he lost his head in Britain's civil war not many years after he began taxing jackpots.*

*A. Kline, *The World of Measurements* (New York: Simon and Schuster, 1975), pp. 32–39.

WEIGHT   The English system has two systems for measuring weight: one for precious metals, in which there is 12 ounces in a pound **(troy unit)**; and one for everyday use, in which there is 16 ounces in a pound **(avoirdupois unit).** We will use the avoirdupois unit. The common English units for weight are shown in Figure 10.7.

ENGLISH UNITS FOR WEIGHT

Ounce	oz	$\frac{1}{16}$ pound
Pound	lb	16 ounces
Ton	tn	2000 pounds

Figure 10.7

Example F

1. 14.3 pounds equals how many ounces?

2. 3200 pounds equals how many tons?

Solution   **1.** 228.8 ounces ($14.3 \times 16 = 228.8$)   **2.** 1.6 tons ($3200 \div 2000 = 1.6$)

TEMPERATURE   In 1714, Gabriel Fahrenheit, a German instrument maker, invented the first mercury thermometer. The lowest temperature he was able to attain with a mixture of ice and salt he called zero degrees (0°). He used the normal temperature of the human body, which he selected to be 96 degrees (96°), for the upper point of his scale. (With today's more accurate thermometers, we know that human body temperature is about 98.6° on the Fahrenheit scale.) On this scale of temperatures, water freezes at 32° and boils at 212°. This scale is called the **Fahrenheit scale** (Figure 10.8).

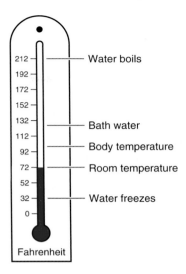

Figure 10.8

Metric Units

In 1790, in the midst of the French Revolution, the metric system was developed by the French Academy of Sciences. To create a system of "natural standards," the scientists subdivided the length of a meridian from the equator to the north pole into 10 million parts to obtain the basic unit of length, the **meter** (Figure 10.9).

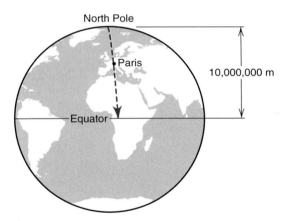

Figure 10.9

Once a basic unit is established in the metric system, smaller units are obtained by dividing the basic unit into 10, 100, and 1000 parts. Larger units are 10, 100, and 1000 times the basic unit. These units are named by attaching prefixes (Figure 10.10) to the name of the basic unit. The prefixes marked with asterisks are commonly used in everyday nonscientific measurement.

METRIC PREFIXES

Greek prefixes	kilo*	1000
	hecto	100
	deka	10
Latin prefixes	deci*	1/10
	centi*	1/100
	milli*	1/1000

Figure 10.10

There are more prefixes for naming both larger and smaller units, each new unit being 10 times or one-tenth the previous one. For example, **mega** is the prefix meaning *million,* and **micro** is the prefix meaning *one-millionth.* This relationship between units is a major advantage of the metric system. Conversion from one type of unit to another can be accomplished by multiplying or dividing by powers of 10, which, since we use a base-ten numeration system, can be accomplished by moving decimal points.

LENGTH   Figure 10.11 shows how the metric system prefixes are used with the meter to obtain other metric units. Notice that as we move from the millimeter to the kilometer, each unit is 10 times greater than the preceding unit. (The common lengths are marked with asterisks.) Several units of length which are less than a millimeter are shown on page 648.

METRIC UNITS FOR LENGTH

Kilometer*	km	1000 m
Hectometer	hm	100 m
Dekameter	dam	10 m
Meter*	m	1 m
Decimeter	dm	1/10 m
Centimeter*	cm	1/100 m
Millimeter*	mm	1/1000 m

Figure 10.11

Measurement lends itself especially well to the use of concrete materials. In fact, it is unlikely that children can gain a deep understanding of measurement without handling materials, making comparisons physically, and measuring with tools.

Standards 2000, p. 44

To acquire a feeling for the metric units of length, it is helpful to visualize objects having a given length. A **meter** is roughly the distance from the floor to the waist of an adult or the distance from one shoulder to the fingertips of the opposite outstretched arm, as shown in Figure 10.12. The distance from the floor to a doorknob is usually a little less than 1 meter. A meter might be used to measure the length of a house, a car, or an athletic field.

Figure 10.12

(a)   (b)   (c)

A **centimeter** is $\frac{1}{100}$ meter. This is the common unit for such body measurements as height, waist, and hat size. The width of a middle school student's thumbnail might be approximately 1 centimeter, as shown in Figure 10.13a. If the thumb is extended, as shown in part b, the length from the tip of the index finger to the bottom of the V shape is approximately 1 decimeter (10 centimeters).

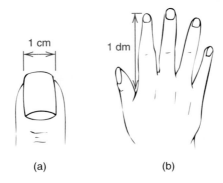

Figure 10.13   (a)   (b)

Occasionally we need a measure smaller than a centimeter. One-tenth of a centimeter is a **millimeter.** The thickness of a pencil lead is approximately 2 millimeters. The ruler shown in Example G has a length between 12 and 13 centimeters, and each centimeter is divided into 10 millimeters.

Example G

1. What is your handspan to the nearest centimeter?

2. Which of your finger widths is approximately 1 centimeter?

3. What is the diameter of a penny to the nearest millimeter?

Since the customary English system of measurement is still prevalent in the United States, students should learn both customary and metric systems and should know some rough equivalences between the metric and customary systems.

Standards 2000, p. 45

Solution   1. The handspans of adults usually range from 18 to 23 centimeters.   2. The little-finger width for an adult is close to 1 centimeter.   3. The diameter of a penny is 1 centimeter and 9 millimeters, or 1.9 centimeters.

A **kilometer** is 1000 meters. Distances between cities and countries (and even planets) are measured in kilometers. A kilometer is shorter than a mile, approximately three-fifths of a mile, as indicated in Figure 10.14.

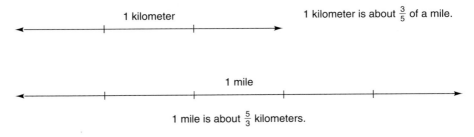

Figure 10.14

Example H

1. If a person walks 3 miles per hour (1 mile every 20 minutes), approximately how many kilometers per hour does the person walk?

2. If a car is traveling 90 kilometers per hour, what is its speed in miles per hour?

Solution   1. Since 1 mile $\approx \frac{5}{3}$ kilometers, 3 miles is 3 times $\frac{5}{3}$ kilometer:

$$3 \times \frac{5}{3} = \frac{15}{3} = 5$$

So the person will walk approximately 5 kilometers per hour.

2. Since 1 kilometer $\approx \frac{3}{5}$ mile, 90 kilometers is 90 times $\frac{3}{5}$ mile:

$$90 \times \frac{3}{5} = \frac{270}{5} = 54$$

So the speed of the car is approximately 54 miles per hour.

VOLUME   The basic unit of volume in the metric system is the **liter.** A liter is slightly larger than a quart. The capacities of fuel tanks, aquariums, and milk containers are measured in liters. For volumes that are less than a liter, such as those of small bottles or jars, the **milliliter** ($\frac{1}{1000}$ liter) is the common measure. Larger volumes, such as a community's reserve water supply, are measured in **kiloliters** (1000 liters).

Figure 10.15 lists the metric system units for volume, which are shown in relationship to the liter. (The common volumes are marked with asterisks.)

METRIC UNITS FOR VOLUME

Kiloliter*	kL	1000 L
Hectoliter	hL	100 L
Dekaliter	daL	10 L
Liter*	L	1 L
Deciliter	dL	1/10 L
Centiliter	cL	1/100 L
Milliliter*	mL	1/1000 L

Figure 10.15

Example I

1. 1.3 liters equals how many milliliters?

2. 245 milliliters equals how many liters?

3. 3487 liters equals how many kiloliters?

Solution   1. 1300 milliliters   2. .245 liters   3. 3.487 kiloliters

Notice in Example I how convenient it is to change from one unit of volume to another. Since 1 liter equals 1000 milliliters, the number of milliliters in 1.3 liters is 1.3 × 1000. Similarly, to change from 245 milliliters to liters, we divide by 1000. With metric units, conversions can be done mentally by multiplying and dividing by powers of 10.

A liter is the volume of a cube whose sides each have a length of 10 centimeters (part a in Figure 10.16). Such a cube is called a **cubic decimeter.** The dimensions of the small cube in part b are each 1 centimeter. This cube is called a **cubic centimeter.**

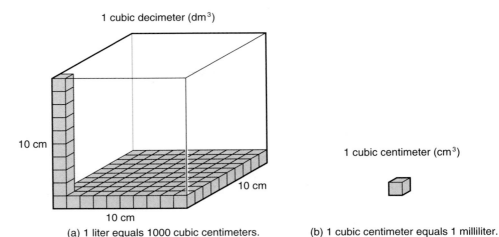

1 cubic decimeter (dm^3)

10 cm

10 cm

10 cm

1 cubic centimeter (cm^3)

Figure 10.16

(a) 1 liter equals 1000 cubic centimeters.

(b) 1 cubic centimeter equals 1 milliliter.

Imagine filling the large cube in Figure 10.16 with the smaller cubes. The floor of the large cube is 10 centimeters × 10 centimeters and can be covered by 100 cubic centimeters. Since 10 layers of 100 cubes will fill the large cube, 1 liter has a volume of 1000 cubic centimeters.

Recall that 1 milliliter is $\frac{1}{1000}$ liter. Since a cubic centimeter is also $\frac{1}{1000}$ liter, 1 cubic centimeter equals 1 milliliter.

Example J

1. 45 cubic centimeters equals how many milliliters?

2. 1.35 liters equals how many cubic centimeters?

3. 800 cubic centimeters equals how many liters?

Solution   **1.** 45 milliliters   **2.** 1350 cubic centimeters   **3.** .8 liter

MASS   In the metric system the word *mass* and *weight* are different, the difference being due to the effect of gravity. We can think of **mass** as the amount of matter that makes up the object. **Weight,** however, is the force that gravity exerts on the object, and it varies with different locations from the center of the earth. An object will weigh more at sea level than on top of a mountain, because the earth's gravity exerts a greater force on it at lower altitudes. The same object in a space-ship would weigh practically nothing. Yet in each of these three locations, the amount of material in the object hasn't changed! Because of this situation, the mass of an object is a measurement that does not change as the object is moved farther from the center of the earth. At sea level the mass and weight of an object are essentially equal, and the variation in an object's weight between sea level and our highest mountains is very small (.1 percent difference).

The basic unit of mass in the metric system is the **gram.** This is a relatively small measure, approximately the mass of a medium-size paper clip or a dollar bill. Many items in grocery stores are measured in grams. Heavier objects are measured in kilograms. A **kilogram** is 1000 grams. To acquire a feeling for this amount, it helps to know the approximate metric measurements of a few objects.

Example K

Use the fact that 1 kilogram is equivalent to approximately 2.2 pounds to determine each mass in kilograms.

1. Your mass

2. The mass of a 10-pound bag of potatoes

3. The mass of 1 pound of hamburger

Solution   1. A person who weighs 125 pounds has a mass of approximately 57 kilograms.   2. Approximately 4.5 kilograms   3. Approximately .5 kilogram

Figure 10.17 shows the metric units for mass and their relationships to the gram. (The common measures are marked with asterisks.) The metric ton, not shown in this table, is 1000 kilograms.

METRIC UNITS FOR MASS

Kilogram*	kg	1000 g
Hectogram	hg	100 g
Dekagram	dag	10 g
Gram*	g	1 g
Decigram	dg	1/10 g
Centigram	cg	1/100 g
Milligram*	mg	1/1000 g

Figure 10.17

A gram is the mass of 1 cubic centimeter of water. (Since water contracts and expands as its temperature changes, the technical definition calls for water to be at its densest state.) Since 1 cubic centimeter equals 1 milliliter ($\frac{1}{1000}$ liter), 1 milliliter of water has a mass of 1 gram. This simple relationship between mass, length, and volume (see Figure 10.18) is another advantage of the metric system over the English system.

Figure 10.18

Example L

1. 1 liter of water has a mass of how many kilograms?

2. 48.2 milliliters of water has a mass of how many grams?

3. 1500 cubic centimeters of water has a mass of how many kilograms?

Solution   1. 1 kilogram   2. 48.2 grams   3. 1.5 kilograms

TEMPERATURE   In 1742, about 50 years before the development of the metric system, the Swedish astronomer Anders Celsius devised a temperature scale by selecting 0 as the freezing point of water and 100 as the boiling point. He called this system the **Centigrade** (100 grades) scale thermometer, but it came to be called the **Celsius scale** in his honor. Some examples of temperatures on the Celsius scale are shown in Figure 10.19.

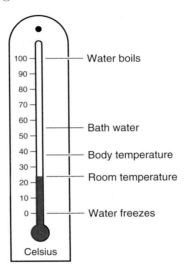

Figure 10.19

Heat is related to the motion of molecules: the faster their motion, the greater the heat. All movement of molecules stops at ⁻273.15° Celsius. The British mathematician and physicist William Thomson, known as Lord Kelvin, called this temperature *absolute zero* and devised the **Kelvin scale,** which increases 1 unit for each increase of 1° Celsius. Thus 273.15 on the Kelvin scale is 0° on the Celsius scale. Both the Celsius and Kelvin scales are part of the metric system. The Celsius scale is used for weather reports, cooking temperatures, and other day-to-day needs; the Kelvin scale is used for scientific purposes.

Example M

1. 270.15 on the Kelvin scale equals how many degrees on the Celsius scale?

2. 100° on the Celsius scale equals how many units on the Kelvin scale?

Solution   **1.** ⁻3°   **2.** 373.15

HISTORICAL

HIGHLIGHT

The metric system was a radical change for the French people and met with widespread resistance. Finally in 1837, the French government passed a law forbidding the use of any measures other than those of the new system. Steadily, other nations adopted the metric system. In 1866 the Congress of the United States enacted a law stating that it was lawful to employ the weights and measures of the metric system and that no contract or dealing could be found invalid because of the use of metric units. Today, less than 200 years after its creation, the metric system has been adopted by almost every country except the United States. The U.S. Metric Conversion Act of 1975 set a policy of voluntary conversion with no overall timetable.

Precision and Small Measurements

The objects in Figure 10.20 are DNA and ribosome molecules in an active chromosome. Each DNA molecule is so small that 100,000 of them lined up side by side will fit into the thickness of this page.

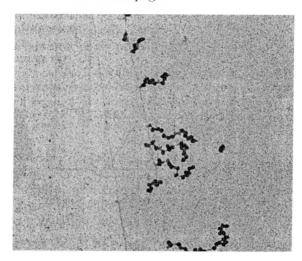

Figure 10.20
DNA and ribosome molecules

In the middle grades, students should also develop an understanding of precision and measurement error. By examining and discussing how objects are measured and how the results are expressed, teachers can help their students to understand that a measurement is precise only to one-half of the smallest unit used in the measurement.

Standards 2000, p. 243

Measurements with this type of precision are possible with the transmission electron microscope. More recently, with the development of the field ion microscope, scientists have been able to view atoms that are one-tenth the size of DNA molecules. The scale in Figure 10.21 shows nine measures in decreasing order from a centimeter down to an **angstrom**, each being one-tenth of the size of the preceding one.

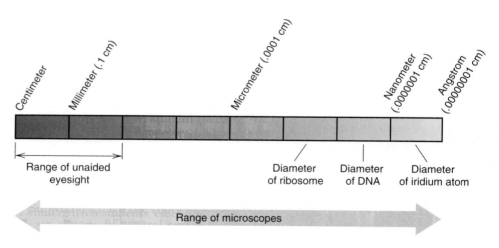

Figure 10.21

The amount of precision that is possible in taking measurements depends on the smallest unit of the measuring instrument. Using a centimeter ruler, we can determine that the paper clip in part (a) of Figure 10.22 has a length of just over 3 centimeters. If a ruler is marked off in millimeters, as in part b, the length of the paper clip can be measured as about 32 millimeters, or 3.2 centimeters. With instruments that are calibrated in smaller units, we might measure the length of this paper clip to be 3.24, 3.241, or 3.2412 centimeters. It would never be possible, however, to measure its length or the length of any other object exactly.

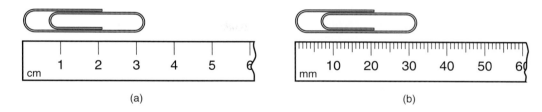

Figure 10.22   (a)   (b)

If the smallest unit on the measuring instrument is a millimeter, then the measurement can be approximated to the nearest millimeter. This means that the measurement could be off by $\frac{1}{2}$ millimeter, either too much or too little. In general, the **precision** of any measurement is to within one-half of the smallest unit of measure being used.

Conversely, if a measurement is given as 14.5 centimeters, we can assume that it was measured to the nearest .1 centimeter and that it is closer to 14.5 centimeters than to 14.4 centimeters or 14.6 centimeters. In other words, it is 14.5 $\pm$ .05 centimeters, as shown in Figure 10.23 (.05 is one-half of one-tenth).

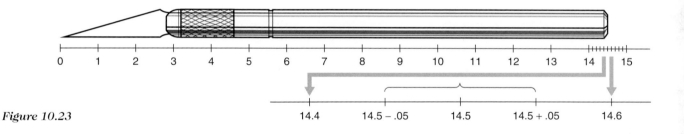

Figure 10.23

Writing a measurement as 7.62 centimeters indicates that the measurement has been obtained to the nearest .01 centimeter and may be off by as much as .005 centimeter (.005 is one-half of one-hundredth). Sometimes you will see a measurement such as 15.0 centimeters. A zero following the decimal point means that the measurement is accurate to the nearest .1 centimeter; 15.0 centimeters implies more precision than does 15 centimeters.

Example N

Find the minimum and maximum measurements associated with each of the following measurements.

1. An oven temperature of 246.3° Celsius

2. A baseball bat with length of 82 centimeters

3. A bag of flour that is labeled 2.27 kilograms

Solution   **1.** One-half of one-tenth is .05, so the temperature is between 246.25 and 246.35° Celsius. **2.** One-half of 1 is .5, so the length of the bat is between 81.5 and 82.5 centimeters.   **3.** One-half of .01 is .005, so the weight of the flour is between 2.265 and 2.275 kilograms.

International System of Units

The **International System of Units** is a modern version of the metric system that was established by international agreement. Officially abbreviated as SI (for Système, International d'Unités), this system is built on the metric units discussed previously, but it also includes units for time **(second)**, electric current **(ampere)**, light intensity **(candela)**, and the molecular weight of a substance **(mole).** This system provides a logical and interconnected framework for all measurements. To enable the type of precision needed in science today, the meter is now defined in SI units as the distance light travels in 1/299,792,458 second, and 1 second of time is defined as the time required for a wave of the cesium-133 atom to complete 9,192,631,770 cycles.

Problem-Solving Application

PROBLEM

This standard set of 11 brass metric measures can be used with a balance scale to weigh any object whose mass is a whole number of grams from 1 to 1600. How can these measures be used to determine that an object has a mass of 917 grams?

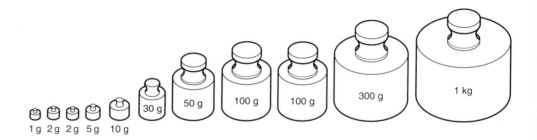

1g 2g 2g 5g 10g   30 g   50 g   100 g   100 g   300 g   1 kg

Understanding the Problem   The object to be weighed must be placed on one side of the scale, as shown. The problem is that the 1-kilogram measure is greater than 917 grams and the sum of the remaining 10 measures is less than 917 grams. **Question 1:** What is the sum of the remaining 10 brass measures?

Devising a Plan   One approach is to *guess and check* by experimenting with the brass measures. If the kilogram measure is placed on the right side of the scale, the scale will tip down on the right. **Question 2:** What additional brass measures will then be needed on the left side of the scale for a balance?

Carrying Out the Plan   The left side of the scale will need measures totaling 83 grams, together with the object weighing 917 grams, to balance 1 kilogram. **Question 3:** How can measures totaling 83 grams be obtained from the set of brass measures?

Looking Back   The key to solving this problem is to place brass measures on both sides of the scale. This is not always necessary. For example, an object with a mass of 18 grams can be balanced by placing measures of 10, 5, 2, and 1 gram on one side of the scale. **Question 4:** What is the lightest object whose mass is a whole number of grams for which brass measures must be placed on both sides of the scale to determine the mass of the object?

Answers to Questions 1–4   **1.** 600 grams   **2.** 83 grams   **3.** 50 grams, 30 grams, 2 grams, 1 gram
4. *Forming an organized list,* beginning with the smallest brass measures, shows that any object whose mass is between 1 and 20 grams can be measured by placing brass measures on just one side of the scale. The first object that requires the brass measures on both sides of the scale is an object whose mass is 21 grams.

MASS OF OBJECTS (GRAMS)	SETS OF MEASURES (GRAMS)
1	1
2	2
3	2, 1
4	2, 2
.	.
.	.
.	.
19	10, 5, 2, 2
20	10, 5, 2, 2, 1

EXERCISES AND PROBLEMS 10.1

Although almost all educators agree that we should not teach the metric system by converting back and forth from English units to metric units, it is sometimes helpful to make rough comparisons between the two systems. Make the comparisons in exercises 1 and 2.

1. **a.** What is a 55-mile-per-hour speed limit approximately equal to in kilometers per hour?
    b. The distance from Jersey City to New York is 24 miles. Approximately what is this distance in kilometers?

2. **a.** It has been suggested that the speed limit be set at 100 kilometers per hour. Approximately what would this speed limit be in miles per hour?
    b. A 10-kilometer race is approximately how many miles?

Measure the length of the scissors shown in the figure, using each of the units in exercises 3 and 4.

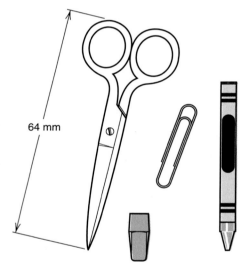

64 mm

3. **a.** The length of the paper clip
    b. The length of the eraser

4. **a.** The length of the crayon
    b. If you had to use one of these three units to measure other lengths, which do you think would consistently give you the most "accurate" measurements? Explain.

5. Express the amount the weight lifter at the top of the next column is raising in each of the following units.
    a. Grams
    b. Milligrams
    c. Pounds (approximately)

THERE WE ARE FOLKS, **202.5** KILOGRAMS!

6. Estimate each of the following to the nearest indicated unit. Then use the metric ruler on page 643 to check your estimate.
    a. The thickness of pencil lead (millimeters)
    b. The width of a pencil (millimeters)
    c. The diameter of a dime (millimeters)
    d. The length of a dollar bill (centimeters)
    e. The width of a standard sheet of typing paper (centimeters)

7. Estimate each item in the preceding exercise, using inches and fractions or decimals for parts of an inch. Then check your estimate by using the inch ruler on page 639.

Recipes that use the English system of measurement include teaspoons (tsp) and tablespoons (tbsp or T) as units of measure. Complete exercises 8 and 9, using 16 tablespoons = 1 cup and 3 teaspoons = 1 tablespoon.

8. **a.** $\frac{1}{2}$ cup = _____ tablespoons
    b. $\frac{1}{3}$ cup = _____ teaspoons
    c. 2 quarts = _____ cups

9. **a.** 1 gallon = _____ pints
    b. 1 gallon = _____ cups
    c. $\frac{1}{2}$ pint = _____ cups

Complete the statements in exercises 10 and 11.

10. **a.** 1 mile = _____ yards
    b. 4800 pounds = _____ tons
    c. 7.5 gallons = _____ quarts

11. a. 12.6 feet = _____ yards
  b. 56 ounces (oz) = _____ pounds
  c. 40 cups = _____ gallons

12. List the following units in order of increasing length: meter, inch, centimeter, kilometer, yard, foot, mile, hectometer.

Choose the most realistic measure for each item in exercises 13 and 14.

13. a. Length of a ski: 200 millimeters, 200 centimeters, 200 meters
  b. Mass of a person: 75 milligrams, 75 grams, 75 kilograms
  c. Volume of an automobile gas tank: 48 milliliters, 48 liters, 48 kiloliters

14. a. Mass of a toothpick: 450 milligrams, 450 grams, 450 kilograms
  b. Height of the Eiffel Tower: 300 centimeters, 300 meters, 300 kilometers
  c. Amount of blood in the human body: 4 milliliters, 4 liters, 4 kiloliters

15. The first unit of measure of which there are historical records is the cubit, which is the distance from elbow to fingertips. This unit was used more than 4000 years ago by the Egyptians and Babylonians. The ancient Egyptian cubit shown below measures 52.5 centimeters and is preserved in the Louvre in Paris.

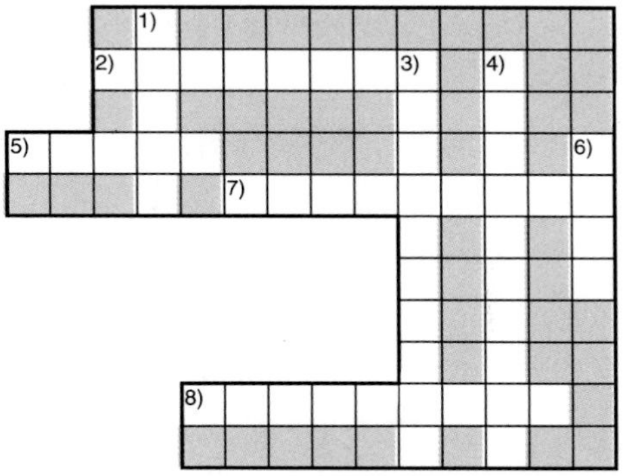

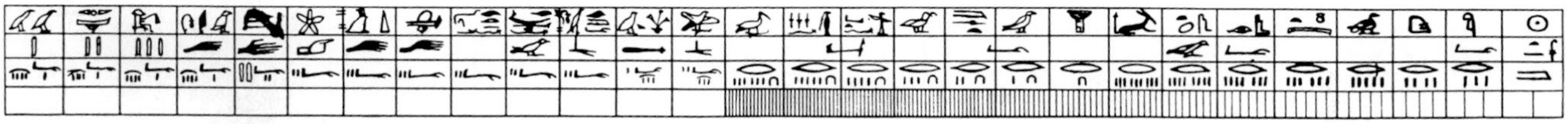

  a. How does the Egyptian cubit compare in length with your cubit? What is the difference to the nearest centimeter?
  b. The dimensions of Noah's Ark, as described in the Bible in the sixth chapter of Genesis, are listed in the table below. Convert these measures to the nearest meter, using the length of the Egyptian cubit. Then convert the measures to the nearest foot (2.54 centimeters = 1 inch).

	CUBITS	METERS	FEET
Length	300		
Breadth	50		
Height	30		

16. Complete the crossword puzzle by determining the most appropriate metric unit to use for the measurement in each clue.

Across
2. Mass of a truck
5. Length of a building
7. Volume of a city water supply
8. Length of a river

Down
1. Volume of a gasoline tank
3. Volume of a perfume bottle
4. Width of a television screen
6. Mass of a 50-cent coin

17. Complete the statement in each clue, and write your answers in the cross-number puzzle, placing one digit in each square.

Across

1. 16.5 cm = _____ mm
4. 3.15 L of water has mass of approximately _____ g
5. .12 L = _____ mL
8. _____ kg = 92,000 g
9. _____ mL of water has mass of approximately 7.920 kg
10. _____ m = 5.55 km

Down

2. 632,000 L = _____ kL
3. 4.5 km = _____ m
6. _____ g is the approximate mass of 432 mL of water
7. _____ kg is the approximate mass of 190 L of water
8. _____ mg = .9 g
9. .75 m = _____ cm

Measurements can be estimated by comparing the unknown quantity with familiar or known measurements. Obtain the estimations in exercises 18 and 19, using the given information.

18. a. Estimate the volume of the glass.

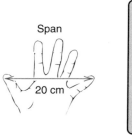

1000 ml

b. Estimate the length and width of the TV screen.

Span

20 cm

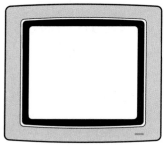

c. Estimate the distance between two towns if a car travels from one town to the other at an average rate of 55 miles per hour and it takes approximately $1\frac{1}{2}$ hours to make the trip.

19. a. Estimate the mass of a dozen eggs, including the mass of the carton.

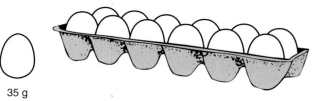

35 g

b. Estimate the length of a garden hose if it is stretched out in a straight line from the house to the flower beds and an adult takes 30 walking steps from the faucet at the house to the end of the hose.

c. Estimate the height of the room shown in the photograph below, assuming that the man is 6 feet tall.

20. The Celsius (C) and Fahrenheit (F) temperature scales are related by the following formulas:

$$C = \frac{5(F - 32)}{9} \quad \text{and} \quad F = \frac{9C}{5} + 32$$

Four temperatures are described in parts a through d below and are indicated on the thermometers on the following page. Convert each temperature to Fahrenheit or Celsius (to the nearest .1°).

a. Highest recorded temperature, Libya, 1922
b. At this body temperature, see a doctor
c. At this temperature, check your car's antifreeze
d. Lowest recorded temperature, Antarctica, 1960

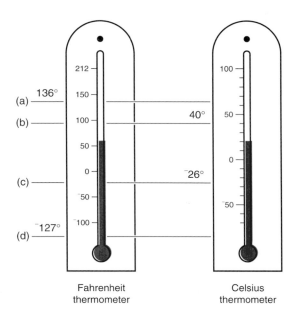

(a) 136°
(b)
(c)
(d) ‾127°

40°

‾26°

Fahrenheit
thermometer

Celsius
thermometer

21. The strand of hair in the following photograph has been magnified 200 times
   a. Measure the thickness of the magnified strand of hair to the nearest millimeter.
   b. Use the results of part a to determine the thickness of a strand of human hair.
   c. How thick is a strand of human hair in micrometers? (1000 micrometers = 1 millimeter.)
   d. Some of the wires in a microcircuit have a thickness (diameter) of 1 micrometer. A human hair is how many times the thickness of a microcircuit wire?

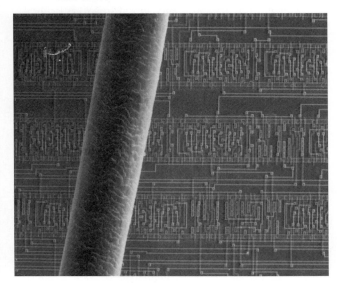

A scanning electron micrograph magnified 200 times shows a microcircuit and a human hair.

22.

Ready or not – metric system is coming

LOS ANGELES (AP) – The mile run and the 100-yard dash, two of track's glamor races, may soon join the horse-drawn carriage and the five-cent beer as relics of days gone by.

The United States soon will be forced to switch from measuring track meets in yards to measuring them in meters. The Amateur Athletic Union and the National Collegiate Athletic Association have long fought such a switch, but both agree it is becoming mandatory.

Under an international rule which went into effect on June 1, an athlete who runs a race in yards may not qualify for the Olympics, whether he sets a record or not.

As a result of an international rule that went into effect in 1975, track events traditionally measured in yards and miles are now measured in meters, as shown in the next table. Using the fact that 1 yard ≈ 91.5 centimeters, determine whether the metric event is longer or shorter, and compute the difference in meters to the nearest tenth.

OLD RACE	NEW RACE	DIFFERENCE
a. 100 yards	100 meters	_____
b. 220 yards	200 meters	_____
c. 440 yards	400 meters	_____
d. 880 yards	800 meters	_____
e. 1 mile	1500 meters	_____

23. A measurement given to a certain unit may be off by as much as $\pm\frac{1}{2}$ of that unit. For example, a can of pineapple juice labeled 1.32 liters is measured to the nearest .01 liter. Its volume is greater than the minimum of 1.315 liters and less than the maximum of 1.325 liters. Find the minimum and maximum numbers associated with each of the following measurements.
   a. A two-speed heavy-duty washing machine with mass of 112 kilograms (to the nearest kilogram)
   b. A patient's temperature of 38.2°C (to the nearest .1°C)
   c. A stereo speaker with a width of 48.3 centimeters (to the nearest .1 centimeter)
   d. A 3-day-old baby has a mass of 3.46 kilograms (to the nearest .01 kilogram)

REASONING AND PROBLEM SOLVING

24. Each of the grocery store items in the photograph is measured either by mass or by volume. Determine which of the following measures goes with each item: 946 milliliters, 4.536 kilograms, 567 grams, 384 milliliters, 40 grams, 59 milliliters.

25. A shopper purchased the following items: tomatoes, 754 grams; soup, 772 grams; potatoes, 3.45 kilograms; sugar, 4.62 kilograms; raisins, 425 grams; vegetable shortening, 1.361 kilograms; and baking powder, 218 grams. What was the total mass of this purchase in kilograms?

26. A curtain for a single window can be made from a piece of material that is 1 meter wide and 120 centimeter long. Suppose you need two curtains per window and have six windows. If the curtain material comes in rolls 1 meter wide, how many meters of length will be needed to make curtains for all six windows?

27. The following amounts of gasoline have been charged on a credit card: 38.2, 26.8, 54.3, 44.7, and 34.0 liters. The price of gasoline is 32 cents per liter.
    a. Use estimation techniques and mental arithmetic to approximate the total cost of the gasoline.
    b. Use a calculator to compute the exact cost.

28. A car owner has her tank filled and notices that the odometer reads 14,368.7 kilometers. After a trip in the country, it takes 34.5 liters to fill the tank, and the odometer reads 14,651.6. How many kilometers per liter is this car getting?

29. A 24-kilogram bag of birdseed is priced at $16.88. If 75 grams of this feed is put in a bird feeder each day, how many days will it be before the bag of seed is empty? Rounded to the nearest penny, how much does it cost to feed the birds each day?

30. The recipe for a fruit punch calls for these ingredients: 3.5 liters of unsweetened pineapple juice, 400 milliliters of orange juice, 300 milliliters of lemon juice, 4 liters of ginger ale, 2.5 liters of soda water, 500 milliliters of mashed strawberries, and a base of sugar, mint leaves, and water which has a total volume of 800 milliliters.

a. How much punch will the recipe make in liters?
b. If you serve the punch at a party of 30 people, how many milliliters of punch will there be per person?
c. This punch was sold at a fair, and each drink of 80 milliliters cost 25 cents. What was the profit on the sale of this punch if the ingredients cost $12.50 and all the punch was sold?

31. Prescription dosages of the antibiotic garamycin vary from 20 milligrams for a child to 80 milligrams for an adult. The garamycin is contained in a vial that has a volume of 2 cubic centimeters (2 milliliters). The garamycin in each vial has a mass of 80 milligrams.
    a. How many cubic centimeters of garamycin are needed for 12 injections of 24 milligrams each?
    b. How many injections of 60 milligrams each can be obtained from 24 vials?

32. **Featured Strategies: Making a Drawing and Working Backward**   When a special ball is dropped perpendicular to the floor, it rebounds to one-half its previous height on each bounce for five bounces. On its fifth bounce, it rebounds to a height of 6 centimeters. What is the total distance the ball has traveled after it bounces the fifth time and falls to the floor. Before reading further, make a drawing and try to work backward to solve this problem.
    a. **Understanding the Problem**   A diagram will help you to visualize the problem. The height of each rebound can be represented by a vertical line that is one-half the height of the preceding line. Here is a diagram of the original distance the ball is dropped and the height of its first rebound. Explain why the height of each rebound must be doubled when the total distance that the ball travels is computed. Draw the complete diagram for this problem.

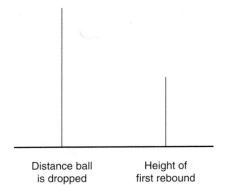

Distance ball   Height of
is dropped   first rebound

b. Devising a Plan Working backward is a natural strategy for solving this problem. After its fourth bounce, how high does the ball rebound?

c. Carrying Out the Plan Continue to work backward to get the height of each rebound and the original distance the ball is dropped. What is the total distance the ball has traveled when it falls to the floor after its fifth bounce?

d. Looking Back For this problem the total distance the ball has traveled is the height from which it was dropped plus 2 times the height of each rebound. Will this statement be true if the problem is changed so that the ball rebounds to one-third its previous height on each bounce?

33. In 1983, at its General Conference on Weights and Measures, the National Institute of Standards and Technology used the speed of light to define the length of a meter. One meter is the distance light travels in 1/299,792,458 second.

a. How many meters does light travel in 1 second?

b. What is the speed of light in kilometers per second?

c. In England in 1956, the speed of light was measured as 299,792.4 ± .11 kilometers per second. Is the speed of light that was used by the General Conference on Weights and Measures within this range?

34. Roof deicers are designed to prevent ice dams from building up on roofs and gutter pipes. An electric heating cable is clipped to the edge of the roof in a sawtooth pattern. In answering the following questions, assume that this pattern is to run along the edges of a roof and that the total length of the edges is 28 meters.

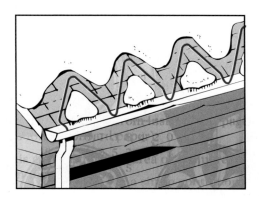

a. How many meters of heating cable will be needed for the edges of the roof if each 1 meter of roof edge requires 2 meters of cable?

b. In addition, heating cable is placed in gutter pipes and downspouts. Two gutter pipes run along the edges of the roof. Each has a length of 14 meters. There are two downspouts, one from each gutter pipe to the ground. Each downspout has a length of 3.2 meters. How many meters of cable will be required to go along the gutter pipes and the downspouts if each 1 meter of gutter pipe or downspout requires 1 meter of cable?

c. The heating cable sells for $1.20 per meter. What is the total cost of the cable for the roof, gutter pipes, and downspouts?

35. The distance around the earth's equator is 40,077 kilometers, and the population of the United States in 2000 was approximately 281,000,000 people. If this many people were spaced equally around the equator, what would be the length of the space each person would have, to the nearest centimeter?

- -

ONLINE LEARNING CENTER   www.mhhe.com/bennett-nelson

• Math Investigation 10.1   *Measuring Angles and Areas*
Section-Related: • Links   • Writing/Discussion Problems   • Bibliography

- -

PUZZLER

A Celsius thermometer and a Fahrenheit thermometer are both placed into a liquid simultaneously. After a time, the temperature measures the same number on both scales. What is the temperature of the liquid? (*Hint:* Guess and check by using the formulas in Exercises and Problems 10.1, exercise 20.)

MATH ACTIVITY 10.2

AREAS OF PATTERN BLOCKS USING DIFFERENT UNITS

Materials: Pattern block pieces in the Manipulative Kit

Research Statement

The 7th national mathematics assessment found that students performed better on questions that were accompanied by manipulatives than on items that asked them to outline figures on a grid.

Martin and Strutchens 2000

*1. Two of the pattern block triangles cover the blue parallelogram. So if the triangle is the unit of area, then the parallelogram has an area of 2.

    a. Use your pattern blocks to find the areas of the trapezoid and the hexagon if the triangle is the unit of area.

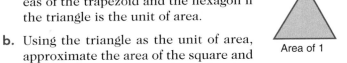

Area of 1   Area of 2

    b. Using the triangle as the unit of area, approximate the area of the square and the white parallelogram. Draw sketches and explain your reasoning. Will the area of the square be greater or less than 2? Will the area of the white parallelogram be greater or less than 1?

2. Suppose the pattern block hexagon is the unit of area.

    a. What are the areas of the trapezoid, blue parallelogram, and triangle?

    b. What are the approximate areas of the square and white parallelogram? Draw diagrams to support your conclusions.

3. Normally a square is used for the unit of area.

    a. Trace a pattern block hexagon on paper, and show that its area is approximately $2\frac{2}{3}$ times the area of the square.

    b. If the square is used as the unit of area and the area of the hexagon is $2\frac{2}{3}$ times the area of the square, find the areas of the trapezoid, blue parallelogram, and triangle.

    c. By placing two white parallelograms and a triangle together as shown below, it can be shown that the total area of two white parallelograms equals the area of the square pattern block. Experiment with the pattern block pieces to find how this can be illustrated. Explain your reasoning.

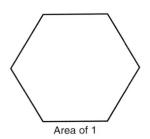

Area of 1

SECTION 10.2

AREA AND PERIMETER

Federal Reserve Bank in Minneapolis

Each of the 10 equilateral triangles in the following figure has sides of length 1 unit, and the perimeter of the entire figure is 12 units. What will the perimeter of the figure be if it is extended to include 50 such triangles?

The design of the Federal Reserve Bank in Minneapolis is based on that of a bridge. In fact, this building can be thought of as a bridge that is 10 stories deep. There was no prototype for its structural design. Each floor has an unobstructed area of 60 × 275 feet. No other building had ever included floors that spanned such a length without internal columns.

This bank was designed to fulfill some unusual zoning restrictions. One of these was that the *coverage,* or ground area occupied by the building, could be only 2.5 percent of the area of the city block on which the bank was to be built. To satisfy this condition, the bank is supported by two towers and its lower floor is 20 feet above the plaza. A 2.5-acre plaza runs under the building and is entirely public space. The building's coverage is the small amount of area occupied by the two towers.

Nonstandard Units of Area

To measure the sizes of plots of land, panes of glass, floors, walls, and other such surfaces, we need a new type of unit, one that can be used to cover a surface. The number of units it takes to cover a surface is called its **area.** Squares have been found to be the most convenient shape for measuring area. If we use the square region in part a of Figure 10.24 as the unit square, the area of the colored region in part b is 4 square units, because it can be covered by 2 squares and 4 half-squares.

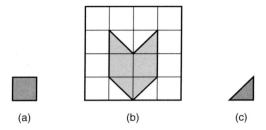

(a)   (b)   (c)

Figure 10.24

The basic concept involved in calculating area—determining the number of units required to cover a region or surface—is often poorly understood by school children. A Michigan State assessment found that fewer than one-half of the seventh-graders examined could calculate the area of the region in part b of Figure 10.24.* Nineteen percent of them thought the area was 6. Can you see why they might have obtained this answer?

Theoretically, the unit for measuring area can have any shape. It can be rectangular, triangular, etc. The only requirement is that the figure used for the unit must tessellate (cover a region without gaps or overlapping).

Example **A**

What is the area of the color region in part b of Figure 10.24 if the gray triangular region in part c is the unit for measuring area?

Solution   Eight triangles are required to cover the color region, so the area is 8 triangular units.

Teachers should provide many hands-on opportunities for students to choose [measurement] tools . . . Although for many measurement tasks students will use nonstandard units, it is appropriate for them to experiment with and use standard measures such as centimeters and meters and inches and feet by the end of grade 2.

Standards 2000, p. 105

The earliest units for measuring area were associated with agriculture. The amount of land that could be plowed in a day with the aid of a team of oxen was called an **acre**. In Germany, a scheffel was a volume of seed, and the amount of land that could be sown with this volume of seed became known as a **scheffel of land**.

Just as nonstandard units for length help children in learning about linear measure, nonstandard units for area help them acquire an understanding of the concept of area.

*T. G. Coburn, Leah M. Beardsley, and Joseph Payne, *Michigan Educational Assessment Program, Mathematics Interpretive Report, 1973 Grade 4 and 7 Tests.* Guidelines for Quality Mathematics Teaching Monograph Series no. 7 (Birmingham, MI: Michigan Council of Teachers of Mathematics, 1975).

Example B

Use each of the following regions as a unit of area to determine the approximate area of the rectangle below.

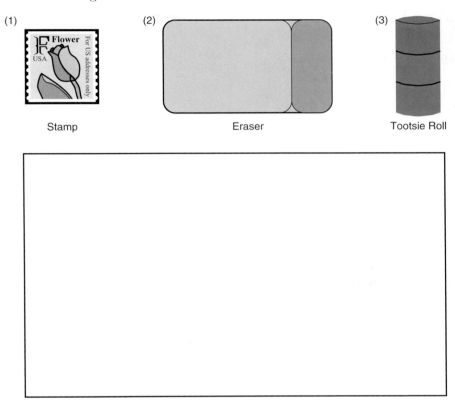

(1) Stamp

(2) Eraser

(3) Tootsie Roll

Solution **1.** Approximately 18 to 19 stamp units **2.** Approximately 6 to 7 eraser units **3.** Approximately 23 to 24 Tootsie Roll units

Standard Units of Area

Eventually more carefully defined units for area were adopted, with the square being the accepted shape of these units.

ENGLISH UNITS In the English system, area is measured by using squares whose sides have lengths of 1 inch, 1 foot, 1 yard, or 1 mile. Each square unit is named according to the length of its sides. The 1 inch × 1 inch square in Figure 10.25 has an area of **1 square inch,** abbreviated 1 sq in or 1 in² (think of the exponent 2 as indicating a square).

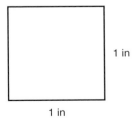

1 in

1 in

Figure 10.25

Similarly, we can measure larger areas by using a **square foot** (1 ft²), a **square yard** (1 yd²), and a **square mile** (1 mi²).

| Example **C** | The different square units are related to one another. |

1. How many square inches equal 1 square foot?

2. How many square feet equal 1 square yard?

Solution   1. 144 square inches   2. 9 square feet

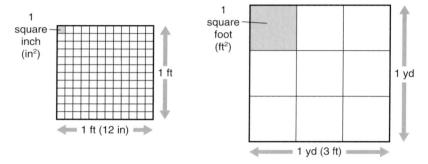

(*Note:* The squares are not drawn to scale.)

The common units for measuring area in the English system are shown in Figure 10.26.

ENGLISH UNITS FOR AREA

Square inch	in²	$\frac{1}{144}$ square foot
Square foot	ft²	144 square inches
Square yard	yd²	9 square feet
Acre		43,560 square feet
Square mile	mi²	27,878,400 square feet

Figure 10.26

METRIC UNITS   In the metric system there is a square unit for area corresponding to each unit for length. For example, a **square meter** (1 m²) is a square whose sides have a length of 1 meter (shown in Figure 10.27, although not to scale). Square meters are used for measuring the areas of rugs, floors, swimming pools, and other such intermediate-size regions. Smaller areas are measured in square centimeters. A **square centimeter** (1 cm²) is a square whose sides have lengths of 1 centimeter. Even smaller areas are measured with the **square millimeter,** a square whose sides have lengths of 1 millimeter. The actual sizes of the square centimeter and the square millimeter are shown in Figure 10.27.

In grades 3–5, students should learn about area more thoroughly, as well as perimeter, volume, temperature, and angle measure. In these grades they learn that measurements can be computed using formulas and need not always be taken directly with a measuring tool.

Standards 2000, p. 44

Figure 10.27

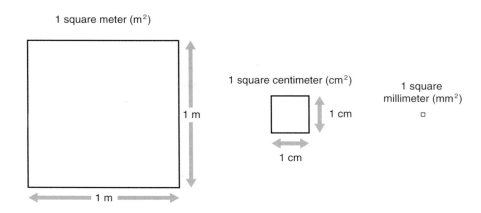

Example D

Determine the following relationships between the metric units for area.

1. How many square millimeters equal 1 square centimeter?

2. How many square centimeters equal 1 square meter?

Solution   1. Since each side of a square centimeter [see figure (1) below] has a length of 1 centimeter, and 1 centimeter = 10 millimeters, a square centimeter can be covered by $10 \times 10 = 100$ square millimeters.   **2.** Since 1 meter equals 100 centimeters, 100 square centimeters can be placed along each side of a square with dimensions of 1 meter × 1 meter [see figure (2) below], and so 10,000 square centimeters will cover the square meter.

Research Statement

Results involving questions on perimeter from the 7th national mathematics assessment reveal that fourth-grade students have difficulty with perimeter concepts, and eighth-grade students show a lack of understanding in more complex contexts that require a conceptual understanding of perimeter.

Martin and Strutchens 2000

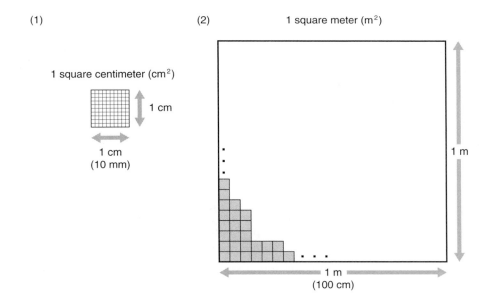

The areas of countries, national forests, oceans, and other such large surfaces are measured with the **square kilometer,** a square whose sides each have a length of 1 kilometer.

Some metric units for area and their relationships are shown in Figure 10.28.

METRIC UNITS FOR AREA

Square millimeter	mm²	$\frac{1}{100}$	square centimeter
Square centimeter	cm²	100	square millimeters
Square meter	m²	10,000	square centimeters
Square kilometer	km²	1,000,000	square meters

Figure 10.28

Perimeter

Another measure associated with a region is its **perimeter**—the length of its boundary. The perimeter of Figure 10.29 is 23 centimeters, which is greater than the width of this page.

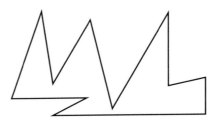

Figure 10.29

Intuitively, it may seem that the area of a region should depend on its perimeter. For example, if one person uses more fence to close in a piece of land than another person, it is tempting to assume the first person has enclosed the greater amount of land. However, this is not necessarily true.

Example E

Each of the following figures has an area of 4 square centimeters. What is the perimeter of each figure?

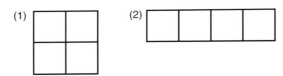

Solution   **1.** The perimeter is 8 centimeters.   **2.** The perimeter is 10 centimeters.

Example E shows that it is possible for two figures to have the same area but different perimeters. It is also possible for two figures to have the same perimeter but different areas.

Example F

Determine the area and perimeter of each figure in square centimeters.

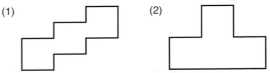

Solution   **1.** The area is 3 square centimeters, and the perimeter is 10 centimeters.   **2.** The area is 4 square centimeters, and the perimeter is 10 centimeters.

Students should begin to develop formulas for perimeter and area in the elementary grades. Middle-grade students should formalize these techniques, as well as develop formulas for the volume and surface area of objects like prisms and cylinders.

Standards 2000, p. 46

Areas of Polygons

RECTANGLES   Rectangles have right angles and pairs of opposite parallel sides, so unit squares fit onto them quite easily. The rectangle in Figure 10.30 can be covered by 24 whole squares and 6 half-squares. Its area is 27 square units. This area can be obtained from the product 6×4.5, because there are $4\frac{1}{2}$ squares in each of 6 columns. In general, if a rectangle has a length l and a width w, the *area of the rectangle* is the product of its length and its width.

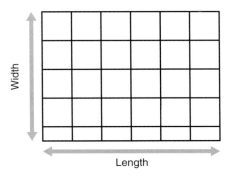

Figure 10.30

For a given perimeter, the dimensions of a rectangle affect its area. In the photographs in Figure 10.31, the same knotted piece of string has been formed into three different rectangles. Using the lengths and widths of the rectangles, you can calculate that their perimeters are 36 centimeters. Yet the area decreases from 80 square centimeters (8×10) to 72 square centimeters (6×12) to 32 square centimeters (16×2), as the shape of the rectangle changes. If we continue to decrease the width of the rectangle, we can make its area as small as we please, although the perimeter will remain 36 centimeters.

Figure 10.31
8 centimeters × 10 centimeters (left); 6 centimeters × 12 centimeters (center); 16 centimeters × 2 centimeters (right)

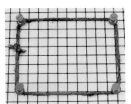 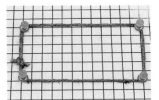 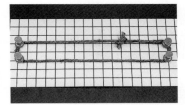

PARALLELOGRAMS   Fitting unit squares onto a figure is a good way for school children to acquire an understanding of the concept of area. However, actually placing squares on a region is usually difficult because of the shape of the boundary (see part a of Figure 10.32).

One of the basic principles in finding area is that *a region can be cut into parts and reassembled without changing its area.* This principle is useful in developing a formula for the area of a parallelogram. The rectangle in part b of Figure 10.32 has been obtained from the figure in part a by cutting triangle A from the left side of the parallelogram and moving it to the right side to create a rectangle. The **base** of the rectangle is 5 centimeters, and its **height** is 2 centimeters, so its area is 10 square centimeters. Since the rectangle was obtained by rearranging the parts of the parallelogram, the area of the parallelogram is also 10 square centimeters. Notice that the **base** of the parallelogram is 5 centimeters and its **height, or altitude** (the perpendicular distance between opposite parallel sides), is 2 centimeters. This suggests that the *area of a parallelogram is the product of its base and its height.*

Area of parallelogram $= b \times h = bh$

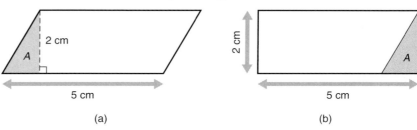

Figure 10.32

(a)   (b)

The notion that shapes that look different can have equal areas is a powerful one that leads eventually to the development of general methods (formulas) for finding the area of a particular shape, such as a parallelogram.

Standards 2000, p. 166

For a given perimeter, the area of a parallelogram depends on its shape. The two parallelograms formed by the inside edges of the linkages in the photograph in Figure 10.33 both have the same perimeter; but as the parallelogram is skewed more to the right, its height decreases. Since the base of both parallelograms is the same and the area of a parallelogram is the base times the height, the parallelogram with the smaller height has the smaller area. The area of the first parallelogram is approximately 72 square centimeters (9×8), and the area of the second one is approximately 45 square centimeters (9×5). The height of the parallelogram, and consequently its area, can be made arbitrarily small by further skewing the linkages while the perimeter stays constant.

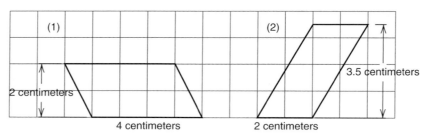

Figure 10.33

Example G

Estimate the area of each parallelogram by visualizing the number of 1 centimeter $\times$ 1 centimeter squares needed to cover the figure. See if you can come within 1 square centimeter of the correct area. Then compute the area.

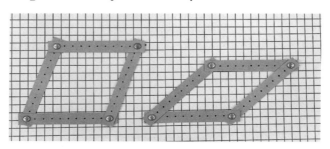

Solution   **1.** 8 square centimeters ($4 \times 2 = 8$)   **2.** 7 square centimeters ($2 \times 3.5 = 7$) Were your estimates close to the areas of these figures?

TRIANGLES   The triangle in Figure 10.34a is covered with 1 centimeter $\times$ 1 centimeter squares and parts of squares. Can you see why this shows that the area of the triangle is more than 4 square centimeters? Since it is inconvenient to cover the triangle with squares, we will use a different approach to find its area. Two copies of a triangle can be placed together to form a parallelogram, as shown in part b. This can be accomplished by reflecting the triangle in part a about side $\overline{AB}$. Since the parallelogram has a base of 5 centimeters and a height of 2 centimeters, its area is 10 square centimeters. Thus the area of the triangle is one-half as much, or 5 square centimeters.

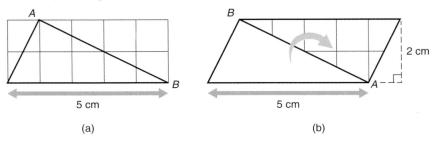

Figure 10.34   (a)   (b)

The preceding example suggests a general approach to finding the area of a triangle: Place two copies of the triangle together to form a parallelogram, and then find the area of the parallelogram. If the length of the **base** of the triangle is b and its **height**, or **altitude** (the perpendicular distance to its base from the opposite vertex), is h, then the base and altitude of the parallelogram are also b and h (Figure 10.35). So the area of the parallelogram is $b \times h$, and since the parallelogram is formed from two triangles,

$$\text{Area of triangle} = \tfrac{1}{2} \times b \times h = \tfrac{1}{2}\,bh$$

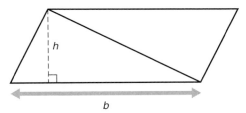

Figure 10.35

Any side of a triangle may be considered the base, and each base has its corresponding altitude. Regardless of the base and altitude chosen, as shown in the next example, the triangle will have the same area.

Example H

Triangle *ABC* is shown below in two positions, with two different bases and altitudes. One of these altitudes falls outside the triangle. Determine the area of each triangle.

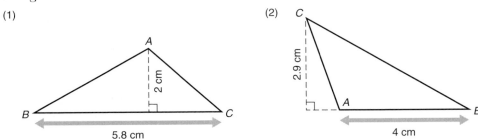

Solution   1. The area is 5.8 square centimeters: $\tfrac{1}{2} \times 5.8 \times 2 = 5.8$.   **2.** The area is 5.8 square centimeters: $\tfrac{1}{2} \times 4 \times 2.9 = 5.8$.

Students can develop formulas for parallelograms, triangles, and trapezoids using what they have previously learned about how to find the area of a rectangle, along with an understanding that decomposing a shape and rearranging its component parts without overlapping does not affect the area of the shape.

Standards 2000, p. 244

TRAPEZOIDS   It is inconvenient to cover a trapezoid with square units because of its sloping sides. However, as with a triangle, we can obtain a parallelogram by placing two trapezoids together.

The trapezoid in Figure 10.36a has a **lower base** of length b and an **upper base** of length u, and its **height,** or **altitude** (the perpendicular distance between its bases), is h. The parallelogram in part b was obtained by placing two copies of the trapezoid side by side. The parallelogram has a base of $b + u$ and a height of h, so its area is $(b + u) \times h$. Since the parallelogram is formed from two trapezoids, this example suggests a general approach for finding the area of a trapezoid:

$$\text{Area of trapezoid} = \tfrac{1}{2} \times (b + u) \times h = \tfrac{1}{2}(b + u)h$$

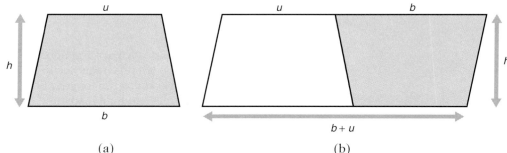

Figure 10.36

(a)   (b)

E x a m p l e

Estimate the area of the trapezoid in Figure 10.36 by visualizing the number of 1-centimeter × 1-centimeter squares needed to cover the figure. See if you can come within 1 square centimeter of obtaining the correct area. Then, using 4 centimeters and 3 centimeters for the lengths of the lower and upper bases and 2.5 centimeters for the height, compute the area of the trapezoid.

Solution   The area of the trapezoid is 8.75 square centimeters: $\tfrac{1}{2} \times (4 + 3) \times 2.5 = 8.75$. Was your estimate between 7 and 10 square centimeters?

Circumferences and Areas of Circles

Circles are part of our natural environment. The sun, the moon, flowers, whirlpools, and cross sections of some trees have circular shapes. The concentric circles in the section of natural pearl in Figure 10.37 were formed by many layers of growth.

Figure 10.37
Concentric circles revealed in a cross section of natural pearl

CIRCUMFERENCE   The perimeter or distance around a circle is called the **circumference.** There is something deceptive about trying to estimate the circumference of a circle, as illustrated in the next example.

Example J

Estimate the circumference of the pearl in Figure 10.37 in centimeters. Is it less than, approximately equal to, or greater than your handspan?

Solution   The circumference is approximately 14.5 centimeters.

Were you surprised at the circumference in Example J? There is a tendency to underestimate the circumferences of circles. Often people estimate the circumference by doubling the diameter. Actually, the circumference is a little greater than 3 times the diameter. This can be illustrated by placing string or a strip of paper around a circular figure, then folding it into three equal parts, and comparing one of these parts to the diameter of the circle. The circumference of the pearl, for example, is approximately 15 centimeters, and its diameter is between 4.5 and 5 centimeters.

The exact ratio of the circumference of a circle to its diameter is the irrational number π **(pi)**, which is 3.1416 rounded to four decimal places. This ratio is expressed in the following equations, where C is the circumference of a circle, d is the diameter, and r is the radius.

$$\frac{C}{d} = \pi \quad \text{or} \quad C = \pi d \quad \text{or} \quad C = 2\pi r$$

 Some calculators have a key for π. Pressing $\boxed{\pi}$ on a calculator with 10 places for digits will give the number shown in the display in Figure 10.38. However, since π is an irrational number, the number in this display is only a rational number approximation of π. For most purposes it is sufficient to approximate π by 3.1416. *Note:* For the exercises and problems in this text, use a calculator value of π or approximate π by 3.1416.

Figure 10.38

```
3.141592654
OFF ■■ ON   DEG ■■ RAD
```

Example K

The following photograph shows a piece of string being stretched around a tennis ball can.

Predict how the length of the string will compare to the height of the can. The can has a diameter of approximately 7 centimeters and a height of approximately 20 centimeters. Compute the length of the string, and compare it to the height of the can.

Solution   It is common for people to predict that the length of the string is less than the height of the can. However, since 3.1416×7 is approximately 22, the length of the string is approximately 22 centimeters, which is 2 centimeters greater than the height of the can.

AREAS   The area of a circle can be approximated by counting unit squares and parts of squares which cover the circle.

Example L

The following circle has been drawn on a centimeter grid. Approximate its area in square centimeters.

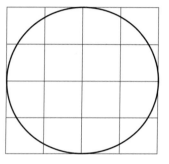

Solution   A first step might be to note that the circle is contained inside a 4×4 grid, which shows that its area is less than 16 square centimeters. Next we can count the squares inside the circle and then combine the parts of the remaining squares, or we can estimate the parts of the squares outside the circle and subtract their area from 16. A reasonable estimate for the area of the circle is 12 square centimeters.

You might have noticed in Example L that one-quarter of the circle is contained in a square whose side has a length that is equal to the radius of the circle. This is illustrated in Figure 10.39, which shows that the area of one-quarter of the circle with radius r is less than the radius times itself, or r^2. Thus the area of the whole circle is less than $4 \times r^2$.

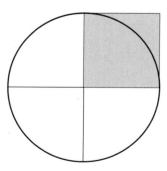

Figure 10.39

Let's consider a method for determining the area of a circle. The circle in part a of Figure 10.40 has been divided into 16 pie-shaped **sectors**. When these 16 sectors are rearranged and placed together, as shown in part b, they form a figure whose shape is close to that of a parallelogram. The length of the base of the parallelogram-like figure is one-half the circumference of the circle, and the height of the figure is approximately the radius of the circle. If the circle is cut into a greater number of sectors, the shape of the resulting parallelogram-like figure will be even closer to that of a parallelogram. Using the formula for the area of a parallelogram, we can approximate the area of the figure in part b:

$$\text{Area} \approx b \times h = \tfrac{1}{2}C \times r = \tfrac{1}{2}(2\pi r) \times r = \pi r^2$$

which is the formula for the area of a circle.

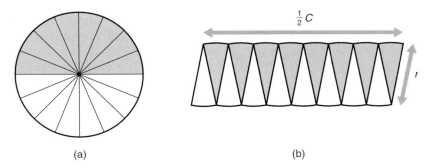

Figure 10.40 (a)   (b)

Notice that since $\pi \approx 3.1416$, the area of a circle is a little more than 3 times the square of the radius of the circle (see Figure 10.39). The *Curriculum and Evaluation Standards for School Mathematics* suggest that students construct such a model to develop the formula for the area of a circle:

Students who can use the relationship between the shape of the "parallelogram" and its area and the circumference of the circle to develop the formula for the area of the circle are demonstrating plausible and deductive reasoning.*

Example M

Approximate the areas of 9-inch and 12-inch pizzas, using a value of 3 for π. If a 9-inch pizza costs $5.40 and the unit cost per square inch of 9-inch and 12-inch pizza is the same, what is the cost of the 12-inch pizza?

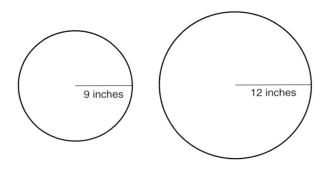

9 inches   12 inches

Curriculum and Evaluation Standards for School Mathematics (Reston, VA: National Council of Teachers of Mathematics, 1989), p. 221.

Solution   The area of a 9-inch pizza is approximately 243 square inches (3×9^2), and the area of a 12-inch pizza is approximately 432 square inches (3×12^2). The cost per square inch of the 9-inch pizza is $2.\overline{2}$ cents ($540 \div 243$), so the cost of the 12-inch pizza is $9.60 ($2.\overline{2} \times 432$).

Pi has had a long and interesting history. In the ancient Orient, π was frequently taken to be 3. This value also occurs in the King James Bible in nearly identical verses (1 Kings 7:23 and 2 Chronicles 4:2) that describe the circumference of a circular container as being 3 times its diameter.

There have been many attempts to compute π. Archimedes computed π to the equivalent of two decimal places, and in 1841 Zacharias Dase computed π to 200 places. In 1873 William Shanks of England computed π to 707 places. In 1946, D. F. Ferguson of England discovered errors starting with the 528th place in Shanks' value for π, and a year later he gave a corrected value of π to 710 places. In recent years electronic computers have calculated π to hundreds of thousands of decimal places. Among the curiosities connected with π are the word devices for remembering the first few decimal places. In the following sentence, the number of letters in each word is a digit in π.

3. 1   4   1   5   9   2   6

May I have a large container of coffee?*

*This mnemonic and others are given by H. W. Eves, *An Introduction to the History of Mathematics,* 3d ed. (New York: Holt, Rinehart and Winston, 1969), p. 94.

Problem-Solving Application

Sometimes it is necessary to find the areas of irregular or nonpolygonal shapes. Some of the water supplied to a leaf by its system of tiny veins is lost through small openings called **stomates.** Botanists collect the water by tying a plastic bag around a branch (Figure 10.41). Then they compute the areas of leaves to determine the amount of water lost for each square centimeter of surface area.

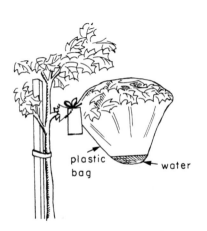

Figure 10.41

PROBLEM

If a certain leaf loses 2 milliliters of water in a 24-hour period, how much water does it lose for each square centimeter of surface area?

Understanding the Problem   First it is necessary to determine the area of the leaf. **Question 1:** If the given leaf has an area of 10 square centimeters, how much water does it lose for each square centimeter?

Devising a Plan   One approach to finding the area of a leaf is to trace the leaf on cardboard and cut it out. Comparing the weight of the cut-out leaf to the weight and area of the original piece of cardboard by using ratios will give an approximation of the leaf's area. Another approach is to trace the leaf on grid paper and count the number of squares that fall inside the boundary of the leaf. **Question 2:** If this approach is used, what can be done with the squares that lie on the boundary?

Carrying Out the Plan   The given leaf has been traced on a centimeter grid in the figure. There are 18 squares, each 1 centimeter × 1 centimeter, that fall inside the boundary. So the area of the leaf is at least 18 square centimeters. To permit a more accurate estimate for the remainder of the leaf's area, each square on the boundary has been divided into four smaller squares. One approach is to count the number of small squares that are half or more than half covered by the leaf. There appear to be 32 such squares. Using the 18 large interior squares and the 32 small boundary squares, we can estimate the area of the leaf. **Question 3:** What is the approximate area, and how much water is lost for each square centimeter?

Research Statement

The 7th national mathematics assessment results indicate that most students primarily experience the concept of area through the memorization of formulas, and that they may never really understand what the concept means in terms of determining the size of a region.

Martin and Strutchens 2000

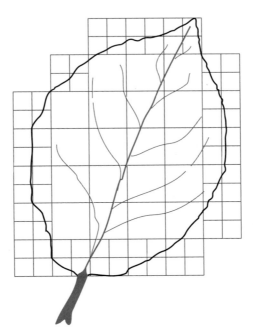

Looking Back   The 32 quarter-squares we counted in the preceding step represent 8 square centimeters of leaf area. The process of subdividing boundary squares can be continued to obtain more accurate estimates. **Question 4:** For

Enrichment

Area of Irregular Shapes

Some shapes are not shaped like squares or triangles. They are irregular shapes.

There are no formulas to help you find areas of irregular shapes, but you can estimate the area.

Look at the shape shown on the grid. What is the area in square units?

- Count the whole squares first. There are 24 whole squares in the shape.

- Now count the partial squares. There are 20 squares where the shape covers $\frac{1}{2}$ of a square. You can think of them as 10 wholes.

- So the area of the shape is about 24 + 10 or 34 square units.

1. **Analyze:** How could you have used the formula for area of a rectangle to help you estimate the area of the shape shown above?

Estimate the area of each shape.

2.
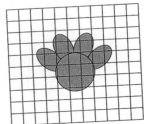

3.

4.
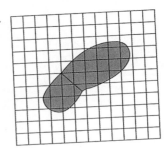

5.
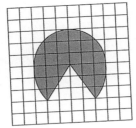

example, if each quarter-square is divided into 4 tiny squares and 136 of these tiny squares are half or more than half covered by the leaf, what is the new estimate of the leaf's area?

Answers to Questions 1–4   1. .2 milliliter   **2.** One approach is to combine parts of squares to obtain whole squares. Another is to subdivide the boundary squares.   **3.** 26 square centimeters; approximately .08 milliliter of water is lost per square centimeter (2 ÷ 26 ≈ .08).   **4.** Since 16 of the tiny squares have an area of 1 square centimeter, 136 of these tiny squares have an area of 8.5 square centimeters (136 ÷ 16 = 8.5). So the new estimate of the area of the leaf is 26.5 square centimeters (18 + 8.5 = 26.5).

PUZZLER

The area of the inscribed square is what percent of the area of the circle?

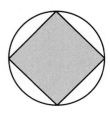

EXERCISES AND PROBLEMS 10.2*

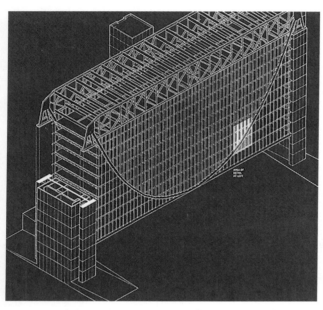

Diagram of the skeletal structure of the Minneapolis Federal Reserve Bank

1. The drawing above shows the skeletal structure of the Minneapolis Federal Reserve Bank. Its 10 floors and the vertical beams partition the front of the bank into congruent rectangles. The dimensions of these rectangles are approximately 2 meters × 4 meters.

    a. How do the width and height of these rectangles compare to the width of your outstretched arms and the height of the average room?

    b. There are 53 rectangles across the front face of the bank. What is the width of the front face of the bank?

    c. There are 10 rectangles running from the bottom to the top of the front face of the bank (one for each floor). What is the height of the front face of the bank?

    d. What is the area of the front face?

The basic unit for measuring area does not have to be a square. Measure the area of the nonconvex octagon on the grid that follows by using the different units given in exercises 2 and 3.

*For computations involving π, use the value on your calculator or approximate π by 3.1416.

2.   a.   b.

3.   a.   b.

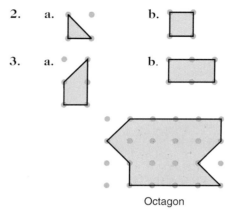

Octagon

Determine the approximate area of the following figure, using the nonstandard units in exercises 4 and 5.

4.

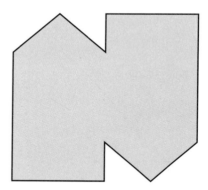

Gum wrapper

5.

Plastic fastener

6. The following question is taken from a mathematics test given to 9-year-olds by the National Assessment of Educational Progress (NAEP).

a. Which of the following figures has the same area as the 4 × 4 square?

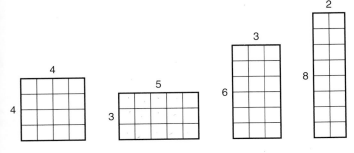

b. Only 44 percent of the students who took the test chose the 8 × 2 rectangle, and almost as many selected the 3 × 5 rectangle. The selection of the 3 × 5 rectangle may indicate confusion about which two concepts of measurement? Explain why students might have made this choice.

7. a. How many square feet are there in 1 square mile?

b. How many acres are there in 1 square mile?

c. Rhode Island has the least land area of the 50 states. Its area is 1049 square miles. How many acres is this?

8. a. How many square millimeters are there in 1 square centimeter?

b. How many square centimeters are in 1 square meter?

c. A standard sheet of paper has dimensions of approximately 28 centimeters × 21.5 centimeters. What is the area of one side of such a sheet of paper?

Each of the figures in exercises 9 and 10 has an area of 3 square units. Using the length of the side of one of these squares as the unit of measure, calculate the perimeter of each figure.

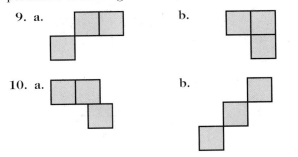

9. a.   **b.**

10. a.   **b.**

Exercises 11 and 12 use the metric units of *are* and *hectare*. The **are** (pronounced as "air") is the unit for measuring the area of house lots, gardens, and other medium-size regions. The *are* is equal to the area of a square whose sides measure 10 meters each. The **hectare** is a unit of area for measuring larger regions. It is the area of a square whose sides measure 100 meters each.

11. a. How many ares equal 1 square kilometer?

b. How many hectares equal 1 square kilometer?

12. a. How many ares equal 1 hectare?

b. How many hectares equal the area of a 2.4-kilometer × 3.5-kilometer rectangle?

Use the value of π from your calculator or π ≈ 3.1416 to compute the perimeter or circumference to the nearest millimeter and the area to the nearest square millimeter of each figure in exercises 13 to 18. Then determine each area to the nearest .01 square centimeter. (*Hint:* In some cases the Pythagorean theorem will be needed to find the length of a side or hypotenuse of a right triangle, see section 6.4.)

13. a. Rectangle   **b.** Parallelogram

14. a. Trapezoid   **b.** Scalene triangle

15. a. Circle   **b.** Trapezoid

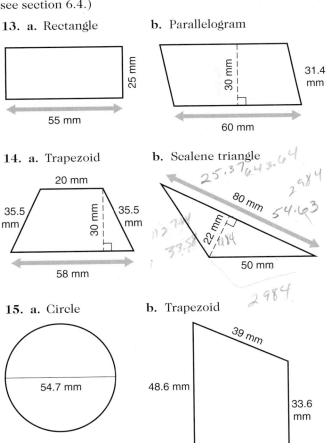

16. a. Parallelogram

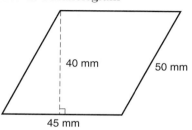

40 mm

50 mm

45 mm

b. Circle

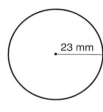

23 mm

17. a. Triangle

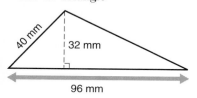

40 mm

32 mm

96 mm

b. Trapezoid

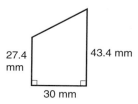

27.4 mm

43.4 mm

30 mm

18. a. Rectangle

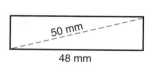

50 mm

48 mm

b. Isosceles triangle

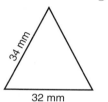

34 mm

32 mm

The area of a polygon can be found by subdividing it into smaller regions. Use this principle to find the area of the polygons in exercises 19 and 20 to the nearest .1 square centimeter.

19.

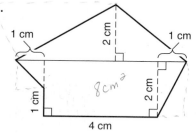

1 cm   2 cm   1 cm

1 cm   8 cm²   2 cm

4 cm

20. Regular pentagon with center *A*

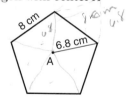

8 cm

6.8 cm

A

Determine the area to the nearest square centimeter of the shaded region of each figure in exercises 21 and 22. (Use the value of π from your calculator or π ≈ 3.146.)

21. a. Trapezoid

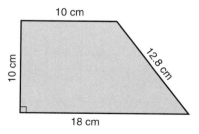

10 cm

10 cm

12.8 cm

18 cm

b. Rectangle with circle and square removed

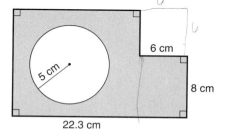

6 cm

5 cm

8 cm

22.3 cm

22. a. Two circles with the same center (**concentric circles**)

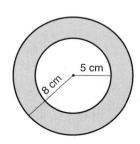

5 cm

8 cm

b. Triangle

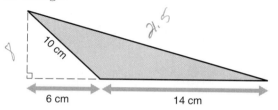

10 cm

6 cm   14 cm

Use these circles in exercises 23 and 24 and the value of π from you calculator or $\pi \approx 3.1416$.

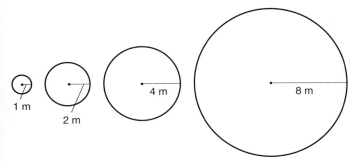

23. Determine the circumference of each circle. What happens to the circumference of a circle when its radius is doubled?

24. Determine the area of each circle. What happens to the area of a circle when its radius is doubled?

25. The common starfish has five arms. Most species grow as large as 20 to 30 centimeters in diameter, but some species reach only 1 centimeter. The starfish shown below, photographed on a centimeter grid, has a diameter of approximately 9.5 centimeters. What is the approximate area of the underside of this starfish in square centimeters? (*Hint:* Enclose the starfish in a large square, and approximate the area that is not covered.)

26. Below is a brief chronology of some early approximations for π. Compare the decimals for these fractions with the value of π to 15 decimal places:

$$\pi \approx 3.141592653589793$$

Which one of the following fractions is closest to the value of π? Which two of these fractions are equal?

a. Archimedes (240 B.C.), $\dfrac{223}{71}$

b. Claudius Ptolemy (A.D. 150), $\dfrac{377}{120}$

c. Tsu Ch'ung-chih (A.D. 480), $\dfrac{355}{113}$

d. Aryabhata (A.D. 530), $\dfrac{62,832}{20,000}$

e. Bhaskara (A.D. 1150), $\dfrac{3927}{1250}$

27. Of all simple closed curves of equal length, the circle encloses the largest area. Consider the following square and circle.

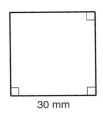 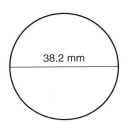

a. What is the perimeter of the square and the circumference of the circle to the nearest millimeter?
b. How much greater (to the nearest square millimeter) is the area of the circle than the area of the square?

28. Rocks are sometimes shaped into disks by the tumbling action of ocean waves. The photograph shows four such rocks on a centimeter grid. Consider the area of the portion of the grid that is occupied by each rock.

a. Estimate the diameter of the large rock. Use this number to find the area occupied by the rock to the nearest square centimeter.
b. What is the difference between the area occupied by the largest rock and the total area occupied by the three smaller rocks?

29. The 1998–99 Manhattan telephone directory had 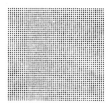 approximately 3400 pages, each with an 8-inch × 10-inch printed surface.

a. If every square inch of printed surface on these pages contained a 50 × 50 array of dots, as shown here, how many dots would there be in this directory?

b. In 1999 the world's population was approximately 6 billion. If each person were represented by one dot, about how many of these telephone directories, to the nearest tenth, would be required to represent everyone in the world?

REASONING AND PROBLEM SOLVING

30. A pane of antique stained glass has dimensions of 30 centimeters × 58 centimeters. If the glass sells for 25 cents per square centimeter, what is the cost of the pane?

31. A store sells two types of Christmas paper. Type A has 4 rolls per package and costs $2.99, and each roll is 75 centimeters × 150 centimeters. Type B has a single roll, costs $3.19, and is 88 centimeters × 500 centimeters. Which type gives you more paper for your money?

32. All-purpose carpeting costs $27.50 per square meter. What is the cost of carpeting a room from wall to wall whose dimensions are 360 centimeters × 400 centimeters?

33. Glass for picture frames sells for $20.00 per square meter. What is the total cost of the glass in two picture frames, of which one is 58 centimeters × 30 centimeters and the other 40 centimeters × 60 centimeters?

34. The length of a kitchen cupboard is 3.5 meters. There are three shelves in the cupboard, each 30 centimeters wide. How many rolls of shelf paper will be needed to cover these shelves if each roll is 30 centimeters × 3 meters?

35. The instructions on a bag of lawn fertilizer recommend that 35 grams of fertilizer be used for each square meter of lawn. How many square meters of lawn can be fertilized with a 50-kilogram bag?

36. Some humidity is necessary in homes for comfort, but too much can cause mold and peeling paint. Paint-destroying moisture can come from walls, crawl spaces, and attics.

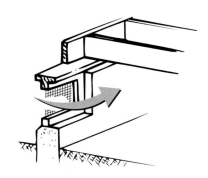

a. An attic should have 900 square centimeters of ventilation for each 27 square meters of floor area. How many square centimeters of ventilation are needed for an attic with a 4-meter × 12-meter floor?

b. A crawl space should have 900 square centimeters of ventilation for each 27 square meters of ceiling area, plus 1800 square centimeters for each 30 meters of perimeter around the crawl space. How many square centimeters of ventilation are needed for a 10-meter × 15-meter crawl space?

37. The wall shown in the following figure has a length of 540 centimeters and a height of 240 centimeters. A few dimensions are also given around the window and fireplace.

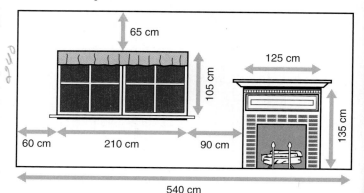

a. How many square centimeters of wallpaper will it take to paper the wall?

b. A standard roll of wallpaper is 12.8 meters × 53 centimeters. A store will not sell partial rolls. How many rolls must be purchased to cover this wall?

Many factors go into assessing the value of a house for tax purposes. Once the proper category has been determined, the assessment rate is per square foot or square meter. Compute the value of the one-floor dwellings in exercises 38 and 39 if the assessment rate is $389 per square meter for the base of the house.

38. a. Ranch-style house with a rectangular base 8 meters × 13.75 meters.
   b. How much tax must be paid on this house if the tax rate is $52 on every $1000 of assessed value?

39. a. L-shaped house consisting of two parts with rectangular bases: 8.7 meters × 11 meters; and 8 meters × 9.5 meters.
   b. How much tax must be paid on the L-shaped house if the tax rate is $73 on every $1000 of assessed value?

40. Featured Strategy: Making a Drawing Draw the largest circle possible on a square piece of paper. Cut out the circle and discard the trimmings. Inside the circle, draw the largest square possible. Cut out the square and discard the trimmings. What fraction of the original square piece of paper has been cut off and thrown away?

   a. Understanding the Problem The shaded portion of this diagram shows the trimmings that will be thrown away in the first step of the paper-cutting process. If the length of the side of the square is 2 centimeters, what percentage of the area of the square is the area of the shaded region?

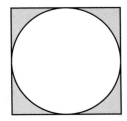

   b. Devising a Plan One approach to the problem is to compute the total area of the trimmings from the two steps separately. A different approach is suggested by inscribing the second square inside the circle. Shade the total region of the following figure that represents the amount that will be cut off from the original square.

   c. Carrying Out the Plan Choose a plan from part b, or devise one of your own; and use it to determine what fraction of the original square piece of paper is cut off.

   d. Looking Back Suppose we begin with a circle, inscribe a square, and then inscribe a smaller circle in the square. How does the area of the small circle compare with the area of the large circle? Will the answer be the same as the answer to the original problem?

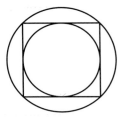

41. A meter trundle wheel is a convenient device for measuring distances along the ground. Every time the wheel makes 1 complete revolution, it has moved forward 1 meter. If you were to cut this wheel from a square piece of plywood, what would be the dimensions of the smallest square you could use? (Use the value of π from your calculator or $\pi \approx 3.1416$.)

42. Physicists study cosmic radiation to learn about properties of our galaxy and levels of sun activity. The proton histogram below contains information on the intensity level of cosmic rays. Region *A* under the histogram, which is called the **background area**, is compared with the total area of regions *A* and *B*.

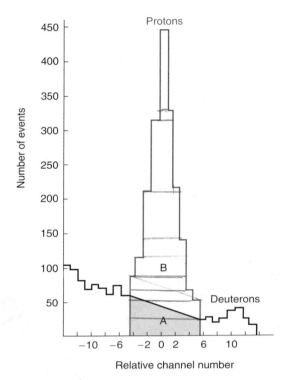

a. What is the approximate area of region *A* in square millimeters?

b. What is the approximate area of region *B*?

c. What is the ratio of the area of region *A* to the total area of regions *A* and *B* to the nearest percent?

43. The 70-story cylindrical building shown in the photograph is the Peachtree Plaza Hotel in Atlanta, Georgia. It contains a seven-story central court with a small pond and over 100 trees. The diameter of this building is 35.36 meters (116 feet). According to its architect, John Portman, cylindrical walls were chosen rather than the more common rectangular walls because a circle encloses more area with less perimeter than any other shape. (Use the value of π from your calculator or π ≈ 3.1416.)

a. What is the area of a horizontal cross section of the cylindrical building (the area of a floor) to the nearest square meter?

Peachtree Plaza Hotel in Atlanta, Georgia

b. What is the perimeter, to the nearest meter, of a square that encloses the same area as you found in part a? (*Hint:* First find the square root of the area in part a.)

c. What is the circumference of the cross section in part a to the nearest meter?

d. How many meters longer is the perimeter of the square in part b than the circumference of the hotel in part c?

e. The Peachtree Plaza Hotel is 230 meters (754 feet) tall. This number multiplied by the correct answer for part d will give the additional wall area that would be needed to enclose the same space if the hotel had a square base rather than a circular one. What is this area?

44. Egyptian scrolls dating from the period between 1850 and 1650 B.C. show many formulas for computing land areas for the purposes of taxation. Does the following formula produce the correct area for a quadrilateral, with successive side lengths of *a*, *b*, *c*, and *d*?

$$Area = \frac{(a + c) \times (b + d)}{4}$$

If not, is the result too large or too small? (*Hint:* Try this formula on some figures.)

45. The wheel has been called the most important invention of all time. Assume that the diameter of each wheel in this cartoon is 75 centimeters and that the distance between opposite pairs of wheels is 300 centimeters. How many revolutions of each wheel will it take to turn this contraption in one complete circle?

"Just because you invented the wheel, it doesn't follow logically that you can go on to the wagon."

46. The height of a tennis ball can is approximately equal to the circumference of a tennis ball. This can be illustrated by rolling a tennis ball along the edge of a can. The ball will make one complete revolution in rolling from one end of the can to the other. Since a can holds three tennis balls, what does this demonstration imply about the diameter of a ball compared to its circumference?

ONLINE LEARNING CENTER   www.mhhe.com/bennett-nelson

• Math Investigation 10.2   *Area Relationships*
Section-Related: • Links   • Writing/Discussion Problems   • Bibliography

PUZZLER

Suppose a cable fits tightly around the equator of the earth. If an additional piece is to be spliced in so that the cable can be raised 6 feet above the earth (at all points), approximately how much additional cable will be needed?

MATH ACTIVITY 10.3

ALGEBRAIC EXPRESSIONS FOR AREAS AND PERIMETERS OF TILE FIGURES

Materials: Color tiles in the Manipulative Kit

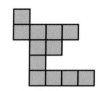

1. Build the figure at the left with the square tiles.
   a. If each edge of the tile has a length of 1 linear unit, what is the perimeter of this figure?
   b. Continue building onto this figure so that tiles only touch along a complete edge (as shown in the figure). Is it possible to obtain all the different whole-number perimeters greater than 24 and less than 40? If not, which perimeters cannot be obtained?
   c. Use the tiles to experiment with building figures so that the tiles only touch along complete edges. Is it possible to build figures having perimeters of 5, 7, 9, or 11?
   d. Write about your observations in parts b and c. In general, what can be said about the perimeters of figures built with tiles when the tiles only touch along complete edges of other tiles? Try to give a reason for any generalization.

*2. Here are the first four figures in a sequence which uses tiles:

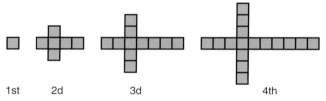

1st   2d   3d   4th

   a. Find a pattern and use the tiles to build the fifth figure. Using one square tile as the unit of area, what is the area of the fifth figure?
   b. What is the perimeter of the fifth figure?
   c. Describe the shape of the 50th figure. For example, how many tiles are in the figure and how many tiles are in each of its four "arms"?
   d. Determine the area and perimeter of the 50th figure.
   e. Write algebraic expressions for the area and perimeter of the nth figure.
   f. Explain how you can tell whether the perimeter of the nth figure is an even number or an odd number.

3. Use the tiles to build the next figure in the following sequence. Sketch the figure and determine its area and perimeter. Don't forget the perimeter on the inside edges. Write formulas for the area and perimeter of the nth figure in this sequence. Explain your reasoning.

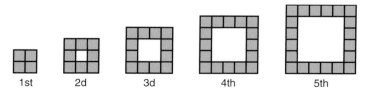

1st   2d   3d   4th   5th

SECTION 10.3

VOLUME AND SURFACE AREA

*Liquefied natural gas
tanker* Aquarius

The numbers of cubes in these U-shaped figures are the beginning of the
sequence

$$5, \quad 28, \quad 81, \quad \ldots$$

If this geometric pattern is continued, how many cubes will there be in the 10th
figure?

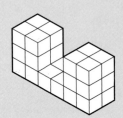

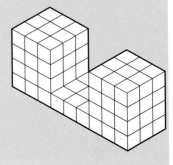

The huge ship in the photograph is the *Aquarius,* one of 12 liquefied natural gas tankers built by the Quincy Shipbuilding Division of General Dynamics. The *Aquarius* is longer than three football fields (285 meters) and carries five spherical aluminum tanks, each with a diameter of 36.58 meters. To appreciate the size of one of these spheres, consider the fact that its diameter is greater than the diameter of one of the floors in the Peachtree Plaza Hotel (page 682) and greater than the length of a professional basketball court. The space inside these spheres is measured by the number of *unit cubes* required to fill it. Each sphere holds the equivalent of 25,000 cubes, each with dimensions of 1 meter × 1 meter × 1 meter.

Nonstandard Units of Volume

To measure the amount of space in tanks, buildings, refrigerators, cars, and other three-dimensional figures, we need units of measure that are also three-dimensional figures. The number of such units needed to fill a figure is its **volume.** Cubes are convenient because they pack together without gaps or overlapping. Using the cube in part a of Figure 10.42 as the unit cube, we can determine that the volume of the box in part b is 24 **cubic units.** The figure shows 12 cubes on the base of the box, and 12 more cubes can be placed above these to fill the box.

The need for a standard three-dimensional unit to measure volume grows out of initial experiences filling containers with items such as rice or packing pieces.

Standards 2000, p. 172

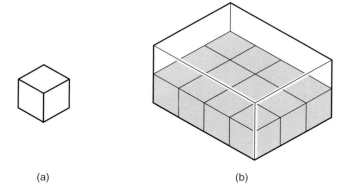

Figure 10.42   (a)   (b)

The first school experiences with measuring volume should involve nonstandard units of measure. Before introducing units of length for the dimensions of a cube, teachers should involve students in activities that require stacking, building, and counting cubes.

Example A

1. Suppose the rectangle at the top of the following page is the base of a box. Determine the approximate number of each of the following units of volume (the die and the cube) that will fit onto this base. (*Hint:* Trace the front face of each unit.)

(1)   (2)

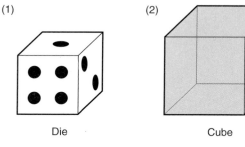

Die   Cube

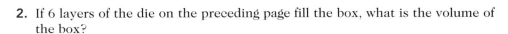

2. If 6 layers of the die on the preceding page fill the box, what is the volume of the box?

3. If 4.5 layers of the cube on the preceding page fill the box, what is the volume of the box?

Solution   1. Approximately 32 dice will cover the base, and approximately 18 of the larger cubes will cover the base.   **2.** The volume of the box is approximately 192 dice units.   **3.** The volume of the box is approximately 81 cube units.

The difficulty that children at all grade levels have in understanding the concept of volume is indicated in the next example. Every 4 years the NAEP (National Assessment of Educational Progress) administers mathematics tests in schools throughout the United States. Example B contains a question on volume from one of these tests.

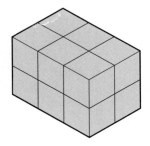

Example **B**

Students were shown the figure at the left and asked how many cubes the box contained. What is the correct answer, and what do you think was the incorrect answer most commonly given by students?

Solution   The box contains 12 cubes. Only 6 percent of the 9-year-olds, 21 percent of the 13-year-olds, and 43 percent of the 17-year-olds answered the question correctly.* The most common incorrect answer was 16. Can you see how students might have obtained this answer?

Standard Units of Volume

For each English unit of length (inch, foot, etc.) and each metric unit of length (centimeter, meter, etc.) there is a corresponding unit of volume, a cube whose three dimensions are the given length.

---

*T. P. Carpenter, T. G. Coburn, R. E. Reys, and J. W. Wilson, "Results and Implications of the NAEP Mathematics Assessment: Elementary School," *Arithmetic Teacher* 22 (October 1975): 438–450.

ENGLISH UNITS   Cubic units are named according to the length of their edges. The most commonly used units for measuring nonliquid volume in the English system are the **cubic inch**, the **cubic foot**, and the **cubic yard**. The cubes for these units are illustrated in Figure 10.43. These cubes are not drawn to scale.

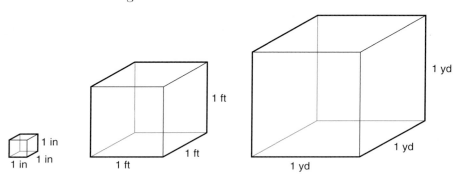

Figure 10.43

The volume of a microwave oven might be measured in cubic inches. A larger volume, such as that of a room or freezer, might be measured in cubic feet. Larger volumes, such as the volume of a truckload of loam or crushed rock, are measured by the cubic yard.

Example C

Determine the following English unit relationships.

1. How many cubic inches equal 1 cubic foot?

2. How many cubic feet equal 1 cubic yard?

3. How many cubic inches equal 1.4 cubic feet?

Solution   **1.** Imagine a box in the shape of a cube whose dimensions are each 1 foot. The base of the box is 12 inches × 12 inches, so the floor of the box can be covered by 144 cubes, each of which is 1 inch × 1 inch × 1 inch. Since 12 such layers will fill the box, its volume is 1728 cubic inches (12 × 144 = 1728).

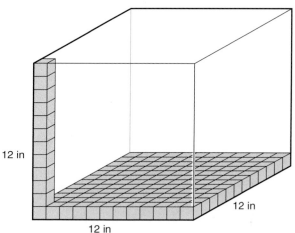

2. Similarly, the floor of a cube-shaped box whose dimensions are each 1 yard can be covered with 9 cubes, each of which is 1 foot × 1 foot × 1 foot. Three such layers will fill the box, so its volume is 27 cubic feet.   **3.** Since 1 cubic foot = 1728 cubic inches, 1.4 cubic feet = 2419.2 cubic inches (1.4 × 1728 = 2419.2).

The English units for volume and their relationships are summarized in Figure 10.44.

ENGLISH UNITS FOR VOLUME

Cubic inch	in³	$\frac{1}{1728}$ cubic foot
Cubic foot	ft³	1728 cubic inches
Cubic yard	yd³	27 cubic feet

Figure 10.44

METRIC UNITS   The common metric units for measuring nonliquid volume are the **cubic millimeter,** the **cubic centimeter,** and the **cubic meter.** Each unit is named according to the length of the edges of its cube. For example, the edges of the cube for the cubic centimeter each have a length of 1 centimeter. The cubes for these three metric units are shown in Figure 10.45. These cubes are not drawn to scale.

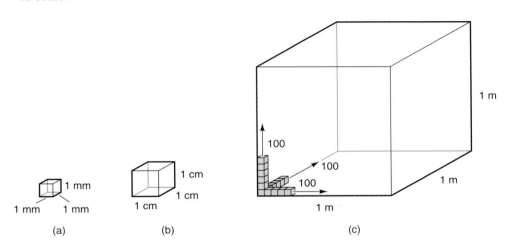

Figure 10.45   (a)   (b)   (c)

Example D

Determine the following relationships.

1. How many cubic centimeters equal 1 cubic meter?

2. How many cubic millimeters equal 1 cubic centimeter?

3. How many cubic millimeters equal 3.4 cubic centimeters?

Solution   **1.** Visualize a cube-shaped box that measures 1 meter on each edge (see part c of Figure 10.45), and imagine filling it with cubes whose edges measure 1 centimeter. The floor of the large cube is 100 centimeters × 100 centimeters, so it can be covered by 10,000 of the smaller cubes. Since there are 100 such layers, the volume of the box is 1,000,000 cubic centimeters (100 × 10,000).   **2.** A cube whose edges each have a length of 1 centimeter has dimensions of 10 millimeters × 10 millimeters × 10 millimeters. So its volume is 1000 cubic millimeters (10 × 10 × 10).   **3.** Since 1 cubic centimeter = 1000 cubic millimeters, 3.4 cubic centimeters = 3400 cubic millimeters.

Some of the metric units for volume and their relationships are shown in the table in Figure 10.46.

METRIC UNITS FOR VOLUME

Cubic millimeter	mm³	$\frac{1}{1000}$ cubic centimeter
Cubic centimeter	cm³	1,000 cubic millimeters
Cubic meter	m³	1,000,000 cubic centimeters

Figure 10.46

Surface Area

Another important measure associated with objects in space is their amount of surface. Just as in the case of two-dimensional figures, **surface area** is expressed as the number of unit squares needed to cover the surface.

Example E

The area of the top of the box in the figure is 9 square centimeters. What is the total surface area, including the base of the box?

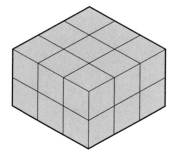

Solution   The top and bottom faces of the box each have an area of 9 square centimeters. The right and left faces each have an area of 6 square centimeters, and the front and back faces each have an area of 6 square centimeters. So the total surface area is 42 square centimeters (2 × 9 + 2 × 6 + 2 × 6).

The surface area of an object cannot be predicted on the basis of its volume, any more than the perimeter of a figure is determined by the area of the figure.

Example F

The box in Example E and the box below each have a volume of 18 cubic centimeters. How do the surface areas of the two boxes compare?

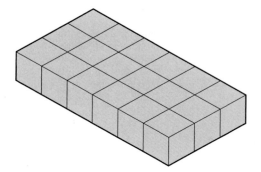

Solution   The top and bottom faces of the box in this figure each have an area of 18 square centimeters, the right and left sides each have an area of 3 square centimeters, and the front and back faces each have an area of 6 square centimeters. So the total surface area is 54 square centimeters. This is 12 square centimeters greater than the surface area of the box in Example E.

Examples E and F show that figures in space can have the same volume but different surface areas. The amount of material you would need to build the box in Example F is about 130 percent of the amount of material you would need to build the box in Example E (130 percent of 42 = 1.3 × 42 ≈ 54), although both have a volume of 18 cubic centimeters.

Volumes and Surface Areas of Space Figures

PRISMS   In Figure 10.47 the length (20) times the width (10) gives the number of cubes (200) on the floor of the box (or base of the rectangular prism). Since the box can be filled with 6 levels of cubes, it will hold 1200 cubes. This volume of 1200 cubic centimeters can be obtained by multiplying the three dimensions of the box: length × width × height. In general, a rectangular prism with length l, width w, and height h has the following volume:

$$\text{Volume} = \text{length} \times \text{width} \times \text{height}$$
$$V = lwh$$

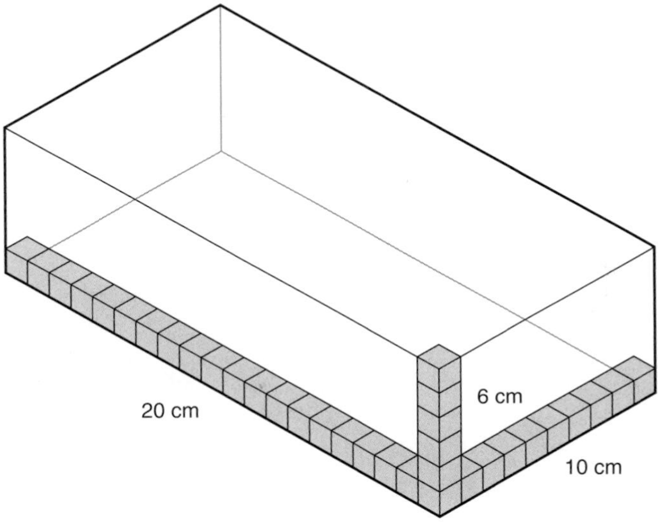

Students in grades 3–5 should develop strategies for determining surface area and volume on the basis of concrete experiences. They should measure various rectangular solids using objects such as tiles and cubes, organize the information, look for patterns, and then make generalizations.

Standards 2000, p. 175

20 cm   6 cm   10 cm

Figure 10.47

The volume of any prism can be found in a similar way. The base of the prism in Figure 10.48 is a right triangle, which is covered by $4\frac{1}{2}$ cubes. Since 6 levels each with $4\frac{1}{2}$ cubes fill the prism, its volume is 6 × 4.5, or 27 cubic centimeters.

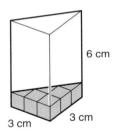

Figure 10.48

6 cm

3 cm   3 cm

3 cm

Make Connections

You can use cubes to help you find volume.

Using Models

Count the cubic units in the shape.

Using Paper and Pencil

There are 3 rows of cubes with 4 cubes in each row. There are 12 cubes in the first layer.

There are 2 layers. There are 24 cubes in all.

The volume is 24 cubic units.

Try It   Find each volume in cubic units.

1.

2.

3.

Sum it Up!   Are all shapes with the same volume always the same shape? Give an example to show why or why not.

Practice   Find each volume in cubic units.

4.

5.

6.

Build shapes that have these numbers of cubes.

	Number of rows	Number in each row	Number of layers	Volume
7.	3	4	4	▨
8.	2	5	3	▨

Journal   9. **Generalize:** How can you use multiplication to find the volume of the figure in problem 7?

Extra Practice, page 521

The number of cubes that cover the base of this prism is the same as the area of the base. Therefore, the volume of the prism can be computed by multiplying the area of the base by the height, or altitude, of the prism. In general, the volume of any right prism having a base of area B and a height of h can be computed by the formula

$$\text{Volume of prism} = \text{area of base} \times \text{height}$$
$$V = Bh$$

The formula for the volume of an oblique prism is suggested by beginning with a stack of cards, as in part a of Figure 10.49, and then pushing them sideways to form an oblique prism, as in part b. If each card in part a is 12.5 centimeters × 7.5 centimeters and the stack is 5 centimeters high, its volume is $12.5 \times 7.5 \times 5$, or 468.75 cubic centimeters. The base of the oblique prism in part b is also 12.5 centimeters × 7.5 centimeters, and its **height**, or **altitude** (the perpendicular distance between its upper and lower bases), is 5 centimeters. Since both stacks contain the same number of cards, their volumes are both 468.75 cubic centimeters. This means that the volume of the oblique prism can be computed by multiplying the area of its base by its height. In general, *the volume of any prism, right or oblique, is the area of its base times its height.*

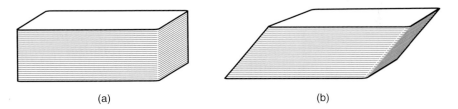

Figure 10.49   (a)   (b)

Example G

Sometimes a prism will have more than one pair of bases, as shown in the following figures. Figure (*1*) is a right prism whose base is a parallelogram. By turning it so that one of its lateral faces becomes the base, as in figure (*2*), we can classify the prism as an oblique prism. Determine the volume of each prism, given the following dimensions:

1. Figure (*1*): area of base, 280 square centimeters; altitude, 6 centimeters

2. Figure (*2*): area of base, 120 square centimeters; altitude, 14 centimeters

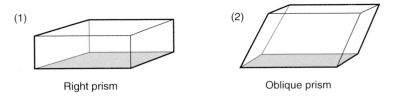

(1)   (2)

Right prism   Oblique prism

Solution   **1.** 1680 cubic centimeters   **2.** 1680 cubic centimeters

---

The surface area of a prism is the sum of the areas of its bases and faces. In right prisms, the faces are rectangles; and in oblique prisms, the faces are rectangles and parallelograms.

CYLINDERS   The cylindrical buildings in Figure 10.50 are part of the Renaissance Center in Detroit. Just as with conventional rectangular buildings, architects need to know the volumes and surface areas of these glass-walled cylinders.

Figure 10.50
Renaissance Center in Detroit

To compute the volumes of cylinders, we continue to use unit cubes even though they do not conveniently fit into a cylinder. More than 33 cubes are needed to cover the base of the cylinder in Figure 10.51. Furthermore, since the cylinder has a height of 12 centimeters, it will take *at least* 12 × 33, or 396, cubes to fill the cylinder.

Although [middle-grade] students may have developed an initial understanding of area and volume, . . . some measurement of area and volume by actually covering shapes and filling objects can be worthwhile for many students.

Standards 2000, p. 242

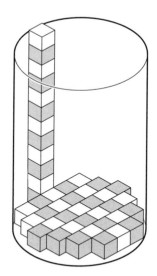

Figure 10.51

If we used smaller cubes in Figure 10.51, they could be packed closer to the boundary of the base and a better approximation would be obtained for the volume of the cylinder. This suggests that the formula for the volume of a cylinder is the same as that for the volume of a prism. For a cylinder with a base of area *B* and a height *h*,

$$\text{Volume of cylinder} = \text{area of base} \times \text{height}$$
$$V = Bh$$

A right cylinder without bases can be formed by joining the opposite edges of a rectangular sheet of paper (Figure 10.52). The circumference of the base of the cylinder is the length of the rectangle, and the height of the cylinder is the height of the rectangle. Therefore, the surface area of the sides of a cylinder is the circumference of the base of the cylinder times its height.

Figure 10.52

For any right cylinder whose base has a radius r and whose height is h, the base has a circumference of $2\pi r$, and the surface area of the side of the cylinder is $2\pi r \times h$. Adding the area of both bases, $2\pi r^2$, to the area of the side of the cylinder produces the total surface area:

$$\text{Surface area of cylinder} = 2\pi rh + 2\pi r^2$$

Example H

Compute the volume and surface area of a tennis ball can if the diameter of its base is 7 centimeters and the height of the can is 20 centimeters.

Solution   Surface area: The radius of the base is 3.5 centimeters, so the top and the base of the can each have an area of $\pi(3.5)^2$ square centimeters, which to two decimal places is 38.48 square centimeters. The circumference of the can is 7π centimeters, which to two decimal places is 21.99 centimeters; so the lateral surface of the can has an area of approximately 21.99×20 square centimeters, which to two decimal places is 439.80 square centimeters. Thus the total surface area of the can is approximately 516.76 square centimeters, or 517 square centimeters when rounded to the nearest whole number. Volume: $20 \times \pi(3.5)^2$ cubic centimeters, which to the nearest whole number is 770 cubic centimeters.

Research Statement

The 7th national mathematics assessment found that questions assessing familiarity with volume and surface area were difficult for fourth and eighth-grade students.

Martin and Strutchens 2000

PYRAMIDS   The Pyramid of Cheops, also known as the Great Pyramid of Egypt, was built about 2600 B.C. and is one of the seven wonders of the ancient world. It has a height of 148 meters. The Transamerica Pyramid in San Francisco (Figure 10.53) has a height of 260 meters and was built in 1972. Even though the Egyptian pyramid is the shorter of these giant pyramids, its volume is several times the volume of the taller pyramid. (See exercise 23 in Exercises and Problems 10.3)

Figure 10.53
Transamerica Pyramid in San Francisco

The pyramid in Figure 10.54d is inside the cube in part b which has a square base *EFGH* and a height *GC*. This pyramid, together with the two pyramids in parts a and c, divide the cube into three congruent pyramids. (Can you see how these fit together?) Therefore, the volume of the pyramid in the cube is one-third of the volume of the cube. That is, the volume of the pyramid is one-third of the area of the base of the cube times the height of the cube.

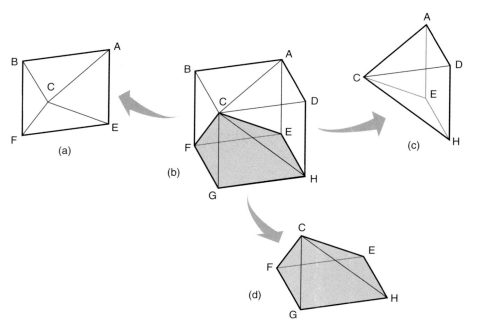

Figure 10.54

In general, if *B* is the area of the base of a pyramid and *h* is the **height,** or **altitude** (perpendicular distance from the apex to the base), of the pyramid, then

$$\text{Volume of pyramid} = \frac{1}{3} \times \text{area of base} \times \text{height}$$

$$V = \frac{1}{3} Bh$$

The surface area of a pyramid is the area of its base plus the area of its lateral (triangular) sides. Exercises and Problems 10.3 has several questions involving the surface area of pyramids.

Example I

Determine the volume of the Pyramid of Cheops to the nearest cubic meter. Its square base has sides of length 232.5 meters, and its height is 148 meters.

Solution   The area of the base is 54,056.25 square meters (232.5 × 232.5), and

$$\frac{1}{3} \times 54,056.25 \times 148 = 2,666,775$$

So the volume of the pyramid is 2,666,775 cubic meters.

CONES   The pile of crude salt in Figure 10.55 has the shape of a cone with a circular base. The conical shape forms as salt is poured from above. The salt has been evaporated from ocean water and awaits further purification.

Figure 10.55

The volume of a cone can be approximated by the volume of a pyramid inscribed in the cone. The hexagonal pyramid in Figure 10.56 has a volume of approximately 430 cubic centimeters, which is slightly less than the volume of the cone. As the number of sides in the base of the pyramid increases, the volume of the pyramid becomes closer to the volume of the cone. Since the volume of the pyramid is one-third the area of its base times its height, we can use the same formula to calculate the volume of a cone. In general, for any cone whose base has area B and whose height is h,

$$\text{Volume of cone} = \frac{1}{3} \times \text{area of base} \times \text{height}$$

$$V = \frac{1}{3} Bh$$

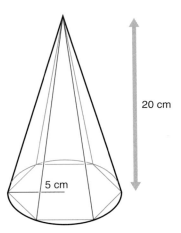

20 cm

5 cm

Figure 10.56

The surface area of the cone in Figure 10.56 is the area of its base, $\pi(5)^2$, plus the area of its lateral surface. The area of the lateral surface can be approximated by the area of the triangular sides of the hexagonal pyramid. The altitude of one of these triangular sides (see Figure 10.57) is approximately equal to the slant height of the cone, which by the Pythagorean theorem is $\sqrt{5^2 + 20^2}$. If s is the length of one side of the hexagonal base, the area of one triangle is $\frac{1}{2}s\sqrt{5^2 + 20^2}$, and the area of the lateral surface is $6(\frac{1}{2}s\sqrt{5^2 + 20^2})$. Notice in Figure 10.57 that $6s$ is the perimeter of the base of the pyramid. Closer approximations can be found by increasing the number of sides of the polygonal base of the pyramid. As the number of sides of the polygon increases, its perimeter $6s$ gets closer to the circumference of the circle, $2\pi(5)$, and the area of the lateral sides of the pyramid gets closer to

$$\frac{1}{2}(2\pi)(5)\sqrt{5^2 + 20^2} = \pi(5)\sqrt{5^2 + 20^2}$$

In general, for a cone of radius r and altitude h, the area of the lateral surface is $\pi r \sqrt{r^2 + h^2}$ and the total surface area is $\pi r \sqrt{r^2 + h^2} + \pi r^2$.

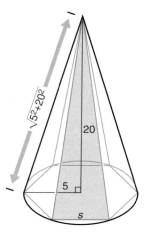

Figure 10.57

Example J

The height of the cone of salt in Figure 10.55 is 12 meters, and the diameter of its base is 32 meters.

1. Determine the number of railroad boxcars this salt will fill if each boxcar has a volume of 80 cubic meters.

2. Determine the number of square meters of plastic sheet needed to cover the lateral surface of this cone of salt.

Solution   1. The area of the base of the cone of salt is approximately 804 square meters. Since

$$\frac{1}{3} \times 804 \times 12 = 3216$$

the volume of the cone to the nearest cubic meter is 3216 cubic meters. This amount of salt will fill about 40 boxcars. **2.** The area of the lateral surface of the cone is approximately

$$\pi(16)\sqrt{16^2 + 12^2} \approx 1005.312$$

So, to the nearest square meter, 1005 square meters of plastic sheet is needed to cover the lateral surface of the cone.

SPHERES   Figure 10.58 shows a view of Earth as seen from the *Apollo 10* spacecraft as it passed over the Moon's surface. Earth, the planets, and their moons are all spherical shapes, spinning and orbiting about a spherical sun. There is considerable variation in the volumes of these objects. Earth has about 18 times the volume of the smallest planet, Mercury. The volume of the largest planet, Jupiter, is 10,900 times the volume of Earth.

Figure 10.58
View from Apollo 10 of Earth over the Moon's surface

The formulas for the volume of a sphere and the surface area of a sphere were known by the ancient Greeks. In fact, Archimedes (ca. 287 to 212 B.C.) discovered some remarkable relationships between a sphere and the smallest cylinder containing it. *The volume of the sphere is two-thirds the volume of the cylinder,* and *the surface area of the sphere is two-thirds the surface area of the cylinder.*

Figure 10.59 shows a sphere of radius *r.* The smallest cylinder that contains the sphere has a height of 2*r.* The volume of this cylinder is

$$\pi r^2 \times 2r = 2\pi r^3$$

Using the relationship discovered by Archimedes, we know that two-thirds of this volume is the volume of the sphere. So,

$$\text{Volume of sphere} = \frac{2}{3} \times 2\pi r^3 = \frac{4}{3}\pi r^3$$

Whenever possible, students should develop formulas and procedures meaningfully through investigation rather than memorize them. Even formulas that are difficult to justify rigorously in the middle grades, . . . , should be treated in ways that help students develop an intuitive sense of their reasonableness.

Standards 2000, p. 244

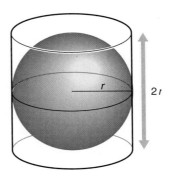

Figure 10.59

The surface area of the cylinder in Figure 10.59 is the sum of the areas of the two bases and the lateral surface of the cylinder. One base has an area of πr^2, and the two bases together have an area of $2\pi r^2$. Since the circumference of the cylinder is $2\pi r$ and the height of the cylinder is 2*r,* the lateral surface area is $2\pi r \times 2r = 4\pi r^2$. So the total surface area of the cylinder is

$$2\pi r^2 + 4\pi r^2 = 6\pi r^2$$

Using Archimedes discovery once again, we know that two-thirds of this area is the area of the sphere. So,

$$\text{Surface area of sphere} = \frac{2}{3} \times 6\pi r^2 = 4\pi r^2$$

Thus the surface area of a sphere is *exactly 4 times* the area of a great circle of the sphere.

The area of a circle and the volume of a sphere can be nicely approximated if we think of π as approximately equal to 3. Then the approximate area of the circle is 3 times the square of the circle's radius,

$$\pi r^2 \approx 3r^2$$

and the volume of the sphere is approximately 4 times the cube of the sphere's radius,

$$\text{Volume of sphere} = \frac{4}{3}\pi r^3 \approx \frac{4}{\cancel{3}}\cancel{3}r^3 = 4r^3$$

The square on the radius of a circle and the cube on the radius of a sphere are shown in Figure 10.60.

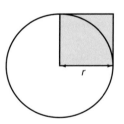

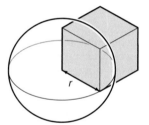

The area of a circle is approximately
3 times the area of the square on its radius.

The volume of a sphere is approximately
4 times the volume of the cube on its radius.

Figure 10.60   (a)   (b)

Example K

Compare the volumes and surface areas of the following two spheres, using the estimations suggested in Figure 10.60.

(1)

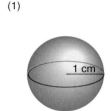

(2)

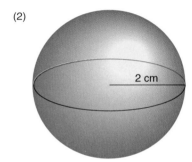

Solution   The volume of sphere (1) is approximately 4 cubic centimeters (4×1^3), and the volume of sphere (2) is approximately 32 cubic centimeters (4×2^3). The sphere whose radius is twice as large has a volume that is 8 times the smaller volume.

The surface area of sphere (1) is approximately 12 square centimeters ($4 \times 3 \times 1^2$), and the surface area of sphere (2) is approximately 48 square centimeters ($4 \times 3 \times 2^2$). The sphere whose radius is twice as large has a surface area that is 4 times the smaller surface area.

NCTM's 5–8 Standard, *Geometry,* recommends that formulas for area and volume be developed gradually:

As students progress through grades 5–8, they should develop more efficient procedures and, ultimately, formulas for finding measures. Length, area, and volume of one-, two-, and three-dimensional figures are especially important over these grade levels. For example, once students have discovered that it is possible to find the area of a rectangle by covering a figure with squares and then counting, they are ready to explore the relationship between areas of rectangles and areas of other geometric figures.*

Curriculum and Evaluation Standards for School Mathematics (Reston, VA: National Council of Teachers of Mathematics, 1989), p. 118.

Archimedes is considered the greatest creative genius of the ancient world. He earned great renown for his mathematical writings and his mechanical inventions. One familiar legend concerns his launching a large ship using pulleys. Archimedes is reported to have boasted that if he had a fixed fulcrum with which to work, he could move anything: "Give me a place to stand and I will move the earth." Archimedes requested that his tomb be inscribed with a figure of a sphere and a cylinder to commemorate his discovery that the volume of a sphere is two-thirds the volume of the circumscribed cylinder. Many centuries later, the Roman orator Cicero discovered the tomb of Archimedes by identifying the inscription honoring Archimedes' request.*

*Archimedes,
ca. 287–212 B.C.*

*D. M. Burton, *The History of Mathematics,* 4th ed. (New York: McGraw-Hill, 1999), pp. 186–199.

Irregular Shapes

The volumes of some figures with irregular shapes can be determined quite easily by submerging them in water and measuring the volume of the water that is displaced. To illustrate this method, we will find the volume in cubic centimeters of the miniature statue in Figure 10.61. Before submerging the statue, we fill the cylinder with water to a height of 700 milliliters. When the statue is placed in the cylinder, the water level rises to the 800-milliliter level. This means that the volume of the statue is equal to the volume of 100 milliliters of water. Since each milliliter equals 1 cubic centimeter, the volume of the statue is 100 cubic centimeters.

Figure 10.61

Creating Surface Area

A potato can be cooked in a shorter time if it is cut into pieces, ice will melt faster if it is crushed, and coffee beans will give a richer flavor if they are ground before they are boiled. The purpose of crushing, grinding, cutting, or, in general, subdividing is to increase the surface area of a substance. You may be aware of this principle and yet be surprised at the rate at which additional surface area is produced.

To illustrate how rapidly surface area can be created, consider a cube that is 2 centimeters on each edge (part a of Figure 10.62). Its volume is 8 cubic centimeters, and its surface area is 24 square centimeters. If this cube is cut into 8 smaller cubes, as in part b, the total volume is still 8 cubic centimeters, but the surface area is doubled, to 48 square centimeters. This can be easily seen by looking at the small cube in the front corner of part b. Faces *a, b,* and *c* contributed 3 square centimeters to the surface area of the original cube; after the cut, 3 more faces of the small cube are exposed, contributing 3 more square centimeters of area. Since this is true for each of the 8 smaller cubes in part b, the total increase in surface area is 8 × 3, or 24 square centimeters. Following this reasoning, when all the small cubes in part b are separated from the large cube, the surface area will be doubled.

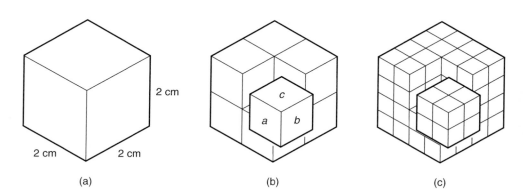

Figure 10.62   (a)   (b)   (c)

If we continue the process, cutting each of the centimeter cubes in Figure 10.62b into 8 smaller cubes, we have 64 cubes whose edges have lengths of $\frac{1}{2}$ centimeter (part c). The total volume of these cubes is still 8 cubic centimeters, but the second cut has again doubled the surface area, increasing it to 96 square centimeters. If the process of halving the dimensions of each small cube is continued, the third set of cuts produces a surface area of $2^3 \times 24 = 192$ square centimeters; after the 12th set of cuts, the surface area has increased to $2^{12} \times 24 = 98,304$ square centimeters! During this splitting process *the volume has remained the same*—8 cubic centimeters.

This process of subdividing can also be used to double the surface area of a sphere. If, for example, a sphere of radius 2 centimeters is formed into 8 smaller spheres, each with a radius of 1 centimeter, the total volume will remain the same, but the surface area will double. As in the case of the cubes, if we continue this subdividing process with the smaller spheres, the surface area will double for each subdivision. Consider the effect when water is sprayed into the air in a fine mist, as from snow-making machines. The surface area of each drop of water is increased many times, allowing the small particles of water to freeze quickly in midair into snowflakes.

Problem-Solving Application

Examples at the beginning of this section showed that, for a given volume, the surface area of a figure can vary. We also saw in the preceding paragraphs how the surface can become arbitrarily large while the volume remains constant. These examples suggest the following question: For a given volume, is there a shape that has the least surface area, and if so, what is this shape?

PROBLEM

If a rectangular solid has a volume of 24 cubic centimeters, what is the smallest surface area it can have?

Understanding the Problem   Figures made of 24 cubes can help us consider different shapes. The following rectangular prisms are two possibilities. **Question 1:** What is the surface area of each, and which has less surface area?

If students move rapidly to using formulas without adequate conceptual foundation in area and volume, many could have underlying confusion. . . . For example, some students may hold the misconception that if the volume of a three-dimensional shape is known, then its surface area can be determined.

Standards 2000, p. 242

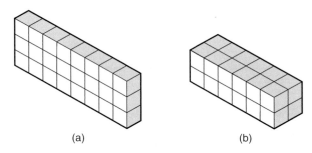

(a)   (b)

Devising a Plan   One approach is to build (or sketch) figures and compute their surface areas. **Question 2:** How many different rectangular prisms can be built using 24 whole cubes, and which has the least surface area?

Carrying Out the Plan   A $2 \times 3 \times 4$ prism [figure (c)] has the least amount of surface area of all the figures that can be built from 24 whole cubes. Imagine that the 24 cubes are made of clay that can be molded into one large cube [figure (d)]. **Question 3:** What is the length of a side of this cube, and what is the cube's surface area?

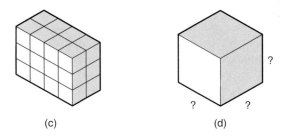

(c)   (d)

Looking Back   Each edge of the cube in figure (d) has a length of $\sqrt[3]{24}$ centimeters, or approximately 2.88 centimeters. Thus the area of 1 face is approximately 8.29 square centimeters ($2.88 \times 2.88 \approx 8.29$), and the total surface area of the cube is approximately 50 square centimeters ($6 \times 8.29 \approx 50$). This is 2 square centimeters less than the area of figure (c). Now imagine the 24 cubes of clay being molded into a sphere of volume 24 cubic centimeters. **Question 4:** What is the surface area of a sphere that has a volume of 24 cubic centimeters?

Answers to Questions 1–4   **1.** Prism (a) has a surface area of 70 square centimeters and prism (b) has a surface area of 56 square centimeters.   **2.** Six such prisms can be built; the $2 \times 3 \times 4$ prism has the least surface area, 52 square centimeters.   **3.** The length of a side is $\sqrt[3]{24}$ centimeters, or

approximately 2.88 centimeters; the cube's surface area is approximately 50 square centimeters.
4. A sphere with a volume of 24 cubic centimeters has a radius of approximately 1.8 centimeters.

$$\frac{4}{3}\pi(1.8)^3 \approx 24.43 \approx 24$$

A sphere with a radius of 1.8 centimeters has a surface area of approximately 41 square centimeters.

$$4\pi(1.8)^2 \approx 40.72 \approx 41$$

Notice that the surface area of the sphere is approximately 9 square centimeters less than the surface area of the cube in figure (*d*). In general, for a given volume, *the sphere is the shape with the least surface area.*

EXERCISES AND PROBLEMS 10.3*

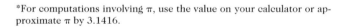

1. a. In the cartoon above, what is the volume of the wheel, to the nearest cubic centimeter, if the wheel has a length and height of 1 meter, a thickness of 20 centimeters, and an inner diameter of 46 centimeters?
 b. If this wheel is made of stone that has a mass of 7 grams per cubic centimeter, what is the mass of the wheel to the nearest kilogram?

The measures of volume and surface area depend on the size of the unit for measuring. Use each of the following cubic units to find the volume and surface area of each figure in 2 and 3.

Unit (i)

Unit (ii)

2. a.

b.

3. a.
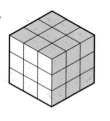
b.
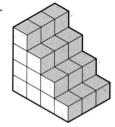

4. a. How many cubic feet equal 5.2 cubic yards?
 b. How many cubic centimeters equal .3 cubic meter?

5. a. How many cubic inches equal 1 cubic yard?
 b. How many cubic millimeters equal 1 cubic meter?

*For computations involving π, use the value on your calculator or approximate π by 3.1416.

6. The liter is a metric unit approximately equal to 1 quart. A 1-quart milk carton has a square base of 7 centimeters × 7 centimeters and vertical sides of height 19.3 centimeters.
a. What is its volume?
b. Which has a greater volume, a quart or a liter?

Compute the volumes of the figures in 7 through 12 to the nearest cubic centimeter, and compute their surface areas to the nearest square centimeter. (*Hint:* The Pythagorean theorem is needed in exercises 7b, 8b, 11b, 12b, 14a, and 14b.)

7. a. Square pyramid

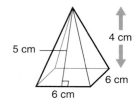

b. Triangular isosceles prism

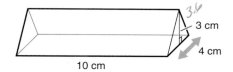

8. a. Trapezoidal prism

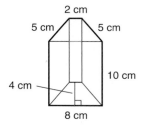

b. Square pyramid

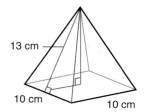

9. a. Sphere

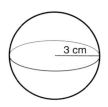

b. Cylinder

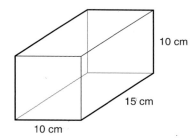

10. a. Rectangular prism

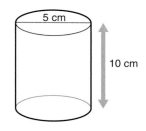

b. Sphere

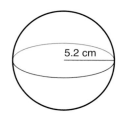

11. a. Trapezoidal prism

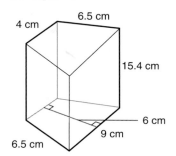

b. Equilateral triangular pyramid

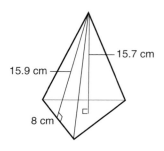

15.7 cm

15.9 cm

8 cm

12. a. Cylinder

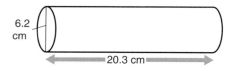

6.2 cm

20.3 cm

b. Hexagonal pyramid

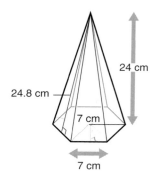

24 cm

24.8 cm

7 cm

7 cm

Compute the volumes to the nearest .1 cubic centimeter for the figures in exercises 13 and 14.

13. a. Cone

4 cm

3 cm

b. Oblique rectangular prism

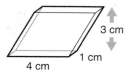

3 cm

4 cm   1 cm

14. a. Cone on a cylinder

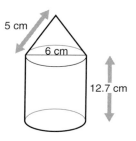

5 cm

6 cm

12.7 cm

b. Cone

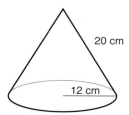

20 cm

12 cm

REASONING AND PROBLEM SOLVING

15. The number of fish that can be put in an aquarium depends on the amount of water the tank holds, the size of the fish, and the capacity of the pump and filter system.

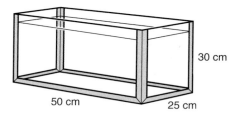

30 cm

50 cm   25 cm

   a. How many liters of water will this tank hold?

   b. The recommended number of tropical fish for this tank is 30. How many cubic centimeters of space would each fish have?

   c. Goldfish need more space and oxygen than tropical fish. Goldfish that are about 5 centimeters long require 3000 cubic centimeters of water. How many goldfish could live in this tank?

   d. How many square centimeters of glass are needed for this tank if there is glass on all sides except the top?

16. The concrete foundation for the office building on the corner of Congress and State streets in Boston required 496 truckloads of concrete and was formed in one continuous pouring carried on over a 30-hour period.
    a. The concrete was poured to a depth of 1.8 meters and covered an area of 2420 square meters. How many cubic meters of concrete were used?
    b. If each truckload was the same size, what was the volume of each load of concrete to the nearest .1 cubic meter?

17. A house with ceilings that are 2.4 meters high has five rectangular rooms with the following dimensions: 4 meters × 5 meters; 4 meters × 4 meters; 6 meters × 4 meters; 6 meters × 6 meters; and 6 meters × 5.5 meters. Which of the following air conditioners will be adequate to cool this house: an 18,000-Btu unit that will cool 280 cubic meters; a 21,000-Btu unit that will cool 340 cubic meters; or a 24,000-Btu unit that will cool 400 cubic meters?

18. A woodshed is 3 meters × 2 meters × 2 meters. If each 1.5 cubic meters of firewood sells for $25, how much will it cost to fill the shed with wood?

19. A catalog describes two types of upright freezers. Type A has a storage capacity of 60 centimeters × 60 centimeters × 150 centimeters and costs $339; type B has a storage capacity of 55 centimeters × 72 centimeters × 160 centimeters and costs $379. Which freezer gives you more cubic centimeters per dollar?

20. A drugstore sells the same brand of talcum powder in two types of cylindrical cans: Can A has a diameter of 5.4 centimeters and a height of 9 centimeters and sells for $1.59; can B has a diameter of 6.2 centimeters and a height of 12.4 centimeters and sells for $2.99. Which can is the better buy?

21. An auditorium has 20 large cylindrical columns. Each column has a height of 22 feet from the floor to the ceiling and a diameter of 2.5 feet. How many gallons of paint, to the nearest whole number, must be purchased to paint these columns if each gallon of paint covers 350 square feet?

22. A cubic box with no top is to be made of plywood. How many square feet of plywood are needed if the box is to hold 64 cubic feet?

23. The Great Pyramid of Egypt has a height of 148 meters and a square base with a perimeter of 930 meters. The Transamerica Pyramid in San Francisco has a height of 260 meters and a square base with a perimeter of 140 meters.
    a. The volume of the Great Pyramid is how many times the volume of the Transamerica Pyramid?

    b. The heights (altitudes) of the triangular faces of the Great Pyramid and Transamerica Pyramid are 188 and 261 meters, respectively. The bases of these triangles are 232.5 and 35 meters, respectively. The surface area of the four faces of the Great Pyramid is about how many times the surface area of the four faces of the Transamerica Pyramid?

24. Swimming pools must be tested daily to determine the pH factor and the chlorine content. Pumps and filters are also necessary, and some pools have heating systems.
    a. What is the depth of a 6-meter × 12-meter pool to the nearest .01 meter that contains 193 kiloliters of water?
    b. If this pool requires 112 grams of chlorine every 2 days, how many kilograms of chlorine should be purchased for a 90-day period?
    c. The Alcoa Solar Heating System for pools has 32 square panels, each 120 centimeters × 120 centimeters. Will this heating system fit onto a 5-meter × 8-meter roof?
    d. Each panel for this system holds 5.68 liters of water. What is the total mass of the water in 32 panels to the nearest kilogram?

25. One of the silos pictured below holds corn, and the other holds hay. Chopped corn and hay are blown into the tops of the silos through pipes running up from the ground.
    a. The silos have a radius of 3 meters and a height of 18 meters. What is the volume, to the nearest cubic meter, of one of these silos?
    b. If a blower can load 1 cubic meter of hay in 3 minutes, how many hours (to the nearest .1 hour) will it take to fill one of these silos?

26. The spheres shown in the photograph were constructed in Charleston, South Carolina, and then towed by tug to Quincy, Massachusetts. Each aluminum sphere for a liquefied natural gas tanker has a diameter of approximately 36.6 meters and a mass of 725,750 kilograms (800 tons).

Spheres for storage of liquefied natural gas

   a. What is the volume, to the nearest cubic meter, of one sphere?

   b. A heavy external coating of insulation on the surface of the sphere enables the sphere to maintain liquefied natural gas at −165°C. How many square meters of insulation, to the nearest whole number, are needed for one sphere?

27. This art form is Alex Lieberman's *Argo*, which is at the Walker Art Center in Minneapolis. The entire display has a mass of about 4535 kilograms.

   a. The cylinder shown in front is 2 meters tall and 1 meter in diameter. What is its surface area (including the bases) to the nearest .01 square meter?

   b. If each square meter of metal in this cylinder has a mass of 92 kilograms, what is the mass of the cylinder to the nearest .1 kilogram?

28. **Featured Strategies: Making a Drawing and Making a Table** An open-top box is to be formed by cutting out squares from the corners of a 50-centimeter × 30-centimeter rectangular sheet of material. The height of the box must be a whole number of centimeters. What size squares should be cut out to obtain the box with maximum volume?

   a. **Understanding the Problem** This diagram shows how the box is to be formed. If 6-centimeter × 6-centimeter squares are cut from the corners, the height of the box will be 6 centimeters. In this case, what will the width and length of the box be?

   b. **Devising a Plan** One plan for solving this problem is to systematically consider corner squares of increasing size. What is the largest square with whole-number dimensions that can be cut from the corners and still produce a box?

   c. **Carrying Out the Plan** Complete the following table, and use inductive reasoning to predict the size of the corner squares needed to obtain the box of maximum volume.

SIZE OF SQUARE (CENTIMETERS)	VOLUME OF BOX (CUBIC CENTIMETERS)
2 × 2	
4 × 4	
6 × 6	
8 × 8	
10 × 10	
12 × 12	
14 × 14	

   d. **Looking Back** The preceding table shows that as the size of the squares at the corners increases, the volume of the box increases for a while and then decreases. Try a few more sizes for the squares, using whole numbers for dimensions, to see if you can obtain a greater volume for the box.

29. Suppose a large cube is built from 1000 small cubes and then painted on all six faces. When the large cube is disassembled, how many of the small cubes will be unpainted? Separate the remaining small cubes into groups according to the number of faces painted, and compute the number in each group. Generalize this result for an $n \times n \times n$ cube.

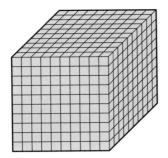

30. A regulation football has a length of approximately
PS 27 centimeters and a diameter of approximately 16
centimeters. Describe two different methods of approximating its volume in cubic centimeters.

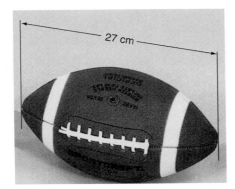

27 cm

31. Assume that a drop of unvaporized gasoline is a
PS sphere with a diameter of 4 milliliters.
   a. If this drop is divided into 8 smaller drops, each
with a diameter of 2 millimeters, the total surface area of the 8 drops is how many times the
surface area of the original drop?
   b. If each drop with a diameter of 2 millimeters is
divided into 8 smaller drops, each with a diameter of 1 millimeter, the total surface area of the
64 drops is how many times the surface area of
the original drop?
   c. If the vaporizing mechanism in a car's engine
carries out this splitting process 20 times, how
many times is the surface area of the original
drop of gasoline increased?

32. An open-top box is to be formed from a sheet of ma-
PS terial 16 inches by 16 inches by cutting out the
squares with whole-number dimensions from the
corners and folding up the edges.

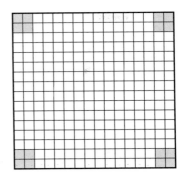

Two such boxes are shown here.

(i) 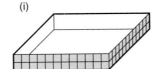   (ii)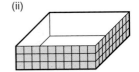

   a. What is the volume of the box in (*i*)?
   b. What is the volume of the box in (*ii*)?
   c. What are the dimensions and volume of the box
having the greatest volume that can be made
from the original sheet of material?

33. A cubic block of cement is tossed into a cylindrical
PS tank of water with a diameter of 2 feet, causing the
water to rise 1.5 inches.
   a. What is the volume of the cube to the nearest cubic inch?
   b. What is the length of the edge of the cube to the
nearest .1 inch?

34. A bank's monthly rental fees for safe deposit boxes
with various dimensions are listed below.

BOX SIZE (INCHES)	FEE ($)
(1) $12\frac{3}{4} \times 4\frac{1}{2} \times 1\frac{1}{2}$	6.80
(2) $22 \times 4\frac{3}{4} \times 1\frac{1}{2}$	10.75
(3) $23\frac{3}{4} \times 4\frac{3}{4} \times 2\frac{1}{2}$	18.40
(4) $21\frac{1}{2} \times 3\frac{5}{8} \times 5$	23.45
(5) $21\frac{1}{4} \times 5\frac{1}{2} \times 4\frac{3}{4}$	32.00
(6) $23\frac{3}{4} \times 10 \times 2\frac{3}{4}$	36.00
(7) $21\frac{1}{4} \times 10\frac{3}{4} \times 3\frac{1}{4}$	38.60
(8) $21\frac{1}{4} \times 10\frac{1}{2} \times 4\frac{1}{2}$	50.00

a. Find the volume of each box to the nearest .01 cubic inch. (*Suggestion:* Change the fractions to decimals.)

b. What is the cost per cubic inch to the nearest .1 cent for renting each box?

c. What happens to the cost per cubic inch as the size of the boxes increase?

. . . .

ONLINE LEARNING CENTER   www.mhhe.com/bennett-nelson

• Math Investigation 10.3 *Approximating Areas and Volumes*
Section-Related: • Links • Writing/Discussion Problems • Bibliography

. . . .

PUZZLER

A cylindrical can such as the one shown here is full of water. If you pour the water from the can, how will you know when one-half the water is gone if you have no measuring device?

CHAPTER REVIEW

1. Systems of measurement
  a. Nonstandard units of length, area, and volume provide background for understanding standard units of measure.
  b. The **English system** arose from natural nonstandard units of measure such as the length of a foot. It is used in the United States.
  c. The **metric system** and the **International System of Units** (SI) are based on the meter and are used in almost all countries.
  d. The **precision** of a measurement is to within one-half of the smallest unit of measure used.
  e. Mass is a measure of a quantity of matter and is not affected by the force of gravity.
  f. Weight is a measure of the force of gravitational pull on a body.

2. English system
  a. Units for length: inch (in), **foot** (ft), **yard** (yd), and **mile** (mi)
  b. Units for volume: ounce (oz), **cup** (c), **pint** (pt), **quart** (qt), and **gallon** (gal)
  c. Units for weight: ounce (oz), **pound** (lb), and **ton** (tn)

  d. Temperature is measured in degrees on the Fahrenheit scale.

3. Metric system
  a. The **metric prefixes** are related by powers of 10. (Those in the following list with asterisks are the most common.)

kilo*	1000
hecto	100
deka	10
deci	1/10
centi*	1/100
milli*	1/1000

  b. Units for length: millimeter (mm), **centimeter** (cm), **meter** (m), and **kilometer** (km)
  c. Units for volume: milliliter (mL), **liter** (L), and **kiloliter** (kL)
  d. Units for mass: milligram (mg), **gram** (g), and **kilogram** (kg)
  e. Temperature is measured in degrees on the Celsius scale.

4. Area and perimeter
   a. The common **English units for area: square inch** (in²), **square foot** (ft²), **square yard** (yd²), **acre**, and **square mile** (mi²)
   b. The common **metric units for area: square millimeter** (mm²), **square centimeter** (cm²), **square meter** (m²), and **square kilometer** (km²)
   c. **Perimeter** is a measure of the length of the boundary of a region.
   d. **Rectangle:** $A = l \times w$, where l is the length and w is the width of the rectangle.
   e. **Parallelogram:** $A = b \times h$, where b is the length of the base and h is the altitude to the base.
   f. **Triangle:** $A = \frac{1}{2} \times bh$, where b is the length of the base and h is the altitude to that base.
   g. **Trapezoid:** $A = \frac{1}{2}(b + u) \times h$, where b and u are the lengths of the bases and h is the altitude between the bases.
   h. **Circle:** $A = \pi r^2$, where r is the radius of the circle.
   i. The **circumference** C of a circle with diameter d and radius r is $C = \pi d = 2\pi r$.

5. Volume and surface area
   a. The common nonliquid **English units for volume: cubic inch** (in³), **cubic foot** (ft³), and **cubic yard** (yd³)
   b. The common nonliquid **metric units for volume: cubic millimeter** (mm³), **cubic centimeter** (cm³), and **cubic meter** (m³)
   c. **Prism and cylinder:** $V = B \times h$, where B is the area of the base of the prism and h is the altitude.
   d. **Pyramid and cone:** $V = \frac{1}{3} \times Bh$, where B is the area of the base and h is the altitude.
   e. **Sphere:** $V = \frac{4}{3} \times \pi r^3$, where r is the radius of the sphere.
   f. The **surface area of a prism or pyramid** is the total area of the faces of these polyhedra.
   g. The **surface area of a right cylinder** is $2\pi rh + 2\pi r^2$, where r is the radius of the base and h is the altitude of the cylinder.
   h. The **surface area of a sphere** is $4\pi r^2$, where r is the radius of the sphere.

CHAPTER TEST

(For all questions involving π, use the value on your calculator or approximate π by 3.1416.)

1. Indicate the most appropriate metric unit to use in measuring each item.
   a. Mass of a bar of soap
   b. Volume of a bottle of eyedrops
   c. Length of a house
   d. Mass of a person
   e. Area of a football field
   f. Volume of a truckload of loam

2. Complete each equality below.
   a. 3.5 feet = _____ inches
   b. 1 square yard = _____ square feet
   c. 3.4 gallons = _____ quarts
   d. 2.5 quarts = _____ ounces
   e. 2.5 cubic yards = _____ cubic feet
   f. 2.75 pounds = _____ ounces

3. Complete each equality below.
   a. 1.6 grams = _____ milligrams
   b. 4.7 meters = _____ centimeters
   c. 5.2 kilometers = _____ meters
   d. 2500 milliliters = _____ liters
   e. 1.6 square centimeters = _____ square millimeters
   f. 1 cubic meter = _____ cubic centimeters

4. Complete each statement below.
   a. 1.6 liters of water has a mass of _____ grams
   b. 32° Fahrenheit equals _____ Celsius
   c. 55 cubic centimeters has a volume of _____ milliliters
   d. 2 cubic decimeters of water has a mass of _____ kilograms
   e. 1 kilometer equals approximately _____ miles
   f. 1 kilogram of water weighs approximately _____ pounds

5. Precision is determined by the smallest unit used for a given measurement. Determine the minimum and maximum measurement for each of the following.
   a. A 5.3-kilogram bag of dog food
   b. An 85-gram tube of toothpaste
   c. A 4.12-ounce box of cake mix

6. Find the area of the dodecagon below, using each of the given units.

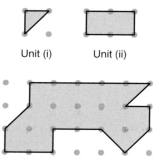

Unit (i)   Unit (ii)

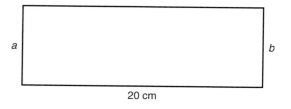

7. Find the area and perimeter or circumference of each figure.

a. Parallelogram   **b.** Isosceles triangle

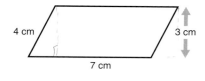

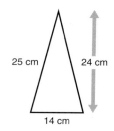

c. Trapezoid   **d.** Circle with diameter

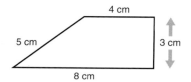

8. Edges a and b of a rectangular sheet of paper are taped together to form a cylinder without bases. What is the diameter of the cylinder to the nearest .1 centimeter?

a b

20 cm

9. Find the area of each shaded region.

a.   **b.**

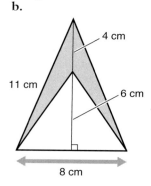

15 cm   4 cm

9 cm   11 cm   6 cm

8 cm

10. Find the volume and surface area of the figure below, using each of the given cubic units. The unit of area is the face of each cube.

Unit (i)   Unit (ii)

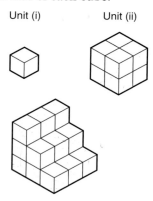

11. Find the volume and surface area of each figure if the figures are solid (that is, no missing cubes) and each single cube has a volume of 1 cubic centimeter.

a.   **b.**

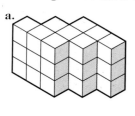

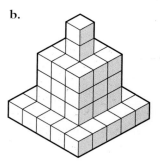

c.

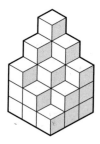

12. Find the volume of each figure to the nearest .1 cubic centimeter.

a. Square pyramid

24 cm

14 cm

b. Right cylinder

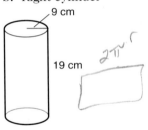

9 cm

19 cm

$2\pi r$

surface
area

c. Sphere

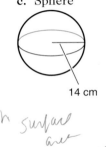

14 cm

d. Square pyramid

14.55

25 cm

top & bott
$2\pi r$, 14 cm

c. Right cone

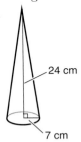

24 cm

7 cm

d. Rectangular prism

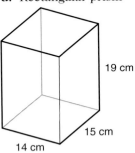

19 cm

15 cm

14 cm

13. Find the surface area of each figure to the nearest .1 square centimeter.

a. Rectangular prism

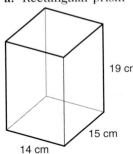

19 cr

15 cm

14 cm

b. Right cylinder

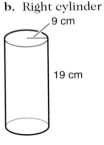

9 cm

19 cm

14. How many cubic yards of concrete (to the nearest .1 cubic yard) are needed to make a base for a square patio if each edge of the square has a length of 11 feet and the cement is poured to a depth of .8 foot?

15. A store sells two types of shelf paper. Type A has dimensions of 5 meters × 30 centimeters and costs $3.70. Type B has dimensions of 4 meters × 35 centimeters and costs $3.50. Which type is the better buy?

16. The cost of a rental car for a two-week 1600-kilometer trip across northern Spain is $414. The cost does not include gasoline, which is 52 cents per liter. If the car uses 1 liter of gasoline per 13 kilometers, what is the total cost for the rental fee plus the gasoline?

MOTIONS IN GEOMETRY

SPOTLIGHT ON TEACHING

Excerpts from NCTM's Standards for School Mathematics Prekindergarten through Grade 2*

Students can naturally use their own physical experiences with shapes to learn about transformations such as slides (translations), turns (rotations), and flips (reflections). They use these movements intuitively when they solve puzzles, turning the pieces, flipping them over, and experimenting with new arrangements. . . .

Teachers should choose geometric tasks that are accessible to all students and sufficiently open-ended to engage students with a range of interests. For example, a second-grade teacher might instruct the class to find all the different ways to put five squares together so that one edge of each square coincides with an edge of at least one other square (see Fig. 4.15). The task should include keeping a record of the pentominoes that are identified and developing a strategy for recognizing when they are transformations of another pentomino. Teachers can encourage students to develop strategies for being systematic by asking, "How will you know if each pentomino is different from all the others? Are you certain you have identified all the possibilities?"

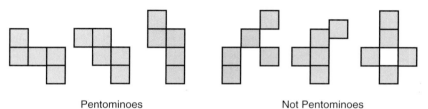

Pentominoes   Not Pentominoes

Figure 4.15

Principles and Standards for School Mathematics (Reston, VA: National Council of Teachers of Mathematics 2000), pp. 99–100.

MATH ACTIVITY 11.1

TRACING FIGURES FROM MOTIONS WITH TILES

Materials: Color tiles in Manipulative Kit

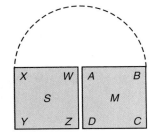

1. The two tiles shown here are labeled S for stationary tile and M for moving tile. Imagine rotating tile M about point A, keeping point A fixed, until side $\overline{AB}$ is next to side $\overline{XW}$; then rotate tile M by keeping point B fixed until side $\overline{CB}$ is next to side $\overline{XY}$; then rotate tile M by keeping point C fixed so that side $\overline{DC}$ is next to side $\overline{YZ}$; finally, rotate tile M by keeping point D fixed so that tile M is back in its starting position.

   a. For the first part of the motion of tile M about tile S, point B traces out the dotted semicircle shown in the figure at the left. Try to visualize the figure traced out by point B for the complete motion of tile M about tile S, and make a prediction about its shape.

   b. Carry out the motion of tile M about tile S, and sketch the path traced by B. You may want to have a classmate help you hold and move the tiles.

   *c. Remove tile M and trace around tile S to mark its position relative to the figure traced by point B. The figure traced by point B can be subdivided into a large right triangle with three semicircles on its legs. Write about relationships between the area of tile S and the area of the right triangle; the area of tile S and the total area of the two small semicircles; and the total area of the two small semicircles and the area of the large semicircle.

2. Each of the figures shown below is created by the path of a point on tile M as tile M is moved about tile S. (*Note:* These figures are smaller than the ones that will be reproduced by your tiles.)

   a. Write detailed directions for moving tile M about tile S so that some point on tile M traces out each figure. Include in your description the location of tile S and the point on tile M which traces out the figure.

   b. Using tile S as the unit of area, determine the area of each figure. Explain with a diagram how you obtained each area.

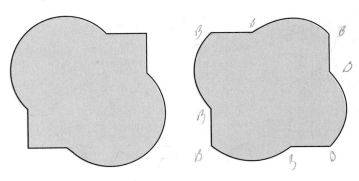

SECTION 11.1

CONGRUENCE AND CONSTRUCTIONS

"WE'RE HERE TO FIX THE COPIER."

PROBLEM OPENER

Cut a 3 × 8 rectangle into two congruent parts, and form a 2 × 12 rectangle.

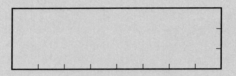

There is an old belief that everyone has a "double"—someone who looks exactly like him or her—somewhere in the world. Two-dimensional and three-dimensional objects often do look exactly alike. Copy machines are able to make reproductions of two-dimensional figures that have the same *size* and *shape* as the originals. The reproductions are said to be *congruent* to the original figures. Intuitively, we think of two plane figures as **congruent** if one can be moved onto the other so that they coincide. The idea of motion or movement is an important concept in mathematics and will be explored in this chapter.

Mappings

If triangle *ABC* in Figure 11.1 is traced on paper and flipped over, it can be placed on triangle *RST* so that the points of each triangle coincide. The correspondence of point *A* with *R*, *B* with *S*, and *C* with *T* is indicated by

$$A \leftrightarrow R \qquad B \leftrightarrow S \qquad C \leftrightarrow T$$

We say that *A* corresponds to *R*, *B* corresponds to *S*, and *C* corresponds to *T*. These pairs of vertices are called **corresponding vertices.**

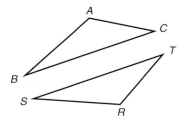

Figure 11.1

If triangle *ABC* is placed onto triangle *RST*, each point on the first triangle corresponds to exactly one point on the second triangle. This one-to-one correspondence of points is a special type of *function*. In Section 2.2 we discussed functions that assign numbers to numbers. In geometry, there are functions that assign points to points, such that to each point in one set there corresponds a unique point, called the **image**, in a second set. Such functions are called **mappings.** In the mapping of △*ABC* to △*RST* in Figure 11.1, the following sides and angles are matched with one another:

Corresponding sides	*Corresponding angles*
$\overline{AB} \leftrightarrow \overline{RS}$	$\angle B \leftrightarrow \angle S$
$\overline{BC} \leftrightarrow \overline{ST}$	$\angle C \leftrightarrow \angle T$
$\overline{AC} \leftrightarrow \overline{RT}$	$\angle A \leftrightarrow \angle R$

Such pairs of sides and angles are called **corresponding** sides and **corresponding angles;** these concepts are used in the following definition.

CONGRUENT POLYGONS   Two polygons are **congruent** if and only if there is a mapping from one to the other such that

1. Corresponding sides are congruent.

2. Corresponding angles are congruent.

In Figure 11.1, triangle *ABC* and triangle *RST* are congruent because their corresponding sides and angles are congruent. This congruence is indicated by writing △*ABC* ≅ △*RST*.

Example A

The following triangles are congruent. Complete the congruence statement △ _____ ≅ △ _____ , and list the pairs of corresponding vertices, sides, and angles.

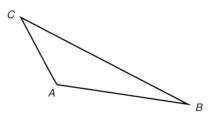
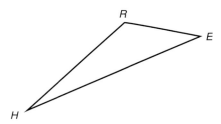

Solution   △*ABC* ≅ △*RHE*

Corresponding vertices: $A \leftrightarrow R$, $B \leftrightarrow H$, $C \leftrightarrow E$

Corresponding sides: $\overline{AB} \leftrightarrow \overline{RH}$,$\overline{BC} \leftrightarrow \overline{HE}$, $\overline{CA} \leftrightarrow \overline{ER}$

(continued on page 718)

Corresponding angles: $\angle A \leftrightarrow \angle R$, $\angle B \leftrightarrow \angle H$, $\angle C \leftrightarrow \angle E$

Notice that the order of the letters in the statement of congruence in Example A indicates which pairs of vertices, sides, and angles correspond.

$$\triangle ABC \cong \triangle RHE$$

To determine if *two* polygons are congruent, we set up a correspondence between their vertices and check to see if their corresponding sides and corresponding angles are congruent. To construct a figure that is congruent to a given figure, we construct corresponding sides and corresponding angles that are congruent to those given. This section introduces techniques for constructing congruent figures.

Constructing Segments and Angles

The study of geometry in grades 3–5 requires thinking *and* doing. As students sort, build, draw, model, trace, measure, and construct, their capacity to visualize geometric relationships will develop. At the same time they are learning to reason and to make, test, and justify conjectures about these relationships.

Standards 2000, p. 165

Geometric figures can be constructed in many ways. One of the more common methods in recent years is the drawing and shading of figures by computers. In Section 9.1 we used paper folding to form perpendicular and parallel lines, angle and line bisectors, and various types of angles and polygons. The Mira, which was introduced in Section 9.4 for locating lines of symmetry, is also useful for certain constructions. A few examples of constructions with the Mira are given at the end of this section and in Exercises and Problems 11.1. Historically, a geometric figure that is produced with only a straightedge and compass is called a **construction**. A **straightedge** is used to draw lines, and unlike a ruler, it has no markings. The compass was introduced in Section 9.2 for constructing circles and regular polygons. A compass opening of length r can be used to draw a circle of radius r (Figure 11.2).

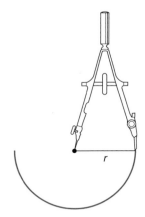

Figure 11.2

To carry out the constructions in this section, you will need a straightedge (or a ruler) and a compass. Try each construction on your own before reading the steps that are given. Attempting each construction will help you to think about the steps that are given, and you may discover a method of your own.

CONSTRUCTING SEGMENTS   Two **line segments** are **congruent** if they have the same length. For example, if $\overline{AB}$ and $\overline{CD}$ have the same length, then $\overline{AB}$ is congruent to $\overline{CD}$, and we write $\overline{AB} \cong \overline{CD}$. The common method of obtaining a line segment that is congruent to a given segment is to measure the given segment with a ruler and then mark off this length on a line. The following example shows how congruent segments can be constructed by using a straightedge and compass.

Example B

Construct a line segment that is congruent to segment $\overline{AB}$.

Original segment

Solution *Step 1* Use a straightedge to draw a line segment that is longer than $\overline{AB}$; label point C.

Step 2 Open the compass to span $\overline{AB}$. Place one end of the compass at point C, and mark point D. Then $\overline{AB} \cong \overline{CD}$.

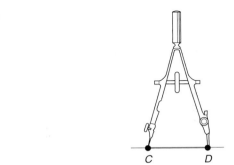

If $\overline{AB}$ in Example B is longer than the opening of the compass, intermediate points can be marked off on $\overline{AB}$. Two such intermediate points are shown in Figure 11.3. The parts of $\overline{AB}$ can then be transferred to the new line by using the compass, as in Example B.

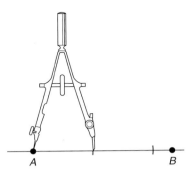

Figure 11.3

CONSTRUCTING ANGLES   Two **angles** are **congruent** if they have the same measure. For example, if $\angle ABC$ and $\angle DEF$ have the same measure, then $\angle ABC$ is congruent to $\angle DEF$, and we write $\angle ABC \cong \angle DEF$. In Section 9.2 we constructed angles of a given number of degrees by measuring the angles with a protractor. Angles can also be reproduced by using a straightedge and compass.

Example C

Construct an angle that is congruent to angle *B*.

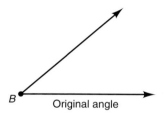

Original angle

Solution   *Step 1* Use a straightedge to draw a line segment and label point *S*.

Step 2 Place the end of the compass at point *B* of the original angle, and draw an arc. Label points *A* and *C* on the sides of the angle, as shown.

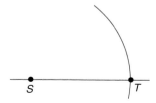

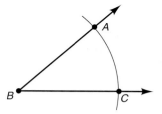

Step 3 Using the same compass opening, place the compass at *S* on the new line and draw an arc. Label point *T* as shown.

Step 4 Place the compass at point *C* of the original angle and adjust the opening to produce an arc through point *A*.

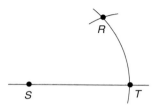

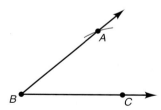

Step 5 Using the same opening, place the compass at point *T* on the new line and draw an arc to locate point *R*.

Step 6 Use a straightedge to connect point *R* to point *S*. Then ∡*ABC* ≅ ∡*RST*.

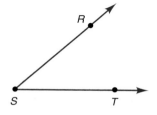

Constructing Triangles

Figure 11.4 shows two congruent triangles: $\triangle ABC \cong \triangle DEF$.

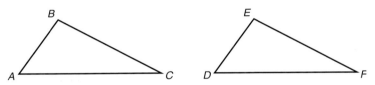

Figure 11.4

The congruence of the triangles implies a correspondence $A \leftrightarrow D$, $B \leftrightarrow E$, and $C \leftrightarrow F$, such that the corresponding sides and corresponding angles of the triangles are congruent. However, to construct a triangle that is congruent to a given triangle, it is not necessary to construct three congruent sides and three congruent angles separately. The following example shows that it is only necessary to construct three congruent sides. The sides of $\triangle ABC$ are used in this example.

Example D

Construct a triangle whose sides are congruent to the three line segments given:

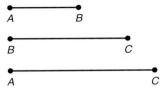

Solution *Step 1* Use a straightedge and compass to construct $\overline{DF}$, which is congruent to $\overline{AC}$.

Step 2 Place the ends of the compass on points A and B of $\overline{AB}$. Then place one end of the compass at point D and draw an arc. All the points on this arc are the distance AB from point D.

Step 3 Place the ends of the compass on points B and C of $\overline{BC}$. Then place one end of the compass on F and draw an arc. The intersection of the two arcs is the third vertex point, E.

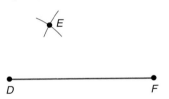

Step 4 Draw segments $\overline{DE}$ and $\overline{EF}$ to form $\triangle DEF$

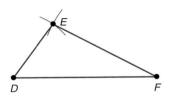

The construction in Example D could have been varied in several ways. For example, we could have begun in step 1 by constructing a segment congruent to either $\overline{AB}$ or $\overline{BC}$. Or in step 2 we could have constructed an arc whose points were the distance BC from point D. However, these variations will all result in a triangle that is congruent to $\triangle DEF$. The following *congruence property of triangles* states that constructing a triangle with three sides that are congruent to three sides of another triangle results in two congruent triangles.

SIDE-SIDE-SIDE (SSS) CONGRUENCE PROPERTY   If three sides of one triangle are congruent to three sides of another triangle, the two triangles are congruent.

Example E

Use the SSS congruence property to show that the following pairs of triangles are congruent. [*Note:* Small slash marks are used to denote congruent segments on geometric figures. For example, in figure *(1)* below, $\overline{AD} \cong \overline{CB}$ and $\overline{AB} \cong$ 721.]

(1)   (2)

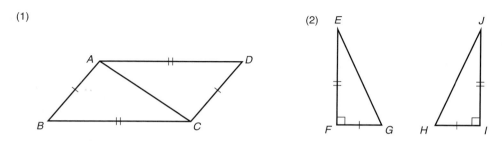

Solution   **1.** Since the third side of both triangles, $\overline{AC}$, is congruent to itself, the two triangles are congruent.   **2.** Since the legs of the right triangles are congruent ($\overline{EF} \cong \overline{JI}$ and $\overline{FG} \cong \overline{IH}$), the Pythagorean theorem guarantees that hypotenuse $\overline{EG}$ is congruent to hypotenuse $\overline{JH}$. Therefore, the two triangles are congruent.

The fact that three line segments determine the *shape and size* of a triangle is of major importance in the construction of a wide range of objects, from bridges and buildings to playground equipment and furniture. Because of this fact, triangular supports are more rigid than supports having other polygonal shapes. This can be illustrated by linkages such as those shown in Figure 11.5. The shapes of all these polygons can be changed, except for that of the triangle. For example, the pentagon can be made nonconvex by pushing one of its vertex points toward the interior of the polygon, or the hexagon can be reshaped into a convex hexagon. The triangle is the only linkage whose shape cannot be changed.

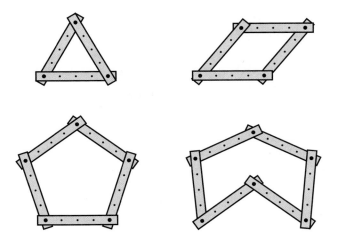

Figure 11.5

Notice the steel frame made up of triangles that is being lifted into place by the crane in the following photograph. What other triangles can you see in the photograph in Figure 11.6?

Figure 11.6
Construction of Lundolm Field House, University of New Hampshire

Example D *should not* lead you to conclude that it is possible to construct a triangle whose sides are congruent to any three given line segments. Consider using the line segments in part a of Figure 11.7. First, set the compass opening by placing it on points C and D, and then draw an arc with center A, as shown in part b. Next, set the compass opening by placing it on points E and F, and then draw an arc with center B. Since the arcs do not intersect, a triangle cannot be constructed from these three segments.

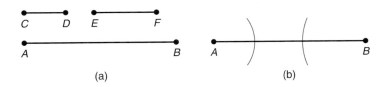

Figure 11.7

The preceding demonstration illustrates a property of triangles known as the **triangle inequality.**

> **TRIANGLE INEQUALITY**   The sum of the lengths of any two sides of a triangle is greater than the length of the third side.

Example F

Can a triangle be constructed whose sides are congruent to the given segments?

(1) ___a___   (2) _____d_____

   ____b____   _____e_____

   _____c_____   _____f_____

Solution   **1.** No, because $a + b < c$. Notice that $b + c > a$ and $c + a > b$, but these conditions are not sufficient for a triangle to be constructed.   **2.** Yes, because the sum of the lengths of any pair of segments is greater than the length of the third segment.

We have seen that if three sides of one triangle are congruent to three sides of another, the triangles are congruent. That is, if three lines segments can be used to form a triangle, they determine a unique triangle. Are there other conditions that can be used to determine a unique triangle? The next example focuses on two sides of a triangle and the **included angle,** that is, the angle formed by the two sides.

Example G

Construct a triangle such that two of its sides and the included angle are congruent to the two line segments and angle shown below.

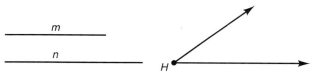

Original segments and angle

Solution *Step 1* Construct line segment $\overline{AB}$ with length m.

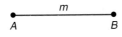

Step 2 Construct an angle congruent to $\angle H$ with A as a vertex.

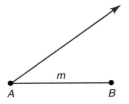

Step 3 Locate point C as shown so that $AC = n$.

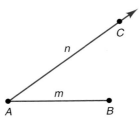

Step 4 Draw segment $\overline{CB}$

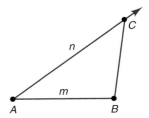

Since the locations of points C and B on the sides of the angle in Example G are determined by the lengths n and m, and since points C and B determine a unique line, it seems reasonable to expect that any triangle constructed by placing $\angle H$ between the two given segments will be congruent to $\triangle ABC$. This result is summarized by the following *congruence property of triangles.*

SIDE-ANGLE-SIDE (SAS) CONGRUENCE PROPERTY If two sides and the included angle of one triangle are congruent to two sides and the included angle of another triangle, the two triangles are congruent.

Example H

Use the SAS congruence property to determine whether the following pairs of triangles are congruent. (*Note:* Small slash marks are used to denote congruent angles. For example, $\angle C \cong \angle E$.)

(1)

(2)

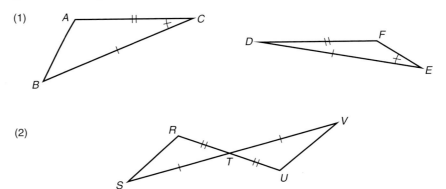

Solution   1. The triangles are not congruent, because $\angle C$ and $\angle D$, which are included between the pairs of congruent sides, are not known to be congruent.   2. The triangles are congruent, because $\angle RTS$ and $\angle UTV$, which are included between the pairs of congruent sides, are vertical angles, and vertical angles are congruent.

There is one other property of triangles that is useful for showing that two triangles are congruent. This property involves the **included side** of two angles, that is, the side that is common to two angles. For example, $\overline{AB}$ is the included side for $\angle A$ and $\angle B$ in Figure 11.8.

Figure 11.8

ANGLE-SIDE-ANGLE (ASA) CONGRUENCE PROPERTY   If two angles and the included side of one triangle are congruent to two angles and the included side of another triangle, the two triangles are congruent.

Example 1

Use the ASA congruence property to show that the following pairs of triangles are congruent. (Remember, slash marks are used to show congruent segments and congruent angles. So $\overline{AH} \cong \overline{EC}$, $\angle A \cong \angle E$, and $\angle K \cong \angle G$.)

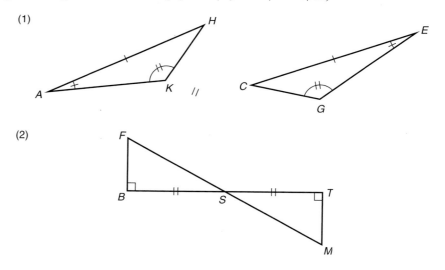

Solution   1. Since there are 180° in every triangle, $\angle H$ must be congruent to $\angle C$. Therefore, $\triangle AKH \cong \triangle EGC$ by the ASA congruence property.   2. Since vertical angles are congruent, $\triangle FSB \cong \triangle MST$ by the ASA congruence property.

Constructing Bisectors

BISECTING SEGMENTS   In the paper-folding examples in Section 9.1, a line segment was bisected by folding the segment onto itself so that the endpoints coincided. In addition to locating the point that bisects the segment, the crease of the paper produces a line perpendicular to the given segment. A line that is perpendicular to a segment at its midpoint is called the **perpendicular bisector** of the segment.

Example J

Construct the perpendicular bisector of the line segment below.

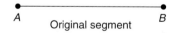

Original segment

Solution *Step 1* Open the compass to span more than one-half the distance from *A* to *B*. Then, with one end of the compass at *A*, draw an arc in each half-plane determined by $\overleftrightarrow{AB}$.

Step 2 With the same compass opening, place the end of the compass at *B* and draw arcs that intersect the arcs created in step 1. Label the points of intersection of the arcs as *C* and *D*.

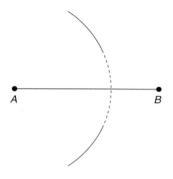

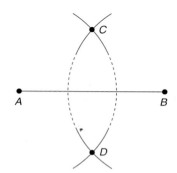

Step 3 Use a straightedge to draw $\overleftrightarrow{CD}$, and label its intersection with $\overline{AB}$ as point *M*. Then $\overleftrightarrow{CD}$, is the perpendicular bisector of $\overline{AB}$, and *M* is the midpoint of $\overline{AB}$.

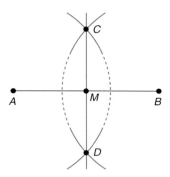

Justification: On the figure in step 3, draw segments $\overline{AC}$, $\overline{BC}$, $\overline{AD}$, and $\overline{BD}$. We know that these segments are all congruent because arcs of the same size were used to locate points *C* and *D*; that is, these segments are radii of circles that are the same size. So, by the SSS congruence property, $\triangle ACD \cong \triangle BCD$. Then $\angle ACD \cong \angle BCD$, because these angles are corresponding parts of congruent triangles. Thus $\triangle ACM \cong \triangle BCM$ by the SAS congruence property. Finally, the parts of $\triangle ACM$ and $\triangle BCM$ correspond: $\overline{AM} \cong \overline{BM}$, so *M* is the midpoint of $\overline{AB}$; $\angle CMA \cong \angle CMB$, and since these angles are supplementary angles, each must be a right angle. So $\overleftrightarrow{CD}$ is the perpendicular bisector of $\overline{AB}$.

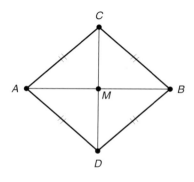

The perpendicular bisector in Example J was constructed by locating two points C and D that were equidistant from the endpoints of $\overline{AB}$. Since this distance was chosen arbitrarily, the justification for this construction proves that any point that is equidistant from the endpoints of a segment will be on the perpendicular bisector of the segment. Conversely, an arbitrary point P on the perpendicular bisector of $\overline{AB}$ is equidistant from the endpoints A and B. These facts are summarized in the following theorem.

> **PERPENDICULAR BISECTOR**   A point is on the perpendicular bisector of a line segment if and only if it is equidistant from the endpoints of the segment.

BISECTING ANGLES   Since $\angle ABD$ in Figure 11.9 is congruent to $\angle DBC$, the ray $\overrightarrow{BD}$ is called the **angle bisector** of $\angle ABC$. If an angle is drawn on paper, the bisector of the angle can be formed by folding one side of the angle onto the other. The crease is the bisector of the angle.

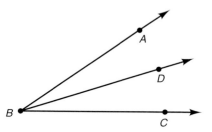

Figure 11.9

Example K   Construct a bisector for the angle below.

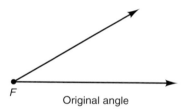

Original angle

Solution *Step 1* Place the end of a compass at point *F* and draw an arc. Label the points where the arc intersects the sides of the angle as *E* and *G*.

Step 2 Place the end of the compass at point *E* and draw an arc. Repeat this step, using point *G* and the same compass opening. Label the intersection of the two arcs as *H*.

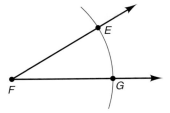

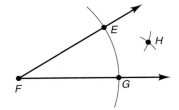

Step 3 Draw $\overleftrightarrow{FH}$, which is the angle bisector of $\angle EFG$.

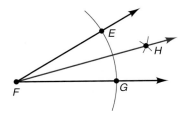

Justification: On the figure in step 3, draw segments $\overline{EH}$ and $\overline{GH}$. Since $\overline{FE} \cong \overline{FG}$ (they were constructed with the same compass opening) and $\overline{EH} \cong \overline{GH}$ (they also were constructed with the same compass opening), $\triangle FEH \cong \triangle FGH$ by the SSS congruence property. Therefore, $\angle EFH \cong \angle GFH$, because these angles are corresponding parts of congruent triangles.

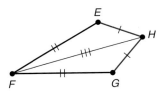

*Evariste Galois
1811–1832*

For 2000 years, beginning with the ancient Greeks, mathematicians sought to solve the following construction problems, using only a straightedge and compass.

1. **Squaring a circle:** Constructing a square whose area equals that of a given circle.

2. **Duplicating a cube:** Constructing a cube whose volume is twice that of a given cube.

3. **Trisecting an angle:** Constructing rays that trisect a given angle.

The results of algebraic developments by the young French mathematician Evariste Galois have been used to prove that these constructions cannot be done by using only a straightedge and compass. Galois died at the age of 20 in a duel, and it wasn't until after his death that his contributions to mathematics were recognized. One important branch of algebra currently bears his name, *Galois theory.**

*E. T. Bell, *Men of Mathematics* (New York: Simon and Schuster, 1965), pp. 362–377.

Constructing Perpendicular and Parallel Lines

Construction of a perpendicular bisector, as in Example J, accomplishes two purposes: It locates the midpoint of a segment, and it creates a right angle. Before you carry out the steps in Example L, think about how the steps in constructing the perpendicular bisector can be used to accomplish the construction.

Example L

Construct a perpendicular to a line through a point that is not on the line.

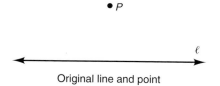

Original line and point

Solution *Step 1* Place one end of a compass at point *P*, and draw an arc that intersects line ℓ in two points. Label these points *A* and *B*.

Step 2 Place the compass at point *A*, and draw an arc in the half-plane not containing *P*. With the same compass opening, place the compass at point *B* and draw an arc in the same half-plane. Label the intersection of these arcs *D*.

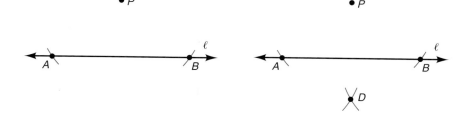

Step 3 Use a straightedge to draw
$\overleftrightarrow{PD}$. Line $\overleftrightarrow{PD}$ is perpendicular to line ℓ.

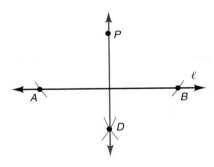

Justification: Since P is the same distance from A as from B (they were constructed with the same compass opening), we know by the perpendicular bisector theorem (page 728) that P is on the perpendicular bisector of $\overline{AB}$. Also, D is the same distance from A and B, so it is on the perpendicular bisector of $\overline{AB}$. Since the two points P and D determine a line, line $\overleftrightarrow{PD}$ is the perpendicular bisector of $\overline{AB}$.

Example M

Construct a line parallel to a given line ℓ and through a point K that is not on ℓ.

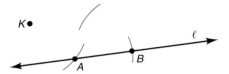

Original line and point

Solution *Step 1* With one end of a compass on point K, draw an arc that intersects ℓ at point A.

Step 2 With the same compass opening and A as center, draw an arc that intersects ℓ at point B.

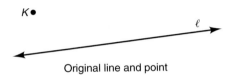

Step 3 With the same compass opening and B as center, draw an arc in the same half-plane as K.

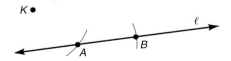

Step 4 With the same compass opening and K as center, draw an arc that intersects the arc drawn in step 3. Label the intersection of the arcs C.

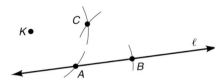

Step 5 Draw line $\overleftrightarrow{KC}$. This line is
parallel to ℓ.

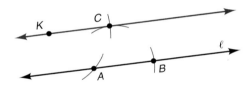

Justification: On the figure in step 5, draw segments $\overline{KA}$, $\overline{CB}$, and $\overline{KB}$. Since $\overline{KA}$, $\overline{AB}$, $\overline{BC}$, and $\overline{KC}$ were constructed as congruent segments, $\triangle KAB \cong \triangle BCK$ by the SSS congruence property. Therefore, $\measuredangle KBA \cong \measuredangle BKC$. Thus since $\measuredangle KBA$ and $\measuredangle BKC$ are congruent alternate interior angles ($\overleftrightarrow{KC}$ is a transversal intersecting $\overleftrightarrow{KC}$ and $\overleftrightarrow{AB}$), line $\overleftrightarrow{KC}$ is parallel to line $\overleftrightarrow{AB}$.

Circumscribing Circles about Triangles

Section 9.2 illustrated two methods of constructing regular polygons. One method involved marking off equal lengths on a circle to obtain an **inscribed polygon** (a polygon whose vertices are points of the circle). The circle for an inscribed polygon is called a **circumscribed circle.** A circumscribed circle for a pentagon is shown in Figure 11.10. The sides of the pentagon, $\overline{AB}$, $\overline{BC}$, etc., are chords of the circle.

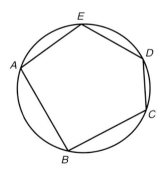

Figure 11.10

Not all polygons will have a circumscribed circle. However, a circumscribed circle can be constructed for any triangle. Consider the triangle in Figure 11.11.

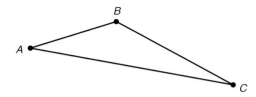

Figure 11.11

If points *A* and *B* are to be on a circle with center *O,* then *OA* must equal *OB* (see Figure 11.12). Thus by the perpendicular bisector theorem, the center of the circumscribed circle must be on the perpendicular bisector of $\overline{AB}$. Similarly, if points *B* and *C* are on the circle, then *OB* = *OC,* and the center of the circle is also on the perpendicular bisector of $\overline{BC}$. So the center of the circle containing *A, B,* and *C* can be located by constructing the perpendicular bisectors of $\overline{AB}$ and $\overline{BC}$, as shown in Figure 11.12. The intersection of the perpendicular bisectors is the center of the circumscribed circle about $\triangle ABC$.

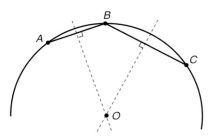

Figure 11.12

The preceding construction can be checked by using a compass to draw a circle with center O and radius OA, to see if points B and C lie on the circle, or by constructing the perpendicular bisector of the third chord $\overline{AC}$ to determine if it passes through point O. Notice that we now have a method for locating the center of any circle if three points of the circle are given: *The center of a circle is the intersection of the perpendicular bisectors of two chords of the circle.*

Constructions with a Mira

The Mira is made of red Plexiglas, which reflects images. It is also transparent so that a drawing on paper in front of the Mira has an image that can be traced on the paper behind the Mira. Figure 11.13 shows the construction of $\triangle A'B'C'$ which is congruent to $\triangle ABC$. To obtain $\triangle A'B'C'$, mark the images of points A, B, C and then connect these points by drawing along a straightedge or the edge of a Mira. (*Note:* The Mira has a beveled edge that should be placed on the paper, facing the viewer.)

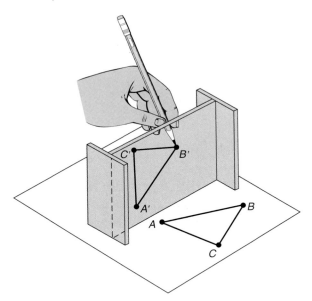

Figure 11.13

BISECTING SEGMENTS AND ANGLES   To bisect $\overline{AB}$ in Figure 11.14a, place the Mira across $\overline{AB}$ (see dotted line) so that the image of point A is point B and draw along the beveled edge. This will produce line ℓ which is the perpendicular bisector of $\overline{AB}$.

To bisect ∡*CDE* in Figure 11.14b, place the beveled edge of the Mira between the two rays of the angle (see dotted line) so that the image of $\overrightarrow{DE}$ is $\overrightarrow{DC}$. Drawing along the beveled edge will produce ray *k*, which bisects ∡*CDE*.

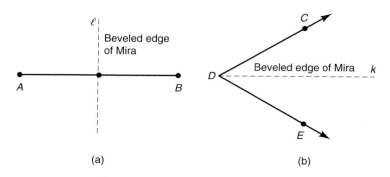

Figure 11.14   (a)   (b)

CONSTRUCTING PERPENDICULAR AND PARALLEL LINES   To construct a line perpendicular to line ℓ at point *P* in Figure 11.15a, place the beveled edge of the Mira on *P* and across ℓ (see dotted line) so that the image of the half-line in front of the Mira falls on the half-line behind the Mira. Drawing along the beveled edge will produce the line perpendicular to ℓ at point *P*.

To construct a line through point *Q* that is parallel to line *k* in Figure 11.15b, place the beveled edge of the Mira perpendicular to line *k* (see dotted line), and mark the image of *Q* as *Q'*. Then use a straightedge or the edge of a Mira to draw $\overline{QQ'}$, which is parallel to line *k*.

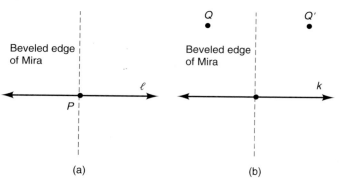

Figure 11.15   (a)   (b)

Problem-Solving Application

PROBLEM

A math club is spending the day at a pond (see the figure below), and the question of the length of the pond arises. One of the club members claims the length can be found by using congruent triangles. How can this be done?

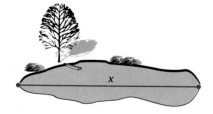

Understanding the Problem   The problem is to determine the distance x by using congruent triangles.

Devising a Plan   One possibility is to select a point C so that points A, B, and C form a triangle in which $\angle ACB$ and side $\overline{BC}$ can be measured (see the figure below). Then select a point D so that $\overline{CD} \cong \overline{CB}$ and $\angle ACD \cong \angle ACB$. **Question 1:** Why is $\triangle ACD \cong \triangle ACB$?

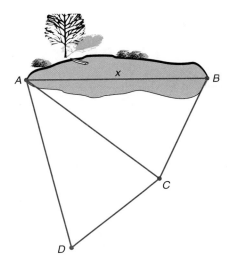

Carrying Out the Plan   Suppose you find that the sides of $\triangle ACD$ have the following lengths: $AC = 2400$ feet, $CD = 1630$ feet, and $AD = 2570$ feet. Because of what we know about corresponding parts of congruent triangles, we know that one of these is the length AB. **Question 2:** Which one?

Looking Back   The length of the pond can also be found by using a right triangle, as shown in the next figure. **Question 3:** If the triangle has legs of 1650 and 1970 feet, what is the length of the pond?

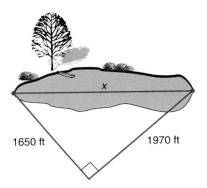

1650 ft

1970 ft

EXERCISES AND PROBLEMS 11.1

Peanuts © UFS. Reprinted by Permission.

1. The following two triangles are congruent. Determine the corresponding angles and sides in a–f for the congruence, and complete the congruence statement in g.

   a. $\angle B \leftrightarrow$ _____   **b.** $\angle M \leftrightarrow$ _____

   c. $\angle K \leftrightarrow$ _____   **d.** $\overline{MB} \leftrightarrow$ _____

   e. $\overline{BK} \leftrightarrow$ _____   **f.** $\overline{MK} \leftrightarrow$ _____

   g. Complete the statement: $\triangle BMK \cong \triangle$ _____ .

2. If $\triangle ABC \cong \triangle DEF$, list the three pairs of corresponding congruent sides and the three pairs of corresponding congruent angles.

The ancient Greeks represented numbers by the lengths of line segments. Addition was represented by placing two line segments end to end and subtraction by comparing the difference between the lengths of two line segments. Use the following segments and a straightedge and compass to construct line segments having the lengths specified in exercises 3 and 4.

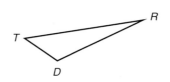

3. a. $r + s$ **b.** $r - t$ **c.** $r + (s - t)$

4. a. $2r - s$ **b.** $(r - s) + t$ **c.** $3t + s$

Show and explain how a straightedge and compass can be used to construct angles that are congruent to the angles in exercises 5 and 6.

5.

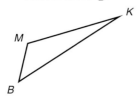

6.

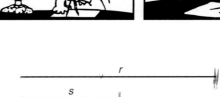

Trace each figure in exercises 7 through 11 on a separate sheet of paper. Then show and explain how a straightedge and compass can be used to obtain the construction listed.

7. The perpendicular bisector of $\overline{AB}$.

8. The bisector of $\angle DEF$.

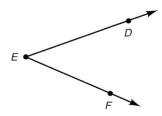

9. A line through K that is perpendicular to line n.

10. A line through Q that is parallel to line m.

11. A line through S that is perpendicular to $\overline{RS}$.

12. Draw a sketch to show how the Mira can be placed to obtain the constructions in exercises 7 and 8. Explain your reasoning.

13. Draw a sketch to show how the Mira can be placed to obtain the constructions in exercises 9 and 10. Explain your reasoning.

Trace the figures in exercises 14 and 15 on a piece of paper and construct a circumscribed circle for each figure. Explain the steps in each construction.

14. a. Scalene triangle

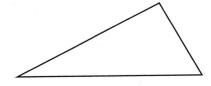

b. Square

15. a. Regular pentagon

b. Regular hexagon

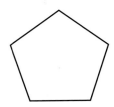

16. a. Construct a triangle whose sides are congruent to these line segments.

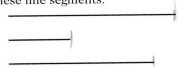

b. Using the line segments in part a, can you construct another triangle that is not congruent to your first triangle? Explain why or why not.

17. The importance of triangles to architecture is due to a basic mathematical fact that is not true of polygons with more than three sides. (Compare the answers to parts a and b with the answer to exercise 16, part b.)

a. Construct two noncongruent quadrilaterals whose sides are congruent to the line segments shown here.

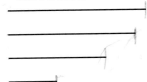

b. How many noncongruent quadrilaterals can be constructed whose sides are congruent to the four line segments used in part a? (*Hint:* Imagine changing the shape of a quadrilateral formed by linkages.)

If a construction is possible, construct triangles in exercises 18 and 19 with the given characteristics. (Use a ruler, compass, or protractor as needed.)

18. a. Three sides of lengths 5, 6, and 7 centimeters
   b. Three sides of lengths 5, 6, and 10 centimeters.
   c. Three sides that are congruent to $\overline{AB}$ below

A   B

19. a. Two sides of lengths 2 and 3 centimeters and a nonincluded angle with a measure of 60°
   b. Two sides of length 5 centimeters and an included angle with a measure of 45°
   c. A right triangle with one leg of length 7 centimeters and one angle of measure 35°

20. In parts a and b, construct a triangle in which one side and two angles are congruent to the line segment and angles below.

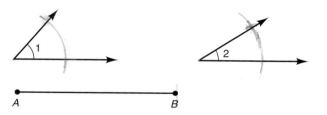

a. Construct the triangle so that the given side is included between the two given angles.
   b. Construct the triangle so that the given side is not included between the two given angles.
   c. Compare the two triangles in parts a and b. Are they congruent?
   d. What conclusion can you draw from your answer in part c?

21. In parts a and b, construct triangles that have one angle and two sides congruent to the angle and segments shown below.

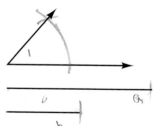

a. Construct the triangle so that the given angle is included between the two given sides.

b. Construct the triangle so that the given angle is not included between the two given sides.
   c. Compare the triangles in parts a and b. Are they congruent?
   d. What conclusion can you draw from part c?

For each case in exercises 22 and 23, determine if the given conditions are sufficient to conclude that △ABC is congruent to △HMS. Draw diagrams and justify your answers.

22. a. $\overline{AB} \cong \overline{HM}$, $\overline{BC} \cong \overline{MS}$, $\overline{AC} \cong \overline{HS}$
   b. $\angle A \cong \angle H$, $\angle B \cong \angle M$, $\angle C \cong \angle S$

23. a. $\overline{AB} \cong \overline{HM}$, $\overline{BC} \cong \overline{MS}$, $\angle B \cong \angle M$
   b. $\overline{AB} \cong \overline{HM}$, $\overline{BC} \cong \overline{MS}$, $\angle A \cong \angle H$

Use a compass and straightedge to construct each of the polygons in exercises 24 through 26 having sides congruent to segment $\overline{AB}$. Explain the steps of each construction.

A   B

24. Square $= .Rtcs$

25. Equilateral triangle

26. Rhombus $= \backslash \mathcal{U}$

27. There are an infinite number of distances to a line from a point that is not on the line.

a. Trace line ℓ and point P on a sheet of paper. Use a ruler and compass to locate points on line ℓ that are the following distances from point P: 3, 2, and 1.5 centimeters.

• P

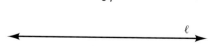

b. To the nearest .1 centimeter, what is the shortest distance from P to ℓ?
   c. Form a conjecture about the shortest distance to a line from a point that is not on the line.

Use the SSS, SAS, or ASA congruence properties to determine which of the pairs of triangles in exercises 28 through 33 are congruent. If these properties cannot be used, explain why. Otherwise, for each pair of triangles state the property which shows they are congruent.

28. a.

b.

29. a.

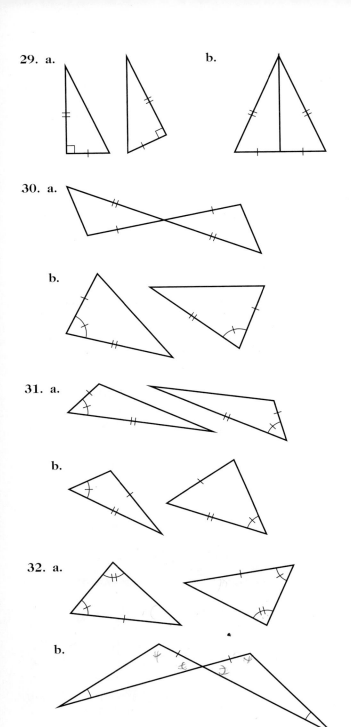

b.

30. a.

b.

31. a.

b.

32. a.

b.

33. a.

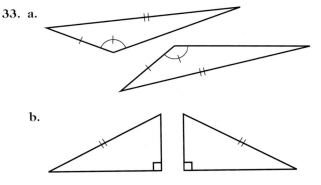

b.

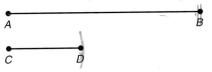

34. Construct an isosceles triangle with two sides congruent to $\overline{AB}$ and one side congruent to $\overline{CD}$. Form a conjecture about the angles that are opposite the two congruent sides of an isosceles triangle.

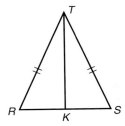

35. In the isosceles triangle below, point K is the midpoint of $\overline{RS}$. What congruence property of triangles can be used to show that $\triangle RKT \cong \triangle SKT$? How can this congruence be used to show that $\measuredangle R \cong \measuredangle S$?

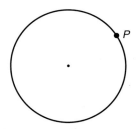

36. A tangent to a point P on a circle is a line through P that is perpendicular to the radius from the center of the circle to point P. Construct a circle and label a point P on its circumference. Using only a straightedge and compass, construct the tangent to the circle at point P. Show and explain the steps of your construction.

REASONING AND PROBLEM SOLVING

37. It has been proved that it is impossible to trisect every angle by using only a straightedge and compass (see Historical Highlight, page 730). However, trisections of certain angles can be constructed. Diagram and list the steps in trisecting a right angle, using only a straightedge and compass.

38. Featured Strategy: Making a Drawing How many different noncongruent triangles can be formed that have two sides and one angle congruent to the line segments and angle below?

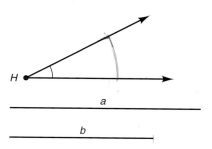

a. Understanding the Problem The third side of the triangle can be any length needed to form a triangle with the given two sides and angle. Construct a triangle with two sides and the included angle congruent to the given segments and angle. If another triangle is constructed using the given segments and the given angle as the included angle, will it be congruent to the triangle you constructed?

b. Devising a Plan One approach is to *make drawings* that will help you consider different combinations of the given segments and angle systematically. For example, suppose the segment of length b is opposite $\angle H$ in one triangle and the segment of length a is opposite $\angle H$ in the second triangle. Are these two triangles congruent?

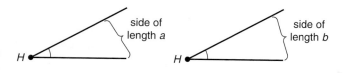

c. Carrying Out the Plan Construct triangles, using different configurations of the given line segments and angle, and determine if they are congruent. How many noncongruent triangles can be constructed?

d. Looking Back Draw a segment of length a, and place the vertex of $\angle H$ at one endpoint, as shown in the following figure. With the point of the

compass on the other endpoint of the line segment, draw an arc of length b. This arc intersects two points on one side of $\angle H$, and these points determine two noncongruent triangles, as shown. Suppose a line segment of length b is drawn and $\angle H$ is placed at one endpoint. Will drawing an arc of length a determine two noncongruent triangles?

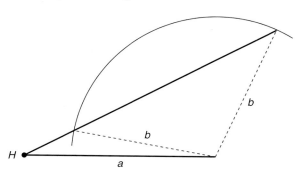

39. To measure the width of a river, a ranger stands across the river directly opposite rock R and places a stake at point A on the river's edge. Then she measures off equal distances and places stakes at points B and C so that $AB = BC$. Finally, the ranger moves directly away from the river to a point D, at which stake B and rock R are in a straight line. The diagram illustrates this information. How can this information be used to measure the width of the river?

40. Jeff and Vonda want to swim from point A to point B on a lake, and they are concerned about the distance (see figure on next page). Vonda suggests laying out triangles ABK and ACK such that $\angle CKA$ is congruent to $\angle BKA$. They pace off $\overline{KC}$ and $\overline{KB}$ to be 380 feet each, and they find that CA is 205 feet. Explain how this information can be used to find the distance from A to B. What is this distance?

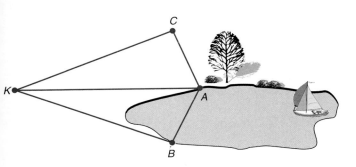

42. There is a mound of dirt and rocks behind the Palumbo house which is to be removed. The Palumbos must supply measurements to determine the number of truckloads needed to remove the mound. Ms. Palumbo puts a stake at point A (see the figure) and moves in a straight line from A through point K, putting a stake at point D so that $AK = KD$. Then she places a stake at point B and moves in a straight line from B through K, placing a stake at point C so that $BK = KC$. Explain how she can find the distance at the base of the mound from A to B. Include any additional information she may need.

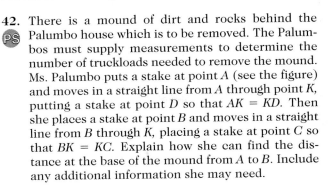

41. An outing club wants to build a rope footbridge across a deep gorge and needs to determine the distance from point A to point B (see the figure). They stretch a line from A to C and from B to C and find that each distance equals 120 feet. They use an altimeter to find that A and B have the same altitudes and that MC equals 96 feet with point M directly above point C. How can they use this information to find the distance from A to B? What is this distance?

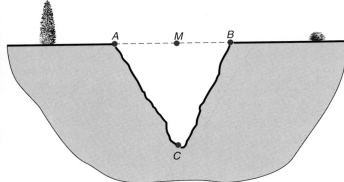

ONLINE LEARNING CENTER   www.mhhe.com/bennett-nelson

• Math Investigation 11.1   *Paper folding*
Section-Related: • Links   • Writing/Discussion Problems   • Bibliography

PUZZLER

The desk calendar at the right consists of two cubes on a stand. How can you number each face on each cube so that the date for each day of any month can be represented above the name of the month? (*Note:* A single-digit day such as day 3 should be represented by 03.)

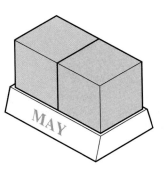

MATH ACTIVITY 11.2

ROTATING, REFLECTING, AND TRANSLATING FIGURES ON GRIDS

Materials: Tracing paper (suggested)

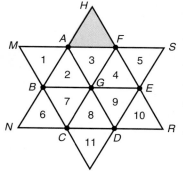

*1. The shaded triangle shown here can be turned (**rotated**) about either point F or point G so that it coincides with (fits exactly on top of) triangle 5. It can also be rotated about the lettered points so that it coincides with all the other numbered triangles except one. Record the letters of the points about which the shaded triangle can be rotated to coincide with these other triangles.

Triangle	1	2	3	4	5	6	7	8	9	10	11
Center of rotation					F, G						

2. The shaded triangle in activity 1 can be flipped (**reflected**) about line $\overleftrightarrow{AG}$ (think of extending $\overline{AG}$) to coincide with triangle 1. Find the seven other triangles to which the shaded triangle can be reflected. Record each triangle that the shaded triangle can be reflected onto, and the line about which it is reflected.

Triangle	1	2	3	4	5	6	7	8	9	10	11
Line of reflection	$\overleftrightarrow{AG}$										

3. The shaded triangle in activity 1 can be slid without any turning motion (**translated**) to coincide with triangle 2. This can be visualized by imagining point H sliding down line $\overleftrightarrow{HB}$ to point A, point F sliding down line $\overleftrightarrow{FG}$ to coincide with point G, and point A sliding down line $\overleftrightarrow{AB}$ to point B. Find the four other triangles that the shaded triangle can be translated onto.

*4. In activity 1, the shaded triangle could not be rotated onto triangle 8. However, it can be rotated about point G onto triangle 11 and then reflected about line $\overleftrightarrow{CD}$ to coincide with triangle 8. Find three other triangles that the shaded triangle can be rotated to and then reflected onto triangle 8.

5. a. The shaded square in the figure shown here can be rotated about a lettered point to coincide with eight of the 11 numbered squares. Find each square to which it can be rotated and the point about which it is rotated.
   b. The shaded square can be reflected onto five of the numbered squares by reflections about lines through the lettered points. Find each of these squares and the lines about which the shaded square can be reflected.
   c. The shaded square cannot be rotated onto square 2 by a rotation about a lettered point, but it can be reflected onto square 1 and then rotated onto square 2. Describe how the shaded square can be reflected and then rotated onto squares 7, 8, 10, and 11. List the lines of reflection and points of rotation.

SECTION 11.2

CONGRUENCE MAPPINGS

M.C. Escher's
"Day and Night"
© 1999 M. C.
Escher/Cordon Art-
Baarn-Holland. All
rights reserved.

PROBLEM OPENER

A hidden rectangle whose area is 12 square units is formed on the grid shown here. The coordinates of each vertex of the rectangle are whole numbers whose sum is either 8 or 12, and the first coordinate is not 8. What is the location of this rectangle?

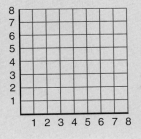

> Students in grades 3–5 should consider three important kinds of transformations: reflections, translations, and rotations (flips, slides, and turns).
>
> Standards 2000, p. 167

In designing the woodcut *Day and Night,* M. C. Escher used geometric mappings. The particular mappings associated with congruence—translations, reflections, and rotations—will be studied in this section, and examples of how Escher used these mappings to create tessellations will be introduced.

Translations

A **translation** is a special kind of mapping that can be described as a sliding motion. Each point is moved the same distance and in the same direction. The translation in Figure 11.16 maps A to A', B to B', C to C', $\overline{BC}$ to $\overline{B'C'}$, and pentagon K to pentagon K'. This translation is completely determined by point A and its image A'. That is, given any point X in this figure, we can find its image X' by moving in the *same direction* as from A to A' and the *same distance* as AA'. Or stated another way, X' can be located by constructing $\overline{XX'}$ so that it is parallel to $\overline{AA'}$ and the distance from X to X' equals the distance from A to A'.

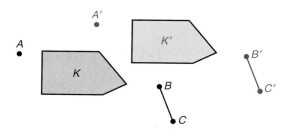

Figure 11.16

Translations occur with space figures as well as with plane figures. Just as in the case of two-dimensional figures, a translation in three dimensions is described as a sliding motion of points in space in the same direction and for the same distance, for example, a box moving on a conveyor belt or a child going down a slide. The photograph in Figure 11.17 shows the results of a sliding motion of the earth's crust, which geologists call a *block fault.* The arrow points to one side of the fault along which the earth's crust has been displaced.

Figure 11.17
Fault line showing displaced rock

Example A

Trace figure (*1*) and determine the image of the pentagon obtained by a translation that maps K to K'. Trace figure (*2*) and determine the image of the three-dimensional figure obtained from a translation that maps P to P'.

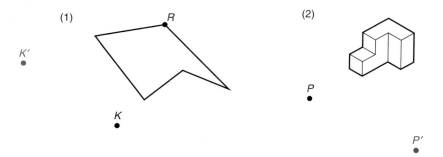

Solution   One method of locating the images of these figures is to use constructions to first find the images of the vertex points. The images of the vertex points can then be connected to obtain the image of the figure. For example, using vertex point R on the pentagon, construct a line through R that is parallel to $\overline{K'K}$. Then, moving in the direction from K to K', locate the image R' of R so that $RR' = KK'$. Similar constructions can be carried out for the remaining vertex points.

Another method of locating the images is to trace the pentagon and the three-dimensional figure on separate sheets of paper. Then slide K along $\overline{KK'}$ so that it coincides with K' to locate the image of the pentagon, and slide P along $\overline{PP'}$ so that it coincides with P' to locate the image of the three-dimensional figure.

Reflections

Research Statement

The **7th** national mathematics assessment found that less than one-half of the eighth-graders could identify the image of a point when folded over an oblique line of reflection.

Martin and Strutchens 2000

A **reflection** about a line is a mapping that can be described by folding. If this page is folded about line ℓ in Figure 11.18, each point will coincide with its image. Point E will be mapped to E', F to F', $\overline{EF}$ to $\overline{E'F'}$, and figure M to figure M'. Line ℓ is called a **line of reflection**. Since point S is on ℓ, it does not move for this mapping. Point S and all other points on ℓ are called **fixed points** for the reflection about ℓ, because each point coincides with (is the same as) its image.

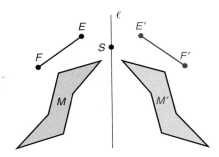

Figure 11.18

Reflections in space take place about planes. Each point to the left of plane P in Figure 11.19 has a unique image on the right side of P. The sphere is mapped to the sphere, point K to K', and tetrahedron T to tetrahedron T'. Point R and all other points on the plane are fixed points of the mapping. That is, each point on the plane is its own image.

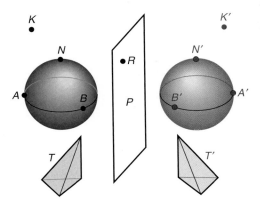

Figure 11.19

Reflections in space can be illustrated by mirrors. If plane P in Figure 11.19 is replaced by a mirror so that the figures to the left of the mirror are reflected, their images will appear to be in the positions of the figures on the right side of the mirror. Plane P is called the **plane of reflection.**

Surprisingly clear images can be created by reflections in pools. Pick out some points on the building and their images in the photograph in Figure 11.20.

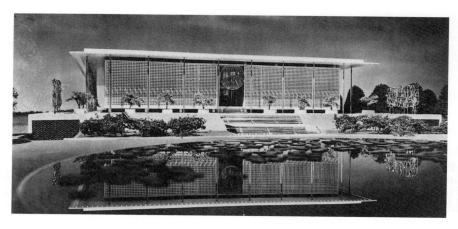

Figure 11.20
Model of the United States Embassy, New Delhi

$\perp$ $90°$
, to ,
distance =

In the mappings about line ℓ (Figure 11.18) and plane P (Figure 11.19), each point and its image are on lines that are perpendicular to the line or plane of reflection. For example, $\overline{EE'}$ in Figure 11.18 is perpendicular to line ℓ, and $\overline{NN'}$ in Figure 11.19 is perpendicular to plane P. Furthermore, each point is the same distance from the line or plane as its image. These two conditions hold for all reflections.

Example B

Trace figure (*1*) and determine the image of the quadrilateral obtained from a reflection about line ℓ. Trace figure (*2*) and determine the image of the "three-dimensional figure" obtained from a reflection about plane P, which is perpendicular to this page.

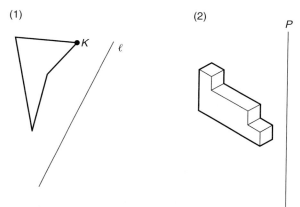

Solution   The image of a polygon can be located by first constructing the images of its vertex points. For example, using vertex point K on the quadrilateral, construct a line through K that is perpendicular to ℓ. Then locate the image K' of K so that K' is on the perpendicular line and the distances from K' to ℓ and from K to ℓ are equal. The images of the vertex points of figure (*2*) can be located in a similar manner by constructing lines perpendicular to "plane" P.

Another method is to fold a paper with the traced figures so that line ℓ coincides with itself (or "plane" P coincides with itself) and trace the image in the opposite half-plane.

Rotations

The third type of mapping is a **rotation,** which for plane figures can be described as turning about a point. As an example, consider a 90° rotation about point O in

Figure 11.21. Place a piece of paper on this figure, and trace $\overline{FG}$ and quadrilateral $ABCD$. Hold a pencil at point O, and rotate the paper 90° in a clockwise direction. (A 90° rotation can be determined by beginning with the edges of the paper parallel to the edges of this page.) Each of the points you trace will coincide with its image after this rotation. Quadrilateral $ABCD$ is mapped to quadrilateral $A'B'C'D'$, and $\overline{FG}$ is mapped to $\overline{F'G'}$. Point O is called the **center of rotation** and is the only fixed point for this mapping. Notice that each point has been rotated 90° to its image. That is, if a line is drawn from any point to the center O, and from the image of the point to the center O, the resulting angle will be a right angle. For example, $\angle COC'$ is a 90° angle.

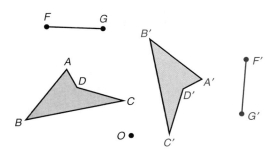

Figure 11.21

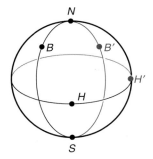

Figure 11.22

Figures in space are rotated about lines. If the sphere shown in Figure 11.22 is rotated 90° about the vertical axis through N and S, point H will be mapped to H' and point B to B'. Each point will be mapped to a new location except for points N and S, which remain fixed.

The earth and other spinning objects such as toy tops rotate about axes. The restaurant and observation deck at the top of the 60-story Space Needle in Seattle, Washington (Figure 11.23), rotate once every 60 minutes about a vertical shaft. Each point on this moving structure traces out a circular path during one complete revolution. These moving points are constantly changing their locations and being mapped to one another.

Figure 11.23
Space Needle, Seattle,
Washington

Example C

Trace the polygon in figure (*1*) on a piece of paper, and determine its image for a 90° clockwise rotation about point *O*. Line ℓ in figure (*2*) passes through the centers of the opposite faces *ABDC* and *HFEG* of the cube. Determine the image of each vertex of the cube for a 90° clockwise rotation about line ℓ.

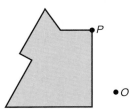

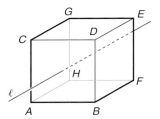

Solution   1. One method of locating the image of the polygon in figure (1) is to use constructions to first find the images of the vertex points. Using vertex point *P* of the heptagon, construct a right angle having *O* as the vertex of the angle and $\overrightarrow{OP}$ as one side. Then locate the image *P′* of *P* on the other ray of the angle so that *OP* = *OP′*. A similar construction can be repeated for the other vertex points.

Another method of finding the image of the polygon is to place a second piece of paper on the traced figure and trace the figure onto this top sheet. Then hold a pencil at point *O* and rotate the paper 90° clockwise. The figure will be rotated to its new location, where it can be imprinted onto the bottom sheet by pressing on the boundary lines of the figure with a ball-point pen. Sometimes shading the back side of the paper with a pencil will help to show the imprinted image on the bottom sheet.

2. The rotation of the cube maps the vertices as follows: *A* → *C*, *C* → *D*, *D* → *B*, *B* → *A*, *H* → *G*, *G* → *E*, *E* → *F*, and *F* → *H*.

Composition of Mappings

Research Statement

The ability to visualize geometric figures and operations on them has been recognized as an important component of mathematical thinking.

Wheatley 1990

The wood engraving by M. C. Escher (Figure 11.24) combines translations and reflections. The white swan *W* can be mapped onto the black swan *B* by a translation followed by a reflection. First trace swan *W* and then slide the traced figure vertically so it is level with swan *B*. The traced swan can now be made to coincide with swan *B* by a reflection about the line parallel to the line of translation (see given line). A *translation* followed by a *reflection* about a line that is parallel to the line of translation is called a **glide reflection**.

Figure 11.24
M. C. Escher's "Swans"

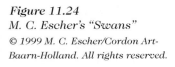

Objective: Identify translations, reflections, and rotations.
Draw all lines of symmetry in a figure.

Transformations and Symmetry

Learn

Math Words

transformation
translation
rotation
reflection
image
glide reflection
line symmetry
line of symmetry

Do you know how cartoons are created? Many separate pictures called cells must be used to make a cartoon character appear to move. Cartoonists sometimes use translations, reflections, and rotations of the characters. What transformation is shown?

Example 1

Transformations change the position of figures. Translations, rotations, and reflections are types of transformations.

A **translation** moves a figure in a straight line without turning or flipping it.

A **rotation** turns a figure about a point.

A **reflection** creates a mirror image of a figure across a line.

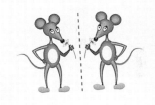

Think: The figures face the same direction. They are congruent.

Think: The figures face different directions. They are congruent.

Think: The figures face each other. They are congruent.

The cartoonist used a reflection.

The **image** of a figure is the new figure made by a transformation. You can combine two transformations as shown at right.

The transformations are a translation and a reflection. A translation and reflection together are called a **glide reflection**.

Image

Original

484 Cluster B

When one mapping is followed by another, the combination is called a **composition of mappings**. Any combination of translations, reflections, rotations, or glide reflections can be used. In Figure 11.25, a 90° clockwise rotation about point O is followed by a translation of each point 3 spaces to the right. Triangle ABC is mapped to triangle $A'B'C'$ by the rotation, and then the translation maps triangle $A'B'C'$ to triangle $A''B''C''$. The composition of the rotation and translation is the single mapping that takes triangle ABC to triangle $A''B''C''$. In this case, the composition is a 90° rotation about point X. Try it.

In grades 3–5 students can investigate the effects of transformations and begin to describe them in mathematical terms.

Standards 2000, p. 43

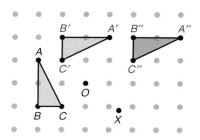

Figure 11.25

Two-dimensional patterns such as those on wallpaper and tiled floors are created by systematic translations, reflections, and rotations of a basic figure, as illustrated by the next example.

Example D

The basic figure in the upper left corner of the following grid has the shape of a mushroom. This figure was repeatedly reflected about the common edge of adjacent squares to obtain the first column of the grid.

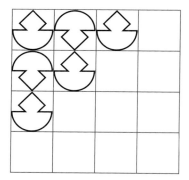

Determine a mapping (translation, reflection, or rotation) that produces each of the following.

1. The top row   **2.** The second column   **3.** The second row

4. The diagonal from upper left to lower right

Solution   1. Rotations of 180° about the midpoints of the edges of adjacent squares in the top row **2.** Reflections about the common edge of adjacent squares in the second column or a 180° rotation about the midpoint of these edges **3.** Rotations of 180° about the midpoints of the edges of adjacent squares in the second row **4.** Translations along the diagonal

Composing mappings is similar to performing an operation on numbers. For example, the product of two integers is always another integer (closure property), and the composition of two congruence mappings is always another congruence mapping. The composition of some pairs of mappings is quite easy to determine. A 30° rotation followed by a 45° rotation can be replaced by a 75° rotation, and two translations can always be replaced by one translation.

The situation for reflections is more interesting, as shown in Figure 11.26. For a reflection about line *m*, figure *H* is mapped to *H'*. Then *H'* is mapped to *H''* by a reflection about line *n*. These two reflections can be replaced by a single rotation about point *O* that maps *H* to *H''*.

<table>
<tr><td>
Students need to learn to physically and mentally change the position, orientation, and size of objects in systematic ways as they develop their understandings about congruence, similarity, and transformations.

Standards 2000, p. 43
</td></tr>
</table>

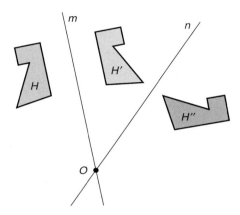

Figure 11.26

Compositions of different types of mappings, such as a rotation followed by a translation or a reflection followed by a rotation, can also be replaced by a single mapping. It can be proved that the composition of any two of the four mappings (rotation, translation, reflection, or glide reflection) is also a rotation, translation, reflection, or glide reflection. In other words, the set of congruence mappings is **closed with respect to composition.**

Congruence

Translations, reflections, rotations, and glide reflections all have something very important in common. If *A* and *B* are any two points and *A'* and *B'* are their respective images, then the distance between *A* and *B* is the same as the distance between *A'* and *B'* (Figure 11.27). That is, for these mappings the lengths of the line segments are the same as the lengths of their images. Such mappings are called **distance-preserving mappings.** This property reflects the simple intuitive notion that as figures are rotated, translated, or reflected, their size and shape do not change.

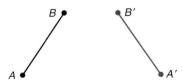

Figure 11.27

Up to this point we have thought of two figures as being congruent if they have the same size and shape or if one can be made to coincide with the other. The need for a more careful definition of congruence becomes evident when we consider congruence in three dimensions. For example, we need a way of defining congruence for the two kitchen grinders in Figure 11.28, and it does not make sense to say that they coincide.

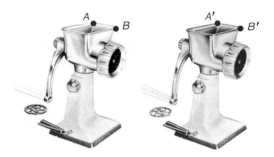

Figure 11.28

A suitable definition of congruence for both plane and space figures can be given in terms of mappings.

> **CONGRUENT FIGURES**   Two geometric figures are **congruent** if and only if there exists a translation, reflection, rotation, or glide reflection of one figure onto the other.

This definition says that for each of these four mappings, a figure is congruent to its image. Conversely, if two figures are congruent, one can always be mapped to the other by one of these mappings. This definition gives us a way of viewing congruence of both plane and space figures. The plane figures H and H'' in Figure 11.26 are congruent because a rotation maps one to the other. The grinders in Figure 11.28 are congruent because a translation maps one to the other. Each point on the left grinder is mapped to a corresponding point on the right grinder. The distances between any two points on the left grinder, such as points A and B, and between their images, A' and B', are equal. Defining congruence in terms of distance-preserving mappings is the mathematical way of saying that two objects have the same size and shape.

Mapping Figures onto Themselves

In their book *Let's Play Math,* Michael Holt and Zoltan Dienes describe the following scheme for coloring pictures of a house.* Cut out a square and color the corners four different colors. Both the front and back sides of each corner should be the same color. Place the square on a piece of paper and draw a frame around it (Figure 11.29). At each corner of the frame, write (or draw pictures for) one of the words *wall, roof, door,* and *window.* The entire configuration is called the Rainbow Toy.

*M. Holt and Z. Dienes, *Let's Play Math* (New York: Walker and Company, 1973), pp. 88–94.

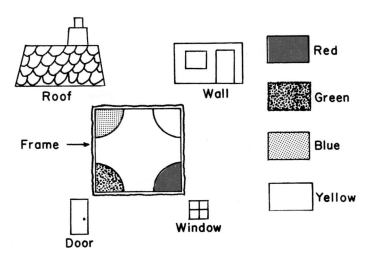

Figure 11.29

The different positions in which the square can be placed on the frame determine different arrangements of colors for the wall, roof, door, and window of the house. With the square in the position shown in Figure 11.29, we get the colors for house (a) in Figure 11.30. Color schemes for houses (b), (c), and (d) are obtained by rotating the square into three different positions; by flipping the square over, we get four more positions for the color schemes for houses (e) through (h).

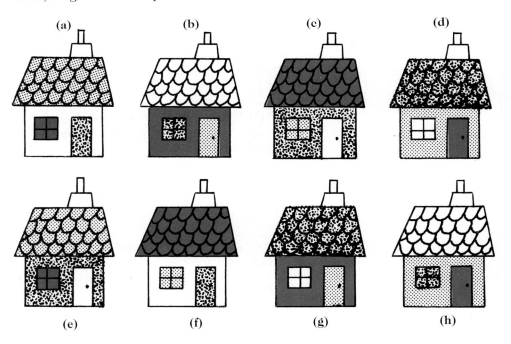

Figure 11.30

The Rainbow Toy provides an elementary way of illustrating the mappings of a square onto itself. Remember from Section 9.4 that a square has four rotational symmetries: 90°, 180°, 270°, and 360°. It also has four lines of symmetry (Figure 11.31): two diagonal lines d_1 and d_2, a horizontal line h, and a vertical line v. Thus there are eight mappings of the square onto itself, and these mappings produce the eight color combinations for the houses in Figure 11.30.

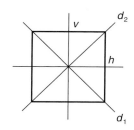

Figure 11.31

In general, the number of mappings of a plane figure onto itself is the total number of lines of symmetry and rotation symmetries.

Example E

Determine the number of mappings of each figure onto itself.

1. A rectangle   **2.** The letter S   **3.** A regular hexagon

Solution   **1.** Four, because it has two lines of symmetry and 2 rotation symmetries   **2.** Two, because it has two rotation symmetries   **3.** Twelve, because it has six lines of symmetry and six rotation symmetries

Escher-Type Tessellations

The Dutch artist M. C. Escher visited the Alhambra in Spain in the 1930s and was inspired by the geometric tilings of the walls and ceilings to create some very unusual tessellations. He used translations, rotations, and reflections to reshape polygons such as squares, equilateral triangles, and regular hexagons, which are known to tessellate, into nonpolygonal figures that also tessellate. In the following paragraphs we will examine the use of mappings in creating tessellations.

TRANSLATION TESSELLATIONS   One of the simplest ways to create a tessellation is to begin with a square (or a rectangle, a rhombus, or other parallelograms) and change its opposite sides. This technique is illustrated in Figure 11.32.

Figure 11.32

Step 1 Draw a curve from *A* to *B*.

Step 2 Translate the curve to the opposite side of the square so that *A* maps to *C* and *B* maps to *D*.

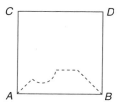

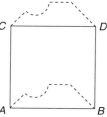

Step 3 Draw a curve from C to A. (Notice that the curve does not have to be within the original figure.)

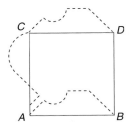

Step 4 Translate the curve to the opposite side of the square so that A maps to B and C maps to D.

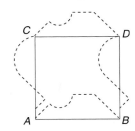

Step 5 Erase the lines of the original square that are not part of the curve to obtain a nonpolygonal figure, and tessellate with this figure.

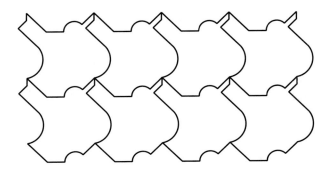

The tessellation in step 5 of Figure 11.32 can be translated onto itself in many ways: move each figure one figure to the right, two to the left, etc.

ROTATION TESSELLATIONS   A rotation tessellation is created below by beginning with a regular hexagon (Figure 11.33, step 1). Rotations are used to alter the sides of the original polygon.

Figure 11.33

Step 1 Draw a curve from A to B.

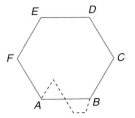

Step 2 Rotate the curve about point B so that A maps to C.

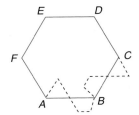

Step 3 Draw a curve from *C* to *D*.

Step 4 Rotate the curve about point *D* so that *C* maps to *E*.

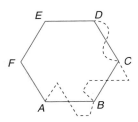

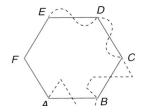

Step 5 Draw a curve from *E* to *F*.

Step 6 Rotate the curve about point *F* so that *E* maps to *A*.

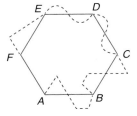

Step 7 Erase the lines of the original hexagon, and form a tessellation with the resulting figure.

The tessellation in step 7 of Figure 11.33, can be rotated on itself. For example, a rotation of 120° or 240° about point *K* maps the tessellation onto itself.

REFLECTION TESSELLATIONS   The steps for creating a reflection tessellation are shown in Figure 11.34. The basic figure in this case is a rhombus.

gure 11.34

Step 1 Draw a curve from *A* to *B*.

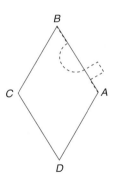

Step 2 Reflect the curve about $\overset{\leftrightarrow}{BD}$ so that *A* maps to *C*.

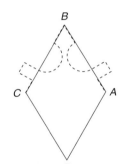

Step 3 Rotate the curve from *B* to *C* about point *C* so that *B* maps to *D*.

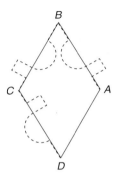

Step 4 Reflect the curve from *C* to *D* about line $\overset{\leftrightarrow}{BD}$ so that *C* maps to *A*.

Step 5 Erase the lines of the original rhombus that are not part of the curve, and tessellate with the resulting figure.

Note that in step 5 of Figure 11.34, the tessellation has many lines about which it can be reflected onto itself. One such line passes through the highest and lowest points of the figure.

Problem-Solving Application

Given any plane figure and its image for a rotation, how can we determine the center of rotation?

Understanding the Problem   The following parallelogram has been rotated a certain number of degrees to its image. The problem is to find the center of rotation.

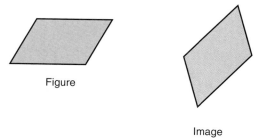

Figure

Image

Devising a Plan   One approach is to trace the original figure and then to *guess and check* to locate a point about which the figure can be rotated to coincide with its image. Another approach is to use two chords of a circle. **Question 1:** How can chords $\overline{AB}$ and $\overline{CD}$ of the following circle be used to locate the center of the circle?

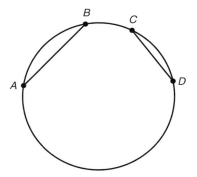

Carrying Out the Plan   Each point of the original figure traces an arc as it is rotated to its image point. So the point and its image lie on a circle whose center is the center of rotation. In the following figure, S maps to S', P maps to P', and the perpendicular bisector of $\overline{PP'}$ is ℓ. **Question 2:** How can the center of rotation be found?

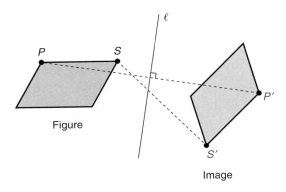

Figure

Image

Looking Back   Check the location of the center of rotation by tracing the original figure and rotating it to its image. **Question 3:** How can the measure of the angle of rotation be determined?

Answers to Questions 1–3   **1.** Draw the perpendicular bisectors of $\overline{AB}$ and $\overline{CD}$. Their intersection is the center of the circle.   **2.** The intersection of ℓ and the perpendicular bisector of $\overline{SS}'$ is the center of rotation.

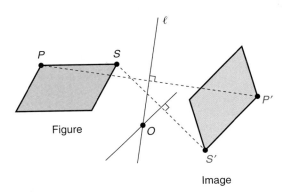

Figure

Image

3. With O as the center of rotation, use a protractor to measure the central angle $\angle POP'$ or $\angle SOS'$.

NCTM's 5–8 Standard, *Geometry,* encourages the constructions and mappings of two- and three-dimensional shapes:

Computer software allows students to construct two- and three-dimensional shapes on a screen and then flip, turn, or slide them to view them from a new perspective. Explorations of flips, slides, turns, stretchers, and shrinkers will illuminate the concepts of congruence and similarity. Observing and learning to represent two- and three-dimensional figures in various positions by drawing and construction also helps students develop spatial sense.*

Curriculum and Evaluation Standards for School Mathematics (Reston, VA: National Council of Teachers of Mathematics, 1989), p. 114.

EXERCISES AND PROBLEMS 11.2

1. The pattern of lines and angles in the above photograph was produced by placing six photographs of a construction staging side by side.
   a. Are these six photographs congruent?
   b. Are the six stagings congruent?
   c. What type of mapping is suggested by this picture?

Copy the dot grid from the inside cover or from the website to use in sketching the images in exercises 2 through 11.

2. For the translation that maps A to A', sketch the image of the hexagon.

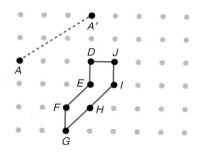

   a. The line through point D and its image is parallel to $\overleftrightarrow{AA'}$. Is this true for every point on the hexagon and its image?

   b. If E' and G' are the respective images of E and G, how does the length $E'G'$ compare with the length EG?
   c. Compare the area of the hexagon with the area of its image.

3. For a translation that maps F to I in exercise 2, sketch the image of the hexagon.
   a. How does the distance from F to I compare with the distance from G to its image for this mapping?
   b. How does the area of the original hexagon compare with the area of its image?

4. Sketch the image of the pentagon in exercise 5 for a reflection about line $\overleftrightarrow{TU}$.
   a. If S' is the image of S, what are the measures of the angles formed by the intersection of $\overleftrightarrow{SS'}$ and $\overleftrightarrow{TU}$?
   b. How does the distance from S to $\overleftrightarrow{TU}$ compare with the distance from S' to $\overleftrightarrow{TU}$?
   c. What are the fixed points of the original pentagon for this mapping?

5. Sketch the image of the pentagon for a reflection about the line ℓ.

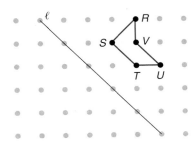

b. Describe the translation that maps C to K.

c. What is the image of quadrilateral $ABCD$ for the composition of the translation which maps B to D and the translation which maps A to C?

9. Map quadrilateral $ABCD$ to quadrilateral $A'B'C'D'$ by a translation that maps point A to A'. Then map quadrilateral $A'B'C'D'$ to quadrilateral $A''B''C''D''$ by a translation that maps A' to A''.

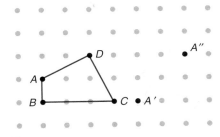

a. The translation that maps A to A' can be described as "right 4 and down 1." The translation that maps A' to A'' is "right 2 and up 2." Describe the translation that maps A to A''.

b. What is the image of quadrilateral $ABCD$ for the composition of the translation that takes A to A' followed by the translation that takes A' to A?

a. If R' is the image of R, what is the measure of the angles formed by the intersection of $\overleftrightarrow{RR'}$ and ℓ?

b. If U' is the image of U, how does the distance from U to ℓ compare with the distance from U' to ℓ?

c. What are the fixed points for this mapping?

6. Sketch the image of the quadrilateral for the 90° clockwise rotation about O that maps A to A'. (Trace the figure on a piece of paper and rotate the paper.)

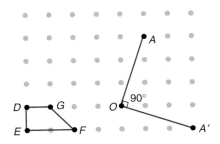

a. If E' is the image of E, what is the measure of $\angle EOE'$?

b. If G' is the image of G, how does the length EG compare with the length $E'G'$?

c. Are there any fixed points for this mapping?

7. Sketch the image of the quadrilateral in exercise 6 for the 90° counterclockwise rotation which maps A' to A.

a. If F' is the image of F for this mapping, what is the measure of $\angle FOF'$?

b. If D' is the image of D, how does the length DF compare with the length $D'F'$?

c. How does the area of the original quadrilateral compare to the area of its image?

8. Map quadrilateral $ABCD$ in exercise 9 to quadrilateral $EFGH$ by a translation that maps B to D. Then map quadrilateral $EFGH$ to quadrilateral $IJKL$ by a translation that maps A to C.

a. The translation that maps B to D can be described as "right 2 and up 2." Describe the translation that maps A to C.

10. Reflect pentagon $RSTUV$ about line m and then reflect its image about line n.

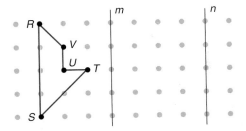

a. What single mapping (rotation, translation, or reflection) is equal to the composition of these two reflections?

b. Let R' be the image of R for the reflection about m, and let R'' be the image of R' for the reflection about n. Compare the distance from R to R'' with the distance from line m to line n. What relationship do you find? Will this relationship hold for other points and their images?

11. Reflect pentagon $RSTUV$ in exercise 10 about line n, and then reflect its image about line m.

a. What single mapping (rotation, translation, or reflection) is equal to the composition of these two reflections?

b. Let R' be the image of R for the reflection about n, and let R'' be the image of R' for the reflection about m. Compare the distance from R to R'' with the distance from line m to line n. What relationship can you find? Will this relationship hold for other points and their images?

12. Sketch the image of hexagon G for a reflection about line n. Label this image G'.

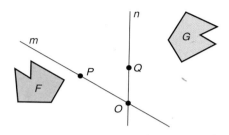

a. What is the image of G' for a reflection about line m?

b. There is a counterclockwise rotation about point O that will map figure G to figure F. How is the number of degrees in the rotation related to $\angle QOP$?

13. Sketch the image of hexagon F in exercise 12 for a reflection about line m.

a. What is the image of the image of F for a reflection about line n?

b. There is a clockwise rotation about point O that will map figure F to figure G. How is the number of degrees in this rotation related to $\angle POQ$?

Trace each figure in exercises 14 and 15 on a sheet of paper. Find the image of the figure for the given transformation by constructing the images of the vertex points. Show each construction and give a brief explanation.

14. a. A translation that maps S to S'

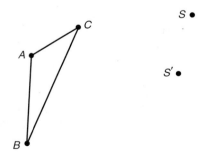

b. A reflection about line ℓ

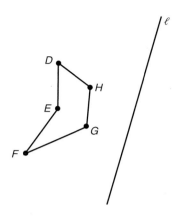

15. a. A 90° clockwise rotation about point O

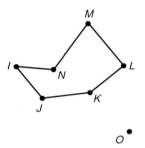

b. A reflection about line k

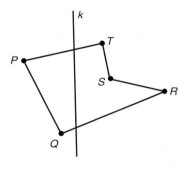

Trace this figure and points R and S on a piece of paper for exercises 16 and 17.

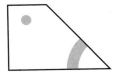

R •

S •

16. a. Locate the image of the figure for the composition of these two mappings: 180° rotation about R followed by a 180° rotation about S.

b. What single mapping (rotation, translation, reflection, or glide reflection) can be used to replace the two rotations in part a so that the figure is mapped to its image?

17. a. Locate the image of the figure for the composition of these two mappings: a 90° clockwise rotation about R followed by a 90° clockwise rotation about S.

b. What single mapping can be used to replace the two rotations in part a?

Complete the pattern in each grid in exercises 18 and 19 by carrying out the mappings on the basic figure in the small square in the upper left corner of the grid. (Copy the rectangular grid from the inside cover or from the website.)

18. Rows: Rotate 180° about the midpoints of the right sides of the squares. Columns: Reflect about the lower side of the squares.

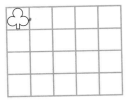

19. Rows: Reflect about the right sides of the squares. Columns: Reflect about the lower sides of the squares.

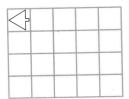

20. Mark off a grid and a square region that can be used as a basic figure to generate this wallpaper pattern. Describe the mappings for obtaining the rows and columns.

21. The design on the nineteenth-century quilt shown here also occurs in the fourteenth-century Moorish palace the Alhambra. The top row can be generated by a sequence of 180° rotations beginning with the white figure in the upper left corner.

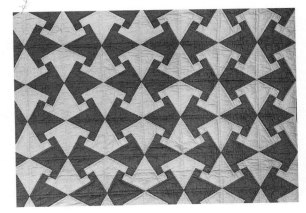

Patchwork quilt with Arabic lattice patterns, ca. 1850.

From the collections of Henry Ford Museum and Greenfield Village

a. Locate the centers of rotation for these mappings.

b. What mapping can be carried out to generate the left column of figures, beginning with the figure in the upper left corner?

Isometric grid paper, such as that shown in exercises 22 through 24, is helpful in drawing three-dimensional figures. Sketch the image of each figure for the given mapping. (Copy the isometric grid from the inside cover or from the website.)

22. A translation that maps P to P'

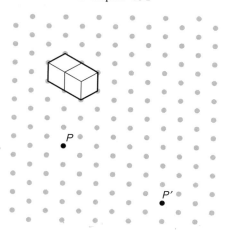

23. A reflection about plane P that is perpendicular to this page

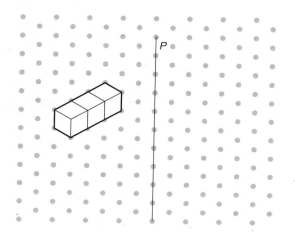

24. A 90° rotation in the indicated direction about line ℓ

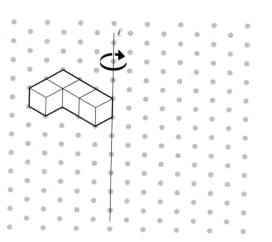

Determine the number of congruence mappings of each polygon onto itself in exercises 25 and 26, and indicate how you determined that number.

25. a. Rhombus
   b. Equilateral triangle
   c. Regular octagon

26. a. Rectangle
   b. Parallelogram
   c. Regular pentagon

Identify the basic figure (rectangle, hexagon, square, or parallelogram) that was used to create the nonpolygonal figure in each tessellation in exercises 27 through 29.

27.

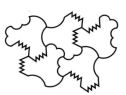

28.

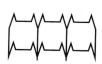

29.

Create a nonpolygonal (Escher-type) tessellation of the given type in exercises 30 through 32.

30. A rotation tessellation

31. A reflection tessellation

32. A translation tessellation

By altering the sides of each polygon in exercises 33 through 35, design a nonpolygonal figure that will tessellate.

33.

34.

35.

Determine the mapping (rotation, translation, or reflection) that maps each figure in exercises 36 and 37 to its image. Locate all lines of reflection and points of rotation.

36. a.

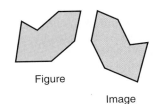

Figure

Image

b.

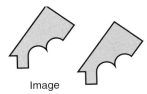

Image

Figure

37. a.

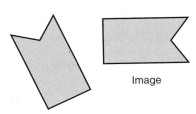

Figure

Image

b.

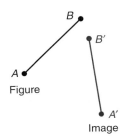

B

B′

A

Figure

A′

Image

REASONING AND PROBLEM SOLVING

38. A translation maps point P with coordinates $(^-2, 1)$ to P' with coordinates $(3, 2)$. Graph these points and draw an arrow from P to P' to indicate the length and direction of the translation. (Copy the coordinate system from the inside cover or from the website.)

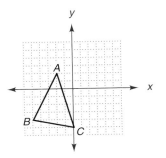

a. Sketch the image of $\triangle ABC$ for this translation.
b. If A', B', and C' are the images of A, B, and C, respectively, what are their coordinates?

39. Draw the image of quadrilateral $DEFG$ for a reflection about the x axis. Label the images of these vertices D', E', F', and G'. (Copy the coordinate system from the inside cover or from the website.)

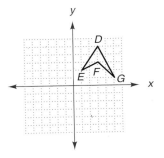

a. What are the coordinates of D', E', F' and G'?
b. Reflect quadrilateral $D'E'F'G'$ about the y axis and label its vertices D'', E'', F'', and G''. What are the coordinates of the vertices of this image?
c. What single rotation will map quadrilateral $DEFG$ to quadrilateral $D''E''F''G''$?

40. Mappings are sometimes given by describing what will happen to the coordinates of each point. For example, the mapping $(x, y) \rightarrow (x + 2, y - 3)$ is a translation that maps each point 2 units to the right and 3 units down. To find the image of a particular point, such as $(1, 7)$, substitute these values for x and y into $(x + 2, y - 3)$. In this case $(1, 7)$ maps to $(3, 4)$. Find the image of each figure for the given mapping. Label each mapping as a translation, rotation, reflection, or glide reflection. (Copy the coordinate system from the inside cover or from the website for the mappings.)

a. $(x, y) \rightarrow (x - 2, y + 1)$

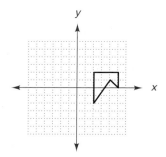

b. $(x, y) \rightarrow (x + 1, {}^{-}y)$

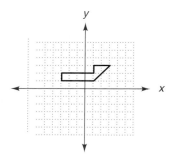

c. $(x, y) \rightarrow ({}^{-}x, {}^{-}y)$

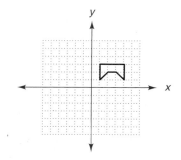

41. It is possible to place the numbers 1, 2, 3, 4, 5, and 6 in the circles of the following figure so that the sum along each side is the same. There are four solutions to this problem which are different, that is, which cannot be obtained from each other by rotations or reflections of the triangle. Find at least two of these solutions.

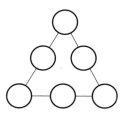

42. Featured Strategy: Making an Organized List How many different ways can five consecutive whole numbers be placed in a row so that no two consecutive whole numbers are next to each other?

a. Understanding the Problem Here is one solution for the first five consecutive whole numbers. If one arrangement can be obtained from another by a reflection, such as the one shown here, then we will consider the two arrangements to be the same. Find another solution.

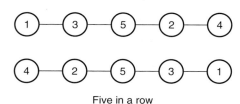

Five in a row

b. Devising a Plan This type of problem can be solved by *making an organized list*. For example, you might begin by listing all the different arrangements with 1 in the first position; then those with 2 in the first position; etc. If you want to eliminate duplication due to reflections, what adjustment must you make in the total number of arrangements?

c. Carrying Out the Plan Follow the system suggested above or one of your own to solve this problem.

d. Looking Back There are several ways to extend this problem. For example, there are 45 different solutions for six consecutive whole numbers; you may want to see if you can find them. Another possibility is to use different configurations. How many different solutions are there for the following figure? (*Reminder:* Two arrangements are the same if they can be obtained from each other by a reflection.)

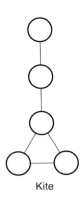

Kite

An ornamental design that extends to the right and left (around rooms, buildings, pottery, etc.) is called a **frieze.** The frieze on the following container is mapped onto itself by a translation.

Container with cover, Attica, Greece, eighth century B.C.

What transformations will map each of the frieze patterns in exercises 43 and 44 onto itself? (Consider these patterns as extending in both directions.)

43. a.

CHINESE ORNAMENT PAINTED ON PORCELAIN

b.

MASONRY FRET, TEMPLE AT MITLA, MEXICO

44. a.

FRENCH RENAISSANCE ORNAMENT FROM CASKET

45. Design a frieze pattern (see exercises 43 and 44) that will be transformed onto itself by all of the following transformations: 180° rotation, translation, horizontal reflection, and vertical reflection.

46. Design a frieze pattern that will be transformed onto itself by a translation and a horizontal reflection, but not by a vertical reflection.

47. A square array of numbers in which the sum of numbers in any horizontal row, vertical column, or diagonal is always the same is called a **magic square.** The two magic squares shown below can be obtained from each other by a reflection about the diagonal from lower left to upper right. How many 3 × 3 magic squares with the numbers in different locations can be obtained from figure (*a*) by using rotations or reflections of the entire square?

4	3	8
9	5	1
2	7	6

(*a*)

6	1	8
7	5	3
2	9	4

(*b*)

48. How many ways can the numbers 1, 2, 3, 4, 5, and 6 be placed in the circles of the figure below so that no two consecutive numbers are next to each other? Two arrangements, such as those shown, are considered the same if one can be obtained from the other by a rotation or reflection.

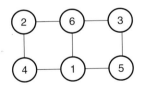 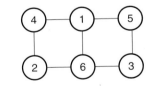

49. The first player to place three X's or three O's in a row, column, or diagonal of a 3 × 3 grid wins the game of Tic-Tac-Toe.
  a. There are nine ways to place the first X (or O) on the grid. The following two grids are congruent because a vertical reflection maps one onto the other. How many noncongruent ways are there of making the first move? Sketch them.

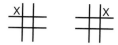

b. After the first move (an X in the upper left corner in this example) there are only eight ways to place the O, but some of these, such as the ones shown in the next two grids, are congruent. Can

you see what transformation maps one onto the other? Sketch all the noncongruent moves for the second turn.

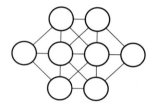

c. Only one of the moves in part b can prevent the player using X's from winning. Which one?

ONLINE LEARNING CENTER   www.mhhe.com/bennett-nelson

- Math Investigation 11.2   *Tessellations*
  Section-Related: • Links   • Writing/Discussion Problems   • Bibliography

PUZZLER

How can the whole numbers from 1 to 8 be placed in the circles of the figure shown here so that any two connected circles do not contain consecutive whole numbers? If we agree that all solutions that can be obtained through rotations and reflections of this diagram are the same, then there is only one solution. Find this unique solution.

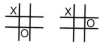

MATH ACTIVITY 11.3

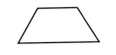

ENLARGEMENTS WITH PATTERN BLOCKS

Materials: Pattern block pieces in the Manipulative Kit

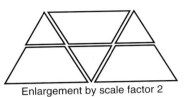

Enlargement by scale factor 2

1. The single pattern block at the upper left is similar to the trapezoid below that is formed with six pattern blocks.

   a. One condition for similarity is that the lengths of the corresponding sides of two figures have the same ratio. What is the ratio of the lengths of the corresponding sides of these two figures?

   b. The second condition for similarity is that the corresponding angles of the two figures have the same measure. Explain which angles are corresponding and how you know they have the same measure.

   c. Because each side of the large trapezoid is 2 times the length of each corresponding side of the small trapezoid, the large trapezoid is an **enlargement** of the small trapezoid by a **scale factor** of 2. The area of the large trapezoid is how many times the area of the small trapezoid? Write a sentence or two to explain your reasoning.

   d. Construct an enlargement by a scale factor of 2 for each of the other pattern blocks. Sketch figures and describe how the area of a figure is related to its enlargement.

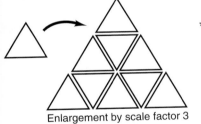

Enlargement by scale factor 3

*2. The large triangle at the left is an enlargement of the small triangle by a scale factor of 3. Build and sketch an enlargement by a scale factor of 3 for each of the other five pattern blocks. (Trace patterns blocks, if there are not enough.) Explain how the area of each enlargement compares to the area of the single pattern block.

3. Build and sketch an enlargement of each of the following figures for the given scale factor. State a conjecture about how you think the area of an enlargement is related to the area of the smaller figure. Write an explanation to support your reasoning.

   a. Enlarge by a scale factor of 3

   b. Enlarge by a scale factor of 4

   c. Enlarge by a scale factor of 3

   d. Enlarge by a scale factor of 2

   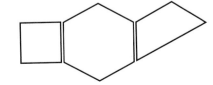

SECTION 11.3

SIMILARITY MAPPINGS

Model of Fort Wayne, Indiana, in a wind tunnel

The following two figures are similar. Each dimension of the larger figure is twice the corresponding dimension of the smaller figure. If this doubling of dimensions is continued, how many cubes will there be in the fifth figure?

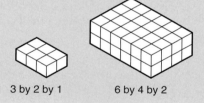

3 by 2 by 1   6 by 4 by 2

An indispensable phase in the design of large objects is the use of models. Research on ship and plane design, for example, is routinely carried out by testing models of ships in water tanks and models of planes in wind tunnels. The above photograph shows a scale model of Fort Wayne, Indiana, in an environmental wind tunnel in the Fluid Dynamics and Diffusion Laboratory at Colorado State University. Environmental engineers will study the effects of wind on the scale model of the city in hopes of solving urban smog and pollution problems.

We say that two figures are **similar** if they have the same shape but not necessarily the same size. For example, models of objects are usually similar to the actual objects. All our familiar optical instruments make use of the principle of similar figures. When you look through a magnifying glass or a microscope, you see an object that is similar to the original figure.

Similarity and Scale Factors

Similar figures can be created by lights and shadows. Hold a flat object perpendicular to a flashlight's rays, and the light will produce a shadow similar in shape to the original figure (see Figure 11.35). Because the light is from a small bulb and spreads out in the shape of a cone, the shadow is larger than the object.

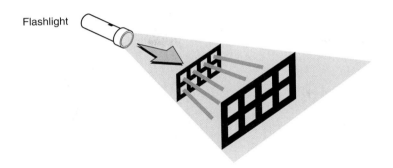

Flashlight

Figure 11.35

Light rays and shadows are analogous to mappings and their images. For each point on the object there is a corresponding "shadow point," which is its image. The rays of light are like lines projecting from a central source to the object. This type of mapping is illustrated in Figure 11.36. Point *O*, which represents the light source, is called the **projection point,** and each point of quadrilateral *ABCD* is mapped to exactly one point on quadrilateral *A'B'C'D'*. This type of mapping is called a **similarity mapping.** In this example, *ABCD* is similar to *A'B'C'D'*, and we write *ABCD* ~ *A'B'C'D'*.

Although students will not develop a full understanding of similarity until the middle grades, when they focus on proportionality, in grades 3–5 they can begin to think about similarity in terms of figures that are related by the transformations of magnifying or shrinking.

Standards 2000, p. 166

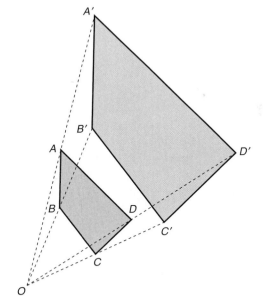

Figure 11.36

Each point on quadrilateral *A'B'C'D'* in Figure 11.36 is twice the distance from point *O* as is its corresponding point on quadrilateral *ABCD*. For instance, distance *OA'* is twice *OA*, *OB'* is twice *OB*, etc. Because of this relationship between points and their images, this mapping is said to have a **scale factor** of 2.

If the scale factor for a similarity mapping is greater than 1, the image is an **enlargement** of the original figure. The mapping from figure *XZW* to figure *X'Z'W'* in

Figure 11.37 has a scale factor of 3. The distance of each image point of figure $X'Z'W'$ from O is 3 times the distance of its corresponding point on figure XZW from O. That is, OX' is 3 times OX, OZ' is 3 times OZ, and OW' is 3 times OW, etc.

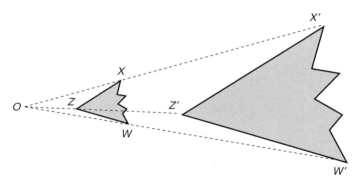

Figure 11.37

When the scale factor is less than 1, the image is a **reduction** of the original figure. In the similarity mapping in Figure 11.38, each of the distances from O to points A, B, C, and D has been multiplied by $\frac{1}{3}$ to get the image points A', B', C', and D'. That is, the larger figure has been reduced by a scale factor of $\frac{1}{3}$.

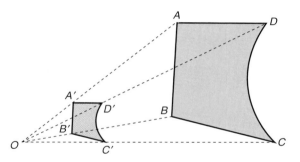

Figure 11.38

It is even possible for a scale factor to be negative. In that case, the original figure and its image are on opposite sides of the projection point, and the image is "upside down" in relation to the original figure. The larger flag shown in Figure 11.39 is projected through point O to the smaller flag using a scale factor of $-\frac{1}{2}$. In particular, A is mapped to A' and G is mapped to G'. As in the previous examples, the scale factor determines the size of the image. With a scale factor of $-\frac{1}{2}$, the distance of each image point from O is half the distance of its corresponding point

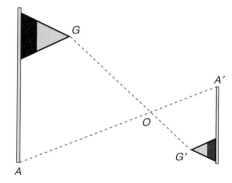

Figure 11.39

on the original figure from O (and the point and its image are on opposite sides of the projection point). For example, OG' is half of OG, and OA' is half of OA.

The lenses of our eyes and of cameras create inverted images of scenes, much like the images from a similarity mapping with a negative scale factor (see Figure 11.40). Such lenses are like projection points, producing a scene upside down on the retinas of our eyes or the film of a camera.

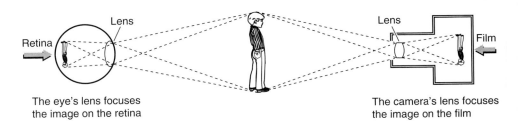

Figure 11.40

The eye's lens focuses the image on the retina

The camera's lens focuses the image on the film

Example **A**

Determine the scale factor for each mapping.

Problems that involve constructing or interpreting scale drawings offer students opportunities to use and increase their knowledge of similarity, ratio, and proportionality. Such problems can be created from many sources, such as maps, blueprints, science, and literature.

Standards 2000, p. 245

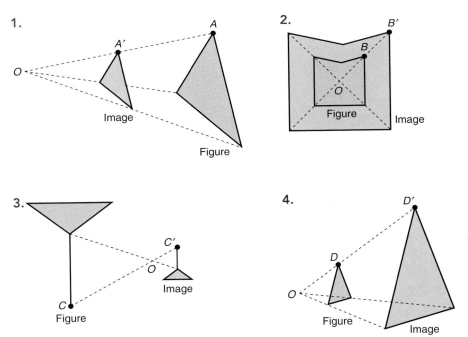

Solution **1.** Each image point is one-half as far from O as is its corresponding point in the figure: $OA'/OA = \frac{1}{2}$. So the scale factor is $\frac{1}{2}$. **2.** Each image point is twice the distance from O as is its corresponding point on the figure: $OB'/OB = 2$. So the scale factor is 2. **3.** $OC'/OC = \frac{1}{3}$, and since the figure and its image are on opposite sides of the projection point, the scale factor is $-\frac{1}{3}$. **4.** $OD'/OD = 3$, so the scale factor is 3.

We have seen several examples of similarity mappings. For each mapping the original figure and its image are similar. We state this fact as the definition of similar figures.

> **SIMILAR FIGURES**   Two geometric figures are **similar** if and only if there exists a similarity mapping of one figure onto the other.

The definition for similarity also holds for space figures. The two boxes in Figure 11.41 are similar because the smaller one can be mapped onto the larger one by using a projection from point O inside the small box. The scale factor for this similarity is 3.6. That is, the distance of each vertex of the larger box from O is 3.6 times the distance of its corresponding vertex of the smaller box from O. As with plane figures, a scale factor greater than 1 produces an enlargement of a three-dimensional figure, and a scale factor between 0 and 1 reduces the original figure.

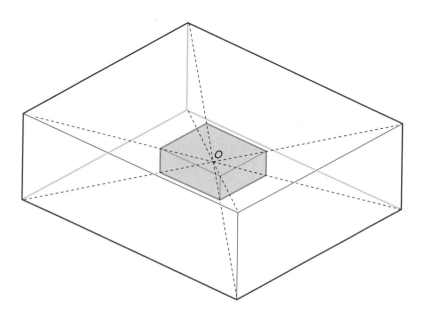

Figure 11.41

In our study of congruence, the mappings we used (rotations, translations, and reflections) *preserved size and shape.* Similarity mappings, on the other hand, except those whose scale factors are ±1 and in which case the figure and its image are congruent, *do not preserve size* but *do preserve shape.*

Similar Polygons

Similarity mappings have two important properties. First, the *sizes of angles do not change.* Consider the similarity mapping in Figure 11.42, which maps $\triangle DEF$ to $\triangle D'E'F'$ with a scale factor of 2. In this case,

$$\angle D \cong \angle D' \qquad \angle E \cong \angle E' \qquad \angle F \cong \angle F'$$

Second, the lengths of line segments all *change by the same multiple,* which is the scale factor. The length of each side of $\triangle D'E'F'$ is twice the length of its corresponding side in $\triangle DEF$. That is,

$$D'E' = 2(DE) \qquad E'F' = 2(EF) \qquad D'F' = 2(DF)$$

Another way of stating this condition is to say that the ratios of the lengths of corresponding line segments are equal.

$$\frac{D'E'}{DE} = \frac{E'F'}{EF} = \frac{D'F'}{DF} = \frac{2}{1}$$

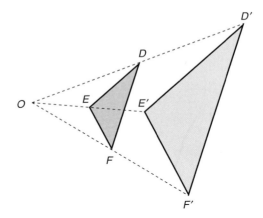

Figure 11.42

In general, for a scale factor of k, where $k > 0$, each line segment will have an image whose length is k times the length of the original line segment.

There are many applications of similar figures in which it is inconvenient to set up similarity mappings by using projection points. A solution to this problem is to produce similar figures from measurements of angles and distances. The construction of maps and charts is an example. The polygon on the chart in Figure 11.43 connects five points and is approximately similar to the large imaginary polygon over the water that connects the actual landmarks. These positions on the chart were plotted by measuring the five vertex angles and five distances between these islands. The following theorem verifies that such measurements are all that is necessary to obtain similar polygons.

Students in grades 3-5 should have opportunities to use maps and make simple scale drawings. Grades 6–8 students should extend their understanding of scaling to solve problems involving scale factors. These problems can help students make sense of proportional relationships and develop an understanding of similarity.

Standards 2000, p. 47

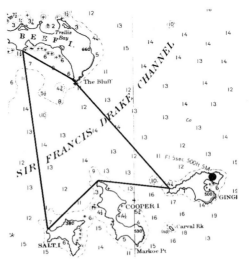

Figure 11.43

Virgin Islands, West Indies, scale factor 139,000

> **SIMILAR POLYGONS**   Two polygons are similar if and only if there is a mapping from one to the other such that
>
> 1. Their corresponding angles are congruent.
> 2. The lengths of their corresponding sides have the same ratio.

Example B

If $\triangle ABC$ is similar to $\triangle DEF$ ($\triangle ABC \sim \triangle DEF$), find the lengths of sides $\overline{AB}$ and $\overline{EF}$.

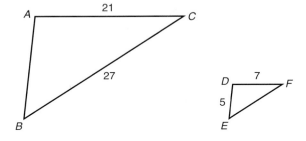

Solution   Since $AC/DF = 21/7 = 3$, the ratio of the lengths of each pair of corresponding sides is 3. Thus,

$$\frac{AB}{DE} = \frac{AB}{5} = 3 \qquad \text{so} \qquad AB = 15$$

$$\frac{BC}{EF} = \frac{27}{EF} = 3 \qquad \text{so} \qquad EF = 9$$

Notice in Example B that the ratio of the lengths of any two sides of the first triangle is equal to the ratio of the lengths of the corresponding two sides of the second triangle. For example,

$$\frac{AC}{AB} = \frac{21}{15} \qquad \text{and} \qquad \frac{DF}{DE} = \frac{7}{5}$$

and these two fractions are equal. In general, if two polygons are similar, *the ratio of the lengths of any two sides of the first polygon is equal to the ratio of the lengths of the corresponding sides of the second polygon.*

To show that two polygons are similar, it is usually necessary to show that both conditions are satisfied: (1) corresponding angles are congruent, and (2) corresponding sides have the same ratio.

Example C

1. Compare the following square and rectangle. Which condition for similarity do they satisfy? Are they similar?

2. Compare the rectangle and the parallelogram. Which condition for similarity do they satisfy? Are they similar?

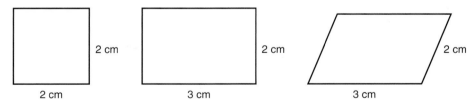

Solution **1.** The square and the rectangle have congruent angles (all 90°), but they do not satisfy the second condition for similar polygons because the ratios of the lengths of their corresponding sides are not equal: 2/2 ≠ 2/3. So these polygons are not similar.   **2.** The rectangle and the parallelogram satisfy the second condition for similar polygons because the ratios of the lengths of their corresponding sides are equal, but the angles in the rectangle are not congruent to those in the parallelogram. Therefore these polygons are not similar.

Similar Triangles

To determine if two triangles are similar, it is not necessary to check both conditions for similar polygons. Minimum conditions for similarity of triangles are examined in the following examples.

Example D

Construct a triangle having two angles congruent to ∡A and ∡B.

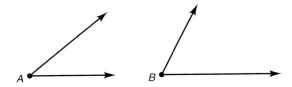

Solution   Draw a line segment of arbitrary length, and label its endpoints C and D.

Then construct an angle at C that is congruent to ∡A and an angle at D that is congruent to ∡B (as shown).

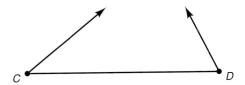

Finally, extend the sides of ∡C and ∡D, and label their intersection E.

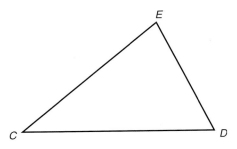

Suppose that instead of beginning with line segment $\overline{CD}$, as in Example D, we begin with $\overline{FG}$, which is one-half as long, and as before construct two angles which are congruent to ∡A and ∡B. The resulting triangle is shown in Figure 11.44 with ∡F ≅ ∡C and ∡G ≅ ∡D.

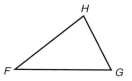

Figure 11.44

Comparing the lengths of the sides of △CDE and △FGH, we see that *FH* is one-half of *CE*, *GH* is one-half of *DE*, and *FG* is one-half of *CD*. So △CDE ~ △FGH. This result suggests the following *similarity property of triangles*.

> **ANGLE-ANGLE (AA) SIMILARITY PROPERTY**   If two angles of one triangle are congruent to two angles of another triangle, the two triangles are similar.

Notice that for two triangles to be similar, it is only necessary that two angles of one triangle be congruent to two angles of the other triangle, because if that is the case, the third angles of the triangles must be equal. Why?

Example E

Find a one-to-one correspondence between the vertices of each pair of triangles in figure (*1*) to show that the triangles are similar. Explain why. Repeat for figure (*2*).

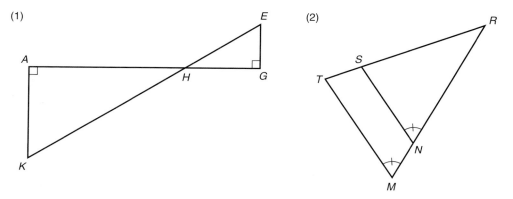

Solution   **1.** △AKH ~ △GEH by the AA similarity property because ∡A ≅ ∡G and ∡AHK ≅ ∡GHE (they are vertical angles).   **2.** △RSN ~ △RTM by the AA similarity property because ∡N ≅ ∡M and both triangles contain ∡R.

We have seen that in order to show that two triangles are similar, it is only necessary to check the measures of their angles. The following example, on the other hand, considers only the measures of the sides of two triangles.

Example F

Two sets of three line segments are shown below. The lengths *r*, *s*, and *t* are 3 times the corresponding lengths *c*, *d*, and *e*. Construct a triangle from each set of segments, and determine if the triangles are similar.

r		*c*
s		*d*
t		*e*

Solution   The following two triangles can be constructed by using the construction techniques described in Section 11.1. If the vertices of these triangles are matched so that $A \leftrightarrow T$, $B \leftrightarrow R$, and $C \leftrightarrow S$, the lengths of the corresponding sides have a ratio of 3. Measuring the corresponding angles of the triangles by using a protractor—or comparing the angles by tracing on paper—shows that angles A, B, and C are congruent, respectively, to angles T, R, and S. Thus $\triangle ABC \sim \triangle TRS$.

Research Statement

Research suggests that students may regard orientation as a salient feature of a geometric figure, since they tend only to see figures in prototypical orientation—for example, with horizontal bases.

Vinner and Hershkowitz 1980

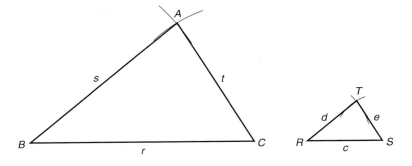

Example F suggests the following *similarity property of triangles.*

SIDE-SIDE-SIDE (SSS) SIMILARITY PROPERTY   If the corresponding sides of two triangles are proportional, then the two triangles are similar.

Example G

Which two of the following three triangles are similar?

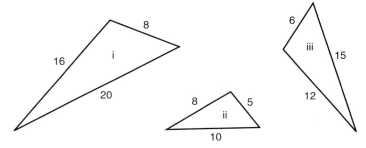

Solution   Triangle i is similar to triangle iii. The ratio of the lengths of their corresponding sides is 4 to 3.

$$\frac{8}{6} = \frac{20}{15} = \frac{16}{12} = \frac{4}{3}$$

Problem-Solving Application

One important application of similar triangles is in making indirect measurements. It is said that the Greek mathematician Thales computed the height of the Great Pyramid of Egypt through indirect measurements. One account describes his use of shadows and similar triangles. The sun is so far away that in a given vicinity the angles formed by its rays and the ground are approximately congruent. If a stick is held perpendicular to the ground, the stick and its shadow form a small right triangle that is similar to the right triangle formed by the pyramid and its shadow. The next problem shows how Thales might have computed the height of the Great Pyramid.

PROBLEM

Suppose that the distance from the base of the Great Pyramid to the tip of its shadow is 342 feet. Also assume that a 6-foot stick placed perpendicular to the ground casts a 9-foot shadow. If the pyramid has a square base with dimensions of 756 feet by 756 feet, what is the vertical height of the pyramid?

Understanding the Problem   The following drawing shows the stick, the pyramid, and the shadows. Point A is the foot of the altitude of the pyramid. The distance from B to C is 342 feet. **Question 1:** What is the distance from A to B?

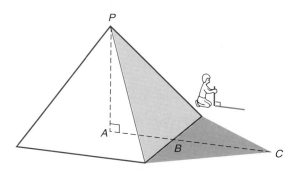

In the middle grades students should build on their formal and informal experiences with measurable attributes like length, area, and volume. . . . They should also become proficient at measuring angles and using ratio and proportion to solve problems involving scaling, similarity, and derived measures.

Standards 2000, p. 241

Devising a Plan   The stick, the pyramid, and the sun's rays form two similar triangles, as shown in the next figure. Using the ratios of the lengths of corresponding sides, we can find the height of the pyramid. **Question 2:** Why is the large triangle similar to the small one?

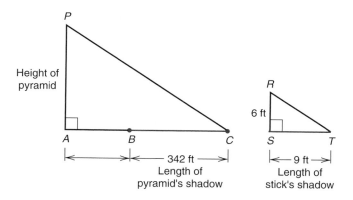

Carrying Out the Plan   **Question 3:** In light of the fact that the corresponding sides of similar triangles are proportional, what is the height of the pyramid?

Looking Back   Once we have the height of the pyramid, the slant height along the face of the pyramid from B to P can be computed by using the Pythagorean theorem. **Question 4:** What is this distance?

Answers to Questions 1–4   1. This distance is one-half the width of the side of the pyramid: $756/2 = 378$. **2.** $\angle A$ and $\angle S$ are both right angles. $\angle C$ and $\angle T$ are congruent angles that are formed by the sun's rays and the ground. Therefore, $\triangle PAC \sim \triangle RST$ by the AA similarity property of triangles.

3. $\dfrac{PA}{RS} = \dfrac{AC}{ST}$, $RS = 6$, $AC = 378 + 342 = 720$, and $ST = 9$. So,

$$\frac{PA}{6} = \frac{720}{9}$$

$$PA = \frac{6(720)}{9}$$

$$PA = 480 \text{ feet}$$

4. $\triangle PAB$ is a right triangle with legs $PA = 480$ and $AB = 378$. So by the Pythagorean theorem,

$$480^2 + 378^2 = (PB)^2$$
$$230{,}400 + 142{,}884 = (PB)^2$$
$$373{,}284 = (PB)^2$$
$$611 \approx PB$$

So, the slant height of the face of the pyramid is 611 feet to the nearest foot.

Thales (636–546 B.C.) was one of the earliest of many famous Greek mathematicians and is regarded by historians as the father of geometry. In his early years he traveled widely, learning geometry from the Egyptians and astronomy from the Babylonians. Thales is generally acknowledged as the first to introduce the use of logical proofs based on deductive reasoning, rather than experiments, to support conclusions. Thales was regarded as unusually shrewd in commerce and science, and many anecdotes are told about his cleverness. On one occasion, according to Aristotle, after several years in which the olive trees failed to produce, Thales suspected weather conditions would change and bought up all the olive presses. When the season came with its abundant crop, he was able to rent the presses for large profits. Thales was known as the first of the Seven Sages of Greece, the only mathematician to be so honored. He is supposed to have coined the maxim "Know thyself."

Scale Factors, Area, and Volume

The smaller of the two knives in Figure 11.45 is a regular-size Scout knife, whose length is about equal to the width of the palm of your hand. The newspaper clipping says that the bigger knife is "three times larger" than the conventional Scout knife. Does this mean that the length of the larger knife is 3 times greater or that its surface area or volume is 3 times greater? Phrases such as *twice as large* and *3 times bigger* can be misleading. They often refer to a comparison of linear dimensions, as in the case of these knives (compare their lengths). The 3 in this example refers to the scale factor. It means that the length, width, and height of the big knife are 3 times the corresponding dimensions of the smaller knife. But what can be said about the relative sizes of the areas or volumes of these knives? In the following paragraphs you will see the effect of scale factors on area and volume.

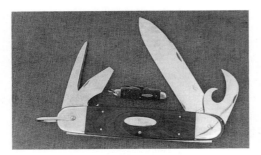

Figure 11.45

Prepared for Anything

What could be the world's largest Scout-type knife is ready for the world's largest potato. Wayne Goddard, a professional knife-maker who works at his home at 473 Durham St., Eugene, turned this one out for Dennis and Raymond Ellingsen, Eugene knife collectors. Completely functional, the knife is $24\frac{1}{2}$ inches long when opened. It weighs $4\frac{1}{4}$ pounds and is three times larger than the conventional Scout knife.

AREA The two rectangles in Figure 11.46 are similar. The scale factor from the smaller to the larger is 3. That is, the length and width of the larger rectangle are 3 times the length and width of the smaller rectangle. How do their areas compare? The area of the small rectangle is 4×2 square units. Because each of its linear dimensions is increased by a multiple of 3, the area of the larger rectangle is $(3 \times 4) \times (3 \times 2)$ square units. Using the commutative and associative properties for multiplication, we find that

$$(3 \times 4) \times (3 \times 2) = (3 \times 3) \times (4 \times 2)$$
$$= 3^2 \times (4 \times 2)$$

So the area of the large rectangle is 9 (the square of the scale factor 3) times the area of the small rectangle. In general, if one plane figure is similar to another figure by a scale factor of k, where k is any positive real number, then the second figure will have an area k^2 times the area of the first figure.

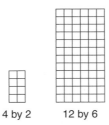

Figure 11.46

4 by 2   12 by 6

The relationship between scale factor and surface area for three-dimensional figures is the same as that for plane figures. Consider the two boxes shown in Figure 11.47. The scale factor from the small box to the large box is 2. That is, the length, width, and height of the large box are each 2 times the corresponding dimension of the small box. Let's compare the surface areas of the sides of these boxes. The front side of the small box has an area of 6, and the front side of the large box has an area of 24. The larger area is 2^2, or 4, times the smaller area. A

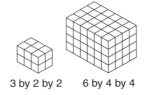

Figure 11.47

3 by 2 by 2   6 by 4 by 4

similar comparison between each face of the small box and the corresponding face of the large box shows that the larger surface area is 4 times the smaller surface area. In general, the surface areas of two similar figures are related by the *square of their scale factor*. If the scale factor is k, where k is any positive real number, then one figure will have a surface area k^2 times the surface area of the other figure.

Example H

1. If the scale factor from a small photograph to its enlargement is 3 and the area of the small photograph is 15 square inches, what is the area of the large photograph?

2. If the surface area of a box is 52 square centimeters and the scale factor from the box to a larger similar box is 2, what is the surface area of the large box?

3. If the scale factor from a figure to its reduction is $\frac{1}{2}$ and the figure has a surface area of 76 square feet, what is the surface area of the smaller figure?

Solution   1. $3^2 \times 15 = 135$, so the area of the large photograph is 135 square inches.   **2.** $2^2 \times 52 = 208$, so the surface area of the large box is 208 square centimeters.   **3.** $(\frac{1}{2})^2 \times 76 = 19$, so the surface area of the smaller figure is 19 square feet.

VOLUME   There is also a relationship between the volumes of two similar space figures. Consider the volumes of the boxes in Figure 11.47. The volume of the small box is $3 \times 2 \times 2$ cubic units. Because each of its linear dimensions is multiplied by a scale factor of 2, the volume of the large box is $(2 \times 3) \times (2 \times 2) \times (2 \times 2)$ cubic units. Using the commutative and associative properties for multiplication,

$$(2 \times 3) \times (2 \times 2) \times (2 \times 2) = (2 \times 2 \times 2) \times (3 \times 2 \times 2)$$
$$= 2^3 \times (3 \times 2 \times 2)$$

So the volume of the large box is 8 (the cube of the scale factor 2) times the volume of the small box. In general, if one space figure is similar to another figure by a scale factor of k, where k is any positive real number, then the second figure will have a volume k^3 times the volume of the first figure.

We are now prepared to examine the relationships between the areas and volumes of the knives in Figure 11.45. The scale factor from the small knife to the large knife is 3. Therefore, the large knife has a surface area that is 3^2, or 9, times the surface area of the small knife. The volume of the large knife is 3^3, or 27, times the volume of the small knife.

Let's apply the relationships between length, area, and volume of similar figures to another example.

Example I

The following photograph shows a nineteenth-century scale model of a cookstove. This miniature stove was used by a traveling salesperson as a sample and has all the features of a life-size stove. The scale factor from this miniature stove to the life-size stove is 5.

1. If the small stove has a surface area of 300 square centimeters, what is the surface area of the life-size stove?

2. If the oven in the small stove has a volume of 1000 cubic centimeters, what is the volume of the oven in the life-size stove?

Nineteenth-century scale model of a cookstove

Solution   1. $5^2 \times 300 = 7500$, so the large stove has a surface area of 7500 square centimeters. 2. $5^3 \times 1000 = 125{,}000$, so the oven in the large stove has a volume of 125,000 cubic centimeters.

Sizes and Shapes of Living Things

The *Curriculum and Evaluation Standards for School Mathematics* state that

Investigations of two- and three-dimensional models foster an understanding of the different growth rates for linear measures, areas, and volumes of similar figures. These ideas are fundamental to measurement and critical to scientific applications.*

One application of growth rates involves the various sizes of animals. For every type of animal there is a most convenient size and shape. One factor that governs the size and shape of a living thing is the ratio of its surface area to its volume. All warm-blooded animals at rest lose approximately the same amount of heat for each unit area of skin. Small animals have too much surface area for their volumes; a major reason they spend so much time eating is to keep warm. For example, 5000 mice may together weigh as much as a person, but their collective surface area and food consumption are each about 17 times greater! At the other end of the scale, large animals tend to overheat because they have too little surface area for their volumes.

Let's take a closer look at the relationship between surface area and volume as the size of an object increases. The table in Figure 11.48 lists the surface areas and volumes of four different cubes. As the size of the cube increases, both the surface area and the volume increase, but the volume increases at a faster rate. One way of viewing this change is to form the ratio of surface area to volume. For a $2 \times 2 \times 2$ cube, the ratio is 3, and as the dimensions of the cube increase, the ratio decreases. For a $10 \times 10 \times 10$ cube, the ratio is less than 1.

> Geometric modeling and spatial reasoning offer ways to interpret and describe physical environments and can be important tools in problem solving.
>
> Standards 2000, p. 41

CUBE	SURFACE AREA	VOLUME	AREA/VOLUME
$2 \times 2 \times 2$	24	8	3
$3 \times 3 \times 3$	54	27	2
$4 \times 4 \times 4$	96	64	1.5
$10 \times 10 \times 10$	600	1000	.6

Figure 11.48

*Curriculum and Evaluation Standards for School Mathematics (Reston, VA: National Council of Teachers of Mathematics, 1989), p. 115.

Another way to compare the changes in surface area and volume as the size of a cube increases is with graphs. If the length, width, and height of a cube are x, its area is $6x^2$ and its volume is x^3. The graphs of $y = 6x^2$ and $y = x^3$ in Figure 11.49 show that for $x < 6$, the area is greater than the volume; for $x = 6$, the area equals the volume; and for $x > 6$, the volume is greater than the area.

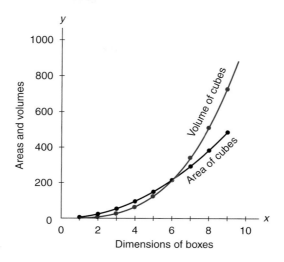

Figure 11.49

To relate these changes in surface area and volume to the problem of maintaining body temperatures, assume that the cubes shown in Figure 11.50 are animals and that the ideal ratio between surface area and volume is 2. In this case the $2 \times 2 \times 2$ animal has too much surface area (it would tend to be too cold), because its area-to-volume ratio is 3 (24/8); the area-to-volume ratio for the $3 \times 3 \times 3$ animal is 2 (54/27), which is just right; and the $4 \times 4 \times 4$ animal has too little surface area (it would tend to be too hot), because its ratio of area to volume is 1.5 (96/64).

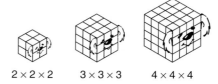

Figure 11.50

$2 \times 2 \times 2$ $3 \times 3 \times 3$ $4 \times 4 \times 4$

EXERCISES AND PROBLEMS 11.3

Determine the scale factor for each mapping from the figure to its image in exercises 1 and 2.

1. a.

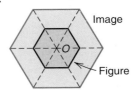

b.

opposite projection

-1/2

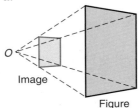

2. a.

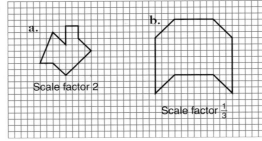

b.

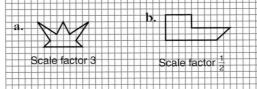

For each figure in exercises 3 and 4, sketch a similar figure using the given scale factor. (Copy the rectangular grid from the inside cover or from the web site to use in your sketches.)

3.

a.   Scale factor 2

b.   Scale factor $\frac{1}{3}$

4.

a.   Scale factor 3

b.   Scale factor $\frac{1}{2}$

5. Use O as a projection point and find the images of triangle T on the following grid, using the three scale factors of 2, 3, and $\frac{1}{2}$. Look for a relationship between the coordinates of the vertices of T and the coordinates of their images. (Copy the rectangular grid from the inside cover or from the website.)

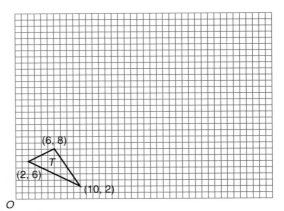

(6, 8)

(2, 6)

T

(10, 2)

O

The pairs of polygons in exercises 6 and 7 are similar. Find the missing length for each side of the polygons.

6. a. $\triangle ABC \sim \triangle DEF$

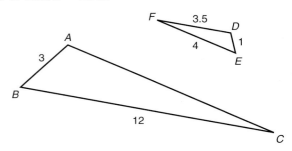

b. $FGHIJ \sim KLMNT$

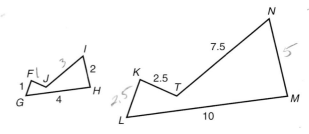

7. a. $WXYZ \sim RSUV$

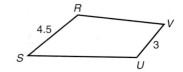

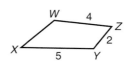

b. $ADCB \sim MONP$

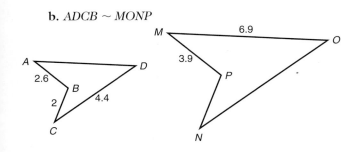

8. Which three of the following triangles are similar to each other? State the reason why.

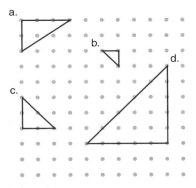

Determine whether the triangles in each pair in exercises 9 and 10 are similar. If so, give a reason and write the similarity correspondence.

9. a.

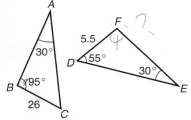

b.

c.

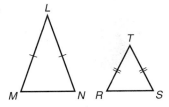

10. a.

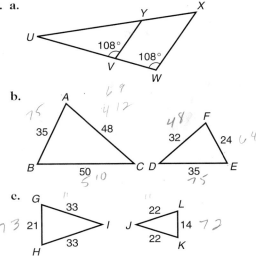

b.

c.

Determine whether the following figures are similar, and if so, explain why. If they are not similar, show a counterexample with measurements.

11. a. Any two squares
   b. Any two isosceles triangles
   c. Any two rhombuses
   d. Any two regular octagons

12. a. Any two equilateral triangles
   b. Any two right triangles
   c. Any two congruent polygons
   d. Any two rectangles

13. Construct the triangles in parts a and b.
   a. A triangle having angles of 42° and 70° and an included side of length 15
   b. A triangle having angles of 42° and 70° and an included side of length 20
   c. Are the triangles in parts a and b similar?
   d. What conjecture about similar triangles is suggested by these constructions?

14. Construct the triangles in parts a and b.
   a. A triangle having sides of 4 and 6 centimeters and an included angle of 45°
   b. A triangle having sides of 2 and 3 centimeters and an included angle of 45°
   c. Are the triangles in parts a and b similar?
   d. What conjecture about similar triangles is suggested by these constructions?

An easy way to test rectangles for similarity is illustrated in exercises 15 and 16. If one rectangle is placed on the other so that their right angles coincide, as shown on the following page, then the rectangles are similar if their diagonals lie on the same line. For example, rectangle $AEFG$ is similar to rectangle $ABCD$, but the two rectangles at the right are not similar.

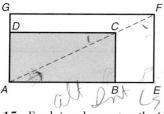

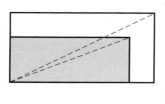

15. Explain why rectangle *ABCD* above is similar to rectangle *AEFG*. (*Hint:* To show the sides are proportional, use similar triangles.)

16. Trace the following rectangles onto another sheet, and use the **diagonal test** to find out which two are similar.

17. The stick and the tree in the following figure form right angles with the ground. Furthermore ∡*CAB* and ∡*STR* are congruent because they are formed by the sun's rays.
a. Why are the triangles in this figure similar?
b. Use the given information to find the height of the tree.

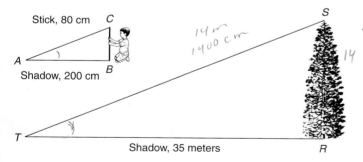

18. Use the figures in exercise 3 to answer these questions.
a. The area of the image of figure a is how many times the area of figure a?
b. The area of the image of figure b is what fraction of the area of the original figure b?

19. Use the figures in exercise 4 to answer these questions.
a. The area of the image of figure a is how many times the area of figure a?
b. The area of the image of figure b is what fraction of the area of figure b?

Triangle *T* in exercise 5 has an area of 16 square units. What is the area of the enlargement or reduction of this triangle for a mapping with the scale factors given in exercises 20 and 21?

20. a. 2   **b.** $\frac{1}{3}$

21. a. $\frac{1}{2}$ **b.** 3

22. A .5-centimeter × .5-centimeter square computer chip is shown in the upper right of this figure. The enlarged scale drawing shows the tiny circuits. Assume that the scale factor from the chip to the scale drawing is 80.

Scale drawing of a computer-on-a-chip; actual chips shown between the fingers in the photograph.

a. What are the dimensions of the drawing?
b. The surface area of the drawing is how many times the surface area of one face of the chip?

23. These two three-dimensional figures are similar. The scale factor from the small figure to the large figure is 2.

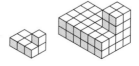

The surface area and volume of the smaller figure on the previous page are given in the top row of the following table. Complete the table for figures which are similar to the smaller figure, using the given scale factors.

SCALE FACTOR	SURFACE AREA (SQUARE UNITS)	VOLUME (CUBIC UNITS)
1	26	7
2	_____	_____
3	_____	_____
4	_____	_____
5	_____	_____

24. A pinhole camera can easily be made from a box. When the pinhole is uncovered, rays of light reflected from an object strike light-sensitive film. These rays of light travel in straight lines from the object to the pinhole of the camera, like lines through a projection point. Without a lens to gather light rays and increase their intensity, it takes from 60 to 75 seconds for enough light to pass through the pinhole for the image to be recorded.

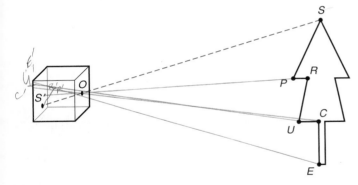

a. Draw lines from the lettered points on this tree through point O, and label their images on the back wall (film) of the camera.

b. Sketch the complete image of the tree.

c. OS is approximately 66 millimeters and OS' is approximately 11 millimeters. What is the scale factor for this projection?

25. Similar figures can be obtained by reproducing a figure from one grid onto another grid of a different size. This procedure is commonly used for enlarging quilting and sewing patterns. What is the scale factor for the enlargement of the patchwork doll?

26. a. Reproduce the figure from grid A below onto grid B by copying one square at a time. What is the scale factor from grid A to grid B?

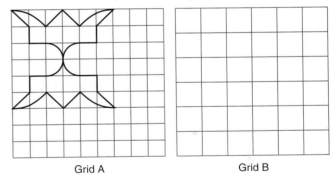

Grid A   Grid B

b. Reproduce the figure from grid B onto grid C below. What is the scale factor from grid B to grid C?

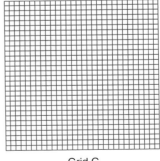

Grid C

c. The scale factor from grid A to grid C is $\frac{3}{10}$. How can this scale factor be obtained from the two scale factors from grid A to grid B and from grid B to grid C?

Similarity mappings are indicated in exercises 27 through 29 by relating the coordinates of each point on the given figure to the coordinates of its image. For example, the mapping in 27 doubles the coordinates of each point: point (⁻1, 1) gets mapped to (⁻2, 2). Sketch the image of each figure. What is the scale factor for each mapping? (Copy the coordinate system from the inside cover or from the website.)

27. $(x, y) \rightarrow (2x, 2y)$

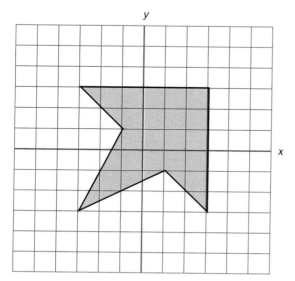

28. $(x, y) \rightarrow \left(\dfrac{x}{2}, \dfrac{y}{2}\right)$

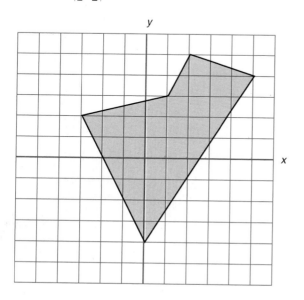

29. $(x, y) \rightarrow (^-3x, ^-3y)$

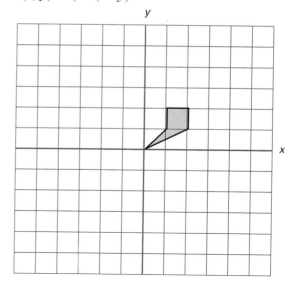

REASONING AND PROBLEM SOLVING

30. A group of scouts formed the triangles with the measurements shown below, in hopes of finding the distance across the river. Will their method work, and if so, what is the width of the river?

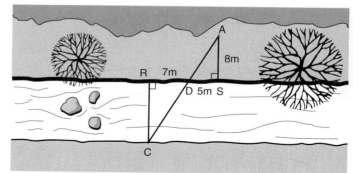

31. During a football game, Beth and her friend were standing next to the goal posts and trying to estimate the height of the posts. Beth noticed that the length of the shadow of the posts was 10 yards, the length of the end zone, and her friend's shadow had a length of 6 feet. Knowing that her friend was 6 feet tall, she quickly computed the height of the goal posts.

a. What is the height of the posts in feet? Explain your reasoning.

b. In 1989, a change in football regulations allowed the height of the goal posts to be increased by 10 feet. If the posts Beth saw had been 10 feet higher, what would have been the length of their shadow in yards?

32. This is not an example of trick photography. There are two average-size adults sitting in this chair, and there is room for several more. The scale factor from the small chair to the large chair is 8.

a. The small chair is 40 centimeters tall, and its seat is 24 centimeters wide. What is the height of the large chair, and what is the width of its seat?

b. The amount of paint required to paint the large chair is how many times the amount of paint required to paint the small chair?

c. The small chair weighs about 1 kilogram. Both chairs are made of the same kind of wood. What is the weight of the large chair?

33. Engineers use models of planes to gain information about wing and fuselage (central body) designs. The scale factor from this model of a Boeing B52 to the full-size plane is 100.

Model of a Boeing B52 being adjusted for wind-tunnel test.

a. The lift of an airplane depends on the surface area of its wings. The surface area of the wings of a B52 is how many times the surface area of the wings of its model?

b. The weight of a plane depends on its volume. The volume of a B52 is how many times the volume of its model?

c. If the tip of the wing of the model flaps a distance of 3 centimeters during a wind-tunnel test, what is the distance that the tip of the wing of a B52 flaps during flight?

34. In *Gulliver's Travels*, by Jonathan Swift, Gulliver went to the kingdom of Lilliput, where he found that he was 12 times the height of the average Lilliputian.

a. The Lilliputians computed Gulliver's surface area to make him a suit of clothes. The amount of material needed for his suit is about how many times the amount of material needed for one of theirs?

b. The Lilliputians computed Gulliver's volume to determine how much food he would need. The amount Gulliver required is about how many times the amount required by a Lilliputian?

c. Tiny people like the Lilliputians can exist only in fairy tales because in real life the ratio of their volume to their surface area would not allow them to maintain the proper body temperature. Would they be too warm or too cold?

35. Alisa is investigating projections by using different projection points, but keeping a constant scale factor of 2. She wonders if using a projection point inside a figure (point M in the figure on the next page) will produce the same-size image as using a projection point outside the figure (point K in the figure). She also wonders what will happen to the size of the image if the projection point is moved farther away from the figure. Sketch a few images of the pentagon for projections with a scale factor of 2, and form a conjecture regarding the location of the projection point.

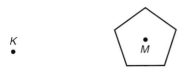

36. Featured Strategy: Making an Organized List   The Xerox 7000 in Mr. Gary's print shop has five switches for determining the size of a reproduction. If switch 1 is used, the reproduction is congruent to the original. Switches 2, 3, 4, and 5 reduce the original size by scale factors of .85, .76, .65, and .58, respectively. Using two switches in sequence, what scale factors can Mr. Gary obtain on this copier?

a. Understanding the Problem   The following copies of hexagons were obtained from the Xerox 7000. The length of the side of hexagon 2 is .85 times the length of the side of hexagon 1. Hexagon 3 was obtained by using switch 2 on hexagon 1 and then using this reproduction and switch 3. What is the scale factor from hexagon 1 to hexagon 3?

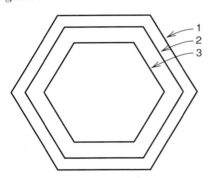

b. Devising a Plan   We could begin by *making an organized list* of the different ways that switches 2, 3, 4, and 5 can be paired (a switch can be paired with itself). What are they? Why isn't switch 1 included in these pairs?

c. Carrying Out the Plan   List the scale factors that can be obtained by using a combination of two switches. Round each scale factor to the nearest hundredth.

d. Looking Back   Mr. Gary also has a copier that enlarges the size of a figure by a scale factor of 2. Using this machine once and a setting on the Xerox 7000 once, what additional scale factors can Mr. Gary obtain?

37. The pages of a book come from the printing press as large, flat rectangular sheets of paper. Each sheet is fed through a series of rollers and folded in half several times. A sheet that has been folded once is called a *folio.* Half of a folio is a *quarto,* and half of a quarto is an *octavo.* Each fold is perpendicular to the previous fold.

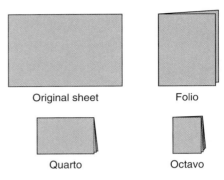

Original sheet   Folio

Quarto   Octavo

a. Which pairs of these rectangles (original, folio, quarto, octavo) are similar? Explain why.

b. If this folding pattern is continued, which of the resulting rectangles will be similar?

38. The setting in the following photograph appears to be life-size except for the nickel on the table. These pieces of furniture and dishes were handcrafted in the early 1800s for a dollhouse collection. The miniature cream pitcher holds 2 milliliters of cream. How much cream would a similar life-size pitcher hold? (*Hint:* Use the nickel on the table to find the scale factor for this photograph.)

39. Loop or knot two elastic bands together, and hold one end fixed at point O. Stretch the bands so that as the knot at point P traces one figure, a pencil at point P' traces an enlargement. Use this method to enlarge the map of the United States. Assume the distance from O to P' is 2.3 times the distance from O to P. How many times greater will the distance from Denver to Kansas City be on the enlarged map than on the small map?

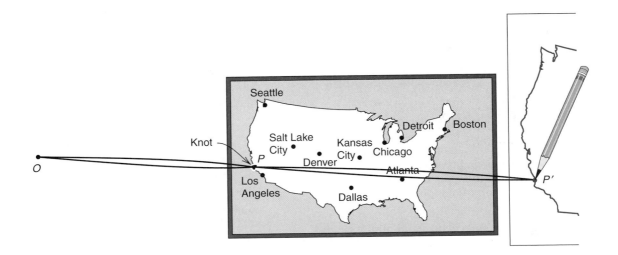

ONLINE LEARNING CENTER   www.mhhe.com/bennett-nelson

- Math Investigation 11.3   *Pantographs*
- Section-Related: • Links • Writing/Discussion Problems • Bibliography

PUZZLER

There is a standard rectangular metric-size sheet of paper which, when cut in half, yields two smaller sheets that are each similar to the original sheet. What is the ratio of the length of the original sheet to the width?*

*"Problems of the Month," *Mathematics Teacher* 80 (October 1987): 555.

CHAPTER REVIEW

1. **Mappings**
   a. A **mapping** is a function that assigns points to points such that to each point in one set there corresponds a unique point, called the **image**, in the second set.
   b. A mapping of $\triangle ABC$ to $\triangle RST$ such that R, S, and T are the images of A, B, and C, respectively, creates the following corresponding parts: **corresponding vertices**, $A \leftrightarrow R$, $B \leftrightarrow S$, $C \leftrightarrow T$; **corresponding sides**, $\overline{AB} \leftrightarrow \overline{RS}$, $\overline{BC} \leftrightarrow \overline{ST}$, $\overline{AC} \leftrightarrow \overline{RT}$; and **corresponding angles**, $\angle A \leftrightarrow \angle R$, $\angle B \leftrightarrow \angle S$, $\angle C \leftrightarrow \angle T$.
   c. If figure A is mapped to figure A' by one mapping and figure A' is mapped to figure A'' by a second mapping, the single mapping that maps A to A'' is called a **composition of mappings.**

2. **Congruence**
   a. Two polygons are **congruent** if and only if there is a mapping from one to the other such that (1) corresponding sides are congruent and (2) corresponding angles are congruent.
   b. For each of the following mappings, a figure and its image are congruent: **translation, reflection, rotation,** or **glide reflection.**
   c. **Side-side-side (SSS)** If three sides of one triangle are congruent to three sides of another triangle, the two triangles are congruent.
   d. **Side-angle-side (SAS)** If two sides and the included angle of one triangle are congruent to two sides and the included angle of another triangle, the two triangles are congruent.
   e. **Angle-side-angle (ASA)** If two angles and the included side of one triangle are congruent to two angles and the included side of another triangle, the two triangles are congruent.

3. **Similarity**
   a. Two polygons are **similar** if and only if there is a mapping from one to the other such that (1) corresponding angles are congruent and (2) lengths of corresponding sides have the same ratio.
   b. **Angle-angle (AA)** If two angles of one triangle are congruent to two angles of another triangle, the two triangles are similar.
   c. **Side-side-side (SSS)** If the lengths of corresponding sides of two triangles are proportional, the two triangles are similar.

   d. If the **scale factor** for a similarity mapping is greater than 1, the image is an **enlargement.** If the scale factor is less than 1, the image is a **reduction.**

4. **Geometric terms**
   a. A line that is perpendicular to a segment at its midpoint is called the **perpendicular bisector** of the segment.
   b. A circle that contains all the vertices of a polygon is called a **circumscribed circle.**
   c. A polygon is called an **inscribed polygon** if all its vertices are points of a circle.
   d. A mapping for which the lengths of line segments is the same as their images is called a **distance-preserving mapping.**

5. **Geometric properties**
   a. The sum of the lengths of any two sides of a triangle is greater than the length of the third side.
   b. A point is on the perpendicular bisector of a line segment if and only if it is equidistant from the endpoints of the segment.
   c. If a plane figure is similar to another figure by a scale factor of k, where k is any positive real number, then the second figure will have an area k^2 times the area of the first figure.
   d. If a figure in space is similar to another figure by a scale factor of k, where k is any positive real number, then the second figure will have a volume k^3 times the volume of the first figure.

6. **Constructions**
   a. A geometric figure produced with a straightedge and compass is called a **construction.**
   b. A few types of constructions:
   Copying a line segment
   Copying an angle
   Bisecting a line segment
   Bisecting an angle
   Constructing a perpendicular to a line through a point not on the line
   Constructing a line parallel to a given line through a point not on the line
   Circumscribing a circle about a triangle

CHAPTER TEST

1. Use a compass and straightedge to carry out each construction. Explain your steps.
   a. The bisector of ∡A

   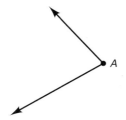

   b. The perpendicular to line *m* through point *Q*

   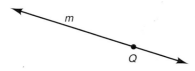

   c. The line through point *P* that is parallel to line ℓ

   d. The perpendicular to line *n* through point *R*

   R •

2. Construct the circumscribed circle about △ABC.

   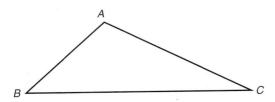

3. Construct a triangle, if possible, whose sides are congruent to the given line segments. If it is not possible, explain why.

   a.

   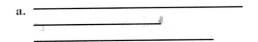

   b.

4. Which of the following pairs of triangles are congruent? For each congruent pair, state the appropriate congruence property of triangles and write the congruence correspondence.
   a.   b.

   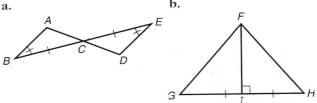

   c.   d.

5. Sketch the image for each mapping.
   a. A translation that maps *R* to *R'*

   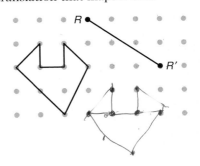

b. A reflection about line ℓ

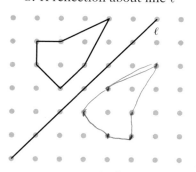

c. A 90° clockwise rotation about point O

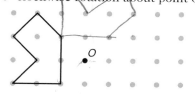

c.

d.

6. Describe the single mapping that is equivalent to the composition of the two given mappings.

a. A clockwise rotation of 45° followed by a counterclockwise rotation of 70° about the same center of rotation

b. A reflection about line ℓ followed by a reflection about line m, when ℓ and m are parallel lines

c. A translation of P to P' that is to the right 12 units and up 8 units, followed by a translation of P' to P'' that is to the right 5 units and down 10 units

7. Determine the number of congruence mappings of each polygon onto itself and explain your reasoning.

a. Isosceles triangle   **b.** Regular hexagon

c. Rectangle

8. Show and explain how to alter the sides of the given polygon to create a nonpolygonal (Escher-type) tessellation.

a. Equilateral triangle   **b.** Parallelogram

9. Name all the transformations that will map each frieze pattern onto itself. (Assume that these patterns extend indefinitely to the right and left.)

a.

b.

10. Using point O as the projection point, determine the image of each figure for the given scale factor.

a. Scale factor of 2

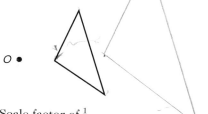

b. Scale factor of $\frac{1}{3}$

c. Scale factor of $\frac{-1}{2}$

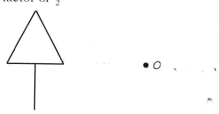

11. Which of the following pairs of triangles are similar? For each similar pair, state the appropriate similarity property of triangles and write the similarity correspondence.

a.   **b.**

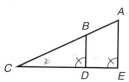

c.

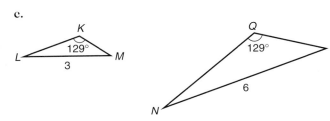

d.

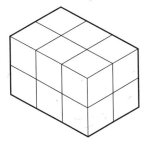

12. If the figures listed below are similar, explain why. If not, sketch a counterexample with measurements.
   a. Two rectangles
   b. Two squares
   c. Two right triangles
   d. Two equilateral triangles
   e. Two congruent quadrilaterals

13. The following figure has a volume of 12 cubic units and a surface area of 32 square units.

   a. What is the volume of an enlargement of the above figure for a scale factor of 3?
   b. What is the surface area of an enlargement with a scale factor of 3?
   c. What is the volume of a reduction with a scale factor of $\frac{1}{2}$?
   d. What is the surface area of a reduction with a scale factor of $\frac{1}{2}$?

14. The scale factor from a model to a life-size table is 4, and the model and table are both made of the same type of wood.

   a. If the life-size table has a height of 28 inches, what is the height of the model?
   b. If the model requires $\frac{1}{32}$ quart (1 fluid ounce) of stain, how many quarts of stain are needed for the life-size table?
   c. If the model weighs $\frac{3}{4}$ pound, what is the weight of the life-size table?

15. A person 6 feet tall standing under a streetlight casts a 10-foot shadow on the ground. If the base of the streetlight is 45 feet from the tip of the shadow, what is the height of the streetlight?

16. Two campers on a beach by a lake want to determine the distance to a small island in the lake. They mark point A with a stake directly across from island I, and walk perpendicular to $\overline{IA}$ to point B where they place another stake. Then they continue in a straight line to point C where they place another stake. Finally, they walk perpendicularly away from the lake to a point D such that points D, B, and I are on a line.

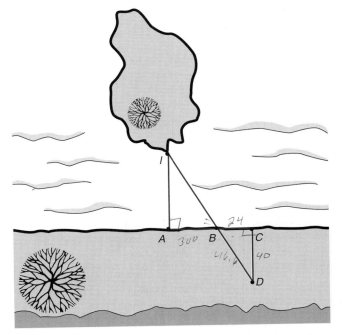

   a. Are triangles AIB and CDB congruent? Are they similar? Explain your reasoning.
   b. If AB = 300 feet, BC = 24 feet, and CD = 40 feet, what is the shortest distance from point A to the island?

REFERENCES FOR RESEARCH STATEMENTS BY CHAPTERS

Chapter 1

Blume, Glendon W., and David S. Heckman. "What Do Students Know About Algebra and Functions?" In *Results from the Sixth Mathematics Assessment of the National Assessment of Educational Progress,* edited by Patricia Ann Kenney and Edward A. Silver, pp. 225–277. Reston, VA: National Council of Teachers of Mathematics, 1997.

MacGregor, Mollie. "How Students Interpret Equations." In *Language and Communication in the Mathematics Classroom,* edited by Heinz Steinbring, Maria G. Bartolini Bussi, and Anna Sierpinska, pp. 262–270. Reston, VA: National Council of Teachers of Mathematics, 1998.

Chapter 2

Friel, Susan, Frances R. Curcio, and George Bright. "Making Sense of Graphs: Critical Factors Influencing Comprehension and Instructional Implications." *Journal for Research in Mathematics Education* 32 (March 2001) 124–158.

Hiebert, James, and Thomas P. Carpenter. "Learning and Teaching with Understanding" In *Handbook of Research on Mathematics Teaching and Learning,* edited by Douglas A. Grouws, pp. 65–97. New York: Macmillan, 1992.

Chapter 3

Kroll, Diana Lambdin, and Tammy Miller. "Insights from Research on Mathematical Problem Solving in the Middle Grades." In *Research Ideas for the Classroom: Middle Grades Mathematics,* edited by Douglas T. Owens, pp. 58–77. New York: Macmillan, 1993.

Resnick, L. B. "A Developmental Theory of Number and Understanding." In *The Development of Mathematical Thinking,* edited by H.P Ginsburg, pp. 110–152. Hillsdale, NJ: Erlbaum, 1983.

Ross, Sharon H. "Parts, Wholes, and Place Value: A Developmental View." *Arithmetic Teacher* 35 (February 1989): 47–51.

Sowder, Judith T., and Judith Kelin. "Number Sense and Related Topics." In *Research Ideas for the Classroom: Middle Grades Mathematics,* edited by Douglas T. Owens, pp. 41–57. New York: Macmillan, 1993.

Chapter 4

Graviss, Tom, and Joanne Greaver. "Extending the Number Line to Make Connections with Number Theory," *Mathematics Teacher* 85 (September, 1992): 418–420.

Sowell, Evelyn J. "Effects of Manipulative Materials in Mathematics Instruction." *Journal for Research in Mathematics Education* 20 (November 1989): 498–505.

Chapter 5

Blume, Glendon W., and David S. Heckman. "Algebra and Functions." In *Results from the Seventh Mathematics Assessment of the National Assessment of Education Progress,* edited by Edward A. Silver and Patricia Ann Kenney, pp. 269–300. Reston, VA: National Council of Teachers of Mathematics, 2000.

Dufour-Janiver, Bernadette, Nadine Bednarz, and Maurice Belanger. "Pedagogical Considerations Concerning the Problem of Representation." In *Problems of Representation in the Teaching and Learning of Mathematics,* edited by Claude Janvier, pp. 109–122 Hillsdale, NJ: Lawrence Erlbaum Associates, 1987.

Kouba, Vicky L., Judith S. Zawojewski, and Marilyn E. Strutchens. "What Do Students Know About Numbers and Operations?" In *Results from the Sixth Mathematics Assessment of the National Assessment of Educational Process,* edited by Patricia Ann Kenney and Edward A. Silver, pp. 33–60. Reston, VA: National Council of Teachers of Mathematics, 1997.

Wearne, Diana, and Vicky L. Kouba. "Rational Numbers." In *Results from the Seventh Mathematics Assessment of the National Assessment of Educational Progress,* edited by Edward A. Silver and Patricia Ann Kenney, pp. 163–191. Reston, VA: National Council of Teachers of Mathematics, 2000.

Chapter 6

Behr, Merlyn, Ipke Wachsmuth, Thomas R. Post, and Richard Lesh. "Order and Equivalence of Rational Numbers: A Clinical Teaching Experiment." *Journal for Research in Mathematics Education* 15 (November 1984): 323–341.

Bell, Alan, Malcolm Swan, and G. Taylor. "Choice of Operation in Verbal Problems with Decimal Numbers." *Educational Studies in Mathematics* 12 (November 1981): 399–420.

Kouba, Vicky L., Catherine A. Brown, Thomas P. Carpenter, Mary M. Lindquist, Edward A. Silver, and Jane 0. Swafford. "Results of the Fourth NAEP Assessment of Mathematics: Number, Operations, and Word Problems." *Arithmetic Teacher* 35 (April 1988): 14–19.

Kouba, Vicky L., Judith S. Zawojewski, and Marilyn E. Strutchens. "What Do Students Know About Numbers and Operations?" In *Results from the Sixth Mathematics Assessment of the National Assessment of Educational Progress,* edited by Patricia Ann Kenney and Edward A. Silver, pp. 33–60. Reston, VA: National Council of Teachers of Mathematics, 1997.

Markovitz, Zvia, and Judith Sowder. "Students Understanding of the Relationship Between Fractions and Decimals." *Focus on Learning Problems in Mathematics* 13 (January 1991): 3–11.

Martin, W. Gary, and Marilyn E. Strutchens. "Geometry and Measurement." In *Results from the Seventh Mathematics Assessment of the National Assessment of Educational Progress,* edited by Edward A. Silver and Patricia Ann Kenney, pp. 193–234. Reston, VA: National Council of Teachers of Mathematics, 2000.

Noelting, Gerald. "The Development of Proportional Reasoning and the Ratio Concept: Part 1—Differentiation of Stages."

Educational Studies in Mathematics 11 (May 1980): 217–253.

Parker, Melanie, and Gaea Leinhardt. "Percent: A Privileged Proportion." *Review of Educational Research* 65 (Winter 1995): 421–481.

Resnick, Lauren B., Pearla Nesher, Francois Leonard, Maria Magone, Susan Omanson, and Irit Peled. "Conceptual Bases of Arithmetic Errors: The Case of Decimal Fractions." *Journal for Research in Mathematics Education* 20 (January 1989): 8–27.

Risacher, Bille F. "Students' Reasoning About Ratio and Percent." In *Proceedings of the Fifteenth Annual Meeting of the North American Chapter of the International Group for the Psychology of Mathematics Education,* edited by Joanne R. Becker and Barbara J. Pence, pp. 261–267. San Jose, CA: San Jose State University, 1993.

Sackur-Grisvard, Catherine, and Francois Leonard. "Intermediate Cognitive Organizations in the Process of Learning a Mathematical Concept: The Order of Positive Decimal Numbers." *Cognition and Instruction* 2 (1985): 157–174.

Vergnaud, Gerard. "Multiplicative Structures." In *Acquisition of Mathematics Concepts and Processes,* edited by Richard Lesh and Marsh Landau, pp. 127–174. New York: Academic Press, 1983.

Chapter 7

Pereira-Mendoza, L., and J. Mello. "Students Concepts of Bar Graphs: Some Preliminary Findings." In *Proceedings of the Third International Congress on Teaching Statistics,* edited by D. Vere-Jones, Vol. I, pp. 150–175. Voorburg, The Netherlands: International Statistics Institute, 1991.

Zawojewski, Judith S., and J. Michael Shaughnessy. "Data and Chance." In *Results from the Seventh Mathematics Assessment of the National Assessment of Educational Progress,* edited by Edward A. Silver and Patricia Ann Kenney, pp. 235–268. Reston, VA: National Council of Teachers of Mathematics, 2000.

Chapter 8

National Research Council. *Adding It Up: Helping Children Learn Mathematics,* edited by J. Kilpatrick, J. Swafford, and B. Findell. Mathematics Learning Study Committee, Center for Education, Division of Behavioral and Social Sciences and Education. Washington, DC: National Academy Press, 2001.

Zawojewski, Judith S., and J. Michael Shaughnessy. "Data and Chance." In *Results from the Seventh Mathematics Assessment of the National Assessment of Educational Progress,* edited by Edward A. Silver and Patricia Ann Kenney, pp. 235–268. Reston, VA: National Council of Teachers of Mathematics, 2000.

Chapter 9

Clements, Douglas H., and Michael T. Battista. "Geometry and Spatial Reasoning." In *Handbook of Research on Mathematics Teaching and Learning,* edited by Douglas A. Grouws, pp. 420–464. New York: Macmillan, 1992.

Geddes, Dorothy, and Irene Fortunato. "Geometry: Research and Classroom Activities." In *Research Ideas for the*

Classroom: Middle Grades Mathematics, edited by Douglas T. Owens, pp. 199–222. New York: MacMillan, 1993.

Martin, W. Gary, and Marilyn E. Strutchens. "Geometry and Measurement." In *Results from the Seventh Mathematics Assessment of the National Assessment of Educational Progress,* edited by Edward A. Silver and Patricia Ann Kenney, pp. 193–234. Reston, VA: National Council of Teachers of Mathematics, 2000.

Strutchens, Marilyn E., and Glendon W. Blume. "What Do Students Know About Geometry?" In *Result from the Sixth Mathematics Assessment of the National Assessment of Educational Progress* edited by Patricia Ann Kenney and Edward A. Silver, pp. 165–193. Reston, VA: National Council of Teachers of Mathematics, 1997.

Chapter 10

Ben-Haim, David, Glenda Lappan, and Richard Houang. "Visualizing Rectangular Solids Made of Small Cubes: Analyzing and Effecting Students' Performance." *Educational Studies in Mathematics* 16 (November 1985): 389–409.

Lindquist, Mary M., and Vicky L. Kouba. "Geometry." In *Results from the Fourth Mathematics Assessment of the National Assessment of Educational Progress,* edited by Mary M. Lindquist, pp. 44–54. Reston, VA: National Council of Teachers of Mathematics, 1989.

Kenney, Patricia Ann, and Vicky L. Kouba. "What Do Students Know About Measurement?" In *Results from the Sixth Mathematics Assessment of the National Assessment of Educational Progress,* edited by Patricia Ann Kenney and Edward A. Silver, pp. 141–164. Reston, VA: National Council of Teachers of Mathematics, 1997.

Martin, W. Gary, and Marilyn E. Strutchens. "Geometry and Measurement." In *Results from the Seventh Mathematics Assessment of the National Assessment of Educational Progress,* edited by Edward A. Silver and Patricia Ann Kenney, pp. 193–234. Reston, VA: National Council of Teachers of Mathematics, 2000.

Strutchens, Marilyn E., and Glendon W. Blume. "What Do Students Know About Geometry?" In *Results from the Sixth Mathematics Assessment of the National Assessment of Educational Progress,* edited by Patricia Ann Kenney and Edward A. Silver, pp. 165–194. Reston, VA: National Council of Teachers of Mathematics, 1997.

Chapter 11

Martin, W. Gary, and Marilyn E. Strutchens. "Geometry and Measurement." In *Results from the Seventh Mathematics Assessment of the National Assessment of Educational Progress,* edited by Edward A. Silver and Patricia Ann Kenney, pp. 193–234. Reston, VA: National Council of Teachers of Mathematics, 2000.

Wheatley, Grayson. "Spatial Sense and Mathematical Learning." *Arithmetic Teacher* 37 (February 1990): 10–11.

Vinner, Shlomo, and Rina Hershkowitz. "Concept Images and Common Cognitive Paths in the Development of Some Simple Geometric Concepts." In *Proceedings of the Fourth International Conference for the Psychology of Mathematics Education,* edited by Robert Karplus, pp. 177–184. Berkeley, CA: Lawrence Hall of Science, 1980.

ANSWERS TO SELECTED MATH ACTIVITIES

MATH ACTIVITY 1.1

2. Two disks take 3 moves; 3 disks take 7 moves
3 and **4**.

NO. OF DISKS	NO. OF MOVES
1	1
2	3
3	7
4	15
5	31
6	63
7	127
8	255
9	511
10	1023

One number pattern that can be seen in the number of moves is that each entry is 1 more than twice the preceding entry. Another pattern is that the number of moves is 1 less than a power of 2. For example, $31 = 2^5 - 1$ and $511 = 2^9 - 1$.

MATH ACTIVITY 1.2

1. **a.** *Pattern:* Starting with a trapezoid, each successive figure is obtained by alternately adding a pair of parallelograms (one at each end) and a pair of trapezoids (one at each end).
   b. 9 trapezoids and 10 parallelograms
2. **b.** The 20th figure would look like seven copies of the third figure, in a row, with the square removed from the right end.
3. **a.** After the first parallelogram you alternately attach triangles (two) and parallelograms (one). The 20th will look like five copies of the fourth figure and will contain 20 triangles and 10 parallelograms.

MATH ACTIVITY 1.3

1. **a.**

Figure number	1	2	3	4	5
Green tiles	2	5	8	13	18
Yellow tiles	2	4	8	12	18

2. **a.**

Figure number	1	2	3	4	5	. . .	10	. . .	25
Red tiles	1	1	6	6	15	. . .	45	. . .	325
Blue tiles	0	3	3	10	10	. . .	55	. . .	300

Starting from the bottom right corner the reds form the number pattern $1 + 5 + 9 + 13 + \cdots$ and the blues form the pattern $3 + 7 + 11 + 15 + \cdots$.

MATH ACTIVITY 2.1

1. There are many ways to continue the pattern that has been started. Here are three ways which use different attribute pieces.
   (1) SYS, LYS, LYC, SYC, SRC
   (2) SRT, LRT, LRH, LRC, LBC
   (3) LYH, LYT, LBT, SBT, SBC
3. Here are the pieces in each region:
   Region 1: LBS, SBS, LBC, SBC, LBT, SBT
   Region 2: LBH, SBH
   Region 3: LRH, SRH, LYH, SYH
   Outside: LRS, SRS, LRT, SRT, LRC, SRC, LYS, SYS, LYT, SYT, LYC, SYC

MATH ACTIVITY 2.2

1. **a.** $\frac{1}{4}$ **b.** $\frac{2}{4}$ **c.** $\frac{3}{4}$ **d.** $\frac{4}{4} = 1$
   As the lines become steeper, the slopes increase.

4. The 12 line segments have the slopes of $\frac{4}{1}, \frac{3}{1}, \frac{2}{1}, \frac{3}{2}, \frac{4}{3}, \frac{1}{1}, \frac{3}{4}, \frac{2}{3}, \frac{1}{2}, \frac{1}{3}, \frac{1}{4}$, and 0, beginning with the line segment on the left side of the board and moving clockwise to the right edge of the board. From least to greatest the slopes are $0, \frac{1}{4}, \frac{1}{3}, \frac{1}{2}, \frac{2}{3}, \frac{3}{4}, 1, \frac{4}{3}, \frac{3}{2}, 2, 3, 4$.

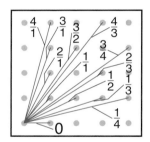

MATH ACTIVITY 2.3

1. Player A's number does not contain the digits 1, 2, or 3.
2. Player A's number contains two of the digits 4, 5, or 6, but no digit is in the correct place-value position.

800

3. Since two of the digits are correct but in the wrong position, switching positions will give us more information.
4. Now player B knows that one of the digits 6 or 4 is in the correct position, but cannot be sure which one. The digit 5 may still be the correct digit but in the incorrect position.

MATH ACTIVITY 3.1

2.

	LONG-FLATS	FLATS	LONGS	UNITS
a.		3	1	4
b.	1	0	4	2
c.	2	0	3	2

4. **a.** 121_{three} **b.** 68 units

MATH ACTIVITY 3.2

1. 2 flats, 1 long, 1 unit
3. After 6 turns the player had 3 flats, 1 long, and 3 units. The player will need 1 flat, 3 longs, and 2 units to obtain 1 long-flat.

MATH ACTIVITY 3.3

2. **a.** 1443_{five} **b.** 2101_{five} **c.** 3231_{five}
5. Base ten. $6_{\text{ten}} \times 373_{\text{ten}} = 2238_{\text{ten}}$

MATH ACTIVITY 3.4

1. The minimal collection consists of 3 longs and 1 unit.
2. **a.** 14_{five}
3. **a.** 20_{five}

MATH ACTIVITY 4.1

1. **a.** A three-digit base-five numeral tells how many flats, longs, and units are in a collection. When divided into groups of 4, there is 1 unit remaining for *each* flat and 1 for *each* long. So the sum of the digits in the numeral also tells us the total number of units remaining in the collection after flats and longs have been grouped by 4s.
   b. When the units in a base-five long-flat are divided into groups of 4 there is 1 unit remaining. The number 1232_{five} is divisible by 4 because $1 + 2 + 3 + 2$ is divisible by 4. A base-five number is divisible by 4 if the sum of its digits is divisible by 4.

MATH ACTIVITY 4.2

1. **a.** 20th is blue; 35th is yellow
   b. Divide the figure number by 4. If there is no remainder, the color is blue. If the remainder is 1, 2, or 3, the color is red, green, or yellow, respectively.

c.

	RED	GREEN	YELLOW	BLUE
Figure 20	45	50	55	60
Figure 35	153	162	171	144

The following chart suggests one way to organize the data and look for patterns.

FIGURE	RED	GREEN	YELLOW	BLUE
1	1			
2	1	2		
3	1	2	3	
4	1	2	3	4
5	1 + 5	2	3	4
6	1 + 5	2 + 6	3	4
7	1 + 5	2 + 6	3 + 7	4
8	1 + 5	2 + 6	3 + 7	4 + 8
9	1 + 5 + 9	2 + 6	3 + 7	4 + 8

MATH ACTIVITY 5.1

3. **a.** $^{-}7$ **b.** $^{-}1$ **c.** 3 **d.** $^{-}8$

MATH ACTIVITY 5.2

3. **a.** $\frac{7}{12}$ **b.** $\frac{1}{4}$ or $\frac{3}{12}$ **c.** $\frac{5}{6}$ or $\frac{10}{12}$ **d.** $\frac{3}{4}$ or $\frac{9}{12}$

MATH ACTIVITY 5.3

2. **a.** $\frac{5}{6} - \frac{1}{2} = \frac{2}{6}$ **b.** $\frac{7}{10} - \frac{2}{5} = \frac{3}{10}$ **c.** $\frac{5}{12} - \frac{1}{4} = \frac{2}{12}$
5. **a.** $\frac{8}{10} \div \frac{2}{5} = 2$ **b.** $\frac{5}{6} \div \frac{2}{12} = 5$ **c.** $\frac{5}{12} \div \frac{1}{4} = 1\frac{2}{3}$

MATH ACTIVITY 6.1

1. **a.** Ten of any one of the pieces have the value of the next larger piece; the pattern of the shapes alternates between nonsquare rectangle and square; there are 100 one-hundredth squares in the unit square and 1000 one-thousandth regions in the unit square.
   b. Here are a few of the many ways:

UNITS	TENTHS	HUNDREDTHS	THOUSANDTHS
1	4	12	
1	5	2	
0	15	2	
0	0	152	
0	0	0	1520
1	0	52	
1	1	42	
1	1	1	410

MATH ACTIVITY 6.2

1. **a.** .76   **b.** .645   **c.** .24   **d.** .26

MATH ACTIVITY 6.3

2. 14 small squares (14 percent of 300) represents
   $14 \times 3 = 42$
   8 small squares (8 percent of 300) represents 24 years

3. One square represents 1.8 skateboards, so 45 percent
   (45 small squares) represents $45 \times 1.8 = 81$
   skateboards. Or, 10 squares represent 18 skateboards,
   so 45 squares represent $4.5 \times 18 = 81$. Fifteen
   squares represent 27 skateboards.

MATH ACTIVITY 6.4

4.

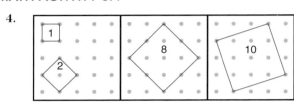
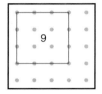

5.

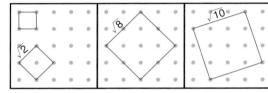

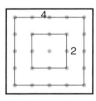

MATH ACTIVITY 7.1

1. First way: Take 6 tiles off the top of the column with
   15 tiles so both columns now have the same height.
   Divide the difference by 2, and put these 3 on top of
   each column.
   Second way: Count all the tiles and divide them
   equally into two columns.
   a. First way: $15 - 9 = 6$ is the difference; $(15 - 9) \div 2 = 3$ is one-half the difference; and $9 + (15 - 9)/2 = 12$ is the average.
      Second way: $15 + 9 = 24$ is the total; $24 \div 2 = 12$ is the average.
   b. One way is $y + (x - y)/2$ and another is $(x + y) \div 2$.
   c. $y + (x - y)/2 = 2y/2 + (x - y)/2 = (x + y)/2$

MATH ACTIVITY 7.2

1. e. Theoretically the average number of yogurts that
      must be purchased to obtain at least one of each
      type of cover is between 8 and 9.

MATH ACTIVITY 7.3

2. a. 1 path each to points *A* and *E*; 4 paths each to
      points *B* and *D*; 6 paths to point *C*

MATH ACTIVITY 8.1

1. b. The chances are slightly better than 60 percent
      that at least one sixth-grader will be chosen.

MATH ACTIVITY 8.2

1. d. Because points are awarded for the total number
      of Xs, this is a fair game. The numbers 1, 2, 3, and
      4 constitute 50 percent of the total outcomes, and
      the numbers 6, 8, 9, 12, and 16 constitute the
      other 50 percent.

MATH ACTIVITY 9.1

1. The triangle has three 60° interior angles. The square
   has four 90° interior angles. The hexagon has six 120°
   interior angles. The trapezoid has two 60° and two
   120° interior angles. The blue parallelogram has two
   60° and two 120° interior angles. The white
   parallelogram has two 30° and two 150° interior
   angles.

MATH ACTIVITY 9.2

3. Different vertices have different numbers of shapes
   surrounding them. For example, one vertex has a
   code of 3,3,3,3,6 while another has code 3,3,6,6.

MATH ACTIVITY 9.3

1. There are many patterns. Here are two:

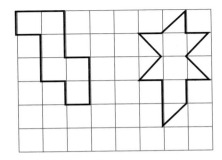

MATH ACTIVITY 9.4

2. a. 360° rotational symmetry
   b. Rotational symmetries of 60°, 120°, 180°, 240°, 300°, and 360°
   c. Rotational symmetries of 90°, 180°, 270°, and 360°
   d. Rotational symmetries of 180° and 360°

MATH ACTIVITY 10.1

3.

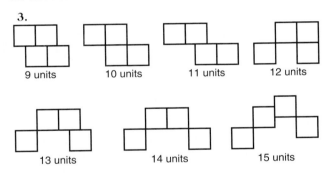

9 units   10 units   11 units   12 units

13 units   14 units   15 units

MATH ACTIVITY 10.2

1. a. Trapezoid 3 units of area; hexagon 6 units of area
   b. Square has slightly more than 2 units of area and white parallelogram slightly more than 1 unit of area

MATH ACTIVITY 10.3

2. a. 21
   b. 44
   c. With one tile as "center," three arms will have 49 tiles each and the fourth arm will have 98 tiles.
   d. Area, 246; perimeter, 494
   e. Expressions equivalent to the following:
   Area: $5n - 4$ or $5(n - 1) + 1$
   Perimeter: $10n - 6$ or $10(n - 1) + 4$
   f. Perimeter will always be an even number.

MATH ACTIVITY 11.1

1. c. Area S is one-half the area of the large right triangle; the total area of the two small semicircles is π times the area of S; the total area of the two semicircles is equal to the area of the large semicircle.

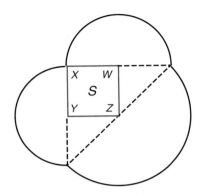

MATH ACTIVITY 11.2

1.

Triangle	1	2	3	4
Center of rotation	A, G	A	A, F	F

5	6	7	8	9	10	11
F, G	G	E, M		B, S	G	G

4. Any of the following: 2, 3, 4, 6, 7, 9, 10

MATH ACTIVITY 11.3

2. The areas of these enlargements are 9 times the areas of the individual pattern blocks.

ANSWERS TO PUZZLERS

p. 34 It is not a spiral but a series of concentric circles. Select a circle and trace it.

p. 73 18 days. There were 5 fine days and 13 days with rain.

p. 116 The first conclusion is invalid.

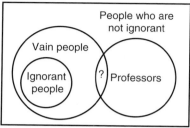

All people

The second conclusion is valid.

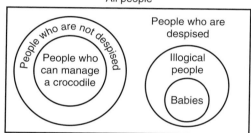

All people

p. 175
$$426 \times 307$$
$$\begin{array}{r} 426 \\ \times\, 307 \\ \hline 2982 \\ 1278 \\ \hline 130{,}782 \end{array}$$

p. 181 There is no missing money. The desk clerk has $25, the bellboy has $2, and each man has $1. The confusion arises when we try to add the $27 (which includes the $2 "tip") to the $2.

p. 199
$$\begin{array}{r} 9087 \\ 39\overline{)354393} \\ 351 \\ \hline 339 \\ 312 \\ \hline 273 \\ 273 \\ \hline \end{array}$$

p. 204 $(22 - 19 + 2) \times 14 \div 10 = 7$
$21 \times 2 - 3 - 12 - 7 = 20$

p. 225 The license plate number is 83173.

p. 245
$$\begin{array}{r} 775 \\ \times\, 33 \\ \hline 2325 \\ 2325 \\ \hline 25{,}575 \end{array}$$

p. 272

⁻4	⁻6	4
6	⁻2	⁻10
⁻8	2	0

p. 295

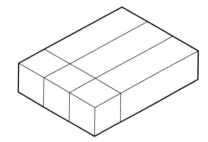

p. 321 84 years

p. 326 The sum of the 3 fractions, $\frac{1}{2} + \frac{1}{3} + \frac{1}{9}$, is $\frac{17}{18}$, not 1, as we would expect. This means that farmer Smith's will accounted for only $\frac{17}{18}$ of his property. Increasing the total number of horses to 18 allowed the boys to take 17 horses ($\frac{17}{18}$ of the total) and left farmer Smith's neighbor the horse he had donated to solve the dilemma.

p. 352 The second odometer reading could have been 73,037, 73,137, or 73,237. For these cases the average speeds in miles per hour are 27.5, 52.5, and 77.5, respectively.

p. 371 25 items, each costing 25 cents

p. 377 This is one of four possible solutions:

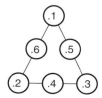

804

p. 400 72 percent

p. 420 Place one plank on $\overline{AB}$ so that $AB = 18.8$ feet. Then (by the Pythagorean theorem) $CD = 9.4$ feet. Since $CE \approx 28.3$ feet, $DE \approx 18.9$ feet, so the second plank will reach across the moat along $\overline{DE}$.

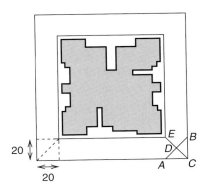

p. 480 48 miles per hour

p. 500 "It is remarkable that a science which began with the consideration of games of chance should be elevated to the rank of the most important subjects of human knowledge."

p. 525 Here is one possibility; there are at least three more.
Die 1: 0, 0, 0, 3, 3, 3
Die 2: 1, 2, 3, 7, 8, 9

p. 545 11/24

p. 567 One possible solution:

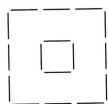

p. 571

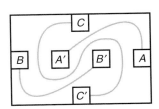

p. 583

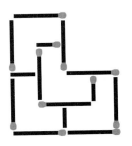

p. 603

p. 610 The bear was white, because the researchers' camp was at the north pole. The researchers could have been in the vicinity of the south pole, except that they would not have seen a white bear, or any bear at all—there are no bears at the south pole. There are, however, an infinite number of locations near the south pole from which the researchers could start out and make the trip described. Imagine a circle with a circumference of 15 miles around the south pole. Suppose the researchers' camp was at a point 15 miles north of the circle. Walking 15 miles south from camp would bring them to a point on the circle. Walking 15 miles east would bring them around to the original point on the circle. Walking 15 miles north would bring them back to the point where they started.

p. 629 1961 and 1881

p. 657 ⁻40°

p. 675 2/π, or approximately 63.7 percent

p. 683 38 feet

p. 710 Watch the surface of the water inside the can as the water is being poured out. Just as the bottom of the can begins to show, the can is half empty.

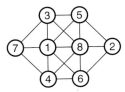

p. 741 Cube 1: 0, 1, 2, 3, 4, 5
Cube 2: 0, 1, 2, 6, 7, 8
(If its cube is rotated 180°, 6 can be used for 9.)

p. 768

p. 793 $\sqrt{2}$ to 1

ANSWERS TO ODD-NUMBERED EXERCISES AND PROBLEMS AND CHAPTER TESTS

EXERCISES AND PROBLEMS 1.1

1. a. 4 feet; 2 feet   **b.** 6 feet   **c.** On day 9
   d. If the snail climbs 4 feet during the day and slips back 3 feet at night, it will take 17 days for it to climb out of the well.

3. 52 and 78 feet

5. a. The old plan   **b.** 58¢
   c. 15 checks   **d.** The difference decreases. 19 checks

7. Six postcards

9. a. One possibility is 46 and 64.
   b. For 64 and 46, the difference is 18.
   c. 82 and 28
   d. 93 and 39

11. a. Dumping 9 gallons into the 4-gallon container twice leaves 1 gallon in the 9-gallon container.
   b. (1) Dump the 1 gallon from part a into the 4-gallon container.
     (2) Fill the 9-gallon container and dump part of it into the 4-gallon container until the 4-gallon container is full.
     (3) There will be 6 gallons left in the 9-gallon container.

13. a. The yellow tiles are touching at the corners.
   b. Each of the other 8 tiles touches the center tile at one or more points.
   c. If only one new color is used for the remaining 4 tiles, then tiles of the same color will meet at their corners.
   d. Yes, it can be done in two colors, with one color along the two diagonals.

15.

	Top		
Front	Right	Back	Left
	Bottom		

		Right	
Top	Front	Bottom	Back
	Left		

17. a. Girl *A* will have 20 chips, girl *B* will have 60 chips, and girl *C* will have 40 chips.
   b, c.

	A	B	C
Beginning	65	35	20
End of first round	10	70	40
End of second round	20	20	80
End of third round	40	40	40

d. No, she would not have enough chips to double the other girls' supplies.

19. 35 tiles

21. The total of 7 squares has a value of 112, so each square has a value of 16. Thus, the numbers are 16, 32, and 64.

23. In the third row, a cup replaces the doughnut above it and the cost increases from 90¢ to $1. So a cup of coffee costs 10¢ more than a doughnut. Thus, replacing the cup in the second row by the doughnut in the first row decreases the cost by 10¢, so that 4 doughnuts cost 80¢. Therefore, 1 doughnut costs 20¢, and a cup of coffee costs 30¢.

25. 6 ships with 4 masts

27. 14 free movie videos

29. The 90- and 110-pound people cross the river, and the 110-pound person returns. Then the 190-pound person crosses the river, and the 90-pound person returns. This requires 4 crossings of the boat. Similarly, another 4 crossings will get the 170-pound person across the river and leave the 110- and 90-pound people left to cross the river in the ninth crossing of the boat. A minimum of 9 crossings is required for the boat.

31. 2 is on back of disk 6; 5 is on back of disk 7; 9 is on back of disk 8.

33. One way: Start both timers at the same time; put the vegetables in the water when the 7-minute timer finishes; turn the 11-minute timer over when it finishes; vegetables will be steamed in 15 minutes, when the 11-minute timer finishes.

35. a. 2 apples
   b. 9 sheep
   c. The other coin is a nickel.
   d. The cider costs 73 cents; the bottle costs 13 cents.
   e. No dirt
   f. 6 pounds
   g. 10 children
   h. Neither; the whites of the egg are white!

EXERCISES AND PROBLEMS 1.2

1. a. Repeats: ▲ + O
   b. Repeats: ✗ ✗ + ✗   **c.** Grows: O ✳ OOOOO ...

3. a. 26, 29, 32
   b. 49, 56, 63
   c. 29, 34, 32

5.a. 91   **b.** Yes
  c. Ten layers of cannonballs: the base is 10×10; the next layers are 9×9, 8×8, etc., up to the top level, which has 1 cannonball. There are 385 cannonballs in the 10th pyramid.

7. a. Arithmetic
  b. There are 58 cubes in the 20th figure, 39 placed in a row and 19 placed in a column on top of the row.

9. The sum divided by 3 is the middle number. The sum of 17, 18, and 19 is 54.

11. The sum divided by 9 is the center number of the array. The numbers 14, 15, 16, 21, 22, 23, 28, 29, and 30 form a 3×3 array whose sum is 198.

13. a. The missing sums equal 5×8, 8×13, and 13×21.
  b. The sum equals the product of the last Fibonacci number times the next Fibonacci number.

15. a. 1, 5, 6, 11, 17, 28, 45, 73, 118, 191
  b. 14, 6, 20, 26, 46, 72, 118, 190, 308, 498
  c. Yes   **d.** Yes
  e. The sum of the first 10 numbers in a Fibonacci-type sequence equals 11 times the seventh number in the sequence.

17. a. $16 + 17 + 18 + 19 + 20 = 21 + 22 + 23 + 24$
  b. $400 + 401 + 402 + \cdots + 420 = 421 + 422 + \cdots + 440$

19. a. 55   **b.** 220

21. 4096

23. a. Arithmetic 59. Add 5 to each number.
  b. Geometric 30,720. Multiply each number by 2.
  c. Arithmetic $^-20$. Subtract 4 from each number.
  d. Geometric 708,588. Multiply each number by 3.

25. a. Yes   **b.** No

27. a. 187   **b.** 103

29. 25, 36, 49, and 10,000

31. a. 30   **b.** 420

33. a. Arithmetic   **b.** Yes

35. Inductive reasoning

37. a. The ninth even number is 18 and can be illustrated by a 2×9 array.
  b. 90

39. This procedure will produce a number which is divisible by 7 for all single-digit numbers but not for all multidigit numbers. For example, beginning with 11, its double is 22, and 2211 is not divisible by 7. However, beginning with 14, its double is 28, and 2814 is divisible by 7.

41. a. The product of two odd whole numbers is not evenly divisible by 2.
  b. 8 cannot be written as the sum of consecutive whole numbers.

43. a. $2 + 3 + 4 + 5$ is not divisible by 4.
  b. True

45. a. 729   **b.** 531,441

47. a. 78   **b.** 364

49. 344
51. 95

EXERCISES AND PROBLEMS 1.3

1. a. 19, 57.7, and 14.7   **b.** 45 and 65
  c. between 120 and 125

3. a. $28m$ **b.** $m + b$ **c.** $28m - 19b$

5. a. $6p = s$
  b. One possible reason for writing $6s = p$ is that the statement says "6 times as many students."

7. a. 2 chips per box; $2x + 5 = 9$
  b. $3\frac{1}{2}$ chips per box; $3x + 4 = x + 11$

9. a. Step 1: Simplification (distributive property)
  Step 2: Addition property of equality
  Step 3: Simplification
  Step 4: Subtraction property of equality
  Step 5: Simplification
  Step 6: Division property of equality
  Step 7: Simplification
  b. Step 1: Simplification
  Step 2: Subtraction property of equality
  Step 3: Simplification
  Step 4: Division property of equality
  Step 5: Simplification

11. a. $x = 323$ **b.** $x = 11$
  c. $x = 719$ **d.** $x = 19$

13. a. Replace each box by 0, 1, 2, or 3 chips; $2x + 5 < 12$.
  b. Replace each box by 4 or more chips; $3x + 2 > 11$.

15. a. Step 1: Subtraction property of inequality
  Step 2: Simplification
  Step 3: Subtraction property of inequality
  Step 4: Simplification
  Step 5: Division property of inequality
  Step 6: Simplification
  b. Step 1: Subtraction property of inequality
  Step 2: Simplification
  Step 3: Multiplication property of inequality
  Step 4: Simplification

17. a. $x < 6$

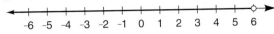

  b. $x > 2$

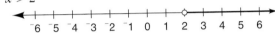

19. a. $.20x$ **b.** $18 - x$
  c. $.33(18 - x)$
  d. $.20x + .33(18 - x) = 4.38$; $x = 12$
  Marci mailed 12 postcards.

21. a. $10.5x$ **b.** $x + 3$ **c.** $8(x + 3)$
  d. $10.5x + 8(x + 3) < 120$; $x < 5.189$
  Merle bought either 1, 2, 3, 4, or 5 compact disks.

23. 60 feet. Let x equal the length of a side of the square.
$$4x + 110 = 350$$
$$x = 60$$

25. Let x equal the unknown number.
$$14 + x < 3x$$
$$7 < x$$
The statement is true for any number greater than 7.

27. a. $n + 1, n + 2, n + 3$
   b. $n + (n + 1) + (n + 2) + (n + 3)$
   c. $n = 86$
   d. $350 = 68 + 69 + 70 + 71 + 72$, and 350 cannot be written as the sum of three consecutive whole numbers.

29. Let x equal an arbitrary number. Add 221:
$$x + 221$$
Multiply by 2652:
$$2652(x + 221) = 2652x + 586,092$$
Subtract 1326:
$$2652x + 586,092 - 1326 = 2652x + 584,766$$
Divide by 663:
$$\frac{2652x + 584,766}{663} = 4x + 882$$
Subtract 870:
$$4x + 882 - 870 = 4x + 12$$
Divide by 4:
$$\frac{4x + 12}{4} = x + 3$$
Subtract x:
$$(x + 3) - x = 3$$
Regardless of the original number, the result will always be 3.

31. 3 nails
33. 1200 miles
35. Yes, the 2744th figure has 8230 tiles.
37. a. Figure 1: 1 yellow, 8 red
   Figure 2: 9 yellow, 16 red
   Figure 3: 25 yellow, 24 red
   Figure 4: 49 yellow, 32 red
   Figure 5: 64 yellow, 40 red
   b. 40,401 tiles: 39,601 yellow and 800 red
   c. Number of yellow tiles: $(2n - 1)^2$
   Number of red tiles: $8n$
   Total number of tiles: $(2n + 1)^2$

CHAPTER 1 TEST

1. Understanding the problem
   Devising a plan
   Carrying out the plan
   Looking back
2. Making a drawing
   Guessing and checking
   Making a table
   Using a model
   Working backward

Finding a pattern
Solving a simpler problem
Using algebra

3. Sums: 3, 8, 21, 55. The sum of the first and third Fibonacci numbers is the fourth Fibonacci number; the sum of the first, third, and fifth Fibonacci numbers is the sixth Fibonacci number; and so forth.
4. 512, or 2^9
5. a. 243   **b.** 18
   c. 30   **d.** 36
   e. 53
6. a. geometric   **b.** arithmetic
   c. arithmetic   **d.** neither
   e. neither
7. a. 91, 140, 204   **b.** 54, 77, 104
8. a. 15   **b.** 25   **c.** 35
9. $2 + 3 + 4 + 5 + 6 + 7 + 8 = 35$, which is not evenly divisible by 4.
10. a. 7 chips   **b.** More than 2 chips
11. a. $x = 68$ **b.** $x = 12$
12. a. $x < 11$ **b.** $x > 12.5$
13. a. Step 1: Subtraction property of equality
   Step 2: Simplification
   Step 3: Addition property of equality
   Step 4: Simplification
   Step 5: Division property of equality
   Step 6: Simplification
   b. Step 1: Simplification (distributive property)
   Step 2: Subtraction property of inequality
   Step 3: Simplification
   Step 4: Division property of inequality
   Step 5: Simplification
14. 201 posts; making a drawing and/or solving a simpler problem
15. Working backward: $170 - 80 = 90$, $90 \times 2 = 180$, $180 - 50 = 130$, $130 \times 2 = 260$. She started with 260 chips.
16. 325 and $n(n + 1)/2$; solving a simpler problem and finding a pattern
17. a. 16   **b.** 200   **c.** $2(n - 1) + 2(n + 1)$ or $4n$; making a drawing, solving a simpler problem, and finding a pattern
18. 78 handshakes and n handshakes; making a drawing, solving a simpler problem, and finding a pattern
19. 9 crossings; making a drawing
20. a. 17 and 452   **b.** $3n + 2$

EXERCISES AND PROBLEMS 2.1

1. Yes
3. a. Row 1
   b. The numbers of marks in row 2 are prime numbers (see Chapter 4). Row 3 has numbers that are just before and just after 10 and 20.
5. *SW* and *SB*; *W* and *L*

7. *W* and *SB*; *SW* and *SB*; *SW* and *L*; *SB* and *L*

9. *lwt, lwr, lwh*

11. a. False   **b.** True   **c.** True

13. a. *swh, sbh*

  b. *lbt, lbr, lbh, sbt, sbr, lwt, lwr, lwh, swt, swr*

  c. *swt, swr, swh, sbt, sbr, sbh, lwt, lwr, lwh*

15. a. {4, 6}   **b.** {0, 1, 2, 3, 5, 7, 8}

17. a.

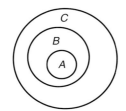

  b.

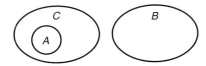

  c.

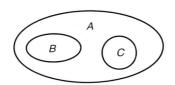

19. a. 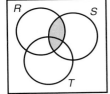   **b.**

  c.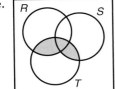

21. Maximum number for $A \cup B$ is 28.
Maximum number for $A \cap B$ is 13.

23.

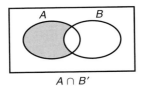

$A \cap B'$

25.

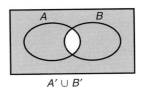

$A' \cup B'$

27. $A' \cap B$

29. a. *d, c*   **b.** *j, i*

31. 2

33. 400

35. 39

37. 43

39. 767

41. a. 8   **b.** 37

EXERCISES AND PROBLEMS 2.2

1. As the level of difficulty increases, the level of motivation decreases.

3. Each element of the domain gets assigned to an element of the range which is 1 less than twice its value.

  a. $f(x) = 2x - 1$

  b.

x	1	2	3	4	5	6	7	8	9	10
$f(x)$	1	3	5	7	9	11	13	15	17	19

  c.

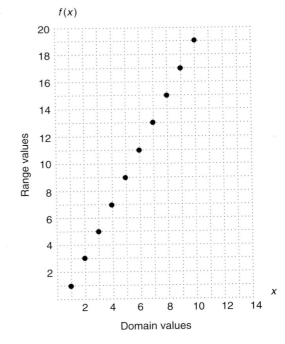

5. a. Function
  b. Function
  c. Not a function, as a person may have more than one telephone number
7. a. $f(x) = x + 17$, where x is a whole number
  b. $f(x) = 3x - 2$, where x is a whole number
9. a. The range values are 1, 4, 9, 16, and 25, respectively.
  b.

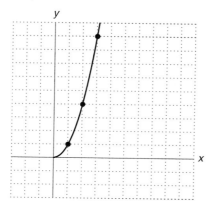

  c. $f(x) = x^2$
  d. nonlinear
11. a. Slope, $^-2$; equation, $y = ^-2x + 2$
  b. Slope, $\frac{1}{4}$; equation, $y = \frac{x}{4} + 2$
13. a. Line i, 10; line ii, 1
  b. Yes. One possibility: $y = 20x$
  c. No. The slope m in $y = mx + b$ can be arbitrarily large.
15. a. $7.50
  b. 17 pounds
  c. $c(x) = 1.5x$
  d.

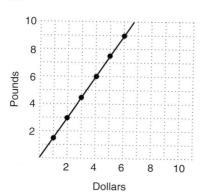

17. a. Middle
  b. $5 more for both 8 hours and 11 hours

c, d.

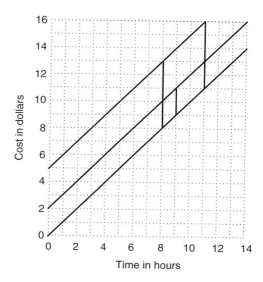

19. a. $c(x) = 12x + 40$
  b. $100
  c.

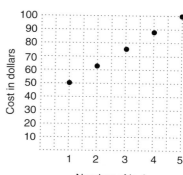

21. a. $g(x) = 6x + 15$
  b. $99
  c.

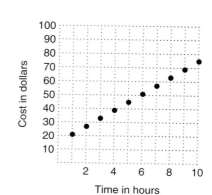

23. a. 12 miles per hour
  b. At the 10- and 20-minute points
  c. 0 to 3 minutes, 6 to 7 minutes, 10 to 13 minutes, and 15 to 16 minutes

25. a. I, Bob; II, Joan; III, Mary; IV, Joel
    b. Joel   **c.** Mary   **d.** Bob   **e.** Joel
27. a. II   **b.** III   **c.** I   **d.** I
29.

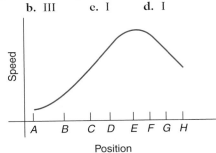

31. a.

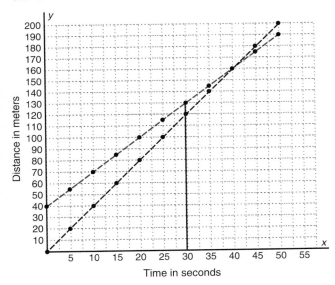

    b. Pat's distance is 120 meters, and Hal's distance is
       130 meters.
    c. 40 seconds   **d.** Pat   **e.** 10 meters
33. a. 4.68 seconds   **b.** .12 second
    c. Approximately .68 second. This is a pulse rate of
       approximately 88 beats per minute.
35. a.

Number of figure	1	2	3	4	5	6	7	8
Number of tiles	3	7	11	15	19	23	27	31

b.

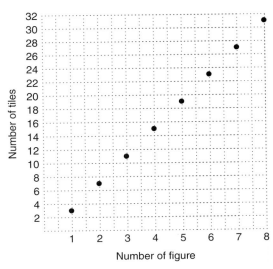

Patterns: The points lie on a line. For each
horizontal increase of 1 unit, there is a vertical
increase of 4 units. With the scales of the axes as
shown above, moving over 2 spaces and up 2
spaces from a given point on the graph locates
another point on the graph.
    c. $f(20) = 79$ **d.** $f(350) = 1399$
37. a. Sequence 1: The number of tiles in the nth figure
       is $2n + 19$.
       Sequence 2: The number of tiles in the nth figure
       is $3n + 2$.
    b.

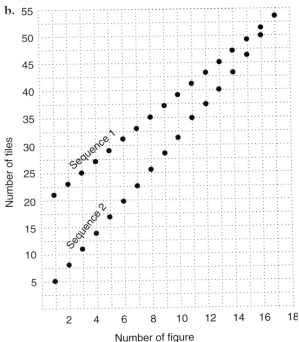

c. $n = 17$

d. The 17th figures in both sequences have the same number of tiles. For $n < 17$, the nth figure in sequence 1 has more tiles than the nth figure in sequence 2. For $n > 17$, the nth figure in sequence 2 has more tiles than the nth figure in sequence 1.

EXERCISES AND PROBLEMS 2.3

1. Yes

3. a. If a person takes a hard line with a bill collector, then it may lead to a lawsuit.

b. If a person is an employee of Tripak Company, then he or she must retire by age 65.

c. If the class is to meet only twice a week, then there must be 2-hour class sessions.

d. If a person is a pilot, then she or he must have a physical examination every 6 months.

5.

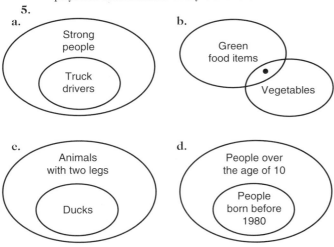

a. Strong people / Truck drivers

b. Green food items / Vegetables

c. Animals with two legs / Ducks

d. People over the age of 10 / People born before 1980

7. Converse: If you itemize your deductions, then you take a deduction for your home office. **Inverse:** If you do not take a deduction for your home office, then you do not itemize your deductions. **Contrapositive:** If you do not itemize your deductions, then you do not take a deduction for your home office.

9. Converse: If the camera focus is on manual, switch B was pressed. **Inverse:** If switch B is not pressed, the camera focus is not on manual. **Contrapositive:** If the camera focus is not on manual, then switch B was not pressed.

11. c.

13. a. If the computer does not reject your income tax return, then you did not subtract $750 for each dependent.

b. If the cards are not dealt again, then there was an opening bid.

c. If the books are not returned at the end of the week's free sing-a-long, then you were delighted with them.

15. You pay the Durham poll tax if and only if you are age 18 or older.

17. If Robinson is hired, then she meets the conditions set by the board. If Robinson meets the conditions set by the board, then she will be hired.

19. Valid reasoning

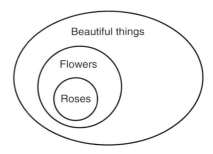

21. Invalid reasoning. The following Venn diagram satisfies the given conditions, but there is not necessarily an intersection between the set of truck drivers and the set of musicians.

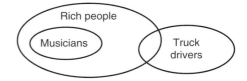

23. This patient does not have anemia.

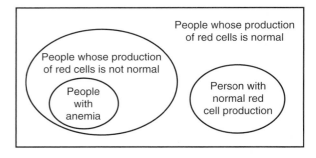

25. Mr. Keene has sufficient vitamin K in his body.

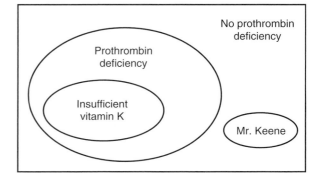

27. Invalid
29. Invalid
31. Valid
33. Dow is a female cook; Eliot is a male singer; Finley is a male appraiser; Grant is a male broker; Harley is a female painter.
35. No, the proof is arranged in logical order.

CHAPTER 2 TEST

1. a. $\{swh\}$ **b.** $\{sbt, sbr, sbh, swt\}$ **c.** $\{sbt, sbh\}$
2. a. $A \cap B = \{2, 4\}$ **b.** $A \cup B = \{1, 2, 3, 4, 6\}$
   c. $A' \cap B = \{1, 3\}$ **d.** $A \cup B' = \{0, 2, 4, 5, 6\}$
3. a.

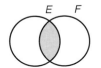

b.

c. **d.**

e. 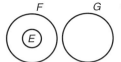 **f.**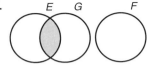

4. a. $A \cap B'$ or $(A' \cup B)'$ **b.** $A' \cup B'$ or $(A \cap B)'$
5. a. Not necessarily

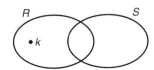

b. Yes

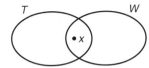

c. No

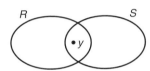

6. For the domain values 1, 2, 3, 4, and 5, the corresponding range values are .5, 1, 1.5, 2, and 2.5, respectively.

b.

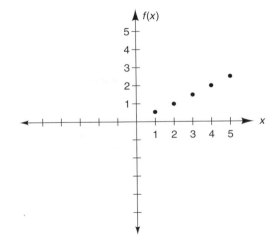

c. $y = \frac{1}{2}x$ **d.** Linear
7. a. $\frac{-1}{2}$ **b.** $\frac{1}{2}$
8. $y = 3x + 4$
9. a. $y = 55x + 120$ **b.** $670   **c.** 13 days
10. a. $24x$ **b.** $60 - x$
   c. $15(60 - x)$ **d.** 18 hours
11. Monday, jogged; Tuesday, walked; Wednesday, biked; and Thursday, roller-bladed.
12. 5 cars
13. 20 men
14. a. If you are denied credit, then you have the right to protest to the credit bureau.
   b. If a child was absent yesterday, then the child was absent today.
   c. If you were at the party, then you received a gift.
15. a. **Converse:** If her husband goes with her, then Mary goes fishing. **Inverse:** If Mary does not go fishing, then her husband does not go with her. **Contrapositive:** If her husband does not go with her, then Mary does not go fishing.
   b. **Converse:** If you receive five free books, then you will join the book club. **Inverse:** If you do not join the book club, then you will not receive five free books. **Contrapositive:** If you do not receive five free books, then you have not joined the book club.
16. Statement 3
17. There will be peace talks if and only if the prisoners are set free.
18. a. Invalid   **b.** Valid   **c.** Invalid
19. a. The people in ward B are not healthy.
   b. The game pieces should be set up as they were before the illegal move was made.
20. a. Invalid   **b.** Valid

EXERCISES AND PROBLEMS 3.1

1. 1241
3. Boolla Boolla Neecha (5)
Boolla Boolla Boolla (6)
5. **a.** 4 hands and 2
b. Hand of hands, 2 hands, and 2
7.

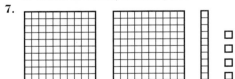

9. **a.**

b.

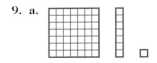

11. **a.** 132_{seven}

b. 242_{five}

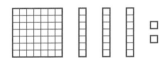

13. **a.** 98 units   **b.** 389 units
15. In each numeration system, the symbol for 1 is repeated to create the symbols for 2, 3, and 4. In the Babylonian and Egyptian systems, the symbol for 1 is repeated in the symbols for 2 through 9. Grouping by 5s occurs in the Roman and Mayan systems. In these systems, a symbol for 5 is used with the symbols for 1, 2, 3, and 4 to form the symbols for 6, 7, 8, and 9; the symbol for 10 can be formed by combining two symbols for the number 5.

17. **a.**

b. M D C C L X X V I
c.

d.

19. Base ten

Hindu-Arabic	1	4	8	16	26
Attic-Greek	I	IIII	ΓIII	ΔΓI	ΔΔΓI

Hindu-Arabic	32	52	57	206	511
Attic-Greek	ΔΔΔII	ΓᴾII	ΓᴾΓII	ΗΗΓI	ΓᴴΔI

21. **a.** $7 \times 10^6 + 0 \times 10^5 + 8 \times 10^4 + 2 \times 10^3 + 5 \times 10^2 + 5 \times 10 + 5$
$7 \times 1,000,000 + 0 \times 100,000 + 8 \times 10,000 + 2 \times 1000 + 5 \times 100 + 5 \times 10 + 5$
b. $5 \times 10^4 + 7 \times 10^3 + 0 \times 10^2 + 2 \times 10 + 0$
$5 \times 10,000 + 7 \times 1000 + 0 \times 100 + 2 \times 10 + 0$
23. **a.** The value is 400; the place value is hundreds.
b. The value is 0; the place value is thousands.
c. The value is 2,000,000; the place value is millions.
25. **a.** Four thousand forty
b. Seven hundred ninety-three million, four hundred twenty-eight thousand, five hundred eleven
c. Thirty million, one hundred ninety-seven thousand, seven hundred thirty-three
d. Five billion, two hundred ten million, nine hundred ninety-nine thousand, six hundred seventeen
27. **a.** 43,700,000   **b.** 43,670,000
c. 43,669,000   **d.** 43,668,900
29. **a.** 108

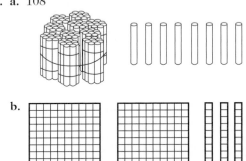

b.

c.

d.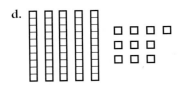

31. a. $\boxplus$ 6,000,000
b. $\boxplus$ 200,000 $\boxplus$ 300
c. $\boxplus$ 3000 $\boxminus$ 50,000 $\boxplus$ 300,000 $\boxminus$ 7,000,000

33. a. 123,456,789   **b.** 111,111,111
35. a. 707,007   **b.** 12,832
37. Yes, this is true.
39. 345
41. 160

EXERCISES AND PROBLEMS 3.2

1. a. Units wheel and hundreds wheel
b. Yes
3. a. $232_{five} + 123_{five} = 410_{five}$
b. $852_{twelve} + 295_{twelve} = B27_{twelve}$, where B represents eleven
5. a. 2 flats, 3 longs, 6 units; $523_{eight} - 265_{eight} = 236_{eight}$
b. 2 flats, 0 longs, 3 units; $342_{five} - 134_{five} = 203_{five}$

7. a. $106 + 38 = 144$

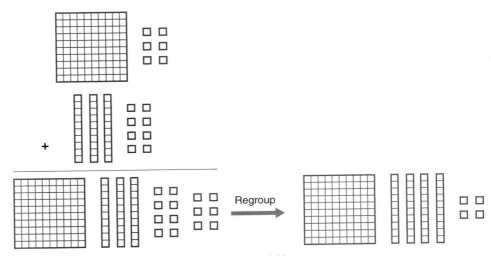

$$106 + 38 = 144$$

b. $41_{five} - 23_{five} = 13_{five}$

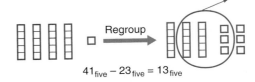

$$41_{five} - 23_{five} = 13_{five}$$

c. $161 - 127 = 34$

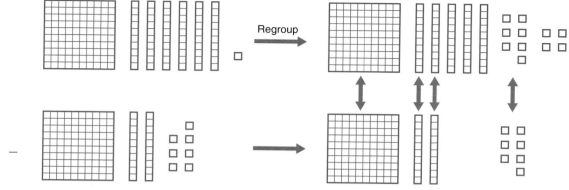

Regroup

$161 - 127 = 34$

d. $142_{\text{five}} + 34_{\text{five}} = 231_{\text{five}}$

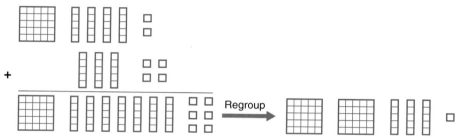

Regroup

$142_{\text{five}} + 34_{\text{five}} = 231_{\text{five}}$

9. a.

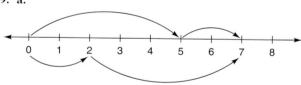

b.

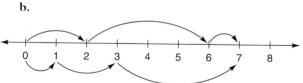

11. a.

b.

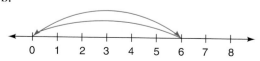

13. a. An advantage of this method is that when the digits of highest place value are added first, a subsequent error will affect only the digits of lower place value.

$$
\begin{array}{r}
726 \\
+\ 508 \\
\hline
1224 \\
\scriptstyle 3
\end{array}
$$

b. An advantage of this method is that all digits of column sums are recorded before regrouping. This eliminates the need to add and regroup in the same step.

$$
\begin{array}{r}
974 \\
+\ 382 \\
\hline
6 \\
15 \\
12 \\
\hline
1356
\end{array}
$$

15. a. Associative property for addition
   b. Commutative property for addition
17. a. No. For example, $3 - 5 \neq 5 - 3$.
   b. Yes
19. a. Ten was not regrouped (1 was not carried) to the tens column.

b. The sum of the units digits is 14. Instead of recording a 4 in the units column and carrying the 1, a 1 was recorded and 4 was carried to the tens column.

21. a. The student computed $6 - 4$ (that is, subtracted the smaller number from the larger).

b. After a 10 in the tens place was regrouped to units, the 5 was not reduced to 4.

23. Other compatible numbers or substitutions are possible.

a. $23 + 25 + 28 = 25 + 23 + (2 + 26)$
$= 25 + 25 + 26$
$= 50 + 26$
$= 76$

b. $128 - 15 + 27 - 50 = 128 + 12 - 50$
$= 140 - 50$
$= 90$

c. $83 + 50 - 13 + 24 = (83 - 13) + 50 + 24$
$= 70 + 74$
$= 144$

25. Other combinations are possible.

a. $6502 - 152 = 6500 - 150 = 6350$
b. $894 - 199 = 895 - 200 = 695$
c. $14,200 - 2700 = 14,000 - 2500 = 11,500$

27. Other combinations are possible.

a. $185 + \quad 15 = 200$
$200 + 200 = 400$
So $185 + 215 = 400$

b. $250 + 250 = 500$
$500 + \quad 35 = 535$
So $250 + 285 = 535$

c. $\quad 47 + \quad 53 = 100$
$100 + \quad 35 = 135$
So $47 + \quad 88 = 135$

29. a. $100 + 40 + 20 = 160$
b. $30 + 40 + 60 = 130$

31. Other compatible numbers are possible.

a. $359 - 192 \approx 360 - 200$
$= 160$
b. $712 + 293 \approx 700 + 300$
$= 1000$
c. $882 + 245 \approx 900 + 245$
$= 1145$
d. $1522 - 486 \approx 1500 - 500$
$= 1000$

33. a. 1600, since $3 + 4 + 9 = 16$
b. 160, since $1 + 4 + 8 + 3 = 16$
c. 20,000, since $7 + 5 + 8 = 20$

35. a. $2800 **b.** No

37. a. 8723, 8823, 8923, 9023, 9123, 9223, 9323, 9423
b. 906, 896, 886, 876, 866, 856, 846

39. a. 2859, 3004, 3149, 3294, 3439, 3584
b. 4164
c. 2569, 2424, 2279, 2134, 1989, 1844

41. a.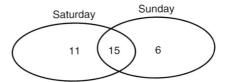
b. 30
c. 20

43. a. 30 cars   **b.** 52 cars
c. 35 cars   **d.** Case b

45. There must be 15 students who watched the Olympics on both Saturday and Sunday to satisfy the given conditions. Therefore, there are 32 students in the class.

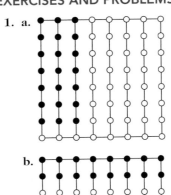

47. a. 665   **b.** 724   **c.** 1143
d. 831   **e.** 1289   **f.** 572

49. Matching pairs of numbers as indicated produces nine pairs, each with a sum of 20. One of each pair can be placed opposite the other on opposite sides of the "circle," and the remaining number 10 can be placed in the center circle to produce sums of 30.

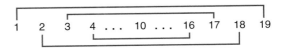

51. 999
$\underline{+ \quad 2}$
1001

EXERCISES AND PROBLEMS 3.3

1. a.

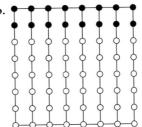

b.

3. a.

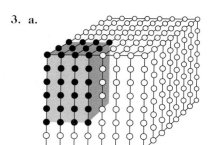

b.

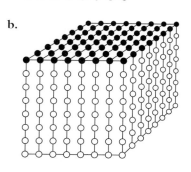

5. a. Three copies of the base-ten pieces that represent 168 have a total of 3 flats, 18 longs, and 24 units. The 24 units regroup to 2 longs and 4 units; and the (18 + 2) longs regroup to 2 flats. The final minimal set contains 5 flats, 0 longs, and 4 units.

  b. Four copies of the base-ten pieces that represent 209 have a total of 8 flats and 36 units. The 36 units regroup to 3 longs and 6 units. The final minimal set contains 8 flats, 3 longs, and 6 units.

  c. Three copies of the base-five pieces that represent 423_{five} have a total of 12 flats, 6 longs, and 9 units. The 9 units regroup to 1 long and 4 units; the (6 + 1) longs regroup to 1 flat and 2 longs. The (12 + 1) flats regroup to 2 long-flats and 3 flats. The final minimal set contains 2 long-flats, 3 flats, 2 longs, and 4 units.

  d. Five copies of the base-eight pieces that represent 47_{eight} have a total of 20 longs and 35 units. The 35 units regroup to 4 longs and 3 units; and the (20 + 4) longs regroup to 3 flats. The final minimal set contains 3 flats, 0 longs, and 3 units.

7. a.

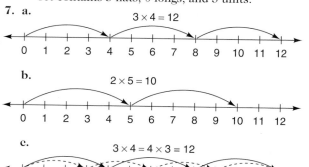

9. a. The 2 that was carried was either multiplied by or added to the 2 in the tens column.

  b. The 2 and 1 in the tens column were added; or the 2 that was carried was ignored.

11.

a.

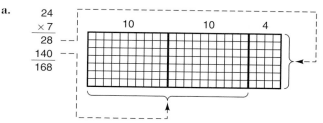

b.

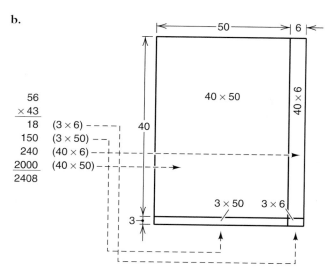

13. a. Commutative property for multiplication
  b. Associative property for multiplication
  c. Distributive property for multiplication

15. a. Closed   **b.** Not closed   **c.** Closed

17. Other combinations and compatible numbers are possible.
  a. 8300 (multiply 83 by 100)
  b. 210 (multiply 21 by 10)

19. a. $25 \times 12 = 25 \times (10 + 2) = 250 + 50 = 300$
  b. $15 \times 106 = 15 \times (100 + 6) = 1500 + 90 = 1590$

21. a. $35 \times 19 = 35(20 - 1) = 700 - 35 = 665$
  b. $30 \times 99 = 30(100 - 1) = 3000 - 30 = 2970$

23. Other products are possible.
  a. Divide 24 by 4 and multiply 25 by 4.
  $24 \times 25 = 6 \times 100 = 600$
  b. Divide 35 by 5 and multiply 60 by 5.
  $35 \times 60 = 7 \times 300 = 2100$

25. Other rounded-number replacements are possible.
  a. $22 \times 17 \approx 20 \times 20 = 400$ (Too big; estimate could be improved by subtracting 20.)
  b. $83 \times 31 \approx 80 \times 30 = 2400$ (Too small; estimate could be improved by adding $3 \times 30 = 90$, or $80 \times 1 = 80$, or adding both.)

27. Other compatible numbers and combinations are possible.

    a. $4 \times 76 \times 24 \approx 4 \times 25 \times 76$
$$= 100 \times 76$$
$$= 7600$$

    This product is greater than the actual product.

    b. $3 \times 34 \times 162 \approx 100 \times 162 = 16200$
Since $100 < 3 \times 34$, the estimated product of 16,200 is less than the actual product.

29. a. Front-end estimation:
$3 \times 5 = 15$, so $36 \times 58 \approx 1500$
Combinations of tens and units digits:
$36 \times 58 \approx 30 \times 50 + (6 \times 50) + (8 \times 30) = 2040$

    b. Front-end estimation:
$4 \times 2 = 8$, so $42 \times 27 \approx 800$
Combinations of tens and units digits:
$42 \times 27 \approx 40 \times 20 + (2 \times 20) + (7 \times 40) = 1120$

31. a. $18 \times 62 \approx 20 \times 60 = 1200$
The gray region shows the increase due to rounding 18 to 20, and the red region shows the decrease due to rounding 62 to 60. Since the increase is greater than the decrease, the estimated product of 1200 is greater than the actual product.

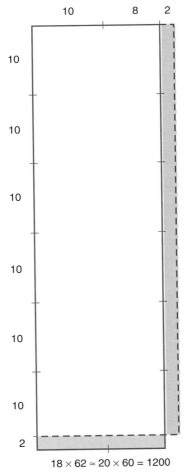

$18 \times 62 \approx 20 \times 60 = 1200$

b. $43 \times 29 \approx 40 \times 30 = 1200$
The gray region shows the increase due to rounding 29 to 30, and the red region shows the decrease due to rounding 43 to 40. Since the increase is less than the decrease, the estimated product of 1200 is less than the actual product.

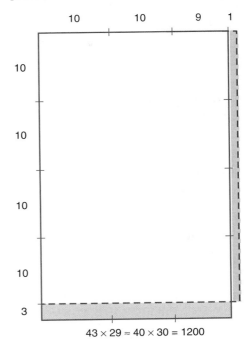

$43 \times 29 \approx 40 \times 30 = 1200$

33. a. $62 \otimes 45 + 14 \otimes 29$
$$\approx 60 \times 50 + 10 \times 30$$
$$= 3000 + 300$$
$$= 3300 \quad \text{Exact answer: } 3196$$

    b. $36 + 18 \otimes 40 + 15$
$$\approx 40 + 20 \times 40 + 15$$
$$= 40 + 800 + 15$$
$$= 855 \quad \text{Exact answer: } 771$$

35. a. 5, 15, 45, 135, 405, 1215, 3645, 10,935, 32,805

    b. 20, 25, 30, 35, 40, 45, 50, 55, 60, 65

37. a. $42,328   **b.** $55,172   **c.** $49,296
    d. $62,296   **e.** $51,792   **f.** $58,500

39. a. 25 or 26   **b.** 18

41. a. Each row increases by a constant amount (each row is an arithmetic sequence). Each column increases by a constant amount. The table is symmetric about the diagonal from upper left to lower right.

    b. The sum of the digits in each product is 9. The tens digits in the products (18, 27, 36, . . . , 81) increased from 1 to 8 while the units digits decreased from 8 to 1.

43. $1570

45. 16

47. This pattern holds for the first nine equations. It does not hold for the 10th equation.
$12,345,678,910 \times 9 + 10 = 111,111,110,200$

49. a. One pattern: The product of 99 and a two-digit number greater than 10 is a four-digit number *abcd* such that *ab* is 1 less than the two-digit number and $ab + cd = 99$. Similarly, the product of 999 and a two-digit number greater than 10 is a five-digit number *abcde* such that *ab* is 1 less than the two-digit number and $ab + cde = 999$.
b, c. Conjectures will vary.

51. 50

53. 8

55. The raised fingers represent 5 tens, or 50, and the product of the numbers of closed fingers is $2 \times 3 = 6$.

57.

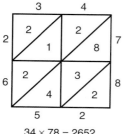

$34 \times 78 = 2652$

EXERCISES AND PROBLEMS 3.4

1. a. Partitive (sharing) concept

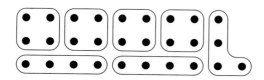

b. Measurement (subtractive) concept

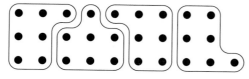

3. a. $68 \div 17 = 4$ if and only if $68 = 17 \times 4$
b. $414 \div 23 = 18$ if and only if $414 = 23 \times 18$

5. a. $336 \div 14 = 24$ **b.** $72 \div 8 = 9$

7. a. Form three groups of 1 flat, 3 longs, and 2 units; $396 \div 3 = 132$

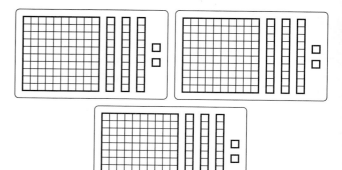

b. Regroup the 3 flats into 15 longs, and regroup 3 of the longs to units so that there are 12 longs and 16 units. Then form 4 groups of 3 longs and 4 units; $301_{\text{five}} \div 4 = 34_{\text{five}}$.

9. a. 392 is represented by 3 flats, 9 longs, and 2 units. Regroup the 3 flats to 30 longs so that there is a total of 39 longs. The 39 longs are divided into 7 groups of 5 longs with 4 longs remaining. This 5 is recorded in the tens place of the quotient. Then the 4 longs are regrouped to 40 units, and the total of 42 units is divided into 7 groups of 6 units each. This 6 is recorded in the units place of the quotient.

$$\overset{56}{7\overline{)392}}$$

b. 320 is represented by 3 flats, 2 longs, and 0 units. Regroup the 3 flats to 30 longs so that there is a total of 32 longs. The 32 longs are divided into 5 groups of 6 longs with 2 longs remaining. This 6 is recorded in the tens place of the quotient. Then the 2 longs are regrouped to 20 units which are divided into 5 groups of 4 units each. This 4 is recorded in the units place of the quotient.

$$\overset{64}{5\overline{)320}}$$

11. a. $72 \div 12 = 6$

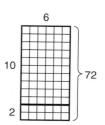

b. $286 \div 26 = 11$

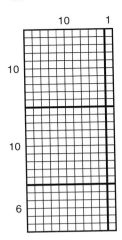

13. a. Regroup 3 flats into 30 longs to obtain 3 flats, 30 longs, and 8 units. Then regroup 1 long into 10 units to obtain 3 flats, 29 longs, and 18 units. These pieces will form a 32×19 rectangle.
Multiplication fact: $32 \times 19 = 608$
Division fact: $608 \div 32 = 19$

b. Regroup 1 flat into 10 longs to obtain 1 flat, 12 longs, and 1 unit. Then regroup 2 longs into 20 units to obtain 1 flat, 10 longs, and 21 units. These pieces will form a 13×17 rectangle.
Multiplication fact: $13 \times 17 = 221$
Division fact: $221 \div 13 = 17$

c. These pieces will form a 21×14 rectangle.
Multiplication fact: $21 \times 14 = 294$
Division fact: $294 \div 21 = 14$

15. a. $0 \div 4 = 0$ **b.** Undefined   **c.** Undefined

17. a. $15 \div 5 = 3$ using the measurement concept, or $15 \div 3 = 5$ using the sharing concept.

b.

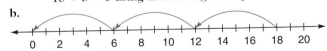

19. a. In the second step of the division algorithm, $5 \div 8$ is 0 with a remainder of 5. The 0 should have been placed in the quotient.

b. The 6 and 8 in the quotient were placed in the wrong columns.

21. a. The two sides of the equation are equal. Division is distributive over addition.

b. Division is not commutative; $8 \div 4 \neq 4 \div 8$

23. a. Not closed   **b.** Not closed   **c.** Closed

25. a. 70 remainder 28
b. 118 remainder 12
c. 2411 remainder 381

27. Other quotients are possible.
a. Divide both numbers by 9; $90 \div 18 = 10 \div 2 = 5$
b. Divide both numbers by 2; $84 \div 14 = 42 \div 7 = 6$

29. Other number replacements are possible.
a. $250 \div 46 \approx 250 \div 50 = 5$ (less than the exact quotient)
b. $82 \div 19 \approx 80 \div 20 = 4$ (less than the exact quotient)
c. $486 \div 53 \approx 500 \div 50 = 10$ (greater than the exact quotient)

31. a. $623 \div 209 \approx 6 \div 2 = 3$
b. $7218 \div 1035 \approx 7 \div 1 = 7$

33. a. 5^{34} **b.** 10^2

35. a. 35   **b.** 38   **c.** 240   **d.** 73

37. a. 10^{13} **b.** 10^{15}

39. Yes, the correct answer is obtained.

41. This sequence produces the correct answer if the calculator follows the rules for the order of operations.

43. a. 1. Q, 4 and R, 4
2. Q, 3 and R, 5
3. Q, 4 and R, 6
4. Q, 4 and R, 2
5. Q, 3 and R, 6
6. Q, 3 and R, 3
b. A total of 27 vans.

45. a. 1. 354294   **2.** 118098
3. 39366   **4.** 13122
5. 4374   **6.** 1458
b. 12, the 13th number is less than 1.

47. a. Q, 510 and R, 13
b. Q, 12 and R, 406

49. a. 500,014   **b.** 6812

51. 4th row $4^2 + 5^2 + 20^2 = 21^2$
12th row $12^2 + 13^2 + 156^2 = 157^2$

53. $133 + 135 + 137 + 139 + 141 + 143 + 145 + 147 + 149 + 151 + 153 + 155 = 1728$

55. a. 8   **b.** 6

57. a. First method. Receiving $\$1 + \$2 + \$4$, etc., for 22 weeks equals $\$4,194,303$.
b. $\$2,194,303$

59. 3 quarts

CHAPTER 3 TEST

1. a.    **b.** CCXXVI

c. ◀◀ ↑↑↑
◀◀ ↑↑↑   **d.** ≐

2. a. The value is 4 million; the place value is millions.
b. The value is 0; the place value is ten thousands.

3. a. 6,300,000   **b.** 6,281,500
c. 6,281,000

4. a.

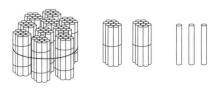

b.

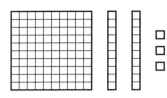

c. 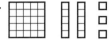   **d.**

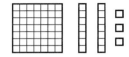

5. a. $245 + 182 = 427$

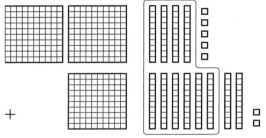

b. $362 - 148 = 214$

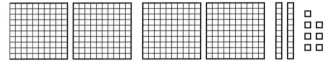

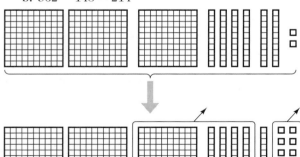

6. a.
$$
\begin{array}{r}
483 \\
+\ 274 \\
\hline
\cancel{6}57 \\
{\scriptstyle 7}
\end{array}
$$

b.
$$
\begin{array}{r}
864 \\
+\ 759 \\
\hline
13 \\
11 \\
15 \\
\hline
1623
\end{array}
$$

7. a. $65 - 19 = 66 - 20 = 46$
b. $843 - 97 = 846 - 100 = 746$

8. a. $321 + 435 + 106 \approx 300 + 400 + 100 = 800$
b. $7410 - 2563 + 4602 \approx 7000 - 2000 + 4000$
$= 9000$
c. $32 \times 56 \approx 30 \times 50 = 1500$
d. $3528 \div 713 \approx 3000 \div 700 \approx 4$

9. a. $18 \times 5 = 3 \times 30 = 90$
b. $25 \times 28 = 100 \times 7 = 700$

10.

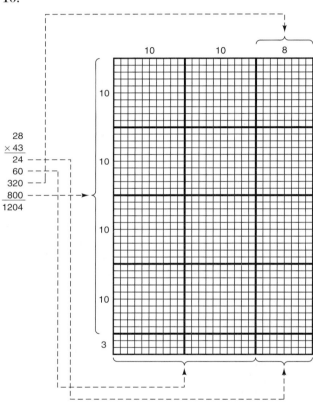

11. a. 117   **b.** 32   **c.** 53
12. a. 3^8 **b.** 7^{10}

13.

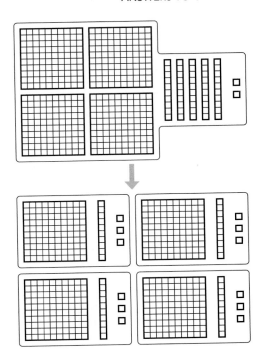

14. Other answers are possible.
  a. $473 + 192 \approx 500 + 200 = 700$
  b. $534 - 203 \approx 500 - 200 = 300$
  c. $993 \times 42 \approx 1000 \times 40 = 40{,}000$
  d. $350 \div 49 \approx 350 \div 50 = 7$
15. **a.** True   **b.** True
  c. False   **d.** False   **e.** False
16. $21^2 + 22^2 + 23^2 + 24^2 = 25^2 + 26^2 + 27^2$
  $36^2 + 37^2 + 38^2 + 39^2 + 40^2 = 41^2 + 42^2 + 43^2 + 44^2$
  $$7230 = 7230$$
  The pattern holds for the fourth equation.
17. 6 players
18. 24 types of pizza

EXERCISES AND PROBLEMS 4.1

1. **a.** Take the escalator to the elevator that serves the even-numbered floors, and deliver to the 26th and 48th floors. Then walk down to the 47th floor, and use the elevator that serves the odd-numbered floors to deliver to the 35th and 11th floors. Return to the street level on the elevator that serves the odd-numbered floors.
  b. Use the top deck elevator to deliver to floors 20, 22, 24, 26, 28, and 30. Then walk down one flight, deliver to floor 29, and use the bottom-deck elevator to deliver to floors 27, 25, 23, and 21.
3. **a.** True   **b.** False   **c.** False
5. **a.** $7 \mid 63$ **b.** $8 \mid 40$
  c. $13 \mid 39$ **d.** $12 \mid 36$

7. **a.**

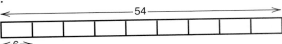

  b.

12 | 60

9. **a.** White, green, purple, dark green
  b. White, green, yellow
  c. One train. The number 1 is the only factor of a prime which is less than the prime.
11. **a.** Prime numbers
  b. 15, 30, 17
  c. Each array will be a rectangle whose sides have two different lengths.
  d. 4. The smallest whole number with eight factors is 24.
13. Both numbers in parts a and b are divisible by 3. When a number is divided by 3, the remainder is equal to the remainder when the sum of the digits is divided by 3.
15. **a.** No. Remainder is 3.
  b. No. Remainder is 2.
17. **a.** Not necessarily, 3 divides 6 but 9 does not divide 6.
  b. Yes, because 3×3 is a factor, so 3 is a factor.
19. **a.** Not divisible by 4. Remainder is 2.
  b. Divisible by 4
21. The base-ten pieces show that each long-flat and each flat can always be divided into four equal parts. So, to determine whether the entire collection of base-ten pieces can be divided into four equal parts, we only need to look at the longs and units.
23. **a.** If a divides b and a does not divide c, then a does not divide the difference $(b - c)$. True.
  b. If a does not divide b and a does not divide c, then a does not divide the sum $(b + c)$. False: $2 \nmid 5$ and $2 \nmid 7$ but $2 \mid (5 + 7)$.
  c. If a divides b and b divides c, then a divides c. True.
25. No number less than 13 divides 173. But if a number n greater than 13 divided 173, there would have to be another number m less than 13 that divided 173. Why?
27. 277 and 683
29. Carry out the process of circling and crossing out multiples until the prime number 17 has been circled. Since every composite number less than 300 has at least one prime factor less than or equal to 17, the process ends when 17 is circled.

31. a. Divisible by 11
  b. Not divisible by 11
  c. Divisible by 11
  d. Yes

33. 47, 59, 73, 89, 107, 127, 149, 173, 199, 227, 257, 289

35. 41, 43, 47, 53, 61, 71, 83, 97

37. True

39. 235 (Every even number between 31 and 501 can be paired with an odd number that is 1 greater. There are 235 odd numbers between 32 and 502.)

41. $3 \times 5 \times 7 \times 11 \times 13 = 15{,}015$

43. Using the fact that if $a \mid b$ and $a \mid c$, then $a \mid (b + c)$, we see that 2 is a factor of $2 \times 3 \times 4 \times 5 \times 6 + 2$ because it is a factor of both $2 \times 3 \times 4 \times 5 \times 6$ and 2. Similarly, 3 is a factor of the next number; 4 is a factor of the next number; etc.
  a. The following 10 numbers have factors of 2, 3, 4, . . . , 11, respectively. Other sequences are possible.
  $2 \times 3 \times 4 \times 5 \times 6 \times 7 \times 8 \times 9 \times 10 \times 11 + 2$
  $2 \times 3 \times 4 \times 5 \times 6 \times 7 \times 8 \times 9 \times 10 \times 11 + 3$
  $2 \times 3 \times 4 \times 5 \times 6 \times 7 \times 8 \times 9 \times 10 \times 11 + 4$
  .
  .
  .
  $2 \times 3 \times 4 \times 5 \times 6 \times 7 \times 8 \times 9 \times 10 \times 11 + 11$
  b. Let n be the product of the whole numbers from 2 through 101. The numbers $n + 2, n + 3, n + 4,$ $\cdots, n + 101$ form a sequence of 100 consecutive composite numbers: $n + 2$ is divisible by 2; $n + 3$ is divisible by 3; $n + 4$ is divisible by 4; etc.

EXERCISES AND PROBLEMS 4.2

1. a. $126 = 2 \times 3 \times 3 \times 7 = 2 \times 3^2 \times 7$
  b. $308 = 2 \times 2 \times 7 \times 11 = 2^2 \times 7 \times 11$
  c. $245 = 5 \times 7 \times 7 = 5 \times 7^2$

3. a.

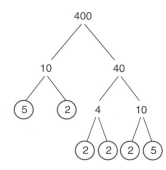

b.

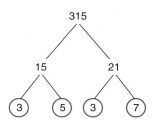

c.

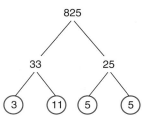

5. 1,000,000,000 has a unique factorization containing only 2s and 5s. Since there is no other factorization, 7 is not a factor.

7. a. 1, 2, 4, 5, 10, 20, 25, 50, 100, 125, 250, 500
  b. 1, 3, 7, 11, 21, 33, 77, 231
  c. 1, 5, 7, 35, 49, 245

9. a. 1, 2, 5, 10
  b. 1
  c. 1, 2, 7, 14

11. a. 56   **b.** 1   **c.** 33

13. a. 28, 56, 84, 112, 140
  b. 24, 48, 72, 96, 120
  c. 204, 408, 612, 816, 1020

15. a. 616   **b.** 912   **c.** 210

17. a. 6 and 9 have common multiple 54
  b. 6 is a common factor of the length of both rods.

19. a. The number of brown rods is a multiple of 5. For every 5 brown rods there are 4 orange rods.
  b. Five

21. a. 2835 seconds, which is less than 1 hour
  b. If you started counting after the lights flashed together, there would be 405 births, 189 deaths, and 35 immigrants. This would be a gain in population of 251 people.
  c. 56,700 seconds, or 945 minutes, or 15.75 hours

23. 28 students on a team and 18 teams

25. a. 12 cookies
  b. 25 piles
  c. 22 piles

27. 150 minutes later, or at 7:30

29. If Cindy and Nicole go together on the first day, then there will be 59 days out of 180 on which neither uses the club.

31. 24 (5 occurs as a factor 24 times and 2 occurs as a factor at least 24 times)

33. a. Yes, 6 is a perfect number.
  b. More deficient numbers

35. a. $\frac{99}{105}$ will be replaced by $\frac{33}{35}$ because their GCF is 3.

b. $\frac{102}{275}$ will be replaced by $\frac{102}{275}$, since the numerator and denominator are relatively prime.

37. The prime numbers less than the square root of 211 are 2, 3, 5, 7, 11, 13. The product of these numbers is 30,030, and the second view screen shows that 211 and 30,030 have no common factors other than 1.

CHAPTER 4 TEST

1. a. False **b.** True **c.** True **d.** False

2. a. 3 | 45 **b.** 12 | 60 **c.** 20 | 140 **d.** 17 | 102

3. a.

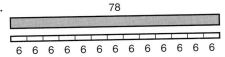

b.

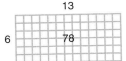

4. a. Exactly one array
b. Two or more arrays
c. One or more arrays, one of which is a square

5. a. False **b.** True **c.** False **d.** False

6. a. Prime **b.** Composite **c.** Composite

7. $1836 = 2^2 \times 3^3 \times 17$

8. 1, 3, 7, 13, 21, 39, 91, 273

9. a. True **b.** False: 2 | (5 + 7) but 2 ∤ 5 and 2 ∤ 7
c. True **d.** False: 2 | (3 × 6) but 2 ∤ 3

10. a. 1, 2, 5, 10
b. The four smallest common multiples are 60, 120, 180, and 240.
c. 1, 3, 5, 15
d. The five smallest common multiples are 260, 520, 780, 1040, and 1300.

11. a. 1 **b.** 154 **c.** 420
d. 5 **e.** 2 **f.** 390

12. a.

b. 15

13. 60 seconds
14. 428
15. 14 inches

EXERCISES AND PROBLEMS 5.1

1. $^-17°$
3. a. $^-3 + 1 = ^-2$ $^-3 < ^-2$

b. $^-14 + 17 = 3$ $3 > ^-14$
c. $^-7 + 8 = 1$ $^-7 < 1$

5.

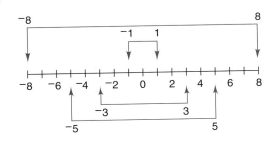

7. a. $^-7°$ **b.** $^-32$ billion dollars

9.

a.

b.

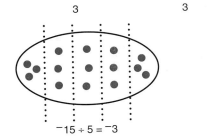

c.

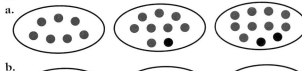

11. a.

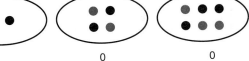

$^-15 \div 5 = ^-3$

b.

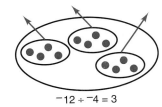

$^-12 \div ^-4 = 3$

c.

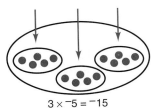

$3 \times ^-5 = ^-15$

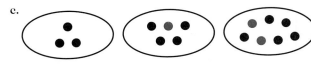

13.

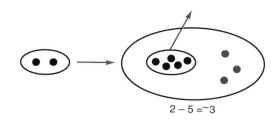

$$2 - 5 = {}^-3$$

15. a. $42°$; $^-2 \times {}^-6 = 12$
    b. $^-12°$, $^-6 \times 4 = {}^-24$

17.

  a.

$$6 + {}^-5 = 1$$

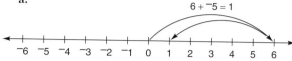

  b.

$$^-4 + 9 = 5$$

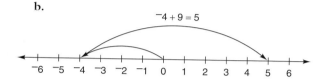

19. a. $^-322$ **b.** $^-12$
    c. $12{,}788$ **d.** 27

21. a. $^-14$ **b.** $^-4$
    c. 2 **d.** 3

23. a. Associative property for multiplication
    b. Commutative property for multiplication

25. a. Closed   **b.** Not closed

27. Other compatible numbers and substitutions are possible.
    a. Compatible numbers:
$$^-125 + 17 + {}^-25 + 13 = {}^-125 + {}^-25 + 17 + 13$$
$$= {}^-150 + 30$$
$$= {}^-120$$
    b.   Substitution:
$$700 + {}^-298 + 135 = 700 + {}^-300 + 2 + 135$$
$$= 400 + 137$$
$$= 537$$

29. Other equal products or equal quotients are possible.
    a. Divide 24 by 4 and multiply $^-25$ by 4:
$$24 \times {}^-25 = 6 \times {}^-100 = {}^-600$$
    b. Divide both numbers by 9:
$$^-90 \div 18 = {}^-10 \div 2 = {}^-5$$
    c. Multiply 5 by 2 and divide $^-28$ by 2:
$$^-28 \times 5 = {}^-14 \times 10 = {}^-140$$
    d. Divide both numbers by 4:
$$400 \div {}^-16 = 100 \div {}^-4 = {}^-25$$

31. a. 20 **b.** $^-100$

33. Other compatible number replacements are possible.
    a. $^-241 \div 60 \approx {}^-240 \div 60 = {}^-4$
    b. $64 \times {}^-11 \approx 64 \times {}^-10 = {}^-640$

35. a. Positive. There are an even number of negative numbers in the product.
    b. Negative. The product of the first three numbers is negative, and this negative number is less than $^-50$, so its sum with 50 is a negative number.

37. a. $5 \times {}^-1 = {}^-5$
       $5 \times {}^-2 = {}^-10$
       $5 \times {}^-3 = {}^-15$
    A positive number times a negative number equals a negative number.
    b. $^-1 \times 6 = {}^-6$
       $^-2 \times 6 = {}^-12$
       $^-3 \times 6 = {}^-18$
    A negative number times a positive number equals a negative number.

39. a. $^-217 - 366 = {}^-583$
    b. $^-483 + 225 = {}^-258$
    c. $2257 \div {}^-37 = {}^-61$
    d. $^-1974 \div 42 = {}^-47$

41. a. Compute $487 + 653$ and negate the answer:
$$^-487 + {}^-653 = {}^-(487 + 653) = {}^-1140$$
    b. Compute $360 + 241$:
$$360 - {}^-241 = 360 + 241 = 601$$
    c. Compute 32×14 and negate the answer:
$$32 \times {}^-14 = {}^-(32 \times 14) = {}^-448$$
    d. Compute $336 \div 16$ and negate the answer:
$$336 \div {}^-16 = {}^-(336 \div 16) = {}^-21$$

43. a. $^-17, {}^-34, {}^-51, {}^-68, {}^-85, {}^-102$
    b. $^-52{,}1352, {}^-35{,}152, 913{,}952, {}^-23{,}762{,}752$

45. Part b produces the correct answer, $^-9$, and part c produces the correct answer on some calculators.

47. a. 51 days   **b.** 17 days 17 hours   **c.** 29 hours

49. $^-8°$

51. $12 - 34 + 5 + 67 = 50$

EXERCISES AND PROBLEMS 5.2

1. a. Some possibilities: $\frac{1}{2}, \frac{1}{3}, \frac{3}{4}, \frac{1}{8}$
    b. Answers vary.

3. a. $\frac{4}{9}$ and $\frac{5}{9}$
    b. $\frac{3}{7}$ and $\frac{4}{7}$
    c. $\frac{5}{12}$ and $\frac{7}{12}$

5. a. $3 \div 2 = 1\frac{1}{2}$

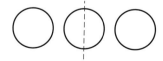

    b. $2 \div 4 = \frac{1}{2}$

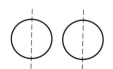

7. a. The brown rod   **b.** $\frac{5}{7}$

9. a. $\frac{1}{3} = \frac{4}{12}$ **b.** $\frac{6}{12} = \frac{1}{2}$

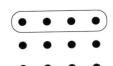

c. $\frac{2}{3} = \frac{8}{12}$ **d.** $\frac{9}{12} = \frac{3}{4}$

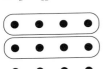

11. a. 28   **b.** 5   **c.** 25   **d.** 4

13. a. $\frac{2}{9}$ **b.** $\frac{4}{9}$ **c.** $\frac{1}{3}$ **d.** $\frac{-2}{3}$

15. a.

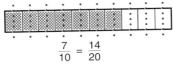

$$\frac{7}{10} = \frac{14}{20}$$

b.

$$\frac{6}{7} = \frac{18}{21}$$

17.

a.

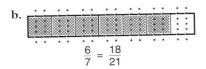

$$\frac{9}{12} = \frac{3}{4}$$

b.

$$\frac{4}{6} = \frac{2}{3}$$

19. a. $\frac{2}{3} = \frac{10}{15}$ **b.** $\frac{1}{6} = \frac{2}{12}$

     $\frac{4}{5} = \frac{12}{15}$ $\frac{-7}{12} = \frac{-7}{12}$

21. a. $\frac{3}{7} < \frac{5}{9}$ **b.** $\frac{1}{4} > \frac{1}{6}$ **c.** $\frac{-5}{6} > \frac{-7}{8}$

23. a. $\frac{3}{40}$ **b.** $\frac{9}{16}$

25. a. $1\frac{2}{3}$ **b.** 1   **c.** $4\frac{1}{6}$

27. a. $\frac{7}{4}$ **b.** $\frac{-11}{5}$ **c.** $\frac{14}{3}$

29.

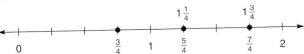

31. a. A bar with 12 equal parts has larger parts than a bar with 20 equal parts. So $\frac{1}{12} > \frac{1}{20}$.

     b. A bar with 10 equal parts has smaller parts than a bar with 8 equal parts. Thus, since $\frac{1}{10} < \frac{1}{8}$, $\frac{9}{10}$ is closer to 1 than $\frac{7}{8}$. So $\frac{7}{8} < \frac{9}{10}$.

     c. The bar for $\frac{5}{12}$ is less than half shaded, and the bar for $\frac{6}{11}$ is more than half shaded. So $\frac{5}{12} < \frac{6}{11}$.

33. a. 0   **b.** 1   **c.** 4

35. Fractions for view screens 2, 3, and 4: $\frac{30}{315}, \frac{10}{105}, \frac{2}{21}$

37. a. $2\frac{3}{4}$ **b.** $2\frac{1}{5}$

39. 67.5 seconds or 1 minute 7.5 seconds

41. $\frac{6}{16}$

43. More iron

45. $\frac{40}{1040} = \frac{1}{26}$

47. 125, since $\frac{1}{125} > \frac{1}{250}$

49. RCA, up 12.5 cents; Xerox, up 18.75 cents; Tyco Lb, down 25 cents

51. a. Less than the day's high

     b. Less than the day's low

53. $\frac{5}{13}; \frac{1}{2}; \frac{3}{8}$

EXERCISES AND PROBLEMS 5.3

1. a. 32 inches   **b.** 18 inches

3. a.

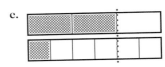

$$\frac{3}{10} + \frac{2}{5} = \frac{7}{10}$$

b.

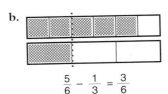

$$\frac{5}{6} - \frac{1}{3} = \frac{3}{6}$$

c.

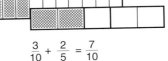

$$\frac{2}{3} \div \frac{1}{6} = 4$$

d.

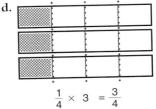

$$\frac{1}{4} \times 3 = \frac{3}{4}$$

e.

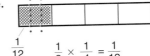

$$\frac{1}{12} \qquad \frac{1}{3} \times \frac{1}{4} = \frac{1}{12}$$

f.

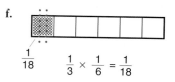

$\frac{1}{18}$ $\frac{1}{3} \times \frac{1}{6} = \frac{1}{18}$

5. a. $\frac{3}{8} \times 24 = 9$

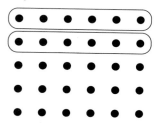

b. $\frac{2}{5} \times 30 = 12$

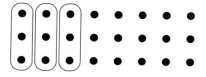

7. a.

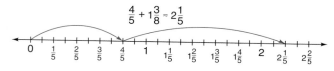

$\frac{4}{5} + 1\frac{3}{8} \approx 2\frac{1}{5}$

b.

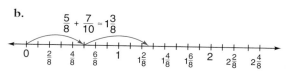

$\frac{5}{8} + \frac{7}{10} \approx 1\frac{3}{8}$

9.

a.

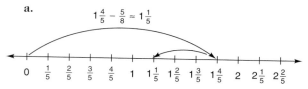

$1\frac{4}{5} - \frac{5}{8} \approx 1\frac{1}{5}$

b. $1\frac{1}{8} - \frac{7}{10} \approx \frac{3}{8}$

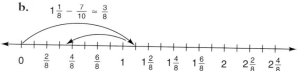

11. a. $1\frac{5}{12}$ **b.** $\frac{13}{24}$ **c.** 4

d. $\frac{-3}{10}$ **e.** $3\frac{7}{12}$ **f.** $1\frac{2}{3}$

g. $7\frac{7}{8}$ **h.** $6\frac{4}{9}$ **i.** $\frac{13}{24}$

13.

Number	$\frac{7}{8}$	$^-4$	$\frac{^-1}{2}$	10
Opposite	$\frac{^-7}{8}$	4	$\frac{1}{2}$	$^-10$
Reciprocal	$\frac{8}{7}$	$\frac{^-1}{4}$	$^-2$	$\frac{1}{10}$

15. a. Obtained common denominators by adding 5 to the numerator and denominator of $\frac{1}{3}$, and adding 4 to the numerator and denominator of $\frac{1}{4}$

b. Subtracted numerators and subtracted denominators

c. Computed 2×4 for the numerator and 1×11 for the denominator

d. Divided 11 by 3 and multiplied by 1.

17. a. Commutative property for addition

b. Inverse for multiplication

c. Associative property for addition

19. a. Closed   **b.** Not closed

21. a. $10\frac{2}{3}$ (Combine mixed numbers with equal denominators.)

b. 7 (First find the difference between the mixed numbers with a denominator of 8.)

c. $^-32$ (First compute $\frac{^-1}{3} \times 12$.)

d. 50 (Follow the order of operations by first computing $\frac{7}{4} \times 24$.)

23. Other substitutions are possible.

a. $215\frac{1}{5} - 11 + \frac{1}{5} = 215\frac{2}{5} - 11 = 204\frac{2}{5}$

b. $4 \times (10 - \frac{1}{7}) = 40 - \frac{4}{7} = 39\frac{3}{7}$

c. $86 + \frac{6}{12} + \frac{5}{12} + 10\frac{1}{2} = 97\frac{5}{12}$

25. Other methods are possible.

a. Equal differences (add $\frac{1}{7}$ to both numbers):

$$8 - 3\frac{6}{7} = 8\frac{1}{7} - 4 = 4\frac{1}{7}$$

b. Adding up:

$$10\frac{9}{10} \xrightarrow{\frac{1}{10}} 11 \xrightarrow{4\frac{3}{10}} 15\frac{3}{10}$$

so $15\frac{3}{10} - 10\frac{9}{10} = 4\frac{4}{10}$

c. Equal quotients (multiply both numbers by 3):

$$\frac{5}{8} \div \frac{1}{3} = 3(\frac{5}{8}) \div 3(\frac{1}{3}) = \frac{15}{8} \div 1 = 1\frac{7}{8}$$

27. a. 9   **b.** 14

29. a. $4\frac{1}{3} \times 6\frac{1}{2} \approx 4 \times 6 + \frac{1}{3} \times 6 + \frac{1}{2} \times 4$
$= 24 + 2 + 2$
$= 28$

b. $5\frac{1}{4} \times 8\frac{2}{5} \approx 5 \times 8 + \frac{1}{4} \times 8 + \frac{2}{5} \times 5$
$= 40 + 2 + 2$
$= 44$

31. a. $\frac{6}{7} \times 34 \approx \frac{6}{7} \times 35$

$\qquad = \frac{6}{7} \times \cancel{35}^{5}$

$\qquad = 30$

b. $9\frac{4}{5} + 5\frac{1}{6} \approx 9\frac{4}{5} + 5\frac{1}{5}$

$\qquad = 15$

33. $\frac{23}{30}$

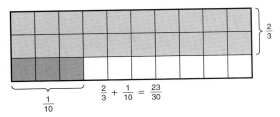

$$\frac{2}{3} + \frac{1}{10} = \frac{23}{30}$$

$\frac{1}{10}$

35. 8 million pounds

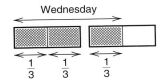

$$\frac{1}{6} \times 48 = 8$$

37. $\frac{1}{2}$ inch. Divide $1\frac{1}{2}$ inches into 3 equal parts:

Wednesday

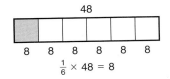

$\frac{1}{3} \quad \frac{1}{3} \quad \frac{1}{3}$

39. a. $1\frac{1}{28}$ **b.** $\frac{5}{24}$

    c. $\frac{2}{7}$ **d.** $\frac{20}{21}$

41. Carl's sequence of steps will not produce the correct answer because $80 \div \frac{3}{5} \neq (80 \div 3) \div 5$. Carl's calculator follows the rules for order of operations, first dividing 80 by 3 and then dividing the result by 5.

43. 1. $7333.33
     2. $2400.00
     3. $9733.33
     6. $688.00
     7. $2752.00
     8. $5070.00

45. a. Drew National, $1\frac{1}{4}$; MEM company, $\frac{5}{8}$; Old Town, $1\frac{3}{8}$
     b. $625

47. a. D, E, A, B
     b. The pairs of notes that are separated by black keys correspond to the pairs of strings in part a in which one string is $\frac{8}{9}$ times the length of the other.

49. 24 students

51. 160 disks

53. Conjecture: This holds for all pairs of fractions except those that are equal.

CHAPTER 5 TEST

1.

a.

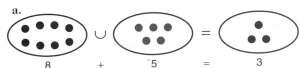

8   +   ⁻5   =   3

b.   **c.**

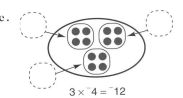

$^{-}7 - {}^{-}3 = {}^{-}4$ $3 \times {}^{-}4 = {}^{-}12$

d.   **e.**

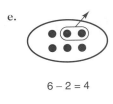

$^{-}20 \div {}^{-}4 = 5$ $6 - 2 = 4$

f.

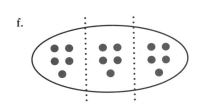

$^{-}15 \div 3 = {}^{-}5$

2.

a.

$^{-}8 + 3 = {}^{-}5$

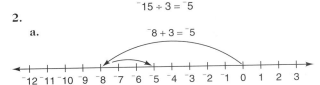

b.

$^{-}8 + {}^{-}6 = {}^{-}14$

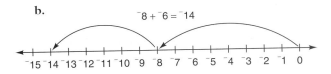

3. a. 42   **b.** ⁻6   **c.** ⁻80   **d.** 5

4. a. $^{-}16 \times 25 = {}^{-}16 \times \frac{1}{4} \times 4 \times 25 = {}^{-}4 \times 100 = {}^{-}400$
     b. $800 \div {}^{-}16 = 200 \div {}^{-}4 = 100 \div {}^{-}2 = {}^{-}50$

5. a. $^{-}271 \div 30 \approx {}^{-}270 \div 30 = {}^{-}9$
     b. $\frac{1}{8} \times 55 \approx \frac{1}{8} \times 56 = 7$
     c. $4 \times 6\frac{1}{5} \approx 4 \times (6 + \frac{1}{4}) = 24 + 1 = 25$
     d. $11 \times {}^{-}34 \approx 10 \times {}^{-}35 = {}^{-}350$

6. a. $6 \div 4 = 1\frac{1}{2}$

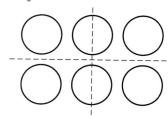

b. $\frac{1}{3} \times 15 = 5$

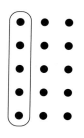

c. $\frac{2}{3} \times \frac{1}{5} = \frac{2}{15}$

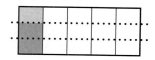

d. $\frac{3}{4} = \frac{6}{8}$

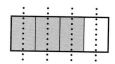

7. a. $\dfrac{3}{14} = \dfrac{24}{112}$ **b.** $\dfrac{1}{24} = \dfrac{1}{24}$

$\dfrac{5}{16} = \dfrac{35}{112}$ $\dfrac{^-7}{8} = \dfrac{^-21}{24}$

8. a. $\frac{6}{11} < \frac{5}{9}$ **b.** $\frac{3}{5} > \frac{6}{11}$ **c.** $\frac{^-4}{9} < \frac{^-3}{7}$

9. a. $\frac{1}{8} > \frac{1}{10}$. For two figures of the same size, 1 out of 10 equal parts is less than 1 out of 8 equal parts.

b. $\frac{4}{7} > \frac{5}{12}$, $\frac{4}{7}$ is greater than $\frac{1}{2}$, $\frac{5}{12}$ is less than $\frac{1}{2}$.

c. $\frac{1}{2} < \frac{7}{12}$, $\frac{7}{12}$ is greater than $\frac{6}{12} = \frac{1}{2}$.

d. $\frac{5}{6} < \frac{7}{8}$. A whole with $\frac{1}{8}$ missing is greater than a whole with $\frac{1}{6}$ missing.

10. a. $6\frac{1}{2}$ **b.** $4\frac{7}{15}$ **c.** $8\frac{7}{24}$ **d.** $5\frac{11}{30}$

11. a. $14\frac{1}{4}$ **b.** $4\frac{12}{85}$ **c.** $^-9\frac{1}{3}$ **d.** 4

12. a. Inverse for multiplication
   b. Distributive property
   c. Commutative property for multiplication
   d. Inverse for addition

13. a. False   **b.** True   **c.** True
   d. False   **e.** False
14. a. 210 inches or 17.5 feet   **b.** $1\frac{3}{5}$ inches
15. $3\frac{1}{3}$ hours

EXERCISES AND PROBLEMS 6.1

1. a. .001   **b.** .000001
3. a. 7 ⓪ 4 ① 6
   b. The 0 was placed between the digits where we now place the decimal point. A small zero could have suggested a point.
5. a. $\frac{7}{100}$ **b.** $\frac{6}{10,000}$
   c. $\frac{3}{1000}$ **d.** $\frac{9}{10}$
7. a. .33 Thirty-three hundredths
   b. .0392 Three hundred ninety-two ten-thousandths
   c. .054 Fifty-four thousandths
   d. 748.1 Seven hundred forty-eight and one-tenth
9. a. Three hundred forty-seven and ninety-six hundredths dollars
   b. Twenty-three and fifty hundredths dollars
   c. One thousand one hundred forty-four and three hundredths dollars
11. A, .65 B, 1.55 C, 2.3

13. a. .40; a square with 100 equal parts, 40 of which are shaded
   b. .470; a square with 1000 equal parts, 470 of which are shaded
15. a. 7 parts out of 10 is equal to 70 parts out of 100. Both decimals are represented by seven shaded columns.
   b. 43 parts out of 100 is equal to 430 parts out of 1000.
   c. 45 parts out of 100 is less than five full columns and 6 parts out of 10 is six full columns.
17. a. 247   **b.** 2.47
19. a. Divide a Decimal Square for hundredths into four equal parts, and shade one of these parts.

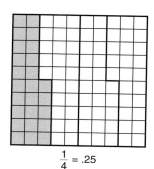

$\frac{1}{4} = .25$

b. Divide a Decimal Square for tenths into five equal parts, and shade one of these parts.

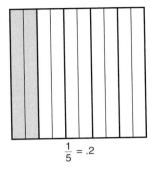

$$\frac{1}{5} = .2$$

21. a. .375   **b.** $.\overline{18}$

    c. $.3\overline{48}$ **d.** 3.75

23. $\frac{1}{3} = .\overline{3}$ $.25 = \frac{1}{4}$

    $\frac{5}{6} = .8\overline{3}$ $.41\overline{6} = \frac{5}{12}$

    $.875 = \frac{7}{8}$ $.0\overline{6} = \frac{1}{15}$

    $\frac{3}{10} = .3$ $\frac{34}{99} = .\overline{34}$

25. The fractions in a and b have repeating decimals. The fraction in c has a terminating decimal.

27. a. Dividing 100 small squares by 3 produces 3 equal groups of 33 small squares each, with 1 small square remaining. Thus the decimal for $\frac{1}{3}$ begins with .33; and since 1 (the number of remaining squares) is less than half of the divisor 3, the decimal for $\frac{1}{3}$ to two decimal places is .33.

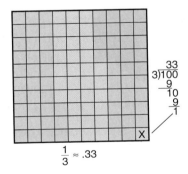

$$\frac{1}{3} \approx .33$$

b. Dividing 100 small squares by 9 produces 9 equal groups of 11 small squares each, with 1 small square remaining. Thus the decimal for $\frac{1}{9}$ begins with .11; and since 1 (the number of remaining squares) is less than half of the divisor 9, the decimal for $\frac{1}{9}$ to two decimal places is .11.

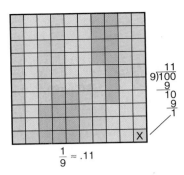

$$\frac{1}{9} \approx .11$$

c. Dividing 100 small squares by 8 produces 8 equal groups of 12 small squares each, with 4 small squares remaining. Thus the decimal for $\frac{1}{8}$ begins with .12, and since 4 (the number of remaining squares) is equal to one-half of the divisor 8, the decimal for $\frac{1}{8}$ to three decimal places is .125, or rounded to two decimal places is .13.

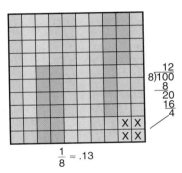

$$\frac{1}{8} \approx .13$$

29. a. .004, or .005 if rounded to the leading nonzero digit

    b. .4, which gives the same result if we round to the leading nonzero digit

    c. .07, which gives the same result if we round to the leading nonzero digit

    d. .002, or .003 if rounded to the leading nonzero digit

31. $\frac{19}{34}, \frac{11}{17}, \frac{38}{52}, \frac{16}{20}, \frac{21}{25}$

33. a. .0625   **b.** .0938

    c. .1094   **d.** .5469

35. a. .37   **b.** .1

    c. 14.372   **d.** .3

37. a. .07 is the smallest. Its Decimal Square has 7 parts shaded out of 100. The Decimal Square for .075 has 75 parts shaded out of 1000 or $7\frac{1}{2}$ parts shaded out of 100; the Decimal Square for .08 has 8 parts shaded out of 100; and the Decimal Square for .3 has 3 parts shaded out of 10, or 30 parts shaded out of 100. 1.003 is represented by 1 whole shaded square and 3 parts shaded out of 1000.

    b. Students may have believed that the more decimal places there are, the smaller the decimal.

39. $.05 = \frac{1}{20}$ $\frac{2}{3} = .\overline{6}$

    $.125 = \frac{1}{8}$ $.4 = \frac{2}{5}$

$.58\overline{3} = \frac{7}{12}$ $\frac{7}{18} = .3\overline{8}$

$.\overline{532} = \frac{532}{999}$ $.2\overline{6} = \frac{4}{15}$

41. a. 579   **b.** 207

43. a. 17.3, 16.3, 15.9, 28.1, 22.6
  b. Knees   **c.** .85

45. a. $\frac{1}{8}$ **b.** No. Her largest drill size is .25.
  c. $\frac{1}{16}$

47. a. 6.92 feet
  b. 6.79 feet

49. The pattern continues to hold for $\frac{4}{9}, \frac{5}{9}, \frac{6}{9}, \frac{7}{9}, \frac{8}{9}$, and $\frac{9}{9}$.
Note that $\frac{9}{9} = .9999\cdots$, which also equals 1. If we
try to continue the pattern, it requires that

$$\frac{10}{9} = .101010\cdots$$

which is not true. However, there is a pattern that
continues:

$$\frac{10}{9} = 1.1111\cdots$$

$$\frac{11}{9} = 1.2222\cdots$$

$$\vdots$$

EXERCISES AND PROBLEMS 6.2

1. a. $^-11.9°C$ **b.** $4.4°C$ ($^-11.9 - {}^-16.3$)

3. a. 3 parts out of 10 has the same amount of shading
  as 30 parts out of 100. So 3 parts out of 10 plus 45
  parts out of 100 equals 75 parts out of 100.

  b. 2 parts out of 10 has the same amount of shading
  as 200 parts out of 1000. So 350 parts out of 1000
  minus 200 parts out of 1000 equals 150 parts out
  of 1000, or 15 parts out of 100.

  c. Using 3 Decimal Squares for .65, the total shaded
  amount has 195 parts. Since 1 whole square has
  100 parts, this amount equals 1 whole square and
  95 parts out of 100.

  d. The Decimal Square for .37 has 37 shaded parts.
  Ten of these squares have 370 shaded parts, which
  is 3 whole squares and 70 parts out of 100 and
  equals 3 whole squares and 7 parts out of 10.

5. a.

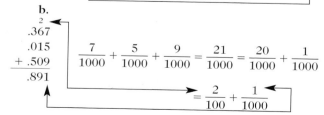

b.

7. a.

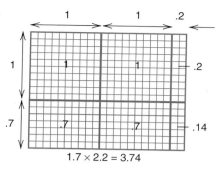

$1.7 \times 2.2 = 3.74$

b.

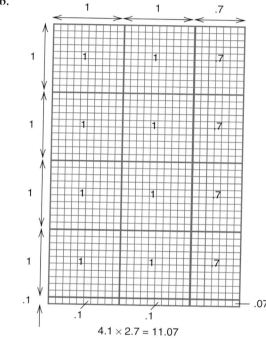

$4.1 \times 2.7 = 11.07$

9. a. 24.96; multiply 32 times 78 and count off two
  decimal places.
  b. 6.43; divide 141.46 by 22.

11. a. .076; move the decimal point two places to the left
  b. .034; move the decimal point three places to
  the left
  c. .0003; move the decimal point two places to
  the left
  d. .004; move the decimal point one place to the left

13. a. $\frac{5}{9}$ **b.** $\frac{14}{99}$ **c.** $\frac{14}{90}$

15. Other answers are possible.
  a. .65   **b.** .0055

17. a. Add 6 thousandths to both numbers to obtain
  $.343 - .300$, and then subtract .300 to obtain .043.
  b. Compute $4.2 + .8 = 5.0$ and then add .1 to
  obtain 5.1.
  c. Compute $2.6 \times 100 = 260$ and add 2.6 to
  obtain 262.6.

   d. Divide both numbers by 3 to obtain $4.3 \div 100$, which equals $.043$.

19. a. $.25 \times 48 = \frac{1}{4} \times 48 = 12$
   b. $.5 \times 40.8 = \frac{1}{2} \times 40.8 = 20.4$
   c. $5.5 \times .2 = 5.5 \times \frac{1}{5} = 1.1$

21. a. Front-end estimation: \$90; rounding to leading digit: \$110
   b. Front-end estimation: \$300; rounding to leading digit: \$400

23. a. $3.1 \times 4.9 \approx 3 \times 5 = 15$

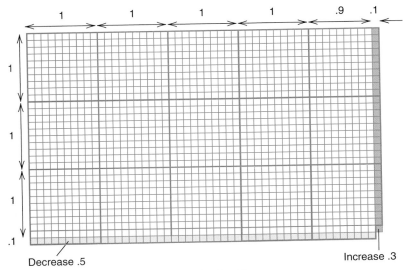

$3.1 \times 4.9 \approx 3 \times 5 = 15$

This estimation is less than the actual product because the decrease due to rounding 3.1 to 3 is greater than the increase due to rounding 4.9 to 5.

b. $5.3 \times 1.6 \approx 5 \times 2 = 10$

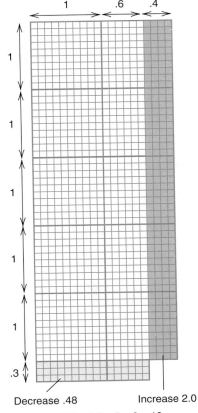

$5.3 \times 1.6 \approx 5 \times 2 = 10$

This estimation is greater than the actual product since the increase due to rounding 1.6 to 2 is greater than the decrease due to rounding 5.3 to 5.

25. a. $8 \div .5 = 16$ **b.** $11.60 + .4 = 12$
   c. $\frac{1}{3} \times 120 = 40$ **d.** $\frac{1}{4} \times 80 = 20$

27. a. 78 percent
   b. By ignoring the decimal points and estimating $304 \times 5 \approx 1600$.

29. a. The 2 should have been written in the tenths column and the 1 in the ones column.
   b. The 6 in the hundredths column was not subtracted (possibly 0 was subtracted from 6). This error caused a subsequent error in the tenths column.
   c. The decimal point in the product was placed under the decimal point in the two given numbers. Perhaps one decimal place was counted off rather than two.
   d. The remainder of 2 was recorded in the quotient.

31. a. Add $.0007$.
   b. Subtract 70.0006.
   c. Subtract $.503$.

33. a. $.41667$ **b.** 2.08333 **c.** 217.39130

35. a. View screen 4; 35.9936; view screen 5; ⁻57.58976
b. View screen 4; 440.2; view screen 5; 423.9
37. a. Geometric with common ratio 1.8; 44.08992
b. Arithmetic with common difference .7; 13.5
39. $4677.98
41. a. $12.66   **b.** $3.76
43. a. 1991   **b.** 1992–1998, 15.0%
c. 1998, coal and petroleum increased
45. a. $1.02   **b.** $27.72   **c.** $39.26
47. a. 6.04 seconds   **b.** 3.33 seconds
49. a. .5 cent   **b.** $325
c. $3250   **d.** $2925

EXERCISES AND PROBLEMS 6.3

1. a. $\frac{4}{5}$ **b.** 2,250,000
3. a. 111   **b.** 150
5. $7.28   **b.** $6.65   **c.** $1.40
7. a. .375; a Decimal Square having $37\frac{1}{2}$ shaded parts out of 100.
b. .065; a Decimal Square having $6\frac{1}{2}$ shaded parts out of 100
c. .283; a Decimal Square having $28\frac{1}{3}$ shaded parts out of 100
9. a. 60 percent (60 parts shaded out of 100)
b. 6 percent (6 parts shaded out of 100)
c. 25.6 percent (25 and 6 tenths parts shaded out of 100, or 256 parts shaded out of 1000)
11. a. 80 percent   **b.** 83.3 percent   **c.** 175 percent
13. a. Since one small square represents 1.6, 27 small squares represent 27 × 1.6 = 43.2. So 27 percent of 160 is 43.2.

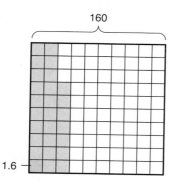

160

1.6

b. Since each small square represents 2, it will require 20 small squares to represent 40. So 40 is 20 percent of 200.

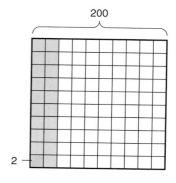

200

2

c. 40   **d.** 91   **e.** 150 percent
15. a. To determine 10 percent of $128.50, move the decimal point one place to the left to obtain $12.85.
b. 75 percent of 32 is $\frac{3}{4} \times 32 = 24$.
c. 10 percent of $60 is $6, so 90 percent of $60 is $54.
d. 10 percent of 80 is 8, so 110 percent of 80 is 88.
17. a. 9 percent of $30.75 ≈ 10 percent of $30.75 = $3.075 ≈ $3.08
b. 19 percent of 60 ≈ $\frac{1}{5} \times 60 = 12$
c. 4.9 percent of 128 ≈ $\frac{1}{2} \times 10$ percent of 128 = $\frac{1}{2}$ of 12.8 = 6.4
d. 15 percent of 241 ≈ 10 percent of 240 + 5 percent of 240 = 24 + 12 = 36
19. a. $\frac{2}{19} \approx \frac{2}{20} = 10$ percent
b. $\frac{408}{1210} \approx \frac{400}{1200} = 33\frac{1}{3}$ percent
c. $\frac{100}{982} \approx \frac{100}{1000} = 10$ percent
21. a. 4.6×10^9 **b.** 2.7×10^{-8}
23. a. .0000000012   **b.** 31,556,900
25. a. 1.58436×10^{18} miles   **b.** 1.49×10^3 seconds
27. a. 51   **b.** 71
29. a. Maine, 13.4; Missouri, 15.1; Oregon, 19.6; Wyoming, 14.3
b. Maine
c. Oregon
31. a. $59.97   **b.** 20 percent
c. $34,400   **d.** 78.6 percent
33. a. Approximately 5.9 cents per ounce
b. The large box
c. Approximately 77 pancakes
35. The identity property for multiplication in the first equation and the distributive property for multiplication over addition in the second equation.
a. $178.08
b. $123.16
c. $61.92
37. a. $21.80   **b.** $118.08
c. 8 years   **d.** $32,992.31
39. a. $13.70
b. $28.77
c. 1276.28 pounds

41.

Mercury	36,002,000	.4 unit
Venus	6.7273×10^7	.7 unit
Earth	93,003,000	1.0 unit
Mars	1.41709×10^8	1.5 units
Jupiter	483,881,000	5.2 units
Saturn	8.87151×10^8	9.5 units
Uranus	1,784,838,000	19.2 units
Neptune	2.796693×10^9	30.1 units
Pluto	3,669,669,000	39.5 units

43. 0, 3, 6, 12, 24, 48, 96
.4, .7, 1.0, 1.6, 2.8, 5.2, 10.0
 a. 2.8 astronomical units
 b. 19.6 astronomical units

EXERCISES AND PROBLEMS 6.4

1. The numbers in b and d are irrational.
3. a. $\sqrt{33} \approx 5.7$ **b.** $\sqrt{113} \approx 10.6$
5. a. $\frac{1}{4}$ **b.** 4   **c.** 3.1   **d.** $^-5$
7. a. Irrational, 4.2
 b. Rational, 6
 c. Rational, $\frac{1}{3}$
9. a. $\sqrt{7} \approx 2.6$
 b. $\sqrt[3]{30} \approx 3.1$
 c. $\sqrt{3} \approx 1.7$

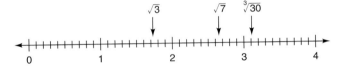

11. a. $a = 4, b = 3, c = 5$
 b. $a = 12, b = 5, c = 13$
 c. $a = 60, b = 11, c = 61$

13.

	WHOLE NUMBERS	INTEGERS	RATIONAL NUMBERS	REAL NUMBERS
$^-3$		✓	✓	✓
$\frac{1}{8}$			✓	✓
$\sqrt{3}$				✓
π				✓
14	✓	✓	✓	✓
$\frac{1.6}{4}$			✓	✓
$.\overline{82}$			✓	✓

15. a. Not closed, $2 - 5$ is not a whole number
 b. Closed
17. a. Commutative property for multiplication
 b. Distributive property
 c. Commutative property for addition
19. a. Irrational   **b.** Irrational   **c.** Rational, 12
21. a. $3\sqrt{5}$ **b.** $4\sqrt{3}$ **c.** $2\sqrt{15}$

23. a. True
 b. False
   $\sqrt{9} - \sqrt{4} = 3 - 2 = 1 \neq \sqrt{9-4} = \sqrt{5} \approx 2.2$
25. a. $\frac{4\sqrt{7}}{7}$ **b.** $\frac{\sqrt{6}}{4}$
27. If the calculator has eight places for digits, 1.0905077 is displayed in step 4. Eventually the number in the view screen will be 1.
29. 1
31. a. $\sqrt[4]{81} = 3$ **b.** $\sqrt{2.25} = 1.5$
   c. $\sqrt{3.0625} = 1.75$ **d.** $\sqrt[3]{-2.197} = ^-1.3$
33. 217 steps
35. 13 feet
37. 17.0×17.0 inches
39. a. 1.5 hours
 b. In this position the satellite takes approximately 24 hours to make 1 orbit of the earth. Therefore, the satellite stays in the same position relative to the earth.
41. a. Here are the first eight ratios for consecutive pairs of Fibonacci numbers: 1, 2, 1.5, $1.\overline{6}$, 1.6, 1.625, 1.6153846, 1.6190476, 1.6176471
 b. $233 \div 144 \approx 1.6180556$

CHAPTER 6 TEST

1. a. The Decimal Square for .4 has four full columns shaded, but the Decimal Square for .27 has less than three full columns shaded.
 b. The Decimal Square with 7 parts shaded out of 10 has the same amount of shading as the Decimal Square with 70 parts shaded out of 100.
 c. The Decimal Square for .225 has less than three full columns shaded, but the Decimal Square for .35 has more than three full columns shaded.
 d. The Decimal Square for .09 has less than one full column shaded, but that for .1 has one full column shaded.
2. a. .75   **b.** .07   **c.** $.\overline{6}$
   d. .875   **e.** $.\overline{4}$ **f.** .24
3. a. $\frac{278}{1000}$ **b.** $\frac{35}{99}$ **c.** $\frac{3}{100}$ **d.** $\frac{7319}{9990}$
4. a. .88   **b.** .4   **c.** .510   **d.** .6667
5. a. 1.3: The total amount of shading in 2 squares, one with 6 columns shaded out of 10 and one with 7 columns shaded out of 10, is 13 shaded columns, or 1 completely shaded square and 3 shaded columns.
 b. 1.2: The total amount of shading in 3 squares, each with 4 columns shaded out of 10, is 12 shaded columns, or 1 completely shaded square and 2 shaded columns.
 c. .14: If a square has 62 parts shaded out of 100 and 48 of the shaded parts are taken away, then 14 shaded parts out of 100 remain.

d. 16: If a square has 80 parts shaded out of 100 and 5 of the 80 shaded parts are removed at a time, the process can be done 16 times, or the 80 shaded parts can be divided into 16 groups, each containing 5 shaded parts.

6. a. .186   **b.** .0496   **c.** .703   **d.** 319

7. a. Move the decimal point in .073 a total of two places to the right to obtain 7.3.
  b. Compute $7 \times 6 = 42$ and count off one decimal place to obtain 4.2.
  c. Move the decimal point in 4.9 a total of three places to the left to obtain .0049.
  d. Move the decimal point in 372 a total of two places to the left to obtain 3.72.
  e. 10 percent of 260 is 26, and one-half of this is 13. So 15 percent of 260 is $26 + 13 = 39$.
  f. 25 percent of 36 is $\frac{1}{4} \times 36 = 9$.

8. a. $\frac{1}{2} \times 310 = 155$ **b.** $\frac{1}{4} \times 416 = 104$
  c. $\frac{1}{3} \times 60 = 20$ **d.** $\frac{3}{4} \times 40 = 30$

9. a. 16.6   **b.** 37.5 percent   **c.** 62.5
  d. 147.5   **e.** 140 percent

10. a. 4.378×10^2 **b.** 1.06×10^{-4}

11. a. Irrational   **b.** Rational   **c.** Irrational
  d. Irrational   **e.** Rational   **f.** Irrational

12. a. 5.8   **b.** 2.6

13. a. Closed by the closure property for rational numbers
  b. Not closed ($\sqrt{2} \times \sqrt{8} = 4$)
  c. Not closed ($^-\sqrt{3} + \sqrt{3} = 0$)

14. a. $9\sqrt{5}$ **b.** $2\sqrt{6}$

15. a. $2\sqrt{13}$ **b.** $\sqrt{319}$

16. $220

17. 16-ounce glass

18. 67.1 feet

19. $7.20

20. 15,664 students

EXERCISES AND PROBLEMS 7.1

1. a. 2.5   **b.** 200,000

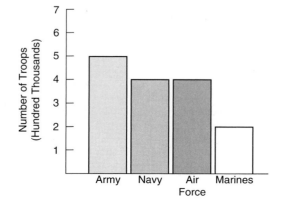

Persons on Active Duty

3. a. 1989, 11 percent
  b. The prime rate increased 1 percent in 1988, 2% in 1989, 1 percent in 1994, and 2 percent in 1995.

5. a.

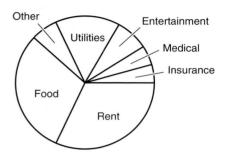

Family's Monthly Budget

b. Rent, 115°; food, 108°; utilities, 54°; insurance, 14°; medical, 18°; entertainment, 29°; other, 22°

7. a. Kansas City
  b. Kansas City, 40 inches; Portland, 38 inches

9. a. Bicycle riding, camping, bowling, fishing, basketball, golf
  b. Golf   **c.** Exercise walking

11. a. 18–19 years old
  b. 35 percent
  c. 18 to 19, 20 to 24, 25 to 29, 30 to 34

13. a.

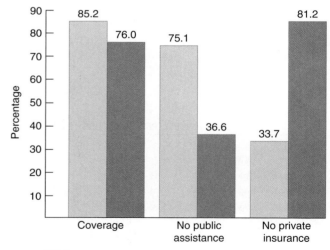

Health care coverage for children under 18

b. 38.5 percent

15. a. 2 percent   **b.** 9.5

17. a.

Percentage of schools of various sizes

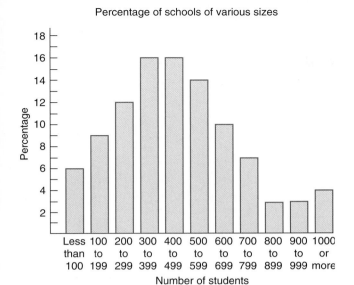

b. 43 percent

19. a.

Number of people involved in auto crashes

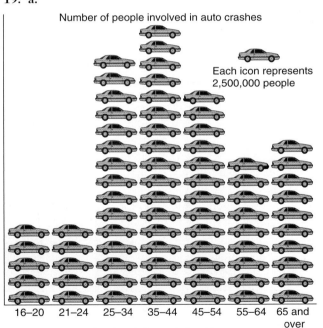

Each icon represents 2,500,000 people

Age level of people in years

b. Fewer people had crashes in these two age groups than in the third age group.

21. a.

1999–2000 salaries of classroom teachers by states

Salaries in thousands of dollars

b. $35,000
c. 66.7 percent

23. a.

STEM	LEAF
9	0, 0
8	3, 5, 0, 8, 1
7	3, 8, 9, 1, 4, 7, 0, 1, 2, 8
6	7, 8, 5, 4, 6, 3, 7, 0, 7, 0, 3, 4
5	3, 6, 7, 8, 7
4	9, 6

b. 19.4 percent   **c.** 19.4 percent

25. a.

STEM	LEAF
27	7
26	
25	1, 3, 0
24	6, 6, 6, 2
23	8, 4, 1, 2, 0, 0
22	3, 5, 7, 0, 1, 0
21	8, 6, 5, 6, 0, 4, 2, 2
20	2, 5, 3, 1, 6, 4, 0, 8, 1, 6
19	3, 7, 0, 9, 7, 8, 1
18	2, 2, 1, 6
17	0, 2, 3
16	6

b. 20   **c.** 27.7 and 16.6 kilograms

27. a.

INTERVAL	FREQUENCY
0–15	1
16–30	14
31–45	8
46–60	7
61–75	3
76–90	2
91–105	2
106–120	1

b.

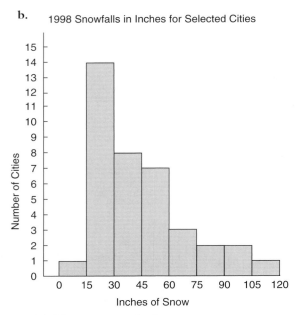

1998 Snowfalls in Inches for Selected Cities

c. 16–30   **d.** 8

29. a. Decreasing
  b. 8000
  c. 1990
  d. 1990 to 1992; 25,000

31. a. Between 7 and 8 percent in 1993 and 1998
  b. Between 12 and 13 percent
  c. Approximately 14 percent
  d. Approximately 1% between 1980 and 1981.

33. a.

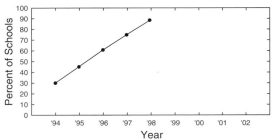

Percents of Elementary Schools with Internet Access

b. 1994 to 1996

35. a.

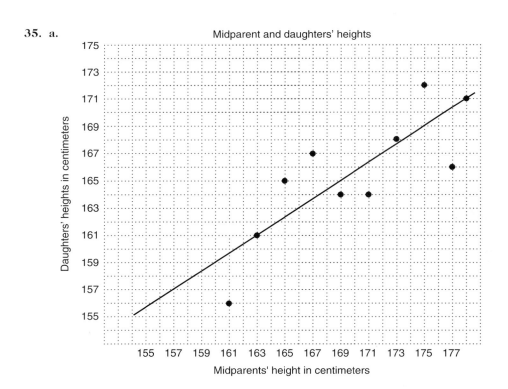

Midparent and daughters' heights

b. Between 158 and 160 centimeters; between 167 and 169 centimeters

c. Between 165 and 167 centimeters; between 175 and 177 centimeters

37. a. 10.7 percent

b. 2 percent

c. Positive

d. Between 20 and 22 percent

39. a. Greatest diameter is 8 inches and oldest age is 42 years.

b. Positive

c. Approximately 5.3 and 6.5 inches

d. Approximately 46 years old

41. a.

Amounts Invested in Advertisements and Corresponding Sales

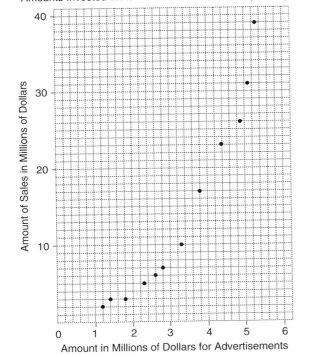

b. Exponential curve

c. Between $12 and $14 million

d. Between $4.0 and $4.5 million

EXERCISES AND PROBLEMS 7.2

1. a. Mean, $4.\overline{6}$; median, 4.5; mode, 4

b. Mean 1.5; median, 1; mode, 0

3. a. Mode   **b.** Mode   **c.** Median

5. a. United States, 977.4; France, 1083.5; Japan, 853.7; Great Britain, 436.3

b. Great Britain

7. a. Mean, 45.9; median, 41.5; modes, 37 and 40

b. Mean, 45.65; median, 45; mode 40

c. 13

d. The home run leaders for the two leagues have about the same records. The means are approximately equal while the median for the American League is higher. The American League's home run leaders hit more home runs in 11 years, and the National League's home run leaders hit more home runs in 7 years. The American League might be considered to have a slightly stronger record.

9. a. 65   **b.** 10

c. 30   **d.** 16

11.

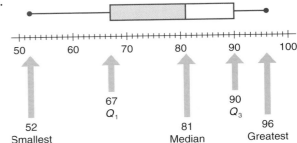

a. 44

b. Approximately 25 percent of the data are greater than or equal to 90, and the middle 50 percent are approximately between 67 and 90.

13. a.

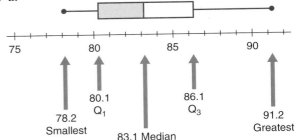

b. The median of 83.1 indicates that approximately half of these states have less than 83 percent of their students completing high school.

c. The upper quartile of 86.1 indicates that approximately 25 percent of these states have more than 86% of their students completing high school.

d. The lower quartile of 80.1 indicates that approximately 25 percent of these states have less than 80.1 percent of their students completing high school.

15. a. Tracer　　**b.** Civic and Golf　　**c.** Justy

d. Golf. It has the greatest lower quartile and the greatest median, and its ratings have less variability than those of the Civic, which has the second-best set of ratings.

17. a. CBS has the best rating. It has the greatest upper quartile, and most of the upper 25 percent of its ratings are above the highest rating received by NBC. ABC has the poorest ratings. It has the smallest lower and upper quartiles.

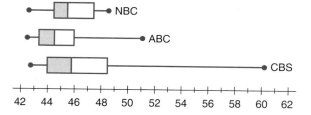

b. The interquartile range for CBS is 4.45, and since 60.2 is greater than 48.5 + (1.5)(4.45) = 55.175, the maximum data value for CBS is an outlier, and indicates an exceptional rating. The maximum data value for ABC is barely an outlier.

19. a. The data for set *B* are less spread out and should have the smaller standard deviation.

b. Standard deviation for set *A* is 4, and standard deviation for set *B* is 2.

c. Yes, the standard deviation for set *A* is twice the standard deviation for set *B*.

21. a. 3.6 percent　　**b.** 5.4 percent

23. a. South: lower quartile, 3.9; median, 4.7; upper quartile, 4.9. West: lower quartile, 4.35; median, 5.1; upper quartile, 5.8

b.

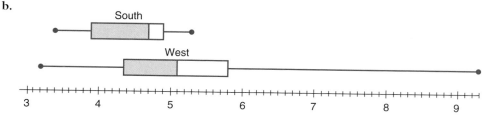

The two quartiles and medians for the south are lower. The upper quartile for the west is greater than the maximum data value for the south.

c. The upper quartile for the south is less than the median for the west. So 75 percent of the states in the south spent less per student than the median amount spent per student by the states in the west.

d. The west has the greater interquartile range, and thus there is greater variability in the amounts of money spent per student by its states.

25. a. West: lower quartile, 16; median, 19; upper quartile, 21. Midwest: lower quartile, 19.5; median, 23; upper quartile, 24

b.

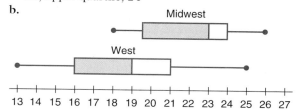

c. The midwest has the higher quartiles and median, which means it has higher percentages of students not finishing high school. Of the states from the west, 50 percent have percentages that are below the lower quartile of the states from the midwest.

d. There are no outliers.

27. a.

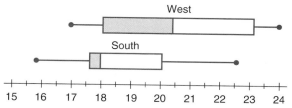

b. West: 5.1; south: 2.4. The smaller interquartile range for the south shows its incomes are less variable.

c. The upper 50 percent of the average incomes for the west are above the upper quartile for the average incomes of the south and the lower 50 percent for the south are below the lower quartile of the west.

d. The lower quartile for the west

e. See part c. In general, the average incomes for the south are significantly lower than the average incomes for the west.

29. a.

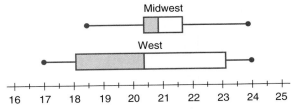

b. Approximately 4

c. The lower 25 percent of the average incomes for the west are below the lowest income for the midwest.

d. The lower quartile for the midwest is equal to the median for the west. Also, the midwest has much less variability in income. However, the top 25 percent of the average incomes for the west are generally greater than the top 25 percent of the average incomes for the midwest.

31. 13 grams

33. 69

35. a. 5.8 grams   **b.** .46 gram   **c.** 60 percent

37. At least 75 percent of Peter's arrow strikes are within 26 inches of the center of the target, and at least 75 percent of Sally's arrow strikes are within 24 inches of the center of the target.

EXERCISES AND PROBLEMS 7.3

1. a. 8908 and 9042   **b.** 8841 and 9109

3. a. Number the names from 1 to 9. Randomly select a number from the table, and continue in the table until you obtain two different numbers less than or equal to 9.

b. Number the questions from 1 to 60. Randomly select a number from the table, and continue in the table until you obtain 10 different numbers less than or equal to 60.

5. Grade K, 10; grade 1, 16; grade 2, 18; grade 3, 16; grade 4, 20

7. a. Skewed right   **b.** Skewed left

9. a. Skewed left

b. Symmetric

c. Skewed left

11. a. 68 percent   **b.** 16 percent   **c.** 2.5 percent

13. a. 1   **b.** 7   **c.** 7

15. a. A normal distribution

b.

DIAMETER (INCHES)	NO. OF TREES
7	2
8	5
9	8
10	10
11	13
12	26
13	12
14	9
15	8
16	4
17	3

c. 70 percent

17.

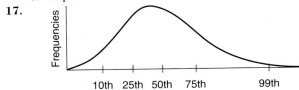

a. 30 percent   **b.** 10 percent

19. a. 54 percent   **b.** 68 percent   **c.** 96 percent

d. The score for mathematics comprehension

e. A lower local percentile means that at the local level fewer students scored below the given student on a given subtest than at the national level.

21. a. 86 percent   **b.** 78 percent

c. 90 percent   **d.** 80 percent

23. a. 5

b. 69th percentile is stanine 6; 62nd percentile is stanine 6; 83rd percentile is stanine 7; 45th percentile is stanine 5

25. Test A, $z \approx {}^{-}.14$ and test B, $z \approx {}^{-}.53$. So A is the better test.

27. Each number from 1 to 6 represents that outcome on the roll of a die. The numbers 0, 7, 8, and 9 are disregarded. The first few random numbers from the table are listed here, and the circled numbers represent the outcomes for 10 rolls of a die.

⑥ ① ④ ④ ③ ④ 0 ③ 0 9 0 ⑤ ⑥ ④

29. a. The z scores to the nearest .01 are ACT, 1.74 and SAT, 1.06.

b. The student performed better on the American College Test.

31. 5 percent

33. 16 percent

35. Since .3 is more than 2 standard deviations below the mean, we may be suspicious of the company's claim.

37. Approximately 11.4 boxes. Label each of five slips of paper with the name of a different color. Place the slips in a container, and randomly select one at a time (with replacement). Compute the average number of selections needed to obtain all five colors.

39. The average number of children a couple must have to be sure of having a child of each sex is 3. Label one slip of paper *boy* and one slip of paper *girl*. Place them in a container, and randomly select one at a time (with replacement). Compute the average number of selections required to select each slip of paper once.

41. Graph (i) gives the impression of substantial increases in sales from 1993 to 1998, whereas graph (ii) gives the impression of slight increases. The top graph is misleading; it suggests that sales doubled from 1994 to 1995 and more than doubled from 1995 to 1997. The bottom graph below better illustrates the true sales increases.

i.

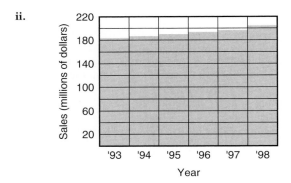

ii.

CHAPTER 7 TEST

1. a. Hawaii **b.** New Hampshire **c.** 83.7 percent
d. 51.7 (the mean of 52.6 and 50.8)
2. a. Sources of Revenue for California Public Schools

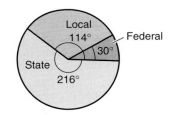

b. Sources of Revenue for Iowa Public Schools

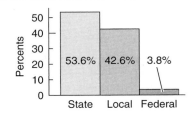

3.

STEM	LEAF
14	1
13	
12	6
11	7, 8
10	2
9	0, 2, 7, 8, 9
8	0, 3, 4, 4, 6
7	1, 3, 4, 4, 5, 6, 8, 9
6	0, 1, 3, 3, 5, 5, 6, 6, 8
5	0, 0, 4, 4, 5, 6, 6, 6, 9, 9
4	0, 1, 2, 4, 4
3	0, 4, 8

4. Frequency Distribution of States in Categories of Local School Revenue

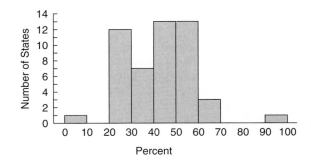

a. 12 **b.** 1
c. The intervals from 40 to 49.95 and 50 to 59.95.
5. a. 68.5 percent **b.** 20.26 percent

6. Using the median-fit line below, if 35 percent of the revenue for schools is from local sources, then approximately 59 percent is from state sources.

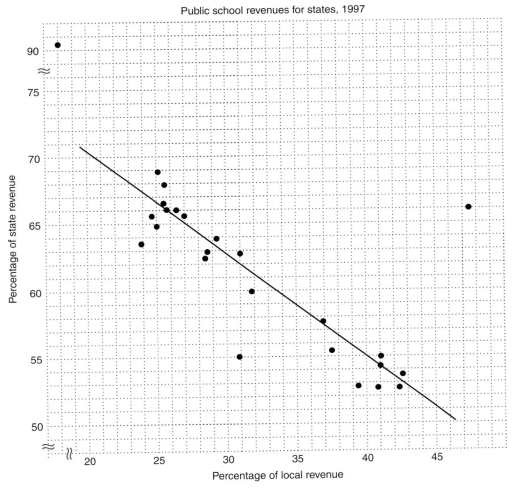

Public school revenues for states, 1997

7. a. Set *B*   **b.** Set *A*   **c.** Set *A*

8. The interquartile range of 23 is greater than half of the range of the data, which is 35.

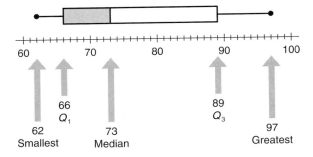

9. a. .8   **b.** 1.3   **c.** On the PSAT

10. a. Skewed to the right   **b.** Normal

11. a. 82.8 percent   **b.** 93 percent

    c. On the Total Math subtest, the scores of 60 percent of local students were lower than this student's score.

    d. This student is performing at grade levels much higher than the fourth grade.

12. a. 68 percent   **b.** 95 percent

13. 70.3

14. 90

EXERCISES AND PROBLEMS 8.1

1.

Sum	2	3	4	5	6	7	8	9	10	11	12
Probability	$\frac{1}{36}$	$\frac{2}{36}$	$\frac{3}{36}$	$\frac{4}{36}$	$\frac{5}{36}$	$\frac{6}{36}$	$\frac{5}{36}$	$\frac{4}{36}$	$\frac{3}{36}$	$\frac{2}{36}$	$\frac{1}{36}$

a. $\frac{5}{12}$ b. $\frac{5}{12}$

3. a. $\frac{2}{3}$ b. 7

5. a. $\frac{4}{7}$ b. $\frac{4}{7}$ c. $\frac{4}{7}$

7. The sample space is the set whose elements are the 18 chips.
   a. $\frac{1}{9}$ b. $\frac{7}{18}$ c. $\frac{8}{9}$

9.

	TETRA-HEDRON	CUBE	OCTA-HEDRON	DODECA-HEDRON	ICOSA-HEDRON
a.	$\frac{1}{4}$	$\frac{1}{6}$	$\frac{1}{8}$	$\frac{1}{12}$	$\frac{1}{20}$
b.	$\frac{1}{4}$	$\frac{1}{2}$	$\frac{5}{8}$	$\frac{3}{4}$	$\frac{17}{20}$

11. a. $\frac{5}{12}$ b. $\frac{3}{4}$
    c. $\frac{1}{4}$ d. $\frac{1}{2}$

13. a. *A, B*   *A, C*   *A, D*   *B, C*   *B, D*   *C, D*
    b. $\frac{1}{2}$ c. $\frac{1}{6}$

15. a. BB, BR, BY, BG, BW, BP, RB, RR, RY, RG, RW, RP, YB, YR, YY, YG, YW, YP, GB, GR, GY, GG, GW, GP, WB, WR, WY, WG, WW, WP, PB, PR, PY, PG, PW, PP
    b. $\frac{1}{36}$ c. $\frac{11}{36}$ d. $\frac{25}{36}$

17. a. $\frac{2}{3}$ and $\frac{5}{6}$
    b. $\frac{5}{6}$ and 1
    c. None. The two sets must be disjoint.

19. a. $\frac{1}{13}$ b. $\frac{1}{4}$ c. $\frac{1}{2}$ d. $\frac{11}{26}$ e. $\frac{3}{52}$

21. a. $\frac{12}{13}$ b. $\frac{10}{13}$ c. $\frac{3}{4}$ d. $\frac{23}{26}$

23. a. $\frac{1}{4}$; 1 to 3   b. $\frac{2}{13}$; 2 to 11
    c. $\frac{1}{2}$; 1 to 1   d. $\frac{1}{2}$; 1 to 1

25. a. 7 to 3   b. 3 to 2   c. 1 to 499   d. 4 to 1

27. a. $\frac{10}{13}$ b. $\frac{1}{5}$

29. a. .21   b. .97

31. a. $6,800,531/7,698,698 \approx .88$
    b. $9,781,958/10,000,000 \approx .98$
    c. $5,592,012/10,000,000 \approx .56$
    d. The probability to five decimal places of a 28-year-old person's not reaching age 29 is .00203 $(19,324/9,519,442)$. Since $.00203 \times 7000 = 14.21$, the insurance company should be prepared to pay approximately 14 death claims.

33. Let even digits represent heads and odd digits represent tails. Arbitrarily select a sequence of 10 digits from the table, and count the number of heads. Carry out this experiment repeatedly, recording the number of heads in each sequence of 10 digits. The probability is approximately .62.

35. Label 3 slips of paper *B* and 2 slips of paper *G*, and put them in a hat. Randomly select these slips one at a time without replacing them, and record the sequence of *B*s and *G*s. Carry out this experiment many times, and divide the number of times that 3 *B*s occur in succession by the total number of experiments. The theoretical probability of having 3 boys in succession is .3.

37. Label 3 slips of paper *H* (for hit) and 7 slips of paper *O* (for out), and put them in a sack. Randomly select 5 slips without replacement and record the number of hits. Carry out this experiment many times. Divide the total number of experiments in which 3, 4, or 5 of the slips of paper represented a hit by the total number of experiments. The theoretical probability is approximately .16.

39. a. Use a table of random digits, letting even digits represent heads and odd digits represent tails. Check sequences of 6 digits, and compute the experimental probability of having exactly 3 heads. The theoretical probability is .3125.
    b. Less than .5. The theoretical probability of obtaining exactly 10 heads in 20 tosses is approximately .18.

41. a.

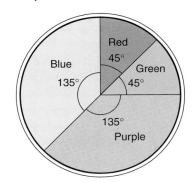

b.

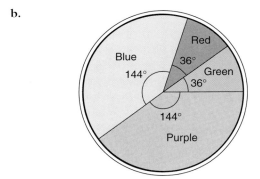

c.

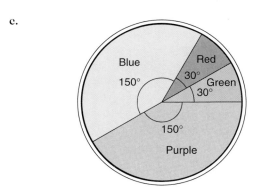

43. .20

45. $\frac{1}{3}$

47. .85

49. a. .49   **b.** .23   **c.** .64

51. a. .12   **b.** .17   **c.** .37

EXERCISES AND PROBLEMS 8.2

1. a. $\frac{1}{4}$ **b.** $\frac{1}{32}$ **c.** $\frac{1}{1024}$

3. a. $\frac{1}{6}$ **b.** $\frac{1}{4}$ **c.** $\frac{1}{6}$

5. a. $\frac{1}{6}$ **b.** $\frac{3}{4}$ **c.** $\frac{1}{2}$

d.

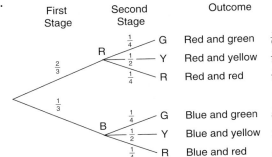

7. a. $\frac{1}{8}$ **b.** $\frac{7}{8}$ **c.** $\frac{1}{2}$

9. a. $\frac{1}{4}$ **b.** $\frac{11}{16}$

c.

First Toss	Second Toss	Third Toss	Fourth Toss	Outcome	
				HHHH	1/16
				HHHT	1/16
				HHTH	1/16
				HHTT	1/16
				HTHH	1/16
				HTTH	1/16
				HTTH	1/16
				HTTT	1/16
				THHH	1/16
				THHT	1/16
				THTH	1/16
				THTT	1/16
				TTHH	1/16
				TTHT	1/16
				TTTH	1/16
				TTTT	1/16

11. a. $\frac{1}{25}$ **b.** $\frac{7}{75}$ **c.** $\frac{1}{15}$

13. a. $\frac{1}{35}$ **b.** $\frac{1}{10}$ **c.** $\frac{1}{14}$

15. a. $\frac{1}{2}$ **b.** $\frac{1}{6}$

17. a. Independent, $\frac{1}{36}$ **b.** Dependent, $\frac{5}{14}$

19. a. $\frac{11}{12}$ **b.** $\frac{5}{6}$ **c.** $\frac{121}{144} \approx .84$

21. a. Approximately .53

    b. Approximately .80

23. a. $\frac{1}{20} \times \frac{3}{20} \times \frac{1}{20} = .000375$

    b. $\frac{5}{20} \times \frac{1}{20} \times \frac{1}{20} = .000625$

25. $\frac{7}{18}$

27. If G_1, G_2, G_3, and G_4 are the four good flashbulbs and B is the bad bulb, the sample space is

    G_1G_2 G_1G_3 G_1G_4 G_1B G_2G_3 G_2G_4

    G_2B G_3G_4 G_3B G_4B

    a. $\frac{3}{5}$ **b.** $\frac{2}{5}$

29. a. $\frac{1}{365}$ **b.** $(\frac{1}{365})^4 \approx 5.6 \times 10^{-11}$

31. Approximately .59; that is $1 - (4/5)^4$. A simulated probability can be obtained by using a random device in which a given number or object has a 1/5 probability of occurring. Many experiments in which this device is used 4 times will produce a simulated probability.

33. a. $(\frac{1}{6})(\$1 + \$2 + \$3 + \$4 + \$5 + \$6) = \$3.50$

    b. $\$3.50$

35. a. $\frac{1}{10,000}(5000) + \frac{1}{100}(25) + \frac{1}{20}(2) + \frac{1}{10}(1) = .95$ (95 cents)

    b. No

37. a. $\frac{37}{38}$ **b.** The expected values are equal.

39. a. $\frac{1}{10}$

    b. .0975 (There is a 19/20 chance of not winning on the first draw and a 19/20 chance of not winning on the second draw. Thus, the chance of not winning is $19/20 \times 19/20 = 361/400 = .9025$, and the chance of winning is .0975.) The chances of winning are better in part a.

41. No   **43.** .996

45. a. .224   **b.** .216   **c.** .856

47. $1/20,736 \approx .00005$

CHAPTER 8 TEST

1. a. AB, AC, AD, AE, AF, BC, BD, BE, BF, CD, CE, CF, DE, DF, EF

    b. $\frac{1}{15}$ **c.** $\frac{1}{3}$

2. a. $\frac{1}{3}$ **b.** $\frac{3}{4}$ **c.** $\frac{2}{3}$

3. a. G_1G_2, G_1G_3, G_1O_1, G_1O_2, G_2G_3, G_2O_1, G_2O_2, G_3O_1, G_3O_2, O_1O_2

    b. $\frac{3}{10}$ **c.** $\frac{1}{10}$ **d.** $\frac{3}{5}$

4. a. 5 to 7   **b.** $\frac{7}{12}$

5. a. 1   **b.** $\frac{2}{5}$ **c.** $\frac{4}{5}$ **d.** $\frac{1}{5}$

6. a. $\frac{4}{9}$ **b.** $\frac{2}{9}$ **c.** $\frac{5}{9}$

7. a. $\frac{2}{5}$ **b.** $\frac{4}{15}$ **c.** $\frac{3}{5}$

8. a.

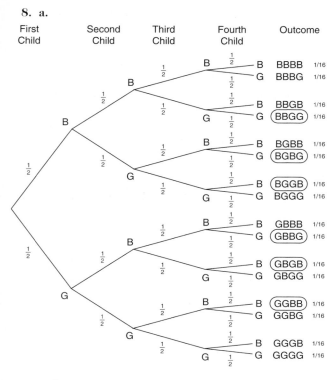

b. $\frac{3}{8}$ **c.** $\frac{11}{16}$

9. $\frac{11}{21}$

10. .488

11. a. $\$2(\frac{1}{2}) + \$1(\frac{1}{6}) + \$3(\frac{1}{6}) + \$5(\frac{1}{6}) = \$2.50$

     b. $\$2.50$

12. .039, or approximately 4 percent $[1 - (.99)^4]$

13. a. .72   **b.** .648   **c.** .998

14. Yes

15. a. .54   **b.** .76

EXERCISES AND PROBLEMS 9.1

1. a. 70°   **b.** It remains the same.

3. *Undefined terms* are words that are undefined, but information can be obtained about these terms from the axioms. They are used in definitions to define other words. *Definitions* use undefined words and other defined words to define new words. *Axioms* are statements which are assumed to be true. *Theorems* are statements which are proved true by using deductive reasoning.

5. a. Edge of a ruler or stretch a piece of string

     b. Angle supports in buildings and bridges or the rack for racking pool balls

     c. Top of a table or wall of a room

7. a. None

     b. Angles A, C, and D

     c. Angles B and E

9. a. $\angle HOK$ and $\angle KOJ$; $\angle KOJ$ and $\angle JOI$; $\angle JOI$ and $\angle IOH$

     b. $\angle HOI$ and $\angle KOJ$; $\angle HOK$ and $\angle IOJ$

     c. $\angle HOK$ and $\angle IOJ$; $\angle HOI$ and $\angle KOJ$

11. a. Diameter $\overline{CD} \perp$ chord $\overline{RS}$

     b. Line ℓ is tangent to radius $\overline{OD}$.

     c. Chords $\overline{AB}$ and $\overline{CD}$ bisect each other.

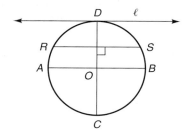

13. a. 145.5°   **b.** 34.5°

     c. 145.5°   **d.** 34.5°

15. a. 120°   **b.** 60°   **c.** 7 minutes

17. a. Simple

     b. None of these

     c. Closed

19. a. Nonconvex   **b.** Convex   **c.** Nonconvex

21. a. 90°   **b.** 60°

23. 0, 1, 4, 5, 6, 7, 8, 9, 10

25. a. True

     b. False; the resulting figure will be a parallelogram if the rectangle is not a square.

     c. True

27. 13

29. 4851

31. a. Yes   **b.** No

33. a. No   **b.** No   **c.** No   **d.** Yes

EXERCISES AND PROBLEMS 9.2

1. a. Hexagons; no, they are not regular.

     b. Hexagons and heptagons

3. a. 1440   **b.** 2340

5. a. Not all angles are congruent.

     b. Not all angles are congruent, and not all sides are congruent.

     c. Not all angles are congruent,

7.

No. of sides	3	4	5	6	7	8	9
Central angle	120°	90°	72°	60°	51.4°	45°	40°

	10	20	100
	36°	18°	3.6°

9. a. Hexagon   **b.** Triangle

11. a. 15   **b.** 18   **c.** 5

13. a. True

     b. True

c. False; beginning with an isosceles triangle whose sides are 20 inches, 20 inches, and 1 inch, connecting the midpoints of the sides will produce a triangle with one side that is shorter than the other two sides.

15. Regular hexagon

17. Every triangle will tessellate because the sum of the measures of the three angles of a triangle is 180° and each angle is used twice at each vertex point of the tessellation.

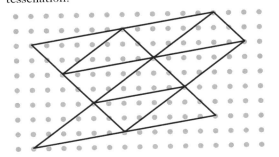

19.

a. b. c.

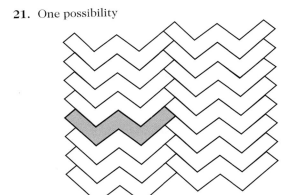

21. One possibility

23. **a.** Not semiregular; some vertices are surrounded by two squares and three triangles, and other vertices are surrounded by two squares, one triangle, and one hexagon.
   b. Semiregular; each vertex has the same arrangement of polygons.

25. Here are three methods: (1) Draw a line segment and use a protractor to draw a 150° angle at one endpoint. Then continue to draw sides for the dodecagon and angles of 150°. (2) Construct a circle with a compass, and draw the central angle for the dodecagon of 30°. Then "pace off" 12 chords of equal length around the circle with a compass. (3) Draw a circle and an inscribed regular hexagon. Then draw the perpendicular bisectors of the sides of the hexagon, and connect the 12 points on the circle.

27. There are six semiregular tessellations that each use two regular polygons. The arrangements of the polygons are octagon, octagon, square; dodecagon, dodecagon, equilateral triangle; square, square, equilateral triangle, equilateral triangle, equilateral triangle; square, equilateral triangle, square, equilateral triangle, equilateral triangle; hexagon and four equilateral triangles; and hexagon, equilateral triangle, hexagon, equilateral triangle. In addition to the one in Figure 9.38a, there is another semiregular tessellation that uses three regular polygons. It is shown in part b of exercise 23.

29. 121

31. The word LOVE

33. Fold paper to obtain $\overline{CD}$ and then place B to coincide with C to obtain an equilateral triangle: $AB = AC = BC$. The desired angles are marked in the following figure. To obtain a 15° angle, bisect twice at $\angle DBC$.

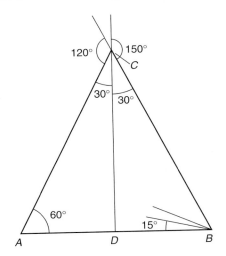

EXERCISES AND PROBLEMS 9.3

1. a. Hexagon   **b.** Hexagonal prisms
3. Part a is the only polyhedron.
5. a. Nonconvex   **b.** Convex
   c. Convex
7. a. Square, triangle, square, triangle
   b. Decagon, square, hexagon
9. a. Square pyramid
   b. Cylinder (or right cylinder)
   c. Triangular prism
11. a. Right cone
   b. Oblique cylinder
   c. Right pentagonal pyramid

13. a. *ABCDEF* **b.** *GLFA*
   c. 90°   **d.** 120°
15. a. Plane
   b. Cylindrical
   c. Conic
17. a. Hands of the clock
   b. Windows
   c. Window on the right and left sides of the front of the building
   d. Windows below the clock
   e. Edges of the roof of the tower
19. a. (20°S, 60°E)
   b. (30°N, 100°W); the United States
21. a. Pentagon   **b.** Rectangle
23. *CFGH, AEFH, ABCF,* and *ACDH*
25. a.

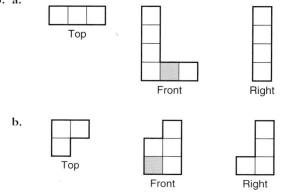

b.

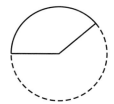

27. a. 1 through 7
   b. 26
29. a. 12 edges; 6   **b.** 10 vertices; 12   **c.** 5 faces; 4
31. a. September 15 (32.5°N, 48°W); September 23 (31°N, 64.5°W); September 30 (35°N, 76°W)
33. Two possibilities: (1) A cylinder that just fits inside a square prism. These objects share a vertical cross section. (2) A sphere that just fits inside a cylinder. These objects share a horizontal cross section.
35. a. Roll up a rectangular sheet of paper and tape the opposite edges.
   b. Cut out and roll up a sector of a disk and tape the radii.

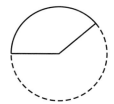

   c. Hold the right cylinder from part a at an angle, dip the ends at the same angle into a liquid, and cut

off the moistened part. Cutting along the taped edges produces the following pattern.

37. a. The first two pentominoes on the left (see exercise 37 in Exercises and Problems 9.3) will fold into an open-top box.
   b. Here are the remaining six pentominoes that will fold into an open-top box.

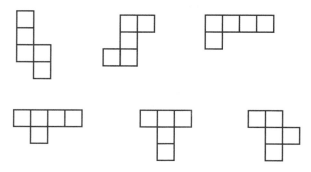

39. a. The number of faces in a cube equals the number of vertices in an octahedron, and the number of faces in an octahedron equals the number of vertices in a cube.
   b. The dodecahedron and icosahedron are duals.
   c. A tetrahedron
41. a. No.
   b. Angle 1 is largest. Angles 2 and 3 are right angles.

EXERCISES AND PROBLEMS 9.4

1. a. The left hedge and right hedge; the window in the left turret and the window in the right turret; the center arch and itself; the arches on the left and the arches on the right; the surface of the pool and itself. In general, nearly every object to the left of the center of the picture has a corresponding object to the right.
   b. The trees and the rectangular window on the right side of the fortress do not have images. There are other windows and openings on the fortress that do not have images for the vertical plane of symmetry.
   c. The rectangular window on the right side of the fortress and the surface of the pool have horizontal lines of symmetry.

3. a. Two lines of reflection and two rotation symmetries

 b. Five lines of reflection and five rotation symmetries

5. a. Four lines of symmetry and four rotation symmetries

 b. No lines of symmetry and two rotation symmetries

 c. Five lines of symmetry and five rotation symmetries

 d. One line of symmetry and one rotation symmetry Polygon c has the highest rating and polygons b and d have the lowest rating.

7. The image of A is not on the figure.

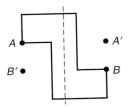

9. Figures a and c do not have lines of symmetry.

11. a. H, X, O, and I have two lines of symmetry.

 b. N, S, and Z have two rotation symmetries but no lines of symmetry.

13. Figure d has no line of symmetry

 a. Two lines of symmetry and two rotation symmetries, 180° and 360°

 b. One line of symmetry

 c. Three lines of symmetry and three rotation symmetries, 120°, 240°, and 360°

 d. Two rotation symmetries, 180° and 360°

15.

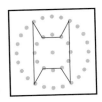 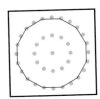 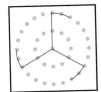

17. a.   **b.**

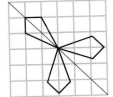 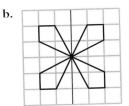

19. a. 16 rotation symmetries and 16 planes of symmetry

 b. One plane of symmetry

21. a. Right cylinder, equilateral prism, sphere, and cube

 b. Right cylinder, 2; equilateral prism, 2; sphere, infinite number; cube, 4

 c. Rectangular prism, 2; equilateral prism, 3; cube, 4

23. Five planes of symmetry and five rotation symmetries

25. a. Four rotation symmetries and four lines of symmetry

 b. Eight rotation symmetries and no lines of symmetry

27. a. 6   **b.** 5

29. a. Four rotation symmetries (Chase Manhattan Bank)

 b. Five lines of symmetry and five rotation symmetries (Texaco)

 c. One line of symmetry (Volkswagen)

 d. Five rotation symmetries and five lines of symmetry (Chrysler Corporation)

 e. One line of symmetry (Shell Oil Company)

31. a. One line of symmetry

 b. Three lines of symmetry and three rotation symmetries

 c. Four lines of symmetry and four rotation symmetries

 d. One line of symmetry

 e. No lines of symmetry and six rotation symmetries

33. 42 feet

35. 48 points. This can be accomplished by beanbags in cups 3, 4, 6, 7, and 8.

37. a. Three possibilities:

 b. Three possibilities:

 c. Three possibilities:

CHAPTER 9 TEST

1. a. (iv)   **b.** (iii)   **c.** (ii)

 d. (i)   **e.** (vi)   **f.** (i) and (v)

2. a.   **b.**

 c.   **d.**

3. a. *C* and *E*   **b.** *D*   **c.** *B*   **d.** *A*

4. a. True   **b.** True   **c.** False
   d. True   **e.** False

5. a. 45°   **b.** 120°   **c.** 72°

6. a. Not all angles are congruent
   b. Not all sides are congruent.
   c. Not all sides are congruent.
   d. Not all angles are congruent.

7. a. No   **b.** Yes   **c.** Yes
   d. Yes   **e.** No

8. No. The measure of a vertex angle of a regular octagon is 135°, and 135 cannot be combined with multiples of 60 and 90 (the degrees in the angles of the equilateral triangle and the square) to equal 360.

9. a. Right pentagonal pyramid
   b. Right rectangular prism
   c. Right hexagonal prism
   d. Oblique cylinder
   e. Right cone
   f. Oblique triangular pyramid

10. a. Nonpolyhedron   **b.** Polyhedron
   c. Polyhedron   **d.** Nonpolyhedron
   e. Polyhedron   **f.** Polyhedron

11. a. 12   **b.** 24

12. a. An equilateral triangle
   b.

   c. A regular pentagon

13. a. 9   **b.** An infinite number   **c.** 5

14.

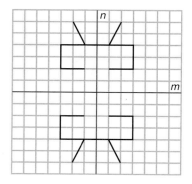

15. a. Two lines of symmetry and two rotation symmetries
   b. Seven lines of symmetry and seven rotation symmetries
   c. Three lines of symmetry and three rotation symmetries
   d. Two rotation symmetries

16. 21

17. 171°

18. a. 11   **b.** 56

EXERCISES AND PROBLEMS 10.1

1. a. 92 kilometers per hour   **b.** 40 kilometers

3. a. Approximately $2\frac{1}{2}$ to $2\frac{2}{3}$ paper clips
   b. Approximately 5 eraser heads

5. a. 202,500 grams
   b. 202,500,000 milligrams
   c. 446 pounds

7. a. $\frac{1}{32}$ inch   **b.** $\frac{1}{4}$ inch
   c. $\frac{11}{16}$ inch   **d.** $6\frac{3}{16}$ inches
   e. $8\frac{1}{2}$ inches

9. a. 8 pints   **b.** 16 cups   **c.** 1 cup

11. a. 4.2 yards   **b.** 3.5 pounds   **c.** 2.5 gallons

13. a. 200 centimeters   **b.** 75 kilograms   **c.** 48 liters

15. a. Most cubits are less than 52.5 centimeters
   b. Length, 158 meters; breadth, 26 meters; height, 16 meters. Or length, 517 feet; breadth, 86 feet; height, 52 feet

17.

^{1}1	^{2}6	5		^{3}4		
	3	^{4}3	1	5	0	
^{5}1	2	0		0		^{6}4
				0		3
			^{7}1		^{8}9	2
		^{9}7	9	2	0	
^{10}5	5	5	0		0	

19. a. Approximately 450 grams
   b. Approximately 60 to 90 feet for a step of 2 to 3 feet
   c. Approximately 8 feet

21. a. 17 millimeters
   b. $\frac{17}{200}$ millimeter = .085 millimeter
   c. 85 micrometers   **d.** 85

23. a. 111.5 to 112.5 kilograms
   b. 38.15 to 38.25° C
   c. 48.25 to 48.35 centimeters
   d. 3.455 to 3.465 kilograms

25. 11.6 kilograms

27. a. Rounding to the nearest multiple of 10 gives 40 + 30 + 50 + 40 + 30 = 190, and one-third of this is approximately $63.
   b. $63.36

29. 320 days; 5 cents per day

31. a. 7.2 cubic centimeters   **b.** 32 injections

33. a. 299,792,458 meters
   b. 299,792.458 kilometers per second
   c. Yes

35. 14 centimeters

EXERCISES AND PROBLEMS 10.2

1. a. The width of these rectangles is greater than the width of the outstretched arms of the average adult, and the height of these rectangles is greater than the height of an average room.
   b. 106 meters
   c. 40 meters
   d. 4240 square meters
3. a. 8   b. 6
5. Approximately 4 plastic fasteners
7. a. 27,878,400 square feet
   b. 640 acres
   c. 671,360 acres
9. a. 10 units   b. 8 units
11. a. 10,000 ares   b. 100 hectares
13. a. Area 1375 square millimeters = 13.75 square centimeters; perimeter 160 millimeters
    b. Area 1800 square millimeters = 18 square centimeters; perimeter 183 millimeters
15. a. Area 2350 square millimeters = 23.50 square centimeters; circumference 172 millimeters
    b. Area 1480 square millimeters = 14.80 square centimeters; perimeter 157 millimeters
17. a. Area 1536 square millimeters = 15.36 square centimeters; perimeter 215 millimeters
    b. Area 1062 square millimeters = 10.62 square centimeters; perimeter 135 millimeters
19. 15.5 square centimeters
21. a. 140 square centimeters
    b. 198 square centimeters
23. The circumferences are $2\pi \approx 6.3$; $4\pi \approx 12.6$; $8\pi \approx 25.1$; $16\pi \approx 50.3$. When the radius is doubled, the circumference is doubled.
25. 40 square centimeters
27. a. Square, 120 millimeters; circle, 120 millimeters
    b. 246 square millimeters
29. a. 6.8×10^8 b. 8.8 directories
31. Type A
33. $8.28
35. Approximately 1428.6 square meters
37. a. 90,675 square centimeters   b. Two rolls
39. a. $66,791.30   b. $4875.76
41. Approximately 31.8 centimeters × 31.8 centimeters
43. a. 982 square meters   b. 125 meters
    c. 111 meters   d. 14 meters
    e. 3220 square meters
45. 4 revolutions

EXERCISES AND PROBLEMS 10.3

1. a. 166,762 cubic centimeters   b. 1167 kilograms
3. a. Unit (i): 54 square units, 27 cubic units
      Unit (ii): $13\frac{1}{2}$ square units, $3\frac{3}{8}$ cubic units
   b. Unit (i): 68 square units, 30 cubic units
      Unit (ii): 17 square units, $3\frac{3}{4}$ cubic units

5. a. 46,656 cubic inches
   b. 1,000,000,000 cubic millimeters
7. a. Volume, 48 cubic centimeters; surface area, 96 square centimeters
   b. Volume, 60 cubic centimeters; surface area, 124 square centimeters
9. a. Volume, 113 cubic centimeters; surface area, 113 square centimeters
   b. Volume, 196 cubic centimeters; surface area, 196 square centimeters
11. a. Volume, 601 cubic centimeters; surface area, 478 square centimeters
    b. Volume, 145 cubic centimeters; surface area, 219 square centimeters
13. a. 9.4 cubic centimeters
    b. 12 cubic centimeters
15. a. 37.5 liters   b. 1250 cubic centimeters
    c. 12   d. 5750 square centimeters
17. 21,000 Btu
19. Type B
21. 10 gallons
23. a. 25   b. 5
25. a. 509 cubic meters   b. 25.5 hours
27. a. 7.85 square meters   b. 722.2 kilograms
29. 512 of the small cubes will be unpainted.

10 by 10 by 10 cube

No. of painted faces	3	2	1	0
No. of cubes	8	12×8	6×8^2	8^3

Here are the results for an n by n by n cube with $n \geq 2$.

No. of painted faces	3	2	1	0
No. of cubes	8	$12(n-2)$	$6(n-2)^2$	$(n-2)^3$

31. a. 2   b. 4
    c. 2^{20} (more than 1 million)
33. a. 679 cubic inches   b. 8.8 inches ($\sqrt[3]{679} \approx 8.8$)

CHAPTER 10 TEST

1. a. Gram   b. Milliliter   c. Meter
   d. Kilogram   e. Square meter   f. Cubic meter
2. a. 42   b. 9   c. 13.6
   d. 80   e. 67.5   f. 44
3. a. 1600   b. 470   c. 5200
   d. 2.5   e. 160   f. 1,000,000
4. a. 1600   b. 0°   c. 55
   d. 2   e. $\frac{3}{5}$ f. 2.2
5. a. Minimum, 5.25 kilograms; maximum, 5.35 kilograms
   b. Minimum, 84.5 grams; maximum, 85.5 grams
   c. Minimum, 4.115 ounces; maximum, 4.125 ounces
6. Area using unit (i): 26 square units; area using unit (ii): 6.5 square units

7. a. 21 square centimeters; 22 centimeters
  b. 168 square centimeters; 64 centimeters
  c. 18 square centimeters; 20 centimeters
  d. 12.5664 square centimeters; 12.5664 centimeters

8. 6.4 centimeters

9. a. 54 square centimeters
  b. 16 square centimeters

10. Unit (i): 18 cubic units; 48 square units
  Unit (ii): 2.25 cubic units; 12 square units

11. a. 27 cubic centimeters; 66 square centimeters
  b. 54 cubic centimeters; 114 square centimeters
  c. 27 cubic centimeters; 66 square centimeters

12. a. 1568 cubic centimeters
  b. 4834.9 cubic centimeters
  c. 1231.5 cubic centimeters
  d. 3990 cubic centimeters

13. a. 1522 square centimeters
  b. 1583.4 square centimeters
  c. 2463.0 square centimeters
  d. 896 square centimeters

14. 3.6 cubic yards

15. Type A

16. $478

EXERCISES AND PROBLEMS 11.1

1. a. $\angle T$ **b.** $\angle D$ **c.** $\angle R$
  d. $\overline{DT}$ **e.** $\overline{TR}$ **f.** $\overline{DR}$
  g. $\triangle TDR$

3.

a.

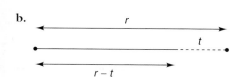

b.

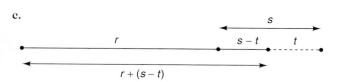

c.

5. See Section 11.1 for the steps to construct an angle which is congruent to a given angle.

7. See steps for bisecting a line segment, pages 727 to 728.

9. See steps for constructing a perpendicular to a line through a given point, pages 730 to 731.

11. Extend $\overline{RS}$ to point B; use a compass and locate point A so that $AS = SB$; use a compass to draw arcs intersecting at point D so that D is equidistant from A and B; $\overline{DS} \perp \overline{RS}$.

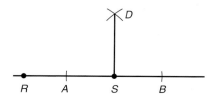

13. Place the edge of the Mira on point K and across line n so that the reflection from one side of line n coincides with the other side of line n.

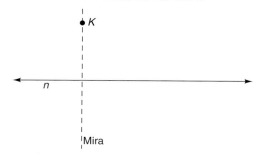

Use the Mira to draw a perpendicular line ℓ through point Q to line m. Then place the edge of the Mira on point Q so that it is parallel to line m. The edge of the Mira and line m will be parallel when the reflection of one side of line ℓ coincides with the other side of line ℓ.

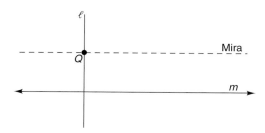

15. For both polygons, construct the perpendicular bisectors of any two sides of the polygon. Their intersection is the center of the circumscribed circle whose radius is the distance from the center to any vertex of the polygon.

17.

a.

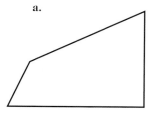
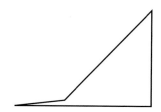

b. An infinite number of quadrilaterals can be constructed.

19. a.

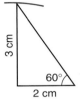

b.

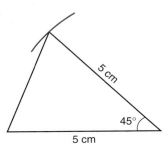

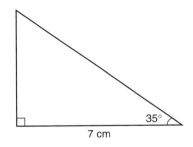

c.

d.

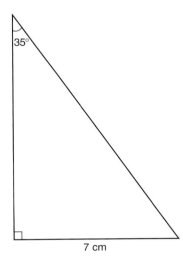

21. a.

b. This is one of two possibilities:

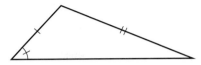

c. No, the triangles are not congruent.

d. Two sides and one angle of a triangle may be congruent to two sides and one angle of a second triangle, and yet the triangles are not necessarily congruent.

23. a. $\triangle ABC \cong \triangle HMS$ by the SAS congruence property.

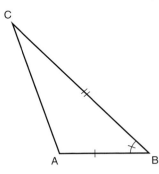
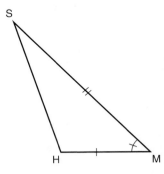

b. One possibility to show $\triangle ABC$ is not necessarily congruent to $\triangle HMS$.

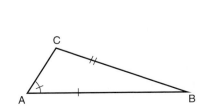
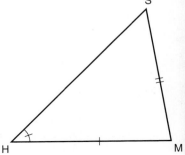

25. Construct $\overline{AB}$ and then with a compass open to span $\overline{AB}$, swing arcs from both A and B. The arcs intersect in the third vertex of the triangle.

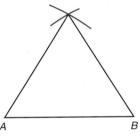

27. a. One of two possible points on line ℓ, for each distance.

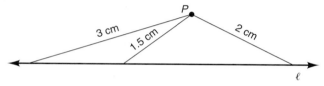

   b. 1.1 centimeters

   c. The shortest distance from a point to a line is the length of the perpendicular line segment from the line to the point.

29. a. The triangles are congruent by SAS.
   b. The triangles are congruent by SSS.

31. a. The triangles are congruent by the SAS congruence property.
   b. The triangles are not necessarily congruent because the congruent angles are not the included angles for the pairs of congruent sides.

33. a. In the answer to exercise 23b (see triangles on preceding page), it was possible to form two noncongruent triangles with the given angle and two given sides in the same relative positions of the two triangles. However, in exercise 33a, it is not possible to form two noncongruent triangles with the given angle and the two given sides in the same relative positions. So, these triangles are congruent.
   b. The triangles are not necessarily congruent.

35. Since $\overline{RT} \cong \overline{ST}$, $\overline{RK} \cong \overline{SK}$, and $\overline{KT}$ is common to both triangles, $\triangle RKT \cong \triangle SKT$ by the SSS congruence property. Since $\triangle RKT \cong \triangle SKT$, the triangles are congruent, and so $\angle R \cong \angle S$ by corresponding parts.

37. To trisect right $\angle ABC$, open a compass to span $\overline{BC}$ and draw an arc with B as the center. With the same compass opening, draw an arc with C as the center and that intersects the first arc at point D. Then $\triangle BDC$ is an equilateral triangle, and $\angle DBC$ has a measure of $60°$. Bisecting this angle will provide a trisection of $\angle ABC$.

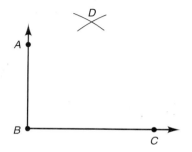

39. Since $\overline{AB} \cong \overline{CB}$, $\angle RAB$ and $\angle DCB$ are right angles, and $\angle RBA \cong \angle DBC$ (because they are vertical

angles), the triangles are congruent by the ASA congruence property. Thus, $\overline{CD}$ can be measured, and by corresponding parts, $\overline{CD} \cong \overline{AR}$.

41. 144 feet

EXERCISES AND PROBLEMS 11.2

1. a. No   **b.** Yes   **c.** Translation mapping
3. a, b. They are equal.
5. a. $90°$
   b. The distances are equal.
   c. All points on ℓ
7. a. $90°$ **b, c.** They are equal.
9. a. Right 6 and up 1
   b. Quadrilateral $ABCD$
11. a. A translation 8 units horizontally to the left
   b. The distance between any point and its image is 8 units, twice the distance between lines m and n.
13.

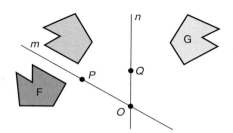

   a. Hexagon G
   b. The number of degrees in the angle of rotation is twice the number of degrees in $\angle POQ$.

15. a. Draw $\overrightarrow{KO}$ and then construct a perpendicular to $\overrightarrow{KO}$ through point O. Use a compass to locate K' on the perpendicular so that $KO = OK'$. Then K' is the image of K. Obtain the images of the remaining five vertex points in a similar manner.

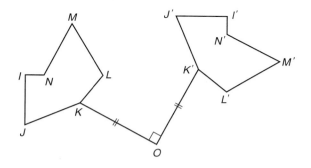

   b. Construct the perpendicular through point Q to line k. Use a compass to locate Q' on the perpendicular so that the distance from Q' to line k equals the distance from Q to line k. Then Q' is the image of Q, and images of the remaining four points can be obtained in a similar manner.

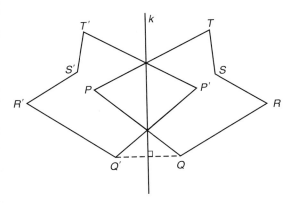

17. a.

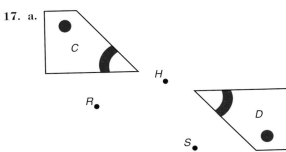

b. Figure *C* can be mapped to figure *D* by a 180° rotation about point *H*.

19.

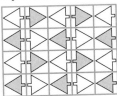

21. a. The centers of rotation are shown in the following figure.

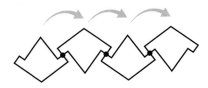

b. Reflections, or 180° rotations about the lower point of the figure.

23.

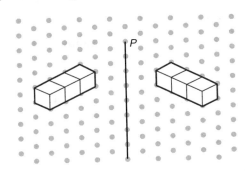

25. a. Four, because a rhombus has rotation symmetries of 180° and 360° and two reflection symmetries.

b. Six; three rotation symmetries and three reflection symmetries

c. Sixteen; eight rotation symmetries and eight reflection symmetries

27. Regular hexagon

29. Rectangle

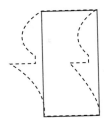

31. See reflection tessellations, pages 756–757.

33. Create a curve from *E* to *F* and translate it to side $\overline{GH}$. Then create a curve from *F* to *H* and translate it to side $\overline{EG}$. This figure can be used to produce a translation tessellation.

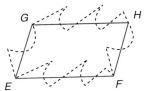

35. Create a curve from P to Q and rotate it about Q so that P maps to R. Similarly, create a curve from R to S and rotate it about S, and create a curve from T to U and rotate it about U. This figure can be used to produce a rotation tessellation.

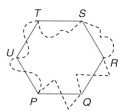

37. a. Rotation about point O, which is the intersection of the perpendicular bisectors of two line segments whose endpoints are pairs of points on the figure and their images.

    b. Rotation about point Q, which is the intersection of the perpendicular bisectors of $\overline{AA'}$ and $\overline{BB'}$.

39. a. $D'\,(3, ^-5), E'\,(1, ^-2), F'\,(3, ^-3), G'\,(5, ^-1)$
    b. $D''\,(^-3, ^-5), E''\,(^-1, ^-2), F''\,(^-3, ^-3), G''\,(^-5, ^-1)$
    c. A $180°$ rotation about the origin

41. There are four solutions which cannot be obtained from each other by rotations or reflections. The sums along their sides are 9, 10, 11, and 12.

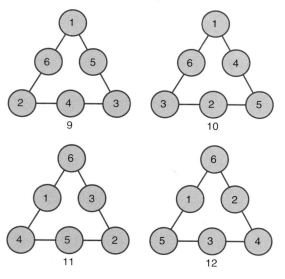

43. a. A translation
    b. A translation, horizontal reflection, or glide reflection

45.

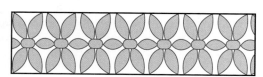

47. Eight, counting the given magic square: four from rotations of $90°$, $180°$, $270°$, and $360°$; one from a reflection about a vertical line; one from a reflection about a horizontal line; and two by reflections about the diagonals.

49. a. 3

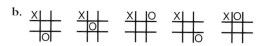

    b.

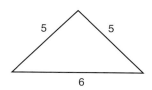

    c.

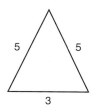

EXERCISES AND PROBLEMS 11.3

1. a. 2   **b.** $^-\frac{1}{2}$

3.

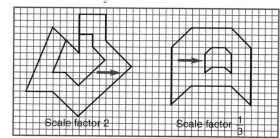

5. For scale factors of 2, 3, and $\frac{1}{2}$, the point $(2, 6)$ is mapped to $(4, 12)$, $(6, 18)$, and $(1, 3)$, respectively. In general, for a scale factor of k, point (a, b) will be mapped to (ka, kb).

7. a. $RV = 6$, $US = 7.5$, $XW = 3$
    b. $AD = 4.6$, $NP = 3$, $NO = 6.6$

9. a. Similar by the AA similarity property: $\triangle ABC \sim \triangle EFD$
    b. Since vertical angles are congruent, the two triangles are similar by the AA similarity property: $\triangle HIG \sim \triangle KIJ$.
    c. Not similar

11. a. Similar (corresponding sides proportional and all angles $90°$)
    b. Not necessarily similar. For example:

c. Not necessarily similar. For example:

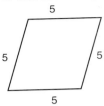 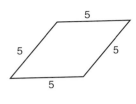

d. Similar (corresponding sides proportional and all angles 135°)

13. a.

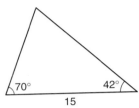

b.

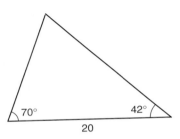

c. Yes

d. If two angles of one triangle are congruent to two angles of another triangle, the two triangles are similar.

15. $\triangle ABC$ is similar to $\triangle AEF$. Therefore, $AB/AE = BC/EF = AC/AF$. Also, $\triangle ACD$ is similar to $\triangle AFG$, so $AD/AG = DC/GF = AC/AF$. All angles in both rectangles equal 90°. Therefore, the corresponding sides of $ABCD$ and $AEFG$ are proportional, and their corresponding angles are equal.

17. a. Since there are 180° in every triangle, the third angles of these triangles are also congruent. Thus the triangles are similar by the AAA similarity property.

b. 14 meters

19. a. 9 **b.** $\frac{1}{4}$

21. a. 4 square units **b.** 144 square units

23.

SCALE FACTOR	SURFACE AREA (SQUARE UNITS)	VOLUME (CUBIC UNITS)
1	26	7
2	104	56
3	234	189
4	416	448
5	650	875

25. 3

27. Scale factor = 2

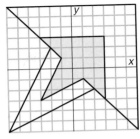

29. Scale factor = ⁻3

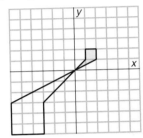

31. a. Since the ratio of the height of her friend to the length of her friend's shadow is 6/6 = 1, the ratio of the height of the goal post to its shadow is also 1. Thus the goal posts are 10 yards or 30 feet in height.

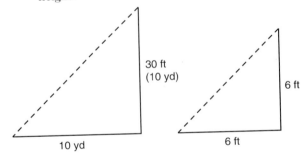

b. $13\frac{1}{3}$ yards

33. a. 10,000
b. 1,000,000
c. 3 meters

35. If the scale factor is 2, all images of the pentagon will be congruent pentagons, regardless of where the projection point is located.

37. a. The original sheet is similar to the quarto with a scale factor of $\frac{1}{2}$, because the two adjacent edges of the original sheet were both folded in half to obtain the quarto; and the folio is similar to the octavo with a scale factor of $\frac{1}{2}$ because two adjacent edges of the folio were both folded in half.
b. Every other rectangle will be similar to the original sheet; and beginning with the folio, every other rectangle will be similar to the folio.

39. 2.3 times greater

CHAPTER 11 TEST

1. a. Using any compass opening and *A* as the center, draw arcs intersecting the sides of ∡*A* in points *B* and *C*. With the same compass opening and points *B* and *D* as centers, draw intersecting arcs at point *D*. Line segment $\overline{DA}$ is the bisector.

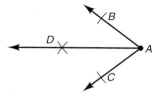

b. Using the same compass opening and point *Q* as center, locate points *A* and *B* on line *m* so that *AQ* = *BQ*. With the same compass opening and *A* and *B* as centers, draw arcs intersecting at point *D* in one half-plane and point *C* in the other half-plane. Then line segment $\overline{DC} \perp m$.

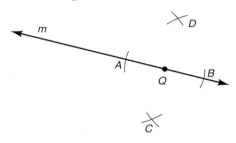

c. Using the same compass opening throughout, draw arcs so that *PA* = *AB* = *BC* = *PC*, as shown in the following figure. Line $\overline{PC} \parallel \ell$.

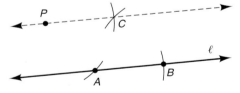

d. With *R* as center, draw arcs intersecting line *n* so that *RA* = *RB*. With *A* and *B* as centers, draw arcs intersecting at *D* so that *AD* = *BD*. Line segment $\overline{RD} \perp n$.

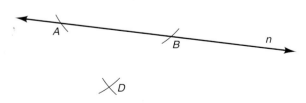

2. Construct the perpendicular bisectors of $\overline{BA}$ and $\overline{AC}$. The intersection of these bisectors is the center of the circle whose radius is the distance from the center to any vertex of the triangle.

3. a.

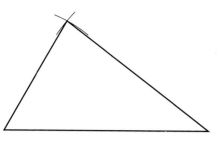

b. A triangle cannot be constructed with the given segments because the sum of the lengths of the two shorter segments is less than the length of the third segment.

4. a. △*ABC* ≅ △*DEC* by the ASA congruence property.
  b. △*FGI* ≅ △*FHI* by the SAS congruence property.
  c. Since the two congruent angles are not included between the pairs of congruent sides, the triangles are not necessarily congruent.
  d. △*RQT* ≅ △*TSR* by the SSS congruence property.

5. a.

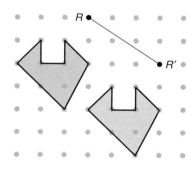

  b.

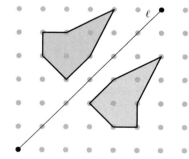

  c.

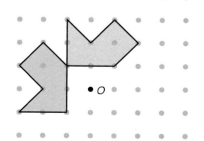

6. **a.** A counterclockwise rotation of 25°
   b. A translation twice the distance between lines ℓ and m
   c. A translation of P to the right 17 units and down 2 units
7. The number of congruence mappings of each figure onto itself is its total number of symmetries.
   a. 2; An isosceles triangle has one line of symmetry and one rotation symmetry.
   b. 12; A regular hexagon has 6 lines of symmetry and 6 rotation symmetries.
   c. 4; A rectangle has 2 lines of symmetry and 2 rotation symmetries.
8. **a.** Alter one side of the triangle by drawing a curve from one vertex to another. Then rotate this curve about these two vertices to the other two sides.
   b. Alter one side of the parallelogram by drawing a curve and then translate this curve to the opposite side. Then alter one of the remaining sides of the parallelogram by a curve and translate this curve to the opposite side.
9. **a.** Translation or reflection about a vertical line
   b. Translation or a 180° rotation
   c. Translation or a glide reflection
   d. Translation, 180° rotation, reflections about horizontal or vertical lines, or glide reflection
10. **a.** Scale factor of 2

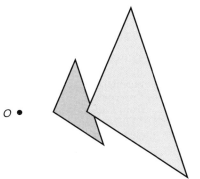

   b. Scale factor of $\frac{1}{3}$

c. Scale factor of $-\frac{1}{2}$

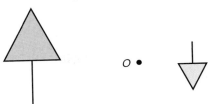

11. **a.** $\triangle BDC \sim \triangle AEC$ by the AAA similarity property.
    b. $\triangle FGH \sim \triangle IJH$ by the AAA similarity property.
    c. These triangles are not necessarily similar.
    d. $\triangle RST \sim \triangle WUV$ by the SSS similarity property.
12. **a.** Not necessarily similar because sides need not be proportional.

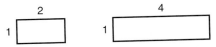

    b. Similar because corresponding sides are proportional and corresponding angles are congruent.
    c. Not necessarily similar because sides need not be proportional, and not all pairs of corresponding angles need be congruent.

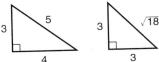

    d. Similar because corresponding sides are proportional and corresponding angles are congruent
    e. Similar because corresponding sides have a proportion of 1 and corresponding angles are congruent
13. **a.** 324 cubic units   **b.** 288 square units
    c. 1.5 cubic units   **d.** 8 square units
14. **a.** 7 inches   **b.** $\frac{1}{2}$ quart   **c.** 48 pounds
15. 27 feet
16. **a.** The triangles are not necessarily congruent and the information in part b shows they are not congruent. The triangles are similar.
    b. 500 feet

CREDITS

TEXT AND ILLUSTRATIONS

Chapter 1

Page 7: PEANUTS reprinted by permission of United Feature Syndicate, Inc. p. 7: From *How to Take a Chance* by Darrell Huff, illustrated by Irving Geis, Copyright © 1959 by W. W. Norton & Company, Inc., renewed 1987 by Darrell Huff & Irving Geis. Reprinted by permission of W. W. Norton & Company, Inc. p. 13: B.C. by permission of Johnny Hart and Field Enterprises, Inc. p. 32: © 1975 by The New York Times Co. Reprinted by permission. p. 33: Reprinted by permission of United Press International. Pages 36 and 47: © 2001 by Sidney Harris, p. 51: Reprinted from the *Arithmetic Teacher* (Oct. 1972), © 1972 by the National Council of Teachers of Mathematics.

Chapter 2

Page 72: Venn diagram from 1977 *Encyclopedia Britannica Book of the Year.* Reprinted by courtesy of Encyclopedia Britannica, Inc. 91: Courtesy of Jim and Lisa Aschbacher. p. 97: Reprinted from *Curriculum and Evaluation Standards for School Mathematics,* © 1989 by the National Council of Teachers of Mathematics. p. 97: Courtesy of Dr. Richard A. Petrie. p. 101: Courtesy of Diane Katrina Demchuck. p. 113: Reproduced from Nuffield Mathematics Project (1972) *Logic,* Wiley/Chambers/Murray. Reprinted by permission.

Chapter 3

Page 134: Reprinted from the Margarita Philosophia of Gregor Reisch, 1503. p. 139: B.C. by permission of Johnny Hart and Field Enterprises, Inc. p. 204: Krypto, produced by M. P. H. Company, Inc. South Bend, Indiana 46624.

Chapter 4

Page 210: B.C. by permission of Johnny Hart and Field Enterprises, Inc. p. 213: Reprinted by courtesy of Agencia J. B., Rio de Janeiro. p. 225: Reprinted from *Aftermath IV,* Dale Seymour et al. Courtesy of Creative Publications. p. 225: Otis Elevator

Illustration reprinted from *Architectural Record,* March 1970. © 1970 by McGraw-Hill, Inc. with all rights reserved. p. 234: Reprinted from the *Mathematics Teacher,* © 1987, 1989 by the National Council of Teachers of Mathematics.

Chapter 5

Page 250: B.C. by permission of Johnny Hart and Field Enterprises, Inc. Figure 5.4: Adapted from the *Book of Popular Science,* courtesy of Grolier Inc. p. 271: Redrawn from a photo by courtesy of National Aeronautics and Space Administration. p. 276: Fraction Bars © 1981 Permission of Scott Resources, Inc. Fort Collins, Colorado. p. 277: From the *Book of Knowledge* © 1960 by permission of Grolier Inc. p. 278: PEANUTS reprinted by permission of United Feature Syndicate, Inc. pp. 321 and 328: Illustrations from Webster's *New International Dictionary,* 2d ed., © 1959 used by permission of G. & C. Merriam Co., publishers of the Merriam-Webster Dictionaries.

Chapter 6

Page 331: Reprinted with permission from the *Mathematics Teacher,* © 1987, 1989 by the National Council of Teachers of Mathematics. Figure 6.5: Decimal Squares © 1981 Permission of Scott Resources, Inc., Fort Collins, Colorado. p. 354: Reprinted from *Activities for Implementing Curricular Themes, Agenda for Action,* © 1986 by the National Council of Teachers of Mathematics. p. 371: Reprinted from the *Mathematics Teacher,* © 1987, 1989 by the National Council of Teachers of Mathematics. p. 372: Redrawn by permission of D. Reidel Publishing Company. p. 376: Reprinted by courtesy of Foster's Daily Democrat, Dover, New Hampshire. Figure 6.37: Redrawn from data by courtesy of the Population Reference Bureau Inc. p. 395: Courtesy U.S. Department of Transportation and the Advertising Council. p. 397 Courtesy of the Stanford Research Institute, J. Grippo (Project Manager).

Chapter 7

Page 426: "Bills of Mortality" from *Devils, Drugs and Doctors* by Howard

W. Haggard. Copyright 1929 by Howard W. Haggard. Copyright renewed 1957 by Howard W. Haggard. Reprinted by permission of HarperCollins Publishers, Inc. p. 444: Copyright 1975. Reprinted by permission of *Saturday Review* and Robert D. Ross. Figure 7.36: Redrawn from the Differential Aptitude Tests. Copyright 1972, 1973, by The Psychological Corporation. Reproduced by special permission of the publisher. p. 495: Reprinted by Courtesy of Washington Post. p. 497: Reproduced by permission from the Stanford Achievement Test, 7th ed. Copyright © 1982 by Harcourt Brace Jovanovich Inc. All rights reserved. p. 500: Reprinted by permission of *Saturday Review* and Ed Fisher. Copyright 1956. p. 503: Reproduced by permission from the Stanford Achievement Test, 7th ed. Copyright © 1982 by Harcourt Brace Jovanovich Inc. All rights reserved.

Chapter 8

Page 506: Courtesy of Leonard Todd. p. 514: Joseph Zeis, Cartoonist. Figure 8.5: Mortality Table from *Principles of Insurance,* 8th ed., by Robert Mehr and Emerson Cammack, Terry Rose © 1985. Reprinted by courtesy of R. D. Irwin, Inc. p. 520: B.C. by permission of Johnny Hart and Field Enterprises, Inc. p. 542: Reprinted from *Ladies Home Journal,* February 1976. Courtesy of Henry R. Martin, cartoonist. p. 544: Reprinted by permission of New Hampshire Sweepstakes Commission.

Chapter 9

Page 550: Reprinted from the *Mathematics Teacher,* © 1987, 1989 by the National Council of Teachers of Mathematics. p. 570: Copyright 1974 by Charles F. Linn. Reprinted by permission of Doubleday & Company, Inc. p. 570: Reprinted by Courtesy of the National Council of Teachers of Mathematics. p. 587: Photos from *Collecting Rare Coins for Profit,* by Q. David Bowers. Courtesy of Harper & Row Publishers 1975. Figure 9.57: Drawings reprinted with permission from *Encyclopedia Britannica,* 14th ed., © 1972 by Encyclopedia Britannica, Inc. Figure 9.58: Reprinted with permission from *Collier's Encyclopedia,* © 1989 Macmillan Educational Corporation. p. 608: Courtesy of National Aeronautics and Space Administration. p. 617: B.C. by permission of Johnny Hart and Field Enterprises, Inc. p. 625: Reprinted from *Early American Design Motifs,* by Suzanne E. Chapman (New York: Dover Publications, Inc., 1974). p. 625: Reprinted from *Symbols, Signs and Signets,* by Ernst Lehner (New York: Dover Publications, Inc., 1950).

Chapter 10

Page 635, Figure 10.1: Courtesy of British Tourist Authority, New York. Figure 10.3: From *The Book of Knowledge,* © 1960, by permission of Grolier Incorporated. p. 652: Reprinted from *Popular Science,* with permission, © 1975 Times Mirror Magazines, Inc. p. 653: Trustees of the Science Museum, London. p. 655: Reprinted with permission from The Associated Press. Figure 10.41: Based on drawing from *Mathematics and Living Things,* Student Text. School Mathematics Study Group, 1965. Reprinted by permission of Leland Stanford Junior University. p. 682: Courtesy of Dr. William Webber, University of New Hampshire. p. 683: by John A. Ruge, reprinted from the *Saturday Review.* p. 704: B.C. by permission of Johnny Hart and Field Enterprises, Inc.

Chapter 11

Page 716: Reprinted by permission *Saturday Review,* © 1976 & V. Gene Meyers. p. 736: PEANUTS reprinted by permission of United Feature Syndicate, Inc. Figure 11.30: Reproduced from *Let's Play Math,* by Michael Holt and Zoltan Dienes. Copyright © 1973 by Michael Holt and Zoltan Dienes, used by permission of Publisher, Walker and Company p. 760: Courtesy John P. Adams, University of New Hampshire. p. 767: Reproduced by permission of the publisher from *Aesthetic Measure* by George D. Birkhoff (Cambridge, MA: Harvard University Press), © 1933 by the President and Fellows of Harvard College; 1961 by Garrett Birkhoff. Figure 11.43: reproduced by permission of the National Ocean Survey, U.S. Department of Commerce. p. 793: Reprinted from the

Mathematics Teacher, © 1987, 1989 by the National Council of Teachers of Mathematics.

PHOTO CREDITS

Chapter 1

Page 3: Courtesy of International Business Machines Corporation. p. 11: © Bettmann/CORBIS. p. 19: California Institute of Technology. Figure 1.2: Negative #320446, Courtesy Department of Library Services, American Museum of Natural History. Figure 1.3: Ron Bergeron. p. 24: Courtesy of British Information Systems. p. 27: Courtesy of the Italian Government Travel Office. p. 34: Reproduced from *An Introduction to Color* by Ralph M. Evans, © 1948 John Wiley and Sons, Inc. Reprinted by Permission. p. 37 STOCK MONTAGE

Chapter 2

Page 58: Courtesy of Dr. Jean de Heinzelin. p. 59: Courtesy of Musee de l'Homme. p. 69: Courtesy of Sylvia Margaret Wiegand. p. 75: Courtesy of U.S. Parachute Association. p. 80: © Bettmann/CORBIS.

Chapter 3

Page 122: Reproduced by Courtesy of the Trustees of the British Museum. p. 154: Reprinted by permission from "More about Computers" © 1974 by International Business Machines Corporation. p. 160: Courtesy of N.Y. State Office of General Services. p. 175: Courtesy of Deutsches Museum, Munich. p. 176: From the exhibition "Mathematica: A World of Numbers and Beyond," made by the Office of Charles and Ray Eames for International Business Machines Corporation. p. 183: Courtesy of TEREX Division, General Motors. p. 188: Courtesy of Texas Instrument, Casio Inc., and Sharp Electronics Corporation.

Chapter 4

Page 230: Courtesy of U.S. Bureau of Census. p. 231: © Bettmann/CORBIS. p. 235: Giraudon/Art Resource, NY.

Chapter 5

Page 268: Official U.S. Navy Photograph. p. 274: Courtesy of the

New York Stock Exchange, Inc. p. 275: Courtesy of the Trustees of the British Museum. p. 277: Official U.S. Navy Photograph. p. 282, Figure 5.26A: Courtesy of Texas Instruments. p. 283, Figure 5.26B: Casio Inc. p. 283: Courtesy of Sharp Electronics Corporation. p. 298: Courtesy of Minolta Corporation. p. 302: Courtesy of Rockwell International. Figure 5.35: Reprinted by Courtesy of Calspan Corporation. p. 303: © Bettmann/CORBIS.

Chapter 6

Page 331: Courtesy of Professor Erwin W. Mueller, The Pennsylvania State University. p. 348: Courtesy of National Institute of Standards and Technology. p. 354: Courtesy of the Bulova Watch Company, Inc. p. 379: Courtesy of NASA. p. 379: © Bettmann/CORBIS. p. 398: By permission of the Pillsbury Company. p. 402: Courtesy of Lehnert and Landrock, Cairo. p. 406: Yale Babylonian Collection.

Chapter 8

Page 507: © Bettmann/CORBIS. p. 527: Courtesy of NASA. p. 540: Ron Bergeron. pp. 539 and 544: Reprinted by permission of The New Hampshire Sweepstakes Commission.

Chapter 9

Page 550: Courtesy of General Motors Research Laboratory. p. 551: © Bettmann/CORBIS. p. 567: Hirshhorn Museum and Sculpture Garden, Smithsonian Institute. p. 567: Reproduced from *Handbook of Gem Identification,* by Richard T. Liddicoat, Jr. Reprinted by permission of the Gemological Institute of America. pp. 569 and 573: B. M. Shaub. p. 579: Negative #286786, Courtesy Department of Library Services, American Museum of Natural History. p. 579: © Bettmann/CORBIS. Figure 9.35: MAS, Barcelona, Spain. p. 583: Reproduced from *Art Forms in Nature* by Ernst Haeckel, © 1974 Dover Publications, Inc. p. 590: © Bettmann/CORBIS. Figure 9.43: B.M. Shaub. Figure 9.45: Talbot Lovering. Figure 9.46: B.M. Shaub. Figure 9.47: Reproduced from *Minerology,* by Ivan Kostov, © 1968 Courtesy of the author. Figure 9.49: Colonial Williamsburg Foundation,

Abby Aldrich Rockefeller Folk Art Center, Williamsburg, VA. Figure 9.52: B.M. Shaub. Figure 9.55: Courtesy of NASA. p. 603: © Bettmann/CORBIS. p. 604 B.M. Shaub. p. 605: Courtesy of John P. Adams, University of New Hampshire. p. 606: Courtesy of Babson College, Wellesley, Massachusetts. p. 612: Courtesy of Government of India Tourist Office. Figure 9.60: Courtesy of University of New Hampshire Media Services. Figure 9.66: Reproduced from *Snow Crystals* by W. A. Bently and W. J. Humphreys. Reprinted by Courtesy of McGraw-Hill Companies. Figure 9.67: Reprinted by Courtesy of the magazine *Antiques*. Figure 9.68: Courtesy of Entomology Department, University of New Hampshire. Photo by Ron Bergeron. p. 619: (*Left* and *right*) Courtesy of Lothrops Ethan Allen, Dover, N.H. Photo by Ron Bergeron. (*Center*) Courtesy of Jamaica Lamp Company, Queensville, New York. Figure 9.69: Courtesy of Lothrops Ethan Allen, Dover, N.H. Photo by Ron Bergeron. p. 621: Courtesy of the Spanish National Tourist Office. p. 621: Courtesy of The American Numismatic Society, New York. p. 622: Reproduced from *Art Forms in Nature,* Ernst Haeckel © 1974 Dover Publications, Inc. p. 623: Ron Bergeron. p. 624, 19a: Courtesy of Erie Glass Company, Parkridge, Illinois. p. 624, 19.b and 20.a,b: Courtesy of Lothrops Ethan Allen, Dover, N.H. Photo by Ron Bergeron. p. 626: B.M. Shaub.

Chapter 10

Page 635: Courtesy of British Tourist Authority. Figure 10.20: Courtesy of O. L. Miller and Barbara A. Hamkalo, Oak Ridge National Library. p. 655: General Electric Research and Development Center. p. 656: Ron Bergeron. p. 659: Courtesy of the Federal Reserve Bank of Minneapolis. Figure 10.31: Ron Bergeron. Figure 10.33: Talbot Lovering. Figure 10.37: Courtesy of Gemological Institute of America. p. 669: Talbot Lovering. p. 676: Courtesy of Gunnar Birkerts and Associates, Architects. Photo by Bob Coyle. p. 679: Ron Bergeron. p. 682: Reprinted by permission of Peachtree Plaza. p. 683: Talbot Lovering. p. 685: Courtesy of General Dynamics, Quincy Shipbuilding Division. Figure 10.50: Courtesy of Renaissance Center, Detroit. Figure 10.53: Reprinted by permission of Transamerica Corporation. Figure 10.55: Courtesy of Leslie Salt Co., Newark, California. Figure 10.58: Courtesy of NASA. p. 701: STOCK MONTAGE, Inc. Figure 10.61: Talbot Lovering. p. 707: Photo by Herb Moyer. Reprinted by permission from Rodney Sanderson. p. 708: (top) Courtesy of General Dynamics, Quincy Shipbuilding Division. p. 708: (below) Collection: Mrs. Harry Lynde Bradley, André Emmerich Gallery. p. 709: Ron Bergeron.

Chapter 11

Figure 11.6: Courtesy University of New Hampshire Media Services. p. 730: Reproduced from *A Concise History of Mathematics,* Dirk J. Struik. © 1984 Dover Publications, Inc. Figure 11.17: Courtesy of U.S. Geological Survey. Figure 11.20: Courtesy of U.S. Department of State. Figure 11.23: Courtesy of Travel Marketing, Inc., Seattle. Figure 11.28: Courtesy of Rival Manufacturing Company. p. 760: Courtesy John P. Adams, University of New Hampshire. p. 767: Catharine Page Perkins Fund. Courtesy, Museum of Fine Arts, Boston. p. 770: Courtesy of J.E. Cermak, Fluid Dynamics and Diffusion Laboratory, Colorado State University. Figure 11.45: Photo by Wayne Goddard. Description of Knife reprinted by permission of the Register Guard, Eugene, Oregon. p. 784: Courtesy of Sally Ann Foley. Photo by Ron Bergeron. p. 788: Courtesy of Rockwell International Corporation. p. 791 (top): Courtesy of Sydney Rogers Chair Company, Georgetown, Massachusetts. p. 791 (bottom): Courtesy of Boeing. p. 792: Courtesy of Sally Ann Foley. Photo by Ron Bergeron.

INDEX

A

Abacus, 134
Abundant numbers, 244
Accuracy. *See* Precision
Acre, 660, 662
Activities for Implementing Curricular Themes from the Agenda for Action, 354
Acute angle, 556, 557
Addends, 139
Adding machine (Pascal), 154
Adding opposites, 257
Addition
  addends, 139
  algorithms, 140–141
  associative property for. *See* Associative property for addition
  base-five pieces, 138
  black and red tiles, 249, 254–255
  closure property, 142, 264, 313, 367, 411
  commutative property. *See* Commutative property for addition
  decimals, 354–355
  distributive property of multiplication, 40, 167–168, 265, 315, 367, 411
  error analysis, 155
  estimation, 150–152
  fractions, 303–306
  geometric method, 736
  identity property for. *See* Identity property for addition
  integers, 254–256, 257
  inverse for, 264, 315
  left-to-right, 141
  mental calculations, 149–150
  models for, 140–141
  number line, 155
  partial sums, 141
  property, 513
  regrouping, 140, 141
  scratch method, 141
  whole numbers, 139–144
Addition property, 513
Additive numeration system, 124
Add-up method, 150, 156, 323, 356
Adjacent
  angle, 557
  sides, 563
  vertices, 563
Aesthetic Measure, 622
Agnesi, Maria Gaetana, 303
Aichele, D. B., 100
Algebra
  algebraic expression, 37
  balance scales, 38–39, 41–42
  equivalent equation, 39

Algebra—*Cont.*
  equivalent inequality, 42
  function, 75–78
  graph, 78–80
  linear function, 80–85
  problem solving, 36–46
  solving equation, 39–41
  variable, 37
Algebraic expression, 37
Algebraic model, 437
Algorithm. *See* Addition; Division; Multiplication; Subtraction
Alternate interior angle, 559
Altitude (height)
  parallelogram, 665
  prism, 693
  trapezoid, 668
  triangle, 585, 667
Ampere, 650
Analogy, reasoning by, 132–133
Angle, 554
  acute, 556, 557
  adjacent, 557
  alternate interior, 559
  bisecting, 728–729, 733–734
  central, 576, 578
  complementary, 557
  congruent, 575, 719
  constructing, 719–720
  corresponding, 568, 717
  degree, 556
  dihedral, 591
  exterior, 576
  included, 724
  measure, 549, 556–558
  minute, 556
  obtuse, 556, 557
  reflex, 556, 557
  right, 556, 557, 564
  second, 556
  sides, 554
  straight, 556
  sum of
    in polygon, 574
    in triangle, 574
  supplementary, 557
  trisecting, 730
  vertex, 554, 576
  vertical, 558
Angle-angle similarity property, 778
Angle-side-angle congruence property, 726
Angstrom, 648
Antipodal points, 606
Apex, 595
Apogee, 419
Approximately equal to ($\approx$), 151
Archimedean solid. *See* Semiregular polyhedron
Archimedes, 672, 679, 701
Are, 677

Area. *See also* Square units
  circle, 670–672
  definition of, 659
  Egyptian formula for, 682
  irregular shape, 673, 679
  parallelogram, 665–666
  polygons, 665–668
  rectangle, 665
  space figure. *See* Surface area
  trapezoid, 668
  triangle, 666–667
Aristotle, 27
Arithmetic, fundamental theorem, 232, 341
Arithmetic sequence, 22
  common difference, 22
Arrow diagrams, 76
Aryabhata, 679
Associative property for addition
  fractions, 314
  integers, 264
  rational numbers, 367
  real numbers, 411
  whole numbers, 143
Associative property for multiplication
  fractions, 315
  integers, 264
  rational numbers, 367
  real numbers, 411
  whole numbers, 166–167
Astronomical unit, 379
Athenaeus, 11
Atomic clock, 348, 635
Attribute pieces, 60
  sorting and classifying, 57
Average. *See* Mean
Avoirdupois unit, 640
Axioms, 551
Axis
  of rotation, 619
  of symmetry, 619
  x, 78
  y, 78
Azimuthal projections, 601

B

Babylonian
  angle measure, 556
  fractions, 275
  geometry, 551
  length measurement, 636
  numerals, 125–126, 135
  stone tablet, 406
Back-to-back stem-and-leaf plot, 433
Balance-scale model
  equation, 38, 39
  inequality, 41–42
Bar graphs, 427–428
Base (exponent), 193

C

TWO-CENTIMETER GRID

DECIMAL SQUARES RECORDING PAPER

Tenths Squares   Hundredths Squares   Thousandths Squares

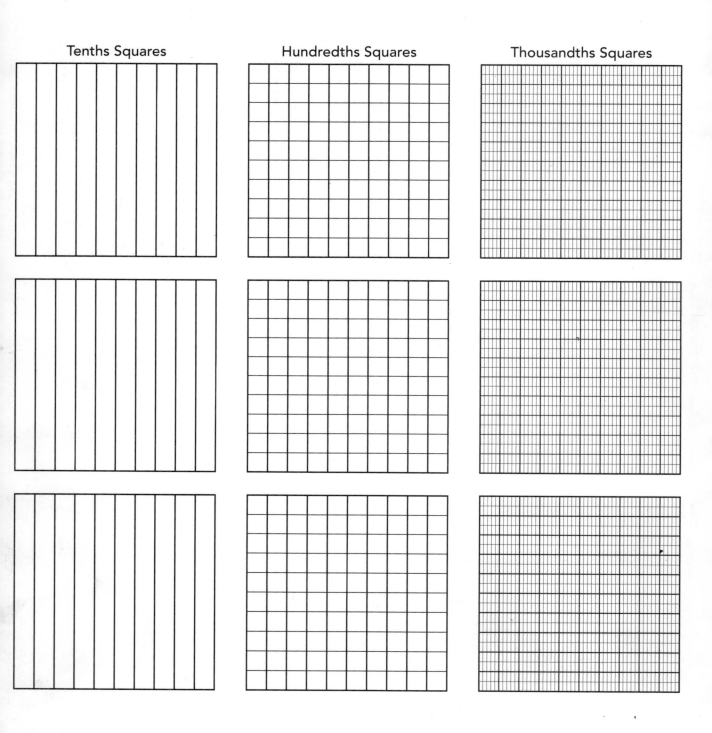